BARRON'S

GUIDE TO
Distance Learning

DEGREES • CERTIFICATES • COURSES

Pat Criscito

All inquiries should be addressed to:
Barron's Educational Series, Inc.
250 Wireless Boulevard
Hauppauge, NY 11788
http://www.barronseduc.com

Library of Congress Catalog Card No. 98-32255

International Standard Book No. 0-7641-0725-9

Library of Congress Cataloging-in-Publication Data

Criscito, Pat, 1953–
     Barron's guide to distance learning : degrees, certificates,
courses / by Pat Criscito.
          p. cm.
     ISBN 0-7641-0725-9
     1. Distance education--United States. 2. Distance education--
Canada. 3. Distance education--United States--Directories
4. Distance education--Canada--Directories.   I. Title.
LC5805.C75   1999
378.1′75′02573--dc21   98-32255
                                                            CIP

PRINTED IN THE UNITED STATES OF AMERICA
9 8 7 6 5 4 3 2 1

Contents

Preface

This book will provide you with all the information you need to find an accredited undergraduate, graduate, or doctoral program that will allow you to complete your course work without sitting in a traditional college classroom. Whether you want to begin a degree program from scratch, finish one you have already begun, earn continuing education credits, stay on the cutting edge of your profession, or take a single class to expand your personal growth, you have selected the right book. Here's what you will find in the following pages:

- An introduction to the concept of distance learning and its terminology.

- Information to help you discern an accredited program from a "diploma mill."

- Tools to assess whether or not you have the personality for nontraditional learning.

- Ways to earn credit for what you already know.

- Means to finance the cost of your education.

- Complete lists of degrees, certificates, and courses to help you evaluate the programs of nearly 800 colleges and universities.

- Indexes listing colleges by geographic location, type of programs offered, individual classes, or on-campus requirements.

Regionally accredited colleges and universities throughout the United States and Canada are profiled here, plus a few international colleges that are accredited by one of the six regional accreditation associations in the United States. Each profile provides contact information (including Web page and e-mail address), program availability (degrees, certificates, and individual classes), admission requirements, costs, teaching methods, financial aid information, and a brief description of the school. An extensive series of indexes follows with breakdowns by location, on-campus requirements, and fields of study. To quickly access the Internet home page for each college, go to *http://www.thespringsmall.com* and click on the little red schoolhouse.

This guide could not have been written without the cooperation of every college listed. My thanks to every person who took the time to complete the survey and to those who graciously answered questions and provided special information about their programs. Morgan Edwards, the Director of Distance Learning at the University of Denver, spent hours providing the foundation for my research. The work would never have been finished without my dedicated assistants—Kathy Traxler and Teri Adams-Fjellman—and the researchers who spent months on the telephone and at computers sending e-mails, entering data, proofreading, and editing the profiles—Melanie Carlston, George Kitkowski, David Huggins, Ruth McConnell, Kathie Cintron, Connie Harrison, Heather Criscito, and Stacey Hightchew. Thanks to each of you and to Mike and Heather for your undying support.

Introduction to Distance Learning

Y ou are just six classes short of a degree, but with a full-time job that requires you to travel two weeks every month, you can't possibly make the time to go back to school! Or so you think. In reality, if you have a computer with a modem, a television set, or a mailbox and a bit of self-discipline, a diploma may be closer than you think.

Online learning, televised classrooms, and home-study courses have revolutionized the way we learn, making it possible to earn college credits from the comfort of our homes or offices without regard for time and geographical barriers. Whether you are a professional who can study for a few hours on an airplane or during a lunch break at work, or a young mother who can "go to school" after the kids are asleep, distance learning may be your answer to completing a degree or acquiring certification.

What Is Distance Learning?

According to Webster, distance is "a measure of separation in space or time." Therefore distance learning is defined as a formal educational process where the majority of the instruction occurs when the learner and instructor are not in the same place and are often separated by time. Education is delivered to people instead of people to education. The definition is as simple as that, but here's a little something of what it means to you as a student.

- Instead of sitting in a lecture hall or attending a seminar, you participate in an online conference through your computer, watch a videotape on your home television set, or join a videoconference at a local teleconferencing center.

- Instead of a team project where a group of students meets together in the same place once a week, you collaborate via computer conferences, e-mail, or audioconferences.

- Instead of searching through the stacks in a dusty library, you surf the Net or use online databases and research librarians.

- Instead of sitting down with your faculty advisor over a cup of coffee, you use e-mail, telephone, or live computer chats.

- Instead of handing in your homework all neatly printed and bound, you return your assignments online or via e-mail, fax, or mail.

- Instead of testing with your class, you go to a local testing center, find a proctor at your local high school or college, or take tests via e-mail, fax, or online.

Many terms in the academic world are used synonymously with distance learning, including distributed learning, nontraditional education, external degree program, innovative program, alternative education, independent study, online program, nonresidential program, faculty-directed courses, guided self-study, and correspondence study, among others. Each of these terms has subtle differences, and a college can choose to call its program whatever it likes, but for the sake of consistency, this book will use the words *distance learning* to describe all of them.

The History of Distance Learning

Distance learning dates back more than 100 years to Europe, Africa, and Asia where open universities offered "external" degrees. In Australia, the University of Queensland offered an external degree program as early as the 1890s. Today, higher education institutions in Australia incorporate distance learning into many of their programs, making Australia a leader in distance education worldwide.

The well-known British Open University began in 1971 and now serves more than 200,000 undergraduate and graduate students worldwide. It is one of the largest distance learning schools in the world and is ranked among the top ten universities in the United Kingdom. At a speech in Ankara, Turkey, Sir John Daniel, the Vice Chancellor of the Open University, reported that his research had discovered eleven distance learning "mega-universities" around the world with more than 100,000 students each. Anadolu University in Turkey was the largest university in the world when measured by the number of degree-level students (570,000). The China TV University System is a close second with more than 550,000 degree-level students in its distance learning programs.

Distance learning in the United States began in the late 19th century with correspondence courses, like the one offered by Isaac Pitman in 1840 to teach his system of shorthand. Columbia University and other colleges offered radio courses in the 1920s and 1930s and televised courses in the 1960s. Since 1890, about 100 million Americans have taken courses at a distance, including such well-known people as Franklin D. Roosevelt, Walter P. Chrysler, Walter Cronkite, Barry Goldwater, and Charles Schulz.

The first exclusively distance degree program in the United States was developed by the University of the State of New York in 1970. Ewald B. Nyquist suggested the formation of the Regents External Degree Program sponsored by the university's Board of Regents. That program has awarded more than 56,000 degrees and is now known as Regents College. In early 1998, Regents College became chartered as an independent member institution with the University of the State of New York.

Today, technology-based distance education has emerged as an increasingly important component of higher education in the United States. Many states have developed innovative distance learning programs that are on the cutting edge of technology. One good example is the Western Governors University (WGU). Formed by the governors of the states in the western United States, WGU is a "virtual university" with no campus and a heavy reliance on technology. It brings the resources of numerous colleges, universities, corporations, and other organizations together to provide degrees and certificates to students around the world.

Canada is a world leader in distance education. Because of its vast expanse and sparsely populated areas, nearly all provinces have developed various media to bring university programs to remote areas that might not otherwise have access to a university education. In addition to the distance learning programs offered by conventional universities, Alberta, British Columbia, and Quebec have each developed an "open university" based on the British model. They have liberal admission policies and use home study, television, teleconferencing, printed materials, audiotapes, and videotapes, among other delivery methods.

Why Distance Learning?

When colleges and universities first began incorporating distance education into their programs, they thought they were tapping into a new market of underserved adult learners who were too busy or lived too far away to come to a traditional campus. It often didn't occur to them that many of their traditional on-campus students would be eager to ease their schedules by taking courses online or would use distance learning to get into courses that had already been closed on campus. Now there are just as many on-campus students taking advantage of distance learning as there are off-campus students. At the State University of New York's Learning Network, 80 percent of the students study full- or part-time on a SUNY campus. At Arizona State University, only 3 percent of the distance education students live in another state. In Canada, Lori Wallace, a senior instructional designer at the University of Manitoba, tracked the demographics of distance education students for more than a decade and found that 66 percent of the students were taking concurrent courses on campus. However, all distance education students have at least one of these things in common:

- ▸ They are trying to finish a degree to get a job or to advance to a better one,

- ▸ Or they need certification for their profession,

- ▸ Or they need continuing education units (CEUs) to stay current in their profession,

- ▸ Or they love learning and take college classes for personal enrichment, intellectual stimulation, socialization, or recreation,

- ▸ Or they want a chance to study with the greatest teachers in the world or to complete a degree program at a prestigious college far from where they live,

- ▸ Or they are high school students wanting to get a jump on a college education,

- ▸ And they need the flexibility that distance learning offers because of where they live, their physical limitations, or the time constraints of work or family commitments.

This flexibility is why people elect to take courses via television, the Internet, or correspondence even when classrooms are just a few minutes away. Online courses are especially popular because students can log on day or night to check e-mail messages, discussion logs, and instructor assignments. Some online courses do require "attendance" at live chats, but according to Morgan Edwards, director of the University of Denver distance learning program, this limits the school's market, so many online courses steer away from real-time activities that require a student to be somewhere at a set time.

Colleges and universities like distance learning because it allows them to accommodate growth without building new facilities and it helps them reach a wider student population. This often helps fulfill the institution's mission of providing education to its students, regardless of their location, diversity, economic status, age, or experience.

For the student, continuing education is often the key to staying current in a rapidly changing job market. According to the Commission for a Nation of Lifelong Learners (CNLL), more than 80 percent of adults believe they need more education to advance their careers. William Hine, Ed.D., dean of the School of Adult and Continuing Education at Eastern Illinois University in Charleston, says:

> The half-life of a college degree is three to five years. If you're not retooling or gaining new knowledge, your education is almost obsolete, especially in the sciences, health, and technology. Those who aren't committed to lifelong learning are unlikely to move ahead in their careers.

In the next decade, 75 percent of the current work force will need significant retraining, and more than half of the new jobs will require higher education and training. In their November 1997 report, the CNLL says that education provides the critical margin of competitiveness in a worldwide economy and, without it, America will not be able to maintain its leadership in the global economy.

> Without a commitment to lifelong learning, America cannot provide its individuals and families with a higher standard of living, assured employability, safe communities, and a better future.

I like how Glenn Jones, the founder and chief executive officer of Jones International, defined *education* in his book, *Cyberschools:*

> Education is a process. Education is how information becomes meaningful. Information without meaning is useless. Education converts information into knowledge, understanding, and wisdom much like changing temperature turns water into ice. Education is the loom through which information is woven into value systems, dignity, self-worth, freedom, and into civilization itself.

With the emergence of today's "knowledge worker," that definition is more true now than at any other time in history. Companies are demanding that their workers be able to produce new designs and concepts instead of just following standard procedures and producing familiar products (Peter Drucker and Robert Reich). This demands effective education.

By developing a love for lifelong learning, you can boost your earning power and make your skills more marketable, giving you that competitive edge so necessary in today's cutthroat corporate world. It is no longer possible to take a job right out of high school, be trained by an employer, and work for the same company until retirement. There is no gold watch at the end of the rainbow, and this trend is unlikely to change. The baby boom generation has already embraced a philosophy of lifetime learning as a result of this dynamic global workplace, and distance learning is the perfect way to incorporate this philosophy into your schedule.

Let's take a look at the U.S. Census Bureau's 1997 mean earning statistics to get an idea of how lifelong learning translates into annual income:

Education Level	Men	Women
High School Diploma	$32,611	$22,656
Associate Degree	$40,465	$29,776
Bachelor's Degree	$55,832	$37,319
Master's Degree	$71,225	$46,072
Professional Degree	$120,052	$74,077
Doctoral Degree	$93,106	$60,468

According to the U.S. Department of Education's National Center for Education Statistics, the average college student today is over the age of 22 and works full time. According to their projections, by the year 2008, nearly 9 million students over the age of 22 will be enrolled in colleges and universities in the United States alone. The Distance Education and Training Council (DETC) surveyed the institutions it accredits and found that the typical student was 31 years old, 48 percent were male, 90 percent were employed, and 31 percent had their tuition paid by their employer. This shift in demographics increases the demand for education that is more accessible and more affordable.

Traditional campus-based universities are accepting the fact that higher education must change with the times. With this change have come distance learning options that meet the needs of adult learners and accept the realities of the new student demographic. These schools are delivering education based on the student's resources (computer, television, or mailbox) and not the resources of the university (manicured lawns and ivy-covered walls). John Sperling put it best when he said:

As we move to meet the educational needs of working adults in a mobile society, our concept of the university must extend beyond place and embrace process. An adult university cannot be campus bound; rather, its borders must be defined by the lives of its students.

Mike Leavitt, the governor of Utah, has said:

For the 21st century, I believe there will be a basic change in higher education. It will move from mass production to mass customization. The educational system will be transformed into a competency-based, versus credit-based system, and higher education will revolve around the student. Where learning takes place will no longer be as important as what a student actually learns.

The majority of regionally accredited colleges and universities today either have distance learning programs now or are seriously considering them. Many have developed full-scale programs that incorporate virtual classrooms via the Internet, interactive computer conferencing, e-mail, newsgroups, LISTSERVs, bulletin boards, fax, videoconferencing, audioconferencing, videotapes, cable/satellite television, and/or correspondence study in various combinations. Others are just dipping their toes into the ocean of possibilities by offering a few classes. Research by the Gartner Group has shown that 65 percent of all colleges and universities were offering their courses over the Internet in 1998, and they project that the number will exceed 80 percent by the year 2001.

Some degree-granting institutions aren't even colleges at all, but are corporations or industry associations that have applied for accreditation to award academic degrees. In 1995, more than $50 billion was spent on training by employers, and some experts estimate that as many as 1,000 corporate universities exist in the United States. Colleges and universities have even teamed up with corporations to form consortia to offer classes, degrees, and certificates.

Types of Distance Learning

Distance learning methods are as numerous as the technologies for delivering the instruction. The three primary delivery mediums are computer, television, and mailbox in various combinations. Let's look at them in more detail.

Correspondence Courses

Distance learning is not a novel concept. Correspondence study (also called home study or independent study) has been around for more than 100 years. The biggest difference between those programs and today's distance learning is technology. However, pure correspondence courses—without the use of technology in some form (e-mail, fax, videotapes, audiotapes, CD-ROMs, satellite/cable television, video/audioconferencing, etc.)—are quickly becoming dinosaurs. Correspondence study, regardless of its delivery method, is included in this book's definition of distance learning.

Accreditation of a correspondence course is critical since most colleges and universities will not accept transfer credits from a school that is not regionally accredited. You will find that the majority of correspondence courses are geared toward undergraduate rather than graduate-level study. Regardless of their level, correspondence courses generally work this way:

1. You complete an application and mail it to a designated address with a check or credit card number for your fees.

2. You receive the course, study guide, instructions, syllabus, etc., in the mail.

3. You order the textbooks listed in the instructions.

4. You receive your textbooks in the mail and begin completing lessons.

5. As each lesson is completed, you return it to your instructor where it is evaluated and graded.

6. The corrected and graded lesson is returned to you in the mail, along with comments from your instructor.

7. You may be required to take a mid-course examination and a final examination. These are usually given at a local testing center provided by the school, although you can make arrangements to pay a local proctor from a list approved by the school.

8. The proctor returns the completed examination to the school.

9. You receive a final grade in the mail.

Virtual Classrooms

If you were a student at the University of Phoenix Online Campus, you would dial into their system via modem, read the instructor's assignment, review your fellow classmates' comments about the current topic in a continuous newsgroup format, and then spend another hour or so online e-mailing other students and your instructor. When you logged off, you would then complete your homework and prepare for the next assignment. Periodically, you would "meet" online with your group members in live chats to collaborate on group projects. These prescheduled live chats (sometimes called computer conferences or IRCs, which stands for Internet Relay Chats) are the closest thing you will get to a live classroom experience in online education.

At the University of Denver, the faculty create their own Internet home pages for each class. These sites contain a wealth of information about the courses, including the syllabus, textbook requirements, detailed learning outcomes, full instructions for completing assignments, and relevant hyperlinks to other sites that the instructor has selected for the course. Students communicate with the instructor and other students via e-mail, and instructors create chat rooms and bulletin boards for idea exchanges and discussions about topics related to the assignments.

While some schools use private computer networks, others use the World Wide Web and bulletin board systems. Some teach entire courses online, and others only parts of courses. Some professors post extensive print materials, video clips, and graphics and use sophisticated messaging systems on their sites, while others use only e-mail. There is no universal approach to online learning, so you need to ask the college or university for more information about its technology before you apply. Most distance learning catalogs and brochures provide clear explanations of the technologies you will be required to use in each class.

Keep in mind, however, that technology is not infallible. Like the proverbial "My dog ate my homework," you are at the mercy of your instructor if your computer crashes! Always back up your files to a floppy disk and set your e-mail software to save any e-mail you send or receive to a "filing cabinet." Then periodically save that filing cabinet to a floppy disk.

This may all seem too "techie" for you, but you don't have to be a computer expert to travel the information superhighway. You will use basic computer skills that can be learned in a day. After all, what is school for if not to teach you what you need to know to be successful using computer-based learning? The university of your choice will have support staff available to walk you through the technology requirements of any class.

Video/Audioconferencing

Videoconferencing and audioconferencing (sometimes called teleconferencing) are now affordable for any school thanks to continuing advances in technology. In fact, a school can hook up a system that lets students and instructors talk to and see each other in remote locations for a few hundred dollars worth of equipment. The more money one spends on teleconferencing equipment, however, the higher the quality of both the video and audio connection, so colleges and universities are spending much more than a few hundred dollars! Unlike other distance learning teaching methods, unless you have a camera and other equipment on your computer, you will have to leave your home or office to join the conference from a location on another college campus or a commercial teleconferencing center.

Videoconferencing allows the class to hold face-to-face discussions and to display visual aids for all to see. It is possible to look at and modify designs on the screen or to make presentations using PowerPoint software. Some programs use teleconferencing to allow students to "sit in" on traditional on-campus classes. The students in class interact with the distance students as if they were sitting in the classroom and vice versa.

If you have a video camera on your computer, a full-duplex sound card, Internet access, and the necessary software (all of which come as standard equipment on many new high-end computers today), you already have your own computerized teleconferencing site. The biggest drawback to Internet-based teleconferencing is the small picture size and slightly jerky motion of the image. In the near future, however, more homes and offices will have access to DSL or ISDN telephone lines, which allow data to move faster and therefore create better sound and picture quality.

A less frequently used medium of communication in distance learning classes is audioconferencing where only conversation is heard. There is no visual element. The students are either speaking individually from their home telephones via a conference call or several small groups of students are sitting around a table with a special speaker in the middle that picks up all of the conversations around the table.

Television

Televised courses were aired over public television stations for many years, but today's televised courses are usually broadcast over special cable channels (like the Learning Channel), via satellite, or from private television stations at universities. Television is a popular method of delivering education, since most homes in developed countries contain at least one television set.

This category of distance learning also includes videotapes of classes that were conducted in special classrooms set up like television studios. These videotapes are often included as a part of correspondence courses today and require only a television set and VCR.

What Is Available

Degree Programs

Most colleges and universities begin their distance learning experiments by offering only individual classes. As their experience with distance learning matures, these schools expand their programs to offer undergraduate, graduate, and sometimes doctoral degrees via this nontraditional format. For a look at the types of degrees available at colleges and universities listed in this guide, check the indexes by fields of study at the end of the book.

Certification Programs

Professional certification is required in many industries, such as teaching, medicine, computer science, hotel management, and quality control. Even where it is not required, certification can help you get a job or promotion, so it is well worth pursuing. Certification is offered in an incredibly diverse number of fields, including business, financial planning, computer networking, theology, human development, child psychology, chemical engineering, transportation planning, and construction management, to name a very few.

Credit Courses

If you are close to finishing a degree but lack a few credits, taking individual classes may help you reach your goal of graduation. Credits from a regionally accredited college or university may be applied toward a degree or transferred to your degree-granting institution, but you should always check first. Don't waste your valuable time and money on a class that won't transfer, if that is your goal.

For those who never attended college or who have earned only a few credits, distance learning classes give the student an opportunity to test the waters before enrolling in a full degree program. If an expensive college requires you to take only the "core courses" from that institution, then you can use community colleges and less-expensive alternatives to complete some of the prerequisite credits before enrolling in the degree program. Again, always check with your degree-granting institution to make sure the credits you are about to earn are transferrable.

Continuing Education Units (CEUs)

If you are a teacher, accountant, physician, nurse, or other licensed professional, most states require you to maintain your certification by continuing your education. Distance learning makes this convenient. A doctor can tape a show from cable television, watch it at her convenience, and then call to request that the short exam be faxed to her office the next morning. A teacher can take classes via the Internet during the summer instead of leaving his family behind while he spends six weeks at summer school in another city.

A single Continuing Education Unit (CEU) is granted for each ten contact hours spent participating in an organized continuing education setting. *Organized* means qualified instructors and responsible programs, which accredited college programs offer. Instead of earning college credits, check with the institution about earning CEUs instead.

Noncredit Courses for Self-Enrichment

If you love to learn but don't care whether you earn college credit for the classes you take, you can audit distance learning classes just like you can when they are offered on campus. Because you don't receive a grade for an audited class, you are not required to turn in homework or take final exams, although many students still do the work because it is part of the learning process.

Besides providing self-enrichment, noncredit courses can help you move ahead in your job as you increase your knowledge of specialized areas in your field. Distance learning is an efficient way to enhance your value as an employee in today's competitive work environment. Recognizing this, many corporations now collaborate with colleges and universities to offer classes at the work site, which benefits both the employer and the employee. If your employer doesn't offer this service, try suggesting it.

Student Services

Learning resources are critical to the success of a student in a distance learning environment. This includes access to tutoring, career counseling, research, technical support, online databases, and libraries. Good distance learning institutions pride themselves on their student-service offerings. They go out of their way to provide toll-free phone numbers for student questions and problems. They provide online or automated registration services, and library services and textbooks are just a phone call or an e-mail away.

The timely availability of research and library resources is very important. The more challenging the course, the more resources you will need. Make sure that you have access to on-campus librarians, databases, periodicals, and the complete library catalog. It should take no more than one to three days to receive requested materials, but you need to plan ahead. You can't procrastinate in distance learning programs!

Graduation

What about graduation? Do you yearn for that cap and gown? Universities understand that graduation is just as important for a distance learning student as it is for the traditional student. In order to provide a traditional finale to the nontraditional educational experience, most schools include their local distance learning students in traditional graduation ceremonies or provide televised or Internet-based ceremonies for students who are too far away to realistically travel to an on-campus event. For instance, International University in Denver held a small ceremony in its corporate offices with university administrators and professors in caps and gowns. Several students traveled to Denver for the ceremony, while the others connected via the Internet. The commencement speaker, Republican Representative Dan Schaefer, joined the ceremony via a separate video link.

Because distance learning students are traditionally older, this event becomes very important to both the students and their families. The sense of accomplishment that comes from completing a long-held dream and sharing it with your family is reinforced with a graduation ceremony, so don't miss it!

By the way, the diploma you will receive from a distance learning program will, in most cases, be identical to those received by students on campus. In fact, diplomas and transcripts rarely mention how a class was completed.

Is Distance Learning Just as Credible?

The answer is yes! When you choose a regionally accredited college or university for your distance education, the quality of the courses, instructors, materials, exams, papers, theses, and dissertations are the same as their on-campus counterparts. The way education is delivered (video, computer, correspondence) has little effect on a student's achievement provided the delivery method is appropriate to the course.

It has long been held that educational quality is linked to the age of the institution, how much money it has at its disposal, how tough it is to get admitted, and how small the classes were. Those standards have changed in the 20th century. It is difficult to evaluate distance learning institutions by the same criteria. They are relatively new, very cost effective, and often offer open admission.

According to a recent study at California State University at Northridge, students learning in a virtual classroom tested 20 percent better across the board than their counterparts who learned in a traditional classroom. There was no significant difference between the sex, age, computer experience, or attitude toward the subject material of the two groups. All of the research published since 1920 indicates that correspondence/distance study students perform just as well as, and in most cases better than, their classroom counterparts. This success stems from several factors, including:

- ▸ Distance learners tend to be self-motivated, disciplined, and higher achievers.

- ▸ Generally, distance students are voluntarily seeking further education and have set goals for themselves that make success more likely.

- ▸ They are usually employed in a career where advancement can be readily achieved through academic achievement.

- ▸ Distance learners in virtual classrooms spend about 50 percent more time collaborating with each other than students in a traditional classroom, which reinforces the learning environment.

- ▸ The most successful students initiate calls to instructors for assistance and possess a more serious attitude toward their classes.

How Much Does Distance Learning Cost?

Tuition rates and textbook costs for distance learning classes are usually the same as their on-campus counterparts, although they are sometimes less and sometimes more. Your savings will not be related to what you pay the school. Instead, you save the costs of commuting, parking, child care, and lost work time. Depending on the teaching method used, you will, of course, need a computer with a modem, television, or a VCR. That means an additional cost if you don't already have these technologies or if you need to update your computer system. However, if you already own or have access to the technology you need, your only additional cost will be an occasional trip to a testing center or to a campus-based seminar or other on-campus meeting required by some programs.

When you think about the incredible amount of time and money it takes to develop these new teaching methods, you can appreciate the fact that the schools are not actually charging you *more* for your distance learning! Not only do colleges and universities pay the additional costs for the development of a new curriculum, but they also must hire computer programmers, Web site developers, videographers, site administrators, distribution clerks, online library resource personnel, specially trained counselors, and technical support staff. On top of that, they must maintain the computer systems, teleconferencing systems, and other equipment necessary to deliver distance learning to the students.

Teaching in front of a camera or via a computer is not the forte of every instructor. Universities must identify faculty members with outstanding presentation abilities and the willingness to consider flexible approaches toward student learning. Training of faculty in the use of technology is vitally important to the success of any distance learning program but, at the same time, it is very expensive. Instead of the traditional weekly office hours, distance learning instructors must give their students daily attention.

Glenn Jones, an innovator in cable television and distance education for more than 30 years, sees the solution to the cost of developing distance learning in "free market fusion" between nonprofit educational entities and private-sector companies. Massive consortia have already been formed between cable companies, four-year universities, community colleges, public broadcasting services, and other for-profit entities to make distance learning available to more students at a reasonable price.

Internet Resources

For more information about distance learning, peruse the following Web sites:

- ▸ The companion site for this book is found by clicking on the little red schoolhouse at: http://www.thespringsmall.com

- ▸ Check under "distance learning," "alternative education," or "adult and continuing education" at Yahoo for related sites: http://www.yahoo.com/Education/Distance_ Learning/Adult_and_ Continuing_Education/

- ▸ A metasite for hyperlinks to Internet sites related to distance education: http://www. cisnet.com/~cattales/Deducation.html

- ▸ The Association of Learning Technologies promotes the use and development of learning technologies for higher education: http://www.csv.warwick.ac.uk/alt-E/

- ▸ The U.S. Distance Learning Association is a nonprofit group formed in 1987 to promote the development and application of distance learning for education and training: http://www.usdla.org

- ▸ The Distance Education Clearinghouse of the University of Wisconsin: http://www. uwex.edu/disted/home.html

- ▸ Educause, an extensive collection of higher education information and technology materials: http://www.educause.edu/

- ▸ Distance Learning Resources Network: http://www.fwl.org/edtech/CollegeDistanceEd. html

- Established in 1983, the Canadian Association of Distance Education (CADE) is a national association of professionals committed to excellence in the provision of distance education in Canada: http://www.cade-aced.ca/

- At the PBS home page, you will find a list of all community colleges participating in PBS's *Going the Distance* program: http://www.pbs.org/learn/als/

- The Distance Education and Training Council has links to its member institutions as well as general information about distance learning: http://www.detc.org

- For lists of accredited college degrees through correspondence, check: http://collegeathome.com/

- The Interactive College Resource Center lists educational programs available to working adults in Southern California: http://www.icrc.com/

- The Commonwealth of Learning, a resource for international distance learning resources: http://www.col.org

- Hamline University's World Education Exchange for international distance learning resources: http://www.hamline.edu/~kjmaier/index.html

- The University of Idaho's overview of distance learning: http://www.uidaho.edu/evo/distglan.html

- For the latest information on the Western Governors University and distance learning out West, check the Web site for the Western Interstate Commission for Higher Education (WICHE): http://www.wiche.edu or http://www.westgov.org/smart/vu/vu.html

- The California Virtual University Foundation offers a central source of information on courses available in California via the Internet, television, or other technologies. It allows users to search the site by college (95 institutions), topic (more than 1,600 courses and 100 full degree or certificate programs), or by delivery method: http://www.california.edu

- The official publication of the Federal Government Distance Learning Association: http://fgdla.org

- Distance education resources from Auburn University: http://www.auburn.edu/administration/horizon/sept_www.html

- The National Education Association: http://www.nea.org

- General distance education resources: http://www.teleeducation.nb.ca/phenom

- Adult Distance Education Internet Surf Shack: http://www.edsurf.net

- Corsortium for Distance Learning: http://www.distlearn.com

- The Globewide Network Academy: http://www.gnacademy.org:8001/uu-gna/index.html

- University of Tennessee's distance learning LISTSERV: http://web.ce.utk.edu/departments/distance_learning/listserv.html

- Distance learning newsgroup: alt.education.distance (check the frequently asked questions first at http://pages. prodigy.com/PAUM88A/)

2 ▶ Is Distance Learning Right for You?

You might think that it will be easier to get better grades when taking distance courses because you will never miss a class or be late while fighting a traffic jam. Or you might think the classes themselves are inherently easier, but that isn't the case. In fact, distance education is often just as time consuming as traditional classroom work. The time you would have spent in class you will spend reading material and writing responses.

Distance learning was designed with highly motivated adults in mind—those who have a clear sense of their goals and can work autonomously. Many younger students seem to have a difficult time succeeding at distance learning. Although generalizations are not true for everyone, younger students frequently have a greater need to be with a live person, to feel the passion of the instructor, and to socialize with fellow students. They find the competition and camaraderie inherent in a classroom full of students motivating, and motivation is the key to success in distance learning. If you are such a student, look for distance learning classes with interactive media (chats, videoconferencing, group work, etc.).

If you are self-motivated and disciplined, regardless of your age, you will have an easier time succeeding in a distance learning setting. You will often be required to be resourceful in thinking through problems and researching solutions on your own. You must be able to set and achieve realistic goals and to work without the supervision or regulations of an instructor. You must be persistent when faced with the choice of watching your favorite television show or doing your homework, which can consume up to 20 hours of your time a week. You will find it a frequent challenge to balance your work, family, school, and recreation time. If you are a social animal who prefers not to be alone, or if you are a procrastinator who always puts off until tomorrow what should be done today, distance learning will be more difficult for you.

The Personality Evaluation

How do you know if you truly have the personality for distance learning? You might never know until you try taking a few classes. If you find that you just prefer to be in a classroom situation where you can bounce ideas off other people or that you need the interaction with a professor and other students in order to learn, then you might have to change course. Here's a little test that might help you determine whether you have the personality for distance learning before beginning, although you will never know until you try it.

The following evaluation is reproduced here with the permission of the Extended Learning Institute of Northern Virginia Community College. It is designed to determine whether a student's circumstances and lifestyles are compatible with distance learning. Choose one answer for each of the ten questions below. Then go to the answer section and assess how well distance learning would fit your needs.

1. My need to take this course now is:
   - ❏ a. High—I need it immediately for degree, job, or other important reason.
   - ❏ b. Moderate—I could take it on campus later or substitute another course.
   - ❏ c. Low—It's a personal interest that could be postponed.

2. Feeling that I am part of a class is:
   - ❏ a. Not particularly necessary to me.
   - ❏ b. Somewhat important to me.
   - ❏ c. Very important to me.

3. I would classify myself as someone who:
   - ❏ a. Often gets things done ahead of time.
   - ❏ b. Needs reminding to get things done on time.
   - ❏ c. Puts things off to the last minute.

4. Classroom discussions are:
   - ❏ a. Rarely helpful to me.
   - ❏ b. Sometimes helpful to me.
   - ❏ c. Almost always helpful to me.

5. When an instructor hands out directions for an assignment, I prefer:
   - ❏ a. Figuring out the instructions on my own.
   - ❏ b. Trying to follow directions on my own, then asking for help as needed.
   - ❏ c. Having the instructions explained orally.

6. I need faculty comments on my assignments:
   - ❏ a. Within a few weeks, since I can review what I did.
   - ❏ b. Within a few days or I forget what I did.
   - ❏ c. Right away or I get very frustrated.

7. Considering my professional and personal schedule, the amount of time I have to work on a course is:
   - ❏ a. More than enough for a campus or distance learning course.
   - ❏ b. The same as for taking a class on campus.
   - ❏ c. Less than for taking a class on campus.

8. When I am asked to use VCRs, computers, voice mail, or other technologies that may be new to me:
   - ❏ a. I look forward to learning new skills.
   - ❏ b. I feel apprehensive but try anyway.
   - ❏ c. I put it off and try to avoid it.

9. As a reader, I would classify myself as:
   - ❏ a. Good—I usually understand the text without help.
   - ❏ b. Average—I sometimes need help to understand the text.
   - ❏ c. Slower than average.

10. If I have to go on campus to take exams or complete lab work:
    - ❏ a. I can go to campus anytime.
    - ❏ b. I may miss some lab assignments or exam deadlines if campus labs are not open evenings and weekends.
    - ❏ c. I will have difficulty getting to the campus even in the evenings or on the weekends.

Scoring

Add 3 points for each "a" that you chose, 2 points for each "b," and 1 point for each "c." If you scored more than 25, distance learning is a real possibility for you. If you scored between 15 and 24, distance learning may work for you, but you may need to make a few adjustments to your schedule to succeed. If you scored 15 or less, distance learning may not currently be a suitable option for you. Here's why:

1. Course work might be neglected because of personal or family circumstances unless there are compelling reasons for completing a course.

2. Some students prefer the independence of distance learning courses; others find it uncomfortable.

3. Distance learning courses give you greater freedom to schedule your work, but they also require more self-discipline.

4. Some people learn best by interacting with other students, but distance learning does not afford as much opportunity for this type of interaction.

5. Distance learning courses require you to work from written directions without face-to-face explanations by the instructor.

6. It may take as long as two weeks to get comments back from your instructor by mail.

7. Distance learning courses require at least as much time as attending classes and completing assignments for campus courses.

8. Distance learning courses frequently use technology for teaching and communication.

9. Print materials are the primary source of directions and information in distance learning.

10. Some distance learning courses require three or four trips to the campus for examinations, and some require lab and library trips. Since evening and weekend lab hours may be limited, schedule flexibility is important.

Reading and Writing Skills

Learning through reading is the primary focus of most distance learning programs. Whether it is a textbook, a Web page, a correspondence course, or an e-mail communication, the ability to read and to absorb facts and ideas from print are critical to the success of a distance learning student. If you have not studied in a while, or if it was never really easy for you, then you will want to find a good book on study skills and read it before you take your first class.

Some people try highlighting key words as they read, or they ask themselves questions about what they just read. Others read the material out loud or review the entire book multiple times. Find what method works best for you and hone it to a fine edge. Taking a study skills class might be very useful, too.

Writing skills are just as important, if not more so, than in traditional education. If you write well, you will find it easier to put your thoughts into writing via e-mail and mailed replies. If writing, spelling, and grammar aren't your strong suits, your written messages may lead your instructor and fellow students to draw inaccurate conclusions about your ability. One nice thing about distance learning in all of its forms is that you can spend more time thinking about and responding to questions from instructors than you can in a traditional classroom setting. And you can use the spell check and grammar features of your e-mail or word processing software to make your replies as correct as possible.

Communication at a Distance

You will find that, in most cases, you will receive more individual attention from your instructors in distance learning courses than in traditional on-campus classes. It is not unusual for a professor to lecture to more than 300 students at a time in an ivy-covered hall. In distance learning, the professor has no choice but to communicate with each student one-on-one.

The same goes for your classmates. Many students have actually found that they interact more via e-mail and take more time to introduce themselves than they would in a classroom. Remember, you can't use first impressions and body language to get to know your classmates, so what you write in your e-mail message is what you are to them.

One of the best things about the Internet is that it is a great social equalizer. You will find yourself communicating with fellow class members without regard for appearance, race, sex, ethnicity, or other common prejudices.

By working long distance on group projects, you will also learn important distance collaboration skills that are real-world necessities when telecommuting or videoconferencing in your job. According to Brian Mueller, Vice President of Distance Education at the University of Phoenix, "There's a lot of talk in the workplace about *virtual teams* working together to complete projects. Our programs really help students develop that skill."

Having the support of your family, friends, and employer is important when you begin a distance learning program. Examine your lifestyle, determine where you can make time for your studies, set aside a private study space with a door that can be closed, and then have a serious discussion with your loved ones. Hold a family meeting to lay the ground rules for your study time and to make sure your children and spouse know how important your studies are to you. Trying to cope with your new schedule may be difficult without that support. If you know where you are heading and how you will get there, then the rewards are a bit more tangible. This advance planning and development of a support structure will help you stick it out to the end. By taking one day and one challenge at a time, you will hold a degree in your hands before you know it.

Special Skills and Resources

If you are participating in online courses, you will need some basic computer skills with word processing, Internet browser, and e-mail software. Like a microwave oven, you don't have to understand how it works to make it work, but it helps if you become generally familiar with your computer's abilities. Some of these skills can be learned as you go, but you will feel more comfortable with online learning if you take some basic computer classes first. Classes in Microsoft Word or Microsoft Office, basic Internet skills, and Internet research using search engines will be the most helpful. Another option would be to ask a knowledgeable friend for help. It shouldn't take more than a day of one-on-one tutoring to get the basics under control. You may feel overwhelmed at first, but every computer expert began by pushing a computer power button the first time.

If you are registered for televised courses, you will need a television set, cable TV connection or satellite dish, and VCR. Take away the cable connection and you will have everything you need to take correspondence courses that include videotapes.

Student Profiles

The average distance learning student works full time, is in his or her early 30s, and has already earned one college degree. But that's just the "average." This author was one of those not-so-average students. As the wife of a career military noncommissioned officer, I spent years living in exotic countries on remote Air Force bases that left few options for finishing a degree other than by distance learning. I know first hand how challenging it can be. In speaking with students all across the United States and Canada, I was inspired by their stories and wanted to share a few with you in the hopes that you would be motivated to lifelong learning.

Christine M. Danner
Business and Marketing Teacher
Institute of Business and Entrepreneurship
Flanagan High School
Broward County, FL

I recently completed my Master of Education in Secondary Education/Computer Technology from the University of North Florida by taking online courses. I earned my undergraduate degree the traditional way at Michigan State University in 1986, which led to a career in marketing for six years. Then I began to wonder about the direction of my life. Something was missing and I began to look for a way to further my education and contribute to society.

I started by taking night courses and working as a full-time high school teacher and part-time waitress. Somehow I managed to juggle all of my responsibilities and still find time for a small social life, which is how I met my future husband. When I was only two courses away from finishing my graduate degree, we were married and moved 300 miles away from the campus. Finding a new teaching position in south Florida wasn't difficult, but I was worried about completing my degree. I had come so far and could not let my dream slip away.

At about the same time, my faculty advisor at the University of North Florida was piloting a distance learning course. At her recommendation, I was allowed to apply the course to my degree program. My first experience with online learning was very challenging and interactive. As a class, we conversed regularly through an online service called Nicenet. Our course requirements were submitted weekly via an online assignment verification form set up by our instructor. Each assignment used different resources and required a variety of learning techniques. During the course of the semester, we videotaped ourselves teaching, conversed with other teachers across the world, reported back to the class, researched topics online, and studied from a textbook.

Over the past year, more professors at the University of North Florida have begun teaching at a distance. I took my final course from a professor who was spending the summer in Wyoming. The students in this course were required to complete individual weekly assignments and submit them via e-mail.

Thanks to these technology advancements, I was able to continue my studies and achieve my goal of graduation.

Patrick A. Kelleher
Lieutenant Colonel
United States Marine Corps
Deputy Chief of Counter-Space Operations
U.S. Space Command
Peterson Air Force Base, CO

As a test pilot in the Marine Corps, I was often required to fly across the country for extended periods of time, making it very difficult to complete my master's degree. While I was attending the U.S. Naval Test Pilot School, I learned of a graduate program offered via distance learning by the University of Tennessee that allowed me to transfer the credits I had earned in test pilot school toward a Master of Science in Aviation Systems.

I had earned my undergraduate degree in mechanical engineering from Gonzaga University in 1980. During my career as a Marine aviator, I had flown nearly 3,000 hours in more than 36 different aircraft models and types, including two and a half years as a test pilot at the Patuxent River test facility in Maryland. Even though I was satisfied with my military career, I wanted to set my sights on a graduate degree, so I enrolled in the University of Tennessee graduate program. This program offered a quality curriculum that didn't conflict with my military responsibilities.

All of the lectures were provided on videotape, which meant I could watch them any time of the day or night even while traveling. The on-base faculty representative and reliable telephone contacts at the home campus made it easy to get the help I needed. Because of this flexibility, I graduated in 1992 without sacrificing any of the quality you would expect from such a program.

Jeanette LeBlanc, Ph.D.
Chief of Program Evaluation
Human Relations Division, Center for Character Development
United States Air Force Academy, CO
Faculty of the University of Phoenix and Central Michigan University
Independent trainer, consultant, and speaker

Distance learning changed my life! I earned my Bachelor of Liberal Arts with a concentration in psychology from Regents College, State University of New York, while living in Germany (1989). It took less than one year from enrollment to earn that degree because of the number of credits I was able to transfer from traditional college classes and earn through examinations such as CLEP, DSST, ACT-PEP, and the advanced GRE.

Completing my undergraduate degree at such a rapid pace empowered me to achieve an even bigger dream—a master's degree in counseling from Georgia State University (1991) through a semi-traditional format of evening and weekend classes. I worked full time as a counselor at a private psychiatric hospital and at a residential program for abused adolescent girls during the two years it took to earn my graduate degree.

Graduate school was challenging and thrilling in so many ways, and I was hooked on learning. Immediately after graduation, I applied to a distance doctoral program at Walden University and was accepted. I was able to condense my residency into "regional intensive sessions" and summer sessions and completed my entire doctoral progam in two years instead of the traditional three to five years. In 1994, I earned a Ph.D. in Administration/Management with a specialization in Psychology of Human Behavior and Organizational Development.

Because of my three college degrees and outstanding external degree programs, I have been able to create a career of my own design. I would recommend nontraditional means of completing a college education to any student who seeks an opportunity for advanced learning, greater self-awareness and discipline, and career advancement.

As the great counselor and educator Eda Le Shan once said, "Excellence in life seems to me to be the way in which each human being makes the most of the adventure of living and becomes most truly and deeply himself, fulfilling his own nature in the context of a good life with other people. . . . What he knows and what he feels have equal importance in his life." May your adventure in life allow you to become most truly and deeply who you are meant to be. Pursue your college dreams boldly as you expand your heart, mind, and sphere of positive influence.

Joseph S. Stanjones
Captain, United States Army
Special Forces Detachment Commander
10th Special Forces Group (Airborne)
Fort Carson, CO

As a Special Forces officer, I spend as many as 200 days per year deployed overseas. At one point in my career I was trying to choose between staying in the Army or taking another path and decided I needed a master's degree either way. After some research, I chose the University of Phoenix Center for Distance Education because it used only the Internet. I began working on my MBA in Global Management in September of 1997 and completed more than one-third of my studies during my travels abroad.

My battalion made annual rotations to Bosnia and Herzogovina and, knowing that I would be stationed in Eastern Europe for extended periods of time, I chose an international Internet provider. I was fortunate to be stationed with the British Multinational Division HQ in Banja Luka, Republika Srpska. I was able to use the first and only Internet server available in the Republic (INECCO) to continue my studies. Even though it was not the fastest server, I was able to maintain contact with my academic advisor to register for classes, conduct research, and contact instructors for submission of all assignments.

Whether I decide to continue with my military career or pursue an international management position in the civilian sector, completing my degree via distance learning has helped me to reach my goal.

3 ▶ *Accreditation of Distance Learning*

Accreditation is simply a recognition, after evaluation, that in the judgment of peers, an institution is providing the educational services at a level of quality that society and the educational world have a right to expect (from the policy statement of the Middle States Association of Colleges and Schools). The focus of accreditation, regardless of the method of instructional delivery or physical location of the learner or the instructor, is on the consistency, quality, and integrity of an institution's academic programs. Distance learning programs must meet the same standards as all other offerings of a college or university.

There are two types of accreditation in the United States—institutional accreditation and specialized accreditation. Institutional accreditation is granted by regional and national accrediting commissions, and specialized accreditation is awarded to professional programs within institutions or to occupational schools. Accreditation is a voluntary process, and those institutions that choose to apply for accredited status undergo a rigorous process of peer review and self-regulation that includes:

1. A self-study conducted by the institution itself over an extended period of time—sometimes years.

2. An evaluation visit by a team of experienced academic colleagues whose function is to review the institution and to give it an informed, searching analysis. The focus of the team's attention is inevitably the intellectual work of the institution. The institution's organization, administration, facilities, and resources are examined for their effect on teaching and learning.

3. The institution studies the team's evaluation and writes a formal response to the accrediting association.

4. The accrediting association studies all the evaluation materials so that it can form its own conclusions relating to the quality of the institution's performance. It examines the institution's self-study document, the evaluation team's report, and the institution's formal response to that report.

5. Accreditation is either granted or denied.

6. Following accreditation, the institution must agree to abide by the standards of its accrediting organization. It must regulate itself and make periodic follow-up reports to ensure the improvement of the institution.

One of the benefits of accreditation is the assurance that you will be able to attain the same educational outcomes as you would in traditional classroom-based programs. You also have the right to the same admissions, registration, advising, counseling, tutoring, placement, and other student services that are available to all other students of a university, regardless of the delivery method of your classes. Without accreditation by a nationally recognized accrediting organization, a school is not eligible to participate in government student assistance programs, which means you, as a student, are not eligible for federal grant or loan money. Those employers who offer tuition assistance to employees will generally insist that a school be regionally accredited before reimbursing a student. Accreditation is also an important factor in the transferability of credits from one institution to another, although it is less important if you are taking courses for self-enrichment.

Who Accredits the Accreditors?

Not all accreditation associations are legitimate. It is not unusual for a diploma mill to create its own accrediting authority and then grant itself "accreditation"! So, how do you know that a college or university is accredited by a legitimate authority? It's really quite easy. There are two oversight organizations that accredit the accreditors. The first is the Council for Higher Education Accreditation (CHEA), a voluntary, nongovernmental organization. The second is a branch of the United States government, the U.S. Department of Education. More than 70 accrediting associations in the United States are recognized by CHEA or the U.S. Department of Education, or both.

CHEA was established in 1996 as a result of the dissolution of its two predecessor organizations, the Council on Postsecondary Accreditation (COPA) and the Commission on Recognition of Postsecondary Accreditation (CORPA). CHEA was established through the efforts of a group of college and university presidents and is accountable to its member institutions of higher learning. CHEA acts as the national policy center and clearinghouse on accreditation for the higher education community.

In Canada, all schools are regulated by provincial governments; no pan-Canadian accrediting body evaluates the quality of general undergraduate university programs. However, a number of agencies do perform this function for some professional programs at both the undergraduate and graduate levels. Membership in the Association of Universities and Colleges of Canada is generally assumed as evidence that an institution is providing programs with acceptable standards. Besides *accreditation,* the terms *university* and *college* are different in Canada, too. Universities are degree-granting institutions. Colleges, community colleges, CEGEPs, and institutes of technology do not grant degrees and tend to be more vocationally oriented.

For more information on accreditation in the United States and Canada, contact:

▸ Council for Higher Education Accreditation (CHEA)
  One Dupont Circle NW, Suite 510
  Washington, DC 20036-1135
  Phone: (202) 955-6126
  Fax: (202) 955-6129
  Web page: http://www.chea.org

▸ U.S. Department of Education
  Office of Postsecondary Education
  Washington, DC 20202-5171
  Phone: (202) 708-7417 or (800) 872-5327
  Fax: (202) 708-9469
  Web page: http://www.ifap.ed.gov/csb_html/agency.htm

- Council of Ministers of Education
  252 Bloor Street West, Suite 5-200
  Toronto, Ontario, Canada M5S 1V5
  Phone: (416) 954-2551
  Fax: (416) 964-2296
  Web page: http://www.cmec.ca/

Who Accredits Colleges and Universities?

Regional Accreditation

Six regional accrediting organizations are responsible for accrediting the majority of colleges and universities in the United States. These associations accredit entire institutions. All of these associations have been approved by both CHEA and the U.S. Department of Education:

- New England Association of Schools and Colleges
  (Connecticut, Maine, Massachusetts, New Hampshire, Rhode Island, and Vermont)
  209 Burlington Road
  Bedford, MA 07130-1433
  Phone: (781) 271-0022
  Fax: (781) 271-0950
  Web page: http://www.neasc.org

- Middle States Association of Colleges and Schools
  (Delaware, District of Columbia, Maryland, New Jersey, New York, Pennsylvania, Puerto Rico, and the Virgin Islands)
  3624 Market Street
  Philadelphia, PA 19104
  Phone: (215) 662-5606
  Fax: (215) 662-5950
  Web page: http://www.msache.org

- North Central Association of Colleges and Schools
  (Arizona, Arkansas, Colorado, Illinois, Indiana, Iowa, Kansas, Michigan, Minnesota, Missouri, Nebraska, New Mexico, North Dakota, Ohio, Oklahoma, South Dakota, West Virginia, Wisconsin, and Wyoming)
  30 North LaSalle, Suite 2400
  Chicago, IL 60602-2504
  Phone: (312) 263-0456
  Fax: (312) 263-7462
  Web page: http://www.ncacihe.org

- Northwest Association of Schools and Colleges
  (Alaska, Idaho, Montana, Nevada, Oregon, Utah, and Washington)
  11130 NE 33rd Place, Suite 120
  Bellevue, WA 98004
  Phone: (425) 827-2005

Fax: (425) 827-3395
Web site: http://www.cocnasc.org

- Southern Association of Colleges and Schools
(Alabama, Florida, Georgia, Kentucky, Louisiana, Mississippi, North Carolina, South Carolina, Tennessee, Texas, and Virginia)
1866 Southern Lane
Decatur, GA 30033-4097
Phone: (404) 679-4500 or (800) 248-7701
Fax: (404) 679-4558
Web page: http://www.sacscoc.org

- Western Association of Schools and Colleges
(California, Guam, and Hawaii)
3402 Mendocino Avenue
Santa Rosa, CA 95403-2244
Phone: (707) 569-9177
Fax: (707) 569-9179
Web page: http://www.wascweb.org

Canadian Accreditation

Since provincial governments control the accreditation of schools in Canada, you can contact the following departments and ministries for more information:

- Newfoundland Department of Education
3rd Floor, Confederation Building, West Block
P.O. Box 8700
St. John's, Canada A1B 4J6
Phone: (709) 729-5097
Fax: (709) 729-5896
Web page: http://public.gov.nf.ca/edu/

- Nova Scotia Department of Education and Culture
P.O. Box 578
Halifax, NS, Canada B3J 2S9
Phone: (902) 424-5605 or (902) 424-5168
Fax: (902) 424-0511
Web page: http://www.ednet.ns.ca/

- Prince Edward Island Department of Education
P.O. Box 2000
Sullivan Building, 2/3 Floors
16 Fitzroy Street
Charlottetown, PE, Canada C1A 7N8
Phone: (902) 368-4600
Fax: (902) 368-4663 or (902) 368-4622
Web page: http://www.gov.pe.ca/educ/

- New Brunswick Department of Education
  P.O. Box 6000
  Fredericton, NB E3B 5H1, Canada
  Phone: (506) 453-3678
  Fax: (506) 453-3325
  Web page: http://www.gov.nb.ca.education

- Quebec Ministry of Education
  Édifice Marie-Guyart
  11e étage, 1035, rue de la Chevrotière
  Quebec, QC G1R 5A5, Canada
  Phone: (418) 643-7095
  Fax: (418) 646-6561
  Web page: http://www.meq.gouv.qc.ca/

- Ontario Ministry of Education and Training
  Mowat Block
  900 Bay Street
  Toronto, ON M7A 1L2, Canada
  Phone: (416) 325-2929 or (800) 367-5514
  Fax: (416) 325-2934
  Web page: http://www.edu.gov.on.ca/

- Manitoba Department of Education
  Legislative Building
  450 Broadway
  Winnipeg, MB R3C 0V8, Canada
  Phone: (204) 945-2211
  Fax: (204) 945-8692
  Web page: http://www.gov.mb.ca/educate/

- Saskatchewan Department of Education
  Department of Post-Secondary Education and Skills Training
  2220 College Avenue
  Regina, SK S4P 3V7, Canada
  Phone: (306) 787-6030
  Fax: (306) 787-2280
  Web page: http://www.sasked.gov.sk.ca/

- Alberta Department of Education
  West Tower, Devonian Building
  11160 Jasper Avenue
  Edmonton, AB T5K 0L2, Canada
  Phone: (403) 427-7219
  Fax: (403) 427-0591
  Web page: http://ednet.edc.gov.ab.ca or http://www.aecd.gov.ab.ca/

- British Columbia Ministry of Education
  P.O. Box 9156, Stn. Prov. Govt.
  Victoria, BC V8W 9H2, Canada

Phone: (250) 387-4611
Fax: (250) 356-5945
Web page: http://www.bced.gov.bc.ca/ or http://www.aett.gov.bc.ca/

Ministry of Advanced Education, Training and Technology
Phone: (250) 356-2771
Fax: (250) 356-3000

▸ Northwest Territories Department of Education, Culture, and Employment
P.O. Box 1320
4501 50th Avenue
Yellowknife, NT X1A 2L9, Canada
Phone: (867) 920-6240
Fax: (867) 873-0456
Web page: http://siksik.learnnet.nt.ca/ece/

▸ Yukon Department of Education
P.O. Box 2703
Whitehouse, YT Y1A 2C6, Canada
Phone: (867) 667-5141
Fax: (867) 393-6339
Web page: http://www.gov.yk.ca/depts/education/

Even though it is not an accrediting organization, the following association represents most of the universities and university-level colleges in the country:

▸ Association of Universities and Colleges of Canada
350 Albert Street, Suite 600
Ottawa, Ontario K1R 1B1, Canada
Phone: (613) 563-1236
Fax: (613) 563-9745
Web page: http://www.aucc.ca

Specialized Accreditation

Some national accrediting bodies accredit only specific kinds of schools, such as religious schools, home study institutions, and some trade and technical schools. Others accredit individual programs or departments within a college. This is more common in the professions where it is sometimes more important that a program or department be accredited by the profession's accrediting body than it is for the entire institution to be accredited by a regional or national accrediting organization. For instance, some school districts hire only teachers who have earned their degrees from schools approved by the National Council for Accreditation of Teacher Education (NCATE).

The following agencies accredit entire schools:

Bible Colleges

‣ American Association of Bible Colleges
P.O. Box 1523
130 F North College Avenue
Fayetteville, AR 72701
Phone: (501) 521-8164
Fax: (501) 521-9202
Web page: http://www.aabc.org

Career and Technology Schools

‣ Accrediting Commission for Career Schools and Colleges of Technology (ACCSCT)
2101 Wilson Boulevard, Suite 302
Arlington, VA 22201
Phone: (703) 247-4212
Fax: (703) 247-4533
Web page: http://www.accsct.org

Distance Education

‣ Distance Education and Training Council (DETC)
1601 18th Street, NW
Washington, DC 20009-2529
Phone: (202) 234-5100
Fax: (202) 332-1386
Web page: http://www.detc.org

Health Education

‣ Accrediting Bureau of Health Education Schools (ABHES)
2700 South Quincy Street, Suite 210
Arlington, VA 22206
Phone: (703) 998-1200
Fax: (703) 998-2550
Web page: http://www.abhes.org

Independent Colleges

‣ Accrediting Council for Independent Colleges and Schools (ACISC)
750 First Street NE, Suite 980
Washington, CD 20002-4241
Phone: (202) 336-6780
Fax: (202) 842-2593
Web page: http://www.acics.org

Occupational Education

▸ Council on Occupational Education (COE)
41 Perimeter Center East, NE, Suite 640
Atlanta, GA 30346
Phone: (770) 396-3898 or (800) 917-2081
Fax: (770) 396-3790

Rabbinical and Talmudic Schools

▸ Association of Advanced Rabbinical and Talmudic Schools
175 Fifth Avenue, Room 711
New York, NY 10010
Phone: (212) 477-0950
Fax: (212) 533-5335

Theology

▸ Association of Theological Schools in the United States and Canada
10 Summitt Park Drive
Pittsburgh, PA 15275-1103
Phone: (412) 788-6505
Fax: (412) 788-6510
Web page: http://www.ats.edu

The following specialized and professional accrediting associations are responsible for evaluating specific programs within a college or university.

Acupuncture

▸ Accreditation Commission for Acupuncture and Oriental Medicine
1010 Wayne Avenue, Suite 1270
Silver Spring, MD 20910
Phone: (301) 608-9680
Fax: (301) 608-9576

Allied Health

▸ Accreditation Review Committee on Education for the Anesthesiologist's Assistant
Emory University School of Medicine
617 Woodruff Memorial Building
Atlanta, GA 30322
Web page: http://www.shoestring.net.com/AAAA/

▸ Accrediting Bureau of Health Education Schools
803 West Broad Street, Suite 730
Falls Church, VA 22046

Phone: (703) 533-2082
Fax: (703) 533-2095
Web page: http://www.abhes.org

- American Association of Blood Banks (AABB)
Committee on Accreditation of Specialists in Blood Bank Technology Schools
8101 Glenbrook Road
Bethesda, MD 30814-2749
Phone: (301) 215-6589
Fax: (301) 951-3729
Web page: http://www.aabb.org

- Commission on Accreditation of Allied Health Education Programs (CAAHEP)
35 East Wacker Drive, Suite 1970
Chicago, IL 60601-2208
Phone: (312) 553-9355
Fax: (312) 553-9616
Web page: http://www.caahep.org

- Joint Review Committee on Educational Programs in Athletic Training
Department of Physical Education
Indiana State University
Terre Haute, IN 47809-1001
Phone: (812) 237-2520
Fax: (812) 237-4338
Web page: http://www.maama.indstate.edu/dls/ug/preprof/athltran.html

- Joint Review Committee on Education in Cardiovascular Technology (JRC-CVT)
3525 Ellicott Mills Drive, Suite N
Ellicott City, MD 21043-4547
Phone: (410) 418-4800, x223
Fax: (410) 418-4805

- Cytotechnology Programs Review Committee
American Society of Cytopathology
400 West Ninth Street, Suite 201
Wilmington, DE 19801-1555
Phone: (302) 429-8802
Fax: (302) 429-8807
Web page: http://www.cytopathology.org

- JRC-Education in Diagnostic Medical Sonography
7108-C South Alton Way
Englewood, CO 80112-2106
Phone: (303) 741-3533
Fax: (303) 741-3655
Web page: http://www.caahep.org/DMS.htm

- Joint Review Committee on Education in Electroneurodiagnostic Technology
Route 1, Box 62A
Genoa, WI 54632

Phone: (608) 689-2058
Fax: (608) 791-9799
Web page: http://www.caahep.org/END.htm

- Joint Review Committee on Educational Programs for the
Emergency Medical Technician-Paramedic
7108-C South Alton Way
Englewood, CO 80112-2106
Phone: (303) 741-3533
Fax: (303) 741-3655
Web page: http://www.caahep.org/EMTP.htm

- Council on Accreditation (American Health Information Management Association)
919 North Michigan Avenue, Suite 1400
Chicago, IL 60611-1683
Phone: (312) 787-2672 x400
Fax: (312) 787-4150
Web page: http://www.ahima.org

- Curriculum Review Board of the American Association of Medical Assistants' Endowment
20 North Wacker Drive, Suite 1575
Chicago, IL 60606
Phone: (312) 899-1500
Fax: (312) 899-1259
Web page: http://www.aama-ntl.org

- Accreditation Review Committee for the Medical Illustrator
University of Illinois at Chicago
1919 West Taylor, Room 213
Chicago, IL 60612-7249
Phone: (312) 996-1303
Fax: (312) 996-8342
Web page: http://medical-illustrators.org

- Committee on Accreditation for Ophthalmic Medical Personnel
JCAHPO
2025 Woodland Drive
St. Paul, MN 55125-2995
Phone: (612) 731-2944
Fax: (612) 731-0410
Web page: http://www.jcahpo.com

- National Commission on Orthotic and Prosthetic Education (NCOPE)
1650 King Street, Suite 500
Alexandria, VA 22314
Phone: (703) 836-7114
Fax: (703) 836-0838
Web page: http://www.cloudnet.com/~oandpnet/NCOPE.html

- Accreditation Committee for Perfusion Education
  7108-C South Alton Way
  Englewood, CO 80112-2106
  Phone: (303) 741-3533
  Fax: (303) 741-3655
  Web page: http://www.caahep.org/PERF.htm

- Accreditation Review Committee on Education for the Physician Assistant
  Marshfield Clinic
  1000 N. Oak Avenue
  Marshfield, WI 54449-5788
  Phone: (715) 389-3785
  Fax: (715) 389-3131
  Web page: http://www.apap.org

- Joint Review Committee for Respiratory Therapy Education
  1701 West Euless Boulevard, Suite 300
  Euless, TX 76040-6823
  Phone: (817) 283-2835
  Fax: (817) 354-8519
  Web page: http://www.coarc.com

- Accreditation Review Committee on Education in Surgical Technology
  7108-C South Alton Way
  Englewood, CO 80112-2106
  Phone: (303) 741-3533
  Fax: (303) 741-3655
  Web page: http://www.ast.org

- Committee on Accreditation of Education Programs for Kinesiotherapy
  100 East Broadway
  Greenwood, IN 46143
  Phone: (317) 554-0000 x2906
  Fax: (317) 554-0070
  Web page: http://www.orst.edu/instruct/exss132/kinprog.html#10part10

Art and Design

- National Association of Schools of Art and Design
  11250 Roger Bacon Drive, Suite 21
  Reston, VA 21090
  Phone: (703) 437-0700
  Fax: (703) 437-6312
  Web page: http://www.arts-accredit.org

Chiropractic Education

- The Council on Chiropractic Education
  7975 North Hayden Road, Suite A-210
  Scottsdale, AZ 85258

Phone: (602) 443-8877
Fax: (602) 483-7333
Web page: http://www.amerchiro.org/webdocs/cce.html

Christian Education

▸ Transnational Association of Christian Schools
P.O. Box 328
Forest, VA 24551
Phone: (804) 525-9539
Fax: (804) 525-9538
Web page: http://www.lynchburg.net/community/tracs

Clinical Laboratory Science

▸ National Accrediting Agency for Clinical Laboratory Science (NAACLS)
8410 West Bryn Mawr Avenue, Suite 670
Chicago, IL 60631
Phone: (312) 714-8880
Fax: (312) 714-8886
Web page: http://www.mcs.net/~naacls/

Clinical Pastoral Education

▸ Association for Clinical Pastoral Education
1549 Claremont Road, Suite 103
Decatur, GA 30033-4611
Phone: (404) 320-1472
Fax: (404) 320-0849
Web page: http://www.acpe-edu.org

Computer Science

▸ Computing Sciences Accreditation Board
Two Landmark Square, Suite 209
Stamford, CT 06901
Phone: (203) 975-1117
Fax: (203) 975-1222
Web page: http://www.csab.org/~csab

Construction Education

▸ American Council for Construction Education
1300 Hudson Lane, Suite 3
Monroe, LA 70201-6054
Phone: (318) 323-2816
Fax: (318) 323-2413
Web page: http://www.calpoly.edu/~cm/acce/

Continuing Education

- Accrediting Council for Continuing Education and Training
  1200 19th Street, NW, Suite 200
  Washington, DC 20036
  Phone: (202) 955-1113
  Fax: (202) 955-1118
  Web page: http://www.accet.org

Cosmetology

- National Accrediting Commission of Cosmetology Arts and Sciences
  901 North Stuart Street, Suite 900
  Arlington, VA 22203
  Phone: (703) 527-7600
  Web page: http://www.naccas.org

Counseling

- American Association for Counseling and Development
  5999 Stevenson Avenue
  Alexandria, VA 22304
  Phone: (703) 823-9800 x301
  Fax: (703) 823-0252
  Web page: http://www.counseling.org

Dance

- National Association of Schools and Dance
  11250 Roger Bacon Drive, Suite 21
  Reston, VA 20190
  Phone: (703) 437-0700
  Fax: (703) 437-6312
  Web page: http://www.arts-accredit.org

Dentistry and Dental Auxiliary Programs

- American Dental Association
  211 East Chicago Avenue, 18th Floor
  Chicago, IL 60611
  Phone: (800) 621-8099 or (312) 440-2500
  Fax: (312) 440-2915
  Web page: http://www.ada.org

Dietetics

- The American Dietetic Association
  216 West Jackson Boulevard, Suite 800
  Chicago, IL 60606-6995
  Phone: (312) 899-4872
  Fax: (312) 899-1758
  Web page: http://www.eatright.org

Engineering

- Accreditation Board for Engineering and Technology
  111 Market Place, Suite 1050
  Baltimore, MD 21202
  Phone: (410) 347-7700
  Fax: (410) 625-2238
  Web page: http://www.abet.org

Environment

- National Environmental Health Science and Protection Accreditation Council
  Environmental Health
  College of Health and Human Services
  102 Health Center
  Bowling Green State University
  Bowling Green, OH 43403-0280
  Phone: (419) 372-7774
  Fax: (419) 372-2897
  Web page: http://www.cdc.gov/nceh/programs/ehserv/EHSA/academic/nehac.htm

Family and Consumer Sciences

- American Association of Family and Consumer Sciences (AAFCS)
  1555 King Street
  Alexandria, VA 22314
  Phone: (703) 706-4600
  Fax: (703) 706-4663
  Web page: http://www.aafcs.org

Forestry

- Society of American Foresters
  5400 Grosvenor Lane
  Bethesda, MD 20814-2198
  Phone: (301) 897-8720 x119
  Fax: (301) 879-3690
  Web page: http://www.safnet.org

Funeral Service Education

- American Board of Funeral Service Education
  13 Gurnet Road, #316
  P.O. Box 1305
  Brunswick, MA 04011
  Phone: (207) 798-5801
  Fax: (207) 798-5988
  Web page: http://www.abfse.org

Health Services Administration

- Accrediting Commission on Education for Health Services Administration
  1911 North Fort Myer Drive, Suite 503
  Arlington, VA 22209-1603
  Phone: (202) 822-8561
  Fax: (202) 822-8555
  Web page: http://monkey.hmi.missouri.edu/acehsa

Interior Design

- Foundation for Interior Design Education Research
  60 Monroe Center NW, #300
  Grand Rapids, MI 49503-2920
  Phone: (616) 458-0400
  Fax: (616) 458-0460
  Web page: http://www.fider.org

Journalism

- Accrediting Council on Education in Journalism and Mass Communications
  School of Journalism
  University of Kansas
  Stauffer-Flint Hall
  Lawrence, KS 66045
  Phone: (913) 864-3986
  Fax: (913) 864-5225
  Web page: http://www.ukans.edu/~acejmc/

Landscaping Architecture

- American Society of Landscape Architects
  4401 Connecticut Avenue NW, Fifth Floor
  Washington, DC 20008-2369
  Phone: (202) 686-2752
  Fax: (202) 686-1001
  Web page: http://www.asla.org/asla/

Law

- American Bar Association
  550 West North Street
  Indianapolis, IN 46202
  Phone: (317) 264-8340
  Fax: (317) 264-8355
  Web page: http://abanet.org/legaled

- Association of American Law Schools
  1201 Connecticut Avenue NW, Suite 800
  Washington, DC 20036-2605
  Phone: (202) 296-8851
  Fax: (202) 296-8869
  Web page: http://www.aals.org

Liberal Education

- American Academy for Liberal Education
  1015 18th Street, NW, Suite 204
  Washington, DC 20036
  Phone: (202) 452-8611
  Fax: (202) 452-8620

Librarianship

- American Library Association
  50 East Huron Street
  Chicago, IL 60611
  Phone: (800) 545-2433, x2436
  Fax: (312) 280-2433
  Web page: http://www.ala.org

Marriage and Family Therapy

- American Association for Marriage and Family Therapy
  1133 15th Street NW, Suite 300
  Washington, DC 20005-2710
  Phone: (202) 452-0109
  Fax: (202) 223-2329
  Web page: http://www.aamft.org

Medicine

- In odd-numbered years beginning each July 1, contact:
  American Medical Association
  515 North State Street
  Chicago, IL 60610

Phone: (312) 464-4933
Fax: (312) 464-5830
Web page: http://www.ama-assn.org

- In even-numbered years beginning each July 1, contact:
Association of American Medical Colleges
2450 North Street, NW
Washington, DC 20037
Phone: (202) 828-0596
Fax: (202) 828-1125
Web page: http://www.aamc.org

Montessori Education

- Montessori Accreditation Council for Teacher Education
Commission on Accreditation
University of Wisconsin – Parkside, Tallent Hall
900 Wood Road, P.O. Box 2000
Kenosha, WI 53141-2000
Web page: http://www.angelfire.com/ma/MACTEcommission

Music

- National Association of Music Schools
11250 Roger Bacon Drive, Suite 21
Reston, VA 22090
Phone: (703) 437-0700
Fax: (703) 437-6312
Web page: http://www.arts-accredit.org

Naturopathic Medicine

- Council on Naturopathic Medical Education
P.O. Box 11426
Eugene, OR 97440-3626
Phone: (541) 484-6028
Web page: http://www.cnme.org

Nuclear Medicine

- Joint Review Committee on Educational Programs in
Nuclear Medicine Technology (JRCNMT)
One Second Avenue East, Suite C
Polson, MT 59860-2320
Phone: (406) 883-0003
Fax: (406) 883-0022

Nurse Anesthesia

- Council on Accreditation of Nurse Anesthesia Educational Programs
  222 South Prospect, Suite 304
  Park Ridge, IL 60068-4010
  Phone: (847) 692-7050
  Fax: (847) 692-7137
  Web page: http://www.aana.com

Nurse Practitioners

- National Association of Nurse Practitioners in Reproductive Health
  Council on Accreditation
  1090 Vermont Avenue NW, Suite 800
  Washington, DC 20005
  Phone: (202) 408-7025
  Fax: (202) 408-0902
  Web page: http://www.nurse.org/nanprh/

Nursing

- National League for Nursing
  350 Hudson Street
  New York, NY 10014
  Phone: (800) 669-1656
  Fax: (212) 898-3710
  Web page: http://www.nln.org

- American College of Nurse-Midwives
  818 Connecticut Avenue NW, Suite 900
  Washington, DC 20006
  Phone: (202) 728-9877
  Fax: (202) 728-9897
  Web page: http://www.midwife.org

Occupational Education

- Accreditation Commission of Career Schools and Colleges of Technology
  2101 Wilson Boulevard, Suite 302
  Arlington, VA 22201
  Phone: (703) 247-4212
  Fax: (703) 247-4533
  Web page: http://www.accsct.org

- Council on Occupational Education
  41 Perimeter Center East NE, Suite 640
  Atlanta, GA 30346
  Phone: (770) 396-3898 or (800) 917-2081

Fax: (770) 396-3790
Web page: http://www.council.org

Occupational Therapy

▸ Accreditation Council for Occupational Therapy Education
American Occupational Therapy Association (AOTA)
4720 Montgomery Lane
P.O. Box 31220
Bethesda, MD 20824-1220
Phone: (301) 652-2682
Fax: (301) 652-7711
Web Page: http://www.aota.org

Opticianry

▸ Commission on Opticianry Accreditation
10341 Democracy Lane
Fairfax, VA 22030-2521
Phone: (703) 352-8028
Fax: (703) 691-3929
Web page: http://www.COAaccreditation.com

Optometry

▸ American Optometric Association
243 North Lindbergh Boulevard
St. Louis, MO 63141
Phone: (314) 991-4100
Fax: (314) 991-4101
Web page: http://www.opted.org or http://www.aoanet.org

Osteopathic Medicine

▸ American Osteopathic Association
142 East Ontario Street
Chicago, IL 60611-2864
Phone: (312) 280-5840
Fax: (312) 280-3860
Web page: http://www.am-osteo-assn.org

Pastoral Education (Clinical)

▸ Association for Clinical Pastoral Education, Inc.
Accreditation Commission
1549 Claremont Road, Suite 103
Decatur, GA 30033-4611

Phone: (404) 320-1472
Fax: (404) 320-0849
Web page: http://www.acpe-edu.org/

Pharmacy

▸ American Council on Pharmaceutical Education
311 West Superior Street, Suite 512
Chicago, IL 60610
Phone: (312) 664-3575
Fax: (312) 664-4652
Web page: http://www.acpe-accredit.org

Physical Therapy

▸ American Physical Therapy Association
1111 North Fairfax Street
Alexandria, VA 22314
Phone: (703) 706-3245
Fax: (703) 684-7343
Web page: http://www.apta.org

Planning

▸ American Institute of Certified Planners
Association of Collegiate Schools of Planning
Planning Accreditation Board
Merle Hay Tower, Suite 302
3800 Merle Hay Road
Des Moines, IA 50310
Phone: (515) 252-0729
Fax: (515) 252-7404
Web page: http://gis2.arch.gatech.edu/acsp/

Podiatry

▸ American Podiatric Medical Association
9312 Old Georgetown Road
Bethesda, MD 20814-2752
Phone: (301) 571-9200
Fax: (301) 581-9299
Web page: http://www.apma.org

Psychology

▸ American Psychological Association
750 First Street NE
Washington, DC 20002-4242
Phone: (202) 336-5979
Fax: (202) 336-5978
Web page: http://www.apa.org/ed/accred.html

Public Affairs and Administration

▸ National Association of Schools of Public Affairs and Administration
1120 G Street NW, Suite 730
Washington, DC 20005
Phone: (202) 628-8965
Fax: (202) 626-4978
Web page: http://cwis.unomaha.edu/~wwwpa/nashome.html

Public Health

▸ Council on Education for Public Health
1015 Fifteenth Street NW, Suite 403
Washington, DC 20005
Phone: (202) 789-1050
Fax: (202) 789-1895

Radiologic Technology

▸ Joint Review Committee on Education in Radiologic Technology
20 North Wacker Drive, Suite 900
Chicago, IL 60606-2901
Phone: (312) 704-5300
Fax: (312) 704-5304
Web page: http://idt.net/~jrcert

Recreation and Parks

▸ National Recreation and Parks Association
22377 Belmont Ridge Road
Ashburn, VA 20148
Phone: (703) 858-0784
Fax: (703) 671-6772
Web page: http://www.nrpa.org

Rehabilitation Counseling

- Council on Rehabilitation Education
1835 Rohlwing Road, Suite E
Rolling Meadows, IL 60008
Phone: (847) 394-1785
Fax: (847) 394-2108
Web page: http://www.core-rehab.org

Social Work

- Council on Social Work Education
1600 Duke Street, Suite 300
Alexandria, VA 22314
Phone: (703) 683-8080
Fax: (703) 683-8099
Web page: http://www.cswe.org

Speech-Language Pathology and Audiology

- American Speech-Language-Hearing Association
10801 Rockville Pike
Rockville, MD 20852
Phone: (301) 897-5700
Fax: (301) 571-0457
Web page: http://www.asha.org

Teacher Education

- National Council for Accreditation of Teacher Education
2010 Massachusetts Avenue NW, Suite 200
Washington, DC 20036-1023
Phone: (202) 466-7496
Fax: (202) 296-6620
Web page: http://www.ncate.org

Veterinary Medicine

- American Veterinary Medical Association
1930 North Meacham Road, Suite 100
Schaumburg, IL 60173-4360
Phone: (847) 925-8070
Fax: (847) 925-1329
Web page: http://www.avma.org

For more information on accreditation, check out the following Web sites:

▶ American Association of Community Colleges (AACC): http://www.aacc.nche.edu

▶ American Association of State Colleges and Universities (AASCU): http://www.aascu.nche.edu

▶ American Council on Education (ACE): http://www.acenet.edu/

▶ Association of Specialized and Professional Accreditors (ASPA): http://www.chea.org/Directories/aspa.html

▶ Association of American Universities (AAU): http://www.tulane.edu~aau/index.html

▶ National Association of State Universities and Land Grant Colleges (NASULGC): http://www.nasulgc.nche.edu

Should You Consider an Unaccredited College?

The decision whether to charter a college or university is the responsibility of individual state governments. Some states are very strict when it comes to authorizing institutions that grant degrees and others are not. California and Louisiana were once famous for their lack of control over educational institutions, but they have improved their regulations within the past few years. At one time, a person could open a school in California for as little as $50,000 in assets and a quick, rubber-stamped government application. This, of course, led to a host of unaccredited schools, many of which were fraudulent. Hawaii now seems to have taken the place of California and Louisiana as the home to the most "diploma mills" in the United States.

On the other end of the spectrum, New York exercises tight control over all educational institutions in its state. Since 1784, the University of the State of New York has acted as an oversight organization to regulate all public and independent colleges and universities in New York. Its Board of Regents determines the state's educational policies and establishes standards for maintaining the quality of schools and the academic programs that lead to college degrees, licenses, and diplomas.

Once an educational institution has been chartered by a state, the school can operate legally without accreditation. As discussed previously in this chapter, regional accreditation is voluntary, and not all legitimate schools choose to go through the long process of accreditation. Remember, too, that all colleges and universities start out as unaccredited, so lack of accreditation does not necessary imply that a school is inferior. However, because of the uncertainty involved in listing unaccredited schools, this book includes only those colleges or universities that have been accredited by one of the six regional accreditation associations or the Distance Education and Training Council's Accrediting Commission.

If you decide that the best opportunity for you lies with an unaccredited college or university, look before you leap! Here are some steps you can take to ensure you are dealing with a legitimate institution:

1. Speak with knowledgeable people in your industry about whether a degree or certification from the school would be acceptable. In fields such as nursing and law, you might not be able to get a license if you attend an unaccredited college or university, even if you have a degree.

2. Call the school and ask why it is not accredited. Perhaps it has applied with one of the approved oversight organizations but has not yet been accepted for accreditation. If so, ask for the name, address, and phone number of the organization. Then call the accrediting body to verify the school's standing.

3. Ask the school for references and talk with former students.

4. Contact one of these state agencies for more information on the school's chartered status and reputation:

Alabama

- Alabama Commission on Higher Education
  Suite 205
  3465 Norman Bridge Road
  Montgomery, AL 36105-2310
  Phone: (334) 281-1998

- State Department of Education
  Gordon Persons Office Building
  50 North Ripley Street
  Montgomery, AL 36130-3901
  Phone: (205) 242-8082

- Department of Postsecondary Education
  401 Adams Avenue
  Montgomery, AL 36104
  Phone: (334) 242-2900

Alaska

- Alaska Commission on Postsecondary Education
  3030 Vintage Boulevard
  Juneau, AK 99801-7109
  Phone: (907) 465-2967

- State Department of Education
  Goldbelt Place
  801 West Tenth Street, Suite 200
  Juneau, AK 99801-1894
  Phone: (907) 465-8715

Arizona

▸ Arizona Commission for Postsecondary Education
2020 North Central Avenue, Suite 275
Phoenix, AZ 85004-4503
Phone: (602) 229-2531

▸ State Department of Education
1535 West Jefferson
Phoenix, AZ 85007
Phone: (602) 542-2147

▸ Arizona Board of Regents
2020 North Central Avenue, Suite 230
Phoenix, AZ 85004
Phone: (602) 229-2500

Arkansas

▸ Arkansas Department of Higher Education
114 East Capitol
Little Rock, AK 72201-3818
Phone: (501) 324-9300

▸ Arkansas Department of Education
4 State Capitol Mall, Room 304A
Little Rock, AK 72201-1071
Phone: (501) 682-4474

California

▸ California Student Aid Commission
3300 Zinfandel Drive
Rancho Cordova, CA 95670
Phone: (916) 526-7590

▸ California Department of Education
721 Capitol Mall
Sacramento, CA 95814
Phone: (916) 657-2451

▸ Postsecondary Education Commission
1303 J Street, Suite 500
Sacramento, CA 958814
Phone: (916) 445-7933

▸ Council for Private Postsecondary and Vocational Education
1027 Tenth Street, Fourth Floor
Sacramento, CA 95814
Phone: (916) 445-3427

Colorado

▸ Colorado Commission on Higher Education
Colorado Heritage Center
1300 Broadway, Second Floor
Denver, CO 80203
Phone: (303) 866-2723

▸ State Department of Education
201 East Colfax Avenue
Denver, CO 80203-1705
Phone: (303) 866-6779

Connecticut

▸ Connecticut Department of Higher Education
61 Woodland Street
Hartford, CT 06105-2391
Phone: (203) 566-3910

▸ Connecticut Department of Education
165 Capitol Avenue
P.O. Box 2219
Hartford, CT 06106-1630

Delaware

▸ Delaware Higher Education Commission
Carvel State Office Building, Fourth Floor
820 North French Street
Wilmington, DE 19801
Phone: (302) 577-3240

▸ State Department of Public Instruction
Townsend Building #279
Federal and Lockerman Streets
P.O. Box 1402
Dover, DE 19903-1402
Phone: (302) 739-4583

District of Columbia

▸ Department of Human Services
Office of Postsecondary Education, Research and Assistance
2100 Martin Luther King Jr. Avenue SE
Suite 401
Washington, DC 20020
Phone: (202) 727-3685

- District of Columbia Public Schools
  Division of Student Services
  4501 Lee Street NE
  Washington, DC 20019
  Phone: (202) 724-4934

- Education Licensure Commission
  717 14th Street NW, Suite 801
  Washington, DC 20005
  Phone: (202) 727-3511

Florida

- Florida Department of Education
  Office of Student Financial Assistance
  1344 Florida Education Center
  325 West Gaines Street
  Tallahassee, FL 32399-0400
  Phone: (850) 488-4234

- State Board of Independent Colleges and Universities
  Department of Education
  212 Collins Building
  Tallahassee, FL 32399
  Phone: (850) 488-8695

Georgia

- Georgia Student Finance Commission
  State Loans and Grants Division
  2082 East Exchange Place, Suite 245
  Tucker, GA 30084
  Phone: (770) 414-3000

- State Department of Education
  2054 Twin Towers East
  205 Butler Street
  Atlanta, GA 30334-5040
  Phone: (404) 656-5812

- Board of Regents of the University System of Georgia
  244 Washington Street SW
  Atlanta, GA 30334
  Phone: (404) 656-6050

- Georgia Nonpublic Postsecondary Education Commission
  2100 East Exchange Place, Suite 203
  Tucker, GA 30084
  Phone: (770) 414-3307

Hawaii

- Hawaii State Postsecondary Education Commission
2444 Dole Street, Room 202
Honolulu, HI 96822-2302
Phone: (808) 956-8213

- Hawaii Department of Education
2530 Tenth Avenue, Room A12
Honolulu, HI 96816
Phone: (808) 733-9103

Idaho

- Idaho Board of Education
P.O. Box 83720
Boise, ID 83720-0037
Phone: (208) 334-2270

- State Department of Education
650 West State Street
Boise, ID 83720
Phone: (208) 334-2113

Illinois

- Illinois Student Assistance Commission
1755 Lake Cook Road
Deerfield, IL 60015-5209
Phone: (708) 948-8500

- Illinois Board of Higher Education
4 West Old Capitol Plaza, Room 500
Springfield, IL 62701
Phone: (217) 782-2551

Indiana

- State Student Assistance Commission of Indiana
150 West Market Street, Suite 500
Indianapolis, IN 46204-2811
Phone: (317) 232-2350

- Indiana Department of Education
Center for Schools Improvement and Performance
Room 229 – State House
Indianapolis, IN 46204-2798
Phone: (317) 232-2305

- Commission for Higher Education
  101 West Ohio Street, Suite 550
  Indianapolis, IN 46204
  Phone: (317) 464-4400

- Commission on Proprietary Education (privately owned, vocational-technical schools)
  302 West Washington Street, Room 201
  Indianapolis, IN 46205-2767
  Phone: (317) 232-1320

Iowa

- Iowa College Student Aid Commission
  914 Grand Avenue, Suite 201
  Des Moines, IA 50309-2824
  Phone: (800) 383-4222

- Iowa Department of Education
  State Board of Regents
  Old Historical Building
  East 12th and Grand
  Des Moines, IA 50319
  Phone: (515) 281-3934

- Association of Independent Colleges and Universities (private institutions)
  505 Fifth Avenue, Suite 1030
  Des Moines, IA 50309-2399
  Phone: (515) 282-3175

Kansas

- Kansas Board of Regents
  700 SW Harrison, Suite 1410
  Topeka, KS 66603-3760
  Phone: (913) 296-3421

- State Department of Education
  Kansas State Education Building
  120 East Tenth Street
  Topeka, KS 66612-1103
  Phone: (913) 296-4876

- Kansas State Board of Education (vocational and community colleges)
  120 SE Tenth Avenue
  Topeka, KS 66612-1182
  Phone: (913) 296-3204

Kentucky

- Kentucky Higher Education Assistance Authority
  1050 U.S. 127 South, Suite 102
  Frankfort, KY 40601-4323
  Phone: (800) 928-8926

- State Department of Education
  500 Mero Street
  1919 Capital Plaza Tower
  Frankfort, KY 40601
  Phone: (502) 564-3421

- Council on Higher Education
  1024 Capital Center Drive, Suite 320
  Frankfort, KY 40601
  Phone: (502) 573-1555

Louisiana

- Louisiana Student Financial Assistance Commission
  Office of Student Financial Assistance
  P.O. Box 91202
  Baton Rouge, LA 70821-9202
  Phone: (800) 259-5626

- State Department of Education
  P.O. Box 94064
  626 North Fourth Street, 12th Floor
  Baton Rouge, LA 70804-9064
  Phone: (504) 342-2098

- Board of Regents
  150 Third Street, Suite 129
  Baton Rouge, LA 70804-9064
  Phone: (504) 342-4411

Maine

- Finance Authority of Maine
  P.O. Box 949
  Augusta, ME 04333-0949
  Phone: (207) 287-3263

- Maine Department of Education
  23 State House Station
  Augusta, ME 04333-0023
  Phone: (207) 287-5800
  TDD/TTY for Hearing-Impaired: (207) 287-2550

Maryland

- Maryland Higher Education Commission
  Jeffrey Building, 16 Francis Street
  Annapolis, MD 21401-1781
  Phone: (410) 974-2971

- Maryland State Department of Education
  200 West Baltimore Street
  Baltimore, MD 21201-2595
  Phone: (410) 767-0480

Massachusetts

- Massachusetts Board of Higher Education
  330 Stuart Street
  Boston, MA 02116
  Phone: (617) 727-9420

- State Department of Education
  350 Main Street
  Malden, MA 02148-5023
  Phone: (617) 388-3300

- Massachusetts Higher Education Information Center
  666 Boylston Street
  Boston, MA 20116
  Phone: (617) 536-0200 x4719

- Higher Education Coordinating Council
  One Ashburton Place, Room 1401
  Boston, MA 02108
  Phone: (617) 727-7785

Michigan

- Michigan Higher Education Assistance Authority
  Office of Scholarships and Grants
  P.O. Box 30462
  Lansing, MI 48909-7962
  Phone: (517) 373-3394

- Michigan Department of Education
  608 West Allegan Street
  Hannah Building
  Lansing, MI 48909
  Phone: (517) 373-3324

- Office of Higher Education Management
  P.O. Box 30008
  Lansing, MI 48909
  Phone: (517) 373-3820

Minnesota

- Minnesota Higher Education Services Office
  Capitol Square Building, Suite 400
  550 Cedar Street
  St. Paul, MN 55101-2292
  Phone: (800) 657-3866

- Department of Children, Families, and Learning
  712 Capitol Square Building
  550 Cedar Street
  St. Paul, MN 55101
  Phone: (612) 296-6104

Mississippi

- Mississippi Postsecondary Education
  3825 Ridgewood Road
  Jackson, MI 39211-6453
  Phone: (601) 982-6611

- State Department of Education
  P.O. Box 771
  Jackson, MS 39205-0771
  Phone: (601) 359-3768

Missouri

- Missouri Coordinating Board for Higher Education
  3515 Amazonas Drive
  Jefferson City, MO 65109-5717
  Phone: (573) 751-2361

- Missouri State Department of Elementary and Secondary Education
  P.O. Box 480
  205 Jefferson Street, Sixth Floor
  Jefferson City, MO 65102-0480
  Phone: (314) 751-2931

Montana

- Montana University System
  2500 Broadway
  Helena, MT 59620-3103
  Phone: (406) 444-6570

- State Office of Public Instruction
  State Capitol, Room 106
  Helena, MT 59620
  Phone: (406) 444-4422

Nebraska

▸ Coordinating Commission for Postsecondary Education
P.O. Box 95005
Lincoln, NE 68509-5005
Phone: (402) 471-2847

▸ Nebraska Department of Education
P.O. Box 94987
301 Centennial Mall South
Lincoln, NE 68509-4987
Phone: (402) 471-2784

Nevada

▸ Nevada Department of Education
400 West King Street
Capitol Complex
Carson City, NV 89710
Phone: (702) 687-5915

▸ Commission on Postsecondary Education
1820 East Sahara Avenue, Suite 111
Las Vegas, NV 89104

New Hampshire

▸ New Hampshire Postsecondary Education Commission
2 Industrial Park Drive
Concord, NH 03301-8512
Phone: (603) 271-2555

▸ State Department of Education
State Office Park South
101 Pleasant Street
Concord, NH 03301
Phone: (603) 271-2632

New Jersey

▸ State of New Jersey
Office of Student Financial Assistance
4 Quakerbridge Plaza, CN 540
Trenton, NJ 08625
Phone: (800) 792-8670

▸ State Department of Education
225 West State Street
Trenton, NJ 08625-0500
Phone: (609) 984-6409

- Commission on Higher Education
  P.O. Box 542
  Trenton, NJ 08625
  Phone: (609) 292-4310

New Mexico

- New Mexico Commission on Higher Education
  1068 Cerrillos Road
  Santa Fe, NM 87501-4925
  Phone: (505) 827-7383

- State Department of Education
  Education Building
  300 Don Gaspar
  Santa Fe, NM 87501-2786
  Phone: (505) 827-6648

New York

- New York State Higher Education Services Corporation
  One Commerce Plaza
  Albany, NY 12255
  Phone: (518) 474-5642

- State Education Department
  111 Education Building
  Washington Avenue
  Albany, NY 12234
  Phone: (518) 474-5705

North Carolina

- North Carolina State Education Assistance Authority
  P.O. Box 2688
  Chapel Hill, NC 27515-2688
  Phone: (919) 821-4771

- State Department of Public Instruction
  Education Building
  Division of Teacher Education
  116 West Edenton Street
  Raleigh, NC 27603-1712
  Phone: (919) 733-0701

- North Carolina System of Community Colleges
  Caswell Boulevard
  2000 West Jones Street
  Raleigh, NC 27603
  Phone: (919) 733-7051

North Dakota

- North Dakota University System
  North Dakota Student Financial Assistance Program
  600 East Boulevard Avenue
  Bismarck, ND 58505-0230
  Phone: (701) 328-2960

- State Department of Public Instruction
  State Capitol Building, 11th Floor
  600 East Boulevard Avenue
  Bismarck, ND 58505-0164
  Phone: (701) 224-2271

Ohio

- Ohio Board of Regents
  P.O. Box 182452
  309 South Fourth Street
  Columbus, OH 43218-2452
  Phone: (888) 833-1133

- State Department of Education
  65 South Front Street, Room 1005
  Columbus, OH 43266-0308
  Phone: (614) 466-2761

Oklahoma

- Oklahoma State Regents for Higher Education
  Oklahoma Guaranteed Student Loan Program
  P.O. Box 3000
  Oklahoma City, OK 73101-3000
  Phone: (405) 858-4300
  Phone: (800) 247-0420

- State Department of Education
  Oliver Hodge Memorial Education Building
  2500 North Lincoln Boulevard
  Oklahoma City, OK 73105-4599
  Phone: (405) 521-4122

Oregon

- Oregon State Scholarship Commission
  Suite 100, 1500 Valley River Drive
  Eugene, OR 97401-2130
  Phone: (503) 687-7400

- Oregon State System of Higher Education
  700 Pringle Parkway, SE
  Salem, OR 97310-0290
  Phone: (503) 378-5585

- Oregon Department of Education
  255 Capitol Street NE, Suite 126
  Salem, OR 97310-0203
  Phone: (503) 378-3921

Pennsylvania

- Pennsylvania Higher Education Assistance Agency
  1200 North Seventh Street
  Harrisburg, PA 17102-1444
  Phone: (800) 692-7435 or (717) 720-2075

- Bureau of Postsecondary Services
  Department of Education
  333 Market Street, 12th Floor
  Harrisburg, PA 17126
  Phone: (717) 783-6769

Rhode Island

- Rhode Island Board of Governors for Higher Education and
  Rhode Island Office of Higher Education
  301 Promenade Street
  Providence, RI 02908-5720
  Phone: (401) 222-6560

- Rhode Island Higher Education Assistance Authority
  560 Jefferson Boulevard
  Warwick, RI 02886
  Phone: (800) 922-9855

- State Department of Education
  22 Hayes Street
  Providence, RI 02908
  Phone: (401) 277-3126

South Carolina

- South Carolina Higher Education Tuition Grants Commission
  1310 Lady Street, Suite 811
  P.O. Box 12159
  Columbia, SC 29201
  Phone: (803) 734-1200

- State Department of Education
  803-A Rutledge Building
  1429 Senate Street
  Columbia, SC 29201
  Phone: (803) 734-8364

- Commission on Higher Education
  1333 Main Street, Suite 200
  Columbia, SC 29201
  Phone: (803) 737-2260

South Dakota

- Department of Education and Cultural Affairs
  Office of the Secretary
  700 Governors Drive
  Pierre, SD 57501-2291
  Phone: (605) 773-3134

- South Dakota Board of Regents
  207 East Capitol
  Pierre, SD 57501
  Phone: (605) 773-3455

Tennessee

- Tennessee Higher Education Commission
  404 James Robertson Parkway
  Suite 1900
  Nashville, TN 37243-0820
  Phone: (615) 741-3605

- State Department of Education
  100 Cordell Hull Building
  Nashville, TN 37219-5335
  Phone: (615) 741-1346 or (800) 342-1663 (TN residents only)

Texas

- Texas Higher Education Coordinating Board
  P.O. Box 12788, Capitol Station
  Austin, TX 78711
  Phone: (800) 242-3062

Utah

- Utah State Board of Regents
  Utah System of Higher Education
  355 West North Temple
  #3 Triad Center, Suite 550
  Salt Lake City, UT 84180-1205
  Phone: (801) 321-7205

- Utah State Office of Education
  250 East 500 South
  Salt Lake City, UT 84111
  Phone: (801) 538-7779

Vermont

- Vermont Student Assistance Corporation
  Champlain Mill
  P.O. Box 2000
  Winooski, VT 05404-2601
  Phone: (800) 642-3177

- Vermont Department of Education
  120 State Street
  Montpelier, VT 05620-2501
  Phone: (802) 828-3147

- Vermont State Colleges
  P.O. Box 359
  Waterbury, VT 05676
  Phone: (802) 241-2520

Virginia

- State Council of Higher Education for Virginia
  James Monroe Building
  101 North 14th Street
  Richmond, VA 23219
  Phone: (804) 786-1690

- State Department of Education
  P.O. Box 2120
  James Monroe Building
  14th and Franklin Streets
  Richmond, VA 23216-2120
  Phone: (804) 225-2072

Washington

▸ Washington State Higher Education Coordinating Board
P.O. Box 43430, 917 Lakeridge Way SW
Olympia, WA 98504-3430
Phone: (206) 753-7800

▸ State Department of Public Instruction
Old Capitol Building, P.O. Box FG 11
Olympia, WA 98504-3211
Phone: (206) 753-2858

West Virginia

▸ State Department of Education
1900 Washington Street
Building B, Room 358
Charleston, WV 25305
Phone: (304) 588-2691

▸ State College and University Systems of West Virginia Central Office
1018 Kanawha Boulevard East, Suite 700
Charleston, WV 25301-2827
Phone: (304) 558-0261

Wisconsin

▸ Higher Educational Aids Board
P.O. Box 7885
Madison, WI 53707-7885
Phone: (608) 267-2206

▸ State Department of Public Instruction
125 South Wester Street
P.O. Box 7841
Madison, WI 53707-7814
Phone: (608) 266-2364

▸ Higher Education Location Program (HELP)
432 North Lake Street, Room 401
Madison, WI 53706
Phone: (800) 442-4621

▸ Wisconsin Association of Independent Colleges and Universities
16 North Carroll Street, Suite 200
Madison, WI 53703-2716
Phone: (608) 256-7761

Wyoming

- Wyoming State Department of Education
  Hathaway Building
  2300 Capitol Avenue, Second Floor
  Cheyenne, WY 82002-0050
  Phone: (307) 777-6265

- Wyoming Community College Commission
  2020 Carey Avenue, Eighth Floor
  Cheyenne, WY 82002
  Phone: (307) 777-7763

American Samoa

- American Samoa Community College
  Board of Higher Education
  P.O. Box 2609
  Pago Pago, AS 96799-2609
  Phone: (684) 699-9155

- American Samoa Government
  Department of Education
  P.O. Box D.O.E.
  Pago Pago, AS 96799
  Phone: (684) 633-5237

Guam

- University of Guam
  303 University Drive
  Mangilao, GU 96923
  Phone: (671) 734-4469

Northern Mariana Islands

- Northern Marianas College
  P.O. Box 1250
  Saipan, Northern Mariana Islands 96950
  Phone: (670) 234-6128

- Commonwealth of the Northern Mariana Islands
  State Board of Public Education
  Public School System
  P.O. Box 1370, CK
  Saipan, Northern Mariana Islands 96950
  Phone: (670) 322-6402

Puerto Rico

▸ Council on Higher Education
Box 23305 – UPR Station
Rio Piedras, PR 00931
Phone: (809) 758-3350

▸ Department of Education
P.O. Box 759
Hato Rey, PR 00919
Phone: (809) 753-2200

Virgin Islands

▸ Virgin Islands Joint Boards of Education
P.O. Box 11900
St. Thomas, VI 00801
Phone: (809) 774-4546

▸ Virgin Islands Department of Education
Office of Federal Programs
44-46 Kongens Gade
St. Thomas, VI 00802
Phone: (809) 774-0100

Byrd Program Representatives for Marshall Islands, Micronesia, and Palau

▸ Federated States of Micronesia
1725 North Street, NW
Washington, DC 20036
Phone: (202) 223-4383

▸ Republic of the Marshall Islands
RMI Scholarship Grant and Loan Board
P.O. Box 1436
3 Lagoon Road
Majuro, Marshall Islands 96960
Phone: (692) 625-3108

▸ Republic of Palau
Ministry of Education Bureau
P.O. Box 9
Koror, Republic of Palau, TT 96940
Phone: (680) 488-1003

Shop! Shop! Shop!

You are spending big money. Potential students often spend more time shopping for a new suit than they spend evaluating their choice of college. It is a buyer's market, and serious students have the right to insist that programs meet their needs in terms of what is taught, when it is taught, and where it is taught. You should expect a school to be serious about the business of providing you with an education. You have the right to know whether a school has a good track record. To help ensure you are getting value for your hard-earned dollars, following is a script you can use to question all the schools you are considering, whether accredited or not:

- Are you accredited and by whom?

- How many students are enrolled?

- How many students graduate each year? (If the attrition rate is 50 percent or more, beware!)

- What are the demographics of your student body?

- What are the job placement rates of students in my area of study?

- What are the credentials of your faculty in my area of study? (i.e., where did they earn their diplomas, how many years have they taught, etc.)

- What is the average student-to-instructor ratio? (It should be no more than 20 students to each instructor, unless it is a one-time seminar.)

- Will I communicate with other students during the course of study in group projects, and if so, how will I communicate with them?

- Can I transfer credits from my previous college work?

- How many credits can I transfer to your college?

- Do you accept credits I have earned from examinations and experiential learning?

- Do you offer students services such as tutoring, financial aid, career placement, libraries, etc.?

- Does the program I am interested in have time limits for completion?

- How much does each credit cost?

- What other costs can I expect?

- Can I get a refund if I decide to withdraw from a course?

- Can I see work done by your students? (This will give you an idea about the quality of the school's instruction.)

- May I have the names and contact information for three former students so I might call them for references?

Before you are finished, call the Better Business Bureau in the city where the school is located, or call the Consumer Protection Division of your state's Attorney General's office. Ask them whether the school has any unresolved complaints or a track record of negative reports. Now you are ready to begin earning credits.

Earning and Transferring Credits

4

Colleges and universities often grant credit for a wide range of prior learning, including standardized proficiency examinations, portfolio assessment of experiential learning, local challenge examinations, assessment by a panel of experts, correspondence courses, and courses offered in your workplace. They now recognize that learning takes place in many environments and not just in the classroom.

The concept of granting college credits for learning, regardless of where it was gained, is not new. Many very famous European universities have granted credits and degrees for centuries based on the knowledge a student demonstrates on examinations and not on the amount of time spent in a classroom.

Credit Banks

Many students do not need to enroll in a degree or certificate program but do need to consolidate their academic records for employment, continuing education, or professional certification purposes. Credit banks provide the means for certifying college-level credits accumulated at various institutions without enrolling in a degree program. Credit earned for examinations, experiential learning, and extrainstitutional learning can be consolidated at a credit bank as well. There is no guarantee, however, that the credits you have been granted elsewhere will be accepted by a credit bank. Those credits accepted by the credit bank will be consolidated on a single transcript with the name of college or university that operates the credit bank, even though you may not have taken a single class at that school. There is, of course, a fee for this service, which can range anywhere from $75 to $335. Contact one of the following sources for more information:

- ▸ Regents College Credit Bank
  7 Columbia Circle
  Albany, NY 12203-5159
  Phone: (518) 464-8500
  Fax: (518) 464-8777
  Web page: http://www.regents.edu

- ▸ Thomas Edison State College Credit Bank
  101 West State Street
  Trenton, NJ 08608-1176
  Phone: (609) 633-6271
  Fax: (609) 984-8447
  Web page: http://www.tesc.edu

▶ Charter Oak State College
Credit Banking
66 Cedar Street
Newington, CT 06111-2646
Phone: (860) 666-4595
Fax: (860) 666-4852
Web page: http://cosc.edu

Credits by Examination

In the 1950s, when experienced adults began returning to colleges and universities after several years of work, they discovered that they knew as much as, if not more than, their instructors. They became bored, lost their motivation, and either dropped out altogether or reluctantly trudged through course after course just to obtain a degree. The colleges were unable to meet their needs because they were teaching them what they already knew, so, during the late 1950s and early 1960s, examinations were developed to test a person's knowledge and equate it to college learning. Depending on the results achieved on these tests, the student could earn college credits and fulfill the requirements for a course without sitting in a single class. This was the first step in meeting the needs of adult learners. Today, these equivalency examination include the CLEP, DANTES, and Regents College Examinations, among others. Credit can also be granted for completing the GRE, GMAT, LSAT, MSAT, and other proficiency examinations. The Proficiency Examination Program (PEP) offered by the American College Testing Program (ACT) was discontinued in 1998, but some colleges still grant credit for passing grades on previous exams.

Examinations are an inexpensive way to accumulate credit toward a degree by demonstrating knowledge gained outside the classroom. Earning credits through examination also allows the student to start studying at a higher level by earning credits for introductory classes, which saves valuable time in earning a degree.

The College-Level Examination Program (CLEP) is the most widely accepted credit-by-examination program in the United States. More than 2,800 accredited institutions of higher learning award credit for satisfactory scores on CLEP examinations in 5 general and 29 subject areas that cover courses typical of the first two years of college. The CLEP examinations include:

▶ *General Examinations:* College Mathematics, English Composition, Humanities, Natural Sciences, and Social Sciences and History.

▶ *Composition and Literature:* American Literature, Analyzing and Interpreting Literature, English Literature, and Freshman College Composition.

▶ *Foreign Languages:* College-Level French Language, German Language, and Spanish Language.

▶ *History and Social Sciences:* American Government, History of the United States I: Early Colonizations to 1877, History of the United States II: 1865 to the Present, Human Growth and Development, Introduction to Educational Psychology, Principles of Macroeconomics, Principles of Microeconomics, Introductory Psychology, Introductory Sociology, Western Civilization I: Ancient Near East to 1648, Western Civilization II: 1648 to the Present.

- *Science and Mathematics:* Calculus with Elementary Functions, College Algebra, College Algebra-Trigonometry, Trigonometry, General Biology, General Chemistry.

- *Business:* Information Systems and Computer Applications, Principles of Management, Principles of Accounting, Introductory Business Law, Principles of Marketing.

Your local bookstore or college library will have CLEP study guides to help prepare you for any of the tests. Barron's produces an excellent study guide, *How to Prepare for the CLEP—College-Level Examination Program, General Examination* (ISBN 0-8120-9007-1), for only $13.95 ($17.95 in Canada).

Advanced Placement (AP) tests are a good way for motivated high school students to earn college credits before they ever set foot in a college classroom. They are offered every May in high schools across the United States in such subjects as biology, calculus, chemistry, English, European history, French, physics, Spanish, statistics, U.S. government and politics, and U.S. history. Check with your high school counselor for testing dates and preparation help. Barron's publishes a series of test preparation guides to help you succeed on these examinations. You can find them in your school library, bookstore, or online at http://www.barronseduc.com.

The Defense Activity for Non-Traditional Education Support (DANTES) serves as a clearinghouse for information about training and testing in the military and Department of Defense. DANTES also provides educational testing and will help military personnel find suitable distance education programs that will minimize the loss of credit transfer. The DANTES Subject Standardized Tests (DSSTs) were developed by the Educational Testing Service under a contract with the Department of Defense. The tests are available to civilian as well as military personnel, and credits are granted for DSSTs at hundreds of colleges and universities in the United States.

You should contact the admissions and/or testing office of a college or university in your local area to determine where exams are being offered. You are not required to take these exams at the distance learning institution where you will be taking classes. The tests are standardized, and you can find convenient testing centers in your area. For instance, Regents College Examinations are given at Sylvan Technology Centers throughout the United States and Canada. The Educational Testing Service oversees most of the testing for CLEP, DANTES, TOEFL, GRE, GMAT, AP, SAT, and Praxis. Their Web site is a good place to start for study resources for all of the exams.

- Educational Testing Service (ETS)
  Rosedale Road
  Princeton, NJ 08541
  Phone: (609) 921-9000
  Fax: (609) 734-5410
  Web page: http://www.ets.org

- College-Level Examination Program (CLEP)
  The College Board
  P.O. Box 6600
  Princeton, NJ 08541-6600
  Phone: (609) 771-7865
  Fax: (609) 771-7088
  Web page: http://www.collegeboard.org

- DANTES, DSSTs
  6490 Saufley Field Road, Code 20A
  Pensacola, FL 32509-5243
  Phone: (904) 452-1745

- Regents College Examinations
  7 Columbia Circle
  Albany, NY 12203-5159
  Phone: (800) 479-5606
  Web page: http://www.regents.edu

Credits for Life Experiences

Besides testing, several other methods can be used to earn college credit for the knowledge you have gained outside a formal classroom. These include assessment of prior learning through essays, portfolio development, and expert panel interview. Whether your knowledge was gained through your work, travel, volunteering, hobbies, reading for personal development, or other activities, it can equate to college-level learning.

It is important, however, for you to differentiate between *learning* and *experience*. You can report for work every day for ten years, perform your job by rote, and never *learn* anything. Just because you experienced something doesn't necessarily mean you developed college-level learning from that experience. That learning must be at least equivalent to what other students have achieved in a comparable college class.

As an example, let's say you manufacture computer chips in a clean room. Every day you etch the same patterns, use the same chemicals, and inspect the finished products the same way. What have you learned besides the mechanics of your job? Probably not much. You have gained *experience*. Now let's say you are interested in getting ahead in your industry, so you grill your boss constantly with questions about the safe handling and disposal of the chemicals. You talk with the design engineers at every opportunity to find out about the functions of the patterns you are etching after they are installed in a computer. You read some books on quality control and develop a new procedure that salvages some of the defective chips. Now, what have you *learned*? You are beginning to master your craft and you are now ready to take a test, develop a portfolio, or be interviewed by a panel of experts.

Colleges and universities that assess experience for credit have developed extensive processes to ensure that students deserve that credit. Those processes are different for every school, so you must ask what each one requires for assessment of experiential learning. At the University of Phoenix, for example, a student can earn a maximum of 30 prior learning credits as a result of professional training (workshops, seminars, licenses, business and professional courses, and other institutionally sponsored course work). This learning must be documented in an "Experiential Learning Portfolio" that contains detailed evidence of learning outcomes, supporting documentation, and descriptions of personal and professional experience. This can include certifications (CPS, CPIM, CFM, CPCU, MSCE, ATC, PFSM, CPhT), diplomas, licenses (pilot, real estate, etc.), awards and citations, taped presentations, written speeches, manuscripts, photographs, newspaper articles, artwork, product samples, patents, musical scores, computer programs, printed programs, letters from third parties, and the list goes on, limited only by your imagination.

Once the portfolio is submitted, it is evaluated by faculty evaluators who hold advanced degrees in their respective disciplines. They are chosen for their educational and professional competence and are assigned according to their expertise. The quality of the evaluation process is assured through internal auditing of evaluations, comprehensive recordkeeping and tracking systems, and well-defined policies and procedures.

Most colleges and universities use the portfolio and essay methods to evaluate prior learning, but occasionally a student is required to undergo an oral interview instead. This is more likely to be required when demonstrating foreign language proficiency or presenting complex ideas. In such cases, an expert or group of experts questions the student, either in person or via audiotape or videotape. Even if the panel submits its questions in writing, the student is always required to respond to the questions orally. Avoid this type of assessment if you are uncomfortable with communicating orally.

Credits earned through portfolio development, essays, and expert panel interviews are often less expensive than taking an equivalent course. They can be as little as $25 or $50 per credit instead of $200 or more. Not only is it less expensive, but earning credit for experience also means you can achieve your degree goals faster. Since learning has already occurred, demonstrating that learning can take much less time, and you won't have to sit through a class covering information you already know.

For more information on assessment of prior learning, contact:

▸ Council for Adult and Experiential Learning (CAEL)
243 South Wabash Avenue #800
Chicago, IL 60604
Phone: (312) 922-5909

Extrainstitutional Learning

The American Council on Education (ACE) has been granting academic credit for military training since the mid-1940s. In 1974, ACE began using the same process to evaluate courses provided by corporations, business associations, labor unions, professional organizations, government agencies, and nonprofit organizations, among others. Under PONSI (Program on Noncollegiate Sponsored Instruction), the American Council on Education has determined the value of thousands of extrainstitutional courses offered by organizations whose primary business is not education.

The Board of Regents of the University of the State of New York sponsors a similar program called the National PONSI (National Program on Noncollegiate Sponsored Instruction). They not only evaluate extrainstitutional programs for credit but also promote the use of those credits with colleges and universities nationwide.

Another organization that assesses credit for extrainstitutional learning is the Service Members Opportunities College (SOC). They have evaluated how service and training in the military can be assessed for college credit. Many military programs have already been evaluated for equivalency to college credits. For more information, contact:

- Service Members Opportunities College
  One Dupont Circle, Suite 680
  Washington, DC 20036-1117
  Phone: (202) 667-0079 or (800) 368-5622

In addition to earning credit for courses you have already taken, you might try participating in some of the courses approved in your area, if they are not restricted to employees or members. Try to get your hands on one of the directories available from any of the following organizations. Since most of these directories are nearly $50, you may want to look for them first at your local library or college admissions office.

- American Council on Education (ACE)
  One Dupont Circle, Suite 250
  Washington, DC 20036
  Phone: (202) 939-9440
  Fax: (202) 833-4730
  Web page: http://www.acenet.edu

- National Program on Noncollegiate Sponsored Instruction
  University of the State of New York
  Cultural Education Center, Room 5A25
  Albany, NY 12230
  Phone: (518) 434-0118
  Fax: (518) 434-0253

- Educational Testing Service (ETS)
  Rosedale Road
  Princeton, NJ 08541
  Phone: (609) 921-9000
  Fax: (609) 734-5410
  Web page: http://www.ets.org

5 ▶ Financing the Cost of Distance Learning

You can finance the cost of higher education in many ways, but not all of them can be used for distance learning. Your first stop should always be the college's financial aid office. The experienced staff will know exactly which degree and certificate programs qualify for what types of financial aid. The school's Web site might also provide some of that information. A simple phone call to the school to request further information can get you started. In the meantime, here is some general information about the types of financing available for your education.

Grants

A grant is an outright gift of money that doesn't have to be repaid. The federal government and most state governments offer grant programs that help pay for tuition, although they rarely pay 100 percent of a student's expenses. The amount of grant money a student receives is based on need. The fewer personal resources you have and the less income you make per year, the more money you can receive from grants.

Federal Pell Grants are awarded only to undergraduate students who have not earned a bachelor's or professional degree. For many students, Pell Grants form the foundation for other financial aid. They are limited to less than $3,000 ($2,000 for 1997–98). You can receive only one Pell Grant in any award year. How much you get depends on financial need, expected family contributions, cost of attendance, and whether you are a full-time or part-time student. When you complete the Free Application for Federal Student Aid (FAFSA), you will automatically be considered for a Pell Grant.

The Federal Supplemental Educational Opportunity Grant (FSEOG) is for undergraduates with exceptional financial need. These grants are for students with the lowest expected family contributions and can range from $100 to $4,000 a year. Much depends on when you apply, your level of need, the funding level of the school you are attending, and the policies of the financial aid office of your school.

Although not a grant, per se, the Federal Work-Study program provides jobs both on and off campus for undergraduate and graduate students with financial need, allowing them to earn money to help pay education expenses. The program encourages community service work and work related to a student's course of study. You must be paid at least the current federal minimum wage, but it may be higher depending on the type of work you do and the skills required. How many hours you are allowed to work is determined by your employer or financial aid administrator who will consider your class schedule and academic progress. The amount you earn cannot exceed your total Federal Work-Study award.

The U.S. Department of Education makes available billions of dollars annually in financial aid to enable millions of students to attend college. Approximately two-thirds of all student financial aid in the United States comes from these federal programs. Individual states also administer grant and loan programs, generally under the oversight of the higher education agency in a student's home state. Even though these dollars are either provided by or guaranteed by the government, the financial aid administrator of your college is the person to contact for information.

Direct and FFEL (Federal Family Education Loan) Stafford Loans are the Department of Education's major form of student financial assistance for both undergraduate and graduate students who are enrolled at least half time. The major difference between these two types of loans is not their terms and conditions but the source of the loan funds. Under the Direct Loan Program, the funds are lent directly by the U.S. government. If a college does not participate in Direct Loans, then the funds are lent from a bank, credit union, or other lender that participates in the FFEL Program.

Direct and FFEL Stafford Loans are either subsidized or unsubsidized. Subsidized loans are interest deferred until you complete your education. The federal government determines your financial need and then pays the interest for you until you begin repayment. An unsubsidized loan is not based on need, and you pay the interest from the time the loan is disbursed until it is paid in full. If you allow the interest to accumulate while you are enrolled, it will be capitalized, meaning the interest will be added to the principal amount of the original loan. To prevent this, you can choose to pay the interest as it accumulates, which means you pay less in the long run.

PLUS Loans are available through both the Direct Loan and FFEL programs to parents of students. PLUS Loans enable parents with good credit histories to borrow money to pay the educational expenses of dependent children who are undergraduate students enrolled at least half time. PLUS Loans can fill in the gaps of other financial aid and make it possible for students to continue their education. Unlike student loans, which do not have to be repaid until you are out of school, parents must begin repaying a PLUS loan 60 days after the final loan disbursement for the academic year. There is no grace period for these loans.

A Federal Perkins Loan is a low-interest loan for undergraduate and graduate students with exceptional financial need. The school itself is the lender of government funds that are matched with school funds. You must repay this loan directly to the school beginning nine months after you graduate, leave school, or drop below half-time status. A student is allowed up to ten years to repay a Federal Perkins Loan.

Remember that these forms of financial aid are borrowed money that must be repaid. You will have to repay the loan even if you drop out or don't receive a passing grade. Defaulting on a school loan can affect your credit rating just like defaulting on any debt. There are ways to defer payment or to consolidate several federal student loans into one smaller payment. For more information, contact the U.S. Department of Education at 800-4-FED-AID (800-433-3243) or through their Web page at http://www.ed.gov. There are even a few cases where a loan can be cancelled if you meet the requirements (certain teachers, for instance).

The AmeriCorps program provides full-time educational awards in return for work in community service. You can work before, during, or after your postsecondary education and use the funds to pay current educational expenses or to repay federal student loans. For more information on this program, call 800-942-2677 or check their Web page at http://www.cns.gov/americorps/.

Veteran and Military Benefits

The Department of Veterans Affairs provides financial aid for veterans, reservists, and active duty military personnel and their families through several programs, including:

- ▸ Montgomery GI Bill

- ▸ Post-Vietnam Era Veterans Educational Assistance Program (VEAP)

- ▸ Old GI Bill

- ▸ Educational Assistance Test Program

- ▸ Educational Assistance Pilot Program

- ▸ Survivors' and Dependents' Educational Assistance Program

- ▸ Restored Entitlement Program for Survivors (REPS)

- ▸ Vocational Rehabilitation

- ▸ Military Tuition Assistance

The basic eligibility for these programs varies from one to the other and usually depends on when the student served on active duty. For instance, the Montgomery GI Bill is generally for military personnel—whether active duty, disabled, or honorably discharged—who entered military service on or after July 1, 1985. VEAP applies to persons who served on or after January 1, 1977, until July 1, 1985. In most cases, eligibility expires ten years from the date of discharge or release from active duty. However, only the Department of Veterans Affairs can determine an applicant's eligibility for educational assistance. Application forms are available at all VA offices, active duty stations, and American embassies. If you are serving on active duty, check with the Educational Service Office on your post, base, or ship. For the nearest VA office contact:

- ▸ Veterans Administration
  810 Vermont Avenue, NW
  Washington, DC 20420
  Phone: (800) 326-8276 (educational loans)
  or (800) 827-1000 (VA benefits)

State governments frequently set up their own educational benefit programs for veterans. In the state of New York, for instance, it is possible to receive financial assistance if you are a Vietnam or Persian Gulf veteran. However, you must also be a resident of New York state and attend an approved college of the University of the State of New York. Talk with your school's financial aid office to get information about programs in your state.

Scholarships

Many organizations offer scholarships and grants to students pursuing their educational goals. If you have access to the Internet, you can visit the Financial Aid Information page (FinAid) at http://www.finaid.org or the Free Scholarship Search and Information Service (FreSch!) at http://www.freschinfo.com/index.phtml or FASTaid's free scholarship search at http://www.fastaid.com. Be careful when surfing the Web for scholarship information. Nearly 95 percent of the scholarship-related sites on the Web are actually advertisements for scholarship search firms that charge anywhere from $30 to $150 for information you can actually find free.

Public and college libraries are good sources for information on scholarships, and don't neglect your college's financial aid office. If you are still in high school, your guidance counselor will also have multiple resources available. Check with foundations, religious organizations, civic groups, and community organizations like the American Legion, YMCA, 4-H Club, Elks, Kiwanis, Jaycees, Chamber of Commerce, Girl Scouts, or Boy Scouts, among many others. Don't overlook aid from professional organizations such as the American Medical Association, the American Bar Association, and others.

Applying for a scholarship is a long and sometimes fruitless endeavor, but it is well worth attempting. Expect to complete lengthy applications; gather recommendation letters, transcripts, and test scores; write essays; and sometimes even complete personal interviews before being seriously considered for a scholarship. Even then, the award might be as small as $500 or $1,000. There are exceptions, though, so don't give up. Be persistent, and steel yourself to face some rejection.

Other Sources of Funds

Local banks and credit unions frequently offer private loans to students outside of federal and state programs. Family and friends might be willing to lend you money, as well.

Vocational rehabilitation assistance is offered through individual states. The Federal government provides funding to each state for retraining of individuals with disabilities. Contact a vocational rehabilitation counselor for information about the benefits available in your state.

Many employers and unions provide financial assistance to their employees and members who wish to earn college credits or complete a degree program. Your human resources office or union representative will have more information. If your employer does not currently offer tuition assistance, you might be the one to get the ball rolling.

Federal and state departments of labor sponsor numerous training and tuition assistance programs for displaced workers and others who wish to access higher education as they pursue career goals. Contact your local labor department to see if you are eligible for such programs.

For more information on loans, grants, scholarships, and other types of college financial aid, look for *Barron's Complete College Financing Guide* (ISBN 0-8120-9523-5) at your local bookstore or library or at http://www.barronseduc.com.

▸ The U.S. Department of Education's Web site is an excellent place to find information on financial aid: http://www.ed.gov/prog_info/SFA/StudentGuide/

▸ Project EASI is a project of the Department Education that provides financial aid information and online application forms: http://easi.ed/gov or http://easi.ed.gov/html/fafsa.html

▸ For links to the financial aid offices of many institutions and for other resources, check the Web site of the National Association of Student Financial Aid Administrators: http://www.finaid.org

▸ Mark Kantrowitz's FinAid site includes a college cost projector, savings growth projector, savings plan designer, annual yield calculator, compound interest calculator, savings plan yield calculator, life insurance needs calculator, federal housing index calculator, and loan discounts calculator, among other valuable information: http://www.FinAid.org

▸ Graduate School Guide: http://www.schoolguides.com/

▸ CollegeSmart financial aid planning software: http://www.collegesmart.com

▸ The National Association of Student Financial Aid Administrators (NASFAA) site with information for students and parents: http://www.nasfaa.org

▸ Educaid, the student loan specialists: http://www.educaid.com

▸ KapLoan, the Kaplan student loan information program: http://www2.kaplan.com/

▸ Sallie Mae gives information on graduate student loans: http://www.salliemae.com

▸ Nellie Mae is a large nonprofit provider of student and parent education loan funds: http://www.nelliemae.org/

▸ The Education Resources Institute (TERI) loan programs and services site: http://www.teri.org

▸ Vermont Student Assistance Corporation: http://www.vsac.org

▸ Access Group provides financial products and services for graduate and professional students: http://www.accessgroup.org/

▸ Citibank student loans: http://www.citibank.com/student/

▸ American Express educational loans: http://www.americanexpress.com/edloans/

▸ College Funding Company: http://www.collegefundingco.org/

▸ Chela Financial: http://www.chelafin.com/

▸ Education Assistant Corporation: http://www.eac-easci.org

▸ Educational Finance Group for medical students: http://www.efg.net/nojava/

- FastWEB Scholarship Search offers a free computer search of more than 275,000 scholarships: http://www.fastweb.com or http://www.studentservices.com/fastWeb

- FASTaid free scholarship service: http://www.fastaid.com/

- Free Scholarship Search and Information Service (FreSch!): http://www.freshinfo.com/index.phtml

- Scholarship Resource Network: http://www.rams.com/srn

- CollegeNET MACH25 scholarship search: http://www.collegenet.com/mach25/

- Fulbright scholarships: http://www.iie.org/fulbright/

- The Chronicle of Higher Education's weekly list of fellowship and grant deadlines: http://chronicle.com/data/infobank.dir/deadline.dir/deadmain.htm

- Graduate study grants site maintained by New York University: gopher://cwis.nyu.edu:3000/7?GIGS/

- Scholarship Foundation of America: http://kent.co.kr/ed/financia/scholar/home.htm

- Cornell Fellowship Competition list of fellowships open to undergraduate students: http://www.cornell.edu/academic/fellowship.html

- A USENET newsgroup for exploring college financial aid issues: news:soc.college.financial-aid

- American Association of University Women (AAUW) fellowships and grants: http://www.aauw.org/3000/felgrawa.html

- The Rotary Foundation scholarship program: http://www.rotary.org/foundation/educational_programs

- The Foundation Center for information on corporate fellowships: http://fdncenter.org

- Internet Nonprofit Center specializing in information about nonprofit organization: http://www.nonprofits.org/

- A metasite for nonprofit organizations: http://www.mindspring.com/~petert/index.htm

6 ► Get Ready, Get Set, Go!

Now that you know what distance learning is, it's time to move! You will need to examine your options (the get ready part), make a plan (get set), and then start the process of being accepted to the college or university of your choice (go!).

Examine Your Options

Look for schools that have the best programs and the best instructors for your area of interest. Does your industry require a prestigious school for success? Then make sure the school has a reputation you would be proud to announce on a bumper sticker. If you want to transfer your distance learning credits to a degree program at another school, make sure you contact that school in advance to ensure that they will accept your credits. Do you have the necessary credentials for admission? Make sure your previous degrees, class prerequisites, and minimum grade point average match the school's requirements. Does the school require that you live within a certain distance of the campus or reside in a certain state? Would a trade or vocational school be a better choice in your career field?

Some programs can be completed totally away from a college campus, while others will require that you attend seminars or other special programs on campus. Some courses will allow you to enroll whenever you want and work at your own pace. Others will be more traditional in structure and have stricter deadlines. So, review each college's catalog and policies closely before making a decision, then make sure you have the funds and commitment to complete the program.

Make a Plan

Once you have narrowed your choices, your first step will be to request an application from each college. Gather your transcripts, complete the application, write the essay (if required), and submit them to the school. You can complete your college application in two ways: (1) by filling out a paper application packet sent through the mail, or (2) by completing an online application form through a college's Web page or an application service like:

- ► CollegeLink: http://www.collegelink.com

- ► CollegeScape: http://www.collegescape.com/

- ► CollegeNet: http://www.collegenet.com

- ► CollegeEdge: http://www.collegeedge.com/

If you choose the electronic route, make sure you don't neglect the quality of your writing. Use your word processing software's spellcheck and grammar features to make your application as error free as possible. Print out a copy before e-mailing your application and then back up your e-mail to a floppy disk. For a hard-copy application, call the college directly and request a catalog, financial aid information, and application package.

To find help on the Internet for completing a graduate school application, check the Rensselaer Polytechnic University's online help with application essays at http://www.rpi.edu/dept/llc/writecenter/web/text/apply.html or the Applicant Support Network at http://www.iglou.com/asn/.

Once you are accepted, you will need to request and complete financial aid forms and take any entrance examinations required. Then you are ready to begin your classes.

Entrance Examinations

If you are a recent high school graduate with little work experience and no previous college credits, you will more than likely be required to submit SAT or ACT scores before admission to most of the schools in this book. Undergraduate distance learning programs will rarely require SAT or ACT testing for acceptance of working adults over the age of 25, but they will often require general aptitude tests in math and communication to assess the student's readiness for college-level learning. If you have difficulty passing these entrance examinations, most schools provide remedial classes that can qualify for your admission.

To help prepare for these examinations, find any of the following Barron's books in your local bookstore or library:

- *How to Prepare for the SAT I*
- *Pass Key to SAT I*
- *SAT I Computer Study Program*
- *Barron's SAT I with CD-ROM*
- *Hot Words for the SAT I*
- *Barron's New Math Workbook for SAT I*
- *Verbal Workbook for SAT I*
- *14 Days to Higher SAT I Scores*
- *SAT I Wordmaster, Level I and Level II*
- SAT II subject preparation books in: American History and Social Studies, Biology, Chemistry, French, Japanese, Literature, Mathematics Level I/IC/IIC, Physics, Spanish, World History, and Writing
- *ACT Computer Study Program*
- *How to Prepare for the ACT* (available with and without computer software)
- *Pass Key to the ACT*

Most graduate programs, on the other hand, generally require applicants to take an examination before acceptance. The GRE (General Aptitude Test of the Graduate Record Examination) is the most commonly used, but some schools also require a GRE Subject Test in a special area of study. The GMAT (Graduate Management Admissions Test) is usually required instead of the GRE for admission into graduate business schools. Speak with the prospective school about its requirements and about testing available in your area. For more information about the GRE and testing sites they sponsor all over the world, contact the Educational Testing Service:

Educational Testing Service (ETS)
Rosedale Road
Princeton, NJ 08541
Phone: (609) 921-9000
Fax: (609) 734-5410
Web page: http://www.ets.org

The General Aptitude Test of the GRE it not an achievement or intelligence test; instead it tests your verbal, quantitative, and analytical abilities. It takes three and one-half hours to complete and is usually given twice a year at test centers in major metropolitan areas.

Each Subject Test is also three and one-half hours long and tests your basic understanding of information in a specific field. Subject Tests are available in the following disciplines, depending on admission requirements: biology, chemistry, computer sciences, economics, education, engineering, French, geology, history, literature in English, mathematics, music, physics, political science, psychology, sociology, and Spanish.

The GMAT is a four-hour test that measures a student's ability to think systematically, as well as reading and analytical skills. A student need not have business experience to pass this test since it does not test knowledge in specific business subjects, although you should have a strong basic knowledge of algebra, geometry, and arithmetic.

If you are not a native English speaker or are applying from a country that does not speak English as its primary language, you will need to prove your ability to communicate in English before being accepted into most American schools. The Test of English as a Foreign Language (TOEFL) is the most frequently used examination for this purpose. For information about dates and locations of tests around the world, write:

TOEFL
P.O. Box 899-R
Princeton, NJ 08541
Phone: (609) 771-7100
Fax: (609) 771-7500
Web page: http://www.ets.org

The Medical College Admission Text (MCAT) and the Law School Admission Test (LSAT) are required for admission to specialized medical or law schools. The LSAT does not measure special knowledge of law, but the MCAT is designed to measure your general knowledge of basic physics, chemistry, and biology. Both exams require good critical thinking skills.

Your local bookstore or library will have some great resources for preparing for the GRE, GMAT, LSAT, MCAT, PCAT, TOEFL, and other examinations. Barron's publishes several excellent study guides, including:

- *How to Prepare for the Graduate Record Exam* (with or without computer software)

- *Pass Key to the GRE*

- *GRE Computer Study Program*

- *How to Prepare for the GRE in Biology*

- *How to Prepare for the GRE: Psychology*

- *How to Prepare for the GMAT* (with CD-ROM)

- *Pass Key to the GMAT*

- *How to Prepare for the TOEFL*

- *TOEFL Strategies*

- *Essential Words for the TOEFL*

- *Practice Exercises for the TOEFL*

- *Pass Key to the TOEFL*

- *TOEFL Computer Study Program*

- *How to Prepare for the Law School Admission Test—LSAT*

- *Pass Key to the LSAT*

- *Law Dictionary*

- *How to Prepare for the Medical College Admission Test (MCAT)*

- *How to Prepare for the PCAT, Pharmacy College Admission Test*

Learning Contracts

Some distance learning programs use learning contracts (or degree plans). The student negotiates the courses and work required to complete a degree and then writes a contract stating the educational goals, learning outcomes, and methods for acquiring that learning, including resources, educational activities, and evaluation procedures. This allows students to tailor a degree program to meet their exact needs.

This legal document is binding on both parties once accepted and signed. That means that, if you fail to complete your part of the bargain, you might forfeit your tuition and be forced to withdraw from the program. On the other hand, the school is equally bound by the contract, and if you satisfactorily complete all elements of the contract, you must be awarded the degree or credits agreed upon. Most learning contracts have a binding arbitration clause that protects both you and the school from breeches of contract.

This contract is extremely important to you and to your future, so don't take its preparation or signing lightly. Certain occasions might even require an attorney's expert eye to review the contract before it is finalized.

Transcripts and Grades

Whenever you complete a course at a college or university, the school records the grade on a transcript and sends a grade report to you for your records. Rarely does a transcript indicate how a course was completed—via distance learning or in a traditional classroom. You can request an official transcript in writing from any institution, although the transcript is not considered "official" if you open the envelope. In your letter, ask the college to send the transcript directly to the requesting institution to avoid any problems of legitimacy.

Course Materials

Every course will require some kind of study materials. Once you register for a course, you will automatically receive a study guide (or instructions for where to get one). This guide will tell you about your instructor, meeting times and places (if any), homework, and will contain an outline of the course. In most cases, you will be required to purchase a textbook and other materials, which might include a workbook, extra reading assignments, lab kits, videotapes, CD-ROMs, audiotapes, and other necessities. These additional costs should be figured into your budget, since they can become significant over time.

Internet Resources

Study and Testing Help

- Links to more than 2,000 Internet study resource sites: http://www.caso.com.
- The College of Education at the University of Illinois Web site for examination preparation: http://www.edu.uiuc.edu/
- Princeton Review's Graduate School and the GRE: http://www.review.com/homepage.html
- Kaplan Educational Centers: http://www.kaplan.com/
- The Graduate Management Admission Council's MBA Explorer: http://www.gmat.org/
- GMAT percentile conversion table: http://haas.berkeley.edu/
- Eisenhower National Clearinghouse for science test preparation: http://www.enc.org
- National Science Teacher's Association site: http://www.nsta.org/
- Mathematics Archives: http://archives.math.utk.edu/index.html
- Geometry: http://www.geom.umn.edu/apps/gallery.html
- Transmath Tutor: http://caliban.eeds.ac.uk
- Chemistry Web Elements: http://www.cchem.berkeley.edu/Table/web-elements-home.html
- Microbiology: http://virtual.class.uconn.edu/MCB/index.html

- World Wide Web Virtual Library subject catalog: http://vlib.org/Overview.html

- Project Gutenberg: http://jg.cso.uiuc.edu/pg/pg_home.html or ftp://uiarchive/cso.uiuc.edu/pub/etext/gutenberg/

- The Library of Congress' National Digital Library Project: http://rs6.loc.gov/amhome.html

- National Library of Canada: http://www.nlc-bnc.ca/confed/e-1867.htm

- Online Computer Library Center, Inc.: http://www.oclc.org

- Alex catalog of electronic texts on the Internet: gopher://rsl.ox.ac.uk/11/lib-corn/hunter

- U.S. National Library of Medicine: http://www.nlm.nih.gov/

- Global Electronic Library: http://www.jec.edu/index.html

- The Voice of the Shuttle: http://humanitas.ucsb.edu/

- Tradewave Gallery Index for Science: http://www.einet.net/galaxy/Science.html

- Astronomy and astrophysics: http://www.stci.edu/astroWeb/astronomy.html

- Art History Visual Guide: http://www.dsu.edu/departments/liberal/

- Carnegie Mellon University history and historiography index: http://eserver.org/history/

- Classics Subject Guide: http://www.ualberta.ca/~slis/guides/classics/home.htm

- Economic History Services of the Cliometric Society: http://cs.muohio.edu/

- Facets of Religion: http://sunfly.ub.uni-freiburg.de/religion

- Historical documents: gopher://gopher.vt.edu:10010/10/33

- National Science Foundation: gopher://stis.nsf.gov/

- TKM's Education Web Search: http://www.alpha.tkm.mb.ca/education

- Search directory for women: http://www.wwwomen.com/

- Michigan State University's search engine for university and informational resources: http://writing.msu.edu/modules/research/engines/default.html

Search Engines

- Altavista: http://www.altavista.digital.com

- Excite: http://www.excite.com/

- Hotbot: http://www.hotbot.com/

- Lycos: http://www.lycos.com

- Yahoo: http://www.yahoo.com

- Web Crawler: http://webcrawler.com

- World Wide Worm: http://www.cs.colorado.edu/wwww

- Savvy Search: http://www.cs.colostate.edu/~dreiling/smartform.html

- Snap: http://www.snap.com

Writing and Style Guides

- Webster's Dictionary: http://c.gp.cs.cmu.edu:5103/prog/webster

- Roget's Thesaurus: http://tuna.uchicago.edu/forms_unrest/ROGET.html

- Roget's Thesaurus: http://web.cs.city.ac.uk/text/roget/thesaurus.html

- Roget's Thesaurus: gopher://odie.niaid.nih.gov/77/.thesaurus/index

- Jack Lynch's Grammar and Style Guides: http://www.english.upenn.edu/~jlynch/grammar.html

- Strunk & White's *Elements of Style*: http://www.columbia.edu/acis/bartleby/strunk/

- Purdue's Online Writing Lab (OWL): http://owl.english.purdue.edu/our-lab/introduction.html

- University of Michigan's OWL: http://www.lsa.umich.edu/ecb/help/owl.html

- Cyber Reference Desk: http://www.devry-phx.edu/lrnresrc/dowsc/refdesk.htm#works

- Rensselaer Polytechnic Institute's basic prose style and mechanics handbook: http://www.rpi.edu/dept/llc/writecenter/web/text/proseman.html

Ethnic, Diversity, and Disability Resources

- Resources for African-American students:
  - http://cnct.com/home/ijblack/BlackExcel.shtml
  - http://eric-web.tc.columbia.edu/hbcu/online.html
  - http://www.webcom.com/~cjcook/SDBP/.hbcu.html
  - http://www.ppsi.org/education-peopleofcolor.htm
  - http://web.fie.com/molis/
  - http://www.nando.net/sproject/colleges
  - http://www.feminist.com/bisas1.htm
  - http://www.gatech.edu/bgsa/blackpages.html

- Resources for Latino and Native American students:
  - http://www.chci.org

- http://www.sacnas.org/

- http://www.unm.edu/~lananet/

- http://latino.sscnet.ucla.edu/Student.html

- http://hanksville.phast.umass.edu/misc/NAschools.html

- http://www.ppsi.org/latino-academic.htm

▸ Resources for Asian American students:

- http://www.igc.apc.org/acon/

- http://www.umiacs.umd.edu/users/sawweb/sawnet

- http://pitcairn.lib.uci.edu/rrsc/asiamer.html

- http://nearnet.gnn.com/gnn/wic/soc.10.html

- http://www.mit.edu:8001/afs/athena.mit.edu/user/:/r/irie/www/aar.html

▸ The Consortium for Graduate Study in Management, a source for merit-based fellowships for minority graduate business students: http://www.cgsm.wustl.edu:8010/

▸ Minorities, education, and job outlook: http://plan.educ.indiana.edu/

▸ Resources for women:

- The Women's Resource Project: http://sunsite.unc.edu/cheryb/women/wshome.html

- Organizations encouraging women in science and engineering: http://www2.nas.edu/cwse/

- Resources for women in science: http://www-ocean.tamu.edu/~wise/women.html

▸ Resource for the sight and hearing impaired:

- American Council of the Blind: http://www.acb.org/index.html

- College and career programs for deaf students: http://www.gallaudet.edu:80/~cadsweb/colleges.html

Metasites of College Web Pages

▸ Christina DeMello's College and University Home Page Directory: http://www.mit.edu:8001/people/cdmello/univ.html

▸ The companion site to this book: http://www.thespringsmall.com (click on the little red schoolhouse)

▸ Yahoo!'s list of universities: http://dir.yahoo.com/Education/Higher_Education/Colleges_and_Universities

▸ List of American universities: http://www.clasufl.edu/CLAS/american-universities.html

▸ Ecola's guide to U.S. colleges: http://www.ecola.com/college/

- Associated Western universities: http://www.awu.org/

- University of Texas' list of community colleges: http://www.utexas.edu/world/comcol/alpha/

- Community colleges Web search: http://www.mcli.dist.maricopa.edu/cc/search.html

- Source Pathways, Inc.: http://www.sourcepath.com/caid/default.html

- Internet College Exchange: http://www.collegenight.com/

- National liberal arts colleges: http://aavc.vassar.edu/libarts.colleges.html

- Shortcuts to American universities: http://www.emich.edu/public/economics/links.htm

- University of Texas at Austin's list of colleges: http://www.utexas.edu/world/univ/

- University pages: http://isl-garnet.uah.edu/Universities/

- Canadian universities: http://www.uwaterloo.ca/~canu/index.html

- Distance education institutions: http://members.tripod.com/~mrasyidi/ola.htm

- The College Information Handbook site with hyperlinks to more than 3,200 colleges and universities in the United States: http://www.collegeboard.org/

- University of Toledo's list of two-year colleges: http://www.sp.utoledo.edu/twoyrcol.html

- CollegeNet college search: http://www.collegenet.com/

- PacificNet: http://www.pacificnet.net/rwm/

- FishNet's college guide: http://www.jayi.com/jayi/ACG/search.html

- Edition XII, a U.K. site with a worldwide directory of schools with MBA programs: http://www.editionxii.co.uk/

- University links to adult education: http://www-net.com/univ/list/adult.html

Other Related Sites

- CSU Mentor to assist students and families in matching needs with colleges: http://www.csumentor.edu

- CollegeView: http://www.collegeview.com/

- U.S. News & World Report's College and Careers page: http://www.usnews.com/usnews/edu/home.htm

- Mapping Your Future: http://www.mapping-your-future.org/

- Best Education Sites Today (BEST): http://www.education-world.com/

- Ohio State University's MBA Page: http://www.scenemaker.com/anon/214/cover.dhtml

- MBA Style Magazine: http://members.aol.com/mbastyle/

► Help for reentry students from a UCSC faculty member: http://www.ucsc.edu/stars/reentry/index.html

7 The Directory

The intent of this guide is to give you a general idea of the types of programs offered by regionally accredited colleges and universities throughout the United States and Canada. It is not an inexhaustible list of schools with distance learning programs. Because more and more distance learning programs will be developed by colleges and universities every month, what was complete yesterday will not be complete today. In addition, not every college that was surveyed chose to respond, although the vast majority of schools did respond. This book will give you enough information, however, to help you narrow down your choices to the programs best suited to your needs without overwhelming you with details.

This guide was current on the date it was published, but exact tuition rates, fees, course availability, entrance requirements, and other details will change often. Some distance learning courses are offered only at certain times of the year or only to students in certain geographic locations, so be sure to check with the school before making your final decision. The catalogs, brochures, and Web pages of colleges and universities are updated several times a year and are the best sources for current information. Remember to shop, shop, shop!

How to Read the Profiles

Each profile begins with *contact information,* including full address, phone number(s), fax number, division responsible for distance learning, Web site, and e-mail address. This information is more dynamic than you might expect, especially the e-mail addresses and Web site URLs (Universal Resource Locators). If you can't get through via e-mail, then the school's mail system has probably changed or the person who was the contact is no longer there. In such cases, simply call the phone number listed and ask for a new e-mail address. Web sites move often, so you will need to use a good Internet search engine to find new addresses when a college moves its site. Try http://www.altavista.digital.com or http://www.yahoo.com. If a URL contains multiple / marks after the first //, then try to delete all of the extensions up to the primary domain name (i.e., http://www.ctc.edu instead of http://www.ctc.edu/~distance). For easy hyperlinks to the colleges of your choice, click on the little red schoolhouse at http://www.thespringsmall.com.

Degree programs are divided into three categories: undergraduate (associate and bachelor's), graduate (master's), and postgraduate (doctoral). *Certificate programs* and individual *class titles* are listed in paragraph form, separated by commas. Remember, other classes might be available via distance learning besides those listed here. Look at the kinds of degree and certificate programs offered by the school and assume that classes are available in the same general subject areas. Ninety-eight percent of colleges allow students to take individual classes without being enrolled in a degree or certificate program, which is great news for those with a love of lifelong learning. You don't need to commit to a degree or certificate program to begin taking college courses now, and distance learning allows busy adults to work around their already-overcommitted time schedules.

Teaching methods (called delivery methods in the academic world) are the technologies used to deliver the classes. The Internet, real-time chats, asynchronous conferencing, electronic classrooms, e-mail, newsgroups, and LISTSERVs all require the use of a computer equipped with a modem. The faster your modem speed, the more satisfied you will be with the quality of your online experience, except for e-mail, of course, which is not as dependent on computer speed. Because each college uses these teaching methods in unique combinations, it is fruitless to give an example of how your class will be delivered. What is more important is that you determine whether you have the technology you need to take the class (computer, modem, VCR, television set, etc.) and then call the schools with programs that interest you to get the details of how they use those technologies.

Here are some of the definitions of the various teaching methods:

- *Internet:* The world's largest network of connected computers, linking government, military, businesses, organizations, educational institutions, and private individuals. The World Wide Web (WWW) is the software that links the information of the Internet, while the Internet is the physical collection of computers and cables by which Web files are transmitted. In order to access the Internet, you will need a computer, modem, browser software, and an Internet Service Provider (ISP). When you subscribe to a commercial online service such as America Online, CompuServe, Microsoft Network, or other ISP, the browser software is installed on your computer's hard drive automatically when you install the ISP software. Most colleges and universities today have a Web site that provides information about the school, much like the catalog that is published every semester. Distance learning programs often use the Internet for much more than just providing information. Professors will set up their own Web pages under the school's domain to give course outlines, assignments, and hyperlinks to related subjects.

- *Electronic classrooms:* By combining live transmission of video and audio, real-time conferencing, and hyperlinks to volumes of printed information on the Internet, electronic classrooms are the closest thing to traditional classroom environments that you will find in distance learning. Electronic classrooms can use the Internet or private networks. Some private networks use Lotus Notes to allow students to see graphics, watch video clips, and communicate with each other and the instructor.

- *Real-time chats:* These are computer conferences in which students and instructors exchange messages in real time. This is synchronous, two-way communication. Study groups will often use real-time chats to communicate about projects.

- *E-mail:* Electronic mail is an electronic message sent from one computer to another via the Internet or a commercial online service. E-mail is used to communicate back and forth between instructors and fellow students.

- *CD-ROM:* Similar to a music compact disk, CD-ROMs can store large volumes of data for access by computers. A single CD-ROM can hold the information from an entire textbook and still have plenty of room left for a set of encyclopedias with photographs. Instructors are making use of this technology to provide valuable resource materials for students in their classes. In order to play a CD-ROM, however, a computer must have a special drive that usually comes standard on most of today's new computers.

- *Newsgroups:* Newsgroups offer students the opportunity to participate in "chats" that are not dependent on "real time." Instead of chatting with someone live, you read a continuous thread of discussion on a certain topic and add your comments whenever you like. Other students in the same class are adding their comments over a period of days or weeks until the discussion ends. Newsgroups can be accessed through the Internet or through a college's local network of computers.

- *LISTSERV:* A LISTSERV is really just a mailing list, an organized form of e-mail that you are sent automatically. You subscribe to a mailing list as part of your class, and mail is sent to you whenever the instructor or a student has something to say to all class members. Like e-mail, you read it at your convenience.

- *Television (videotape, cable, satellite, PBS):* Some correspondence courses are accompanied by videotapes that make the subject as alive as if the student were in a traditional classroom. To participate in such a course, you must, of course, have access to a videocassette player/recorder (VCR) and a television set. PBS, cable, and satellite television program are one-way video. In other words, the instruction is coming to you, but you can't interact with the instructor in real time. This is asynchronous communication, meaning the interaction between student and instructor occurs before and/or after, but not during, the instruction, usually by e-mail or telephone.

- *Videoconferencing:* This is interactive video in which the students and instructors can see and hear each other. As a general rule, video cameras and monitors are placed in the rooms, and operators in each classroom work the equipment. Students can see the teacher and any visual aids on one monitor and see students at other sites on the other monitors. The instructor can choose not to watch the classes when they are shown in multiple locations. Video allows students and instructors to pick up on the nuances of a discussion, including body language, movement, and personal interaction.

- *Audioconferencing:* Also known as teleconferencing, this technology allows students to use a telephone to listen to and join classes in real time, but the participants cannot see one another. A bridge operator sets up a telephone connection between all of the parties, like a party line. You should have a good telephone with a mute button and a speaker for audioconferencing.

- *Audiographics:* This type of audio-based technology uses telephone lines to transmit visual information such as charts and illustrations. Fax machines, electronic black boards, telewriters, electronic pens, compressed video, and freeze-frame video are good examples of this technology. Some of these technologies require computers or special equipment at the student's end of the telephone line and are more likely to be used in a group setting at a remote meeting place. These technologies are used when visual demonstrations are an important part of the learning, such as in mathematics, science, and art subjects, but they're not used as frequently as videoconferencing.

- *Radio Broadcast:* Prerecorded or live broadcasts are made using radio signals that can be picked up by anyone within broadcast range with a radio receiver. Radio broadcasts are more popular overseas than in the United States, but they are a great delivery method for highly verbal subjects like psychology or auditory subjects like music appreciation.

- *Audiocassette Tapes:* Audiotapes contain prerecorded instruction and are delivered to the student with the print study materials. Audiotapes are generally used when the number of students is too small to justify a radio broadcast or in cases where students are outside the range of a radio signal. Students with very visual or kinaesthetic learning styles may find it difficult to learn in an auditory learning environment.

- *Independent Study (also called Correspondence Study):* Traditional correspondence courses fall into this category. You are truly alone in this type of program; there is no classroom or group interaction. It is just you and your instructor, corresponding back and forth until the work is done. Correspondence isn't always via the post office anymore and includes such technologies as fax, e-mail, and telephone conferences with the instructor.

- *Learning Contracts:* You will find information about learning contracts at the end of Chapter 6 of this book.

Credits Granted for: Many colleges and universities grant credit for life experiences, examinations, and extrainstitutional learning (corporate and professional association seminars and workshops). These were discussed in detail in Chapter 4.

The *admission requirements* listed in this book are the bare essentials. They include age, employment status, prerequisites, and restrictions such as state residency and time limits for completion. Once you have narrowed down your choices, call each college to request a catalog or check the Web page for full details.

On-Campus Requirements: Some degree and certificate programs require that students spend a certain number of hours or percentage of study time in a traditional classroom setting, either on their campus, in an off-campus classroom, or at seminars. If you live a long distance from the campus, the requirement of on-campus time becomes a very important part of your decision-making process.

Tuition and fees will rarely be exactly what they are quoted in this guide because of the lead-time required in producing such a book and because of the shelf-life of the printed word. The real advantage of showing prices in this guide is that it helps you compare the relative price ranges of different schools. You will know whether a school offers the highest prices, the lowest prices, or prices in between. Always call the school or check the Web page before making a decision.

Credit by: The last item in the tuition and fees section of each profile indicates whether an institution's credits are measured by semester or quarter. Transferring credits earned under a quarter system to a college that awards credits by the semester can sometimes be difficult, since quarters equate to partial credits under a semester system. Speak with your admissions counselor about how these credits will appear on your transcript.

Financial Aid: Various financing options are listed for each college. Read more about financial aid in Chapter 5.

Accreditation is explained more fully in Chapter 3, but suffice it to say that every institution listed in this book has been accredited by one of the six regional accreditation associations or the Distance Education and Training Council.

Description: The last item in each profile is a brief description of the school in its own words. The number in parentheses in the first sentence of the profile is the year the school was founded.

Following the profiles is a series of indexes that cross-references schools by state/province, fields of study, and on-campus requirements. Use these indexes to narrow down your choice if location, subjects, or travel time are important to you.

Acadia University

42 University Avenue	Phone: (902) 585-1434
Wolfville, NS, Canada B0P 1X0	(800) 565-6568
	Fax: (902) 585-1068

Division(s): Continuing and Distance Education
Web Site(s): http://conted.acadiau.ca
E-mail: shawna.smith@acadiau.ca

Certificate Programs: Computer Science, Business Administration, Business Administration Diploma.

Class Titles: Accounting, Management, Managerial Finance, Marketing, Operations Management, Organizational Change, Business Law, Change Management, Computer-Based Intelligence, Computer Programming, Systems Programming, Digital Systems, Assembly Language/Computer Organization, Data Structures/File Processing, Object Oriented Systems, Economics, History of Education, Philosophy of Education, Literature, Reading/Writing Texts, Shakespeare, Romantics, 18th Century Novel, Short Story, Canadian Short Story, Frankenstein to Dracula, Oceanography, Atmosphere/Weather/Climate, Western Civilization, Canadian History, U.S. History, Maritime Provinces, Women in Modern World, Environmental Law, Latin Prose/Poetry, Precalculus Math, Math Functions, Calculus, Math Sets/Functions/Algorithms, Graph Theory/Matrix Algebra, Nutrition, Politics/Government, Experimental Psychology, Applied Psychology, Drugs/Behaviour, Stress/Coping, Personality, Sociology, Sociology of Aging, Criminology, Sociology of Education, Spanish.

Teaching Methods: *Computers:* Internet, electronic classroom, e-mail, CD-ROM, newsgroup, LISTSERV. *TV:* videotape. *Other:* videoconferencing, audiographics, correspondence.

Admission Requirements: *Undergraduate:* high school completion. *Certificate:* high school completion.

On-Campus Requirements: None.

Tuition and Fees: *Undergraduate:* $425/credit. *Application Fee:* $25. *Other Costs:* $80 distance education fee. *Credit by:* open entry.

Financial Aid: Federal Student Loans, Provincial Student Loans.

Accreditation: Association of Universities and Colleges of Canada.

Description: Acadia University (1838) is a fully accredited institution with a long tradition of offering accessible postsecondary education. Every year, more than 2,000 students access Acadia University through its worldwide distance learning program, which began in 1965. Acadia offers credit courses toward degrees in all branches of university work. More than 200 curriculum combinations lead to degrees, diplomas, and certificates in Faculties of Arts, Pure and Applied Science, Professional Studies, and Theology.

Adams State College

208 Edgemont	Phone: (719) 587-7671
Alamosa, CO 81102	(800) 548-6679
	Fax: (719) 587-7974

Division(s): Extended Studies
Web Site(s): http://www.adams.edu
E-mail: ascextend@adams.edu

Class Titles: Education courses; vary by semester.

Teaching Methods: *Computers:* Internet, real-time chat, e-mail. *TV:* satellite broadcasting, PBS. *Other:* videoconferencing, fax, correspondence, audiotapes, independent study.

On-Campus Requirements: None.

Tuition and Fees: *Undergraduate:* $70/credit independent study. *Other Costs:* books extra. *Credit by:* semester.

Accreditation: North Central Association of Colleges and Schools, National Council for Accreditation of Teacher Education, National Association of School of Music, Council for Accreditation of Counseling and Related Education Programs.

Description: The Division of Extended Studies at Adams State College (1925) provides continuing education opportunities to students who can benefit from them, and has been offering high quality distance education courses via print-based correspondence study for 10 years.

Adelphi University

1 South Avenue	Phone: (516) 877-3165
Garden City, NY 11530	Fax: (516) 877-6873

Division(s): Provost Office
Web Site(s): http://Adelphi.Edu
E-mail: Kraeger@adlibv.adelphi.edu

Undergraduate Degree Programs:
Bachelor Business Administration in Management (pending New York state approval)

Graduate Degree Programs:
Master of Business Administration in Management (pending New York state approval)

Teaching Methods: *TV:* 2-way audio/video room systems. *Other:* None.

Admission Requirements: *Undergraduate:* application, ACT/SAT, high school graduate or equivalent, upper 1/3 of class, application fee, transfer transcripts. *Graduate:* bachelor's degree, transcripts, application fee.

On-Campus Requirements: None.

Tuition and Fees: *Undergraduate:* $430/credit. *Graduate:* $485/credit. *Application Fee:* $35 undergraduate, $50 graduate. *Other Costs:* home computer required for video-enabled courses, costs for ISDN systems are student's responsibility. *Credit by:* semester.

Financial Aid: Federal Pell Grant, Supplemental Educational Opportunity Grant, Federal Work-Study, New York resident programs, Adelphi scholarships, awards, grants, loans.

Accreditation: Middle States Association of Colleges and Schools.

Description: Adelphi (1896) is a liberal arts institution chartered by the State Board of Regents in 1896. Initially located in Brooklyn with 57 students and 16 faculty members. In 1929, it moved to its current location in Garden City. It became a women's college in 1912 for 3 decades. The university, over the years, added several programs and schools besides the liberal arts courses of study including Nursing (1944), Social Work (1949), doctoral level Clinical Psychology (Derner Institute, 1951), and the Schools of Education, Management and Business, and University College (in the 1960s and 1970s). In the 1990s, the Honors College and the Center for Health and Human Services were added to the university.

Alaska Pacific University

4101 University Drive	Phone: (907) 564-8222
Anchorage, AK 97508	Fax: (907) 562-4276

Division(s): RANA (Rural Alaska Native Adult) Program
Web Site(s): http://www.alaskapacific.edu
E-mail: gsmith@alaskapacific.edu

Undergraduate Degree Programs:
Bachelor of Arts degree with a Business Administration major with a focus on Health Services Administration

Teaching Methods: *Computers:* Internet, real-time chat, e-mail, CD-ROM, newsgroup, LISTSERV. *TV:* videotape, satellite broadcasting. *Other:* videoconferencing, audioconferencing, audiographics, audiotapes, fax, correspondence, independent study, individual study, learning contracts.

Credits Granted for: experiential learning, portfolio assessment, extrainstitutional learning, examination (CLEP, ACT-PEP, DANTES, GRE).

Admission Requirements: *Undergraduate:* RANA application.

On-Campus Requirements: Yes, one week residency at beginning of each semester.

Tuition and Fees: *Undergraduate:* $285/credit. *Credit by:* semester.

Financial Aid: Federal Stafford Loan, Federal PLUS Loan, Federal Pell Grant, Federal Work-Study, VA, Alaska resident programs.

Accreditation: Northwest Association of Schools and Colleges.

Description: Alaska Pacific University (1957) is a private, independent university that promotes the fullest development of its students through liberal arts and professional programs while emphasizing individual attention to students, the development of leadership abilities, and the nurturing of spiritual and moral values consistent with its Christian heritage, while still respecting the religious convictions of all. The university emphasizes personal growth through student-centered, experiential education using Alaska, the Arctic, and the Pacific Rim as laboratories for learning. The university develops and maintains academic excellence by combining the breadth, integrative understanding, and critical thinking of the liberal arts with practical and focused knowledge for professional careers. The Rural Alaska Native Adult Program, implemented in 1998, marks APU's advent into distance learning. RANA is designed to allow rural Alaskans to complete bachelor's degrees in several professional fields without lengthy absences from their home communities.

Alverno College

3401 South 39th Street	
PO Box 343922	Phone: (414) 382-6000
Milwaukee, WI 53234-3922	Fax: (414) 382-6354

Division(s): Office of the Academic Dean
Web Site(s): http://www.alverno.edu
E-mail: institute@alverno.edu

Class Titles: Challenges of Supervising Teacher (graduate credit).

Teaching Methods: *TV:* videoconferencing. *Other:* None.

Admission Requirements: *Undergraduate:* courses supplement undergraduate programs—current requirements apply.

Graduate: same as undergraduate.

On-Campus Requirements: None.

Tuition and Fees: *Undergraduate:* the course for cooperating teachers is provided at no cost to the participants, who are site mentors for our student teachers. *Credit by:* semester

Financial Aid: Federal Stafford Loan, Federal Perkins Loan, Federal PLUS Loan, Federal Pell Grant, Federal Work-Study, VA, Wisconsin resident programs.

Accreditation: North Central Association of Colleges and Schools.

Description: Alverno College (1887) is an undergraduate liberal arts college for women. We also offer a Master of Arts in Teaching Learning and Assessment that is open to women and men. We are just beginning to use distance learning and plan to do so in programmatic response to our current students. Alverno will open a new building, a Teaching, Learning and Technology Center, in January 1999. We have committed ourselves to offering the Cooperating Teachers course as noted above, plus other courses in the near future.

American Academy of Nutrition

3408 Sausalito	Phone: (800) 290-4226
Corona Del Mar, CA 92625-1638	Fax: (949) 760-1788

Other Campus: 1212 Kenesaw, Knoxville, TN 37919-7736
Web Site(s): http://www.nutritioneducation.com
E-mail: aancal@aol.com

Undergraduate Degree Programs:
Associate of Science in Applied Nutrition

Certificate Programs: Diploma in Comprehensive Nutrition.

Class Titles: Understanding Nutrition, Environmental Challenges/Solutions, Eating Disorders/Weight Management, Vegetarian Nutrition, Medicinal Herbs/Other Alternative Therapies, Nutrition Counseling Skills, Women's Special Health Concerns, Pregnancy, Pediatric/Adolescent Nutrition, Clinical Nutrition, Sports Nutrition, Community Nutrition, Managing Small Business, Direct Marketing (Selling) Skills, Child Development, Anatomy/Physiology, Human Biology, General Chemistry, Organic/Biochemistry, Psychology, English: Reading Enhancement, Public Speaking, Business Mathematics.

Teaching Methods: *TV:* videotape. *Other:* audioconferencing, audiotapes, fax, correspondence, independent study, individual study.

Credits Granted for: examination (CLEP, DANTES, GRE).

Admission Requirements: *Undergraduate:* age 18, high school graduate or equivalent, 15-month limitation for

completion of diploma program, 12-month limitation for completion of each degree segment, 4-month completion for an individual course.

On-Campus Requirements: None.

Tuition and Fees: *Undergraduate:* $97/credit. *Other Costs:* $20/course fee for final exam (proctored).

Financial Aid: DANTES approval, employer paid tuition, group rates.

Accreditation: Distance Education and Training Council.

Description: For more than a decade, the American Academy of Nutrition (1984) has been dedicated to providing students from all walks of life with the most accessible, convenient, and comprehensive nutrition distance education in the world. We offer certificate, diploma, and degree programs that maintain the highest academic standards. Our faculty is comprised of respected nutrition educators providing the learning materials used by highly regarded universities. Our guided curriculum offers traditional and scientifically sound alternative approaches to thinking and nutrition. We are fully committed to helping people help others.

American College of Prehospital Medicine

365 Canal Street, Suite 2300	Phone: (800) 735-2276
New Orleans, LA 70130-1135	Fax: (800) 350-3870

Division(s): All
Web Site(s): http://www.acpm.edu
E-mail: ceo@acpm.edu or admit@acpm.edu

Undergraduate Degree Programs:
Associate of Science in Emergency Medical Services
Bachelor of Science in Emergency Medical Services

Certificate Programs: Emergency Medical Technology.

Teaching Methods: *Computers:* Internet, electronic classroom, e-mail, CD-ROM, LISTSERV. *TV:* videotape. *Other:* audiotapes, fax, correspondence, independent study, individual study.

Credits Granted for: experiential learning, portfolio assessment, extrainstitutional learning, examination (CLEP, ACT-PEP, DANTES, GRE).

Admission Requirements: *Undergraduate:* high school graduate, completion of EMT-Basic certification or military equivalent. For bachelor's degree, completion of paramedic training before graduation. *Certificate:* age 18.

On-Campus Requirements: The Certificate Course in Emergency Medical Technology requires 32 hours minimum of local seminar work for psychomotor skills and 10 hours of clinical exposure that will also be arranged by the Instructor/Coordinator appointed by the college.

Tuition and Fees: *Undergraduate:* $235/semester hour for single course enrollment, flat tuition for the 2 degree programs: $5,200 for the Associate of Science in Emergency Medical Services, $6,800 for the Bachelor of Science in Emergency Medical Services (we finance these amounts internally at 12% APR). *Application Fee:* $50. *Other Costs:* Students are required to have a CD-ROM equipped and Internet capable computer. Can be purchased locally or ACPM will refer them to the corporate sales department of PC Connection. Students who mail work to the college will incur postage expenses. No costs for telephone as all faculty have toll-free access for U.S./U.S.-possession students. No other costs. Tuition includes all course materials, books, software, videotapes, audiotapes, etc. *Credit by:* semester.

Financial Aid: VA, DANTES, military tuition assistance.

Accreditation: Distance Education and Training Council.

Description: ACPM (1991) was founded exclusively as a distance education institution dedicated to providing undergraduate, degree-completion opportunities to those involved in the civilian emergency medical services community and the military medical community. Our certificate course in Emergency Medical Technology was launched in 1997. We are becoming more heavily dependent upon electronic communication for which our students are now required to have computers that are CD-ROM equipped and Internet capable.

American Graduate University

| 733 North Dodsworth Avenue | Phone: (626) 966-4576 |
| Covina, CA 91724 | Fax: (626) 915-1709 |

Division(s): Student Services
Web Site(s): http://www.agu.edu
E-mail: agu@ix.netcom.com
Info@agu.edu

Graduate Degree Programs:
Master of Project Management
Master of Acquisition Management

Certificate Programs: Project/Program Management, Acquisition and Contracting, Financial Management and Pricing, Management.

Class Titles: Program Management, Government Program Management, Project Management, Technical Program Management, Earned Value Management Systems, Contracting/Procurement for Project Managers/Technical Personnel, Project Scheduling Techniques, Risk Analysis/Management, Building/Managing Project Teams, Marketing/Pricing/Management of Government Contracts/Subcontracts, Pricing/Negotiation of Government Contracts/Subcontracts, Contract Management/Administration, Subcontract Management/Advanced Procurement Techniques, Government Contract Law, Price/Cost Analysis, Negotiation Principles/Practices, Government Contracting, Financial Management of Government Contracts, Essentials of Management, Law/Contracts, Business Research Methods, Management Accounting/Control, Organizational Behavior/Human Resources, Financial Management, Management Economics.

Teaching Methods: *Computers:* e-mail. *Other:* correspondence, fax, live instruction.

Credits Granted for: transfer credits.

Admission Requirements: *Graduate:* accredited undergraduate degree, employed in subject area field. No requirements to take individual courses. *Certificate:* high school graduate, employed in subject area field.

On-Campus Requirements: None.

Tuition and Fees: *Graduate:* $550–$650/distance education course, $895–$1095/course for 3-day, 4-day, or 5-day live courses (12 courses in master's degree programs, 6 courses in professional certificate programs). *Credit by:* equivalent to semester; enrollment and completion take place continuously throughout the year.

Financial Aid: VA pending, DANTES pending.

Accreditation: Distance Education and Training Council.

Description: American Graduate University (1958) and its affiliate, Procurement Associates, Inc., have been developing and conducting public and distance education courses in all aspects of program/project management, contracts/procurement, and business management. AGU's distance education courses, offered since 1969, have attracted 100,000 industry and government representatives worldwide. AGU presently offers Master of Project Management and Master of Acquisition Management degree programs; Professional Certificate programs in project/program management, acquisition and contracts management, financial management, and business management; and individual professional development. The university is accredited and has full institutional approval from the California Bureau for Private Postsecondary and Vocational Education to grant its degrees.

American Health Science University

| 1010 South Joliet, #107 | Phone: (303) 340-2054 |
| Aurora, CO 80012 | Fax: (303) 367-2577 |

Division(s): None.
Web Site(s): http://healthynine@earthlink.net

E-mail: nuted@aol.com

Certificate Programs: Nutritionist.

Teaching Methods: *Computers:* e-mail. *Other:* fax, correspondence, independent study, individual study.

Credits Granted for: experiential learning, portfolio assessment, extrainstitutional learning (all on individual case basis).

Admission Requirements: *Certificate:* prerequisite college degree or equivalent work experience.

On-Campus Requirements: None.

Tuition and Fees: *Credit by:* 6 courses, 18 college semester hours for certificate program.

Accreditation: Distance Education and Training Council, courses validated by American Council on Education.

Description: American Health Science University (1980) is an accredited, adult distance education institution whose mission is to provide educational solutions for life's most precious quality—good health. Its courses are designed for individuals interested in profitably meeting the needs of the new kind of health care consumer who is asking questions about nutrition, nutritional supplements, herbs, and diets, and who has other lifestyle concerns.

American Military University

| 9104-P Manassas Drive | Phone: (703) 330-5398 |
| Manassas Park, VA 20111 | Fax: (703) 330-5109 |

Division(s): Academic Department
Web Site(s): http://www.amunet.edu
E-mail: amugen@amunet.edu or amuadmsn@amunet.edu

Undergraduate Degree Programs:
Bachelor of Arts in:
    Military History
    Military Management
    Intelligence Studies

Graduate Degree Programs:
Master of Arts in:
    Military Studies/Air Warfare
    Military Studies/Land Warfare
    Military Studies/Naval Warfare
    Military Studies/Unconventional Warfare
    Military Studies/Intelligence
    Military Studies/Defense Management
    Military Studies/Civil War Studies

Certificate Programs: Foreign Policy/Great Decisions.

Class Titles: All classes may be taken individually.

Teaching Methods: *Computers:* Internet, real-time chat, electronic classroom, e-mail, CD-ROM, newsgroup, LIST-SERV. *TV:* videotape. *Other:* videoconferencing, audioconferencing, fax, correspondence, independent study, individual study, learning contracts, internships.

Credits Granted for: experiential learning, portfolio assessment, extrainstitutional learning, examination (CLEP, ACT-PEP, DANTES, GRE).

Admission Requirements: *Undergraduate:* high school diploma/GED, age 18, 10 years to complete program. *Graduate:* accredited bachelor's degree, 2.7 GPA in final 60 undergraduate hours, references, 7 years to complete program. *Certificate:* complete local Great Decisions Program.

On-Campus Requirements: None.

Tuition and Fees: *Undergraduate:* $133/credit. *Graduate:* $200/credit. *Application Fee:* $50. *Credit by:* semester.

Financial Aid: Military Tuition Assistance, Federal Government Tuition Reimbursement, Corporate/Private Tuition Reimbursement, VA GI Bill, AMU Tuition Payment Plan

Accreditation: National/Distance Education and Training Council.

Description: AMU began in January 1993, offering graduate programs in military studies. From 4 original majors (Air/Land/Naval Warfare, Defense Management), AMU expanded in 1995 to include Unconventional Warfare, Intelligence, and Civil War Studies. AMU added its upper-level bachelor's program in January 1996 and recently expanded it to a full 4-year program offering majors in Military History, Military Management, and Intelligence Studies. AMU offers its military studies curriculum exclusively through distance learning. Students study independently under faculty member guidance, following a 15-week course guide. Extensive reading (100 pages/week), research, writing, and conferencing are required, along with at least 4 one-on-one student/professor contacts. These conferences are conducted by phone or e-mail through the Electronic Classroom. Online courses feature newsgroups, chatrooms, and discussion lists that enhance communication and collegiality between students and professors. AMU accepts transfer credits of up to 15 graduate (against a 36-hour program) and 90 (out of 120) undergraduate hours. More than 100 professors, most with PhDs, teach the 250+ courses AMU offers.

American River College

| 4700 College Oak Drive | Phone: (916) 484-8456 |
| Sacramento, CA 95841 | Fax: (916) 484-8018 |

Division(s): Learning Resources (located in ARC library)
Web Site(s): http://www.arc.losrios.cc.ca.us/learnres/distance.html
E-mail: ondricd@arc.losrios.cc.ca.us

Class Titles: Foundations of Biology, Business, Business Mathematics, Principles of Marketing, Small Business Management, Health Science, College Composition, Tutor Training.

Teaching Methods: *Computers:* Internet, e-mail. *TV:* videotape, cable program, satellite broadcasting, PBS. *Other:* audiotape.

Credits Granted for: Credit by examination, CLEP, DANTES.

Admission Requirements: *Undergraduate:* Open-door policy to high school graduates or people over age 18 with application. Fees for nonresidents of state/country.

On-Campus Requirements: Some meetings for TV classes, one meeting for online class.

Tuition and Fees: *Undergraduate:* $13/credit unit. *Other Costs:* Transfer Academy's Foundations of Biology class has $40 videotape rental, $20 refunded when tapes returned. *Credit by:* semester.

Financial Aid: Federal Stafford Loan, Federal Pell Grant, Federal Work-Study, VA, California resident programs.

Accreditation: Western Association of Schools and Colleges.

Description: American River College (1955) is among the 10 largest community colleges in the state and is looked upon as a leader in innovative programs and services. Each semester, ARC offers college credit courses for students at home via TV. Course selection is based on curriculum and the availability of suitable courses through the Consortium for Distance Learning. The staff chooses books and materials, and students must attend approximately 5 campus meetings. This nontraditional offering has provided transfer and general education courses to thousands of students without everyday campus access.

Andrew Jackson University

10 Old Montgomery Highway	Phone: (800) 429-9300
Birmingham, AL 35209	(205) 871-9288
	Fax: (205) 871-9294

Division(s): Distance Learning
Web Site(s): http://www.aju.edu
E-mail: info@aju.edu

Undergraduate Degree Programs:
Bachelor of Arts in Communication
Bachelor of Science in Business
Bachelor of Science in Criminal Justice

Graduate Degree Programs:
Master of Business Administration
Master of Public Administration

Master of Science in Criminal Justice

Teaching Methods: *Computers:* e-mail, software, CD-ROM. *TV:* videotape. *Other:* audiotapes, fax, correspondence, independent study, individual study.

Credits Granted for: experiential learning, portfolio assessment, extrainstitutional learning, examination (CLEP, ACT-PEP, DANTES).

Admission Requirements: *Undergraduate:* high school diploma or equivalent. *Graduate:* accredited bachelor's degree.

On-Campus Requirements: None.

Tuition and Fees: *Undergraduate:* $3,350/30-credit module (equivalent of 2 semesters) includes $150 enrollment fee. *Graduate:* $4,950/entire 36-credit program includes $150 enrollment fee. *Application Fee:* $25 (applicable to enrollment fee). *Software:* optional for some courses. *Other Costs:* $850–$1,350 textbooks, $100 graduation fee. *Credit by:* semester.

Financial Aid: interest-free tuition payment plan, PLATO loans.

Accreditation: Distance Education and Training Council.

Description: Andrew Jackson University's (1994) degree programs are designed for those whose circumstances demand flexible study. Courses are available only through off-campus, directed learning. No class schedules or assignment deadlines are imposed. Students may enroll and begin their program at any time and proceed as quickly as their desire, time, and ability permit. Degree programs are textbook-based, and study guides include learning objectives, assignment description, and detailed instructions. Some course materials also include audiotapes or videotapes and software or CD-ROM exercises. Each lesson is submitted as completed to allow for frequent faculty feedback. Midterm and final exams are proctored.

Andrews University

Berrien Springs, MI 49104	Phone: (800) 471-6210
	Fax: (616) 471-6236/6374

Division(s): Distance Education, undergraduate
School of Education Distance Education, graduate
Web Site(s): http://www.andrews.edu/AUHSI
http://www.educ.andrews.edu/DLC
E-mail: zork@andrews.edu
dlc@andrews.edu (graduate)

Undergraduate Degree Programs:
Associate of Arts in General Studies, Personal Ministry emphasis

Bachelor of Arts in:
   Religion
   General Studies, Humanities emphasis
Bachelor of Science in General Studies:
   Cross-Cultural Relations emphasis
   Human Organization and Behavior emphasis

Graduate Degree Programs:
variable; contact school.

Class Titles: 50 courses in areas of: Behavioral Science, Psychology, Sociology, Communication, Composition, American Literature, Cultural Geography, World Civilization, American History, Church History, American Government, College Algebra, Statistics, Enjoyment of Music, Nutrition, Astronomy, Greek, Biblical Studies, Religion. Graduate titles: Managing Behavior in Diverse Classroom, Technology/Learning in Today's Classroom, Helping Students Become Self-Directed Learners, Learning Differences: Effective Teaching with Learning Styles/Multiple Intelligence, Building Your Repertoire of Teaching Strategies, Including Students with Special Needs in Regular Classroom, Motivating Today's Learner, Teaching Students to Get Along, Strategies for Preventing Conflict/Violence, Succeeding with Difficult Students, High-Performing Teacher, How to Get Parents on Your Side, Assertive Discipline/Beyond, Assessment to Improve Student Learning.

Teaching Methods: *TV:* videotape, satellite broadcast. *Other:* correspondence.

Credits Granted for: experiential learning, portfolio assessment, extrainstitutional learning, examination (CLEP, ACT-PEP, DANTES, GRE).

Admission Requirements: *Undergraduate:* official documentation of completion of secondary school studies with a minimum of 13 units of solid subjects. Minimum GPA and college-bound percentile on ACT/SAT of (a) 2.75 overall GPA (b) or 2.5 overall GPA and 35th percentile on ACT/SAT (c) or 2.25 overall GPA and 50th percentile on ACT/SAT. A GED certification with a minimum average score of 60 on 5 sections and no section lower than 50 will also meet minimum admission requirements. *Graduate:* Students complete the admissions forms for Andrews University and are processed as Permission to Take Classes students. Students are encouraged to have a study partner or partners or participate in the course activities. The regular standards for admission do not apply to PTC students at Andrews University on the main campus, extension campuses, or distance learning settings. If students subsequently wish to enroll in the university for degree programs, they are processed through regular admission channels and standards with a maximum of 32 credits PTC transferrable to a degree.

On-Campus Requirements: None.

Tuition and Fees: *Undergraduate:* $165/credit. *Graduate:*

$350/course. Discounts offered for 2 or more registering for same course together. Call to verify current/discounted rates. *Application Fee:* $30, degree-seeking student. *Other Costs:* extra for shipping/handling of textbooks and study guides, $60 enrollment processing fee (one or more classes). *Credit by:* quarter basis: courses offered on semester basis but converted to quarter credits before they are transcripted. Most courses are 3 semester hours (4.5 quarter credits); 5 quarter credits (equal to 3.3 semester hours) per course.

Financial Aid: Students must be accepted into a degree-seeking program at Andrews University and be attending at least half-time. Eligibility is determined through the standard FAFSA process. Students must adhere to the same academic calendar as on-campus students. If students are Michigan residents and meet other eligibility requirements, state funding is available.

Accreditation: North Central Association of Colleges and Schools, National Council for Accreditation of Teacher Education.

Description: Andrews University (1874) is a Christian university in the Seventh-Day Adventist tradition. It was first established in 1874 in Battle Creek, Michigan as Battle Creek College. Andrews University is comprised of the College of Arts and Sciences, the College of Technology, the School of Business, the School of Education, the Seventh-Day Adventist Theological Seminary, and the Division of Architecture. Course and degree offerings through the undergraduate distance education program are primarily offered through College of Arts and Sciences. The university offers more than 180 education programs on campus with a general education component rooted in the strong liberal arts tradition. The undergraduate distance education program at Andrews University functions in partnership with Home Study International, a distinguished and accredited distance education delivery institution since 1909. Our partnership is new, having established the AU/HSI Distance Education program in 1997. The graduate distance education program is housed in the School of Education and was established in 1989.

Angelina College

PO Box 1768	Phone: (409) 639-1301
Lufkin, TX 75902-1768	Fax: (409) 639-4299

Division(s): Registration
Web Site(s): http://angelina.cc.tx.us
E-mail: jhill@angelina.cc.tx.us

Undergraduate Degree Programs:
Associate of Science in many areas
Associate of Arts in many areas
Associate of Applied Science in many areas

Certificate Programs: Business, some vocational programs.

Class Titles: Psychology, Sociology, Government, History.

Teaching Methods: *TV:* videotape, satellite broadcasting. *Other:* Off-site classrooms.

Credits Granted for: examination (CLEP, ACT-PEP, DANTES).

Admission Requirements: *Undergraduate:* application, transcripts, TASP test results.

On-Campus Requirements: None.

Tuition and Fees: *Undergraduate:* $19/credit in-district, $25/credit out-of-district, $30/credit out-of-state. *Other Costs:* $66 in fees. *Credit by:* semester.

Financial Aid: Federal Pell Grant, Federal Work-Study, VA.

Accreditation: Southern Association of Colleges and Schools.

Description: Angelina College opened the doors of its original 7 buildings to students in the fall of 1968. Distance learning programs began around 1993, allowing students to study off-campus. Credits earned at Angelina may be transferred to senior colleges throughout the nation.

Anne Arundel Community College

101 College Parkway	Phone: (410) 541-2464
Arnold, MD 21012	Fax: (410) 541-2874

Division(s): Distance Learning Center
Web Site(s): http://web.aacc.cc.md.us/diseduc
E-mail: pmmccarthyoneill@mail.aacc.cc.md.us

Undergraduate Degree Programs:
Associate of Science in Business Administration Transfer
Associate of Applied Science in Business Management
Associate of Arts in General Studies Transfer
Associate of Applied Science in Computer Information Systems Personal Computer Systems Technology Option

Certificate Programs: Business Management (Communications Option), Computer Information Systems Personal Computer Specialist Option.

Teaching Methods: *Computers:* Internet, real-time chat, electronic classroom, e-mail, CD-ROM, LISTSERV. *TV:* videotape, cable program, PBS. *Other:* videoconferencing, audioconferencing, fax, independent study.

Credits Granted for: examination (CLEP, DANTES).

Admission Requirements: *Undergraduate:* academic credentials, SAT, ACT, AACC assessment tests and/or equivalent college courses.

On-Campus Requirements: None.

Tuition and Fees: *Undergraduate:* $63/credit. *Other Costs:* $35/telecourse; $20 registration fee. *Credit by:* semester.

Financial Aid: Federal Stafford Loan, Federal PLUS Loan, Federal Pell Grant, Federal Work-Study, VA, Maryland resident programs.

Accreditation: Middle States Association of Colleges and Schools.

Description: Anne Arundel Community College began in 1961 with teaching as its central mission. It is an accredited, public, open-admission institution of higher learning located in the Washington-Baltimore-Annapolis triangle. In academic year 1996–1997, 16,999 credit students and 25,574 noncredit students enrolled for classes on the centrally located 230-acre campus, at 2 off-campus centers, or at one of more than 100 additional sites throughout the county. The distance learning program began in 1981 with telecourses. Its original charge was to serve students unable to attend traditional classroom courses because of scheduling conflicts, lack of transportation, home responsibilities, etc. In February 1995 the Going the Distance Agreement was signed, committing the college to develop degree and program completion pathways for its distance learning students. Currently, the distance learning program offers telecourses, online courses, and teleweb courses.

Anoka-Ramsey Community College Coon Rapids Campus

11200 Mississippi Boulevard NW	Phone: (612) 427-2600
Coon Rapids, MN 55433	Fax: (612) 422-3341

Division(s): Education Services–Instruction
Web Site(s): http://www.an.cc.mn.us
E-mail: None.

Undergraduate Degree Programs:
Associate in Arts
Associate in Science
Associate in Applied Science

Certificate Programs: Business-related.

Class Titles: Business, Accounting, Marketing, Management, Economics, Geography.

Teaching Methods: *Computers:* Internet, real-time chat, electronic classroom, e-mail, newsgroup, LISTSERV. *Other:* independent study.

Credits Granted for: experiential learning, examination (CLEP, ACT-PEP).

Admission Requirements: *Undergraduate:* application and fees, assessment tests.

On-Campus Requirements: Faculty determine on-campus meetings—up to 3.

Tuition and Fees: *Undergraduate:* $78/credit. *Application Fee:* $20. *Other Costs:* $3 transcripts. *Credit by:* semester.

Financial Aid: Federal Stafford Loan, Federal Perkins Loan, Federal PLUS Loan, Federal Pell Grant, Federal Work-Study, VA, Minnesota resident programs.

Accreditation: North Central Association of Colleges and Schools, Association of Collegiate Business Schools and Programs.

Description: Anoka-Ramsey Community College, Coon Rapids Campus (1965), a multicampus college just north of Minneapolis/St. Paul, offers associate degrees in transfer and career areas and certificates through its business program and its continuing education department. In 1978, this publicly supported institution added its Cambridge campus about 35 miles away. More than 8,500 students of all ages and backgrounds enroll in transfer and career programs each semester at the 2 campuses. Another 4,000 participate annually in continuing education and community service activities. Appropriate Anoka-Ramsey credits are transferable to all Minnesota colleges and universities and are accepted by out-of-state schools as well. Distance learning through Internet classes began 2 years ago and has grown to 6 offerings/semester in 1998.

Arizona State University

PO Box 870501	Phone: (602) 965-6738
Tempe, AZ 85287-0501	Fax: (602) 965-1371

Division(s): Distance Learning Technology
Web Site(s): http://www.dlt.asu.edu
http://asuonline.asu.edu (Internet courses)
E-mail: distance@asu.edu

Graduate Degree Programs:
Master of Science in Engineering, Electrical Engineering major (available in metro Phoenix area over TV)

Class Titles: Accounting Lab, Qualitative Methods in Cultural Art Contexts, Groundwater Hydrology, Intelligent Transport Systems, Principles of Process Control, Voice Improvement, Communication Technology in Everyday Life, Operating Systems, Computer Networks, Artificial Intelligence, Natural Language Processing, Database Management, Parallel Processing, Software Engineering, Software Verification/Validation/Testing, Dance, Cross-cultural Dance Perspectives, Patterns in Nature, Electrical Networks, Electronic Devices/Instrumentation, Properties of Electronic Materials, Outdoor/Environmental Education, Signals/Systems, Electromagnetic Engineering, Random Signal Analysis, Comp Electromagnetics, Digital Image Processing/Compression, Artificial Neural Computation Systems, Analog Integrated Circuits, VLSI Design, Semiconductor Device Theory, Solid State Electronics, Electromagnetic Fields/Guided Waves, Antenna Analysis/Design, Transform Theory/Applications, Error Correcting Codes, Random Signal Theory, Digital Communications, Power System Transients, Power Engineering Operations/Planning, Digital Control Systems, Optimal Control Systems, Fiber Optics, Error Correct Code, Communication Systems, Digital Signal Processing, Digital Systems/Circuits, Electrical Machine, Electrical Power Device, Electrical Power Plant Systems, Filter Design, State Space, Analog Integrated Circuits, Solid State Devices, Analog CMOS, Low Power Electronics, Multidimensional Signal Processing, A to D Converters, Wireless Networks, Adaptive Signal Processing, Microwave Solid State Circuit Design, Current Issues/Problems in Media/Computer Ed, Instructional Media Design, Internet for Teachers, Understanding Teaching, Distance Education Theory/Practice, Medieval/Renaissance Paleography, Physical Activity/Healthy Lifestyles, Fitness for Living, Fitness for Life, Parenting, Personal Growth in Human Relationships, Family Development, Nutrition, Global Change, Global/Environmental Change, Middle Ages, Renaissance, 19th-Century Europe, U.S. Immigration/Ethnicity, Arizona, Contemporary Issues in Humanities, Technology Management, Prod Control Information Systems, Business/Industrial Publications, Consumer Perspective/Business Law, Teaching with Technology, Optimal Control, Mechanical Design/Failure Prevention, Rotary Wing Aerodynamics, Conduction Heat Transfer, Comp Methods Eng. Mech., Media Statistics, Media/Politics, Advertising/Marketing Communication, Southwest Home Horticulture, Purchasing/Supplier Management, Hispanic Literature, Theater, Women/Social Action, Women in Contemporary Society.

Teaching Methods: *Computers:* Internet, real-time chat, electronic classroom, e-mail, CD-ROM, newsgroup, LISTSERV. *TV:* videotape, cable program, satellite broadcasting, PBS. *Other:* videoconferencing, audioconferencing, audiographics, audiotapes, fax, correspondence, independent study.

Credits Granted for: examination (CLEP, ACT-PEP, DANTES, GRE).

Admission Requirements: *Undergraduate:* high school graduate and/or sufficient ACT/SAT scores. *Graduate:* application to Graduate Admissions Office; visit http://www.asu.edu. *Certificate:* variable.

On-Campus Requirements: Students must complete 30 hours (may be at a distance) through ASU.

Tuition and Fees: *Undergraduate:* $110; other tuition/fees may apply. *Graduate:* $110; other tuition/fees may apply. *Application Fee:* $40 nonresident undergraduate, nonrefundable; $15 nondegree graduate, nonrefundable. *Other Costs:* $35 graduation application fee, $10 nondegree studies. *Credit by:* semester.

Financial Aid: Federal Stafford Loan, Federal Perkins Loan,

Federal PLUS Loan, Federal Pell Grant, Federal Work-Study, VA, Arizona resident programs.

Accreditation: North Central Association of Colleges and Schools.

Description: Arizona State University (1885) began offering classes at a distance in 1935 with the introduction of correspondence study. In 1955, ASU offered the first tele-course in Arizona over a local TV station. In 1982 the Arizona Board of Regents adopted guidelines for developing educa-tional telecommunications systems. In the fall of 1982, the Instructional Television Fixed Service (ITFS) system began sending engineering and business courses to corporate sites in Phoenix. The ITFS system also connects to various educational access channels, allowing students to receive some live interactive courses in their homes. Shortly after National Technological University (NTU) began in 1988, ASU contributed courses via satellite. The university also uses NAUNet, a microwave network connecting the 3 state universities. For several years ASU has offered CD-ROM courses and, since the spring of 1996, has offered courses via the Internet.

Arizona State University West

4702 West Thunderbird Road	Phone: (602) 543-4577
Phoenix, AZ 85069	Fax: (602) 543-7012

Division(s): Extended Instruction
Web Site(s): http://www.west.asu.edu/asuw/acprogs/exted.html

Class Titles: contact school.

Teaching Methods: *Computers:* Internet, e-mail. *TV:* cable program, local TV. *Other:* correspondence.

Admission Requirements: *Undergraduate:* contact school or see http://www.west.asu.edu/asuw/acprogs/app.html.

On-Campus Requirements: only allow an average of 2 correspondence courses.

Tuition and Fees: *Undergraduate:* $105/credit in-state, $360/credit nonresident. *Graduate:* same. *Doctoral:* same. *Application Fee:* $12 undergraduate, $17 graduate. *Credit by:* semester.

Financial Aid: Federal Perkins Loan, Federal Pell Grant, Federal Supplemental Educational Opportunity Grant, William D. Ford Federal District Loan Program, Federal Family Educational Loan Program (graduate students only), Federal PLUS Loan, Federal Work-Study, VA. State/local: Financial Aid Trust Grant, State Student Incentive Grant, Regents' Merit, ASU West Regents, ASU West Book, ASU West Honeywell Engineering, Community Leadership, Devil's West, J.W. Mirandon Memorial, Ruth Zornew, Provost's Club, Vernon E.

Lattin Cultural Diversity.

Accreditation: North Central Association of Colleges and Schools.

Description: Arizona State University West (1984), an upper-level, nonresidential campus of Arizona State University, is located in the rapidly growing northwestern area of metropol-itan Maricopa County. ASU West offers quality academic programs through the College of Arts and Sciences, School of Management, College of Education, College of Human Services, and the Division of Collaborative Programs. The campus is committed to encouraging the educational, economic, cultural, and social development of the metropoli-tan area. ASU West prepares students to be successful in the global society of the 21st century by engendering a respon-siveness to change and an appreciation of intellectual, cultural, gender, and generational diversity.

Arkansas State University

2004 East Nettleton	Phone: (870) 972-3052
Jonesboro, AR 72401	Fax: (870) 972-3849

Division(s): Regional Programs
Web Site(s): http://www.astate.edu
E-mail: linnstaedter@caddo.astate.edu

Undergraduate Degree Programs:
Bachelor of Science in:
  Accounting
  Business Administration
  Elementary Education
  Criminology
  Nursing

Graduate Degree Programs:
Master of Science in:
  Educational Administration
  Elementary Education
  Nursing (not all programs available at every site)

Teaching Methods: *TV:* compressed video networking. *Other:* None.

Credits Granted for: experiential learning, portfolio assess-ment, examination (CLEP).

Admission Requirements: *Undergraduate:* contact admis-sions@chickasaw.astate.edu. *Graduate:* contact Graduate School at gradsch@choctaw.astate.edu.

On-Campus Requirements: must be on the campus of one of our partner schools.

Tuition and Fees: *Undergraduate:* contact school. *Credit by:* semester.

Financial Aid: available only to students on ASU-J campus or the campus of one of our partner schools.

Accreditation: North Central Association of Colleges and Schools.

Description: Arkansas State University (1909) started distance learning to provide nursing education to parts of rural Arkansas. Distance learning is presently available only at 8 off-campus sites—partner colleges—in Arkansas: ASU-Beebe, ASU-Mountain Home, Mid-South Community College, Mississippi County Community College, East Arkansas Community College, Westark Community College, Ozarka Technical College, and Black River Technical College.

Art Instruction Schools

3309 Broadway Street NE	Phone: (612) 362-5075
Minneapolis, MN 55413	Fax: (612) 362-5260

Division(s): Education
Web Site(s): None.
E-mail: None.

Certificate Programs: Fundamentals of Art.

Teaching Methods: *Other:* correspondence, independent study, individual study, telephone.

Credits Granted for: portfolio assessment for advanced college placement.

Admission Requirements: *Certificate:* review of personal artwork competence, 2-year completion limit.

On-Campus Requirements: None.

Tuition and Fees: *Undergraduate:* $1,785/28 lessons included in the Fundamentals of Art certificate program. *Credit by:* self-paced learning schedule.

Accreditation: Distance Education and Training Council.

Description: Art Instruction Schools (1914) began as an in-house training department for commercial artists in the Minneapolis printing industry. Today we enroll students throughout the U.S., Canada, and several other foreign countries, making AIS the premier home-study art school in the world. Some of our students just want to become more familiar with basic art concepts and techniques. But many others have gone on to become famous, supporting the Hollywood film industry, Disney, or their private careers, like Charles Schulz, creator of "Peanuts" cartoons. Many graduates work in commercial art or sell their work in galleries worldwide. Some use our training as a foundation for advanced placement into a college art program. Whatever your motivation, AIS instructors will guide you through the Fundamentals of Art—from shapes to shading, pencil to color, muscle structure to figure drawing, perspective to

building your portfolio—so you can learn at home, on your own schedule, as a class of one.

Ashland Community College

1400 College Drive	Phone: (606) 329-2999
Ashland, KY 41101	Fax: (606) 324-9951

Division(s): Academic Affairs
Web Site(s): http://www.ashcc.uky.edu
E-mail: lshytle@pop.ashcc.uky.edu

Graduate Degree Programs:
Master of Science in Education

Doctoral Degree Programs:
Education Doctorate in:
    Education Administration
    Course Work Rehabilitation Counseling

Class Titles: Aerosols, Algorithms-Theory/Practice, Seminar in Administration, Issues in EDS, Severe Developmental Disabilities, Family Studies, Special Education, Coal Preparation.

Teaching Methods: *Computers:* Internet, real-time chat, electronic classroom, e-mail, CD-ROM, newsgroup, LIST-SERV. *TV:* videotape, cable program, satellite broadcasting, PBS. *Other:* radio broadcast, audioconferencing, videoconferencing, audiographics, audiotapes, fax, correspondence, independent study, individual study, learning contracts.

Credits Granted for: experiential learning, portfolio assessment, extrainstitutional learning, examination (CLEP, ACT-PEP, DANTES, GRE).

Admission Requirements: *Graduate:* application, accredited bachelor's degree, 2.5 undergraduate GPA, 3.0 graduate GPA, 2 official transcripts from all colleges/universities, GRE, letter of recommendation. *Doctoral:* Same as graduate.

On-Campus Requirements: None.

Tuition and Fees: *Graduate:* $147/credit. *Doctoral:* $147/credit. *Other Costs:* $6/credit technology fee, $36 (full-time). *Credit by:* semester.

Financial Aid: Federal Stafford Loan, Federal Perkins Loan, Federal PLUS Loan, Federal Pell Grant, Federal Work-Study, VA, Kentucky resident programs.

Accreditation: Southern Association of Colleges and Schools.

Description: Ashland Community College (1938) provides education without barriers to all citizens in its service area. Emerging technologies in the early 1990s allowed us to enter distance learning via compressed video. For many years prior, we had accessed the satellite network. Currently we are moving toward the virtual classroom via the Web.

Athabasca University

1 University Drive
Athabasca, Alberta, Canada T9S 3A3

Phone: (403) 675-6100
(800) 788-9041
Fax: (403) 675-6145

Division(s): None.
Web Site(s): http://www.athabascau.ca
E-mail: auinfo@athabascau.ca

Undergraduate Degree Programs:
Bachelor of Administration in:
  Health Administration
  Industrial Relations
  Management
  Organization
  Public Administration
Bachelor of Arts in:
  Anthropology
  Canadian Studies
  English
  French
  History
  Humanities
  Information Systems
  Labour Studies
  Psychology
  Sociology
  Women's Studies
Bachelor of Commerce
Bachelor of General Studies in Arts/Science, Applied Studies
Bachelor of Nursing (post Registered Nurse)
Bachelor of Professional Arts in Communications, Criminal Justice
Bachelor of Science, with or without Human Science major
Bachelor of Science in Computing/Information Systems

Graduate Degree Programs:
Master of Business Administration
Master of Distance Education
Advanced Graduate Diploma in Community Nursing Practice, Management

Certificate Programs: Accounting, Advanced Accounting, Administration, Career Development, Computers/Management Information Systems, Counseling Women, English Language Studies, French Language Proficiency, Health Development Administration, Home Health Nursing, Information Systems, Labour Relations, Labour Studies, Public Administration, Rehabilitation Practice, Diploma in Arts, Diploma in Inclusive Education.

Class Titles: Accounting, Administration, Anthropology, Applied Studies, Art History, Astronomy/Astrophysics, Biology, Career Development, Chemistry, Communications, Communication Studies, Computers/Management Information Systems, Computer Science/Information Systems, Criminal Justice, Counseling, Economics, Educational Psychology, English, Environmental Studies, Finance, French, Geography, Geology, German, Global Studies, Health, Health Administration, Health Studies, History, Humanities, Industrial Relations, Information Systems, Labour Studies, Legal Studies, Management Science, Marketing, Mathematics, Music, Native Studies, Nursing, Nutrition, Organizational Behavior, Philosophy, Physics, Political Economy, Political Science, Psychology, Public Administration, Religious Studies, Science, Small Business Management, Social Science, Sociology, Spanish, Taxation, Women's Studies. (Over 430 undergraduate courses available for home study without degree or credential enrollment; call (800) 788-9041 or visit www.athabascau.ca for list.)

Teaching Methods: *Computers:* Internet, electronic classroom, e-mail, CD-ROM, newsgroup. *TV:* videotape, cable program, satellite broadcasting. *Other:* radio broadcast, videoconferencing, audiotapes, correspondence, independent study, individual study.

Credits Granted for: experiential learning, portfolio assessment, extrainstitutional learning. Along with its Centre for Prior Learning Assessment, the university has collaboration and articulation agreements with several colleges, universities, and professional associations, often giving diploma-holders or members advanced standing in Athabasca via block transfer credit.

Admission Requirements: *Undergraduate:* age 18 (some exceptions). Some courses/programs have specific academic requirements. *Graduate:* For Master of Business Administration or Advanced Graduate Diploma in Management call (800) 561-4650. For Master of Distance Education call (800) 788-9041 x6179.

On-Campus Requirements: None.

Tuition and Fees: *Undergraduate:* $372/3-credit course (includes tuition, textbooks, materials/handling, student/alumni fees). *Graduate:* $19,550 for entire MBA program, $9,950 for entire MDE program. *Application Fee:* $50 (one-time, nonrefundable, for undergraduates). *Credit by:* by course (3- or 6-credit).

Financial Aid: Provincial Student Finance Boards; various awards/scholarships.

Accreditation: Association of Universities and Colleges of Canada, Association of Commonwealth Universities, International Council for Distance Education, Canadian Association for Distance Education.

Description: Athabasca University is a world leader in distance education, offering a university education since 1970 to all people regardless of location or educational background. With more than 430 undergraduate and graduate courses and more than 45 degree and certificate programs, the university offers an alternative to traditional campus-based study. More than 14,000 students worldwide register for courses annually. Most study part-time in their communities while working full- or part-time, employing learning methods and course materials such as textbooks and study guides, audiotapes, videotapes, science lab kits, computer software, and the Internet.

Atlantic Union College

338 Main Street	Phone: (978) 368-2300
South Lancaster, MA 01561	(800) 282-2030
	Fax: (978) 368-2514

Division(s): Adult Degree Program
Web Site(s): http://atlanticuc.edu
E-mail: adp@atlanticuc.edu

Undergraduate Degree Programs:
Bachelor of Science
Bachelor of Arts

Graduate Degree Programs:
Master of Education

Teaching Methods: *Computers:* e-mail. *Other:* audiotapes, fax, correspondence, independent study, individual study, learning contracts.

Credits Granted for: prior learning credit portfolios, examination (CLEP).

Admission Requirements: *Undergraduate:* high school graduation or equivalent (GED with no score below 50 in any subtest or 5 GCE passes). Students who do not have high school equivalency may prepare portfolio to demonstrate the necessary competencies for college admission have been met. TOEFL score of 550 is required for applicants whose native language is not English. Completed application, essay, letter of recommendation, transcripts, application fee. *Graduate:* application, essay, recommendations, application fee, GRE scores, transcript of bachelor's degree.

On-Campus Requirements: 8–11 day seminars offered in January and July or each time they start a new unit of study.

Tuition and Fees: *Undergraduate:* $3,500/unit of study (16 credits). *Graduate:* $3,950/unit of study. *Application Fee:* $15 undergraduate, $25 graduate. *Other Costs:* $50 graduation fee, $40 student fees. *Credit by:* semester.

Financial Aid: Federal Stafford Loan, Federal Pell Grant.

Accreditation: New England Association of Schools and Colleges.

Description: Atlantic Union College is an accredited coeducational, liberal arts/professional institution. Founded in 1882 by the Seventh-Day Adventist Church for the purpose of preparing trained workers for its worldwide organization, the college now educates students for many professions and occupations in the church, community, and larger society. The campus welcomes qualified students who are interested in an education structured on Christian and liberal arts principles. The college draws its students from all over the world, encouraging a varied and cosmopolitan campus atmosphere. The Adult Degree Program is based on 2 beliefs held by the college faculty: that many adults whose college work has been interrupted by marriage, work, military service, or other personal circumstances should have the opportunity of completing their degrees, and that there are many ways of doing reputable academic work other than being enrolled in on-campus courses. The program was founded in 1972 for adults who wished to complete degrees started years before, for college graduates who are changing their professions, and for life-long learners.

Auburn University

204 Mell Hall	Phone: (334) 844-3103
Auburn, AL 36849	Fax: (334) 844-4731

Division(s): Distance Learning
Web Site(s): http://www.auburn.edu/outreach/dl
E-mail: audl@uce.auburn.edu

Graduate Degree Programs:
Master of:
    Business Administration
    Aerospace Engineering
    Chemical Engineering
    Civil Engineering
    Computer Science
    Industrial/Systems Engineering
    Materials Engineering
    Mechanical Engineering
    Hotel/Restaurant Management

Class Titles: American Government, Biology, Criminal Justice, Economics, Entomology, Film, Geography, Horticulture, Math, Political Science, Psychology, Vocational Education.

Teaching Methods: *Computers:* Internet, real-time chat, electronic classroom, e-mail, CD-ROM, LISTSERV. *TV:* videotape, satellite broadcasting. *Other:* videoconferencing, audioconferencing, audiotapes, fax, correspondence, individual study.

Credits Granted for: examination (CLEP, ACT-PEP, DANTES, GRE).

Admission Requirements: *Graduate:* GRE, 5-year limit, etc.

On-Campus Requirements: Some days required for Graduate Degrees.

Tuition and Fees: *Undergraduate:* $46/quarter hour. *Graduate:* $185–$225/quarter hour. *Application Fee:* $25 (graduate). *Software:* variable. *Other Costs:* materials, etc. *Credit by:* quarter.

Financial Aid: Federal Stafford Loan, Federal Perkins Loan, Federal PLUS Loan, Federal Pell Grant, Federal Work-Study, VA, Alabama resident programs.

Accreditation: Southern Association of Colleges and Schools.

Description: Auburn University (1859) today enrolls 21,778 students, the largest on-campus enrollment in Alabama. The university's mission is to embrace the interrelation of instruction, research, and outreach. For instruction, Auburn offers the baccalaureate in more than 130 areas that span the disciplines, providing the state's only publicly supported programs in many fields. The graduate school provides master's level programs in more than 64 areas and the doctorate in more than 40. Auburn's successes in research within its 12 schools and colleges have been recognized by the National Science Foundation and the Carnegie Foundation, among others. Many outreach programs use the Auburn University Conference Center, with advanced audio/visual and computer technology. The Auburn University Satellite Uplink provides capabilities for national and international video programming. Through this comprehensive university instruction, research, and outreach, Auburn is having a positive impact on people's lives.

Aurora University

347 South Gladstone Avenue
Aurora, IL 60506

Phone: (630) 844-5401
Fax: (630) 844-7830

Division(s): School of Business and Professional Studies
Web Site(s): http://www.aurora.edu
E-mail: lquick@aurora.edu

Certificate Programs: Quality and System Management Program.

Teaching Methods: *Computers:* Internet, e-mail. *Other:* None.

Admission Requirements: *Undergraduate:* advanced undergraduates. *Graduate:* graduate students.

On-Campus Requirements: None.

Tuition and Fees: *Undergraduate:* $1,300/3-semester-hour course. *Graduate:* $1,300/3-semester-hour course. *Doctoral:* $1,300/3-semester-hour course. *Application Fee:* $100. *Software:* included. *Credit by:* semester.

Accreditation: North Central Association of Colleges and Schools.

Description: Aurora University (1893) began as Mendota

Seminary to train ministers and lay workers in the Advent Christian Church. The seminary quickly became a college, providing a full, liberal arts, collegiate curriculum. By 1911 the college had outgrown its facilities and moved closer to Chicago. Citizens of Aurora donated land and funds to cover the cost of erecting the first 3 buildings of Aurora College, which grew substantially over the years. In 1938 it was one of the first small colleges to achieve regional accreditation. In 1947 the college instituted an evening program, one of the nation's first adult education programs at a liberal arts college. The college became legally independent of the Advent Christian Church in 1971. In 1985 the college reorganized as Aurora University, reflecting the increased size of the institution and the breadth of its many new programs. The university serves 3,500 degree-seeking students in 34 undergraduate majors, 30 undergraduate minors, and 7 graduate programs. The main campus is located in Aurora, Illinois, with a 200-acre campus in Lake Geneva, Wisconsin, and instructional sites in Chicago and Waukegan, Illinois, and New Berlin, Wisconsin. The university began distance learning in 1997.

Austin Community College

7748 Highway 290 West
Austin, TX 78736

Phone: (888) 223-8026
Fax: (512) 223-8988

Division(s): Open Campus
Web Site(s): http://opc.austin.cc.tx.us
E-mail: kruch10@austin.cc.tx.us

Teaching Methods: *Computers:* Internet, electronic classroom, e-mail. *TV:* videotape, cable program, satellite broadcasting, PBS. *Other:* videoconferencing, independent study.

Credits Granted for: examination (CLEP, ACT-PEP, DANTES, GRE).

Admission Requirements: *Undergraduate:* high school graduate.

On-Campus Requirements: None.

Tuition and Fees: *Undergraduate:* $38/credit in-district, $71/credit Texas out-of-district, $143/credit out-of-state and international. *Other Costs:* $28/semester. *Credit by:* semester.

Financial Aid: Federal Stafford Loan, Federal Perkins Loan, Federal Pell Grant, Federal Work-Study, VA, Texas resident programs.

Accreditation: Southern Association of Colleges and Schools.

Description: In the fall of 1973, Austin Community College offered its first classes to 2,363 students. Since then ACC has grown to 6 campuses, a district administration office building, and numerous community sites throughout its 8-

county service area. More than 26,000 students attended during the fall of 1997. ACC offered its first distance learning course in the spring of 1979. It now offers more than 100 courses each semester and generates 13,000 enrollments annually. Open Campus is rapidly expanding the courses using the Internet and interactive compressed video.

Aviation and Electronic Schools of America

7940 Silverton Avenue, Suite 101	Phone: (619) 566-2184
San Diego, CA 92126	Fax: (619) 684-3583

Division(s): Jamie Doyle
Web Site(s): http://www.aesa.com
E-mail: aesa@aesa.com

Certificate Programs: FCC General Radiotelephone Operator's License, Airframe and Powerplant License, FCC General Telephone Operator's License.

Teaching Methods: *TV:* videotape. *Other:* correspondence, independent study, individual study.

On-Campus Requirements: Some programs require the student to attend a seminar portion that will be equal to 49% or less of the total course length.

Tuition and Fees: *Undergraduate:* Contact school. *Graduate:* Contact school. *Doctoral:* Contact school. *Application Fee:* Contact school. *Software:* Contact school. *Other Costs:* Contact school.

Financial Aid: VA (pending).

Accreditation: Distance Education and Training Council.

Description: Aviation and Electronic Schools of America (1988) specializes in short-term career advancement programs leading to certification or higher skills in the aviation maintenance, telecommunications, electronic, and computer fields. Originally founded by James P. Doyle, the school has grown to 55 current employees. To better serve our military and other frequently traveling students, the company developed the FCC General Radiotelephone Operator's License course in a distance format. Current plans call for the addition of a distance version of the Airframe and Powerplant License course as well as combination distance/seminar versions of the Airframe and Powerplant and FCC General Radiotelephone Operators license courses.

Baker College Center for Graduate Studies and Baker College On-Line

1050 West Bristol Road	Phone: (800) 469-3165
Flint, MI 48507-5508	Fax: (810) 766-4399

Division(s): Graduate Studies
Web Site(s): http://www.baker.edu
E-mail: gurden_c@corpfl.baker.edu

Undergraduate Degree Programs:
Associate of Business Administration
Bachelor of Business Administration.

Graduate Degree Programs:
Master of Business Administraiton.

Certificate Programs: Certified Financial Planning, Microsoft Certified Professional.

Class Titles: Contact school for list.

Teaching Methods: *Computers:* electronic classroom, e-mail. *Other:* None.

Credits Granted for: experiential learning, portfolio assessment, examination (CLEP, ACT-PEP, DANTES, GRE).

Admission Requirements: *Undergraduate:* high school graduate, with work experience. *Graduate:* accredited bachelor's degree and 3 years of work experience. *Certificate:* high school graduate or equivalent.

On-Campus Requirements: None.

Tuition and Fees: *Undergraduate:* $140/credit. *Graduate:* $215/credit. *Application Fee:* $25. *Software:* $100. *Other Costs:* books. *Credit by:* quarter.

Financial Aid: Federal Stafford Loan, Federal Perkins Loan, Federal PLUS Loan, Federal Pell Grant, Federal Work-Study, VA, Michigan resident programs.

Accreditation: North Central Association of Colleges and Schools.

Description: Baker College (1888) is a private, nonprofit, educational institution. Currently Baker College has 13 campuses throughout Michigan and is currently the largest private school system in the state. Baker entered distance education through its graduate school in 1994. Since many MBA candidates are busy with work, family, etc., Baker designed a degree to fit their needs.

Baker University

6600 College Boulevard, Suite 340
Overland Park, KS 66211

Phone: (913) 491-4432
Fax: (913) 491-0470

Division(s): School of Professional and Graduate Studies
Web Site(s): http://www.bakerspgs.edu
E-mail: jtdriski@apollogrp.edu

Undergraduate Degree Programs:
Associate of Arts in Business
Bachelor of Science in Management
Bachelor of Business Administration

Graduate Degree Programs:
Master of Business Administration
Master of Science in Management
Master of Liberal Arts
Master of Arts in Education

Teaching Methods: *Computers:* Internet, real-time chat, e-mail. *Other:* None.

Credits Granted for: experiential learning, portfolio assessment, extrainstitutional learning, examination (CLEP, ACT-PEP, DANTES, GRE).

Admission Requirements: *Undergraduate:* AAB degree: age 21, one year of work experience; BBA/BSM: age 23, 2 years of work experience. *Graduate:* age 25, 3 years of work experience.

On-Campus Requirements: None.

Tuition and Fees: *Undergraduate:* $180/credit—AAB degree; $260/credit—BSM and BBA degrees. *Graduate:* $280/credit—MSM degree; $300/credit—MBA degree. *Application Fee:* $20. *Credit by:* semester.

Financial Aid: Federal Stafford Loan, Federal Perkins Loan, Federal PLUS Loan, Federal Pell Grant, Federal Work-Study, VA, Kansas resident programs.

Accreditation: North Central Association of Colleges and Schools.

Description: With the introduction of adult-centered programs in 1975, Baker University (1858) continues to be a pioneer in higher education. The formation of the School of Professional and Graduate Studies in 1988 formalized the commitment to the metropolitan communities throughout Kansas. It also provided a vehicle for responsiveness to business and industry throughout the state in the form of graduate and undergraduate programs in business. In 1997 Baker offered the first online course to students who needed additional elective hours to complete their undergraduate degrees. The course provided feedback to the administration that gave direction to future forays into distance learning opportunities. Today Baker provides programs to specialized groups unable to complete degree programs without the benefit of online courses. The future looks promising as Baker looks closely at providing online, educational opportunities to students in more-remote areas of Kansas.

Bakersfield College

1801 Panorama Drive
Bakersfield, CA 93305

Phone: (805) 395-4011
Fax: (805) 395-4241

Division(s): Distance Learning Office
Web Site(s): http://www.bc.cc.ca.us
E-mail: kloomis@bc.cc.ca.us

Undergraduate Degree Programs:
Associate of Arts
Associate of Science

Teaching Methods: *Computers:* Internet, real-time chat, electronic classroom, e-mail. *TV:* videotape, cable program. *Other:* independent study (not at-a-distance).

Admission Requirements: *Undergraduate:* high school diploma or certificate of proficiency. Persons age 18+ without diploma may be admitted based on other experience. High school students may apply for the "Concurrent Enrollment" program. Students from foreign institutions may contact the International Education Research Foundation in Los Angeles.

On-Campus Requirements: Orientation, examinations, and review sessions held on campus. Only online courses are "geography free."

Tuition and Fees: *Undergraduate:* $12/unit. *Application Fee:* $118/unit nonresidents, up to 15 units/semester. *Other Costs:* It is estimated that the cost of books and supplies will be $250–$275/semester for a 15-unit schedule. *Credit by:* semester.

Financial Aid: Federal Stafford Student Loan, Federal PLUS Loan, Federal Pell Grant, Federal Work-Study, California resident programs-Board of Governor's Enrollment Fee Waiver, CAL Grants, Extended Opportunities Programs Services, Cooperative Agencies Resources for Education, Federal Supplemental Educational Opportunity Grant.

Accreditation: Western Association of Schools and Colleges.

Description: Bakersfield College is one of the oldest 2-year community colleges in the nation. The initial program offered a one-year curriculum, and in 1915 the trustees of the Kern County High School and Junior College District authorized a second year of junior college and normal school courses. The college opened its present 153-acre campus on Panorama Drive in 1956. As a member of the INTELECOM, a consortium of 32 Southern California community colleges, Bakersfield offers a wide variety of telecourses. BC began offering online courses in the fall of 1997, and now offers numerous online courses.

Barstow College

2700 Barstow Road
Barstow, CA 92311

Phone: (760) 252-2411 x7220
Fax: (760) 252-1875

Division(s): Learning Resources and Distance Education Department
Web Site(s): http://www.bcconline.com
E-mail: jaclark@barstow.cc.ca.us

Undergraduate Degree Programs:
Associate in Science with an emphasis in Business Technology (Business Administration, Business Technology, Computer Science and Management) is expected by 12/98; in Business Administration and in Management by 6/99.

Class Titles: Art History/Appreciation, Biology (nonlab), Computers, Internet, Online Courses, Business, Business Communications, English Composition, Survey of English Literature, Creative Writing, Basic English, Health Education, Survey of U.S. History to 1877, Elements of Supervision, Human Resource Management, American Political Institutions, Descriptive College Physics (nonlab), Career/Life Planning, Business Law, Business English, Economics, Psychology of Management, Ideas of Math, Comparative Religion, Earth Sciences, Interpersonal Communications.

Teaching Methods: *Computers:* Internet, real-time chat, electronic classroom, e-mail, news group, LISTSERV. *TV:* videotape, cable program, PBS. *Other:* correspondence, independent study, individual study, learning contracts.

Credits Granted for: experiential learning, portfolio assessment, extrainstitutional learning, examination (CLEP, ACT-PEP, DANTES, GRE). Up to 30 credits may be earned through experiential learning and assessment. Another 30 credits may be earned through examination. Only 12 credits of residential course units is required for graduation and these may be earned strictly online. Military evaluations conducted upon receipt of all transcripts and completion of 6 units with the Institution.

Admission Requirements: *Undergraduate:* age 18 and application completion. No entrance exams (SAT, ACT, TABE) required. Transfer students must submit transcripts.

On-Campus Requirements: While a student must complete 12 units with the institution in order to establish residency, these can be accomplished strictly through online enrollments.

Tuition and Fees: *Undergraduate:* $13/unit for California residents or military personnel assigned to California. All others, $127/unit. *Credit by:* semester.

Financial Aid: Federal Pell Grant, Federal Work-Study, VA, California resident programs, Military Tuition Assistance (TA).

Accreditation: Western Association of Schools and Colleges.

Description: Barstow College (1962) is a public community college serving the Eastern Mojave Desert area. It is centrally located 2 hours from Los Angeles and the southern California beaches and 2½ hours from Las Vegas. The college has 3,500 students, making it one of the state's smallest community colleges. Because of its proximity to surrounding military bases, Barstow has a long history of working closely with the military. It is a member of the Servicemembers' Opportunity College, actively supporting SOCAD, SOCMAR, and SOCNAV programs. About 28% of its annual graduates are soldiers, sailors, and marines stationed at Ft. Irwin, USMC-MCLB, and USMC-MWTC. An early pioneer with ITV, the college has long been involved in nontraditional instruction. Ultimately, Barstow intends to offer online access to all of its associate degrees.

Bastyr University

14500 Juanita Drive NE
Bothell, WA 98011-4995

Phone: (425) 602-3154
Fax: (425) 823-6222

Division(s): Distance Learning
Web Site(s): http://www.bastyr.edu/continuing/distance.html
E-mail: dlcourses@bastyr.edu

Undergraduate Degree Programs:
Classes may apply toward degree programs.

Class Titles: Nutrition, Nutritional Aspects of Herbs, Diet/Behavior, Nutrition in Natural Medicine, Nutrition in NP Industry, Chinese Medicine, Homeopathic Medicine.

Teaching Methods: *Computers:* Internet, e-mail. *Other:* fax, correspondence, audiotapes.

On-Campus Requirements: None.

Tuition and Fees: *Undergraduate:* $170/credit. *Application Fee:* $25. *Other Costs:* course materials, $15 shipping/handling ($60 overseas). *Credit by:* quarter.

Accreditation: Northwest Association of Schools and Colleges.

Description: Bastyr University (1978) is a progressive, accredited, nonprofit university internationally recognized as a pioneer in natural healing study. The university was founded to train naturopathic physicians with a scientific approach. Since then, Bastyr has added degree programs in Nutrition, Acupuncture/Oriental Medicine, and Applied Behavioral Sciences, expanding its mission to serve as a leader and vital force in improving the health and well-being of the human community. Bastyr began its Distance Learning Program in 1992 to meet the education needs of people who are interested in learning more about natural health and nutrition but who cannot become full-time, resident students at our Seattle campus. This program allows students to explore topics related to natural medicine and to earn academic credits from home.

Bates Technical College

1101 South Yakima Avenue	Phone: (253) 502-4024
Tacoma, WA 98405	(888) 872-7221
	Fax: (253) 502-4044

Division(s): Paraeducation Training Program
Web Site(s): http://www.batestc.ctc.edu
E-mail: jpearson@ctc.edu

Class Titles: Beginning Sign Language, Education of Students with Disabilities, School Law, Child Growth/Development.

Teaching Methods: *Computers:* e-mail. *TV:* videotape. *Other:* fax, toll-free phone number.

Admission Requirements: *Undergraduate:* contact department.

On-Campus Requirements: None.

Tuition and Fees: *Undergraduate:* $90/5 credits Sign Language, $65/3 credits Education of Students with Disabilities, $65/3 credits School Law, $65/3 credits Child Growth/Development.

Accreditation: Northwest Association of Schools and Colleges.

Description: Bates Technical College (1948) has been in the business of training people for careers for more than 50 years. Bates is Washington state's largest technical college, with more than 25,000 class registrations per year. Bates Technical College is creating a statewide distance learning opportunity for individuals currently working as paraeducators or those wishing to enter the field. Although the target audience is paraeducators, other school employees, people working with children in the private sector, or anyone interested in education would benefit. The program, which will eventually lead to an Associate of Technology in Education degree, is designed to meet the Washington state core competencies for paraeducators.

Bay Mills Community College

| 12214 West Lakeshore Drive | Phone: (906) 248-3354 |
| Brimley, MI 49715 | Fax: (906) 248-3351 |

Division(s): Nishnaabek Kinoomaadewin Virtual College
Web Site(s): http://www.bmcc.org
E-mail: register@bmcc.org
sbertram@bmcc.org

Class Titles: Art Appreciation, History of World Civilization, Learning on Internet, Pre-College Algebra, Head Start Performance Standards, Children's Literature, Evaluation/Continuous Improvement, Partners in Decision Making, Strategic Planning/Proposal Writing.

Teaching Methods: *Computers:* Internet, real-time chat, electronic classroom, e-mail. *Other:* None.

Admission Requirements: *Undergraduate:* open enrollment, placement testing.

On-Campus Requirements: None.

Tuition and Fees: *Undergraduate:* $85/credit. *Other Costs:* $50 registration fee (12 hours or more), $30 registration fee (1–11 hours), $50 computer fee (12 hours or more), $25 computer fee (1–11 hours), $50 student activity fee (12 hours or more) $20 building fee (12 hours or more). *Credit by:* semester.

Financial Aid: Federal Pell Grant, Federal Work-Study, VA.

Accreditation: North Central Association of Colleges and Schools.

Description: Bay Mills Community College (1984) is Michigan's only tribally controlled community college. It is chartered by the Bay Mills Indian Community pursuant to the Tribally Controlled Community College Act of 1978. The college serves the tribes of Michigan and neighboring communities. A Board of Regents elects administrative officers and establishes policy. In 1994, BMCC was declared a land grant college. In 1996, Dr. Helen Scheirbeck, Chief of the American Indian Program Branch, held a series of brainstorming sessions in Washington, DC. Dr. Scheirbeck wanted to examine technology to see if training and educating American Indian Head Start employees could be done in an innovative way. Those sessions resulted in a plan that eventually became the Nishnaabek Kinoomaadewin Virtual College at Bay Mills Community College.

Beaver College

| 450 South Easton Road | Phone: (888) 232-8373 |
| Glenside, PA 19038-3295 | Fax: (215) 572-4049 |

Division(s): Continuing Education
Web Site(s): http://www.beaver.edu
E-mail: admiss@beaver.edu

Undergraduate Degree Programs:
Bachelor of Fine Arts
Bachelor of Arts
Bachelor of Science

Graduate Degree Programs:
Master of:
Education
Counseling
Psychology
Health Education
Physician Assistant Studies
Health Counseling

Doctoral Degree Programs:
Doctorate of Physical Therapy

Certificate Programs: Post-baccalaureate programs in Computer Science, Health Sciences, Health Administration Management, Information Systems.

Teaching Methods: *Computers:* Internet, real-time chat, electronic classroom, e-mail, CD-ROM, newsgroup, LIST-SERV. *TV:* videotape, cable program, PBS. *Other:* videoconferencing, audioconferencing, fax, correspondence, independent study, individual study, learning contracts.

Credits Granted for: experiential learning, extrainstitutional learning, examination (CLEP, ACT-PEP, DANTES, GRE).

Admission Requirements: *Undergraduate:* high school transcript, college transcript, recommendations. *Graduate:* undergraduate college transcript, recommendations, GRE. *Doctoral:* same. *Certificate:* official transcripts.

On-Campus Requirements: None.

Tuition and Fees: *Undergraduate:* $300/credit. *Graduate:* $365/credit. *Application Fee:* $30. *Credit by:* semester.

Financial Aid: Federal Stafford Loan, Federal Perkins Loan, Federal PLUS Loan, Federal Pell Grant, Federal Work-Study, VA, Pennsylvania resident programs.

Accreditation: Middle States Association of Colleges and Schools.

Description: Beaver College (1853), a small, comprehensive college, offers a wide array of liberal arts and professional programs in a personalized setting. Building on 143 years of academic achievement, this coeducational, independent institution is committed to forging a synthesis of liberal education and career preparation in its undergraduate programs. Recognizing the pluralism of our nation and the increasing internationalism in business and other institutions, the college also is committed to expanding students' horizons, and preparing them to prosper in a world of cultural diversity. Students may pursue undergraduate study at Beaver College on a full-time or part-time basis; day, evening or weekend; for credit or not for credit. The college offers high quality, undergraduate degree programs in more than 30 fields of study, as well as graduate degrees and certificates of advanced study. History: Founded in Beaver, Pennsylvania, Beaver College was one of the country's first institutions to provide women with an education equivalent to that offered men in private schools. In 1972, the college became coeducational. Originally under the auspices of the Methodist Episcopal Church, Beaver College is now one of the church-related colleges of the Presbyterian Church (USA), but it independently controlled and ecumenical in spirit. In 1925, with the purchase of the property owned by the Beechwood School in suburban Philadelphia, the college moved to Jenkintown. In 1928, it acquired the former country estate of

William Welsh Harrison in Glenside. After operating on 2 campuses for many years, the college consolidated all its activities in Glenside in 1962. The Beaver College campus today takes its special character from the original buildings of the estate in a naturally beautiful setting. Above its wooded slopes and open, rolling lawns rise the massive towers of Grey Towers Castle, inspired by the famous Alnwick Castle in England. Winding, tree-lined drives lead to the smaller stone buildings of the original estate, now converted into classrooms and studios which preserve the old-world charm.

Bellevue Community College

3000 Landerholm Circle SE   Phone: (425) 641-2438
Bellevue, WA 98007-6484   Fax: (425) 562-6186

Division(s): Distance Education, Room D-261
Web Site(s): http://distance-ed.bcc.ctc.edu/
E-mail: landerso@bcc.ctc.edu

Undergraduate Degree Programs:
Associate of Arts Transfer Degree

Certificate Programs: Web Authoring

Class Titles: Written Expression, Programming, Mathematical Models/Applications, Age of Exploration, Exploring Digital Future, Global History: Neanderthal to Nukes, Techniques/Technology of Persuasion, Washington/Pacific Northwest, Accounting, Archeology, Economics (macro/micro), Psychology, Sociology, Ecology/Biosphere, Nutrition/Human Body, Weather/Climate/Vegetation/Soils, Grammar/Sentence Structure, Powerpoint 97, Internet, Multimedia Foundations, Digital Imaging, Web Design, Web Tools, Web Multimedia, Animation for Multimedia, Internet Objects, Programming for Web Authors, Portfolio/Employment, Internship in Media.

Teaching Methods: *Computers:* Internet, real-time chat, electronic classroom, e-mail. *TV:* videotape, cable program. *Other:* videoconferencing, fax, correspondence.

Credits Granted for: examination.

Admission Requirements: *Undergraduate:* high school diploma, age 18.

On-Campus Requirements: Weekly review sessions at instructor's discretion.

Tuition and Fees: *Undergraduate:* $52/credit (5-credit classes). *Other Costs:* $20/class distance education, lab. *Credit by:* quarter.

Financial Aid: Federal Stafford Loan, Federal Perkins Loan, Federal Pell Grant, Federal Work-Study, VA, Washington resident programs.

Accreditation: Northwest Association of Schools and College.

Description: Bellevue Community College, founded in 1966, began offering Annenberg-funded telecourses in 1986, added PBS offerings as they became available, and began producing its own telecourses in 1992. BCC began offering the 90-credit transfer degree in 1993, adding online and correspondence courses in 1997. Bellevue also participates in the Washington Online College Program and is planning an online business transfer degree by 1999.

Bellevue University

1000 Galvin Road South	Phone: (402) 293-2044
Bellevue, NE 68005	Fax: (402) 293-2020

Division(s): Center for Distributed Learning
Web Site(s): http://www.bellevue.edu
E-mail: bellevue_u@scholars.bellevue.edu

Graduate Degree Programs:
Master of Arts in Leadership
Master of Business Administration

Class Titles: courses for accelerated undergraduate degree completion programs for bachelor of science degrees in criminal justice administration, management, global business management, business information systems, as well as for graduate degree programs listed above.

Teaching Methods: *Computers:* Internet, real-time chat, electronic classroom, e-mail, CD-ROM, newsgroup, LISTSERV. *TV:* videotape, satellite broadcasting. *Other:* videoconferencing, audioconferencing, audiotapes, fax, correspondence, independent study, individual study, learning contracts.

Credits Granted for: experiential learning, portfolio assessment, extrainstitutional learning, examination (CLEP, ACT-PEP, DANTES, GRE).

Admission Requirements: *Graduate:* accredited bachelor's degree, 2.5+ GPA last 60 hours, 3 years of work experience.

On-Campus Requirements: None.

Tuition and Fees: *Undergraduate:* $250/credit. *Graduate:* $275/credit. *Application Fee:* $50. *Software:* no additional charge. *Other Costs:* $150 college fees, textbooks purchased on Web site. *Credit by:* semester.

Financial Aid: Federal Stafford Loan, Federal Perkins Loan, Federal PLUS Loan, Federal Pell Grant, Federal Work-Study, VA, Nebraska resident programs.

Accreditation: North Central Association of Colleges and Schools.

Description: Bellevue University (1966) is an information-age learning institution committed to creating optimum learning environments and assisting students in an accelerated process of lifelong learning. Bellevue provides more diverse access to classes and degrees and is more productive and cost efficient than traditional institutions. The university's online programs serve the economic and citizenship development needs of communities locally and globally. Bellevue University listens, is accountable, very flexible, and responsive to student needs.

Bemidji State University

1500 Birchmont Drive Northeast D-3D	Phone: (218) 755-2068
Bemidji, MN 56601-2699	Fax: (218) 755-4048

Division(s): Center for Extended Learning
Web Site(s): http://cel.bemidji.msus.edu/cel/
E-mail: cel@vax1.bemidji.msus.edu

Undergraduate Degree Programs:
Associate Degrees in Arts, Science (Criminal Justice)
Bachelor of Science in Criminal Justice

Teaching Methods: *Computers:* Internet, electronic classroom, e-mail, CD-ROM, LISTSERV. *TV:* videotape. *Other:* videotape.

Credits Granted for: experiential learning, extrainstitutional learning, examination (CLEP, ACT-PEP, DANTES).

Admission Requirements: *Undergraduate:* U.S. citizen, high school diploma or GED.

On-Campus Requirements: None.

Tuition and Fees: *Undergraduate:* $96/credit resident, $199/credit nonresident. *Graduate:* $140/credit resident. *Application Fee:* $20. *Software:* variable. *Other Costs:* textbooks, materials such as videotapes or audiotapes, CD-ROMs. *Credit by:* semester.

Financial Aid: Federal Stafford Loan, Federal Perkins Loan, Federal PLUS Loan, Federal Pell Grant, Federal Work-Study, VA, Minnesota resident programs (may require enrollment of 6+ in-class credits before distance enrollment determines eligibility).

Accreditation: North Central Association of Colleges and Schools.

Description: Bemidji State Normal School was chartered in 1919 by the Minnesota State Legislature in response to a growing need for public school teachers. In 1921 it became Bemidji State Teachers College and offered a 4-year degree. In 1975, in recognition of its growing role as a multipurpose educational institution, it became Bemidji State University. Bemidji established its External Studies Program in 1974 to provide university study and educational services to adults unable to participate in programs on campus in rural, northern Minnesota. The program, which offers most university courses, allows individuals who are place-bound or have barriers such as distance or work schedule to pursue their educational goals.

Berean University of the Assemblies of God

1445 Boonville Avenue	Phone: (417) 862-9533
Springfield, MO 65802	(800) 443-1083
	Fax: (417) 862-5318

Division(s): None.
Web Site(s): http://www.berean.edu
E-mail: berean@ag.or

Undergraduate Degree Programs:
Bachelor of Arts

Graduate Degree Programs:
Master of Arts

Certificate Programs: Diploma in Ministerial Studies, Bible/Doctrine, Church Ministries, Specialized Ministries.

Class Titles: All 50+ courses may be taken individually.

Teaching Methods: *Computers:* Internet, real-time chat, electronic classroom, e-mail. *Other:* audiotapes, correspondence, independent study, individual study.

Credits Granted for: experiential learning, portfolio assessment, extrainstitutional learning, examination (CLEP, ACT-PEP, DANTES, GRE).

Admission Requirements: *Undergraduate:* high school diploma. *Graduate:* accredited college degree, prerequisites.

On-Campus Requirements: only for MA in Christian Counseling.

Tuition and Fees: *Undergraduate:* $69/credit. *Graduate:* $129/credit. *Application Fee:* $35. *Other Costs:* textbooks. *Credit by:* semester.

Financial Aid: VA.

Accreditation: Distance Education and Training Council.

Description: Berean University (1948) provides training for ministers and missionaries, as well as enrichment studies for others interested in Bible, ministry, and related subjects. The school originally provided reading courses for those unable to attend a residence school. Later it expanded to a full set of curricula for ministerial studies for the Assemblies of God. In 1985 the school added a college program and became accredited through the Distance Education and Training Council.

Bergen Community College

400 Paramus Road	Phone: (201) 612-5254
Paramus, NJ 07652	Fax: (201) 612-8225

Division(s): Instructional Support Services and Center for Instructional Technology
Web Site(s): http://www.bergen.cc.nj.us

Class Titles: U.S. History to (and since) Reconstruction, Sociology, General Psychology, Psychology of Family, Child Psychology, Business Math, Business Administration, Personal Finance/Money Management.

Teaching Methods: *Computers:* Internet, real-time chat, electronic classroom, e-mail, CD-ROM, newsgroup, LISTSERV. *TV:* videotape, cable program, satellite broadcasting, PBS. *Other:* radio broadcast, audioconferencing, videoconferencing, audiographics, audiotapes, fax, correspondence, independent study, individual study, learning contracts.

Credits Granted for: experiential learning, portfolio assessment, extrainstitutional learning, examination (CLEP, ACT-PEP, DANTES, GRE).

Admission Requirements: *Undergraduate:* open-door policy.

On-Campus Requirements: 5 lectures.

Tuition and Fees: *Undergraduate:* $65/credit. *Application Fee:* $50. *Other Costs:* $10/credit general fee, $4/credit technology fee. *Credit by:* semester.

Financial Aid: Federal Stafford Loan, Federal PLUS Loan, Federal Pell Grant, Federal Work-Study, VA, New Jersey resident programs.

Accreditation: Middle States Association of Colleges and Schools. In addition, 4 programs are accredited by American Medical Association Commission on Accreditation of Allied Health Education Programs (Diagnostic Medical Sonography, Medical Office Assistant, Respiratory Therapy, and Surgical Technology).

Description: Bergen Community College (1965) registered its first class with day and evening students in 1968. Its first phase of expansive construction was completed in 1973. Since then, the college has expanded its facilities to include additional classrooms, laboratories, library space, a theater arts center, and a student center.

Bismarck State College

1500 Edwards Avenue
PO Box 5587
Bismarck, ND 58506-5587

Phone: (701) 224-5404
Fax: (701) 224-5550

Division(s): Office of the Vice President of Instruction
Web Site(s): http://www.bsc.nodak.edu/dised/dised.htm
E-mail: gabriel@gwmail.nodak.edu

Undergraduate Degree Programs:
2-year general education requirements

Class Titles: English, Sociology, Computers, Native American Studies, Adult Farm Management, Psychology, Speech, History, Algebra
Teaching Methods: *Computers:* Internet, real-time chat, electronic classroom, e-mail, LISTSERV. *TV:* videotape, satellite broadcasting. *Other:* audioconferencing, audiotapes, fax, correspondence, independent study, individual study.

Credits Granted for: extrainstitutional learning, examination (CLEP, ACT-PEP).

Admission Requirements: *Undergraduate:* ACT/COMPASS entrance scores, dual credit offered to high school seniors, no residency requirements for online computer instruction.

On-Campus Requirements: None.

Tuition and Fees: *Undergraduate:* $72/credit. *Application Fee:* $25. *Other Costs:* $25 online computer instruction to provide online academic support (remediation). *Credit by:* semester.

Financial Aid: Federal Stafford Loan, Federal Perkins Loan, Federal PLUS Loan, Federal Pell Grant, Federal Work-Study, VA, North Dakota resident programs.

Accreditation: North Central Association of Colleges and Schools.

Description: As a community college, Bismarck State College's (1993) purpose is to provide high-quality, student-centered learning opportunities. Students may earn college credits for transfer to a 4-year college, complete training in a vocational-technical program, keep job skills current, or take noncredit courses in subjects of personal interest. Bismarck has been involved in the distance learning field since its founding. Since that time, we have provided interactive video instruction and offered a variety of general education requirements. In 1995 we began offering online computer instruction in English Composition, and in 1998 we began offering several general education courses in English, sociology, computers, psychology, and agriculture.

Black Hills State University

1200 University Street, USB 9508
Spearfish, SD 57799-9508

Phone: (605) 642-6771
Fax: (605) 642-6031

Division(s): Extended Services
Web Site(s): http://www.bhsu.edu/academics/distlrn/distlrn.html
E-mail: vfish@mystic.bhsu.edu

Class Titles: Undergraduate and graduate courses rotate by semester, with Human Experience offered most semesters.

Teaching Methods: *Computers:* Internet, electronic classroom. *TV:* satellite broadcasting. *Other:* videoconferencing, correspondence.

Credits Granted for: examination (CLEP, ACT-PEP, DANTES, GRE).

Admission Requirements: *Undergraduate:* admission form/fees, course prerequisites, and completion limits. *Graduate:* admission form/fees, course prerequisites, and completion limits.

On-Campus Requirements: Final 30 undergraduate hours. 6 graduate hours.

Tuition and Fees: *Undergraduate:* Costs are reasonable; contact school for details. *Graduate:* Costs are reasonable; contact school for details. *Application Fee:* contact school. *Software:* contact school. *Other Costs:* contact school. *Credit by:* semester.

Financial Aid: Contact university for available distance learning assistance.

Accreditation: North Central Association of Colleges and Schools, National Council for Accreditation of Teacher Education.

Description: Founded in 1885, Black Hills State University is located in Spearfish (pop. 11,000), home to the famed Black Hills Passion Play, in a picturesque mountain valley near the Montana/Wyoming border. Distance education by correspondence and extension has been a major part of the school's delivery for many years. In 1992 BHSU began offering technology-based distance learning and is currently increasing this delivery through an audio/visual interactive network, the Internet, and satellite.

Blackfeet Community College

PO Box 819
Browning, MT 59417

Phone: (406) 338-5441/5411
Fax: (406) 338-3272

Division(s): Distance Learning (University of Great Falls/NorthNet MSU Northern)
Web Site(s): http://www.bcc/ana.edu/ or http://www.bcc

Undergraduate Degree Programs:
Bachelor of Science in:
  Education
  Business
  Humanitarian Services

Graduate Degree Programs:
Master of Science in:
  Education
  Business
  Humanitarian Services

Certificate Programs: Building Trades, General Office Clerk, Tribal Management.

Teaching Methods: *TV:* videoconferencing. *Other:* independent study.

Credits Granted for: experiential learning, extrainstitutional learning.

Admission Requirements: *Undergraduate:* open-admission. *Graduate:* contact school. *Certificate:* open-admission.

On-Campus Requirements: 2 years at BCC Campus, at least 30 credits.

Tuition and Fees: *Undergraduate:* $30/credit. *Graduate:* contact school. *Application Fee:* $15. *Other Costs:* $107 computer, registration, building, activity fees. *Credit by:* quarter.

Financial Aid: Federal Pell Grant, Federal Work-Study, VA.

Accreditation: Northwest Association of Schools and Colleges.

Description: Blackfeet Community College (1985) has 2-year degree programs, but also offers 4-year and master's programs on the district level. We do not offer distance learning programs but are a site for 2 universities that offer distance learning: University of Great Falls, Great Falls, Montana; and NorthNet MSU Northern, Havre, Montana. We have been carrying their programs since 1993. We plan to offer our own distance education in the next 2–4 years.

Blinn College

902 College Avenue	Phone: (409) 830-4130
Brenham, TX 77833	Fax: (409) 830-5334

Division(s): Distance Learning
Web Site(s): http://www.blinncol.edu
E-mail: cschaefer@acmailroom.blinncol.edu

Class Titles: Anthropology (Peoples/Cultures of World), Child Development/Early Childhood, American Government (Federal), American Government (State), American History, General Psychology, Sociology, Business, Philosophy, Composition/Rhetoric, Composition/Literature, Technical Writing, Microcomputer Applications/Lab.

Teaching Methods: *Computers:* Internet, real-time chat, e-mail. *TV:* videotape, cable program, broadcasting. *Other:* audioconferencing, fax, correspondence, independent study, individual study, learning contracts.

Credits Granted for: examination (CLEP, ACT).

Admission Requirements: *Undergraduate:* high school degree, GED. TASP for new students.

On-Campus Requirements: Orientation and 3–4 semester study sessions/test dates for telecourse or Web-based students.

Tuition and Fees: *Undergraduate:* $28/credit. *Graduate:* $28/credit. *Application Fee:* $40. *Software:* $12 technology fee/3-hour class. *Other Costs:* $15 student services. *Credit by:* semester.

Financial Aid: Federal Stafford Loan, Federal Perkins Loan, Federal PLUS Loan, Federal Pell Grant, Federal Work-Study, VA.

Accreditation: Southern Association of Colleges and Schools.

Description: Blinn College (1883) is located in Brenham and serves a 13-county area with campuses in Bryan and Schulenburg. The school was founded by the Methodist denomination. In 1937 Washington County made Blinn the first county-owned junior college district in Texas. To further open its resources to immediate and prospective constituency, Blinn began a distance learning telecourse program in the spring of 1996. Currently Blinn offers 9 telecourses for credit and 3 Internet courses with 2 more to follow in the fall of 1999. Our distance learning program continues to grow.

Bluefield State College

219 Rock Street	Phone: (304) 327-4059
Bluefield, WV 24701	Fax: (304) 327-4106

Division(s): Center for Extended Learning
Web Site(s): http://www.bluefield.wvnet.edu
E-mail: tblevins@bscvax.wvnet.edu

Undergraduate Degree Programs:
Associate of Arts in Liberal Arts

Class Titles: Tests/Measurements, Business Law, Health Promotion/Protection, Composition. BSC offers various PBS and Interactive Video (2-way, audio/video, live instruction) courses each semester.

Teaching Methods: *Computers:* e-mail, Web materials. *TV:* videotape, PBS (in West Virginia), interactive video. *Other:* workbooks.

Credits Granted for: Prior education, life experience through portfolio assessment, CLEP scores.

Admission Requirements: *Undergraduate:* high school diploma, GED, or individual classes without formal enrollment.

On-Campus Requirements: Attendance at Bluefield, Beckley, or Lewisburg, West Virginia, required for interactive video.

Tuition and Fees: *Undergraduate:* $71/credit hour, $193/credit hour out-of-state. Several Distance Learning courses are available at in-state rates through the Southern Regional Electronic Campus. *Credit by:* semester.

Financial Aid: Federal Stafford Loan, Federal Perkins Loan, Federal Pell Grant, Federal Work-Study, VA, West Virginia resident programs.

Accreditation: North Central Association of Colleges and Schools (national organization accreditation for 12 specialty area degree programs).

Description: Bluefield State College was established as a black teachers' college by the West Virginia Legislature in 1895 and was integrated after 1954. By the 1960s, the college had a comprehensive 4-year program of teacher education, arts and sciences, and engineering technology. Today BSC focuses primarily on career and technical 2- and 4-year programs and secondarily on liberal arts offerings. The college offers baccalaureate and associate degrees, with instructional programs in engineering technologies, business, teacher education, arts and sciences, nursing and health science professions, and a variety of career fields. Students may also complete the nontraditional Regents Bachelor of Arts degree. BSC began offering instructional television courses in the mid-1970s through the West Virginia Higher Education ITV Consortium, which produced satellite-delivered courses on the West Virginia Satellite Network (SATNET) in the late 1980s. In 1996 the college installed an Interactive Video Network between its 3 campuses and created the Center for Extended Learning. This effort now includes asynchronous delivery of distance courses to the Southern Regional Education Board Virtual Campus.

Boise State University

1920 University Drive	Phone: (208) 385-1709
Boise, ID 83725	Fax: (208) 385-3467

Division(s): Continuing Education
Web Site(s): http://www.idbsu.edu/conted/
E-mail: showell@bsu.idbsu.edu

Graduate Degree Programs:
Master of Science in Instructional/Performance Technology

Class Titles: Accounting, Business, Math, Theater Arts, Music, Economics, Engineering, Communications, Information Sciences, English, Spanish, Geography, Nursing, Physical Science, Sociology, Teacher Education, Nutrition, Instructional/Performance Technology, Income Taxation, History, Child Psychology, C++ Programming, Pathophysiology, Pharmacotherapeutics, Humanities, Psychology, Philosophy, Communication Studies, Telecommunications, Archeology, Speech, Law/Justice.

Teaching Methods: *Computers:* Internet, real-time chat, electronic classroom, e-mail, LISTSERV. *TV:* videotape, cable program, satellite broadcasting, PBS. *Other:* radio broadcast, 2-way compressed video with 2-way audio.

Credits Granted for: Experiential learning, portfolio assessment, examination.

Admission Requirements: *Undergraduate:* regular university admission for full-time distance education students. Part-time distance students must meet course prerequisites. *Graduate:* call (208) 385-1312 for MS catalog. Distance class requirements similar to undergraduate.

On-Campus Requirements: Some undergraduate distance classes have on-campus meetings. None for MS program.

Tuition and Fees: *Undergraduate:* part time undergraduate $107/credit in-state. *Graduate:* part time graduate $135/credit in-state, $315/credit MS degree. *Application Fee:* $20. *Software:* Varies. *Other Costs:* $20 some classes have telecommunications fee. *Credit by:* semester.

Accreditation: Northwest Association of Schools and Colleges.

Description: With humble beginnings as a junior college in 1932, Boise State University now enrolls 15,000 students each semester in its academic and applied technology programs. BSU students come from every county in Idaho, nearly every state in the nation, and from numerous foreign countries. Boise State's 8 colleges offer 180 major fields, many of which have been offered through distance education since 1989. For telecourses, Boise utilizes TV networks, cable systems, and a PBS channel. In addition, its Radio Classroom combines teleconferencing with a radio talk-show. Instructors can create a virtual classroom in students' homes. Using a special receiver developed by BSU Radio, students can access these courses, which are piggy-backed onto regular BSU broadcast signals. Students can phone in responses to instructor questions or ask questions themselves. Students also may participate in Internet courses 24 hours a day, 7 days a week, from anywhere in the world.

Boston University

15 Saint Mary's Street
Boston, MA 02215

Phone: (617) 353-2842
Fax: (617) 353-5548

Division(s): Manufacturing Engineering
Web Site(s): http://eng.bu.edu/MFG/grad_prog.html
E-mail: esd@bu.edu

Graduate Degree Programs:
Master of Science in Manufacturing Engineering

Class Titles: Production Systems Analysis, Product Development, Materials/Processes in Manufacturing, Operations Management, Computational Problem Solving.

Teaching Methods: *Computers:* Internet (for course materials). *Other:* videoconferencing (interactive compressed video).

Admission Requirements: *Graduate:* GRE or GMAT, undergraduate engineering degree.

On-Campus Requirements: None.

Tuition and Fees: *Graduate:* $713/credit. *Application Fee:* $50. *Credit by:* semester.

Accreditation: New England Association of Schools and Colleges.

Description: Founded in 1839 and incorporated in 1869, Boston University is an independent, coeducational, nonsectarian university open to women and all members of minority groups. The Department of Manufacturing Engineering offers BS, MS, and PhD degrees and was the country's first department with an ABET-accredited BS program in manufacturing engineering. The Interactive-Compressed Video (ICV) graduate program in manufacturing engineering may be completed in about 3 years and leads to the Master of Science in Manufacturing Engineering. Concentrations are offered in: Manufacturing Systems, Manufacturing Operations Management, and Process Design. Students may take up to 3 courses before applying to the program. ICV permits the department to conduct live classes concurrently at many industrial sites with complete 2-way video and audio interaction. The department is a pioneer in distance learning, graduating its first MS degree earned entirely by ICV in May 1992.

Brenau University

One Centennial Circle
Gainesville, GA 30501

Phone: (770) 534-2699
Fax: (770) 538-4306

Division(s): individual departments
Web Site(s): http://www.brenau.edu
E-mail: jupchurch@lib.brenau.edu

Class Titles: Operations Management, Accounting, Psychology, Human Growth/Development, School/Society, Spanish, Survey of American Literature, Conceptual Basis/Professional Nursing, Nursing Research, Computer Literacy.

Teaching Methods: *Computers:* Internet, e-mail. *TV:* videotape, cable program, satellite broadcasting. *Other:* independent study.

Credits Granted for: experiential learning, portfolio assessment, examination (CLEP, ACT-PEP, DANTES, GRE).

Admission Requirements: *Undergraduate:* application packet, official high school transcript, SAT/ACT or placement tests. *Graduate:* application packet, all official college/university transcripts, high school transcript if fewer than 30 college credits.

On-Campus Requirements: program completion requires classroom course work. Contact school for information.

Tuition and Fees: *Undergraduate:* $247/credit. *Graduate:* $208/credit education, $249/credit MBA, $411/credit health-related. *Application Fee:* $30. *Credit by:* semester.

Financial Aid: Federal Stafford Loan, Federal Perkins Loan, Federal Pell Grant, Federal Work-Study, VA, Georgia resident programs.

Accreditation: Southern Association of Colleges and Schools.

Description: Brenau University (1878) has just initiated a limited program of distance learning courses. Individual courses are in the process of being developed for delivery soon. Our intention is to use distance education to supplement programs of evening and weekend college students already enrolled in degree programs at the university. As a supplement to our existing programs, we offer "special students" an opportunity to enroll in courses without enrolling in a specific Brenau program.

Brevard Community College

1519 Clearlake Road
Cocoa, FL 32922

Phone: (407) 632-1111 x6470
Fax: (407) 633-4565

Division(s): Dean of Student Development
Web Site(s): http://www.brevard.cc.fl.us
E-mail: harrisp@brevard.cc.fl.us

Undergraduate Degree Programs:
Associate of Arts
Associate of Science in Legal Assisting

Class Titles: All courses can be taken individually, without degree program enrollment.

Teaching Methods: *Computers:* Internet, electronic classroom, e-mail. *TV:* videotape, cable program, PBS. *Other:* correspondence and independent study (only with instructor consent).

Credits Granted for: experiential learning, portfolio assessment, examination (CLEP, ACT-PEP, DANTES).

Admission Requirements: *Undergraduate:* high school diploma or GED (USAFI accepted for individual classes, placement testing required for AA degree courses).

On-Campus Requirements: None.

Tuition and Fees: *Undergraduate:* $47/credit in-state, $150/credit out-of-state. *Application Fee:* $20. *Software:* Internet Service Provider Fee. *Other Costs:* videotapes up to $50. *Credit by:* semester.

Financial Aid: Federal Stafford Loan, Federal Pell Grant, Federal Work-Study, VA, Florida resident programs.

Accreditation: Southern Association of Colleges and Schools.

Description: Established in 1960 by dedicated local citizens, Brevard Community College is a vital part of America's Space Coast. BCC is recognized nationwide as one of America's leading community colleges in institutional excellence, financial management, student development, culture, equal opportunity, service to the community, and use of technology. BCC began offering telecourses in 1987 and online courses in 1995. Today the college offers 50 courses online and a full 2-year curriculum through TV. Its mission is to meet the educational needs of its students, area businesses, and industry through quality, affordable education.

Bridgewater State College

100 Burrill Avenue
Bridgewater, MA 02325

Phone: (508) 279-6145
Fax: (508) 279-6121

Division(s): Moakley Center
Web Site(s): http://www.bridgew.edu/DEPTS/MOAKLEY
E-mail: mfuller@bridgew.edu

Graduate Degree Programs:
Master of Library Media Studies

Class Titles: Learners with Special Needs in School/Society, Seminar on Educational Leadership for Future, Research Methods, Selection/Development of Educational Personnel, Legal Issues in Special Education, Inclusion Classroom, Curriculum Development for Learners with Special Needs, Exceptional Child in School, Management, Irish Literature, Ethnic Experience in America.

Teaching Methods: *Computers:* Internet, e-mail. *TV:* videotape, PBS. *Other:* videoconferencing, fax.

Admission Requirements: *Undergraduate:* high school degree or equivalent, SAT or ACT. *Graduate:* bachelor's degree, 2.5 GPA, GRE, letters of recommendation. *Doctoral:* master's degree, 3.0 GPA, letters of recommendation. *Certificate:* undergraduate degree, GRE, letters of recommendation.

On-Campus Requirements: None.

Tuition and Fees: *Undergraduate:* $121/credit resident, $316/credit nonresident. *Graduate:* $138/credit resident, $318/credit nonresident. *Doctoral:* $137/credit resident. *Application Fee:* $20 (undergraduate), $25 (graduate). *Other Costs:* $12 (less than 12 semester hours) or $24 (12 semester hours or more) for student government association, $25 late registration fee. *Credit by:* semester.

Financial Aid: Federal Perkins Loan, Federal Pell Grant, Federal Work-Study, Federal Ford Direct Subsidized and Unsubsidized Loans, Federal Ford Direct Plus Loan, Mass Plan, Federal Supplemental Educational Opportunity Grant, BSC Tuition Waiver, BSC Tuition Grant, BSC Fee Grant, Massachusetts State Scholarship.

Accreditation: New England Association of Schools and Colleges.

Description: Bridgewater State College (1840) is one of America's oldest public colleges, rich in tradition and pride. Today, Bridgewater is a multipurpose liberal arts institution that enrolls 8,700 full- and part-time students, offers 100 undergraduate and graduate academic programs, has a full-time faculty of 256 teacher-scholars, and occupies a 235-acre campus with 29 academic and residential buildings. Distance learning programs began in the fall of 1997.

Brigham Young University

206 Harman Continuing Education Building
Box 21514
Provo, UT 84602-1514

Phone: (801) 378-2868
Fax: (801) 378-5817

Division(s): Independent Study
Web Site(s): http://coned.byu.edu/is/
E-mail: roy_schmidt@byu.edu

Certificate Programs: Family History

Class Titles: call (801) 378-4351.

Teaching Methods: *Computers:* Internet, e-mail, CD-ROM. *Other:* correspondence, audiotapes, independent study.

Admission Requirements: *Undergraduate:* open-enrollment. *Certificate:* open-enrollment.

On-Campus Requirements: None.

Tuition and Fees: *Undergraduate:* $81/credit. *Other Costs:* $20/course extension, or transfer. *Credit by:* semester.

Financial Aid: limited Independent Study scholarships.

Accreditation: Northwest Association of Schools and Colleges.

Description: Brigham Young University's (1875) mission is to assist individuals in their quest for perfection and eternal life. The mission of the Division of Continuing Education is to help people improve their lives by offering quality educational programs. The mission of the Department of Independent Study is to make quality educational experiences available to all who can benefit from individualized learning.

Bristol Community College

777 Elsbree Street	Phone: (508) 678-2811 x2850
Fall River, MA 02720	Fax: (508) 676-7146

Division(s): Academic Computing and Distance Learning
Web Site(s): http://www.bristol.mass.edu
E-mail: distance@bristol.mass.edu

Class Titles: Psychology, Technical Math, Coastal Zone Management, Environment, Computer Tools for Engineers, Clinical Laboratory Science, Electrical Engineering, Statistics.

Teaching Methods: *Computers:* Internet, real-time chat, electronic classroom, e-mail. *TV:* videotape, PBS. *Other:* videoconferencing, audiotapes, fax, correspondence, independent study, learning contracts.

Credits Granted for: examination (CLEP, ACT-PEP, DANTES, GRE).

Admission Requirements: *Undergraduate:* open-admission; high school diploma or equivalent for associate degree. This may be waived for adults who pass a BCC-approved exam.

On-Campus Requirements: Yes.

Tuition and Fees: *Undergraduate:* $74/credit. *Credit by:* semester.

Financial Aid: Federal Stafford Loan, Federal Perkins Loan, Federal PLUS Loan, Federal Pell Grant, Federal Work-Study, VA, Massachusetts resident programs.

Accreditation: New England Association of Schools and Colleges.

Description: Bristol Community College (1965) is a 2-year, comprehensive community college offering career and transfer programs that lead to associate degrees or certificates.

Brookdale Community College

735 Newman Springs Road	Phone: (732) 224-2000
Lincroft, NJ 07738	Fax: (732) 224-2060

Division(s): Telecommunication Technologies
Web Site(s): http://www.brookdale.cc.nj.us
E-mail: lpullano@brookdale.cc.nj.us

Undergraduate Degree Programs:
Associate of Arts in:
    Liberal Education
    Business Administration
    Social Sciences

Class Titles: Cultural Anthropology, Business, Principles of Management, Money Management/Personal Finance, Cycles of Life, Macroeconomics, Writing Process, Writing/Research, Living with Health, World Civilization, American Civilization, Italian, French, Spanish, Marketing, Music Appreciation, Ethics, Psychology, Human Growth/Development, Sociology, Human Geography, Musical Theater

Teaching Methods: *TV:* videotape, cable program, satellite broadcasting, PBS. *Other:* radio broadcast, videoconferencing, audioconferencing, audiographics, audiotapes, fax, correspondence, independent study, individual study, learning contracts.

Credits Granted for: experiential learning, portfolio assessment, extrainstitutional learning, examination (CLEP, ACT-PEP, DANTES, GRE).

Admission Requirements: *Undergraduate:* Age 18+.

On-Campus Requirements: For ITV Courses.

Tuition and Fees: *Undergraduate:* $72/credit. *Application Fee:* $25. *Other Costs:* $13/credit General Service Fee. *Credit by:* term. Fall/spring: 15 weeks each, Summer I: 6 weeks, Summer II: 10 weeks, Summer III: 6 weeks.

Financial Aid: Federal Stafford Loan, Federal PLUS Loan, Federal Pell Grant, Federal Work-Study, VA.

Accreditation: Middle States Association of Colleges and Schools.

Description: Brookdale (1967) is an open admission college available to anyone 18 years older who is a high school graduate or holder of an equivalency diploma. (Health programs have additional admission criteria.) In keeping with the college's dedication to open and innovative education, learning at Brookdale is oriented toward success. Each course has printed objectives explaining student assignments unit by unit. In effect, students select the grades they wish to attain and are told clearly and concisely how to earn them. Along with teaching and counseling, faculty members, Learning Assistants, and Lab Assistants in each major area of the college assist students in completing classwork. Telecourse and distance learning classrooms provide educational opportunities free of time and location constraints. Since 1978, Brookdale has offered credit courses via radio and cable television through its Telecourse Program. Brookdale has been a participant in "Going the Distance," an Annenberg/CPB Pathways to a Degree, since 1995, and now offers an AA Liberal Education Program and an AAS in Business Administration Program strictly through distance learning. The recently completed Interactive Video (ITV) Classroom allows interactive distance teaching and videoconferencing. A fiber optic network currently under construction throughout New Jersey will allow full transmission of courses from one site to another. The ITV system allows a host site (Brookdale) to interact simultaneously with 3 distant locations with full-motion video and audio response. Additional sites are able to watch programs solely in broadcast mode.

Bucks County Community College

Swamp Road	Phone: (215) 968-8052
Newtown, PA 18940	Fax: (215) 968-8005

Division(s): Distance Learning Office
Web Site(s): http://www.bucks.edu/distance
E-mail: learning@bucks.edu

Undergraduate Degree Programs:
Associate of Arts in Business
Associate of Arts in Liberal Arts

Certificate Programs: Yes.

Class Titles: Art History, Business, Communication, Composition, Computer Science, History, Health, Law, Literature, Math, Music, Political Science, Psychology, Science, Sociology.

Teaching Methods: *Computers:* Internet, real-time chat, electronic classroom, e-mail, CD-ROM, newsgroup, LISTSERV. *TV:* videotape, PBS. *Other:* audiotapes, fax, correspondence, independent study, individual study, learning contracts.

Credits Granted for: experiential learning, portfolio assessment, extrainstitutional learning, examination (CLEP, ACT-PEP, DANTES, GRE).

Admission Requirements: *Undergraduate:* Open admissions.

On-Campus Requirements: variable (see www.bucks.edu/distance).

Tuition and Fees: *Undergraduate:* varies by residency. $71/credit state residents in Bradford, Bucks, Pike, Wayne, Tioga counties. *Application Fee:* (See www.bucks.edu/distance). *Credit by:* semester.

Financial Aid: Federal Stafford Loan, Federal Perkins Loan, Federal PLUS Loan, Federal Pell Grant, Federal Work-Study, VA, PHEA.

Accreditation: Middle States Association of Colleges and Schools.

Description: Bucks County Community College (1965) is one of the largest community colleges in Pennsylvania. The Distance Learning Program began in 1994 and involves more than 90 courses with complete AA degrees in Business and Liberal Arts, as well as degree completions in many other areas.

Burlington College

95 North Avenue	Phone: (800) 862-9616
Burlington, VT 05401	Fax: (802) 658-0071

Division(s): Independent Degree Program
Web Site(s): http://www.burlcol.edu
E-mail: tkahan@burlcol.edu

Undergraduate Degree Programs:
Bachelor of Arts in:
    Writing and Literature
    Transpersonal Psychology
    Cinema Studies
    Fine Art
    Individualized Major

Teaching Methods: *Computers:* e-mail, LISTSERV. *Other:* fax, independent study, individual study, learning contracts.

Credits Granted for: experiential learning, portfolio assessment, extrainstitutional learning, examination (CLEP, ACT-PEP, DANTES).

Admission Requirements: *Undergraduate:* 45 college credits minimum, writing sample, 2 references, phone interview with director of program.

On-Campus Requirements: None.

Tuition and Fees: *Undergraduate:* $2,000/semester part-time (6–9 credits), $3,400/semester full-time (12–15 credits). *Application Fee:* $50. *Credit by:* semester.

Financial Aid: Federal Stafford Loan, Federal Perkins Loan, Federal PLUS Loan, Federal Pell Grant, Federal Work-Study, VA, institution scholarships.

Accreditation: New England Association for Schools and Colleges.

Description: Burlington College (1972) was founded by Dr. Stewart LaCasce as an alternative college for nontraditional students emphasizing individualized education and community involvement. From 1972–1992 the college was primarily oriented around its campus program though it had always had contract-based learning for students wanting to do independent study. In 1993 the Independent Degree Program was conceived and has operated ever since. The primary areas for study are in the liberal arts, specifically, Transpersonal Psychology, Psychology, and Writing and Literature. The program also works with what is called individualized majors, wherein each student's program is individually designed.

Burlington County College

Route 530
Pemberton, NJ 08068

Phone: (609) 894-9311 x7790
Fax: (609) 894-4189

Division(s): Office of Distance Learning
Web Site(s): http://www.bcc.edu
E-mail: sespensh@bcc.edu

Undergraduate Degree Programs:
Associate of Arts
Associate of Science

Class Titles: Cultural Anthropology, Art, Biology/Human Affairs with Lab, Human Ecology, Human Ecology Lab, Business Administration, Management, Personal Finance/ Money Management, Business Law, Marketing, Small Business Management, American Cinema, Computers, Computer Science, Internet Literacy, Microeconomics, Macroeconomics, Whole Child, College Composition, French, Earth Revealed, Geology with Lab, U.S. History, Ancient/Medieval Foundations, History of Modern East Asia, Children's Literature, Statistics, Music, American Government/Politics, Project Universe, Oceanus, Psychology, General Psychology, Child Psychology, Developmental Psychology, Sociology, Spanish, Marriage/Family.

Teaching Methods: *Computers:* Internet, electronic classroom, e-mail, CD-ROM. *TV:* videotape, cable program, ETN, PBS. *Other:* radio broadcast, audioconferencing, videoconferencing, audiotapes, fax.

Credits Granted for: examination (CLEP, DANTES).

Admission Requirements: *Undergraduate:* Must be at least a high school junior and take New Jersey Basic Skills Test.

On-Campus Requirements: We offer optional but very helpful seminars and an orientation.

Tuition and Fees: *Undergraduate:* $57/credit plus $6/credit in general classes, $4/credit in technology, $25/course license fee (all for Burlington County residents, part-time); $70 plus fees/credit out-of-county; $135 plus fees/credit out-of-state. *Application Fee:* $20. *Credit by:* semester.

Financial Aid: Federal Stafford Loan, Federal Perkins Loan, Federal PLUS Loan, Federal Pell Grant, Federal Work-Study, VA, New Jersey resident programs.

Accreditation: Middle States Association of Colleges and Schools.

Description: Burlington County College (1969) is a community college that awards associate degrees and certificates. Many students go on to other colleges for a bachelor's degree after completing their work at BCC. Distance education began in 1978 through telecourses. The program blossomed in 1995 when the college became a pilot school for PBS' *Going the Distance* program. The Distance Learning Department now offers 40 video, radio, and Internet courses each semester.

Butte Community College

3536 Butte Campus Drive
Oroville, CA 95965

Phone: (530) 895-2430
Fax: (530) 895-2380

Division(s): Center for Media and Distance Learning
Web Site(s): http://www.butte.cc.ca.us
E-mail: jack@bctv.net

Class Titles: Math, Science, Agricultural Science, History, Political Science, Anthropology, Latin, Business, Child Development, Administration of Justice, Art, Telecommunications, Sociology.

Teaching Methods: *Computers:* Internet. *TV:* videotape, cable program. *Other:* videoconferencing.

Admission Requirements: *Undergraduate:* age 18.

On-Campus Requirements: depends on course.

Tuition and Fees: *Undergraduate:* $13/credit. *Application Fee:* $40. *Other Costs:* out-of-state tuition. *Credit by:* semester.

Financial Aid: Federal Stafford Loan, Federal Perkins Loan, Federal PLUS Loan, Federal Pell Grant, Federal Work-Study, VA, California resident programs.

Accreditation: Western Association of Schools and Colleges.

Description: Butte Community College (1968) is located in northern California and serves a primarily rural, 2-county area. We began distance learning using telecourses in 1986 and have expanded into 2-way, live interactive and the Internet.

Cabrillo Community College

6500 Soquei Drive
Aptos, CA 95003

Phone: (831) 479-6477
Fax: (831) 479-5092

Division(s): Transfer Education
Web Site(s): http://www.cabrillo.cc.ca.us
E-mail: glgaring@cabrillo.cc.ca.us

Class Titles: telecourses within region: Anthropology, English as Second Language, Geography, Psychology, Spanish. Internet courses: Allied Health, Criminal Justice. Live Interactive (within region): Medical Assistant, Business, ECE. Visit http://www. cabrillo.cc.ca.us/schedule.

Teaching Methods: *Computers:* Internet, e-mail, LISTSERV. *TV:* videotape, cable program. *Other:* audiotapes, fax, correspondence.

Admission Requirements: *Undergraduate:* Age 18; high

school diploma, GED, or equivalent certificate.

On-Campus Requirements: Varies with course.

Tuition and Fees: *Undergraduate:* California residents: $24 for one credit, $37 for 2 credits, $50 for 3 credits, $66 for 4 credits. Out-of-state students: $145 for one credit, $279 for 2 credits, $413 for 3 credits, $547 for 4 credits. International students: $149 for one credit, $287 for 2 credits, $425 for 3 credits, $563 for 4 credits. *Credit by:* semester.

Financial Aid: Federal Stafford Loan, Federal PLUS Loan, Federal Pell Grant, Federal Work-Study, VA, California resident programs: California Grant A, B, C, ELOPS/Care.

Accreditation: Western Association of Schools and Colleges.

Description: Cabrillo Community College (1959) is one of California's top 10 community colleges for number of students who transfer to the University of California system. Almost 70% of the courses offered to Cabrillo's 13,000 students are transferable. CCC began its distance education program in 1994.

Caldwell College

9 Ryerson Avenue	Phone: (973) 618-3285
Caldwell, NJ 07006	Fax: (973) 618-3690

Division(s): Continuing Education, External Degree Program
Web Site(s): http://www.caldwell.edu
E-mail: jalbalah@caldwell.edu

Undergraduate Degree Programs:
Bachelor of Science in:
  Accounting
  Business Administration
  Computer Information Systems
  International Business
  Marketing and Management
Bachelor of Arts in:
  Art*
  Communications Art*
  Criminal Justice
  English
  History
  Political Science
  Psychology
  Religious Studies
  Sociology
  Social Studies

Class Titles: Contact school for complete listing of courses offered.

Teaching Methods: *Computers:* Internet, e-mail. *TV:* videotape. *Other:* audiotapes, fax, correspondence, independent study.

Credits Granted for: experiential learning, portfolio assessment, extrainstitutional learning, examination (CLEP, ACT-PEP, DANTES, GRE).

Admission Requirements: *Undergraduate:* 12 transferable college credits.

On-Campus Requirements: External degree students are required to be on campus only for the external degree weekend at the beginning of each semester. *Some on-campus course work is required for majors in Art and Communications Art.

Tuition and Fees: *Undergraduate:* $298/credit. *Application Fee:* $25. *Credit by:* semester.

Financial Aid: Federal Stafford Loan, Federal Perkins Loan, Federal PLUS Loan, Federal Pell Grant, Federal Work-Study, VA, New Jersey resident programs.

Accreditation: Middle States Association of Colleges and Schools.

Description: Caldwell College (1939) is a Catholic, coeducational, 4-year liberal arts institution committed to intellectual rigor, individual attention, and the ethical values of the Judeo-Christian academic tradition. Caldwell College offers a 12:1 student-faculty ratio, small classes, and individual attention. Professors know their students by name, challenge them to strive for excellence, and provide the support needed to achieve it. This close relationship between faculty members and students also leads to a spirit of friendship throughout the campus community. Caldwell College pioneered the external degree concept in 1979, becoming the first higher education institution in the state of New Jersey to offer students the option of completing their degrees without attending on-campus classes. The external degree program offers 16 majors.

Calhoun State Community College

Highway 31 North	Phone: (256) 306-2755
PO Box 2216	(256) 306-2621
Decatur, AL 35609	Fax: (256) 306-2507

Division(s): Dean of Instruction, Distance Education Coordinator
Web Site(s): http://www.calhoun.cc.al.us
E-mail: registration: mwt@calhoun.cc.al.us
answer questions: cfb@calhoun.cc.al.us

Class Titles: Business, Chemistry, Computer Information Systems, Health, History, Math, Music, Philosophy, Physical Science, Psychology, Sociology, Spanish, French, Speech, Theatre Appreciation, English.

Teaching Methods: *Computers:* Internet, e-mail, CD-ROM. *TV:* videotape. *Other:* audiotapes, fax, correspondence.

Credits Granted for: examination.

Admission Requirements: *Undergraduate:* application, high school graduation or GED.

On-Campus Requirements: The distance education courses (college by cassette, college by CD, or Web-based) do require some visits to campus, either for exams, labs, etc.

Tuition and Fees: *Undergraduate:* $52/credit. *Other Costs:* $3 for facility, $1 for technology. *Credit by:* semester.

Financial Aid: Federal Stafford Loan, Federal Pell Grant, Federal Work-Study, VA, Alabama resident programs, Federal Supplemental Educational Opportunity Grant.

Accreditation: Southern Association of Colleges and Schools.

Description: Calhoun State Community College (1947) began as a technical college and expanded to academic offerings. In 1992 we began offering telecourses via cable broadcast, PBS, and college by cassette. The college by cassette was the preferred format by students. In the past year, we added Web-based college and college by CD courses.

California College for Health Sciences

222 West 24th Street   Phone: (619) 477-4800
National City, CA 91950   Fax: (619) 477-4360

Division(s): Correspondence Institution
Web Site(s): http://www.cchs.edu
E-mail: cchsinfo@cchs.edu

Undergraduate Degree Programs:
Vocational Programs:
    Dental Assisting
    Medical Assisting
    Pharmacy Technician
    Physical Therapy Aide
    EKG Technology
    Home Health Aide
Associate of Science in:
    Business
    Respiratory Technician
    Respiratory Therapist
    EEG
    Medical Transcription
    Allied Health
    Early Childhood Education
Bachelor of Science in:
    Health Services Management
    Respiratory Care
    Business

Graduate Degree Programs:
Master of Science in:
    Health Services with Community Health or Wellness Promotion
    Health Care Administration
Master of Public Health

Certificate Programs: Business Essentials, Community Health Education, Gerontology, Health Psychology, Health Care Ethics, Polysomnography.

Class Titles: English, Sociology, Sciences, Math, Management, Business.

Teaching Methods: *Computers:* e-mail *Other:* fax, correspondence, independent study, individual study.

Credits Granted for: experiential learning, portfolio assessment, extrainstitutional learning, examination (CLEP, ACT-PEP, DANTES, GRE).

Admission Requirements: *Undergraduate:* Associate and Vocational: minimum of high school diploma. Entrance to Respiratory varies. BS degrees: 60 semester credits. *Graduate:* accredited BS degree. *Certificate:* 60 semester credits of lower-division work.

On-Campus Requirements: None.

Tuition and Fees: *Undergraduate:* $100 + $35 enrollment fee/course *Graduate:* $100 + $35 enrollment fee/course *Credit by:* semester.

Financial Aid: VA.

Accreditation: Distance Education and Training Council.

Description: California College for Health Sciences (1975) is a private postsecondary institution originally founded as a resident campus for respiratory care education. In 1978 the school launched a distance education component in the field of respiratory care. Since that time, the distance education curriculum has expanded to include programs in medical transcription, EEG, health services management, wellness promotion, and early childhood education. Associate, bachelor's, and master's degrees are offered. The mission of the college is "to assist prospective and working health and human services professionals in the achievement of their individual career objectives with comprehensive, highly accessible and practical education that meets national professional academic standards." The independent study format of distance education enables students to design a study schedule that meets their individual needs, taking into consideration career and family obligations.

California National University for Advanced Studies

16909 Parthenia Street
North Hills, CA 91343

Phone: (800) 782-2422
(818) 830-2411
Fax: (818) 830-2418

Division(s): Distance Learning
Web Site(s): http://www.cnuas.edu
E-mail: cnuadms@mail.cnuas.edu

Undergraduate Degree Programs:
Bachelor of Science in:
  Business Administration
  Engineering
Bachelor of Computer Science
Bachelor of Quality Assurance Science

Graduate Degree Programs:
Master of Business Administration
Master of Human Resource Management
Master of Science in Engineering

Teaching Methods: *Computers:* Internet, real-time chat, e-mail, CD-ROM. *Other:* audioconferencing, videotape, audiotapes, fax, telephone contact, correspondence, independent study, individual study.

Credits Granted for: transfer credits, challenge exams, portfolio assessment towards pre-requisite requirements, extrainstitutional learning, examination (CLEP, ACT-PEP, DANTES, GRE).

Admission Requirements: *Undergraduate:* high school graduate or GED, Math Placement Test when appropriate, TOEFL when appropriate. *Graduate:* bachelor's degree, 3.0 cumulative undergraduate GPA, TOEFL when appropriate.

On-Campus Requirements: None.

Tuition and Fees: *Undergraduate:* $195/credit (U.S./Canadian residents), $210/credit (non U.S./Canadian residents). *Graduate:* $210/credit (U.S./Canadian residents), $230/credit (non U.S./Canadian residents). *Application Fee:* $50 U.S./Canadian, $100 non-U.S./non-Canadian. *Other Costs:* $100 registration fee nonrefundable of tuition/course, $25 extension program registration, software/textbooks, shipping costs variable, $15 late payment, $100 change of degree program. *Credit by:* trimester (15 weeks).

Financial Aid: VA, DANTES tuition assistance, GI Bill.

Accreditation: Distance Education and Training Council.

Description: California National University (1993) was founded to provide quality degree programs in a flexible environment so that midcareer professionals could meet contemporary challenges to re-think and re-tool. CNU has adopted an innovative approach to a traditional education: combining correspondence with direct personal contact and technology. A unique aspect to CNU programs is the one-on-one instruction students receive from a distinguished, national faculty. Although the university has taken advantage of advancements in technology to improve instruction, technology is regarded as an enhancement rather than a replacement for good teaching and relevant content. Students enjoy an educational climate typical of one found on a small traditional campus. This is accomplished at a distance through a centralized learning network that emphasizes committed student service and open communication. CNU offers bachelor's and master's degrees in business administration and engineering.

California School of Professional Psychology, Fresno

5130 East Clinton Way
Fresno, CA 93727

Phone: (209) 456-2777
Fax: (209) 253-2267

Division(s): Administration for Master's in Applied Human and Community Development
Web Site(s): http://www.cspp.edu
E-mail: admissions@mail.cspp.edu

Graduate Degree Programs:
Master's in Applied Human and Community Development

Teaching Methods: *Computers:* Internet, real-time chat, electronic classroom, e-mail. *Other:* audiographics, audiotapes, fax, correspondence, independent study, individual study.

Admission Requirements: *Graduate:* bachelor's degree in related field, 2+ years of field experience working with communities.

On-Campus Requirements: Classwork organized into 3–4 day intensive sessions run 6 extended weekends (Thursday evening through Sunday afternoon) annually for 2 years.

Tuition and Fees: *Graduate:* $9,000/year. *Application Fee:* $35. *Credit by:* semester.

Financial Aid: Federal Stafford Load, Federal Perkins Loan, Federal Work-Study, VA.

Accreditation: Western Association of Schools and Colleges.

Description: The California School of Professional Psychology (CSPP) is one of the world's largest human services professional schools. Dedicated to excellence in training and education and to innovative programs that meet community and individual needs, CSPP-Fresno has offered a diverse set of scholar- and practitioner-based programs since 1973.

Programs include multicultural psychology, criminal justice, public policy, clinical psychology, organizational behavior, health-care-related psychology, and community health. To provide increased flexibility for working adults, CSPP is offering its first distance learning program, the Master's in Applied Human and Community Development, in early 1999. The interdisciplinary work and study program will provide a practical integration of the related disciplines of community psychology, community development, health promotion, adult education, applied anthropology, community economics, and sustainable development studies. Classwork is organized into 3–4 day intensive sessions over 6 extended weekends annually for 2 years. Internet, e-mail, bulletin boards, and teleconferencing connect learners to each other and to faculty.

California State University, Bakersfield

9001 Stockdale Highway	Phone: (805) 664-2441
Bakersfield, CA 93311-1099	Fax: (805) 664-2447

Division(s): Extended University
Web Site(s): http://www.csubak.edu/ExtUniversity/
E-mail: bbell@csubak.edu
torr@csubak.edu
jdslack@csubak.edu
dtorres@csubak.edu

Certificate Programs: Attorney Assistant, Drug and Alcohol Studies, Geographical Information Systems, Managing Human Resources, Purchasing and Supply Management, Safety Management, Total Quality Management, Workers' Compensation Law.

Class Titles: General education courses, Business Administration, Communicative Sciences/Disorders, Nursing, Master's Social Work.

Teaching Methods: *Computers:* Internet, real-time chat, electronic classroom, e-mail, CD-ROM, newsgroup, LIST-SERV. *TV:* videotape, cable program, satellite broadcasting, PBS. *Other:* videoconferencing, audioconferencing, audiographics, audiotapes, fax, correspondence, independent study, individual study, learning contracts.

Credits Granted for: experiential learning, portfolio assessment, extrainstitutional learning, examination (CLEP, ACT-PEP, DANTES, GRE).

Admission Requirements: *Undergraduate:* high school graduate, have a qualifiable eligibility index (see section of Eligibility Index in catalog) and have completed with grades of C or better each of the courses in the comprehensive pattern of college preparatory subject requirements (see subject requirements in catalog). Courses must be completed prior to the first enrollment in the California State University. *Graduate:* program-specific. *Certificate:* program-specific.

On-Campus Requirements: Yes.

Tuition and Fees: *Undergraduate:* $502/quarter, 6.1 or more units. *Graduate:* $306/quarter, 0.1 to 6.0 units, $528/quarter, 6.1 or more units. *Application Fee:* $55. *Credit by:* quarter.

Financial Aid: Federal Stafford Loan, Federal Perkins Loan, Federal PLUS Loan, Federal Pell Grant, Federal Work-Study, VA, California resident programs.

Accreditation: Western Association of Schools and Colleges.

Description: The individual California State Colleges were brought together as a system by the Donahoe Higher Education Act of 1960. In 1972 the system became The California State University and Colleges and in 1982 the system became The California State University.

California State University, Chico

Center for Regional and Continuing Ed	Phone: (530) 898-6105
Chico, CA 95929-0250	Fax: (530) 898-4020

Division(s): Center for Regional and Continuing Education
Web Site(s): http://rce.csuchico.edu
E-mail: jlayne@csuchico.edu

Undergraduate Degree Programs:
Bachelor of Science in:
    Computer Science (available to employees of participating companies)
    Social Science
    Sociology
    Political Science
Minors available in:
    Business Administration
    Career and Life Planning
    Family Relations
    Political Science
    Psychology
    Sociology

Graduate Degree Programs:
Master of Science—Interdisciplinary Studies: Telecommunications (available to employees of participating companies)
Master of Science in Computer Science (available to employees of participating companies)

Certificate Programs: Greater Avenues for Independence, Resource Specialist.

Class Titles: courses toward Bachelor of Science in Liberal Studies and toward Certificate in Paralegal Studies.

Teaching Methods: *Computers:* Internet, e-mail, video-streaming. *TV:* videotape, satellite. *Other:* None.

Credits Granted for: examination (CLEP).

Admission Requirements: *Undergraduate:* CSUSAT*CHICO students must meet the same university admissions requirements and deadlines as those students on-campus. Only students who have already been admitted to the university (prior to the beginning of classes) will be allowed to register for CSUSAT*CHICO classes. Early application to the university is encouraged. For more information, please contact the school. *Graduate:* same as undergraduate. *Certificate:* same as undergraduate.

On-Campus Requirements: Courses are delivered live via satellite to off-campus learning centers. Off-campus students are required to attend class regularly.

Tuition and Fees: *Undergraduate:* same as on-campus students. Fall 1997 fees were $703 for 0–6 units and $1,035 for 6.1 units or more. All fees are subject to change by action by the Board of Trustees of the California State University. *Graduate:* Please call the Center for Regional and Continuing Education for information regarding this corporate program. *Application Fee:* $55. *Credit by:* semester.

Financial Aid: Federal Stafford Loan, Federal Perkins Loan, Federal Pell Grant, VA, California resident programs (financial aid DOES NOT apply to the Computer Science degrees).

Accreditation: Western Association of Schools and Colleges.

Description: California State University, Chico (1887), is located in northern California, 99 miles north of the state capital of Sacramento. It was established as California's second State Normal School. CSU, Chico, is the second oldest institution in the 23-campus California State University System. The university has been active in distance education since 1975. CSU, Chico, offers 2 distinct distance education programs.

California State University, Fullerton

800 North State College Boulevard	Phone: (714) 278-3156
Fullerton, CA 92834	Fax: (714) 278-3892

Division(s): University Extended Education
Web Site(s): http://www.takethelead.fullerton.edu
E-mail: bthomas@fullerton.edu

Undergraduate Degree Programs:
Bachelor of Science in Nursing

Graduate Degree Programs:
Master of Science in Electrical Engineering
Master of Business Administration.

Doctoral Degree Programs:
Partial degree program in:
    Liberal Studies

Elementary Education
Education Administration

Certificate Programs: Mortgage Lending.

Class Titles: Math, Christian Thought, Accounting, Finance, Business, Communications, Marketing, Physics, Electrical Engineering, Nursing.

Teaching Methods: *Computers:* yes. *TV:* cable program, satellite broadcasting. *Other:* audioconferencing.

Admission Requirements: *Undergraduate:* application. *Graduate:* same. *Doctoral:* same. *Certificate:* same.

On-Campus Requirements: None.

Tuition and Fees: *Undergraduate:* $137/lecture unit, $175/activity unit, $217/laboratory unit. *Credit by:* semester.

Financial Aid: Federal Stafford Loan, Federal Perkins Loan, Federal PLUS Loan, Federal Pell Grant, Federal Work-Study, VA, California resident programs.

Accreditation: Western Association of Schools and Colleges.

Description: California State University, Fullerton (1957) became the 12th state college in California. Once part of a vast orange grove, California State Fullerton's attractively landscaped main campus now consists of 225 acres. Today there is much dramatic evidence of additional rapid growth. Beginning in 1986, CSU Fullerton began delivering 4 classes to 6 high schools in Orange County via the Titan Interactive Network on cable TV. During the past year, 44 credit classes, numerous conferences, and noncredit extended education classes have been offered. In the future, the university will be working on maintaining and building the programs already in place. The campus will also be developing online courses in support of existing degree programs, with selected courses delivered on the Internet.

California State University, Northridge

18111 Nordhoff Street	Phone: (818) 677-2355
Northridge, CA 91330-8324	(800) 882-0128
	Fax: (818) 677-2316

Division(s): Extended Learning
Web Site(s): http://www.csun.edu/exl/online.html
E-mail: sheri.kaufmann@csun.edu

Graduate Degree Programs:
Master of Science in Communicative Disorders

Certificate Programs: Contract Management, Production and Inventory Control, Accounting, Bookkeeping and Taxation, Purchasing, Management and Leadership, International Quality Standard.

Class Titles: Electrical Engineering, Mechanical/Aerospace

Engineering, Foreign Languages (French, Spanish, German, etc.), Health Science, Art.

Teaching Methods: *Computers:* Internet, real-time chat, electronic classroom, e-mail, CD-ROM, newsgroup, LIST-SERV. *TV:* microwave broadcasting (ITFS). *Other:* None.

Credits Granted for: experiential learning, portfolio assessment, extrainstitutional learning, examination (CLEP, ACT-PEP, DANTES, GRE).

Admission Requirements: *Graduate:* contact admissions at (818) 677-3786. *Certificate:* contact admissions at (818) 677-3786.

On-Campus Requirements: attendance at designated receive sites for 2-way video.

Tuition and Fees: *Undergraduate:* $631/0–6 units, $946/6.1 or more units. *Graduate:* $652/0–6 units, $985/6.1 or more units. *Application Fee:* $55. *Other Costs:* $50 TV surcharge in addition to noncredit course fee, $150/unit Open University. *Credit by:* semester.

Financial Aid: Federal Stafford Loan, Federal Perkins Loan, Federal PLUS Loan, Federal Pell Grant, Federal Work-Study, VA, California resident programs.

Accreditation: Western Association of Schools and Colleges.

Description: The Educational Technologies and Distance Learning Services program at California State University, Northridge (1958) is a university outreach program providing quality education for the distant learner. This is accomplished using multiple technologies including online-based courses, interactive ISDN based 2-way video, and a 14,000 square mile 4-channel interactive microwave broadcasting system. The microwave system enables the university to establish an electronic network and to provide training and education to students in the Los Angeles, Orange, Kern, and Ventura counties. Educational Technologies and Distance Learning Services offers credit courses and extension courses from studio class rooms to telecommute centers, schools, and industrial corporations.

California State University, San Marcos

| Extended Studies | Phone: (760) 750-4020 |
| San Marcos, CA 92096 | Fax: (760) 750-3138 |

Division(s): Department of Distance Learning
Web Site(s): http://www.csusm.edu/es
E-mail: es@mailhost1.csusm.edu

Class Titles: History of California, Riding Information Superhighway, Sociology of Ethnicity/Racism, Sociology of Law, Sociology: Postmodern Thought, Mainstreaming, Using

Database Instruction in Special Education, Teaching Reading in K-8 Classroom.

Teaching Methods: *Computers:* Internet. *Other:* None.

On-Campus Requirements: None.

Tuition and Fees: *Undergraduate:* $105/unit tuition. No other costs. *Graduate:* same. *Credit by:* semester.

Financial Aid: No financial aid through Extended Studies.

Accreditation: Western Association of Schools and Colleges.

Description: California State University, San Marcos (1989) offers excellence in undergraduate and graduate education to a diverse citizenry in an increasingly interdependent world. As the 20th campus in the California State System, CSU San Marcos provides an academic environment in which students, taught by active scholars, researchers, and artists, can achieve a foundation in the liberal arts and sciences and acquire specific competencies appropriate to major disciplines or graduate/professional study.

California State University, Stanislaus

| 801 West Monte Vista Avenue | Phone: (209) 667-3319 |
| Turlock, CA 95380-0299 | Fax: (209) 667-3333 |

Division(s): Coordinator of Regional Distance Learning, Department of History
Web Site(s): http://lead.csustan.edu
E-mail: oppenhei@toto.csustan.edu

Undergraduate Degree Programs:
Bachelor of Arts in Communications Studies
Bachelor of Arts in History (Stockton)

Graduate Degree Programs:
Master of Business Administration (Stockton)

Class Titles: Students must be regularly enrolled students at CSU Stanislaus in order to take a distance learning course. Accounting, Auditing, Computer in Accounting, Anthropology/Modern Social Issues, Cultures of Pacific, Native Americans, Comparative Religion, Folk Literature/Arts, American Art, Frontiers in Biology, Business Law, Child Abuse/Neglect, Chemicals in Your Life, Biochemistry, Computer Information Systems, Administration of Corrections, Language/Speech Development, Communications Research Methods, Communication Colloquium, Communication Theory, Organizational Communication, Persuasion/Social Influence, Mass Communication Perspectives, Public Relations, Personal Computing, Business/Economic Environment, Applied Writing, Rhetoric, Linguistic Theory, Masterpieces of World Literature, English Grammar, Contemporary World History, Medieval Europe, Renaissance/Reformation History, 19th Century Europe, 20th Century Europe, Great Teachings, Contemporary America, Women in American History, East Asia in Traditional Times,

Islamic Civilization, Colonialism/States of Asia/Africa, European Intellectual History, Judaism/Jewish History, Hitler/Nazi Era, Directed Reading Seminar, Senior Thesis, History of Journalism, Applied Mathematical Models, Gerontology, International Business, Marketing, Health Assessment, Nursing Leadership/Management, Community Health Nursing, Nursing Research, Operations Management, Productivity Management, Psychological Testing, Behavior Genetics, Learning Disabilities, Cross-Cultural Social Issues, Treatment of Offender, Sociology of Death, Sociology of Mental Health, Social Science Interdisciplinary Seminar.

Teaching Methods: *Computers:* All courses are live and interactive. CSU Stanislaus currently has 2 channels of Instructional TV Fixed Service microwave, which is 2-way audio and one-way video to all locations. We also have one channel of compressed video (CODEC) between Turlock and Stockton. That channel is both 2-way audio and 2-way video. The instructional TV rooms are computer-equipped. Some instructors use Web materials, but that is not standard. *Other:* None.

Credits Granted for: All courses are for letter grade or pass/fail. They are all part of the regular degree programs of the University.

Admission Requirements: *Undergraduate:* high school graduate in top 1/3 of class. *Graduate:* bachelor's degree. *Doctoral:* master's degree.

On-Campus Requirements: Except in Stockton, and then only for the programs mentioned above, most distance learners will take some or much of their course work on the Turlock campus. Stockton has a large site at which 200 courses/year are taught "live" in addition to the 80 or so ITV courses. At the Stockton Center, therefore, many degrees are offered.

Tuition and Fees: *Undergraduate:* $540 for in-state undergraduate for 0–6 units, $854 (fall and spring) for 7 or more units. Out-of-state undergraduates pay same as in-state PLUS $246/unit. *Graduate:* $540 for graduates carrying 0–6 units, $855 (fall and spring, so double that for the year) for 7 or more units. Out-of-state graduates pay same as above PLUS $246/unit. *Doctoral:* See "Graduate" above. *Application Fee:* $55. *Software:* might vary and apply in certain courses. *Credit by:* We have a 4-1-4. This includes 2 13-week terms and a 1-month winter term. All courses are regular 3- and 4-unit semester courses, meeting extra minutes during the 13-week terms to be the equivalent of a 15-week term.

Financial Aid: Federal Stafford Loan, Federal Perkins Loan, Federal PLUS Loan, Federal Pell Grant, Federal Work-Study, VA, California resident programs.

Accreditation: Western Association of Schools and Colleges.

Description: California State University, Stanislaus (1960) is located in the heart of the San Joaquin Valley and currently has a College of Arts, Letters, and Science; a School of Business; and a School of Education. It offers a full array of bachelor's and master's degrees in English, History, Psychology, Social Work, Education, Business Administration, and Public Administration. Stanislaus began offering live, interactive, distance learning courses to sites in its service area in the fall of 1981. It currently has 3 channels of operation that televise 75–95 courses/academic year.

Cambridge Academy

3855 SE Lake West Avenue	Phone: (352) 401-3688
Ocala, FL 34480	Fax: (352) 401-9013

Division(s): all departments
Web Site(s): under development; search under Cambridge Academy
E-mail: CamAcad@aol.com

Undergraduate Degree Programs:
high school diploma, grades 6–12

Class Titles: English, Math, Science, Social Studies, electives for grades 6–12; general and college preparatory programs.

Teaching Methods: *Computers:* e-mail. *TV:* videotape. *Other:* fax, correspondence, independent study, individual study, learning contracts.

Credits Granted for: portfolio assessment.

Admission Requirements: *Undergraduate:* completion of prior grade level.

On-Campus Requirements: None.

Tuition and Fees: *Other Costs:* $75/5 credit. *Credit by:* semester.

Accreditation: Southern Association of Colleges and Schools.

Description: Cambridge Academy (1978) provides instruction via distance education for grades 6–12. Accredited by the Southern Association of Colleges and Schools, Cambridge offers an accredited high school diploma to its graduates. Programs include general and college preparatory courses of study. Students work independently, and work is assessed by Cambridge instructors. Core academic subjects are taught with traditional textbooks and Cambridge study guides. Elective subjects are designed by the student with the guidance of an electives instructor. Students who are traveling, homebound, in need of make-up credits, or wishing to accelerate their learning enroll in Cambridge Academy.

Camden County College

Box 200 College Drive
Blackwood, NJ 08012

Phone: (609) 227-7200 x4271
Fax: (609) 374-5017

Division(s): Extended Education Services
Web Site(s): http://www.camdencc.edu/
E-mail: breveal@erols.com

Undergraduate Degree Programs:
Associate in Arts/Liberal Arts and Sciences

Class Titles: American Cinema, American Federal Government, Anthropology, Business Law, Business Math, Business, Economics, Composition, Ethics, French, Health/Wellness, History of American Education, History of Western Civilization, U.S. History, Journalism, Literature, Management, Small Business Management, Marketing, Math Skills, Abnormal Psychology, Psychology, Child Psychology, Selling, Sociology of Family, Sociology, Spanish

Teaching Methods: *Computers:* Internet, electronic classroom, e-mail, CD-ROM. *TV:* videotape, cable program, satellite broadcasting, PBS. *Other:* independent study, individual study, learning contracts.

Credits Granted for: experiential learning, portfolio assessment, extrainstitutional learning, examination (CLEP, ACT-PEP, DANTES, GRE).

Admission Requirements: *Undergraduate:* rolling admissions for accredited secondary or preparatory school graduates, State Equivalency Certificates, or age 18, plus application. Camden acceptance does not guarantee admission to restricted programs in Allied Health and Automotive Technology. CCC is authorized to issue I-20's and F-1 student visas with proper documentation and satisfactory academic progress.

On-Campus Requirements: None.

Tuition and Fees: *Undergraduate:* $57/credit in-county, $61/credit out-of-county, $111/credit foreign students. *Other Costs:* $19 general service fee 1–11 credits, $32 general service fee 12 or more credits, $25/course-$193/credit lab and material fees for applicable courses, $25/course distance learning course fee. *Credit by:* semester.

Financial Aid: Federal Stafford Loan, Federal Perkins Loan, Federal PLUS Loan, Federal Pell Grant, Federal Work-Study, New Jersey resident programs.

Accreditation: Middle States Association of Colleges and Schools.

Description: More than 30 years ago, the Salvatorian Fathers sold their Mother of the Savior Seminary and its 320 acres to Camden County College (1967). Today, Camden enrolls 13,000 credit students in 75 degree programs encompassing technical fields and liberal arts and sciences. A national leader in technology instruction with programs such as robotics, computer-integrated manufacturing, and laser/electro-optics technology, the college is also recognized as a vital resource for transfer education, customized training for business and industry, and community-based cultural arts programming. The Blackwood campus now includes 26 buildings, and an innovative new campus building opened in 1991 in Camden to house junior- and senior-year programs for Rowan College, allowing students to earn associate and bachelor's degrees at the Camden campus. A third campus in Cherry Hill will begin construction soon. Distance learning programming recognizes the need to serve those who have transportation, child-care, and employment-related issues that make it difficult or impossible to participate in the traditional college experience.

Capitol College

11301 Springfield Road
Laurel, MD 20708

Phone: (301) 369-2800
Fax: (301) 953-1442

Division(s): Office of the Academic Vice President
Web Site(s): http://www.capitol-college.edu
E-mail: admissions@capitol-college.edu
graduate school: ken@capitol-college.edu

Undergraduate Degree Programs:
Bachelor of Science in:
 Software
 Computer
 Electrical Engineering
 Software and Internet Applications
 Management of Information Technology
 Computer Electronics
 Telecommunications Engineering Technology

Graduate Degree Programs:
Master of Science in:
 Systems Management
 Telecommunications Systems Management
 Global Business Technology
 Global Commerce Technology

Certificate Programs: all degree programs have a certificate component.

Teaching Methods: *Computers:* Internet, real-time chat, electronic classroom, e-mail, CD-ROM, newsgroup. *Other:* None.

Admission Requirements: *Undergraduate:* contact admissions@capitol-college.edu *Graduate:* contact, Graduate School of Systems Management at (703) 998-5503. *Certificate:* same as above.

On-Campus Requirements: None.

Tuition and Fees: *Undergraduate:* $392+/credit. *Graduate:* $296/credit. *Application Fee:* $25. *Credit by:* semester.

Financial Aid: Federal Stafford Loan, Federal Perkins Loan, Federal PLUS Loan, Federal Pell Grant, Federal Work-Study, VA, Maryland resident programs (must be degree-seeking).

Accreditation: Middle States Association of Colleges and Schools; Accrediting Board for Engineering and Technology for programs in EE, Electronics, Computer and Telecommunications Engineering Technology.

Description: Capitol College (1927) is an accredited independent college which focuses on undergraduate and graduate programs in information technology, engineering and management. Undergraduate programs range from electrical engineering, computer engineering, and telecommunications to software engineering and Internet applications. Students are guaranteed job placement. The graduate school offers evening degree programs in systems management and telecommunications systems management for the working adult. All students studying online receive the same instruction from the same professors as do students on our resident campuses. Online courses are interactive and taught in synchronous and asynchronous modes.

Carl Sandburg College

2232 South Lake Storey Road	Phone: (309) 341-5290
Galesburg, IL 61401-9576	Fax: (309) 344-3526

Division(s): Learning Resource Services
Web Site(s): http://www.csc.cc.il.us/
E-mail: ckreider@csc.cc.il.us

Undergraduate Degree Programs:
Associate of Arts
Associate of Science
Associate of Fine Arts
Associate of Applied Science
Associate in General Education

Certificate Programs: Yes.

Class Titles: History, Sociology, Psychology, English, Music, Math, Child Development, Economics, Art, Liberal Arts, Business, Health, Agriculture, Industrial.

Teaching Methods: *Computers:* Internet, electronic classroom, e-mail. *TV:* videotape. *Other:* videoconferencing, fax.

Credits Granted for: extrainstitutional learning (CLEP, PEP, DANTES).

Admission Requirements: *Undergraduate:* open admissions.

On-Campus Requirements: 15 hours or 25%.

Tuition and Fees: *Undergraduate:* $57/credit. *Credit by:* semester.

Financial Aid: Federal Stafford Loan, Federal Perkins Loan,

Federal Pell Grant, Federal Work-Study, VA, Illinois resident programs.

Accreditation: North Central Association of Colleges and Schools.

Description: Carl Sandburg College (1966) is a comprehensive, 2-year community college. We offer selected courses in a variety of disciplines via distance learning; however, an entire program cannot be completed by distance.

Carroll College

100 N East Avenue	Phone: (414) 524-7216
Waukesha, WI 53186	Fax: (414) 650-4851

Division(s): Professional Studies
Web Site(s): http://www.cc.edu
E-mail: pstudies@carroll1.cc.edu

Undergraduate Degree Programs:
Bachelor of Arts

Certificate Programs: World Wide Web, Client Server Database, Marketing/Sales Promotion, Nonprofit Management, Piano Pedagogy; only a few courses can be taken as Web courses.

Class Titles: Computer Science.

Teaching Methods: *Computers:* Internet, e-mail. *Other:* None.

Credits Granted for: portfolio assessment, examination (CLEP).

Admission Requirements: *Undergraduate:* high school diploma, 2.0 average in college course work.

On-Campus Requirements: First and last class of each course.

Tuition and Fees: *Undergraduate:* $180/credit. *Credit by:* semester.

Financial Aid: Federal Stafford Loan, Federal Perkins Loan, Federal PLUS Loan, Federal Pell Grant, Federal Work-Study, VA, Wisconsin resident programs.

Accreditation: North Central Association of Colleges and Schools.

Description: Nearly 2,500 students attend Carroll College (1846) and its partner school, Columbia College of Nursing in Milwaukee. The college, affiliated with the Presbyterian Church, also collaborates with U.S. Speedskating, Up With People, AFS, Quad Graphics, and Hawaiian Pacific University. Students can earn degrees from Carroll while working with these organizations. Divisions include Humanities and Fine Arts (English, History, Modern Language, Philosophy, Religious Studies, Art, Music, Theater Arts), Sciences (Biology,

Chemistry, Computer Science, Geography, Math, Physics, Physical Therapy, Psychology), and Social Sciences (Communication, Politics, Sociology/Social Work, Business Administration, Accounting/Economics, Education/Physical Education). The Professional Studies Department offers evening and Saturday classes, in addition to distance learning for adults able to learn independently.

Carroll Community College

1601 Washington Road	Phone: (410) 386-8100
Westminster, MD 21157	Fax: (410) 876-5869

Division(s): Extended Learning and Workforce Development
Web Site(s): http://www.carroll.cc.md.us
E-mail: jnickles@carroll.cc.md.us

Class Titles: Veterinary Technology, Chemical Dependency Counseling, Languages, Advanced Math, Nutrition for Nursing, Computers, Sciences, Sociology, History, English, Psychology, Philosophy, Business.

Teaching Methods: *Computers:* Internet, real-time chat, electronic classroom, e-mail. *TV:* videotape, cable program, satellite broadcasting, PBS. *Other:* videoconferencing, fax, correspondence, independent study, individual study, learning contracts.

Credits Granted for: experiential learning, portfolio assessment, examination (CLEP, ACT-PEP, DANTES, GRE).

Admission Requirements: *Undergraduate:* completed admission application, high school transcripts or GED scores, ACT/SAT results if available, and other transcripts if possible, completion of placement tests and meeting with a student advisor.

On-Campus Requirements: currently, Maryland Higher Education Commission is in the process of changing the guidelines. The changes will allow students to complete entire degrees at a distance.

Tuition and Fees: *Undergraduate:* $67/credit county residents. *Application Fee:* $25. *Other Costs:* 10% of tuition college service fee; $2/billable hour student activity fee; $75/semester/1/2 hour applied music lab fee; $25/applicable life fitness course fee; $10, $20, or $25 technology fee depending on applicable courses; $2/request transcript fee; ½ course tuition credit-by-exam fee. *Credit by:* semester.

Financial Aid: Federal Stafford Loan, Federal Perkins Loan, Federal PLUS Loan, Federal Pell Grant, Federal Work-Study, Maryland resident programs.

Accreditation: Middle States Association of Colleges and Schools.

Description: Carroll Community College (1976) began as a campus of Catonsville Community College, became an independent community college on July 1, 1994, and fully accredited in the spring of 1996. CCC entered into the distance education arena first with telecourses. In 1995, the college purchased a compressed video system as part of a grant awarded to 5 community colleges. This system is linked via a T-1 line and has ISDN capabilities. In 1997, the college added a second live interactive system that provides a statewide link via fiber to other colleges, universities, and public school systems. The college also provides noncredit courses for the professions via the live interactive video systems. The college began offering courses via the Internet in 1997.

Casper College

125 College Drive, Suite AD 298	Phone: (307) 268-2617 or 2110
Casper, WY 82601	Fax: (307) 268-2224

Division(s): Academic Affairs
Web Site(s): http://www.cc.whecn.edu
E-mail: steinle@acad.cc.whecn.edu

Undergraduate Degree Programs:
Associate of Arts
Associate of Science
Associate of Applied Science
Associate of Applied Arts
Associate of Business

Certificate Programs: one-year certificates of completion.

Teaching Methods: *Computers:* Internet, real-time chat, e-mail, LISTSERV. *TV:* videotape, cable program, satellite broadcasting, PBS. *Other:* independent study, individual study.

Credits Granted for: extrainstitutional learning, examination (CLEP, ACT-PEP, DANTES, GRE).

Admission Requirements: *Undergraduate:* high school graduate or GED. No admission requirement if special nondegree student. *Certificate:* same as undergraduate.

On-Campus Requirements: None.

Tuition and Fees: *Undergraduate:* $47/credit resident, $131/credit nonresident. *Credit by:* semester.

Financial Aid: Federal Stafford Loan, Federal PLUS Loan, Federal Pell Grant, Federal Work-Study, VA, Wyoming resident programs.

Accreditation: North Central Association of Colleges and Schools.

Description: Casper College (1945) was established as Wyoming's first community college and has grown in size and reputation into one of the West's outstanding 2-year colleges. Casper offers 70 academic transfer degrees and 30 technical/career programs. Distance education classes were added to the curriculum 3 years ago to meet the needs of a sparsely populated geographic region. CC currently offers a wide variety of telecourses and Internet course offerings and continues to grow each year.

Central Baptist Theological Seminary

741 North 31st Street	Phone: (913) 371-5313
Kansas City, KS 66102-3964	Fax: (913) 371-8110

Division(s): Academic
Web Site(s): http://www.cbts.edu
E-mail: rejohnson@cbts.edu

Undergraduate Degree Programs:
Diploma in Theological Studies

Graduate Degree Programs:
Master of Divinity
Master of Arts in Religious Studies

Teaching Methods: *Computers:* Internet, e-mail. *TV:* videotape. *Other:* videoconferencing, audioconferencing, audiographics, audiotapes, fax, correspondence, independent study, individual study, learning contracts.

Credits Granted for: extrainstitutional learning (pre-approved workshops).

Admission Requirements: *Undergraduate:* 2.3 undergraduate GPA, must matriculate within 2 years of admission. *Graduate:* accredited bachelor's degree, 2.3 GPA for undergraduate and graduate work, must matriculate within 2 years of admission.

On-Campus Requirements: yes, required opening and closing intensives are held on campus for each distance learning class. In addition, only 25% of the total hours for any degree program may be taken off campus.

Tuition and Fees: *Undergraduate:* $180/credit part-time, $1800 full-time tuition flat rate. *Graduate:* same as undergraduate. *Application Fee:* $30-MDiv., MA, diploma; $20-special, audit, continuing education. *Other Costs:* $66 audit or continuing education; $75/semester registration; $600 one-year internship; $305 summer internship; $455 military chaplain internship; $100 for 1st semester MDiv. assessment, $25 following completion of 30 hours, $100 following completion of 60 hours; $25 MA, diploma and special student assessment; $45 electronic telecommunication (nonresident LDL only); $55/6-hr unit of CPE. *Credit by:* semester.

Financial Aid: Federal Stafford Loan; VA; scholarships—Presidential, Honor, Tuition, and Matching Funds; American Indian students are guaranteed full tuition grants; special tuition rate for couples; 50% tuition discount for children of alumni/alumnae; spouses of degree program students may audit courses for $10/semester hour.

Accreditation: Association of Theological Schools in the U.S. and Canada, North Central Association of Colleges and Schools.

Description: Central Baptist Theological Seminary (1901) was chartered to offer professional graduate training for ministers and laypeople, without regard for race, color, national origin, gender, age, or disability. Initially a cooperative effort between Northern and Southern Baptists, the school now enjoys a longstanding covenant relationship with the American Baptist Churches in the U.S. The new Cooperative Baptist Fellowship, for which the seminary has expressed full support, is also well represented among our faculty, staff, students, and board of directors. Indeed, Baptists of every kind make up more than half of the student body, with the rest drawn from Christian denominations of similar theology and heritage. The distance learning program began in 1989 and has evolved into one of the few distance education programs serving graduate theological education in America. It has offered 23 courses since that time by using videotaped lectures and telephone conference calls linking on-campus students and students at remote locations—for up to 24 participants per class. In the fall of 1995, an Internet dimension was added, allowing students with e-mail capabilities to converse with other students and professors.

Central Community College

PO Box 4903	Phone: (308) 389-6441
Grand Island, NE 68801	Fax: (308) 389-6398

Division(s): Community Education
Web Site(s): http://www.cccneb.edu
E-mail: hargced@cccadm.gi.cccneb.edu

Undergraduate Degree Programs:
Associate of Arts
Associate of Applied Sciences

Teaching Methods: *Computers:* Internet, real-time chat, electronic classroom, e-mail, CD-ROM, newsgroup, LISTSERV. *TV:* videotape, cable program, satellite broadcasting, PBS. *Other:* radio broadcast, videoconferencing, audioconferencing, audiographics, audiotapes, fax, correspondence, independent study, individual study, learning contracts.

Credits Granted for: experiential learning, portfolio assessment, extrainstitutional learning, examination (CLEP, ACT-PEP, DANTES, GRE).

Admission Requirements: *Undergraduate:* please contact school for information. *Graduate:* please contact school for information. *Doctoral:* please contact school for information. *Certificate:* please contact school for information.

On-Campus Requirements: None.

Tuition and Fees: *Undergraduate:* $44/credit. *Other Costs:* vary for special tools/supplies. *Credit by:* semester.

Financial Aid: Federal Stafford Loan, Federal Perkins Loan, Federal PLUS Loan, Federal Pell Grant, Federal Work-Study, VA, Nebraska resident programs.

Accreditation: North Central Association of Colleges and Schools.

Description: Central Community College (1973) as it exists today was formed with the enactment of legislation that established 6 technical community college areas in the state of Nebraska. This enabling legislation merged the Hastings campus (including its practical-nursing program in Kearney), which was established in 1966 as Nebraska's first vocational-technical college (serving a 17-county area), and the Platte campus, established at Columbus in 1969 as Nebraska's first county-supported community college. The Grand Island campus began offering courses in 1976. Central Community began offering courses at a distance through its learning centers almost from the beginning, with individualized curriculum offerings as its strength.

Central Florida Community College

PO Box 1388	Phone: (352) 854-2322 x1348
Ocala, FL 34478	Fax: (352) 873-5870

Division(s): Office of Instruction
Web Site(s): http://www.cfcc.cc.fl.us
E-mail: flemingp@cfcc.cc.fl.us

Undergraduate Degree Programs:
Associate in Arts
Associate in Science

Certificate Programs: Criminal Justice Bridge, Radiation Protection Technology

Class Titles: Humanities, English Composition, Personal Wellness, Nutrition, Health Practice, Economics (macro/micro), Microcomputer Applications, Ornamental Horticulture, Sociology, Social Science, Physics, Freshwater Ecology, Chemistry, World Civilizations, Geology, Spanish, Geography.

Teaching Methods: *Computers:* Internet, real-time chat, electronic classroom, e-mail, CD-ROM, newsgroup, LIST-SERV. *TV:* videotape, cable program, satellite broadcasting, PBS. *Other:* radio broadcast, videoconferencing, audiotapes, fax, correspondence, independent study, individual study, learning contracts.

Credits Granted for: experiential learning, portfolio assessment, extrainstitutional learning, examination (CLEP, ACT-PEP, DANTES, GRE).

Admission Requirements: *Undergraduate:* open-enrollment.

Certificate: open-enrollment.

On-Campus Requirements: subject to instructor discretion (0–4/course).

Tuition and Fees: *Undergraduate:* $47/credit in-state, $171/credit out-of-state. *Application Fee:* $20. *Other Costs:* $5–$20 laboratory fees/course. *Credit by:* semester.

Financial Aid: Federal Stafford Loan, Federal Perkins Loan, Federal PLUS Loan, Federal Pell Grant, Federal Work-Study, VA, Florida resident programs.

Accreditation: Southern Association of Colleges and Schools.

Description: Central Florida Community College (1958) is located in the gentle, rolling hills of Ocala, with branch campuses in Citrus and Levy counties. The college is one of 28 in the Florida Community College system and offers a full range of degree and certificate programs for students seeking to advance to a 4-year institution or to hone skills for the job market. Located a half-hour from the University of Florida and 2 hours from 4 other state schools, the college provides ready, articulated access to future transfer students. Although relatively small, the institution prides itself on its personal touch to students and its ability to react to a changing educational and vocational marketplace. If the college does not have a desired program, it will soon find a way to create it. Distance learning has existed mainly through telecourses for 15 years. However, CFCC Online has recently emerged as a significant player in online education, developing a slate of 24 courses ranging from physics to humanities. These courses take advantage of the ever-increasing capabilities of students and teachers to interact electronically through e-mail and the Internet.

Central Methodist College

411 CMC Square	Phone: (660) 248-6286
Fayette, MO 65248	Fax: (660) 248-2622

Division(s): Academic Dean's Office
Web Site(s): http://www.cmc.edu
E-mail: aoberhau@cmc2.cmc.edu

Undergraduate Degree Programs:
Bachelor of Arts
Bachelor of Science

Graduate Degree Programs:
Master of Education

Class Titles: Nursing, Education, German, Religion.

Teaching Methods: *Computers:* Internet, CD-ROM, LIST-SERV. *TV:* videotape. *Other:* videoconferencing, audioconferencing, fax, correspondence, independent study, individual study.

Credits Granted for: examination (CLEP, ACT-PEP, DANTES, GRE).

Admission Requirements: *Undergraduate:* 2.5 GPA, 20 ACT. *Graduate:* 2.75 GPA.

On-Campus Requirements: yes, students cannot complete programs with distance learning only

Tuition and Fees: *Undergraduate:* $431 and $120. *Graduate:* $165. *Application Fee:* $20–$25. *Credit by:* semester.

Financial Aid: Federal Stafford Loan, Federal Perkins Loan, Federal PLUS Loan, Federal Pell Grant, Federal Work-Study, VA, Missouri resident programs.

Accreditation: North Central Association of Colleges and Schools.

Description: Central Methodist College (1855) is located midway between St. Louis and Kansas City in a region of exceptional natural beauty. The 52-acre campus is a National Historic District distinguished by its majestic plantation of shade and ornamental trees. During the last decade, CMC began cooperative programs that allow regional citizens who have completed their AA degree (or who have 62 credits) to earn a bachelor's degree at nearby Mineral Area College and East Central College. In 1996 the college began offering its first master's degree program, the Master of Education, on all 3 campuses.

Central Missouri State University

Humphreys 403	Phone: (660) 543-8480
Warrensburg, MO 64093	Fax: (660) 543-8333

Division(s): Extended Campus—Distance Learning
Web Site(s): http://www.cmsu.edu/extcamp/
E-mail: criswell@cmsu1.cmsu.edu
bassore@cmsu1.cmsu.edu

Undergraduate Degree Programs:
Bachelor of Science in Electronics Technology

Graduate Degree Programs:
Master of Science in:
 Occupational Safety Management
 Criminal Justice
 Aviation Safety

Doctoral Degree Programs:
Doctor of Philosophy in Technology

Certificate Programs: Certified Financial Planner (for members of Missouri Bankers Association only); state certification requirements for teachers of the severely developmentally disabled.

Class Titles: Public Speaking, Early Childhood Nutrition/Health, Contemporary Math, Media Literacy, Marketing Policy, Contemporary Family, Study Skills/ACT Preparation, Interactive TV Training, Comparative Education, Elementary School Curriculum, Community/Family Resources, Cooperative Learning.

Teaching Methods: *Computers:* Internet, real-time chat, electronic classroom, e-mail, CD-ROM, newsgroup, LISTSERV. *TV:* 2-way interactive TV, videotape, satellite broadcasting, PBS. *Other:* audioconferencing, videoconferencing, fax, correspondence, independent study.

Credits Granted for: extrainstitutional learning, examination (CLEP, ACT-PEP, DANTES, GRE).

Admission Requirements: *Undergraduate:* ACT of 20, high school diploma or GED, transcript. *Graduate:* GRE/GMAT, undergraduate degree, transcripts, 8-year completion time. *Doctoral:* master's degree, transcripts, 8-year completion time. *Certificate:* variable.

On-Campus Requirements: None.

Tuition and Fees: *Undergraduate:* $121/credit. *Graduate:* $187/credit. *Doctoral:* $158/credit. *Application Fee:* $25. *Other Costs:* vary for books plus $4/book mailing charge. *Credit by:* semester.

Financial Aid: Federal Stafford Loan, Federal Perkins Loan, Federal PLUS Loan, Federal Pell Grant, Federal Work-Study, VA, Missouri resident programs.

Accreditation: North Central Association of Colleges and Schools.

Description: Central Missouri State University (1871) is a state university offering 150 areas of study to 11,800 undergraduate and graduate students. The wide range of academic programs, people with varied backgrounds and experiences, a friendly and inviting environment, skilled professors, and excellent facilities combine to make Central Missouri State an outstanding institution of higher education. Central, charged with a statewide mission in academic and professional technology, meets the needs of students physically located off campus through its commitment to distance education. Classes are conducted via 2-way interactive TV, the Internet, and satellite delivery systems. A charter member of Missouri's largest educational consortium, Central currently offers 3 full master's degree programs, a variety of undergraduate and high school dual-credit classes, and specified courses of a cooperative doctoral degree using distance learning technologies.

Central Piedmont Community College

PO Box 35009
Charlotte, NC 28235

Phone: (704) 330-6883
Fax: (704) 330-6945

Division(s): College Without Walls
Web Site(s): http://cww.cpcc.cc.nc.us
E-mail: dave_flanagan@cpcc.cc.nc.us

Undergraduate Degree Programs:
Associate of Arts

Teaching Methods: *Computers:* Internet, electronic class-room, e-mail, CD-ROM, newsgroup, LISTSERV. *TV:* video-tape, cable program, PBS. *Other:* None.

Credits Granted for: examination (CLEP).

Admission Requirements: *Undergraduate:* open-door policy.

On-Campus Requirements: None.

Tuition and Fees: *Undergraduate:* $20/semester credit. *Other Costs:* $14 activity fee/semester. *Credit by:* semester.

Financial Aid: Federal Pell Grant, Federal Work-Study, VA, North Carolina resident programs.

Accreditation: Southern Association of Colleges and Schools.

Description: Central Piedmont Community College (1963) is an innovative, comprehensive, public, 2-year college with a mission to advance the lifelong educational development of adults. Central Piedmont has offered telecourses for a number of years and has recently begun offering online courses.

Central Virginia Community College

3506 Wards Road
Lynchburg, VA 24502

Phone: (804) 832-7600
Fax: (804) 386-4531

Division(s): Learning Resources Center
Web Site(s): http://www.cv.cc.va.us
E-mail: cvbeass@cv.cc.va.us

Certificate Programs: Occupations/Technical areas.

Class Titles: Business, Health, Sociology, Biology, Economics, Math, Psychology, Marketing.

Teaching Methods: *Computers:* Internet, electronic class-room, e-mail, CD-ROM. *TV:* videotape, PBS. *Other:* video-conferencing, audioconferencing, audiotapes, fax, correspondence, independent study, individual study.

Credits Granted for: experiential learning, examination (CLEP, ACT-PEP, DANTES, GRE).

Admission Requirements: *Undergraduate:* please contact school for information.

On-Campus Requirements: None.

Tuition and Fees: *Undergraduate:* $47/credit in-state, $156/credit out-of-state. *Other Costs:* $10 general student fee. *Credit by:* semester.

Financial Aid: Federal Stafford Loan, Federal Perkins Loan, Federal PLUS Loan, Federal Pell Grant, Federal Work-Study, VA, Virginia resident programs.

Accreditation: Southern Association of Schools and Colleges.

Description: Central Virginia Community College (1967) is part of the Virginia Community College System. It offers associate degrees, diplomas, and certificate programs in Occupations/Technical areas as well as for college transfer. In 1987 the college began offering distance education courses in several disciplines. The program and course offerings have grown to include Web-based and compressed-video offerings.

Central Washington University

400 East 8th Avenue
Ellensburg, WA 98926

Phone: (509) 963-3001
Fax: (509) 963-3022

Division(s): Office of the Provost
Web Site(s): http://www.cwu.edu
E-mail: schwindt@cwu.edu

Undergraduate Degree Programs:
Business Administration
Education
Organization Development

Class Titles: Personal Finance via Internet, a variety of Professional Development, Education, Accounting, Business courses.

Teaching Methods: *Computers:* Internet, electronic class-room, e-mail, CD-ROM. *TV:* videotape, cable program, satellite broadcasting. *Other:* videoconferencing, fax, independent study, individual study.

Admission Requirements: *Undergraduate:* 1st-year students (under 45 credits): transcripts from high school or college (if attended), ACT/SAT scores that meet the mission index, required high school core (contact school for details). Transfer students (over 45 credits): all college transcripts, meet minimum GPA standard (alternate admission possible for low GPA). *Graduate:* official copies of all undergraduate and graduate study at other institutions, 3 recommendation letters, personal statement of education objectives and professional aims (500 words or less). For some programs, acceptable GRE, 3.0 GPA for last 90 quarter hours (60 semester hours).

On-Campus Requirements: Students are required to attend

the satellite broadcast session or participate in an evening orientation for Internet course.

Tuition and Fees: *Undergraduate:* $88/credit (2-credit minimum). *Graduate:* $140/credit (2-credit minimum). *Application Fee:* $35. *Other Costs:* $25 technology fee, $40 health and counseling fee, other software or lab-related fees may apply. Tuition and fees are always subject to change. *Credit by:* quarter.

Financial Aid: Federal Stafford Loan, Federal Perkins Loan, Federal PLUS Loan, Federal Pell Grant, Federal Work-Study, VA.

Accreditation: Northwest Association of Schools and Colleges.

Description: Central Washington University (1890) is one of 6 state-supported institutions offering bachelor's and graduate degrees. The words *Docendo Discimus*, "by teaching we learn," remain today as in the past the cornerstone of the university's mission. As a comprehensive university, Central offers programs in an environment that means to nurture a student's physical, intellectual, social, and ethical development, and this environment is marked by small classes, residential and recreational programs, and concern for each student as an individual. Instruction is organized into degree and certificate programs providing theoretical and practical education in the liberal arts/sciences, visual/performing arts, professional/technical fields, education, business, applied sciences, and engineering technologies. Continued assessment and accreditation reviews ensure vitality of all university programs. Central has 5 university-center programs in addition to on-campus programs. Distance learning originated 2 years ago when we broadcast our Wenatchee Site to ensure that students met their degree requirements.

Central Wyoming College

2660 Peck Avenue	Phone: (307) 855-2187
Riverton, WY 82501	Fax: (307) 855-2065

Division(s): Distance Education
Web Site(s): http://www.cwc.whecn.edu/
E-mail: mgores@Interserve1.cwc.whecn.edu

Undergraduate Degree Programs:
Associate of Arts
Associate of Science

Class Titles: several individual courses are offered every semester

Teaching Methods: *Computers:* Internet, real-time chat, electronic classroom, e-mail, CD-ROM. *TV:* videotape, PBS. *Other:* audioconferencing, videoconferencing.

Credits Granted for: examination (CLEP, DANTES).

Admission Requirements: *Undergraduate:* under age 16 with permission; COMPASS/ACT; plans underway for open-entry, open-exit courses.

On-Campus Requirements: None.

Tuition and Fees: *Undergraduate:* $59/credit. *Other Costs:* $7/credit for computer-based courses. *Credit by:* semester.

Financial Aid: Federal Stafford Loan, Federal PLUS Loan, Federal Pell Grant, Federal Work-Study, VA, Wyoming resident programs.

Accreditation: North Central Association of Colleges and Schools.

Description: The Central Wyoming College (1966) campus is located in a city of 10,000 on the banks of Wind River. The campus and community lie in the Wind River Valley, bounded by mountains on 3 sides. Lakes and streams are abundant, and recreational opportunities are unlimited. Yellowstone National Park, Grand Teton National Park, Hot Springs State Park, and extensive forested lands are within easy driving distance. Outdoor activities include skiing, snowmobiling, snowshoeing, ice skating, hiking, backpacking, hunting, fishing, photography, horseback riding, golf, and swimming. The valley has a rich and varied history, with a large portion presently occupied by an Indian reservation housing Shoshone and Arapahoe tribes. CWC has offered distance education since 1983 through a campus-based PBS station and the student-run FM radio station. Recently the program has expanded to include courses via the Internet; CD-ROM; electronic classrooms; and live, 2-way, interactive audio/video connections.

Centralia College

600 West Locust	Phone: (360) 736-9391
Centralia, WA 98531	Fax: (360) 330-7502

Division(s): Distance Learning (Correspondence)
Web Site(s): http://www.centralia.ctc.edu or http://www. webmaster@centralia.ctc.edu
E-mail: ckimbel@centralia.ctc.edu

Undergraduate Degree Programs:
Associate in Arts
Associate in Liberal Arts
Associate in Science
Associate in Technical Arts
Associate Degree Programs in:
   Anthropology
   Business Administration
   Civil Engineering Technology
   Computer Network Technology
   Diesel Equipment Technology
   Dramatic Arts

Earth Sciences
Early Childhood Education (also ATA degree)
Electronics Technology
English Literature
English, Writing
Physical Education, Teacher Education
Physical Education, Health and Recreation
Fine Arts
Foreign Languages
Forestry Technology
Natural Resources/Forest Technology
General Engineering
Graphic Design
Humanities
Biology
Botany
Pre-Chiropractic
Pre-Physical Therapy
Pre-Dentistry
Pre-Pharmacy
Pre-Medicine
Pre-Veterinary Science
Law Enforcement
Legal Office Assistant
Marketing/Management Training
Mathematics
Medical Office Assistant
Music
Office Assistant
Nursing (Practical or Transfer)
Chemistry
Physics
Radio and Television Broadcasting
History
Psychology
Sociology
Welding

Certificate Programs: Accounting Clerk, Basic Computer Applications, Computer Aided Drafting, Corrections Officer, Early Childhood Education, Electronics Assembly, Individualized Certificate of Proficiency, Industrial Plant Service, Legal Office Assistant, Medical Office Assistant, Office Assistant, Office Receptionist, Retail Management, Welding.

Class Titles: Accounting, Pharmacology/Physiology of Alcohol/Drugs, Astronomy, Business, Business Law, Transcription Fundamentals, Filing, Legal Terminology, Medical Terminology, Education, Physical Geography, Health/Wellness, Exercise/Nutrition, Nutrition, U.S. History, Pacific Northwest History, Algebra, Technical Mathematics, Probability/Statistics, Plane Trigonometry, Pre-Calculus, Survey of Calculus, Elementary Math Concepts, Oceanography, Philosophy, Political Science, American Government, Meteorology, Biology

of Aging, Cultural Botany.

Teaching Methods: *Computers:* Internet, e-mail. *TV:* videotape, satellite broadcasting, PBS. *Other:* videoconferencing, fax, correspondence, independent study, individual study.

Credits Granted for: examination (CLEP, Advanced Placement), military credit and experience, articulation agreements, law enforcement/fire protection training.

Admission Requirements: *Undergraduate:* age 18 and/or a high school (or GED program) graduate. Special considerations may be given to individuals not meeting these criteria. Some programs have additional requirements that must be met.

On-Campus Requirements: at this time, it is not possible to earn all credits for a degree off-campus, although many of a student's credits may be earned through correspondence courses.

Tuition and Fees: *Undergraduate:* $51/credit Washington state residents, $199/credit nonresidents. *Other Costs:* $5 student activities fee, $10 placement testing (ASSET), $11 or $23 video program fee for correspondence students, $4/credit with $40 maximum/quarter technology fee, varied fees for specialized programs. Fees and tuition subject to change; please check for current rates. *Credit by:* quarter.

Financial Aid: Federal Stafford Loan, Federal Perkins Loan, Federal PLUS Loan, Federal Pell Grant, Federal Work-Study, VA, Washington resident programs.

Accreditation: Northwest Association of Schools and Colleges, Washington State Board for Community College Education, State Approving Agency for the Training of Veterans, U.S. Department of Education.

Description: Centralia College (1925) is the oldest continuously operating community college in the state of Washington. It is located on the I-5 corridor in an area that is a combination of forest and farmland. The community is mostly rural, but also has 2 cities with a combined population of about 18,000 people. The service area of Centralia College covers 2,409 square miles which includes Lewis County and south Thurston County. Our Distance Learning Program began in 1976 in the form of video courses. It later progressed to other correspondence courses in 1980. This program was created in answer to requests by students for distance learning and individual study programs. It was modeled after a successful program at Everett Community College. The need for these classes has grown due to work schedules, cost and time of commuting, and convenience for the student. We currently offer 42 correspondence courses, with 2 additional courses on the Internet.

Cerritos College

| 11110 Alondra Boulevard | Phone: (562) 860-2451 x2833 |
| Norwalk, CA 90650 | Fax: (562) 467-5005 |

Division(s): Distributed Education Program
Web Site(s): http://www.cerritos.edu
E-mail: de-info@cerritos.edu

Class Titles: Reading, English, History, Political Science, Business, Technology, Spanish.

Teaching Methods: *Computers:* Internet, real-time chat, electronic classroom, e-mail, CD-ROM, newsgroup, LIST-SERV. *TV:* videotape, cable program, satellite broadcasting, PBS. *Other:* radio broadcast, audioconferencing, videoconferencing, audiographics, audiotapes, fax, correspondence, independent study, individual study, learning contracts.

Credits Granted for: examination (CLEP, ACT-PEP, GRE).

Admission Requirements: *Certificate:* some have prerequisites.

On-Campus Requirements: None.

Tuition and Fees: *Undergraduate:* $13/credit. *Credit by:* semester.

Financial Aid: Federal Stafford Loan, Federal Perkins Loan, Federal PLUS Loan, Federal Pell Grant, Federal Work-Study, VA, California resident programs.

Accreditation: Western Association of Schools and Colleges.

Description: Cerritos College (1955) symbolizes many things to many people. This defining fact is reflected in the large number of courses, programs of study and other opportunities available to students of all backgrounds and ages. We are committed to helping every student succeed and to that end, we provide a wide range of support services to ensure your success.

Cerro Coso Community College

| 3000 College Heights Boulevard | Phone: (760) 384-6100 |
| Ridgecrest, CA 93555 | Fax: (760) 375-4776 |

Division(s): Office of Instruction
Web Site(s): http://www.cc.cc.ca.us
E-mail: mhightow@cc.cc.ca.us

Undergraduate Degree Programs:
Associate of Arts
Associate of Science

Certificate Programs: Business Administration, Computer Information Systems

Class Titles: dozens—see Web site for current class descriptions.

Teaching Methods: *Computers:* Internet, real-time chat, electronic classroom, e-mail, CD-ROM, newsgroup, LIST-SERV. *Other:* None.

Credits Granted for: examination (CLEP, USAFI, DANTES).

Admission Requirements: *Undergraduate:* accredited high school graduates, holders of CHSPE or GED certificates, or age 18 and able to profit from college instructional programs.

On-Campus Requirements: None.

Tuition and Fees: *Undergraduate:* $12/credit. *Other Costs:* variable materials fees. *Credit by:* semester.

Financial Aid: Federal Stafford Loan, Federal Perkins Loan, Federal PLUS Loan, Federal Pell Grant, Federal Work-Study, VA, California resident programs.

Accreditation: Western Association of Schools and Colleges.

Description: Cerro Coso Community College (1973) is a comprehensive community college serving the eastern Sierra Nevada and eastern Kern County regions of California. Cerro Coso has 4 instructional sites that together form the largest geographical service area (12,000 square miles) of any community college in California, serving a population of approximately 85,000. A leader in distance learning online classes and degree programs, Cerro Coso offers 3 dozen online classes each semester leading to an Associate in Arts or Associate in Science in Business Administration, Computer Information Systems, or General Education. Online classes serve students in other states and nations.

Chabot College

| 25555 Hesperian Boulevard | Phone: (510) 786-6758 |
| Hayward, CA 94545 | Fax: (510) 264-1506 |

Division(s): Distance Education Center
Web Site(s): http://www.clpccd.cc.ca.us/cc/dised/index.html
E-mail: egrant@clpccd.cc.ca.us

Undergraduate Degree Programs:
Various courses are offered, almost enough to complete an Associate of Arts Degree.

Class Titles: Anthropology, Cultural Anthropology, Business, Business Law, Business Management, Excel for PC, Chemistry, General Economics, World Regional Geography, Holistic Health, Western Civilization Since 1600, U.S. History Through Reconstruction, U.S. History Since Reconstruction, Mass Communications, Reading/Publishing on Web, Algebra Review, Stress Management/Health Psychology/Lab, General Psychology, Principles of Sociology, Cultural/Racial Minorities, Marriage/Family Relations.

Teaching Methods: *Computers:* Internet, real-time chat, electronic classroom, e-mail, LISTSERV. *TV:* videotape, cable program. *Other:* audioconferencing, videoconferencing, fax, correspondence, independent study.

Admission Requirements: *Undergraduate:* high school diploma or GED equivalent.

On-Campus Requirements: Depends on the course curriculum.

Tuition and Fees: *Undergraduate:* $13/semester unit. *Credit by:* semester units.

Financial Aid: Federal Stafford Loan, Federal Perkins Loan, Federal PLUS Loan, Federal Pell Grant, Federal Work-Study, VA, California resident programs.

Accreditation: Western Association of Schools and Colleges. The College is approved by the California State Department of Education and is a member of the American Association of Community and Junior Colleges and the Community College League of California.

Description: Chabot College (1961) has been serving southern Alameda County for almost 4 decades. It shares a diverse learning environment of 12,500 students, of which 27% are enrolled full time and 73% are enrolled part time. Almost 45% take courses only during the day, 22% take both day and evening, while 30% take evening or evening/Saturday courses. Clearly, our student population needs an alternative mode of accessing education in the midst of working full time in a very congested Bay Area. To meet this need, we began offering telecourses in 1990, having offered independent study for some time before then. As with many colleges, Chabot has struggled to improve the image of distance education and obtain the necessary funding. Despite this, we have increased the number of courses every term. We have a distance education group consisting of faculty, administrators, and staff who meet every week to discuss issues of quality and other concerns. We have just begun to offer courses live via cable.

Chadron State College

1000 Main Street	Phone: (308) 432-6376
Chadron, NE 69337	Fax: (308) 432-6473
	or (308) 432-6299

Division(s): Regional Programs
Web Site(s): http://www.csc.edu
E-mail: alangford@csc1.csc.edu

Undergraduate Degree Programs:
Bachelor of Science in Interdisciplinary Studies

Class Titles: Software Application/Aviation, Business Law, Keyboarding, Records Management, Earth Science, Environmental Geology, Physical Geology, Historical Geology, Hydrogeology, Survey of Economics, Economics (micro/ macro), Teaching, Play/Art/Music, Composition, Child Growth/Development, Parenting in Contemporary Society, Program Management, Individualized Fitness, Foundations of P.E., Personal Health/Wellness, History of P.E., Theory/Reading Elementary Physical Education, Adapted Physical Education, U.S. History to 1877, U.S. History Since 1877, Western Civilization, Driver Education, Computer Science Curriculum, Management, Marketing, Buyer Behavior, Math, Algebra, College Algebra, Applied Statistics, American National Government, International Politics, Child Psychology, Developmental Psychology, Adolescent Psychology, Psychopharmacology, Abnormal Psychology, Real Estate, Sociology.

Teaching Methods: *Computers:* Internet, real-time chat, electronic classroom, e-mail. *TV:* videotape, cable program, satellite broadcasting, PBS. *Other:* audioconferencing, videoconferencing, audiographics, audiotapes, fax, correspondence, independent study.

Credits Granted for: experiential learning, portfolio assessment, examination (CLEP).

Admission Requirements: *Undergraduate:* high school graduate or GED.

On-Campus Requirements: None.

Tuition and Fees: *Undergraduate:* $142/credit. *Application Fee:* $15. *Credit by:* semester.

Accreditation: North Central Association of Colleges and Schools, National Council for the Accreditation of Teacher Education, Council on Social Work Education, American Association of University Women.

Description: Founded as a teacher's college, Chadron State College (1911) now offers degrees in 21 areas to a student body of 3,000. All distance learning faculty are full-time and have served distance learners from the beginning. The college has 50 correspondence courses, 8 online courses, 35 courses per semester by ground line videoconferencing to selected sites, and 8 interactive satellite transmission courses per semester.

Champlain College

163 South Willard Street	Phone: (888) 545-3459
Burlington, VT 05402-0670	Fax: (802) 865-6447

Division(s): Online Distance Learning Program
Web Site(s): http://online.champlain.edu
E-mail: online@champlain.edu

Undergraduate Degree Programs:
Accounting
Business
Computer Programming
Hotel-Restaurant Management

Management
Telecommunications
Travel and Tourism

Certificate Programs: Accounting, Business, Computer Programming, Hotel-Restaurant Management, Management, Telecommunications.

Class Titles: Accounting, Art, Computers, Communications, Early Childhood Education, Economics, English, Geography, History, Hospitality, Legal Field, Management, Marketing, Math, Philosophy, Social Sciences, Telecommunications

Teaching Methods: *Computers:* Internet, electronic classroom, e-mail. *Other:* videoconferencing.

Credits Granted for: extrainstitutional learning.

Admission Requirements: *Undergraduate:* application form—online courses may be taken without degree or certificate program admittance. *Certificate:* see undergraduate.

On-Campus Requirements: None.

Tuition and Fees: *Undergraduate:* $305/credit (1998/99 academic year). *Application Fee:* $30. *Credit by:* semester.

Financial Aid: Federal Stafford Loan, Federal Perkins Loan, Federal PLUS Loan, Federal Pell Grant, Federal Work-Study, VA, Vermont resident programs.

Accreditation: New England Association of Schools and Colleges.

Description: Champlain College (1878) has carried out its mission of preparing students for successful careers since its founding. Today Champlain is recognized as an outstanding institution with programs in career disciplines chosen for their relevance to the needs of the workplace. Champlain College's World Wide Web delivery system provides students with convenient access to online classes 24 hours a day, 7 days a week, from anywhere in the world. The unique Virtual Campus that Champlain created gives access to all the support services that busy people are likely to require, all from the convenience of their own homes or offices. Champlain College has been providing online distance learning classes, certificates, and degree programs since 1993.

Charter Oak State College

| 66 Cedar Street | Phone: (860) 666-4595 x21 |
| Newington, CT 06111-2646 | Fax: (860) 666-4852 |

Division(s): Academic
Web Site(s): http://cosc.edu
E-mail: mwoodman@commnet.edu

Undergraduate Degree Programs:
Associate in Arts
Associate in Science

Bachelor of Arts
Bachelor of Science

Class Titles: Anthropology, Biology, Business, Critical Thinking, Earth Science, Economics, English, Fine Arts, History, Math, Philosophy, Psychology, Sociology.

Teaching Methods: *Computers:* Internet, real-time chat, electronic classroom, e-mail, CD-ROM, newsgroup. *TV:* videotape. *Other:* learning contracts.

Credits Granted for: experiential learning, portfolio assessment, extrainstitutional learning, examination (CLEP, ACT-PEP, DANTES, GRE).

Admission Requirements: *Undergraduate:* age 16, must have completed 9 college credits.

On-Campus Requirements: None.

Tuition and Fees: *Undergraduate:* $65/video-based credit, resident; $98/video-based credit, nonresident. $95/online credit, resident; $130/online credit nonresident. Military personnel pay resident tuition/fees. *Application Fee:* $40. *Other Costs:* $15/semester nonresident nonrefundable registration fee; $30/year technology fee; $397 enrollment fee/first-year advising fee, resident, $595 nonresident; $265 annual advising fee/records maintenance, resident; $400 nonresident; $245 baccalaureate concentration proposal review fee. *Credit by:* semester.

Financial Aid: fee waivers.

Accreditation: New England Association of Schools and Colleges.

Description: Charter Oak State College (1973) was established as a virtual university to provide an alternate way for adults to earn a degree. Charter Oak does not offer classroom instruction and has no residency requirements. Instead, students earn credits based on Charter Oak faculty evaluation of courses transferred from regionally accredited colleges and universities, distance courses offered by Charter Oak, noncollegiate-sponsored instruction, college-level exams, special assessment, contract learning, and portfolio review. Degrees are offered at the associate and bachelor's levels.

Chesapeake College

1000 College Avenue	
PO Box 23	Phone: (410) 822-5400
Wye Mills, MD 21679	Fax: (410) 827-7057

Division(s): Academic Support Services
Web Site(s): http://www.chesapeake.edu
E-mail: mary_celeste_alexander@crabpot.chesapeake.edu
kathy_petrichenko@crabpot.chesapeake.edu

Class Titles: Accounting, Business, Computer Information

Systems, Early Childhood Development, Economics, English, History, Paralegal Studies, Math, Sociology, Psychology

Teaching Methods: *Computers:* Internet, e-mail, LISTSERV, electronic classroom. *TV:* videotape, PBS, interactive video classroom. *Other:* audiotapes, correspondence, independent study, individual study, self-guided instruction.

Credits Granted for: examination (CLEP, ACT-PEP).

Admission Requirements: *Undergraduate:* open admissions, prerequisite testing for some classes.

On-Campus Requirements: most distance classes require attendance at 3 seminars during the semester.

Tuition and Fees: *Undergraduate:* $65/credit. *Other Costs:* $10 for distance education classes, $15 full-time/$4 part-time service fee; $5 registration fee; $10/$5 parking fee; $2/credit student activity fee. *Credit by:* semester.

Financial Aid: Federal Stafford Loan, Federal Perkins Loan, Federal PLUS Loan, Federal Pell Grant, Federal Work-Study, VA, Maryland resident programs.

Accreditation: Middle States Association of Colleges and Schools.

Description: Chesapeake College (1965), a nonresidential community college serving the 5-county, mid-shore region on Maryland's eastern shore, was established as the state's first regional community college in 1965. Chesapeake offers career and transfer programs in a wide variety of fields, including accounting, business management technology and business administration, computer information systems and computer transfer, criminal justice, engineering, teaching education, nursing, and liberal arts and sciences. Chesapeake, which has always strived to be on the cutting edge of technology, opened its first distance learning classroom in 1994. The college's main campus in Wye Mills is networked with fully interactive, fiber-optic distance learning classrooms at 4 other mid-shore sites.

Christopher Newport University

| 1 University Place | Phone: (757) 594-7607 |
| Newport News, VA 23606 | Fax: (757) 594-7481 |

Division(s): CNU ONLINE
Web Site(s): http://www.cnuonline.cnu.edu
E-mail: info@cnu.edu

Undergraduate Degree Programs:
Bachelor of Science in Governmental Administration with concentrations in:
    Public Management
    Criminal Justice
    International Studies

Bachelor of Arts in Philosophy with concentration in Religious Studies

Class Titles: Accounting, Business, Computer Science, Economics, English, Government, Health, Philosophy, History, Mathematics, Physics, Religious Studies, Spanish.

Teaching Methods: *Computers:* Internet, World Wide Web, CD-ROM (for Spanish ONLY). *Other:* None.

Credits Granted for: examination (CLEP, DANTES); contact the Admissions Office.

Admission Requirements: *Undergraduate:* contact Admissions Office at admit@cnu.edu *Graduate:* contact Admissions Office at admit@cnu.edu

On-Campus Requirements: None.

Tuition and Fees: *Undergraduate:* $145/credit (in-state). *Graduate:* $145/credit. *Application Fee:* $25, degree-seeking. *Credit by:* semester.

Financial Aid: Federal Stafford Loan, Federal Perkins Loan, Federal PLUS Loan, Federal Pell Grant, Federal Work-Study, VA, Virginia resident programs.

Accreditation: Southern Association of Colleges and Schools.

Description: Christopher Newport University (1961), a state-supported comprehensive institution, first offered computer-based distance learning courses in 1993. In the fall of 1998, a total of 800 students enrolled in approximately 50 distance learning courses.

Church Divinity School of the Pacific

| 2451 Ridge Road | Phone: (510) 204-0720 |
| Berkeley, CA 94709-1217 | Fax: (510) 644-0712 |

Division(s): Center for Anglican Learning and Life (CALL)
Web Site(s): http://www.cdsp.edu/call.html
E-mail: call@cdsp.edu

Class Titles: variable; have included classes on Anglican/Christian Spirituality, How to Teach Bible, Dead Sea Scrolls, Book of Revelation, Who is Jesus?, Small Church Ministry, Julian of Norwich, Sacred Space.

Teaching Methods: *Computers:* Internet, Web pages, e-mail, LISTSERV. *Other:* None.

On-Campus Requirements: None.

Tuition and Fees: *Undergraduate:* $175/7-week course. *Credit by:* Continuing Education Units.

Accreditation: Graduate Theological Seminary of the Episcopal Church, member of Ecumenical Graduate Theological Union in Berkeley.

Description: The Church Divinity School of the Pacific (1895) is the seminary of the Episcopal Church's western province. Originally founded to prepare individuals for ordained ministry, it now offers a variety of degrees and programs for clergy, laity, and the general public. Launched in 1995, the school's Center for Anglican Learning and Life acknowledges its partnership with the wider Church in addressing today's issues. CALL offers on-campus classes, forums, conferences, and online programs through the Internet. CALL began offering online courses and an annual online book club partly in response to a perceived need among rural and isolated congregations and clergy and among laity for accessible opportunities for ministry development and personal spiritual deepening.

Cincinnati Bible College and Seminary

2700 Glenway Avenue	Phone: (513) 244-8100
Cincinnati, OH 45204-3200	Fax: (513) 244-8140

Division(s): College Academic Dean's Office
Web Site(s): http://www.cincybible.edu/index.htm
E-mail: Priscilla.Berry@cincybible.edu

Class Titles: Foundations for Morals, Epistles of James/John, I/II Thessalonians, Acts of Apostles, I Corinthians.

Teaching Methods: *Other:* correspondence.

Admission Requirements: *Undergraduate:* none, other than the desire to study a Bible course, a 2-credit hour course must be completed in 6 months.

On-Campus Requirements: None.

Tuition and Fees: *Undergraduate:* $180/credit. *Other Costs:* textbooks/syllabus. *Credit by:* semester.

Accreditation: North Central Association of Colleges and Schools, Accrediting Association of Bible Colleges.

Description: On September 23, 1924, Cincinnati Bible Seminary came into existence through the merging of 2 institutions who were similar in purpose and beliefs. CBS came into being to meet the pressing leadership needs of the Restoration Movement fellowship at that time. The founding principle and ultimate purpose of the school was to provide church leaders who were well-grounded in the word of God. In 1987 the corporate name of the school was changed to Cincinnati Bible College and Seminary. The undergraduate division was designated as Cincinnati Bible College, and the graduate division as Cincinnati Bible Seminary. Correspondence studies were developed to provide a home study opportunity for those who were not able to attend classes on campus.

Citrus Community College

1000 Foothill Boulevard	Phone: (626) 963-0323
Glendora, CA 91741	Fax: (626) 914-8574

Division(s): Distance Education
Web Site(s): http://www.citrus.cc.ca.us
E-mail: kguttman@citrus.cc.ca.us

Undergraduate Degree Programs:
General Education, Associate of Arts in fall 1999

Class Titles: Psychology, Physiological Psychology, Developmental Psychology, Behavioral Science Statistics, Sociology, College Algebra, Cultural Anthropology, Composition, Nursing Nutrition, Nursing Social Psychology, Technical Writing, College Reading

Teaching Methods: *Computers:* Internet, real-time chat, e-mail, CD-ROM, newsgroup, LISTSERV. *TV:* videotape, PBS. *Other:* audioconferencing, audiotapes, fax, correspondence, independent study, individual study, learning contracts.

Admission Requirements: *Undergraduate:* open enrollment.

On-Campus Requirements: per California regulations.

Tuition and Fees: *Undergraduate:* $12/credit. *Credit by:* semester (units).

Financial Aid: Federal Stafford Loan, Federal Perkins Loan, Federal PLUS Loan, Federal Pell Grant, Federal Work-Study, VA, California resident programs.

Accreditation: Western Association of Schools and Colleges.

Description: Citrus College (1915) is located in the foothills of the San Gabriel Mountains, 25 miles northeast of Los Angeles. The 104-acre campus has the distinction of being the oldest community college in Los Angeles County and the fifth oldest in the state. The college, which opened with 28 students, currently enrolls 10,000. Citrus offers transfer programs to 4-year colleges and universities, a 2-year college degree, and 30 career and technical training programs to prepare students for the job market. Distance education began in 1996 and has grown from one class of 17 students to 15 classes with 500. In the fall of 1999, we will be offering an online AA degree in general education as well as a partially online vocational nursing program.

City College of San Francisco

50 Phelan Avenue	Phone: (415) 239-3885
San Francisco, CA 94112	Fax: (415) 239-3694

Division(s): Telecourses
Web Site(s): None.
E-mail: PKBrown@TELIS.006

Class Titles: contact school for more information.

Teaching Methods: *Computers:* e-mail, LISTSERV-BBS. *TV:* cable program. *Other:* None.

Admission Requirements: *Undergraduate:* age 18.

On-Campus Requirements: 2-hour orientation, 2-hour midterm, 2-hour final.

Tuition and Fees: *Undergraduate:* $12/unit. *Credit by:* semester.

Financial Aid: Federal Stafford Loan, Federal Perkins Loan, Federal PLUS Loan, Federal Pell Grant, Federal Work-Study, VA, California resident programs.

Accreditation: Western Association of Schools and Colleges.

Description: City College of San Francisco is a 2-year community college that has offered distance education for more than 10 years. CCSF currently provides 19 telecourses each semester, with an average enrollment of 55.

City University

919 SW Grady Way
Renton, WA 98055

Phone: (425) 637-1010
(800) 426-5596
Fax: (425) 277-2437

Division(s): Admissions and Student Affairs
Web Site(s): http://www.cityu.edu
E-mail: www.info@cityu.edu

Undergraduate Degree Programs:
Associate of Science in:
    General Studies
    General Studies (Medical Office/Lab Technology specialty)
    Management
Bachelor of Arts in:
    General Studies
    International Studies
    Management
    Marketing
    Mass Communications and Journalism
    Multi-Science
    Philosophy
    Psychology
    Sociology
Bachelor of Science in:
    Accounting
    Business Administration
    Computer Systems
    General Studies
    Management Specialty
    Marketing
Graduate Degree Programs:
Master of Arts in:
    Management
    Marriage and Family Counseling
    Mental Health Counseling
    Vocational Rehabilitation
Master of Business Administration in:
    Business Administration
    Financial Management
    Individualized Study
    Information Systems
    Managerial Leadership
    Marketing
    Personal Financial Planning
Master of Education in:
    Curriculum and Instruction
    Educational Technology
    Special Education
    ESL Instructional Methods
Master of Public Administration
Master of Science in Computer Systems

Certificate Programs: Undergraduate: Accounting, Computer Programming, Internetworking, Network/Telecommunications, Paralegal Studies. Graduate: Financial Management, Information Systems, Management, Managerial Leadership, Marketing, Personal Financial Planning, Public Administration.

Teaching Methods: *Computers:* Internet, real-time chat, e-mail, CD-ROM. *Other:* fax, correspondence, independent study, individual study, learning contracts.

Credits Granted for: experiential learning, portfolio assessment, extrainstitutional learning, examination (CLEP, ACT-PEP, DANTES).

Admission Requirements: *Undergraduate:* age 18, high school or GED diploma, application. *Graduate:* accredited bachelor's degree or equivalent, application. The MEd and MA programs have additional requirements. *Certificate:* application.

On-Campus Requirements: None.

Tuition and Fees: *Undergraduate:* $157/credit. *Graduate:* $280/credit. *Application Fee:* $75. *Software:* variable. *Other Costs:* books. *Credit by:* quarter.

Financial Aid: VA, Washington resident programs, private alternative loans.

Accreditation: Northwest Association of Schools and Colleges.

Description: City University (1973) is a private, nonprofit institution of higher learning founded to serve working adults who want to build on their experience through education but cannot interrupt their careers to become full-time students. In keeping with its mission of providing convenient, accessible education, the university offers most of its degree programs through distance learning. CU currently serves 4,600 distance students worldwide. Distance learning courses, added in 1985, make degree programs available through traditional correspondence and through the Internet. Students also have the option of combining traditional classroom courses with distance courses. Students can complete course work through the university's online instructional center using computers and the Internet. In the center, students may access course-specific video, audio, animation, and interactive assignments, as well as instructor notes. Students can communicate with instructors by e-mail, phone, mail, or fax. Technology requirements include a computer with a modem and Internet access. Students may begin distance learning courses on the first of any month as long as registration and payment take place by the 20th of the preceding month.

Clackamas Community College

19600 South Molalla Avenue	Phone: (503) 657-6958
Oregon City, OR 97045	Fax: (503) 655-8925

Division(s): Instructional Support Services
Web Site(s): http://www.clackamas.cc.or.us
E-mail: cyndia@clackamas.cc.or.us

Undergraduate Degree Programs:
Yes.

Class Titles: Child Abuse, Career Exploration, Computing, Reporting, Health GED, Marketing, Business, Anthropology, Autocad (Drafting), Print Reading, Geometric Dimensioning, Chemistry.

Teaching Methods: *Computers:* Internet, electronic classroom, e-mail, CD-ROM, newsgroup, LISTSERV. *TV:* videotape, cable program, satellite broadcasting, PBS. *Other:* videoconferencing, audioconferencing, fax, correspondence, independent study, individual study, 2-way interactive TV.

Credits Granted for: experiential learning, extrainstitutional learning, examination (CLEP, ACT-PEP, DANTES, GRE).

Admission Requirements: *Undergraduate:* age 16, open-admission process, some programs have special admissions.

On-Campus Requirements: 12 credit hours required for full-time status, 3 classroom hours weekly for 11 weeks for 3 (term) credits.

Tuition and Fees: *Undergraduate:* $35/credit for 1–14 credits, $490/credit for 14–18 credits, $35/credit above 18 credits. *Other Costs:* general fee of $2/credit, distance learning fee $30/course/term. *Credit by:* quarter.

Financial Aid: Federal Stafford Loan, Federal Perkins Loan, Federal PLUS Loan, Federal Pell Grant, Federal Work-Study, VA, Oregon resident programs, Federal Supplemental Educational Opportunity Grants.

Accreditation: Northwest Association of Schools and Colleges.

Description: Clackamas Community College (1966) is a small, rural/suburban college offering transfer, technical, professional, and adult supplemental education. Located near the major metropolis city of Portland, Clackamas offers associate transfer degrees, several technical/professional programs, and a 2-year certificate Honors Program. The college's 4,700 full-time students can participate in athletics, student government, clubs, intramurals, and foreign student programs. Testing, advising, registration, and tutorial assistance are available, and some free special support services/accommodations are available for students with disabilities. Clackamas has offered distance learning telecourses since 1979 and online courses since 1997.

Clarion University of Pennsylvania

108 Carrier	
Clarion University	Phone: (814) 226-1838
Clarion, PA 16214-1232	Fax: (814) 226-2722

Division(s): Office of Distance Learning and Extended Studies
Web Site(s): http://www.clarion.edu/academic/venango/itvsched.htm
E-mail: cmuschweck@mail.clarion.edu

Undergraduate Degree Programs:
Real Estate

Graduate Degree Programs:
Library Science
Nursing

Class Titles: graduate classes in Library Science, undergraduate and graduate classes in Nursing, and undergraduate classes in Communication and various other departments. Course offerings vary by semester; visit Web site.

Teaching Methods: *Other:* videoconferencing.

Credits Granted for: examination (CLEP, ACT-PEP, DANTES, GRE).

Admission Requirements: *Graduate:* bachelor's degree, 2.75 undergraduate GPA.

On-Campus Requirements: None.

Tuition and Fees: *Undergraduate:* $144/credit resident, out-of-state $325. *Graduate:* $193/credit resident, out-of-state $346. *Application Fee:* $25. *Other Costs:* approximately 10% of student's tuition (support, health, activities, student center, etc.). *Credit by:* semester.

Financial Aid: Federal Stafford Loan, Federal Perkins Loan, Federal PLUS Loan, Federal Pell Grant, Federal Work-Study, VA, Pennsylvania resident programs.

Accreditation: Middle States Association of Colleges and Schools.

Description: Clarion University of Pennsylvania is a member of the State System of Higher Education of Pennsylvania. Clarion began offering distance education courses in 1996 using videoconferencing between the Clarion campus and the Venango campus in Oil City. In 1997–1998, Clarion offered 18 distance learning classes at 6 sites in western Pennsylvania and Harrisburg. Distance learning classes are offered only at specified sites including Clarion University campus, Venango campus, Clarion University Pittsburgh site, Slippery Rock University, and Dixon Center (Harrisburg). Classes are not available via the Internet.

Clark College

1800 East McLoughlin Boulevard	Phone: (360) 992-2314
Vancouver, WA 98663	Fax: (360) 992-2870

Division(s): Office of Instruction
Web Site(s): http://www.clark.edu
E-mail: swolff@clark.edu

Class Titles: Cinema, Wildlife Conservation, Elements of Business, Entrepreneurship, Personal Finance, Professional Selling, Principles of Marketing, Preparatory Inorganic Chemistry, Economies of Pacific Rim, Economies of Americas, International Economics, English Composition, Technical Report Writing, Creative Writing, Poetry, HP Graphing Calculator, General Engineering, Statistics, Strength of Materials, Dynamics, German, Electronic Publishing, Health for Adult Living, Middle Ages-Age of Absolutism, Business Environment, College Trigonometry, Finite Math, Linear Algebra, Independent Fitness, General Psychology, Human Development.

Teaching Methods: *Computers:* Internet, real-time chat, electronic classroom, e-mail, CD-ROM, newsgroup, LISTSERV. *TV:* videotape, cable program, satellite broadcasting, PBS. *Other:* videoconferencing, audiotapes, fax, correspondence.

Admission Requirements: *Undergraduate:* course prerequisites.

On-Campus Requirements: in most cases, students are required to come on campus for an orientation, to take tests, and to submit assignments.

Tuition and Fees: *Undergraduate:* $52 with a 2-credit minimum. *Other Costs:* telecourses—$20 fee in addition to tuition; online courses—$2/credit in addition to tuition. Students who do not have their own computer hardware and software will need to purchase a $20 computer lab pass if they intend to use the computer facilities on the Clark College campus. *Credit by:* quarter.

Financial Aid: Federal Stafford Loan, Federal Perkins Loan, Federal PLUS Loan, Federal Pell Grant, Federal Work-Study, VA, Washington resident programs.

Accreditation: Northwest Association of Schools and Colleges.

Description: Clark College (1933) has occupied 6 Vancouver campuses since its founding as a private junior college. In 1967 Clark became an entity of a state system of 24 community college districts. Its district now includes Clark, Skamania, and west Klickitat counties. During the 1996–1997 school year, the college served 10,700 students on its 80-acre campus.

Clark State Community College

100 South Limestone Street	
PO Box 570	Phone: (937) 328-6028
Springfield, OH 45501	Fax: (937) 328-3853

Division(s): Information Technology
Web Site(s): http://www.clark.cc.oh.us
E-mail: JonesT@clark.cc.oh.us

Class Titles: English, Fiction, History, Medical Terminology, Psychology, Western Civilization, Spanish

Teaching Methods: *Computers:* Internet, real-time chat, e-mail. *TV:* videotape. *Other:* None.

Credits Granted for: experiential learning, portfolio assessment, examination (CLEP, ACT-PEP, DANTES, GRE).

Admission Requirements: *Undergraduate:* high school graduate, GED, or ability to benefit.

On-Campus Requirements: None.

Tuition and Fees: *Undergraduate:* $55/credit resident, $104/credit nonresident. *Application Fee:* $15. *Other Costs:* $5/term auxiliary fee, $2/credit technology fee up to 14 credits. *Credit by:* quarter.

Financial Aid: Federal Stafford Loan, Federal Perkins Loan, Federal PLUS Loan, Federal Pell Grant, Federal Work-Study, VA, Ohio resident programs.

Accreditation: North Central Association of Colleges and Schools.

Description: The mission of Clark State Community College (1962), a public, 2-year, open-admissions institution, is to provide quality prebaccalaureate and technical 2-year associate degree programs, educational support programs and services, and community services for a broad spectrum of students ranging from recent high school graduates to adults pursuing the goals of lifelong education. Distance learning options are a growing part of our offerings to our learning community. New courses are being developed each quarter. Check our Web site for more details.

Clarkson College

101 South 42nd Street
Omaha, NE 68131

Phone: (800) 647-5500
Fax: (402) 552-3575

Division(s): Distance Education
Web Site(s): http://www.clarksoncollege.edu
E-mail: alaniz@clrkcol.crhsnet.edu

Undergraduate Degree Programs:
Bachelor of Science in:
Business
Nursing (for RNs only)
Medical Imaging (for Radiographers only)

Graduate Degree Programs:
Master of Science in:
Health Services Management
Nursing (for BSNs only)

Doctoral Degree Programs:
Family Nurse Practitioner (post-master's certificate)

Teaching Methods: *Computers:* Internet, electronic classroom, e-mail. *Other:* audioconferencing, audiotapes, fax, correspondence, independent study, individual study, learning contracts.

Credits Granted for: portfolio assessment, extrainstitutional learning, examination (CLEP, ACT-PEP, DANTES, GRE).

Admission Requirements: *Undergraduate:* high school transcripts, ACT/SAT scores, college transcripts. *Graduate:* college transcripts, 3 letters of reference, admission essay. *Doctoral:* same as graduate.

On-Campus Requirements: 1–3 three-week clinicals for BSN, 3 weekends for clinical evaluation for MSN students in Family Nurse Practitioner major, one day to defend thesis or for comprehensive exams for graduate students.

Tuition and Fees: *Undergraduate:* $272/credit. *Graduate:* $314/credit. *Doctoral:* $314/credit. *Application Fee:* $15. *Other Costs:* $200/year for distance education courses. *Credit by:* semester.

Financial Aid: Federal Stafford Loan, Federal Perkins Loan, Federal PLUS Loan, Federal Pell Grant, Federal Work-Study, VA.

Accreditation: North Central Association of Colleges and Schools, National League for Nursing.

Description: Clarkson College (1888) is a private, nonprofit, coeducational, Episcopal institution that offers undergraduate and graduate health science degrees. Clarkson began as a School of Nursing before branching out into other areas of health care including business, physical therapy, occupational therapy, radiography, medical imagining, and health services management. The distance program was started in 1989 when the college offered courses at satellite campuses in rural Nebraska. Today, distance courses are available to students in all 50 states. Our mission is to provide high-quality education to prepare competent, thoughtful, ethical, and compassionate health care professionals for service to individuals, families, and communities. We accomplish this mission by emphasizing teaching, research, and service.

Clayton College and State University

5900 North Lee Street
Morrow, GA 30260-0285

Phone: (770) 961-3634
Fax: (770) 961-3630

Division(s): Office of Distance Learning
Web Site(s): http://www.clayton.edu/distancelearning
E-mail: moton@gg.clayton.edu

Undergraduate Degree Programs:
Associate of Arts in Integrative Studies

Class Titles: Accounting, Biology, Business Administration, Critical Thinking, Citizenship, Dental Hygiene, English, Finance, History, Health Sciences, Management, Marketing, Math, Music, Political Science, Psychology, Sociology

Teaching Methods: *Computers:* Internet, real-time chat, electronic classroom, e-mail, CD-ROM, newsgroup, LIST-SERV. *TV:* videotape, cable program, satellite broadcasting, PBS. *Other:* videoconferencing, audiotapes, fax, correspondence.

Credits Granted for: examination (CLEP, ACT-PEP).

Admission Requirements: *Undergraduate:* standard university policies apply to distance programs. Please contact school for complete information.

On-Campus Requirements: None.

Tuition and Fees: *Undergraduate:* $72/credit resident, $290/credit nonresident. *Application Fee:* $20. *Other Costs:* $300 technology fee, $147 other fees. *Credit by:* semester.

Financial Aid: Federal Stafford Loan, Federal PLUS Loan, Federal Pell Grant, Federal Work-Study, VA, Georgia resident programs, SEOG, SIG.

Accreditation: Southern Association of Colleges and Schools.

Description: Clayton College and State University (1969) is a distinctive institution with a mission to prepare graduates for the world of work in the 21st century and to improve the quality of life for the people and communities of Atlanta and Georgia. Located 15 miles south of Georgia's state capital, CCSU resides in metro Atlanta's "Southern Crescent"—home to 650,000 residents. CCSU holds a distinctive position as the state's only member of the University System of Georgia, the Georgia Department of Technical and Adult Education, and the Atlanta Regional Consortium for Higher Education. This means that CCSU students and faculty are able to draw upon a wide array of resources. At CCSU, students can prepare for 40 majors and earn bachelor's degrees in several areas. CCSU is the third public university in the U.S. to equip each student with a powerful multimedia notebook computer. CCSU's newest venture represents the first comprehensive, competency-based, 3-tiered Information Technology Career Ladder program at an American university, providing students with certificate, associate, and bachelor's degrees in 6 areas.

Cleary College

3750 Cleary Drive	Phone: (517) 548-3670
Howell, MI 48843	Fax: (517) 547-2170

Division(s): Vice President of Academic Affairs
Web Site(s): http://www.cleary.edu
E-mail: cbono@cleary.edu

Class Titles: undergraduate areas: Business Administration Management, Marketing, Management Information Technology, Computer Information Systems, Finance, Quality Management.

Teaching Methods: *Computers:* Internet, real-time chat, e-mail, CD-ROM. *Other:* None.

Credits Granted for: experiential learning, portfolio assessment, extrainstitutional learning, examination (CLEP, ACT-PEP).

Admission Requirements: *Undergraduate:* Some programs require 3 years of work-related experience. Prerequisites vary by program.

On-Campus Requirements: on-campus classes along with distance learning classes. We have 2 main campuses in Howell and Ypsilanti, Michigan and 7 extension sites throughout Southeastern Michigan including Farmington Hills, Auburn Hills, Southfield, Garden City, Dearborn, Waterford, and Lansing.

Tuition and Fees: *Undergraduate:* $166/credit. *Application Fee:* $25. *Other Costs:* the Direct Degree Program is an all inclusive fee based on the number of credits a student transfers in. *Credit by:* quarters.

Financial Aid: Federal Stafford Loan, Federal Perkins Loan, Federal PLUS Loan, Federal Pell Grant, Federal Work-Study, VA, Michigan resident programs.

Accreditation: North Central Association of College and Schools.

Description: Cleary College (1883) is unique: the college of choice for busy people who need just one thing to enhance their career—a business degree. At Cleary College, students master contemporary business concepts. Practical experience

is recognized, valued, and can earn academic credit. Students and employers are our customers and are important, both inside and outside the classroom. Our graduates get results—a credential guaranteed to improve their career potential.

Cleveland Institute of Electronics

1776 East 17th Street	Phone: (216) 781-9400
Cleveland, OH 44114	Fax: (216) 781-0331

Division(s): Entire School
Web Site(s): http://www.cie.wc.edu
E-mail: instruct@cie.wc.edu

Undergraduate Degree Programs:
Associate in Applied Science in Electronic Engineering Technology
Bachelor in Electronic Engineering Technology

Certificate Programs: 10 programs in Electronics/Computer Technology.

Class Titles: CET Exam Review, FCC Exam Review, Programmable Controllers, Television Diagnosis/Repair, Computers, Database Management, Computer Aided Design/Drafting, Oscilloscope Fundamentals, Automotive Electricity/Electronics, Mobile Equipment, Microprocessor Theory/Applications, AC/DC Basic Electronics with Lab, Fiber Optics, Soldering with Lab.

Teaching Methods: *Computers:* Internet, real-time chat, electronic classroom, e-mail, CD-ROM, newsgroup, LISTSERV *TV:* videotape, cable program, satellite broadcasting, PBS *Other:* independent study.

Credits Granted for: extrainstitutional learning (DANTES).

On-Campus Requirements: independent study.

Tuition and Fees: *Credit by:* Independent Study.

Financial Aid: VA.

Accreditation: Distance Education and Training Council.

Cleveland State University

2344 Euclid Avenue	Phone: (216) 687-2149
Cleveland, OH 44115	Fax: (216) 687-9399

Division(s): Continuing Education
Web Site(s): http://www.csuohio.edu/ce/
E-mail: j.bradford@csuohio.edu

Graduate Degree Programs:
Master of Social Work (cooperative with University of Akron)
Master of Education in Educational Technology (at Lorain Community College)

Certificate Programs: Employee Benefit Specialist, Certified Public Manager

Class Titles: for credit—Art, Education, English, Philosophy, Psychology, Sociology, Spanish, Engineering; noncredit—Business, Computers, Construction, Engineering, Hazardous Materials, Landscaping, Nursing/Health Professions

Teaching Methods: *Computers:* Internet, electronic classroom, e-mail, LISTSERV. *TV:* videotape, cable program, satellite broadcasting, PBS. *Other:* videoconferencing, audioconferencing, fax, correspondence, independent study, faculty at remote site classroom.

Credits Granted for: portfolio assessment, examination (CLEP, ACT-PEP, DANTES, GRE).

Admission Requirements: *Undergraduate:* application and fees, transcripts, appropriate test scores (SAT/ACT/others), special for international students. *Graduate:* 2.75 GPA or 50th percentile on standardized admission test (may include GRE, GMAT, MAT); additional requirements vary by colleges and departments.

On-Campus Requirements: programs generally include some courses taught on campus.

Tuition and Fees: *Undergraduate:* $144/credit or $1,728/12–18 credits resident, $288/credit or $3,456/12–18 credits nonresident. *Graduate:* $194/credit or $2,525/13–16 credits resident, $388/credit or $5051/13–16 credits nonresident. *Application Fee:* $25. *Credit by:* semester.

Financial Aid: Federal Stafford Loan, Federal Perkins Loan, Federal PLUS Loan, Federal Pell Grant, Federal Work-Study, Ohio resident programs, cooperative education, student employment, scholarships, grants.

Accreditation: North Central Association of Colleges and Schools.

Description: Established as a state-assisted university, Cleveland State University (1964) assumed a tradition for excellence when it adopted Fenn College. Five years later, the university merged with the Cleveland-Marshall College of Law. Today Cleveland State continues to grow, offering quality, diversity, and flexibility in its programs and course offerings. Courses leading to degrees are offered though CSU's 7 colleges—5 for undergraduates and 2 for graduates. The campus consists of 80 acres with 35 buildings used for teaching, research, housing, and recreation. CSU supports students, faculty, and staff use of computing, telecommunications, and electronic media for teaching, learning, and administration. University courses have been taught for a number of years at off-campus locations. Over the past several years, partnerships and cooperative agreements have been developed with area colleges and universities, community colleges, public schools, government agencies, and companies to provide an increasing number of courses using video and electronic distance learning technologies.

Clinton, Muscatine, and Scott Community Colleges

306 West River Drive	Phone: (319) 336-3300
Davenport, IA 52801	Fax: (319) 336-3350

Division(s): Academic Affairs
Web Site(s): http://www.eiccd.cc.ia.us
E-mail: eiccdinfo@eiccd.cc.ia.us

Undergraduate Degree Programs:
Associate of Arts in General Studies
Associate of Applied Science in Environmental Technology

Class Titles: wide variety of classes.

Teaching Methods: *Computers:* Internet, electronic classroom, e-mail, CD-ROM. *TV:* videotape, PBS. *Other:* audioconferencing, videoconferencing, correspondence, independent study, individual study.

Credits Granted for: experiential learning, examination (CLEP).

Admission Requirements: *Undergraduate:* open-admissions

On-Campus Requirements: None.

Tuition and Fees: *Undergraduate:* $62/credit. *Other Costs:* variable. *Credit by:* semester.

Financial Aid: Federal Stafford Loan, Federal Perkins Loan, Federal PLUS Loan, Federal Pell Grant, Federal Work-Study, VA.

Accreditation: North Central Association of Colleges and Schools.

Description: Clinton, Muscatine, and Scott Community Colleges (1965) are located along the Mississippi River in the Iowa communities of Clinton, Muscatine, and Bettendorf. The colleges also have additional sites in Davenport and Maquoketa. The colleges offer 100 Associate in Arts and Associate in Applied Science programs as well as certificate and diploma options. Length of study ranges from one semester to 2 years.

Coastline Community College

11460 Warner Avenue, Third Floor	Phone: (714) 241-6208
Fountain Valley, CA 92708	Fax: (714) 241-6287

Division(s): Distance Learning Department
Web Site(s): http://vcs.ccc.cccd.edu
E-mail: http://vcs.ccc.cccd.edu

Undergraduate Degree Programs:
Associate of Arts

Class Titles: Anthropology, Astronomy, Biology, Business, Chemistry, Communications, Computer, Computer Services

Technology, Computer Science, Ecology, English, French, Geology, Health, History, Humanities, International Business, Management/Supervision, Marine Science, Math, Philosophy, Political Science, Psychology, Social Science, Sociology, Spanish.

Teaching Methods: *Computers:* Internet, real-time chat, discussion forums, chat-room, electronic classroom, e-mail, CD-ROM. *TV:* videotapes (pre-produced), cablecast programs, satellite broadcasting, PBS, KOCE. *Other:* codec-interactive videoconferencing, audiocassette tapes, fax, independent study, independent study-labs.

Credits Granted for: portfolio assessment, by examination (CLEP, ACT-PEP, DANTES, GRE) and professional credit (to be evaluated).

Admission Requirements: *Undergraduate:* individuals age 18+ who can profit from instructional qualify for admission. If under 18, you will qualify for admission if one of the following has been satisfied: graduated from high school, passed the California High School Certificate of Proficiency Test or equivalent, completed the 10th grade and received permission from your high school. (Note: students who have not completed the 10th grade may be eligible to enroll in certain advanced courses not available at their high schools. Permission of the dean of student services or designee, the parent and the high school principal or designee is required.)

On-Campus Requirements: All distance learning courses have examinations (midterm, essay exam and/or final exam). These examinations are administered on site by the instructor or administered at an on-site location by a department approved proctor. Some courses may require student attendance for workshops, review sessions or field trips. Students may transfer units from other accredited 2- or 4-year institutions; however, if the student wants to graduate from Coastline, the student would need to take 12 units from Coastline.

Tuition and Fees: *Undergraduate:* $12/unit resident, $133/unit nonresident, $142/unit international. *Software:* students enrolled in Internet or CD-ROM-based courses must have access to a multimedia computer with a full-service connection to an Internet provider to participate. Students who enroll in telecourse or cablecast courses must have access to a TV and/or access to the cable station carrier. For students who do not have access to a TV or cable station carrier, they can view video lessons at one of seven Coastline Viewing Centers located in the Coast Community College District. *Other Costs:* course materials ($75–$175), varies for shipping, approximately $60/semester course video rental, $7/semester mandatory health fee. Tuition and fees subject to change. *Credit by:* semester.

Financial Aid: Federal Pell Grant, Federal Supplemental Educational Opportunity Grant, Federal Perkins Loan, Federal Stafford Loan, Cal Grants A, B and C.

Accreditation: Western Association of Schools and Colleges.

Description: Coastline Community College (1976) is committed to accessible, flexible, student-centered education within and beyond the traditional classroom. Our distance learning combines technology—television, computers, fax/modems, telephone—with textbooks and printed materials to bring course content, instructor, and students together. With more than 20 years' experience in distance learning, Coastline offers a variety of college-credit course options to meet educational needs.

Coconino Community College

3000 North 4th Street, Suite 17	Phone: (520) 527-1222
Flagstaff, AZ 86003-8000	Fax: (520) 526-8693

Division(s): Education Services
Web Site(s): http://www.coco.cc.az.us
E-mail: smiller@coco.cc.az.us

Undergraduate Degree Programs:
Associate of Arts
Associate of Science
Associate of Applied Science
Associate of General Studies

Certificate Programs: Accounting Technician, Clerical, Computer Software, Construction Technology, Drafting, Fire Science, Hospitality Administration, Legal Secretary, Manufacturing, Medical Transcription.

Teaching Methods: *Computers:* Internet, real-time chat, electronic classroom, e-mail, CD-ROM. *TV:* videotape, cable program. *Other:* audiotapes, fax, correspondence, independent study, individual study, learning contracts.

Credits Granted for: extrainstitutional learning, examination (currently under consideration).

Admission Requirements: *Undergraduate:* open campus, with minimal restrictions.

On-Campus Requirements: None.

Tuition and Fees: *Undergraduate:* $27/credit in-state, $42/credit out-of-state. *Other Costs:* vary/course. *Credit by:* semester.

Financial Aid: Federal Pell Grant, Federal Work-Study, VA, Arizona resident programs, Navajo Nation programs, Hopi Nation programs.

Accreditation: North Central Association of Colleges and Schools.

Description: The multicampus Coconino Community College (1991) primarily serves the residents of 18,000-square-mile Coconino County. We initiated our first Web-based course,

Art History, in 1997. We also use PLATO courseware for delivery to extension sites, and on-site instruction in specific public and private sector organizations. The voters of the county passed a construction bond in 1997, which will help develop extensive distance delivery resources countywide. This system is currently being developed.

Cogswell Polytechnical College

1175 Bordeaux Drive	Phone: (408) 541-0100 x105
Sunnyvale, CA 94089-1299	(800) 264-7955 x105
	Fax: (408) 747-0764

Division(s): Open Learning for Fire Services
Web Site(s): http://www.cogswell.edu
E-mail: olfs@cogswell.edu

Undergraduate Degree Programs:
Bachelor of Science Fire Administration
Bachelor of Science Fire Prevention/Technology

Certificate Programs: Fire Administration, Fire Prevention/Technology

Class Titles: Core curriculum of upper division Fire Science courses, concentration courses in Fire Science

Teaching Methods: *Computers:* Internet (one course, 1999-2000, with more to follow). *Other:* fax, correspondence, independent study.

Credits Granted for: extrainstitutional learning (professional association seminars/workshops), examination (CLEP, DANTES).

Admission Requirements: *Undergraduate:* 12 units of lower-division Fire Science and English Composition.

On-Campus Requirements: None.

Tuition and Fees: *Undergraduate:* $325/3-unit course. *Application Fee:* $50. *Other Costs:* vary, textbooks when required. *Credit by:* semester.

Financial Aid: modest scholarships.

Accreditation: Western Association of Schools and Colleges.

Description: Cogswell College (1887) was founded as a San Francisco polytechnical school. The college is now located in the Silicon Valley, between San Francisco and San Jose. Cogswell offers on-campus programs with degrees in Electrical Engineering, Software Engineering, and Computer and Video Imaging. The Open Learning for Fire Services program with Bachelor of Science degrees in Fire Administration and Fire Prevention/Technology is the school's only distance learning. Cogswell is part of a consortium of 7 colleges and universities across the country that offer this program sponsored by the National Fire Academy.

College for Financial Planning

4695 South Monaco Street	Phone: (800) 237-9990
Denver, CO 80237	Fax: (303) 220-5146

Division(s): All
Web Site(s): http://www.fp.edu
E-mail: mih@fp.edu

Graduate Degree Programs:
Master of Science in Financial Planning

Certificate Programs: Certified Financial Planner, Paraplanner, Accredited Tax Preparer, Accredited Tax Advisor, Accredited Asset Management Specialist, Chartered Mutual Fund Counselor, Chartered Retirement Planning Counselor, Chartered Retirement Plans Specialist.

Class Titles: Investments, Taxes, Estate Planning, Insurance, Retirement.

Teaching Methods: *Computers:* Internet, e-mail. *Other:* phone, fax, correspondence, independent study, classroom study available in some locations.

Admission Requirements: *Graduate:* BA; experience in financial services recommended. *Certificate:* Certified Financial Planner Program—high school diploma or GED (BA recommended), 3-year completion limit. For information on all other programs, please call (800) 237-9990.

On-Campus Requirements: None.

Tuition and Fees: *Graduate:* $600/course (includes tuition, an interim exam, final exam, and study guides). *Application Fee:* $225 application processing fee. *Other Costs:* Certified Financial Planner Program is $1,670 (includes tuition, study materials, educational testing, and a review course); enrollment fee is an additional $325. Paraplanner Program is $450 with an additional enrollment fee of $125. Accredited Tax Preparer Program, Accredited Tax Advisor Program, Accredited Asset Management Specialist Program, Chartered Mutual Fund Counselor Program, Chartered Retirement Planning Counselor Program, Chartered Retirement Planning Specialist Program all cost $450 with additional enrollment fees of $125. *Credit by:* semester.

Accreditation: Distance Education and Training Council, North Central Association of Colleges and Schools.

Description: The College for Financial Planning (1972) was founded on the principle of providing a comprehensive solution to consumers' financial needs by developing a new level of professional counselor. The college's pioneering course work—the Certified Financial Planner or CFP Professional Education Program—established the framework for the entire profession. The resultant CFP mark, which enables consumers to identify a professional financial, is today the most widely recognized and respected financial planning credential. The college's current programs and courses represent the growth and evolution of the financial services industry. Programs now range from an introductory financial program to an MS degree. For 26 years, all course work has adhered to an independent study approach; however, some courses are offered in a classroom setting for students who prefer that environment.

College for Lifelong Learning

175 Ammon Drive, Room 215	Phone: (603) 669-7997
Manchester, NH 03103	Fax: (603) 627-5103

Division(s): Educational Technology and Computing
Web Site(s): http://usnh.unh.edu/CLL/itvhome.html
E-mail: NHETN-ITV.CLL@unh.edu

Undergraduate Degree Programs:
Associate of Arts in General Studies
Associate of Science
Bachelor of General Studies
Bachelor of Science

Certificate Programs: core courses via distance learning for advanced-level Health Care Management, Health Care Case Management

Class Titles: courses in Behavior Sciences, Health Care, Adult Learning/Development, Computing

Teaching Methods: *TV:* videoconferencing. *Other:* classroom instruction, individual study, learning contracts.

Credits Granted for: portfolio assessment, extrainstitutional learning, examination (CLEP, ACT-PEP, DANTES, GRE).

Admission Requirements: *Undergraduate:* for AA and AS: high school diploma or GED; ability to succeed in college work, either by college-level work completed as a nondegree learner or by achievement test results. For BS: high school diploma or GED, 2 years of work experience including homemaking, ability to complete college-level learning. For BGS: for learners who haven't studied full time for 2 years or who have 2 years of work experience and a) 60 acceptable, college-level, semester credits; b) an associate degree; or c) are registered nurses with diplomas from hospital schools of nursing, and successful completion of state board exams. *Certificate:* variable.

On-Campus Requirements: residency is a requirement of graduation: 16 semester hours for the associate degree, 30 semester hours for the bachelor's degree.

Tuition and Fees: *Undergraduate:* $155/credit resident, $172/credit nonresident. *Graduate:* $182/credit. *Application Fee:* $35 Associate Degree, $35 Bachelor of Science Degree, $135 Bachelor of General Studies Degree, $10 Certificate.

Software: variable. *Other Costs:* $300–$650, assessment of prior learning fee, $125 continuation of assessment fee. *Credit by:* quarter.

Financial Aid: Federal Stafford Loan, Federal Pell Grant, Federal Work-Study, VA, NH Charitable foundation.

Accreditation: New England Association of Schools and Colleges.

Description: The University System of New Hampshire created the College for Lifelong Learning (1972) to serve the higher educational needs of citizens, primarily adults, who required alternatives to campus-based programs. CLL administers the state's Educational TV Network for USNH. The 5-site, 2-way video and audio system began in 1992, offering individual courses and full academic degree programs. State departments, nonprofit agencies, and the business community use the facilities to deliver meetings, in-service training sessions, public forums, etc. The college's mission is to "be a leader serving the higher education needs of New Hampshire adults by aggressively using innovative technology to add value to teaching, learning, access, and support services." Future plans include Web-based courses combining asynchronous and synchronous components, while utilizing the outstanding educational and learner-support resources available at our 9 regional centers.

College of DuPage

425 22nd Street	Phone: (630) 942-3326
Glen Ellyn, IL 60137	Fax: (630) 942-3764

Division(s): Centers for Independent Learning
Web Site(s): http://www.cod.edu/cil
http://www.cod.edu/online
E-mail: schiesz@cdnet.cod.edu

Undergraduate Degree Programs:
Associate in Arts
Associate in Science
Associate in Applied Science
Associate in General Studies
Associate in Engineering Science

Certificate Programs: 125 certificate programs.

Class Titles: 140 courses.

Teaching Methods: *Computers:* Internet, real-time chat, electronic classroom, e-mail, CD-ROM. *TV:* videotape, local cable broadcast, local radio broadcast. *Other:* telecourses using audiotape and videotape, independent study, individual study, learning contracts.

Credits Granted for: experiential learning, examination (CLEP, credit by proficiency examination through an instructor).

Admission Requirements: *Undergraduate:* open-door, age 18, high school graduate who can benefit from college-level instruction.

On-Campus Requirements: None.

Tuition and Fees: *Undergraduate:* $30/credit in-district, $104/credit out-of-district, $141/credit out-of-state. *Application Fee:* $10. *Other Costs:* $30/credit for all Internet-delivered courses, vary for lab fees. *Credit by:* quarter (11 weeks in length).

Financial Aid: Federal Stafford Loan, Federal Perkins Loan, Federal PLUS Loan, Federal Pell Grant, Federal Work-Study, VA, Illinois resident programs.

Accreditation: North Central Association of Colleges and Schools.

Description: The College of DuPage (1966) is a comprehensive 2-year community college that serves a district population of 950,000 in the far-western suburbs of Chicago. The college has an overall enrollment of 34,000 students each fall term. The Centers for Independent Learning offer a variety of distance learning formats in 140 courses serving an enrollment of 5,000 distance learners each academic term.

College of Lake County

| 19351 West Washington | Phone: (847) 223-6601 |
| Grayslake, IL 60030 | Fax: (847) 223-0934 |

Division(s): Educational Affairs
Web Site(s): http://www.clc.cc.il.us/applic.htm
E-mail: curtdenny@clc.cc.il.us

Class Titles: Business, Computer/Information Systems, History, English, Humanities, Spanish, Multimedia.

Teaching Methods: *Computers:* Internet, real-time chat, e-mail, CD-ROM, newsgroup. *TV:* videotape, cable program, satellite broadcasting, PBS. *Other:* videoconferencing, fax, independent study, individual study, learning contracts.

Credits Granted for: experiential learning, portfolio assessment, extrainstitutional learning, examination (CLEP, DANTES), AP.

Admission Requirements: *Undergraduate:* meet prerequisites for credit courses.

On-Campus Requirements: not for Internet courses, some telecourses may require an orientation.

Tuition and Fees: *Undergraduate:* $47/credit, $4 comprehensive fee, $1 tech fee in-district, $225 out-of-district, $301 out-of-state. *Credit by:* semester.

Financial Aid: Federal Stafford Loan, Federal Perkins Loan, Federal PLUS Loan, Federal Pell Grant, Federal Work-Study, VA, Illinois resident programs.

Accreditation: North Central Association of Colleges and Schools.

Description: College of Lake County (1969) offers its students a variety of options. They can enroll as transfer students, career students, basic skills students, or as students interested in lifelong learning. CLC is committed to the needs of all students who can benefit from postsecondary instruction. The college understands that many students have busy schedules and live far from campus but want to take college courses. This commitment that learning need not be limited to constraints of time and place has been an important source of the commitment to distance learning.

College of San Mateo

| 1700 West Hillsdale Boulevard | Phone: (650) 574-6120 |
| San Mateo, CA 94402 | Fax: (650) 574-6506 |

Division(s): Instruction/Distance Learning
Web Site(s): http://www.kcsm.org/adultlearn.html and http://gocsm.net
E-mail: csmdl@kcsm.pbs.org

Undergraduate Degree Programs:
Associate of Arts courses
Associate of Science courses

Class Titles: Art of Western World, Astronomy, Contemporary American Business, Small Business Management, Salesmanship, Marketing, Business Management, Business Law, Career/Life Planning, Chemistry, Nutrition, American Cinema, Geology, Health Science, History of Western Civilization, History of Modern Latin America/Caribbean, Italian, Ethics, Political Science-Race to Save Planet, Psychology, Courtship/Marriage/Family, Abnormal Psychology, Child Psychology, Sociology, Spanish, Family Communications, Internet/Windows Platform, Hypertext Markup Language, Chinese Writing Skills, Computer/Information Science, California State/Local Government, Composition/Reading, Composition/Fiction, Creative Writing, Writing for Non-native Speakers, College Reading, French.

Teaching Methods: *Computers:* Internet, real-time chat, electronic classroom, e-mail, CD-ROM, newsgroup, LISTSERV. *TV:* videotape, cable program, PBS. *Other:* audiotapes, fax.

Admission Requirements: *Undergraduate:* age 18, high school graduate or passed California Proficiency Examinations. High school juniors or equivalent may be admitted concurrently with permission.

On-Campus Requirements: introductory meeting and exams for some classes.

Tuition and Fees: *Undergraduate:* $12/unit, California residents; $128/unit, nonresidents. *Other Costs:* $1 student representation fee, $5 refundable student body fee, no health fee if only registered in distance learning, parking permits. *Credit by:* semester.

Financial Aid: Federal Stafford Loan, Federal Perkins Loan, Federal PLUS Loan, Federal Pell Grant, Federal Work-Study, VA, Federal SOP grant, Cal Grant, EOPS, Board of Governors Enrollment Fee Waiver, local scholarships.

Accreditation: Western Association of Schools and Colleges.

Description: Starting with just 35 students when it first opened its doors, San Mateo County Community College District (1922) has grown to a complex of 3 modern campuses serving 25,000 day and evening students. The College of San Mateo, the oldest of the 3 colleges, entered the field of distance learning 30 years ago by providing college credit for telecourses broadcast on KCSM-TV, a public TV station licensed to SMCCCD and located on the College of San Mateo campus. Programs are broadcast throughout the Bay Area via UHF and cable. The college offers an average of 28 telecourses in the fall and spring semesters and 15 in the summer. CSM has offered classes online since 1996. The ever-expanding online course selection has grown to 12 courses for fall of 1998. The College of San Mateo serves 3,000 students/year through distance learning, and all courses are transferable to California State University.

College of St. Scholastica

1200 Kenwood Avenue   Phone: (218) 733-2236
Duluth, MN 55811-4199   (218) 723-6448 (HIM Graduate)
     (218) 723-6116 (HIM ART)
     Fax: (218) 723-6709/2239

Division(s): Education
Health Information Management (HIM)
Web Site(s): http://www.css.edu
E-mail: chuber@css.edu
seichenw@css.edu (HIM)
vvruno@css.edu (HIM ART)

Undergraduate Degree Programs:
Bachelor of Arts in Health Information Management/Accredited Record Technician (ART) Progession Program

Graduate Degree Programs:
Master of Education in Curriculum and Instruction
Master of Arts in Health Information Management

Class Titles: Chemistry, Computer Science/Information Systems, Education (undergraduate/graduate), Health Information Management (undergraduate/graduate), Management, Religious Studies.

Teaching Methods: *Computers:* Internet, real-time chat, electronic classroom, e-mail. *TV:* videotape, cable program, satellite broadcasting. *Other:* audiotapes, fax, correspondence, independent study, individual study, learning contracts.

Credits Granted for: experiential learning, portfolio assessment, examination (CLEP, ACT-PEP, DANTES, GRE).

Admission Requirements: *Undergraduate:* ART certification. *Graduate:* 2 years of professional experience in educational setting, undergraduate degree with transcripts, prior graduate course transcripts, 2 letters of recommendation, essay, letters of recommendation, interview.

On-Campus Requirements: Orientation Seminary and Colloquium at various sites including CSS Campus, 2 weeks in June.

Tuition and Fees: *Undergraduate:* $312/quarter credit, $468/semester credit. *Graduate:* $332/quarter credit, $498/semester credit, $240/semester credit. *Application Fee:* $50. *Software:* variable. *Other Costs:* textbooks, etc. *Credit by:* quarters converting to semesters beginning 1999–2000 academic year.

Financial Aid: Federal Stafford Loan, Federal Perkins Loan, Federal PLUS Loan, Federal Pell Grant, Federal Work-Study, VA, Minnesota resident programs.

Accreditation: North Central Association of Colleges and Schools, Commission on Accreditation of Allied Health Education Programs.

Description: The College of St. Scholastica (1912) is an independent, coeducational, comprehensive college with programs in the liberal arts and sciences and professional career fields. Founded in the Catholic intellectual tradition and shaped by the Benedictine heritage, the college stresses intellectual and moral preparation for responsible living and meaningful work. The Master of Education (Distance Learning program) (1995) provides graduate level professional development to teachers. We developed a distance learning program that provides access to a high-quality graduate education a time and location convenient to the student. The graduate program in Health Information Management began in 1997, and the Health Information Management/Accredited Record Technician Progression Program began in 1981.

College of the Canyons

26455 Rockwell Canyon Road   Phone: (805) 259-7800
Santa Clarita, CA 91355   Fax: (805) 253-1845

Division(s): Learning Resources
Web Site(s): http://www.coc.cc.ca.us
E-mail: keller_j@mail.coc.cc.ca.us

Class Titles: Anthropology, Astronomy, American Cinema, Economics, Western World History, U.S. History, Health,

Political Science, Psychology, Sociology.

Teaching Methods: *TV:* cable program, PBS. *Other:* None.

Credits Granted for: experiential learning, examination (CLEP).

Admission Requirements: *Undergraduate:* age 18 or high school diploma.

On-Campus Requirements: usually 4–6 2-hour sessions on Saturdays.

Tuition and Fees: *Undergraduate:* $12/credit in-state, $133/credit out-of-state. *Application Fee:* $100 out-of-state only. *Other Costs:* $10 parking/semester, $10 health fee/semester. *Credit by:* semester.

Financial Aid: Federal Stafford Loan, Federal Pell Grant, Federal Work-Study, VA, California Community Colleges Board of Governors Fee Waiver, California CAL Grants A, B and C.

Accreditation: Western Association of Schools and Colleges.

Description: College of the Canyons (1969) is a 2-year, public community college located 30 miles north of Los Angeles, California. Our College by TV program began in 1989.

College of the Desert

43-500 Monterey Avenue	Phone: (909) 346-8041
Palm Desert, CA 92260	Fax: (760) 776-7382

Division(s): Communications, Business and Hospitality
Web Site(s): http://desert@dccd.cc.ca.us
E-mail: see Web site.

Class Titles: Composition, World Wide Web Publishing.

Teaching Methods: *Computers:* Internet, real-time chat, e-mail, newsgroup. *Other:* None.

Admission Requirements: *Undergraduate:* high school diploma or age 18.

On-Campus Requirements: None.

Tuition and Fees: *Undergraduate:* $12/credit California residents. $140/credit nonresidents, $155/credit foreign students. *Other Costs:* varies for books/materials. *Credit by:* semester.

Financial Aid: Federal Stafford Loan, Federal PLUS Loan, Federal Pell Grant, Federal Work-Study, VA, California resident programs.

Accreditation: Western Association of Schools and Colleges.

Description: College of the Desert (1962) is a California community college offering 2-year academic transfer, occupa-

tional and vocational programs. COD is located in Palm Desert with centers in Joshua Tree and Indio and has a student body of 10,000 students. The college began offering credit courses on the Internet in 1997.

College of the Sequoias

915 South Mooney Boulevard	Phone: (209) 730-3790
Visalia, CA 93277	Fax: (209) 730-3894

Division(s): Liberal Arts
Web Site(s): http://sequoias.cc.ca.us
E-mail: diannes@giant.sequoias.cc.ca.us

Undergraduate Degree Programs:
Associate of Arts
Associate of Science

Class Titles: English, Child Development, Nutrition, Math.

Teaching Methods: *Computers:* Internet, real-time chat, e-mail, LISTSERV. *TV:* videotape, cable program, satellite broadcasting, microwave, 2-way interactive TV. *Other:* None.

Admission Requirements: *Undergraduate:* English/math prerequisites.

On-Campus Requirements: 5 hours of face-to-face contact.

Tuition and Fees: *Undergraduate:* $12/unit. *Credit by:* semester.

Financial Aid: Federal Stafford Loan, Federal Perkins Loan, Federal PLUS Loan, Federal Pell Grant, Federal Work-Study, VA, California resident programs.

Accreditation: Western Association of Schools and Colleges.

Description: College of the Sequoias, a community college in Visalia, was instituted in 1926 and is known for its academic excellence, high transfer rate, and award-winning vocational programs. Distance learning is new to this institution, beginning in the spring of 1997 with 2 online English courses. It has expanded to include television and other distance classes. The college has also begun broadcasting from its own TV studio.

The College of West Virginia

609 South Kanawha Street	Phone: (304) 253-7351
Beckley, WV 25802-2830	(800) 766-6067 x366
	Fax: (304) 253-3485

Division(s): School of Academic Enrichment and Lifelong Learning
Web Site(s): http://www.cwv.edu/saell
E-mail: saell@cwv.edu

Undergraduate Degree Programs:
Associate of Arts in General Studies
Associate of Science in:
    Secretarial Science (Administrative)
    Secretarial Science (Medical)
    Business Administration (General Business
    Business Administration (Office Management)
    Business Administration (Management)
    Secretarial Science (Legal)
    Business Administration (Accounting)
    Environmental Studies
Bachelor in Business Administration (General Business)
Bachelor in RN-BSN Pathway
Bachelor in Business Administration:
    Accounting
    Office Management
    Management
Bachelor in Health Care Management (Health Care Administration)

Certificate Programs: General Business (Management), Office Technology (Word Processing), Office Technology (Secretarial Skills), Travel.

Class Titles: Accounting, Biology, Business Law, Chemistry, Computer Information Systems (CIS), Communications, Diagnostic Medical Sonography (DMS), Economics, English, Environmental Studies, Finance, Geography, Geology, Healthcare Administration, History, Interdisciplinary Studies (IDS), Math, Management, Marketing, Medical Assisting, Office Management, Nursing, Philosophy, Physical Science, Physics, Politics, Psychology, Respiratory Care, Secretarial Science, Social Work, Sociology, Travel.

Teaching Methods: *Computers:* Internet, e-mail. *TV:* videotape. *Other:* fax, correspondence, independent study, individual study, learning contracts.

Credits Granted for: experiential learning, portfolio assessment, extrainstitutional learning, examination (CLEP, ACT-PEP, DANTES, GRE).

Admission Requirements: *Undergraduate:* open admission policy, high school diploma or equivalency. *Certificate:* Same.

On-Campus Requirements: To earn a degree a student must complete a minimum of 18 hours through traditional or Directed Independent Study courses. (Does not have to be completed on campus).

Tuition and Fees: *Undergraduate:* $155/credit. *Application Fee:* $25. *Credit by:* semester.

Financial Aid: Federal Stafford Loan, Federal PLUS Loan, Federal Pell Grant, Federal Work-Study, VA.

Accreditation: North Central Association of Colleges and Schools.

Description: The College of West Virginia (1933) is a private, not-for-profit college located in Southern West Virginia. The college began as Beckley College in 1933 with 97 students. Founded as a 2-year institution during the Great Depression, Beckley College sought to provide affordable and quality education in marketable business skills for the youth of Southern West Virginia. Today, as a bachelor degree-granting institution, The College of West Virginia continues to provide programs that will lead to gainful employment for its graduates. The College remains committed to the founding philosophy of Beckley College that every individual should have the opportunity to obtain an education and maximize his/her human potential. The School of Academic Enrichment and Lifelong Learning (1995) offers many progressive degree completion programs specifically designed for individuals who wish to begin and/or complete a college degree, but find it difficult or impossible to attend traditional classes. By providing diverse and alternative methods for learning and earning college-level credit, SAELL is uniquely suited to meet the educational needs of busy adults with varied degree needs and lifestyles.

College Universitaire de Saint-Boniface

| 200 Avenue de la Cathedrale | Phone: (204) 235-4408 |
| Saint-Boniface, MB, Canada R2H OH7 | Fax: (204) 235-4485 |

Division(s): Faculty of Arts
Web Site(s): http://www.ustboniface.mb.ca
E-mail: registra@ustboniface.mb.ca

Undergraduate Degree Programs:
Psychology, Translation

Class Titles: Psychology (French), Translation courses—Traduction (French).

Teaching Methods: *Computers:* Internet, LISTSERV. *TV:* videotape, cable program, satellite broadcasting, PBS. *Other:* radio broadcast, videoconferencing, audioconferencing, audiographics, audiotapes, fax, correspondence, independent study, individual study, learning contracts.

Credits Granted for: experiential learning, portfolio assessment, extrainstitutional learning, examination (CLEP, ACT-PEP, DANTES, GRE).

Admission Requirements: *Undergraduate:* high school diploma, entrance exams.

On-Campus Requirements: None.

Tuition and Fees: *Undergraduate:* $610/6-credit course. *Credit by:* semester.

Financial Aid: VA.

Accreditation: Association of Universities and Colleges of Canada.

Description: Then and now, excellence in French and English language skills has always been a College Universitaire de Saint-Boniface (1818) trademark. The bilingual skills and excellent liberal arts education of many CUSB alumni have made them natural candidates for important positions in Manitoba's and Canada's civil services and enterprises. The university's French-language and francophone literature programs have made it Manitoba's window on the world's francophone communities. BS programs and an honours BA in translation are also offered. The university's community college division, l'Ecole Technique et Professionnelle, offers one- and two-year programs in business administration, bilingual secretarial services, and in training French-language day care, health service, and business workers. CUSB's Department of Continuing Education offers courses to francophone adults and to adults wanting to learn French, Spanish, and German. Continuing Education and the University of Manitoba are now offering Spanish-language training to 2,000 volunteers of the 1999 Pan American Games. CUSB will soon offer a Bachelor of Business Administration program capitalizing on bilingual skills by stressing international/intercultural administration and acquiring another business language. The university began its distance learning program in 1996.

Colorado Electronic Community College

9075 East Lowry Boulevard	Phone: (800) 801-5040
Denver, CO 80220	Fax: (303) 365-8803

Division(s): None.
Web Site(s): http://www.cecc.cccoes.edu
E-mail: sb_mike@cccs.cccoes.edu

Undergraduate Degree Programs:
Associate of Arts

Teaching Methods: *Computers:* Internet, real-time chat, e-mail, CD-ROM, newsgroup, LISTSERV. *TV:* videotape, cable program, satellite broadcasting, PBS. *Other:* audiotapes, fax, correspondence, independent study, individual study.

Credits Granted for: extrainstitutional learning, examination (CLEP, ACT-PEP, DANTES, GRE).

Admission Requirements: *Undergraduate:* age 16 and entrance exam, or prior college education.

On-Campus Requirements: None.

Tuition and Fees: *Undergraduate:* $120/credit. *Other Costs:* $25 for voice mail. *Credit by:* semester.

Financial Aid: Federal Stafford Loan, Federal PLUS Loan, Federal Pell Grant, Federal Work-Study, VA, Colorado resident programs.

Accreditation: North Central Association of Colleges and Schools.

Description: Colorado Electronic Community College (1995)

is a unique and new college in the Colorado system. The school uses distance education methods and electronic technology to bring college courses to your home and place of work. We have the courses to deliver a full Associate of Arts degree for transfer to 4-year colleges and universities. These courses fulfill the typical requirements of Composition, Speech, Math, Sciences, Behavioral Sciences, Humanities, and Open Electives. Twenty courses are needed to graduate, representing about 60 semester-hour credits. Your degree plan might be much shorter if you have transfer credits.

Colorado State University

Spruce Hall	Phone: (970) 491-5288
Fort Collins, CO 80523-1040	(800) 525-4950
	Fax: (970) 491-7885

Division(s): Educational Outreach
Web Site(s): http://www.colostate.edu/Depts/CE
E-mail: info@learn.colostate.edu

Graduate Degree Programs:
Master of Science in:
   Statistics
   Computer Science
   Human Resource Development
   Bioresource and Agricultural Engineering
   Chemical Engineering
   Civil Engineering
   Electrical Engineering
   Engineering Management
   Environmental Engineering
   Industrial Engineering
   Industrial Hygiene
   Mechanical Engineering
   Systems Engineering and Optimization
Master of Business Administration

Certificate Programs: Gerontology

Teaching Methods: *Computers:* Internet, e-mail, newsgroup, LISTSERV. *TV:* videotape, PBS. *Other:* fax, correspondence, independent study, individual study.

Credits Granted for: examination (CLEP, ACT-PEP, DANTES, GRE).

Admission Requirements: *Graduate:* residing in the U.S. or Canada or in the U.S. Military. For the MBA, must have 4 years of experience in management.

On-Campus Requirements: None.

Tuition and Fees: *Graduate:* $328/credit Colorado sites, $368/credit non-Colorado sites, $384/credit individual delivery. *Credit by:* semester.

Financial Aid: Federal Stafford Loan, Federal Perkins Loan,

Federal PLUS Loan, Federal Pell Grant, VA if admitted to a degree seeking program.

Accreditation: North Central Association of Colleges and Schools, American Assembly of Collegiate Schools of Business.

Description: Colorado State University (1879) has a unique mission in the state of Colorado. The land-grant concept of a balanced program of teaching, research, extension, and public service provides the foundation for the university's teaching and research programs, the Agricultural Experiment Station, Cooperative Extension, and the Colorado State Forest Service. The university has long been a leader in recognizing the rapidly changing global environments and has a commitment to excellence in international education in all its instructional, research, and outreach programs. The Distance Degree Program (formerly known as SURGE) was started in 1967. Since that time, more than 530 degrees have been conferred through the program, and numerous individual courses have been completed.

Columbia Basin College

2600 North 20th Avenue	Phone: (509) 547-0511
Pasco, WA 99301	Fax: (509) 544-8790

Division(s): Communications Technology
Web Site(s): http://www.cbc2.org
http://www.ctc.edu/~distance
http://www.waol.org
E-mail: rcummins@cbc2.org

Undergraduate Degree Programs:
Associate of Arts in General Studies

Class Titles: Accounting, Business Law, Computer Science, Research Writing, Literature, Technical Writing, Math, History, Sociology, Anthropology, Economics, World Civilization, Psychology, Internet, Computer Applications, Business Technology, Medical Technology.

Teaching Methods: *Computers:* Internet, real-time chat, electronic classroom, e-mail, CD-ROM, newsgroup, LIST-SERV. *TV:* videotape, satellite broadcasting, PBS. *Other:* videoconferencing, correspondence, independent study, individual study.

Admission Requirements: *Undergraduate:* open-admission, placement testing. *Certificate:* open-admission, placement testing.

On-Campus Requirements: None.

Tuition and Fees: *Undergraduate:* $514/10–18 credits, residential. *Other Costs:* $20 distance education fee; $2/credit technology fee. *Credit by:* quarter.

Financial Aid: Federal Stafford Loan, Federal Perkins Loan, Federal PLUS Loan, Federal Pell Grant, Federal Work-Study, VA, Washington resident programs.

Accreditation: Northwest Association of Schools and Colleges, National Accrediting Commission, American Association of Community and Junior Colleges, Washington Association of Community Colleges, Washington Association of Colleges.

Description: Columbia Basin College (1955) is a 2-year, comprehensive community college that held its first classes in a temporary quarters at Pasco Naval Base. The first permanent building was completed in 1957, and ongoing capital construction has added an additional 21 buildings in southeastern Washington state. Enrollment has increased from 299 students in 1955 to nearly 12,000 students in 1998. The faculty includes 107 full-time and 300 part-time instructors. Columbia Basin has offered videotaped telecourses since 1985 and began providing classes on the Internet in 1997. In 1998, an AA degree, transferable to state institutions, became available for students desiring to complete online course work leading to a general studies Associate of Arts degree.

Columbia International University

7435 Monticello Road	Phone: (803) 754-4100 x3710
Columbia, SC 29203	(800) 777-2227 x3710
	Fax: (803) 786-4209

Division(s): Columbia Extension
Web Site(s): http://www.ciu.edu
E-mail: extoff@ciu.edu

Certificate Programs: Biblical Studies

Class Titles: Undergraduate: Christian Evidences, Old Testament, Gospels/Life of Christ, Acts—Revelation, Galatians, Living Your Faith: Studies in Amos, Mark: Cross in Our Lives, Ephesians, Philippians: How to Study/Teach, Colossians/Philemon, Bible Interpretation, Progress of Redemption, Historical Perspectives on Church/Mission, Biblical Counseling by Encouragement, Bible Doctrine, Bibliology: Inerrancy/Authority, Ethics/Sanctification; Graduate: Genesis-Poetical Books, Prophetic Books, Gospels/Life of Christ, Acts—Revelation, Conquest/Settlement, Biblical Hermeneutics, Psalms, Upper Room Discourse, Acts in Perspective, Progress of Redemption, Christian/Old Testament Theology, Romans, Messianic Prophecy, Leadership/Administration, Role of Women in Ministry, Urban Mission/Ministry, Personal Evangelism, Field Education: Personal Evangelism, Greek Exegesis of Romans, Early/Medieval Church: 30 AD–1517, Reformation/Modern Church: 1517–Present, American Christianity, Islam, Cultural Anthropology, Social Anthropology for Missionaries, Women in Islam, China/Chinese Ministry, Ministry of Encouragement,

Field Education: Foundations of Ministry, Missions, History of Missions, Biblical Theology of Missions, Folk Religions, Theologies of Liberation, Doctrine: Survey, Doctrine: Church, Christian Life, Theology of Jonathan Edwards

Teaching Methods: *Computers:* e-mail. *TV:* videotape. *Other:* audiotapes, fax, correspondence, independent study.

Credits Granted for: examination (CLEP, DANTES, GRE).

Admission Requirements: *Undergraduate:* independent learning credit courses (undergraduate and graduate): admittance to Columbia Bible College or Columbia Biblical Seminary Graduate School of Missions. Special nondegree student: application and fee; may earn 12 Independent Learning semester credits before completing full application. Note: Application fee waived for students already admitted to a CIU program. *Graduate:* see undergraduate. *Certificate:* see undergraduate.

On-Campus Requirements: Undergraduate: Columbia Bible College requires bachelor's degree students to complete a minimum of 32 semester hours in residence at CBC including a minimum of 2 consecutive regular semesters in which they are registered for at least 6 semester hours credit. Of the remaining hours, up to 30 credit hours earned through IDL may be applied toward a bachelor's degree from CBC. Up to 15 credit hours earned through IDL may be applied toward an Associate of Arts degree. Consult the College Admissions Office for more information on earning a CBC degree. Graduate: Columbia Biblical Seminary requires at least half of any seminary degree to be earned while on campus. Intensive 2–3 week courses offered on campus during January or the summer months are applied toward satisfying this residency requirement. Because of the many options available to help you complete a CBS degree, and because of varying limits on the number of credits earned through IDL which may be applied toward a degree, begin planning your academic program with counsel from the Seminary Admissions Office.

Tuition and Fees: *Undergraduate:* $100/credit. *Graduate:* $165/credit. *Application Fee:* $10. *Other Costs:* materials (textbooks, lectures, study guides, etc.). *Credit by:* semester.

Financial Aid: only for resident study.

Accreditation: Southern Association of Colleges and Schools, Accrediting Association of Bible Colleges, Association of Theological Schools.

Description: Columbia International University (1923) is a multidenominational, biblically based, Christian institution with one of the leading missionary training programs in the world. Although CIU is denominationally unaffiliated, it serves students from many denominations and independent churches. CIU is the parent company encompassing Columbia Biblical Seminary Graduate School of Missions, Columbia Bible College, Ben Lippen Schools, and Christian radio stations WMHK (Columbia, SC) and WRCM (Wingate/Charlotte, NC).

Columbia State Community College

PO Box 1315　　　　　　　　　　　Phone: (931) 540-2665
Columbia, TN 38402-1315　　　　　Fax: (931) 540-2795

Division(s): Extended Services
Web Site(s): http://www.coscc.cc.tn.us
E-mail: jonesd@coscc.cc.tn.us

Undergraduate Degree Programs:
Associate of Arts
Associate of Science
Associate of Applied Science

Certificate Programs: Business Management, Commercial Performance, Customer Service, Dance Studio Management, Early Childhood Education, Electronics Engineering Technology, EMT-Paramedic, Industrial Technology, Musical Instrument Digital Interface, Workforce Preparedness.

Class Titles: Psychology, Business, Accounting, Personal Finance, Medical Terminology, Technology/Society, Humanities Seminar, Composition, Mass Communications

Teaching Methods: *Computers:* Internet, e-mail. *TV:* videotape, PBS. *Other:* audiotapes.

Credits Granted for: experiential learning, portfolio assessment, extrainstitutional learning, validated by examinations.

Admission Requirements: *Undergraduate:* high school diploma or GED; ACT for degree-seeking students under age 21 and for selected programs; placement exams in math, reading, and writing for students with ACT scores under 19. Dual enrollment for exceptional high school students. *Certificate:* high school diploma or GED.

On-Campus Requirements: Associate degrees and certificates cannot be earned entirely at a distance.

Tuition and Fees: *Undergraduate:* $50/credit in-state ($585 maximum/semester), $198/credit out-of-state ($2,258/semester maximum). *Application Fee:* $5 payable on first registration. *Software:* $5/credit (maximum $50/semester). *Other Costs:* $8/semester student fees. *Credit by:* semester.

Financial Aid: Federal Stafford Loan, Federal Perkins Loan, Federal PLUS Loan, Federal Pell Grant, Federal Work-Study, VA, Tennessee resident programs.

Accreditation: Southern Association of Colleges and Schools.

Description: Columbia State Community College (1966) is located in south-central Tennessee and serves a 9-county area. It is an open-door commuter institution with one main campus and 4 off-campus sites dedicated to enhancing the region's educational, cultural, economic, and social life. The college has established for its constituents: a university-parallel general transfer program with a strong core curriculum, industrial and business programs with a strong emphasis on computer technologies to serve the growing business and industrial community, nursing and allied health programs to serve the need for health care professionals, a strong developmental studies program to serve the needs of open-admission students, and noncredit and community service programs to provide lifelong personal and professional development. The college began distance education in 1990 with an interactive TV system connecting the main campus with a branch site. Videotape courses were added in 1994, and compressed video was introduced in 1995. An average of 25 courses per semester are offered via distance learning.

Columbia Union College

7600 Flower Avenue	Phone: (800) 782-4769
Takoma Park, MD 20912	(301) 891-4119
	Fax: (301) 891-4121

Division(s): Home Study International
Web Site(s): http://www.cuc.edu
E-mail: 74617.74@compuserve.com

Undergraduate Degree Programs:
Associate of Arts
Associate of Science
Bachelor of Arts
Bachelor of Science

Class Titles: at least 50 classes in general areas of Health, Nutrition, History, Business, Business Administration, Psychology, Theology/Religion, General Studies, Respiratory Program, French, Spanish, Greek, Biology, Communications, Computer Science, Education, English, Fine Arts (Music Appreciation), Math, Sociology.

Teaching Methods: *Computers:* Internet, real-time chat, electronic classroom, e-mail, CD-ROM, newsgroup, LISTSERV. *TV:* videotape, satellite broadcasting. *Other:* audioconferencing, videoconferencing, audiographics, audiotapes, fax, correspondence, independent study, individual study, learning contracts.

Credits Granted for: experiential learning, portfolio assessment, extrainstitutional learning, examination (CLEP, ACT-PEP, DANTES, GRE).

Admission Requirements: *Undergraduate:* high school graduate or equivalent, 2.5 high school GPA, 2.0 college GPA (if attended), must finish distance education courses within one year or pay to extend. No requirements for nondegree seeking students.

On-Campus Requirements: if degree requires.

Tuition and Fees: *Undergraduate:* $150/credit. *Application Fee:* $50. *Other Costs:* $60 enrollment fee, supplies vary. *Credit by:* semester.

Accreditation: Middle States Association of Colleges and Schools, Maryland Higher Education Commission, The Adventist Accrediting Association of the Department of Education of the General Conference of Seventh-Day Adventists.

Description: Columbia Union College is a Christian institution operated by the Seventh-Day Adventist Church. The heart of Columbia Union College is a Christocentric vision, with its affirmation of the goodness of life, the sacredness of earth, and the dignity of all people and cultures. The mission of the college, carried out in the spirit of this vision, is: to make learning a pleasure and a joy, to embrace the adventure of truth, to link scholarship and service, to develop talent through an ethos of excellence, to seize the challenge and opportunity of the nation's capital, and to produce graduates who bring competence and moral leadership to their communities. Columbia's External Degree Program, established in 1969, meets the needs of adult students who find it difficult to finish a college degree during traditional, weekday hours or within fixed class schedules. It is not intended to replace traditional, on-campus learning; approximately half of all credits should be earned in the classroom. Students may pursue a degree or supplement a program elsewhere without being confined to class schedules or to a campus. They can live anywhere, move anytime, start anytime during the year, and study on their own time at their own pace without interfering with their course work.

Columbia-Greene Community College

4400 Route 23	Phone: (518) 828-4181
Hudson, NY 12534	Fax: (518) 822-2015

Division(s): Academic Support
Web Site(s): http://www.sunycgcc.edu
E-mail: hallenbeck@vaxa.sunycgcc.edu

Class Titles: contact school.

Teaching Methods: *Computers:* Internet, electronic classroom, e-mail, LISTSERV. *TV:* cable program. *Other:* None.

Credits Granted for: experiential learning, examination (CLEP, ACT-PEP, DANTES).

Admission Requirements: *Undergraduate:* proof of prerequisite skill/knowledge. Contact school for complete information.

On-Campus Requirements: None.

Tuition and Fees: *Undergraduate:* $90/credit. *Credit by:* semester.

Accreditation: Middle States Association of Colleges and Schools.

Description: Columbia-Greene Community College (1969) is a small, rural, public community college. Columbia-Greene is a unique college, large enough to offer a broad array of dynamic programs in the technologies, the humanities and the arts, yet small enough to nurture students. We are a comprehensive, 2-year college offering a variety of transfer and career programs leading to associate degrees.

Columbus State Community College

550 East Spring Street	Phone: (614) 227-5353
Columbus, OH 43215	Fax: (614) 227-5123

Division(s): Instructional Technologies and Distance Learning
Web Site(s): http://www.cscc.edu and http://global.cscc. edu
E-mail: global@cscc.edu

Undergraduate Degree Programs:
Associate of Science in Business Management
Associate of Arts

Class Titles: Accounting, Organizational Behavior, Management Decisions, Case Studies in Business Seminar, Visual Basic, Economics (micro/macro), Technical Writing, Writing About American Experience, Images of Men/Women in Literature, Shakespeare, Survey of British Literature, Business Finance, Managed Care Trends, Medical Terminology, Human Resource Management, Labor Relations, Civilization, Computer Literacy, Internet, Nursing Skills, Gerontological Nursing, Business Grammar Usage, Business, Management, Business Ethics, Small Business Development, Small Business Operations, Speech, Composition, Essay/Research, Business Communication, French, Personal Finance, Nutrition, Business Law, Legal Environment of Business, Marketing, Business Math, Natural Science, Spanish

Teaching Methods: *Computers:* Internet, real-time chat, electronic classroom, e-mail, CD-ROM, newsgroup, LIST-SERV. *TV:* videotape, cable program, satellite broadcasting, PBS. *Other:* videoconferencing, audioconferencing, audiotapes, fax, independent study, individual study.

Credits Granted for: experiential learning, portfolio assessment, extrainstitutional learning.

Admission Requirements: *Undergraduate:* open. *Certificate:* open.

On-Campus Requirements: None.

Tuition and Fees: *Undergraduate:* $2,461/credit. *Credit by:* quarter.

Financial Aid: Federal Stafford Loan, Federal Perkins Loan, Federal PLUS Loan, Federal Pell Grant, Federal Work-Study, VA, Ohio resident program.

Accreditation: North Central Association of Colleges and Schools.

Description: As a comprehensive community college, Columbus State (1963) has a strong commitment to technical education, offering the Associate of Applied Science and the Associate of Technical Studies degree programs in Business, Health, Public Service, and Engineering Technologies to prepare graduates for immediate employment. The transfer programs, Associate of Arts and Associate of Science, meet the majority of freshman and sophomore course requirements of bachelor's degree programs offered by 4-year colleges and universities in central Ohio and throughout the state. Columbus State has been offering distance learning for more than 2 decades in the area of TV and video-based learning. The college began its Web-based course offering 4 years ago.

Columbus State University

4225 University Avenue	Phone: (706) 568-2410
Columbus, GA 31907	Fax: (706) 565-3529

Division(s): Computer Science
Web Site(s): http://csuonline.edu
E-mail: bell_leary@colstate.edu

Graduate Degree Programs:
MS in Applied Computer Science

Class Titles: Computer Science: Programming Languages, Computer Networks, Operating Systems, Databases, Object-Oriented Design, Graphical User Interfaces, Software Design

Teaching Methods: *Computers:* Internet, real-time chat, electronic classroom, e-mail, CD-ROM, newsgroup, LIST-SERV. *Other:* None.

Admission Requirements: *Graduate:* accredited undergraduate degree, 2.5 undergraduate cumulative GPA, 800 on GRE (verbal and math), or undergraduate degree in computer science or closely related field or 50 percentile on computer science of GRE.

On-Campus Requirements: None.

Tuition and Fees: *Graduate:* contact school for more information. *Credit by:* semester.

Accreditation: Southern Association of Colleges and Schools.

Description: Columbus State University (1998) is a public, comprehensive, senior university that serves 6,000 students on its 132-acre main campus and many more on its off-campus centers. CSU is located 100 miles southwest of Atlanta and serves diverse educational needs with a mixture of liberal arts and professional programs leading to associate, bachelor's, and graduate degrees. The university fosters several programs that have achieved a national reputation of excellence. Columbus State has also received national acclaim for its programs in computer education, economic development, and regional services. The university has educated more than 1,000 computer professionals for local corporate partners. The first degree program to be delivered on online is the Master of Science in Applied Computer Science. CSU Online will continuously strive to keep this program and all additional programs academically sound and pertinent to the changing needs of today's workplace.

Community College of Philadelphia

1600 Callowhill Street, 2nd Floor	Phone: (215) 751-8370
Philadelphia, PA 19130-3991	Fax: (215) 751-8954

Division(s): Community Services and Continuing Education
Web Site(s): http://www.ccp.cc.pa.us
E-mail: tcampbell@fcis.whyy.org
rkulba@ccp.cc.pa.us

Undergraduate Degree Programs:
Associate of Arts in:
Architecture and Interior Design, Architecture Option
Architecture and Interior Design, Interior Design Option
Art
Art, Photography Option
Business
Communication Arts, Speech
Communication Arts, Theater
Culture, Science and Technology
Education
Liberal Arts, General Option
Liberal Arts, Humanities Option
Liberal Arts, International Studies Option
Liberal Arts, Social/Behavioral Science Option
Music
Associate of Science in:
Computer Science
Engineering Science
Science
Associate of Applied Science in:
Accounting
Automotive Technology
Chemical Technology
Clinical Laboratory Technician
Computer Assisted Design Technology, Architectural Documentation Option
Computer Assisted Design Technology, Engineering Documentation Option
Construction Technology
Data Processing, Business Programming Option
Data Processing, PC Applications Option
Dental Hygiene
Dietetic Nutrition Care Technician
Early Childhood Education
Electronics Engineering Technology
Electronics Engineering Technology, Biomedical Electronics Technology Option
Electronics Engineering Technology, Digital/Communications Option
Environmental Technology
Finance
Fire Science
Health Information Technology
Hospitality Technologies, Hotel and Restaurant Management Program
Hospitality Technologies, Culinary Arts Program, Chef Option
Hospitality Technologies, Culinary Arts Program, Chef Apprenticeship Option
International Trade
Interpreter Education
Justice
Management
Marketing
Medical Assisting and Office Management
Mental Health/Social Service
Nursing
Office Technology
Paralegal Studies
Photography
Radiologic Technology
Railroad Operations
Respiratory Care Technology
Retail Management
Retail Management, Fashion Buying Option
Secretarial Science, Business Education Option

Certificate Programs: Alcohol and Drug Abuse, Children in Crisis, Computer Assisted Design Technology, Computer Operations, Dental Assisting, Dietary Manager, Electronics Engineer Technology, Family Home Visiting, Justice, Management, Marketing, Office Skills, Retail Management, Retail Management—Fashion Buying, Sign Language, Social Gerontology

Class Titles: Anthropology, Chemistry, Earth Science, Economics, English, French, History, Marketing, Management, Math, Philosophy, Political Science, Psychology, Sociology, Spanish

Teaching Methods: *Computers:* Internet, real-time chat, electronic classroom, e-mail. *TV:* videotape, cable program, satellite broadcasting, PBS. *Other:* None.

Credits Granted for: experiential learning, portfolio assessment, examination (CLEP, ACT-PEP, APP).

Admission Requirements: *Undergraduate:* open admission for all who may benefit; accredited secondary school diploma or state equivalency for some programs. Call the College Information Center at (626) 751-8010 for more details.

On-Campus Requirements: certain programs require attendance on campus or at an off-campus location.

Tuition and Fees: *Undergraduate:* $72/credit. *Application Fee:* $20. *Software:* $4/credit technology fee. *Other Costs:* $3/credit general fee, $5 registration fee. *Credit by:* semester.

Financial Aid: Federal Stafford Loan, Federal Perkins Loan, Federal PLUS Loan, Federal Pell Grant, Federal Work-Study, VA, Pennsylvania resident programs, Federal Supplemental Educational Opportunity Grant.

Accreditation: Middle States Association of Colleges and Schools.

Description: More than 400,000 students have passed through the Community College of Philadelphia's (1964) classrooms since the college opened its doors to its first class of 1941 students. The year 1983 was important in the school's history, for that was when the college moved to its newly constructed campus in the former U.S. Mint Building. The structure has been renovated to include administrative offices, a library, laboratories, and classrooms. Distance learning via telecourses has been available at CCP for 2 decades on the college's own broadcast station. Today, Cable Channel 53 and WHYY Channel 12 (PBS) broadcast all of the distance learning telecourses. Since 1996, Internet English courses have been offered, and plans are in progress to expand the Internet courses to other disciplines such as business management.

Community College of Rhode Island

One Hilton Street	Phone: (401) 455-6113
Providence, RI 02905-2304	Fax: (401) 455-6047

Division(s): Instructional Technology and Distance Education
Web Site(s): http://www.ccri.cc.ri.us
E-mail: ykadelski@ccri.cc.ri.us

Class Titles: Biology, Business, English, Math, Law, Social Science, Psychology

Teaching Methods: *Computers:* Internet. *TV:* videotape, cable program, satellite broadcasting, PBS. *Other:* None.

Credits Granted for: experiential learning, portfolio assessment, cooperative education, examination (CLEP, GRE).

Admission Requirements: *Undergraduate:* age 18. *Certificate:* age 18.

On-Campus Requirements: final exam.

Tuition and Fees: *Undergraduate:* $73/credit. *Application Fee:* $20. *Other Costs:* $25 for general fees. *Credit by:* semester.

Financial Aid: Federal Stafford Loan, Federal Perkins Loan, Federal PLUS Loan, Federal Pell Grant, Federal Work-Study, VA, Rhode Island resident programs.

Accreditation: New England Association of Schools and Colleges, National League of Nursing, National Accrediting Agency for Clinical Laboratory Sciences, Commission on Dental Accreditation, Joint Review Committee on Education in Radiologic Technology, Committee for Accreditation of Respiratory Care Programs, Commission on Accreditation in Physical Therapy Education, American Chemical Society, Granted Developing Program Status by the American Council of Occupational Therapy Education.

Description: Community College of Rhode Island (1964) is the largest public, 2-year, degree-granting college in New England. It provides a variety of career, technical, and academic programs at campuses in Warwick (1972), Lincoln (1976), and Providence (1990) and offers courses at satellite facilities in East Providence, Middletown, Newport, and Westerly. From its modest beginning with 325 students to its present enrollment of 15,000, CCRI has grown to meet the goals of its founders. In 1987, CCRI began offering distance education courses delivered by TV, using the local cable companies. CCRI's telecourses, with enrollment around 1,000, offer accessibility and flexibility to learners who have personal or professional challenges and responsibilities that prohibit travel to a campus on a regular basis for traditional classes.

Community College of Southern Nevada

6375 West Charleston W1B	Phone: (702) 651-5619
Las Vegas, NV 89146	Fax: (702) 651-5069

Division(s): Community Education
Web Site(s): http://ccsn.nevada.edu/academics/DistanceEd/
E-mail: distanceed@ccsn.nevada.edu

Undergraduate Degree Programs:
Associate of Arts in General Studies

Certificate Programs: Cardio-Respiratory Therapy

Class Titles: American Sign Language, Astronomy, Business, Education, English, History, Library Skills, Mathematics, Music, Philosophy, Political Science, Psychology, Sociology, Study Skills.

Teaching Methods: *Computers:* Internet, real-time chat, e-mail. *TV:* videotape, PBS. *Other:* videoconferencing, fax.

Admission Requirements: *Undergraduate:* application and fees, age 16 with signature of parent or legal guardian, placement tests for Math and English.

On-Campus Requirements: None.

Tuition and Fees: *Undergraduate:* $40/credit for certificate or associate degree. *Application Fee:* $5. *Credit by:* semester.

Financial Aid: Federal Stafford Loan, Federal Perkins Loan, Federal PLUS Loan, Federal Pell Grant, Federal Work-Study, VA, Nevada resident programs.

Accreditation: Western Association of Schools and Colleges.

Description: The Community College of Southern Nevada consists of 4 distinct campuses: Charleton Campus (1988), Cheyenne Campus (1974), Henderson Campus (1981), and Summerlin Center (1998). The mission of Nevada's community colleges as institutions of the university and community college system of Nevada is to provide superior student-centered educational opportunities for the citizens of the state within designated service areas of each college. The community college mission encompasses a belief that education and training are the chief means of developing human capital for investment in the economic health of the state of Nevada.

Community College of Vermont

38 Main Street	Phone: (802) 748-6673
St. Johnsbury, VT 05860	Fax: (802) 748-5014

Division(s): Office of On-line Learning
Web Site(s): http://online.ccv.vsc.edu/welcome.html
E-mail: christej@mail.ccv.vsc.edu

Class Titles: vary with term: Abnormal Psychology, Creative Writing Poetry, America Between Wars, Critical Issues of Holocaust, Foundations of Western Civilization, Bioethics, Environmental Science, Philosophy, Programming in C++, Mythology, Current Issues in Management, Word Processing, Criminology/Criminal Behavior, Modern Poetry, Women's Utopian Literature, Elementary Statistics, Sociology, Principles of Accounting, Women in Management, Web Site Design/ Management, Internet.

Teaching Methods: *Computers:* Internet, real-time chat, electronic classroom, e-mail, CD-ROM, newsgroup, LIST-SERV. *Other:* None.

Credits Granted for: experiential learning, portfolio assessment, extrainstitutional learning, examination (CLEP, ACT-PEP, DANTES, GRE).

Admission Requirements: *Undergraduate:* high school diploma, on-site assessment of basic skills.

On-Campus Requirements: None.

Tuition and Fees: *Undergraduate:* $103 (in-state) $210 (out-of-state)/credit. *Other Costs:* $50 registration, $6/credit academic services, varying materials fees. *Credit by:* semester.

Financial Aid: Federal Stafford Loan, Federal Perkins Loan, Federal PLUS Loan, Federal Pell Grant, Federal Work-Study, VA, Vermont resident programs.

Accreditation: Northeast Association of Colleges and Schools.

Description: Community College of Vermont (1970) began offering online courses via Web Crossing discussion forums in 1995. CCV's courses—online and traditional—are designed for students residing in Vermont or in nearby areas of New York, Massachusetts, and New Hampshire.

Concordia University

7400 August Street	Phone: (708) 209-3024
River Forest, IL 60305	Fax: (708) 209-3176

Division(s): College of Continuing Education
Web Site(s): http://www.curf.edu
E-mail: crfconted@crf.cuis.edu

Class Titles: Theology, Psychology.

Teaching Methods: *Computers:* Internet, e-mail, LISTSERV. *TV:* interactive TV. *Other:* videoconferencing, audioconferencing, audiotapes, fax, correspondence, independent study

Credits Granted for: experiential learning, portfolio assessment, extrainstitutional learning, examination (CLEP, ACT-PEP, DANTES, GRE).

Admission Requirements: *Undergraduate:* high school diploma.

On-Campus Requirements: None.

Tuition and Fees: *Undergraduate:* variable. *Credit by:* semester.

Financial Aid: Federal Stafford Loan, Federal Perkins Loan, Federal PLUS Loan, Federal Pell Grant, Federal Work-Study, VA, Illinois resident programs.

Accreditation: North Central Association of Colleges and Schools.

Description: Concordia University (1864) is a church-related (Lutheran) liberal arts institution offering bachelor's and master's degrees. Concordia has offered courses via correspondence since 1950 and is now in the process of making these courses available on the Web.

Concordia University, Austin

3400 IH35 North
Austin, TX 78705-2799

Phone: (512) 452-7661
Fax: (512) 459-8517

Division(s): School of Nontraditional Studies
Web Site(s): http://www.concordia.edu
E-mail: meissner@concordia.edu

Undergraduate Degree Programs:
Bachelor of Arts in:
   Early Childhood Education
   Accounting
   Behavioral Sciences
   Business
   Management
   Church Music/Conducting
   Church Music/Organ
   Communications
   Elementary Education
   Secondary Education
   English
   Environmental Science
   Liberal Arts
   Mexican American Studies
   History
   Pre-Seminary Spanish

Graduate Degree Programs:
Master in Education

Class Titles: Communications/Human Communication Theory, Mass Media History/Theory, English/Short Story, Government/American Government, History/Western Civilization from 1715, Math/Finite Math, Psychology/Personality Theory, Religion/New Testament, Religion/Old Testament, Religion/History/Philosophy of Reformation, Religion/American Christianity.

Teaching Methods: *TV:* videotape, cable program, satellite broadcasting. *Other:* None.

Credits Granted for: experiential learning, portfolio assessment, extrainstitutional learning, examination (CLEP, ACT-PEP, DANTES, GRE).

Admission Requirements: *Undergraduate:* high school graduation or equivalent, ACT/SAT scores.

On-Campus Requirements: attend orientation.

Tuition and Fees: *Undergraduate:* $325/credit distance learning; validated prior learning, administrative fee $75; evaluation fee/semester hour requested $50. *Application Fee:* $25. *Other Costs:* adult degree program modules $910. *Credit by:* semester.

Financial Aid: Federal Stafford Loan, Federal Pell Grant, Federal Work-Study, VA, Texas resident programs.

Accreditation: Southern Association of Colleges and Schools.

Description: Concordia University at Austin (1925) opened as Concordia Academy to train young men for ministry in the Lutheran Church. The junior college department, added in 1951, became coeducational in 1955. Concordia received authorization to implement a 4-year liberal arts program in 1979, and its first BA students graduated in 1982. The current student population includes various cultural, religious, and ethnic backgrounds. Distance learning was started in 1992 to help students reach their educational goals by providing more convenient access and flexibility to classes off campus.

Concordia-New York

171 White Plains Road
Bronxville, NY 10708

Phone: (914) 337-9300
Fax: (914) 395-4500

Division(s): None.
Web Site(s): http://www.concordia-ny.edu
E-mail: meb@concordia-ny.edu

Undergraduate Degree Programs:
Bachelor of Liberal Arts
Bachelor of Science in:
   Education
   Social Work
   Business

Class Titles: call (914) 337-9300 x2103 or e-mail blanco@concordia-ny.edu.

Teaching Methods: *TV:* videoconferencing (compressed video). *Other:* None.

Credits Granted for: portfolio assessment, extrainstitutional learning, examination (CLEP, ACT-PEP, DANTES, GRE).

Admission Requirements: *Undergraduate:* high school graduate with strong college-prep curriculum, application, SAT/ACT scores, official transcripts from high school and all colleges or universities, recommendations. *Certificate:* variable.

On-Campus Requirements: one year in residence.

Tuition and Fees: *Undergraduate:* $400/year. *Credit by:* semester.

Financial Aid: Federal Stafford Loan, Federal PLUS Loan, Federal Pell Grant, Federal Work-Study, VA, New York resident programs.

Accreditation: Middle States Association of Colleges and Schools, Council on Social Work Education.

Description: Concordia-New York (1881) is a liberal arts, church-related college that offers majors in the liberal arts as well as in education, social work, and business. The college is small (600), located in a beautiful NYC suburb, and two-thirds of its students are residential. Distance learning at Concordia began in 1996 as part of the Concordia University System, a group of 10 schools nationwide. It allows member schools to send and receive classes via compressed video.

Concordia University, St. Paul

275 Syndicate Street N	Phone: (651) 641-8897
St. Paul, MN 55104	(800) 211-3370
	Fax: (651) 603-6144

Division(s): Department of Human Services and Professional Development
Web Site(s): http://www.csp.edu/hspd
E-mail: gradstudies@luther.csp.edu

Undergraduate Degree Programs:
Bachelor of School-Age Care
Bachelor of Youth Development
Bachelor of Human Services

Graduate Degree Programs:
Master of Arts in Education:
    Early Childhood
    School-Age Care
    Youth Development

Certificate Programs: Areas for School-Age Care: Proficiency, Site Leadership, Special Needs, Physical Recreation, Programming for Young Adolescence.

Teaching Methods: *Computers:* Internet, chat rooms, e-mail, bulletin boards. *TV:* videotapes. *Other:* audiotapes, phone conferences.

Credits Granted for: examination (CLEP or DANTES), life experience essays, military training.

Admission Requirements: *Undergraduate:* 60 accredited semester credits. *Graduate:* accredited baccalaureate degree, resume/portfolio of experience/leadership. *Certificate:* high school diploma or GED.

On-Campus Requirements: Initial 5-day residency at St. Paul campus.

Tuition and Fees: *Undergraduate:* $185/credit. *Graduate:* $225/credit. *Application Fee:* $20. *Software:* varies. *Other Costs:* travel/lodging for 5-day residency. *Credit by:* semester.

Financial Aid: Federal Stafford Loan, Federal Perkins Loan, Federal PLUS Loan, Federal Pell Grant, Federal Work-Study, VA, Minnesota resident programs.

Accreditation: North Central Association of Colleges and Schools.

Description: Founded in 1893, Concordia University is a private, liberal arts university owned and operated by the Lutheran Church-Missouri Synod. Concordia began distance learning programs in 1997 with BA and MA degrees in school-age care. Graduate degrees in Human Services will be available soon. Concordia admits students of any race, color, sex, and national or ethnic origin to all rights, privileges, programs, and activities generally accorded to university students.

Concordia University, Wisconsin

12800 North Lake Shore Drive	Phone: (414) 243-4257
Mequon, WI 53097	(800) 665-6564
	Fax: (414) 243-4459/4545

Division(s): Distance Learning Graduate Admissions
Web Site(s): http://www.cuw.edu
E-mail: brooke_konopacki@cuw.edu (prospective students)
sweaver@bach.cuw.edu (enrolled students)

Graduate Degree Programs:
Master of Business Administration
Master of Science in:
    Education Administration
    Education Counseling
    Education Reading
    Nursing Education Curriculum and Instruction

Class Titles: Education, Business, Religion, Psychology, Nursing.

Teaching Methods: *Computers:* Internet, e-mail. *TV:* videotape. *Other:* videoconferencing, fax, correspondence.

Admission Requirements: *Graduate:* bachelor's degree from an accredited university with minimum GPA of 3.0; international students must have 550+ on TOEFL, specific programs have specific prerequisites/special restrictions.

On-Campus Requirements: Yes, we offer 1–3 week summer courses, students complete a specific course (3 credits) while on-campus, room/board available.

Tuition and Fees: *Graduate:* $300/credit. *Application Fee:* $25. *Other Costs:* books and communication $50–$100/course. *Credit by:* semester.

Financial Aid: Federal Stafford Loan, Federal Perkins Loan, Federal PLUS Loan, Federal Pell Grant, Federal Work-Study, VA, Wisconsin resident programs.

Accreditation: North Central Association of Colleges and Schools.

Description: Concordia University Wisconsin (1881) was founded as a school of the Lutheran Church, Missouri Synod. Concordia gained university status in 1989. Located in suburban Mequon, Wisconsin, just north of metropolitan Milwaukee, Concordia serves more than 4,000 students at the main campus, 8 campus sites, and through distance learning. It is the third largest private school in the education-rich State of Wisconsin, making it an academic leader both regionally and globally. Concordia attracts a wealth of culturally diverse students and faculty, which enriches the learning process. Distance learning courses were started in 1993.

Connors State College

RR 1, Box 1000	Phone: (918) 463-2931
Warner, OK 74469	Fax: (918) 463-2233

Division(s): Director, Distance Education
Web Site(s): http://www.connors.cc.ok.us
E-mail: rramming@connors.cc.ok.us

Class Titles: Agriculture, Math, History, Spanish, Criminal Justice, Geography, Political Science, Psychology.

Teaching Methods: *TV:* interactive video, videotape, PBS. *Other:* None.

Credits Granted for: examination (CLEP, departmental, Advanced Placement), military credit evaluation.

Admission Requirements: *Undergraduate:* open-admission; testing (ACT/CPT) for advising/course placement. *Certificate:* same as undergraduate.

On-Campus Requirements: None.

Tuition and Fees: *Undergraduate:* $41/credit Oklahoma resident. *Other Costs:* $5/semester student ID, $10/semester parking permit, $3–$20/course instructional fees/lab fees. *Credit by:* semester.

Financial Aid: Federal Stafford Loan, Federal Perkins Loan, Federal Pell Grant, Federal Work-Study, VA, Oklahoma resident programs.

Accreditation: North Central Association of Colleges and Schools, National League of Nursing, Oklahoma State Board of Nursing Registration and Nursing Education.

Description: The mission of Connors State College (1908) is to provide undergraduate education leading to associate degrees or certificates of achievement in arts and sciences, business, agriculture and technology, pre-professional and service professions. Being sensitive to the educational needs of Eastern Oklahoma and believing education is a life-long process, Connors State College is committed to providing a general education curricula consistent with the first 2 years of a bachelor's degree program, developmental education for college preparation or for self-development purposes. Continuing education for personal enrichment and occupational development is also offered along with technical

programs that prepare individuals to enter the labor market, and organizations/activities to promote leadership, citizenship and social enhancement. The college has 2 sites: Warner, Oklahoma, and Muskogee, Oklahoma.

Corcoran School of Art

500 Seventeenth Street, NW	Phone: (202) 639-1820
Washington, DC 20006-4804	Fax: (202) 639-1821

Division(s): The Open Program
Web Site(s): http://www.corcoran.edu/online
E-mail: harry@st-ours.com

Undergraduate Degree Programs:
Bachelor of Fine Arts

Certificate Programs: Computer Graphics

Class Titles: Computer Art, Photoshop, Illustrator, Web Design, Explorations in 3D Design.

Teaching Methods: *Computers:* Internet, real-time chat, electronic classroom, e-mail. *Other:* None.

Credits Granted for: experiential learning, portfolio assessment.

Admission Requirements: *Undergraduate:* high school graduate. *Certificate:* high school graduate.

On-Campus Requirements: None.

Tuition and Fees: *Undergraduate:* $337/credit. *Application Fee:* $25. *Software:* variable. *Other Costs:* $30/course optional certificate fee, $25 late registration fee, 50% discount on tuition for full-time K–12 art teachers, 60% discount for recent (within 3 years) Corcoran BFA Alumni. *Credit by:* semester basis.

Financial Aid: Federal Stafford Loan, Federal Perkins Loan, Federal PLUS Loan, Federal Pell Grant, Federal Work-Study, Supplemental Educational Opportunity Grant, VA, Washington DC resident programs, DC State Student Initiative Grant.

Accreditation: Middle States Association of Colleges and Schools, Association of Independent Colleges of Art and Design.

Description: Officially founded in 1890, some 15 years after William Wilson Corcoran established Washington, DC's first museum, The Corcoran School of Art ranks today among America's oldest and most distinguished colleges of the visual arts. Offering a Bachelor of Fine Arts in 3 disciplines, Fine Arts, Graphic Design, and Photography, the college enrolls 300 full-time degree candidates, maintaining an intimate community of students and faculty. Graduates and faculty of The Corcoran have traditionally been leaders of the Washington art community, and their contributions have been critical to the artistic values and creative life of the nation. To make available this high-caliber education in the visual arts to the greater community at large, The Corcoran offers a wide range of courses through its Division of Continuing Education, well known as the Open Program, including the Computer Graphics Certificate. The Corcoran again leads the way in educational alternatives in the art and design community online, on America Online since 1995 (keyword: Corcoran) and now on the Internet at http://www.corcoran.edu/online.

Cornell University

| 149 Warren Hall | Phone: (607) 255-3028 |
| Ithaca, NY 14852-4320 | Fax: (607) 254-5122 |

Division(s): Agricultural Resources and Managerial Economics and Food Industry Management Distance Education Program
Web Site(s): http://distance-ed.arme.cornell.edu
E-mail: distance-ed@cornell.edu

Certificate Programs: Food Industry Management Distance Education

Class Titles: 40 courses in Supermarket, Convenience Store/Distribution Series.

Teaching Methods: *Computers:* e-mail, CD-ROM. *TV:* videotape. *Other:* fax, correspondence, independent study, workshops.

Credits Granted for: articulation agreements with some colleges—our students' transcripts are evaluated by outside schools for credit. Cornell college credit is not awarded.

Admission Requirements: *Undergraduate:* open enrollment. *Certificate:* open enrollment.

On-Campus Requirements: None.

Tuition and Fees: *Undergraduate:* $60–95/course certificate program (students work at their own pace).

Accreditation: Middle States Association of Colleges and Schools.

Description: The Cornell University (1964) Food Industry Management Distance Education Program serves the food industry, supermarkets, wholesalers, and convenience stores. This certificate program offers 40 courses in an independent study format. Companies often teach our courses in-house in a workshop format. The program offers bachelor's, master's, and PhDs on campus, executive development programs on campus and globally, applied research for the food industry, and the Distance Education Program.

County College of Morris

| 214 Center Grove Road | Phone: (973) 328-5184 |
| Randolph, NJ 07869-2086 | Fax: (973) 328-5082 |

Division(s): Distance Education
Web Site(s): http://www.ccm.edu
E-mail: sstout@ccm.edu

Undergraduate Degree Programs:
Associate in:
Arts
Science
Applied Science

Certificate Programs: college credit programs of varying lengths that lead to certificates.

Teaching Methods: *Computers:* Internet, real-time chat, electronic classroom, e-mail, CD-ROM. *TV:* videotape, cable program, satellite broadcasting, PBS. *Other:* videoconferencing, audioconferencing, audiographics, audiotapes, fax, correspondence, independent study, individual study.

Credits Granted for: experiential learning, extrainstitutional learning, examination (CLEP, ACT-PEP, DANTES, GRE).

Admission Requirements: *Undergraduate:* high school diploma or GED.

On-Campus Requirements: None.

Tuition and Fees: *Undergraduate:* $77/credit. *Application Fee:* $25. *Software:* variable. *Credit by:* semester.

Financial Aid: Federal Stafford Loan, Federal Perkins Loan, Federal PLUS Loan, Federal Pell Grant, Federal Work-Study, VA, New Jersey resident programs.

Accreditation: Middle States Association of Colleges and Schools.

Description: County College of Morris (1968) is located on 218 acres of rolling terrain. The college is dedicated to meeting the needs of area residents and employers for educational advancement and career training and to fostering social and cultural enlightenment within the community it serves. The college believes that enlightened self-interest and the public good are synonymous, and that all citizens are worthy of the opportunity to develop their potential to the fullest. CCM Online brings the college to you through classes in your own home on days and times convenient for you. You'll find no physical boundaries or limitations with CCM Online. We're as close as your home or office computer!

Covenant Theological Seminary

12330 Conway Road   Phone: (800) 264-8064
Saint Louis, MO 63141   (314) 434-4044
     Fax: (314) 434-4819

Division(s): Seminary Extension Training
Web Site(s): http://www.covenantseminary.edu
E-mail: admissions@covenantseminary.edu

Graduate Degree Programs:
Master of Divinity
Master of Arts in:
     General Theological Studies
     Counseling
Master of Theology

Certificate Programs: Christianity and Contemporary Culture, Biblical and Theological Studies, Counseling, Missions Studies (all graduate certificates).

Class Titles: Though courses are not available to those not in degree/certificate programs, materials (audio- or video-tapes/syllabus) are available for purchase through our Curriculum Resource Bank.

Teaching Methods: *Computers:* (in development) Internet, e-mail, newsgroup, LISTSERV. *TV:* videotape. *Other:* corre-spondence, independent study, individual study, learning contracts, regular telephone contact with a mentor.

Admission Requirements: *Undergraduate:* bachelor's degree or equivalent.

On-Campus Requirements: A student may complete up to 18 hours through the individual program, or 30 hours through the SET site program.

Tuition and Fees: *Undergraduate:* $150/credit by SET. *Application Fee:* $25. *Credit by:* semester.

Financial Aid: Federal Stafford Loan, VA.

Accreditation: North Central Association of Colleges and Schools, Association of Theological Schools.

Description: Covenant Theological Seminary (1956) was established by concerned Christians in what was then known as the Evangelical Presbyterian Church. These believers recognized that their denomination needed a strong theologi-cal school of its own. In 1989, Covenant recognized the need and opportunity to provide the same biblically founded, theological education to men and women who for various reasons could not relocate to its Saint Louis campus. Since then, the program has continued to grow and become available to more and more people throughout the country and the world.

Crowder College

601 Laclede   Phone: (417) 451-3223
Neosho, MO 64850   Fax: (417) 451-4280

Division(s): Information Technology Office
Web Site(s): http://www.crowder.cc.mo.us
E-mail: rspencer@mail.crowder.cc.mo.us
rbriggs@mail.crowder.cc.mo.us
lsimek@mail.crowder.cc.mo.us

Class Titles: French, Literature, Math, Theater.

Teaching Methods: *Computers:* Internet. *TV:* videotape, satellite broadcasting. *Other:* None.

Credits Granted for: experiential learning, examination (CLEP).

Admission Requirements: *Undergraduate:* accredited high school graduate or GED, ACT. *Certificate:* same as undergrad-uate.

On-Campus Requirements: None.

Tuition and Fees: *Undergraduate:* $42/credit in-district (Newton and McDonald Counties in Missouri), $61/credit out-of-district, $81/credit out-of-state and international. *Other Costs:* $6/credit technology/facilities use fees. *Credit by:* semester.

Financial Aid: Federal Stafford Loan, Federal Pell Grant, Federal Work-Study, VA, Missouri resident programs.

Accreditation: North Central Association of Colleges and Schools.

Description: Crowder College (1963) is a public, 2-year institution located in southwest Missouri. Recognized nationally for innovative work in the alternative-energy field, Crowder boasts of a strong transferability rate and offers coadmission programs with various 4-year institutions. Crowder's student to faculty ratio is 16:1, with an enrollment of 1,800. Crowder College has been moving forward in the field of distance learning since 1995 and has several program expansion plans in place for the future.

Cuesta College

Highway 1   Phone: (805) 546-3122
San Luis Obispo, CA 93403   Fax: (805) 546-3966

Division(s): Instructional Services
Web Site(s): http://www.cuesta.cc.ca.us
E-mail: cuestainfo@bass.cc.ca.us

Class Titles: Chemistry, Health Education, Physics. Students may take classes as long as prerequisites are met.

Teaching Methods: *Computers:* Internet, e-mail, CD-ROM. *Other:* None.

On-Campus Requirements: varies by course.

Tuition and Fees: *Undergraduate:* $12/credit in summer, $12/credit in fall (California residents), $118/credit in summer, $129/credit in fall (nonresident tuition). *Other Costs:* varies for material fees. *Credit by:* semester.

Financial Aid: Board of Governor's Fee Waiver (BOGFW), Federal Pell Grant, Federal Stafford Loan program, Federal SEOG grant, Federal Work Study, Cal Grant B and C, campus-based scholarships, recommend use of the Free Application for Federal Student Aid.

Accreditation: Western Association of Schools and Colleges.

Description: The original junior college was initiated as a postgraduate division of San Luis Obispo High School in 1916 and was terminated when the U.S. entered World War I. The district again formed a junior college in 1936, which remained in operation until 1959. The San Luis Obispo County Junior College District was established by the electorate of the county in 1963. In the fall of 1998, the college opened its North County campus, serving approximately 2,000 students in day and evening classes. Cuesta College offered its first distance education classes in 1998.

Cumberland County College

| College Drive | Phone: (609) 691-8600 |
| Vineland, NJ 08360 | Fax: (609) 691-8813 |

Division(s): Learning and Technology Resources
Web Site(s): http://cccnj.net
E-mail: ttirrell@cccnj.net

Undergraduate Degree Programs:
Associate in General Liberal Arts

Class Titles: English Composition, Spanish, Statistics, Economics, Psychology, Sociology, Human Growth/Development, Child Psychology. Gerontology, U.S. History, Western Civilization, Mass Media, Business, Marketing, Management.

Teaching Methods: *Computers:* Internet, real-time chat, electronic classroom, e-mail, CD-ROM, newsgroup, LISTSERV. *TV:* videotape, cable program, PBS. *Other:* None.

Credits Granted for: examination (CLEP, ACT-PEP, DANTES, GRE).

Admission Requirements: *Undergraduate:* high school diploma or GED.

On-Campus Requirements: None.

Tuition and Fees: *Undergraduate:* $70/credit. *Application Fee:*

$25. *Other Costs:* $9/credit comprehensive fee, $5/credit technology fee. *Credit by:* semester.

Financial Aid: Federal Stafford Loan, Federal Perkins Loan, Federal PLUS Loan, Federal Pell Grant, Federal Work-Study, VA, New Jersey resident programs.

Accreditation: Middle States Association of Colleges and Schools.

Description: Cumberland County College (1966) was the first community college in New Jersey to open its own campus. The 100-acre campus features 9 buildings and an excellent educational and social atmosphere. Cumberland offers 46 career and transfer programs of study. Degrees conferred: Associate of Arts, Associate in Science, Associate in Applied Science, Certificate. Opportunity: 70% of Cumberland's graduates are the first in their families to earn a college degree. Enrollment: 2900 students per semester during the academic year. Class Size: The average class size is 23 students. Financial Aid: About half of our students receive some form of financial aid. Last year, $3,162,000 in financial assistance was awarded to 1394 students from the various grant, scholarship, and loan programs.

Cuyahoga Community College

| 2900 Community College Avenue | Phone: (216) 987-4257 |
| Cleveland, OH 44114 | Fax: (216) 987-3675 |

Division(s): Distance Learning Center
Web Site(s): http://dlc.tri-c.cc.oh.us
E-mail: distance@tri-c.cc.oh.us

Undergraduate Degree Programs:
Associate of Arts

Class Titles: course areas: Business Administration, English, Medical Terminology, Philosophy, Psychology, Information Literacy, Marketing, Sociology, Computer Science.

Teaching Methods: *Computers:* Internet, real-time chat, e-mail, CD-ROM, newsgroup, LISTSERV. *TV:* videotape, cable program, PBS. *Other:* videoconferencing, independent study, individual study.

Credits Granted for: experiential learning, portfolio assessment, examination (CLEP, ACT-PEP, DANTES, GRE).

Admission Requirements: *Undergraduate:* high school graduates or GED equivalent or age 18. In some instances, certain courses may be restricted to program majors. Admission to a specific program may be competitive or require specific minimum qualifications. Some students may be requested to enroll in special courses to eliminate deficiencies in academic preparation.

On-Campus Requirements: None.

Tuition and Fees: *Undergraduate:* $62/credit Cuyahoga County resident, $82/credit Ohio resident, $163/credit nonresident. *Other Costs:* $25 additional fee for some distance learning courses. *Credit by:* semester.

Financial Aid: Federal Stafford Loan, Federal Perkins Loan, Federal PLUS Loan, Federal Pell Grant, Federal Work-Study, VA.

Accreditation: North Central Association of Colleges and Schools.

Description: Cuyahoga Community College (Tri-C)(1963) is Ohio's first and largest public community college. Since its founding, the college has served more than 425,000 county residents. Today, Tri-C serves nearly 58,000 credit and noncredit students at its Eastern, Metropolitan and Western campuses, off-campus sites located throughout the county, and through multiple distance learning options. The college offers 70 career/technical options, and its arts and science courses transfer to state universities and private colleges throughout the U.S.

D-Q University

PO Box 409	Phone: (530) 758-0470
Davis, CA 95617	Fax: (530) 758-4891

Division(s): MIS
Web Site(s): http://dqu.cc.ca.us
E-mail: stiwari@dqu.cc.ca.us

Class Titles: Environmental Science, Business English

Teaching Methods: *Computers:* Internet, real-time chat, e-mail. *TV:* satellite broadcasting. *Other:* fax, correspondence, independent study, learning contracts.

Credits Granted for: experiential learning, portfolio assessment.

Admission Requirements: *Undergraduate:* age 18 with high school diploma or GED, or the ability to benefit with passing scores on the Test of Adult Basic Education.

On-Campus Requirements: None.

Tuition and Fees: *Undergraduate:* $25/credit. *Application Fee:* $10. *Credit by:* semester.

Financial Aid: Federal Stafford Loan, Federal Pell Grant, Federal Work-Study.

Accreditation: Western Association of Schools and Colleges.

Description: D-Q University (1971) is the only Native American-controlled postsecondary institution in California. Our mission is to serve the educational needs of Native American students while respecting their traditional cultures. A founding member of the American Indian Higher Education Consortium, a consortium of 29 tribal colleges, D-Q University is located near Sacramento. D-Q offers AA and AS degrees in 9 areas, including Indigenous Studies. Many Native students begin their studies here and transfer to California state colleges and universities. Our distance education program is in its beginning stages, with courses being added each semester.

Dakota State University

201A Karl Mundt Library	Phone: (605) 256-5049
Madison, SD 57042-1799	(800) 641-4309
	Fax: (605) 256-5208

Division(s): Office of Distance Education
Web Site(s): http://www.courses.dsu.edu/disted/
E-mail: dsuinfo@columbia.dsu.edu

Undergraduate Degree Programs:
Information Systems and Health Information Administration

Graduate Degree Programs:
Information Systems and Computer Education and Technology (starting fall 1999)

Class Titles: Basic Programming, Principles of Programming, COBOL, Composition, Career Planning, Sociology, Fund Raising, Health Care Courses, Literature, Native American Studies, Psychology, Information Systems.

Teaching Methods: *Computers:* Internet, e-mail. *Other:* None.

Credits Granted for: experiential learning, examinations, etc.

Admission Requirements: *Undergraduate:* must meet prerequisites; international students must have a TOEFL of 550. *Graduate:* same.

On-Campus Requirements: None.

Tuition and Fees: *Undergraduate:* $133/credit in-state, $156/credit out-of-state. *Graduate:* $161/credit in-state, $182/credit out-of-state. *Credit by:* semester.

Accreditation: North Central Association of Colleges and Schools, National Council on Accreditation of Teacher Education.

Description: The primary purpose of Dakota State University (1881) is to provide instruction in computer management, computer information systems, electronic data processing, and other related undergraduate and graduate programs. Secondarily, the school offers authorized 2-year, one-year, and short courses for application and systems training, and elementary and secondary teachers are trained to use computers and information processing. Distance courses have been offered online since 1991, and DSU is planning to expand its distance programs soon by offering degrees online.

Dalhousie University

Registrar's Office
Arts and Administration Building
Halifax, NS, Canada B3H 4H6

Phone: (902) 494-2450
Fax: (902) 494-1630

Division(s): various departments
Web Site(s): http://www.dal.ca
E-mail: registrar@dal.ca

Graduate Degree Programs:
Master of Business Administration (Financial Services)
Master of Information Technology Education
Master of Occupational Therapy (proposed)

Certificate Programs: Adult Education, Business Management, Financial Management, Fire Service Administration, Fire Service Leadership, Human Resources Management, Local Government Administration, Police Leadership, Public Sector Management, Small Business Management.

Class Titles: Anatomy/Neurobiology, Nursing, Business Administration, Physiology/Biophysics, Health Services Administration, Social Work, Occupational Therapy.

Teaching Methods: *Computers:* Internet, real-time chat, electronic classroom, e-mail, CD-ROM, newsgroup, LISTSERV. *TV:* videotape, cable program. *Other:* radio broadcast, videoconferencing, audioconferencing, audiographics, audiotapes, tax, correspondence, independent study, individual study, learning contracts.

Credits Granted for: experiential learning, portfolio assessment, extrainstitutional learning, examination (CLEP, ACT-PEP, DANTES, GRE).

Admission Requirements: *Undergraduate:* contact registrar's office for specific requirements outside the U.S.

On-Campus Requirements: variable.

Tuition and Fees: *Undergraduate:* variable, contact registrar's office or Henson College directly.

Financial Aid: Dalhousie has a leading student assistance program, for enrolled students.

Accreditation: Association of Universities and Colleges of Canada, Atlantic Association of Universities.

Description: Dalhousie University (1818) is a comprehensive teaching and research university located in the provincial capital of Nova Scotia, a major regional center for Atlantic Canada. The university offers special expertise in Ocean Studies and Health Studies and has a growing involvement in Advanced Technical Education. Dalhousie offers 3,600 courses to 13,500 full-time students in programs that include 60 degree and advanced diplomas in diverse specialties at the undergraduate level, 71 master's degrees, and 41 doctoral-level areas of study. Professional programs are available in Architecture, Dentistry, Engineering, Law, and Medicine. Students consistently earn awards from external agencies, including 72 Rhodes Scholars since 1904. Dalhousie provides continuing education for 15,000 additional part-time students. Henson College of Public Affairs and Continuing Education plays a leadership role in the provision of programs for the adult student. Dalhousie's 180 years of history provide a solid foundation for the development of exciting, new learning opportunities for the 21st century.

Dallas TeleCollege

9596 Walnut Street
Dallas, TX 75243

Phone: (972) 669-6400
Fax: (972) 669-6409

Division(s): Distance Education and College Services
Web Site(s): http://dallas.dcccd.edu
E-mail: None.

Undergraduate Degree Programs:
Associate of Arts and Sciences

Class Titles: Accounting, Algebra, Anthropology, Astronomy, Biology, Business, Business Communications, Business English, Business Law, Calculus, Child Development courses, College Skills, Composition, Computer-Aided Design/Electrical Drafting courses, Computer Software/Hardware courses, Economics, Electronics courses, English as Second Language, Ethics, Government, History, Humanities, Import Customs Regulations, Geometry, Literature, Management, Marketing, Medical Office Procedures, Medical Terminology, Multimedia courses, Music Appreciation, Nutrition, Office Procedures, Physical Fitness, Psychology, Sociology, Spanish, Speech, Trigonometry.

Teaching Methods: *Computers:* Internet, real-time chat, e-mail, CD-ROM. *TV:* videotape, cable program, PBS. *Other:* audioconferencing, audiotapes, fax, correspondence.

Credits Granted for: credits earned through other education programs, such as credit-by-examination, military experience, and the U.S. Armed Forces Institute, are reviewed by the Registrar and credit may be granted if applicable.

Admission Requirements: *Undergraduate:* open-door, assessment procedures, high school diploma or GED, age 18 or approval, TASP or alternative, TOEFL of 525.

On-Campus Requirements: None.

Tuition and Fees: *Undergraduate:* $366/3-credit course. *Other Costs:* varies for textbooks/other materials (usually less than $100/course). *Credit by:* semester.

Financial Aid: most financial aid programs are offered to distance learning students. A financial aid officer will be able to direct students appropriately.

Accreditation: Southern Association of Colleges and Schools.

Description: The Dallas Community College District (1972) is composed of 7 colleges in Dallas, Texas, with 46,000 credit and 45,000 noncredit enrollments per semester and 2,000 full-time faculty and staff members. The distance learning program, Dallas TeleCollege, draws its strength from the faculty of these colleges as well as from 26 years of experience in the development and delivery of distance learning courses worldwide. 230,000 students have enrolled in the DALLAS program since it began in 1972. Courses enroll 10,000 each year. Dallas TeleCollege provides greater access to educational opportunities for learners worldwide through the delivery of flexible, cost-effective courses. Ninety courses are offered and coordinated by the LeCroy Center for Educational Telecommunications, which also houses Dallas Tele-Learning, the producer of telecourse and online courses.

Dallas Theological Seminary

3909 Swiss Avenue	Phone: (800) 992-0998
Dallas, TX 75204	Fax: (214) 841-3565

Division(s): External Studies
Web Site(s): http://www.dts.edu
E-mail: External_Studies@dts.edu

Graduate Degree Programs:
Master of Arts in Biblical Studies

Certificate Programs: Graduate Studies

Teaching Methods: *Computers:* Internet, e-mail, LISTSERV. *TV:* videotape. *Other:* videoconferencing, audiotapes, fax, correspondence, independent study, individual study, learning contracts.

Credits Granted for: graduate transfer, experiential learning, portfolio assessment, extrainstitutional learning, examination (on-site Advanced Standing).

Admission Requirements: *Graduate:* regionally accredited bachelor's degree. *Certificate:* regionally accredited bachelor's degree.

On-Campus Requirements: students must complete at least 50% of their program either at the main campus (Dallas) or one of the extension sites (San Antonio, TX; Houston, TX; Tampa, FL; or Chattanooga, TN/Atlanta, GA regional site).

Tuition and Fees: *Graduate:* $260/credit. *Application Fee:* $30. *Credit by:* semester.

Financial Aid: Grants (San Antonio, Houston, Tampa), VA (Texas only).

Accreditation: Southern Association of Colleges and Schools, Association of Theological Schools.

Description: Dallas Theological Seminary (1924) entered the distance learning field in 1987 when the first extension site was launched. Since then, extension sites in Houston, Tampa, San Antonio, and Chattanooga/Atlanta have grown into fully accredited sites offering the Master of Arts degree in Biblical Studies with more than 350 students enrolled. Helping to fulfill the mission of the school, the extension program seeks to deliver graduate theological education to lay-oriented ministers and professional ministers desiring a Bible-centered curriculum and to encourage students toward professional programs offered on the main campus in Dallas (1,450 students).

Danville Area Community College

2000 East Main Street	Phone: (217) 443-8577
Danville, Il 61832	Fax: (217) 443-3178

Division(s): Instructional Media
Web Site(s): http://www.dacc.cc.il.us/distancelearning
E-mail: jspors@dacc.cc.il.us

Undergraduate Degree Programs:
yes. Contact school for a complete list of degrees offered via long distance.

Certificate Programs: Yes.

Class Titles: Latin American History, U.S. History since 1865, Contemporary Health, Poetry, Film, Social Psychology of Aging, Psychology, Sociology, Philosophy.

Teaching Methods: *Computers:* Internet, real-time chat, electronic classroom, e-mail, newsgroup, LISTSERV. *TV:* videotape, cable program, satellite broadcasting, PBS. *Other:* videoconferencing, audiotapes, fax, correspondence, independent study, individual study.

Credits Granted for: examination (CLEP, ACT-PEP, DANTES, GRE).

Admission Requirements: *Undergraduate:* contact school. *Certificate:* contact school.

On-Campus Requirements: None.

Tuition and Fees: *Undergraduate:* $42/credit in-district, additional fees for out-of-district and out-of-state. *Credit by:* semester.

Financial Aid: Federal Stafford Loan, Federal Perkins Loan, Federal PLUS Loan, Federal Pell Grant, Federal Work-Study, VA, Illlinois resident programs.

Accreditation: North Central Association of Colleges and Schools.

Description: Danville Area Community College (DACC) is a 2-year community college. Associate degrees are offered in a wide array of disciplines. About half of our students go on for 4-year degrees. DACC has been involved in distance learning for about 4 years.

Danville Community College

1008 South Main Street	Phone: (804) 797-2222
Danville, VA 24541	Fax: (804) 797-8541

Division(s): Learning Resources
Web Site(s): http://www.dc.cc.va.us
E-mail: bfoster@dc.cc.va.us

Undergraduate Degree Programs:
Associate in Arts
Associate in Science
Associate in Applied Science

Class Titles: Math, English, Statistics, Music Appreciation, Chemistry, Personal Wellness, Natural Science

Teaching Methods: *Computers:* Internet, electronic classroom, e-mail. *TV:* videotape, cable program. *Other:* videoconferencing, individual study.

Admission Requirements: *Undergraduate:* open enrollment.

On-Campus Requirements: None.

Tuition and Fees: *Undergraduate:* $48/credit in-state, $161/credit out-of-state. *Software:* $1. *Other Costs:* $4 activity fee. *Credit by:* semester.

Financial Aid: Federal Perkins Loan, Federal Pell Grant, Federal Work-Study, VA, Virginia resident programs.

Accreditation: Southern Association of Colleges and Schools.

Description: Danville Community College (1967) is a 2-year institution of higher education established under a statewide system of community colleges. The college, located on a 76-acre campus, offers Associate in Arts, Associate in Science, Associate in Applied Science, diplomas, and certificate programs. As part of the Virginia Distance Education Network, DCC began offering distance learning courses in 1995. Courses are delivered using a variety of formats including telecourses, interactive TV, and the Internet.

Darton College

2400 Gillionville Road	Phone: (912) 430-6759
Albany, GA 31707	Fax: (912) 430-6910

Division(s): Continuing Education
Web Site(s): http://www.dartnet.peachnet.edu/~distlrn/dlhome.htm
E-mail: bquattro@dmail.dartnet.peachnet.edu

Class Titles: French, German, Japanese, Spanish, English, Business, Real Estate.

Teaching Methods: *Computers:* Internet, real-time chat, electronic classroom, e-mail, CD-ROM, newsgroup. *TV:* videotape, cable program, satellite broadcasting, PBS. *Other:* radio broadcast, videoconferencing, audioconferencing, audiographics, audiotapes, fax, correspondence, independent study, individual study.

Credits Granted for: examination (CLEP, ACT-PEP, DANTES).

Admission Requirements: *Undergraduate:* GED, age 17, placement exam depending on SAT/ACT scores. *Certificate:* same as undergraduate.

On-Campus Requirements: None.

Tuition and Fees: *Undergraduate:* $49/credit. *Credit by:* semester.

Financial Aid: Federal Stafford Loan, Federal Perkins Loan, Federal PLUS Loan, Federal Pell Grant, Federal Work-Study, VA, Georgia HOPE scholarship.

Accreditation: Southern Association of Colleges and Schools.

Description: Darton College (1963) is a 2-year unit of the University System of Georgia, located in Albany (population 100,000), the hub of southwest Georgia, surrounded by rural cotton, pecan, and peanut farms. Darton prides itself on student success, as measured by its 2-year graduates' high pass rates on state licensing tests and their success after transferring to 4-year institutions. Students pursue 73 2-year transfer and career associate degrees. Darton is currently pursuing an aggressive distance learning program, with plans to offer new distance education classes each semester. Darton's Distance Learning program has received 2 awards from the National Council of Instructional Administrators in the past 2 years and encompasses 4 main areas: Georgia Statewide Academic and Medical System, Cable Telecasts, Satellite Downlinks, Internet-Based Courses. Our goal is to offer an associate degree through distance education in the not too distant future.

Davenport Educational System, Inc.

415 East Fulton Street	Phone: (616) 451-3511
Grand Rapids, MI 49503	(800) 632-9569
	Fax: (616) 742-2076

Division(s): Learning Network
Other colleges: Davenport College, Detroit College of Business, Great Lakes College
Web Site(s): http://www.learningnetwork.davenport.edu
E-mail: epung@davenport.edu
dzoet@davenport.edu

Class Titles: Management, Marketing, International Business, Computer Information Systems, Healthcare Administration, Business Law, Communications, Social Sciences.

Teaching Methods: *Computers:* Internet, real-time chat, electronic classroom, e-mail, net meeting. *Other:* None.

Credits Granted for: experiential learning, portfolio assessment, extrainstitutional learning, examination (CLEP, ACT-PEP, DANTES, GRE).

Admission Requirements: *Undergraduate:* open-enrollment.

On-Campus Requirements: one course for associate degree, 3 courses for bachelor's degree.

Tuition and Fees: *Undergraduate:* $745/course. *Application Fee:* $20. *Other Costs:* under $75, online orientation. *Credit by:* quarter.

Financial Aid: Federal Stafford Loan, Federal Perkins Loan, Federal PLUS Loan, Federal Pell Grant, Federal Work-Study, VA.

Accreditation: North Central Association of Colleges and Schools.

Description: The Davenport Educational System Learning Network (1866) offers the combined educational excellence of Davenport College, Detroit College of Business, and Great Lakes College. The North Central Association of Colleges and Schools accredits all 3 Davenport Educational System, Inc. colleges. The colleges have been offering online courses since 1995. In March of 1998 the Learning Network was developed to expand and enhance the online learning options. The Learning Network offers a variety of courses in business and general education for students to gain knowledge and skills while applying their learning experience toward the completion of their degree at either Davenport College, Detroit College of Business, or Great Lakes College. The courses are the same world-class courses that have been developed and refined since 1866. However, now you can take your course at home, work, or even in your hotel room.

De Anza College

21250 Stevens Creek Boulevard	Phone: (408) 864-8969
Cupertino, CA 95014	Fax: (408) 864-8245

Division(s): Distance Learning Center
Web Site(s): http://dadistance.fhda.edu
E-mail: information@dadistance.fhda.edu

Undergraduate Degree Programs:
Associate of Arts

Certificate Programs: Business

Class Titles: Accounting, Algebra, American Government/Politics, Anatomy/Physiology, Biology, Business, Business Law, Child Development, Computers/Data Processing/Applications, Economics, English Literature, English Writing, Health, History, Humanities, Intercultural Studies, Library Skills, Management, Marketing, Mass Communication, Medical Terminology/Common Diseases, Microsoft Windows NT Administration, Music, NCLEX Practice/Analysis, Newswriting, Nutrition, Parenting, Philosophy, Psychology, Religion, Sociology, Statistics, World Wide Web Page Development

Teaching Methods: *Computers:* Internet, chat rooms, bulletin boards, e-mail, CD-ROM, LISTSERV, Web pages. *TV:* videotape, cable programs, PBS. *Other:* None.

Admission Requirements: *Undergraduate:* age 18 or high school graduate, younger students allowed with permission of high school and guardian. *Certificate:* same as undergraduate.

On-Campus Requirements: Business certificate program requires one course on campus. Some courses require on-campus testing.

Tuition and Fees: *Undergraduate:* $8/credit California residents, $93/credit nonresidents, $101/credit foreign citizens. *Other Costs:* $23/quarter term. *Credit by:* quarter.

Financial Aid: Federal Stafford Loan, Federal Perkins Loan, Federal PLUS Loan, Federal Pell Grant, Federal Work-Study, VA, California resident programs, Federal Supplemental Educational Opportunity Grant Program, Extended Opportunity Program Grant, Bureau of Indian Affairs, Board of Governors Fee Waivers, Cal Grant A, Cal Grant B, Cal Grant C, De Anza College Book loans.

Accreditation: Western Association of Schools and Colleges.

Description: De Anza College (1967), located in the Silicon Valley area of northern California, is one of more than 100 public community colleges in the state and has gained a national reputation for its responsiveness to community needs, including students with physical and learning disabilities, minorities, re-entry students, and distance learning students. De Anza offers educational opportunities in a range of programs including the first 2 years of 4-year degree programs that parallel the requirements of the University of California, California State University, and private colleges and universities. The distance learning program at De Anza has been in operation since 1974 and offers courses via TV, video, Internet, and mixed media. All distance courses are equivalent to the on-campus courses and are taught by De Anza College instructors. The Distance Learning Center offers more than 55 lower-division courses per term in a variety of subject areas.

Delaware County Community College

901 South Media Line Road	Phone: (610) 359-5158
Media, PA 19063	Fax: (610) 359-5343

Division(s): Distance Learning
Web Site(s): http://www.dccc.edu or http://www.whyy.org
E-mail: tmurray@dcccnet.dccc.edu

Undergraduate Degree Programs:
Associate

Class Titles: Biological Science, Business, Small Business Management, Management, Marketing, Business Law, Business Math, Economics (micro/macro), Composition, American History, Western Civilization, American Cinema, Contemporary Moral Problems, American National Government, Psychology, Abnormal Psychology, Child Psychology, Sociology, Sociology of Marriage/Family, Cultural Anthropology, Spanish.

Teaching Methods: *Computers:* Internet, real-time chat, electronic classroom, e-mail, CD-ROM, newsgroup, LISTSERV. *TV:* videotape, cable program, satellite broadcasting, PBS. *Other:* videoconferencing, audiotapes, fax, correspondence, independent study, individual study.

Credits Granted for: portfolio assessment, extrainstitutional learning, examination (CLEP).

Admission Requirements: *Undergraduate:* contact school. *Graduate:* contact school. *Doctoral:* contact school. *Certificate:* contact school.

On-Campus Requirements: orientation and testing only.

Tuition and Fees: *Undergraduate:* $62/credit sponsoring school district, $124/credit nonsponsoring school districts, $187/credit out-of-state. *Application Fee:* $20. *Other Costs:* $9/credit instructional support fee, $15/semester records fee. *Credit by:* semester.

Financial Aid: Federal Stafford Loan, Federal Perkins Loan, Federal PLUS Loan, Federal Pell Grant, Federal Work-Study, VA, Pennsylvania resident programs.

Accreditation: Middle States Association of Colleges and Schools.

Description: Delaware County Community College (1967) is dedicated to providing high-quality, low-cost educational opportunities that meet the needs of our students. Programs include college and university parallel programs equivalent to the first 2 years of a bachelor's degree, career programs to prepare graduates for employment, and short-term certificate programs in specific occupational fields. DCCC's competency-based curriculum ensures that our students are really prepared for employment or further education. Our faculty, from instructors to full professors, are committed to being there for their students. Counselors, tutors, librarians, and the entire DCCC staff are dedicated to providing the support and services our students need. DCCC has an extensive distance learning program with courses offered online and through TV and independent study. The true measure of DCCC's value can be gauged only by what happens to DCCC students when they leave. They meet their goals—98% seeking jobs are employed within 3 months after graduation and 89% of those who intend to transfer do.

Delaware Technical and Community College

400 Stanton/Christiana Road
Newark, DE 19711

Phone: (302) 453-3747
Fax: (302) 453-3025

Division(s): Corporate and Community Programs
Web Site(s): http://www.dtcc.edu
E-mail: poplos@hopi.dtcc.edu

Class Titles: Algebra, College Algebra/Trigonometry, College Math/Statistics, Calculus, Math for Behavioral Sciences, Biomedical Statistics, Math of Finance, Precalculus, Business Statistics, Business Law, Business, Customer Service, Consumer Behavior, Economics (macro/micro), Principles of Management, Principles of Marketing, Salesmanship, Medical Terminology, Electricity, Composition, Technical Writing, Critical Reading/Thinking, Oral Communications, Post-Industrial American Literature, American History, History of Technology, Health Careers, Political Science, General Psychology, Industrial Psychology, Child Development, Human Development, Psychology of Aging, Abnormal Psychology, Family Structures, Sociology, Adult Learner Success Strategies.

Teaching Methods: *Computers:* Internet, electronic classroom, e-mail, newsgroup. *TV:* videotape, satellite broadcasting, fiber-optic cable, PBS. *Other:* videoconferencing, audioconferencing, fax.

Credits Granted for: experiential learning, extrainstitutional learning, examination (CLEP, ACT-PEP, DANTES, GRE).

Admission Requirements: *Undergraduate:* open admissions. *Certificate:* open admissions.

On-Campus Requirements: orientation is conducted on campus, via videotape, and via interactive classroom. Attendance or completion of the videotape is mandatory. Tests are scheduled with the instructor, in a test center, or through a proctor at a distant location.

Tuition and Fees: *Undergraduate:* $58/credit. *Application Fee:* $10. *Other Costs:* $17 distant learning fee; $5 materials fee; plus appropriate lab fees, textbooks/materials, and student services fees. *Credit by:* semester.

Financial Aid: Federal Stafford Loan, Federal Perkins Loan, Federal PLUS Loan, Federal Pell Grant, Federal Work-Study, VA, Delaware resident programs.

Accreditation: Middle States Association of Colleges and Schools.

Description: Delaware Technical and Community College (1966) is a statewide institution of higher education providing basic, technical, and industrial training opportunities and continuing education to every resident of Delaware at 4 conveniently located campuses. Several degree programs are offered, and the Associate in Applied Science degree is granted upon successful completion of specific curriculum requirements. The college is committed to using distance learning to enhance the instructional processes at all of its campus locations. Telecourses developed by various community college networks and by Delaware Tech faculty are recorded in our 2 state-of-the-art TV studios.

Delgado Community College

615 City Park Avenue	Phone: (504) 483-4173
New Orleans, LA 70119-4399	Fax: (504) 483-4895

Division(s): Community Campus
Web Site(s): http://www.dcc.edu
E-mail: knmix@dcc.edu

Class Titles: Psychology, Philosophy, History, Business, Speech, Sign Language, Allied Health.

Teaching Methods: *TV:* videotape, cable program. *Other:* compressed video.

Credits Granted for: experiential learning, portfolio assessment, examination (CLEP, ACT).

Admission Requirements: *Undergraduate:* placement test, immunization form, transfer transcript.

On-Campus Requirements: varies with class.

Tuition and Fees: *Undergraduate:* $240/1–3 credits, $282/4 credits, $324/5 credits, $366/6 credits, $408/7 credits, $450/8 credits, $492/9 credits, $534/10 credits, $576/11 credits, $618/12 or more credits. *Application Fee:* $15. *Credit by:* semester.

Financial Aid: Federal Stafford Loan, Federal PLUS Loan, Federal Pell Grant, Federal Work-Study, VA, Louisiana resident programs (TOPS, merit scholarships).

Accreditation: Southern Association of Colleges and Schools.

Description: Delgado Community College (1929) is a comprehensive, multicampus, public community college with strong undergraduate programs as well as occupational and technical programs. The college is dedicated to providing educational opportunities for all people in a free and open society. Through an open-door admissions policy, the college welcomes students from diverse racial, religious, economic, educational, and cultural backgrounds. Central to the college curriculum is a commitment to the integration of arts and sciences, career education, and technology. In recognition of the diverse needs of the individual and the demands of a democratic society, the college provides a comprehensive educational program that helps students clarify values and develop skills in critical thinking, self-expression, communication, decision making, and problem solving.

Delta State University

Box C-1	Phone: (601) 846-4027
Cleveland, MS 38733	Fax: (601) 846-4313

Division(s): Continuing Education
Web Site(s): http://www.deltast.edu
E-mail: mataylor@dsu.deltast.edu

Class Titles: 45 courses in areas of Art, Music, English, Speech Communication, History, Social Sciences, Business, Education, all by correspondence.

Teaching Methods: *Other:* None.

On-Campus Requirements: None.

Tuition and Fees: *Undergraduate:* $91/credit for correspondence. *Graduate:* same as above. *Credit by:* semester.

Accreditation: Southern Association of Colleges and Schools.

Description: Delta State University (1924) was created as Delta State Teachers College. Delta State is a public institution, receiving primary funding from the state; however, it also seeks and receives support from private and federal sources, as well as tuition revenue. The university provides a comprehensive undergraduate curriculum, offering 15 bachelor's degrees in 45 majors. It also seeks to meet the need for advanced training in certain fields by providing programs of study for 9 master's degrees, the Educational Specialist degree and the Doctor of Education degree.

Denver Seminary

3401 South University Boulevard	Phone: (303) 761-2482
Englewood, CO 80110	Fax: (303) 761-8060

Division(s): Academic Dean
Web Site(s): http://www.gospelcom.net/densem/
E-mail: billk@densem.edu

Graduate Degree Programs:
Master of Arts
Master of Divinity

Certificate Programs: Theology, Leadership, Christian Studies

Teaching Methods: *Computers:* Internet, e-mail. *Other:* audiotapes, fax, correspondence, independent study, individual study.

Admission Requirements: *Graduate:* undergraduate degree.

On-Campus Requirements: one-third of degree must be taken on the Denver campus.

Tuition and Fees: *Graduate:* $199/credit; but $125/credit for distance students. *Application Fee:* $5 short application, $25 full application. *Other Costs:* $75–$125/course materials.

Credit by: semester.

Financial Aid: Federal Stafford Loan, Federal Perkins Loan, Federal PLUS Loan, Federal Pell Grant for regular students, but not for specials.

Accreditation: North Central Association of Colleges and Schools, Association of Theological Schools, Council for Accreditation of Counseling and Related Education Programs (MA Counseling—Licensure only).

Description: Denver Seminary (1950) is a graduate theological seminary in the evangelical Christian tradition educating men and women for a variety of ministries in this country and abroad. Our mission is "To glorify God in partnership with his church to equip leaders to know the truth, practice godliness and mobilize ministry." Started by a group of Baptist churches, the seminary now serves students from 50 Christian denominations. In the mid-1990s, the seminary began offering audio courses in a distance education mode. Plans are currently underway to expand the distance offerings and modes to capitalize on new technologies. The Distance Learning Institute has been founded as a subsidiary of Denver Seminary to expand the seminary's presence in this arena.

DePaul University

| 25 East Jackson | Phone: (312) 362-6314 |
| Chicago, IL 60604 | Fax: (312) 362-6309 |

Division(s): Distance Learning
Web Site(s): http://www.lifelearn.depaul.edu
E-mail: dlevin@wppost.depaul.edu

Certificate Programs: Prior Learning Assessment.

Class Titles: Nursing, Computer Science, Management, School for New Learning (a nontraditional degree program for adults).

Teaching Methods: *Computers:* Internet, real-time chat, electronic classroom, e-mail, CD-ROM, newsgroup, LISTSERV *TV:* videotape. *Other:* videoconferencing.

Credits Granted for: experiential learning, portfolio assessment, extrainstitutional learning, examination (CLEP, ACT-PEP, DANTES, GRE).

Admission Requirements: *Undergraduate:* age 24 for the School for New Learning.

On-Campus Requirements: None.

Tuition and Fees: *Undergraduate:* $275/credit. *Graduate:* $275/credit. *Credit by:* quarter.

Financial Aid: Federal Stafford Loan, Federal Perkins Loan, Federal PLUS Loan, Federal Pell Grant, Federal Work-Study, VA, Illinois resident programs.

Accreditation: North Central Association of Colleges and Schools.

Description: DePaul University (1898) is a comprehensive Catholic university serving more than 17,000 students. Through its 8 schools and colleges, DePaul is committed to offering students a wide range of programming in a manner that respects learners' need to achieve their personal goals. Through innovative programming such as its competence-based degree programs for adults and its distance learning programs, DePaul attempts to offer programming that is relevant to and convenient for working adults.

Diablo Valley College

| 321 Golf Club Road | Phone: (510) 685-1230 |
| Pleasant Hill, CA 94523 | Fax: (510) 687-2527 |

Division(s): All academic departments
Web Site(s): http://www.dvc.edu
E-mail: fmarce@dvc.edu

Undergraduate Degree Programs:
Associate of Arts in Liberal Arts

Certificate Programs: Administration of Justice, Alcohol and Drug Studies, Architecture Technology, Accounting, Office Professional, Real Estate, Real Estate—Salesperson's License (license only), Real Estate—Broker's License (license only), Retailing, Small Business Management, Computer and Information Science, Computer Hardware Support, Microcomputer Hardware Support, Construction and Building Inspection, Construction Supervision and Superintendency, Construction Management, Dental Assisting, Dental Hygiene, Dental Laboratory Technology, Early Childhood Assistant–Basic, Early Childhood Assistant–Children's Center Instruction, Early Childhood Assistant–Family Day Care Provider/Foster Care Provider, Electronic Service Technology, Advanced Electronic Technology, Civil Drafting, Mechanical Drafting, General Drafting, Materials Testing, Surveying, Environmental Hazardous Materials Technology, Facilities Maintenance Technology, Horticulture—Basic, Landscape Construction, Landscape Design, Landscape Maintenance, Hotel and Restaurant Management: Baking and Pastry, Culinary Arts, Restaurant Management, Hotel Administration; Library and Information Technology, Machine Technology, Management Studies, Multimedia, Music Industry Studies, Respiratory Therapy, TV Arts, Women's Programs and Services

Teaching Methods: *Computers:* Internet, real-time chat, electronic classroom, e-mail, CD-ROM, newsgroup, LISTSERV. *TV:* videotape. *Other:* videoconferencing, audioconferencing, audiotapes.

Credits Granted for: experiential learning, examination (CLEP, ACT-PEP, DANTES).

Admission Requirements: *Undergraduate:* open admission, 2 hours of study required for every hour of instruction.

On-Campus Requirements: None.

Tuition and Fees: *Undergraduate:* $12/unit. *Credit by:* semester.

Financial Aid: Federal Stafford Loan, Federal Perkins Loan, Federal PLUS Loan, Federal Pell Grant, Federal Work-Study, VA, CalWorks.

Accreditation: Western Association of Schools and Colleges.

Description: Diablo Valley College (1949), located in Contra Costa County, is a California community college. The college offers an Associate of Arts Degree in Liberal Arts and Certificates of Achievement in various occupational programs. The publicly supported college offers low-cost access to quality higher education. Diablo Valley serves 20,000 students of all ages each year and remains the college of choice for students seeking transfer to the University of California and the California State University systems.

Dickinson State University

291 Campus Drive	Phone: (701) 227-2129
Dickinson, ND 58601	Fax: (701) 227-2028

Division(s): Department of Extended Campus
Web Site(s): http://www.dsu.nodak.edu
E-mail: thupp@eagle.dsu.nodak.edu

Certificate Programs: Yes.

Class Titles: Internet, e-mail, LISTSERV.

Teaching Methods: *Computers:* videotape, cable program, satellite broadcasting, PBS. *TV:* videoconferencing, audio-conferencing, fax, correspondence, independent study, individual study, learning contracts. *Other:* experiential learning, portfolio assessment, extrainstitutional learning, examination (CLEP, ACT-PEP, DANTES, GRE).

Credits Granted for: contact school for complete admission requirements.

Admission Requirements: *Doctoral:* Contact school for complete admission requirements.

Tuition and Fees: *Undergraduate:* $91 resident tuition includes all fees. *Application Fee:* $25. *Software:* included in tuition ($50/semester). *Credit by:* semester.

Financial Aid: Federal Stafford Loan, Federal Perkins Loan, Federal PLUS Loan, Federal Pell Grant, Federal Work-Study, VA, North Dakota resident programs.

Accreditation: North Central Association of Schools and Colleges, National Council for Accreditation of Teacher Education, National League for Nursing.

Description: Dickinson State University (1918) is a regional 4-year institution within the North Dakota University System, whose primary role is to contribute to intellectual, social, economic, and cultural development, especially in West River, North Dakota. The university's mission is to provide high quality accessible programs; to promote excellence in teaching and learning; to support scholarly and creative activities; and to provide service relevant to the economy, health, and quality of life of the citizens of North Dakota.

Dixie College

225 South 700 East	Phone: (435) 652-7652
St. George, UT 84770	Fax: (435) 652-7873

Division(s): Continuing Education
Web Site(s): http://www.dixie.edu
E-mail: booth@dixie.edu

Undergraduate Degree Programs:
Associate of Arts
Associate of Science
Applied Associate of Science

Class Titles: English, Music, Math, Computer Science, Economics

Teaching Methods: *Computers:* Internet, real-time chat, electronic classroom, e-mail, CD-ROM, newsgroup, LIST-SERV. *TV:* videotape, cable program. *Other:* correspondence, independent study.

Credits Granted for: examination (CLEP).

Admission Requirements: *Undergraduate:* open admission, ACT scores for degree-seeking students. *Certificate:* same as undergraduate.

On-Campus Requirements: None.

Tuition and Fees: *Undergraduate:* $46/credit resident, $202/credit nonresident. Currently negotiating a single fee for all students for distance learning courses regardless of residency. *Application Fee:* $25. *Other Costs:* Some courses have additional fees. *Credit by:* semester.

Financial Aid: Federal Stafford Loan, Federal Perkins Loan, Federal PLUS Loan, Federal Pell Grant, Federal Work-Study, VA, Utah resident programs.

Accreditation: Northwest Association of Schools and Colleges.

Description: Dixie College (1911) is a state-supported, comprehensive community college located 300 miles south of Salt Lake City and 110 miles northeast of Las Vegas. The combination of a semitropical climate and cotton-raising efforts by the first colonizers in 1861 caused the early settlers to refer to the area as Utah's Dixie—hence the name

Dixie College. Dixie offers academic instruction for the completion of associate degree programs as well as certificates in vocational/technical programs. The college offered an Internet-based course in 1995 and has continued to add online courses and other distance learning options including cable TV and video-based courses.

Dodge City Community College

2501 North 14th Avenue	Phone: (316) 227-9325
Dodge City, KS 67801	Fax: (316) 227-9113

Division(s): None.
Web Site(s): http://www.dccc.cc.ks.us
E-mail: None.

Class Titles: Medical Terminology, Computer Science, Furniture Refinishing, Education, Emergency Medical Technician, English, History, Spanish, Math, Philosophy, Psychology, Speech, Zoology, Art, Geography, Government, Political Science, Mass Communications, Physical Education, Sociology, Child Care, French, Administration Assistant, Technology, Business, Developmental Studies, Electives, Health, Human Development, Social Work; also noncredit courses.

Teaching Methods: *Other:* live, full-motion interactive TV.

Credits Granted for: examination (CLEP).

Admission Requirements: *Undergraduate:* open admission.

On-Campus Requirements: 100% in ITV.

Tuition and Fees: *Undergraduate:* $30. *Other Costs:* $5/credit for incidental fees. *Credit by:* semester.

Financial Aid: Federal Stafford Loan, Federal Perkins Loan, Federal PLUS Loan, Federal Pell Grant, Federal Work-Study, VA.

Accreditation: North Central Association of Colleges and Schools.

Description: As a student, every day will be an opportunity for you to develop new skills, new knowledge, and new relationships. Working with competent caring faculty and staff, you can achieve your personal, academic, and career goals. What you accomplish will depend primarily on the effort you make, but there are great people here to work with you. We are committed to learning, personal growth, and community development.

Duquesne University

600 Forbes Avenue	Phone: (412) 396-4593
Pittsburgh, PA 15212	Fax: (412) 396-6577

Division(s): Center for Academic Technology
Web Site(s): http://www.duq.edu/DistanceLearning

E-mail: virtualcampus@duq.edu

Undergraduate Degree Programs:
Bachelor of Science in Nursing

Graduate Degree Programs:
Master of Science in Nursing
Master of Music Education
Master of Science Environmental Science Management
Master of Business Administration

Doctoral Degree Programs:
Doctor of Pharmacy
Doctor of Philosophy in Nursing

Certificate Programs: Online Teaching and Learning, Conflict Resolution and Peace Studies, Pastoral Ministry, Instructional Technology.

Class Titles: Thinking/Writing Across Curriculum, Social/Political/Economic Systems, History, Fine Arts Appreciation, Philosophical Questions, Foundations of Modern Science, Speech/Communication Disorders, Leadership/ Organizations, Multimedia, Action Research Seminar, Technology/Leadership, Epidemiology, Educators in Workplace, Instructional Techniques.

Teaching Methods: *Computers:* Internet, real-time chat, electronic classroom, e-mail, CD-ROM, newsgroup, LISTSERV. *Other:* videoconferencing, audioconferencing.

Credits Granted for: experiential learning, portfolio assessment, examination (CLEP).

Admission Requirements: *Graduate:* accredited RN certificate for BSN degree. *Doctoral:* accredited bachelor's degree. *Certificate:* accredited bachelor's degree.

On-Campus Requirements: vary according to program. Most graduate level programs require some on-campus residency.

Tuition and Fees: *Undergraduate:* $314–$596/credit. *Graduate:* $450–$569/credit. *Application Fee:* $40. *Software:* variable. *Other Costs:* $30/course technology fee. *Credit by:* semester.

Financial Aid: Federal Stafford Loan, Federal Perkins Loan, Federal PLUS Loan, Federal Pell Grant, Federal Work-Study, VA, Pennsylvania resident programs.

Accreditation: Middle States Association of Colleges and Schools.

Description: Duquesne University (1878) first opened its doors as the Pittsburgh Catholic College of the Holy Ghost with an enrollment of 40 students and a faculty of 7. Today Duquesne is a progressive educational facility that was recently named one of the top ten Catholic universities in the U.S. The university's academics are recognized both nationally and internationally. As a result of its worldwide academic excellence, Duquesne has signed agreements with institutions in Belgium, Germany, France, Spain, Ireland, England, China, Japan, and Italy, as well as the new Commonwealth of Independent States. To support these international collaborations and to extend the opportunity for access to the same rigorous Duquesne quality education to prospective students from more remote regional and national sites, Duquesne initiated distance learning activities in 1995. The programs and offerings expand each year.

Dutchess Community College

53 Pendell Road	Phone: (914) 431-8000
Poughkeepsie, NY 12601	Fax: (914) 431-8993

Division(s): Academic Affairs
Web Site(s): http://www.sunydutchess.edu
E-mail: registrar@www.sunydutchess.edu

Undergraduate Degree Programs:
Associate of Arts
Associate of Science
Associate of Applied Science

Teaching Methods: *Computers:* Internet, electronic classroom, e-mail, CD-ROM. *TV:* videotape, cable program, satellite broadcasting. *Other:* videoconferencing, audiotapes, fax, correspondence, independent study.

Credits Granted for: experiential learning, portfolio assessment, extrainstitutional learning, examination (CLEP, ACT-PEP, DANTES, GRE).

Admission Requirements: *Undergraduate:* high school diploma or GED.

On-Campus Requirements: None.

Tuition and Fees: *Undergraduate:* $89/credit resident, $178/credit nonresident. *Credit by:* semester.

Financial Aid: Federal Stafford Loan, Federal Perkins Loan, Federal PLUS Loan, Federal Pell Grant, Federal Work-Study, VA, New York resident programs.

Accreditation: Middle States Association of Colleges and Schools.

Description: Dutchess Community College (1958) began distance learning in the mid-1970s with telecourses. Approximately 8 courses are offered each semester. In the mid-1990s, the college began offering asynchronous courses and currently offers 5 different courses each semester utilizing this computer technology. Dutchess Community College is a founding member of the SUNY Learning Network.

D'Youville College

320 Porter Avenue	Phone: (716) 881-7607
Buffalo, NY 14201	Fax: (716) 881-7760

Division(s): None.
Web Site(s): http://www.dyc.edu
E-mail: disibira@dyc.edu

Class Titles: Education, Business, Occupational Therapy, Physical Therapy, Health Services Administration, Chemistry, Physics.

Teaching Methods: *Computers:* Internet, real-time chat, e-mail, CD-ROM, LISTSERV. *TV:* videotape, cable program. *Other:* audioconferencing, correspondence, independent study, individual study, learning contracts.

Credits Granted for: examination (CLEP, ACT-PEP, DANTES, GRE).

Admission Requirements: *Undergraduate:* SAT or ACT, 80 grade average, top 25% of class. *Graduate:* 30 transfer credits.

On-Campus Requirements: Yes. Normally 1st and last class plus exam on campus.

Tuition and Fees: *Undergraduate:* $285. *Graduate:* $357. *Credit by:* semester.

Financial Aid: Federal Stafford Loan, Federal Perkins Loan, Federal PLUS Loan, Federal Pell Grant, Federal Work-Study, VA, New York resident programs.

Accreditation: Middle States Association of Colleges and Schools; other programs accredited by their own governing bodies.

Description: D'Youville College (1908) is an independent, urban, coeducational college providing liberal arts and professional programs for 1,900 graduate and undergraduate students through day, evening, weekend, and summer sessions. D'Youville was founded by the Grey Nuns as the first college for women in western New York. It became coeducational in 1971, and a graduate program in Community Health Nursing was introduced in 1983. Since then, other graduate programs have been developed in Elementary Education, Secondary Education, Special Education, Health Services Administration, and Family Nurse Practitioner. Additionally 5-year programs leading to BS/MS degrees have been established in Dietetics, International Business, Nursing, Occupational Therapy, and Physical Therapy. An RN-BS/MS degree is also offered in Nursing.

East Carolina University

Erwin Building
Greenville, NC 27858

Phone: (800) 398-9275
(252) 328-6346
Fax: (252) 328-4350

Division(s): Continuing Studies
Web Site(s): http://www.dcs.ecu.edu/
E-mail: byrdj@mail.ecu.edu

Undergraduate Degree Programs:
Bachelor of Science in Business Education
Bachelor of Science in Industrial Technology

Graduate Degree Programs:
MSIT-Manufacturing
MSIT-Occupational Safety
MSIT-Environmental Planning and Management
MSIT-Digital Communication Technology
MAEd-Instructional Technology
MSA-School Administration

Doctoral Degree Programs:
PhD-Industrial Technology

Teaching Methods: *Computers:* Internet, real-time chat, electronic classroom, e-mail, LISTSERV. *Other:* videoconferencing, audioconferencing, independent study.

Credits Granted for: examination (CLEP).

Admission Requirements: *Undergraduate:* variable. *Graduate:* variable. *Doctoral:* variable.

On-Campus Requirements: no, MSA and some MAEd classes are limited to NC locations.

Tuition and Fees: *Undergraduate:* $95/credit. *Graduate:* $115/credit. *Doctoral:* $115/credit. *Application Fee:* $40 graduate, $35 undergraduate. *Software:* variable. *Credit by:* semester.

Financial Aid: Federal Stafford Loan, Federal Perkins Loan, Federal PLUS Loan, Federal Pell Grant, Federal Work-Study, VA, North Carolina resident programs.

Accreditation: Southern Association of Colleges and Schools.

Description: The state-supported, public East Carolina University (1907) is part of the 16-institution University of North Carolina. Since 1994, East Carolina has offered courses and degrees by distance learning to students residing in North Carolina, the U.S., and all over the world. In 1998 ECU was number 25 in *Yahoo Internet Life* magazine's top 100 most-wired schools, reflecting the institution's high degree of information technology development. Currently ECU offers several degree programs and 100 courses by distance learning, taught mostly on the Internet. East Carolina continues to develop new distance learning programs.

East Central College

1964 Prairie Dell Road
Union, MO 63084

Phone: (314) 583-5193
Fax: (314) 583-1897

Division(s): Media Services
Web Site(s): http://www.ecc.cc.mo.us
E-mail: haysdr@ecmail.ecc.cc.mo.us

Undergraduate Degree Programs:
Associate of Arts
Associate of Science
Associate of Applied Science

Certificate Programs: Administrative Assistant, Auto Technology, Legal Secretary, Medical Information Technology—Secretary or Transcription (all 2-year certificates); Accounting Clerk, Accounting (Evening), Administrative Assistant, Air Conditioning and Refrigeration Technology, Auto Technology, Banking, Building Construction Technology, Business Management/Marketing, Computer Information Systems, Criminal Justice, Dental Assisting, Electronics, EMT-Paramedic, Fire Technology, Floral Design/Flower Shop Management, Hospitality Management, Legal Assistant, Legal Secretary, Medical Information Technology—Secretary or Transcription, Welding (all one-year certificates).

Class Titles: American Adventure, Art of Western World, It's Strictly Business, Cycles of Life, Living with Health, Psychology—Study of Human Behavior, Taking Lead, Time to Grow, Marketing, Finite Math.

Teaching Methods: *TV:* videotape, cable program, PBS. *Other:* independent study, individual study.

Credits Granted for: portfolio assessment, examination (CLEP, ACT).

Admission Requirements: *Undergraduate:* high school transcript or GED scores, math/English assessment, proof of immunity to measles and rubella if born after 1956. *Certificate:* same as undergraduate.

On-Campus Requirements: orientation session at beginning of each telecourse.

Tuition and Fees: *Undergraduate:* $41/credit in-district, $55/credit out-of-district, $82/credit out-of-state. *Software:* variable. *Other Costs:* vary for field trips, tickets, supplies, usage fees for special courses. *Credit by:* semester.

Financial Aid: Federal Stafford Loan, Federal SEOG, Federal PLUS Loan, Federal Pell Grant, Federal Work-Study, VA, Missouri State Grants, A+ Program, college and community scholarships.

Accreditation: North Central Association of Colleges and Schools.

Description: East Central College (1968) was established to provide a postsecondary educational resource for the people of East Central Missouri. The college held its first classes in 1969 in temporary quarters. That same year a 114-acre campus site was purchased. An additional 92 acres were purchased in 1994 to accommodate expansion and growth. District voters have approved $14.7 million in bonds to build the administration building in 1971, the multipurpose building in 1973, the vocational-technical building in 1978, the classroom building in 1985 and the auditorium/classroom building in 1998. Since 1968, East Central College has helped 80,000 area residents prepare for jobs and careers, begin work on college degrees, and take part in enrichment programs and cultural activities.

East Central Community College

Broad Street	Phone: (601) 635-2111
Decatur, MS 39327	Fax: (601) 635-4060

Division(s): Adult and Continuing Education
Web Site(s): http://www.eccc.cc.ms.us
E-mail: rlee@eccc.cc.ms.us

Undergraduate Degree Programs:
Associate of Arts

Class Titles: Art, Government, Sociology, Nutrition, Psychology, Philosophy, Spanish.

Teaching Methods: *Computers:* electronic classroom. *TV:* PBS. *Other:* None.

Credits Granted for: examination (CLEP, DANTES).

Admission Requirements: *Undergraduate:* high school diploma or equivalent. *Certificate:* same as undergraduate.

On-Campus Requirements: None.

Tuition and Fees: *Undergraduate:* $50/credit. *Credit by:* semester.

Financial Aid: Federal Stafford Loan, Federal PLUS Loan, Federal Pell Grant, Federal Work-Study, VA, Mississippi resident programs.

Accreditation: Southern Association of Colleges and Schools.

Description: East Central Community College (1928) is a public 2-year college with a credit enrollment of more than 2,100 students. We offer university transfer curricula and terminal vocational/technical curricula. Our distance education program is several years old and is mainly via educational TV in Mississippi.

Eastern Kentucky University

521 Lancaster Avenue	Phone: (606) 622-2001
Richmond, KY 40475	Fax: (606) 622-1177

Division(s): Office of Extended Programs
Web Site(s): http://www.eku.edu
E-mail: sosnelso@acs.eku.edu

Class Titles: Accounting, Algebra, Art, Biology, Business, Computer Information Systems, Economics, Education, English, Environmental Health Science, Finance, Geography, Health, History, History of Science, Insurance, Library Science, Loss Prevention/Safety, Management, Marketing, Mass Communications, Music, Nursing, Occupational Therapy, Philosophy, Police Studies, Political Science, Psychology, Real Estate, Religion, Sociology, Spanish, Special Education, Theater, Trigonometry.

Teaching Methods: *Computers:* Internet, real-time chat, electronic classroom, e-mail, LISTSERV. *TV:* cable program, satellite broadcasting, PBS. *Other:* audiotapes, correspondence.

Credits Granted for: examination (CLEP, ACT-PEP, DANTES, GRE).

Admission Requirements: *Undergraduate:* high school diploma or GED, ACT, precollege curriculum. *Graduate:* bachelor's, GRE scores, letters of recommendation.

On-Campus Requirements: yes for television courses, no for correspondence and Web-based courses.

Tuition and Fees: *Undergraduate:* $92/credit *Graduate:* $133/credit. *Credit by:* semester.

Financial Aid: Federal Stafford Loan, Federal Perkins Loan, Federal PLUS Loan, Federal Pell Grant, Federal Work-Study, VA, Kentucky resident programs.

Accreditation: Southern Association of Colleges and Schools.

Description: Eastern Kentucky University (1906), originally founded as a teacher's college, is a regional, coeducational, public institution of higher education offering general and liberal arts program, preprofessional and professional training in education, and various other fields at the undergraduate and graduate levels. It currently enrolls 15,000 students and continues to prepare quality teachers for the elementary and secondary schools of the state. However, a strong liberal arts curriculum leading to appropriate degrees, together with preprofessional courses in several areas and graduate programs, enable Eastern to serve Kentucky as a regional university. For 60 years the university has offered distance learning through correspondence courses. In the past few years it has used modern technology to deliver telecourses through the statewide public TV network and its own cable-linked network. Web-based courses on the Internet were first offered in 1998.

Eastern Maine Technical College

1 Industrial Drive
East Millinochet, ME 04430

Phone: (207) 746-5741
Fax: (207) 746-9389

Division(s): Outreach Services Division
Web Site(s): http://www.emtc.org
E-mail: tconroy@maine.edu

Class Titles: Becoming Maine Guide, Catering as Small Business.

Teaching Methods: *TV:* TV. *Other:* videoconferencing.

Admission Requirements: *Undergraduate:* contact school for complete information.

On-Campus Requirements: None.

Tuition and Fees: *Undergraduate:* courses vary in price. *Credit by:* semester.

Financial Aid: Federal Stafford Loan, Federal Perkins Loan, Federal PLUS Loan, Federal Pell Grant, Federal Work-Study, VA, Maine resident programs.

Accreditation: New England Association of Schools and Colleges.

Description: Eastern Maine Technical College, formerly Eastern Maine Vocational Institute was established in 1966 by the Maine State Legislature, under the authority of the State Board of Education. Today the college offers one-year certificates, and one- and two-year diplomas and Associate degrees in 18 technologies. Programs of study are developed in cooperation with experts currently working in representative areas of technology.

Eastern Michigan University

611 West Cross Street
Ypsilanti, MI 48197

Phone: (734) 487-1081
Fax: (734) 487-6695

Division(s): Continuing Education
Web Site(s): http://emich.edu
E-mail: distance.education@emich.edu

Class Titles: English, Literature, Math, History, Sociology, Psychology, Management, Philosophy, Industrial Technology.

Teaching Methods: *Computers:* Internet, e-mail. *TV:* videotape. *Other:* audiotapes, fax, correspondence.

Credits Granted for: experiential learning, portfolio assessment, extrainstitutional learning, examination (CLEP, ACT-PEP, DANTES, GRE).

Admission Requirements: *Undergraduate:* open-admission.

On-Campus Requirements: None.

Tuition and Fees: *Undergraduate:* $99/credit. *Credit by:* semester.

Financial Aid: all classes must be prepaid by credit card, check, or employer voucher.

Accreditation: North Central Association of Colleges and Schools.

Description: Eastern Michigan University is a multipurpose university whose roots date back to 1849, when the State Legislature designated it as Michigan's first institution to educate teachers to serve the public schools. For its first 100 years, Michigan State Normal School, as EMU was conceived, certified thousands of teachers and developed the broad-based academic curricula that prepared it for its evolution to university status in 1959. Within the new university, 3 colleges emerged: the College of Education, the College of Arts and Sciences, and the Graduate School. The university expanded again in 1964 with a College of Business, in 1975 with a College of Health and Human Services, and in 1980 with a College of Technology. EMU's campus also extends into downtown Ypsilanti, where its new College of Business building is located. The rapid college matriculation experienced in the late 1960s peaked in 1970 at 19,965, stabilized at 18,500 plus in 1979, and then began its upward climb again, totaling 25,936 in the fall of 1991. Today's student body represents both full-time and part-time students, indicative of the national trend of mature adults returning to complete their college education and to prepare for new careers in a changing society. Program development has consistently adapted to the needs of entering and returning students as the world greets the new era of high technology. More opportunities are being offered to those seeking practical experience through business-industry internships and cooperative education experiences. Courses are provided in 180 fields of study for the ever-diversifying student body. EMU's perspective also has grown larger, not only in on-campus program developments but also in regular or special courses offered in 14 counties through its Office of Continuing Education and in cooperative agreements with nearby community colleges. The Office of International Studies plans spring/summer travel-study credit programs abroad and student-faculty exchanges with the University of Warwick, the Bulmershe College of Higher Education, and Nonington College, all in England. In addition, the Corporate Education Center provides a vital link between research theory and practical application as it is called upon by businesses, schools, industries, and agencies to lend its expertise. Eastern Michigan University today is known worldwide for its educational contributions. Its 125,000 graduates are scattered among many countries as well as coast-to-coast in the U.S., both strengthening and supporting the foundation that is the multipurpose university in Ypsilanti, Michigan.

Eastern New Mexico University

Station 9
Portales, NM 88130

Phone: (505) 562-2166
Fax: (505) 562-2168

Division(s): Extended Learning
Web Site(s): http://www.enmu.edu
E-mail: Renee.Neely@enmu.edu

Undergraduate Degree Programs:
Completion programs for:
Nursing
Business Administration
Communicative Disorders

Graduate Degree Programs:
Master of Science in:
Business Administration
Communicative Disorders
Bilingual Education
Special Education
English

Class Titles: Accounting, Bilingual Education, Business, Communicative Disorders, Computer Information Systems, Criminal Justice, Economics, Education Administration, Education Foundations, English, Finance, History, Management, Marketing, Nursing, Political Science, Psychology, Reading, Religion, Sociology, Spanish, Special Education.

Teaching Methods: *Computers:* Internet, real-time chat, e-mail, LISTSERV. *TV:* ITFS. *Other:* None.

Credits Granted for: examination.

Admission Requirements: *Undergraduate:* open-enrollment; 2.0 GPA, high school graduate or equivalent, ACT/SAT, transfer students in good standing, some program restrictions apply. *Graduate:* accredited bachelor's degree, 3.0 GPA (2.5 conditional), some program restrictions/examinations apply.

On-Campus Requirements: 2–3 times/semester for some programs.

Tuition and Fees: *Undergraduate:* $107/credit. *Graduate:* $115/credit. *Application Fee:* $15 undergraduate, $10 graduate. *Credit by:* semester.

Financial Aid: Federal Stafford Loan, Federal Perkins Loan, Federal PLUS Loan, Federal Pell Grant, Federal Work-Study, VA, New Mexico resident programs.

Accreditation: North Central Association of Colleges and Schools.

Description: Eastern New Mexico University's (1934) main campus of more than 400 acres is located in Portales on the eastern side of the state. The institution operated as a 2-year college from 1934 to 1940 when the third and fourth years of college were added. Graduate work leading to the master's degree was added in 1949. ENMU has a branch campus in Roswell and an instructional center in Ruidoso. ENMU has 30 years of experience in alternative delivery systems for education programs. In 1957 it began offering courses on-site in other communities, and in 1978 it began offering instruction through educational TV. More recently, a limited number of Internet courses have been developed. Programs are offered in a variety of liberal arts and professional areas.

Eastern Oregon University

1410 L Avenue
La Grande, OR 97850-2899

Phone: (541) 962-3378
Fax: (541) 962-3627

Division(s): Extended Programs
Web Site(s): http://www.eou.edu/dep
E-mail: dep@eou.edu

Undergraduate Degree Programs:
Associate of Science in Office Administration
Bachelor of Arts/Bachelor of Science in:
Liberal Studies
Business/Economics
Politics/Philosophy/Economics
Physical Education/Health
Fire Services Administration

Graduate Degree Programs:
Master of Teacher Education (not available outside Oregon)

Class Titles: 200 courses in a variety of subject areas including Business, Economics, English, Geography, Philosophy, Political Science, Psychology, Science, Writing.

Teaching Methods: *Computers:* Internet, real-time chat, electronic classroom, e-mail, CD-ROM, newsgroup, LISTSERV. *TV:* videotape, cable program, satellite broadcasting, PBS. *Other:* videoconferencing, audioconferencing, audiotapes, fax, correspondence, independent study, individual study.

Credits Granted for: experiential learning, portfolio assessment, agency-sponsored learning, examination (CLEP).

Admission Requirements: *Undergraduate:* high school diploma, SAT (recommended). *Graduate:* undergraduate diploma.

On-Campus Requirements: Master of Teacher Education and Fire Services Administration require some on-campus training.

Tuition and Fees: *Undergraduate:* $85/credit. *Graduate:* $132/credit. *Software:* $15. *Other Costs:* $50 admission fee, $4/credit tech fee, $25 computer conferencing account. *Credit by:* quarter.

Financial Aid: Federal Stafford Loan, Federal Perkins Loan,

Federal PLUS Loan, Federal Pell Grant, Federal Work-Study, VA, Oregon resident programs.

Accreditation: Northwest Association of Schools and Colleges.

Description: Eastern Oregon University (1929) has been involved in distance learning programs since 1978 as part of its mission to provide education to the eastern half of the state. Currently Eastern is Oregon's pilot provider to the Western Governors University and is involved in creating a model virtual institution through the Eastern Oregon Collaborative Colleges Center. Eastern does not charge out-of-state tuition to non-Oregon residents. The emphasis of the distance learning program is on helping students obtain degrees; however, students can take up to 8 quarter credits per term without being admitted to Eastern. Admission is required to pursue a degree at Eastern and to be eligible for financial aid.

Eastern Washington University

526 Fifth Street, MS-162	Phone: (509) 359-2268
Cheney, WA 99004	Fax: (509) 359-2220

Division(s): Distance and Extended Learning
Web Site(s): http://deo@mail.ewu.edu
E-mail: jtait@mail.ewu.edu

Class Titles: General education core requirement courses, Black Culture, African American History, Literature, Modern Government in American Context, Western Heritage: Origins to 18th Century, Western Heritage: 18th Century to Present, American Experience: Survey, Great World Views, Attention Deficit/Hyperactivity In Schools, Child Abuse: Recognition/Intervention Strategies, Accounting, Personnel Management, Creative Writing, Short Story Writing, Writing Poetry, Thematic Teaching, Literature of Bible, American Literature to Whitman, American Literature: Twain to Dreiser, 20th Century American Literature, Facts About HIV/AIDS, Adolescent Health, History/Government of Pacific Northwest, Women in American History, Finite Math, Sport Psychology, Physical Education, Time Management, Psychology, Abnormal Psychology, Social Psychology, Human Communication, Educating Able Learners, Computer Fundamentals with Program Concepts, Cultural Events Seminar, Internet in Classroom, Art in Humanities, Art Gallery Visits, New Europe, Effective Thinking/Writing

Teaching Methods: *Computers:* Internet, e-mail, LISTSERV. *TV:* videotape, cable program. *Other:* independent learning, correspondence.

Credits Granted for: portfolio assessment, examination (CLEP).

On-Campus Requirements: None.

Tuition and Fees: *Undergraduate:* $175/1–2 credits + $87/additional credit resident, $621/1–2 credits + $311/additional credit nonresident. *Graduate:* $280/1–2 credits + $140/additional credit resident, $852/1–2 credits + $426/additional credit nonresident. *Doctoral:* same as graduate. *Software:* student will need software to access WWW/Internet for online classes. *Other Costs:* $75/credit independent learning/correspondence/telecourse/cable, $75 tape rental fee (12 tapes) or $8/tape. *Credit by:* quarter.

Financial Aid: Federal Stafford Loan, Federal Perkins Loan, Federal PLUS Loan (if enrolled as a degree seeking student), Federal Pell Grant, Federal Work-Study, VA.

Accreditation: Northwest Association of Schools and Colleges.

Description: Eastern Washington University (1882) is a comprehensive regional university with educational facilities in Cheney and Spokane. The university serves a large traditional and nontraditional student population. EWU provides high-quality liberal arts and professional education and maintains a strong commitment to excellence in instruction. Distance education in the form of correspondence courses have been offered at EWU since the 1930s, telecourses for the past decade, and online Internet courses since 1998. In the fall of 1998, the university joined in a consortial arrangement with other state institutions to offer a distance learning degree in business. This consortium will allow the Washington state higher education institutions to join resources to provide multiple statewide degrees in coming years.

Edison Community College

8099 College Parkway	Phone: (941) 489-9455
Ft. Myers, FL 33919	Fax: (941) 489-9021

Division(s): Distance Learning
Web Site(s): http://www.edison.edu
E-mail: lbronder@edison.edu

Undergraduate Degree Programs:
General Education Degree

Class Titles: courses toward associate degrees in—Agriculture, Anthropology, Art, Astronomy, Biology, Business, Chemistry, Criminal Justice, Ecology, Economics, Education, Engineering, English, Geology, Pre-Medical Technology, Pre-Nursing, Pre-Physical Therapy, Pre-Occupational Therapy, Health/Wellness, History, Hospitality, Human Services, Humanities, Languages, Literature, Music, Philosophy, Physics, Political Science, Pre-Law, Pre-Medicine, Pre-Dentistry, Psychology, Radio/TV, Sociology, Speech, Theater Arts, Accounting, Technology, Business Administration/Management, Banking/Finance, Customer Service Technology,

Hospitality/Tourism Management, International Business, Marketing/Management, Small Business/Entrepreneurship, Cardiovascular Technology, Citrus Production Technology, Computer Programming Applications, Networking, Programming, Criminal Justice Technology, Management, Dental Hygiene, Drafting/Design Technology, CAD, Civil Engineering/Land Surveying, Electronics Engineering Technology, Emergency Medical Services Technology, Fire Science Technology, Golf Course Operations, Legal Assisting, Nursing RN, Nursing Advanced Placement Option, Radiologic Technology, Respirator Care; and toward certificates in Accounting Applications, Business Data Processing, Small Business Management, Emergency Medical Services-Basic, Emergency Medical Services-Paramedic, Fire Apparatus Operator, Fire Officer, Fire Safety Inspector, Special Fire Safety Inspector, Arson Investigator.

Teaching Methods: *Computers:* Internet, real-time chat, electronic classroom, e-mail. *TV:* videotape, satellite broadcasting, PBS. *Other:* videoconferencing, independent study, individual study, learning contracts.

Credits Granted for: experiential learning, portfolio assessment, extrainstitutional learning, examination (CLEP, ACT-PEP).

Admission Requirements: *Undergraduate:* Degree-Seeking Students: (1) Contact your high school for an official transcript and/or our GED office for official GED scores. Your social security number should be included on all documents. These must be on file in the Admissions Office before you register for your second term. (2) If you have taken the ACT or SAT in the last 2 years, please submit your scores to the Counseling Center. If you have not, you will need to take the FCELPT (placement test) at Edison. (3) Schedule an orientation and advising session at the Counseling Center. This session is required of all new degree-seeking students. (4) Arrange to have each college/university you have attended send an official transcript directly to Edison Admissions Office on the Lee County campus. All transcripts should include your Social Security Number. CLEP and AP scores are official transcripts and must be sent from The College Board. Nondegree Seeking Students: (1) Orientation is strongly recommended. (2) Students are limited to a maximum academic loan of 11 semester hours during the fall/spring sessions and 5 semester hours during the Summer A/B sessions. (3) Testing is required for most English and math courses. Nondegree-seeking students who are college graduates may be exempt from testing. Early admission, accelerated, and dual-enrollment high school students: (1) Part-time and full-time dual-enrollment high school students must complete testing before registering. (2) Submit completed/signed dual-enrollment forms indicating which courses are approved by the high school for dual enrollment or early admission and test scores. Early admission students must also submit a letter of recommendation for college-campus

early admission. (3) Accelerated students are admitted by letter of recommendation from their high school principal and counselor. The letter must specify the course(s) requested. Testing is required for most English and math courses. (4) Parents/guardians must co-sign the admissions applications if students are under age 18. *Certificate:* see undergraduate.

On-Campus Requirements: None.

Tuition and Fees: *Undergraduate:* $44/credit in-state, $165/credit out-of-state. *Other Costs:* $6–$25 health and science fees, $30 health technologies fee, $25–$50 applied music fees, $6–$11 telecourse fees, $5–$15 workforce programs fees, $30 visual arts fee, $15–$100 health and wellness fees, $10–$30 public services fees. All fees are subject to change if approved by the Florida Legislature. *Credit by:* semester.

Financial Aid: Federal Stafford Loan, Federal Perkins Loan, Federal PLUS Loan, Federal Pell Grant, Federal Work-Study, VA, Florida resident programs.

Accreditation: Southern Association of Colleges and Schools.

Description: Edison Community College (1962) celebrates 37 years of service to southwest Florida this year. Since the first students were admitted to Edison, the college has enrolled more than 150,000 students in credit courses. Associate in Art and Associate in Science degrees are offered at Edison as well as one-year certificate programs. Edison's 3 campuses—Lee County, Charlotte County, and Collier County—bring higher education within reach of the entire 5-county district. As a student-centered learning college, we recognize the importance of distance education. Our Department of Distance Learning has been active for 18 years. We continually expand educational opportunities for students in outlying areas of southwest Florida as well as nontraditional students in our immediate area. At this time a student may earn a General Education Degree completely through distance learning telecourses.

Edison Community College

1973 Edison Drive	Phone: (937) 778-8600
Piqua, OH 45356	Fax: (937) 778-1920

Division(s): Learning Information Systems
Web Site(s): http://www.edison.cc.oh.us
E-mail: eccreg@edison.cc.oh.us

Undergraduate Degree Programs:
Associate of:
   Arts
   Science
   Applied Science
   Applied Business
   Technical Study

Class Titles: English Composition, Literature, Humanities, Technical Writing, Economics, Psychology, Desktop Publishing, Archaeology, Art, Business, Sociology, Speech.

Teaching Methods: *Computers:* Internet, e-mail, CD-ROM. *TV:* videotape. *Other:* independent study, individual study, learning contracts.

Credits Granted for: experiential learning, portfolio assessment, extrainstitutional learning, examination (CLEP, ACT-PEP, DANTES, GRE).

Admission Requirements: *Undergraduate:* open admissions.

On-Campus Requirements: None.

Tuition and Fees: *Undergraduate:* $81/credit in-state, $162/credit out-of-state. *Application Fee:* $15. *Software:* variable. *Credit by:* semester.

Financial Aid: Federal Stafford Loan, Federal Perkins Loan, Federal PLUS Loan, Federal Pell Grant, Federal Work-Study, VA, Ohio resident programs.

Accreditation: North Central Association of Colleges and Schools.

Description: Edison Community College (1973) is a comprehensive community college serving western Ohio. Learning is our business. Because we are learner-centered, we provide multiple opportunities for students to succeed. Edison uses a combination of online, cassette, and flexibly scheduled courses to serve students with time and place barriers. Whether students are dealing with family, work, or community activities, Edison's schedule fits students' schedules. Students currently may receive telephone advising, and online advising is planned. Registration is possible in person, by phone, or by mail, and the bookstore will mail books to online students. Faculty, Learning Lab, and Student Development professionals will work with students to meet their other distance learning needs. Edison's courses transfer to 4-year colleges and universities.

El Camino College

16007 Crenshaw Boulevard	Phone: (310) 660-6453
Torrance, CA 90506	Fax: (310) 660-3513

Division(s): Instructional Services
Web Site(s): http://www.elcamino.cc.ca.us
E-mail: jshannon@admin.elcamino.cc.ca.us

Class Titles: courses toward Associate of Arts, Associate of Science, and toward Certificate of Completion and Certificate of Competence in a variety of fields: Anthropology, Astronomy, Child Development, Computer Information Systems, Contemporary Health, English, English as Second Language, History, Humanities, Music, Political Science, Psychology, Sociology, Japanese, Philosophy, Real Estate.

Teaching Methods: *Computers:* Internet, real-time chat, e-mail, LISTSERV. *TV:* videotape, cable program, PBS. *Other:* None.

Admission Requirements: *Undergraduate:* age 18. Students under age 18 may qualify if graduated from high school or passed the California High School Certificate of Proficiency Test. El Camino College may admit anyone in grades K–12 who, in the opinion of the college president, may benefit from instruction taken.

On-Campus Requirements: 6 on-campus meetings are required (1 hour, 50 minutes each meeting).

Tuition and Fees: *Undergraduate:* $12/unit. *Software:* Required for some online courses; cost varies. *Other Costs:* textbooks, cost varies. *Credit by:* semester.

Financial Aid: Federal Stafford Loan, Federal Pell Grant, Federal Work-Study, Federal Supplemental Educational Opportunity Grant, Federal Parents Loans, VA, Board of Governors Waiver, California Grants B and C, Aid for American Indians.

Accreditation: Western Association of Schools and Colleges.

Description: El Camino College (1947) has taken its mission most seriously since its founding more than a half-century ago. Recognizing the ever-changing population of the South Bay area along with the diversity of educational needs and advances in technology, the college continually refocuses its courses and programs to stay in the vanguard of America's higher education.

Elizabethtown Community College

600 College Street Road	Phone: (502) 769-2371
Elizabethtown, KY 42701	Fax: (502) 769-0736

Division(s): Distance Learning Programs
Web Site(s): http://www.uky.edu/CommunityColleges/Eli
E-mail: jburk1@pop.uky.edu
grsuth1@pop.uky.edu

Undergraduate Degree Programs:
Associate in Arts
Associate in Applied Science

Graduate Degree Programs:
Through the University of Kentucky and Western Kentucky University.

Class Titles: History, Psychology, Business, Sociology, Music, French.

Teaching Methods: *Computers:* Internet, e-mail, CD-ROM. *TV:* videotape, cable program, satellite broadcasting, PBS,

KET. *Other:* videoconferencing.

Credits Granted for: examination (CLEP, ACT-PEP, DANTES, GRE).

Admission Requirements: *Undergraduate:* open-admission.

On-Campus Requirements: exams usually administered on campus.

Tuition and Fees: *Undergraduate:* $45/credit resident, $135/credit nonresident. *Other Costs:* $4/credit technology fee, $20/TV course KET fee, $10/school year parking fee. *Credit by:* semester.

Financial Aid: Federal Stafford Loan, Federal Perkins Loan, Federal PLUS Loan, Federal Pell Grant, Federal Work-Study, VA, Kentucky resident programs.

Accreditation: Southern Association of Colleges and Schools.

Description: Elizabethtown Community College (1963) is one of 13 community colleges in the Kentucky Community and Technical College System. Formerly a branch of the University of Kentucky, the school was founded in 1963, offering transfer programs, associate degree programs, and community service and education. Those areas of focus remain today, along with the addition of local workforce training and development. ECC has partnered with the University of Kentucky and Kentucky Educational TV since the late 60s to provide distance learning to students in the area. Earlier access was achieved via microwave transmissions and open-air broadcasts. Today, students are served using cable, computers, interactive TV, satellite delivery, as well as the traditional open-air broadcasts. ECC is currently exploring all possible avenues to provide quality educational opportunities to all potential students.

Elmhurst College

190 Prospect Avenue	**Phone: (630) 617-3153**
Elmhurst, IL 60126-3296	**Fax: (630) 617-3739**

Division(s): Instructional Media
Web Site(s): http://www.elmhurst.edu
E-mail: bonniee@elmhurst.edu

Undergraduate Degree Programs:
Bachelor of Arts
Bachelor of Liberal Studies
Bachelor of Music
Bachelor of Science

Graduate Degree Programs:
Master of Education in Early Childhood Special Education
Master of Science in Computer Network Systems
Master of Arts in Industrial/Organizational Psychology
Master of Arts in Professional Writing and Culture

Master in Professional Accountancy

Certificate Programs: Church Music, Music Performance, Management, Teaching, Piano Pedagogy

Teaching Methods: *Computers:* Internet. *Other:* videoconferencing, independent study, individual study, learning contracts.

Credits Granted for: experiential learning, portfolio assessment, extrainstitutional learning, examination (CLEP, ACT-PEP, DANTES, GRE).

Admission Requirements: *Undergraduate:* ability to complete college-level work based on secondary-school and college/university performance (see catalog for specifics). *Graduate:* academic success at undergraduate level, recommendations, test scores, interview, resume, and statement of purpose. *Certificate:* nondegree; walk-in registration.

On-Campus Requirements: None.

Tuition and Fees: *Undergraduate:* $1,500/course, $375/semester hour. *Graduate:* $410/semester hour. *Application Fee:* $15. *Credit by:* course system (one full course equals 4 semester hours).

Financial Aid: Federal Stafford Loan, Federal Perkins Loan, Federal PLUS Loan, Federal Pell Grant, Federal Work-Study, VA, Illinois resident programs.

Accreditation: North Central Association of Colleges and Schools.

Description: Elmhurst College (1871) is a 4-year college offering undergraduate and graduate programs where the traditions of liberal arts education and preparation for professional life come together with a synergy that gives the college its identity and focus. Elmhurst is affiliated with the United Church of Christ. The college is located on a 38-acre arboretum campus 16 miles west of downtown Chicago. In 1995 Elmhurst used a grant from the Illinois Board of Higher Education to convert a classroom into a distance education classroom.

Embry-Riddle Aeronautical University

600 South Clyde-Morris Boulevard	**Phone: (800) 359-3728**
Daytona Beach, FL 32114-3900	**(800) 866-6271 (Graduate)**
	Fax: (904) 226-7627

Division(s): Center for Distance Learning
Web Site(s): http://www.ec.erau.edu
E-mail: holubj@cts.db.erau.edu (Undergraduate)
galloglyj@cts.db.erau.edu (Graduate)

Undergraduate Degree Programs:
Associate in Science in Aviation Business Administration
Associate of Science in Professional Aeronautics

Bachelor of Science in Professional Aeronautics
Bachelor of Science in Management of Technical Operations

Graduate Degree Programs:
Master in Aeronautical Science

Teaching Methods: *Computers:* Internet, real-time chat, electronic classroom, e-mail. *TV:* videotape. *Other:* independent study.

Credits Granted for: experiential learning, portfolio assessment, extrainstitutional learning, examination (CLEP, ACT-PEP, DANTES, GRE).

Admission Requirements: *Undergraduate:* must be out of high school 3 years and meet nontraditional status. *Graduate:* bachelor's degree.

On-Campus Requirements: None.

Tuition and Fees: *Undergraduate:* $134/credit. *Graduate:* $280/credit. *Application Fee:* $30. *Software:* $20 graduate program only. *Credit by:* semester.

Financial Aid: Federal Direct Stafford Loan, Federal Perkins Loan, Federal Direct PLUS Loan, Federal Pell Grant, Federal Work-Study, VA.

Accreditation: Southern Association of Colleges and Schools.

Description: Embry-Riddle Aeronautical University (1926) is an independent, nonsectarian, nonprofit, coeducational institution with a history dating back to the early days of aviation. Residential campuses in Daytona Beach, Florida, and in Prescott, Arizona, provide education in a traditional setting. The Extended Campus network of education centers throughout the U.S. and Europe and the Distance Learning Program serve civilian and military working adults around the world. Embry-Riddle established the Distance Learning Program in the early 1980s to meet the needs of working professionals. The university has served the public and private sectors of aviation through education for 70 years and is the only accredited not-for-profit university in the world totally oriented to aviation/aerospace. Alumni are employed in all facets of civilian and military aviation.

Emporia State University

1200 Commercial Street
Campus Box 4052
Emporia, KS 66801

Phone: (316) 341-5385
Fax: (316) 341-5744

Division(s): Office of Lifelong Learning
Web Site(s): http://www.emporia.edu/lifelong/home.htm
E-mail: lifelong@emporia.edu

Undergraduate Degree Programs:
Bachelor of General Studies

Graduate Degree Programs:
Master of Science in Health, Physical Education, and Recreation

Class Titles: Career/Technical Education, Business/Computer Curriculum Development, Personal Law, Employment Law, Using World Wide Web, Conflict Resolution, Shakespeare Online, Health/Wellness for Children, Activity Ideas for Elementary Physical Education, Internet for Math Educators, Internet Resources/Tools for Educators, Instructional Design, Computer Programming with PASCAL, Computer Networks/Internets, Research Problems in Earth Science, Remote Sensing, Information Retrieval/Repackaging, Technology Institutions/Policies/Operations, Information Needs of Seniors, Scenarios/Information Planning.

Teaching Methods: *Computers:* Internet, real-time chat, electronic classroom, e-mail, newsgroup, LISTSERV. *TV:* videotape. *Other:* videoconferencing, independent study, individual study.

Credits Granted for: examination (CLEP, CEEB).

Admission Requirements: *Undergraduate:* open-admission for in-state; 2.0 GPA, 16 ACT score for out-of-state. *Graduate:* 2.5 GPA, undergraduate degree, transcripts, GRE or GMAT scores.

On-Campus Requirements: None.

Tuition and Fees: *Undergraduate:* $76/credit. *Graduate:* $105/credit. *Application Fee:* $20 undergraduate, $30 graduate. *Other Costs:* $25 average media fee. *Credit by:* semester.

Financial Aid: Federal Stafford Loan, Federal Perkins Loan, Federal PLUS Loan, Federal Pell Grant, Federal Work-Study, VA, Kansas resident programs, scholarships, Supplemental Educational Opportunity Grant, Jones fund (Jones Institute).

Accreditation: North Central Association of Colleges and Schools.

Description: Emporia State University (1863) was established as the state's first school for training teachers. With an enrollment of 5,400 students, the university is a public, comprehensive university which confers bachelor, master, and specialist degrees in the College of Liberal Arts and Sciences, the School of Business, the School of Library and Information Management, and The Teachers College. ESU also offers a bachelor of general studies online degree completion program, international business degree, and a joint nursing degree program with Newman Memorial County Hospital. It offers the only doctoral degree in library and information management in the 18-state Great Plains region. ESU offers a wide array of courses via the Internet and desktop videoconferencing.

Essex Community College

7201 Rossville Boulevard   Phone: (410) 780-6715
Baltimore, MD 21237   Fax: (410) 686-9503

Division(s): Dean of Instruction, Office for Extended Learning
Web Site(s): http://www.essex.cc.md.us
E-mail: llb2@eccmain.essex.cc.md

Class Titles: French, Spanish, English, Political Science, Psychology, Math, Management, Veterinary, Technology, Sociology.

Teaching Methods: *Computers:* Internet, electronic classroom, e-mail, CD-ROM. *TV:* videotape, cable program, satellite broadcasting, PBS. *Other:* videoconferencing, audioconferencing, audiotapes, fax, correspondence, independent study, individual study, learning contracts.

Credits Granted for: experiential learning, portfolio assessment, extrainstitutional learning, examination (CLEP, ACT-PEP, DANTES, GRE).

Admission Requirements: *Undergraduate:* application; some programs have competitive criteria. Contact Admissions for more information.

On-Campus Requirements: None.

Tuition and Fees: *Undergraduate:* $60/credit in-county, $108/credit out-of-county, $166/credit out-of-state. *Application Fee:* $15. *Other Costs:* $3/credit activity fee, $4/credit technology fee. *Credit by:* semester.

Financial Aid: Federal Stafford Loan, Federal Perkins Loan, Federal PLUS Loan, Federal Pell Grant, Federal Work-Study, VA, Maryland resident programs.

Accreditation: Middle States Association of Colleges and Schools.

Description: Essex Community College (1957) is one of 3 colleges that currently comprise the Community Colleges of Baltimore County system. The Community Colleges of Baltimore County—Catonsville, Dundalk and Essex Community Colleges—are a system of 3 public colleges that anticipate and respond to the educational, training, and employment needs of Baltimore County and the region. Together, the colleges offer a broad array of transfer and career programs and services, including basic skills instruction, general education, arts and science courses, career education, employment skills training, student and community services, and economic development activities.

Everett Community College

801 Wetmore   Phone: (425) 388-9501
Everett, WA 98201   Fax: (425) 388-9144

Division(s): Library-Media Services
Web Site(s): http://www.evcc.ctc.edu
E-mail: sstier@ctc.edu

Undergraduate Degree Programs:
Associate in Arts and Sciences
Associate in Technical Arts

Certificate Programs: various

Class Titles: Computer Science, English, Spanish, Literature, Geology, Early Childhood Education, Nutrition, History, Music, Psychology

Teaching Methods: *Computers:* Internet, real-time chat, e-mail, newsgroup, LISTSERV. *TV:* telecourse. *Other:* correspondence.

Credits Granted for: experiential learning, portfolio assessment, extrainstitutional learning, examination (CLEP, ACT-PEP, DANTES, GRE).

Admission Requirements: *Undergraduate:* accredited high school graduate, age 18, or apply for options program. Skills assessment test if taking more than 7 credits.

On-Campus Requirements: None.

Tuition and Fees: *Undergraduate:* $99/credit resident, $384/credit nonresident. *Application Fee:* $20. *Other Costs:* telecourse tape rental, online services, lab fees. *Credit by:* quarter.

Financial Aid: Federal Stafford Loan, Federal Perkins Loan, Federal PLUS Loan, Federal Pell Grant, Federal Work-Study, VA, Washington resident programs.

Accreditation: Northwest Association of Schools and Colleges.

Description: Everett Community College (1941) has grown from modest beginnings in a converted elementary school to become an institution of stature in the community and within the Washington state community college system. Everett offers programs for students who intend to transfer to a college or university as well as a variety of occupational and professional-technical programs. The college has offered distance learning opportunities for many years to provide students with flexibility in scheduling and increased access to college programs.

Ferris State University

1301 South State Street, IRC-204
Big Rapids, MI 49307

Phone: (616) 592-3802
Fax: (616) 592-2785

Division(s): Extended Learning
Web Site(s): http://www.ferris.edu
E-mail: hardmanc@ferris.edu
perrinj@ferris.edu

Graduate Degree Programs:
Master of Science in Information Systems Management

Certificate Programs: Heating, Ventilating, and Air Conditioning; Optometry Professional Continuing Education, Summer Computer Institute.

Class Titles: Microcomputer Classroom Applications, World of Information Systems, Internet as Instructional Resource, Placing Course Materials on Internet, Teaching Structured Programming, Midrange Computing, Programming, Microcomputer Applications, Information Systems, Visual Basic, Internet.

Teaching Methods: *Computers:* Internet, real-time chat, electronic classroom, e-mail, CD-ROM. *TV:* interactive TV, videotape, cable program. *Other:* fax, correspondence, independent study, individual study, learning contracts.

Credits Granted for: experiential learning, portfolios, transfer credits, extrainstitutional learning, examination (CLEP, ACT-PEP, DANTES, GRE)—all depending on program.

Admission Requirements: *Undergraduate:* program-specific. *Graduate:* program-specific. *Certificate:* program-specific.

On-Campus Requirements: final 30 credits must be from Ferris State.

Tuition and Fees: *Undergraduate:* $165/credit part-time resident, $350/credit part-time nonresident, $3,998/academic year full-time resident, $8,350/academic year full-time nonresident. *Graduate:* $220/credit resident, $450/credit nonresident. *Other Costs:* books/supplies. *Credit by:* semester.

Financial Aid: Federal Stafford Loan, Federal Perkins Loan, Federal PLUS Loan, Federal Pell Grant, Federal Work-Study, VA, Michigan resident programs.

Accreditation: North Central Association of Colleges and Schools.

Description: Ferris State University (1884) is a national leader in providing opportunities for innovative teaching and learning in career-oriented, technological, and professional education. Distance education technologies and modes of delivery are used most frequently to support and enhance existing on-campus and off-campus course certificate and degree offerings.

Fielding Institute

2112 Santa Barbara Street
Santa Barbara, CA 93105

Phone: (800) 340-1099
Fax: (805) 687-9793

Division(s): None.
Web Site(s): http://www.fielding.edu
E-mail: admissions@fielding.edu

Graduate Degree Programs:
Master of Arts in Organizational Design and Effectiveness

Doctoral Degree Programs:
Doctorate in Clinical Psychology (PhD)
Doctorate in Human and Organization Development (PhD, EdD)
Doctorate in Educational Leadership and Change (EdD)

Certificate Programs: Neuropsychology

Teaching Methods: *Computers:* Internet, electronic classroom, e-mail, LISTSERV. *Other:* networked learning, fax, correspondence, independent study, individual study, learning contracts.

Credits Granted for: competency-based assessment.

Admission Requirements: *Doctoral:* accredited bachelor's degree, midcareer status, professional and academic experience in desired field, interest and ability in graduate-level research and writing, critical thinking skills. Applicants to Psychology Program must reside within the 48 contiguous states.

On-Campus Requirements: one-week orientation session; other face-to-face opportunities at various times and locations.

Tuition and Fees: *Graduate:* $12,250 Psychology and Human and Organizational Development, $11,550 Educational Leadership and Change, $12,750 Organizational Design and Effectiveness, $5,500 Neuropsychology (all annual tuitions). *Doctoral:* same as undergraduate. *Application Fee:* $75. *Other Costs:* variable. *Credit by:* semester.

Financial Aid: Federal Stafford Loan.

Accreditation: Western Association of Schools and Colleges, American Psychological Association.

Description: The Fielding Institute (1974) was founded on the principles of adult learning and the best practices of distance education. Its scholar-practitioner model serves midcareer professionals by offering opportunities for self-directed, mentored study with the flexibility of time and location that enables students to maintain commitments to family, work, and community. An active, geographically dispersed learning community is formed from dynamic scholarly and intellectual interactions by means of electronic communication combined with periodic face-to-face events at various locations.

Fitchburg State College

160 Pearl Street
Fitchburg, MA 01420-2697

Phone: (978) 665-3181
Fax: (978) 665-3658

Division(s): Graduate and Continuing Education
Web Site(s): http://www.fsc.edu/~distance
E-mail: dgce@fsc.edu

Undergraduate Degree Programs:
Bachelor of Business Administration
Bachelor of General Studies

Graduate Degree Programs:
Master of Education

Class Titles: Writing, Drugs/Alcohol, U.S. History, Managerial Accounting, Economics (micro/macro), Math. Note: over next 3 years FSC will make 120 credits available online.

Teaching Methods: *Computers:* Internet, electronic classroom, e-mail, CD-ROM, newsgroup, LISTSERV. *TV:* videotape, PBS. *Other:* None.

Credits Granted for: experiential learning, portfolio assessment, extrainstitutional learning, examination (CLEP, ACT-PEP, DANTES, GRE).

Admission Requirements: *Undergraduate:* high school diploma or GED, SAT/ACT, applicant essay, recommendation, for returning students—resume of work and academically related activities. *Graduate:* bachelor's degree in appropriate field, applicant essay, MAT or GRE score.

On-Campus Requirements: None.

Tuition and Fees: *Undergraduate:* $110/credit. *Graduate:* $140/credit. *Other Costs:* $62/semester in fees. *Credit by:* semester.

Financial Aid: Federal Stafford Loan, Federal Perkins Loan, Federal PLUS Loan, Federal Pell Grant, Federal Work-Study, Massachusetts State Grant, Massachusetts resident programs, Massachusetts No Interest Loan.

Accreditation: New England Association of Schools and Colleges.

Description: Fitchburg State College (1894) was initially formed as a teacher preparation institution. It currently offers undergraduate degree programs in 30 majors and specialties and graduate degrees in 20 areas, in addition to graduate and postgraduate certificate programs. Fitchburg State has been providing online distance learning courses for 2 years on both the graduate and undergraduate level.

Flathead Valley Community College

777 Grandview Drive
Kalispell, MT 59901

Phone: (406) 756-3822
Fax: (406) 756-3815

Division(s): Educational Services
Web Site(s): http://fvcc.cc.mt.us
E-mail: mstoltz@fvcc.cc.mt.us

Class Titles: World Regional Geography.

Teaching Methods: *TV:* TV broadcast, videotape. *Other:* None.

Credits Granted for: experiential learning, examination (CLEP), military credits, advanced placement, service learning, Tech Prep.

On-Campus Requirements: None.

Tuition and Fees: *Undergraduate:* $72/credit county resident, $97/credit Montana resident, $197/credit nonresident. *Other Costs:* $15 for equipment, $3/credit computer fee. *Credit by:* semester.

Financial Aid: Federal Stafford Loan, Federal Perkins Loan, Federal PLUS Loan, Federal Pell Grant, Federal Work-Study, VA, Montana resident programs.

Accreditation: Northwest Association of Schools and Colleges.

Description: Flathead Valley Community College (1967) is a comprehensive community college, providing college transfer, vocational, and community service classes for residents of northwestern Montana. In 1984–85 the college added the Glacier Institute program in Glacier Park and the Lincoln County Center, which provides classes to the residents of Lincoln County. In the fall of 1998 we began offering World Regional Geography via local TV broadcast. Students can also come into our instructional media center and view the tapes. We are planning to develop courses to be offered over the Internet.

Florence-Darlington Technical College

2715 West Lucas Street
Florence, SC 29501

Phone: (843) 661-8031
Fax: (843) 661-8358

Division(s): Distance Learning
Web Site(s): http://www.flo.tec.sc.us
E-mail: kirvenp@flo.tec.sc.us

Undergraduate Degree Programs:
Associate in Arts

Certificate Programs: Opticianry

Class Titles: Electricity for HVAC/R, Wiring Diagrams for HVAC/R, Special Projects in Business, Microcomputer

Applications, Composition, American Literature, English Literature, Creative Writing, Technical Communications, American History: Discovery to 1877, American History: 1877–Present, Algebra, College Algebra, Management, Marketing, Music Appreciation, Physical Science, American Government, Psychology, Human Growth/Development, Sociology, Public Speaking.

Teaching Methods: *Computers:* Internet, e-mail. *TV:* video-tape, satellite broadcasting. *Other:* videoconferencing, audioconferencing, audiotapes, fax, correspondence, independent study.

Credits Granted for: examination (CLEP, ACT-PEP, DANTES).

Admission Requirements: *Undergraduate:* age 18 or high school diploma or GED certificate, college entrance requirements, SAT/ACT or Computerized Placement Tests.

On-Campus Requirements: None.

Tuition and Fees: *Undergraduate:* $55/credit. *Application Fee:* $15. *Credit by:* semester.

Financial Aid: Federal Stafford Loan, Federal Perkins Loan, Federal PLUS Loan, Federal Pell Grant, Federal Work-Study, VA, South Carolina resident programs.

Accreditation: Southern Association of Colleges and Schools.

Description: Founded to attract industry to the state to provide employment for South Carolinians, the South Carolina Technical Education System began with legislation enacted in 1961 to create the South Carolina Advisory Committee for Technical Education. The committee identified strategic locations throughout the state for technical education training centers to train people for industrial employment. The Florence-Darlington Technical Education Center was established in 1963 and presently serves Florence, Darlington, and Marion counties. In 1974, the Florence-Darlington Technical Education Center received accreditation from the Southern Association of Colleges and Schools and changed its name to Florence-Darlington Technical College. The college's initial enrollment of 250 students now stands at 3,000 curriculum students. Its original campus of 10 acres has expanded to 100 acres with a modern complex of 7 major buildings totaling 300,000 square feet. The college also operates sites in Hartsville and Lake City and will soon open a large medical education complex in downtown Florence.

Florida Atlantic University

777 Glades Road	Phone: (561) 297-3690
Boca Raton, FL 33431	Fax: (561) 297-3668

Division(s): Information Resource Management/University Learning Resources
Web Site(s): http://www.fau.edu
E-mail: disted@fau.edu

Certificate Programs: Financial Planner, Human Resource Management, Conflict Resolution, Business Communications Using Computer Technology.

Class Titles: Quantitative Methods, Educational Research, Educational Statistics, Methods of Teaching, Introduction to Medical Technology, Pathophysiology, Medical Complex Child, Modes of Helping, Advanced Pharmacotherapeutics, Math/Science Fractals, Exploring Chemistry, Chemistry in Modern Life, Aging Considerations, Engineering Multimedia Systems, Engineering ISDN Systems, Engineering Wavelets, Engineering Software Testing, Introduction to Ocean Engineering.

Teaching Methods: *Computers:* Internet, ITFS microwave, electronic classrooms, e-mail, CD-ROM. *TV:* videotape, microwave. *Other:* videoconferencing, independent study.

Credits Granted for: experiential learning determined by assessment and examination (CLEP, etc.).

Admission Requirements: *Undergraduate:* see electronic catalog on Web site. *Graduate:* see electronic catalog on Web site. *Certificate:* program-specific; see electronic catalog on Web site.

On-Campus Requirements: program-specific; contact school.

Tuition and Fees: *Undergraduate:* $67/credit resident, $263/credit nonresident. *Graduate:* $132/credit resident, $4382/credit nonresident. *Credit by:* semester.

Financial Aid: contact school, call FICET Office at (954) 229-4187, or see Web site.

Accreditation: Southern Association of Colleges and Schools.

Description: Florida Atlantic University (1961) consists of 7 beautiful campuses distributed across southeastern Florida and serves a population of approximately 2.5 million residents. It offers a wide range of superior programs and courses in Palm Beach, Broward, Martin, St. Lucie, Indian River, and Okeechobee Counties. It is recognized as one of the "top 100 best college buys in the U.S." by an independent consumer magazine. It has been one of the leading distance learning providers for more than 15 years and is currently expanding that role to deliver a wider variety of courses through new technologies. Above all, FAU is student oriented and cares about the people it serves.

Florida Community College, Jacksonville

101 West State Street, Room 1195	Phone: (904) 633-8281
Jacksonville, FL 32202	Fax: (904) 633-8435

Division(s): Distance Learning Office
Web Site(s): http://www.fccj.org/DistanceLearning
E-mail: aguiler@fccj.org

Undergraduate Degree Programs:
Associate of Arts
Associate of Science

Class Titles: Accounting, Anthropology, Biological/Physical Sciences, Business, Computer Science, Economics, English, French, Geography, History, Humanities, Literature, Math, Nutrition, Political Science, Psychology, Religion, Speech, Sociology.

Teaching Methods: *Computers:* Internet, real-time chat, e-mail, CD-ROM, LISTSERV. *TV:* videotape, cable program. *Other:* None.

Credits Granted for: extrainstitutional learning, examination (CLEP, ACT-PEP, DANTES, GRE).

Admission Requirements: *Undergraduate:* application form, application fee, official transcripts, placement exams.

On-Campus Requirements: only for the Associate of Science degree, TV courses—24 hours maximum.

Tuition and Fees: *Undergraduate:* $44/credit in-state, $168/credit out-of-state. *Application Fee:* $25. *Other Costs:* variable. *Credit by:* semester.

Financial Aid: Federal Stafford Loan, Federal Perkins Loan, Federal PLUS Loan, Federal Pell Grant, Federal Work-Study, VA, Scholarships, Florida resident programs, Talent Grants.

Accreditation: Southern Association of Colleges and Schools.

Description: Florida Community College at Jacksonville (1966) is a public, 2-year comprehensive community college enrolling 94,000 students annually in a variety of academic, training, and enrichment courses and programs. FCCJ is the second largest community college in the state and the 10th largest in the nation. Starting in 1980 with 2 telecourses on educational access cable TV, the distance learning program at FCCJ now includes 55 credit courses via cable TV and the Internet, educational and informational TV series, and technological innovations. In 1997, FCCJ was the recipient of the annual Telecourse People Award for exemplary uses of telecourses in their educational programs and that has become a nationally recognized leader in providing students with increased educational opportunities. In 1998, a distance education faculty member received the Instructional Telecommunications Council Southeast Regional Award for providing quality academic instruction and service to distance learning students.

Florida State University

University Center, Suite 3500	Phone: (850) 644-8004
Tallahassee, FL 32306-2550	Fax: (850) 644-4952

Division(s): Center for Academic Support and Distance Learning

Web Site(s): http://www.idl.fsu.edu
E-mail: sfell@lsi.fsu.edu

Graduate Degree Programs:
Master of Information Studies
Master of Open and Distance Learning
Master of Speech Pathology and Communication Disorders

Certificate Programs: Financial Planning

Class Titles: Criminology, Music, Geography, Education, Nursing, Speech Pathology

Teaching Methods: *Computers:* Internet, real-time chat, electronic classroom, e-mail, CD-ROM, newsgroup, LISTSERV. *TV:* videotape, cable program, satellite broadcasting, PBS. *Other:* None.

Admission Requirements: *Undergraduate:* FTIC: Florida students with "B" average in all academic subjects grades 9-12, ACT of 24 (composite) or SAT I of 100 (verbal plus math). Non-Florida applicants ordinarily held to a higher standard. Transfer students: acceptable high school GPA, academic units, and test scores; 2.5 college GPA. Transfer AA degrees from Florida public institutions admitted for nonlimited access programs. *Graduate:* accredited bachelor's degree, good standing in the last higher-learning institution, and GRE. Some programs may have additional requirements. *Certificate:* variable.

On-Campus Requirements: variable.

Tuition and Fees: *Undergraduate:* $66/credit in-state, $263/credit out-of-state. *Graduate:* $131/credit in-state, $436/credit out-of-state. *Other Costs:* Technology and other fees may be assessed on a course-by-course basis for distance learning delivery. *Credit by:* semester.

Financial Aid: scholarships, federal and state assistance.

Accreditation: Southern Association of Colleges and Schools.

Description: Florida State University (1857) is the oldest site of continuous higher education in the state. It is a public university; one of 10 state universities. FSU has a statewide charter for excellence in undergraduate education and research. FSU has, for decades, delivered an outreach educational program at the master's level to other areas within the state by sending faculty members to other cities for face-to-face instruction and interaction with students. In the last 3 years, however, the university has been migrating many of its courses and degree programs to an interactive mode of delivery that does not require synchronous or face-to-face activities. The university has also partnered with The Open University of the United Kingdom to provide quality distance education programs to FSU students. In this regard, by the fall of 1999 FSU will add bachelor's degree programs in Computer Science and in Information Technology.

Floyd College

3175 Cedartown Highway	Phone: (706) 802-5000
Rome, GA 30161	Fax: (706) 295-6610

Division(s): Instructional Technology Support
Web Site(s): http://www.fc.peachnet.edu
E-mail: marsha_welch@fc.peachnet.edu

Class Titles: Chemistry, Geology, English Literature, English Composition, American History, Political Science, Pre-Calculus, Math I, American Sign Language Interpreter Training, Economics, Psychology, Medical Terminology, Clinical Calculations.

Teaching Methods: *Computers:* Internet, real-time chat, electronic classroom, e-mail, CD-ROM, LISTSERV, digital video. *TV:* videotape, cable program, satellite broadcasting. *Other:* videoconferencing.

Credits Granted for: examination (CLEP, ACT-PEP).

Admission Requirements: *Undergraduate:* traditional freshman: application, high school transcript, SAT/ACT, immunization for MMR, possible entrance exam, college prep curriculum recommended. Nontraditional freshman: application, high school diploma or GED, MMR immunization, entrance exam. Transfers: application, official transcripts and good standing from all colleges/universities, MMR immunization; might need: high school transcripts, SAT/ACT, entrance exam; must live in Georgia for one year prior to registration for resident rate (some waivers may be allowed). *Certificate:* high school transcript or GED.

On-Campus Requirements: No; however, students must compete 20 semester hours of Floyd College credit level course work in order to receive a degree.

Tuition and Fees: *Undergraduate:* $49/hour. *Software:* $300 technology fee for laptop lease required of all students. *Other Costs:* $23 student activity fee, $17 data card fee, $2 parking fee, various courses may have lab or course participation fees required. *Credit by:* semester.

Financial Aid: Federal Pell Grant, Work-Study, Stafford Loans, Supplemental Educational Opportunity Grant, Veterans' Assistance, Georgia Student Incentive Grant, Regents' Scholarship, HOPE Scholarships, Vocational Rehabilitation, Service Cancelable Loans.

Accreditation: Southern Association of Colleges and Schools.

Description: Floyd College (1970) has 3 ways to deliver courses at a distance, and each live telecourse airs 3 times—once live, once on tape the same evening, and once in a weekly block during the following weekend. During the live classes, students can call in to ask questions of the instructors. In addition to telecourses, Floyd College produces several weekly informational shows through GSAMS, a 2-way, audio/visual, interactive classroom. Students must attend all sessions at a GSAMS classroom. Eventual plans are for more than 300 classrooms to be on the GSAMS network, with up to 8 sites from around the state able to link simultaneously. College by Cassette courses are contained on a series of videotapes that can be checked out from the library. Students watch these videotaped lectures and travel to campus for reviews, exams, etc. In addition, the college operates 3 off-campus centers: Cartersville, Haralson County, and Acworth North Metro Technical Institute.

Fond du Lac Tribal and Community College

2101 14th Street	Phone: (218) 879-0800
Cloquet, MN 55720	(800) 657-3712
	Fax: (218) 879-0814

Division(s): Instructional Services—Interactive TV Network
Web Site(s): http://www.fdl.cc.mn.us
E-mail: admissions@asab.fdl.cc.mn.us

Undergraduate Degree Programs:
Associate in Arts
Associate in Science
Associate in Applied Science.

Certificate Programs: Anishinaabe, Child Development, Customer Service, Management Development, Microcomputer Software Specialist, Office Technology.

Class Titles: Anishinaabe Language, Federal Laws/American Indian, Survey of Bilingual American Indian Education, Chippewa of Lake Superior, Contemporary Indian Concerns, American Indian Studies, Chemical Dependency/Addiction, Chemical Dependency Counseling/Assessment, College Writing, American Indian Literature, American Indian History, Family Counseling, American Indian Philosophy, Transition to College.

Teaching Methods: *Computers:* Internet, electronic classroom. *TV:* Interactive TV Network, satellite broadcasting. *Other:* independent study, individual study by arrangement.

Credits Granted for: examination (CLEP, Advanced Placement Program), International Baccalaureate program, Evaluation of Educational Experiences in the Armed Services.

Admission Requirements: *Undergraduate:* open-door institution; all individuals, regardless of prior academic preparation, have the opportunity to advance their education at Fond du Lac Tribal and Community College. *Certificate:* same as undergraduate.

On-Campus Requirements: The Interactive TV Network is a collection of off-campus interactive classrooms. Broadcasts originate from the main campus but can be delivered to many locations.

Tuition and Fees: *Undergraduate:* $74/credit. *Application Fee:* $20. *Other Costs:* $35–$45 average textbook(s) cost/course. *Credit by:* semester.

Financial Aid: Federal Stafford Loan, Federal PLUS Loan, Federal Pell Grant, Federal Work-Study, VA, Minnesota State Grant for Minnesota residents, American Indian College Fund, Alliss Grant, Supplemental Educational Opportunity Grants, Child Care Grant.

Accreditation: North Central Association.

Description: When you walk in the door at Fond du Lac Tribal and Community College (1987), you feel like you're home. The campus is nestled among 60-foot-tall red pines, making you feel like you're in your own private forest. As part of the Minnesota State College and University system, FDLTCC awards 2-year AA, AS, and AAS degrees, plus fully transferrable degree program credits that meet the lower-division and general education requirements in most 4-year programs in the state. Several occupational and certificate options are available, including computer-related careers. As one of the newest and most technologically advanced campuses in Minnesota, the school boasts a student-computer ratio of only 6 to 1, with Internet and individual e-mail accounts available to all students. FDLTCC also offers continuing education for credit and noncredit courses, workshops, and seminars in business, communications, human services, public service, social science, arts, and recreation. FDLTCC will be adding on-campus housing and more classroom and office space. The U.S. Department of Agriculture has designated FDLTCC a Center of Excellence to provide education, employment, and research opportunities in soil science and related areas. Without a doubt, FDLTCC is a comfortable and affordable place to start a college program. With approximately 700 students, you won't get lost in the crowd.

Fort Peck Community College

| PO Box 398, Highway 2 | Phone: (406) 768-3231 |
| Poplar, MT 59255 | Fax: (406) 768-5475 |

Division(s): Community Services
Web Site(s): None.
E-mail: donnab@FPCC.CC.mt.us

Undergraduate Degree Programs:
Bachelor of Science in:
   Elementary Education
   Applied Business Management

Graduate Degree Programs:
Master of Learning Development

Certificate Programs: Automotive Mechanics, Bookkeeper/Accountant Technician, Building Traces, Computer Opera-

tor/Office Clerk, Foster Home Parenting, Hazardous Materials/Waste Technology, Paraprofessional Education, Pre-Nursing Preparation, Truck Driving/Heavy Equipment, Visual Fine Arts.

Class Titles: Elementary Education, Applied Business Management (cohort structured in modular format).

Teaching Methods: *Computers:* Internet, real-time chat, electronic classroom, e-mail, CD-ROM, newsgroup, LIST-SERV. *TV:* videotape, cable program, satellite broadcasting, PBS. *Other:* radio broadcast, videoconferencing, audioconferencing, audiographics, audiotapes, fax, correspondence, independent study, individual study, learning contracts, Picture Tel VisionNet.

Credits Granted for: experiential learning, portfolio assessment, extrainstitutional learning, examination (CLEP, ACT-PEP, DANTES, GRE).

On-Campus Requirements: None.

Tuition and Fees: *Undergraduate:* $260. *Graduate:* $147. *Application Fee:* $25. *Credit by:* semester.

Financial Aid: Federal Pell Grant, Federal Work-Study, VA, Montana resident programs.

Accreditation: Northwest Association of Schools and Colleges.

Description: Fort Peck Community College (1969) is a tribally-controlled institution chartered by the governments of the Fort Peck Assiniboine and Sioux tribes. Although FPCC does not deny anyone the opportunity for higher education, the school's primary purpose is to serve the Indian population of the Fort Peck Reservation. To preserve Indian culture, history, and beliefs and to perpetuate them among all Indian people are important functions of the college. Since many of the people choose not to leave their homeland, education must be brought to them. FPCC's programs enable students to earn transferrable college credits. The college also maintains occupational programs based on the needs of the local people and on local employment opportunities.

Fort Scott Community College

| 2108 South Horton | Phone: (316) 223-2700 |
| Fort Scott, KS 66701 | Fax: (316) 223-4927 |

Division(s): Deans of Instruction and Interactive Distance Learning Facilitator
Web Site(s): http://www.ftscott.cc.ks.us
E-mail: judyh@fsccax.ftscott.cc.ks.us

Class Titles: English, Sociology, Algebra, History, Psychology, Music Appreciation, varies with semester.

Teaching Methods: *TV:* interactive TV, videotape. *Other:* fax, telephone, U.S. postal services.

Admission Requirements: *Undergraduate:* open-enrollment; high school juniors/seniors with principal's permission.

On-Campus Requirements: None.

Tuition and Fees: *Undergraduate:* $31/credit resident, $87/credit nonresident, $109/credit international. *Other Costs:* $12/credit fees. *Credit by:* semester.

Financial Aid: Federal Stafford Loan, Federal Plus Loan, Federal Pell Grant, Federal Work-Study, VA, Single Parent, Supplemental Educational Opportunity Grants, endowed and institutional scholarships.

Accreditation: North Central Association of Colleges and Schools.

Description: Fort Scott Community College (1919) is the oldest community college in Kansas, founded as Fort Scott Junior College. In 1965, we became a separate institution and were renamed Fort Scott Community College. We moved to the present 147-acre site in 1967. Early in 1982, the college completed Arnold Arena. One side is an agricultural and rodeo arena with earth floor and welded pipe pens. The other half contains a basketball gym, weight training area, athletic dressing rooms, classrooms, and athletic offices. N. Jack Burris Hall was built in 1989 for the Environmental Water Technology program. It also houses our Interactive Distance Learning Lab where we teach ITV college courses to area high school students and other community colleges, including our own Paola, Kansas extension site. The IDL lab began operation in 1996. We also receive courses from Pittsburg State University, and the lab is used by the community for satellite downlinks and videoconferences. We can interact with 3 sites simultaneously through the use of video cameras, microphones, monitors, and asynchronous transmission over fiber optic cables.

Fox Valley Technical College

1825 North Bluemound Drive	Phone: (920) 735-5600
Appleton, WI 54913-2277	Fax: (920) 735-2582

Division(s): Instructional Support Services
Web Site(s): http://www.foxvalley.tec.wi.us
E-mail: admissions@foxvalley.tec.wi.us

Undergraduate Degree Programs:
More than 60 associate degree and technical diploma programs

Certificate Programs: more than 35 short-term certificate offerings

Teaching Methods: *Computers:* Internet, real-time chat, electronic classroom, e-mail, CD-ROM. *TV:* videotape, cable program, satellite broadcasting. *Other:* videoconferencing,

audioconferencing, fax, correspondence, independent study, individual study, learning contracts.

Credits Granted for: portfolio assessment, seminars/workshops, examination (CLEP, ACT-PEP, DANTES, GRE).

Admission Requirements: *Undergraduate:* for career programs—high school graduate or demonstrated ability to master subject matter, academic assessment or ACT scores. Some programs have additional requirements. High school students can begin applying in February of their junior year.

On-Campus Requirements: None.

Tuition and Fees: *Undergraduate:* $57/credit. *Application Fee:* $25. *Credit by:* semester.

Financial Aid: Federal Stafford Loan, Federal PLUS Loan, Federal Pell Grant, Federal Work-Study, VA, Wisconsin Higher Education Grant, Talent Incentive Program Grant, Indian Student Assistance, Fox Valley Technical College Foundation Scholarships.

Accreditation: North Central Association of Colleges and Schools.

Description: Established in 1967 as one of 16 districts in the Wisconsin Technical College System, the Fox Valley Technical College district encompasses a 5-county area in northeastern Wisconsin. Each year 46,000 people enroll in at least one course through FVTC. The college has been involved in distance learning since 1985 when the FVTC interactive TV network was established to connect all campuses and regional centers. In 1992, FVTC joined the Wisconsin Overlay Network for Distance Education Resources (WONDER), a consortium of Wisconsin Technical College and University of Wisconsin system schools. Area K–12 schools, FVTC, and the University of Wisconsin-Oshkosh formed the K–12 Schools/College Alliance for Distance Education (KSCADE) Network in 1997. With its ATM/MPEG technology, KSCADE is the largest, most technologically advanced network in the nation. In 1998 the Wisconsin Technical College Network was created for the 16 member schools. FVTC will have 25 courses available over the Internet in 1998–99.

Franciscan University of Steubenville

1235 University Boulevard	Phone: (740) 283-6517
Steubenville, OH 43952	(800) 466-8336
	Fax: (740) 284-7037

Division(s): Distance Learning
Web Site(s): http://gabriel.franuniv.edu/disted/distance.html
E-mail: lcampana@franuniv.edu

Graduate Degree Programs:
Master of Theological Studies proposed, but not yet available

Class Titles: Theology, Philosophy, History

Teaching Methods: *Other:* audiotapes with corresponding study guides.

Admission Requirements: *Undergraduate:* official copies of high school transcript and all college work. *Graduate:* undergraduate degree, official copies of college transcripts, 3 recommendations, and possible undergraduate prerequisites.

On-Campus Requirements: None.

Tuition and Fees: *Undergraduate:* $150/credit. *Graduate:* $150/credit. *Application Fee:* $20. *Other Costs:* $50 for media package audiotapes and study guide. Shipping and textbooks are extra. *Credit by:* Each course is worth 3 semester credits.

Accreditation: North Central Association of Colleges and Schools.

Description: Over the years, Franciscan University of Steubenville (1946) has received numerous requests for distance learning courses in Catholic theology, philosophy, and history. Under the persevering leadership of Fr. Michael Scanlan, TOR, president of the university, we have responded to those requests by establishing Franciscan University Distance Learning. In 1994 the Distance Learning department began recording graduate theology courses live in the classroom. Several undergraduate theology, philosophy, and history courses were also recorded to provide graduate students with the prerequisites necessary for successful graduate study. Undergraduate theology electives were also made available through the Distance Learning program. We are currently in the proposal process for a Master of Theological Studies earned primarily at a distance. We hope to have approval for this by the fall of 1999.

Franklin University

201 South Grant Avenue	Phone: (877) 341-6300 x6256
Columbus, OH 43215-5399	Fax: (614) 224-4025

Division(s): Distance Education
Web Site(s): http://www.alliance.franklin.edu
E-mail: alliance@franklin.edu

Undergraduate Degree Programs:
Completion degrees in:
    Business Administration
    Technical Administration
    Computer Science
    Management Information Systems
    Health Services Administration
Subsequent degrees in:
    Computer Science
    Management Information Systems

Teaching Methods: *Computers:* Internet, real-time chat, electronic classroom, e-mail, CD-ROM, newsgroup, LIST-SERV. *Other:* audioconferencing, fax.

Admission Requirements: *Undergraduate:* completion programs—accredited associate degree or 60 credit hours, 2.5 GPA, enrollment in an Alliance Partnership. Subsequent degree programs—accredited bachelor's degree.

On-Campus Requirements: students enrolled in a completion degree program will complete some of their required course work through a local Alliance Partner that may include a traditional classroom setting. Students enrolled in the subsequent degree programs can complete all of the required course work outside of the traditional classroom setting.

Tuition and Fees: *Undergraduate:* $206/credit, standard courses; $250/credit, Computer Science courses. *Credit by:* semester.

Financial Aid: Financial Aid, Federal Stafford Loan, Federal PLUS Loan, Federal Pell Grant, Federal Work-Study, VA, Federal Supplemental Educational Opportunity Grant, Franklin University Transfer Grant, Ohio resident programs, Lifetime Learning Credit.

Accreditation: North Central Association of Colleges and Schools.

Description: Franklin University (1902) has served 20,000 alumni since 1902. Annually, 5,000 students pursue programs leading to Bachelor of Science degrees. Franklin University is a student-centered, independent institution of lifelong higher education, working in partnership with central Ohio's business, Alliance Partnerships nationwide, and the professional business community in a global context. The university promotes excellence in teaching and the use of appropriate technology to deliver accessible, innovative, measurably effective learning, which integrates theory and develops the ability of students to become lifelong learners. To accomplish this goal, Franklin University's Distance Education program is designed and faculty are prepared to develop the following skills and abilities of students: problem finding and problem solving, active researcher, collaborative thinker/worker/team member, strategist, leader, communicator and critical thinker. Students will discover that online courses are interactive, inquiry-based, focused on real-world learning and taught by faculty who are experienced practitioners.

Front Range Community College

3645 West 1112th Avenue	Phone: (303) 404-5554
Westminster, CO 80030	Fax: (303) 404-5156

Division(s): Distance Learning
Web Site(s): http://frcc.cc.co.us
E-mail: gertrude@cccs.cccoese.edu

Undergraduate Degree Programs:
Associate

Certificate Programs: Paralegal.

Class Titles: Anthropology, Art, Biology, Business, Computer Science, Early Childhood Professions, English, Electronics, Geography, Geology, History, Humanities, Literature, Management, Marketing, Math, Paralegal, Philosophy, Physics, Political Science, Psychology, Speech, Sociology.

Teaching Methods: *Computers:* Internet, real-time chat, e-mail, CD-ROM, newsgroup, LISTSERV. *TV:* videotape, PBS. *Other:* audiotapes, independent study.

Credits Granted for: experiential learning, portfolio assessment, extrainstitutional learning, examination (CLEP, ACT-PEP, DANTES, GRE).

Admission Requirements: *Undergraduate:* assessment test, differential tuition for nonresident. *Certificate:* variable, certificate-specific.

On-Campus Requirements: lab/field trip for a few courses.

Tuition and Fees: *Undergraduate:* $55/credit. *Software:* variable. *Other Costs:* $9/semester registration fee, $5/credit college fee, $3/credit student fees, $45/telecourse, $5/audiocourse, $20/online course. *Credit by:* semester.

Financial Aid: Federal Stafford Loan, Federal PLUS Loan, Federal Pell Grant, Federal Work-Study, VA, Colorado resident programs.

Accreditation: North Central Association of Colleges and Schools.

Description: Front Range Community College (1968) is the largest 2-year college in Colorado, a member of the Colorado Community College and Occupational Education system. We offer traditional classes in a wide variety of programs and areas at our 4 campuses in Westminster, Boulder, Longmont, and Fort Collins, thus covering the northern Front Range area of the state from the northern suburbs of Denver to the Wyoming border. We began offering PBS-licensed and broadcast telecourses in the late 1980s, and these continue to constitute a substantial part of our distance learning offerings. Our first online, computer-based course was offered in 1994, and the online program has grown rapidly ever since. FRCC currently offers 60 technology-based courses in fall and spring semester, and 1,500 enrollments per term.

Frostburg State University

101 Braddock Road
Frostburg, MD 21532

Phone: (301) 687-4353
Fax: (301) 687-3025

Division(s): Instructional Technology Support Center

Web Site(s): http://www.fsu.umd.edu
E-mail: fsuweb@fre.fsu.umd.edu

Class Titles: Accounting, Business Administration, Criminal Justice, Education, Engineering, English, French, Political Science, Recreation

Teaching Methods: *Computers:* Internet, real-time chat, electronic classroom, e-mail. *TV:* videotape. *Other:* audiotapes, fax, independent study, extended classroom using compressed and full motion video.

Credits Granted for: pass-by-examination.

Admission Requirements: *Undergraduate:* see Web site: (http://www.fsu.umd.edu/ungrad/unadmiss.htm). *Graduate:* see Web site: (http://www.fsu.umd.edu/grad/gradmiss.htm).

On-Campus Requirements: Combination of distance learning and traditional to complete degrees.

Tuition and Fees: *Undergraduate:* $131/credit in-state part-time, $226 out-of-state part-time, $1,546 full-time in-state, $3,676 full-time out-of-state. *Graduate:* $170/credit in-state, $197/credit out-of-state. *Application Fee:* $30 graduate application. *Other Costs:* vary for athletic fee, Student Union operating fee, auxiliary facilities fee, transportation fee, and optional activity fee depending on status as full/part-time, in-state/out-of-state, undergraduate/graduate. *Credit by:* semester.

Financial Aid: Federal Stafford Loan, Federal Perkins Loan, Federal PLUS Loan, Federal Pell Grant, Federal Work-Study, VA, Maryland resident programs.

Accreditation: Middle States Association of Colleges and Schools, Council on Social Work Education, Interorganizational Board of Master's in Psychology Programs.

Description: Frostburg State University (1898) is a comprehensive constituent of the University System of Maryland. Originally established to train elementary school teachers, Frostburg now offers 30 undergraduate programs to 4,000 undergraduates and 11 master's degree programs to 1,000 graduate students. FSU consists of a main campus in Frostburg and off-campus centers in Hagerstown and Frederick. A recently established program site in Baltimore provides a master's degree in Parks and Recreation Resource Management through traditional classes and distance education. Since 1970, FSU has sponsored off-campus courses and programs at various sites in the state. Distance education emerged in 1995 when faculty applied technology that linked classrooms at different locations. In 1998, FSU added to its array of alternative delivery mechanisms through online courses.

Fuller Theological Seminary

| 135 North Oakland Avenue | Phone: (626) 584-5266 |
| Pasadena, CA 91182 | Fax: (626) 584-5313 ATTN: IDL |

Division(s): Continuing and Extended Education
Web Site(s): http://www.fuller.edu
E-mail: idl@fuller.edu

Certificate Programs: Christian Studies, Youth Ministry.

Class Titles: courses toward degrees in our School of Theology MA and MDiv programs and our School of World Mission MA and ThM programs.

Teaching Methods: *Computers:* e-mail, LISTSERV. *TV:* videotape. *Other:* audiotapes, fax, correspondence, independent study, individual study.

Credits Granted for: accredited graduate level credit.

Admission Requirements: *Graduate:* accredited BA degree or equivalent. Admission is granted to a specific program, not to Fuller Seminary or its schools at large. Fuller depends on factors beyond applicant's academic record, including theological development, Christian experience, spiritual growth, call to service, and gifts for ministry. Men and women of God are qualified for Christian ministry by faith, moral character, experience, and academic achievement. *Doctoral:* see graduate requirements; possibly GRE. *Certificate:* see graduate requirements; see Fuller's catalog for complete details.

On-Campus Requirements: consult Fuller's catalog.

Tuition and Fees: *Graduate:* consult catalog or contact Admissions Department, (800) 238-5537. *Doctoral:* see graduate. *Credit by:* quarter.

Financial Aid: Federal Stafford Loan, Federal Perkins Loan, Federal Work-Study, VA, California resident programs.

Accreditation: Western Association of Schools and Colleges, ATS.

Description: Fuller Theological Seminary resulted from the dreams of 2 well-known evangelical leaders, Charles E. Fuller, famous radio evangelist, and Harold John Ockenga, pastor of Boston's Park Street Church. As the result of announcements made on the "Old Fashioned Revival Hour," students enrolled in the first class in 1947. FTS, embracing the Schools of Theology, Psychology, and World Mission, is an evangelical, multidenominational, international, and multiethnic community dedicated to preparing men and women for the manifold ministries of Christ and His Church. Fuller has been involved in distance learning since the mid-1970s. The roots of its Individualized Distance Learning program come from the School of World Mission's heart for "bringing the classroom" to those on the mission field. Fuller now offers courses to students in SWM and the School of Theology, enabling students to complete some of their degree program before coming to our Pasadena or Extended Education sites.

Fullerton College

| 321 East Chapman Avenue | Phone: (714) 992-7487 |
| Fullerton, CA 92832-2095 | Fax: (714) 879-3972 |

Division(s): Media Services/Distance Education
Web Site(s): http://www.fullcoll.edu
E-mail: admiss.reg@fullcoll.edu

Class Titles: History, Oceanography, Business, Psychology, Stress Management, Sociology, Cinema, Geography, English as Second Language.

Teaching Methods: *Computers:* Internet, real-time chat, electronic classroom, e-mail, CD-ROM, newsgroup, LISTSERV. *TV:* videotape, cable program, PBS. *Other:* videoconferencing, audiotapes, fax, correspondence, independent study, individual study, VHS tapes.

Credits Granted for: examination.

Admission Requirements: *Undergraduate:* please see catalog on Web site.

On-Campus Requirements: orientation and testing (usually).

Tuition and Fees: *Undergraduate:* $12/credit (maximum $60/semester). *Credit by:* semester.

Financial Aid: Federal Stafford Loan, Federal Perkins Loan, Federal PLUS Loan, Federal Pell Grant, Federal Work-Study, California resident programs.

Accreditation: Western Association of Schools and Colleges.

Description: Fullerton College (1913) is a Southern California community college with a history as the oldest existing college in the state. Fullerton began distance education in 1981 with the cablecasting of telecourses to the North Orange County area. We now serve 165,000 households in 8 cities.

Fuqua School of Business, Duke University

One Towerview Drive	
Box 90127	Phone: (919) 660-7804
Durham, NC 27708-0127	Fax: (919) 660-8044

Division(s): Executive MBA Programs
Web Site(s): http://www.fuqua.duke.edu
E-mail: fuqua-gemba@mail.duke.edu

Graduate Degree Programs:
Master of Business Administration, Global Executive

Teaching Methods: *Computers:* Internet, real-time chat, e-mail, CD-ROM, newsgroup. *Other:* fax, correspondence.

Admission Requirements: *Graduate:* 10 years of professional experience with international managerial responsibilities, undergraduate degree, achievement in quantitative areas, proficiency in written and spoken English.

On-Campus Requirements: students spend a total of 11 weeks in residency in the U.S. Europe, Asia, Latin America.

Tuition and Fees: *Graduate:* $25,250/year full-time in- or out-of-state. *Application Fee:* $150. *Other Costs:* students are responsible for their travel cost to the residencies. *Credit by:* terms of 17 weeks each.

Financial Aid: Federal Stafford Loan

Accreditation: American Association of Collegiate Schools of Business.

Description: Duke University's Fuqua School of Business (1996) is an established leader among MBA and executive education programs in the world. Founded in 1969 as the Duke Graduate School of Business Administration, the school was renamed in honor of entrepreneur and philanthropist J. B. Fuqua in 1980. As a front-runner in curricular innovation and integration of global issues throughout its programs, Fuqua is widely recognized as a worldwide leader in management education and research. Today, more than one-quarter of the school's MBA student body is international and more than half of Fuqua's faculty have taught outside the U.S. Fuqua launched its groundbreaking Global Executive MBA program in May 1996. GEMBA was created expressly to meet the needs of high-potential managers of globally oriented corporations. GEMBA's unique format, which combines residential classroom sessions on 4 continents with distance education via advanced Internet-based technologies, allows students to earn a world-class MBA degree while living and working anywhere in the world.

Galveston College

4015 Avenue Q	Phone: (800) 305-6226
Galveston, TX 77550	Fax: (409) 762-9367

Division(s): Distance Education
Web Site(s): http://www.gc.edu
E-mail: syoung@gc.edu

Undergraduate Degree Programs:
Associate of Arts
Associate of Applied Sciences

Class Titles: Anthropology, Economics, English, Government, History, Humanities, Nutrition, Psychology, Sociology, Statistics

Teaching Methods: *Computers:* Internet, real-time chat, electronic classroom, e-mail. *TV:* videotape, PBS. *Other:* independent study, individual study, learning contracts.

Credits Granted for: examination (CLEP).

Admission Requirements: *Undergraduate:* high school graduate or GED.

On-Campus Requirements: None.

Tuition and Fees: *Undergraduate:* $115/3-credit course. *Application Fee:* included. *Software:* $30/course for videotapes. *Other Costs:* $50–$80 for books. *Credit by:* semester.

Financial Aid: Federal Stafford Loan, Federal Perkins Loan, Federal PLUS Loan, Federal Pell Grant, Federal Work-Study, VA, Texas resident programs.

Accreditation: Southern Association of Colleges and Schools.

Description: Galveston College (1967) is a 2-year, comprehensive community college located on 32-mile-long Galveston Island 45 miles south of Houston. It is part of the 55-college network of publicly supported community colleges blanketing the state of Texas. Distance learning programs have been offered by Galveston College since 1987. All of the distance education courses entail transferrable college credit.

Garland County Community College

101 College Drive	Phone: (501) 760-4155
Hot Springs, AR 71913-9174	Fax: (501) 760-4100

Division(s): Community Services/Continuing Education
Web Site(s): http://www.gccc.cc.ar.us
http://www.educationtogo.com/garland
E-mail: rjeffery@admin.gccc.cc.ar.us
ahoffman@admin.gccc.cc.ar.us

Class Titles: a variety of computer classes and supervisory management classes for noncredit. For-credit telecourses: Small Business Management, Geography, Health/Safety, Psychology, Sociology, History, Literature, Art Appreciation, others. Schedule changes each semester, and we offer more telecourses each semester.

Teaching Methods: *Computers:* Internet, real-time chat, electronic classroom, e-mail, CD-ROM, newsgroup, LISTSERV. *TV:* videotape, cable program, satellite broadcasting, PBS. *Other:* videoconferencing, audioconferencing, audiotapes, fax, correspondence, independent study, individual study, learning contracts.

Credits Granted for: experiential learning (corporate or professional association seminars/workshops), portfolio assessment, examination (CLEP, ACT-PEP, DANTES, GRE).

Admission Requirements: *Undergraduate:* application, high school transcript or GED, proof of immunization, ASSET/ACT/SAT. *Certificate:* same as undergraduate.

On-Campus Requirements: 18 hours.

Tuition and Fees: *Undergraduate:* contact school or visit Web site (costs are per class and include books, etc.). *Credit by:* semester.

Financial Aid: Federal Stafford Loan, Federal Perkins Loan, Federal PLUS Loan, Federal Pell Grant, Federal Work-Study, VA, Arkansas resident programs, Emergency Secondary Education Loan Program, Garland County Community College Scholarships, JTPA, Single Parent/Homemaker Program.

Accreditation: North Central Association of Colleges and Schools, National League for Nursing Accrediting Commission, Commission on the Accreditation of Allied Health Educational Programs, Joint Review Committee in Education on Radiologic Technology, Association of Collegiate Business Schools and Programs, National Accrediting Agency for Clinical Laboratory Sciences.

Description: Garland County Community College (1973) was established as a public 2-year college to provide postsecondary educational opportunities to the citizens of Garland County and surrounding areas. The college is located in Mid-American Park, just outside the city limits of Hot Springs, America's oldest national park. The average enrollment is 1,800 per semester at this commuter college. While the majority of our students are Garland County residents, many students from surrounding counties also enroll. A profile shows that 44.4% of all students attend full time. Some 65% are female, 7.13% are minority, and 5.4% are dual-enrolled high school/college students. A majority (61.9%) receive some form of financial aid. The average age of our graduates is 30. Since 80% of our students work and attend college, many of them find the early morning, evening, and weekend classes an advantage. As an integral part of this community GCCC recognizes the necessity of providing services to meet the needs of the area's business, industry, and schools. Distance Education at GCCC is relatively new, but our goal is to work toward providing courses any time and any place to meet the needs of our students.

Gavilan College

5055 Santa Teresa Boulevard	Phone: (408) 848-4705
Gilroy, CA 95020-9578	Fax: (408) 848-3077

Division(s): Learning Center
Web Site(s): http://gavilan.cc.ca.us
E-mail: vestrada@gavilan.cc.ca.us

Class Titles: Telecourses: Child Development, English, Humanities, Archaeology, Marketing, Anthropology.

Teaching Methods: *Computers:* Internet, real-time chat, electronic classroom, e-mail, CD-ROM, newsgroup, LISTSERV (in development). *TV:* videotape, cable program. *Other:* audioconferencing, videoconferencing, audiotapes, fax, independent study, individual study, learning contracts.

Credits Granted for: examination (CLEP, ACT-PEP, DANTES, GRE).

Admission Requirements: *Undergraduate:* age 18, high school graduate, or able to profit from instruction. *Certificate:* varies.

On-Campus Requirements: Telecourse orientations, exams.

Tuition and Fees: *Undergraduate:* $12/credit. *Other Costs:* $10 Health Fee, $5 Campus Center Use. *Credit by:* semester.

Financial Aid: Federal Pell Grant, Federal Work-Study, VA.

Accreditation: Western Association of Schools and Colleges.

Description: Gavilan College is a small community college founded in 1919. It has offered telecourses each semester since 1994, with online courses/programs coming soon. San Jose State University also conducts some upper division and graduate courses, especially in education, by microwave through the Gavilan campus.

Gemological Institute of America

5345 Armada Drive	Phone: (760) 603-4000
Carlsbad, CA 92008	(800) 421-7250 x4100
	Fax: (760) 603-4080

Division(s): Distance Education
Web Site(s): http://www.gia.edu
E-mail: selliott@gia.edu

Certificate Programs: Diamonds, Diamond Grading, Colored Stones, Colored Stone Grading, Gem Identification, Diamond Essentials, Fine Jewelry Sales, Advanced Fine Jewelry Sales, Insurance Replacement Appraisal, Gold and Precious Metals, Pearl and Bead Stringing, Jewelry Display, Counter Sketching, Gemologist Diploma, Graduate Gemologist Diploma.

Teaching Methods: *Computers:* Internet, real-time chat, e-mail, CD-ROM, newsgroup. *TV:* videotape. *Other:* individual study.

On-Campus Requirements: 3 extension classes to earn Graduate Gemologist Diploma—these classes travel to various cities throughout the U.S. annually.

Tuition and Fees: *Undergraduate:* [program tuitions] $3,150 or $3,750 w/audiotapes Gemologist Program (5 courses), $1,195 or $1,550 w/audiotapes Diamonds Program (2 courses), $2,095 or $2,395 w/audiotapes Colored Stones Program (3 courses); [course tuitions] $655 or $845 w/audiotapes Diamonds, $755 or $945 w/audiotapes Diamond Grading, $755 or $1,055 w/audiotapes Colored Stones, $655 Colored Stones Grading, $955 Gem Identification, $525 Pearl and Bead Stringing, $525 Counter Sketching, $349 Diamond Essentials, $245 or $295 w/audiotapes Fine Jewelry Sales, $425 Advanced Fine Jewelry Sales, $425 Jewelry Display,

$325 or $425 w/audiotapes Gold and Precious Metals, $525 Insurance Replacement Appraisal.

Accreditation: Distance Education Training Council.

Description: Gemological Institute of America (1931) is the leading education, research, and information source for the international gem and jewelry industry. Since its founding, GIA has provided gemological and jewelry manufacturing arts training to 200,000 jewelers with classes and programs offered at its 12 campuses around the world, through distance education programs, and through traveling extension classes. GIA's mission is to ensure the public trust by educating and serving the jewelry industry worldwide.

Genesee Community College

College Road	Phone: (716) 343-0055 x6595
Batavia, NY 14020-9704	Fax: (716) 343-0433

Division(s): Learning Resources
Web Site(s): http://www.sunygenesee.cc.ny.us
E-mail: jwcianfrini@sunygenesee.cc.ny.us

Class Titles: Accounting, Anthropology, Art, Biology, Business, Marketing, Management, Sales, Writing, English, Creative Writing, Technical Writing, Cinema, History, Western Civilization, Personal Health, Gerontology, Literature, Algebra, Medical Terminology, Paralegal, Psychology, Sociology, Physics, Coaching, Retailing.

Teaching Methods: *Computers:* Internet, electronic classroom, e-mail. *TV:* videotape, cable program. *Other:* videoconferencing, audioconferencing, audiotapes, fax, correspondence, individual study, learning contracts.

Admission Requirements: *Undergraduate:* open-door; some specific majors do have restrictions, i.e., allied health fields, paralegal, etc. *Certificate:* same as undergraduate.

On-Campus Requirements: one orientation visit to main campus. Optional orientations to off-campus support sites recommended and much used. These are where distance learning students are based.

Tuition and Fees: *Undergraduate:* $97/credit, lower division. *Other Costs:* $25 technology fee, full-time (prorated for part-time). *Credit by:* semester.

Financial Aid: Federal Stafford Loan, Federal Perkins Loan, Federal Pell Grant, Federal Work-Study, VA, New York resident programs, Tuition Assistance Plan.

Accreditation: Middle State Association of Colleges and Schools.

Description: Genesee Community College (1967) is a comprehensive community college with 3,000 full-time students in a rural area of western New York state, serving a 4-county area and beyond, with 45 certificate, AAS, AS and AA degrees. The main campus in Batavia, 4 campus centers in towns 25–50 miles distant, and distance learning offerings serve both traditional age college students and working adults. The distance learning program is exemplified by a wide diversity of delivery media, course design parameters, support infrastructure and curricula. Student support services (advising, tutoring, technical training and support, etc.) are centrally administered but decentrally provided. Fifty-five course sections serve 1,400 students/year in both synchronous and asynchronous delivery modes (telecourses, Internet courses, live interactive video courses) and an on-time student course completion rate of better than 80% is consistently maintained.

George Washington University

2134 G Street NW, Suite B-06	Phone: (202) 994-1701
Washington, DC 20052	Fax: (202) 994-2145

Division(s): Graduate School of Education and Human Development
Web Site(s): http://www.gwu.edu/~etl
E-mail: etladmin@www.gwu.edu

Graduate Degree Programs:
Master of Science in Educational Technology Leadership

Certificate Programs: Distance Learning

Class Titles: Required courses: Managing Computer Applications, Educational Hardware Systems, Applying Educational Media/Technology, Computers in Education/Human Development, Design/Development of Educational Software, Power/Leadership/Education, Education Policy, Quantitative Methods/Research Methods. Elective Courses: Needs Assessment, Program Evaluation, Managing Multimedia Production, Critical Issues in Distance Education, Effective Presentations for Education/Training, Technology/Disabilities, Technology/Organizations, Telecommunications in Education, History of Media/Technology, Instructional Systems/Design, Human Computer Interaction in Education.

Teaching Methods: *Computers:* Internet, asynchronous and synchronous conferencing, video, audio, e-mail, CD-ROM, LISTSERV. *Other:* None.

Admission Requirements: *Graduate:* bachelor's degree with 2.75 GPA, 2 letters of recommendation, resume, statement of purpose, GRE or MAT. *Certificate:* same as graduate.

On-Campus Requirements: None.

Tuition and Fees: *Graduate:* $259/credit. *Application Fee:* $50. *Software:* variable. *Other Costs:* $35 registration fee. *Credit by:* semester (and a summer session).

Financial Aid: Federal Stafford Loan, Federal Perkins Loan.

Accreditation: American Association of Colleges for Teacher Education, Middle States Association of Colleges and Schools.

Description: The George Washington University (1821) is a private, nonsectarian, coeducational institution located in the heart of the nation's capital. The Educational Technology Leadership (ETL) program at The George Washington University was the first educational technology oriented Master of Arts program to be delivered at a distance throughout the U.S. The program has remained at the forefront of communications technology (including satellite, cable, Internet, multimedia) in delivering distance learning to students throughout North America and the world. The ETL program is also available in a distance learning supported face-to-face environment in Alexandria, Virginia. The faculty and staff of ETL believe that distance education offers unparalleled opportunities in high quality graduate study for self-motivated high potential students. The ETL program has been in existence for 9 years and graduates find jobs in various education and training arenas in public agencies and the private sector. ETL students are very competitive and regularly report that they are hired because of their degree or simply their participation in the ETL program. Highly motivated students with basic computer skills will find the ETL program worth their time and energy.

Georgia Perimeter College

| 555 North Indian Creek Drive | Phone: (404) 298-3954 |
| Clarkston, GA 30021-2396 | Fax: (404) 298-3955 |

Division(s): Center for Continuing and Distance Education
Web Site(s): http://www.gpc.peachnet.edu
E-mail: rclark@gpc.peachnet.edu

Undergraduate Degree Programs:
Associate of Arts in Health Information Management
Associate of Science in Health Information Management

Teaching Methods: *Computers:* Internet, real-time chat, electronic classroom, e-mail, CD-ROM, newsgroup, LIST-SERV. *TV:* videotape, cable program, satellite broadcasting, PBS. *Other:* radio broadcast, videoconferencing, audioconferencing, audiographics, audiotapes, fax, correspondence, independent study, individual study, learning contracts.

Admission Requirements: *Undergraduate:* ACT/SAT, immunization.

On-Campus Requirements: None.

Tuition and Fees: *Undergraduate:* $44/credit. *Application Fee:* $20. *Other Costs:* $38 technology fee. *Credit by:* semester.

Financial Aid: Federal Stafford Loan, Federal PLUS Loan, Federal Pell Grant, Federal Work-Study, VA, Georgia resident programs, Georgia Hope Scholarships.

Accreditation: Southern Association of Colleges and Schools.

Description: A regional multi-campus unit of the university system of Georgia, Georgia Perimeter College (1964) strives to meet the changing expectations of our diverse collegiate and community constituencies by providing effective, innovative, lifelong educational opportunities. We are committed to diversity, continuous improvement, high academic standards, and the efficient use of the resources. In decision making at all levels, the enhancement of our students' lives is our first priority. GPC supports one of the oldest and largest distance learning programs in the state, serving 2,500 learners every year.

Glendale Community College

| 1500 North Verdugo Road | Phone: (818) 240-1000 |
| Glendale, CA 91208 | Fax: (818) 549-9436 |

Division(s): Letters, Arts and Sciences
Web Site(s): http://glendale.cc.ca.us
E-mail: See Web site

Undergraduate Degree Programs:
Associate of Arts
Associate of Science

Certificate Programs: Yes.

Teaching Methods: *Computers:* Internet, electronic classroom, e-mail, CD-ROM, newsgroup. *TV:* videotape, cable program, PBS. *Other:* independent study

Credits Granted for: examination (CLEP, ACT-PEP, DANTES, GRE).

Admission Requirements: *Undergraduate:* age 18 and/or ability to benefit.

On-Campus Requirements: None.

Tuition and Fees: *Undergraduate:* $12 residents, $117 out-of-state *Other Costs:* $10 technology fee, other fees $30 (first time student). *Credit by:* Semester.

Financial Aid: Federal Pell Grant, Federal Work-Study, California resident programs.

Accreditation: Western Association of Schools and Colleges.

Description: Glendale Community College (1927) has long served Glendale, Burbank, Pasadena, and Los Angeles with quality academic and career education. The college has extensive credit and noncredit programs. Contract education and an extensive array of software courses are provided through the Professional Development Center. Glendale is implementing a carefully designed plan to expand facilities and renovate existing structures in response to the increased demands of technology and enrollment. Students currently have access to more than 20 specialized computer laboratories for subjects from business to science as well as for general use. The college has a long-standing telecourse program and added Internet-based instruction in 1998. GCC expects to have a breadth of Internet-based courses available within the year.

Goddard College

123 Pitkin Road	Phone: (802) 454-8311
Plainfield, VT 05667	(800) 468-4888
	Fax: (802) 454-1029

Division(s): Admissions Office
Web Site(s): http://www.goddard.edu
E-mail: ellenc@earth.goddard.edu

Undergraduate Degree Programs:
Bachelor of Science in:
   Education
   Psychology
   Social Ecology
   Individualized Study
   Health Arts

Graduate Degree Programs:
Master of Science in:
   Education
   Psychology
   Social Ecology
   Individualized Study
Master of Fine Arts in:
   Creative Writing
   Interdisciplinary Arts
   Health Arts

Teaching Methods: *Computers:* Internet, real-time chat, e-mail, newsgroup, LISTSERV. *Other:* fax, correspondence, independent study, individual study, learning contracts.

Credits Granted for: experiential learning, portfolio assessment, examination (CLEP, ACT-PEP, DANTES).

Admission Requirements: *Undergraduate:* adult students, high school diploma or GED. *Graduate:* adult students, accredited undergraduate degree.

On-Campus Requirements: 7-day residency at beginning of each semester.

Tuition and Fees: *Undergraduate:* $4,115/semester. *Graduate:* $4,825/semester. *Application Fee:* $40. *Credit by:* semester.

Financial Aid: Federal Stafford Loan, Federal Perkins Loan, Federal PLUS Loan, Federal Pell Grant, Federal Work-Study, VA.

Accreditation: New England Association of Schools and Colleges.

Description: As an heir to Goddard Seminary, Goddard College (1938) was chartered as an experimental and progressive institution of higher learning. In 1959 Goddard was accredited by the New England Association of Schools and Colleges. We have consistently shown a commitment to education of adults as well as younger students, a recognition that education and vocation are inseparable, and the understanding of learning as an individual process. In 1963 Goddard pioneered the first low-residency undergraduate program, acknowledging the need of working adults to be served by a workable program. In the 1970s, graduate programs were also developed in this mode.

Gogebic Community College

E4946 Jackson Road	Phone: (906) 932-4231 x343
Ironwood, MI 49938	Fax: (906) 932-2129

Division(s): Dean of Instruction's Office
Web Site(s): http://gogebic.cc.mi.us
E-mail: nancyk@admin1.gogebic.cc.mi.us

Undergraduate Degree Programs:
Certificate and Associate Degree

Class Titles: vary with semester; call or e-mail for current offerings.

Teaching Methods: *Computers:* Internet, real-time chat, electronic classroom, e-mail, CD-ROM, newsgroup, LISTSERV. *TV:* videotape, cable program, satellite broadcasting, PBS. *Other:* videoconferencing, audioconferencing, fax, correspondence, independent study.

Credits Granted for: in exceptional circumstances: experiential learning, portfolio assessment, extrainstitutional learning, examination (CLEP, ACT-PEP, DANTES, GRE).

Admission Requirements: *Undergraduate:* open-door policy. *Certificate:* same as undergraduate.

On-Campus Requirements: None.

Tuition and Fees: *Undergraduate:* $41/credit in-district, $57/credit out-of-district, $59/credit out-of-state reciprocity area, $80/credit out-of-state. *Other Costs:* $160 estimated total annual fees based on full-time load of 31 credits. *Credit by:* semester.

Financial Aid: Federal Stafford Loan, Federal Perkins Loan, Federal PLUS Loan, Federal Pell Grant, Federal Work-Study, VA, Michigan resident programs.

Accreditation: North Central Association of Colleges and Schools.

Description: Gogebic Community College (1932) is a small, rural, full-service community college located in Michigan's western Upper Peninsula. The college offers liberal arts, technical, and community service programming. GCC's primary service district is Gogebic County, but it also serves the western 6 counties in the Upper Peninsula. Because this large service area is rural, the barriers of time and distance are often a hindrance to those pursuing a college education. The college initially entered distance learning as a way of addressing these barriers, and over time has broadened its offerings.

Golden Gate University

536 Mission Street	Phone: (888) 874-2923
San Francisco, CA 94105	(415) 442-7060
	Fax: (415) 896-2394

Division(s): CyberCampus
Web Site(s): http://cybercampus.ggu.edu
E-mail: cybercampus@ggu.edu

Graduate Degree Programs:
Master of Finance
Executive Master of Public Administration

Certificate Programs: Arts Administration, Accounting, Healthcare Administration, Taxation, Finance and Personal Financial Planning (all are graduate certificates).

Class Titles: Computer Information Systems, Hotel Restaurant/Tourism Management, Math, Management, Marketing, Telecommunications Management, International Relations.

Teaching Methods: *Computers:* Internet, electronic classroom, e-mail, interactive discussion conference. *Other:* None.

Credits Granted for: examination (CLEP, ACT-PEP, DANTES, GRE).

Admission Requirements: *Graduate:* MBA programs—statement of purpose, official GMAT score report, official transcript. Other master's degree programs—statement of purpose, undergraduate GPA of 2.5 (except MAC requires 3.0 and MS Taxation requires 3.2). *Certificate:* An official transcript documenting the equivalent of a college/university degree from an approved institution. Some certificate programs have prerequisite courses that students must meet. Admitted certificate-program students must maintain normal academic standards, including GPA. All units applied to a certificate program must be earned at Golden Gate University. Transfer credit is not applicable.

On-Campus Requirements: The student never has to attend a class meeting. The course is taught entirely over the Internet. All courses require at least one supervised exam. The student must select an exam supervisor for this exam. Some examples of supervisors are employers, local librarians, other universities or any GGU campus location.

Tuition and Fees: *Undergraduate:* $960/course. *Graduate:*

$996/Arts Administration, English, Executive Master of Public Administration, Health Care Administration/PAD course; $1,200/Accounting, Computer Information Systems, Finance, Management, Marketing, Telecommunications Management course; $1,494/Tax course. *Application Fee:* $55 degree, $25 certificate, $70 degree or certificate for international students. *Credit by:* quarter.

Financial Aid: Federal Stafford Loan, Federal Perkins Loan, Federal PLUS Loan, Federal Pell Grant, Federal Work-Study, VA, California resident programs.

Accreditation: Western Association of Schools and Colleges.

Description: Golden Gate University (1853) has been a leader in quality, practical training for working professionals for more than a century. The university is dedicated to providing an educational environment and curricula that simulate the professional workplace. This dedication inspired Cyber-Campus, the university's Online Campus. In existence since the fall of 1997, the online university began with 13 courses. Now it offers 30 courses and, by the fall of 1998, will offer almost 50. The program's success is a reflection of a thorough development cycle and a commitment to quality.

Gonzaga University

East 502 Boone Avenue	Phone: (800) 533-2554 x5912
Spokane, WA 99258-0001	Fax: (509) 323-5965

Division(s): Off-Campus Education Services
Other Contacts: Nursing: (800) 533-2554 x5542
Organizational Leadership: (800) 533-2554 x6645
Fax for Nursing and Organizational Leadership:
(509) 323-5827
Web Site(s): http://www.gonzaga.edu
E-mail: aruff@soe.gonzaga.edu (Off-Campus Education)
norwood@gu.gonzaga.edu (Nursing)
albert@gu.gonzaga.edu (Organizational Leadership)

Graduate Degree Programs:
Master of Initial Teaching (includes teacher certification)
Master of Arts in:
Computer Education
Administration, Curriculum, and Instruction
Teaching: Teaching At-Risk Kids
Counseling (Canadian program only)
Organizational Leadership
Master of Science in Nursing

Certificate Programs: Postgraduate Family Nurse Practitioner.

Teaching Methods: *Computers:* Internet, electronic classrooms, e-mail, CD-ROM, LISTSERV. *TV:* videotape. *Other:* audioconferencing, fax, correspondence, independent study, individual study, learning contracts, face-to-face instruction.

Credits Granted for: portfolio assessment.

Admission Requirements: *Graduate:* program-specific, written statement of purpose, 2 letters of recommendation, transcripts, GRE or Miller Analogies Test. *Doctoral:* same as graduate.

On-Campus Requirements: Off-Campus Education: Our programs are comprised of face-to-face instruction offered in a community over a 2-year period. Classes typically meet twice a week every other week. Our Master of Arts in Counseling program (Canadian only) requires on-campus residency the first year for one summer session (4 weeks). All other programs are offered in the community year-round. Nursing and FNP Certificate: 2 days/month. Organizational Leadership: no on-campus requirement.

Tuition and Fees: *Graduate:* $310/credit Off-Campus Education, $410/credit Nursing. *Application Fee:* $40. *Other Costs:* $60 Miller Analogies Test, $100-$250 practicum fee (for supervisor honorarium), $40 orals fee, $40 readers travel fee, $25 summer session administrative fee, $10 technology fee/semester. *Credit by:* semester.

Financial Aid: Federal Stafford Loan, Federal PLUS Loan.

Accreditation: National Council of Accreditation for Teacher Education, National League for Nursing, Private Postsecondary Education Commission of British Columbia, Advanced Education and Career Development.

Description: Gonzaga University (1968) has provided distance graduate degrees to 1,800 students from northern Canada to the Hawaiian Islands in its 30 years of extended service. The university will continue to offer its graduate program as long as a need exists for Jesuit-inspired education. The mission of the university is to develop knowledgeable and competent professionals. Gonzaga is committed to providing excellence without elitism, to blending contemporary and innovative theory and practice, and to appreciating wide-range views and ideologies. The School of Education offers graduate-level, off-campus programs in teacher certification, administration and curriculum, teaching at-risk kids, educational technology, and sports administration. Counseling programs are offered only in Canada and require a summer residency. Programs are designed around a typical work schedule, through weekly courses or through evening courses twice every other week over a 2-year period. The School of Professional Studies offers a blend of distant and on-campus study and experiences for the nursing programs. This format combines videotapes of current campus classes and student interaction by region with campus attendance periods. The student can proceed at his or her own pace in this format. The organizational leadership program is offered in an evening and/or weekend class format.

Gordon-Conwell Theological Seminary

130 Essex Street   Phone: (877) 736-5465 (toll free)
South Hamilton, MA 01982   Fax: (978) 468-1791

Division(s): Ockenga Institute
Web Site(s): http://www.gcts.edu/semlink
E-mail: semlink@gcts.edu

Certificate Programs: Ockenga Institute Diploma—nondegree program in which a diploma is awarded for the completion of 6 courses.

Class Titles: Christian Ethics, Christian/Old Testament Theology, Church History to Reformation, Church History Since Reformation, Church History Survey, Church Leadership/Administration, Epistle to Romans, Christian Apologetics, Pastoral Care/Counseling, Marriage Counseling, Modern Theology, New Testament Survey, Pastoral Epistles, Reformation Church History, Systematic Theology, Spiritual Formation for Ministry, Tentmaking Witness at Home/Abroad, Theology of Jonathan Edwards, Theology Survey, Urban Mission/Ministry.

Teaching Methods: *Computers:* Internet, CD-ROM. *TV:* videotapes. *Other:* audiotapes.

Admission Requirements: *Graduate:* accredited bachelor's degree, recommendations. *Certificate:* application, recommendations.

On-Campus Requirements: a student may complete up to a third of a master's degree (10 of 30 courses towards a Master of Divinity and 4 of 20 courses towards a Master of Arts degree) through the Semlink distance education program. The degree must then be completed in residence. Gordon-Conwell does not offer correspondence degrees.

Tuition and Fees: *Graduate:* $450/3-credit course. *Application Fee:* $25. *Credit by:* semester.

Financial Aid: Semlink students may be eligible to defer prior loans or be eligible for a federal loan if taking 2 courses simultaneously.

Accreditation: Association of Theological Schools in the U.S. and Canada, New England Association of Schools and Colleges.

Description: Gordon-Conwell Theological Seminary (1987) has a rich, century-long heritage. The school's roots are founded in 2 institutions which have long provided evangelical leadership for the Christian church in a variety of ministries. The Conwell School of Theology was founded in Philadelphia in 1884 by the Rev. Russell Conwell, a prominent Baptist minister who was well known for his famous sermon and book, *Acres of Diamonds*. The Conwell School later developed into Temple University in Philadelphia. In 1889, out of a desire to equip "men and women in practical religious work and to furnish them with a thoroughly biblical training," the Boston Missionary Training School was founded by another prominent Baptist minister, the Rev. A. J. Gordon. Based in Boston, Massachusetts, the school shared Gordon's deep concern for missions abroad and in New England urban centers. Upon his death, the institution was given his name, and the Gordon Divinity School eventually moved to Boston's North Shore. The Conwell School of Theology and Gordon Divinity School merged in 1969 through the efforts of philanthropist J. Howard Pew, Dr. Harold J. Ockenga, and Dr. Billy Graham. Their vision was for an institution "established within a strong evangelical framework, an independent, interdenominational seminary whose constituents are united in the belief that the Bible is the infallible, authoritative Word of God . . . consecrated to educating men and women in all facets of gospel outreach." Semlink is a personalized learning method which allows you to study at your own pace when and where it is most convenient for you. Each course is structured around cassette-taped lectures with a course syllabus and study guide supplemented by textbooks, reference materials and, in some cases, video, Internet, and CD-ROM formats. If taken for credit, you will receive individual attention from both a Gordon-Conwell mentor and faculty advisor as you proceed through each course. Inviting friends to join you in regular sessions enriches your experience and adds accountability.

Goucher College

1021 Dulaney Valley Road	Phone: (410) 337-6200
Baltimore, MD 21204	(800) 697-4646
	Fax: (410) 337-6085

Division(s): Center for Graduate and Continuing Studies
Web Site(s): http://goucher.edu/
E-mail: nmack@goucher.edu

Graduate Degree Programs:
Master of Arts in:
  Historic Preservation
  Arts Administration
Master of Fine Arts in Creative Nonfiction

Teaching Methods: *Computers:* Internet, real-time chat, electronic classroom, e-mail, CD-ROM, newsgroup, LISTSERV. *Other:* fax, correspondence, independent study, individual study, learning contracts.

Admission Requirements: *Graduate:* accredited bachelor's degree, 2 years of paid or volunteer post-graduate work experience.

On-Campus Requirements: 2-week summer residencies.

Tuition and Fees: *Graduate:* varies; contact school for details. *Credit by:* varies; contact school for details.

Financial Aid: Federal Stafford Loan

Accreditation: Middle States Association of Colleges and Schools.

Description: Since its founding in 1885, Goucher College has been known for its commitment to excellence in liberal arts and sciences education. The limited-residency, distance-learning graduate programs began in 1995. These programs offer an opportunity to students, living anywhere, to earn further knowledge and credentials which will make them valuable in their fields. The limited-residency format allows the programs to include nationwide experts in the fields.

Governors State University

Stuenkel Road	Phone: (800) 478-8478
University Park, IL 60486	Fax: (708) 534-8458

Division(s): Extended Learning
Web Site(s): http://www.govst.edu.bog
E-mail: gtvstudy@govst.edu
gsubog@govst.edu

Undergraduate Degree Programs:
Board of Governors Bachelor of Arts

Class Titles: Financial Accounting, Alcoholism: Study of Addiction, Substance Abuse: Current Concepts, Addictions Counseling: Multicultural Perspective, Managing Health Behaviors, Adolescent Substance Abuser: School/Family/Treatment/Prevention Strategies, Alcoholism: Employee Assistance in Business/Industry, Beliefs/Believers, Anthropology in Film, Worlds of Art, Human Evolution, Models of Intervention for Substance Abusing Offender, Concepts in Communication, Communication Workshop: Family Communication, Macroeconomics, Foundations of Education, Living Literature: Classics/You, Composition: Structure/Style, Writing, Modern American Poetry: Voices/Visions, Shakespeare's Plays, Native American Authors, World Regional Geography, Key Issues in State/Federal Constitutional Government, History of Illinois/Its Constitution, Modern Chinese History, Russia in 20th Century, Hispanic Experience in U.S., Ethnicity/Culture/Politics, African Civilizations, Latin American Culture/Society, American Cinema, Management Strategies, Production Management, Organizational Behavior, Marketing Management, Public Administration, Religion, Urban Politics, Psychology, Personality Theories, Social Psychology, Child Development, Adulthood, Seasons of Life, Cognitive Development Through Life Cycle, Urban Studies, Family History: Legacies, Women/Social Action, Urban Dynamics, Survey of Social Science, Dealing with Diversity, Survey of Exceptional Students, Statistics.

Teaching Methods: *Computers:* Internet, electronic classroom, e-mail, CD-ROM. *TV:* videotape, cable program, PBS.

Other: audioconferencing, audiotapes, correspondence.

Credits Granted for: experiential learning, portfolio assessment, extrainstitutional learning, examination (CLEP, ACT-PEP, DANTES, USAFI), ACE-approved training.

Admission Requirements: *Undergraduate:* Governors State University is an upper-division and graduate public university in Illinois. The Board of Governors BA degree completion program is a program for adult learners that can be completed at a distance. It is not organized by traditional academic disciplines. Students may design their own degree program to fit their career goals. Students with 60 semester hours from a regionally accredited institution will be readily admitted into the program. Students with 30–59 semester credit hours and substantial experiential learning may be admitted on a conditional basis until they reach 60 hours. Students must have a GPA of 2.0 or better. The BOG program accepts transfer credit with passing grades from any regionally accredited college or university in the U.S. There are no time limits to when the credits were earned. Students may transfer up to 80 hours of lower division credit into the program.

On-Campus Requirements: students must take 15 semester hours of course work from Governors State. Students may select course work from the 55 media-based distance learning courses that are offered by GSU (TV, correspondence, Internet, CD-ROM) to fulfill this requirement.

Tuition and Fees: *Undergraduate:* $100/credit. *Graduate:* $105/credit. *Software:* variable. *Other Costs:* fee for portfolio assessment. *Credit by:* trimester (semester).

Financial Aid: Federal Direct Loan, Federal Perkins Loan, Federal Pell Grant, Federal Work-Study, VA, Illinois resident programs.

Accreditation: North Central Association of Colleges and Schools.

Description: Governors State University (1969), located in the southern suburbs of Chicago, serves 9,000 adult students each year. GSU, an upper-division and graduate-level university, has 4 colleges (Arts and Sciences, Business and Public Administration, Education, and Health Professions) with 172 full-time faculty. GSU is known for its adult-oriented Board of Governors BA degree program, which can be completed at a distance, as well as its production of TV courses. There are 12,000 graduates of the BOG BA degree program. The average age is 40; 95% of BOG BA graduates in the job market are employed; and 42% of BOG alumni enroll in a graduate program after completing their BOG BA degree.

Grace University

1311 South 9th Street
Omaha, NE 68108

Phone: (402) 449-2999
Fax: (402) 341-9587

Division(s): Grace College of Continuing Education
Web Site(s): http://www.graceu.edu
E-mail: guconed@graceu.edu

Class Titles: Life of Christ, I Corinthians, Romans, Philosophy, Apologetics, Church History, Biblical Counseling.

Teaching Methods: *Computers:* Internet, e-mail. *Other:* correspondence, independent study.

Credits Granted for: experiential learning, portfolio assessment, examination (CLEP).

Admission Requirements: *Undergraduate:* application, references, transcripts, health form, ACT scores.

On-Campus Requirements: None.

Tuition and Fees: *Undergraduate:* $236/credit. *Application Fee:* $25. *Credit by:* semester.

Financial Aid: Federal Stafford Loan, Federal PLUS Loan, Federal Pell Grant, VA, state programs for residents of all states, institutional scholarships and grants, alternative loans.

Accreditation: North Central Association of Colleges and Schools, AABC.

Description: Originally founded as Grace Bible Institute, then renamed as Grace College of the Bible, Grace University (1943) adopted its new identity by adding 2 more colleges in 1995. Grace College of the Bible continues to be the university's primary undergraduate college, offering associate's and bachelor's degrees. Grace is a distinctly Christian university with an interdenominational identity and a curriculum shaped by the university's conservative, evangelical heritage. All undergraduates complete a double major: the first in Biblical Studies and the second in a chosen major field. For students completing a degree at a different college or university, Grace's Independent Studies program offers "electives" required by most colleges. Taking a couple of Christ-centered courses and transferring them into another program is an ideal way to inject some biblical learning into your overall college experience.

Graceland College

700 College Avenue
Lamoni, IA 50140

Phone: (515) 784-5324
Fax: (515) 784-5405

Division(s): Continuing Education/Distance Learning
Web Site(s): http://graceland.edu/home.html
E-mail: rriley@graceland.edu

Undergraduate Degree Programs:
Bachelor of Arts in Accounting
Bachelor of Science in:
    Business Administration
    Elementary Education
    Information Technology
    Nursing
    Sociology/Criminal Justice

Graduate Degree Programs:
Master of Science in Nursing

Teaching Methods: *Computers:* Internet, CD-ROM, e-mail. *TV:* videotape, Iowa Communication Network (interactive fiberoptic cable). *Other:* audioconferencing, fax, correspondence, independent study, individual study, by arrangement.

Credits Granted for: experiential learning, extrainstitutional learning, examination (CLEP, ACT-PEP, DANTES, GRE).

Admission Requirements: *Undergraduate:* associate degree or 60 college credits. *Graduate:* varies.

On-Campus Requirements: variable.

Tuition and Fees: *Undergraduate:* $165/credit. *Graduate:* varies. *Application Fee:* $25. *Other Costs:* varies. *Credit by:* semester.

Financial Aid: Federal Stafford Loan, Federal Perkins Loan, Federal PLUS Loan, Federal Pell Grant, Federal Work-Study, VA, Iowa Tuition Grant, Canadian Student Loan Plan.

Accreditation: North Central Association of Colleges and Schools, National Council for Accreditation of Teacher Education, National League for Nursing.

Description: Graceland College (1895), delivering distance education for more than a decade, is committed to lifelong learning. Graceland's curriculum, firmly rooted in the liberal arts tradition and enhanced by career-oriented practical experiences, is ideally suited to the distance learner. The majority of the college's continuing and distance education students participate in the Partnership Program between Graceland and 4 regional community colleges. A student with the equivalent of an associate degree takes day, evening, or weekend classes delivered traditionally by Graceland faculty or through the innovative medium of live, interactive fiberoptic TV at one of these partnership sites. Independent study courses and courses scheduled by arrangement with the instructor allow students to tailor a program of study to their modern lifestyle. This structured yet flexible approach allows students to complete their bachelor's degree in as few as 2 years. (Nursing degrees may be obtained from the Outreach Program in Independence, MO. Phone (800) 833-0524 for information.)

The Graduate School of America

330 2nd Avenue S, Suite 550   Phone: (800) 987-1133
Minneapolis, MN 55401   (612) 339-8650
                      Fax: (612) 339-8022

Division(s): None.
Web Site(s): http://www.tgsa.edu
E-mail: tgsainfo@tgsa.edu

Graduate Degree Programs:
Master of Science in:
    Education
    Management
    Human Service/Psychology
Doctor of Philosophy in:
    Education
    Organization/Management
    Human Services/Psychology

Certificate Programs: Instructional Design, Forensic Psychology, Clinical Supervision, Geriatric Care, Psycho-Neurological Testing.

Class Titles: all classes can be taken individually.

Teaching Methods: *Computers:* Internet, real-time chat, electronic classroom, e-mail, CD-ROM, newsgroup, LIST-SERV. *TV:* videotape. *Other:* audioconferencing, audiotapes, fax, correspondence, independent study, individual study, learning contracts.

Credits Granted for: graduate credits from accredited institutions will be reviewed for credit.

Admission Requirements: *Graduate:* application, official transcripts, 2.7 cumulative GPA for MS (3.0 for PhD), academic goal statement, and professional resume; letters of recommendation and interview for some programs. *Certificate:* application, transcripts.

On-Campus Requirements: residency requirements will vary depending on degree and program. Some MS programs do not require attendance at residency seminars. All PhD programs require attendance at some residency seminars.

Tuition and Fees: *Graduate:* MS $845/course (4 quarter credits) or $1,995/quarter, PhD $3,295/quarter. *Application Fee:* $50. *Other Costs:* residency seminars may be required for some programs. Cost/seminar ranges from $325 to $695. *Credit by:* quarter.

Financial Aid: Federal Stafford Loan, Federal PLUS Loan, VA, Minnesota resident programs, SELF loan is available to all learners (not just Minnesota residents).

Accreditation: North Central Association of Colleges and Schools.

Description: The Graduate School of America (1993) is an institution of higher education that offers graduate degree programs to adult learners who seek to integrate advanced study with their professional lives. Our mission is to deliver high-quality programs that provide traditional and contemporary knowledge through flexible and innovative forms of distance learning. TGSA explicitly recognizes adult learners as active partners in the design and implementation of their academic experience.

Grand Rapids Baptist Seminary

1001 East Beltline NE	Phone: (616) 222-1422
Grand Rapids, MI 49525	Fax: (616) 222-1414

Division(s): Academic Office
Web Site(s): http://www.cornerstone.edu/grbs
E-mail: jverberkmoes@cornerstone.edu

Class Titles: Biblical Hermeneutics, Old Testament Biblical Theology, Acts of Apostles, Pastoral Epistles, Hebrews, Life of Christ, Gospel of Luke, Post-Exilic Prophets, Parables of Jesus, Historical Theology: Ancient Church, Historical Theology: Reformation Church, Historical Theology: Christianity in America, Theologies of Liberation, Radical Reformation, Doctrine of Man/Sin, Christian Worldview, Christian Ethics, Theology of Jonathan Edwards, Theology of Martin Luther, Doctrine of Salvation, Contemporary Theology, Doctrine of Trinity, Apologetics, Spiritual Formation, Role of Women in Ministry, Adult Ministries in Church, Urban Mission/Ministry, History/Philosophy of Christian Missions, Missionary Encounter with World Religions, Muslim Evangelism, Interpersonal Conflict Management, Administration/Care of Church, History/Philosophy of Christian Education.

Teaching Methods: *Computers:* e-mail. *Other:* audiotapes, fax, correspondence, independent study, individual study, learning contracts.

Credits Granted for: portfolio assessment, transfer credit, advanced standing by exam.

Admission Requirements: *Graduate:* admission into the In-Ministry Master of Religious Education degree program (part resident, part extension) requires a bachelor's degree from a regionally accredited college with a 2.5 cumulative GPA, statement of Christian faith commitment, 3 years of full-time professional ministry experience and current professional ministry involvement, and fulfillment of all other application requirements as outlined in the Grand Rapids Baptist Seminary academic catalog. Contact school.

On-Campus Requirements: most degree programs at Grand Rapids Baptist Seminary are designed as resident programs, with the exception of the In-Ministry Master of Religious Education and Doctor of Ministry degree programs. The resident degree programs do allow up to 30% completion through distance education. The In-Ministry Master of Religious Education degree program is a 32 semester hour program consisting of 20 hours of distance education and a 12 semester hour residency requirement. The 12-hour resident study requirement is typically fulfilled through various 2-week sessions offered on campus in early January and throughout the summer months.

Tuition and Fees: *Graduate:* $245/credit. *Application Fee:* $25. *Other Costs:* $60/set of lecture tapes (estimated). *Credit by:* semester.

Financial Aid: institution grants and scholarships, Federal Stafford Loan, Federal PLUS Loan, Federal Work-Study, VA.

Accreditation: North Central Association of Colleges and Schools, Associate Member of Association of Theological Schools.

Description: Grand Rapids Baptist Seminary (1949) is a graduate school of biblical studies, theology, and ministry which serves individuals preparing for vocational ministry. The seminary is located in Grand Rapids, Michigan. Currently some 225 students are enroled in residence and through distance education in the various graduate degree programs. Grand Rapids Baptist Seminary maintains a strong commitment to its Baptistic theological heritage and historical biblical Christianity, while seeking to serve the broader evangelical community with a distinctively conservative theological education.

Grantham College of Engineering

34641 Grantham College Road	Phone: (800) 955-2527
Slidell, LA 70469-6815	Fax: (504) 649-4183

Division(s): None.
Web Site(s): http://www.grantham.edu
E-mail: gce@grantham.edu

Undergraduate Degree Programs:
Associate of Science in:
    Computer Science
    Computer Engineering
    Electronics Engineering

Graduate Degree Programs:
Bachelor of Science in:
    Computer Science
    Computer Engineering
    Electronics Engineering

Class Titles: all classes offered by school; check catalog.

Teaching Methods: *Computers:* Internet, e-mail, CD-ROM, LISTSERV. *TV:* videotape, cable program, satellite broadcasting, PBS. *Other:* radio broadcast, fax, correspondence, independent study, individual study.

Credits Granted for: experiential learning, portfolio assessment, extrainstitutional learning, examination (CLEP, ACT-PEP, DANTES, GRE).

Admission Requirements: *Undergraduate:* high school diploma, GED, or equivalent.

On-Campus Requirements: None.

Tuition and Fees: *Undergraduate:* contact school (changes often). *Application Fee:* $150. *Other Costs:* $65 evaluation fee, books and software are included in price. *Credit by:* semester.

Financial Aid: VA.

Accreditation: Distance Education and Training Council.

Description: Grantham College of Engineering (1951) has been in distance education since its founding. Grantham became a member of the Distance Education and Training Council in 1961. Our goal from the start was to give those workers in the computer and electronic fields without a college degree the opportunity to earn one while they still held down their jobs. We have many graduates who have benefitted from this unique concept of distance education in the past. Now we have an increasing number of traditional students taking advantage of the cost- and timesaving distance education offers. Grantham College continues to be a leader in the distance education field, offering individual courses in addition to our degree programs.

Grays Harbor College

1620 Edward P. Smith Drive	Phone: (360) 532-9020
Aberdeen, WA 98520	Fax: (360) 538-4293

Division(s): Continuing Education
Web Site(s): http://ghc.ctc.edu
E-mail: admissions@ghc.ctc.edu

Undergraduate Degree Programs:
Associate of Arts
Associate of Science
Associate of Applied Science or Technology
Associate of General Studies

Certificate Programs: Accounting/Bookkeeping, Aquaculture Technician, Business Management, Corrections, Criminal Justice, Early Childhood Education, Geographic Information Systems, Health Promotion and Fitness Technician, Legal Secretary, Medical Office Assistant, Microcomputer Maintenance and Service Technician, Network Technician, Office Technology, Pharmacy Technician, Practical Nursing, Related Welding, Small Business/Entrepreneurship, Software Applications, Trim Carpentry, Watershed Restoration, Welding

Technology.

Teaching Methods: *Computers:* Internet, real-time chat, electronic classroom, e-mail, LISTSERV. *TV:* videotape. *Other:* videoconferencing, independent study.

Credits Granted for: examination (CLEP).

Admission Requirements: *Undergraduate:* age 18 with high school diploma or GED, complete a placement exam. *Certificate:* same as undergraduate.

On-Campus Requirements: None.

Tuition and Fees: *Undergraduate:* $51/credit. *Other Costs:* $60 parking, technology, and lab fees. *Credit by:* quarter.

Financial Aid: Federal Stafford Loan, Federal PLUS Loan, Federal Pell Grant, Federal Work-Study, VA, Washington resident programs, scholarships.

Accreditation: Northwest Association of Schools and Colleges.

Description: Grays Harbor College (1930) continues to operate quality programs at an affordable price. We offer classes in several formats and many areas of interest. Classes can be delivered via Internet, video, and teleconferencing. Our Internet site is constantly being updated as we upgrade and adapt our courses with new technology and methods.

Great Basin College

1500 College Parkway	Phone: (702) 738-8493
Elko, NV 89801	Fax: (702) 738-8771

Division(s): Office of Academic Affairs
Web Site(s): http://www.scs.edu/gbc/
E-mail: cholt@gbcnv.edu

Undergraduate Degree Programs:
Education

Class Titles: Biology, Construction, Computer Science, Criminal Justice, Education, English, Environmental, Fire Science, Mathematics, Mining, Music, Political Science, Sociology Accounting, Economics, Philosophy.

Teaching Methods: *Computers:* Internet, real-time chat, electronic classroom, e-mail, LISTSERV. *TV:* videotape, satellite broadcasting, PBS. *Other:* videoconferencing, audioconferencing, audiotapes, fax, independent study, individual study, learning contracts.

Credits Granted for: experiential learning, extrainstitutional learning, examination (CLEP, ACT-PEP, DANTES, GRE).

Admission Requirements: *Undergraduate:* ACT or placement exams.

On-Campus Requirements: None.

Tuition and Fees: *Undergraduate:* $40/credit. *Application Fee:* $5. *Credit by:* semester.

Financial Aid: Federal Stafford Loan, Federal Perkins Loan, Federal PLUS Loan, Federal Pell Grant, Federal Work-Study, VA, Nevada resident programs.

Accreditation: Northwest Association of Schools and Colleges.

Description: Great Basin College (1968) is a community college with selected 4-year programs serving a largely rural region of 45,000 square miles. Distance education is utilized to reach individuals and small groups of people residing throughout the region. GBC has delivered the curriculum through distance education for many years. The college now offers a variety of distance education formats including telecourses, interactive video courses, and Web-based courses.

Green River Community College

12401 Southeast 320th Street	Phone: (253) 288-3354
Auburn, WA 98092	Fax: (253) 288-3455

Division(s): Distance Learning
Web Site(s): http://www.greenriver.ctc.edu
E-mail: pallen@grcc.ctc.edu

Undergraduate Degree Programs:
Associate of Arts

Certificate Programs: Water Supply Technology, Wastewater Technology (both vocational training programs are under planning and development)

Class Titles: Humanities, History, Composition, Technical Writing, Math, Music Appreciation, Psychology, Earth Science, Astronomy, American Literature, Sociology, Anthropology, Chemistry, Philosophy, Cinema, Health/Wellness, Art Appreciation, Economics, Biology, World Literature, Learning for 21st Century (How to do Online Library Research/Take Online Courses), Career Exploration, Water Distribution, Water Treatment.

Teaching Methods: *Computers:* Internet, real-time chat, electronic classroom, e-mail, CD-ROM, newsgroup, LISTSERV. *TV:* videotape, cable program, PBS. *Other:* videoconferencing.

Credits Granted for: examination (CLEP, DANTES), enlisted military experience, advanced placement.

Admission Requirements: *Undergraduate:* age 18, high school diploma, official transcripts. *Certificate:* same as undergraduate.

On-Campus Requirements: None.

Tuition and Fees: *Undergraduate:* $505/10–18 credits, $51/credit part-time. *Other Costs:* $.50/credit special services fee, $2/credit technology fee (maximum $20), $10–$20 facilities fee, $40/student/quarter Washington On-Line (WAOL) enrollment fee, $7/student/year WAOL library fee, $20/telecourse license fee, variable lab fees. *Credit by:* quarter.

Financial Aid: Federal Stafford Loan, Federal Supplemental Educational Opportunity Grant, Federal PLUS Loan, Federal Pell Grant, Federal Work-Study, VA, Washington State Need Grants, State Work-Study, GRCC College Tuition Waiver.

Accreditation: Northwest Association of Schools and Colleges.

Description: Green River Community College (1964) is a 2-year public college offering degrees and certificates in academic and professional/technical programs, as well as courses in continuing and developmental education. The college has roots dating to 1945 with adult evening education at the Auburn School District. GRCC began delivering telecourses in 1994 and over the past 2 years has delivered courses online over the Internet and using videoconferencing equipment. Green River is focused on providing quality distance learning for academic transfer, professional/vocational degrees and certificates, and for continuing education.

Greenville Technical College

506 South Pleasantburg Drive	Phone: (864) 250-8164
Greenville, SC 29606-5616	Fax: (864) 250-8085

Division(s): Distance Learning
Web Site(s): http://www.college-online.com
http://www.greenvilletech.com
E-mail: moreinfo@college-online.com

Undergraduate Degree Programs:
A variety of one-year diploma and 2-year associate degree programs in a wide choice of fields including industrial/engineering technologies, nursing/allied health sciences, business, criminal justice, and culinary arts. Associate in Sciences and Associate in Arts degrees are available through the University Transfer program.

Certificate Programs: Programs in a wide choice of fields including industrial and engineering technologies, nursing and allied health sciences, business, criminal justice, and culinary arts.

Class Titles: Accounting, Art History/Appreciation, Astronomy, Biology, Chemistry, Computers/Programming, English Composition, English Literature, Ethics, History, Hospitality, Internet Communications, Logic, Math, Management, Marketing, Microcomputer Applications, Office Systems Technology, Operating Systems Psychology, Public Speaking, Sociology, Spanish, Total Quality Management.

Teaching Methods: *Computers:* Internet/online, e-mail. *TV:* videotape, cable program. *Other:* videoconferencing.

Admission Requirements: *Undergraduate:* open admission policy. This does not mean, however, that there are no entrance requirements. The state of South Carolina imposes general restrictions governing all admissions practices. Various residency requirements exist. See online catalog.

On-Campus Requirements: None.

Tuition and Fees: *Undergraduate:* full-time tuition/semester (12 hours or more): Greenville County Resident $525, out-of-county South Carolina Resident $570. *Credit by:* semester.

Financial Aid: Federal Stafford Loan, Federal PLUS Loan, Federal Pell Grant, Federal Work-Study, Federal HOPE Tax Credit, VA, South Carolina Resident Needs-based Grant, South Carolina Resident Palmetto Life Scholarships.

Accreditation: Southern Association of Colleges and Schools.

Description: Greenville Technical College (1963) is a comprehensive community college offering a wide variety of educational opportunities to the citizens of the upstate region of South Carolina. For-credit enrollment during fall semester 1998 totaled just more than 9,400 students. For 35 years the college has continuously updated and tailored educational programs to meet the needs of the students and the needs of local business and industry. The college has played a major role in the rapid and diverse economic growth in the upstate region of South Carolina. The college is dedicated to an aggressive distance learning program in an effort to provide students with as much class scheduling flexibility as possible. The college began offering distance learning telecourses in 1991 and courses via the Internet in 1997. Fall semester 1998 found more than 1,600 students taking advantage of the various distance learning course offerings.

Hadley School for the Blind

| 700 Elm Street | Phone: (847) 446-8111 |
| Winnetka, IL 60093 | Fax: (847) 446-0855 |

Division(s): All departments
Web Site(s): http://www.hadley-school.org
E-mail: info@hadley-school.org

Undergraduate Degree Programs:
High school level courses/diploma; continuing adult education.

Graduate Degree Programs:
Continuing Education Units or Carnegie units.

Class Titles: 6 core course areas: Academic/High School Studies, Braille/Other Communication Skills, Technology, Independent Living/Life Adjustment, Recreation/Leisure Time, Parent/Family Education

Teaching Methods: *Computers:* e-mail. *Other:* audiotapes, fax, correspondence, individual study.

Credits Granted for: course work.

Admission Requirements: *Undergraduate:* proof of legal blindness, family member of a legally blind person, or a professional or paraprofessional in the field of blindness/visual impairment.

On-Campus Requirements: None.

Tuition and Fees: *Undergraduate:* All of Hadley's services are tuition-free. *Credit by:* year-round; credit is awarded upon completion of a course.

Accreditation: Distance Education and Training Council, North Central Association of Colleges and Schools.

Description: The Hadley School for the Blind (1920) was founded by William A. Hadley and Dr. E. V. L. Brown as a distance education institution to teach braille to blind adults. Today, Hadley offers more than 90 tuition-free courses in 6 core course areas to more than 11,000 blind/visually impaired students, their families, and professionals throughout the world. The mission of The Hadley School for the Blind is to enable blind persons during all stages of life to acquire specialized skills, attitudes, and knowledge needed to enhance their participation in personal, family, and community life. The school accomplishes this mission by providing lifelong learning opportunities in a home setting through distance education with the support of family, friends, and blindness professionals.

Hamilton College

| 1924 D Street SW | Phone: (319) 363-0481 |
| Cedar Rapids, IA 52404 | Fax: (319) 363-3812 |

Division(s): Center for Distance Learning
Web Site(s): http://www.hamiltonia.edu
E-mail: fairs@aicedu.com

Undergraduate Degree Programs:
Associate of Science in Applied Management
Associate of Science in Interdisciplinary Studies

Class Titles: Accounting, Communications, Literature, Composition, Keyboarding, Information Technology, Developmental English, Developmental Math, Literature, History, Management, Mathematics, Environmental Sciences, Chemical Sciences, Anatomy/Physiology, Ethics, Social Problems, Economics, Sociology, Psychology, Government.

Teaching Methods: *Computers:* Internet, real-time audio and text chat, electronic classroom, e-mail, CD-ROM, peer group projects, research components, interactive Web sites to supplement texts. *Other:* audioconferencing, audiotapes are used to supplement other course materials.

Credits Granted for: extrainstitutional credit (work or life experiences and/or participation in formal courses, following guidelines of ACE, DANTES, SOC), other college or university transfer credit, nationally standardized exams (CLEP, ACE).

Admission Requirements: *Undergraduate:* official high school transcript or GED scores; brief essay describing work, educational experiences, and objectives for enrollment; and brief essay demonstrating how the student will succeed in a distance course or program. International students must demonstrate a 490 TOEFL score in written English.

On-Campus Requirements: None.

Tuition and Fees: *Undergraduate:* $210/credit. *Application Fee:* $25 one-time fee. *Software:* $30/semester technology fee. *Other Costs:* books and supplies are additional. Evaluation of transfer credit or extrainstitutional credit; fees are available in the catalog. *Credit by:* semester.

Financial Aid: Federal Stafford Loan, Federal Perkins Loan, Federal PLUS Loan, Federal Pell Grant, Federal Work-Study, VA, Iowa resident programs.

Accreditation: Accrediting Council for Independent Colleges and Schools, North Central Association of Colleges and Schools.

Description: Hamilton College (1900) has been a leader in private education for almost a century. Residentially, the 3-campus system provides educational and career training to Iowa residents. Nationally, the Center for Distance Learning was established early in 1998 after several years of development, research, and planning. The college believes in the learner-centered model of instruction and in the use of multimedia in delivering course content. Students are empowered through this model by being active participants in their educational success. The combination of highly credentialed, extensively trained faculty and students involved in their own educational goals form a strong and innovative distance education program.

Harold Washington College

30 East Lake Street	**Phone: (312) 553-5975**
Chicago, IL 60601	**Fax: (312) 553-5987**

Division(s): Open Learning
Web Site(s): http://www.ccc.edu
E-mail: plattimore@ccc.edu

Undergraduate Degree Programs:
Associate

Teaching Methods: *Computers:* Internet, e-mail, CD-ROM (for programs for military). *TV:* videotape, satellite broadcasting, PBS. *Other:* videoconferencing, audioconferencing.

Credits Granted for: experiential learning, portfolio assessment, examination (CLEP, ACT-PEP, DANTES, GRE).

Admission Requirements: *Undergraduate:* age 18, high school graduate or GED, college entrance exam, prerequisites may apply depending on course.

On-Campus Requirements: None.

Tuition and Fees: *Undergraduate:* $48/credit Chicago resident, $145/credit Illinois resident. *Other Costs:* $25 registration fee, $20/course packet. *Credit by:* semester.

Financial Aid: Federal Stafford Loan, Federal Perkins Loan, Federal PLUS Loan, Federal Pell Grant, Federal Work-Study, VA, Illinois resident programs.

Accreditation: North Central Association of Colleges and Schools.

Description: Harold Washington College (1962) was founded as The Loop College. The name was changed in 1985. Harold Washington College is a member of The City Colleges of Chicago which have offered media-based instruction since 1958. Early course delivery methods included print, audio, and TV. With the acquisition of WYCC-Channel 20, a PBS affiliate station, the Center for Open Learning became the central coordinating department for distance learning in 1975. Today the Center for Open Learning enrolls approximately 3,000 individuals each semester in telecourses, courses on videocassette, or computer assisted instruction. Plans are in progress for teleweb courses and Web-based instruction.

Harper College

1200 Algonquin Road	**Phone: (847) 925-6000**
Palatine, IL 60067	**Fax: (847) 925-6037**

Division(s): Distance Learning/Media Services
Web Site(s): http://www.harper.cc.il.us
E-mail: scatlin@harper.cc.il.us (registrar), bbohrer@harper.cc.il.us (admissions)

Undergraduate Degree Programs:
Associate of:
   Arts
   Science
   Applied Science

Class Titles: 26 telecourses; Internet courses expanding.

Teaching Methods: *Computers:* Internet, e-mail, CD-ROM, LISTSERV. *TV:* videotape, cable program, satellite broadcasting, PBS. *Other:* interactive video, independent study.

Credits Granted for: examination (CLEP, ACT-PEP).

Admission Requirements: *Undergraduate:* assessment testing after 6 credit hours.

On-Campus Requirements: None.

Tuition and Fees: *Undergraduate:* $50/credit. *Application Fee:* $20. *Other Costs:* $24 Student Activity Fee full-time ($12 part-time), $5 registration, $15 telecourse. *Credit by:* semester.

Financial Aid: Federal Stafford Loan, Federal Perkins Loan, Federal PLUS Loan, Federal Pell Grant, Federal Work-Study, VA, Illinois resident programs.

Accreditation: North Central Association of Colleges and Schools.

Description: Founded in 1965, Harper College has been offering telecourses since 1982 and is expanding into Web-based offerings.

Harrisburg Area Community College

One HACC Drive	Phone: (717) 780-2541
Harrisburg, PA 17110-2999	Fax: (717) 780-3250

Division(s): Distance Education
Web Site(s): http://www.hacc.edu
E-mail: distance@vm.hacc.edu

Class Titles: Accounting, Anthropology, Biology, Business, Economics, Composition, Finance, Geology, Geography, Government/Politics, Health, History, Nutrition, Humanities, Management, Marketing, Math, Philosophy, Physical Science, Psychology, Sociology.

Teaching Methods: *Computers:* Internet, real-time chat, electronic classroom, e-mail, CD-ROM. *TV:* videotape. *Other:* videoconferencing, audiotapes, fax, correspondence.

Credits Granted for: extrainstitutional learning (corporate or professional association seminars/workshops), examination (CLEP, ACT-PEP, DANTES, GRE).

Admission Requirements: *Undergraduate:* entrance exams for math and English. *Certificate:* same as undergraduate.

On-Campus Requirements: attend course orientation meeting or watch a copy in our library on tape, 3 exams.

Tuition and Fees: *Undergraduate:* $67–$131/credit depending on residency. *Application Fee:* $25. *Software:* variable. *Other Costs:* $20 videotape rental, $18 copyright fee (videocourses). *Credit by:* semester.

Financial Aid: Federal Stafford Loan, Federal Perkins Loan, Federal PLUS Loan, Federal Pell Grant, Federal Work-Study, VA, Pennsylvania resident programs.

Accreditation: Middle States Association of Colleges and Schools.

Description: Established in 1964 as the first community college in Pennsylvania, Harrisburg Area Community College welcomed its first class of 426 students on September 21. In seeking to fulfill its mission of "providing educational and cultural opportunities to the community it serves," HACC has become one of the largest undergraduate colleges in Pennsylvania, with 11,000 students enrolling in credit programs and courses each semester. Currently, our program consists of videocourse offerings. We will be offering several online (Internet) courses in the spring 1999 semester. Our distance education courses award the same academic credit as traditional classroom sections. No distinction is made on a student's transcript. These credits can be applied to college degree programs and transfer the same as on-campus sections of the same course.

Hawkeye Community College

1501 East Orange Road	Phone: (319) 296-4017
Waterloo, IA 50704	Fax: (319) 296-4018

Division(s): Academic Telecommunications
Web Site(s): http://www.hawkeye.cc.ia.us/academic/distance/distance.htm
E-mail: distance@hawkeye.cc.ia.us or rrezabek@hawkeye.cc.ia.us

Undergraduate Degree Programs:
Associate in Arts

Class Titles: Intro to Business, General Psychology, Intro to Sociology, Principles of Marketing, Composition, Calculus, Western Civilization, Non-parenteral Med Aide (continuing ed), Intro to Criminal Justice, Human Growth/Development.

Teaching Methods: *Computers:* Internet, real-time chat, electronic classroom, e-mail, CD-ROM, newsgroup, LISTSERV. *TV:* videotape telecourse, cable program, satellite broadcasting, PBS, live interactive TV, videoconferencing. *Other:* independent study, individual study, learning contracts.

Credits Granted for: examination (CLEP, ACT-PEP, DANTES, GRE).

Admission Requirements: *Undergraduate:* high school diploma or GED.

On-Campus Requirements: None.

Tuition and Fees: *Undergraduate:* $66/credit in-state, $128/credit out-of-state or international. *Other Costs:* $9/credit for student activities, registration, and computers. *Credit by:* semester.

Financial Aid: Federal Stafford Loan, Federal PLUS Loan, Federal Pell Grant, Federal Work-Study, VA, SEOG, Iowa resident programs.

Accreditation: North Central Association of Colleges and Schools.

Description: Hawkeye Community College (1966) was originally founded as a Vocational/Technical School. The college serves Black Hawk County and all or part of 10 other counties in northeast Iowa. The student population has doubled during the past 5 years to 4,000 students. Hawkeye's distance learning program and its Telecommunications System were established in 1993. Live interactive TV courses are provided over the state's DS-3 fiber-optics system (the Iowa Communications Network) and a 5-county Instructional TV Fixed Service (ITFS) system. In addition, Hawkeye offers credit telecourses that can be viewed on Iowa Public TV or by videocassette lease, and online courses are provided over the Internet. The distance learning Web site was established in 1996.

Hebrew College

43 Hawes Street	Phone: (617) 232-8710
Brookline, MA 02446	Fax: (617) 734-9769

Division(s): Center for Information Technology/Academic Programs
Web Site(s): http://www.hebrewcollege.edu
E-mail: None.

Graduate Degree Programs:
Master of Jewish Studies
Master of Jewish Education

Certificate Programs: Family Education, Early Childhood, Early Childhood Directors, Jewish Music Institute.

Class Titles: Finding Your Jewish Voice—Creative Writing Workshop, Women in Jewish History—Rabbinic Discourse/Social Reality, Justice/Forgiveness/Reconciliation in Jewish/Christian Thought, Jews Among Christians/Muslims, Playwriting on Jewish Themes.

Teaching Methods: *Computers:* Internet, e-mail, LISTSERV. *Other:* fax, correspondence, independent study, individual study.

On-Campus Requirements: None.

Tuition and Fees: *Undergraduate:* $750/course. *Graduate:* $1,000/course. *Other Costs:* $250 for noncredit students. *Credit by:* semester.

Accreditation: New England Association of Schools and Colleges.

Description: Founded to educate teachers for Jewish schools, Hebrew College (1921) is a nonsectarian, transdenominational institution that offers instruction in Jewish history, literature, language, religion, culture, and civilization and provides library, research, and other programmatic resources to the academic and general communities. Hebrew College today serves more than 20,000 students directly through its undergraduate and graduate degree programs and its institutes for family and early childhood educators, Jewish music practitioners, and other professional educators. In its life-span approach to Jewish education, the college also educates Jewish youth through its Prozdor high school and its overnight Camp Yavneh. Hebrew College believes that research, analysis, and strategic planning are vital in shaping its own programs as well as in building the Jewish community for tomorrow.

Henderson State University

1100 Henderson Street	Phone: (870) 230-5134
Arkadelphia, AR 71999-0001	Fax: (870) 230-5479

Division(s): Academic Affairs
Web Site(s): http://www.hsu.edu
E-mail: hardwrv@oaks.hsu.edu

Undergraduate Degree Programs:
Associate of Science in:
    Office Administration
    Child Care
Bachelor of Science in:
    Accounting
    Art
    Aviation
    Biology
    Business Administration
    Business Computer Science
    Chemistry
    Communication
    Computer Science–Mathematics
    Elementary Education
    English
    Family and Consumer Sciences
    History
    Human Services
    Mass Media Communication
    Mathematics
    Music
    Nursing
    Physical Education
    Physics
    Psychology
    Political Science
    Public Administration
    Recreation
    Social Science
    Sociology
    Spanish
    Vocational Business Education

Bachelor of Arts in:
   Studio Art
   Theater Arts

Graduate Degree Programs:
Master of Arts in Art
Master of Arts in Liberal Arts
Master of Science in:
   Biology
   Business Administration
   Community Counseling
   Early Childhood-Special Education
   Elementary Education
   English
   Mathematics
   Physical Education
   School Administration
   School Counseling
   Social Science
   Special Education

Teaching Methods: *Computers:* Internet, real-time chat, electronic classroom, e-mail, CD-ROM, LISTSERV. *TV:* videotape. *Other:* videoconferencing, independent study, individual study, learning contracts.

Credits Granted for: examination (CLEP, ACT-PEP, GRE).

Admission Requirements: *Undergraduate:* 19 on ACT, 2.5 high school GPA, 2.0 GPA for transfer students. *Graduate:* discipline-specific, 2.7 undergraduate GPA, entrance exam.

On-Campus Requirements: last 30 hours.

Tuition and Fees: *Undergraduate:* $89/credit. *Graduate:* $120/credit. *Other Costs:* $20 activity fee, $15 health fee, $13 technology fee, $10 infrastructure fee, $5 publications fee, $2/credit student center fee, $.25/credit band fee, $.25/credit library fee. *Credit by:* semester.

Financial Aid: Federal Stafford Loan, Federal Perkins Loan, Federal PLUS Loan, Federal Pell Grant, Federal Work-Study, VA, Arkansas resident programs.

Accreditation: North Central Association of Colleges and Schools, American Assembly of Collegiate Schools of Business, International Association for Management Education, National Council for Accreditation of Teacher Education, National League for Nursing, National Association of Schools of Music.

Description: Henderson State University (1890) is Arkansas' public, liberal arts university. True to the century-long tradition that has distinguished Henderson since its founding, the university remains dedicated to providing excellent undergraduate curricula in the arts and sciences. Further, the university is committed to offering strong professional programs in teacher education and business administration at both the undergraduate and graduate levels. Henderson State University began offering distance learning in 1995.

Heriot-Watt University

6921 Stockton Avenue	Phone: (800) 622-9661
El Cerrito, CA 94530	(510) 528-3777
	Fax: (510) 528-3555

Division(s): Edinburgh Business School
North American Distributor
Web Site(s): http://www.eachwmba.edu
E-mail: hwmba@degree.net

Graduate Degree Programs:
Master of Business Administration

Teaching Methods: *Other:* independent study, individual study.

Credits Granted for: Professional credentials such as CPA; graduate-level business courses, undergraduate degree in business; or a series of single subject, undergraduate business courses. Up to 2 compulsory courses may be waived for prior learning.

Admission Requirements: *Graduate:* accredited bachelor's degree or testing into program.

On-Campus Requirements: One final exam/course at local testing center.

Tuition and Fees: *Graduate:* $885/course. *Software:* $200/course optional supplementary software. *Other Costs:* $85/course exam registration fee. *Credit by:* semester.

Financial Aid: A payment plan is available to qualified students in the U.S.

Accreditation: Royal Charter, the highest level of British accreditation, equivalent to full U.S. accreditation.

Description: Heriot-Watt University was originally established in 1821 as an engineering college. Now located on a modern, 280-acre campus in Edinburgh, Scotland, the school is well-established as a premier business and technical university. Each year 2,500 graduates earn degrees in science, engineering, business, and technology. The Edinburgh Business School is Heriot-Watt University's graduate school of business. EBS administers the closely linked, on-campus and distance learning MBA programs. Students can pursue the MBA on campus, entirely by distance learning, or in combination, making it one of the most flexible programs available. Currently the Heriot-Watt MBA by distance has 7,000 students in 120 countries. The Heriot-Watt office opened in 1991 to serve North American students.

Herkimer County Community College

100 Reservoir Road	Phone: (315) 866-0300 x211
Herkimer, NY 13350	Fax: (315) 866-0876

Division(s): Distance Learning Coordinator
Web Site(s): http://www.hccc.ntcnet.com
E-mail: wmpelz@borg.com

Undergraduate Degree Programs:
Associate of Arts
Associate in Science
Associate in Applied Science

Graduate Degree Programs:
Master of Adult Education

Teaching Methods: *Computers:* Internet, electronic classroom, e-mail. *Other:* videoconferencing.

Credits Granted for: examination (CLEP, ACT, GRE).

Admission Requirements: *Undergraduate:* open admissions. *Graduate:* 4-year degree.

On-Campus Requirements: minimum of 30 hours credit from Herkimer County Community College required for associate degree. All may be via distance learning.

Tuition and Fees: *Undergraduate:* $80/credit. *Graduate:* $213/credit. *Other Costs:* variable, but minimal. *Credit by:* semester.

Financial Aid: Federal Stafford Loan, Federal Perkins Loan, Federal PLUS Loan, Federal Pell Grant, Federal Work-Study, VA, New York resident programs.

Accreditation: Middle States Association of Colleges and Schools.

Description: Herkimer County Community College (1967) is a full-service, open-door college. We are affiliated with the State University of New York and have a population of about 2,500 students. Our distance learning opportunities are extensive, with both closed-circuit videoconferencing for local students and Internet-based classes for anytime/anyplace student access.

Highland Community College

2998 West Pearl City Road	Phone: (815) 235-6121 x256
Freeport, IL 61032	Fax: (815) 235-1366

Division(s): Learning Resource Center
Web Site(s): http://highland.userworld.com/telecour
E-mail: ewelch@admin.highland.cc.il.us

Class Titles: History, Accounting, Business, Nutrition, Photography, Sociology, Poetry, Statistics, Literature, Economics.

Teaching Methods: *Computers:* electronic classroom. *TV:* videotape, cable program, satellite broadcasting. *Other:* None.

Credits Granted for: examination (CLEP, ACT-PEP, DANTES, GRE).

Admission Requirements: *Undergraduate:* high school graduate.

On-Campus Requirements: None.

Tuition and Fees: *Undergraduate:* $43/credit. *Other Costs:* assorted fees. *Credit by:* semester.

Financial Aid: Federal Stafford Loan, Federal Perkins Loan, Federal PLUS Loan, Federal Pell Grant, Federal Work-Study, VA, Illinois resident programs.

Accreditation: North Central Association of Colleges and Schools.

Description: Highland Community College (1963) is a small student-oriented, publicly funded community college in northwestern Illinois that serves a 4-county district. Distance learning activities are primarily limited to videotape-based programs.

Highline Community College

2400 South 240th	Phone: (206) 878-3700 x3011
Des Moines, WA 98000	Fax: (206) 870-3776

Division(s): Distance Education
Web Site(s): http://hcc.ctc.edu/~high/
E-mail: dsteussy@hcc.ctc.edu
slilley@hcc.ctc.edu

Undergraduate Degree Programs:
Associate Degree

Certificate Programs: Occupational Programs—Accounting, Administration of Justice/Law Enforcement, Administrative Assistant, Bookkeeping, Business, Career Transition, Child Care Provider, Chiropractic Technician, Client-Server Specialist, Dental Assistant, Drafting/Design Technology, Education: Early Childhood, Special Ed/Ed Paraprofessional, Freight Forwarding, Hotel/Tourism, Interactive Media, Interior Design, Jewelry/Goldsmithing, Library Technician, Legal Secretary, Legal Word Processor, Manufacturing Engineering Technology, Marketing/Selling, Medical Assistant, Medical Secretary and Receptionist, Medical Transcriptionist/Word Processor, Microcomputer Information Specialist, Network Specialist, Nursing, Nursing Articulation (Ladder), Office Assistant, Offset Printing, Paralegal, Parent Education, Physical Education, Plastics Manufacturing, Production Illustration, Respiratory Care, Retailing, Small Business Entrepreneurship, Transportation Agent, Travel/Transportation, Word Processing Operator, Word Processing Specialist.

Class Titles: Biology, Business, General Science, History,

Education, Literature, Social Science, Humanities, Mathematics, Computer Programming.

Teaching Methods: *Computers:* Internet, real-time chat, electronic classroom, e-mail, CD-ROM, newsgroup, LISTSERV. *TV:* videotape, cable program, satellite broadcasting, PBS. *Other:* radio broadcast, audioconferencing, videoconferencing, audiographics, audiotapes, fax, correspondence, independent study, individual study, learning contracts.

Credits Granted for: experiential learning, portfolio assessment, extrainstitutional learning, examinations (CLEP, ACT-PEP, DANTES, GRE).

Admission Requirements: *Undergraduate:* Advisors help with this process. They are: Denny Steussy at (206) 878-3710 x3534 and Siew Lai Lilley at (206) 878-3710 x3295. For the 2-year associate degree: high school graduate or age 18; U.S. citizen, refugee, or immigrant; foreign students are enrolled through the admissions office; prerequisites for all classes; time limits for completion.

On-Campus Requirements: None.

Tuition and Fees: *Undergraduate:* $51/credit. *Other Costs:* $20/quarter for e-mail accounts. *Credit by:* quarter.

Financial Aid: Federal Pell Grant, Supplementary Educational Opportunity Grant, Federal Work-Study, Federal Stafford Loan, Stafford Student Loan Program, student employment, State Need Grant, State Work Study, Highline Community College Grant, and Tuition Waiver.

Accreditation: American Association of Community Colleges.

Description: Highline Community College (1961) offers high-quality transfer, occupational, and continuing education programs to a diverse campus population and a wide array of community residents. Highline has offered distance courses for more than 20 years. The college offers a wide variety of programs designed to teach the technical, professional, and personal skills needed for employment in today's competitive world. Faculty are joined by representatives of business and labor in their specific fields to develop and review curricula to maintain high quality.

Hillsborough Community College

39 Columbia Drive
PO Box 31127
Tampa, FL 33631-3127

Phone: (813) 253-7000
Fax: (813) 253-7868

Division(s): Distance Learning
Web Site(s): http://www.hcc.cc.fl.us/DistanceLearning
E-mail: cominsm@mail.firn.edu

Class Titles: American History, Florida History, American Government, Art Appreciation, English, Humanities, Asian Humanities, Astronomy, Biology, Earth Science, Child Development, Psychology, Sociology, Marriage, Economics (micro/macro), Personal Finance, Business, Management, Marketing, College Algebra, Algebra, Computer Literacy for Teachers, Computers/Technology, Internet.

Teaching Methods: *Computers:* Internet, real-time chat, electronic classroom, e-mail, CD-ROM, newsgroup, LISTSERV. *TV:* videotape, cable program, PBS. *Other:* radio broadcast, videoconferencing, audiographics, fax, correspondence, independent study,

Credits Granted for: examination (CLEP, DANTES).

Admission Requirements: *Undergraduate:* high school diploma; college-level reading, writing, and math for most distance learning courses.

On-Campus Requirements: 5 meetings (optional) each term. A majority of work that determines student's grades must be completed in the presence of the instructor or an approved proctor. Some 75% of Associate of Arts and 75% of Associate of Science degrees earned at a distance; the other 25% are on site.

Tuition and Fees: *Undergraduate:* $46/credit resident, $167/credit nonresident. *Credit by:* semester.

Financial Aid: Federal Stafford Loan, Federal Perkins Loan, Federal PLUS Loan, Federal Pell Grant, Federal Work-Study, VA, Florida resident programs.

Accreditation: Southern Association of Colleges and Schools.

Description: Hillsborough Community College (1968) is embarking on its 30th year of providing contemporary educational programs to a highly diverse population. HCC's facilities include campuses in Tampa, Brandon, Plant City, and Ybor City. Courses are also offered at many off-campus sites throughout Hillsborough County. More than 45,000 students attend HCC each year. Of Florida's 28-member community college system, HCC ranks 7th in size. Students at HCC embody the spirit of diversity. In addition to a multitude of ethnic backgrounds and age groups, HCC students include individuals who are pursuing a college degree for the first time to those returning to college to increase their knowledge and skills. Because there is no "typical" HCC student, newcomers quickly fit right in. HCC is committed and continuously strives to anticipate technological, economic, and demographic trends to ensure that its graduates are well prepared to achieve success in their next ventures.

Hocking College

3301 Hocking Parkway   Phone: (740) 753-3591
Nelsonville, OH 45764   Fax: (740) 753-4097

Division(s): Academic Affairs
Web Site(s): http://www.hocking.edu
E-mail: dabelko_e@hocking.edu

Class Titles: Anatomy/Physiology, Human Organism, Psychology, Corrections, Real Estate, Health Information Management, Marketing, Job Communications, Technical Writing

Teaching Methods: *Computers:* e-mail. *Other:* videoconferencing.

Credits Granted for: experiential learning, portfolio assessment.

Admission Requirements: *Undergraduate:* high school diploma or GED. Some programs have special admission requirements.

On-Campus Requirements: 30 credit hours.

Tuition and Fees: *Undergraduate:* $63/credit part-time in-state, $126/credit out-of-state, $755/12–18 credits in-state, $1510/12–18 credits out-of-state, additional for international. *Application Fee:* $30. *Other Costs:* varying lab fees. *Credit by:* quarter.

Financial Aid: Federal Stafford Loan, Federal PLUS Loan, Federal Pell Grant, Federal Work-Study, VA, Ohio Instructional Grant.

Accreditation: North Central Association of Colleges and Schools.

Description: Hocking College (1968) is a 2-year technical college in which the accent is on "learning by doing." Located in southeastern Ohio about 60 miles from Columbus, the college offers associate degrees and certificates in more than 30 programs. It also provides the state-approved Transfer Module for students planning to transfer to a 4-year college. The 6,000 students are diverse in age, background, geographic origin, and interests and represent 88 Ohio counties, 20 states, and 47 foreign countries. Students may enroll in day or evening classes and may choose traditional classroom or self-paced instruction. Hocking's 2-way, interactive, audio-video distance learning program was established with funding from the Rural Utilities Services in 1994. Additionally, new, asynchronous, online distance learning offerings are being developed.

Holy Names College

3500 Mountain Boulevard   Phone: (510) 436-1321
Oakland, CA 94619-1699   (800) 430-1321
     Fax: (510) 436-1325

Division(s): Nursing
Web Site(s): http://www.hnc.edu
E-mail: vanderlaag@admin.hnc.edu

Undergraduate Degree Programs:
Bachelor of Science in Nursing

Teaching Methods: *Computers:* computer software, e-mail, CD-ROM. *TV:* interactive TV. *Other:* videoconferencing, telephone, fax, print, mail. Adjunct faculty are at each videoconferencing site.

Credits Granted for: examination (CLEP), ACE/PONSI evaluated military training programs, ACE/PONSI evaluated business training programs, transfer credits.

Admission Requirements: *Undergraduate:* for transfer students, good standing at last institution, 2.2 GPA in 30 transferable units, Associate Degree in Nursing or hospital school of nursing diploma, currently licensed as RN in California or eligibility for NCLEX, completion of lower-division prerequisites including Anatomy/Physiology, Microbiology, Sociology or Anthropology, Psychology, and freshman English Composition.

On-Campus Requirements: classes are telecast to multiple sites at selected Kaiser Hospital facilities throughout California on Wednesdays and Thursdays from 6:00 to 9:00 P.M.

Tuition and Fees: *Undergraduate:* $250/credit. *Application Fee:* $35. *Credit by:* semester.

Financial Aid: Federal Stafford Loan, Federal Pell Grant, VA, Cal Grant.

Accreditation: National League for Nursing, Western Association of Schools and Colleges.

Description: Holy Names College (1868) is a cosmopolitan institution of innovative higher learning offering men and women of all faiths and ages the opportunity to obtain an outstanding education in liberal arts, preparation for many careers, and an enriched life. A leader in providing degree completion opportunities for working adults, Holy Names has offered a campus-based nursing program for Registered Nurses seeking BSN degrees since 1971. Since 1995 the college has offered its accredited NLN program via teleconferencing and in partnership with Kaiser Permanente.

Home Study International
(Griggs University)

| 12501 Old Columbia Pike | Phone: (800) 782-4769 |
| Silver Spring, MD 20904-6600 | Fax: (301) 680-5157 |

Division(s): entire school
Web Site(s): http://www.griggs.edu
E-mail: 74617.74@compuserve.com

Undergraduate Degree Programs:
Bachelor of Science in:
    Church Business Management
    Religious Education
Bachelor of Arts in:
    Religion
    Theological Studies

Class Titles: all classes are available via distance learning. Call college for complete list.

Teaching Methods: *Computers:* Internet. *TV:* videotape. *Other:* audiotapes, correspondence.

Credits Granted for: experiential learning, portfolio assessment, examination (CLEP, ACT-PEP, DANTES, GRE).

Admission Requirements: *Undergraduate:* accredited secondary school graduate or equivalent, completion of adequate pattern of high school subjects, 2.5 high school GPA; if native language is not English, must submit exam results for TOEFL or Michigan Test for English Language Proficiency with scores of 550 (TOEFL) or 90 (Michigan).

On-Campus Requirements: None.

Tuition and Fees: *Undergraduate:* $165/credit. *Application Fee:* $60. *Other Costs:* varies for textbooks, supplies, materials. *Credit by:* semester.

Accreditation: Distance Education and Training Council.

Description: Since 1909 Home Study International has helped students achieve their educational goals through distance learning. The mission of HSI is to provide students with a well-balanced education that will enrich the quality of their lives and their church.

Hope International University

| 2500 East Nutwood Avenue | Phone: (714) 879-3901 |
| Fullerton, CA 92831 | Fax: (714) 879-1041 |

Division(s): Distance Learning
Web Site(s): http://www.hiu.edu
E-mail: llenz@hiu.edu

Graduate Degree Programs:
Master of Business Administration
International Development
Nonprofit Organization
Master of Ministry Intercultural Studies

Class Titles: Theology of Ministry, Life of Christ, World Civilization, Perspectives in World Christian Movement, Violent Encounters in Family, History of Hebrew People (in Spanish only), Intercultural Studies, Marriage/Family/Child Counseling, Biblical Interpretation (Theology/Hermeneutics), Bible Survey, Cross Cultural Mores/Values, World Christian Movement, Missiological Exegesis, Apostolic Hermeneutics.

Teaching Methods: *Computers:* Internet, real-time chat, electronic classroom, e-mail, CD-ROM, newsgroup, LISTSERV. *TV:* videotape. *Other:* audiotapes, fax, correspondence, independent study, individual study, learning contracts.

Credits Granted for: experiential learning, examination (CLEP, ACT-PEP, DANTES, GRE).

Admission Requirements: *Graduate:* bachelor's degree, 3.0 GPA for full admission, TOEFL.

On-Campus Requirements: None.

Tuition and Fees: *Undergraduate:* $600/course. *Graduate:* $600/individual videocourse, $341/unit for full degree program (MBA and Intercultural Studies). *Application Fee:* $30 for graduate and undergraduate courses as well as graduate degree program. *Other Costs:* $100 videotape deposit (refunded upon videotape's return). *Credit by:* semester.

Financial Aid: Federal Stafford Loan, Federal Perkins Loan, Federal PLUS Loan, Federal Pell Grant, Federal Work-Study, CAL Grant, FEOG.

Accreditation: Western Association of Schools and Colleges.

Description: Hope International University (1928) is built upon the historic and solid foundations of Pacific Christian College, which was called Pacific Bible Seminary at its inception. The university is composed of 3 schools: Pacific Christian College—the traditional undergraduate college; the School of Professional Studies—with an adult degree completion program and international programs; and the School of Graduate Studies—offers several graduate programs to enhance professional and church-related management careers. Distance Learning began in 1994 with individual courses delivered via videotape; student progress is monitored by university faculty. The program has since grown to include 2 complete online degree programs at the graduate level. The Master of Business Administration and the Master of Intercultural Studies are offered online to students worldwide.

Hospitality Training Center

220 North Main Street
Hudson, OH 44236

Phone: (330) 653-9151
Fax: (330) 650-2833

Certificate Programs: Medical Office Computer Specialist, Motel Management.

Teaching Methods: *Other:* correspondence, independent study, individual study, learning contracts.

Credits Granted for: experiential learning, portfolio assessment, extrainstitutional learning, examination (CLEP, ACT-PEP, DANTES GRE).

Admission Requirements: *Certificate:* open enrollment.

On-Campus Requirements: None.

Tuition and Fees: *Undergraduate:* $1,995 Motel Management, $2,395 Medical Office Computer Specialist (includes software). *Credit by:* hours.

Accreditation: Distance Education and Training Council.

Description: Hospitality Training Center (1961) was founded by Dr. Robert W. McIntosh at Michigan State University. In 1963, Duane Hills purchased the school, originally known as Modern School, and changed the name to Motel Managers School. This name was changed in 1985 to Hospitality Training Center to better reflect what the school is doing. Currently 2 courses are being offered and are accredited by DETC. The school is now over 35 years old. It is the only school in the U.S. to train for Motel Management by distance learning. Duane Hills is the President of DETC and serves on the Board of Trustees.

Houston Community College

4310 Dunlavy Room 215G
Houston, TX 77006

Phone: (713) 718-5275
Fax: (713) 718-5388

Division(s): Distance Education
Web Site(s): http://distance.hccs.cc.tx.us
E-mail: paul_c@hccs.cc.tx.us

Undergraduate Degree Programs:
Associate Degree

Class Titles: Accounting, Anthropology, Art, Business, Child Development, Criminal Justice, Computer Science, Drafting, Economics, Electronic Engineering Technology, English, Geology, Government, History, Math, Marketing, Mental Health, Philosophy, Photography, Psychology, Real Estate, Records Management, Sociology, Spanish.

Teaching Methods: *Computers:* Internet, real-time chat, electronic classroom, e-mail, CD-ROM, BBS. *TV:* videotape, cable program, PBS. *Other:* videoconferencing, audiotapes, fax, correspondence, independent study, print based.

Credits Granted for: examination (CLEP).

Admission Requirements: *Undergraduate:* open door, high school graduate or GED, TASP/ASSET testing, see catalog for exemptions.

On-Campus Requirements: Some classes have weekly on-campus labs.

Tuition and Fees: *Undergraduate:* $107/3 credits in-district, $164/3 credits out-of-district, $366/3 credits out-of-state. *Other Costs:* $24/course distance education fee. *Credit by:* semester.

Financial Aid: Federal Stafford Loan, Federal Pell Grant, Federal Work-Study, VA, Texas resident programs.

Accreditation: Southern Association of Colleges and Schools.

Description: The Houston Community College System (1971) was created as a public open-admission institution of higher education offering associate degrees, certificates, workforce training, and lifelong learning opportunities for all people in the communities it serves. In an effort to make education more accessible to all students, HCCS has offered a regular schedule of telecourses since 1985, and in 1987 it introduced the first computer-modem course. The distance education department currently offers 120 courses to 3,000 students each semester: telecourses airing on PBS-TV, HCCS cable, and Stafford cable, videocassette courses, print-based (textbook only) courses, and computer courses (computer/modem-based and on the Internet).

Hutchinson Community College

1300 North Plum
Hutchinson, KS 67501

Phone: (316) 665-3536
Fax: (316) 665-3310

Division(s): Instructional Technology Department
Web Site(s): http://www2.hutchcc.edu
http://www.hutchcc.edu
E-mail: hortonl@hutchcc.edu

Undergraduate Degree Programs:
Associate of Arts

Class Titles: English, Literature, Psychology, Abnormal Psychology, Human Relations, Spanish, Personal Finance, Nutrition, Sociology, Anthropology, Aerobics, Business Communications, Leadership, Microcomputer Applications, Internet, Art Appreciation, Business Law, U.S. History.

Teaching Methods: *Computers:* Internet, real-time chat, e-mail, CD-ROM, LISTSERV. *TV:* videotape, cable program, PBS, telecourse, interactive TV. *Other:* fax, correspondence, independent study, individual study.

Credits Granted for: transfer courses, challenge examinations.

Admission Requirements: *Undergraduate:* high school

graduate or GED, high school transcript, transfer transcripts.

On-Campus Requirements: 16 hours of class time on campus or ITV site for telecourse; Internet and cable courses are competency based.

Tuition and Fees: *Undergraduate:* $37/credit plus $30 fee telecourse/Internet/cable, $37/credit cable course. *Other Costs:* $5 art appreciation. *Credit by:* semester.

Financial Aid: Federal Pell Grants, Federal Supplemental Education Opportunity Grants, Federal College Work-Study, Federal Direct Stafford Loan, VA.

Accreditation: North Central Association of Colleges and Schools.

Description: Hutchinson Community College (1928) Area Vocational School is a comprehensive community college offering a wide variety of course work for transfer and 26 vocational programs. HCC serves 125,000 residents in a 3½ county service area. Some 1,600 students attend the institution full-time, with a full-time student equivalency of 2,257 students (fall 1997 statistics). HCC entered the world of distance education in the early 1990s. Six businesses contributed toward the construction of an interactive television classroom to connect the college to a 4-high-school ITV consortium. Day and evening classes have been offered on this full-motion system each semester since 1992. Two additional area schools became ITV sites in 1997 and a 7th will come on board in the fall of 1998. HCC is also capable of interacting with a wide variety of sites via compressed motion videoconferencing and serves as a satellite receive site for a broad array of educational programming.

Hypnosis Motivation Institute

| 18607 Ventura Boulevard, Suite 310 | Phone: (800) 682-4464 |
| Tarzana, CA 91356 | Fax: (818) 344-2262 |

Division(s): Extension School
Web Site(s): http://www.HypnosisMotivation.com
E-mail: None.

Certificate Programs: Hypnotherapy.

Class Titles: Hypnotherapy

Teaching Methods: *TV:* videotape. *Other:* audiotapes, fax, correspondence, tutorial.

Admission Requirements: *Undergraduate:* age 18.

On-Campus Requirements: None.

Tuition and Fees: *Undergraduate:* $4,400/300 clock hours. *Credit by:* clock hour.

Accreditation: Distance Education and Training Council.

Description: Hypnosis Motivation Institute (1968) is America's only accredited college of hypnotherapy.

ICI University

| 6300 North Belt Line Road | Phone: (972) 751-1111 |
| Irving, TX 75063 | Fax: (972) 714-8185 |

Division(s): Certificate Programs: Global Operations Degree Programs: Global Enrollment
Web Site(s): http://www.ici.edu
E-mail: enroll@ici.edu

Undergraduate Degree Programs:
Associate of Arts in Religious Studies
Diploma in Theology
Diploma in Ministry
Bachelor of Arts in:
    Bible and Theology
    Religious Education
    Missions

Graduate Degree Programs:
Master of Arts in Biblical Studies:
    Old Testament
    New Testament
    Ministerial Studies
    Leadership

Certificate Programs: Christian Life, Christian Service.

Class Titles: All courses are available through distance learning.

Teaching Methods: *Computers:* Internet, electronic classroom, e-mail, LISTSERV. *Other:* audioconferencing, video conferencing, audiotapes, fax, correspondence, independent study, individual study.

Credits Granted for: experiential learning, portfolio assessment, extrainstitutional learning, examination (CLEP, DANTES).

Admission Requirements: *Undergraduate:* open-enrollment. The basic requirement for matriculation into a degree program is the possession of a high school diploma, GED certificate, GCE 'O' level certificate or equivalent. *Graduate:* Bachelor of Arts Degree, 24 credit hours of undergraduate course work in Bible/Theology, and the ability to study and communicate in English.

On-Campus Requirements: None.

Tuition and Fees: *Undergraduate:* $75/credit. *Graduate:* $126/credit. *Application Fee:* $35. *Credit by:* semester.

Financial Aid: VA benefits, Free Interest Tuition payment plan.

Accreditation: Distance Education and Training Council.

Description: ICI University (1967) was founded as the International Correspondence Institute by the Division of Foreign Missions of the Assemblies of God. ICI is an independent study and extension instruction school for all levels and types of religious instruction. ICI has developed evangelism and Christian education courses for preachers, teaching new Christians, and training workers for the local church. Certificates are awarded in evangelism, Christian life, and Christian service programs for completion of courses and units of study. For ministerial training, ICI has developed the Christian ministry program for the completion of a diploma in Christian ministry. The college degree program offers the bachelor of arts and associate of arts degrees. In addition, graduate courses are available leading to a master of arts degree.

Illinois Eastern Community Colleges
Frontier Community College
Lincoln Trail College
Olney Central College
Wabash Valley College

233 East Chestnut Street
Olney, IL 62450

Phone: (618) 393-2982
Fax: (618) 392-4816

Division(s): Information Technology
Web Site(s): http://www.iecc.cc.il.us
E-mail: hubblee@iecc.cc.il.us

Class Titles: Sign Language, Telecommunications Technology, Composition, Statistics, Spanish, Economics, Sociology

Teaching Methods: *TV:* videotape, videoconferencing. *Other:* correspondence, independent study, individual study.

Credits Granted for: experiential learning, portfolio assessment, examination (CLEP, ACT-PEP, DANTES, GRE).

Admission Requirements: *Undergraduate:* ASSET test.

On-Campus Requirements: None.

Tuition and Fees: *Undergraduate:* $36/credit. *Application Fee:* $10. *Credit by:* semester.

Financial Aid: Federal Stafford Loan, Federal Perkins Loan, Federal PLUS Loan, Federal Pell Grant, Federal Work-Study, VA, Illinois resident programs.

Accreditation: North Central Association of Colleges and Schools.

Description: The mission of Illinois Eastern Community Colleges District (1967) is to provide educational opportunities and public services to the citizens of southeastern Illinois. IECC is a system of 4 public institutions of higher education supported by a district office. By offering quality educational and public service programs, the colleges work together to better the cultural, social, and economic futures of the citizens of southeastern Illinois.

Independent Study at Portland State University

School of Extended Studies
1633 SW Park Avenue
Portland, OR 97201

Phone: (503) 725-4865
(800) 547-8887 x4865
Fax: (503) 725-4840

Division(s): Distance Learning
Web Site(s): http://extended.pdx.edu/study
E-mail: xsis@ses.pdx.edu

Class Titles: Criminal Justice Process, Juvenile Justice Process, Criminal Law/Legal Reasoning, Constitutional Criminal Procedures, Court Procedures, Drawing, Atmospheric Science, Projects-Weather Analysis Lab (Synoptic Meteorology), Accounting, Cost Accounting, Accounting for Not-For-Profit Organizations, Auditing, Nutrition, Principles of Economics (Micro/Macro), Shakespeare, American Literature, American Fiction, Contemporary Literature, American Folklore, Corrective English (noncredit), English Composition, Short Story Writing (Fiction or Nonfiction), Poetry Writing, Introductory Geography, General Geology, Volcanoes/Earthquakes, Oceanography, Geology of Oregon, Fossil Record, Geology of Pacific Northwest, History of Western Civilization, History of U.S., Algebra (noncredit), College Mathematics, Calculus for Management/Social Sciences, Calculus, Probability/Statistics, Psychology as Natural Science, Psychology as Social Science, Human Development, Psychopathology, World Religions, Sociology, Social Problems/Issues.

Teaching Methods: *Computers:* e-mail, CD-ROM. *TV:* videotape. *Other:* correspondence, independent study.

Credits Granted for: undergraduate credits based on a quarter system.

Admission Requirements: *Undergraduate:* No admission/residency requirements.

On-Campus Requirements: Students complete independent study courses from their home/hometown. Office of Independent Study approves proctor and exam site. No on-campus time required.

Tuition and Fees: *Undergraduate:* $75/credit. *Other Costs:* $15 registration fee, textbooks/materials. *Credit by:* quarter.

Financial Aid: Some packages fund correspondence study.

Accreditation: Northwest Association of School and Colleges.

Description: Independent Study at Portland State University, established in 1907 by the Oregon University System, offers 68 correspondence courses in 15 areas ranging from Business Administration to Sociology. This one-to-one experience allows students to pace themselves during the 12-month program. Enrollment is open, students may register any day in any term, and Portland State University admission is not necessary to take independent study courses. Independent study credits are transferrable and are held in the Portland State University Registrar's Office.

Indiana College Network

957 West Michigan Street	Phone: (800) 426-8899
Indianapolis, IN 46202	Fax: (812) 855-9380

Division(s): Student Services Center
Web Site(s): http://www.icn.org
E-mail: ICN@ihets.org

Undergraduate Degree Programs:
Associate of Applied Science in:
  Accounting
  Business Administration (Restaurant Management Specialty)
  Design Technology (CAD Option)
Associate of Arts in:
  Biblical Studies
  General Arts
  Justice Administration (Ministry Concentration)
  Justice Administration (Public Policy Concentration)
  Liberal Arts (General Studies)
Associate of General Studies
Associate of Science in:
  Business Administration
  Labor Studies
  General Aviation Flight Technology
  General Studies
  Behavioral Sciences
  Business Administration (Management Option)
  Communications
  Histotechnology
  Social Science
  Law Enforcement
Bachelor of General Studies
Bachelor of Science in:
  Electronics Technology
  General Industrial Supervision
  General Industry Technology
  Human Resource Development
  Labor Studies
  Nursing
  Health Services
  Nursing (RN Baccalaureate Completion Track)

Graduate Degree Programs:
Master of Arts in:
  Education in Elementary Education
  Education in Special Education
  Executive Development for Public Service
Master of Business Administration

Master of Science in:
  Adult Education
  Computer Science
  Education in Language Education
  Electrical Engineering
  Industrial Engineering
  Mechanical Engineering
  Interdisciplinary Engineering
  Human Resource Development
  Nursing
  Recreation (Therapeutic Recreation Emphasis)
  Health and Safety (Specialization in Occupational Safety Management)
Master of Arts in Health and Safety (Specialization in Occupational Safety Management

Certificate Programs: Distance Education, General Studies, Labor Studies, Public Library (Librarian V and IV), School Library/Media and Information Technology, Christian Worker.

Teaching Methods: *Computers:* Internet, e-mail, CD-ROM, newsgroup, LISTSERV. *TV:* videotape, cable TV, satellite broadcasting, PBS. *Other:* videoconferencing, audioconferencing, correspondence, independent study.

Credits Granted for: variable.

Admission Requirements: *Undergraduate:* variable. *Graduate:* variable. *Certificate:* variable.

On-Campus Requirements: some courses may require a student to attend a specific number of on-campus sessions; most courses do not.

Tuition and Fees: *Undergraduate:* tuition and fees are established independently by each participating institution. *Software:* variable. *Credit by:* Most participating institutions are on the semester system, although many are offering courses with open enrollment throughout the year.

Financial Aid: Financial aid is determined independently by each participating institution, and may include the Federal Stafford Loan, Federal Perkins Loan, Federal PLUS Loan, Federal Pell Grant, Federal Work-Study, VA, etc.

Accreditation: All participating institutions are accredited.

Description: The Indiana College Network (1992) is a not-for-profit service of the Indiana Partnership for Statewide Education, a unique state-funded consortium of 39 public and private universities and colleges whose mission is to ensure that higher education is available to Indiana citizens wherever they may live or work. It was created as a vehicle for Indiana's postsecondary institutions to collaborate on the development and delivery of distributed learning. The network's Student Service Center serves prospective students as a clearinghouse for information about admissions, registration, career counseling, and financial aid. It is the students' first stop in registering for distance education courses.

Partnership institutions include: Ball State University, Independent Colleges of Indiana, Inc., Indiana State University, Indiana University, Ivy Tech State College, Purdue University, University of Southern Indiana, and Vincennes University.

Indiana Institute of Technology

1600 East Washington Boulevard	Phone: (888) 666-8324
Fort Wayne, IN 46803	(219) 422-5561
	Fax: (219) 422-1518

Division(s): Extended Studies Division
Web Site(s): http://www.indtech.edu
E-mail: stahl@indtech.edu

Undergraduate Degree Programs:
Associate of Science in:
  Business Administration
  Concentrations in Management of Finance
Bachelor of Science in:
  Business Administration
  Concentrations in Management, Marketing, Finance or Human Resources

Class Titles: Accounting, Business, English, Humanities or Social Science classes.

Teaching Methods: *Computers:* e-mail. *Other:* fax, correspondence, independent study, individual study.

Credits Granted for: experiential learning, portfolio assessment, extrainstitutional learning, examination (CLEP, ACT-PEP, DANTES, GRE).

Admission Requirements: *Undergraduate:* application fee, official copy of high school transcript/GED.

On-Campus Requirements: None.

Tuition and Fees: *Undergraduate:* $193/credit. *Application Fee:* $50. *Credit by:* semester.

Financial Aid: Federal Stafford Loan, Federal PLUS Loan, Federal Pell Grant, VA.

Accreditation: North Central Association of Colleges and Schools.

Description: Indiana Institute of Technology (1930) is a private, not-for-profit institution offering undergraduate degrees in engineering, computer science, and business. The Extended Studies Division was founded in 1981 to deliver the traditional, quality business education. Indiana Tech has become known for its emerging number of adult students. ESD offers students 2 degree programs: the Accelerated Degree Program (classroom environment) and the Independent Study Program (self-study). The Independent Study Program offers you the opportunity to complete your entire college degree without attending formal classes. Via mail, you are provided with the detailed materials to guide you through the course work at your own pace. The established completion period for courses is 6 months.

Indiana University

620 Union Drive	
Union Building 129	Phone: (317) 274-4178
Indianapolis, IN 46202-5171	Fax: (317) 278-0895

Division(s): School of Continuing Studies, Office of Distance Learning
Web Site(s): http://www.indiana.edu/~iudisted/
E-mail: scs@indiana.edu

Undergraduate Degree Programs:
Associate of General Studies
Associate of Science in Labor Studies
Bachelor of General Studies
Bachelor of Science in Labor Studies

Graduate Degree Programs:
Master of Science in:
  Adult Education
  Language Education
  Nursing
  Therapeutic Recreation
Master of Recreation and Park Administration

Certificate Programs: Labor Studies, Distance Education (in Indiana only), Public Library—Librarian IV, Public Library—Librarian V, School Library/Media and Information Technology.

Class Titles: university-level and high school-level independent study courses, professional development programs, African Studies, American Studies, Anthropology, Astronomy, Biology, Business, Classical Studies, College of Arts/Sciences, Communication/Culture, Computer Science, Criminal Justice, Economics, Education, English, Fine Arts, Folklore, French, Geography, Geological Sciences, Health/Physical Education/Recreation, History, History/Philosophy of Science, Italian, Journalism, Labor Studies, Linguistics, Math, Music, Nursing, Philosophy, Physics, Political Science, Psychology, Religious Studies, School of Public/Environmental Affairs, Sociology, Spanish, Speech Communication, Telecommunications.

Teaching Methods: *Computers:* Internet, real-time chat, electronic classroom, e-mail, CD-ROM, newsgroup, LIST-SERV. *TV:* videotape, cable program, satellite broadcasting, PBS. *Other:* audioconferencing, videoconferencing, audiographics, audiotapes, fax, correspondence.

Credits Granted for: experiential learning, portfolio assessment, examination (CLEP, DANTES), military service, accredited transfer credits.

Admission Requirements: *Undergraduate:* variable. *Graduate:* variable.

On-Campus Requirements: for some programs.

Tuition and Fees: *Undergraduate:* $109/credit resident, $357/credit nonresident, $94/credit correspondence. *Graduate:* $147/credit resident, $428/credit nonresident. *Application Fee:* variable. *Software:* variable. *Other Costs:* variable. *Credit by:* semester.

Financial Aid: varies; not available for correspondence courses.

Accreditation: North Central Association of Colleges and Schools.

Description: Indiana University (1820) is both an internationally ranked institution of higher education and a great public university. It has 90,000 students on its 8 campuses and 400,000 alumni worldwide. IU is committed to providing high-quality education to traditional and nontraditional students. At Indiana University, students who cannot attend traditional, on-campus classes may still earn certification, certificates, and undergraduate and graduate degrees through traditional classroom courses and hundreds of distance courses. Distance programs incorporate such technologies as computers, the Internet, online conferencing, e-mail, CD-ROM, videotape, virtual reality software, and interactive TV, in addition to independent study by correspondence. IU has offered independent study by correspondence since 1912, and its use of technology to deliver academic programs has earned it a reputation as one of America's most "electronically wired" universities.

Indiana University of Pennsylvania

Keith 100	Phone: (724) 357-2209
Indiana, PA 15701	Fax: (724) 357-7597

Division(s): School of Continuing Education
Web Site(s): http://www.iup.edu/contin/
E-mail: ce-ocp@@grove.iup.edu

Certificate Programs: Web-based instruction for Physics Certification (Graduate credit)

Teaching Methods: *Computers:* Internet, electronic classroom, e-mail, LISTSERV *TV:* videotape. *Other:* correspondence, independent study, individual study

Admission Requirements: *Undergraduate:* state certification in science or math, 8 credits of physics at introductory college level, math background including calculus. NOTE: state requirements also include one course in biology, 2 in chemistry, and one course in geoscience.

On-Campus Requirements: Two laboratory courses will be offered in the summers of 1999 and 2000.

Tuition and Fees: *Undergraduate:* Tuition and fees subject to change without notice, resident $144/credit, nonresident 151/credit *Graduate:* resident $193/credit, nonresident $197/credit *Application Fee:* $30 *Other Costs:* instruction fee $87, registration fee $20/person *Credit by:* semester.

Financial Aid: Federal Stafford Loan, Federal Perkins Loan, Federal PLUS Loan, Federal Pell Grant, Federal Work-Study, VA, Pennsylvania resident programs.

Accreditation: Middle States Association of Colleges and Schools.

Description: Indiana University of Pennsylvania (1875), opening with only 225 students in a single building, has experienced continuous growth that has made it Pennsylvania's fifth-largest university. The current enrollment is more than 13,000, with students from 36 states and more than 50 countries. More than 100 degree programs are available. Although access has been provided for many years to the citizens of western/central Pennsylvania through off-campus degree programs, 1998 marks the beginning of the use of distance education technologies for this purpose.

Indiana University, South Bend

1700 Mishawaka Avenue	Phone: (219) 237-4872
South Bend, IN 46634-7111	Fax: (219) 237-6549

Division(s): Off-Campus Programs
Web Site(s): http://www.iusb.edu
E-mail: jwierick@iusb.edu

Class Titles: History, Psychology, Communications, General Studies, Philosophy, Labor Studies, Chemistry, Education, Personal Finance.

Teaching Methods: *TV:* 2-way audio/video interactive, PBS. *Other:* None.

Admission Requirements: *Undergraduate:* good standing at another higher education institution. Please contact school for complete information.

On-Campus Requirements: programming is available only at TV receive sites in Indiana.

Tuition and Fees: *Undergraduate:* $96/credit Indiana resident. *Other Costs:* $25/3 credits technology fee. *Credit by:* semester.

Financial Aid: Federal Stafford Loan, Federal Perkins Loan, Federal PLUS Loan, Federal Pell Grant, Federal Work-Study, VA, Indiana resident programs.

Accreditation: North Central Association of Colleges and Schools.

Description: Indiana University at South Bend (1966), with 100 certificate, associate, bachelor's, and master's degree programs, is northern Indiana's primary resource for lifelong learning. Approximately 7,500 students are enrolled in degree and certificate programs in South Bend and at off-campus sites in Elkhart and Plymouth. Graduate students comprise 20% of enrollment, and some 9,000 area residents enroll in IUSB's Continuing Education programs. For the past 5 years, IUSB has offered distance education classes through the Virtual Indiana Campus, a 2-way, interactive audio/video system connecting IU campuses and centers throughout the state. Some additional programming is offered through PBS to the local service area.

Indiana Wesleyan University

4301 South Washington Street	Phone: (800) 621-8667 x2343
Marion, IN 46953	Fax: (765) 677-2380

Division(s): Adult and Professional Studies
Web Site(s): http://www.indwes.edu
E-mail: cleonard@indwes.edu

Graduate Degree Programs:
Online Master of Business Administration

Class Titles: Biblical Literature, Music Appreciation, Ethics, Composition, Earth Science, Drivers Ed on Information Superhighway, Internet Tools, Building Your www.Home. page, Computer Concepts; various online electives in the following programs: Bachelor of Science in Business Administration, Bachelor of Sciene in Management, Bachelor of Science in Organizational Leadership, Bachelor of Science in Nursing.

Teaching Methods: *Computers:* Internet, electronic bulletin board, real-time chat. *Other:* None.

Credits Granted for: experiential learning, portfolio assessment, examination (CLEP, ACT-PEP, DANTES), extrainstitutional learning, American Council on Education Guide to the Evaluation of Educational Experiences in Armed Services.

Admission Requirements: *Undergraduate:* high school graduate or GED, 60 accredited transferable credits (40 hours may be equivalent training), 2.0 overall GPA (2.5 for Bachelor of Science in Nursing), minimum of 2 years of full-time work experience beyond high school. *Graduate:* online MBA: bachelor's degree; 2.5 overall college GPA; 3 years of full-time, related work experience; prerequisites in math, economics, finance, and accounting.

On-Campus Requirements: For the online MBA, students must take 2 3-day courses offered in Indianapolis.

Tuition and Fees: *Undergraduate:* $175/credit (online elective courses). *Graduate:* $18,000 for entire online MBA program,

which includes all books and fees. *Application Fee:* $20. *Other Costs:* $200 educational resource fee, $25/credit examination transcription fee, $150 portfolio application fee plus $25/credit transcription fee. *Credit by:* semester.

Financial Aid: Federal Stafford Loan, Federal Pell Grant, Indiana resident programs, VA.

Accreditation: North Central Association of Colleges and Schools.

Description: Indiana Wesleyan University (1890) is a Christian, liberal arts, coeducational university related to The Wesleyan Church. The original campus was well known in Indiana for teacher education before it annexed the Fairmount Bible School. Today the university prepares students for service and leadership roles in teacher education, health care, social work, business, industry, government, Christian ministries, and other areas. Indiana Wesleyan was the fastest-growing college in Indiana over the past 5 years. More than 1,800 students are enrolled in traditional programs on the Marion campus, and 4,250 working men and women take Adult and Professional Studies Division classes throughout the state. In 1997 we began offering online, elective courses within the APS undergraduate programs, and we began the Online Master of Business Administration program in late 1998.

Institute of Transpersonal Psychology

744 San Antonio Road	Phone: (650) 493-4430 x40
Palo Alto, CA 94303	Fax: (650) 493-6835

Division(s): Global
Web Site(s): http://www.tmn.com/itp/
E-mail: itpinfo@best.com

Graduate Degree Programs:
Master of Arts in Transpersonal Studies
Master of Transpersonal Psychology
Master of Arts in Transpersonal Studies, Learning in Network Knowing (LINK)

Certificate Programs: Transpersonal Studies, Spiritual Psychology, Women's Spiritual Development, Creative Expression, Wellness Counseling and Bodymind Consciousness, LINK Certificate in Transpersonal Studies.

Teaching Methods: *Computers:* Internet, real-time chat, electronic classroom, e-mail, CD-ROM, newsgroup, LISTSERV. *Other:* fax, correspondence, independent study, individual study, learning contracts.

Admission Requirements: *Graduate:* emotional maturity and experience in self-exploration are essential factors for admission to any program. Master of Transpersonal Psychology: bachelor's degree with 8 semester psychology credits

(12 quarter) with a "B" GPA for upper-level course work. Master of Arts in Transpersonal Studies and LINK Master of Arts in Transpersonal Studies: may include general social sciences courses.

On-Campus Requirements: for each certificate, 2 4-day seminars are required. For Wellness Certificate, 3 4-day seminars are required. For the LINK Certificate, 3 seminars are required.

Tuition and Fees: *Graduate:* $878/3-credit course, $,7896 for the Certificate Programs, $6,328 for the MA in Transpersonal Studies, $8,736 for the MA in Transpersonal Psychology. *Application Fee:* $55. *Software:* $640/LINK Certificate program, $1,080/LINK Master in Transpersonal Psychology. *Other Costs:* $100 registration fee. *Credit by:* quarter.

Financial Aid: Federal Stafford Loan.

Accreditation: Western Association of Schools and Colleges.

Description: The Institute of Transpersonal Psychology (1975) provides graduate programs in psychology. ITP offers whole-person learning with traditional and nontraditional psychological and spiritual models of learning and teaching. Course work integrates experiential work with theory and research. Campus Programs offers a PhD in Transpersonal Psychology, a Master of Arts in Transpersonal Psychology, and a Master of Arts in Counseling Psychology. Global Programs give students the opportunity to study at any location in the world. Each Global Program is designed to allow maximum flexibility to mature students who have the desire, ability, and motivation to work independently and in relationship with the support of a Global Faculty Mentor.

Inter-American University of Puerto Rico

500 Road 830	Phone: (787) 279-1912
Bayamon, PR 00957	Fax: (787) 279-2205

Division(s): None.
Web Site(s): http://bc.inter.edu
E-mail: http://mail.bc.inter.edu

Undergraduate Degree Programs:
Associate of Science in:
    Secretarial Sciences
    Accounting
    Business Administration
    Audiovisual Communications Technology
    Computer Sciences
    Telecommunications Technology
    Installation and Repair of Computer Systems
Bachelor of Arts in:
    Mathematics

    Secretarial Sciences
        Information Processing
        Executive Secretary
Bachelor of Business Administration in:
    Accounting
    Managerial Economics
    Management
    Human Resources Management
    Industrial Management
    Marketing
    Computer Management Information Systems
Bachelor of Science in:
    Industrial Engineering
    Electrical Engineering
    Mechanical Engineering
    Airway Sciences
        Management
        Electronic Systems
        Computer Sciences
        Aircraft Management
    Computer Sciences
        Commercial
        Systems
        Scientific Applications
    Communications Technology
    Mathematics
    Biology
        General
        Microbiology
        Public Health
        Environmental Sciences
        Environmental

Class Titles: all courses (ask for list).

Teaching Methods: *Computers:* Internet, e-mail, CD-ROM. *TV:* videotape. *Other:* audioconferencing, videoconferencing, audiotapes, independent study, learning contracts, portfolio assessment, individual research, seminar, special topics, COOP Program.

Credits Granted for: portfolio assessment (3–9 credits/portfolio submitted), learning contracts (maximum 15 credits for associate degrees, maximum 25 credits for bachelor degrees), independent study (maximum 6 credits for associate degrees, maximum 12 credits for bachelor degrees), individual research (maximum 3 credits for associate degrees, maximum 6 credits for bachelor degrees), seminar (1–6 credits/course), special topics (1–6 credits/course), COOP Program (maximum 4 credits for associate degrees, maximum 7 credits for bachelor degrees).

Admission Requirements: *Undergraduate:* evidence of graduation from an accredited secondary school or its equivalent with a minimum GPA of 2.00, present scores of the College Entrance Examination Board Test, Scholastic

Aptitude Test (English language students) or the "Prueba de Aptitud Académica" (Spanish language students), obtain a minimum admission index of 800, interview (if necessary), application, transcript of secondary school record, nonrefundable fee of $19, an updated certificate of vaccination (if the student is under 21 years old), medical form completed by a licensed physician (before May 1 for admission in August).

On-Campus Requirements: to obtain a degree, at least 50% of the credits must be taken at the campus.

Tuition and Fees: *Undergraduate:* $105/credit. *Application Fee:* $19. *Credit by:* semester.

Financial Aid: Federal Stafford Loan, Federal Perkins Loan, Federal Pell Grant, Federal Work-Study, VA.

Accreditation: Middle States Association of Colleges and Schools.

Description: Inter-American University of Puerto Rico (1912) is a private, nonprofit organization founded as the Polytechnic Institute of Puerto Rico by Rev. John W. Harris. In 1944, the IAUPR was accredited by the Middle States Association. It was the first 4-year liberal arts college to be accredited outside the USA. It is also the largest private university of Puerto Rico, with an enrollment of 41,300 students in 1997. The Bayamon campus was established in 1956 as an extension of the San German campus. In 1984, the Bayamon University College (former name) was converted into an independent academic unit of the entire system. In 1991 its name was changed to Inter-American University of Puerto Rico, Bayamon campus and its mission also changed to a focus on science and technology programs. In January 1997, the Bayamon campus was moved to its new facilities in Southern Bayamon. The engineering programs were established and the campus was inaugurated in October 1997.

International Aviation and Travel Academy

4846 South Collins	Phone: (817) 784-7000
Arlington, TX 76018-1110	Fax: (817) 784-7022

Division(s): Travel and Tourism
Web Site(s): http://www.iatac.com
E-mail: info@iatac.com

Certificate Programs: Airline/Travel Industry Extension/Residency Program.

Class Titles: Careers in Travel Industry, Professional Development/Career Planning, Airport Related Operations, Lodging Industry, Travel Agency Operations/Sales/Marketing, Rail/Bus/Rent-a-Car/Cruises, Customer Service Skills/Telephone Sales Techniques, Selling Domestic/International Travel, U.S. Travel Geography/Airlines of North America, World Travel Geography/International Airlines, How To Use Official Airline Guides/Travel Planners, Domestic/International Tariff Skills, Ticket Writing/Travel Industry Automation, Basic Sabre Computer Skills/Travel Project/Review.

Teaching Methods: *Computers:* Internet, e-mail. *Other:* correspondence.

Admission Requirements: *Certificate:* high school diploma prior to residency.

On-Campus Requirements: None.

Tuition and Fees: *Credit by:* program.

Accreditation: Distance Education and Training Council.

Description: At International Aviation and Travel Academy (1971), training makes the difference. With state-of-the-art equipment, experienced staff, and a broad-ranged curriculum, we are committed to providing industry employers with high-caliber personnel. Our graduates have been recruited by more than 300 airline and service companies. IATA's mission is to recognize and fulfill the needs of the aviation and travel industry and those pursuing careers in these industries. IATA's educational mission is to meet the training need for entry-level skills required in the travel and transportation industry. Our perspective includes personal as well as career and professional growth. Standards are high and they match the levels of success our graduates are trained to achieve. Working in this thriving industry, you'll have the chance to meet fascinating people, go places you've always dreamed of, and enjoy the personal and professional rewards that are unique to this career path.

Iowa Lakes Community College

300 South 18th Street	Phone: (712) 362-2604
Estherville, IA 51334	Fax: (712) 362-8363

Division(s): Chief Academic Officer
Technology Center
Web Site(s): http://www.ilcc.cc.ia.us
E-mail: info@ilcc.cc.ia.us

Class Titles: Psychology, Math, Economics, general education courses.

Teaching Methods: *Computers:* Internet, real-time chat, e-mail, LISTSERV. *TV:* videotape, cable program, satellite broadcasting, PBS. *Other:* audioconferencing, videoconferencing, fax, correspondence, independent study, individual study, learning contracts.

Credits Granted for: experiential learning, portfolio assessment, extrainstitutional learning, examination (CLEP, ACT-PEP).

Admission Requirements: *Undergraduate:* open-door.

On-Campus Requirements: None.

Tuition and Fees: *Undergraduate:* $59/credit Iowa/Minnesota residents, $99/credit nonresidents/international students. *Other Costs:* $4/credit technology fee, $2/credit activity fee, $5–$10 processing fee. *Credit by:* semester.

Financial Aid: Federal Stafford Loan, Federal Perkins Loan, Federal PLUS Loan, Federal Pell Grant, Federal Work-Study, VA, Iowa Grant, Iowa Vocational Technical Grant, ILCC scholarships.

Accreditation: North Central Association of Colleges and Schools.

Description: The picturesque Iowa Great Lakes Region provides the setting for Iowa Lakes Community College (1967). The college provides quality, affordable education through traditional methods as well as distance education. The focus of Iowa Lakes is to provide for the first 2 years of college work, including preprofessional education, vocational and technical training, in-service and retraining programs, and high school completion. During the 1980s, Iowa Lakes established an interactive TV network linking the 5 counties it serves in northwest Iowa. In 1998 the college received a $225,000 "Working Connections" grant from Microsoft Corporation and the American Association of Community Colleges, which helped launch distance education via the Internet.

Iowa State University

102 Scheman Building	Phone: (515) 294-6222
Ames, IA 50011-1112	Fax: (515) 294-6146

Division(s): Extended and Continuing Education
Web Site(s): http://www.exnet.iastate.edu/Pages/ece/
E-mail: lspicer@iastate.edu

Undergraduate Degree Programs:
Bachelor of Science in Electrical Engineering
Bachelor of Science in Professional Agriculture

Graduate Degree Programs:
Master of Agriculture
Master of Engineering in Systems Engineering
Master of Family and Consumer Sciences
Master of School Mathematics
Master of Science in:
    Microbiology
    Computer Engineering
    Electrical Engineering

Certificate Programs: Public Management, Advanced Studies (Superintendency)

Teaching Methods: *Computers:* Internet, real-time chat, e-mail, CD-ROM, LISTSERV. *TV:* videotape, satellite broad-casting, fiber optic 2-way videoconferencing. *Other:* independent study.

Credits Granted for: examination (CLEP, ACT-PEP, AP, IB, GRE and departmental exams).

Admission Requirements: *Undergraduate:* high school diploma or GED. *Graduate:* vary by degree. *Doctoral:* vary by degree. *Certificate:* vary by certificate.

On-Campus Requirements: None.

Tuition and Fees: *Undergraduate:* $112/credit. *Graduate:* $176/credit. *Doctoral:* $176/credit. *Application Fee:* $20. *Software:* variable. *Other Costs:* various. *Credit by:* semester.

Financial Aid: Federal Stafford Loan, Federal Perkins Loan, Federal PLUS Loan, Federal Pell Grant, Federal Work-Study, VA, Iowa resident programs.

Accreditation: North Central Association of Colleges and Schools.

Description: Outreach at Iowa State University (1859) has its history as far back as 1904 when agriculture agents traveled by train to several sites in Iowa offering short courses and lectures on topics ranging from plant breeding to manure management. Today, Iowa has a dedicated fiber optic video system connecting ISU with more than 600 towns and cities. Within our rich heritage of outreach, we have a strong vision for the future, keeping ISU at the forefront of educational excellence for the 21st century.

Iowa Wesleyan College

601 N Main Street	Phone: (319) 385-6247
Mt. Pleasant, IA 52641	Fax: (319) 385-6296

Division(s): Office of Continuing Education
Web Site(s): http://www.iwc.edu
E-mail: conted@iwc.edu

Undergraduate Degree Programs:
Bachelor of Arts
Bachelor of Science

Class Titles: Organizational Behavior, Life Health, Art Appreciation, Sociology, Modern World Religions, Developmental Psychology, Abnormal Psychology.

Teaching Methods: *Computers:* e-mail. *TV:* PBS. *Other:* videoconferencing, fax, independent, study, individual study.

Credits Granted for: experiential learning, extrainstitutional learning, examination (CLEP, ACT-PEP, DANTES, GRE)

Admission Requirements: *Undergraduate:* high school equivalency.

On-Campus Requirements: None.

Tuition and Fees: *Undergraduate:* $180/credit. *Application Fee:* $15. *Credit by:* semester.

Financial Aid: Federal Stafford Loan, Federal Perkins Loan, Federal PLUS Loan, Federal Pell Grant, Federal Work-Study, VA, Iowa resident programs.

Accreditation: North Central Association of Colleges and Schools.

Description: Iowa Wesleyan College (1842) is the oldest coeducational liberal arts college west of the Mississippi River. It serves southeast Iowa and the bordering areas in Illinois and Missouri. A distinctive program of required service-learning, field experience, and emphasis on lifeskills (communication, reasoning, valuing, and social effectiveness) characterizes the curriculum. Many graduates enter the teaching, business, social services, and nursing professions. Distance learning began in the early 1990s.

ISIM University

501 South Cherry Street, Room 350	Phone: (303) 333-4224
Denver, CO 80246	Fax: (303) 336-1144

Division(s): Admissions
Web Site(s): http://www.isimu.edu
E-mail: admissions@isimu.edu

Graduate Degree Programs:
Master of Business Administration
Master of Science in Information Management
Master of Science in Information Technology

Certificate Programs: Project Management and Project Management for Information Systems Professionals, Fundamentals of Information Systems, Business Management, Finance.

Class Titles: All courses can be taken individually through ISIM's executive education program. Visit http://www.isimu.edu for course information.

Teaching Methods: *Computers:* Internet-based electronic classroom, e-mail. *Other:* guided self-study program via fax, correspondence, e-mail, independent study.

Credits Granted for: experiential learning, portfolio assessment, examination, transfer credit.

Admission Requirements: *Graduate:* evidence of bachelor's degree (20 years of experience may qualify candidates for ISIM's MBA program), all official college transcripts, resume, goals statement, 3 letters of recommendation.

On-Campus Requirements: None.

Tuition and Fees: *Graduate:* $415/credit. *Application Fee:* $75. *Other Costs:* $1,500–$2,000 for books, shipping (based on completion of 36 credits). *Credit by:* 5 terms/year.

Accreditation: Distance Education and Training Council.

Description: Founded in 1987, ISIM University, formerly known as the International School of Information Management, serves both individuals and organizations in providing its distance education offerings worldwide. ISIM is accredited by the Distance Education and Training Council and recognized by Colorado Commission of Higher Education to offer graduate degree programs and continuing education. ISIM is also a member of the U.S. Distance Learning Association and a member of the American Association of Collegiate Registrars and Admissions Officers. ISIM brings education and training curriculum to individuals over the Internet and through guided self-study. Three times in the last 8 years, ISIM has earned top industry honors. In 1991, 1994, and 1996, the U.S. Distance Learning Association conferred on ISIM its "Best Distance Learning Program in Higher Education" award. ISIM offers graduate degrees in Business Administration, Information Management, and Information Technology as well as certificate and executive education programs to students worldwide with an eye on the global marketplace.

Ivy Tech State College

7999 U.S. Highway 41 South	Phone: (812) 299-1121
Terre Haute, IN 47802	Fax: (812) 299-5723

Division(s): Instruction
Web Site(s): http://ivytech7.cc.in.us/distance-education/
E-mail: cwymer@ivy.tec.in.us

Undergraduate Degree Programs:
Business Administration
Design Technology
Accounting

Class Titles: Accounting, Business, Physics, Physical Science, Algebra, English, CAD, Speech, Design, Drafting, Fiber Optics, Psychology.

Teaching Methods: *Computers:* Internet, real-time chat, e-mail. *Other:* None.

Credits Granted for: experiential learning, extrainstitutional learning, examination (CLEP, ACT-PEP, DANTES, GRE).

Admission Requirements: *Undergraduate:* high school diploma or GED.

On-Campus Requirements: None.

Tuition and Fees: *Undergraduate:* $65/credit. *Software:* depends on course. *Other Costs:* depends on course. *Credit by:* semester.

Financial Aid: Federal Stafford Loan, Federal Perkins Loan, Federal PLUS Loan, Federal Pell Grant, Federal Work-Study, VA, Indiana resident programs.

Accreditation: North Central Association of Colleges and Schools.

Description: Ivy Tech State College (1968) is a public, state-supported, 2-year college serving the state of Indiana. The college offers transfer-oriented AS and occupationally oriented AAS degrees. Situated in the Wabash Valley Region, Ivy Tech serves the 13 regions of the state from its main campus in West Central Indiana. The college began distance education in the fall of 1997 and received approval to grant distance degrees in business, accounting, and design in the spring of 1998. Currently more than 500 students are enrolled in ITSC's Internet-based distance education.

Ivy Tech State College, Central Indiana

One West 26th Street	Phone: (317) 921-4800
Indianapolis, IN 46208	Fax: (317) 921-4753

Division(s): Information Technology
Web Site(s): http://www.ivy.tec.in.us/indy/
E-mail: None.

Undergraduate Degree Programs:
Associate Degrees and Technical Certificates

Class Titles: Torts/Claims Investigation, Family Law, Legal Terminology, Sanitation/First Aid.

Teaching Methods: *Computers:* Internet, real-time chat, electronic classroom, e-mail, CD-ROM, newsgroup, LISTSERV. *TV:* videotape, cable program, satellite broadcasting, PBS. *Other:* radio broadcast, videoconferencing, audioconferencing, audiographics, audiotapes, fax, correspondence, independent study, individual study, learning contracts.

Credits Granted for: experiential learning, portfolio assessment, extrainstitutional learning, examination (CLEP; ACT-PEP, DANTES, GRE).

Admission Requirements: *Undergraduate:* open-admissions policy.

On-Campus Requirements: None.

Tuition and Fees: *Undergraduate:* $67/credit. *Credit by:* semester.

Financial Aid: Federal Stafford Loan, Federal Perkins Loan, Federal PLUS Loan, Federal Pell Grant, Federal Work-Study, VA, Indiana resident programs.

Accreditation: North Central Association of Colleges and Schools.

Description: Ivy Tech State College, Central Indiana (1963) was created with the support of the Indiana AFL-CIO, the Indiana Farm Bureau, and the Indiana Chamber of Commerce.

The college soon learned that technical and occupational education and training needs differed in each area of the state. As a result, the college recommended that the General Assembly create 13 administrative regions that could determine the unique needs of each area and respond to them in the most cost-effective way. The General Assembly approved the college's plan, and, between 1966 and 1969, all 13 Ivy Tech Regions were chartered. Ivy Tech, Central Indiana opened its doors in 1966 to serve residents of Indianapolis and Marion, Morgan, Hancock, Johnson, Shelby, Boone, Hendricks, and Hamilton counties. In 1966 the college enrolled 367 students in 3 technical programs. By the fall of 1997, the college enrolled 7,075 students in 31 areas of study.

J. Sargeant Reynolds Community College

1636 East Parham Road	
PO Box 85622	Phone: (804) 371-3612
Richmond, VA 23285-5622	Fax: (804) 371-3822

Division(s): Center for Distance Education
Web Site(s): http://www.jsr.cc.va.us
E-mail: smarshall@jsr.cc.va.us

Undergraduate Degree Programs:
Liberal Arts
Business Administration
Social Sciences
Management
Respiratory Therapy (at selected sites in Virginia)

Certificate Programs: Management Development.

Class Titles: Accounting, African-American Literature, Business, Creative Writing, Developmental Biology, Developmental Chemistry, Computer Science, Economics, English, Finance, French, History, Information Systems, Mathematics, Medical Terminology, Political Science, Psychology, Sociology.

Teaching Methods: *Computers:* Internet, real-time chat, forums, e-mail, LISTSERV. *TV:* videotape, cable program. *Other:* videoconferencing, audiographics, audiotapes, fax, correspondence, independent study.

Admission Requirements: *Undergraduate:* high school diploma or equivalent, or age 18 and able to benefit from a program at the college. See catalog for more information. *Certificate:* Same as undergraduate.

On-Campus Requirements: Some courses may require labs to be completed on campus. Most courses offer the opportunity for an on-campus orientation meeting with the instructor.

Tuition and Fees: *Undergraduate:* $50/credit for Virginia residents; $163/credit for out-of-state residents. *Software:* Technology fee included in undergraduate tuition fee listed above. *Other Costs:* lab fees for selected music courses. *Credit by:* semester.

Financial Aid: FFEL Stafford Loans, FFEL Federal PLUS Loans, FFEL Consolidation Loans, Federal Pell Grant, FSEOG, Federal Work-Study, VA, Virginia resident programs, various private scholarships.

Accreditation: Southern Association of Colleges and Schools.

Description: J. Sargeant Reynolds Community College (1972) is a 3-campus institution and the third-largest college in the Virginia Community College System. The college offers 30 degree programs (including 6 transfer programs); 13 one-year certificate programs; and 54 career studies certificate programs requiring less than one year of full-time study. JSRCC has been delivering print-based, distance education courses since 1980, with its first telecourse in 1984. Audiographics, compressed video, and computer-based deliveries were added in 1994.

Jacksonville State University

700 Pelham Road N	Phone: (256) 782-5616
Jacksonville, AL 36265	Fax: (256) 782-5169

Division(s): Instructional Services Unit
Web Site(s): http://www.jsu.edu/depart/distance/
E-mail: fking@jsucc.jsu.edu

Class Titles: Concepts of Wellness, American Government, Western Civilization, U.S. History, Anthropology, College Algebra, Child Psychology, Survey of English Literature, World Regions, Geography, Physical Geology, EFD Tests/Measurements, Management of Student Services, Psychological Principles of Learning, Law/Politics of Education.

Teaching Methods: *Computers:* Internet. *TV:* videotape, cable program. *Other:* videoconferencing.

Credits Granted for: examination (CLEP).

Admission Requirements: *Undergraduate:* call Admissions and Records at (256) 782-5400.

On-Campus Requirements: may apply to courses using videocassettes and videoconferencing.

Tuition and Fees: *Undergraduate:* $85/hour. *Graduate:* $102/hour. *Application Fee:* $20. *Other Costs:* $20 undergraduate/graduate degree fee, $5 degree (current) reprint fee, $10/student identification card fee, $5 identification card replacement processing fee, $20/student late registration fee, $15 change-in-course-schedule fee, $20/student teaching certificate fee, $5/transcript for transcript of records, $10/student residence hall deposit. *Lab fees charged in some

courses when applicable. Note: information subject to change without prior notice to individual students. *Credit by:* semester.

Financial Aid: Federal Stafford Loan, Federal Perkins Loan, Federal Pell Grant, Federal Work Study, VA.

Accreditation: Southern Association of Colleges and Schools.

Description: From modest beginnings, Jacksonville State University (1883) has evolved into the educational center of northeast Alabama. After acquiring 12 acres of land and a 2-story building, Jacksonville became a teacher's college, added a master's degree in elementary education, and has now developed into a modern regional university on a 318-acre campus with 58 buildings. In addition, the university operates off-campus centers in Gadsden, Fort McClellan, Anniston, and Oxford. The Distance Learning Program was added in 1994.

Jamestown Community College

525 Falconer Street	Phone: (716) 665-5220
Jamestown, NY 14702-0020	Fax: (716) 665-5518

Division(s): Huctauist Library
Web Site(s): http://www.sunyjcc.edu
E-mail: None.

Class Titles: Music, Computer Science, Business, Sociology, SUNY Learning Network/Computer Courses.

Teaching Methods: *Computers:* Internet, real-time chat, electronic classroom, e-mail, LISTSERV. *TV:* videotape, cable program, satellite broadcasting, PBS. *Other:* videoconferencing, independent study, individual study, learning contracts.

Credits Granted for: experiential learning, portfolio assessment.

Admission Requirements: *Undergraduate:* age 18 or high school diploma.

On-Campus Requirements: None.

Tuition and Fees: *Undergraduate:* $88 resident, $154 out-of-state. *Other Costs:* various fees $20–$50. *Credit by:* semester.

Financial Aid: Federal Stafford Loan, Federal Perkins Loan, Federal PLUS Loan, Federal Pell Grant, Federal Work-Study, VA, New York resident programs.

Accreditation: Middle States Association of Colleges and Schools.

Description: Jamestown Community College (1950) began distance learning in 1996. JCC is also a receive site for the Pennsylvania State MBA program, the SUNY Fredonia BS in Business, and the SUNY University, Buffalo, BS in Nursing.

JEC College Connection

9697 East Mineral Avenue
Englewood, CO 80112

Phone: (800) 777-6463
Fax: (303) 799-0966

Division(s): None.
Web Site(s): http://www.jec.edu
E-mail: edcenter@jec.edu

Undergraduate Degree Programs:
Associate of Arts
Bachelor of Arts in Social Sciences with concentrations in:
  Anthropology
  Criminal Justice
  Psychology
  Sociology
  Political Science
  History
  Women's Studies
Bachelor of Arts in Business Communication
Bachelor of Science in:
  Business Administration
  Nursing
  Human Resources (concentration in Hotel, Restaurant and Institutional Management)

Graduate Degree Programs:
Master in Business Administration
Master of Arts in Business Communication
Master of Arts in Education and Human Development (concentration in Educational Technology Leadership)

Certificate Programs: Essential Oral and Written Communication Skills for Managers, Telecommunications Applications for Managers, Using Human Communication Skills to Motivate Performance, Practical Communication Technology Tools for Managers, Marketing in Today's Electronic Business Environment, Public Relations for New Media Manager, Human Resource Management for Changing Environments, Communication Management for Global Marketplace, Telecommunications in Business, Productive Organization—Communication Skills for Management Effectiveness, Early Reading Instruction, New Business Solutions Through Communications Technologies, Leadership and Influence Through the Spoken and Written Word, Management Skills with a Human Directive, Cyber Marketing—Competitive Advantages Using the Internet, Team Strategies for the Effective Manager, Advanced Public Relations for the Wired World.

Teaching Methods: *Computers:* Internet, real-time chat, electronic classroom, e-mail, LISTSERV. *TV:* videotape, cable program, satellite broadcasting. *Other:* audiotapes, correspondence, independent study.

Credits Granted for: experiential learning, portfolio assessment, extrainstitutional learning, examination (CLEP, ACT-PEP, DANTES, GRE).

Admission Requirements: *Undergraduate:* high school diploma or equivalent, previous undergraduate course work for some bachelor's degree programs. *Graduate:* bachelor's degree, GMAT or GRE for some programs. *Certificate:* undergraduate degree for some graduate- and master's-level certificates.

On-Campus Requirements: No (one week on campus for the Bachelor of Science in Human Resources).

Tuition and Fees: *Undergraduate:* $120–$245/credit. *Graduate:* $233–$275/credit. *Application Fee:* $0–$75. *Other Costs:* books, materials, etc. *Credit by:* semester (except for Associate of Arts program in quarter credits).

Financial Aid: Federal Stafford Loan, Federal Perkins Loan, Federal PLUS Loan, Federal Pell Grant, VA, Colorado resident programs.

Accreditation: JEC affiliated institutions are accredited by their appropriate regional accrediting agency (except for International University which is a candidate for accreditation with the North Central Association of Colleges and Schools).

Description: Jones Education Company (1987) College Connection is a private, for-profit company that contracts with colleges and universities to help students take courses and degree programs at a distance. Currently, College Connection works with 11 colleges and universities who provide 2 associate, 5 bachelor's, and 3 master's degree programs, along with a variety of certificate programs. Students taking courses or degrees through these affiliated institutions receive the same credits and degrees as the on-campus students. They also complete the same course work by watching lectures on videotape and communicating with instructors and classmates via the Internet and telephone.

Jefferson College

1000 Viking Drive
Hillsboro, MO 63050

Phone: (314) 789-3000
Fax: (314) 789-4012

Division(s): Extended and Nontraditional Learning
Web Site(s): http://www.jeffco.edu
E-mail: bthomas@gateway.jeffco.edu

Class Titles: Algebra, Biology, Business, Children's Literature, Economics, English, French, History, Personal Health, Psychology, Sociology, Spanish, Geography.

Teaching Methods: *TV:* videotape, cable program, satellite broadcasting, PBS, ITV. *Other:* None.

Credits Granted for: examination (CLEP, ACT-PEP, departmental proficiency exams), military experience.

Admission Requirements: *Undergraduate:* Official high school graduate transcript or GED (high school equivalency) scores, completion of ASSET or official ACT scores for placement purposes.

On-Campus Requirements: None.

Tuition and Fees: *Undergraduate:* $40/credit in-district, $52/credit out-of-district/in-state, $64/credit out-of-district/out-of-state (Tuition and fees are subject to change without prior notice.). *Application Fee:* $15 (one-time fee for new students only). *Other Costs:* $4/credit Facilities Use Fee, $2 (first-time-student only) Student Identification Fee, $25 Lab Fees (vary by course), $40/course telecourse fee. *Credit by:* semester.

Financial Aid: Federal Stafford Loan, Federal Perkins Loan, Federal PLUS Loan, Federal Pell Grant, Federal Work-Study, VA, Missouri resident programs.

Accreditation: North Central Association of Colleges and Schools.

Description: Jefferson College (1963) is a student-centered, comprehensive community college on 450 beautifully wooded acres located 25 miles south of St. Louis. Jefferson offers its 4,000 students Associate of Arts and Associate of Science degrees, along with an Associate of Applied Science degree in more than 20 vocational-technical programs.

Jewish Theological Seminary

3080 Broadway	Phone: (212) 678-8897
New York, NY 10027	Fax: (212) 749-9085

Division(s): The Melton Research Center for Jewish Education

Web Site(s): http://www.jtsa.edu
http://www.jtsa.edu/melton/courses/

E-mail: mistarr@jtsa.edu

Class Titles: Talmud, Translating Jewish Theology for Educational Settings, Methods of Teaching Prayer, Women in Rabbinic Literature.

Teaching Methods: *Computers:* Internet, real-time chat, electronic classroom, e-mail. *Other:* None.

Admission Requirements: *Undergraduate:* contact school.

On-Campus Requirements: None.

Tuition and Fees: *Undergraduate:* $422/credit. *Graduate:* $511/credit. *Application Fee:* $35. *Other Costs:* $185 registration fee. *Credit by:* semester.

Accreditation: Middle States Association of Colleges and Schools.

Description: The Jewish Theological Seminary (1886) is the center of an international network of academic, research, education, and community programs at the service of world Jewry; the premier North American center for the academic study of Judaism; and the spiritual center of Conservative Judaism worldwide. Its New York City campus houses the undergraduate Albert A. List College of Jewish Studies, the Graduate School, the Rabbinical School, the William Davidson Graduate School of Jewish Education, the H. L. Miller Cantorial School and College of Jewish Music, and the Rebecca and Israel Ivry Prozdor honors high school program. JTS faculty constitutes the largest assembly of Judaica scholars in the United States; the renowned JTS library houses the largest collection of Judaica and Hebraica outside Israel. JTS began its distance learning program in late 1996 thanks to a generous grant from the Kaminer Family Foundation. Currently, JTS offers courses for academic credit, professional development, adult education, and high school education. The distance learning program is housed in the Melton Research Center for Jewish Education.

John Tracy Clinic

806 West Adams Boulevard	Phone: (213) 748-5481
Los Angeles, CA 90007	Fax: (213) 749-1651

Division(s): Academy for Professional Studies

Web Site(s): http://www.johntracyclinic.org

E-mail: jtclinic@aol.com

Class Titles: Typical/Atypical Infant/Child Development, Methods of Auditory Learning/Teaching Speech to Children with Hearing Loss, Professional as Facilitator: Working with Children with Hearing Loss Infancy–Preschool (Methods), Public Policy/Service Delivery Systems for Infants/Toddlers with Special Needs, Working with Families of Children with Special Needs: Parent-Professional Teams, Audiology for Teachers of Children with Hearing Loss, First Language: It's Nature/Acquisition/Development in Typical Children.

Teaching Methods: *Computers:* Internet, asynchronous discussion forum, e-mail. *TV:* audiotapes and videotapes. *Other:* commercial texts, syllabus.

Admission Requirements: *Graduate:* bachelor's degree, working in or access to educational setting with young deaf children.

On-Campus Requirements: None.

Tuition and Fees: *Graduate:* $150/credit. *Application Fee:* $25. *Other Costs:* $25/proctored examination; vary for texts, materials, postage. *Credit by:* semester.

Accreditation: Distance Education and Training Council.

Description: In 1942, Mrs. Spencer (Louise Treadwell) Tracy and 12 other mothers of young deaf children established a place where such parents could receive information and support. The nonprofit institution was officially named "John Tracy Clinic" (1943) for the deaf son of Mr. and Mrs. Spencer Tracy. Mrs. Tracy and the Board of Directors understood the need to have well-trained teachers to work with the children and to demonstrate to parents how to facilitate a positive learning environment for their children. For this reason, John Tracy Clinic and the University of Southern California soon began a joint master's-level, resident program in teacher education in the area of deaf and hard-of-hearing. In 1996, John Tracy Clinic Academy for Professional Studies was established to offer distance education courses for professionals who work with deaf and hard-of-hearing children.

Johns Hopkins School of Hygiene and Public Health

615 North Wolfe Street	Phone: (410) 223-1830
Baltimore, MD 21205	Fax: (410) 223-1832

Division(s): Professional Education and Programs
Web Site(s): http://distance.jhsph.edu
E-mail: alentz@jhsph.edu

Graduate Degree Programs:
Master of Public Health

Certificate Programs: Graduate Public Health

Teaching Methods: *Computers:* Internet, real-time chat, electronic classroom, e-mail, CD-ROM. *TV:* videoconferencing, audiotapes, fax. *Other:* independent study, individual study.

Credits Granted for: academic standards committee may approve courses.

Admission Requirements: *Graduate:* GRE. Preference given to applicants with clearly identified career goals consistent with anticipated training, strong academic record and preparation, and impressive references stating potential success as a public health professional. Consideration given to: doctoral professional graduates of medicine, dentistry, veterinary medicine, or law; graduates of bachelor's or master's programs such as nursing, engineering, or natural or social sciences; bachelor's program graduates pursuing joint degree programs.

On-Campus Requirements: Three 2-week sessions in 18-month program.

Tuition and Fees: *Graduate:* $473/credit. *Application Fee:* $60. *Credit by:* quarter.

Financial Aid: Federal Direct loans, Federal Perkins Loan, Federal Work-Study, VA, Maryland resident programs.

Accreditation: Council on Education for Public Health.

Description: Founded in 1916, the Johns Hopkins University School of Hygiene and Public Health is dedicated to the education of research scientists and public health professionals, a process inseparably linked to the discovery and application of new knowledge, and through these activities to the improvement of health and prevention of disease and disability worldwide.

Johnson County Community College

12345 College Boulevard	Phone: (913) 469-8500
Overland Park, KS 66210	Fax: (913) 469-4417

Division(s): Computer Instruction and Media Resources
Web Site(s): http://www.johnco.cc.ks.us
http://www.johnco.cc.ks.us/acad/dl/courses.htm
E-mail: dludwig@johnco.cc.ks.us

Class Titles: Accounting, Criminal Justice System, Word Processing on Micros, Spreadsheets on Micros, Databases on Micros: MS Access, Personal Computer Applications: Office 97, MS/DOS 6.22, Windows for Micros, UNIX, Internet, Web Pages, Visual Basic for Windows, CAD Concepts: AutoCAD LT, Composition, Technical Writing, U.S. History to 1877, Library Research, Trigonometry, Computerized Keyboarding, Psychology, Sociology, Cultural Anthropology, Biology: Cycles of Life, Oceanus: Marine Environment, Environmental Science: Race to Save Planet, Business: It's Strictly Business, Marketing, Computers: New Literacy, Economics, Writer's Exchange, Writer's Stage, Geology, Aerobics, Personal/Community Health: Living with Health, Humanities Through Arts, Survey of Mathematics, Philosophy: Socrates-Sartre, American National Government, Child Development: Time to Grow, Sociological Imagination, Marriage/Family.

Teaching Methods: *Computers:* Internet, electronic classroom, e-mail, CD-ROM, newsgroup, LISTSERV. *TV:* videotape, cable program, interactive microwave, compressed video. *Other:* videoconferencing, independent study.

Credits Granted for: experiential learning, portfolio assessment, examination (CLEP, ACT-PEP, DANTES, GRE).

Admission Requirements: *Undergraduate:* may have to complete an assessment exam.

On-Campus Requirements: telecourses: 3 meetings.

Tuition and Fees: *Undergraduate:* $46/credit resident, $122/credit nonresident. *Credit by:* semester.

Financial Aid: Federal Stafford Loan, Federal Perkins Loan, Federal PLUS Loan, Federal Pell Grant, Federal Work-Study.

Accreditation: North Central Association of Colleges and Schools.

Description: Johnson County Community College (1969) has emerged as one of the premier community colleges in the U.S. and earned a reputation for high-quality, comprehensive and flexible programming to meet the needs of the citizens of Johnson County. The college began its distance learning programming in 1976 with the introduction of telecourse instruction. These offerings continue while other courses are being developed and delivered in a Web-based environment.

Joliet Junior College

1215 Houbolt Road	Phone: (815) 773-6613
Joliet, IL 60431	Fax: (815) 773-6603

Division(s): Distance Education
Web Site(s): http://www.jjc.cc.il.us/98FALL/DL.html
http://www.jjc.cc.il.us/98FALL/tele.html
E-mail: rsterlin@jjc.cc.il.us
Dsitar@jjc.cc.il.us

Class Titles: Astronomy, Biology, Business, Economics, History, Marketing, Math, Political Science, Psychology, Sociology, English, General Studies Development, Horticulture, Hotel/Restaurant Management, Spanish, Speech.

Teaching Methods: *TV:* videotape. *Other:* videoconferencing, fax, correspondence, independent study.

Credits Granted for: portfolio assessment, examination (CLEP).

Admission Requirements: *Undergraduate:* open door policy, high school graduate/GED, college transfer student, gifted high school student.

On-Campus Requirements: None.

Tuition and Fees: *Undergraduate:* $42/credit, $149/credit out-of-district, $185/credit out-of-state, $217/credit out-of-country. *Other Costs:* $3/credit service fee, $4/credit technology fee, $2/credit ITV class fee, $4/credit telecourse fee. *Credit by:* semester.

Financial Aid: Federal Stafford Loan, Federal PLUS Loan, Federal Pell Grant, Federal Work-Study, VA.

Accreditation: North Central Association of Colleges and Schools.

Description: Joliet Junior College (1901) is committed to providing a quality education that is affordable and accessible to the diverse student population it serves. Through a rich variety of educational programs and support services, JJC prepares its students for success in higher education and employment. As part of this college's commitment to lifelong learning and services to its community, it also provides a broad spectrum of transitional, extension, adult, continuing and work force education.

Judson College

1151 North State Street	Phone: (847) 695-2500 x2221
Elgin, IL 60123-1498	Fax: (847) 695-4880

Division(s): Continuing Education
Web Site(s): http://judsonil.edu
E-mail: djameson@judsonil.edu

Undergraduate Degree Programs: Bachelor of Arts and Professions

Certificate Programs: Management Information Systems, various.

Class Titles: Criminal Justice, Management Information Systems.

Teaching Methods: *Computers:* Internet, real-time chat, electronic classroom, e-mail, CD-ROM, newsgroup, LISTSERV. *TV:* videotape, cable program, satellite broadcasting, PBS. *Other:* radio broadcast, videoconferencing, audioconferencing, audiographics, audiotapes, fax, correspondence, independent study, individual study, learning contracts.

Credits Granted for: experiential learning, portfolio assessment, examination (CLEP, ACT-PEP, DANTES, GRE).

Admission Requirements: *Undergraduate:* rank in the upper 50th percentile, ACT 18, SAT 840, GPA 2.0.

On-Campus Requirements: varies.

Tuition and Fees: *Undergraduate:* varies. *Credit by:* semester or individualized.

Financial Aid: call for information.

Accreditation: North Central Association of Colleges and Schools, Coalition for Christian Colleges and Universities.

Description: Judson College (1963) is an evangelical Christian college that represents the Church at work in higher education. Judson's mission is to equip its students to be fully developed, responsible persons who glorify God by the quality of their personal relationships, their work, and their citizenship within the community, the nation, and the world. Through a broadly based education in the liberal arts, sciences, and professions, the college enables its students to acquire ideas and concepts that sharpen their insights, develop skills appropriate for their career goals, and foster a commitment to lifelong learning.

Juniata College

1700 Moore Street	Phone: (814) 641-3594
Huntingdon, PA 16652	Fax: (814) 641-3685

Division(s): Teaching and Learning Technology
Web Site(s): http://www.juniata.edu
E-mail: info@juniata.edu

Class Titles: Communication, Music, Technical Writing, International Business.

Teaching Methods: *Computers:* e-mail, LISTSERV. *Other:* videoconferencing, fax, correspondence.

Credits Granted for: examination (CLEP, ACT-PEP, DANTES, GRE).

Admission Requirements: *Undergraduate:* Credit courses limited to students enrolled at Juniata or another "CAPE" Consortium college; noncredit courses open to all individuals.

On-Campus Requirements: videoconferencing requires special facilities.

Tuition and Fees: *Undergraduate:* $750/credit (part-time); $17,500/year standard tuition for full-time students. *Application Fee:* $30 (standard application fee for all students). *Credit by:* semester.

Financial Aid: Federal Stafford Loan, Federal Perkins Loan, Federal PLUS Loan, Federal Pell Grant, Federal Work-Study, Pennsylvania resident programs.

Accreditation: Middle States Association of Colleges and Schools.

Description: Juniata College (1876) is an independent, coeducational college of liberal arts and sciences committed to providing an education that awakens students to the empowering richness of the mind and enables them to lead fulfilling and useful lives. Located in the small town of Huntingdon in the scenic central Pennsylvania mountains, the college occupies 110 acres with 31 buildings. Additional land holdings include a 365-acre Environmental Studies Field Station, the 315-acre Baker-Henry Nature Preserve, and the 70-acre Juniata College Conference Center. Primarily residential, Juniata maintains an enrollment of 1250 students. To supplement its regular programs, Juniata began to use distance learning technology in 1995. Through the Consortium for Agile Pennsylvania Education, the college exchanges videoconference courses with CAPE members. Online instruction is also offered. Future plans include increasing the number of courses imported and exported and further collaboration with international sites.

Kankakee Community College

River Road
PO Box 888　　　　　　　　Phone: (815) 933-0345
Kankakee, IL 60901　　　　　Fax: (815) 933-0217

Division(s): Instruction and Workforce Development
Web Site(s): http://www.kcc.cc.il.us
E-mail: rmanuel@kcc.cc.il.us

Class Titles: Psychology, Managerial Accounting, Legal Environment in Business, Calculus, Transition for LPNs, Humanities, Business.

Teaching Methods: *TV:* videotape. *Other:* videoconferencing.

Admission Requirements: *Undergraduate:* contact school.

On-Campus Requirements: None.

Tuition and Fees: *Undergraduate:* $38/credit. *Credit by:* semester.

Financial Aid: Federal Stafford Loan, Federal Perkins Loan, Federal PLUS Loan, Federal Pell Grant, Federal Work-Study, VA, Illinois resident programs.

Accreditation: North Central Association of Colleges and Schools.

Description: Kankakee Community College (1966) serves as an educational, vocational, and recreational center for 130,000 residents of an area encompassing all or part of Kankakee, Iroquois, Ford, Grundy, Livingston, and Will counties. Kankakee County is located only 50 miles south of Chicago. For several years, KCC has offered a limited number of videotaped courses. Four years ago, the college began offering courses via interactive TV as a member of a network with 9 other institutions. The network has now expanded to include some high schools and medical centers. Although KCC does not offer a complete degree via distance, an increasing number of distance courses are being offered.

Kansas City, Kansas Community College

7250 State Avenue　　　　　　Phone: (913) 596-9660
Kansas City, KS 66112　　　　Fax: (913) 596-9663

Division(s): Continuing Education/Community Services
Web Site(s): http://www.kckcc.cc.ks.us
E-mail: ltrumbo@toto.net

Undergraduate Degree Programs:
Associate of Arts
Associate of Science
Associate of Applied Science
Associate in General Studies

Certificate Programs: Business, Child Care, Education, Engineering Technology, Fire Science, Law Enforcement, Long Term Care Administration, Recreation Therapy, Special Education for Paraprofessionals, Victim/Survivor, Wellness/Fitness, Women's Studies, Addiction Counseling.

Teaching Methods: *Computers:* Internet, electronic classroom, e-mail, CD-ROM, newsgroup, LISTSERV. *TV:* videotape, cable program, satellite broadcasting, PBS. *Other:* videoconferencing, audiotapes, fax, correspondence, independent study, individual study, learning contracts.

Credits Granted for: experiential learning, portfolio assessment, examination (CLEP, ACT-PEP, DANTES, GRE), service learning.

Admission Requirements: *Undergraduate:* high school graduate or age 18 and GED. *Certificate:* high school graduate or age 18 and GED.

On-Campus Requirements: telecourses require some on-campus hours, online courses do not.

Tuition and Fees: *Undergraduate:* $40/credit resident, $108/credit out-of-state. *Other Costs:* additional fees are required in some classes. *Credit by:* semester.

Financial Aid: Federal Stafford Loan, Federal Perkins Loan, Federal PLUS Loan, Federal Pell Grant, Federal Work-Study, VA, Kansas resident programs.

Accreditation: North Central Association of Colleges and Schools.

Description: Kansas City, Kansas Community College (1923) is a public, 2-year institution located in northeast Kansas. Our college serves more than 6,000 students annually. The average age of students at the college is 30 (60% female, 39% male). Culturally, 63% are white, 21% African American, 5% Hispanic, 2% Asian/Pacific Islander, 1% American Indian, 8% are other. Students are 28% full time, 72% part time.

Kansas State University

13 College Court Building	Phone: (785) 532-5687
Manhattan, KS 66506	(800) 622-2KSU
	Fax: (785) 532-5637

Division(s): Division of Continuing Education
Web Site(s): http://www.dce.ksu.edu
E-mail: info@dce.ksu.edu

Undergraduate Degree Programs:
Bachelor of Science in:
   Interdisciplinary Social Sciences
   Animal Sciences and Industry
Bachelor in Dietetics

Graduate Degree Programs:
Master of Engineering in:
   Electrical and Computer Engineering
   Civil Engineering
   Chemical Engineering
   Software Engineering
   Engineering Management
Master of Agribusiness

Certificate Programs: Food Science

Class Titles: Farm/Ranch Management, Range Management, Animal Science, Food Science, Food Processing, Nutrition, Meat Science, Food Chemistry, Problems: Food Microbiology, Meat Selection/Utilization, Quality Assurance of Food Products, Food Analysis, Food Science Seminar, Food Science Problems, Cereal Science, Human Dimensions in Horticulture, Horticulture for Special Populations, Dealing with Diversity, Earth in Action, Earth Through Time, Geology Lab, College Algebra, General Calculus/Linear Algebra, Political Thought, World Politics, International Relations, Latin American Politics, Ideologies: Their Origins/Impact, Why Big Government?, Women's Studies.

Teaching Methods: *Computers:* Internet, real-time chat, electronic classroom, e-mail, CD-ROM, newsgroup, LISTSERV. *TV:* videotape, cable program, satellite broadcasting, PBS. *Other:* audioconferencing, videoconferencing, audiographics, audiotapes, fax, correspondence, independent study, individual study.

Credits Granted for: experiential learning, portfolio assessment, extrainstitutional learning, examination (CLEP, ACT-PEP, DANTES, GRE).

Admission Requirements: *Undergraduate:* contact Office of Admissions. *Graduate:* contact Ellen Stauffer, Engineering Program Coordinator at (785) 532-2562 or e-mail, engineering@dce.ksu.edu or see Web site at http://www.dce.ksu.edu/dce/engg. *Certificate:* contact Office of Admissions.

On-Campus Requirements: None.

Tuition and Fees: *Undergraduate:* $90/credit. *Graduate:* $132/credit. *Application Fee:* $30 for bachelor degree programs. *Other Costs:* media fees vary with course, textbooks, and materials. *Credit by:* semester.

Financial Aid: Federal Stafford Loan, Federal Perkins Loan, Federal PLUS Loan, Federal Pell Grant, Federal Work-Study, VA.

Accreditation: North Central Association of Colleges and Schools.

Description: Kansas State University (1863) was founded as a land-grant institution under the Morrill Act. It was initially located on the grounds of the old Bluemont Central College, which was chartered in 1858. The university moved to its present site in 1875. The 664-acre campus is in Manhattan, 125 miles west of Kansas City via Interstate 70 in the rolling Flint Hills of northeast Kansas. The campus is convenient to both business and residential sections of the city. Under an enactment of the 1991 Kansas Legislature, the Salina campus, 70 miles west of Manhattan, was established through a merger of the former Kansas College of Technology with the university. Additional university sites include 18,000 acres in the 4 branch locations of the Agricultural Experiment Station (Hays, Garden City, Colby, and Parsons) and 8,600 acres in the Konza Prairie Research Natural Area jointly operated by the AES and the Division of Biology. One of the 6 universities governed by the Kansas Board of Regents, Kansas State University continues to fulfill its historic educational mission in teaching, research, and public service.

Kansas Wesleyan University

100 East Claflin Avenue	Phone: (785) 827-5541
Salina, KS 67401-6196	Fax: (785) 827-0927

Division(s): Academic Dean's Office
Web Site(s): http://www.kwu.edu
E-mail: kjeffm@acck.edu

Class Titles: Business Law, Working Successfully with Attention Deficit Disorder, Changing Face of Education

Teaching Methods: *Computers:* Internet, e-mail. *TV:* cable program. *Other:* independent study.

Credits Granted for: experiential learning, portfolio assessment, examination (CLEP, ACT-PEP, DANTES, GRE).

Admission Requirements: *Undergraduate:* application and fee; 2.5 GPA, 50 GED, or rank in upper 50% of class; 18 Enhanced ACT composite or 850 Recentered SAT. *Graduate:* bachelor's degree, transcripts, essay.

On-Campus Requirements: limit of 30 hours correspondence, extension for bachelor's; limit of 15 hours correspondence, extension for associate, residence requirements: bachelor's—at least 48 hours of the last 62 credits or 24 of the last 33 at KWU; at least 12 hours of major at KWU, associate—at least 12 hours of major at KWU; 15 of last 20 at KWU.

Tuition and Fees: *Undergraduate:* $160/credit (up to 6 hours). *Graduate:* $340/credit. *Application Fee:* $15 undergraduate, $30 graduate. *Credit by:* semester.

Financial Aid: Federal Stafford Loan, Federal Perkins Loan, Federal PLUS Loan, Federal Pell Grant, Federal Work-Study, VA, Kansas resident programs, Kansas Tuition Grant, institutional scholarships.

Accreditation: North Central Association of Colleges and Schools.

Description: Kansas Wesleyan University (1886) is a liberal arts institution that maintains a covenant relationship with the United Methodist Church and is supported by the Kansas West Conference. The mission of Kansas Wesleyan is to promote and integrate academic excellence, spiritual development, personal well-being, and social responsibility.

Kellogg Community College

450 North Avenue	Phone: (616) 965-3931 x2248
Battle Creek, MI 49017	Fax: (616) 965-4133

Division(s): Learning Resources/Distance Learning
Web Site(s): http://www.kellogg.cc.mi.us
E-mail: marzf@kellogg.cc.mi.us

Class Titles: Anthropology, Art History, General Business, Business Statistics, Business Management, Business Law, Marketing, Economics (Macro/Micro), American History, World History, Political Science, Psychology, Environmental Science, Sociology, International Business, Calculus, Cost Accounting, Criminal Justice Management, French, Information Processing, Organic Chemistry, World Literature, Electronic Devices.

Teaching Methods: *Computers:* Internet, real-time chat, electronic classroom, e-mail, CD-ROM. *TV:* videotape, satellite broadcasting, PBS. *Other:* audioconferencing, videoconferencing, audiotapes, fax, correspondence, independent study, individual study, learning contracts.

Credits Granted for: experiential learning, portfolio assessment, extrainstitutional learning, examination (CLEP, ACT-PEP, DANTES, GRE).

Admission Requirements: *Undergraduate:* open admissions. *Doctoral:* open admissions. *Certificate:* open admissions.

On-Campus Requirements: None.

Tuition and Fees: *Undergraduate:* $51/credit for residents, $83/credit for nonresidents, $127/credit for international students. *Doctoral:* same as undergraduate. *Other Costs:* lab fees for some courses. *Credit by:* semester.

Financial Aid: Federal Pell Grant, Federal Work-Study, VA, Michigan resident programs, Ford Direct Loan, Direct PLUS Loan.

Accreditation: North Central Association of Colleges and Schools.

Description: Kellogg Community College (1956) is a public institution of higher learning that provides academic, occupational, general, and lifelong learning opportunities for all people in its district and contiguous service area. The institution offers a comprehensive range of curricula, courses, activities, and services while maintaining open-door admissions. Current enrollment is approximately 11,000. The institution has offered telecourses since 1990, and in 1997 it began interactive video courses via a fiber optic loop linking 23 secondary and postsecondary sites in a 2-county area. In the fall of 1998, Kellogg began offering interactive-video courses to additional sites via Codec technology. Efforts are currently underway to enhance traditional and distance courses through the Internet. Beginning January, 1999, Kellogg will offer 2 online courses.

Kettering University

1700 West Third Avenue	Phone: (810) 762-7494
Flint, MI 48504-4898	Fax: (810) 762-9935

Division(s): Office of Graduate Studies
Web Site(s): http://www.gmi.edu/acad/grad/
E-mail: bbedore@kettering.edu

Graduate Degree Programs:
Master of Science in:
 Manufacturing Management
 Engineering
 Operations Management

Teaching Methods: *Computers:* Internet, e-mail. *TV:* videotape. *Other:* fax, correspondence.

Admission Requirements: *Graduate:* application, transcripts, 2 letters of recommendation; MS in Engineering requires GRE; MS Management degrees require GMAT. International requirements include TOEFL.

On-Campus Requirements: None.

Tuition and Fees: *Graduate:* $375/credit. *Other Costs:* $45, registration. *Credit by:* quarter.

Financial Aid: Federal Stafford Loan, Graduate Access Loan, Michigan Tuition Grant.

Accreditation: North Central Association of Colleges and Schools.

Description: Founded in 1919, General Motors Corporation agreed to underwrite the school in 1926, and General Motors Institute, a totally cooperative undergraduate school was born. In 1982 GMI became independent of General Motors and the private corporation "GMI Engineering and Management Institute" was established. In January 1998, GMI changed its name to Kettering University. Kettering continues to maintain a close affiliation with industry, as it has throughout its history. In the fall of 1982 Kettering began a video-based, distance learning graduate program leading to a Master of Science in Manufacturing Management degree. In 1990 the Master of Science in Engineering degree was initiated and in 1998 the Master of Science in Operations Management degree was implemented.

Kingwood College

20000 Kingwood Drive	**Phone: (281) 312-1674**
Kingwood, TX 77339	**Fax: (281) 312-1438**

Division(s): Teaching and Learning Center
Web Site(s): http://kcweb,nhmccd.cc.tx.us/kc_home.html
E-mail: pwhitley@nhmccd.edu

Undergraduate Degree Programs:
Associate in Arts

Class Titles: Office Administration, Physical Education, Psychology, Sociology, Spanish, Accounting, Biology, Geography, Geology, Government, History, Business, Child Development, Communications, Computer Sciences, English, Human Development, Legal Assistant.

Teaching Methods: *Computers:* Internet, real-time chat,

electronic classroom, e-mail, CD-ROM, newsgroup, LIST-SERV. *TV:* videotape, satellite broadcasting, PBS. *Other:* videoconferencing, audioconferencing, fax, correspondence, independent study, individual study, learning contracts.

Credits Granted for: experiential learning, portfolio assessment, extrainstitutional learning, examination (CLEP, ACT).

Admission Requirements: *Undergraduate:* Open admission. *Certificate:* open-admission.

On-Campus Requirements: None.

Tuition and Fees: *Undergraduate:* $24/credit. *Other Costs:* $12–$50 lab fees. *Credit by:* semester.

Financial Aid: Federal Stafford Loan, Federal Perkins Loan, Federal PLUS Loan, Federal Pell Grant, Federal Work-Study, VA, Texas resident programs.

Accreditation: Southern Association of Colleges and Schools.

Description: Kingwood College (1984) is one of 4 colleges in the North Harris Montgomery Community College District. It opened in fall of 1984. Its current enrollment is 3,400. The college began distance learning in 1990 with telecourses. Now the distance enrollment is 900 and includes courses via telecourses, video, Internet, and print-based. Effective 1997 students can complete an Associate of Arts degree solely by distance.

Kirkwood Community College

6301 Kirkwood Boulevard SW	**Phone: (319) 398-4974**
Cedar Rapids, IA 52406-2068	**Fax: (319) 398-5492**

Division(s): Distance Learning and Learning Initiatives
Web Site(s): http://www.kirkwood.cc.ia.us
E-mail: jeadie@kirkwood.cc.ia.us

Undergraduate Degree Programs:
Associate of Arts

Class Titles: Composition, Literature, Business Writing, Humanities, Music Appreciation, Sociology, Anthropology, Psychology, History, Math, Chemistry, Accounting, Business, Medical Terminology, Nutrition, Keyboarding, MS Word

Teaching Methods: *Computers:* Internet, e-mail, CD-ROM, newsgroup. *TV:* videotape, cable program, satellite broadcasting, PBS, live interactive instructional TV. *Other:* audiotapes, correspondence,

Credits Granted for: examination (CLEP).

Admission Requirements: *Undergraduate:* open door. *Certificate:* open door.

On-Campus Requirements: Students must complete 16 credits from Kirkwood. These may be in distance delivered formats.

Tuition and Fees: *Undergraduate:* $60/credit. *Other Costs:* textbooks and other course materials. *Credit by:* semester.

Financial Aid: Federal Stafford Loan, Federal Perkins Loan, Federal PLUS Loan, Federal Pell Grant, Federal Work-Study, VA, Iowa resident programs.

Accreditation: North Central Association of Colleges and Schools.

Description: Kirkwood Community College (1966) is a publicly supported, 2-year college with a current enrollment of 11,000 credit students. The college offers diplomas, certificates, and degrees including associate of arts, associate of science, and associate of applied science degrees. Kirkwood pioneered interactive TV instruction in the early 1980s and has offered classes in asynchronous distance learning formats since 1984. Twenty percent of our students each semester are enrolled in one or more distance-delivered courses. Student support services such as advising, counseling, and tutoring for selected classes are available through the college's Web site.

Kirtland Community College

10775 North St. Helen Road	Phone: (517) 275-5121
Roscommon, MI 48653	Fax: (517) 275-6789

Division(s): None.
Web Site(s): http://kirtland.cc.mi.us
E-mail: loseed@kirtland.cc.mi.us

Undergraduate Degree Programs:
25 vocational (technical career oriented) associate degree programs and
Associate in (transfer programs):
  Arts
  Business Administration
  Criminal Justice, General
  Fine Arts
  Science

Certificate Programs: contact school.

Class Titles: contact school.

Teaching Methods: *Computers:* Internet. *TV:* videotape. *Other:* None.

Credits Granted for: examination (CLEP, ACT-PEP, DANTES).

Admission Requirements: *Undergraduate:* high school graduate or GED completer.

On-Campus Requirements: 15 credits.

Tuition and Fees: *Undergraduate:* $50/credit in-district plus fees. *Credit by:* semester.

Financial Aid: Federal Stafford Loan, Federal Perkins Loan, Federal PLUS Loan, Federal Pell Grant, Federal Work-Study, VA, Michigan resident programs.

Accreditation: North Central Association of Colleges and Schools.

Description: On March 7, 1966, in accordance with provision of Public Act 188 of the Michigan Public Acts of 1955, Kirtland Community College was created by a vote of the electorate from 6 local K–12 school districts (Crawford-AuSable, Fairview Area, Gerrish-Higgins, Houghton Lake, Mio-AuSable and West Branch-Rose City). With this approval, the largest Michigan Community College District was formed. The college's district totals 2,500 square miles and consists of all or part of 9 counties.

Knowledge Systems Institute

3420 Main Street	Phone: (847) 679-3135
Skokie, IL 60076	Fax: (847) 679-3166

Division(s): None.
Web Site(s): http://www.ksi.edu
E-mail: office@ksi.edu

Graduate Degree Programs:
Master of Science in Computer and Information Sciences

Certificate Programs: Computer and Information Sciences

Teaching Methods: *Computers:* Internet, e-mail. *Other:* None.

Admission Requirements: *Graduate:* BS degree or equivalent, open-admission for individual courses (see Web site: http://www.ksi.edu). *Certificate:* same as undergraduate.

On-Campus Requirements: limited number of courses by distance, see Web site.

Tuition and Fees: *Graduate:* $275/credit (all graduate courses are 3 credits). *Application Fee:* $40. *Credit by:* semester.

Financial Aid: Federal Stafford Loan, VA, Federal Work-Study.

Accreditation: North Central Association of Colleges and Schools.

Description: Knowledge Systems Institute (1978) is a Graduate School of Computer and Information Sciences dedicated to the training and education of professional people in the fields of computers and management information systems. KSI offers an MS degree in Computer and Information Sciences and an MS degree with specialization in Management Information Systems, Computer Networks, Software Engineering, and other areas. Most of KSI's courses can be taken on campus or via the Internet. This approach greatly facilitates working professionals completing their education. However, there are limitations on the number of courses that can be taken by distance learning. For further information please consult our Web site www.ksi.edu, or send e-mail message to: office@ksi.edu.

Kutztown University

PO Box 700	Phone: (610) 683-4212
Kutztown, PA 19530	Fax: (610) 683-4398

Division(s): Academic Affairs
Web Site(s): http://www.kutztown.edu
E-mail: admission@kutztown.edu

Class Titles: American Literature, Current Health Issues, Personal Fitness.

Teaching Methods: *Computers:* Internet, real-time chat, e-mail, CD-ROM, newsgroup, LISTSERV, Web. *TV:* videotape, cable program, PBS. *Other:* audioconferencing, videoconferencing, audiotapes, fax, correspondence.

Credits Granted for: examination (CLEP, ACT-PEP, DANTES, GRE).

On-Campus Requirements: per instructor basis.

Tuition and Fees: *Undergraduate:* $171/credit in-state, $417/credit out-of-state. *Graduate:* $225/credit in-state, $393/credit out-of-state. *Credit by:* semester.

Financial Aid: Federal Stafford Loan, Federal Perkins Loan, Federal PLUS Loan, Federal Pell Grant, Federal Work-Study, VA, state grant programs for Pennsylvania, Delaware, Ohio, Rhode Island, Maine, Virginia, Massachusetts, Vermont, West Virginia residents. Private loans are also available.

Accreditation: Middle States Association of Colleges and Schools, Pennsylvania Department of Education, State System of Higher Education, National Council for Accreditation of Teacher Education, National League for Nursing, Inc., Council on Social Work Education.

Description: Kutztown University (1866) began as Keystone State Normal School in response to a local need for more teachers. Since those early times, KU has grown into a university that serves 7,900 students in 5 colleges: Business, Education, Liberal Arts and Sciences, Visual and Performing Arts, and Graduate Studies and Extended Learning. The campus sits on 326 acres of rural countryside near Kutztown (population 4,500), in the heart of the state's southeastern "Pennsylvania Dutch" area. Kutztown University first offered distance learning classes in 1996 and plans to expand its offerings in the future. The first classes used Internet technology, and a videoconferencing classroom and conference room have since been added. Kutztown, as a member of the Pennsylvania State System of Higher Education, collaborates with its sister institutions as well as with the community colleges, school districts, and various consortiums to enhance academic offerings and access.

Labette Community College

200 South 14th Street	Phone: (316) 421-6700
Parsons, KS 67357	Fax: (316) 421-4481

Division(s): Instructional Office
Web Site(s): http://www.labette.cc.ks.us
E-mail: chrisb@labette.cc.ks.us

Undergraduate Degree Programs:
Associate in:
    Arts
    Science
    Applied Science
    General Studies

Certificate Programs: Business, Technology, Paraprofessional, and more.

Teaching Methods: *Computers:* Internet, electronic classroom, e-mail. *TV:* videotape, satellite broadcasting. *Other:* audiotapes, independent study, practicums, internships.

Credits Granted for: military (if course identified in American Council on Education Guide), CLEP, CEEB.

Admission Requirements: *Undergraduate:* high school graduate or GED, age 18 as a special student, high school juniors and seniors with permission of principal, "gifted" students (with copy of IEP).

On-Campus Requirements: 15 hours of "seat time"/credit.

Tuition and Fees: *Undergraduate:* $41/credit. *Application Fee:* $15 plus $41/credit nontraditional. *Other Costs:* $25 graduation fee, $45/week private music lessons, lab fees. *Credit by:* semester.

Financial Aid: Federal Pell Grants, Federal Supplemental Educational Opportunity Grants, Federal Work-Study, Federal Family Educational Loans, institutional work, scholarships.

Accreditation: North Central Association of Colleges and Schools, National League for Nursing Council of Associate Degree Programs, Joint Review Committee on Education in Radiologic Technology, Joint Review Committee for Respiratory Therapy Education.

Description: Labette Community College originated as Parsons Junior College in 1923 and attained county college district status in 1965. In 1981 the college expanded, adding an extension campus in the former Oswego Hospital Building. Labette has evolved from a city college primarily serving future transfer students to a comprehensive community college offering transfer degrees, vocational degrees and certificates, continuing education, customized training for business and industry, lifelong learning opportunities, and many other programs and services.

Lackawanna Junior College

501 Vine Street
Scranton, PA 18509

Phone: (717) 961-7840
Fax: (717) 961-7858

Division(s): Distance Learning
Web Site(s): http://members.aol.com/grifflew/ljc/dlc.html
E-mail: grifflew@aol.com

Class Titles: Classes vary by semester depending on demand from our satellite centers (see description). For example, an accounting course was offered from Scranton to Towanda via distance learning. It usually is not known until the beginning of a semester what courses may be offered via teleteaching.

Teaching Methods: *Other:* videoconferencing.

Credits Granted for: experiential learning, portfolio assessment, extrainstitutional learning, examination (CLEP, ACT-PEP, DANTES, GRE).

Admission Requirements: *Undergraduate:* open-admission. *Certificate:* open-admission.

On-Campus Requirements: None.

Tuition and Fees: *Undergraduate:* $230/credit. *Application Fee:* $25. *Credit by:* semester.

Financial Aid: Federal Stafford Loan, Federal Perkins Loan, Federal PLUS Loan, Federal Pell Grant, Federal Work-Study, VA, Pennsylvania resident programs.

Accreditation: Middle States Association of Colleges and Schools.

Description: Lackawanna Junior College (1894) is an accredited, private, nonprofit, educational institution providing opportunities for career and personal development within selected associate degree, certificate, and continuing education programs. Degree programs are accredited by the Commission on Higher Education of the Middle States Association of Colleges and Schools. Lackawanna Junior College is an Equal Opportunity/Affirmative Action educational institution. Distance Learning at Lackawanna began in 1993. They have offered courses to satellite centers in Towanda, Honesdale, and Hazleton (all in Pennsylvania). In addition, they have teletaught courses to Monument Valley High School in Arizona. Lackawanna is a member of the Northern Tier (PA) Distance Learning Consortium.

Lafayette College

Skillman Library
Lafayette College
Easton, PA 18042

Phone: (610) 330-5632
Fax: (610) 252-0370

Division(s): Instructional Technology
Web Site(s): http://www.lafayette.edu
E-mail: benginif@lafayette.edu

Undergraduate Degree Programs:
Bachelor of Science
Associate of Business

Class Titles: German, French, Political Science, Engineering, Religion, Anthropology/Sociology.

Teaching Methods: *Computers:* Internet, electronic classroom, e-mail, CD-ROM. *TV:* videotape, PBS. *Other:* videoconferencing, fax, correspondence, independent study, individual study, learning contracts.

Credits Granted for: examination (CLEP, ACT-PEP, DANTES, GRE).

Admission Requirements: *Undergraduate:* high school graduate; admission is competitive.

On-Campus Requirements: Yes.

Tuition and Fees: *Undergraduate:* $22,049/1998–1999 academic year, part-time is $950/4-credit class. *Credit by:* semester.

Financial Aid: Federal Stafford Loan, Federal Perkins Loan, Federal PLUS Loan, Federal Pell Grant, Federal Work-Study, VA, Pennsylvania resident programs.

Accreditation: Middle States Association of Colleges and Schools.

Description: Lafayette College (1826) offers a challenging, broad-based curriculum with strong programs in liberal arts, sciences, and engineering. With about 2,000 students, Lafayette offers a small-college environment with large-college resources and an exceptionally qualified faculty committed to each student's success. Lafayette is a residential college, and students enjoy living in the college's uniquely friendly community with its exciting social life and broad spectrum of extracurricular activities. In 1995 Lafayette began to explore the use of videoconferencing to enhance its students' educational experiences and to share resources with other colleges and universities. The college has 2 state-of-the-art videoconferencing centers that share courses and other programs with similar institutions, bring in guest speakers from distant places, and teach courses to Lafayette students studying abroad.

Lake Land College

5001 Lake Land Boulevard
Mattoon, IL 61938

Phone: (217) 234-5450
Fax: (217) 234-5400

Division(s): Continuing Education Department
Web Site(s): http://www.lakeland.cc.il.us
E-mail: lpoffinbarger@lakeland.cc.il.us

Class Titles: Anthropology, Small Business Management, Business, Financial Accounting, Managerial Accounting, Legal Environment of Business, Principles of Marketing, Principles of Salesmanship, Business Law, Human Resource Management, Business Statistics, Composition, Speech, Principles of Health, U.S. History, Western Civilization to 1660, Literature, Algebra, College Algebra, Statistics, Ethics, Philosophy, State/Local Government, Psychology, Human Development/Life Span, Child Development, Principles of Economics, Interpersonal Communications.

Teaching Methods: *Computers:* Internet, electronic classroom, e-mail, CD-ROM, LISTSERV. *TV:* videotape, satellite broadcasting. *Other:* videoconferencing, fax, correspondence, independent study, individual study.

Credits Granted for: experiential learning, portfolio assessment, extrainstitutional learning, examination (CLEP, ACT-PEP, DANTES, GRE).

Admission Requirements: *Undergraduate:* age 16, entrance exams.

On-Campus Requirements: Most classes on and off campus require 2,250 minutes seat time, although our Internet classes do not require actual classroom time.

Tuition and Fees: *Undergraduate:* This varies with the classes taken due to additional class fees. The average cost is $50/credit. *Application Fee:* $10. *Credit by:* semester.

Financial Aid: Federal Stafford Loan, Federal Perkins Loan, Federal PLUS Loan, Federal Pell Grant, Federal Work-Study, VA, Illinois resident programs.

Accreditation: North Central Association of Colleges and Schools.

Description: Lake Land College (1966) began with classes held in temporary facilities. The first building on the present campus was completed in 1971. That campus now includes 3 temporary buildings that house cosmetology, civil engineering, maintenance, and a bookstore. Four other buildings house academic offices, admissions and records, administration, and classrooms. Funds were recently approved to begin construction on a new classroom building in the fall of 1998. The distance learning program began in 1994 through a collaborative effort by the Illinois Prairie Higher Education Consortium comprised of Lake Land College, Danville Area Community College, Parkland College, Richland Community College, Eastern Illinois University, University of Illinois U-C, and Lakeview College of Nursing.

Lake-Sumter Community College

| 9501 Highway 441 | Phone: (352) 365-3566 |
| Leesburg, FL 34788 | Fax: (352) 365-3501 |

Division(s): Television Studio and V.P. Educational Services
Web Site(s): http://www.lscc.cc.fl.us
E-mail: huntp@lscc.cc.fl.us

Class Titles: Marine Science, Earth Revealed, Business/Law, Business, Psychology, Psychology of Child Development, Basic Nutrition, Trends/Issues in Health, American National Government.

Teaching Methods: *Computers:* Internet, electronic classroom, e-mail, CD-ROM. *TV:* videotape, satellite, broadcasting, PBS. *Other:* videoconferencing, audiotapes, fax, correspondence, independent study, individual study.

Credits Granted for: examination (CLEP, ACT-PEP, DANTES, GRE).

Admission Requirements: *Undergraduate:* high school diploma or GED. GPA of 2.5 or better, application.

On-Campus Requirements: students, logistically, must spend time on campus in a traditional classroom setting.

Tuition and Fees: *Undergraduate:* $39/credit resident, $145/credit nonresident. *Application Fee:* $20. *Software:* $15. *Other Costs:* $20 late registration, $16 nursing fee (insurance), $20/credit exemption exam fee, $20 international student processing fee. *Credit by:* semester.

Financial Aid: Federal Stafford Loan, Federal Perkins Loan, Federal PLUS Loan, Federal Pell Grant, Federal Work-Study, VA, Florida resident programs.

Accreditation: Southern Association of Colleges and Schools.

Lake Superior State University

| 650 West Easterday | Phone: (906) 635-2802 |
| Sault Ste. Marie, MI 49783 | Fax: (906) 635-2762 |

Division(s): Continuing Education
Web Site(s): http://www.lssu.edu
E-mail: csd@lakers.lssu.edu

Undergraduate Degree Programs:
Bachelor of Arts/Bachelor of Science in:
    Business Administration
    Engineering Management
    Accounting
    Criminal Justice
    Nursing, BSN Completion

Graduate Degree Programs:
Master of Business Administration

Teaching Methods: *Other:* interactive TV.

Credits Granted for: previous academic work.

Admission Requirements: *Undergraduate:* average high school GPA: 2.88, ACT 21. *Graduate:* undergraduate GPA, GMAT.

On-Campus Requirements: At the present time all of our

distance education courses are offered via Interactive TV, so all students must participate from an ITV classroom at one of 4 distant sites. Some classes require participation in concentrated labs on the campus of LSSU.

Tuition and Fees: *Undergraduate:* $155/credit. *Graduate:* $172/credit. *Application Fee:* $20 undergraduate, $25 graduate. *Credit by:* semester.

Financial Aid: Federal Stafford Loan, Federal Perkins Loan, Federal PLUS Loan, Federal Pell Grant, Federal Work-Study, VA, Michigan resident programs.

Accreditation: North Central Association of Colleges and Schools.

Description: Lake Superior State University (1946) is located in the beautiful and rugged, eastern upper peninsula. Distance education at Lake Superior State consists of interactive TV courses and degree programs available at 4 community colleges in northern Michigan in Alpena, Escanaba, Petoskey, and Traverse City. A variety of degrees are available at these sites, including bachelor's degrees in accounting, business administration, criminal justice, engineering management, and BSN nursing completion. A Master of Business Administration is also available. Each degree can be completed entirely by distance. LSSU is also in the process of developing other courses for alternative delivery. Future Internet courses are planned, along with self-contained, asynchronous courses on CD-ROM and videotape, with student/teacher interaction available over the Web.

Lake Tahoe Community College

One College Way	Phone: (530) 541-4660
South Lake Tahoe, CA 96150	Fax: (530) 541-7852

Division(s): Instruction Office
Web Site(s): http://www.ltcc.cc.ca.us
E-mail: stevenson@ltcc.cc.ca.us

Undergraduate Degree Programs:
Associate of Arts in:
Art
English
Fine Arts
Health, Physical Education, and Dance
Humanities
Liberal Arts
Natural Science
Psychology
Social Science
Spanish
Addiction Studies
Business
Business Office Administration
Computer Studies

Criminal Justice
Early Childhood Education
Fire Science
Medical Office Assistant: Administrative
Medical Office Assistant: Clinical
Real Estate

Certificate Programs: Addiction Studies, Art, Business, Business Office Administration, Computer Studies: Programming, Computer Studies: Applications, Criminal Justice, Early Childhood Education, Fire Science, Legal Assistant, Medical Office Assistant: Administrative/Clinical, Photography, Real Estate.

Class Titles: Research Paper, Composition, Java Script

Teaching Methods: *Computers:* Internet, real-time chat, electronic classroom, e-mail, CD-ROM, newsgroup, LISTSERV. *Other:* None.

Admission Requirements: *Undergraduate:* open-access. *Certificate:* open-access.

On-Campus Requirements: None.

Tuition and Fees: *Undergraduate:* $8/credit California resident, $28/credit nonresident (less than 6 units). *Credit by:* quarter.

Financial Aid: Federal Stafford Loan, Federal Perkins Loan, Federal Pell Grant, Federal Work-Study, VA, California resident programs.

Accreditation: Western Association of Schools and Colleges.

Description: Lake Tahoe Community College (1975) is a public, 2-year college located at 6,000 feet in the Sierra Nevada mountain range. We offer lower-division, transfer programs as well as a wide range of occupational programs. We have just started to offer distance education and have several classes available. Visit our home page for more information.

Lakehead University

RC 0009, 955 Oliver Road	Phone: (807) 346-7730
Thunder Bay, ON, Canada P7E 5E1	Fax: (807) 343-8008

Division(s): Part-Time Studies
Web Site(s): http://www.lakeheadu.ca/~disedwww/menu.html
E-mail: parttime@lakeheadu.ca

Undergraduate Degree Programs:
Bachelor of Arts (General)
Bachelor of Science in Nursing for Registered Nurses

Graduate Degree Programs:
Master of Forestry

Certificate Programs: Environmental Assessment

Teaching Methods: *Computers:* Internet, e-mail, LISTSERV. *TV:* videotape, cable program. *Other:* audioconferencing, videoconferencing, audiographics, audiotapes, fax, correspondence, independent study, individual study.

Admission Requirements: *Undergraduate:* see university calendar. *Graduate:* see university calendar. *Certificate:* see university calendar.

On-Campus Requirements: one-term residency for Master of Forestry.

Tuition and Fees: *Undergraduate:* $730/credit. *Other Costs:* $6–$100 for manuals, $40 Audio/Visual deposit. *Credit by:* semester.

Financial Aid: Ontario Student Assistance Program

Accreditation: Association of Universities and Colleges of Canada.

Description: At Lakehead University (1965), our faculty, staff, programs, and services team up to provide an extensive range of learning choices and alternatives. The university evolved from Lakehead Technical Institute, which was established in 1946. Lakehead serves a dual role with the responsibility for bringing knowledge and an understanding of a broad range of the basic disciplines to Northwestern Ontario, while striving to be a good general university for the purpose of regional accessibility.

Lakeland Community College

7700 Clocktower Drive	Phone: (440) 953-7000
Kirtland, OH 44094	Fax: (440) 953-9710

Division(s): Instructional Technologies
Web Site(s): http://www.lakeland.cc.oh.us
E-mail: wryan@lakeland.cc.oh.us

Undergraduate Degree Programs:
Associate of:
　Arts
　Science
　Applied Business
　Applied Science
　Technical Studies

Certificate Programs: can be earned in any program.

Class Titles: Voices in Democracy, Power of Place, Economics, Portrait of Family, Sociological Imagination, Faces of Culture, Cycles of Life, Ethics in America, Taking the Lead, By the Numbers, World of Art, Living with Health, American Cinema, American Vision, It's Strictly Business, Personal Finance, Marketing, Against All Odds.

Teaching Methods: *Computers:* Internet, e-mail, CD-ROM, LISTSERV. *TV:* videotape, cable program, satellite broadcast-

ing, PBS. *Other:* videoconferencing, fax.

Credits Granted for: certification, examination (CLEP), experience, articulation.

Admission Requirements: *Undergraduate:* application, official high school transcript, college transcripts if applicable.

On-Campus Requirements: class orientation for telecourses.

Tuition and Fees: *Undergraduate:* $43/credit in-county, $53/credit out-of-county, $112/credit out-of-state. *Other Costs:* $20/distance learning class. *Credit by:* quarter (converting to semester in 2000).

Financial Aid: Federal Stafford Loan, Federal Perkins Loan, Federal PLUS Loan, Federal Pell Grant, Federal Work-Study, VA, Ohio resident programs, scholarships, grants, loans, work-study.

Accreditation: North Central Association of Colleges and Schools.

Description: Lakeland Community College's (1967) mission is to provide transfer programs to begin studies toward a 4-year degree, career programs leading to immediate employment, and training and retraining programs to update job skills. Lakeland offers more than 1,000 classes in 76 degree and certificate programs.

Lamar University

PO Box 10008, LU Station	Phone: (409) 880-8431
Beaumont, TX 77710	Fax: (409) 880-8683

Division(s): Continuing Education
Web Site(s): http://www.lamar.edu
E-mail: brownok@lub002.lamar.edu

Class Titles: Nutrition/Diet, U.S. History, American Government, Microcomputers/Business, Humanities.

Teaching Methods: *Computers:* Internet, e-mail. *TV:* videotape, cable program, PBS. *Other:* videoconferencing, fax.

Credits Granted for: experiential learning, portfolio assessment, extrainstitutional learning, examination (CLEP, ACT-PEP, DANTES, GRE).

Admission Requirements: *Undergraduate:* accredited high school graduate, SAT/ACT, TASP, college transcripts if transfer student (18 hours). *Graduate:* contact school. *Doctoral:* contact school.

On-Campus Requirements: exams only.

Tuition and Fees: *Undergraduate:* $283/credit. *Graduate:* $283/credit. *Doctoral:* $283/credit. *Credit by:* semester.

Financial Aid: Federal Stafford Loan, Federal Perkins Loan, Federal PLUS Loan, Federal Pell Grant, Federal Work-Study,

VA, Texas resident programs.

Accreditation: Southern Association of Colleges and Schools.

Description: Lamar University (1923) opened as "a Junior College of the first class" with 125 students and a faculty of 14. In 1932 the name of the institution was changed to Lamar College, to honor Mirabeau B. Lamar, second president of the Republic of Texas and the "Father of Education" in Texas. Lamar was the first junior college in Texas to become a 4-year, state-supported college. Lamar continued to grow, building strong programs in engineering, the sciences, business, and education. In 1962, a graduate school was established offering master's degrees in several fields. The Doctorate in Engineering was established in 1971, at which time Lamar boasted an enrollment of 10,874. New programs were added, including Technical Arts, Allied Health, Office Technology, and Restaurant/Institutional Food Management. The Doctorate of Education in Deaf Education was established in 1993. Lamar's growth has been steady and progressive, anticipating the evolving needs of its students.

Laney College

900 Fallon Street	Phone: (510) 446-7368
Oakland, CA 94607	Fax: (510) 464-3231

Division(s): Distance Learning
Web Site(s): http://www.peralta.cc.ca.us
E-mail: lmnelson@metro.net

Undergraduate Degree Programs:
Associate in Arts
General Curriculum

Class Titles: Anthropology, Astronomy, Biology, Business, Health Education, History, Humanities, Journalism, Philosophy, Psychology, Sociology, Spanish.

Teaching Methods: *Computers:* Internet, e-mail, CD-ROM. *TV:* videotape, cable program, PBS. *Other:* audiotapes, fax, correspondence, learning contracts, project-based learning, portfolio assessment.

Credits Granted for: all except computer classes over the Internet.

Admission Requirements: *Undergraduate:* all over age 18 admitted.

On-Campus Requirements: None.

Tuition and Fees: *Undergraduate:* $13/credit resident. *Credit by:* semester.

Financial Aid: Federal Stafford Loan, Federal Perkins Loan, Federal PLUS Loan, Federal Pell Grant, Federal Work-Study, VA, California resident programs.

Accreditation: Western Association of Schools and Colleges.

Description: Laney College (1953) is the largest of the 4 colleges in the Peralta Community College District. Laney offers a positive view of what is right about a diverse America. The college offers intense academic learning, modern occupational training, and a sophisticated, dedicated faculty whose teaching and caring are the heart of the college. Laney is well known for its outstanding student newspaper, *The Laney Tower,* its Transfer Opportunity Center, and its array of quality academic and vocational course offerings.

Lansing Community College

528 North Capitol Avenue	Phone: (517) 483-9940
Lansing, MI 48933	Fax: (517) 483-9750

Division(s): Virtual College
Web Site(s): http://vcollege.lansing.cc.mi.us
E-mail: advising_vcollege@lansing.cc.mi.us

Undergraduate Degree Programs:
Associate in General Studies (emphasis in Business)

Certificate Programs: Internet for Business

Class Titles: A majority of courses offered can be used for other degrees as well.

Teaching Methods: *Computers:* Internet, real-time chat, electronic classroom, e-mail, CD-ROM, LISTSERV, bulletin board. *TV:* videotape, cable program, interactive TV. *Other:* fax, correspondence.

Credits Granted for: experiential learning, portfolio assessment, extrainstitutional learning, examination (CLEP, ACT-PEP, DANTES, GRE).

Admission Requirements: *Undergraduate:* open-enrollment: age 18, high school diploma or GED, dual enrollment for high school students, TOEFL for international students.

On-Campus Requirements: None.

Tuition and Fees: *Undergraduate:* $48/credit in-district, $77/credit out-of-district, $106/credit out-of-state and international. *Application Fee:* $10. *Other Costs:* $20 registration fee. *Credit by:* semester.

Financial Aid: Federal Stafford Loan, Federal PLUS Loan, Federal Pell Grant, Federal Work-Study, VA, Michigan resident programs.

Accreditation: North Central Association of Colleges and Schools.

Description: Lansing Community College (1957) has been committed to excellence in education for 40 years. We've grown from a small technical college to one of the largest, most comprehensive community colleges in the nation. We offer classes year-round on our 28-acre campus in the heart of Michigan's capital. You can choose from 150 degree and certificate programs and 2,500 courses, or complete the first 2 years of a liberal arts education. LCC first offered distance learning in 1979 through telecourses, later adding a Child Development Series on a cable TV access channel. Since then, more than 18,000 students have enrolled in telecourses. LCC continues to be a leader in distance learning by offering a complete degree online. Currently, students may choose from 40 online courses.

Laramie County Community College

1400 East College Drive	Phone: (307) 778-5222
Cheyenne, WY 82007	Fax: (307) 778-1344

Division(s): Community Outreach
Web Site(s): http://www.lcc.whecn.edu
E-mail: mollyc@mail.lcc.whecn.edu

Class Titles: Business, Economics, English, Geology, U.S. History, Humanities, Political Science, Psychology, Child Growth/Development, Communications, Education, American Studies, Anthropology, Astronomy, Biology, Geography, Management, Philosophy, Sociology.

Teaching Methods: *Computers:* Internet, real-time chat, e-mail. *TV:* telecourses, videotape. *Other:* independent study (instructor approval only), compressed video and videoconferencing to branch campus only.

Credits Granted for: departmental examination program, military service credits.

Admission Requirements: *Undergraduate:* high school graduate, age 18, or can benefit from a college's programs. Degree-seeking students need high school diploma or equivalent. All new students, unless otherwise exempted, must undergo assessment in reading, writing, and math prior to class registration. Prerequisites must be passed with a C or exempted through a higher-level course or through placement scores. *Certificate:* same as undergraduate.

On-Campus Requirements: To receive a degree from Laramie County Community College, a student must complete 15 semester hours in residence (distance education courses can count) at Laramie County Community College.

Tuition and Fees: *Undergraduate:* $50/credit resident, $134/credit out-of-state. *Application Fee:* $15 *Other Costs:* $20/telecourse. *Credit by:* semester.

Financial Aid: Federal Stafford Loan, Federal PLUS Loan, Federal Pell Grand, Federal Work-Study, VA, Wyoming resident programs.

Accreditation: North Central Association of Colleges and Schools.

Description: The main campus of Laramie County Community College (1968) consists of 20 modern buildings. Outreach programs/facilities are also available at the Albany County Campus in Laramie, the Eastern Laramie County Campus in Pine Bluffs, and at F.E. Warren Air Force Base in Cheyenne. LCCC serves 4,500 credit and noncredit students each semester and has an annualized full-time enrollment of 2,770. The college first offered telecourses in 1982 and consistently offers 12–15 telecourses each semester. Internet courses were offered for the first time in the fall of 1996. Although only 4 Internet courses are presently offered, this number is growing for upcoming semesters. Each semester the college serves 400 distant learners.

Las Positas College

3033 Collier Canyon Road	Phone: (925) 373-5800
Livermore, CA 94550-7650	Fax: (925) 373-4967

Division(s): Learning Resources
Web Site(s): http://www.laspositas.cc.ca.us
E-mail: llucas@clpccd.cc.ca.us

Undergraduate Degree Programs:
Associate of Arts
Associate of Science

Class Titles: Anthropology, Philosophy, Psychology, Religious Studies, Spanish.

Teaching Methods: *TV:* videotape, cable program, PBS. *Other:* videoconferencing, independent study, individual study.

Admission Requirements: *Undergraduate:* age 18, able to benefit from instruction; completion limit/course is one semester.

On-Campus Requirements: None.

Tuition and Fees: *Undergraduate:* $12/credit; out-of-state and international tuition set annually. *Credit by:* semester.

Financial Aid: Federal Stafford Loan, Federal Pell Grant, Federal Work-Study, VA, California resident programs.

Accreditation: Western Association of Schools and Colleges.

Description: Las Positas College (1975) is a 2-year community college enrolling about 6,300 students. The college has a small distance learning program designed to help working adults complete their college education while working full time. Most classes are offered as telecourses and facilitated with Internet-based newsgroups, videoconferencing, or some combination of media. Online courses are planned for 1999–2000.

Laurentian University

935 Ramsey Lake Road	Phone: (705) 673-6569
Sudbury, ON, Canada P3E 2C6	Fax: (705) 675-4897

Division(s): Continuing Education
Web Site(s): http://www.laurentian.ca
E-mail: cce_l@nickel.laurentian.ca

Undergraduate Degree Programs:
Bachelor of Arts in:
  Native Studies
  Psychology
  Religious Studies
  Sociology
  Women's Studies
Bachelor of Social Work (Native Human Services)
Bachelor of Liberal Science

Certificate Programs: Family Life Studies and Human Sexuality/Gerontology.

Teaching Methods: *Computers:* Internet, electronic classroom, e-mail, LISTSERV. *TV:* videotape, cable program, satellite broadcasting, PBS. *Other:* audioconferencing, videoconferencing, audiotapes, fax, correspondence, independent study, individual study.

Credits Granted for: examination (CLEP, ACT-PEP, DANTES, GRE).

Admission Requirements: *Undergraduate:* contact school for information. *Certificate:* contact school for information.

On-Campus Requirements: 3 hours/week winter, 6 hours/week summer.

Tuition and Fees: *Undergraduate:* $712/credit on-campus, $747/credit by distance. *Graduate:* $995/credit. *Application Fee:* $35. *Other Costs:* $35 for distance education manual. *Credit by:* semester.

Financial Aid: Ontario Student Assistance Program, Part-time Canada Student Loan, Special Opportunity Grants, Laurentian University Bursaries.

Accreditation: Association of Universities and Colleges of Canada.

Description: Laurentian University was founded in 1960. Its distance education program, Envision, was launched in September 1972 to reach the 600,000 northeastern Ontario students scattered in an area twice the size of France. Courses are designed to respond to students' needs for autonomous learning along with student and faculty interaction. The first courses were TV-based, with subsequent productions through audiocassette, teleconferencing, and computer-based systems. All courses include a strong print component and utilize media according to stated learning objectives. Complete degree programs include 7 bachelor's in English, 6 in French, and a master's in Humanities in English. Bachelor's degrees in History and Liberal Science and Language and Linguistics are being developed. More than 250 courses exist, with 15–25 new courses every year. Laurentian offers Canada's largest bilingual distance education program, with a greater degree selection than most open universities. Laurentian University is a founding member of the Canadian Association for Distance Education and a member of the International Council for Distance Education. The university is also involved with the Commonwealth of Learning and provides all distance education courses free of charge to developing nations.

Laval University

Pavillon Louis-Jacques-Casault (4731)	Phone: (418) 656-3202
Quebec City, Quebec, Canada G1K 7P4	Fax: (418) 656-5538

Division(s): Continuing Education Division
Web Site(s): http://www.ulaval.ca
E-mail: dgfc@dgfc.ulaval.ca

Undergraduate Degree Programs:
Diploma in:
  Personal Financial Planning
  Computer Science
  Horticulture and Landscape Management
  Food Science and Quality Food Merchandising

Teaching Methods: *Computers:* Internet, electronic classroom, e-mail, newsgroup. *TV:* videotape, cable program. *Other:* audioconferencing, videoconferencing, audiotapes, fax, correspondence, individual study.

Admission Requirements: *Undergraduate:* high school certificate.

On-Campus Requirements: None.

Tuition and Fees: *Undergraduate:* $55/credit (Quebec resident). *Application Fee:* $30. *Other Costs:* $=FD100 for study material. *Credit by:* semester.

Accreditation: Association of Universities and Colleges of Canada, American Assembly of Collegiate Schools of Business.

Description: Laval University (1663) holds the distinction of being Canada's first university. Today it is recognized in program assessment and strategic planning. Laval is a leading institution of higher education that offers more than 350 programs to more than 34,000 students, and the school has an international presence, with more than 300 agreements with more than 50 countries.

Lehigh Carbon Community College

4525 Education Park Drive
Schnecksville, PA 18078

Phone: (610) 799-1196
Fax: (610) 799-1159

Division(s): Distance Education Programs
Web Site(s): http://www.lccc.edu
E-mail: admis@lex.lccc.edu

Undergraduate Degree Programs:
Associate of Arts in:
  Business Administration
  Criminal Justice Administration
  Education
  Fine Arts/Studio Arts
  Humanities/Arts
  Liberal Arts
  Social Sciences
Associate of Science in:
  Computer Science
  Engineering
  Mathematics
  Mechanical Engineering Tech
  Natural Science
Associate of Applied Science
  (contact school for listing)

Certificate Programs: Accounting, Art, Business, Computer Servicing, Computer Specialist in Information Systems, Computer Specialist in Multimedia, Computer Specialist in Network, Construction Technology, Corrections, Drafting, Early Childhood Education, Electrical Technology, Electronics, Gerontology, Indoor Environmental Technology, Industrial Automation–Robotic, Law Enforcement, Management, Medical Transcriptionist, Paramedic (Credit and Credit-Fee), Practical Nursing, Real Estate, Retailing, Tool and Die/Machinist Apprenticeship, Travel and Tourism, Word Processing.

Teaching Methods: *Computers:* Internet, real-time chat, electronic classroom, e-mail. *TV:* videotape, cable program, satellite reception, PBS. *Other:* videoconferencing, correspondence, independent study, individual study.

Credits Granted for: experiential learning, portfolio assessment, examination (CLEP, ACT-PEP, DANTES, GRE).

Admission Requirements: *Undergraduate:* anyone who can profit from furthering their education. *Certificate:* same as undergraduate.

On-Campus Requirements: None.

Tuition and Fees: *Undergraduate:* $72/credit resident, $144/credit nonresident. *Other Costs:* $45 distance learning course fee. *Credit by:* semester.

Financial Aid: Federal Stafford Loan, Federal Perkins Loan, Federal PLUS Loan, Federal Pell Grant, Federal Work-Study, VA, Pennsylvania resident programs.

Accreditation: Middle States Association of Colleges and Schools.

Description: Lehigh Carbon Community College (1966) is a vibrant, responsive, and diverse institution. From business and industry training to literacy and job training, from degree and certificate credit programs to community education classes, LCCC addresses significant educational needs. As a community college, we have a broad responsibility to help educate the community, and LCCC has delivered results to our region for more than 30 years. This means we seek to offer course work that is interesting and useful at convenient times and locations that fit into students' busy schedules. Toward that aim, the college developed creative learning opportunities through distance learning.

Lehigh University

205 Johnson Hall
36 University Drive
Bethlehem, PA 18015

Phone: (610) 758-5794
Fax: (610) 758-6269

Division(s): Office of Distance Education
Web Site(s): http://www.lehigh.edu/~indis/indis.html
E-mail: mak5@lehigh.edu

Graduate Degree Programs:
Master of Science in:
  Chemistry
  Chemical Engineer
  Polymer Science/Engineering
  Molecular Biology
  Quality Engineering
Master of Business Administration

Teaching Methods: *Computers:* Internet access, real-time chat, electronic classroom bulletin boards, e-mail, newsgroup, LISTSERV. *TV:* satellite broadcasting (live via digital KU-band satellite transmission into corporate sites). *Other:* None.

Admission Requirements: *Graduate:* accredited bachelor's degree. MBA requires GMAT scores. Each department has its own criteria.

On-Campus Requirements: Students must view classes live at their work site. MBA requires 2 Saturday campus participations.

Tuition and Fees: *Graduate:* $570/credit (1998/99). *Application Fee:* $30 one-time. *Other Costs:* textbooks. *Credit by:* semester.

Financial Aid: Federal Stafford Loan

Accreditation: Middle States Association of Colleges and Schools. MBA by AACSB.

Description: Lehigh University was founded in 1865 in

Bethlehem, Pennsylvania, by industrialist and philanthropist Asa Packer, whose vision for the university—"a classical education for a useful life"—is still adhered to today. An independent, coeducational university with programs in the arts and humanities, business, education, engineering, and the natural and social sciences, Lehigh is small enough to be personal, yet large enough to provide stimulating diversity and to play important national and international roles. Lehigh is known for its integration of teaching, research, and service to industry. The integrating element of that teaching, research, and service is learning, which is the principal mission of all members of the Lehigh community. Whether serving students on campus or at off-site locations, Lehigh is an intellectually unified community of learners. Since 1992, the Lehigh Educational Satellite Network has aspired to provide educational opportunities at locations accessible for students and cost-effective for their employers. Distance education students are as important to the university as traditional students, and the program strives to maintain the high quality and character of education found on the Lehigh campus. The Office of Distance Education and its staff view distance students and their employers as clients of the university, deserving the best efforts in all areas, including technology, programming, academic support, and customer service. In short, the guiding principles of Lehigh University distance education are convenience, cost-effectiveness, academic excellence, and client satisfaction.

Leicester University, UK and North American Distributor

University Road	Phone: UK (44) 116-252-2522
Leicester, UK IE1 7RH	UK (44) 116-292-5960
6921 Stockton Avenue	US (888) 534-2378
El Cerrito, CA 94530	US (510) 528-3020
	Fax: (510) 528-3555

Division(s): UK Departments: School of Archeological Studies; Management Center; Scarman Center for the Study of Public Order; International Center for Management, Law and Industrial Relations; Center for Applied Psychology; Center for Mass Communications Research; Center for Research into Sport and Society; Center for Labor Market Studies; School of Education; Educational Management Development Unit; Labor Market Studies, North American Distributor

Web Site(s): http://www.clms.le.ac.uk
E-mail: (UK) eeg1m@admin.le.ac.uk
(UK) mb19@1e.ac.uk
(US/Canada) luhrm@vickery.net

Undergraduate Degree Programs:
Diploma in Training and Development
Diploma in Human Resource Management

Diploma in Managment (Banking and Finance)
Graduate Degree Programs:
United Kingdom:
Master of Arts in:
    Applied Linguistics and TESOL
    Archeology and Heritage
    Mass Communications
Master of Business Administration (MBA)
    MBA in Sports Management
Law (LLM) and Master of Arts in:
    European Union Law
    Law and Employment Relations

UK/US/Canada:
Master of Science in:
    Criminal Justice Studies
    Training
    Training and Human Resource Management
    Training and Performance Management
    Finance
    Forensic and Legal Psychology
    Museum Studies
    Public Order Studies
    Risk, Crisis and Disaster Management
    Security and Crime Risk Management
    Sociology of Sport (Physical Education)
    Sociology of Sport (Sports Management)

Doctoral Degree Programs:
Cooperative Management and Organizational Development, Human Resource Management, Management (Banking and Financial Services), Training and Development

Certificate Programs: Supervision and Mentorship (Child Care), Diplomas in Management, Banking and Financial Services, Training and Development, Human Resource Management, and Cooperative Management.

Teaching Methods: *Computers:* Internet, real-time chat, e-mail, newsgroup, LISTSERV. *TV:* videotape (supplementary), fax. *Other:* independent study, individual study, correspondence, learning contracts.

Admission Requirements: *Undergraduate:* age 21, high school diploma, 3 years of relevant experience. *Graduate:* age 21, bachelor's degree, 3.0 GPA, or 3 years of relevant professional experience plus academic credentials. Also, B+ in one-year Leicester University Diploma program (see above). *Doctoral:* UK Honors Bachelor's degree (2.2 minimum) or equivalent, professional qualifications and substantial professional experience, for applicants whose first language is not English, an IELTS score of 6.5 or a TOEFL score of 575 minimum.

On-Campus Requirements: (For UK students) Optional, annual, residential, weekend seminar in North America.

Tuition and Fees: *Undergraduate:* $2,750/one-year program. *Graduate:* $2,400/module (semester). *Application Fee:* $25 master's program. *Other Costs:* $30 shipping in U.S., travel/lodging optional for residential weekend. *Credit by:* semester.

Financial Aid: Federally insured U.S. student loans, tuition payment plan.

Accreditation: Distance Education and Training Council for Center for Labor Market Studies.

Description: Leicester University (1921) was founded as a university college that provided for students studying for the University of London external degrees. It was granted a Royal Charter by Her Majesty the Queen in 1957, which transformed the college into Leicester University. More than 12,000 students study on campus, with thousands more in the U.S., Canada, Europe, and Asia enrolled in distance learning programs. The first distance course (MA/LLM in Employment Law) was offered in 1987 and the university is now one of the largest providers of distance learning postgraduate courses in the UK, with students throughout the world. LU first offered the Master's in Training and Human Resource Management program in 1991 to distance students in the UK and Europe. In 1994 the university received the Queen's Anniversary Prize for "outstanding educational achievement." By 1996 a North American version of the program became available to students in the U.S., Canada, and the Caribbean. Leicester designed its master's and diploma programs for distance students employed while pursuing part-time studies. These programs draw from sociology, psychology, management studies, economics, and adult education.

Lesley College

29 Everett Street	**Phone: (617) 349-8421**
Cambridge, MA 02138	**Fax: (617) 349-8169**

Division(s): Technology in Education, School of Education
Web Site(s): http://www.lesley.edu
E-mail: myoder@mail.lesley.edu

Graduate Degree Programs:
Master of Education

Class Titles: Computers/Technology/Education, Telecommunications: Curriculum In Global Context, Teaching/Learning with Multimedia, Integrating Technology into School Curriculum, Microworlds/Models/Simulation, Computer Structure, Technology/Special Needs, Technology: Impact on Society/Schools, Technology in Mathematics Curriculum, Technology in Language Arts Curriculum, Authoring with HTML—Weaving World Wide Classroom Webs, Video as Educational Technology.

Teaching Methods: *Computers:* Internet, e-mail, CD-ROM, newsgroup, LISTSERV. *Other:* None.

Credits Granted for: students may transfer up to 6 graduate credits from other institutions, provided they meet with our criteria.

Admission Requirements: *Graduate:* 7-year completion limit for master's degree.

On-Campus Requirements: None.

Tuition and Fees: *Graduate:* $300/credit. *Application Fee:* $45. *Software:* variable. *Other Costs:* $30–$60 materials fees, $15/semester registration fee. *Credit by:* 33 credits (11 3-credit courses, fall, spring, and summer semesters).

Financial Aid: Federal Stafford Loan, Federal Perkins Loan, Federal PLUS Loan, Federal Pell Grant, Federal Work-Study, VA, Massachusetts resident programs.

Accreditation: New England Association of Schools and Colleges.

Description: Lesley College's (1909) Technology in Education program, founded in 1979, is one of the oldest in the country. The program provides state-of-the-art technology courses with a mixture of practical classroom applications and educational theory. Our distance learning program began in 1997 and has a diverse student body from all over the world. Classes are small, under 20 students, and students are encouraged to work collaboratively. Most students are K–12 classroom teachers and administrators. Classes are rigorous and students rarely take more than 6 credits per semester. Eleven 3-credit courses are required, though students can transfer up to 6 approved graduate credits.

Lewis-Clark State College

500 Eighth Avenue	**Phone: (208) 799-2239**
Lewiston, ID 83501	**Fax: (208) 799-2444**

Division(s): Center for Individualized Programs
Web Site(s): http://www.lcsc.edu/cip/
E-mail: kmartin@lcsc.edu

Undergraduate Degree Programs:
Associate of Arts in Liberal Arts
Bachelor of Science in:
    Interdisciplinary Studies
    Business/Communication

Class Titles: Biology, Business, Communications, Computer/Information Sciences, Education, English Language/Literature, History, Math, Physical Sciences, Psychology, Social Sciences, Visual/Performing Arts.

Teaching Methods: *Computers:* Internet, real-time chat, electronic classroom, e-mail, CD-ROM, newsgroup, LIST-

SERV. *TV:* videotape, satellite broadcasting, PBS. *Other:* audioconferencing, videoconferencing, audiotapes, fax, correspondence, individual study, compressed video.

Credits Granted for: experiential learning, portfolio assessment, extrainstitutional learning, examination, military training.

Admission Requirements: *Undergraduate:* high school transcripts or GED; ACT, SAT, or CPT scores if degree-seeking.

On-Campus Requirements: limited for some classes.

Tuition and Fees: *Undergraduate:* $102/credit part-time, $1,022 full-time. *Application Fee:* $20 degree-seeking. *Credit by:* semester.

Financial Aid: Federal Stafford Loan, Federal Perkins Loan, Federal PLUS Loan, Federal Pell Grant, Federal Work-Study, VA, Idaho resident programs.

Accreditation: Northwest Association of Schools and Colleges.

Description: Lewis-Clark State College (1893) is a regional undergraduate institution providing an alternative learning environment. An integral part of the college's mission is to provide outreach courses and programs to meet the educational and training needs of a diverse population. Since 1995, the college's flexible distance learning program has offered credit courses for students with time and geographic constraints. While many courses have required due dates for assignments and exams, they usually have no structured class meeting times. Course offerings follow the same academic calendar dates and registration procedures as on-campus classes. Some of the 50 distance courses offered include the general education core, electives, and major concentrations in business and communications, with additional courses developed annually. Most courses require e-mail and Internet access to complete assignments, participation in individual and group discussions with the instructor, and participation in peer group activities.

Liberty University

1971 University Boulevard	Phone: (804) 582-2183
Lynchburg, VA 24502	Fax: (800) 628-7977

Division(s): External Degree/Distance Education Program
Web Site(s): http://www.liberty.edu
E-mail: dtfoutz@liberty.edu

Undergraduate Degree Programs:
Associate of Arts in General Studies
Associate of Arts in Religion
Bachelor of Science in:
   Multidisciplinary Studies

Religion
Business
Psychology

Graduate Degree Programs:
Master of Arts in Religion
Master of Arts in Counseling

Teaching Methods: *Computers:* Internet, e-mail. *TV:* videotape. *Other:* correspondence, independent study, individual study.

Credits Granted for: experiential learning, portfolio assessment, extrainstitutional learning, examination (CLEP, ACT-PEP, DANTES, GRE).

Admission Requirements: *Undergraduate:* high school diploma or accredited bachelor's degree. *Graduate:* bachelor's from accredited institution and prerequisites appropriate to desired course. *Certificate:* SAT, ACT scores.

On-Campus Requirements: for every 30 credits, students must spend one week on campus.

Tuition and Fees: *Undergraduate:* $180/credit. *Graduate:* $195/credit. *Application Fee:* $35. *Software:* varies. *Other Costs:* books and videos. *Credit by:* semester.

Financial Aid: Federal Stafford Loan, Federal Pell Grant, Federal Work-Study, VA, Virginia resident programs.

Accreditation: Southern Association of Colleges and Schools, Transnational Association of Christian Schools.

Description: Founded in 1971 as a liberal arts institution of higher learning, Liberty entered the field of distance education in 1985. Since then, more than 90,000 students have benefitted from its programs. Liberty's distance education program currently has more than 5,000 students enrolled in video-based curricula in associate, bachelor's, and master's degrees.

LIFE Bible College

1100 Covina Boulevard	Phone: (909) 599-5433 x314
San Dimas, CA 91773	Fax: (909) 599-6690

Division(s): School of Correspondence Studies
Web Site(s): http://www.lifebible@edu
E-mail: correspo@lifebible.edu

Undergraduate Degree Programs:
Associate of Arts Degree

Teaching Methods: *Other:* correspondence, independent study.

Admission Requirements: *Undergraduate:* high school diploma or GED, must be a Christian for at least one year.

On-Campus Requirements: None.

Tuition and Fees: *Undergraduate:* $65/unit. *Application Fee:* $35 (for AA program). *Credit by:* semester.

Financial Aid: VA.

Accreditation: AABC, ACCESS, UCEA.

Description: Aimee Semple McPherson, founder of the Foursquare Denomination, established the School of Correspondence Studies at LIFE Bible College in 1924. She believed that every dedicated person should have an opportunity to study God's Word even if separated from the college by great distances. Today her vision is allowing people worldwide to study the Word of God through LIFE. LIFE Bible College provides flexible college-level training, providing students the freedom to set their own schedule and pace. After recently expanding its program, LIFE now offers an AA in Biblical Studies.

Lifetime Career Schools

101 Harrison Street	Phone: (717) 876-6340
Archbald, PA 18403	Fax: (717) 876-8179

Division(s): Instruction
Web Site(s): http://lifetime-career.com
E-mail: lcslearn@aol.com

Certificate Programs: Flower Arranging and Floristry, Doll Repair, Sewing/Dressmaking, Computer Support Specialist, Secretarial, Bookkeeping, Cooking, Landscaping, Small Business Management (all diplomas).

Class Titles: Doll Repair, Secretarial, Bookkeeping, Cooking, Landscaping, Small Business Management, Floristry.

Teaching Methods: *Computers:* Internet, electronic classroom, e-mail. *Other:* correspondence, independent study, individual study, learning contracts.

Admission Requirements: *Certificate:* 10th grade education.

On-Campus Requirements: None.

Tuition and Fees: *Undergraduate:* $300–$500/program (diploma).

Accreditation: Distance Education and Training Council.

Description: From its beginning, Lifetime Career Schools' (1944) charter has been to offer vocationally oriented diploma programs through correspondence. Using an open-enrollment philosophy, the institution offers programs that cater to the needs of working men and women desiring to change careers, upgrade workplace-related skills, or simply to learn more about a hobby. Beginning in 1998, LCS established a Web site and began supplementing traditional course material and student support with various forms of electronic publishing and communications.

Lima Technical College

4240 Campus Drive	Phone: (419) 995-8870
Lima, OH 45804	Fax: (419) 995-8096

Division(s): Alternative Learning Systems
Web Site(s): http://www.ltc.tec.oh.us
E-mail: als@ltc.tec.oh.us

Undergraduate Degree Programs:
Associate of Technical Studies in:
    Business Studies
    Emergency Medical Services Technology
Associate of Applied Science in Industrial Engineering

Certificate Programs: Distribution/Logistics Methods Study, Facilities Planning, Production Planning, Industrial Relations, Advance Topics, Distribution/Logistics Management (all part of Industrial Engineering Technology program)

Class Titles: Accounting, English, Developmental Writing, Economics, Sociology, Psychology, Childhood Development, Community Health/Safety, Phlebotomy, Intravenous Line Insertion, Quality Assurance in Health Care, Patient Education, Legal Issues in Health Care, Sanitation/Safety, Management, Marketing, Pre-algebra, Business Math, Fundamentals of Quality, Office Administration, Computer Applications, Law Enforcement, Corrections, Industrial Engineering, Blueprint Reading, Retail/Fashion Merchandising, Medical Terminology.

Teaching Methods: *Computers:* Internet, real-time chat, e-mail, CD-ROM, LISTSERV. *TV:* videotape, cable program, PBS. *Other:* videoconferencing, audiotapes, fax, correspondence, independent study, individual study.

Credits Granted for: experiential learning, portfolio assessment, extrainstitutional learning, examination (CLEP, ACT-PEP, DANTES, GRE).

Admission Requirements: *Undergraduate:* open-door; application, $25 nonrefundable fee, official high school transcript from each high school attended or certificate of GED score report along with the official high school transcripts showing work completed, sent directly to the Student Advising and Development Center; official college, university, or any other postsecondary institution transcript, sent directly from previous institution to the SAD; evidence of ACT scores (required of all students who seek admission to health programs except EMP P certification candidates); any other material required for admission to a specific program; finally, applicants to the college are required to take the ASSET Placement Test; Ohio high school students may earn credit applied toward graduation in the Postsecondary Enrollment Options Program—specific enrollment and application requirements are listed in the catalog.

On-Campus Requirements: testing for some distance learning courses.

Tuition and Fees: *Undergraduate:* $66/credit. *Application Fee:* $25. *Other Costs:* $20/quarter registration fee, lab fee for selected courses, $6/telecourse credit fee. *Credit by:* quarter.

Financial Aid: Federal Stafford Loan, Federal PLUS Loan, Federal Pell Grant, Federal Work-Study, VA, Ohio resident programs, Ohio Instructional Grant Program, academic scholarship, BVR, JTPA, Hauss-Helms Foundation.

Accreditation: North Central Association of Colleges and Schools.

Description: In 1971 Lima Technical College was chartered as a state, public-assisted associate degree granting institution of higher education. LTC has served 40,000 students in the area. Distance learning was initiated with the creation of an Office Administration self-paced program in 1990; in 1993 the distance learning initiative was taken a step further with the creation of the Alternative Learning Systems. Through the years the original self-paced program has continued to expand beyond its original program area; telecourses are broadcast via local cable channels; a videotape take-home program is available for those students not receiving the cable channel; numerous online courses are available through the college's Virtual College, and ALS is now venturing into the realm of interactive classrooms. ALS students are supported in the ALS Center located on campus, with instructor support and multimedia computers for their use. E-mail accounts with Internet access are also provided upon registration.

Linfield College

900 SE Baker Street	Phone: (503) 434-2447
McMinnville, OR 97128	Fax: (503) 434-2215

Division(s): Continuing Education
Web Site(s): http://www.linfield.edu/dce
E-mail: tdwilli@linfield.edu

Undergraduate Degree Programs:
Bachelor of Arts in Arts and Humanities
Bachelor in Science in:
> Accounting
> Business Information Systems
> International Business
> Management
> Social and Behavioral Sciences

Certificate Programs: Accounting, Computer Information Systems, Human Resource Management, Marketing.

Teaching Methods: *Computers:* electronic classroom, e-mail. *TV:* satellite broadcasting. *Other:* videoconferencing, correspondence, independent study, individual study.

Credits Granted for: experiential learning, portfolio assess-

ment, extrainstitutional learning, examination (CLEP, ACT-PEP, DANTES, GRE).

Admission Requirements: *Undergraduate:* high school completion, 2.0 college GPA.

On-Campus Requirements: 30 semester credits of Linfield course work.

Tuition and Fees: *Undergraduate:* $175/credit. *Application Fee:* $100. *Credit by:* semester.

Financial Aid: Federal Stafford Loan, Federal Pell Grant, VA, Oregon resident programs.

Accreditation: Northwest Association of Schools and Colleges.

Description: Linfield College (1849) is an independent, 4-year, liberal arts institution with an active off-campus program for working adults. Distance learning technologies are used effectively to enhance opportunities for site-bound students and for traditional on-campus students as well.

Lock Haven University of Pennsylvania

Fairview Street	Phone: (717) 893-2121
Lock Haven, PA 17745	Fax: (717) 893-2540

Division(s): Learning Technology and Distance Education
Web Site(s): http://www.lhup.edu
E-mail: jsmalley@eagle.lhup.edu

Undergraduate Degree Programs:
contact school.

Graduate Degree Programs:
contact school.

Certificate Programs: Biology, Chemistry, Driver/Safety Education, Early Childhood Education, Earth/Space Science, Elementary Education, English, English/Foreign Language, French, General Science, Geography, Social Science, German, Health, Physical Education, Math, Physics, Secondary Education, Social Science, Sociology, Special Education.

Class Titles: Accounting, Applied Geology, Art, Applied Science in Management, Biology, Chemistry, Computer Information Science, Computer Science, Cooperative Engineering, Curriculum/Instruction, Driver/Safety Education, Early Childhood Education, Earth-Space Science, Economics, Elementary Education, English, English/Foreign Language, Environmental Geology, French, General Science, General Studies, Geography, German, Health/Physical Education, Health Sciences, History, Humanities, International Studies, Journalism/Mass Communication, Latin American Studies, Liberal Arts, Management, Mathematics, Music, Natural

Sciences, Nursing, Philosophy, Physics, Political Science, Psychology, Recreation, Secondary Education, Social Sciences, Social Work, Sociology, Spanish, Special Education, Speech Communication, Theater.

Teaching Methods: *Computers:* Internet, electronic classroom, e-mail, CD-ROM. *TV:* videotape, cable program, satellite broadcasting, PBS. *Other:* radio broadcast, videoconferencing, audiographics, audiotapes, correspondence, independent study, individual study, learning contracts.

Credits Granted for: experiential learning, advanced placement, examination (CLEP).

Admission Requirements: *Undergraduate:* high school graduate, satisfactory command of the English language, CEEB/ACT examination. All applicants are required to take the Scholastic Aptitude Test (SAT).

On-Campus Requirements: most classes are conducted in traditional classroom settings with exceptions of independent and individual instruction, and interns.

Tuition and Fees: *Undergraduate:* $144/credit resident, $285/credit out-of-state, $368/credit international. *Graduate:* resident $193/credit, out-of-state $346/credit. *Application Fee:* $25. *Other Costs:* contact school for more information. *Credit by:* semester.

Financial Aid: Federal Stafford Loan, Federal Perkins Loan, Federal PLUS Loan, Federal Pell Grant, Federal Work-Study, VA, Pennsylvania resident programs, Federal Supplemental Educational Opportunity Grant.

Accreditation: Middle States Association of Colleges and Schools.

Description: Located in a rural setting in north central Pennsylvania, Lock Haven University (1870) is one of 14 institutions that make up the Commonwealth's State System of Higher Education. The university emphasizes active learning and the use of technology, individual attention from faculty, strong ties between curricular and cocurricular learning, and open interaction among all members of the academic community. Students experience the multicultural and global dimensions of our changing society and are provided with opportunities to acquire, clarify, and demonstrate those skills and values that are necessary for active participation in a democracy. Among the Commonwealth's universities, Lock Haven University has been in the fore of the development and utilization of distance learning. With assistance from major Link-to-Learn grants and a university commitment to advance the use of all available technology in its delivery of instruction, Lock Haven University does all it can to accomplish this. Faculty are afforded the opportunity to become skilled in the use of distance learning and incorporate this where desired.

Long Beach City College

4901 East Carson Street
Long Beach, CA 90808

Phone: (562) 938-4136
Fax: (562) 938-4651

Division(s): Learning Resources
Web Site(s): http://www.lbcc.cc.ca.us
E-mail: rschultz@lbcc.cc.ca.us

Undergraduate Degree Programs:
Distance learning classes count toward the Associate of Arts and Associate of Science degrees.

Class Titles: Astronomy, Biology, Child Development, History, Political Science, Psychology, Sociology, English, Counseling, Computer/Office Technologies.

Teaching Methods: *Computers:* Internet, e-mail. *TV:* videotape, cable program, PBS. *Other:* None.

On-Campus Requirements: Most telecourses require 6–7 on-campus meetings. Online courses require 2–3 meetings on campus.

Tuition and Fees: *Undergraduate:* $12/credit for California residents, $130/credit for out-of-state U.S. residents, $137/credit for international students. *Other Costs:* $7 for health fee, $15 parking fee. *Credit by:* semester.

Financial Aid: Federal Perkins Loan, Federal Pell Grant, Federal Work-Study, VA, California resident programs.

Accreditation: Western Association of Schools and Colleges.

Description: Long Beach City College (1927), a 2-year community college, is one of the largest of 107 community colleges in California and serves an area encompassing Long Beach, Signal Hill, Lakewood, and Santa Catalina Island. The college enrolls approximately 24,000 students each semester. A 1993 study, reported in *Black Issues in Higher Education*, found that only 9 other 2-year colleges in the nation award more associate degrees to minority students.

Longview Community College
Metropolitan Community College District

500 Southwest Longview Road
Lee's Summit, MO 64081

Phone: (816) 672-2369
Fax: (816) 672-2426

Division(s): There is a distance learning area at Penn Valley in addition to the PACE and Internet Classes offered through each division at each campus.
Web Site(s):
http://www.kcmetro.cc.mo.us/longview/lvhome.html
http://www.kcmetro.cc.mo.us/programs/pace.html
http://www.kcmetro.cc.mo.us/pacetv.html

E-mail: millert@longview.cc.mo.us

Undergraduate Degree Programs:
Associate in Arts

Class Titles: contact school for complete listing of course titles.

Teaching Methods: *Computers:* Internet, e-mail. *TV:* videotape, cable program, PBS. *Other:* videoconferencing, fax.

Credits Granted for: examination (CLEP).

Admission Requirements: *Undergraduate:* open admission policy. Students must be at least 17. Placement exam is required.

On-Campus Requirements: some classes require campus time. That is determined by individual instructors and the subject matter of the course.

Tuition and Fees: *Undergraduate:* $49/credit in district, $83/credit out-of-district, $117/credit out-of-state. *Other Costs:* cable courses have an additional $10/credit charge. Textbooks are not included in the costs. *Credit by:* semester.

Financial Aid: Federal Stafford Loan, Federal Perkins Loan, Federal PLUS Loan, Federal Pell Grant, Federal Work-Study, VA, Missouri resident programs.

Accreditation: North Central Association of Colleges and Schools.

Description: MCC was founded in 1964 with roots in the Kansas City Polytechnic Institute which was founded in 1915. There are 4 campuses that comprise the district, Longview, Blue River, Maple Woods and Penn Valley. In addition there are satellite campuses in Independence and at the Park Hill Education Center. The district offers Associate in Arts, Associate in Applied Science and Certificate programs. PACE, the Program for Adult College Education, piloted the first distance learning using local cable programming in 1992. Distance learning now accounts for approximately one third of the students in PACE. PACE was the logical choice for the pilot as they already had alternate delivery systems in place for their students. PACE classes are grouped by discipline and full-time students attend one night each week and one weekend each month. The initial distance learning that PACE piloted has been expanded to the other campuses in the district and now includes Internet classes and closed circuit classes.

Los Angeles Pierce College

6201 Winnetka Avenue	Phone: (818) 719-6444
Woodland Hills, CA 91371-6201	Fax: (818) 710-9844

Division(s): Academic Affairs
Web Site(s): http://www.lapc.cc.ca.us

E-mail: None.

Class Titles: Chemistry, Statistics.

Teaching Methods: *Computers:* Internet, real-time chat, electronic classroom, e-mail, CD-ROM. *Other:* audioconferencing, videoconferencing, fax.

Admission Requirements: *Undergraduate:* open-admission.

On-Campus Requirements: labs for chemistry classes.

Tuition and Fees: *Undergraduate:* $13/credit. *Credit by:* semester.

Financial Aid: Federal Stafford Loan, Federal Perkins Loan, Federal PLUS Loan, Federal Pell Grant, Federal Work-Study, VA, California resident programs.

Accreditation: Western Association of Schools and Colleges.

Description: Los Angeles Pierce College (1947) is one of 9 community colleges in the Los Angeles Community College District. In 1997/1998, Pierce College entered the distance education arena with videoconferenced agricultural offerings in collaboration with Cal Poly. The fall of 1998 marked the college's entry into the field of Internet class offerings.

Lower Columbia College

1600 Maple Street	Phone: (360) 577-3458
Longview, WA 98632	Fax: (360) 577-3400

Division(s): Distance Education
Web Site(s): http://www.lcc.ctc.edu
E-mail: akaneko@lcc.ctc.edu

Undergraduate Degree Programs:
Associate in Arts and Science
Associate in Applied Science

Class Titles: Astronomy, Wildlife Conservation, Geology, Nutrition, Spanish, Windows 95, Microsoft Word, Microsoft Excel, Microsoft PowerPoint, Internet Fundamentals, Microcomputer Applications, Medical Terminology, English Composition, World Literature, Understanding Financial Statements, Survey of Chemical Dependency, Finite Math.

Teaching Methods: *Computers:* Internet, e-mail, CD-ROM. *TV:* videotape, cable program. *Other:* videoconferencing, correspondence, independent study.

Credits Granted for: examination (CLEP, AP).

Admission Requirements: *Undergraduate:* open-door; special admissions for nursing (RN) and Medical Assisting.

On-Campus Requirements: Some courses have lab requirements.

Tuition and Fees: *Undergraduate:* $51/credit. *Application Fee:* $11. *Other Costs:* various lab fees. *Credit by:* quarter.

Financial Aid: Federal Stafford Loan, Federal Perkins Loan, Federal PLUS Loan, Federal Pell Grant, Federal Work-Study, VA, Washington resident programs.

Accreditation: Northwest Association of Schools and Colleges.

Description: Lower Columbia College (1934) is a comprehensive community college serving Cowlitz and Wahkiakum counties in Washington. Programs at the college include 2-year transfer and vocational degrees as well as community and basic adult education. Our distance education program began 2 years ago with correspondence and videotape courses and has expanded to include online, Web-based, and interactive CD courses.

Loyola College, Maryland

4501 North Charles Street	Phone: (410) 617-2000
Baltimore, MD 21210	Fax: (410) 617-5130

Division(s): Information Services
Web Site(s): http://www.loyola.edu/
E-mail: admissions@mailgate.loyola.edu

Undergraduate Degree Programs:
Bachelor of Science in Business

Graduate Degree Programs:
Master of Science in Education
Master of Business Administration

Class Titles: Accounting, Education, MBA courses.

Teaching Methods: *Computers:* Internet, real-time chat, electronic classroom, e-mail, CD-ROM, newsgroup, LIST-SERV. *TV:* videotape. *Other:* videoconferencing, audioconferencing, independent study.

Credits Granted for: extrainstitutional learning, $342/credit part-time undergraduate (less than 12 credits).

Admission Requirements: *Undergraduate:* applications are evaluated according to their academic qualifications. The most important academic criteria include the secondary school record and performance on the SAT-I Reasoning Test, which is the required college entrance examination. *Graduate:* application form, nonrefundable fee, official transcripts from all postsecondary institutions that have awarded the applicant a degree or advanced certification. Additional requirements may be determined necessary based on specific program requirements.

On-Campus Requirements: vary by professor.

Tuition and Fees: *Undergraduate:* $18,200/annual full-time, $342/credit part-time. *Graduate:* $222/credit Education, $365/credit Engineering Science, $222/credit Modern Studies, Pastoral Counseling—contact Dept. Chair, $278/credit

Psychology (MA/MS/CAS), $365/credit School of Business and Management, $278/credit Speech-Language Pathology (part-time CAGS students), Speech-Language Pathology (full-time students)—contact Dept3. Chair. *Doctoral:* Psychology (PsyD)—contact Dept. Chair. *Application Fee:* $30 undergraduate. *Credit by:* semester.

Financial Aid: Federal Stafford Loan (Federal Direct Loan Participant), Federal Perkins Loan, Federal PLUS Loan, Federal Pell Grant, Federal Supplemental Educational Opportunity Gant, Federal Work-Study, VA, Maryland, Massachusetts, Vermont and Rhode Island resident programs.

Accreditation: The International Association of Management Education, American Association of Pastoral Counselors, American Speech-Language-Hearing Association, Middle States Association of Colleges and Schools, Council for Accreditation of Counseling and Related Educational Programs, U.S. Catholic Conference, Accreditation Board for Engineering and Technology (BSES Program only), American Chemical Society, Computer Science Accreditation Commission.

Description: Loyola College in Maryland (1852) is a comprehensive, liberal arts, Jesuit university comprised of a College of Arts and Sciences and a School of Business and Management. Loyola teaches its approximately 3,200 undergraduates and approximately 3,000 graduates to lead and serve in a diverse and changing world. In 1996 Loyola received its first grant for the flagship campus in Baltimore to join the Maryland Interactive Video Distance Learning Network, a full-motion, 2-way interactive video distance learning delivery system based on digital fiber-optic technology. In 1997 and 1998, Loyola received 2 additional grants to connect its graduate campuses in Columbia and Timonium. In 1998 Loyola introduced its first class offered via the Internet. Now students in an introductory accounting course can use an asynchronous approach to receive lectures anytime, anywhere they have access to the Internet.

Loyola University, New Orleans

6363 St. Charles Avenue, Box 14	Phone: (504) 865-3250
New Orleans, LA 70118	Fax: (504) 865-3883

Division(s): City College
Web Site(s): http://www.loyno.edu/City College
E-mail: scheuer@loyno.edu

Undergraduate Degree Programs:
Bachelor of Criminal Justice
Bachelor of Nursing Science

Teaching Methods: *TV:* videotapes. *Other:* None.

Credits Granted for: experiential learning, portfolio assessment, extrainstitutional learning, examination (CLEP, ACT-

PEP, DANTE, GRE).

Admission Requirements: *Undergraduate:* to enter the RN-to-BSN program, you must be a registered nurse and live in the state of Louisiana.

On-Campus Requirements: must attend one class on-campus; contact school for information.

Tuition and Fees: *Undergraduate:* $197. *Application Fee:* $20.

Financial Aid: Federal Stafford Loan, Federal Perkins Loan, Federal PLUS Loan, Federal Pell Grant, General Work-Study, VA, Louisiana resident programs.

Accreditation: National League for Nursing.

Description: Created in 1991, the Off-Campus Learning Program at Loyola University, New Orleans (1912) provides access for Louisiana adult residents who, because of their work schedules or distance from campus, cannot attend on-campus classes. The off-campus groups, located within the state, meet regularly to view classes on videotape at a location and time of their choosing. All assignments, exams, and papers correspond exactly to those of the on-campus students. Students have access to the campus professor through telephone conferences via our 800 line and through individual meetings. Off-campus students complete courses in the same semester as campus students.

Luther Seminary

2481 Como Avenue	Phone: (651) 641-3456
St. Paul, MN 55108	(800) LUTHER-3
	Fax: (651) 641-3425

Division(s): Cross-Cultural Education
Web Site(s): http://www.luthersem.edu
E-mail: rdolson@luthersem.edu

Graduate Degree Programs:
Master of Arts
Master of Theology
Master of Religious Education
Master of Sacred Music
Master of Divinity

Doctoral Degree Programs:
Doctor of Philosophy
Doctor of Ministry

Certificate Programs: Islamic Studies

Teaching Methods: *Computers:* Internet, electronic classroom, e-mail, CD-ROM, LISTSERV. *TV:* videotape, cable program, satellite broadcasting, PBS. *Other:* radio broadcast, videoconferencing, audioconferencing, audiographics, audiotapes, fax, correspondence, independent study, individual study, learning contracts. Listed teaching methods are subject to discretion of instructor.

Credits Granted for: For detailed information, call: (651) 641-3456 or toll-free: (800) LUTHER-3.

Admission Requirements: *Graduate:* accredited bachelor's degree or equivalent, 2.8 GPA. *Doctoral:* Doctor of Philosophy: bachelor's degree in divinity, accredited master's degree in arts or divinity (or equivalent), and 3.25 GPA. Doctor of Ministry: master of divinity degree, 3.0 GPA, transcripts of professional graduate degree(s). *Certificate:* accredited bachelor's degree (or equivalent), 2.8 GPA.

On-Campus Requirements: None.

Tuition and Fees: *Graduate:* $5,950 full-time annual tuition for Master of Arts, Master of Divinity, Master of Religious Education, Master of Sacred Music, Nondegree Students/Certificate Students/Auditors, $595/part-time full course, $298/part-time half course, $35 application fee. $255 Applied Lessons (for master of sacred music). $8,950 full-time annual tuition for Master of Theology, Post-Master of Divinity Nondegree Students, $595/part-time full course, $298/part-time half course, $35 application fee, $150 continuation fee. *Doctoral:* $8,950 full-time annual tuition for Doctor of Philosophy, $1,350/course part-time, $35 application fee, $500 annual continuation fee. $5,400 basic tuition for Doctor of Ministry (summer program), $50 application fee, $400 confirmation fee, $600 thesis fee. *Application Fee:* see specific degree categories. *Other Costs:* contact school. *Credit by:* semester (2 semesters and one January term).

Financial Aid: Federal Stafford Loan, Federal Perkins Loan, Federal PLUS Loan, Federal Pell Grant, Federal Work-Study, Presidential Scholarships (full tuition for first year of study for Master of Arts, Master of Religious Education, Master of Sacred Music, and Master of Divinity students who have recently graduated from college); Leadership Scholarships (full tuition for first year of study for Master of Divinity students seeking ordination through ELCA); Heritage Scholarships (full tuition awards for first year of study for Master of Sacred Music or Master of Divinity students); Quest Scholarship (partial tuition for first year of study for second career students); Spectrum Scholarships (for students of color).

Accreditation: North Central Association of Colleges and Schools, Association of Theological Schools in the U.S. and Canada, affiliated with the Evangelical Lutheran Church in America.

Description: Luther Seminary (1869), through a series of mergers covering more than half a century, represents the consolidation of 6 institutions. Today the Minnesota-based seminary is the largest of 8 Evangelical Lutheran Church in America seminaries in the U.S. providing theological education to equip people for ministry. The seminary's campus grounds consist of more than 40 acres of rolling wooded land in the small-town atmosphere of St. Anthony Park, one of the Twin Cities' oldest and most pleasant residential neighborhoods. The seminary's mission is to educate leaders called and sent by the Holy Spirit to witness salvation through Jesus Christ and to serve in God's world. LS supports a wide spectrum of distance study opportunities and programs designed to help students pursue areas of special interest and/or gain experience directly related to their ministry.

Lutheran Theological Seminary at Philadelphia

7301 Germantown Avenue	Phone: (215) 248-6378
Philadelphia, PA 19119	Fax: (215) 248-4577

Division(s): Director of Distance Learning
Web Site(s): http://www.ltsp.edu
E-mail: Registrar@ltsp.edu or MKyrch@ltsp.edu

Graduate Degree Programs:
Master of Divinity
Master of Arts in Religion

Doctoral Degree Programs:
Master of Theological Studies
Doctor of Ministry

Certificate Programs: Social Ministry and Church

Class Titles: Communication in Congregation, Christian Education, Theology, Evangelism, Stewardship.

Teaching Methods: *Computers:* Web-based instruction, Internet (using Convene Software), real-time chat, electronic classroom, e-mail, CD-ROM, newsgroup, LISTSERV. *TV:* videotape, videoconferencing. *Other:* audioconferencing, audiographics, audiotapes, fax, correspondence, independent study, individual study, learning contracts.

Credits Granted for: examination.

Admission Requirements: *Graduate:* bachelor's degree, completion limits, credits older than 10 years not accepted for degree completion. *Doctoral:* Master of Divinity or Master of Arts in Religion. *Certificate:* bachelor's degree.

On-Campus Requirements: No full degree completion via Distance Learning.

Tuition and Fees: *Graduate:* $716/unit (3 semester hours). *Doctoral:* $716/unit (3 semester hours). *Application Fee:* $25. *Software:* $11/month Ecunet Access, Netscape Navigator/Internet Explorer (free). *Other Costs:* $1,250 Health Insurance for full-time students. *Credit by:* semester.

Financial Aid: Federal Stafford Loan, VA.

Accreditation: Middle States Association of Colleges and Schools, Association of Theological Schools.

Description: Lutheran Theological Seminary at Philadelphia's (1864) roots go back to 1747 with the colonial church and the first Lutheran Synod. Lutheran leaders like the notable Franklin Clark Fry and the current ELCA Bishop, H. George Anderson, are a part of the Philadelphia tradition. The first Lutheran graduate school was begun at Philadelphia in 1913. In 1938, "Mt. Airy" seminary, as it was then dubbed, was one of the first three Lutheran schools accredited by the American Association of Theological Schools. The first full-capacity TV studio was inaugurated in 1965. In 1998–1999, distance learning capabilities will be fully functional, increasing opportunities for learning at the campus and away from it. In partnership with the Eastern Cluster of Seminaries, opportunities for theological education will be made available to areas up and down the East Coast.

Madison Area Technical College

3550 Anderson Street	Phone: (608) 246-6282
Madison, WI 57704	Fax: (608) 246-6880

Division(s): Instructional Medical Services/Distance Education
Web Site(s): http://www.madison.tec.wi.us
E-mail: None.

Class Titles: variable: Abnormal Psychology, Anthropology, Corporate Finance, Drawing Interpretation, Effective Listening, Insurance, Real Estate Appraisal, Small Business, Spanish, Tax, Time Management, Accounting, Center Director, Cost Accounting, Employee Involvement, Psychology, Making Meetings Work, Morale/Work Place Ethics, OSHA/Hazardous, Real Estate Brokerage, Real Estate Law, Statistics, Business Statistics, Communication Skills, Speech, Contemporary American Society, Dealing with Diversity, Developmental Psychology, Economics, International Economics, Management Techniques, Mathematics of Finance, Small Business Management, GED via TV.

Teaching Methods: *Computers:* Internet, e-mail, LISTSERV. *TV:* videotape, interactive TV. *Other:* None.

Credits Granted for: experiential learning, portfolio assessment, extrainstitutional learning, examination (CLEP, ACT-PEP, DANTES, GRE).

Admission Requirements: *Undergraduate:* age 16, assessment test if joining a program; certain programs have higher requirements.

On-Campus Requirements: contact school.

Tuition and Fees: *Undergraduate:* $95/credit (college transfer). *Other Costs:* textbooks. *Credit by:* semester.

Financial Aid: Federal Stafford Loan, Federal Perkins Loan, Federal PLUS Loan, Federal Pell Grant, Federal Work-Study, VA, Wisconsin resident programs.

Accreditation: North Central Association of Colleges and Schools.

Description: Madison Area Technical College (1912) offers 2-year transfer associate degrees, along with job training to meet the demands of area employers. We also offer Adult Basic Education.

Madonna University

36600 Schoolcraft Road	Phone: (734) 432-5300
Livonia, MI 48150	Fax: (734) 432-5393

Division(s): School of Business, Social Work.
Web Site(s): http://www.munet.edu
E-mail: muinfo@smtp.munet.edu

Undergraduate Degree Programs:
Bachelor of Social Work
Bachelor of Science in Business

Graduate Degree Programs:
Master of Science in Business Administration

Class Titles: contact school for more information.

Teaching Methods: *Computers:* Internet, real-time chat, electronic classroom, e-mail, CD-ROM, newsgroup, LIST-SERV. *TV:* videotape, cable program, satellite broadcasting, PBS. *Other:* radio broadcast, videoconferencing, audioconferencing, audiographics, audiotapes, fax, correspondence, independent study, individual study, learning contracts.

Credits Granted for: experiential learning, portfolio assessment, extrainstitutional learning, examination (CLEP, ACT-PEP, DANTES, GRE).

Admission Requirements: *Undergraduate:* variable. *Graduate:* variable.

On-Campus Requirements: variable.

Tuition and Fees: *Undergraduate:* variable. *Graduate:* variable. *Credit by:* semester.

Financial Aid: Federal Stafford Loan, Federal Perkins Loan, Federal PLUS Loan, Federal Pell Grant, Federal Work-Study, VA, Michigan resident programs.

Accreditation: North Central Association of Colleges and Schools, Council on Social Work Education.

Description: Madonna University (1947) is an independent-religious, Roman Catholic, comprehensive institution. It first offered distance learning telecourses in 1983. Our current distance learning degree programs in business feature online instruction and videotapes. Our social work degree program features live, 2-way interactive TV. Individual credit and noncredit courses in a number of subjects (business, liberal arts, social sciences) are available to matriculants and nonmatriculants.

Maharishi University of Management

1000 North 4th Street	Phone: (515) 472-1110
Fairfield, IA 52557	Fax: (515) 472-1179

Division(s): School of Business and Public Administration
Web Site(s): http://www.mum.edu/SBPA/distance.html
E-mail: admissions@mum.edu

Graduate Degree Programs:
Master of Business Administration

Class Titles: Accounting, Economics, Finance, Human Resources Management, Marketing, Management Information Systems, Statistics.

Teaching Methods: *Computers:* Internet, real-time chat, e-mail, newsgroup. *TV:* videotape. *Other:* fax, correspondence.

Credits Granted for: experiential learning, extrainstitutional learning, prior work experience (based on examination).

Admission Requirements: *Graduate:* undergraduate degree and official transcripts, GMAT or equivalent, completed application to MBA program, and professional recommendations. (More emphasis is placed on academic record, work experience, etc.). TOEFL of 550 (or approved equivalent proficiency test) where English is student's second language. Technology requirements include TV, VCR, Internet access, and computer for word processing functions.

On-Campus Requirements: None.

Tuition and Fees: *Graduate:* $370/credit ($1,480/4-credit course). *Application Fee:* $40. *Credit by:* semester.

Financial Aid: Federal Stafford Loan, Federal Perkins Loan, university scholarships.

Accreditation: North Central Association of Colleges and Schools.

Description: Maharishi University of Management (1971) was founded by Maharishi Mahesh Yogi as Maharishi International University to make education complete, so that every student enjoys great success and fulfillment in life. In 1995 the name was changed to emphasize the importance for students to gain the knowledge and experience they need to successfully manage the personal and professional areas of their lives. Academic programs include bachelor's, master's, and doctoral programs in a broad range of disciplines, including programs in Management, Physics, Physiology, and Neuroscience (the science of creative intelligence). The educational approach in each discipline—in the sciences, applied sciences, humanities, arts, government, and business—applies the knowledge of the field to practical, professional values.

Manatee Community College

PO Box 1849
Bradenton, FL 34206

Phone: (941) 755-1511 x4267
Fax: (941) 727-6050

Division(s): Academic Affairs
Web Site(s): http://www.mcc.cc.fl.us

Undergraduate Degree Programs:
Associate of Arts
Associate of Science

Certificate Programs: numerous, contact school for more information.

Teaching Methods: *Computers:* Internet, electronic classroom, e-mail, CD-ROM, newsgroup, LISTSERV. *TV:* videotape, cable program, PBS. *Other:* videoconferencing, independent study, individual study, learning contracts.

Credits Granted for: experiential learning, portfolio assessment, examination (CLEP, ACT-PEP, DANTES, GRE).

Admission Requirements: *Undergraduate:* high school diploma or GED, placement tests. *Certificate:* high school diploma or GED, placement tests.

On-Campus Requirements: None.

Tuition and Fees: *Undergraduate:* $40/credit resident, $148/credit out-of-state. *Application Fee:* $15. *Other Costs:* varying textbooks costs. *Credit by:* semester.

Financial Aid: Federal Stafford Loan, Federal Perkins Loan, Federal PLUS Loan, Federal Pell Grant, Federal Work-Study, VA, Florida resident programs.

Accreditation: Southern Association of Schools and Colleges.

Description: Manatee Community College (1958), a public, multicampus institution, is accredited by the Commission on Colleges of the Southern Association of Colleges and Schools to award Associate in Art and Associate in Science degrees. Manatee's enrollment exceeds 8,000 students, with individuals attending classes at 2 campuses and at many sites in the community. The college offers parallel programs for those seeking a bachelor's degree or higher; occupational-technical programs to prepare students to enter the job market or continue their education; and responsive, noncredit courses and activities for continuing education, upgrading skills, and enriching personal and cultural life.

Mansfield University

Clinton Street
Mansfield, PA 16933

Phone: (717) 662-4244
(800) 661-3640
Fax: (717) 662-4120

Division(s): Center for Lifelong Learning
Web Site(s): http://www.mnsfld.edu
E-mail: knorton@mnsfld.edu

Class Titles: varies by semester—examples: Microcomputers, Supervision/Improvement of Instruction, Psychology of Exceptional Children, Marketing, Methods/Materials Research, Oral Communication, Creative Teaching Materials With Internet, Pharmacological Basis for Nursing Practice, Women's Health Issues, Composition, Statistics, Family Nursing, Philosophy, General Psychology, Life Span Development, Sociology, Theater, Accounting.

Teaching Methods: *Computers:* Internet, electronic classroom, e-mail, CD-ROM, newsgroup, LISTSERV. *TV:* videotape, satellite broadcasting. *Other:* audioconferencing, videoconferencing, audiographics, audiotapes, fax, correspondence, independent study, individual study.

Credits Granted for: examination (CLEP), credit by exam.

Admission Requirements: *Undergraduate:* high school diploma or GED, SAT. *Graduate:* GRE, official transcripts.

On-Campus Requirements: As we offer no complete programs through distance education, all students take traditional classes on- or off-campus in addition to distance education classes.

Tuition and Fees: *Undergraduate:* $144/credit state residents, $368/credit nonresidents. *Graduate:* $193/credit state residents, $346/credit nonresidents. *Application Fee:* $25. *Other Costs:* $15/credit education fee for undergraduate state residents, $37/credit education fee for undergraduate nonresidents, $20/credit education fee for graduate state residents, $35/credit education fee for graduate nonresidents. Other fees may apply. *Credit by:* semester.

Financial Aid: Federal Stafford Loan, Federal Perkins Loan, Federal PLUS Loan, Federal Pell Grant, Federal Work-Study, VA, Pennsylvania resident programs.

Accreditation: Middle States Association of Colleges and Schools.

Description: Mansfield University (1857) is located in north-central Pennsylvania and has an enrollment of approximately 3,000 students. The university serves the region and the national and international communities by developing human and material resources. Mansfield is committed to providing optimum learning opportunities for students of a variety of ages, backgrounds, and needs. Distance education courses were instituted in 1995 to meet the needs of learners who were geographically isolated from the university or who could not, for a number of reasons, attend traditional classes. All distance course work meets academic, departmental standards and earns Mansfield University credits.

Marist College

290 North Road	Phone: (914) 575-3800
Poughkeepsie, NY 12601-1387	Fax: (914) 575-3640

Division(s): School of Graduate and Continuing Education
Web Site(s): http://www.marist.edu
http://www.marist.edu/graduate
http://www.marist.edu/adulted

Undergraduate Degree Programs:
Bachelor of Arts
Bachelor of Science in:
    Business Administration
    Organizational Communications
    Information Systems
    Law

Graduate Degree Programs:
Master of Business Administration

Certificate Programs: Systems Analysis/Design, Paralegal, Legal Nurse Consultant.

Teaching Methods: *Computers:* Internet, real-time chat, electronic classroom, e-mail, newsgroup, LISTSERV. *TV:* videotape, PBS. *Other:* independent study, individual study, learning contracts.

Credits Granted for: experiential learning, portfolio assessment, extrainstitutional learning, examination (CLEP, ACT-PEP, DANTES, GRE).

Admission Requirements: *Undergraduate:* rank in top half of high school class, 3.0 GPA. *Graduate:* formal application, transcripts of undergraduate degree, letters of recommendation, personal statement, interview, GRE or GMAT.

On-Campus Requirements: one course.

Tuition and Fees: *Undergraduate:* $315/credit. *Graduate:* $419/credit. *Application Fee:* $20. *Credit by:* semester.

Financial Aid: Federal Stafford Loan, Federal Perkins Loan, Federal PLUS Loan, Federal Pell Grant, Federal Work-Study, VA, New York resident programs.

Accreditation: Middle States Association of Colleges and Schools.

Description: Located on the east bank of the Hudson River, Marist College (1946) is an independent, private, liberal arts institution. Its modern 130-acre campus and 2 extension centers serve some 5,000 students. Marist has become known as one of the most technologically advanced institutions of higher education in the country as a result of its partnership with the IBM Corporation. Marist has been recognized as one of the top 4 colleges in the U.S. in using technology in and out of the classroom.

Marshall University

400 Hal Greer Boulevard	Phone: (304) 696-4723
Huntington, WV 25755	Fax: (304) 696-6419

Division(s): School of Extended Education
Web Site(s): http://www.marshall.edu
http://www.marshall.edu/aee/
E-mail: combsd@marshall.edu

Undergraduate Degree Programs:
Regents Bachelor of Arts (for adults)
Bachelor of Business Administration

Graduate Degree Programs:
Master of Business Administration

Doctoral Degree Programs:
Master of Science in Management Technology

Class Titles: courses in areas of nursing, communications (varies by semester).

Teaching Methods: *Computers:* Internet, electronic classroom, e-mail, CD-ROM, LISTSERV. *TV:* videotape, cable program, satellite broadcasting, PBS. *Other:* videoconferencing, audioconferencing.

Credits Granted for: portfolio assessment, extrainstitutional learning, examination (CLEP, ACT-PEP, DANTES, GRE).

Admission Requirements: *Undergraduate:* high school curriculum, application, official high school transcript or GED scores or 2.0 GPA or ACT/SAT-I verbal and math 810, transfer transcripts. *Graduate:* bachelor's degree, official undergraduate transcripts, application, information sheet, GRE/GMAT, department-specific requirements.

On-Campus Requirements: None.

Tuition and Fees: *Undergraduate:* (estimated) $1,092/semester West Virginia residents; $2,038/semester residents of Lawrence and Gallia Counties in Ohio, and Boyd, Carter, Floyd, Greenup, Johnson, Lawrence, Martin, Pike Counties, Kentucky; $3,033/semester out-of-state. *Graduate:* department-specific. *Application Fee:* varies. *Software:* varies. *Credit by:* semester.

Financial Aid: Federal Stafford Loan, Federal Perkins Loan, Federal PLUS Loan, Federal Pell Grant, Federal Work-Study, VA, West Virginia resident programs.

Accreditation: North Central Association of Colleges and Schools.

Description: Marshall University (1837) is a state university under the University of West Virginia Board of Trustees. It is an urban-oriented university which functions through 9 colleges and divisions. It has a very high level of commitment to the use of technology in its academic program and its administrative functions. Enrollment is 15,000, including 4,000 graduate students. Marshall has been involved in distance education since 1987.

Marylhurst University

17600 Pacific Highway (Highway 43)	
PO Box 261	Phone: (503) 636-8131
Marylhurst, OR 97036-0261	Fax: (503) 636-9526

Division(s): Instructional Technology
Web Site(s): http://www.marylhurst.edu
E-mail: Studentinfo@marylhurst.edu
wbird@marylhurst.edu
npeterson@marylhurst.edu
admission@marylhurst.edu

Undergraduate Degree Programs:
Humanities
Business Management
Telecommunications
Communications
Life Planning
Organization Communication
Science
Math
Environmental Science
Social Sciences (Psychology, Sociology, Anthropology, Political Science, Economics)

Graduate Degree Programs:
Master of Business Administration

Certificate Programs: Public Relations, Telecommunications

Class Titles: Psychology, Biology, Business Finance, Economics, History of Film, Selling.

Teaching Methods: *Computers:* Internet, real-time chat, e-mail, newsgroup, bulletin boards. *Other:* directed study, independent study, individual study, learning contracts, internships, travel study.

Credits Granted for: experiential learning, portfolio assessment, extrainstitutional learning, examination (CLEP, ACT-PEP, DANTES, GRE).

Admission Requirements: *Undergraduate:* open-enrollment, assessment testing. *Graduate:* bachelor's degree, GRE, GMAT, MAT, references, interviews, essays, portfolios, resumes. *Doctoral:* master's degree, references, interviews, essays, portfolios, resumes. *Certificate:* open-enrollment.

On-Campus Requirements: None.

Tuition and Fees: *Undergraduate:* $217/credit. *Graduate:* $250/credit. *Application Fee:* $50. *Other Costs:* $16 technology fee. *Credit by:* quarter.

Financial Aid: Federal Stafford Loan, Federal Perkins Loan, Federal PLUS Loan, Federal Pell Grant, Federal Work-Study, VA, Marylhurst specific scholarships.

Accreditation: Northern Association of Schools and Colleges, National Association of Schools of Music.

Description: Marylhurst University (1893) is a dynamic educational institution serving students who want to be actively engaged in the learning process. The institution's collaborative learning environment fosters student development at all levels. Educational programs are constructed and taught with the intention of assisting students in becoming active learners who embrace not only the knowledge and skill competencies mastered, but also the process of continual change. Marylhurst has been a pioneer in innovative education methods, from credit-for-life experience to Internet-based courses. Our newest online offerings include a degree completion program with a BS in Management, a BA in Organizational Communication, and online MBA programs. Marylhurst University—see the future, be the future.

Marywood University

2300 Adams Avenue	Phone: (717) 348-6235
Scranton, PA 18509	Fax: (717) 961-4751

Division(s): Office of Distance Education
Web Site(s): http://www.marywood.edu
E-mail: kdom@ac.marywood.edu or matthias@ac.marywood.edu

Undergraduate Degree Programs:
Bachelor of Science in:
Accounting
Business Administration with concentrations in:
Management
Marketing
Financial Planning

Certificate Programs: Professional Communications, Comprehensive Business Skills, Office Administration

Teaching Methods: *Computers:* Internet, real-time chat, electronic classroom, e-mail, CD-ROM, newsgroup, LIST-SERV. *Other:* videoconferencing, audioconferencing, audiographics, audiotapes, fax, correspondence, independent study, individual study.

Credits Granted for: experiential learning, portfolio assessment, extrainstitutional learning, examination (CLEP, ACT-

PEP, DANTES, GRE).

Admission Requirements: *Undergraduate:* not within 25-mile radius, should have graduated from high school at least 3 years prior to applying, GED score of 250, good academic standing from most recent institution, minimum GPA of 2.50 on 12 credits or between 2.25 and 2.49 on 12 credits for probationary status.

On-Campus Requirements: 12 credits for degree programs.

Tuition and Fees: *Undergraduate:* $266/credit. *Application Fee:* $40. *Other Costs:* $50/3 credits, registration; $90/more than 3 credits, registration; $85 text and material fee/course. *Credit by:* semester.

Financial Aid: Federal Stafford Loan, Federal Perkins Loan, Federal PLUS Loan, Federal Pell Grant, Federal Work-Study, VA, Pennsylvania resident programs.

Accreditation: Middle States Association of Colleges and Schools.

Description: Marywood University (1915) is an independent, comprehensive Catholic university owned and sponsored by the Congregation of the Sisters, Servants of the Immaculate Heart of Mary, and collaboratively staffed by lay and religious personnel. Its mission is the education of men and women of all ages in undergraduate, graduate, and continuing education programs. The university serves a wide range of students, both nationally and internationally, while maintaining a concern for the education of women, culturally diverse persons, and first generation students. Committed to spiritual, ethical, and religious values and a tradition of service, Marywood University provides a framework that enables students to develop fully as persons and to master the professional and leadership skills necessary for meeting human needs on regional and global levels.

Massachusetts Institute of Technology

| 77 Massachusetts Avenue, Room 9-234 | Phone: (617) 253-7408 |
| Cambridge, MA 02139 | Fax: (617) 253-8301 |

Division(s): Center for Advanced Educational Services
Web Site(s): http://caes.mit.edu
E-mail: caes-courses@mit.edu

Certificate Programs: yes, contact school for complete information.

Class Titles: Economics, System Dynamics, Data Informed Networks, Internet Commerce, Java Programming, Interactive Design, Strategic Planning, Desktop Learning, Welding.

Teaching Methods: *Computers:* Internet, real-time chat, electronic classroom, e-mail, CD-ROM, newsgroup, LIST-SERV. *TV:* videotape, cable program, satellite broadcasting, PBS. *Other:* videoconferencing, audioconferencing, fax, correspondence, individual study.

Credits Granted for: extrainstitutional learning

Admission Requirements: *Graduate:* Applicants seeking for-credit courses are admitted based on their official transcripts from the college(s) which they earned their degree(s) and a record of other graduate work they have completed. A letter of nomination written by a principle executive in the applicant's organization, confirming approval of their candidacy and the organization's willingness to provide the appropriate support must be included. In addition, a summary of professional experience and a statement indicating the applicants immediate and ultimate objectives in taking the course are required. Applicants seeking noncredit courses will be accepted based upon their academic training and professional experience. In order to maintain the highest standards, CAES reserves the right to select those applicants whose qualifications and experiences suggest that they will receive the most benefit from a given program. *Certificate:* same as graduate.

On-Campus Requirements: None.

Tuition and Fees: *Graduate:* $4,750/course, credits vary. Tuition in MIT's distance learning programs is based on the type of academic credit provided. For-credit courses, delivered live through the Advanced Study Program, carry full MIT tuition for qualified candidates. Academic credit from our "Strategic Partner Relationships" with other universities using MIT professors is based on tuition arrangements established by those institutions. *Credit by:* semester.

Accreditation: Northeast Association of Schools and Colleges.

Description: The Massachusetts Institute of Technology (1865) is one of the world's outstanding universities. MIT is independent, coeducational, and privately endowed. It is organized into 5 schools containing 21 academic departments as well as many interdepartmental programs, laboratories, and centers whose work extends beyond traditional departmental boundaries. The Institute was founded by William Barton Rogers, whose philosophy envisioned a new kind of institution relevant to the times and the nation's need, where students would be educated in the application as well as the acquisition of knowledge. A distinguished natural scientist, Rogers stressed the importance of basic research and believed that professional competence was best fostered by coupling teaching, research, and attention to real-world problems. Today MIT's programs in engineering, the sciences, economics, management, linguistics, architecture, and other areas are internationally recognized, and leaders in industry and government routinely draw upon the expertise of MIT faculty. MIT began its distance learning programs in 1995.

McCook Community College

| 1205 East 3rd | Phone: (308) 345-6303 x223 |
| McCook, NE 69001 | Fax: (308) 345-3305 |

Division(s): Distance Learning
Web Site(s): http://www.mccook.cc.ne.us/mcc/
E-mail: jhaney@mcc.mccook.cc.ne.us

Undergraduate Degree Programs:
Individual courses

Class Titles: Contact school for complete course listing.

Teaching Methods: *Computers:* Internet, real-time chat, electronic classroom, e-mail, CD-ROM, newsgroup, LISTSERV. *TV:* videotape, cable program, satellite broadcasting, PBS. *Other:* radio broadcast, videoconferencing, audioconferencing, audiographics, audiotapes, fax, correspondence, independent study, individual study, learning contracts.

Credits Granted for: experiential learning, portfolio assessment, extrainstitutional learning, examination (CLEP, ACT-PEP, DANTES, GRE).

Admission Requirements: *Undergraduate:* open enrollment.

On-Campus Requirements: None.

Tuition and Fees: *Undergraduate:* $43/credit. *Application Fee:* $13. *Credit by:* semester.

Financial Aid: Federal Stafford Loan, Federal Perkins Loan, Federal PLUS Loan, Federal Pell Grant, Federal Work-Study, Nebraska resident programs.

Accreditation: North Central Association of Colleges and Schools.

Description: McCook Community College (1926) is the oldest 2-year institution in the state of Nebraska. We are primarily a transfer institution with a light offering of vocational courses. We have a fiber-optic system that is connected to all of the public schools in southwestern Nebraska plus Mid-Plains community colleges and NCTA in Curtis. We are in the process of developing courses to be offered via Internet. These should be available sometime in 1999.

McDowell Technical Community College

| Route 1, Box 170 | Phone: (828) 652-6021 |
| Marion, NC 28752 | Fax: (828) 652-1014 |

Division(s): Educational Programs
Web Site(s): http://www.mcdowelltech.cc.nc.us
E-mail: KmL@mail.mcdowell.cc.nc.us

Class Titles: Business, Economics, Psychology, History.

Teaching Methods: *Computers:* Internet, electronic class room. *TV:* videotape, cable program, satellite broadcasting, PBS. *Other:* videoconferencing, fax, correspondence, independent study, individual study.

Admission Requirements: *Undergraduate:* open-door policy, GED or high school diploma, placement test.

On-Campus Requirements: Yes, student must maintain course work as traditional student does which includes video, readings, written papers/research, etc.

Tuition and Fees: *Undergraduate:* $20/credit. *Other Costs:* activity fee $8, full time insurance $1, part time $4. *Credit by:* semester.

Financial Aid: Federal Pell Grant, General Work-Study, VA, North Carolina resident programs, local scholarships.

Accreditation: Southern Association of Colleges and Schools.

Description: McDowell Technical Community College (1964) offered its first distance learning course in the 1991–1992 academic term with one telecourse. We now offer a variety of telecourses and information highway classes, and we have just begun online classes.

McGill University

3700 McTavish Street (A)	Phone: (514) 398-3457 (A)
Montreal, QC, Canada H3A 1Y2 (A)	(514) 398-6989 (B)
1140 Pine Avenue West (B)	Fax: (514) 398-2182 (A)
Montreal, QC Canada H3A 1A3 (B)	(514) 398-7153 (B)

Division(s): Faculty of Education (A)
Occupational Health, Faculty of Medicine (B)
Web Site(s): http://www.education.mcgill.ca/distance (A)
http://www.mcgill.ca/occh (B)
E-mail: distance@education.mcgill.ca (A)
distocch@epid.lan.mcgill.ca (B)

Graduate Degree Programs:
Master of Science in Occupational Health Sciences (B)

Certificate Programs: Educational Technology, Second Language Teaching (A)

Class Titles: Education, Music/Art Education, Culture/Values Education, Educational Computing, Educational Media, Educational Studies, First Nations/Unit Education, Inclusive Education, Teaching Second Languages (A). Occupational Health, Physical Health Hazards, Biological/Chemical Hazards, Work Environment Epidemiology, Occupational Diseases, Occupational Diseases: Occupational Health Nurses Focus, Occupational Health Practice, Occupational Hygiene, Occupational Safety Practice, Physiology of Work/Ergonomics, Toxicology, Social/Behavioural Aspects of Occupational Health (B).

Teaching Methods: *Computers:* Internet, e-mail, LISTSERV (A/B). *TV:* videotape (A/B). *Other:* audiotapes, fax, correspondence (A/B).

Admission Requirements: *Graduate:* doctorate in medicine or bachelor's degree in nursing, industrial hygienist must have a Bachelor of Science (any major) and 3 years of experience in industrial hygiene and/or in occupational safety. All candidates must have maintained a 3.0 GPA (B). *Certificate:* university degree and teacher certification. Mature students accepted. TESL requires language test. Five-year limit for certificate programs (A).

On-Campus Requirements: practicums and examinations (usually 3 days/term)(B).

Tuition and Fees: *Undergraduate:* Canadian (Cdn) $106/credit Quebec resident, Cdn $156/credit Canadian resident, Cdn $325/credit international. Fees include instructional materials (A). *Graduate:* Cdn $167/3-credit course Quebec resident, Cdn $317/3-credit course Canadian resident, Cdn $440/credit international, $440/credit nondegree seeking (B). *Application Fee:* $40 (A), $60 (B). *Other Costs:* Cdn $50 refundable deposit for videotapes (A), Cdn $325–$375 materials/course (B). *Credit by:* semester.

Accreditation: Association of Universities and Colleges of Canada.

Description: McGill University (1821) is an English-language university located in Montreal, Canada and was originally established as the Royal Institute for the Advancement of Learning. Our mission is the advancement of learning through teaching, scholarship and service to society by offering to outstanding undergraduate and graduate students the best education available, by carrying out scholarly activities judged to be excellent when measured against the highest international standards, and by providing service to society in those ways for which we are well suited by virtue of our academic strengths. Distance education dates back to radio broadcasting in the late 1930s, and in recent years to the establishment of correspondence and Web-based courses for experienced professionals in education and occupational health.

The McGregor School of Antioch University

800 Livermore Street
Yellow Springs, OH 45387-1609

Phone: (937) 767-6325 or 6321
Fax: (937) 767-6461

Division(s): Individualized Master of Arts program
Web Site(s): http://www.mcgregor.edu
E-mail: admiss@mcgregor.antioch.edu

Graduate Degree Programs:
Master of Arts

Class Titles: dependent on student design and degree committee approval.

Teaching Methods: *Computers:* Internet, real-time chat, electronic classroom, e-mail, CD-ROM, newsgroup, LISTSERV. *TV:* videotape, cable program, satellite broadcasting, PBS. *Other:* radio broadcast, audioconferencing, videoconferencing, audiographics, audiotapes, fax, correspondence, independent study, individual study, learning contracts.

Credits Granted for: experiential learning, portfolio assessment.

Admission Requirements: *Undergraduate:* accredited bachelor's degree or, if outside the U.S., its equivalency; relevant experience in the chosen field; ability to travel for limited residential sessions.

On-Campus Requirements: one or 2 weeks, once or twice a year, depending on the field of interest. Conflict Resolution: one 2-week session and several weekend workshops each year during the 2½ year program. Intercultural Relations: one 1-week and one 2-week session each year during the 2½ year program. Self-designed topics: one week of orientation at the beginning of the program, and one week of thesis review prior to the thesis year.

Tuition and Fees: *Graduate:* $1,486/quarter for self-designed topics; Conflict Resolution is $2,178/quarter, and Intercultural Relations is $2,032/quarter. *Application Fee:* $50. *Other Costs:* approximately $50–100/credit for individual learning components, travel costs, and room and board during the residential periods. *Credit by:* 60 quarter credits; 10 of which are thesis.

Financial Aid: Federal Stafford Loan, Federal Perkins Loan, Federal PLUS Loan.

Accreditation: North Central Association of Colleges and Schools.

Description: From its origins more than a century ago, Antioch University (1852) has been a pioneer in higher education. Under the leadership of its first president, Horace Mann, Antioch was the first college to offer equal opportunities to women and was one of the first to admit black students. Throughout the last century, Antioch continued to break ground in many areas, including the co-op program, independent and interdisciplinary study, distance learning, self-designed majors, study abroad, learning assessment, and community governance, which have been adopted by other institutions and have resulted in significant contributions to higher education. True to Antioch's heritage, The McGregor School of Antioch University (1988) aims to challenge adult students with a dynamic, holistic curriculum designed to help graduates make a better living and make a difference where the world needs it. McGregor's distance learning program, the Individualized Master of Arts, was developed as a limited residency program in which adults could design and implement a graduate degree in a chosen field of interest. The program, established in 1975, allows students to use resources in their own communities to earn their master's degree, and provides them with a means by which they can tailor their education to match their professional goals.

Memorial University of Newfoundland

| E2000, G.A. Hickman Building | Phone: (709) 737-8700 |
| St. John's, NF, Canada A1B 3X8 | Fax: (709) 737-7941 |

Division(s): School of Continuing Education
Web Site(s): http://www.ce.mun.ca
E-mail: cstudies@morgan.ucs.mun.ca

Undergraduate Degree Programs:
Nursing (post-RN)
Social Work (2nd degree)
Technology (post-diploma)

Certificate Programs: Criminology, Library Studies, Municipal Administration, Public Administration, Business, Newfoundland Studies.

Class Titles: 100 courses in Arts, Science, or professional studies.

Teaching Methods: *Computers:* Internet, e-mail, asyncronous conferencing, LISTSERV. *TV:* videotape, satellite broadcasting. *Other:* audioconferencing, audiographics, audiotapes, fax, correspondence.

Credits Granted for: Please contact registrar for details (709) 737-4425.

Admission Requirements: *Undergraduate:* high school diploma, official high school/college transcripts, letters of recommendation. Students may apply via Web site.

On-Campus Requirements: Please contact registrar for details (709) 737-4425.

Tuition and Fees: *Undergraduate:* $110/credit Canadian citizens/residents, $220/credit non-Canadians. *Graduate:* Please contact School of Graduate Studies (709) 737-2445. *Application Fee:* $40 Canadians ($80 transfers, non-Canadians). *Other Costs:* varies. *Credit by:* semester.

Financial Aid: Federal/Provincial Canada Student Loan Program.

Accreditation: Association of Universities and Colleges of Canada.

Description: Memorial University College was established in 1925 as a memorial to Newfoundlanders who had lost their lives during World War I. Memorial University then became a degree-conferring institution in 1949. In 1969 MUN first offered distance education courses around the province.

Merced College

| 3600 M Street | Phone: (209) 384-6000 |
| Merced, CA 95348 | Fax: (209) 384-6338 |

Division(s): Instruction
Web Site(s): http://www.merced.cc.ca.us
E-mail: blenz@merced.cc.ca.us

Class Titles: English Composition, Reading.

Teaching Methods: *Computers:* Internet, real-time chat, electronic classroom, e-mail. *Other:* None.

Admission Requirements: *Undergraduate:* high school diploma or equivalent; if you are enrolled in K–12 you may also be admitted as a special student with the written recommendation of the principal of the school which you attend with parental consent and the approval of a college administrator. *Certificate:* cach certificate program has individual requirements. See Merced College's Web page for a list of certificates and then contact the appropriate department.

On-Campus Requirements: face-to-face instruction with the faculty is required for the English 1A class. The meeting place is the campus writing lab, and the required hours are set by the instructor.

Tuition and Fees: *Undergraduate:* $12/unit resident, $121/unit nonresident. *Other Costs:* $10/semester health fee, $7/semester Associated Students of Merced College, $500/year required International Student Insurance Policy, $20/semester auto parking fee, $10/semester motorcycle parking fee. *Credit by:* semester.

Financial Aid: Federal Pell Grant, Federal Work-Study.

Accreditation: Western Association of Schools and Colleges.

Description: Merced College (1962) is a California public community college operated by the Merced Community College District. It was formed by a vote of the people of the Merced and Le Grand High School Districts on February 27, 1962. College classes were first conducted at the Merced County Fairgrounds and were moved completely to the newly constructed campus in the spring semester, 1967. Merced College offers transfer, vocational, developmental studies, and community services classes. Associate of Science and Associate of Arts degree programs are offered as well as several vocational and occupational certificate programs. Its student population of 7,000 is one of the most diverse in the U.S. Merced College has offered only a few experimental distance educational classes. The Office of Instruction and the Curriculum Committee have approved English 1A for the 1998–99 academic year, and one more course is in the planning stages.

Mercy College

555 Broadway   Phone: (914) 674-7527
Dobbs Ferry, NY 12550   Fax: (914) 674-7518

Division(s): Distance Learning
Web Site(s): http://MerLIN.Mercynet.edu
E-mail: Admission@MerLIN.Mercynet.edu

Undergraduate Degree Programs:
Associate of Arts in Liberal Arts
Bachelor of Science in:
     Computer Science
     International Business
     Psychology
Bachelor of Arts in Psychology

Doctoral Degree Programs:
Acupuncture and Oriental Medicine (CEU for Licensed Acupuncturists)

Certificate Programs: Direct Marketing

Class Titles: Behavioral Science, Civic/Cultural Studies, Economics, Education, Literature, Mathematics, Psychology, Science, Sociology.

Teaching Methods: *Computers:* Internet, real-time chat, electronic classroom, e-mail. *Other:* None.

Admission Requirements: *Undergraduate:* interview, placement exam, programs have additional requirements. Contact school. *Doctoral:* Licensed Acupuncturist. Contact school for more information. *Certificate:* Contact school.

On-Campus Requirements: None.

Tuition and Fees: *Undergraduate:* $300/credit or $3,800/semester (12–18 credits). *Application Fee:* $35. *Credit by:* semester.

Financial Aid: Federal Stafford Loan, Federal Perkins Loan, Federal PLUS Loan, Federal Pell Grant, Federal Work-Study, VA, New York resident programs.

Accreditation: Middle States Association of Colleges and Schools, New York State Board of Education.

Description: Mercy College (1950) is a comprehensive college offering both undergraduate and graduate degrees. Founded by the Sisters of Mercy, the college became independent in 1969. The guiding principles of the college are: service to the community through education of both traditional and nontraditional students, reliance on the foundation of education, and dedication to teaching and the advancement of knowledge.

Metropolitan Community College

PO Box 3777   Phone: (402) 457-2416
Omaha, NE 68103   Fax: (402) 457-2255

Division(s): Student and Instructional Services
Web Site(s): http://www.mccneb.edu
E-mail: ismith@metropo.mccneb.edu

Undergraduate Degree Programs:
Programs lead to:
     Associate in Applied Science
     Associate of Arts
     Associate of Science in Nursing
     Certificate of Achievement

Teaching Methods: *Computers:* Internet, electronic classroom, e-mail, CD-ROM, LISTSERV. *TV:* videotape, cable program, satellite broadcasting, PBS. *Other:* audioconferencing, videoconferencing, audiographics, audiotapes, fax, independent study, individual study, learning contracts.

Credits Granted for: experiential learning, portfolio assessment, extrainstitutional learning, examination (CLEP, ACT-PEP, DANTES, GRE).

Admission Requirements: *Undergraduate:* age 18, assessment testing.

On-Campus Requirements: None.

Tuition and Fees: *Undergraduate:* $27/credit residents, $33/credit nonresidents. *Other Costs:* $2/credit technology fee. *Credit by:* quarter.

Financial Aid: Federal Stafford Loan, Federal Perkins Loan, Federal PLUS Loan, Federal Pell Grant, Federal Work-Study, VA, Nebraska resident programs.

Accreditation: North Central Association of Colleges and Schools.

Description: Now in its 25th year, Metro is the third-largest, higher-learning institution in Nebraska. With a 1997–1998 enrollment of 25,374 students, Metro is also one of the state's fastest growing postsecondary institutions. MCC is a comprehensive public community college providing high quality education in 100 programs, including vocational technical education and many general education classes. Metro also continues to be a distance education leader.

Metropolitan State College of Denver

11990 Grant Street #102   Phone: (303) 450-5111
Northglenn, CO 80233   Fax: (303) 450-9973

Division(s): Extended Campus
Web Site(s): http://clem.mscd.edu/~options
E-mail: juergens@mscd.edu

Class Titles: Survey of African History, Ecology for Non-majors, Chicano Studies, Private Security, Constitutional Law, Juvenile Law, Probation/Parole, Penology, Crime Prevention/Loss Reduction, Computers, Technical Writing, Industrial Editing/Production, Elementary Education in U.S., Survey of American History, Issues in European History—Spain, Women in European History, Western Heroes/Villains, American Revolution, Modern Middle East, World War II 1939–1948, Pharmacology Drugs/Alcohol, Educational Exceptionality/Human Growth, Exceptional Learner in Classroom, Diversity, Disability/Education, Spanish, Communication Disorders, Voice Science—Pathology/Technology, Boundary Law, Women in Transition.

Teaching Methods: *Computers:* Internet, real-time chat, electronic classroom, e-mail, CD-ROM, newsgroup, LIST-SERV. *TV:* videotape, cable program, satellite broadcasting, PBS. *Other:* radio broadcast, videoconferencing, audioconferencing, audiographics, audiotapes, fax, correspondence, independent study, individual study, learning contracts.

Credits Granted for: extrainstitutional learning, examination (CLEP, ACT-PEP, DANTES, GRE).

On-Campus Requirements: None.

Tuition and Fees: *Undergraduate:* $80/credit. *Other Costs:* tapes/slides $100. *Credit by:* semester.

Financial Aid: Federal Stafford Loan, Federal Perkins Loan, Federal PLUS Loan, Federal Pell Grant, Federal Work-Study, VA, Colorado resident programs.

Accreditation: North Central Association of Colleges and Schools.

Description: With no class meetings, correspondence courses at Metropolitan State College of Denver (1963) allow students to set an independent learning pace at home. Students may register for correspondence courses at any time and are given one calendar year to complete a course (unless they are financial aid recipients). Note that registration, financial aid processes, and tuition are different for correspondence courses. Please call for a registration form and a "Student Guide for Taking Correspondence Courses." Applicability of correspondence courses to majors may vary with department.

Michigan State University

216 Administration Building	**Phone: (517) 353-8977**
East Lansing, MI 48824	**Fax: (517) 432-2069**

Division(s): Vice Provost University Outreach
Web Site(s): http://www.vu.msu.edu
E-mail: Vertrees@pilot.msu.edu or MSUMIDMI@pilot.msu.edu

Undergraduate Degree Programs:
Bachelor of Science in Nursing
Bachelor of Science in Interdisciplinary Social Science (both offered at regional offices—see Master's offerings)

Graduate Degree Programs:
The following are degrees offered off-campus at regional offices in Birmingham, Grand Rapids, Kalamazoo, Marquette, Midland, Novi, Traverse City, Michigan:
Master of Arts in:
  K–12 Administration
  Educational Technology and Instructional Design
  Advertising
  Curriculum and Teaching
  Telecommunications
  Social Work
  Adult and Continuing Education
  Community Services
  Family Studies
Master of Science in:
  Chemical Engineering
  Computer Science
  Electrical Engineering
  Mechanical Engineering
  Nursing
The following are full programs offered via the Internet:
Master of Arts in Criminal Justice/Security Management Specialization
Master of Science in Beam Physics

Certificate Programs: Applied Plant Science (in-state-only), Educational Technology (in-state-only), Medical Technology (in-state-only), Literacy (in-state-only), Instructional Design (in-state-only), Social Work (Internet), Telecommunication (Internet and in-state).

Class Titles: Material/Energy Balance, Law Enforcement, Proseminar in Criminal Justice, Design/Analysis in CJ Research, Security Management, Security Administration, Independent Study, Internship/Practicum, Home Computing, Concept of Learning Society, Computer/Technology, CAD for Design, Applied Pharmacology, APN in Managed Health, Aging/Health in U.S., Issues in Health Care, Physics, Beam Physics, Topics in Beam Physics, Social Psychology, Applied SW Research, Special Needs Children in School Settings, Social Work in Schools, Testing/School Social Work, Information Society, Telecommunication Applications, Telecommunication Network Management, Special Topics in TC: Policy. All courses via Internet.

Teaching Methods: *Computers:* Internet, real-time chat, e-mail, LISTSERV. *TV:* satellite, Interactive TV (CODEC). *Other:* None.

Credits Granted for: examination (CLEP, Advanced Placement tests).

Admission Requirements: *Undergraduate:* grades, tests scores, caliber of high school program, principal and counselor comments, leadership qualities, exceptional talents, citizenship record, and high school achievement. *Graduate:* academic record, experience, personal qualifications, and proposed program of study.

On-Campus Requirements: Required for the satellite programs, some certificate programs, and CODEC programs. Not required for the following programs: MS in Computer Science, MS in Electrical Engineering, MS in Mechanical Engineering. Not required for Internet courses or programs.

Tuition and Fees: *Undergraduate:* $141/credit (plus $283 matriculation fees/semester) lower-level undergraduates, $157/credit (plus $283 matriculation fees/semester) upper-level undergraduates. *Graduate:* $216/credit (plus $283 matriculation fees/semester). *Application Fee:* $30 for degree programs. *Other Costs:* all costs are from the 1997/98 school year. *Credit by:* semesters.

Financial Aid: Federal Stafford Loan, Federal Perkins Loan, Federal PLUS Loan, Federal Pell Grant, Federal Work-Study, VA, Michigan resident programs (financial aid available for degree-seeking students only, if they qualify).

Accreditation: Association of American Universities.

Description: Founded as an autonomous, public institution of higher learning, Michigan State University (1855) became one of the earliest land-grant institutions in the U.S. Since then, Michigan State has evolved into an internationally esteemed university that offers a comprehensive spectrum of programs and attracts gifted professors, staff members, and students. The university's land-grant and service mission originated in agriculture and the mechanic arts. While these emphases remain essential to the school's purpose, the land-grant commitment now encompasses health, human relations, business, communications, education, and government, extending to urban and international settings. MSU has offered Distance Learning degree programs since 1992 via 2-way, interactive TV. In 1995 it also began offering courses and degree programs via the Internet.

Michigan Technological University

1400 Townsend Drive	Phone: (906) 487-3170
Houghton, MI 49931-1295	Fax: (906) 487-2463

Division(s): Extended University Programs
Web Site(s): http://www/admin.mtu.edu/eup
E-mail: disted@mcu.edu

Undergraduate Degree Programs:
Bachelor of Science in:
 Engineering (Mechanical Design)*
 Engineering (Manufacturing)*
 Surveying

Graduate Degree Programs:
Master of Science in Mechanical Engineering*
Doctor of Philosophy in Mechanical Engineering-Engineering Mechanics*
*corporate sponsorship required

Teaching Methods: *Computers:* Internet, e-mail, LISTSERV. *TV:* videotape. *Other:* audioconferencing, videoconferencing, fax, independent study.

Credits Granted for: examination (CLEP, ACT-PEP, DANTES, GRE).

Admission Requirements: *Undergraduate:* transcripts from high school, C+ GPA. *Graduate:* MS: undergraduate degree, transcripts, essay or personal statement, letter(s) of recommendation. PhD: graduate degree, transcripts, essay or personal statement, letter(s) of recommendation.

On-Campus Requirements: BS in Surveying has some lab assignments.

Tuition and Fees: *Undergraduate:* $200–$300/credit *Graduate:* $500–$700/credit *Application Fee:* $30 ($35 international). *Credit by:* quarter (semester in fall 2000).

Financial Aid: Federal Stafford Loan, Federal Perkins Loan, Federal PLUS Loan, Federal Pell Grant, VA.

Accreditation: Accreditation Board of Engineering and Technology (BSE degrees).

Description: Michigan Technological University was founded in 1885. As the demand for engineers grew, so did MTU's reputation as a leader among technology-oriented educational institutions. Today, students from many states and foreign countries pursue degrees in science, engineering, forestry, business, liberal arts, social sciences, and technology. Considered one of the four Michigan research institutions (with MSU, UM, and WSU), Michigan Tech offers one of the largest engineering programs in the nation. Based on undergraduate engineering enrollment, MTU recently ranked 11th nationwide in BS degrees granted. Tech has offered individual courses via distance education for many years. A large corporation interested in furthering its employees' education initiated MTU's first BSE degree program in 1989. Today MTU is also offering distance BSS, MS, and PhD programs.

Mid-America Bible College

3500 Southwest 119th Street	Phone: (405) 691-3800
Oklahoma City, OK 73170	Fax: (405) 692-3165

Division(s): Admissions
Web Site(s): http://www.concentric.net/~rkriesel/MBC/MBC.shtml
E-mail: mbcok@cris.com

Undergraduate Degree Programs:
Bachelor of Arts in Pastoral Ministry
Bachelor of Science in Pastoral Ministry or
  Specialized Ministry (Youth, Christian Education)

Class Titles: New Testament, Old Testament, Gospel of John, Acts, Romans, Life of Jesus, Psychology, Sociology, American Literature, U.S. History, World History.

Teaching Methods: *Other:* audiotapes, fax, correspondence, independent study, individual study, learning contracts.

Credits Granted for: experiential learning, portfolio assessment, extrainstitutional learning, examination (CLEP, ACT-PEP, DANTES, GRE).

Admission Requirements: *Undergraduate:* age 25, 60 credit hours, working in ministry capacity at local church.

On-Campus Requirements: None.

Tuition and Fees: *Undergraduate:* $199/credit. *Application Fee:* $20. *Other Costs:* $150/semester books. *Credit by:* semester.

Financial Aid: Federal Stafford Loan, Federal Perkins Loan, Federal PLUS Loan, Federal Pell Grant, Federal Work-Study, VA, Oklahoma resident programs.

Accreditation: North Central Association of Colleges and Universities, Accrediting Association of Bible Colleges.

Description: Mid-America Bible College was founded in 1953 in Houston, Texas. The college moved to Oklahoma City, OK in 1985 and became the first 4-year private college to move across state lines and keep its accreditation. In 1991, we started a distance learning program to go along with our already successful correspondence program. We chose the area of Pastoral Ministry and Specialized Ministry because of the many ministers who are unable to leave their present churches to pursue a college degree. Many of our graduates from the TELOS program go on to pursue master's and doctoral programs. For more information about our programs please call or write.

Mid-Plains Community College

601 West State Farm Road	Phone: (308) 532-8980
North Platte, NE 69101	Fax: (308) 532-8590

Division(s): Instruction
Web Site(s): http://www.mpcc.cc.ne.us/mpcc/index.html
E-mail: jmridnou@ziggy.mpcc.cc.ne.us

Undergraduate Degree Programs:
Associate of Arts
Associate of Applied Science

Class Titles: English, Algebra, History, Sociology, Criminal Justice, Communication.

Teaching Methods: *Computers:* Internet, real-time chat, electronic classroom, e-mail, newsgroup, LISTSERV. *TV:* videotape, satellite broadcasting, PBS, fiber optics. *Other:* fax, correspondence, independent study, individual study.

Credits Granted for: examination (CLEP, ACT-PEP).

Admission Requirements: *Undergraduate:* high school diploma or GED, or high school junior/senior with permission from school.

On-Campus Requirements: None.

Tuition and Fees: *Undergraduate:* $40. *Other Costs:* $3/hour tech fee. *Credit by:* semester.

Financial Aid: Federal Stafford Loan, Federal Perkins Loan, Federal PLUS Loan, Federal Pell Grant, Federal Work-Study, VA, Nebraska resident programs.

Accreditation: North Central Association of Colleges and Schools.

Description: Mid-Plains Community College (1974) entered the distance learning arena in 1994 by providing interactive classes over the Nebraska satellite system, primarily to schools in the designated 18-county region in west central Nebraska. However, delivery could be anywhere in the world. In 1996 interactive televised classes through a fiber-optic system were added to the college's capability. The fiber-optic system delivers classes to 36 sites, primarily high schools, in the region. Independent study courses can be arranged by individuals requesting classes from the college's instructors. Mid-Plains is a member of the Going the Distance Consortium delivering classes through PBS programming.

Middle Tennessee State University

1500 East Main Street	Phone: (615) 898-5611
Murfreesboro, TN 37132	Fax: (615) 898-5141

Division(s): Continuing Studies
Web Site(s): http://www.mtsu.edu
E-mail: ozeh@mtsu.edu

Class Titles: Criminal Justice Administration, Nutrition, Drug/Violence Education, Sociology, Media Writing, Behavioral Science, Learning Theories, Experience of Literature, Community Relations, Effective Living, U.S. Presidency, Women's Studies, Mass Media Law, Sensation/Perception, African-American Studies, American Literature.

Teaching Methods: *Computers:* Internet, real-time chat, electronic classroom, e-mail, newsgroup, LISTSERV. *TV:* videotape, cable program, satellite broadcasting, PBS. *Other:* videoconferencing, audioconferencing, audiotapes, fax, correspondence, independent study, individual study.

Credits Granted for: portfolio assessment, extrainstitutional learning, examination (CLEP, ACT-PEP, DANTES, GRE).

On-Campus Requirements: maximum amount of correspondence allowed is 1/4 the total number of credits for the degree. No more than 66 hours awarded by correspondence, credit by exam, etc.

Tuition and Fees: *Undergraduate:* $85/credit resident, $296/credit out-of-state. *Graduate:* $129/credit resident, $340/credit out-of-state. *Application Fee:* $15 undergraduate, $26 graduate. *Other Costs:* $4/hour debt service fee, $8/hour technology fee, $5/hour student activity fee, $15 recreation fee, $8 postal fee (12+ hours), $5 SGA fee (7+ hours). *Credit by:* semester.

Financial Aid: Federal Stafford Loan, Federal Perkins Loan, Federal PLUS Loan, Federal Pell Grant, Federal Work-Study, VA, Tennessee resident programs.

Accreditation: Southern Association of Colleges and Schools.

Description: Middle Tennessee State University (1911) opened with a 2-year program for training teachers. It evolved into a 4-year teacher's college in 1925. In 1965 the institution was granted university status, and in 1992 its 6 schools—5 undergraduate and one graduate—became colleges. MTSU began distance learning in 1994 with compressed video courses. Soon after, telecourses, correspondence courses, and online courses followed. In academic year 1997–1998, more than 3,000 students were served by distance learning.

Midland College

3600 North Garfield	Phone: (915) 685-4749
Midland, TX 79705	Fax: (915) 685-6412

Division(s): Distance Learning
Web Site(s): http://www.midland.cc.tx.us
E-mail: cduchesne@midland.cc.tx.us

Undergraduate Degree Programs:
Associate of Arts
Associate of Science
Associate of Applied Science

Certificate Programs: Accounting; Air Conditioning, Heating and Refrigeration Technology; Alcohol and Drug Abuse Counseling; Automotive Technology; Aviation Maintenance—Airframe and Powerplant; Building Science Technology; Child Care and Development; Coding; Computer Graphics Technology; Computer Information Systems with Business and Electronic Emphasis; Electronics Technology; Environmental Technology; Emergency Medical Services; Horticulture Technology; Law Enforcement; Legal Assistant; Management; Medical Imaging; Medical Transcription; Nursing-Vocational; Office Systems Technology; Respiratory Care; Welding.

Teaching Methods: *Computers:* Internet, e-mail. *Other:* videoconferencing, fax.

Credits Granted for: experiential learning, portfolio assessment, examination (CLEP, ACT-PEP, DANTES, GRE).

Admission Requirements: *Undergraduate:* open-door, high school graduate or GED, TASP. *Certificate:* same as undergraduate.

On-Campus Requirements: 25% of major course work.

Tuition and Fees: *Undergraduate:* $109/credit in-district, $117/credit out-of-district, $241/credit out-of-state, prorated increase/each additional credit. *Other Costs:* variable laboratory fees. *Credit by:* semester.

Financial Aid: Federal Pell Grant, Federal Work-Study, VA, Texas resident programs.

Accreditation: Southern Association of Colleges and Schools.

Description: Midland College (1972) is an open-door, comprehensive, public community college committed to educational excellence. The college strives to provide citizens of its region with the opportunity to learn through diverse and flexible programs. The faculty is committed to instruction that provides students with occupational and professional skills, encourages creative and critical thinking, and promotes individual development. In 1996, distance learning became a reality at Midland College with the development of both an interactive videoconferencing classroom and computer communication-based instruction. Since that time, course offerings and enrollments have increased, and Web-based instruction is now available. Indeed, Midland College strives to enhance the quality of life in its "community."

Miles Community College

2715 Dickinson	Phone: (406) 233-3553
Miles City, MT 59301	Fax: (406) 233-3598

Division(s): PC Services and Telecommunications
Web Site(s): http://www.mcc.cc.mt.us
E-mail: mcc@po.mcc.cc.mt.us

Class Titles: Spanish, Psychology.

Teaching Methods: *Other:* videoconferencing.

Credits Granted for: experiential learning.

Admission Requirements: *Undergraduate:* if enrolling for 9 or fewer credits and do not plan to earn a degree or certificate, you need only to register for each class. Contact school for other information.

On-Campus Requirements: None.

Tuition and Fees: *Undergraduate:* contact school for all tuition and fee information. *Credit by:* semester.

Tuition and Fees: *Undergraduate:* contact school for all tuition and fee information. *Credit by:* semester.

Financial Aid: Federal Stafford Loan, Federal Perkins Loan, Federal PLUS Loan, Federal Pell Grant, Federal Work-Study, VA, Montana resident programs.

Accreditation: Northwest Association of Schools and Colleges.

Description: Miles Community College (1939) is located in Miles City, Montana, a town with a colorful history. Citizens of the area are friendly, hard-working people who enjoy a good time and are proud of their western heritage. It is expected that the college reflect the wonderful culture of this unique American community. We call ourselves "Pioneers." It's a concept that exudes ruggedness, individualism, tremendous perseverence, and most of all a willingness to explore the unknown. We are looking for students who possess such qualities and want to be challenged. MCC is a small college with caring faculty and staff who dedicate themselves to helping people succeed.

Milwaukee School of Engineering

1025 North Broadway	Phone: (414) 277-7176
Milwaukee, WI 53202	Fax: (414) 277-7453

Division(s): Marketing and Public Affairs
Web Site(s): http://www.msoe.edu/
E-mail: vandeyac@msoe.edu

Graduate Degree Programs:
Master of Science in Engineering Management

Class Titles: Organizational Behavior, Principles of Research/Writing, New Product Management, International Market.

Teaching Methods: *Computers:* Internet, e-mail, LISTSERV. *TV:* videotape. *Other:* None.

Credits Granted for: examination (CLEP)

Admission Requirements: *Undergraduate:* high school graduate, ACT scores. *Graduate:* college degree, 2.80 GPA. *Certificate:* open admissions.

On-Campus Requirements: Courses taken via distance education must be less than 50% of the total program credits.

Tuition and Fees: *Undergraduate:* $300/credit *Graduate:* $365/credit *Application Fee:* $30 (waived when applying online) *Credit by:* quarter.

Financial Aid: Federal Stafford Loan, Federal Perkins Loan, Federal PLUS Loan, Federal Pell Grant, Federal Work-Study, VA, Wisconsin resident programs, Federal Supplemental Educational Opportunity Grant, institutional grants, loans, and scholarship programs.

Accreditation: North Central Association of Colleges and Schools.

Description: The independent, coeducational Milwaukee School of Engineering (1903) was founded by Oscar Werwath, a practicing engineer and graduate of European technical schools. He was the first man to plan an American engineering educational institution based on an application-oriented curriculum. Today, MSE offers 14 bachelor's degrees, 3 associate degrees, and several certificate programs. Instructional TV materials including telecourses are produced under the name PROFNET, which began in 1989 after careful study of other programs and selection of the best techniques for use in these video presentations. Telecourse students work fairly independently, watching the videotapes and completing assignments at home or at work. Guidance from professors can be obtained through multiple communication techniques. Online courses have been offered since 1996.

Minot State University

500 University Avenue W	Phone: (800) 777-0750 x3822
Minot, ND 58707	Fax: (701) 858-4343

Division(s): Continuing Education
Web Site(s): http://www.misu.nodak.edu/conted
http://online.misu.nodak.edu
E-mail: conted@warp6.cs.misu.nodak.edu

Class Titles: Accounting, Advertising, Cultural Studies, Business, Business Administration/Management, Business Information/Technology, Creative Writing, Composition, English Language/Literature, History, Human Resources Management, Math, Philosophy/Religion, Sociology, Teacher Education.

Teaching Methods: *Computers:* Internet, real-time chat, e-mail, CD-ROM, LISTSERV. *TV:* videotape, satellite broadcasting. *Other:* correspondence, independent study.

Credits Granted for: extrainstitutional learning (seminars/workshops), examination (CLEP, ACT-PEP, DANTES, GRE).

Admission Requirements: *Undergraduate:* immunization records, ACT, high school diploma, official high school transcripts or GED. *Graduate:* bachelor's degree, official college/university transcripts, 3 letters of recommendation, immunization records, autobiography.

On-Campus Requirements: None.

Tuition and Fees: *Undergraduate:* $95/credit IVN/Correspondence, $139/credit online courses. *Graduate:* $108/credit IVN/Correspondence, $161/credit online courses. *Application Fee:* $25 online study. *Credit by:* semester.

Financial Aid: Federal Stafford Loan, Federal Perkins Loan,

Federal PLUS Loan, Federal Pell Grant, Federal Work-Study, VA, North Dakota resident programs.

Accreditation: North Central Association of Colleges and Schools.

Description: Founded in 1913, Minot State University is a comprehensive, public university whose twofold mission is to foster the intellectual, personal, and social development of its students, and to promote the public good through excellence in teaching, research, scholarly activity, and public service. Minot State is an integral part of the state and region it serves, and its mission is linked inextricably to the needs, aspirations, and commonwealth of the people of North Dakota. Since its founding, MSU has evolved steadily in serving North Dakota and creating opportunities for its citizens. In the late 1970s, Minot saw a need for students to take nontraditional courses. The school then developed the Office of Continuing Education and offered correspondence courses. Continuing Education expanded its distance program in 1996 by offering courses via the Internet through MSU Online.

Mississippi Delta Community College

Cherry Street/Highway 3	Phone: (601) 246-6304
Moorhead, MS 38761	Fax: (601) 246-6321

Division(s): Academic
Web Site(s): http://www.mdcc.cc.ms.us
E-mail: lsteele@mdcc.cc.ms.us

Class Titles: courses toward Associate of Arts and Associate of Applied Science degrees.

Teaching Methods: *Computers:* Internet, real-time chat, electronic classroom, e-mail, CD-ROM, newsgroup. *TV:* videotape, cable program, satellite broadcasting, PBS. *Other:* radio broadcast, videoconferencing, audioconferencing, audiographics, audiotapes, fax, correspondence, independent study, individual study, learning contracts.

Credits Granted for: experiential learning, portfolio assessment, extrainstitutional learning, examination (CLEP, ACT-PEP).

Admission Requirements: *Undergraduate:* ACT, high school diploma with 19 acceptable credits. *Certificate:* application; medical form; high school diploma, GED, or Tabe Test Level of 4948.

On-Campus Requirements: None.

Tuition and Fees: *Undergraduate:* $50 (full-time), $55 (part-time). *Other Costs:* room reservation fee $50. *Credit by:* semester

Financial Aid: Federal Pell Grant, Federal Work-Study, VA,

Mississippi resident programs, SSIG, MTAG, MESG, HELP

Accreditation: Southern Association of Colleges and Schools.

Description: Mississippi Delta Community College's (1926) philosophy is to provide qualifying students with quality, affordable educational experiences that include intellectual, academic, vocational, technical, social, cultural, and recreational learning opportunities. Specifically, the college seeks to provide: I) an academic program that leads to Associate of Arts/Science degrees and/or meets transfer requirements for students planning to complete a degree at a senior college or university; II) vocational and technical programs that, upon completion, will qualify students for entry-level employment in business or industry and/or for additional educational opportunities; III) activities and/or facilities that will foster productive citizenship, enhance personal growth, enrich the quality of life, and promote economic development in MDCC's service communities; IV) educational opportunities for business and industries requesting employee skills training and occupational enhancements; V) continuing and adult education for those desiring to extend their education, achieve a general education or associate degree, or to improve their basic educational skills; and VI) assistance to students in program identification and design for attaining personal, academic, vocational, and technical goals.

Mississippi State University

1 Barr Avenue	
PO Box 5247	Phone: (601) 325-1558
Mississippi State, MS 39762	Fax: (601) 325-8578

Division(s): Continuing Education
Web Site(s): http://www.msstate.edu or http://distance.ce.msstate.edu
E-mail: distance@ce.msstate.edu

Undergraduate Degree Programs:
Bachelor of Business Administration

Graduate Degree Programs:
Master of Business Administration
Master of Science in:
    Systems Management
    Physical Education, Emphasis: Health Education/Promotion
    Counselor Education, Emphasis: Vocational Rehabilitation
    Instructional Technology
    Civil Engineering
    Chemical Engineering
    Electrical Engineering
    Industrial Engineering
    Mechanical Engineering
Doctor of Philosophy in:
    Civil Engineering

Chemical Engineering
Electrical Engineering
Industrial Engineering
Mechanical Engineering

Certificate Programs: Vocational Teacher Licensure, Computer Application, Broadcast Meteorology, Operational Meteorology.

Class Titles: 70 courses in following areas (besides degree and certificate programs): Accounting, Business Statistics, Computer Science, Counselor Education, Economics, Educational Psychology, Elementary Education, Finance, Food Science/Technology, Foreign Languages, History, Home Economics, Marketing, Math, Microbiology, Physical Education, Physics, Political Science, Psychology, Real Estate/Mortgage Financing, Sociology, Special Education, Wildlife/Fisheries.

Teaching Methods: *Computers:* Internet, real-time chat, electronic classroom, e-mail, newsgroup, LISTSERV. *TV:* videotape. *Other:* videoconferencing, audioconferencing, audiotapes, fax, correspondence, independent study, individual study.

Credits Granted for: examination (CLEP, DANTES, Advanced Standing Exam, Advanced Placement Exam).

Admission Requirements: *Undergraduate:* (1) fill out an application for admission and send it to the university (If you are applying over the Web, you must also mail in a signed certification form and, if you are an out-of-state student, a $25 application fee), (2) request that your ACT or SAT scores be sent to Mississippi State (not required for transfer students), and (3) request that your high school send to the university a 6-semester high school transcript or, if appropriate, transcripts from other institutions attended. *Graduate:* submit the following items (note that some academic departments have additional requirements): Graduate School Application for Admission, written "Statement of Purpose," 3 letters of recommendation, and official transcripts sent directly from the registrar of all colleges attended. *Certificate:* students who do not wish to seek a degree may apply to the university as a nondegree-seeking student or a transient student. However, if a student wishes to apply the certificate courses toward a degree, students must gain full admission into the university.

On-Campus Requirements: some on-campus work for Master of Science in Instructional Technology.

Tuition and Fees: *Undergraduate:* $128/credit (average). *Graduate:* $192/credit (average). *Application Fee:* $25 out-of-state. *Other Costs:* videotape rental and postage. *Credit by:* semester.

Financial Aid: Federal Stafford Loan, Federal Perkins Loan, Federal PLUS Loan, Federal Pell Grant, Federal Work-Study, VA, Mississippi resident programs.

Accreditation: Southern Association of Colleges and Schools.

Description: Mississippi State University (1878) was founded as a land-grant institution to meet the needs of the people, institutions, and organizations of the state and nation through undergraduate and graduate education. MSU enrolls more than 15,000 students on the main campus, branch campus, off-campus centers, and through distance learning. The university is a Doctoral I institution and is among the top 100 universities in the nation in federal research support received. The Division of Continuing Education is a service arm of the university that extends nontraditional programs to individuals, groups, and agencies. The DCE is committed to meeting the needs of students unable to attend classes on campus due to geographic location and/or career and personal commitments. Through its expertise in applying a variety of advanced telecommunication technologies, the DCE continues to be a leader in distance learning. Beginning in 1989, MSU offered physics and math courses via satellite. In 1992 Mississippi State was involved in the world's first publicly switched, fiber optic, 2-way audio and video network. Distance learning now includes a variety of media to deliver 15 degrees and 4 certificate programs.

Modesto Junior College

435 College Avenue	Phone: (209) 575-6893
Modesto, CA 95350	Fax: (209) 575-6025

Division(s): Dean of Instructional Services
Web Site(s): http://virtual.yosemite.cc.ca.us
E-mail: bob@trex.ccc-infonet.edu (online courses); margo.sasse@trex.ccc-infonet.edu (telecourses)

Undergraduate Degree Programs:
Associate of Arts
Associate of Science

Certificate Programs: Many available.

Class Titles: Chemistry, Nursing, English, Statistics, Psychology, Group/Organizational Communication, etc. More than 20 telecourses on many topics.

Teaching Methods: *Computers:* Internet, real-time chat, electronic classroom, e-mail, CD-ROM, newsgroup, LISTSERV. *TV:* videotape, cable program, satellite broadcasting, direct broadcast (interhome network). *Other:* audioconferencing, videoconferencing, fax, correspondence, independent study, individual study, learning contracts.

Credits Granted for: experiential learning, portfolio assessment, extrainstitutional learning, examination (CLEP, ACT-PEP, DANTES), credit by examination.

Admission Requirements: *Undergraduate:* age 18 or high school graduate (permission needed if not a graduate).

On-Campus Requirements: None.

Tuition and Fees: *Undergraduate:* $12/unit residents, $118/unit nonresidents. *Other Costs:* Books, supplies, etc. *Credit by:* semester.

Financial Aid: Federal Perkins Loan, Federal Pell Grant, Federal Work-Study, VA, California resident programs.

Accreditation: Western Association of Schools and Colleges.

Description: Since 1921 Modesto Junior College has aspired to meet diverse educational, cultural, student, and community needs by offering open access to excellence in higher education and cultural activities. To accomplish this, college staff are committed to helping students with responsive and diverse career preparation, personal development, and lifelong learning opportunities. Modesto strives to provide excellence in instruction and support services, creating an intellectually and culturally stimulating atmosphere for students, staff, and the community. To aid continuing personal and professional development for all employees, Modesto offered telecourses in 1986, then entered the field of online instruction (Internet) in 1994.

Monroe Community College

1000 East Henrietta Road	Phone: (716) 292-2200
Rochester, NY 14623	Fax: (716) 292-3860

Division(s): Academic Services
Web Site(s): http://monroecc.edu
E-mail: rhanson@monroecc.edu

Undergraduate Degree Programs:
Associate in Science
Associate in Arts
Associate in Applied Science

Class Titles: Biomechanics, Career Development, Coaching, Computer-Aided Drafting, Dental Assisting, Emergency Medical Services, English, Fire Protection Technology, Nutrition, Golf Management, Law, Personal Fitness, Stress Management, Sport Science, Adventure Bound, Sports Medicine, Philosophy/Physical Education, Physics, Sport Psychology, Sports Management, Retailing, Travel/Tourism, Business, Chemistry, Economics, History, Philosophy, Political Science, Psychology, Sociology, Speech/Theater.

Teaching Methods: *Computers:* Internet, e-mail, CD-ROM. *TV:* cable program, PBS. *Other:* None.

Credits Granted for: experiential learning, portfolio assessment, extrainstitutional learning, examination (CLEP, ACT-PEP, DANTES).

Admission Requirements: *Undergraduate:* high school diploma or equivalent, degree-specific.

On-Campus Requirements: None.

Tuition and Fees: *Undergraduate:* $105/credit. *Application Fee:* $20. *Software:* To Be Determined. *Other Costs:* $8 health and insurance. *Credit by:* semester.

Financial Aid: Federal Stafford Loan, Federal Perkins Loan, Federal PLUS Loan, Federal Pell Grant, Federal Work-Study, VA, New York resident programs.

Accreditation: Middle States Association of Colleges and Schools.

Description: Monroe Community College (1961) is a comprehensive college offering a full variety of technical, business, health, and transfer curricula. The college enrolls 28,000 students annually in credit and noncredit courses. Distance learning began 15 years ago and currently includes 40 Internet courses, offered in association with the State University of New York Learning Network, as well as a dozen telecourses offered on PBS and cable TV.

Montana State University

128 EPS Building	
PO Box 173860	Phone: (406) 994-6812
Bozeman, MT 59717-3860	Fax: (406) 994-7856

Division(s): Burns Telecommunications Center/individual departments
Web Site(s): http://btc.montana.edu
http://btc.montana.edu/nten
http://btc.montana.edu/ceres
http://www.montana.edu/btc/sciedmasters.html
http://math.montana.edu
E-mail: kboyce@montana.edu

Graduate Degree Programs:
Master of Science in:
  Science Education
  Mathematics, Math Education Option
  Nursing, Family Nurse Practitioner
  Technology Education

Class Titles: Mountain Streams/Lakes, Infection/Immunity, Agricultural/Medical Biotechnology, Designing Technology-Based Solutions, 12 Principles of Soil Science, Exploration of Food Biotechnology, Internet-Based K-14 Earth System Science Instruction, Nutrition for Fitness/Performance, Special Relativity, Astronomy for Teachers, Comparative Planetology: Establishing Virtual Presence in Solar System, Demystifying Quantum Mechanics, Science/Photography, Studying Universe with Space Observatories, Visualization/Communication Tools for Mathematics/Science Teaching, General Relativity, Plains Landscape, Life in Streams/Ponds of Northern Great Plains, Hydrology of Streams/Ponds of Northern Great Plains, Conceptual Physics, Biology of Riparian Zones/Wetlands,

Terrestrial Ecology of Plains/Prairies, Chemistry Concepts, Mountains/Plains Riparian Processes, Electronic Snow, Advanced Mathematical Modeling for Teachers, Physics of Energy, Water Quality.

Teaching Methods: *Computers:* Internet, real-time chat, electronic classroom, e-mail, CD-ROM. *TV:* videotape, cable program, satellite broadcasting, PBS. *Other:* videoconferencing, audioconferencing, audiotapes, fax.

Credits Granted for: extrainstitutional learning, examination (CLEP, ACT-PEP, DANTES, GRE).

Admission Requirements: *Graduate:* call school for details.

On-Campus Requirements: most individual courses are delivered entirely at a distance. Program-specific.

Tuition and Fees: *Graduate:* variable; call school for details. *Credit by:* semester.

Financial Aid: Federal Stafford Loan, Federal Perkins Loan, Federal PLUS Loan, Federal Pell Grant, Federal Work-Study, VA, Montana resident programs.

Accreditation: Northwest Association of Colleges and Schools.

Description: Montana State University, Bozeman (1893) is a 4-year public, comprehensive, land-grant university with undergraduate and graduate programs in liberal arts, basic sciences, the professional areas, agriculture, architecture, business, nursing, education and engineering. Founded in 1893 as Montana's land-grant institution, MSU-Bozeman is a multipurpose research university with 11,600 students. Its affiliated campuses are MSU-Billings, MSU-Northern in Havre, and MSU College of Technology-Great Falls. As a land-grant institution, Montana State University has a long history of outreach and distance learning experience. Courses and programs have been delivered throughout the state for more than a decade using videotape, public TV broadcast, satellite uplink and downlink, audioconferencing and face-to-face delivery. More recently MSU distance learning reaches beyond state borders and includes videoconferencing and Internet-based course delivery.

Montana State University College of Technology, Great Falls

2100 16th Avenue South	Phone: (406) 771-4300
Great Falls, MT 59405	(800) 446-2698
	Fax: (406) 771-4317

Division(s): Outreach
Web Site(s): http://www.msucotgf.montana.edu
E-mail: zgf1014@maia.oscs.montana.edu

Class Titles: Composition, Human Biology, Medical Terminol-

ogy, Business/Technical Communications, Physical Science, Introduction to Computers, Introduction to Business, General Psychology, Fitness for Life.

Teaching Methods: *Computers:* Internet, real-time chat, electronic classroom, e-mail. *Other:* fax.

Credits Granted for: examination (CLEP, DANTES).

Admission Requirements: *Undergraduate:* after 7 credits, education assessment, immunization documents.

On-Campus Requirements: None.

Tuition and Fees: *Undergraduate:* $249/3-credit course Montana resident, $567/3-credit course nonresident. *Application Fee:* $30. *Other Costs:* $45/course distance learning fee. *Credit by:* semester.

Financial Aid: Federal Stafford Loan, Federal PLUS Loan, Federal Pell Grant, Federal Work-Study, VA, Montana resident programs.

Accreditation: Northwest Accreditation of Schools and Colleges.

Description: Montana State University College of Technology, Great Falls (1969) offers students several instructional formats: (1) 2-year Associate of Applied Science degrees, as well as associate degrees; (2) a Specialized Endorsements option for those who wish to move rapidly into the job market with a core of job skills; (3) short-term training in seminars and workshops, as well as customized training to fit the specific needs of companies; and (4) courses and programs through distance technologies, such as compressed video and computer-mediated instruction, that provide learning opportunities for those without access to regular college courses.

Montana State University, Northern

300 West 11th Street	Phone: (406) 265-3747
PO Box 7751	(800) 662-6132
Havre, MT 59501	Fax: (406) 265-3570

Division(s): Extended Education
Web Site(s): http://nmclites.edu
E-mail: oveson@msun.nmclites.edu

Class Titles: general education classes and courses leading to the following degrees: Associate of Science in Business Technology, Bachelor of Science in Business Technology, Bachelor of Science in Nursing—Nursing Completion Program, Master of Education in Learning Development.

Teaching Methods: *Computers:* Internet, e-mail, CD-ROM. *TV:* videotape, satellite broadcasting, videoconference, interactive TV. *Other:* fax, correspondence, individual study.

Credits Granted for: experiential learning/portfolio assessment, corporate or professional association seminars/workshops, work experience, examination (CLEP, DANTES).

Admission Requirements: *Undergraduate:* placement exams; measles, mumps, rubella immunizations, see catalog. *Graduate:* see undergraduate.

On-Campus Requirements: None.

Tuition and Fees: *Undergraduate:* $133/credit resident, $310/credit nonresident. *Graduate:* $147/credit resident, $317/credit nonresident. *Application Fee:* $30. *Credit by:* semester.

Financial Aid: Federal Stafford Loan, Federal Perkins Loan, Federal PLUS Loan, Federal Pell Grant, VA, Montana resident programs.

Accreditation: Northwest Association of Schools and Colleges.

Description: Montana State University, Northern (1929) is a state-supported, coeducational university with affiliate campuses in Bozeman, Billings, and Great Falls. Northern serves a vast area of 32,000 square miles, including 4 Indian reservations. Constituencies include undergraduate students with traditional goals, students seeking specific knowledge or skills, and graduate students seeking master's degrees. Northern is a statewide resource for technology education and economic development, and it functions as a cultural resource and continuing education center for north central Montana. Through NorthNet, MSU–Northern is the primary provider of higher education to rural place-bound Montana residents in its 53 service communities. During the day, public schools use VisionNet to share teachers and special classes. Then MSU–Northern uses the system for college courses at night. Also, through MSU–Northern's QuickStart program, high school students may take our college-level courses during their school day.

Montana Tech of the University of Montana

1300 West Park Street	Phone: **(406) 496-4311**
Butte, MT 59701	Fax: **(406) 496-4116**

Division(s): Continuing Education and Extended Studies
Web Site(s): http://www.mtech.edu
E-mail: kburgher@po1.mtech.edu
suanderson.mtech.edu

Undergraduate Degree Programs:
Occupational Safety/Health

Class Titles: Industrial Hygiene, Engineering/Tech, Sampling/Evaluation of Health Hazards, Safety Administration, Construction Safety, Industrial Toxicology, Fire Protection, Hazardous Material Management, Business/Professional

Writing, Web-Based Accel Introduction to Computer Science.

Teaching Methods: *Computers:* Internet, electronic classroom, e-mail. *Other:* videoconferencing, fax, correspondence, independent study.

Credits Granted for: examination (CLEP, DANTES), ACE/PONSI military training program, ACE/PONSI business training program.

Admission Requirements: *Undergraduate:* application and fee, high school transcript. *Doctoral:* same as undergraduate.

On-Campus Requirements: currently under review.

Tuition and Fees: *Undergraduate:* resident $147, out-of-state $380. *Doctoral:* add 20% to undergraduate tuition. *Application Fee:* $30. *Software:* variable. *Other Costs:* all OSH classes: $800/class, lab fee: variable. *Credit by:* semester.

Financial Aid: Federal Stafford Loan, Federal Perkins Loan, Federal PLUS Loan, Federal Pell Grant, Federal Work-Study, VA, Montana resident programs.

Accreditation: Northwest Association of Schools and Colleges, ABET, ACS.

Description: Montana Tech of the University of Montana (1881) is one of six institutions that comprise the Montana University System. Montana Tech enrollment remains on a steady upward track, currently approaching 2,000 students, and school officials predict 2,300 students by the end of the century. Two-thirds of the student body receive some form of financial aid. Montana Tech features a 15:1 student-to-faculty ratio, providing ample opportunity for individual attention. Classes are taught by professors who possess a unique blend of academic and industrial experience. Graduates traditionally enjoy a 95% placement rate and garner starting salaries that exceed national averages in their respective degree areas.

Monterey Peninsula College

980 Fremont Street	Phone: **(831) 646-4000**
Monterey, CA 93940	Fax: **(831) 655-2627**

Division(s): Community Education

Undergraduate Degree Programs:
contact school for more information.

Certificate Programs: contact school for more information.

Class Titles: contact school for more information.

Teaching Methods: *Computers:* Internet, CD-ROM. *TV:* videotape, satellite broadcasting. *Other:* correspondence, independent study.

Credits Granted for: experiential learning, examination (CLEP, ACT-PEP, DANTES, GRE).

Admission Requirements: *Undergraduate:* contact school for more information. *Certificate:* contact school for more information.

On-Campus Requirements: None.

Tuition and Fees: *Undergraduate:* contact school for complete fee and tuition information. *Credit by:* semester.

Financial Aid: Federal Stafford Loan, Federal Perkins Loan, Federal PLUS Loan, Federal Pell Grant, Federal Work-Study, VA, California resident programs.

Accreditation: Western Association of Colleges and Schools.

Description: Monterey Peninsula College (1947), one of 107 colleges in the California Community College System, is the focal point for learning beyond secondary school. The college offers courses to prepare students for transfer to 4-year institutions, to prepare for the workplace, to update their work skills or prepare for a new career, to provide students with a general education, and to improve their basic skills.

Montgomery College

51 Mannakee Street	Phone: (301) 251-7518
Rockville, MD 20850-1195	Fax: (301) 251-7516

Division(s): Visual Communications
Web Site(s): http://www.montgomerycollege.edu/online
http://www.mc.cc.md.us/online
E-mail: hsaint@montgomerycollege.edu

Undergraduate Degree Programs:
Associate of Arts

Certificate Programs: Graphic Design with the Computer

Class Titles: Graphic Design with Computer, Photoshop, Illustrator, Web Design, 3D Design.

Teaching Methods: *Computers:* Internet, real-time chat, electronic classroom, e-mail. *Other:* None.

Credits Granted for: experiential learning, portfolio assessment.

Admission Requirements: *Undergraduate:* secondary school graduate or GED or age 18 or meet the early placement requirements. *Certificate:* same as undergraduate.

On-Campus Requirements: None.

Tuition and Fees: *Undergraduate:* $69/credit, Montgomery County resident, $140/credit out-of-county, $187/credit nonresident. *Application Fee:* $25. *Software:* variable. *Other Costs:* $50 consolidated fee. *Credit by:* semester.

Financial Aid: Federal Stafford Loan, Federal Perkins Loan, Federal PLUS Loan, Federal Pell Grant, Federal Work-Study, VA, Federal Supplemental Educational Opportunity Grant,

Board of Trustees Grant, DC State Student Incentive Grant, MC Foundation Scholarship, Student Assistantship, Maryland resident programs, Lifetime Learning Tax Credit, Hope Scholarship Tax Credit, National Guard Tuition Waiver.

Accreditation: Middle States Association of Colleges and Schools.

Description: Originally the higher education division of Montgomery County Public Schools, Montgomery College (1946) achieved independent status in 1969, and operates under a 9-member Board of Trustees. Montgomery College deems the success of its students the highest priority. All aspects of the institution's academic programs and administration are guided by a mandate to provide an environment and opportunities for student success. Long a leader in providing remote education solutions for its students, Montgomery College was the first college in the mid-Atlantic region to offer this unique opportunity in live-online distance learning. The Advertising Art Program's popular Graphic Design with the Computer classes are offered on the Internet with the same content as our on-site classes. Students can participate for full college credit, or noncredit, and a complete Certificate in Graphic Design with the Computer is available entirely online. Visit http://www.montgomerycollege.edu/online for details.

Montgomery College

7600 Takoma Avenue	Phone: (301) 650-1551
Takoma Park, MD 29012	Fax: (301) 650-1550

Division(s): Continuing Education—Distance Learning Programs
Web Site(s): http://www.mc.cc.md.us
E-mail: bmuse@mc.cc.md.us

Class Titles: Business Administration, Chemistry, Civil Rights History, Economics, English, U.S. History, Management, Marketing, Nutrition, Oceanography, Philosophy, Psychology, Abnormal Psychology, Spanish, Sociology.

Teaching Methods: *Computers:* Internet, electronic classroom, e-mail, CD-ROM. *TV:* videotape, cable program, PBS. *Other:* videoconferencing.

Credits Granted for: examination (CLEP, GRE).

Admission Requirements: *Undergraduate:* open enrollment. *Certificate:* open enrollment.

On-Campus Requirements: 5 one-hour seminars for TV courses.

Tuition and Fees: *Undergraduate:* $69/credit. *Application Fee:* $25. *Other Costs:* 20% of tuition for consolidated fee. *Credit by:* semester.

Financial Aid: Federal Stafford Loan, Federal Perkins Loan, Federal PLUS Loan, Federal Pell Grant, Federal Work-Study, VA, Maryland resident programs.

Accreditation: Maryland Higher Education Commission.

Description: Montgomery College (1946) is Maryland's largest and oldest community college. For more than 50 years, Montgomery has helped nearly half a million students earn a degree, prepare to transfer to a 4-year school, complete an apprenticeship, or retrain for a new career. The continuing education program provides a wide range of quality noncredit and credit educational offerings and services through a planned, diversified program that includes forums, lectures, exhibits, short courses, and activities for county businesses and residents.

Montgomery County Community College

340 Dekalb Pike	**Phone: (215) 641-6440**
Blue Bell, PA 19422	**Fax: (215) 619-7161**

Division(s): Dean of Academic Affairs
Web Site(s): http://www.mc3.edu
E-mail: bgottfr@admin.mc3.edu

Undergraduate Degree Programs:
Associate of General Studies
Associate of Liberal Studies

Class Titles: Accounting, Environmental Biology, Information Systems for Management, Internet, Engineering Technology, A.C./D.C. Circuits, Basic Writing, Composition, Writing for Business/Industry, Survey of American Literature, History of Western Civilization (Modern European), History of U.S. from 1877, Management, Philosophy, Psychology, Cultural Anthropology, Economics (macro/micro), French, Western Civilization, History of U.S. to 1877, Statistics, Business, Health/Wellness for Whole Person, American National Government, Child Psychology, Abnormal Psychology, Sociology, Marriage/Family, Spanish.

Teaching Methods: *Computers:* Internet, real-time chat, electronic classroom, e-mail, CD-ROM, newsgroup, LIST-SERV. *TV:* videotape, cable program, Pennsylvania Cable Network, satellite broadcasting, PBS. *Other:* videoconferencing, correspondence, independent study, individual study.

Credits Granted for: experiential learning, portfolio assessment, extrainstitutional learning, examination (CLEP, ACT-PEP, DANTES, GRE).

Admission Requirements: *Undergraduate:* high school diploma.

On-Campus Requirements: None.

Tuition and Fees: *Undergraduate:* $70/credit in-county, $140/credit out-of-county. *Application Fee:* $20. *Software:* $3/credit computing fee. *Credit by:* semester.

Financial Aid: Federal Stafford Loan, Federal Perkins Loan, Federal PLUS Loan, Federal Pell Grant, Federal Work-Study, VA, Pennsylvania resident programs.

Accreditation: Middle States Association of Colleges and Schools.

Description: Founded in 1964, Montgomery County Community College is a comprehensive institution offering transfer and career programs in 40 fields. The college offers a growing distance learning program in which students can enroll in 17 online courses and 20 telecourses, some with videoconferencing.

Moraine Park Technical College

235 North National Avenue	**Phone: (920) 922-8611**
Fond du Lac, WI 54935	**(800) 221-6430**
	Fax: (920) 924-3391

Division(s): Academic Affairs
Other Campuses: 700 Gould Street, Beaver Dam, WI 53916
2151 North Main Street, West Bend, WI 53090
Web Site(s): http://moraine.tec.wi.us
E-mail: coehmcke@moraine.tec.wi.us

Class Titles: Accounting, Creating Web Site, Water/Wastewater Treatment, Health Information Technology, General Education.

Teaching Methods: *Computers:* Internet. *TV:* videotape, cable program, satellite broadcasting, PBS. *Other:* correspondence, independent study.

Credits Granted for: experiential learning, portfolio assessment, extrainstitutional learning (examination, CLEP).

Admission Requirements: *Undergraduate:* application and fee, ASSET test. *Certificate:* application and fee, ASSET test.

On-Campus Requirements: No program is currently available completely via distance education.

Tuition and Fees: *Undergraduate:* $57/credit, Wisconsin residents; $67/credit, nonresidents taking courses via the Internet; $441/credit nonresidents for all other courses. *Application Fee:* $25. *Other Costs:* $10 graduation fee. *Credit by:* semester.

Financial Aid: Federal Stafford Loan, Federal Perkins Loan, Federal PLUS Loan, Federal Pell Grant, Federal Work-Study, VA.

Accreditation: North Central Association of Colleges and Schools.

Description: Moraine Park Technical College is a 2-year college offering associate degree and technical diploma programs with an occupational focus, as well as a variety of certificate options. It has 3 campuses located in east-central Wisconsin and is part of the Wisconsin Technical College System. Selected courses are offered worldwide via the Internet. All courses are learner-centered and taught using performance-based curricula. They are designed to prepare students for entry into or advancement in the workforce.

Moraine Valley Community College

| 10900 South 88 Avenue | Phone: (708) 974-5288 |
| Palos Hills, IL 60465 | Fax: (708) 974-1184 |

Division(s): Academic Services and Learning Technologies
Web Site(s): http://www.mv.cc.il.us
E-mail: grund@moraine.cc.il.us

Class Titles: see Web site.

Teaching Methods: *Computers:* Internet, electronic classroom. *TV:* videotape. *Other:* None.

Credits Granted for: experiential learning, examination (CLEP).

Admission Requirements: *Undergraduate:* placement tests for math and English.

On-Campus Requirements: one-fourth of degree on campus.

Tuition and Fees: *Undergraduate:* $44. *Credit by:* semester.

Financial Aid: Federal Pell Grant, Federal Work-Study, VA, Illinois resident programs.

Accreditation: North Central Association of Colleges and Schools.

Description: Moraine Valley Community College (1965) is a public community college in southwest Cook County.

Mortgage Bankers Association of America

| 1125 15th Street NW | Phone: (202) 861-6578 |
| Washington, DC 20005 | Fax: (202) 429-9526 |

Division(s): Education
Web Site(s): http://www.mbaa.org
E-mail: education@mbaa.org

Class Titles: all courses offered by MBAA; all classes pertain to mortgage banking industry.

Teaching Methods: *Computers:* Internet (Web-based training). *Other:* audioconferencing, videoconferencing, correspondence.

Credits Granted for: MBAA does not grant college credit.

Admission Requirements: *Undergraduate:* no prerequisites.

On-Campus Requirements: None.

Tuition and Fees: *Undergraduate:* $185/Web-based course, $300/Web-based seminar module, $260/correspondence course. Students employed by a company that is a member of the Mortgage Bankers Association of America receive substantial discounts. *Credit by:* College credit is not granted by the MBAA.

Accreditation: Distance Education and Training Council.

Description: The Mortgage Bankers Association of America (1914) is the premiere trade association for real estate finance. The association began training mortgage banking professionals in 1948, later offering correspondence courses in the 1960s. For more than 30 years, mortgage banking professionals have gained the necessary knowledge and skills required to stay on top of their field without leaving their home or office. The MBAA now offers a wide range of courses to students desiring to learn more about the mortgage banking industry in various distance learning formats. In addition to offering correspondence courses, the MBAA also provides the convenience of Web-based training courses and seminars.

Mott Community College

1401 East Court Street	Phone: (800) 398-2715
Flint, MI 48503	(810) 762-5686
	Fax: (810) 762-0282

Division(s): College in the Workplace
Web Site(s): http://edtech.mcc.edu/cwp
E-mail: lfrance@edtech.mcc.edu

Undergraduate Degree Programs:
Associate in General Studies
Associate in Applied Science:
    General Business
    Computer Occupations Technology

Teaching Methods: *Computers:* Internet, e-mail, CD-ROM, LISTSERV. *TV:* videotape, broadcasting, PBS. *Other:* videoconferencing, audiotapes, fax, independent study.

Credits Granted for: transfer credits from regionally accredited colleges only.

Admission Requirements: *Undergraduate:* online registration at http://edtech.mcc.edu/cwp/start.html or call 800-398-2715.

On-Campus Requirements: None.

Tuition and Fees: *Undergraduate:* $450/course regardless of credit hours. *Other Costs:* $35/semester registration fee. *Credit by:* semester.

Financial Aid: Federal Stafford Loan, Federal PLUS Loan, Federal Pell Grant, Federal Work-Study, VA, Michigan resident programs.

Accreditation: North Central Association of Colleges and Schools.

Description: Mott Community College (1923) began its distance learning offerings in 1981, expanding into the College in the Workplace program in 1992 in order to better serve employees of manufacturing companies by delivering distance learning degrees totally campus-free. This program offers associate degrees through video-based and online courses. Convenient home study with flexible worksite testing allows students to earn their degrees while working full-time.

Mount Hood Community College

26000 Southeast Stark Street	Phone: (503) 669-6953
Gresham, OR 97030	Fax: (503) 667-7389

Division(s): Library Resource Center
Web Site(s): http://www.mhcc.cc.or.us
http://www.lbcc.cc.or.us/occdec/chart.html
E-mail: vogtc@mhcc.cc.or.us

Class Titles: Medical Terminology, Psychology, Health, Speech, Science, Management, Accounting, Computer Concepts, Literature, Keyboarding, Nutrition, Stress Management, Weight Management, Report Writing, Study Skills, Child Abuse.

Teaching Methods: *Computers:* Internet, e-mail, LISTSERV. *TV:* videotape, cable program, satellite broadcasting, PBS. *Other:* audioconferencing, videoconferencing, audiotapes, fax, correspondence, independent study, individual study, learning contracts.

Admission Requirements: *Undergraduate:* placement exams, state identification showing residency and birth date, social security number. *Certificate:* same as undergraduate.

On-Campus Requirements: some meetings for telecourses, proctored tests for online classes arranged throughout the community.

Tuition and Fees: *Undergraduate:* $39/credit in-state, $128/credit out-of-state. *Application Fee:* $15. *Other Costs:* $15 distance education course fees. *Credit by:* quarter.

Financial Aid: Federal Stafford Loan, Federal Perkins Loan, Federal PLUS Loan, Federal Pell Grant, Federal Work-Study, VA, Oregon resident programs.

Accreditation: Northwest Association of Schools and Colleges.

Description: Mount Hood Community College (1966) offers classes to its 30,000 students at the 200-acre main campus in Gresham, the MHCC Maywood Park Center, the Thompson Center, and at evening education centers in district public schools. MHCC offers general education instruction that permeates each of the college's 3 degrees: AAS, AGS, and AAOT, plus a variety of vocational certificates. The college strives to maintain effective, quality education within a comprehensive range of learning experiences that include traditional and nontraditional offerings. In the early 1980s, MHCC began offering distance education through telecourses over the local cablecast access channel and now offers courses online. With the growing demand placed on colleges to offer alternatives to the traditional way of learning, MHCC has dedicated itself to expanding and strengthening its distance education program.

Mount St. Vincent University

166 Bedford Highway	Phone: (902) 457-6437
Halifax, NS, Canada B3M 2J6	(800) 665-3838 (in Canada)
	Fax: (902) 457-6455

Division(s): Duet and Open Learning
Web Site(s): http://www.msvu.ca or http://www.msvu.ca/distance
E-mail: mary.hart-baker@msvu.ca
or distance@msvu.ca

Undergraduate Degree Programs:
Arts
Sciences
Tourism and Hospitality Management
Business Administration
Gerontology

Graduate Degree Programs:
Master of Education in Literacy Education
Master of Adult Education

Certificate Programs: Proficiency in French, Marketing, Tourism and Hospitality Management, Gerontology, Business, Information Management, Human Ecology.

Class Titles: over 50 courses offered in general fields of English, Gerontology, Marketing, Math, French, History, Business, Tourism/Hospitality, Psychology, Adult Education, Literacy Education.

Teaching Methods: *Computers:* Internet, real-time chat, electronic classroom, e-mail, CD-ROM, newsgroup, LISTSERV. *TV:* videotape, cable program, satellite broadcasting. *Other:* audioconferencing, audiographics, fax, correspondence, independent study, individual study, learning contracts.

Credits Granted for: experiential learning, portfolio assessment, extrainstitutional learning, examination (CLEP, ACT-PEP, DANTES, GRE), transfer from other institutions.

Admission Requirements: *Undergraduate:* high school graduate or mature admission. *Graduate:* undergraduate degree. *Certificate:* similar to other undergraduate admission requirements; i.e., high school completion, or mature admission if out of school for more than 5 years. We are very flexible; professors can choose to admit students at their discretion, even if the above criteria are not met.

On-Campus Requirements: None.

Tuition and Fees: *Undergraduate:* $850 Canadian/credit. *Graduate:* $1,135 Canadian/credit. *Application Fee:* $30. *Other Costs:* varies for books and course materials. *Credit by:* semester.

Financial Aid: scholarships and bursaries.

Accreditation: Association of Universities and Colleges of Canada.

Description: Mount St. Vincent University (1873) currently offers more than 50 distance education courses, many that lead to certificates, degrees, and diplomas. These courses are delivered through several modes, including TV broadcast, videotapes, audiographics, and recently via the Web. All distance courses include print materials, and sophisticated technology allows abundant interaction between students and professors. The university pioneered distance education in Maritime Canada, and for nearly 20 years has been expanding its offerings, employing increasingly user-friendly technology and reaching students ever further afield. Today, distance enrollment exceeds 1,000 and includes students from across Canada, the U.S., the Caribbean, the Middle East, and Africa. The language of instruction is English.

Mount Wachusett Community College

444 Green Street	Phone: (978) 632-6600 x275
Gardner, MA 01440	Fax: (978) 632-6155

Division(s): Division of Continuing Education and Community Services
Web Site(s): http://www.mwcc.mass.edu
E-mail: L_Cogswell@mwcc.mass.edu

Undergraduate Degree Programs:
Associate of Science in:
    Business Administration Transfer
    Business Administration Career
    Computer Information Systems
    Executive Office Administration (Administrative Assistant Option)
    Medical Assisting
    Automotive Technology
    Electronic Technology
    Fire Science Technology
    Nursing
    Plastics Technology
    Physical Therapist Assistant

    American Sign Language and Deaf Studies
    Child Study
    Criminal Justice
    General Studies
    General Human Services
Associate of Arts in:
    Computer Graphic Design
    Art
    Art (Professional Track)
    Broadcasting and Telecommunications
Associate of Liberal Arts and Sciences in:
    Liberal Arts
    Pre-Engineering Concentration
    Global Studies
    Liberal Studies
    Liberal Studies, Theater Arts Option

Certificate Programs: Administrative Computer Skills, Business Administration Career, Business Administration, Computer Assisted Accounting, Computer Information Systems, Information Processing, Medical Office, Paralegal, Small Business, Computer Graphic Design, Automotive Technology, Computer Aided Drafting, Massage Therapy, Plastics Technology, Corrections, Early Childhood Education, Gerontology, Human Services Technician, Integrated Health Care, American Sign Language.

Teaching Methods: *Computers:* Internet, electronic classroom, e-mail, CD-ROM, LISTSERV. *TV:* videotape, cable program, satellite broadcasting, PBS. *Other:* radio broadcast, audioconferencing, videoconferencing, audiographics, audiotapes, fax, correspondence, independent study, individual study, learning contracts.

Credits Granted for: experiential learning, portfolio assessment, extrainstitutional learning, examination (CLEP, DANTES).

Admission Requirements: *Undergraduate:* application, official high school transcript or copy of GED certificate. For selected programs, letters of recommendation, personal essay, or work/volunteer experience. *Certificate:* same as for undergraduate.

On-Campus Requirements: None.

Tuition and Fees: *Graduate:* $97/credit. *Other Costs:* $20/semester registration fee, $30/semester technology fee, $5/semester Masspirg (an environmental agency, optional), $395/full calendar year for health insurance, $265 Spring semester only, $50–$75/semester for books (estimate/course). *Credit by:* semester.

Financial Aid: Federal Stafford Loan, Federal Perkins Loan, Federal PLUS Loan, Federal Pell Grant, Federal Work-Study, VA.

Accreditation: New England Association of Schools and Colleges.

Description: Mount Wachusett Community College (1963) was established in response to a statewide plan to create a system of community colleges throughout Massachusetts. Located on 269 scenic acres, the main campus includes fully equipped classrooms, laboratories, studios, a library, and a theater to serve 29 cities and towns in north central Massachusetts. In addition, the Fitness and Wellness Center offers a gymnasium, athletic field, running track, racquetball courts, pool, weight room, and fitness center. Distance learning programs began 3 years ago to sustain a learning environment responsive to the needs of a population diverse in culture and life experiences. The college continues to develop innovative methods to deliver its services to students who cannot physically attend classes and lectures.

Mt. San Antonio College

| 1100 North Grand Avenue | Phone: (909) 594-5611 x5658 |
| Walnut, CA 91789 | Fax: (909) 468-3992 |

Division(s): Learning Resources
Web Site(s): http://vclass.mtsac.edu/distance/
E-mail: kstern@ibm.mtsac.edu

Class Titles: Business Organization/Management, Small Business Management, Principles of Business, General Psychology, Sociology, Marriage/Family, Physical Anthropology, General Cultural Anthropology, Child Growth/Development, Creative Writing-Poetry.

Teaching Methods: *Computers:* Internet, e-mail, newsgroup, LISTSERV. *TV:* videotape, cable program, PBS. *Other:* fax.

Admission Requirements: *Undergraduate:* some courses have prerequisites. Must complete within a semester.

On-Campus Requirements: Students must be on campus for midterms and finals.

Tuition and Fees: *Undergraduate:* $13/unit in-state, $117/unit out-of-state. $148/unit Nonresident F-1 Visa Foreign Students. *Application Fee:* $30. *Credit by:* semester.

Financial Aid: Federal Perkins Loan, Federal Pell Grant, Federal Work-Study, VA, California resident programs.

Accreditation: Western Association of Schools and Colleges.

Description: Mt. San Antonio College opened in 1946. The 421-acre college site was originally part of the 48,000-acre La Puente Rancho. With an enrollment of 38,544, MSAC is the ninth largest overall district and largest single-campus, 2-year college district in California. The Distance Learning Program began with televised courses in 1993 and introduced Internet courses in the fall of 1997.

Mt. San Jacinto College

| 1499 North State Street | Phone: (909) 672-6752 x2508 |
| San Jacinto, CA 92583 | Fax: (909) 672-0454 |

Division(s): Office of Instruction
Web Site(s): http://www.msjc.cc.ca.us
E-mail: pspencer@msjc.cc.ca.us

Undergraduate Degree Programs:
Associate of Arts
Associate of Science

Teaching Methods: *TV:* videotape, cable program. *Other:* videoconferencing.

Credits Granted for: examination (CLEP).

Admission Requirements: *Undergraduate:* A complete admission application may be obtained from the Mt. San Jacinto or Menifee Valley campuses, the Temecula Valley MSJC Outreach office, or in each Schedule of Classes. For additional information, please call (909) 672-6752 x2452.

On-Campus Requirements: Each telecourse requires 15 hours of on-campus attendance.

Tuition and Fees: *Undergraduate:* $12/credit. *Other Costs:* book costs vary. *Credit by:* semester.

Financial Aid: Federal Stafford Loan, Federal PLUS Loan, Federal Pell Grant, Federal Work-Study, VA, California resident programs.

Accreditation: Western Association of Schools and Colleges.

Description: Mt. San Jacinto College (1963) is a community college offering a wide variety of degree, certificate, occupational, developmental, and community services courses. The college began offering courses via TV and videoconferencing in 1997.

Murray State University

| PO Box 9 | Phone: (502) 762-4229 |
| Murray, KY 42071 | Fax: (502)762-3593 |

Division(s): Continuing Education and Academic Outreach
Web Site(s): http://ceao.mursuky.edu
E-mail: kendra.marsh@murraystate.edu

Undergraduate Degree Programs:
Bachelor of Independent Studies

Class Titles: Correspondence Study, Animal Science, Poultry Science, World Civilizations, Personal Health, American Experience to 1865, American Experience Since 1865, New Technologies, Business Law, College Algebra, Records Management, Office Administration, Logic, American National Government, International Relations, Recreation/Leisure

Services, Internet courses, Agribusiness, Records/Analysis, Advanced Computer Applications for Agriculture, Pathophysiology, Ethics/Environment of Business, CAD Applications, Script Writing, Information Technology Marketing, Music Theory/Aural Skills, Public Planning/Evaluation, Social Problems.

Teaching Methods: *Computers:* Internet, real-time chat, electronic classroom, e-mail, CD-ROM, newsgroup, LISTSERV. *TV:* videotape, cable program, satellite broadcasting, PBS. *Other:* radio broadcast, videoconferencing, audioconferencing, audiographics, audiotapes, fax, correspondence, independent study, individual study, learning contracts.

Credits Granted for: portfolio assessment, extrainstitutional learning, examination (CLEP, ACT-PEP, DANTES, GRE).

Admission Requirements: *Undergraduate:* application for admission, official transcripts from all colleges attended, official ACT test score reports, official high school transcript or GED test score. If you already have more than 24 semester hours of college credits, you need not submit high school transcripts or ACT test score. You can be admitted to the Bachelor of Independent Studies degree program only if you have 12 semester hours of college credits and attend a one-day seminar titled "Introduction to the Bachelor of Independent Studies Degree." The purpose of the seminar is to provide students with enough information to decide whether the B.I.S. degree will meet their educational goals. Gain admission to Murray State University from the Admissions and Registrar's Office. Please note that your application must include the application form, required transcripts, and report of ACT scores if required. The admissions office will admit you only after your application is complete. At that time you may also register for classes. When you are admitted to Murray State University, you may register for BIS 101.

On-Campus Requirements: degree requirements: 128 semester hours required, 32 hours at Murray State, 40 upper-division hours, 61 4-year college hours. Persons who can schedule classes on the Murray State campus can usually complete the 32 hours of Murray State courses in almost any subject, but students at a greater distance will find their choice of courses limited. BIS advisers will provide information by telephone to prospective students.

Tuition and Fees: *Undergraduate:* $84/credit in-state, $245/credit out-of-state. *Graduate:* $124/credit in-state, $357/credit out-of-state. *Application Fee:* $25. *Other Costs:* $20 extended campus fees. *Credit by:* semester.

Financial Aid: Federal Stafford Loan, Federal Perkins Loan, Federal PLUS Loan, Federal Pell Grant, Federal Work-Study, VA, Kentucky resident programs.

Accreditation: Southern Association of Colleges and Schools.

Description: Murray State University (1922) recognizes its responsibility to its designated service regions and to nontraditional students who desire educational opportunities.

The function of the Center for Continuing Education and Academic Outreach is to organize all extended campus courses, correspondence, educational TV activities, workshops, conferences, noncredit courses, community education, military programs and adult outreach programs. Murray State University is a member of the Association for Continuing Higher Education.

Nassau Community College

One Education Drive
Garden City, NY 11530-6793

Phone: (516) 572-7883
Fax: (516) 572-7503

Division(s): College of the Air
Web Site(s): http://sunynassau.edu
E-mail: friedma@sunynassau.edu

Undergraduate Degree Programs:
Associate

Class Titles: Accounting, Art History, Business, Communications, Economics, English Literature, Film History/Appreciation, History, Italian, Business Law, Mathematics, Marketing, Music Appreciation, Health, Psychology, Sociology, Spanish, French, Social Problems.

Teaching Methods: *Computers:* Internet, e-mail. *TV:* videotape, PBS. *Other:* radio broadcast, audiotapes, fax, correspondence, independent study.

Credits Granted for: experiential learning, portfolio assessment, examination (GRE).

Admission Requirements: *Undergraduate:* high school graduate (GED).

On-Campus Requirements: Yes, for degree.

Tuition and Fees: *Undergraduate:* $86/credit. *Application Fee:* $20. *Other Costs:* $6/credit student fee (maximum = $55/semester). *Credit by:* semester.

Financial Aid: Federal Stafford Loan, Federal Perkins Loan, Federal PLUS Loan, Federal Pell Grant, Federal Work-Study, VA, New York resident programs.

Accreditation: Middle States Association of Colleges and Schools.

Description: Nassau Community College (1959) is a comprehensive full-opportunity institution of higher education created as part of the State University of New York. The college is dedicated to high-quality, low-cost education and career preparation. The college offers Associate of Arts, Associate of Science, and Associate of Applied Science degrees, certificates, and continuing education programs. The 225-acre campus is located in central Nassau County. Nassau Community College has a long history in distance learning activities, beginning with its participation in the University of the Air program in the early 1970s. Course offerings at off-campus sites and the development of the College of the Air program in 1991 continue this tradition. Additional courses have been added to the program each semester. In the 1997–1998 academic year, distance learning registrations exceeded 1,600 units.

National Genealogical Society

4527 17th Street N	Phone: (703) 525-0050 x223
Arlington, VA 22207-2399	(800) 473-0060 x223
	Fax: (703) 525-0052

Division(s): Education
Web Site(s): http://www.ngsgenealogy.org
E-mail: education@ngsgenealogy.org

Class Titles: American Genealogy (correspondence), Introduction to Genealogy (online).

Teaching Methods: *Computers:* Internet, e-mail. *Other:* fax, correspondence.

On-Campus Requirements: None.

Tuition and Fees: *Undergraduate:* $295/correspondence course if member, $375 if nonmember; $60/online course if member, $75 if nonmember.

Accreditation: Distance Education and Training Council.

Description: The National Genealogical Society (1903) is a nonprofit national, membership organization for those interested in genealogy and family history. The society's programs and services include a library, library loan program, quarterly journal, bimonthly newsletter, bimonthly computer interest group digest, distance education courses, annual conference, and publications sales. Its first distance education course, American Genealogy: A Basic Course, was launched in 1981. The society will offer a short course for beginners on its Web site in late 1998.

National Technological University

700 Centre Avenue	Phone: (970) 495-6433
Fort Collins, CO 80526	Fax: (970) 498-0601

Division(s): Admissions and Records
Web Site(s): http://www.ntu.edu
E-mail: Lisa@ntu.edu

Graduate Degree Programs:
Master of Science in:
 Chemical Engineering
 Computer Engineering
 Computer Science
 Electrical Engineering
 Engineering Management
 Environmental Systems Management
 Health Physics
 International Master of Business Administration
 Management of Technology
 Manufacturing Systems Engineering
 Materials Science and Engineering
 Software Engineering
 Special Majors Program
 Transportation Systems Engineering

Certificate Programs: Available for NTU's Fast Track Program in Computer Science and for other areas.

Teaching Methods: *Computers:* Internet, e-mail. *TV:* videotape, satellite broadcasting. *Other:* fax, correspondence, telephone.

Admission Requirements: *Graduate:* bachelor's degree in appropriate major.

On-Campus Requirements: None.

Tuition and Fees: *Graduate:* $585–$900/credit. *Application Fee:* $50. *Credit by:* semester.

Financial Aid: VA.

Accreditation: North Central Association of Colleges and Schools.

Description: National Technological University is a private, nonprofit institution founded in 1984 to serve the advanced educational needs of today's busy, highly mobile engineers, scientists, and technical managers. On a national and international basis, NTU offers a wide range of satellite-delivered instructional television courses taught by a faculty selected from 50 of the nation's top engineering schools and from other leading organizations and institutions.

National Training, Incorporated

188 College Drive	Phone: (904) 272-4000
Orange Park, FL 32065	Fax: (904) 272-6702

Division(s): Student Services
Web Site(s): http://www.truckschool.com
E-mail: truckschool@worldnet.att.net

Certificate Programs: Commercial Driver's License Preparation, Accelerated Commercial Driver's License Preparation, CDL Prepared Independent Trucker's program.

Teaching Methods: *Other:* correspondence, independent study, individual study, resident training.

Credits Granted for: Confirmed Tractor Trailer Driving classes at an accredited institution.

Admission Requirements: *Certificate:* age 21, valid motor vehicle operator's license, acceptable driving record—Florida

Commercial Driver's License, instructional permit, pass DOT physical examination.

On-Campus Requirements: Resident training requires some classroom hours.

Tuition and Fees: *Undergraduate:* $1,995–$3,395 (tuition prices can be subject to change). *Credit by:* year-round.

Financial Aid: VA, Florida resident programs—job training partnership programs, vocational rehabilitation; in-house financing available based on credit criteria.

Accreditation: Distance Education and Training Council.

Description: National Training, Inc., (1978) was established to provide basic, year-round training needed to help supply the trucking industry with knowledgeable, safety-conscious, and industrious truck driving personnel. National Training attempts to instill in its students an awareness of all the factors that will enable them to accomplish and maintain a level of proficiency that will prove to be an ongoing asset after they graduate. This is accomplished through a study of the rules, safety elements, and the complexities and versatility of the trucks they drive. Through a dedicated faculty, a varied and multifaceted curriculum, and facilities capable of providing a multitude of practical experiences, our graduates develop the confidence and skills to begin a rewarding career. The combination of distance education and the resident training portion of the programs has met with much success.

National University

11255 North Torrey Pines Road	Phone: (800) 628-8648
La Jolla, CA 92037	Fax: (619) 563-7299

Division(s): School of Management and Technology, School of Education and Human Services, School of Arts and Sciences
Web Site(s): http://www.nu.edu
E-mail: pmontroy@nu.edu

Undergraduate Degree Programs:
Bachelor of Science in Global Studies

Graduate Degree Programs:
Global Master of Business Administration

Certificate Programs: Crosscultural Language Academic Development.

Teaching Methods: *Computers:* Internet, real-time chat, electronic classroom, e-mail, CD-ROM, newsgroup, LIST-SERV. *TV:* videotape. *Other:* videoconferencing, fax, correspondence, independent study, individual study, learning contracts.

Credits Granted for: experiential learning, portfolio assessment, extrainstitutional learning.

Admission Requirements: *Undergraduate:* open. *Graduate:* open. *Certificate:* open.

On-Campus Requirements: None.

Tuition and Fees: *Undergraduate:* $775/credit. *Graduate:* $825/credit. *Application Fee:* $60. *Credit by:* quarter.

Financial Aid: Federal Stafford Loan, Federal Perkins Loan, Federal PLUS Loan, Federal Pell Grant, Federal Work-Study, VA, California resident programs.

Accreditation: Western Association of Schools and Colleges.

Description: National University (1971) is a nonprofit, accredited institution of higher education that specializes in meeting the educational needs of adult learners. Classes are designed to meet the time constraints of its working, adult students, who average 34 years old. NU offers a unique one-course-per-month format, and its distance education programs were designed to be an even more flexible alternative for students. With 11,300 FTE students, NU is the third-largest private university in California.

Native American Educational Services College

2838 West Peterson	Phone: (773) 761-5000
Chicago, IL 60659	Fax: (773) 761-3808

Division(s): Chicago Campus
Web Site(s): http://naes.indian.com
E-mail: DAVENAES@aol.com

Undergraduate Degree Programs:
Community Studies

Class Titles: Internet: Finding American Indian-Related Resources.

Teaching Methods: *Computers:* Internet, real-time chat, electronic classroom, e-mail. *Other:* videoconferencing, fax, correspondence, independent study, individual study, learning contracts.

Credits Granted for: experiential learning, examination (CLEP).

Admission Requirements: *Undergraduate:* involvement in American Indian community; degree candidates must make special request to enroll if under age 23 with no college experience. *Graduate:* involvement in American Indian community, accredited bachelor's degree.

On-Campus Requirements: 54 credits in residency for degree candidates.

Tuition and Fees: *Undergraduate:* $208/credit. *Graduate:* $225/credit. *Other Costs:* $70/semester. *Credit by:* semester.

Financial Aid: Federal Pell Grant; Federal Work-Study; Illinois, Wisconsin, Montana, Minnesota resident programs; tribal programs for tribal members (depends on tribe).

Accreditation: North Central Association of Colleges and Schools.

Description: Native American Educational Services College (1974) is the only private, American-Indian-controlled, BA-granting institution in the U.S. We have 2 urban campuses, in the Chicago and Minneapolis Indian communities, and 2 reservation campuses, at Menominee in Wisconsin and Fort Peck in eastern Montana. We offer one degree: a BA in Community Studies. The focus of instruction is community building, which is accomplished by understanding the community's history and culture, understanding how public policy works in the local arena, understanding social change, and working to make it happen. The liberal-arts education is project-based in a majority of the course work. We are constantly trying to find the balance between incorporating traditional tribal knowledge and conventional, Western-based knowledge into the curriculum. Though the students work in small communities, their knowledge base must spread far beyond those communities to include the problems, solutions, and situations of other communities throughout Indian country in the U.S., in indigenous communities throughout the hemisphere, and indeed throughout the world. We entered distant learning in the spring of 1998 to help our students learn modern technology and to offer our courses at several campuses simultaneously. Besides computer courses, we will offer public policy and tribal language courses via videoconferencing in the future.

Neumann College

One Neumann Drive	Phone: (610) 558-5507
Aston, PA 19014-1298	Fax: (610) 459-1370

Division(s): Academic Affairs
Web Site(s): http://www.neumann.edu
E-mail: mosborn@smtpgate.neumann.edu

Class Titles: Foreign Languages, Literature.

Teaching Methods: *Computers:* electronic classroom, e-mail. *TV:* cable program, PBS. *Other:* videoconferencing via PictureTel, fax, independent study.

Credits Granted for: experiential learning, portfolio assessment, examination (CLEP, ACT-PEP, DANTES, GRE).

On-Campus Requirements: None.

Tuition and Fees: *Undergraduate:* $310/credit. *Graduate:* $410/credit. *Application Fee:* Undergraduate $35, Graduate $50. *Credit by:* semester.

Financial Aid: Federal Stafford Loan, Federal Perkins Loan, Federal PLUS Loan, Federal Pell Grant, Federal Work-Study, VA, Pennsylvania resident programs.

Accreditation: Middle States Association of Colleges and Schools.

Description: Neumann College (1965) is a Catholic, Franciscan institution of higher education.

New College of California

50 Fell Street	Phone: (415) 241-1377
San Francisco, CA 94102	Fax: (415) 626-5171

Division(s): Media Studies and Teleducation
Web Site(s): http://www.newcollege.edu/mediastudies/
E-mail: dcaploe@ncgate.newcollege.edu

Undergraduate Degree Programs:
Bachelor of Arts

Graduate Degree Programs:
Master of Arts

Class Titles: Global Media Society—Theoretical Context, World Politics, World Political Economy—Theory/History 1789–Present, Cultural History of Western World—Renaissance–MTV.

Teaching Methods: *Computers:* Internet, real-time chat, electronic classroom, e-mail. *TV:* videotape. *Other:* telephone, audiotapes, fax, correspondence, independent study, individual study.

Credits Granted for: experiential learning, portfolio assessment, extrainstitutional learning, examination (CLEP, ACT-PEP, DANTES, GRE).

Admission Requirements: *Undergraduate:* high school transcripts, letters (SAT is optional). *Graduate:* accredited BA or BS, GRE strongly recommended, transcripts. *Doctoral:* same as graduate.

On-Campus Requirements: None.

Tuition and Fees: *Undergraduate:* contact admissions@ncgate.newcollege.edu. *Graduate:* $15,000 for MA program. *Application Fee:* $40. *Software:* to be decided. *Other Costs:* books/videotapes. *Credit by:* module (all courses are counted as double courses, i.e., 6 credits).

Financial Aid: Federal Stafford Loan, Federal Perkins Loan, Federal PLUS Loan, Federal Pell Grant, Federal Work-Study, VA, California resident programs.

Accreditation: Western Association Schools and Colleges.

Description: New College of California (1971) was established as part of this country's alternative-school tradition. The name dates back to New College of Oxford, England (1479), whose purpose was to turn away from the ossified and compartmentalized educational establishment of its day. The Media Studies and Teleducation programs seek, above all, to link the traditional grounding of a humanities-based approach with the concerns and technologies of the 21st century "global media society."

New Hampshire College

2500 North River Road	Phone: (603) 645-9766
Manchester, NH 03106-1045	Fax: (603) 645-9706

Division(s): Distance Education
Web Site(s): http://de.nhc.edu or www.dist-ed.nhc.edu
E-mail: kbyrne@nhc.edu

Undergraduate Degree Programs:
Business (pending)

Graduate Degree Programs:
Business (pending)

Certificate Programs: Accounting, Computer Programming, Human Resource Management, Small Business Management, Healthcare.

Class Titles: See projected schedule for year on Web site at http://de.nhc.edu, click on courses, then projected schedule.

Teaching Methods: *Computers:* Internet, real-time chat, e-mail, newsgroup, file transfer. *Other:* None.

Credits Granted for: experiential learning, portfolio assessment, examination (CLEP, ACT-PEP, DANTES, GRE), institutional exams.

Admission Requirements: *Undergraduate:* equal opportunity institution. Distance Education has open-admissions policy. Must maintain GPA standard. Residency requirement (taking courses "through" rather than "at" NHC): 30 credits, including 12 from major for bachelor's and 9 from major field for associate. Final 24 credits must be through NHC. Exceptions made for active-duty military personnel and dependents. Transfer credits are accepted. See undergraduate or graduate catalog for details. *Graduate:* see undergraduate.

On-Campus Requirements: None.

Tuition and Fees: *Undergraduate:* $184/credit. *Graduate:* $315/credit. *Software:* varies/course. *Other Costs:* varies for texts and supplemental material. *Credit by:* term: undergraduate: 6 8-week terms/year; graduate: 4 12-week terms/year.

Financial Aid: Federal Stafford Loan, Federal Perkins Loan, Federal PLUS Loan, Federal Pell Grant, Federal Work-Study, VA, Federal and New Hampshire resident programs, vocational rehabilitation programs, military programs, etc. Contact our financial aid office for more details at (603) 645-9645.

Accreditation: New England Association of Schools and Colleges, Association of Collegiate Business Schools and Programs, New England Postsecondary Education Commission.

Description: New Hampshire College (1932) is hub to a wheel of progress with industrial and business growth. The college is a nonprofit, coeducational institution with a great international population on campus. The college offers business, liberal studies, and hospitality degrees at the Undergraduate School, with MBA, MS, and doctorate degrees through the Graduate School. Distance Education began in 1996 and is an innovative, nontraditional delivery of education to meet the changing demands of students, without compromising the integrity of its academic content. The program began with 12 students and has grown to more than 300 students per term, averaging 1,800 per year, in the undergraduate division. Many undergraduate and graduate courses are offered through distance education.

New Jersey City University

2039 Kennedy Boulevard	Phone: (201) 200-3449
Jersey City, NJ 07305	Fax: (201) 200-2188

Division(s): Continuing Education
Web Site(s): http://conted4.njcu.edu
E-mail: conted@njcu.edu

Graduate Degree Programs:
Courses only

Class Titles: Using Internet in Education, Using Integrated Software Across Curriculum, Hypermedia, Publishing on Web: Design/Theory/Application, Technology in Social Studies Curriculum, Technology in Special Education Curriculum, selected offerings in Special Education/Literacy Education.

Teaching Methods: *Computers:* Internet, real-time chat, electronic classroom, e-mail, LISTSERV. *Other:* None.

Admission Requirements: *Graduate:* accredited bachelor's degree, transcripts demonstrating completion of such degree.

On-Campus Requirements: None.

Tuition and Fees: *Graduate:* $190/credit. *Other Costs:* variable for textbooks. *Credit by:* semester.

Financial Aid: Federal Stafford Loan, Federal Perkins Loan, Federal PLUS Loan, Federal Pell Grant, Federal Work-Study, VA, New Jersey resident programs.

Accreditation: Middle States Association of Colleges and Schools, National Council for Accreditation of Teacher Education.

Description: New Jersey City University (1927) was founded as New Jersey Normal School. In 1935 it became the Jersey State Teacher's College, and in 1958 the name was changed to Jersey City State College. In 1998 the college was granted university status, and its name was changed to reflect its mission as New Jersey's urban university. Distributed learning at off-campus sites began during the 1970s, with electronic delivery of courses over the Internet beginning in 1997.

New Mexico State University

Box 3WEC	Phone: (505) 646-5837
Las Cruces, NM 88003	Fax: (505) 646-2044

Division(s): Office of Distance Education
Web Site(s): http://www.nmsu.edu/~distance/
E-mail: tenevare@nmsu.edu

Undergraduate Degree Programs:
Bachelor of Business Administration in General Business

Graduate Degree Programs:
Master of Arts in Education
Master of Science in Engineering

Teaching Methods: *Computers:* Internet, e-mail, LISTSERV. *TV:* videotape, satellite broadcasting. *Other:* videoconferencing, independent study.

Credits Granted for: examination (CLEP, ACT-PEP, DANTES).

Admission Requirements: *Undergraduate:* high school graduate or GED, ACT. *Graduate:* accredited bachelor's degree.

On-Campus Requirements: None.

Tuition and Fees: *Undergraduate:* $125/credit. *Graduate:* $125/credit. *Application Fee:* $15. *Credit by:* semester.

Financial Aid: Federal Stafford Loan, Federal Perkins Loan, Federal Pell Grant, Federal Work-Study, VA, New Mexico resident programs.

Accreditation: North Central Association of Colleges and Schools.

Description: New Mexico State University, which began in 1888 as an agricultural college and preparatory school, is a comprehensive institution dedicated to teaching, research, and service. The main campus is in the southern New Mexico city of Las Cruces, population 75,000. With a current enrollment of nearly 15,000 and a regular faculty of about 700, the faculty/student ratio is 1 to 18.2. Almost 80% of the full-time faculty hold PhDs. The university offers 75 bachelor's, 50 master's, 4 Specialist in Education, and 20 doctoral degrees. NMSU is a Carnegie Foundation Level One research institution, anchoring the southern end of the Rio Grande Research Corridor. The campus has 2 of the state's 5 Centers for Excellence—in computing and in plant genetics—as well as a Physical Science Laboratory.

New Mexico State University, Alamogordo

2400 North Scenic Drive	Phone: (505) 439-3714
Alamogordo, NM 88310	Fax: (505) 439-3800

Division(s): Office of Distance Learning
Web Site(s): http://alamo.msu.edu
E-mail: conro@nmsua.nmsu.edu

Undergraduate Degree Programs:
Bachelor of Business Administration

Class Titles: Accounting, Business Administration, Business Computer Systems, Business Law, Economics, Finance, Management, Marketing, Nursing, Health Sciences, English, Counseling

Teaching Methods: *Computers:* Internet, real-time chat, electronic classroom, e-mail, CD-ROM, newsgroup, LISTSERV. *TV:* videotape. *Other:* videoconferencing, fax, independent study, individual study.

Admission Requirements: *Undergraduate:* all applicants: select degree- or nondegree-seeking status and have high school diploma with official transcripts or GED scores (GED applicants must be 18 to apply). Transfer students: 2.0 cumulative GPA, good standing from last college/university attended, application, official transcripts from all colleges.

On-Campus Requirements: variable.

Tuition and Fees: *Undergraduate:* $125/credit (2-way interactive courses). *Graduate:* $135/credit (2-way interactive courses). *Application Fee:* $15 first time admission, $20/ Associate Degree, $10/Certificate. *Other Costs:* $5–$40 laboratory fees, if applicable. *Credit by:* semester.

Financial Aid: Federal Stafford Loan, Federal Perkins Loan, Federal PLUS Loan, Federal Pell Grant, Federal and New Mexico Work-Study, New Mexico resident programs.

Accreditation: North Central Association of Colleges and Secondary Schools.

Description: New Mexico State University, Alamogordo (1958) is a 2-year branch campus of NMSU in Las Cruces. NMSU at Alamogordo is a 500-acre campus with an enrollment of 2,250 students served by 55 regular, 85 adjunct, 50 classified, and 22 professional, full-time staff members. The university's service area is 7,000 square miles, roughly the size of Massachusetts. The student population includes recent high school graduates, military personnel (including members of the German Air Force unit stationed at Holloman) and their family members, and students returning after a long hiatus. Distance learning began on campus in 1996 with offerings of 2-way interactive videoconferencing courses, satellite broadcasts, Internet-based, and on-site instruction from the New Mexico State University main campus in Las Cruces.

New River Community College

PO Box 1127
Dublin, VA 24084

Phone: (540) 674-3614
Fax: (540) 674-3626

Division(s): Distance Education and Off-Campus Services
Web Site(s): http://www.nr.cc.va.us
E-mail: nrshelt@nr.cc.va.us

Undergraduate Degree Programs:
Associate of Applied Science in Education
Associate of Applied Science in General Studies

Class Titles: English, History, Math, Biology, Geology, Business, Economics, Psychology, Sign Communication, Public Speaking, Health, Marketing, Music, Philosophy, Religion, Statistics, Library Skills.

Teaching Methods: *Computers:* Internet, electronic classroom, e-mail, CD-ROM. *TV:* videotape, cable program, satellite broadcasting, PBS. *Other:* audioconferencing, videoconferencing, audiotapes, fax, correspondence, independent study.

Admission Requirements: *Undergraduate:* application; English/math placement test.

On-Campus Requirements: None.

Tuition and Fees: *Undergraduate:* $47/credit in-state, $156/credit out-of-state. *Other Costs:* $3/semester Student Fee, $3/semester-hour (up to $9/semester) Facilities Fee, $1/semester-hour Technology Fee. *Credit by:* semester.

Financial Aid: Federal Stafford Loan, Federal Perkins Loan, Federal PLUS Loan, Federal Pell Grant, Federal Work-Study, VA, Virginia resident programs.

Accreditation: Southern Association of Colleges and Schools.

Description: New River Community College is a 2-year, state institution founded in 1969 and operating under a statewide system of community colleges. The college has a growing distance education program that began in 1980. Currently the college offers more than 65 distance education courses per semester in many formats.

New School

66 West 12th Street
New York, NY 10011

Phone: (212) 229-5880
Fax: (212) 989-2928

Division(s): Distance Instruction for Adult Learning (DIAL)
Web Site(s): http://www.dialnsa.edu
E-mail: dialexec@dialnsa.edu

Undergraduate Degree Programs:
Bachelor of Arts in Liberal Arts

Graduate Degree Programs:
Master of Arts in Media Studies

Class Titles: over 300 courses each year; examples: Foundations of Feminism, Decadent Feminist–Rethinking Feminism for 1990s, Political Theory for 21st Century, Multiculturalism in American Politics, Bill of Rights/Supreme Court, Situating Victim–Study of Crimes Against Women, Economic Theory/Transformation, Pacific Century, 1920s–Emergence of Modern America, Sociology–Tools for Understanding World, Ethics/Family, Foundations of Psychology, Depression/Melancholia–Humorous History, Theorizing Intellect, Social Psychology, Understanding Gender, Hysteria–Her Story, Jung, Insanity/Psychiatry/Society, Mother Earth/Father Sky–Feminine/Masculine in Native America, Society/Rights of Animals, Crime/Punishment, Borders of Identity, Celebrating Differences–Disability Culture, William Blake, 4 American Classics, 4 European Classics, Women's Autobiographical Writing, 7 Visionary Poets, Race/Sex in American Life: 6 African-American Women Writers, Psychoanalysis/Literature–Plumbing Literary Unconscious, D.H. Lawrence/Language of Love, Forbidden Literature, Secrets of South, Buddhas/Bards/Beatniks–Buddhist Influences in American Literature, Memorializing Vietnam, Lesbian Literary Tradition, Seeking (M)other–Mother/Daughter Theme in Literature, Environmental Geology, Observing Night Sky–Astronomy, Statistics for Everyone, Italian for Italian Speakers, Graduate Reading Course, Linguistics, Learner Assessment, Family Literacy, Methods/Techniques of Teaching ESL/EFL, English Grammar for ESL Teachers, Teaching Sound System of English, Teaching Writing, Published ESL/EFL Materials, Teaching ESL Writing Online, Business Writing (ESL), Fundamentals of English, Grammar of Business Writing, Fundamentals of Copy Editing, Elements of Business Writing, Preparatory Writing, Writing with Power–Language as Listening Tool, Silence to Poem, Rendering Ordinary Extraordinary–Poetry Workshop, Fiction Writing–Memory/Imagination/Desires, Accidental Realities–Writing Experimental Fiction, Harlem Writers Guild Online Fiction Workshop, Writing Creative Nonfiction, Family Narrative–How/Why My Family Came to This Country, Playwriting, Documentary Fiction–Multigenre Writing from Multicultural Roots, Hypertext Poetry/Fiction, Electronic Studio–Photoshop for Artists, Drawing–Online Workshop for Beginners, Basic Photography–Critique/Response, Intermediate Photography–Critique/Response, Electronic Studio–Photoshop for Photographers, Whose Story Is It? Media in Developing Countries, How To Do Research Online, Screenwriting– Fundamentals, Screenwriting–Facing Blank Page, Business Management, Investment Basics, Fundamental Principles of Financial Freedom, UNIX Operating System, C Language Programming, Microsoft PowerPoint, MS Word (Windows 95), QuarkXPress (Macintosh), Adobe Illustrator (Macintosh), Photoshop 4.0 (Macintosh), Live Picture, World Wide Web Page Design/Construction Mac Platform, PC Platform, Webmaster, Troubleshooting Web Graphics, MacroMedia DreamWeaver, How to Open a Restaurant, Marcus Apicius to Julia Child–Culinary History.

Teaching Methods: *Computers:* Internet, CD-ROM. *Other:* None.

Credits Granted for: experiential learning, portfolio assessment.

Admission Requirements: *Undergraduate:* for a distance, liberal arts BA: 60 transferable credits, application, official college transcripts, 2 related essays, and an interview. No graduate programs are currently available fully online; however, students with undergraduate degrees may be allowed to take a graduate DIAL course with department permission.

On-Campus Requirements: None.

Tuition and Fees: *Undergraduate:* $500/credit for degree students. A typical 12-week course costs $420. *Graduate:* $616/credit. *Other Costs:* $100 university services fee/semester for degree students. *Credit by:* semester.

Financial Aid: Federal Stafford Loan, Federal Perkins Loan, Federal PLUS Loan, Federal Pell Grant, Federal Work-Study, VA, New York resident programs.

Accreditation: Middle States Association of Colleges and Schools.

Description: The New School (1919) was established as a center for discourse and learning for adult students. It is the leader in American adult education. Established in 1994 with only 7 courses, Distance Instruction for Adult Learning has grown to more than 300 courses annually, ranging from music and writing to business and communications. The New School is the only accredited university in the world that offers credit, noncredit, and degree courses that can be taken anytime, anywhere through the Internet. "Using any personal computer with Internet access, students can enter the classroom whenever they choose; it's open 24 hours a day, 7 days a week," notes Elizabeth Dickey, Dean of The New School. "Online education is one of the great advents in education, and we have worked hard to be on the cutting edge of the movement." The DIAL environment is very much like a traditional university. Each DIAL course is taught by a New School faculty member who provides lectures, asks and answers questions, gives assignments, assesses student work, and gives feedback in class or privately. Students discuss topics by posting comments, questions, and observations which become part of the ongoing text-based seminar instruction. DIAL also provides a place for extracurricular discussions and personal exchanges. "The program is designed to provide maximum flexibility to students who might not be able to attend courses at The New School, either due to distance or schedule conflicts," says Stephen Anspacher, Director of The New School's DIAL program. "DIAL is asynchronous, so students can access, the online campus at any time, as often as they choose. We have found that students log on to their courses 3 to 5 times/week at the beginning of a semester, and up to 3 to 5 times/day near the end of a course because of the ease of use and evolution of the dialogue taking place online." Many DIAL students have little or no online experience prior to enrolling in the program. "They are interested in the courses, not the technology per se," according to Mr. Anspacher. DIAL provides extensive instruction and materials to students, including: orientation sessions, 24-hour technical assistance, student handbook and video guide to DIAL, course guides (with syllabi), structural overview, instructions for student advising, inter-library access and online textbook ordering. Faculty members are required to participate in an intensive 3-month Faculty Development Conference prior to teaching through DIAL. Several New School special events are accompanied by free, online dialogues with program participants. Programs range from discussions of art and politics to simultaneous multisite concerts.

New York Institute of Technology

PO Box 9029
Central Islip, NY 11722

Phone: (800) 222-6948
Fax: (516) 348-0299

Division(s): On-Line Campus
Web Site(s): http://www.nyit.edu/olc
E-mail: olc@iris.nyit.edu

Undergraduate Degree Programs:
Bachelor of Science in:
　　Psychology
　　Sociology
　　Criminal Justice
　　Community Mental Health
　　Interdisciplinary Studies
　　Business Administration

Graduate Degree Programs:
Master of Business Administration
Master of Professional Studies in Human Relations
Master of Science in Energy Management

Teaching Methods: *Computers:* Internet, e-mail. *Other:* None.

Credits Granted for: experiential learning, portfolio assessment, extrainstitutional learning, examination (CLEP, ACT-PEP, DANTES, GRE).

Admission Requirements: *Undergraduate:* high school degree or equivalent. *Graduate:* GRE and GMAT.

On-Campus Requirements: None.

Tuition and Fees: *Undergraduate:* $345/credit. *Graduate:* $413/credit. *Application Fee:* $50. *Credit by:* semester.

Financial Aid: Federal Stafford Loan, Federal Perkins Loan, Federal PLUS Loan, Federal Pell Grant, VA, New York resident programs (TAP).

Accreditation: Middle States Association of Schools and Colleges.

Description: The On-Line Campus of New York Institute of Technology (1955) is an innovative degree program that allows students to acquire a 4-year college degree entirely through Web-based computer conferencing with no campus residency required. It is a convenient and flexible alternative for those who cannot attend a traditional campus because of job schedule, geography, personal commitments, or other limitations. The OLC method of delivery requires the student to have a computer, a modem, and an Internet provider. Upon enrolling, the student's personal academic advisor will suggest classes based upon individual degree needs. The school year is divided into 4 semesters of 15 weeks, with a wide variety of courses from which to choose. Students "attend class" by logging on at their convenience, day or night.

New York University

48 Cooper Square	Phone: (212) 998-9112
New York, NY 10003	Fax: (212) 995-3550

Division(s): The Virtual College
Web Site(s): http://www.sce.nyu.edu/virtual
E-mail: sce.virtual@nyu.edu

Graduate Degree Programs:
Master of Science in Management and Systems (36 credits)

Certificate Programs: Advanced Professional Certificate (APC) in Information Technology (16 credits)

Teaching Methods: *Computers:* Internet, computer conferencing, e-mail, digital video, hypertext readings. *Other:* None.

Admission Requirements: *Graduate:* bachelor's degree, GMAT or GRE, 2 letters of recommendation. *Certificate:* bachelor's degree.

On-Campus Requirements: None.

Tuition and Fees: *Graduate:* $637/credit. *Application Fee:* $50. *Credit by:* semester.

Financial Aid: Federal Stafford Loan, Federal Perkins Loan.

Accreditation: Middle States Association of Colleges and Schools.

Description: New York University was founded in 1831 to meet the educational needs of persons aspiring to careers in business, industry, science, and the arts, as well as in law, medicine, and the ministry. NYU pioneered distance learning in the 1950s with its *Sunrise Semester* TV series, which aired nationally for 25 years. In the spirit of *Sunrise Semester*, NYU introduced the Virtual College in 1992 to expand the spatial and temporal boundaries of learning and to respond to the increasing professional education needs of working adults. Through the Virtual College, students receive instruction, ask questions, conduct analyses, manage projects, and complete assignments—all at their own convenience and from practically anywhere. The teleprogram network provides an electronic workplace for students and faculty, allowing them to go from just talking about course projects to actually completing them. All Virtual College course work is conducted from the student's home or office PC; no on-campus sessions are required.

Newman University

3100 McCormick Avenue	Phone: (316) 942-4291 x241
Wichita, KS 67060	Fax: (316) 942-4483

Division(s): Community Education
Web Site(s): http://www.newmanu.edu
E-mail: nortons@newmanu.edu

Undergraduate Degree Programs:
Bachelor of Science in:
    Business Management
    Nursing, RN completion

Graduate Degree Programs:
Master of Science Education in:
    Adult Education
    Elementary Education
    Middle Level Education
    English as a Second Language

Certificate Programs: Pastoral Ministries (in conjunction with the Diocese of Dodge City), Catholic Building Leadership (in conjunction with the Diocese of Oklahoma City).

Teaching Methods: *Computers:* e-mail. *TV:* videotape. *Other:* videoconferencing.

Credits Granted for: portfolio assessment, extrainstitutional learning, examination (CLEP, ACT-PEP, DANTES, GRE).

Admission Requirements: *Undergraduate:* contact school for specific requirements. *Graduate:* contact school for specific requirements. *Certificate:* contact Sr. Margaret Knoeber, Director of the Pastoral Ministry program at (316) 227-9616.

On-Campus Requirements: certain components of these programs are taught in a traditional classroom setting at our outreach sites as well as on campus. Consult school for program specifics.

Tuition and Fees: *Undergraduate:* please consult with the school for specific program costs. *Credit by:* semester.

Financial Aid: Federal Stafford Loan, Federal Perkins Loan, Federal PLUS Loan, Federal Pell Grant, Federal Work-Study, VA, Kansas resident programs.

Accreditation: North Central Association of Colleges and Schools.

Description: Newman University (1933 as Sacred Hearts College) is an independent, coeducational Catholic college which incorporates career-oriented disciplines within its liberal arts curriculum. As an institution of higher learning, the university challenges individuals to come to an ever expanding awareness of themselves and their world through reason and experience.

North Arkansas College

1515 Pioneer Drive	Phone: (870) 391-3217
Harrison, AR 72601	Fax: (870) 391-3250

Division(s): Vice President of Instruction
Web Site(s): http://pioneer.northark.cc.ar.us
E-mail: gwatts@northark.cc.ar.us

Class Titles: courses toward Associate of Arts, Associate of Science, Associate of Applied Science, and toward certificates in Business: Auto Body Repair, Automotive Mechanics, Construction Equipment Operation, Electronics, Carpentry, Heating/Ventilation/Air Conditioning, Machine Shop, Practical Nursing, Surgical Technology, Welding.

Teaching Methods: *Computers:* Internet, e-mail. *TV:* videotape, cable program, 2-way interactive TV, PBS. *Other:* independent study.

Credits Granted for: extrainstitutional learning, examination (CLEP, ACT-PEP, DANTES, GRE).

Admission Requirements: *Undergraduate:* application, ACT/COMPASS Test scores.

On-Campus Requirements: None.

Tuition and Fees: *Undergraduate:* $36/credit in-county, $45/credit out-of-county, $91/credit out-of-state. *Other Costs:* $3/credit activity fee. *Credit by:* semester.

Financial Aid: Federal Stafford Loan, Federal Perkins Loan, Federal PLUS Loan, Federal Pell Grant, Federal Work-Study, VA, Arkansas resident programs.

Accreditation: North Central Association of Colleges and Schools, Commission on Institute of Higher Education.

Description: North Arkansas College (1974) is a public, comprehensive community college serving 7 counties in Northern Arkansas. The college offers 2-year transfer and technical degree programs, one-year technical certificates, certificates of proficiency, customized business and industry training, ABE-GED classes, and noncredit community education courses. Since 1995, Northark has expanded its distance learning program to include the following: college level courses offered to area high schools via interactive TV, bachelor's degrees in nursing and human resource development, master's degrees in adult and vocational education, master's level courses in nursing and education via interactive TV from AR universities, and Internet-based courses.

North Carolina State University

218 McKimmon Center	
Campus Box 7401	Phone: (919) 515-7730
Raleigh, NC 27695	Fax: (919) 515-5778

Division(s): Instructional Telecommunications
Web Site(s): http://www2.ncsu.edu/oit/
E-mail: oit@ncsu.edu

Certificate Programs: Training and Development

Class Titles: Accounting, Adult/Community College Education (graduate level), Biology, Botany, Business, Calculus, Chemistry, Communication, Economics, English, French, History, Horticulture, Logic, Mathematics, Music, Nutrition, Parks/Recreation/Tourism Management, Philosophy, Physical Education, Political Science, Psychology, Spanish, Statistics, Textiles.

Teaching Methods: *Computers:* Internet. *TV:* videotape, cable program. *Other:* None.

Admission Requirements: *Undergraduate:* high school diploma or GED, or admissions office permission. *Graduate:* bachelor's degree. *Certificate:* bachelor's degree.

On-Campus Requirements: Many courses completed without campus visits; lab courses require campus attendance.

Tuition and Fees: *Undergraduate:* $409/3-credit video course. *Graduate:* $538/3-credit course. *Other Costs:* textbooks. *Credit by:* semester.

Financial Aid: Available for students in degree programs or admittance courses.

Accreditation: Southern Association of Colleges and Schools.

Description: Founded in 1887, North Carolina State University serves the people of the state and nation under the provisions of the national Land Grant Act. As part of its commitment to public education, the university began offering distance education in 1976 to those unable to enroll in on-campus courses due to time, schedule, location, or other constraints. Students complete their degree or other educational goals through a diverse course selection offered via cable, Internet, and video.

North Central Bible College

910 Elliot Avenue S	Phone: (612) 343-4433
Minneapolis, MN 55424	Fax: (612) 343-4435

Division(s): The Carlson Institute for Church Leadership
Web Site(s): None.
E-mail: Carlinst@NCBC.edu

Undergraduate Degree Programs:
Associate of Arts in:
   Christian Studies
   Church Ministries

Bachelor of Arts in:
Christian Studies
Church Ministries

Certificate Programs: One-Year Bible.

Teaching Methods: *TV:* videotape. *Other:* audiotapes, fax, correspondence, independent study, individual study, learning contracts.

Credits Granted for: experiential learning, portfolio assessment, extrainstitutional learning, examination (CLEP, ACT-PEP, DANTES, GRE).

Admission Requirements: *Undergraduate:* no admissions; just fill out an order form for the courses. *Certificate:* see undergraduate.

On-Campus Requirements: None.

Tuition and Fees: *Undergraduate:* $79/credit. *Application Fee:* $30. *Other Costs:* books/materials (approximately $60/course). *Credit by:* semester.

Financial Aid: VA.

Accreditation: North Central Association of Colleges and Schools.

Description: North Central Bible College (1930) is an independent, religious, 4-year college affiliated with the Assemblies of God. The first distant learning courses were offered in 1991.

North Central Technical College

| 1441 Kenwood Circle | Phone: (888) 755-4899 |
| Mansfield, OH 44906 | Fax: (419) 755-4750 |

Division(s): Vice President for Academic Services
Web Site(s): http://www.nctc.tec.oh.us
E-mail: pmoir@nctc.tec.oh.us

Undergraduate Degree Programs:
Associate of Applied Business
Associate in Applied Science

Certificate Programs: Business, Engineering/Corporate Services, Health Sciences.

Class Titles: Accounting, Business Administration, Computer Information Systems, Criminal Justice, Early Childhood Education, Paralegal Studies, Restaurant/Hotel Management, Culinary Arts, Drafting/Design Technology, Electronic Engineering Technology, Electrical Maintenance, Heating/Ventilation/Air Conditioning Manufacturing Engineering Technology, Mechanical Engineering Technology, Operations Management Technology, Tool/Die, Welding, Nursing, Human Services, Massage Therapy, Pharmacy Technology, Physical Therapist Assistant, Practical Nursing, Radiological Sciences, Respiratory Therapy Technology, Therapeutic Recreation, Basic Police Training Academy, Business Management, Certified Purchasing Manager, Child Development Associate, Firstline Leadership, Food Preparation, General Banking, Institutional Food Service, International Trade, Microcomputer Applications, Microsoft Office, Networking, Office Computer Skills, PC Repair, Sales/Marketing, Transportation, Biomedical Equipment, Drafting/Design Technology, Electrical Maintenance Technician, Electrical Maintenance Technology, Advanced Telecommunications, Heating/Ventilation/Air Conditioning, Manufacturing, Operations Management, Tool/Die, Tool/Die Management, Welding, Alcohol/Drug Counseling, Behavior Management Aide, Family Service Worker, Mental Retardation, Nonprofit Grant Writing, Pharmacy Technician, Practical Nursing.

Teaching Methods: *Computers:* Internet, e-mail, CD-ROM, LISTSERV. *TV:* videotape. *Other:* videoconferencing, independent study.

Credits Granted for: portfolio assessment, examination (CLEP, ACT-PEP).

Admission Requirements: *Undergraduate:* open admission with placement testing; some programs have limited enrollment. *Certificate:* same as undergraduate.

On-Campus Requirements: contact school for more information.

Tuition and Fees: *Undergraduate:* $54/credit. *Other Costs:* variable lab fees. *Credit by:* quarter.

Financial Aid: Federal Stafford Loan, Federal Perkins Loan, Federal PLUS Loan, Federal Pell Grant, Federal Work-Study, VA, Ohio resident programs.

Accreditation: North Central Association of Colleges and Schools.

Description: North Central Technical College (1969), a public institution of higher education, is committed to providing comprehensive, occupationally oriented associate degree programs, certificate programs, customized business and industry training, noncredit courses, and other educational and community services. The primary mission of the college is to respond with continued excellence to the varied educational needs and interests of the citizens in the communities we serve. Since this is an ever-changing condition, we are constantly reviewing, improving, and expanding our programs, services, activities, and structure in order to maintain relevancy and responsiveness. Currently the course offerings via distance learning are limited, but the numbers are increasing. Call for a listing of the available courses.

North Central University

910 Elliot Avenue S
Minneapolis, MN 55404

Phone: (800) 446-1176
(612) 343-4430
Fax: (612) 343-4435

Division(s): Carlson Institute
Web Site(s): http://www.ncbc.edu
E-mail: carlinst@ncbc.edu

Undergraduate Degree Programs:
Associate of Arts in Bible/Theology
Associate of Arts in Christian Education
Bachelor of Arts in:
    Christian Education
    Christian Studies
    Church Ministries

Certificate Programs: One-Year Bible.

Teaching Methods: *TV:* videotape. *Other:* audiotapes, textbooks, study guides, individual study.

Credits Granted for: portfolio assessment, examination (CLEP).

Admission Requirements: *Undergraduate:* age 22, live outside the 100-mile radius of our campus, high school diploma or GED. *Certificate:* same as undergraduate.

On-Campus Requirements: None.

Tuition and Fees: *Undergraduate:* $79/credit. *Application Fee:* $30. *Other Costs:* $40 orientation fee. *Credit by:* semester (students may enroll at any time through our distance education program).

Financial Aid: VA benefits, GI Bill.

Accreditation: North Central Association of Schools and Colleges.

Description: Carlson Institute is the distance education department of North Central University (1930), formerly the North Central Bible College. The institute is named in honor of G. Raymond Carlson, former general superintendent of the Assemblies of God, our school's affiliation. Reverend Carlson is also a past president of North Central University. Since 1991, the purpose of the Carlson Institute has been to contribute to the overall mission of NCU by providing nontraditional programs of adult education with a Christian world view for those who cannot participate on the main campus, thus equipping them for ministry in the church and marketplace through excellence in curricula and services.

North Dakota State University

1320 Albrecht Boulevard
Fargo, ND 58105

Phone: (701) 231-7100
(701) 231-1090/8944
Fax: (701) 231-7016/8520

Division(s): Continuing Education, Information Technology Services, Extension
Web Site(s): http://www.ndsu.nodak.edu/conted
http://www.ndsu.nodak.edu/ndsu/resources/infores/ivn.html
http://www.ag.ndsu.nodak.edu/
E-mail: nolson@plains.nodak.edu
tacummin@badlands.nodak.edu

Graduate Degree Programs:
Master of Business Administration
Master of Education Administration

Class Titles: Math, Computer Science, Counseling, Education, Child Development/Family Science, Speech/Communications, Business, University Studies, Health/Physical Education, Animal/Range Science, English, Physics, Engineering, Food/Nutrition, Anthropology, Nursing, Pharmacy, Zoology, Botany, Geology, Architecture, Art, Music.

Teaching Methods: *Computers:* Internet, real-time chat, electronic classroom, e-mail, CD-ROM, LISTSERV. *TV:* videotape. *Other:* videoconferencing, fax, correspondence, independent study, individual study.

Credits Granted for: experiential learning, portfolio assessment, examination (CLEP, ACT-PEP, DANTES, GRE).

Admission Requirements: *Graduate:* degree-specific, acceptance into graduate school; contact school.

On-Campus Requirements: None.

Tuition and Fees: *Undergraduate:* variable. *Graduate:* $115/credit variable. *Doctoral:* variable. *Application Fee:* $35 variable. *Other Costs:* variable. *Credit by:* semester.

Financial Aid: Federal Stafford Loan, Federal Perkins Loan, Federal PLUS Loan, Federal Pell Grant, Federal Work-Study, VA, North Dakota resident programs.

Accreditation: North Central Association of Colleges and Schools.

Description: North Dakota State University (1890), a land-grant institution, provides instruction, research, and public service through its colleges, experiment station, and extension service. People are educated and served by the discovery, communication, application, and preservation of knowledge. The personal growth of individuals is fostered by creating an environment that nurtures intellectual, social, and cultural development. Academic and professional programs are offered that lead to bachelor's through doctorate degrees. NDSU assumes a coordinating role in the North Dakota University System for academic computing and economic development. Mission values include people, scholarship, the idea of a university, and the land-grant ideal. As a land-grant institution, NDSU has offered outreach programs throughout most of its history. This effort is broadening as technologies develop to provide quality educational opportunities.

North Georgia College and State University

South Chestatee	Phone: (706) 864-1844
Dahlonega, GA 30597	Fax: (706) 864-1886

Division(s): Information Technology, Education Building
Web Site(s): http://www.ngc.peachnet.edu/
E-mail: temoseley@nugget.ngc.peachnet.edu

Class Titles: Graduate School of Education—Foundations of Education, Classroom Psychology, Educational Research, Educational Leadership; Graduate School of Business/Government—Master of Public Administration core courses, Seminar in Public Administration, Statistics for Public Administration, Policy Analysis, Public Budgeting.

Teaching Methods: *Computers:* Internet, electronic classroom, e-mail, CD-ROM, LISTSERV. *TV:* videotape, satellite broadcasting (including PBS satellite programs). *Other:* audioconferencing, videoconferencing, fax.

Credits Granted for: examination. For further information contact school or see catalog.

Admission Requirements: *Undergraduate:* age 16 with good moral character, approved high school graduate, CPC exam, entrance exam, college preparatory classes (students may be able to make up credit deficiency), immunization certification, NGC/SU medical report. For more information, transfer students and others may contact Dr. Tom Davis at: tdavis@nugget.ngc.peachnet.edu *Graduate:* bachelor's degree, GPA, application, MAT or GRE, immunization certification, official transcripts. For more information, write: Dean of Graduate Programs, North Georgia College and State University, Dahlonega, GA 30597.

On-Campus Requirements: No complete degree programs are offered at this time. Students attend classes here, on the main campus, or at a collaborative institution.

Tuition and Fees: *Undergraduate:* $865/credit. *Graduate:* $1,000/credit. *Application Fee:* $25. *Software:* course specific. *Other Costs:* see catalog, or for more information, contact the director of admissions, Dr. Tom Davis, at tdavis@nugget.ngc.peachnet.edu. *Credit by:* semester.

Financial Aid: Federal Pell Grants, Grants, Federal Supplemental Educational Opportunity Grant, Student Incentive Grant, Regent's Opportunity Grant, North Georgia College and State University Music Scholarships, Gloria Shott Scholarship,

Georgia Military Scholarship, North Georgia College and State University Scholarships, Gordon Elwood Crowfoot Rotary Scholarship, Eugene C. Patterson Scholarship, Regents' Scholarship, Federal Perkins Loan, Brown Loan Fund, Federal Family Education Loan SGS and Class of '62 Loan Fund, Service-Cancellable Loan, Pickett and Hatcher Education Federal Work-Study Program. For more information, contact the director of admissions, Dr. Tom Davis, at: tdavis@nugget.ngc.peachnet.edu

Accreditation: Southern Association of Colleges and Schools, National Council for Accreditation of Teacher Education, Georgia Professional Standards Commission.

Description: North Georgia College and State University (1873) is a traditional liberal arts college nestled in the Blue Ridge Mountains and is one of an elite group of publicly supported, coeducational, military, liberal arts colleges. NGCSU began as a land-grant school of agriculture and mechanical arts, particularly mining engineering. Its mission evolved to emphasize arts and sciences as gold resources diminished and the University of Georgia assumed agricultural education. Georgia has developed an audio/video, 2-way, interactive, compressed TV network with 400 sites. With online courses and other resources, this statewide effort provides educational opportunities to all citizens. The school is one of 34 schools in the University System of Georgia.

North Iowa Area Community College

500 College Drive	Phone: (515) 422-4326
Mason City, IA 50401	Fax: (515) 423-1711

Division(s): Academic Affairs/Telecommunications
Web Site(s): http://www.niacc.cc.ia.us
E-mail: mozaclar@niacc.cc.ia.us

Undergraduate Degree Programs:
Associate in Arts

Class Titles: Communication, Geography of Non-Western World, Ethics, Human Growth/Development, Management, Statistics, Psychology, U.S. Government, American History to 1865, American History 1865–Present, Cultural Anthropology.

Teaching Methods: *Computers:* Internet, real-time chat, electronic classroom, e-mail, CD-ROM, newsgroup, LISTSERV. *TV:* videotape, cable program, satellite broadcasting, PBS. *Other:* radio broadcast, audioconferencing, videoconferencing, audiographics, audiotapes, fax, correspondence, independent study, individual study, learning contracts.

Credits Granted for: experiential learning, portfolio assessment, examination (CLEP, ACT-PEP, DANTES, GRE).

Admission Requirements: *Undergraduate:* Open-door policy.

On-Campus Requirements: None.

Tuition and Fees: *Undergraduate:* $75/credit. *Credit by:* semester.

Financial Aid: Federal Stafford Loan, Federal Perkins Loan, Federal PLUS Loan, Federal Pell Grant, Federal Work-Study, VA, Iowa resident programs.

Accreditation: North Central Association of Colleges and Schools.

Description: Founded in 1918, North Iowa Area Community College is the first public 2-year college in Iowa and one of the first in the country. The college has long been an innovator in 2-year higher education. NIACC has offered distance education since 1980 utilizing telecourses, directed study (correspondence), interactive TV, and most recently the Internet.

Northampton Community College

3835 Green Pond Road	Phone: (610) 861-5300
Bethlehem, PA 18020	Fax: (610) 861-5373

Division(s): Instructional Services/Distance Learning
Web Site(s): http://www.nrhm.cc.pa.us
E-mail: chh@mail.nrhm.cc.pa.us

Undergraduate Degree Programs:
Bachelor of Science in:
  Business Administration
  General Studies

Certificate Programs: Specialized diplomas in Library Technical Assistant and Home-Based Child Care.

Class Titles: contact school.

Teaching Methods: *Computers:* Internet, Spring 1999. *TV:* videotape, cable program, PBS. *Other:* videoconferencing, correspondence.

Credits Granted for: experiential learning, portfolio assessment, CLEP.

Admission Requirements: *Undergraduate:* open admission.

On-Campus Requirements: None.

Tuition and Fees: *Undergraduate:* $63 county, $126 out-of-county. *Application Fee:* $13 county, $32 out-of-county. *Credit by:* semester.

Financial Aid: Federal Stafford Loan, Federal Perkins Loan, Federal PLUS Loan, Federal Pell Grant, Federal Work-Study.

Accreditation: Middle States Association of Colleges and Schools.

Description: Northampton Community College (1965) began distance education 20 years ago with correspondence courses. Today more than 60 courses open every week. Ten years ago telecourses were added. Today there are 16 telecourses.

For spring 1999, 20 Internet courses and tele-webs will join the offerings. Two degree and two specialized diplomas may be achieved through distance learning.

Northeast Louisiana University

101 University Avenue	Phone: (318) 342-1030
Monroe, LA 71209	Fax: (318) 342-1049

Division(s): Continuing Education
Web Site(s): http://www.nlu.edu
E-mail: cetownsend@alpha.nlu.edu or ceupshaw@alpha.nlu.edu

Undergraduate Degree Programs:
Associate Degree in General Studies/College of Liberal Arts

Teaching Methods: *Computers:* Internet, real-time chat, electronic classroom, e-mail, CD-ROM, LISTSERV. *TV:* videotape, cable program, satellite broadcasting, PBS. *Other:* videoconferencing, audiotapes, fax, compressed video.

Credits Granted for: extrainstitutional learning, examination (CLEP, ACT-PEP, DANTES, GRE).

Admission Requirements: *Undergraduate:* open-admissions, accredited high school diploma, ACT score of 17 or higher. See Web site at http://www.nlu.edu.

On-Campus Requirements: depends on the course and the instructor. Arrangements can generally be made at an off-campus site.

Tuition and Fees: *Undergraduate:* $80/credit. *Graduate:* $80/credit. *Doctoral:* $80/credit. *Application Fee:* $15. *Software:* $15. *Other Costs:* $40 distance education fee. *Credit by:* semester.

Financial Aid: Federal Stafford Loan, Federal Perkins Loan, Federal PLUS Loan, Federal Pell Grant, Federal Work-Study, VA, Louisiana resident programs (TOPS).

Accreditation: Southern Association of Colleges and Schools.

Description: Northeast Louisiana University (1932) entered distance education in 1983 with LPB and PBS.

Northeastern State University

600 North Grand	Phone: (918) 456-5511 x2060
Tahlequah, OK 74464	Fax: (918) 458-2061

Division(s): Office of Academic Affairs
Web Site(s): http://www.nsuok.edu
E-mail: nowlin@cherokee.nsuok.edu

Undergraduate Degree Programs:
Courses only

Class Titles: Accounting, Business Law, Marketing, Management, Meetings/Destination Management, Nursing (+2), Education.

Teaching Methods: *Computers:* e-mail, LISTSERV. *Other:* videoconferencing, audioconferencing.

Credits Granted for: examination (CLEP, ACT-PEP, DANTES, GRE).

Admission Requirements: *Undergraduate:* high school graduate or GED; high school GPA of 2.70; ranked in upper 50% of graduating class, or ACT composite of 20. Need 15 units of required high school courses (4 English, 2 Lab Science, 3 Math, 2 History, 1 Citizenship, 3 other subjects). *Graduate:* bachelor's degree, scores no more than 5 years old on appropriate aptitude test (Miller Analogies Test or GRE), undergraduate GPA of 2.5 (or 2.75 in the last 60 hours), proof of citizenship for U.S. citizens born outside U.S. and for resident aliens, TOEFL score of 550 for all U.S. citizen applicants or international applicants for whom English is a second language.

On-Campus Requirements: 30 hours of residency with Northeastern State University.

Tuition and Fees: *Undergraduate:* $59/credit, lower division; $138/credit, nonresident lower division; $60/credit, upper division; $148/credit, nonresident upper division. *Graduate:* $75/credit, resident; $177/credit, nonresident. *Other Costs:* $25 records fee, $2 cultural scholastic fee, $20/credit remedial course fee. *Credit by:* semester.

Financial Aid: Federal Stafford Loan, Federal Perkins Loan, Federal PLUS Loan, Federal Pell Grant, Federal Work-Study, VA, Oklahoma resident programs.

Accreditation: North Central Association of Colleges and Schools.

Description: Northeastern State University (1909) is one of six regional universities in Oklahoma. It offers 65 undergraduate degrees, 13 graduate degrees, and one doctoral degree in Optometry. Northeastern State University began offering distance education courses to limited sites in Oklahoma by interactive videoconferencing in the fall of 1997.

Northeastern University

360 Huntington Avenue, 328 C.P.	Phone: (617) 373-5620
Boston, MA 02115	Fax: (617) 373-5625

Division(s): Network Northeastern
Web Site(s): http://www.neu.edu/network-nu
E-mail: Mperkins@lynx.neu.edu

Graduate Degree Programs:
Master of Science in:
  Electrical and Computer Engineering

Computer Science
Information Systems

Certificate Programs: UNIX/C++, Webmaster Technology and Internet Technologies (online).

Class Titles: Algebra, Calculus, Physics.

Teaching Methods: *Computers:* Internet, real-time chat, electronic classroom, e-mail, CD-ROM, newsgroup, LISTSERV. *TV:* videotape, cable program, satellite broadcasting, PBS. *Other:* radio broadcast, audioconferencing, videoconferencing, audiographics, audiotapes, fax, correspondence, independent study, individual study, learning contracts.

Credits Granted for: experiential learning, portfolio assessment, association seminars/workshops, examination (CLEP, ACT-PEP, DANTES, GRE).

Admission Requirements: *Undergraduate:* open enrollment. *Graduate:* GRE in some cases.

On-Campus Requirements: None.

Tuition and Fees: *Undergraduate:* $210/credit. *Graduate:* $465/credit. *Application Fee:* $50. *Credit by:* quarter.

Financial Aid: Federal Stafford Loan, Federal Perkins Loan, Federal PLUS Loan, Federal Pell Grant, Federal Work-Study, VA, Massachusetts resident programs.

Accreditation: Accreditation Board for Engineering and Technology.

Description: Northeastern University (1898) is located in the heart of Boston and is a practice-oriented, student-centered, urban university dedicated to high-quality teaching and research.

Northern Kentucky University

Nunn Drive	Phone: (606) 572-5601
Highland Heights, KY 41099	Fax: (606) 572-5174

Division(s): Credit Continuing Education and Distance Learning
Web Site(s): http://www.nku.edu
E-mail: hedgesb@nku.edu

Class Titles: call (606) 572-5601 or e-mail hedgesb@nku.edu.

Teaching Methods: *Computers:* Internet, real-time chat, electronic classroom, e-mail, LISTSERV. *TV:* videotape, cable program, PBS. *Other:* videoconferencing.

Credits Granted for: experiential learning, portfolio assessment, extrainstitutional learning, examination (CLEP).

Admission Requirements: *Undergraduate:* ACT, high school diploma or GED, Kentucky PreCollege Curriculum Requirements. *Graduate:* varies by program.

On-Campus Requirements: orientation/testing for some courses.

Tuition and Fees: *Undergraduate:* $94/credit resident, $254/credit nonresident. *Graduate:* $132/credit resident, $368/credit nonresident. *Application Fee:* $25. *Other Costs:* $1/credit (support of learning surcharge). *Credit by:* semester.

Financial Aid: Federal Stafford Loan, Federal Perkins Loan, Federal PLUS Loan, Federal Pell Grant, Federal Work-Study, VA, Kentucky and Indiana resident programs.

Accreditation: Southern Association of Colleges and Schools.

Description: Northern Kentucky University's (1968) distance learning options are currently limited, but significant growth is expected during the next 5 years.

Northern State University

1200 South Jay Street	Phone: (605) 626-2568
Aberdeen, SD 57401	Fax: (605) 626-2542

Division(s): Continuing Education
Web Site(s): http://lupus.northern.edu
E-mail: winthert@wolf.northern.edu

Class Titles: Algebra, College Algebra, Trigonometry, Calculus, Foundations of Math, Algebra/Geometry for Elementary Schools, U.S. History, State/Local Government, Sociology, Courtship/Marriage, Family, Technology/Society, Special Problems in Metric Measurement, Survey of Business, Math for Business, Personal Finance, Human Resources Management, Educational Psychology.

Teaching Methods: *Computers:* Internet, e-mail. *TV:* videotape, cable program, satellite broadcasting. *Other:* fax, correspondence.

Credits Granted for: examination (CLEP, ACT-PEP, DANTES, GRE).

Admission Requirements: *Undergraduate:* high school diploma, GED.

On-Campus Requirements: yes for regular degrees.

Tuition and Fees: *Undergraduate:* $83/credit. *Other Costs:* $25/course processing fee, deposit for tapes. *Credit by:* semester.

Accreditation: North Central Association of Colleges and Schools, National Council for Accreditation of Teacher Education, institutional member of University Continuing Education Association.

Description: Northern State University (1901) is a multipurpose regional institution of higher education founded as a normal and industrial school to serve the northern part of the state. The university has since diversified its offerings to address the emerging needs of the students, community, and region. Teacher preparation remains an important feature of the institutional mission, as do programs in the arts and sciences, business, and fine arts. Through undergraduate and graduate programs, the university provides quality teaching and learning. Offering students a breadth and depth in the liberal arts and in professional studies, NSU develops effective and productive professionals and citizens. Further, the university creates and nurtures a community of students, faculty, and staff, supporting communication, student and faculty research, and professional growth. Northern State has designed programs to meet academic, social, cultural, and economic needs of the community and area, providing lifelong learning opportunities, a center for the arts and recreation, and support for regional development.

Northern Virginia Community College

8333 Little River Turnpike	Phone: (703) 323-3368
Annandale, VA 22003-3796	(800) 627-5443
	Fax: (703) 323-3392

Division(s): Extended Learning Institute
Web Site(s): http://eli.nv.cc.va.us
E-mail: nvtownj@nv.cc.va.us

Undergraduate Degree Programs:
Associate in Science in Business Administration
Associate in Science in Engineering
Associate in Science in General Studies

Certificate Programs: Health Information Technology

Class Titles: see Web site for 120 courses offered.

Teaching Methods: *Computers:* Internet, e-mail, CD-ROM, computer conferencing. *TV:* videotape, cable program, PBS, compressed video (only in Virginia). *Other:* voice-mail conferencing, audiotapes, fax, correspondence, independent study, individual study.

Credits Granted for: experiential learning, portfolio assessment, extrainstitutional learning (military service school courses), examination (CLEP, ABLE, AP, DANTES, GED, ABLE).

Admission Requirements: *Undergraduate:* high school diploma or equivalent, age 18, specific requirements to each individual curriculum.

On-Campus Requirements: Average of 3 proctored activities (e.g., exams, laboratories); local proctoring possible.

Tuition and Fees: *Undergraduate:* $48/credit in-state, $162/credit out-of-state. *Credit by:* semester.

Financial Aid: William D. Ford Federal Direct Loan, Federal Perkins Loan, Federal Pell Grant, Federal Work-Study, Federal

Supplemental Educational Opportunity Grant, VA, Virginia residents (CSAP, VCCS grants).

Accreditation: Southern Association of Colleges and Schools.

Description: Northern Virginia Community College, founded in 1964, began its Extended Learning Institute in 1975, making it one of the nation's oldest, largest, and most successful distance education programs. ELI's purpose was to extend educational opportunities to the northern Virginia community. Since then, ELI has enrolled more than 160,000 students nationwide, and it currently offers 120 courses with 10,000 students annually. ELI provides courses for those who cannot or prefer not to attend regular classes on campus. Instruction includes TV, computers, audiocassettes, videocassettes, and printed materials designed especially for independent study. ELI also offers continuous enrollment for most courses; students can register any day the college is open.

Northwest Iowa Community College

603 West Park Street	Phone: (712) 324-5061
Sheldon, IA 51201	Fax: (712) 324-4136

Division(s): Iowa Communications Network
Web Site(s): http://nwicc.cc.ia.us
E-mail: cscott@nwicc.cc.ia.us

Undergraduate Degree Programs:
Associate of:
    Arts
    Science
    Technical Programs

Certificate Programs: Contact us for program list.

Teaching Methods: *TV:* satellite broadcasting, PBS. *Other:* independent study, individual study, learning contracts, videoconferencing via the fiber optic Iowa Communications Network.

Credits Granted for: corporate or professional association seminars/workshops, examination (CLEP, ACT-PEP, DANTES, GRE).

Admission Requirements: *Undergraduate:* high school or other transcripts, ASSET test, ACT or SAT.

On-Campus Requirements: None.

Tuition and Fees: *Undergraduate:* $56/credit. *Other Costs:* $3/credit Student Fee. *Credit by:* semester.

Financial Aid: Federal Stafford Loan, Federal PLUS Loan, Federal Pell Grant, Federal Work-Study, VA, Iowa Vocational Technical grants, SEOG grants.

Accreditation: North Central Association of Colleges and Schools.

Description: NCC is a 2-year community college providing a wide range of services to the communities and citizens of northwest Iowa. The college offers a comprehensive educational program, including many vocational-technical programs and a solid core of academic offerings that help develop a broadly educated person.

Northwest Missouri State University

800 University Drive	Phone: (660) 562-1113
Maryville, MO 64468	Fax: (660) 562-1900

Division(s): Northwest Missouri Educational Consortium
Web Site(s): http://www.nwmissouri.edu/nmec/
E-mail: FVEEMAN@mail.nwmissouri.edu

Undergraduate Degree Programs:
Bachelor of Science in Business

Graduate Degree Programs:
Master of Science in Education

Doctoral Degree Programs:
Doctorate of Education (EdD)

Teaching Methods: *Computers:* Internet (being developed), real-time chat, electronic classroom, e-mail, CD-ROM. *Other:* radio broadcast, videoconferencing.

Credits Granted for: experiential learning, portfolio assessment, extrainstitutional learning, examination (CLEP, ACT-PEP, DANTES, GRE).

Admission Requirements: *Undergraduate:* 2.0 high school GPA, 21 ACT composite (or SAT equivalent). Northwest accepts students regardless of age, race, creed, sex, color, religion, national origin, or handicap. *Graduate:* 2.5 undergraduate GPA, GRE/GMAT. Students with 2.2 cumulative undergraduate GPA may be admitted but must achieve a 3.0 GPA in first 8 semester hours. Accredited bachelor's degree needed for students seeking nondegree admission for professional growth.

On-Campus Requirements: None.

Tuition and Fees: *Undergraduate:* $91/credit Missouri resident, $158/credit nonresident. *Graduate:* $113/credit Missouri resident, $197/credit nonresident. *Software:* $90/ year. *Other Costs:* $3,890/year room and board. *Credit by:* semester.

Financial Aid: Federal Direct Loan (subsidized), Federal Direct Loan (unsubsidized), Federal Perkins Loan, Federal PLUS Loan, Federal Pell Grant, Federal Work-Study, Missouri resident programs.

Accreditation: North Central Association of Colleges and Schools.

Description: Northwest Missouri State University has distinguished itself among American universities in at least 2 areas: our electronic campus and our "Culture of Quality" initiative to continuously improve every aspect of our institution. Northwest Missouri State is a moderately selective, learner-centered, regional university offering a focused range of undergraduate and graduate programs. The university serves 19 northwest Missouri counties, emphasizing programs related to agriculture, business, and education.

Northwest Technical College

2022 Central Avenue NE	Phone: (218) 773-4575
East Grand Forks, MN 56721	Fax: (218) 773-4502

Division(s): Distance Education
Web Site(s): http://www.ntconline.com
E-mail: thompsonl@mail.ntc.mnscu.edu

Undergraduate Degree Programs:
Associate of Applied Science

Class Titles: Accounting, Algebra, Medical, Electronics, General Education.

Teaching Methods: *Computers:* Internet, e-mail, CD-ROM, virtual classroom software. *Other:* fax, correspondence, independent study, individual study.

Credits Granted for: experiential learning, portfolio assessment.

Admission Requirements: *Undergraduate:* entrance exam. *Certificate:* entrance exam.

On-Campus Requirements: None.

Tuition and Fees: *Undergraduate:* $68/credit in-state, $137/credit out-of-state. *Application Fee:* $20. *Other Costs:* $2/credit state fees, varies for books/course materials. *Credit by:* semester.

Financial Aid: Federal Stafford Loan, Federal Perkins Loan, Federal Pell Grant, Federal Work-Study, VA, Minnesota resident programs.

Accreditation: North Central Association of Colleges and Schools.

Description: Northwest Technical College (1992) is a regional technical college with 5 campuses serving northwestern Minnesota. Its primary mission is to provide quality occupational education to individuals, business, industry, and society in response to a changing world. The college provides industry-validated technical and general education curricula that are designed to meet a variety of career choices and that lead to the award of certificates, diplomas, or associate in applied science degrees. Distance Education was born in 1995 out of our changing societal needs and the rural area we live in. Knowing students would travel 2 hours round trip to attend classes everyday, we needed to find a better way. We began by writing general education curriculum in corre-

spondence delivery. In 1997 we then upgraded to Internet delivery. Last year we began implementing virtual classroom software. Our course offerings now include 58 courses, and we are slated to deliver 3 AAS programs by the fall of '99.

Northwestern College

1441 North Cable Road	Phone: (419) 227-3141
Lima, OH 45875	Fax: (419) 998-3080

Division(s): Vice President for Academic Affairs
Web Site(s): http://www.nc.edu
E-mail: info@nc.edu

Undergraduate Degree Programs:
Associate of Applied Business in:
 Business Administration
 Marketing
 Automotive Management
 Accounting
 Agribusiness Marketing/Management Technology
 Business Computer Applications
 Medical Office Assistant Technology
 Travel Management
Bachelor degrees (approval pending)

Certificate Programs: Agribusiness Management, Retail Merchandising, Travel/Tourism, Medical Office Assistant.

Teaching Methods: *Computers:* Internet, real-time chat, e-mail. *Other:* fax, correspondence, independent study, individual study, learning contracts.

Credits Granted for: experiential learning, portfolio assessment.

Admission Requirements: *Undergraduate:* age 22+, preferably employed, personal or telephone interview. *Certificate:* same as undergraduate.

On-Campus Requirements: None.

Tuition and Fees: *Undergraduate:* $126/credit. *Application Fee:* $50. *Credit by:* quarter.

Financial Aid: Federal Stafford Loan, Federal PLUS Loan, Federal Pell Grant, Federal Work-Study, VA, Ohio resident programs.

Accreditation: North Central Association of Colleges and Schools.

Description: Founded in 1920, Northwestern College is a private, coeducational, not-for-profit institution that began offering distance learning in 1993. The Ohio Board of Regents authorizes the college to grant associate degrees and diplomas in applied science in the Technological Division and applied business in the Business Division. Northwestern's enrollment averages 1,800 with approximately 982 students living in residence halls. Students can enjoy an on-campus gymnasium, baseball diamond, restaurant, student lounges, and picnic areas.

Northwestern College

3003 Snelling Avenue North	Phone: (651) 631-5494
Saint Paul, MN 55113-1598	(800) 308-5495
	Fax: (651) 631-5133

Division(s): Center for Distance Education
Web Site(s): http://www.nwc.edu/disted/
E-mail: distance.ed.dpt@nwc.edu

Undergraduate Degree Programs:
Intercultural Ministries

Certificate Programs: Bible.

Teaching Methods: *Computers:* Internet, real-time chat, e-mail. *TV:* videotape. *Other:* audiotapes, fax, correspondence, independent study.

Credits Granted for: experiential learning, portfolio assessment, examination (CLEP, ACT-PEP, DANTES, GRE).

Admission Requirements: *Undergraduate:* Evidence of new birth in Jesus Christ, willingness to subscribe to the patterns of life and conduct of the Northwestern community, likelihood of academic success at Northwestern, high school diploma or GED certificate, ACT/SAT scores, financial capability to meet college expenses.

On-Campus Requirements: None.

Tuition and Fees: *Undergraduate:* $120/credit. *Application Fee:* $25 one-time. *Other Costs:* $60/course materials fee. *Credit by:* quarter.

Financial Aid: Federal Stafford Loan, Federal Perkins Loan, Federal PLUS Loan, Federal Pell Grant, Federal Work-Study, VA, Minnesota resident programs.

Accreditation: North Central Association of Colleges and Schools.

Description: Northwestern College (1902) is the only nondenominational private college in Minnesota. The college is an independent enterprise that takes a biblically Christian ethical and moral position with a theologically conservative doctrine. The alumni and its growing radio audience are the college's primary constituencies. The Center for Distance Education provides Christ-centered education and training at college and professional levels. NC's mission is to meet the needs of all students who aspire to an intellectual, reasoned, and healthy Christian worldview, and to help them prepare for productive ministry and occupational performance.

Northwestern Community College

500 Kennedy Drive	Phone: (970) 675-3273
Rangely, CO 81648	Fax: (970) 675-3291

Division(s): Distance Learning
Web Site(s): http://www.cncc.cc.co.us
E-mail: klangston@cncc.cc.co.us

Class Titles: Criminal Justice, Composition, Spanish, Math/Calculus, Forestry, Psychology, Statistics, Computer Science, Economics, Education, Business, Child Development, Sociology, Geography, Anthropology.

Teaching Methods: *Computers:* electronic classroom, e-mail. *TV:* videotape, cable program, satellite broadcasting, PBS. *Other:* videoconferencing, audioconferencing, fax, correspondence, independent study, Individual study.

Credits Granted for: experiential learning, portfolio assessment, examination (CLEP, ACT-PEP).

Admission Requirements: *Undergraduate:* GED or high school graduate, dual enrollments. *Certificate:* interview.

On-Campus Requirements: orientation and testing, some courses have associated labs.

Tuition and Fees: *Undergraduate:* $0/credit in-district residents of one year, $264/semester affiliated district residents, $552/semester in-state residents. *Other Costs:* $35/distance learning course. *Credit by:* semester.

Financial Aid: Federal Stafford Loan, Federal Perkins Loan, Federal PLUS Loan, Federal Pell Grant, Federal Work-Study, VA, Colorado resident programs.

Accreditation: North Central Association of Colleges and Schools.

Description: Colorado Northwestern Community College (1967) is a small district community college serving the northwest region of Colorado. We anticipate joining the state community college system in early 1999. The college began distance learning activities in the form of audio bridge and telecourses. Recently we became a member of the WestCel Consortium and began delivering interactive video courses via a compressed video network. We also distribute Utah State University satellite courses to our campuses and communities via a cable TV educational and community access channel.

Northwestern Michigan College

1701 East Front Street	Phone: (616) 922-8985
Traverse City, MI 49686	Fax: (616) 922-1080

Division(s): Media Services and Distance Education Systems
Web Site(s): http://www.nmc.edu
E-mail: redwards@nmc.edu

Class Titles: Psychology, Sociology, Anthropology, Child Development, Marriage/Family, Business, Marketing, Management, Government, History, Art History, Biology, Business Law, Business Writing, English Composition, Computers in Art, Music Appreciation.

Teaching Methods: *Computers:* Internet, real-time chat, electronic classroom, e-mail, CD-ROM, newsgroup, LISTSERV. *TV:* videotape, cable program, PBS. *Other:* videoconferencing.

Credits Granted for: experiential learning, portfolio assessment, extrainstitutional learning, examination (CLEP).

Admission Requirements: *Undergraduate:* Open access enrollment—must take ASSET test.

On-Campus Requirements: For online courses there is a 2-hour orientation before the course begins. For telecourses there are between 3–6 on-campus sessions through the semester. For ITV courses there are no requirements to come on campus.

Tuition and Fees: *Undergraduate:* $53/contact hour (in-district), $88/contact hour (in-state), $99/contact hour (out-of-state). *Application Fee:* $15 one time only. *Software:* $10–$50/course. *Other Costs:* $8/semester registration fee, $5/semester campus maintenance fee, $11/semester health fee for anyone taking 6 or more credits, $3/contact hour general fee (student government) up to a maximum of 12 contact hours. *Credit by:* semester.

Financial Aid: Federal Stafford Loan, Federal Perkins Loan, Federal PLUS Loan, Federal Pell Grant, Federal Work-Study, VA, Michigan resident programs.

Accreditation: North Central Association of Colleges and Schools.

Description: Northwestern Michigan College (1951) is a comprehensive community college founded by local citizens who wanted to provide an affordable college education for area residents. Starting out in temporary headquarters at the Traverse City airport terminal, NMC now has a spacious, 80-acre main campus. From 65 students and a staff of 6, NMC has grown to 4,000 students and 100 full-time faculty. In 1981 NMC began its distance education program with one telecourse, and now it offers courses in 4 delivery methods including telecourses, online courses, open entry/open exit independent courses, and Interactive TV that connects the main campus to the surrounding 16 high schools with a fiber optic network for voice, video, and data.

Northwestern State University of Louisiana

Williamson Hall	Phone: (318) 357-5682
Natchitoches, LA 71459	Fax: (318) 357-6125

Division(s): Continuing Education
Web Site(s): http://www.nsula.edu
E-mail: yvonne@nsula.edu

Graduate Degree Programs:
Master of Arts in English

Class Titles: Educational Technology, Adult Education, Education, Computer, Math, English, Nursing, more soon.

Teaching Methods: *Computers:* Internet, real-time chat, electronic classroom, e-mail, newsgroup, LISTSERV, compressed video. *TV:* PBS. *Other:* videoconferencing, fax, independent study, individual study.

Credits Granted for: examination (CLEP, ACT, DANTES, GRE).

Admission Requirements: *Undergraduate:* high school graduate/GED, over age 21 can be provisional without either. *Graduate:* GRE, prerequisites for degree. *Certificate:* high school grad/GED, over age 21 can be provisional without either.

On-Campus Requirements: policy in review.

Tuition and Fees: *Undergraduate:* based on hours enrolled; contact school. *Graduate:* based on hours enrolled; contact school. *Application Fee:* $15 U.S., $25 international. *Other Costs:* activity, technology included in tuition. *Credit by:* semester.

Financial Aid: Federal Stafford Loan, Federal Perkins Loan, Federal PLUS Loan, Federal Pell Grant, Federal Work-Study, VA, Louisiana resident programs, Supplemental Educational Opportunity Grant.

Accreditation: Southern Association of Colleges and Schools.

Description: Northwestern State University (1884), originally created for training teachers, has steadily expanded its resources and curricula to meet the increasingly diverse requirements of Louisiana's expanding population. Northwestern is located between Shreveport and Alexandria on a 916-acre site that serves a city of 25,000. NSU is known for its education and nursing programs. Its Nursing Center is located in Shreveport, and the university has 3 satellite campuses (Alexandria, Shreveport, Fort Polk) and 8 off-campus sites within its service region. The university serves a large nontraditional student population that demands nontraditional methods of receiving an education. Thus, technology is the answer.

Northwood University

3225 Cook Road
Midland, MI 48640

Phone: (800) 445-5873
Fax: (517) 837-4457

Division(s): University College
Web Site(s): http://www.northwood.edu
E-mail: beyer@northwood.edu

Undergraduate Degree Programs:
Bachelor of Business Administration

Graduate Degree Programs:
Master of Business Administration (Michigan only)

Class Titles: degree plans available for Management, International Business, Marketing, others.

Teaching Methods: *Other:* fax, correspondence, independent study, individual study, learning contracts. Outreach/extension centers offer nontraditional classroom delivery at more than 30 locations across the U.S.

Credits Granted for: experiential learning, portfolio assessment, extrainstitutional learning, examination (CLEP, ACT-PEP, DANTES, GRE).

Admission Requirements: *Undergraduate:* high school diploma or GED. *Graduate:* GMAT.

On-Campus Requirements: two 3-day seminars and a written/oral examination with campus faculty for independent study students.

Tuition and Fees: *Undergraduate:* $70/credit for independent study. *Graduate:* Michigan residents, call for more information. *Application Fee:* $15. *Other Costs:* $225/credit for on-campus seminars. *Credit by:* quarter.

Financial Aid: Federal Stafford Loan, Federal Perkins Loan, Federal PLUS Loan, Federal Pell Grant, Federal Work-Study, VA, Michigan resident programs.

Accreditation: North Central Association of Colleges and Schools.

Description: Four decades ago, 2 young men with an idea, a goal, and a philosophy created Northwood University (1959). Today, the Northwood idea of incorporating the teachings of the American free enterprise system into college courses is a success. Besides the campus in Midland, other campuses thrive in Cedar Hill, Texas, and West Palm Beach, Florida, with extension centers across the U.S. Northwood is a private, tax-exempt, independent, accredited, coeducational, business- and management-oriented university allied to both business and the arts. Northwood translates its philosophy into practical, useful curriculums designed to prepare students for the working world. Instructors of business are professionals who have chosen to direct their business talents toward preparing students for the work world. Graduates of Northwood have practical, useful management skills and a solid understanding of business, and they immediately become part of the business world.

Notre Dame College

2321 Elm Street
Manchester, NH 03104

Phone: (603) 669-4298
Fax: (603) 644-8316

Division(s): Graduate Theology
Web Site(s): http://www.notredame.edu
E-mail: NDCMinInst@aol.com

Class Titles: Bible, Systematics, Ethics, Ministry (all graduate courses).

Teaching Methods: *Computers:* Internet, real-time chat, e-mail. *Other:* fax.

Admission Requirements: *Graduate:* apply as special student for online courses. Students must be able to access AOL. Contact school for more information.

On-Campus Requirements: None.

Tuition and Fees: *Graduate:* $299/credit. *Other Costs:* $30 late registration fee. *Credit by:* semester and 6-week summer sessions.

Financial Aid: Federal Stafford Loan, Federal Perkins Loan, Federal PLUS Loan, Federal Pell Grant, Federal Work-Study, VA, New Hampshire resident programs.

Accreditation: New England Association of Schools and Colleges.

Description: Notre Dame College (1950) is a 4-year, Catholic, coeducational liberal arts college, founded and sponsored by the Sisters of Holy Cross. The college community includes approximately 1,400 full- and part-time, graduate, undergraduate, and life-long learning students and more than 100 full- and part-time faculty. The mission of the college is education of the whole person, mind, heart, body, spirit. This holistic education is geared toward preparing students for leadership and service to their profession, their local community, their church, and society-at-large. Since its beginnings in 1950, the college has been a leader in teacher preparation, and, more recently, in programs in health science. It was the first and remains the only college in New Hampshire with a program in Graduate Theology. The college initiated distance education in fall 1997 when it began to offer Graduate Theology courses online.

Nova Southeastern University

3100 SW 9th Avenue
Ft. Lauderdale, FL 33315-3025

Phone: (954) 262-2000
(800) 986-2247 x2000
Fax: (954) 262-3872

Division(s): School of Computer and Information Sciences
Web Site(s): http://www.scis.nova.edu
E-mail: scisinfo@scis.nova.edu

Graduate Degree Programs:

Master of Science in:
    Computer Science
    Computer Information Systems
    Management Information Systems
    Computing Technology in Education

Doctoral Degree Programs:

PhD in:
    Computer Science
    Computer Information Systems
    Information Systems
    Information Science
PhD or EdD in Computing Technology in Education

Certificate Programs: Information Resources Management

Teaching Methods: *Computers:* Internet, electronic classroom, e-mail, electronic assignment submission, electronic forums, and bulletin boards. *Other:* None.

Admission Requirements: *Undergraduate:* application, fees, proof of high school graduation, official college transcripts. *Graduate:* application and fee, 500-word essay, portfolio or GRE (minimum score of 550/exam area, no more than 5 years old), 3 letters of recommendation, official transcripts of all graduate and undergraduate work with a 2.5 undergraduate GPA (3.0 in a major field), minimum of accredited bachelor's degree with appropriate major. Applicants whose native language is not English must pass the Test of English as a Foreign Language with a minimum 550 score. *Doctoral:* application and fee, 500-word essay, portfolio or GRE (minimum score of 550/exam area; no more than 5 years old), 3 letters of recommendation, official transcripts of all graduate and undergraduate work with a minimum 3.25 graduate GPA and an accredited master's degree with appropriate major. Applicants whose native language is not English must pass the Test of English as a Foreign Language with a minimum 550 score. *Certificate:* Application and fee, official transcripts of all graduate and undergraduate college credits, 2.8 GPA in a major field or a 3.0 graduate GPA, accredited bachelor's degree.

On-Campus Requirements: Master of Science degree programs require a weekend orientation on campus. All course work can be completed online. Doctoral programs are offered in 2 formats: institute and cluster. Institute requires students to attend sessions on campus one week each 5-month term, while cluster requires students to attend 2 weekends each 5-month term.

Tuition and Fees: *Undergraduate:* $345/credit. *Graduate:* $370/credit. *Doctoral:* $4,150/semester. *Application Fee:* $50. *Other Costs:* $30 for registration; $60 for master's orientation. *Credit by:* semester.

Financial Aid: Federal Stafford Loan, Federal Perkins Loan, Federal PLUS Loan, Federal Pell Grant, Federal Work-Study, VA, Florida resident programs.

Accreditation: Southern Association of Colleges and Schools.

Description: The School of Computer and Information Sciences at Nova Southeastern University (1964) is a major force in educational innovation, distinguished by its ability to offer both traditional and nontraditional choices in educational programs and formats that enable professionals to pursue advanced degrees without career interruption. SCIS offers programs leading to the Master of Science, Doctor of Philosophy, and Doctor of Education in several disciplines to its 900 graduate students from across the U.S. and other countries. The school pioneered online graduate education and has been offering programs with an online component since 1983. Forbes and the Wall Street Journal have recognized NSU as one of the top universities offering distance learning programs.

Oakland University

205 Wilson Hall	Phone: (248) 370-2191
Rochester, MI 48326	Fax: (248) 370-4475

Division(s): Academic Units
Web Site(s): http://www.oakland.edu/
E-mail: gilroy@oakland.edu

Undergraduate Degree Programs:

Bachelor of Arts in:
    Communications
    Music
Bachelor of General Studies

Teaching Methods: *TV:* videotape, cable program, satellite broadcasting. *Other:* audioconferencing, videoconferencing.

Credits Granted for: examination (CLEP).

Admission Requirements: *Undergraduate:* ACT for freshmen. If out of school for 3 years, sustained employment record; recommendations from employers, educators, or other professionals; and/or standardized tests.

On-Campus Requirements: undergraduate must complete 32 credits at Oakland University, which includes any of its locations.

Tuition and Fees: *Undergraduate:* $115/lower-division credit, resident; $128/upper-division credit, resident; $340/lower-division credit, nonresident; $366/upper-division credit, nonresident. *Graduate:* $214/credit resident, $474/credit nonresident. *Other Costs:* variable. *Credit by:* semester.

Financial Aid: Federal Stafford Loan, Federal Perkins Loan, Federal PLUS Loan, Federal Pell Grant, Federal Work-Study, VA, Michigan resident programs, William D. Ford Federal Direct Loan, Federal Supplemental Educational Opportunity

Grant, Michigan Competitive Scholarships, Michigan Educational Opportunity Grants, Michigan Adult Part-Time Grants, Michigan Work-Study, Oakland University grants, Oakland University Institutional Scholarships.

Accreditation: North Central Association of Colleges and Schools.

Description: Oakland University (1957) currently offers its 14,000 students 71 undergraduate degree programs and 45 graduate programs. It includes the College of Arts and Sciences, School of Business Administration, School of Education and Human Services, School of Engineering and Computer Science, School of Health Sciences, and the School of Nursing. About 95% of OU's undergraduate students were employed within 4 months after graduation in 1996. OU firsts: The Network Management Program, which upgrades the skills of information system professionals, and a health care/academic alliance with the Henry Ford Health System to prepare nurses for a rapidly changing health care environment. OU is moving up to Division I and is a new member of the Mid-Continent Conference in Intercollegiate Athletics. The university is an equal opportunity and affirmative action institution. We started distance learning in 1995.

Ohio University

302 Tupper Hall	Phone: (740) 593-2910
Athens, OH 45701	(800) 444-2910
	Fax: (740) 593-2901

Division(s): Office of Independent Study
Web Site(s): http://www.ohiou.edu/~indstu/
E-mail: indstudy@ouvaxa.cats.ohiou.edu

Undergraduate Degree Programs:
Associate of Arts
Associate of Science
Associate of Individualized Studies
Bachelor of Specialized Studies

Class Titles: see catalog.

Teaching Methods: *Computers:* Internet, e-mail, LISTSERV. *TV:* videotape. *Other:* audiotapes, fax, correspondence, independent study, individual study, learning contracts.

Credits Granted for: experiential learning, portfolio assessment, extrainstitutional learning, examination (CLEP).

Admission Requirements: *Undergraduate:* Enrollment in independent study courses is open to anyone who can profit from the learning. Enrollment in a course does not constitute formal admission to Ohio University or any of its degree programs. Degree-seeking students must have a high school diploma to be admitted to the External Student Program; transfer students must have a minimum 2.0 cumulative GPA.

Admission to the External Student Program does not guarantee admission to any on-campus degree program.

On-Campus Requirements: None.

Tuition and Fees: *Undergraduate:* $64/credit. *Application Fee:* $15/course. *Credit by:* quarter.

Financial Aid: VA.

Accreditation: North Central Association of Schools and Colleges.

Description: Ohio University (1804) was the first institution of higher learning in the Northwest Territory. Today it enrolls 20,000 students in 10 colleges, offering degrees in 325 subject areas. The university holds membership in several professional organizations, and many of its programs are individually accredited by their respective associations. The Independent Study program, begun in 1924, serves students at a distance through correspondence courses, course credit by examination, and individual learning contracts. Course materials may be presented via print, audiotape or videotape, computer disk, or Internet site. Assignments may be submitted by postal mail, fax, or e-mail. Credit earned through any of these options is considered resident credit. Almost 5,000 students take 350 courses annually through independent study.

Ohlone College

43600 Mission Boulevard	Phone: (510) 659-6160
Fremont, CA 94539	Fax: (510) 659-6265

Division(s): Learning Resources and Instructional Technology Division
Web Site(s): http://www.ohlone.cc.ca.us/
E-mail: dchapman@ohlone.cc.ca.us

Class Titles: Anthropology, Computer Studies, English, English as Second Language, American Government, Nursing, Photography, Art, Business, Mass Media.

Teaching Methods: *Computers:* Internet, real-time chat, e-mail, CD-ROM, newsgroup, LISTSERV. *TV:* videotape, cable program. *Other:* videoconferencing.

Credits Granted for: examination (CLEP, ACT-PEP, DANTES, GRE), military service, noncollege courses.

Admission Requirements: *Undergraduate:* high school graduate or equivalency certificate, or age 18, or meets high school special admission requirements.
On-Campus Requirements: varies by class.

Tuition and Fees: *Undergraduate:* $12/credit California residents, $120/credit all others. *Credit by:* semester.

Financial Aid: Federal Stafford Loan, Federal Perkins Loan, Federal PLUS Loan, Federal Pell Grant, Federal Work-Study,

VA, California resident programs.

Accreditation: Western Association of Schools and Colleges.

Description: Ohlone College (1966) is a 2-year, public, coed community college. Ohlone is a commuter, suburban campus located on a 534-acre hillside site (300 acres are reserved for open space) that is only 15 miles from San Jose and 40 miles from San Francisco. The college is on a semester calendar with a limited summer session that offers both general education and occupational education classes; extensive evening and early morning classes are available. Degrees offered by the college include AA and AS; more than 500 associate degrees were awarded in 1997. The college library has 65,000 books, an online catalog, and 4 CD-ROM periodical databases. Plus, there are 57 microcomputers located in the library, classrooms, computer centers, and learning/tutoring centers. The college has a state-of-the-art fine/performing arts center.

Oklahoma City University

2501 North Blackwelder	Phone: (405) 521-5265
Oklahoma City, OK 73106	Fax: (405) 521-5447

Division(s): Prior Learning and University Studies (PLUS)
Web Site(s): http://www.okcu.edu/plus
E-mail: plus@frodo.okcu.edu

Undergraduate Degree Programs:
Bachelor of Science in Technical Management
Bachelor of Arts in:
    Liberal Arts
    Business

Teaching Methods: *Other:* correspondence, independent study.

Credits Granted for: experiential learning, portfolio assessment (ACE), extrainstitutional learning, examination (CLEP, ACT-PEP, DANTES).

Admission Requirements: *Undergraduate:* high school diploma or GED, no minimum number of credit hours, appropriate for age 22.

On-Campus Requirements: one weekend class required (Friday evening and all day Saturday; this class is offered 4 times/year).

Tuition and Fees: *Undergraduate:* $149/credit plus fees for most distance studies. $297 plus fees for weekend class (current for 98–99 academic year). *Application Fee:* $25. *Other Costs:* $20/semester enrollment fee. $25/term record maintenance. *Credit by:* semester.

Financial Aid: Federal Stafford Loan, Federal Perkins Loan, Federal PLUS Loan, Federal Pell Grant, VA, Federal Work-

Study.

Accreditation: North Central Association of Colleges and Schools.

Description: Oklahoma City University (1904) is an independent institution affiliated with the United Methodist Church. The university is committed to a strong education in the liberal arts tradition. The PLUS program is an alternative way for busy, working adults to complete a bachelor of science or bachelor of arts degree. PLUS allows individuals the opportunity to earn course credit for knowledge students have already gained and helps them in attaining credits without spending unnecessary hours in the classroom. While the PLUS curriculum is as rigorous as traditional degree programs, it operates differently in that students may achieve credit through a variety of methods.

Oklahoma State University

470 Student Union	Phone: (405) 744-6390
Stillwater, OK 74078	Fax: (405) 744-7793

Division(s): Independent and Correspondence Study and University Extension
Web Site(s): http://www.okstate.edu/education/inc.html (for I&CS) http://www2.okstate.edu/xtra (for University Extension)
E-mail: ics-inf@okway.okstate.edu

Graduate Degree Programs:
Master of Business Administration
Master of Science in:
    Computer Science
    Electrical/Computer Engineering
    Mechanical/Aerospace Engineering
    Natural/Applied Sciences Specialization in Health Care
      Administration
    Telecommunications Management
    Agriculture Education

Certificate Programs: Fire Protection Technology

Class Titles: all; see Web site or request current catalog.

Teaching Methods: *Computers:* Internet, real-time chat, e-mail, CD-ROM, LISTSERV. *TV:* videotape, cable program, satellite broadcast. *Other:* videoconferencing, compressed video, audiotapes, ISDN/BRI desktop video, fax, correspondence, independent study, individual study, extrainstitutional learning, examination (CLEP, ACT-PEP, DANTES, GRE).

Admission Requirements: *Undergraduate:* variable.

On-Campus Requirements: None.

Tuition and Fees: *Undergraduate:* $70/credit. *Graduate:* contact individual program. *Application Fee:* $15 undergraduate, $25 graduate. *Other Costs:* $10/course shipping and

handling, varies for course materials. *Credit by:* semester.

Financial Aid: Federal Stafford Loan, Federal Perkins Loan, Federal PLUS Loan, Federal Pell Grant, Federal Work-Study, VA, Oklahoma resident programs.

Accreditation: North Central Association of Colleges and Schools.

Description: Oklahoma State University (1890) was founded as Oklahoma Agricultural and Mechanical College just 20 months after the Land Run of 1889. OSU is now a modern, comprehensive land-grant university that provides exceptional academic experiences, conducts scholarly research and other creative activities, and disseminates knowledge to the people of Oklahoma and throughout the world through its extension endeavors. Distance learning opportunities are coordinated by University Extension and offered by Independent and Correspondence Study and the various college extension units. More than 130 undergraduate distance courses are available, along with 12 accredited graduate-level degree and certificate programs. With technology changing daily, we aggressively stay on the cutting edge with delivery methods that utilize state-of-the-art equipment and the most advanced technology currently available.

Oklahoma State University, Oklahoma City

900 North Portland	Phone: (405) 945-3376
Oklahoma City, OK 73107	Fax: (405) 945-3325

Division(s): Academic Affairs
Web Site(s): http://www.osuokc.edu
E-mail: davenpo@okway.okstate.edu

Undergraduate Degree Programs:
Associate of Applied Science in:
  Quality Management
  Nursing
  Interpreter Training
Associate of Science in:
  Drug and Alcohol Abuse
  Fire Protection Technology

Class Titles: Mathematics, English, Political Science, Computer Information Science, Quality Assurance.

Teaching Methods: *Computers:* Internet, real-time chat, electronic classroom, e-mail, CD-ROM, newsgroup, LISTSERV. *TV:* videotape, cable program. *Other:* videoconferencing, fax, correspondence.

Credits Granted for: experiential learning, extrainstitutional learning, examination (CLEP, ACT-PEP, DANTES, GRE).

Admission Requirements: *Undergraduate:* application, high school transcript (college transcript for transfer students),

and ACT (or similar battery).

On-Campus Requirements: None.

Tuition and Fees: *Undergraduate:* $54/credit resident, $127/credit nonresident. *Other Costs:* $25 distance learning fee, $10/credit development course fee. *Credit by:* semester.

Financial Aid: Federal Stafford Loan, Federal Perkins Loan, Federal PLUS Loan, Federal Pell Grant, Federal Work-Study, VA, Oklahoma resident programs.

Accreditation: North Central Association of Colleges and Schools, Oklahoma State Regents for Higher Education, National League for Nursing.

Description: Oklahoma State University, Oklahoma City (1961) is a state-assisted, public, 2-year college serving 4,500 students each semester in one of the fastest growing metropolitan cities in the country. The mission of the institution is to provide collegiate-level career and transfer educational programs and supportive services to prepare individuals to live and work in an increasingly technological and global community. OSU-OKC offers more than 30 certificate and degree programs including Nursing, Fire Protection Technology, Alcohol and Substance Abuse Counseling, Interpreter Training, and Quality Management. The distance learning program, which began in 1996, has grown to include courses and programs online, via interactive TV, and through Western Governors University.

Open Learning Agency

4355 Mathissi Place	Phone: (604) 431-3300
Burnaby, BC, Canada V5G 4S8	(800) 663-9711
	Fax: (604) 431-3381

Division(s):
Open University and Open College (postsecondary) Workplace
  Training Systems
Knowledge Network (educational TV)
Open School (K–12)
Web Site(s): http://www.ola.bc.ca
E-mail: studentserv@ola.bc.ca

Undergraduate Degree Programs:
Bachelor of Arts, General Program
Bachelor of Arts, Major Program
Bachelor of Business Administration
Bachelor of Business Administration (Public Sector Management)
Bachelor of:
  Fine Art
  Design
  General Studies
  Health Science (Physiotherapy)
  Health Science (Psychiatric Nursing)

Music Therapy
Music (Jazz Studies)
Music (Performance)
Science (General Program)
Science (Major Program)
Technology (Technology Management)
Tourism Management

Graduate Degree Programs:
Master of Music Therapy

Certificate Programs: Business Skills, Management of Workplace Instruction, Workplace Leadership Foundation, Management Studies, General Studies, Certified Dental Assisting, Home Support Attendant, Nurse Refresher, Practical Nurse Refresher, Social Service Worker, Adult Basic Education, College Basic Education/Career Preparation Courses: Intermediate (Adult Grade 10), Advanced (Adult Grade 11).

Class Titles: Accounting, Administration, Agricultural Studies, Animal Science, Anthropology, Apiculture, Applied Science, Archaeology, Asian Studies, Astronomy, Biological Sciences, Business/Management, Calculus, Canadian Studies, Career Planning, Certified Dental Assisting, Chemistry, Child Care, Commerce, Communication, Community Economic Development, Computer Applications, Computer Science, Computer Studies, Counseling, Criminology, Economics, Education, Adult Education, Curriculum Development, Early Childhood Education, Law for Teachers, Educational Psychology, Engineering, English, English as Second Language, Environmental Studies, Film, Finance, Fine Art, First Nations Studies, Food Science, Forestry, French, Geography, Geology, German, Gerontology, Health, History, Home Care Nursing, Home Support Attendant, Humanities, Japanese, Kinesiology, Languages Education, Law, Library Studies, Linguistics, Literature, Math, Museum Studies, Music, Nursing, Oceanography, Philosophy, Physics, Plant Science, Political Science, Practical Nursing, Psychology, Science, Social Sciences, Social Service, Soil Science, Spanish, Statistics, Urban Studies, Women's Studies, Workplace Leadership.

Teaching Methods: *Computers:* Internet, computer conferencing, e-mail. *TV:* broadcast, videotape. *Other:* independent study, some face-to-face and classroom-based methods, fax, telephone, audioconferencing, audiotapes, videotape.

Credits Granted for: experiential learning, portfolio assessment, extrainstitutional learning, transfer credit.

Admission Requirements: *Undergraduate:* open-admission. Students may register at any time throughout the year. For some programs, students must meet specific criteria and apply for admission. *Graduate:* students must fulfil specific admission requirements for Master of Music Therapy. *Certificate:* same as undergraduate.

On-Campus Requirements: None.

Tuition and Fees: *Undergraduate:* Canadian $51/credit for 100 and 200 level courses, Canadian $64/credit for 300 and 400 level courses. *Graduate:* TBA. *Application Fee:* Canadian $45/course. *Other Costs:* textbooks/supplies, long distance costs (outside BC and the Yukon Territory). *Credit by:* semester, although continuous registration is offered.

Financial Aid: Adult Basic Education Student Assistance Program (part-time bursaries and grants), British Columbia Student Assistance Program (full-time student loans), student loans, BC Grant and Loan Remission, private bursaries and scholarships.

Accreditation: Association of Universities and Colleges of Canada, Association of Community Colleges of Canada.

Description: The government of British Columbia established the "Open Learning Institute" (1978) to develop and deliver distance education to British Columbians living outside urban centers. In 1988 the OLI merged with Knowledge Network (BC's educational broadcaster) and formed the Open Learning Agency. In the fall of 1998, this organization took another step toward the future, incorporating Workplace Training Systems, Open School (K–12), Knowledge Network, and Open University and Open College. As part of the Open Learning Agency, both Open University and Open College are committed to providing innovative learning opportunities for British Columbians, Canadians, and others around the world. Through flexible admissions policies, established distance learning methods, and new educational technologies, Open University students may earn credits toward associate, bachelor's, or master's degrees, or for transfer to other institutions. Through the same range of services, Open College students may pursue a range of certificates and diplomas, many of which may be applied to Open University programs.

Oral Roberts University

7777 South Lewis Avenue	Phone: (888) 900-4678
Tulsa, OK 74171	(918) 495-6236
	Fax: (918) 495-7965

Division(s): School of Life Long Education
Web Site(s): http://www.oru.edu (university home page), http://oru.edu/slle/ (SLLE Home Page)
E-mail: jantoine@oru.edu (Jacque Antoine, SLLE Distance Recruiter)
dschnacker@oru.edu (Darby Schnacker, Director of Distance Education)

Undergraduate Degree Programs:
Bachelor of Science in:
Business Administration
Christian Care/Counseling
Church Ministries

Elementary Christian School Education
Liberal Studies

Graduate Degree Programs:
(Distance Education and modular combination)
Master of Arts in:
Christian School Administration
Christian School Teaching
Christian School Curriculum

Doctoral Degree Programs:
Call Graduate Recruiter at (888) 900-4678 for details. Homeschool College Program, call (800) 678-8876 x4.

Certificate Programs: Theology/Home Bible Study Series (noncredit).

Class Titles: The school offers more than 150 courses for individual study.

Teaching Methods: *Computers:* Internet, e-mail, CD-ROM. *TV:* videotape, cable program, satellite broadcasting. *Other:* audiotapes, fax, correspondence, independent study, individual study, learning contracts.

Credits Granted for: experiential learning, portfolio assessment, extrainstitutional learning, examination (CLEP, ACT-PEP, DANTES, GRE).

Admission Requirements: *Undergraduate:* application, high school transcripts, signed Honor Code, Minister's recommendation, essay, age 22+. *Graduate:* application, college transcripts, signed Honor Code, Minister's recommendation, essay, GRE/MAT. *Doctoral:* same as graduate.

On-Campus Requirements: *Undergraduate:* fully through distance education. *Graduate:* about half through modular format.

Tuition and Fees: *Undergraduate:* $105/credit, $5/course administrative fee. *Graduate:* $135/credit, $25/term administrative fee. *Doctoral:* $55/credit Homeschool; call for details. *Application Fee:* $35. *Other Costs:* $15/course proctor fee, $10/term postage fee. *Credit by:* semester.

Financial Aid: Federal Stafford Loan, Federal Perkins Loan, Federal PLUS Loan, Federal Pell Grant, VA. Aid available only for degrees.

Accreditation: North Central Association of Colleges and Schools.

Description: Founded in 1965, ORU has been offering distance courses since 1974. In 1992 the program became a school, known as the School of Life Long Education, within the university. Oral Roberts University is a charismatic liberal arts university fully accredited and recognized by applicable professional societies.

Oregon Health Sciences University
School of Nursing

3181 SW Sam Jackson Park Road	Phone: (503) 494-3668 (A)
Portland, OR 97201 (A)	(541) 552-6703 (B)
1250 Siskiyou Boulevard	(541) 962-3803 (C)
Ashland, OR 97520 (B)	(541) 885-1665 (D)
1410 L Avenue	Fax: (503) 494-4350 (A)
LaGrande, OR 97850 (C)	(541) 552-6055 (B)
3201 Campus Drive	(541) 962-3737 (C)
Klamath Falls, OR 97601 (D)	(541) 885-1855 (D)

Division(s): School of Nursing on 4 campuses:
OHSU Portland (A)
OHSU at Southern Oregon University (B)
OHSU at Eastern Oregon University (C)
OHSU at Oregon Institute of Technology (D)
Web Site(s): http://www.ohsu.edu
E-mail: proginfo@ohsu.edu (A)
williams@sou.edu (B)
lstout@eou.edu (C)
manning@oit.edu (D)

Undergraduate Degree Programs:
Bachelor of Science in Nursing

Graduate Degree Programs:
Master of Science (selected specialties) from Portland only to selected sites

Doctoral Degree Programs:
Doctorate of Philosophy from Portland only to selected sites

Certificate Programs: Post Master's Certificate Option in selected specialties.

Class Titles: selected nursing courses. Please contact individual campuses.

Teaching Methods: *Computers:* Internet, real-time chat, electronic classroom, e-mail, CD-ROM, newsgroup, LIST-SERV. *TV:* videotape (delayed tape of classes offered in selected sites and courses). *Other:* videoconferencing, audioconferencing (rare; may be used in selected courses), fax, correspondence, independent study, individual study.

Credits Granted for: bachelor's degree (Registered Nurses): portfolio assessment, articulation credit (29 quarter credits) for graduates of NLN accredited Associate Degree Nursing Programs. Graduates of diploma programs must take NLN Mobility II Exams for the awarding of 29 quarter credits. Credit by examination offered in selected courses.

Admission Requirements: *Undergraduate:* must be a Registered Nurse licensed in Oregon, pre-admission GPA of 2.5, possess computer skills. *Graduate:* BS in Nursing from an NLN accredited program, undergraduate GPA of 3.0, GRE 1,000 or above combined score. *Doctoral:* For PhD MS in Nursing or MN from NLN accredited program, graduate GPA of 3.5, GRE 1,000 or above combined score. *Certificate:* MS in Nursing or MN from an NLN accredited program, graduate GPA of 3.0.

On-Campus Requirements: each program has different requirements for the number of credits that must be taken from OHSU for a degree. No distance learning class has on-campus requirements. Distance learning is offered only in the state of Oregon.

Tuition and Fees: *Undergraduate:* varies from campus to campus; please contact School of Nursing at campus of choice. *Graduate:* same as undergraduate. *Doctoral:* same as undergraduate. *Application Fee:* $60. *Other Costs:* $25 technology fee. *Credit by:* quarters.

Financial Aid: Federal Stafford Loan, Federal Perkins Loan, Federal PLUS Loan, Federal Pell Grant, Federal Work-Study, VA; contact Financial Aid Office for eligibility of students in distance education programs.

Accreditation: National League for Nursing (NLN) Accrediting Commission, Commission on Collegiate Education.

Description: The Oregon Health Sciences University School of Nursing (1926) has been involved in outreach education since the 1970s. At that time faculty traveled to distance sites to deliver courses. In the early 1990s the state of Oregon developed 2-way audio/video technology (Oregon ED-NET) so that classes could be offered to distance sites in real time. This system also provided technology for asynchronous computer conferencing. In 1992 the School of Nursing began teaching courses using this technology to distance learning sites throughout the state. As the technology becomes more efficient, more courses will be offered in this way. In 1998, the school has embarked on offering the PhD to selective sites in Montana in conjunction with Montana State University using newer PolyCom technology. It is expected that this type of distance learning program will expand for all distance learning programs.

Otero Junior College

1802 Colorado Avenue	Phone: (719) 384-6831
La Junta, CO 81050	Fax: (719) 384-6935

Division(s): Instructional Services
Web Site(s): http://www.ojc.cccoes.edu

Undergraduate Degree Programs:
Associate of Applied Science in Business

Class Titles: Accounting, Business, Human Resource Management, Legal Environment of Business, Business Communication/Report Writing, Business Statistics, Computer Information Systems, PC Applications, Spreadsheets, Economics (micro/macro), Composition, Small Business Management, Management, Sales, Marketing, College Algebra, Speech

Communication, Psychology, Sociology, Western Civilization, Art Appreciation, Business, Mass Media, Human Growth/Development, Belief/Believers.

Teaching Methods: *Computers:* Internet. *TV:* videotape. *Other:* independent study.

Credits Granted for: portfolio assessment, examination (CLEP, DANTES).

Admission Requirements: *Undergraduate:* full-time students: age 16; high school diploma, GED, or college degree; basic skills assessment test (exceptions: college degree or ACT of 22 on individual subjects). Must be resident of Colorado for 12 months, possess a driver's license, or have paid previous year taxes.

On-Campus Requirements: the student must be enrolled in 16 semester credit hours of course work at Otero Junior College.

Tuition and Fees: *Undergraduate:* $55/credit. *Credit by:* semester.

Financial Aid: Federal Stafford Loan, Federal PLUS Loan, Federal Pell Grant, Federal Work-Study, VA, Colorado resident programs.

Accreditation: North Central Association of Colleges and Schools.

Description: Otero Junior College (1941) has been in existence for more than half a century, first as a junior college and now as a modern, comprehensive community college. In its current role, the college offers a variety of means by which students can access the first 2 years of a higher education. In the 1960s, OJC embarked on meeting the needs of nontraditional students through alternative learning methods. In 1997 these methods were expanded to include distance learning, specifically the Internet, as a means to provide educational programming to individuals who were simply unable to attend campus classes.

Ottawa University, Kansas City

10865 Grandview Drive	Phone: (913) 451-1431
Overland Park, KS 66210	Fax: (913) 451-0806

Division(s): individual departments
Web Site(s): http://www.ott.edu/~oukc/main.html
E-mail: ottawainfo@aol.com

Undergraduate Degree Programs:
Bachelor of Arts in Management of Health Services

Graduate Degree Programs:
Master of Arts in Human Resources

Teaching Methods: *Computers:* Internet, real-time chat, electronic classroom, e-mail. *Other:* correspondence, independent study, individual study.

Credits Granted for: experiential learning, portfolio assessment, extrainstitutional learning, examination (CLEP, ACT-PEP, DANTES, GRE).

Admission Requirements: *Undergraduate:* allied health service background and education. *Graduate:* accredited bachelor's degree.

On-Campus Requirements: undergraduate Friday and Saturday sessions 4 times/year in Overland Park, Kansas; Wilmington, Delaware; or New Orleans, Louisiana. Graduate Thursday through Sunday sessions 3 times/year in Overland Park, Kansas.

Tuition and Fees: *Undergraduate:* $195/credit. *Graduate:* $275/credit. *Application Fee:* $50. *Credit by:* semester.

Financial Aid: Federal Stafford Loan, Federal PLUS Loan, Federal Pell Grant, VA.

Accreditation: North Central Association of Colleges and Schools.

Description: Established as the university's first nonresidential campus, Ottawa University, Kansas City (1974) serves the educational needs of adults. Its programs, consistent with those of the residential campus, include individual educational planning, full-time faculty advisors, interdisciplinary approaches, and resources for lifelong learning. Additionally, these programs are directed to the unique circumstances of adult learners who must balance their quests for higher education with competing claims of work and family responsibility.

Owens Community College

PO Box 10000	Phone: (419) 661-7355
Toledo, OH 43699-1947	Fax: (419) 661-7662

Division(s): Academic Affairs
Web Site(s): http://www.owens.cc.oh.us
E-mail: mrocher@owens.cc.oh.us

Undergraduate Degree Programs:
Associate of Arts

Teaching Methods: *Computers:* Internet, real-time chat, electronic classroom, e-mail, CD-ROM. *TV:* videotape, cable program, satellite broadcasting, PBS. *Other:* videoconferencing, audiotapes, fax, correspondence, independent study, individual study, learning contracts.

Credits Granted for: Education, work experience, etc.

Admission Requirements: *Undergraduate:* open-admission.

On-Campus Requirements: None.

Tuition and Fees: *Undergraduate:* $79/credit. *Software:*

varies. *Other Costs:* $10 registration fee/semester, $25 waivers/course. *Credit by:* semester.

Financial Aid: Federal Stafford Loan, Federal Perkins Loan, Federal Pell Grant, Federal Work-Study, VA, Ohio resident programs.

Accreditation: North Central Association of Colleges and Schools.

Description: Owens Community College began in 1965 as a technical institute. Its mission is to provide quality technical and general education for students and employers in its service area. The college is committed to preparing every graduate to succeed in the world of technical service, to make a positive contribution to society, and to support—as well as survive—change. As part of the Owens mission, distance learning began in the early 1990s through a partnership with Ameritech, which provided a fiber optic link between the 2 campuses and a number of businesses in Toledo and Findlay. Since then, the Board of Regents has approved a grant to expand that technology capability.

Ozarks Technical Community College

933 East Central	Phone: (417) 895-7746
Springfield, MO 65802	Fax: (417) 895-7366

Division(s): Academic Services
Web Site(s): http://www.otc.cc.mo.us
E-mail: slawler@emh1.otc.cc.mo.us

Class Titles: Philosophy, German, Sociology, various courses available each semester on "as needed" basis.

Teaching Methods: *Computers:* e-mail. *TV:* videotape, cable program, satellite broadcasting, PBS. *Other:* videoconferencing, audioconferencing, audiographics, audiotapes, fax, correspondence.

Credits Granted for: experiential learning, examinations.

Admission Requirements: *Undergraduate:* age 16, high school junior or senior. *Certificate:* same as undergraduate.

On-Campus Requirements: None.

Tuition and Fees: *Undergraduate:* $49/credit in-district, $69/credit out-of-district. *Credit by:* semester.

Financial Aid: Federal Stafford Loan, Federal Pell Grant, Federal Work-Study, VA, Missouri resident programs (A+).

Accreditation: North Central Association of Colleges and Schools.

Description: Ozarks Technical Community College (1991) offered its first classes in the fall of 1991. It has since grown from 1,200 students to 5,000, making it the fastest growing community college in Missouri. The primary purpose of

Ozarks Technical Community College is to provide technical education programs supported by essential foundation and basic skills courses, which are responsive to the education needs of the community and its industrial, commercial, and service organizations. In response to the educational needs of the surrounding area, OTC began to offer ITV courses in the spring of 1998. These interactive courses are offered to college students as well as secondary students in the area who are interested in being dually enrolled in high school and college courses.

Pacific Oaks College

5 Westmoreland Place	Phone: (800) 684-0900
Pasadena, CA 91103	Fax: (626) 577-6144

Division(s): Distance Learning
Web Site(s): http://www.pacificoaks.edu
E-mail: postmaster@pacificoaks.edu

Undergraduate Degree Programs:
Bachelor of Arts in Human Development

Graduate Degree Programs:
Master of Arts in Human Development

Doctoral Degree Programs:
Human Development/Early Childhood.

Certificate Programs: Human Development/Early Childhood (postgraduate)

Class Titles: Early Childhood Themes/Life Cycle Issues, Communication for Empowerment, Leadership in Education, Working with Adults, Administration/Supervision: Fieldwork, College Teaching: Fieldwork, Parent/Community Work: Fieldwork, Reflective Teaching, Play in Childhood, Parent Involvement, Observation, Sociolinguistics, Emergent Curriculum, Cognitive Development, Earliest Years, Working with Children, Anti-Bias Curriculum, Developmental Assessment/Program Planning, Assessment of Experience, Thesis Development.

Teaching Methods: *Computers:* Internet, e-mail, LISTSERV. *Other:* None.

Credits Granted for: experiential learning, portfolio assessment, examination (CLEP).

Admission Requirements: *Undergraduate:* 60 acceptable semester credits. *Graduate:* accredited bachelor's degree, OR 60 credits and age 35, with 5 years of leadership experience. *Doctoral:* master's degree. *Certificate:* master's degree.

On-Campus Requirements: 2–3 classes in a week-long intensive or weekend format at Southern CA, Northern CA, or Seattle campus.

Tuition and Fees: *Undergraduate:* $475/credit. *Graduate:*
$475/credit. *Doctoral:* $475/credit. *Application Fee:* $55. *Software:* included. *Other Costs:* $30/semester Student Activity. *Credit by:* semester.

Financial Aid: Federal Stafford Loan, Federal Perkins Loan, Federal PLUS Loan, Federal Pell Grant, Federal Work-Study, VA, California resident programs, Pacific Oaks Graduate Fellowships.

Accreditation: Western Association of Schools and Colleges.

Description: Pacific Oaks College (1945) began as a community education center and nursery school and soon added a teacher education program, out of which the college grew. Upper division and graduate programs available to distance students lead to BA and MA degrees in Human Development, with specializations in Early Childhood Education, Bicultural Development, and Leadership in Education and Human Services. The college also offers on-campus, elementary teacher and family counselor certification programs. Online, as on campus, experiential learning is at the heart of Pacific Oaks' curriculum for adults as well as for children. Pacific Oaks believes people learn both theory and practice through action and interaction; thus the college encourages its students to work together and learn from each other. Through e-mail "meetings," lively discussion-in-writing involves students and faculty. Distance learning online has been available since 1996, and the course offerings are growing steadily.

Palo Alto College

1400 West Villaret Boulevard	Phone: (210) 921-5103
San Antonio, TX 78224-2499	Fax: (210) 921-5412

Division(s): Instructional Innovation
Web Site(s): http://www.accd.edu/pac/pacmain/pachp.htm
E-mail: izuniga@accd.edu

Undergraduate Degree Programs:
Associate

Certificate Programs: Computer Skills, Entry-Level Supervision, Customer Service Representative, Financial Customer Service Representative, Loan Processing Specialist, Mortgage Banking Specialist, General Office, Administrative Assistant, Office Systems Technology/Tech-Prep Enhanced Skills, Environmental Regulations Technician, Environmental Compliance Technician, Warehouse Specialist, Distribution Logistics Specialist, Product Marketing Specialist, Animal Health Specialist, Food System Specialist, Food Science and Technology/Enhanced Skills, Agribusiness Operations/Enhanced Skills.

Class Titles: variable by semester. Biology, Economics (macro/micro), American Government: National/State/Local, American Government: Problems/Policies, History of U.S.,

Psychology, Humanities, Sociology, British Literature, American Literature, Software Applications: PowerPoint, Computer Literacy, Engineering Mechanics—Statics.

Teaching Methods: *Computers:* Internet, real-time chat, electronic classroom, e-mail, CD-ROM, LISTSERV. *TV:* videotape, cable program, satellite broadcasting, PBS. *Other:* videoconferencing, audiotapes, fax.

Credits Granted for: examination (CLEP, DANTES, Subject Examination, Advanced Placement, standardized, departmental challenge), Army/ACE Registered Transcripts System through Service Members Opportunity Colleges for Active Army, military training, transfer transcripts. Credit by nontraditional methods must be applicable to a Palo Alto degree program.

Admission Requirements: *Undergraduate:* high school graduate with official transcript, GED, or transcript of last school attended if transferring; placement test scores; meet minimum scholastic standards of Palo Alto; TASP scores if taken. Contact the school for international student requirements. Conditional admission with permission. High school students may apply for Dual-Credit Program and earn college credit while in high school. No admission credentials needed for audit status. *Certificate:* same as undergraduate.

On-Campus Requirements: variable.

Tuition and Fees: *Undergraduate:* $120/1–6 hours, $168/7 hours, $192/8 hours, $216/9 hours, $240/10 hours, $264/11 hours, $288/12 hours, $312/13 hours, $336 14/hours, $360/15 hours, $384/16 hours, $408/17 hours, $432/18 hours, $456/19 hours, $480/20 hours, $504/21 hours in-district. Out-of-district Texas residents: $230/1–6, $322/7, $368/8, $414/9, $460/10, $506/11, $552/12, $598/13, $644/14, $690/15, $736/16, $782/17, $828/18, $874/19, $920/20, $966/21. Nonresidents and international: $460/1–6, $644/7, $736/8, $828/9, $920/10, $1,012/11, $1,104/12, $1,196/13, $1,288/14, $1,380/15, $1,472/16, $1,564/17, $1,656/18, $1,748/19, $1,840/20, $1,932/21. *Other Costs:* $3/credit instructional technology fee, $40 general summer fee, $60–$65 general fall/spring fee, $10 library fee, $6 summer registration fee, $10 fall/spring registration fee, $4 insurance fee except for international student, $10 auditing fee, lab and special fees depend on individual courses, $25 late registration fee, $5–$10 vehicle registration and parking permits (depending on time of year), $10 returned check fee, $4/schedule change. Note: summer tuition differs from fall/spring tuition given above; contact school if interested. *Credit by:* semester.

Financial Aid: Federal Stafford Loan, Federal PLUS Loan, Federal Pell Grant, Federal Work-Study, VA, Texas Public Educational Grant, State Student-Incentive Grant.

Accreditation: Southern Association of Colleges and Schools.

Description: Palo Alto College (1983) is one of four colleges in the Alamo Community College District. It serves students from an immediate service area in the southern sector of San Antonio, other parts of Bexar County, and the outlying rural counties south of Bexar County. Palo Alto is one of the fastest-growing institutions of higher education in Texas. The college is an open-admission, public, 2-year college dedicated to the pursuit of excellence in its educational programs and services. PAC provides the foundation skills and workplace competencies that empower students to pursue their goals of entering the workforce, continue formal education at other colleges and universities, develop additional skills for their chosen occupations, or acquire learning for personal enjoyment and satisfaction. Palo Alto began distance learning 6 years ago via telecourses.

Palomar Community College

1140 County Mission Road   Phone: (760) 744-1150 x2431
San Marcos, CA 92069-1487   Fax: (760) 761-3519

Division(s): Educational TV
Web Site(s): http://www.ETV.palomar.edu
E-mail: shargrav@palomar.edu

Undergraduate Degree Programs:
Associate of Arts
Intersegmental General Transfer program

Certificate Programs: Certificate of Achievement

Class Titles: Financial Accounting, Race/Class/Ethnic Groups in America, Cultural Anthropology, Art, American Sign Language, Awareness of Deaf Culture, Business, Business Math, Business Law, Personal Finance, Small Business Management, Child Development, Time to Grow, College Success Skills Career Search, English As Second Language, Painter, Humanities, Fundamentals of Music, Fundamentals of Vocal Skills, Contemporary Legal Issues, Psychology, Marriage/Family, Abnormal Psychology, Refrigeration/Heat/Air Conditioning—Electric, Refrigeration/Heat/Air Conditioning—Mechanical, Sociology, Spanish.

Teaching Methods: *TV:* videotape, cable program, satellite broadcasting, PBS. *Other:* videoconferencing

On-Campus Requirements: None.

Tuition and Fees: *Undergraduate:* $13/unit, California resident one year. *Credit by:* semester.

Financial Aid: Federal Stafford Loan, Federal Perkins Loan, Federal PLUS Loan, Federal Pell Grant, Federal Work-Study, VA, California resident programs.

Accreditation: Community and Junior Colleges of the Western Association of Schools and Colleges.

Description: The history of Palomar College (1946) is rich in tradition, educational achievements, and personalities. Exactly 100 persons showed up on the first day of classes. Enrollment has grown steadily over the last half century, with more than 25,000 full- and part-time students currently studying on Palomar's 200-acre campus. The college provides the first 2 years of regular 4-year college course work, a 2-year liberal arts AA, and training programs in semiprofessional and vocational fields. Outreach locations now include 4 high schools and 3 centers at the Pauma Indian Reservation.

Park College

8700 River Park Drive
Parkville, MO 64152

Phone: (816) 741-2000 x6240
Fax: (816) 741-6138

Division(s): School for Extended Learning
Web Site(s): http://www.park.edu
http://www.park.edu/dist/course.htm
E-mail: carolh@mail.park.edu

Class Titles: Human Ecology, Managing Information Systems, Computers in Society, World Political Geography, American Civil War, Principles of Supervision, Organizational Behavior, Production/Operations Management, Senior Seminar-Management, Labor Relations, Business Ethics, Compensation Management, Small Business Management, Earlier American Literature, Networks/Data Communications, Programming, Financial Institutions/Markets, Business, Marketing, Computers, Management, Complex Organizations, Human Resource Development, Personal Financial Management, Chemistry/Society, Computers, Financial Management, Criminal Law, Organization Development/Change, U.S. Foreign Policy in 20th Century, Social Psychology, Business Writing, Scientific/Technical Writing (the preceding are Internet courses), Human Ecology (CD-ROM), Business Ethics, Evolution, EC.

Teaching Methods: *Computers:* Internet, real-time chat, electronic classroom, e-mail, CD-ROM. *Other:* audioconferencing, videoconferencing.

Credits Granted for: experiential learning, portfolio assessment, examination (CLEP, ACT-PEP, DANTES, GRE).

Admission Requirements: *Undergraduate:* high school graduate.

On-Campus Requirements: None.

Tuition and Fees: *Undergraduate:* $114/credit. *Application Fee:* $25. *Other Costs:* See http://www.park.edu/catalog/cost.htm. *Credit by:* semester.

Financial Aid: Federal Stafford Loan, Federal Perkins Loan, Federal PLUS Loan, Federal Pell Grant, Federal Work-Study, VA.

Accreditation: North Central Association of Colleges and Schools.

Description: The School for Extended Learning is the outreach arm of Park College (1875). It is dedicated to serving learners with quality educational programs whenever need is demonstrated. The service is accomplished through these extended learning programs: (1) the Resident Center Program delivers degree completion programs on U.S. military and federal installations, (2) a Community College cooperative program allows students to obtain a bachelor's degree, and (3) Distance Learning provides students access to current educational technologies. The School for Extended Learning takes very seriously the task of educating persons to use knowledge beneficially for economic, social, and moral purposes. It regards cultivating literary and critical intelligence, understanding human cultural context, and developing artistic and moral sensibilities as important education purposes. The school is also dedicated to sound innovation and experimentation in its programs to meet people's needs in extended learning settings. Finally, since it views education as both the acquisition and utilization of knowledge, the school recognizes verifiable educational accomplishment regardless of how or where it was acquired. (See http://www.park.edu/catalog/mission.htm.)

Parkland College

2400 West Bradley Avenue
Champaign, IL 61821-1899

Phone: (217) 373-3893
Fax: (217) 353-2241

Division(s): Distance and Virtual Learning
Web Site(s): http://www.parkland.cc.il.us
E-mail: ramage@parkland.cc.il.us

Class Titles: Pathophysiology, Intro Chemistry, News Writing, Basic Web Page Design, Composition, Nursing, Sports Psychology, Sociology, Speech, Business, Philosophy, Psychology, Anatomy/Physiology, Statistics, Geometry, Marketing.

Teaching Methods: *Computers:* Internet, real-time chat, electronic classroom, e-mail, CD-ROM, LISTSERV. *TV:* videotape, cable program, satellite broadcasting. *Other:* videoconferencing, audioconferencing, fax, correspondence, independent study, individual study.

Credits Granted for: experiential learning, portfolio assessment, extrainstitutional learning, examination (CLEP, ACT-PEP, DANTES, GRE).

Admission Requirements: *Undergraduate:* please call for information.

On-Campus Requirements: None.

Tuition and Fees: *Undergraduate:* $49/credit residents, $89/credit nonresident. *Credit by:* semester.

Accreditation: North Central Association of Colleges and Schools.

Description: Parkland College (1965) is dedicated to providing for the comprehensive educational needs of its students with accessible and flexibly scheduled programs and high-quality services. Further, the college values and works toward the economic and cultural well-being of the local residents. Parkland recognizes the dignity and worth of each person, the contributions of diverse cultures, the value of creativity, and the need to rely on reason and cooperation to achieve our goals. The college's mission includes guiding and assisting students in becoming active, responsible, self-disciplined citizens; providing up-to-date technical-vocational and career education for students, business, and industry; providing developmental programs, courses, and services to prepare students for college-level work; preparing students for transfer to 4-year colleges/universities; assisting the district economic through services to the public, business, industry, agriculture, and labor; providing lifelong opportunities that include continuing and adult education; engaging students actively in developing a perspective on and an appreciation for cultural diversity; providing support services that enhance students' personal growth and supply employment information and placement; and expanding students' global awareness through international studies and experiences.

Pasadena City College

1570 East Colorado Boulevard	Phone: (626) 585-7108
Pasadena, CA 91106-2003	Fax: (626) 585-7916

Division(s): Learning Resources/Telecourse Administration
Web Site(s): None.
E-mail: iomartinez@paccd.cc.ca.us

Undergraduate Degree Programs:
Associate of Science
Associate of Arts

Class Titles: Anthropology, Biology, History, Humanities, Political Science, Psychology, Sociology.

Teaching Methods: *TV:* videotape, cable program. *Other:* independent study (part of ITV)

Credits Granted for: extrainstitutional learning

On-Campus Requirements: None.

Tuition and Fees: *Credit by:* semester.

Financial Aid: Federal Stafford Loan, Federal Perkins Loan, Federal PLUS Loan, Federal Pell Grant, Federal Work-Study, VA, California resident programs.

Accreditation: Western Association of Schools and Colleges.

Description: Pasadena City College (1924) is the third-largest single-campus community college in the U.S., currently enrolling 21,000 credit and 3,350 noncredit students. PCC is located on a 53-acre campus in a district of 370,000, though the college draws 60% of its students from outside the district. The new Community Education Center, just a few miles from the campus, serves 11,000 clients per year, and Continuing Education offers courses to 7,500 students. Pasadena also owns and operates a Child Development Center within a few blocks of the campus. The District employs 363 faculty, librarians, counselors, and administrators and 334 maintenance, trade, professional, clerical, and management workers.

Penn State University

207 Mitchell Building	Phone: (814) 865-5403
University Park, PA 16802	(800) 252-3592
	Fax: (814) 865-3290

Division(s): Distance Education/World Campus
Web Site(s): http://www.outreach.psu.edu/de/
http://www.worldcampus.psu.edu
E-mail: psude@cde.psu.edu or psuwd@psu.edu

Undergraduate Degree Programs:
Associate Degrees in:
  Letters, Arts, and Sciences
  Business Administration
  Human Development
  Family Studies
  Dietetic Food Systems Management
LionHawk (joint bachelor's program between Penn State and
  University of Iowa)

Certificate Programs: Administration of Justice, Writing Social Commentary, Business Management, Small Business Management, Advanced Business Management, Management, Logistics/Supply Chain Management, Retail Management, Senior Retail Management, Purchasing Management, Marketing Management, Human Resources, Dietary Manager, Dietetics/Aging, Adult Development/Aging, Children-Youth-Family Services, Nursing Management, Chemical Dependency, Turfgrass Management; noncredit: Paralegal, Legal Issues for Business Professionals, Noise Control Engineering, Geographical Information Systems.

Teaching Methods: *Computers:* Internet, real-time chat, electronic classroom, e-mail, CD-ROM, newsgroup, LISTSERV. *TV:* videotape, satellite broadcasting. *Other:* audioconferencing, videoconferencing, audiotapes, fax, correspondence.

Credits Granted for: extrainstitutional learning, examination (CLEP, DANTES).

Admission Requirements: *Undergraduate:* high school diploma or GED, SAT or ACT. *Certificate:* high school diploma or GED for most; more education for some in World Campus.

On-Campus Requirements: None.

Tuition and Fees: *Undergraduate:* $115/credit Distance Education, $266/credit World Campus. *Application Fee:* $40 undergraduate degree. *Software:* varies for World Campus courses. *Credit by:* semester.

Financial Aid: Federal Stafford Loan, Federal Perkins Loan, Federal PLUS Loan, Federal Pell Grant, Federal Work-Study (previous programs may soon be available for Distance Education/World Campus), VA.

Accreditation: Middle States Association of Colleges and Schools.

Description: Penn State University was chartered in 1855 as the Farmer's High School. In 1953 the name was changed to The Pennsylvania State University to recognize that the school had become one of the nation's leading universities. Since 1892 Penn State has been a pioneer and international leader in distance education, originally offering noncredit correspondence courses to farmers mastering new techniques in crop growing. Today more than 20,000 adults choose Distance Education to begin or continue their college education or to find personal enrichment. Penn State University's prime purpose has always been to serve the people and interests of the Commonwealth and the nation.

Pensacola Junior College

1000 College Boulevard	Phone: (850) 484-1238
Pensacola, FL 32504	Fax: (850) 484-1838

Division(s): Distance Learning
Web Site(s): http://www.distance.pjc.cc.fl.us
E-mail: dlearn@pjc.cc.fl.us

Class Titles: American History, Humanities Art, Descriptive Astronomy, Biological Principles for Non Majors, Child Development, Human Growth/Development, Economics, English Composition, Marriage/Family Living, Personal Finance/Money Management, Business, Earth Science, Nutrition, Algebra, Trigonometry, Principles of Management, Psychology, Public Speaking, Statistics, Sociology, Social Problems, Music Appreciation, Internet Research.

Teaching Methods: *Computers:* Internet, real-time chat, electronic classroom, e-mail, CD-ROM, LISTSERV. *TV:* videotape, cable program, PBS. *Other:* videoconferencing, audiotapes, fax, correspondence.

Credits Granted for: examination (CLEP, departmental exemption, CPS), military credit, Prior Learning Assessment, Servicemembers Opportunity College, transfer correspondence college credit, CPS Examination.

Admission Requirements: *Undergraduate:* official high school transcript with graduation date, or official GED score report with diploma issue date.

On-Campus Requirements: 5–10 hours/term covering reviews and testing.

Tuition and Fees: *Undergraduate:* $43/credit state residents, $156/credit nonresidents. *Application Fee:* $30. *Other Costs:* $20–30 for lab fees; fees subject to change at the discretion of the Board of Trustees. *Credit by:* semester.

Financial Aid: Federal Stafford Loan, Federal PLUS Loan, Federal Pell Grant, Federal Work-Study, VA, Florida resident programs.

Accreditation: Southern Association of Colleges and Schools.

Description: Pensacola Junior College (1948) is a student-centered, comprehensive community college dedicated to providing educational opportunities that develop its students' personal, academic, career, and aesthetic capabilities so they may achieve self-fulfillment and participate fully and positively in a democratic society. PJC began offering telecourses in 1968 through the school's PBS station. Distance learning courses, using a variety of delivery modes, continue to increase as the college seeks to be flexible in meeting the needs of adult learners.

Peralta Community College District Alameda, Laney, Merritt, and Vista Colleges

333 East Eighth Street	Phone: (510) 466-7268
Oakland, CA 94606	Fax: (510) 466-7304

Division(s): Information Technology Management Information Systems
Web Site(s): http://www.peralta.cc.ca.us
E-mail: hperdue@peralta.cc.ca.us or lmnelson@mail.metro.net

Undergraduate Degree Programs:
Associate

Certificate Programs: numerous; call for listing.

Class Titles: Astronomy, Biology, Human Nutrition, Geology, Marine Environment, Physics, Archaeology, Social/Cultural Anthropology, Business, Economics USA (macro/micro), Cultural Geography, Health Issues, History of U.S. to 1877, History of U.S. Since 1865, History of Mexico, Media/Mass Society, Government/Politics in U.S., Psychology, Psychology of Childhood, Sociology, Minority Groups, Sociology of Family, Poetry, French, Human Values/Ethics, Arts/Ideas of West Culture, Religions of World, Destinos (Spanish course), Composition, Statistics, Math for Liberal Arts Students, Elementary Algebra, College Algebra, Computer Literacy, Speech.

Teaching Methods: *Computers:* Internet. *TV:* videotape, cable program, satellite broadcasting, PBS. *Other:* None.

Admission Requirements: *Undergraduate:* age 18.

On-Campus Requirements: None.

Tuition and Fees: *Undergraduate:* $12/credit. *Credit by:* semester.

Financial Aid: California Community Colleges Board of Governor's Enrollment Fee Waiver, Federal Pell Grant, Federal Supplemental Educational Opportunity Grant, Federal Work-Study, Student Loan Cal Grants B and C, Extended Opportunity Programs and Services.

Accreditation: Western Association of Colleges and Schools.

Description: The Peralta Community College District (1953), comprised of 4 colleges, is one of 71 community college districts in California. The colleges serve 23,000 students and offer the first 2 years of undergraduate education as well as numerous certificates. The mission of the colleges is to meet the educational needs of their communities by providing comprehensive and flexible programs that will enable students to transfer to 4-year institutions, to earn degrees and certificates in selected academic and occupational fields, to prepare for entry-level positions in specific careers, to improve their basic learning skills, and to expand their general knowledge. The distance education program was started in 1995.

Philadelphia College of Textiles and Science

School House Lane and Henry Avenue	Phone: (215) 951-2700
Philadelphia, PA 19144	Fax: (215) 951-2615

Division(s): Academic Affairs
Web Site(s): http://www.philacol.edu
E-mail: kennyl@philacol.edu

Graduate Degree Programs:
Master of Science in Midwifery (for certified nurse midwives)

Teaching Methods: *Computers:* Internet *Other:* None.

Admission Requirements: *Graduate:* contact department for complete admission information.

On-Campus Requirements: 5 days at beginning of course work, for Master of Science in Midwifery.

Tuition and Fees:

Accreditation: Middle States Association of Schools and Colleges.

Description: Philadelphia College (1884) is the nation's first school to offer a Master of Science in Midwifery. Since the students are already experienced, practicing midwives, the program focuses on research and classes in health care policy and theory.

Piedmont College

PO Box 10	Phone: (706) 778-8500 x169
Demorest, GA 30535	Fax: (706) 776-2811

Division(s): None.
Web Site(s): None.
E-mail: admit@piedmont.edu

Class Titles: Quantitative Methods, Economics (micro/macro), English Composition/Literature, World History, Japanese, Algebra, Precalculus, Statistics, U.S. Government, Psychology, Spanish, History, Holocaust, Senior Seminar.

Teaching Methods: *Computers:* Internet, real-time chat, e-mail, LISTSERV. *Other:* videoconferencing, independent study, individual study, learning contracts.

Credits Granted for: experiential learning, portfolio assessment, examination (CLEP, ACT-PEP, DANTES, GRE).

Admission Requirements: *Undergraduate:* high school diploma or GED (except transfers with 24 hours), all official transcripts, SAT, 2.0 GPA.

On-Campus Requirements: depends on course.

Tuition and Fees: *Undergraduate:* $342/credit. *Graduate:* $160/credit. *Application Fee:* $20. *Credit by:* semester.

Financial Aid: Federal Stafford Loan, Federal Perkins Loan, Federal PLUS Loan, Federal Pell Grant, Federal Work-Study, VA, Georgia resident programs.

Accreditation: Southern Association of Colleges and Schools.

Description: Piedmont (1897) is an independent, private, liberal arts college offering undergraduate degrees in 23 major areas and Master of Arts Teaching degrees in early childhood and secondary education. Enrollment is 1,600 in its Demorest and Athens campuses. In 1994 Piedmont installed an interactive distance learning lab under the Georgia Statewide Academic and Medical System. Through its use, the college offers courses to local and distant high schools, and today provides classes between the college's Demorest campus and Athens center. In 1997 the college began offering classes on the Web, with many more offerings planned.

Pierce College

9401 Farwest Drive SW	Phone: (253) 964-6244
Lakewood, WA 98498-1999	Fax: (253) 964-6713

Division(s): Developmental Education
Web Site(s): http://www.pierce.ctc.edu
E-mail: smartens@pierce.ctc.edu

Class Titles: Social Anthropology, Human Anatomy/Physiology, Economics, Composition, Exposition, Composition-

Argumentation/Research, Literature, Poetry, Creative Writing, Environmental Science, French, Physical Geology, Wellness, Far East, Arithmetic, Algebra, Contemporary Moral Problems, Physical Science, Survey of Physics, Psychology, Human Development, Abnormal Psychology.

Teaching Methods: *Computers:* Internet, e-mail. *TV:* videotape, PBS. *Other:* correspondence, independent study, individual study.

Admission Requirements: *Undergraduate:* application, assessment testing and/or transcripts from other institutions.

On-Campus Requirements: None.

Tuition and Fees: *Undergraduate:* $248–$263/5-credit course. *Other Costs:* varies for books, study guides, videotape rentals. *Credit by:* quarter.

Financial Aid: Federal Stafford Loan, Federal Perkins Loan, Federal PLUS Loan, Federal Pell Grant, Federal Work-Study, VA, Washington resident programs.

Accreditation: Northwest Association for Schools and Colleges.

Description: Pierce College (1967) is a public, 2-year community college with major campuses in Lakewood and Puyallup. Pierce is one of the state's largest colleges, serving more than 40,000 full-time and part-time students each year.

Pikes Peak Community College

5675 South Academy Boulevard	**Phone: (719) 540-7539**
Colorado Springs, CO 80906	**Fax: (719) 540-7532**

Division(s): Office of Distance Education and Division of Learning Technologies
Web Site(s): http://www.ppcc.cccoes.edu
E-mail: Distance.Ed@ppcc.cccoes.edu

Undergraduate Degree Programs:
Associate of General Studies

Class Titles: Accounting, Business Math, Business, Biology, Developmental English, Composition, Technical Writing, Writing for Radio/TV, U.S. History, U.S. Government, Psychology, Developmental Mathematics, Algebra, Statistics, Criminal Justice, Spaceflight, Satellite Communication.

Teaching Methods: *Computers:* Internet, real-time chat, electronic classroom, e-mail, CD-ROM, newsgroup, LISTSERV. *TV:* videotape, cable program, satellite broadcasting, PBS. *Other:* correspondence, independent study, individual study, learning contracts.

Credits Granted for: experiential learning, portfolio assessment, examination (CLEP, ACT-PEP, DANTES).

Admission Requirements: *Undergraduate:* Age 16, high school diploma or GED, assessment tests in English, reading, math/study skills (college work or ACT/SAT may allow test exemptions).

On-Campus Requirements: None.

Tuition and Fees: *Undergraduate:* $54/credit. *Other Costs:* $35 Student Fee (fewer than 4 credits), $56 (4 or more); $9/term registration; $35/course distance education. *Credit by:* semester.

Financial Aid: Federal Stafford Loan, Federal Perkins Loan, Federal PLUS Loan, Federal Pell Grant, Federal Work-Study, VA, Colorado resident programs, PPCC Foundation Scholarships.

Accreditation: North Central Association of Colleges and Schools.

Description: Pikes Peak Community College (1968) is a 2-year public institution that provides occupational and liberal arts curricula allowing students to obtain employment in technical and vocational fields and/or transfer to 4-year colleges and universities. It also provides personal and avocational curricula to allow students throughout the community to pursue individual areas of interest for personal growth. Independent study opportunities have been available since the school opened, but distance learning that employs technology began in 1990 with interactive televised courses. The current program also includes telecourses and Internet courses.

Pine Technical College

1000 4th Street	**Phone: (320) 629-6764**
Pine City, MN 55063	**(800) 521-7463**
	Fax: (320) 629-7603

Division(s): Distance Education
Web Site(s): http://www.ptc.tec.mn.us
E-mail: hutchinsj@ptc.tec.mn.us

Class Titles: Locksmithing Technology, Security Management.

Teaching Methods: *Computers:* Internet, real-time chat, electronic classroom, e-mail, CD-ROM, newsgroup, LISTSERV. *Other:* fax.

Admission Requirements: *Undergraduate:* application and fees, contact information@ptc.tec.mn.us or call (800) 521-7463 for specific programs.

On-Campus Requirements: None.

Tuition and Fees: *Undergraduate:* $74/credit plus $20/course residents of Minnesota, Wisconsin, North Dakota, South Dakota; $107/credit plus $20/course residents of Kansas, Michigan, Nebraska, Missouri; $140/credit plus $20/course residents of other states/other countries. *Credit by:* semester.

Accreditation: North Central Association of Colleges and Schools.

Description: Pine Technical College's (1965) mission as an institution of higher education is to serve individuals and society by providing occupational, educational, and technical expertise that enhances personal development, increases economic opportunity for both employees and employers, and contributes to the global community.

Pitt Community College

Highway 11 South, PO Drawer 7007	Phone: (252) 321-4200
Greenville, NC 27835-7007	Fax: (252) 321-4404

Division(s): Distance Education
Web Site(s): http://sphynx.pitt.cc.nc.us:8080/home.htm
E-mail: pjones@pcc.pitt.cc.nc.us

Undergraduate Degree Programs:
Information Systems
Business

Certificate Programs: Accounting, Basic Law Enforcement Training, Business Administration, Business Administration/Human Resources Technology, Business Administration/Marketing and Retailing, Cardiovascular Sonography, Computed Tomography and Magnetic Resonance Imaging Technology, Health Unit Coordinator, Healthcare Management Technology.

Class Titles: General Biology, Business, Business Law, Computers, Programming/Logic, Spreadsheet, Survey of Operating Systems, Operating System-Windows, Database Concepts/Applications, Technical Support Functions, Internet, Network Theory, Trends in Technology, Systems Analysis/Design, Systems Project, Visual BASIC Programming, Advanced C, Internet Programming, Expository Writing, Health Law/Ethics, Coding/Classification, Quality Management, Medical Terminology, Data Comm/Networking, History of Philosophy, Sociology, Sonographic Physics, Abdominal Sonography, Gynecological Sonography. several in Information Systems, Arts, Sciences, Health Sciences.

Teaching Methods: *Computers:* Internet, real-time chat, electronic classroom, e-mail, CD-ROM, newsgroup, LISTSERV, Web board. *TV:* videotape, cable program, PBS. *Other:* audioconferencing, videoconferencing, fax, correspondence, independent study, individual study, learning contracts.

Credits Granted for: experiential learning, portfolio assessment, extrainstitutional learning, examination (CLEP, ACT-PEP, DANTES, GRE).

Admission Requirements: *Undergraduate:* entrance exam.

On-Campus Requirements: None.

Tuition and Fees: *Undergraduate:* $20/hour in-state, $163/hour out-of-state. *Software:* as needed. *Credit by:* semester.

Financial Aid: JTPA, Federal Stafford Loan, Federal PLUS Loan, Federal Pell Grant, Federal Work-Study, VA, private scholarships, Pitt Community College scholarships, Day Care Grant for eligible students who are parents of day care age children.

Accreditation: Southern Association of Colleges and School.

Description: Pitt Community College (1961) can trace its roots back to Pitt Technical Institute, which opened in 1964 with 96 students in 9 curricula. Since then, the school has added 2-year college transfer programs. The Learning Resources Center, which provides 33,000 square feet of Individualized Instruction Center services, opened in 1987. Then in 1990 a vocational education and lab/shop building opened to house these programs: Machinist, Electronic Servicing, Electronic Engineering Technology, Architectural Technology, Manufacturing Engineering Technology, and Industrial Construction Technology. PCC began Distance Education with the mission to educate additional students without regard to time or space and inform the workforce about the technology used in day-to-day business operations.

Plattsburgh State University of New York

101 Broad Street	
Sibley Hall 418A	Phone: (518) 564-4234
Plattsburgh, NY 12901	Fax: (518) 564-4236

Division(s): Center for Lifelong Learning/Distance Learning Office
Web Site(s): http://www.plattsburgh.edu
E-mail: marshaca@splava.cc.plattsburgh.edu

Undergraduate Degree Programs:
Bachelor of Science major in Nursing/RN completion program

Class Titles: upper-level nursing courses, general education courses which vary by semester.

Teaching Methods: *Computers:* Internet. *Other:* videoconferencing—limited to sites in northern New York State.

Credits Granted for: Examination (CLEP, ACT-PEP, DANTES).

Admission Requirements: *Undergraduate:* for RN-BSN must be licensed RN, GPA 2.5.

On-Campus Requirements: Students must complete 36 Plattsburgh credits delivered by videoconferencing to sites across northern New York State.

Tuition and Fees: *Undergraduate:* $137/credit. *Graduate:*

$213/credit. *Application Fee:* $30. *Other Costs:* $.85/credit College Fee; $5/credit Technology Fee. *Credit by:* semester.

Financial Aid: Federal Stafford Loan, Federal Perkins Loan, Federal PLUS Loan, Federal Pell Grant, VA, New York resident programs, Tuition Assistance Program (TAP).

Accreditation: Middle States Association of Colleges and Schools.

Description: Plattsburgh State University (1889) is a state-supported comprehensive institution. Its nursing programs are accredited by the National League for Nursing. It first offered distance learning courses in 1994 and currently offers courses in northern New York state by live, interactive videoconferencing and by Internet. In 1997 Plattsburgh offered 14 courses at a distance, and in the fall of 1997, 210 students enrolled in distance learning courses.

Polytechnic University

6 Metrotech Center	Phone: (718) 260-3600
Brooklyn, NY 11201	Fax: (718) 260-3755

Division(s): Life Long Learning Program in the Provost's Office
Web Site(s): http://www.poly.edu
E-mail: admitme@poly.edu (S. Kerge, Dean of Admissions)

Undergraduate Degree Programs:
Bachelor of Science

Graduate Degree Programs:
Master of Science

Doctoral Degree Programs:
Doctorate

Certificate Programs: Chemical Engineering, Chemistry/Materials Science, Polymeric Materials, Civil Engineering, Hazardous Waste Management, Traffic Engineering, Transportation Management/Economics, Transportation Planning, Computer/Information Science, Software Engineering, Electrical Engineering, Wireless Communications, Humanities/Social Sciences, Technical Communications, Management, Construction Management, Financial Engineering, Information Management, Operations Management, Technology Management, Telecommunications Management, Mechanical/Aerospace/Manufacturing Engineering, Achieving World Class Quality, Computational Methods for Engineering Design/Analysis, Manufacturing Engineering/Production Science, Manufacturing Excellence By Design: Holistic Approach.

Class Titles: Probability, Signals/Systems/Transforms, Web Site Authoring/Development, Writing Technical Manuals/Procedures, Technical Translation/Locational Practices, Internet Informatics.

Teaching Methods: *Computers:* Internet, real-time chat,

electronic classroom, e-mail, newsgroup. *TV:* videotape. *Other:* audioconferencing, videoconferencing, audiographics, audiotapes, fax, correspondence.

Credits Granted for: special project, internship.

Admission Requirements: *Undergraduate:* SAT, high school average. *Graduate:* undergraduate records.

On-Campus Requirements: None.

Tuition and Fees: *Undergraduate:* $620/credit. *Graduate:* $675/credit. *Application Fee:* $40 undergraduate, $45 graduate. *Credit by:* semester.

Financial Aid: Federal Stafford Loan, Federal Perkins Loan, Federal PLUS Loan, Federal Pell Grant, Federal Work-Study, VA, New York resident programs.

Accreditation: Middle States Association of Colleges and Schools, Accreditation Board for Engineering and Technology, Computer Science Accreditation Board.

Description: Polytechnic University (1854) is New York's major metropolitan educational resource in science and technology education and research. A private, coeducational institution known for many years as "Brooklyn Poly," Polytechnic has a distinguished history of excellence in electrical engineering, polymer chemistry, aerospace, and microwave engineering. Today it is a leader in telecommunications and information technology, urban infrastructure, materials, polymers, transportation, the environment, and management of technology. The university is also known for its outstanding research centers and outreach programs to encourage math and science education in New York schools. Polytechnic University comprises 3 campuses: (1) Brooklyn: Polytechnic's campus in downtown Brooklyn is at Metrotech Center, a 16-acre, $1 billion academic/research complex spearheaded and codeveloped by Polytechnic. Metrotech has attracted major corporations as tenants and partners in education, research, and development projects. The address is 6 Metrotech Center, Brooklyn, NY 11201, (718) 260-3600; (2) Long Island: Polytechnic's campus on Long Island is at 901 Route 110, Farmingdale, NY 11735, (516) 755-4400; (3) Westchester: Polytechnic's Westchester Graduate Center is at 36 Saw Mill River Road, Hawthorne, NY 10532, (914) 323-2000.

Porterville College

100 East College Avenue	Phone: (209) 791-2320
Porterville, CA 93257	Fax: (209) 791-2487

Division(s): Office of Instruction
Web Site(s): http://www.pc.cc.ca.us
E-mail: yschultz@pc.cc.ca.us

Undergraduate Degree Programs:
Liberal Studies

Sociology
Social Science
Political Science

Graduate Degree Programs:
Master of Business Administration, Behavioral Science

Class Titles: Speech, Political Science, Health, English, Information Systems, Sociology.

Teaching Methods: *Computers:* Internet, real-time chat, electronic classroom, e-mail, CD-ROM, newsgroup, LIST-SERV. *TV:* satellite broadcasting of bachelor's and master's programs. *Other:* None.

Admission Requirements: *Undergraduate:* admission application form online. *Graduate:* application to Satellite University. *Doctoral:* application to Satellite University.

On-Campus Requirements: None.

Tuition and Fees: *Undergraduate:* $12/credit. *Graduate:* handled by university. *Credit by:* semester for undergraduate, both semester and quarter for graduate.

Financial Aid: Federal Stafford Loan, Federal Perkins Loan, Federal PLUS Loan, Federal Pell Grant, Federal Work-Study, VA, California resident programs.

Accreditation: Western Association of Schools and Colleges.

Description: Porterville College (1927) is a 2-year community college situated in the rural foothills of the Sierra Nevada Mountains in central California. This is Porterville's second year of offering online courses to make education more accessible to nontraditional students.

Portland State University

1633 Southwest Park Avenue	Phone: (503) 725-4865
Portland, OR 97201	(800) 547-8887 x4865
	Fax: (503) 725-4840

Division(s): Independent Study
Distance Learning
School of Extended Studies
Web Site(s): http://extended.pdx.edu/istudy
E-mail: xsis@ses.pdx.edu

Class Titles: Criminal Justice Process, Juvenile Justice Process, Criminal Law/Legal Constitutional Criminal Procedures, Court Procedures, Drawing, Atmospheric Science, Projects-Weather Analysis Lab (Synoptic Meteorology), Advanced Project in Synoptic Meteorology, Accounting, Cost Accounting, Accounting for Not-For-Profit Organizations, Auditing, Nutrition, Principles of Economics (micro/macro), Shakespeare, Survey of American Literature, American Fiction, Contemporary Literature, Contemporary Literature (Drama), American Folklore, Corrective English (noncredit),

English Composition, Short Story Writing (Fiction or Nonfiction), Poetry Writing, Geography, Geology, History of U.S., Algebra (noncredit), College Math, Calculus for Management/Social Sciences, Calculus, Probability/Statistics, Psychology as Natural Science, Psychology as Social Science, Human Development, Psychopathology, Quests for Meaning—World Religions, Sociology, Social Problems/Issues, Women in China.

Teaching Methods: *Computers:* e-mail, CD-ROM. *TV:* videotape. *Other:* correspondence, independent study.

Admission Requirements: *Undergraduate:* open enrollment.

On-Campus Requirements: None.

Tuition and Fees: *Undergraduate:* $69/credit plus a nonrefundable $15 registration fee *Other Costs:* textbook and/or additional course materials. Prices vary. *Credit by:* quarter.

Financial Aid: students must check whether or not correspondence study will be funded by their financial aid package.

Accreditation: Northwest Association of Schools and Colleges.

Description: Independent Study at Portland State University (1907) offers 68 courses that earn college credit in an array of 15 areas of study ranging from Business Administration to Sociology through correspondence providing a one-to-one learning experience for students who wish to set their own pace for course completion within a 12-month (maximum) time frame. Enrollment is open; students may register any day in any term; they do not need to be admitted by Portland State University to take Independent Study courses. The credits earned by students through Independent Study are held in the student's permanent record in the Portland State University Registrar's Office and may be transferred to the school of the student's choice.

Prairie State College

202 South Halsted Street	Phone: (708) 709-3551
Chicago Heights, IL 60411	Fax: (708) 709-3940

Division(s): Learning Resources Center
Web Site(s): http://www.prairie.cc.il.us
E-mail: pgaitskill@prairie.cc.il.us

Undergraduate Degree Programs:
All distance education classes are part of the Associate of Arts degree

Class Titles: Varies by semester, but usually in subjects such as business, social sciences, humanities, astronomy, interior design, dental hygiene, Italian, Spanish, languages.

Teaching Methods: *Computers:* electronic classroom (in development). *TV:* videotape, cable program, PBS. *Other:*

independent study, individual study.

Credits Granted for: portfolio assessment, proficiency examinations (CLEP).

Admission Requirements: *Undergraduate:* assessment exams and official transcripts.

On-Campus Requirements: None.

Tuition and Fees: *Undergraduate:* $56/credit. *Application Fee:* $10. *Other Costs:* various lab fees. *Credit by:* semester.

Financial Aid: Federal Stafford Loan, Federal PLUS Loan, Federal Pell Grant, Federal Work-Study, VA, Illinois resident programs.

Accreditation: North Central Association of Colleges and Schools.

Description: Prairie State College (1957), originally established to offer transfer and occupational-technical courses, now encompasses 5 high school districts. In 1979 a vocational/technical building and a dental studies building were completed, and in 1990 a conference and performance center opened. Prairie State's latest addition is its Community Instructional Center, a multipurpose facility with state-of-the art capabilities. It holds a 487-seat auditorium for lectures, concerts, and other events; 4 breakout rooms for meetings; and an art gallery. Groundbreaking for the new Health Education Center took place in April 1998. This facility will enhance the dental center and add teaching classrooms for dental and nursing students.

Pratt Community College and Area Vocational School

348 North East S.R. 61	Phone: (316) 672-5641
Pratt, KS 67124	(800) 794-3091
	Fax: (316) 672-2519

Division(s): Instruction
Web Site(s): http://www.pcc.cc.ks.us
E-mail: donh@pcc.cc.ks.us

Teaching Methods: *Computers:* Internet, e-mail, newsgroup, LISTSERV. *TV:* videotape, cable program, satellite broadcasting, PBS video courses. *Other:* radio broadcast, audioconferencing, videoconferencing, audiographics, audiotapes, fax, correspondence, independent study, individual study, learning contracts.

Credits Granted for: experiential learning, portfolio assessment, extrainstitutional learning, examination (CLEP, ACT-PEP, DANTES, GRE).

Admission Requirements: *Undergraduate:* ASSET placement test or ACT exemption for degree student.

On-Campus Requirements: some campus time required.

Tuition and Fees: *Undergraduate:* $43/credit. *Credit by:* semester.

Financial Aid: Federal Stafford Loan, Federal Perkins Loan, Federal PLUS Loan, Federal Pell Grant, Federal Work-Study, VA, Kansas resident programs.

Accreditation: North Central Association of Colleges and Schools.

Description: Pratt Community College (1938) installed its first ITV studio in the fall of 1995. Interactive TV is the most readily used means of distance education at the school. A second studio was added in the fall of 1996. Audio and video signals from all sites are generally live and interactive, although filmed lessons, as well as commercial and educational films, can also be presented over ITV. PCC also has a Coder-Decoder system that allows the school to receive audio and video signals and to transmit such signals over telephone lines. Other distance education services available at PCC include satellite downlinks, which provide a one-way audio and video feed to several of the school's classrooms. PCC is also connected to Telenet 2, a statewide audio/video network connecting computers at various sites across Kansas.

Presentation College

1500 North Main	Phone: (605) 225-1634
Aberdeen, SD 57401	Fax: (605) 229-8518

Division(s): Academic Dean
Web Site(s): http://www.presentation.edu
E-mail: admit@presentation.edu

Undergraduate Degree Programs:
Bachelor of Science in:
  Business
  Nursing

Teaching Methods: *Computers:* Internet, e-mail, LISTSERV. *TV:* videotape, closed-circuit cable program. *Other:* videoconferencing, audioconferencing, fax, correspondence, independent study, learning contracts.

Credits Granted for: portfolio assessment, examination (CLEP, ACT-PEP, DANTES, GRE).

Admission Requirements: *Undergraduate:* completed application form with $15 nonrefundable application fee, official high school transcript or GED, all official college and/or vocational technology transcripts, placement test scores, and ACT or SAT scores. *Certificate:* same as undergraduate.

On-Campus Requirements: None.

Tuition and Fees: *Undergraduate:* $3,410/block (12–18 credits), $225/credit regular tuition. *Application Fee:* $15.

Other Costs: $20 technology fee. *Credit by:* semester.

Financial Aid: Federal Stafford Loan, Federal Perkins Loan, Federal PLUS Loan, Federal Pell Grant, Federal Work-Study, VA, South Dakota resident programs.

Accreditation: North Central Association of Colleges and Schools, National League for Nursing Accrediting Commission, Commission on Accreditation of Allied Health Education Programs, Council on Social Work Education.

Description: Presentation College (1922) is an independent, Catholic educational institution conducted by the Sisters of the Presentation of the Blessed Virgin Mary. The college has a satellite nursing program, the Cheyenne River Lakota Nursing School at Eagle Butte, South Dakota, that began in 1980. Presentation College's mission is to offer women and men the opportunity of education toward self-actualization, professional excellence, and lifelong learning. As a Catholic-Christian community, Presentation College challenges its members in the pursuit of Christian values and in responsive relationships with the human community and with God. Distance learning was initiated in response to rural education needs. Many individual courses are offered via videoconferencing. A Bachelor of Science Nursing completion program is offered almost in its entirety over the system. Dual-enrollment credit courses are offered to area high schools.

Prince George's Community College

301 Largo Road	Phone: (301) 322-0642
Largo, MD 20774	Fax: (301) 386-7502

Division(s): Telecommunications and Weekend Programs
Web Site(s): http://pgweb.pg.cc.md.us/pgdocs/distlern/index.htm
E-mail: distance_learning@pgstumail.pg.cc.md.us

Undergraduate Degree Programs:
Associate of Arts in:
General Studies
Business Management

Certificate Programs: General Management.

Teaching Methods: *Computers:* Internet, real-time chat, electronic classroom, e-mail, CD-ROM, LISTSERV. *TV:* videotape, cable program, PBS. *Other:* audioconferencing, audiographics, audiotapes, fax, correspondence, independent study, individual study.

Credits Granted for: experiential learning, examination (CLEP, ACT-PEP, DANTES, GRE).

Admission Requirements: *Undergraduate:* high school graduate or equivalent, age 16 who has graduated, talented and gifted student, or high school student who may benefit from attending college. *Certificate:* same as undergraduate.

On-Campus Requirements: None.

Tuition and Fees: *Undergraduate:* in county rates only: $74/credit. *Application Fee:* free. *Other Costs:* $20 registration fee, $15/credit instructional services fee, $1/credit student activity fee, $30/course telecredit fee, $30 late registration fee. *Credit by:* semester.

Financial Aid: Federal Stafford Loan, Federal Perkins Loan, Federal PLUS Loan, Federal Pell Grant, Federal Work-Study, VA, Maryland resident programs.

Accreditation: Middle States Association of Colleges and Schools.

Description: Prince George's Community College (1958) is located on a beautiful 150-acre campus. In 1976 PGCC began offering courses via distance learning. Today we offer more than 60 distance courses, including 6 via the BBS (Bulletin Board System) and some via the Web.

Professional Career Development Institute

430 Technology Parkway	Phone: (770) 729-8400
Norcross, GA 30092	Fax: (770) 729-9296

Division(s): Education
Web Site(s): http://pcdi.com

Certificate Programs: Diploma.

Class Titles: Real Estate Appraisal, Property Management, Paralegal, Bookkeeping/Accounting, Animal Care, Interior Decorating, VCR Repair, Travel, Gun Smithing, Computer Training, Hotel/Restaurant Management, Medical/Dental Office Assisting, Home Inspection, PC Repair, Fitness/Nutrition, Auto Mechanics, Medical Transcription, Conversation, Floral, Legal Transcriptionist, Electrician, Tax Preparation, Motorcycle Repair, Locksmith, Child Day Care, High School, Computer Applications, Visual BASIC, Electronics, Teacher Assisting, Private Investigator, Landscaping Design, Medical Billing, Carpentry, Fashion Merchandising, Small Business Management.

Teaching Methods: *Other:* audiotapes, correspondence, independent study, individual study.

Credits Granted for: GRE.

On-Campus Requirements: None.

Tuition and Fees: *Credit by:* semester.

Accreditation: Distance Education and Training Council.

Description: Professional Career Development Institute (1983) creates and markets distance education (home study) training courses. The diploma programs provide basic vocational or avocational skills that help people build a foundation of knowledge on which to start and advance their careers. PCDI is the nation's second-largest and fastest-growing distance education institute of its kind. The institute has delivered top-quality career training to 400,000 students in the U.S. and in 125 countries around the world. PCDI has grown from only one course, in real estate appraisal, to 36 diploma programs.

Pueblo Community College

900 West Orman Avenue	Phone: (719) 549-3343
Pueblo, CO 81004	Fax: (719) 549-3453

Division(s): Educational Technology and Telecommunications
Web Site(s): http://www.pcc.cccoes.edu; www.ccconline.org
E-mail: mcpheeters@pcc.cccoes.edu (for telecourses), admissions@pcc.cccoes.edu (for online courses at PCC-Admissions), townley_r@pcc.cccoes.edu (for Internet courses, Dr. Rod Townley).

Undergraduate Degree Programs:
AAS in Business (CCC Online)

Class Titles: Course offerings vary each semester and may have prerequisites. U.S. Cinema, Race to Save Planet, Nutrition Pathways, Child Development, Economics USA, Writer's Exchange, Power of Place, Earth Revealed, Literary Visions, Voices/Visions, College Algebra, Discovering Psychology, Sociological Imagination, Spanish, Biology, Human Anatomy/Physiology, Pathophysiology, Chemistry, Creativity/Young Child, Guidance Strategies for Young Children, Conceptual Physics, Clinical Nutrition, Language/Cognitive Development, Health Information Technology, Coding, Management of Health Information Systems, Medical Terminology, CP4m UCD9 Coding, Nutrition/Young Child, Health Statistics, Legal Aspects, Pharmacology.

Teaching Methods: *Computers:* Internet. *TV:* videotape, cable program, satellite broadcasting, PBS. *Other:* radio broadcast, audioconferencing, videoconferencing, audiotapes, fax, independent study, individual study.

Credits Granted for: portfolio assessment, examination (CLEP, ACT-PEP, Post-Secondary Enrollment Options, Advanced Vocational Education Program).

Admission Requirements: *Undergraduate:* age 18, admission application, high school graduate or GED, or ability to benefit demonstrated by examination.

On-Campus Requirements: Student must attend semester orientations to receive class syllabi and meet with course instructor. Telecourses require some lab work and testing and on-campus meetings.

Tuition and Fees: *Undergraduate:* $73/credit resident, $271/credit nonresident. *Other Costs:* $115/credit online courses, $35/course Telecourse Fee, $10 Student ID, $8/ credit hour fees, $3 College Fee, $9 Registration. *Credit by:* semester.

Financial Aid: Federal Stafford Loan, Federal Perkins Loan, Federal PLUS Loan, Federal Pell Grant, Federal Work-Study, VA, Colorado resident programs, scholarships. See www.financialaid@pcc.cccoes.edu

Accreditation: North Central Association of Colleges and Schools.

Description: Pueblo Community College (1933) is located in the city of Pueblo, Colorado, population 102,000. PCC provides educational programs at its Pueblo campus, its Fremont County campus in Canon City, and at its Southwest Center, which serves Cortez and Durango. The mission of the college is to develop and support lifetime learning that leads to positive change in individuals, families, and communities. PCC's Educational Technology and Telecommunications Division provides telelearning to Pueblo and Southern Colorado through interactive TV, telecourses, and CBC (College by Cassette). Pueblo Community also offers high quality educational programming via the college's educational cable channel. This channel carries standard academic courses to students and teletraining programs to industry. These training programs can be delivered to work stations, corporate training centers, or to students' homes. PCC is also helping provide an Internet degree through Colorado Community College and Occupational Education System's (CCCOES) CCC Online. Currently, faculty from all Colorado community colleges collaborate through CCC Online to offer an AAS in Business via the Internet.

Purdue University

1137 Engineering Administration Building, Rm 301	Phone: (765) 496-3337
West Lafayette, IN 47907-1137	Fax: (765) 496-3339

Division(s): Office of Distance Learning
Web Site(s): http://www.purdue.edu/distance
E-mail: cmlawson@reg.purdue.edu

Graduate Degree Programs:
Master of Science in Engineering

Doctoral Degree Programs:
Cohort Doctoral Program in Educational Administration

Certificate Programs: Digital Signal Processing

Teaching Methods: *Computers:* Internet, real-time chat, electronic classroom, e-mail, CD-ROM, newsgroup, LISTSERV. *TV:* videotape, cable program, satellite broadcasting, PBS. *Other:* videoconferencing, audioconferencing, audiotapes, fax, correspondence, independent study, individual study, learning contracts.

Credits Granted for: experiential learning, portfolio assessment, extrainstitutional learning, examination (CLEP, ACT-PEP, GRE), credit by exam, credit established/awarded on the basis of CEEB Match Achievement test score or Purdue Composite Score, transfer credit.

Admission Requirements: *Undergraduate:* SAT/ACT unless over age 25 with 12 credits, rank in or near upper half of high school class. Permission needed for high school student or younger. Contact individual schools for high school classes required.

On-Campus Requirements: determined on a course-by-course basis.

Tuition and Fees: *Undergraduate:* resident $126, nonresident $387. *Graduate:* resident $126, nonresident $387. *Doctoral:* resident $126, nonresident $387. *Application Fee:* resident $30, nonresident $30. *Other Costs:* $3 technology fee; $100–$2,518 differential fees depending on program; some courses assess a special fee ranging from $40–$4,130 depending on course. Full fees at 8+ hours $1,750 (resident) and $5,860 (nonresident). 1–7 credits/semester assessed at the above rates. *Credit by:* semester.

Financial Aid: Federal Stafford Loan (subsidized and unsubsidized), Federal Perkins Loan, Federal PLUS Loan, Federal Pell Grant, Federal Work-Study, VA, Indiana resident programs, Lilly Awards, Purdue Loans, University Fee Remissions, Supplemental Grants, State awards, 4-H and other scholarships, ROTC, Merit Scholars, 21st Century Scholars, Hoosier Scholars, Special Education Services Scholarship, Minority Teachers Scholarship, Nursing Scholarship, Higher Education Award, Presidential Scholarship, departmental scholarships.

Accreditation: North Central Association of Colleges and Schools.

Description: Purdue University (1922) already has a significant track record in technology-enhanced distance learning. In 1922, Purdue's WBAA—Indiana's first radio station—began broadcasting electronic engineering courses. Since then, more schools and departments have provided educational opportunities to learners across Indiana and beyond. And today, the innovative use of distance learning to enhance teaching, learning, research, and outreach has become an institutional strategic priority. The office of distance learning was established in 1997.

Queen's University

F1 Mackintosh-Corry Hall
Kingston, ON, Canada K7L 3N6

Phone: (613) 533-2471
Fax: (613) 533-6805

Division(s): Continuing and Distance Studies
Web Site(s): http://www.queensu.ca/cds
E-mail: cds@post.queensu.ca

Undergraduate Degree Programs:
Bachelor of Arts with minor concentrations in:
 History
 Psychology
 German
 English
 Political Studies
 Women's Studies

Class Titles: Drama, Economics, English Language/Literature, French Studies, Geography, German Language/Literature, History, Math/Statistics, Microbiology/Immunology, Pharmacology/Toxicology, Philosophy, Political Studies, Psychology, Religious Studies, Sociology, Spanish/Italian Languages/Literatures, Women's Studies, Effective Writing.

Teaching Methods: *Computers:* Internet, e-mail, CD-ROM. *TV:* videotape. *Other:* audioconferencing, audiotapes, fax, correspondence.

Admission Requirements: *Undergraduate:* high school diploma (university preparation program) or equivalent.

On-Campus Requirements: None.

Tuition and Fees: *Undergraduate:* Canadian (Cdn) $730/credit domestic, Cdn $2,020 international. *Application Fee:* Cdn $30. *Software:* variable. *Credit by:* semester and quarter.

Accreditation: Association of Universities and Colleges of Canada.

Description: The Queen's University (1841) main campus is located on the shores of Lake Ontario in historic Kingston, Ontario, Canada. The university was established by Royal Charter and has the oldest distance education program in North America, with the first correspondence courses being offered in 1889. Our students include those wanting to complete a degree or take university courses for interest, personal enrichment, or upgrading purposes. Print-based and CD-ROM/Internet-based correspondence courses provide students who are unable to attend classes an opportunity to complete Queen's degree credit courses from anywhere in the world. Each course consists of a series of assignments and either a final examination or final term paper. Queen's has more than 1,000 established exam centers around the globe, and if there is not a center within 60 miles of your home, one will be established for you.

Rancho Santiago Community College District Santa Ana and Santiago Canyon Colleges

1530 West Seventeenth Street
Santa Ana, CA 92706

Phone: (714) 564-6725
Fax: (714) 564-6158

Division(s): Distance Education
Web Site(s): http://www.rancho.cc.ca.us/rsccd/rsccd.htm
E-mail: oleabj@mail.rancho.cc.ca.us

Class Titles: Anatomy, Physiology, Anthropology, Astronomy, Biology, Business, Computer Science, Geology, Human Development, Humanities, Nutrition, Philosophy, Psychology, Real Estate, Sociology.

Teaching Methods: *Computers:* Internet, real-time chat, electronic classroom, e-mail, CD-ROM, LISTSERV. *TV:* videotape, cable program, satellite broadcasting, PBS. *Other:* videoconferencing, audiotapes, fax.

Credits Granted for: experiential learning, portfolio assessment, extrainstitutional learning, examination (CLEP, ACT-PEP, DANTES, GRE).

Admission Requirements: *Undergraduate:* age 18.

On-Campus Requirements: None.

Tuition and Fees: *Undergraduate:* $12/credit. *Credit by:* semester.

Financial Aid: Federal Stafford Loan, Federal Perkins Loan, Federal PLUS Loan, Federal Pell Grant, Federal Work-Study, VA, California resident programs.

Accreditation: Western Association of Schools and Colleges.

Description: Rancho Santiago Community College District (1915), located in central Orange County in southern California, comprises an area of 193 square miles with a population of 650,000. Santa Ana College is California's 4th oldest of 107 community colleges, and Santiago Canyon College (1985) is the newest. The mission of the RSCCD is to provide educational programs and services that reflect the needs of our multifaceted communities. Santa Ana College is fully accredited by the Western Association of Schools and Colleges and has been a member of Intelecom, the Southern California Consortium for Community College TV. Distance education has been offered since 1970.

Red Rocks Community College

13300 West 6th Avenue
Lakewood, CO 80228

Phone: (303) 914-6704
Fax: (303) 914-6716

Division(s): Learning and Resource Center
Web Site(s): http://www.rrcc.cccoes.edu

Undergraduate Degree Programs:
Associate of Applied Science in Business

Class Titles: Microcomputer Operating Systems, Computer, Microcomputer Applications, Word Processing, Presentation Graphics, Windows, Microcomputer Database, Electronic Spreadsheets, Project Management (currently based on Microsoft Office '97), Philosophy, Ethics.

Teaching Methods: *Computers:* Internet, e-mail, CD-ROM. *TV:* videotape, PBS. *Other:* audioconferencing, videoconferencing, fax, individual study, self-paced online instruction. RRCC is also a consortium partner in ccconline (see http://www.ccconline.org for more information).

Credits Granted for: experiential learning, portfolio assessment, examination (CLEP, ACT-PEP, DANTES, GRE).

Admission Requirements: *Undergraduate:* open-entry; assessment test for new students.

On-Campus Requirements: None.

Tuition and Fees: *Undergraduate:* $56/credit. *Other Costs:* $9 registration, $7/credit student fees. *Credit by:* semester.

Financial Aid: Federal Stafford Loan, Federal Perkins Loan, Federal PLUS Loan, Federal Pell Grant, Federal Work-Study, VA, Colorado resident programs.

Accreditation: North Central Association of Colleges and Schools.

Description: The mission of Red Rocks Community College (1971) is to develop and support lifelong learners so they may live fuller lives and add value to the communities in which they live and work. Providing learning options is essential for our students. We began offering self-paced courses 20 years ago to meet the needs of students. In 1991 we began offering videoconferencing courses to one site. We now offer an AA degree through videoconferencing to 4 sites. We also offer a variety of courses achieved through online instruction, including the AAS in Business.

Redlands Community College

1300 South Country Club Road	Phone: (405) 262-2552 x2420
El Reno, OK 73036-5304	Fax: (405) 422-1200

Division(s): Alternative and Off-campus
Web Site(s): http://www.redlands.cc.ok.us
E-mail: hobsont@redlands.cc.ok.us

Class Titles: History, English, Political Science, Humanities, Psychology, Sociology, Math, Business.

Teaching Methods: *Computers:* Internet, electronic classroom, e-mail, CD-ROM, newsgroup, LISTSERV. *TV:* videotape, cable program. *Other:* fax, correspondence, independent study, individual study, learning contracts.

Credits Granted for: experiential learning, portfolio assessment, extrainstitutional learning, examination (CLEP, ACT-PEP, DANTES, GRE).

Admission Requirements: *Undergraduate:* ACT 19 or secondary assessment.

On-Campus Requirements: None.

Tuition and Fees: *Undergraduate:* $30 tuition, fees $26. *Credit by:* semester.

Financial Aid: Federal Stafford Loan, Federal Perkins Loan, Federal PLUS Loan, Federal Pell Grant, Federal Work-Study, VA, Oklahoma resident programs.

Accreditation: North Central Association of Colleges and Schools.

Description: Redlands Community College (1939) is a 2-year coeducational public institution of higher education specializing in general and technical education. The collegiate experience is, in RCC's, opinion, the next level. The next level of your education, the next level in self-betterment, and the next level in the experiences you can gain by going to college.

Reformed Theological Seminary

2101 Carmel Road	Phone: (704) 366-5066 x232
Charlotte, NC 28226	Fax: (704) 366-9295

Division(s): Distance Education
Web Site(s): http://www.rts.edu
E-mail: distance.education@rts.edu

Graduate Degree Programs:
Master of Arts in:
   Biblical Studies
   Theological Studies
Master of Divinity

Certificate Programs: Missions, Biblical Studies, Historical Studies, Theological Studies, General Studies.

Class Titles: all courses.

Teaching Methods: *Computers:* Internet, e-mail, CD-ROM. *Other:* audiotapes, notebooks, fax, correspondence, learning contracts.

Credits Granted for: transfer credits from other institutions.

Admission Requirements: *Graduate:* accredited bachelor's degree.

On-Campus Requirements: Students pursuing the Master of Arts degrees are required to take 50% of their course work on campus. In addition, students pursuing the Master of Divinity degree are required to take 80% of their course work on campus.

Tuition and Fees: *Graduate:* $220/credit. *Application Fee:* $25. *Credit by:* semester.

Financial Aid: Individual and local scholarships are available on a first come, first served basis.

Accreditation: Southern Association of Colleges and Schools, Association of Theological Schools in the U.S. and Canada.

Description: Reformed Theological Seminary was established in 1966 to provide serious, realistic training for those interested in pursuing opportunities in ministry. Our purpose is to serve the Church in all branches of Evangelical Christianity by training its leaders, with a priority on pastors, missionaries, educators, and counselors. From its humble beginnings in Jackson, Mississippi, RTS has grown to 5 campuses, including a "virtual" campus that began in 1991. Theological students worldwide currently take courses by distance, adding a new dimension to the educational scope of RTS.

Regent University

1000 Regent University Drive	Phone: (800) 373-5504
Virginia Beach, VA 23464-9800	Fax: (757) 226-4388

Division(s): Distance Education and Information
Web Site(s): http://www.regent.edu
E-mail: admissions@regent.edu

Graduate Degree Programs:
Master's and/or Doctoral degrees in:
   Communication
   Business
   Education
   Government
   Law (LLM in International Taxation)
   Organizational Leadership
   Divinity

Doctoral Degree Programs:
Post-master's endorsement programs in Education:
   Reading Specialist

Learning Disabilities
Mild Mental Retardation
Emotional/Behavioral Disorders

Certificate Programs: Administrator, Advanced Graduate Studies (CAGS)

Teaching Methods: *Computers:* Internet, real-time chat, electronic classroom, e-mail, CD-ROM, newsgroup, LIST-SERV. *Other:* audiotapes, videotapes, correspondence, independent study, individual study, field-based ministry programs.

Admission Requirements: *Graduate:* accredited 4-year bachelor's degree (nonaccredited degrees considered on an individual basis), cumulative undergraduate GPA of 2.75 (3.0 in desired area), submission of test scores (MAT, GMAT, GRE, etc., depending on school requirement), maturity in spiritual and/or character qualities, and personal goals consistent with Regent's mission and goals (individual schools may have additional admissions criteria). Accelerated Scholars and Professionals Program allows some students to enter master's program without a bachelor's degree—must have 90 credits toward undergraduate degree and have significant life experience (determined by admissions committee) in a professional area relevant to master's program. *Doctoral:* same as graduate. *Certificate:* same as graduate.

On-Campus Requirements: vary among Regent schools; contact individual schools.

Tuition and Fees: *Graduate:* $325/credit, Business; $350/credit, Communication; $295/credit, Education; $385/credit, Government; $263/credit, Divinity; $2,400/semester, Organizational Leadership, Law (LLM). *Credit by:* semester.

Financial Aid: Federal Stafford Loans, school-specific scholarships and grants, VA.

Accreditation: Southern Association of Colleges and Schools, Association of Theological Schools, American Bar Association.

Description: Regent University (1977) is a graduate institution offering 22 master's and doctoral degrees. Each professional area of study is approached from a moral and ethical perspective found in Judeo-Christian tradition. This perspective seeks to foster a sense of moral responsibility in each student. Relevant, ethical values are applied to professional pursuits within a rigorous, scholarly framework. Regent has grown to an enrollment of 1,830 students. In addition to main campus programs, Regent offers several degree programs in its northern-Virginia/Washington, DC, area extension. Today, 15 graduate degree programs serve students worldwide via the Internet and Distance Learning.

Regents College

7 Columbia Circle
Albany, NY 12203-5159

Phone: (518) 464-8500
Fax: (518) 464-8777

Division(s): None.
Web Site(s): http://www.regents.edu
E-mail: rcinfo@regents.edu

Undergraduate Degree Programs:
Associate and Bachelor's Degrees in:
    Business
    Liberal Arts
    Nursing
    Technology

Graduate Degree Programs:
Master of Arts in Liberal Studies (MLS)

Certificate Programs: Home Health Care Nursing

Teaching Methods: *Computers:* students and advisors develop programs using appropriate teaching methods. *Other:* None.

Credits Granted for: experiential learning, portfolio assessment, extrainstitutional learning, college-level proficiency examination (CLEP, Regents College Examinations, DANTES, GRE), ACE-evaluated military training.

Admission Requirements: *Undergraduate:* open-admissions, except nursing. *Graduate:* bachelor's degree, enrollment essay. *Certificate:* licensed RN.

On-Campus Requirements: None.

Tuition and Fees: *Undergraduate:* $650 associate enrollment fee first year, $750 bachelor's enrollment fee first year, $325 each additional year. *Graduate:* $1,500 for first core assessment. *Application Fee:* $100 for MLS program. *Other Costs:* $390 associate degree graduation fee, $415 bachelor's degree graduation fee, other fees vary. *Credit by:* semester.

Financial Aid: VA, New York resident programs, institutional scholarships, private grants/scholarships, private (alternative) loans.

Accreditation: Middle States Association of Colleges and Schools, National League for Nursing Accrediting Commission, American Council on Education, Center for Adult Learning and Education Credentials, Home Health Care Nursing (66 CEU units approved by New York State Nurses Association).

Description: Regents College was established in 1971 as "America's First Virtual University." Created to remove barriers to education for adult learners, Regents has more than 80,000 graduates worldwide. Founded on the belief that what you know is more important than where or how you learned it, the school offers flexibility in earning degrees. All degrees are designed to be completed independently, at a distance. Regents college examinations are available around the world, and most urban areas in the U.S. are within 30 miles of a testing site. Exams are computer-delivered via Sylvan Technology Centers and are a means to earn undergraduate credit.

Rensselaer Polytechnic Institute

| 110 8th Street - CII 4011 | Phone: (518) 276-7787 |
| Troy, NY 12180-3590 | Fax: (518) 276-8026 |

Division(s): Continuing and Distance Education
Web Site(s): http://rsvp.rpi.edu/
E-mail: gregac@rpi.edu

Graduate Degree Programs:
Master of Business Administration in Management/Technology
Mechanical Engineering
Master of Engineering in Electrical Engineering, Microelectronics concentration
Master of Science in:
Computer Science
Electrical Engineering, Microelectronics concentration
Engineering Science, concentrations in:
Manufacturing Systems
Engineering
Microelectronics Manufacturing Engineering
Industrial and Management Engineering, Service Systems concentration
Management/Technology
Mechanical Engineering
Professional Master's in Information Technology, tracks in:
Microelectronics
Computer Networks
Computer Graphics
Software Engineering Design
Computational Science

Certificate Programs: Human Computer Interaction, Polymer Chemistry, Information Science, Management/Technology, Manufacturing Systems Engineering, Mechanical Engineering, Microelectronics Manufacturing, Reliability, Service Systems.

Class Titles: Specific to degree program offerings each semester.

Teaching Methods: *Computers:* Internet, real-time chat, electronic classroom, e-mail, CD-ROM, newsgroup, LISTSERV. *TV:* videotape, satellite broadcasting. *Other:* videoconferencing (room-based and desktop), audioconferencing, fax.

Credits Granted for: approved transfer of college credit.

Admission Requirements: *Graduate:* completed graduate application, bachelor's degree, 3.0 undergraduate GPA, brief statement of background and goals, 2 supporting letters of recommendation, 2 official transcripts from all colleges and universities. *Certificate:* application form, transcript of bache-

lor's degree (or highest degree earned).

On-Campus Requirements: None.

Tuition and Fees: *Graduate:* $630/credit. *Application Fee:* $35. *Software:* varies. *Other Costs:* $25. *Credit by:* semester.

Accreditation: Middle States Association of Colleges and Schools.

Description: Rensselaer Polytechnic Institute (1824) is America's first engineering university and a leader in technological innovation. Today Rensselaer has grown into an internationally respected technological university offering graduate and undergraduate degrees in engineering, science, management, architecture, humanities, and social sciences. Founded by Stephen Van Rensselaer "for the purpose of instructing persons in the application of science to the common purposes of life," Rensselaer is located on a handsome, historic campus high above the Hudson River. Widely respected for the quality of its education, Rensselaer is also highly regarded as a prominent research institution with strong ties to industry and business. After Rensselaer began its graduate distance education program with 60 registrations in 1987, it now attracts 900 per semester. The program offers participants the same quality educational experience received by those who attend the campus, and it can be directly delivered and tailored to companies' specific needs.

Renton Technical College

| 3000 NE 4th Street | Phone: (425) 235-2352 |
| Renton, WA 98055 | Fax: (425) 235-7832 |

Division(s): Technical Programs
Web Site(s): http://www.renton.tc.ctc.edu
E-mail: cdaniels@ctc.ctc.edu

Class Titles: English, Psychology.

Teaching Methods: *Computers:* Internet, e-mail *Other:* None.

Credits Granted for: experiential learning, portfolio assessment, extrainstitutional learning, examination (CLEP, ACT-PEP, DANTES, GRE).

On-Campus Requirements: None.

Tuition and Fees: *Credit by:* quarter.

Financial Aid: Federal Stafford Loan, Federal Perkins Loan, Federal Pell Grant, Federal Work-Study, VA, Washington resident programs.

Accreditation: Northwest Association of Schools and Colleges.

Description: For more than 55 years, Renton Technical College (1941) has made dreams a reality for students training, retraining, and upgrading their skills for rewarding careers. As the community has grown and changed, Renton

Technical College has followed suit, offering exciting new programs and keeping abreast of cutting edge technologies that have reshaped the workplace. As we stand on the cusp of the 21st century, what remains constant is our commitment to service the community and help make dreams come true.

The Richard Stockton College of New Jersey

| PO Box 195 | Phone: (609) 652-4580 |
| Pomona, NJ 08240-0195 | Fax: (609) 748-5543 |

Division(s): Office of Distance Learning, General Studies
Web Site(s): http://loki.stockton.edu/~fergusoc/dist.html
E-mail: lopatto@pollux.stockton.edu

Class Titles: Ethnic/Cultural Studies, Business, Communications, Conservation/Natural Resources, Education, English Language/Literature, Foreign Language/Literature, Health Professions/Related Sciences, History, Family Studies, Mathematics, Philosophy/Religion, Physical Sciences, Psychology, Social Sciences, Visual/Performing Arts.

Teaching Methods: *Computers:* Internet, electronic classroom, e-mail. *Other:* audiotapes, fax, correspondence, independent study, individual study.

Admission Requirements: *Undergraduate:* for fewer than 16 accepted credits: application, SAT/ACT, 16 units college preparatory, assessment tests in writing and reading, mathematics, and critical thinking; Transfer students: transcripts, 16 accepted credits, application; nonmatriculating student: application for nonmatriculating status. Can take up to 8 credits/term.

On-Campus Requirements: Varies, but all students must attend an in-person orientation.

Tuition and Fees: *Undergraduate:* $130/credit. *Application Fee:* $25 nonmatriculating students. *Other Costs:* $50 Technology Fee. *Credit by:* semester.

Financial Aid: Federal Stafford Loan, Federal Perkins Loan, Federal PLUS Loan, Federal Pell Grant, Federal Work-Study, VA, New Jersey resident programs.

Accreditation: Middle States Association of Colleges and Schools; Social Work: Council on Social Work Education; Education: New Jersey Department of Education and the National Association of State Directors of Teacher Education and Certification; Nursing: National League for Nursing, New Jersey Board of Nursing; Chemistry: American Chemical Society; Physical Therapy: American Physical Therapy Association; Environmental Health track: National Environmental Health Sciences and Protection Accreditation Council.

Description: The Richard Stockton College of New Jersey (1969) is an undergraduate college of arts and sciences and professional studies, providing distinctive undergraduate pro-

grams that combine traditional and alternative approaches to education, along with some graduate programs. The Office of Distance Learning (1995) provides access to quality and affordable higher education through alternative delivery methods.

Richland Community College

| One College Park | Phone: (217) 875-7200 |
| Decatur, IL 62521 | Fax: (217) 875-6961 |

Division(s): Learning Resource Center
Web Site(s): http://www.richland.cc.il.us
E-mail: ncooper@richland.cc.il.us

Undergraduate Degree Programs:
Associate in Arts
Associate in Science
Associate in Engineering Science
Associate in Liberal Studies
Associate in Applied Science (occupational training programs)

Certificate Programs: basic certificate and 2-year degrees.

Teaching Methods: *Computers:* Internet, electronic classroom, e-mail. *TV:* videotape, satellite broadcasting. *Other:* videoconferencing, audiotapes, fax, correspondence, learning communities, independent study, extended learning program.

Credits Granted for: Examination (CLEP, APP), Proficiency Examination, Proficiency by Advanced Course.

Admission Requirements: *Undergraduate:* High school graduate or GED equivalent, or may qualify as high school student or "gifted" high school student. Possible placement testing in English, math, foreign language, or other areas. *Certificate:* same as undergraduate.

On-Campus Requirements: None.

Tuition and Fees: *Undergraduate:* $45*/hour (in-district students), $142*/hour (out-of-district students), $231*/hour (out-of-state students) (*includes academic fee). *Other Costs:* $10 semester registration fee (nonrefundable and payable at time of registration); lab fees vary depending on type of class and are payable at time of registration). *Credit by:* semester.

Financial Aid: Grants: Pell Grant, Supplemental Educational Opportunity Grant (SEOG). Illinois State Monetary Award Program Scholarships: Merit Recognition Scholarship, National Guard/Naval Militia Program, Policeman/Fireman Scholarship, Correctional Workers' Scholarship, MIA/POW Scholarship, Illinois Veterans' Grant, Department of Rehabilitation Services, Richland Community College Foundation, Private, and institutional scholarships.

Accreditation: North Central Association of Colleges and Schools.

Description: The primary purpose of Richland Community College (1972) is to improve the quality of life in Central Illinois by actively serving the educational needs of its people, organizations, and institutions. Richland offers bachelor's, technical, continuing education, and community service programs. In 1994 Richland first offered its Distance Learning Program to enable students to take classes from several district sites through an interactive-video system. Area universities and other community colleges also use Richland's distance program.

Rio Salado College

2323 West 14th Street	Phone: (800) 729-1197
Tempe, AZ 85281	Fax: (602) 517-8129

Division(s): Academic Programs and Applied Programs
Web Site(s): http://www.rio.maricopa.edu/
E-mail: mills@rio.maricopa.edu

Undergraduate Degree Programs:
Associate of Arts
Associate of General Studies
Associate of Applied Science

Certificate Programs: Computer Usage and Technology, Water/Wastewater Management

Class Titles: Accounting, Anthropology, Biology, Business, Child/Family Studies, Communication, Computers, Counseling/Personal Development, Education, English, English Humanities, Geography, Geology, Health Science, History, Humanities, Integrated Studies, Management/Supervision, Mathematics, Medical Terminology, Office Automation Systems, Philosophy, Political Science, Psychology, Reading, Small Business, Sociology, Spanish, Theater, Total Quality Management, Water/Wastewater Management.

Teaching Methods: *Computers:* Internet, e-mail, CD-ROM, computer disk. *TV:* videotape. *Other:* audioconferencing, videoconferencing, audiotapes, fax, correspondence.

Credits Granted for: examination (CLEP, ACT-PEP, DANTES, GRE).

Admission Requirements: *Undergraduate:* classifications: college transfer, high school graduate, GED certified, age 18, international, or special admission (for students not qualifying in any other classification).

On-Campus Requirements: None.

Tuition and Fees: *Undergraduate:* $38/credit state and county residents, $38/credit plus an additional $25/credit out-of-state. *Other Costs:* $5/semester registration fee for all students; variable for lab fees, etc. *Credit by:* semester.

Financial Aid: Federal Pell Grant, Federal Work-Study, VA.

Accreditation: North Central Association for Colleges and Schools.

Description: From its beginning, Rio Salado College (1978) has been recognized for its innovative, educational delivery systems. "Let the College come to you," is the prevailing philosophy of Rio Salado's distance learning program. Students can earn a complete associate degree via distance. By the fall of 1998, Rio Salado will offer 212 distance learning courses via Internet, mixed media, and print. All distance courses encourage maximum interaction between student and instructor. Students choose their own study times and submit assignments by mail, fax, or computer. All major student services are online, including registration, career and academic counseling, tutoring, book ordering, and scholarship application. Almost all distance courses begin every other week, allowing initial enrollment 26 times throughout the year!

Riverside Community College

4800 Magnolia Avenue	Phone: (909) 222-8000
Riverside, CA 92506	Fax: (909) 222-8036

Division(s): Instructional TV/Learning Technologies
Web Site(s): http://www.rccd.cc.ca.us
E-mail: sharonm@rccd.cc.ca.us

Class Titles: History, Anthropology, Astronomy, Business, Business Law, Business Math, Small Business Organization, Early Childhood Studies, Economics, French Listening Comprehension, Principles of Management, Techniques of Selling, Philosophy, Oceanography, Elementary Arithmetic, Political Science, Geography, Psychology, Sociology, Spanish Listening Comprehension, Athletic Training.

Teaching Methods: *TV:* videotape, cable program, satellite broadcasting, PBS. *Other:* None.

Admission Requirements: *Undergraduate:* open admission. *Certificate:* open admission.

On-Campus Requirements: 5 on-campus meetings required for 3-unit class.

Tuition and Fees: *Undergraduate:* $13/credit. *Credit by:* semester.

Financial Aid: Federal Pell Grant, Federal Work-Study, VA, California resident programs, Board of Governors.

Accreditation: Western States Association of Schools and Colleges.

Description: Riverside Community College (1916) is an accessible, comprehensive school committed to providing an affordable postsecondary education (including student and community services) to a diverse student body. Located 60 miles east of Los Angeles, the RCC District has 3 campuses—Riverside, Moreno Valley, and Norco—serving more than 21,000 students. RCCD's values are expressed in student centeredness, teaching excellence, learning environment, and tradition.

Rochester Community and Technical College

851 30th Avenue SE
Rochester, MN 55904

Phone: (507) 285-7256
Fax: (507) 285-7108

Division(s): Academic Affairs
Web Site(s): http://www.roch.edu
E-mail: nancy.schumaker@roch.edu

Class Titles: English Composition, French, History, Physics for Nonmajors, Technical Math, Graphic Design. Spanish, Child Development.

Teaching Methods: *Computers:* Internet, real-time chat, electronic classroom, e-mail, newsgroup, LISTSERV. *TV:* videotape, cable program, satellite broadcasting, PBS. *Other:* independent study.

Credits Granted for: examination (CLEP), Advanced Placement high school courses.

Admission Requirements: *Undergraduate:* high school diploma, basic skills testing and placement in developmental courses if needed (developmental courses not available as distance education at this time).

On-Campus Requirements: 25% of credits at this institution, but no restrictions on how many credits must be on-campus as opposed to distance-earned. No complete degree programs via distance learning, currently.

Tuition and Fees: *Undergraduate:* $75/credit (includes technology fee). *Credit by:* semester.

Financial Aid: Federal Stafford Loan, Federal Perkins Loan, Federal PLUS Loan, Federal Pell Grant, Federal Work-Study, VA, Minnesota resident programs.

Accreditation: North Central Association of Colleges and Schools.

Description: Rochester Community and Technical College (1915) is one partner in the University Center Rochester, which also houses sites for the University of Minnesota and Winona State University. For more than 5 years, the 2 universities have been delivering bachelor's and graduate programs here in Rochester, with substantial portions of the curriculum delivered via ITV. The ITV mode is also used by RCTC to share delivery of courses in foreign languages, law enforcement, and mathematics with a nearby community college and area high schools. All 3 institutions are currently developing courses, and eventually degree programs, for delivery online.

Rochester Institute of Technology

Bausch and Lomb Center
58 Lomb Memorial Drive
Rochester, NY 14623-5604

Phone: (716) 475-2229
(800) 225-5748
Fax: (716) 475-7164

Division(s): Part-time and Graduate Enrollment Services
Web Site(s): http://www.distancelearning.rit.edu
E-mail: OPES@rit.edu

Undergraduate Degree Programs:
Bachelor of Science in:
Applied Arts and Science, concentrations in:
Technical Communication
Telecommunications
Management
Health Systems Administration
Emergency Management
Environmental Management
Electrical/Mechanical Engineering Technology
Environmental Management and Technology

Graduate Degree Programs:
Master of Science in:
Environmental, Health and Safety Management
Health Systems Administration
Information Technology
Software Development/Management
Cross-Disciplinary Professional Studies

Certificate Programs: Basic Quality, Basic Technical Communication, Emergency Management, Environmental Management Science, Health Systems Administration, Industrial Environmental Management, Data Communication, Network Management, Voice Communications; Advanced (Graduate): Health Systems Finance, Integrated Health Systems, Statistical Quality.

Teaching Methods: *Computers:* Internet, real-time chat, electronic classroom, e-mail, CD-ROM, LISTSERV. *TV:* videotape, cable program. *Other:* audioconferencing, videoconferencing, audiographics, audiotapes, fax.

Credits Granted for: experiential learning, portfolio assessment, extrainstitutional learning, examination (CLEP, ACT-PEP, DANTES, GRE).

Admission Requirements: *Undergraduate:* 2-year degree or equivalent in credit for E/MET degree, TOEFL: 550. *Graduate:* accredited BS/BA/BTech, TOEFL: 550 or above.

On-Campus Requirements: Labs for E/MET program completed at predetermined site or in summer residence.

Tuition and Fees: *Undergraduate:* $240/credit 200, 300 courses; $263/credit 400, 500, 600 courses. *Graduate:* $527/credit. *Application Fee:* $40 undergraduate/graduate degrees (nonmatriculation study accepted). *Other Costs:* books. *Credit by:* RIT—quarter, bachelor's degrees—180 quarter credits, graduate degrees—48 quarter credits, certificates vary.

Financial Aid: Federal Stafford Loan, Federal Perkins Loan,

Federal PLUS Loan, Federal Pell Grant, Federal Work-Study, VA, New York resident programs (TAP, APTS).

Accreditation: Middle States Association of Colleges and Schools, New York State Education Department Office of Higher Education and the Professions (Other programs hold individual, professional accreditations.).

Description: *U.S. News and World Report* lists Rochester Institute of Technology (1829) as the number one comprehensive university in the East for science and technology and calls it one of America's most imitated institutions. Located on a 1,300-acre suburban campus in New York, RIT enrolls 13,230 full- and part-time students, including 1,000 distance learning students and 2,180 graduate students in 7 colleges. RIT is New York's fifth largest private college/university and the 15th largest in the nation. Since 1979 RIT has offered distance learning courses and has been a leader in using electronic forms of communication for course interaction. The Annenberg/CPB project, *New Pathways to a Degree*, chose RIT as one of its 7 projects because it offers students the flexibility needed to complete a college degree or professional education. With a computer, VCR, and telephone, students can pursue an RIT degree anytime, anywhere.

Rockland Community College

145 College Road, Room 4104	Phone: (914) 574-4732
Suffern, NY 10901	Fax: (914) 356-5811

Division(s): Instructional Technology
Web Site(s): http://rocink.sunyrockland.edu
E-mail: rechevarria@sunyrockland.edu

Undergraduate Degree Programs:
Associate of Liberal Arts
Associate of Science

Teaching Methods: *Computers:* e-mail. *TV:* videotape, cable program, satellite broadcasting, PBS. *Other:* audiotapes, correspondence, independent study, individual study, learning contracts.

Credits Granted for: experiential learning, work, volunteer and community service, military, portfolio assessment, examination (CLEP).

Admission Requirements: *Undergraduate:* after completing 11 credits, an English and Math Placement Exam is required.

On-Campus Requirements: None.

Tuition and Fees: *Undergraduate:* $97/credit. *Application Fee:* $25 first-time student. *Other Costs:* $20/course for supplies, $3/credit activity fee. *Credit by:* semester.

Financial Aid: Federal Stafford Loan, Federal Perkins Loan, Federal PLUS Loan, Federal Pell Grant, Federal Work-Study, VA, New York resident programs, RCC institutional scholarships.

Accreditation: Middle States Association of Colleges and Schools.

Description: Rockland Community College (1959) is located on a 175-acre campus, with extension sites in Nyack, Haverstraw, and Spring Valley. The Rockland experience includes mingling with a diverse student population and studying with an experienced, award-winning faculty. The college pays special attention to individual needs through small class sizes, alternate learning modes, and a variety of student services. In addition, flexible scheduling enables many of the 5,000 Rockland students to earn credits or a degree through the Distance Learning program.

Roger Williams University

One Old Ferry Road	Phone: (401) 254-3530
Bristol, RI 02809	Fax: (401) 254-3560

Division(s): Open Program, University College
Web Site(s): http://www.rwu.edu
E-mail: eac@alpha.rwu.edu

Undergraduate Degree Programs:
Bachelor of Science in:
　Business Management
　Criminal Justice
　Industrial Technology
　Public Administration

Class Titles: Biology, Financial Accounting, Enterprise, Business Ethics, Economics (micro/macro), Money/Banking, Management, Human Resource Management, Small Business Management, Business Policy, Marketing, Sales Management, Insurance, Investments, Financial Management, Stock Market, Computers, Spreadsheets (EXCEL), Computers Applications in Business, Criminal Justice, Policing in America, Substantive Criminal Law, Criminal Procedure, Constitutional Law, Evidence, Police Community Relations, Drugs/Society/ Behavior, Criminology, Courts/Criminal Justice, Corrections in U.S., Correctional Administration, Community-Based Corrections, Juvenile Justice, Organized Crime, Law in Contemporary Society, Law of Contracts, Law of Business Organization, Man/Technology, Environment/Technology, ISO 9000, TQM, World Class MFG, Time/Motion, Production Planning, Manufacturing Processes, Workplace Safety, Quality Control, Facilities Plan/Design, Evolution of Jazz, Psychology, Psychology of Stress Management, American Government/ Politics, Public Administration, State/Local Government, Public Policy, Public Personnel Administration, Public Financial Administration, Organizational Theory/Management, City Management, Social Science Research Methods, Perspectives on Peace, Sociology, Juvenile Delinquency, Theater.

Teaching Methods: *Computers:* Internet, e-mail. *TV:* videotapes, audiotapes. *Other:* fax, correspondence, independent study, individual study, internships, etc.

Credits Granted for: Up to 2 years (60 credits) allowed for experiential learning, portfolio assessment, extrainstitutional learning, examination (CLEP, ACT-PEP, DANTES, GRE); up to 3 years (90 credits) allowed for transfer credit, military service and training.

Admission Requirements: *Undergraduate:* high school diploma/GED. Advanced standing based on college credits, military training, creditable employment experiences, and/or CLEP exams. (Note: 60 credits required for Criminal Justice degree program.) Possible access to libraries, local college courses, local proctors, potential sites for internship placements, computers, etc.

On-Campus Requirements: No campus residency is required. In addition to academic and program requirements, students in the Open Program must complete 30 credits at the university, although these do not need to be completed in the classroom or on campus. Normally, students need to meet with advisors and complete some activities on the main campus. These activities may include assisting in developing an educational plan, submitting student record materials, reviewing credit documentation, meeting with adjunct faculty, etc. However, the on-campus visit may be waived for distance students by an academic advisor.

Tuition and Fees: *Undergraduate:* $210–$385/credit. *Application Fee:* $35. *Credit by:* semester.

Financial Aid: Federal Stafford Loan, Federal Perkins Loan, Federal PLUS Loan, Federal Pell Grant, VA, military tuition assistance programs, some adult education scholarships.

Accreditation: New England Association of Schools and Colleges.

Description: Roger Williams University (1948) is a comprehensive, coeducational, private university offering degrees at the bachelor's and first professional levels. It has a waterfront campus in Bristol and an educational center in Providence. Roger Williams also offers undergraduate degree programs in liberal arts, engineering, architecture, business management, and other areas of professional studies, along with its new school of law. RWU's Open Program began in 1974 as a comprehensive external degree program enabling working adults to study with minimal interference to family or job commitments; distance students have been enrolled since the program's beginning. It is a time-shortened degree program available part- or full-time, with continuous advisement services throughout the year. Special programs exist for students affiliated with the military.

Rogers State University

1701 West Will Rogers Boulevard
Claremore, OK 74017

Phone: (918) 341-7510
Fax: (918) 343-7595

Division(s): Distance Learning
Web Site(s): http://www.ruonline.edu
http://www.rogersu.edu
E-mail: online@rogersu.edu

Undergraduate Degree Programs:
Associate of Arts in:
    Humanities
    Liberal Arts
    Business Administration
Associate of Science in Computer Science
All totally online. Partial requirements for other degree programs can be completed online.

Class Titles: Accounting, Financial Accounting, Managerial Accounting, Principles of Management, Marketing, Business Statistics, Business, Business Communications, Criminal Justice, Visual Basic, Computer Programming, Microcomputer Applications, Software Engineering (Systems Analysis/Design), Operating Systems (UNIX), Seminar in Computer Science (Web Site Design/Development), Seminar in Computer Science (Java Programming), C Programming, C++ Programming, Microsoft Access, Microsoft Excel, Macro Economics, Micro Economics, Basic Writing, Composition, American Literature, Human Geography, U.S. History to 1865, Humanities, Basic Mathematics, Elementary Algebra, College Algebra, Statistics, Anatomy, American Federal Government, Psychology, Reading in Disciplines.

Teaching Methods: *Computers:* Internet, real-time chat, electronic classroom, e-mail, newsgroup. *TV:* videotape, cable program, compressed video, interactive video. *Other:* audiotapes, independent study.

Credits Granted for: examination (CLEP, APP).

Admission Requirements: *Undergraduate:* High school transcripts (or GED or equivalent) and ACT scores for students with no college course work, all college transcripts. Students over age 21 do not need to submit ACT scores. *Certificate:* Same as undergraduate.

On-Campus Requirements: None.

Tuition and Fees: *Undergraduate:* $47–$82/credit in-state, $110–$145/credit out-of-state. *Credit by:* semester.

Financial Aid: Federal Stafford Loan, Federal Perkins Loan, Federal PLUS Loan, Federal Pell Grant, Federal Work-Study, VA, Oklahoma resident programs.

Accreditation: North Central Association of Colleges and Schools, The Oklahoma State Regents for Higher Education.

Description: Rogers State University's history is nearly as old as Oklahoma. The institution began as prep school, changed to the Oklahoma Military Academy in 1919, then became a community college in 1972. In addition to providing a traditional classroom experience, Rogers State University offers academic programs designed to fit the busiest schedule by providing classes live from its own KRSC-TV or through RU Online. In 1993 the university designed a program to bring the best distance learning to students across Oklahoma, the U.S., and the world. This program gives RSU students access to all important student services and classroom learning strategies online. No matter what degree program or learning option is chosen, Rogers State University students receive high-quality education that is convenient, flexible, and affordable. Rogers State University has been accredited since 1950.

Roosevelt University

430 South Michigan Avenue	Phone: (312) 341-3866
Chicago, IL 60605-1394	Fax: (312) 341-2417

Division(s): External Studies Program
Web Site(s): http://www.roosevelt.edu/distance-learning
E-mail: areichle@roosevelt.edu

Class Titles: Accounting, General Studies, Women's Studies, Social Sciences, Natural Sciences, Computer Science, Humanities, Economics, English, Finance, Geography, History, Hospitality Management, Management, Psychology, Information Sciences.

Teaching Methods: *Computers:* Internet, e-mail. *Other:* fax, correspondence, independent study, individual study, learning contracts.

Admission Requirements: *Undergraduate:* high school diploma and be in good standing at Roosevelt or another institution.

On-Campus Requirements: None.

Tuition and Fees: *Undergraduate:* $380. *Application Fee:* $100 registration fee. *Credit by:* semester

Financial Aid: Federal Stafford Loan, Federal Perkins Loan, Federal PLUS Loan, Federal Pell Grant, Federal Work-Study, VA, Illinois resident programs.

Accreditation: North Central Association of Colleges and Schools.

Description: Roosevelt University (1945) was founded to provide opportunities for learning and teaching in conditions of freedom and equality. Since 1947, the home of Roosevelt's Chicago campus has been the famous auditorium building overlooking Grant Park and Lake Michigan. The Schaumburg Campus has become the largest and most comprehensive university in the northwest suburban area of Chicago. The university seeks to develop individuals who will be dedicated to the essential themes of a democratic society, who possess an understanding of human history and the basic ideas of the humanities and sciences, and who will accept their responsibilities as citizens of a vital nation and a changing world. Roosevelt serves 6,600 undergraduate and graduate students in 5 colleges and schedules classes days, evenings, and weekends so students may work while attending school. The external studies program was founded by a Lilly Foundation grant and began offering courses in 1976.

Rose State College

6420 Southeast 15th Street	Phone: (405) 733-7393
Midwest City, OK 73110	Fax: (405) 736-0339

Division(s): Academic Affairs
Web Site(s): http://www.rose.cc.ok.us
E-mail: bbrown@ms.rose.cc.ok.us

Undergraduate Degree Programs:
Library Technical Assistant

Certificate Programs: Library Technical Assistant

Class Titles: 38 courses. Current semester offerings provided upon request.

Teaching Methods: *Computers:* Internet, real-time chat, electronic classroom, e-mail, LISTSERV. *TV:* videotape, cable program, PBS Affiliate Station. *Other:* videoconferencing, independent study.

Credits Granted for: extrainstitutional learning, examination (CLEP, ACT-PEP, DANTES, GRE).

Admission Requirements: *Undergraduate:* open-door policy.

On-Campus Requirements: None.

Tuition and Fees: *Undergraduate:* $42/credit. *Application Fee:* $15. *Software:* $3/credit. *Credit by:* semester.

Financial Aid: Federal Stafford Loan, Federal Perkins Loan, Federal PLUS Loan, Federal Pell Grant, Federal Work-Study, VA, Oklahoma resident programs.

Accreditation: North Central Association of Colleges and Schools, Oklahoma State Regents for High Education.

Description: Rose State College (1970) is a public, 2-year institution located a short distance from downtown Oklahoma City. The college, originally named Oscar Rose Junior College, accepted its first students in September 1970. Curriculum consists of both terminal and transfer programs. Degrees granted include the Associate in Arts, Associate in Applied Science, and Associate in Science. The college provides opportunities for students outside traditional service areas through telecourses, Internet courses, and courses delivered through an interactive state telecommunications network. Semester schedules for both traditional and distance learning courses are provided upon request.

Rosemont College

1400 Montgomery Avenue	Phone: (610) 527-0200
Rosemont, PA 19010	Fax: (610) 526-2964

Division(s): Technology in Education
Web Site(s): http://techined@rosemont.edu
E-mail: roscolgrad@rosemont.edu

Graduate Degree Programs:
Master's of Education in Technology in Education

Certificate Programs: Professional Study in Technology in Education

Teaching Methods: *Computers:* Internet, real-time chat, electronic classroom, e-mail, CD-ROM, newsgroup, LIST-SERV. *TV:* videotape, cable program, satellite broadcasting, PBS. *Other:* radio broadcast, audioconferencing, videoconferencing, audiographics, audiotapes, fax, correspondence, independent study, individual study, learning contracts.

Admission Requirements: *Graduate:* bachelor's degree; MAT or GRE.

On-Campus Requirements: A student must take half of the credits during the summer on campus.

Tuition and Fees: *Graduate:* $360/credit. *Credit by:* semester.

Financial Aid: Federal Stafford Loan.

Accreditation: Middle States Association of Colleges and Schools.

Description: Rosemont College (1921) established its Master of Education program in 1986. The program offers programs of study leading to the Professional Study in Technology in Education and the Master of Education in Technology in Education, both of which are constantly evolving to meet the needs of educators working with the technologies of today's classrooms.

Rutgers, The State University of New Jersey

83 Somerset Street	Phone: (732) 932-5935
New Brunswick, NJ 08901-1281	Fax: (732) 932-9225

Division(s): Continuous Education and Outreach
Web Site(s): http://ce1766.rutgers.edu
E-mail: Rnovak@rci.rutgers.edu

Certificate Programs: Communication Management

Class Titles: Nursing, Law, History, Chinese, Education, Biomaterials, Human Resource Management, Business, Music Studies.

Teaching Methods: *Computers:* Internet, real-time chat, electronic classroom, e-mail, CD-ROM, newsgroup, LIST-SERV. *TV:* videotape. *Other:* 2-way interactive videoconferencing, fax.

Admission Requirements: *Undergraduate:* vary according to discipline and school. No special admission requirements for distance learning students.

On-Campus Requirements: The majority of the distance learning courses are interactive videoconferenced courses between campuses or between campus and an off-campus site. The Internet-based certificate in Communication Management has a limited on-campus requirement.

Tuition and Fees: *Undergraduate:* $4,262/academic year, New Jersey residents; $8,676/academic year, nonresidents. Tuition for the College of Engineering, College of Pharmacy, and Cook College (our school of life, environmental, marine, and agricultural sciences) is about 10% higher. These costs do not include books, travel, recreation, and personal expenses. Yearly tuition increases over the past 3 years have averaged 5%. *Graduate:* Total estimated educational and living expenses for the 1998–1999 academic year (excluding costs for the schools of management and law) are $16,400 for New Jersey residents and $19,350 for out-of-state residents. Expenses for international students are approximately $21,800 for the calendar year. *Application Fee:* $50, nonrefundable. *Other Costs:* $168–$816 student fee (depending on school and part-time/full-time status), $40–$150 computer fee (part-time/full-time), $257 major medical insurance (mandatory for foreign students), $1,014 average fees residents/nonresidents. Contact school for details of tuition and fees. *Credit by:* semester.

Financial Aid: university, governmental, corporate, and individual sources—merit-based financial aid; university fellowships, scholarships, assistantships; Rutgers Excellence Fellowship Awards; special programs for students of underrepresented populations (Minority Advancement Program, Ralph Johnson Bunche Fellowships); part-time employment; New Jersey State Grants, Educational Opportunity Fund Grants, Federal Perkins Loans, Federal Stafford Loans, Federal Supplemental Educational Opportunity Grant, Federal Work-Study.

Accreditation: Middle States Association of Colleges and Schools.

Description: Established as Queen's College to train ministers for the Dutch Reformed Church, today Rutgers, the State University of New Jersey (1766) is one of the largest educational institutions in the U.S., with 3 campuses, 29 degree-granting schools, and 48,000 students. As New Jersey's land-grant institution and home to a host of centers, bureaus and institutes, Rutgers serves the evolving needs of the state and its citizens. Rutgers began offering distance learning courses several years ago to provide access to its many resources for students throughout the state. Most of the distance learning courses are offered through state-of-the-art, interactive video classrooms. Various courses are shared among the 3 campuses as well as with off-campus sites. In addition, the School of Communication, Information, and Library Science offers a 4-course, Internet-based certificate in Communication Management (for details consult: http://www.scils.rutgers.edu/de/commgt.html).

Saddleback College

| 28000 Marguerite Parkway, LIB 218 | Phone: (949) 582-4515 |
| Mission Viejo, CA 92692 | Fax: (949) 582-4753 |

Division(s): Learning Resources
Web Site(s): http://www.saddleback.cc.ca.us
E-mail: snelson@saddleback.cc.ca.us

Class Titles: Accounting, Cultural Anthropology, Business, Business Management, Marketing, Salesmanship, Small Business Management, American History, Music Appreciation, History of Rock (music), American Government, Psychology, Developmental Psychology, Real Estate, Sociology, Marriage/Family, Marine Science, Creative Writing, Computer/Information Systems.

Teaching Methods: *Computers:* Internet, e-mail, CD-ROM. *TV:* videotape, cable program. *Other:* radio broadcast (broadcast area restricted).

Credits Granted for: experiential learning.

Admission Requirements: *Undergraduate:* high school diploma.

On-Campus Requirements: Some courses require on-campus meetings and computer lab work. Real estate courses are on campus at students' convenience. All courses must be completed within the semester offered.

Tuition and Fees: *Undergraduate:* $12/credit residents and military; $131/credit nonresidents. *Graduate:* same. *Doctoral:* same. *Application Fee:* $46 for citizens and residents of a foreign country. *Other Costs:* $3–$14 for health and material fees, as applicable. *Credit by:* semester.

Financial Aid: Federal Stafford Student Loans, Federal Perkins Loan, Federal Pell Grant, Federal Work-Study, Federal Supplemental Educational Opportunity Grant, Saddleback Emergency Loan Funds, Board of Governors Fee Waiver, California Student Aid Commission Program, Saddleback College Scholarships.

Accreditation: Western Association of Schools and Colleges, Accrediting Commission for Community and Junior Colleges.

Description: Saddleback College (1967) is committed to providing a high-quality, postsecondary education to all people, with nondiscriminatory recognition of the dignity and worth of the individual in a free society. To that end, Saddleback provides rigorous degree and certificate curricula in lower-division arts and sciences and in vocational and occupational fields. In addition, personal attention is extended through tutoring, remedial instruction, English as a second language, and support services such as counseling, career guidance, and assistance for the disabled. Finally, the college provides lifelong learning through Community Education seminars, credit and noncredit courses, workshops, etc., to support nontraditional community needs.

Saint Francis College

| 1 Evergreenway | Phone: (814) 472-3130 |
| Loretto, PA 15940 | Fax: (814) 472-3377 |

Division(s): Center of Excellence for Remote and Medically Underserved Areas (CERMUSA)
Web Site(s): http://www.sfcpa.edu
E-mail: mstasik@sfcpa.edu

Graduate Degree Programs:
Master of Medical Science

Class Titles: Ethical Issues in Practice, Seminar in Selected Medical Topics, Essentials of Research Methodology, Advanced Pharmacology, Practicum for Underserved Populations, Clinical Residency Project.

Teaching Methods: *Computers:* e-mail, CD-ROM, newsgroup, LISTSERV. *TV:* videotape, cable program, satellite broadcasting, PBS. *Other:* radio broadcast, videoconferencing, audioconferencing, audiographics, audiotapes, fax, correspondence, independent study, individual study, learning contracts.

Credits Granted for: experiential learning, portfolio assessment, extrainstitutional learning, examination (CLEP, ACT-PEP, DANTES, GRE), up to 10 credits of advanced standing may be granted for prior ER and FP.

On-Campus Requirements: MMS program is designed to allow physician assistants the flexible schedule needed.

Tuition and Fees: *Graduate:* $460/credit. *Application Fee:* $50. *Credit by:* semester.

Accreditation: Middle States Association of Colleges and Schools.

Description: Saint Francis College (1847) since its beginning, has established an exceptional track record of success. Standing the test of time, the college upholds its commitment—now 150 years strong—to offering high quality academic programs, an active student life, leadership opportunities, and personalized attention from dedicated professionals—all within a Franciscan tradition.

Saint Joseph's College

| 278 Whites Bridge Road | Phone: (800) 752-4723 |
| Standish, ME 04084-5263 | Fax: (207) 892-7480 |

Division(s): Continuing and Professional Studies
Web Site(s): http://www.sjcme.edu
E-mail: eandrews@sjcme.edu
lrobinso@sjcme.edu

Undergraduate Degree Programs:
Health Care
Business
Professional Studies
Criminal Justice
Nursing

Graduate Degree Programs:
Master of Science in Health Care
Master of Science in Nursing

Certificate Programs: Long Term Care, Project Management, Health Care, Professional Studies, Women's Studies, self-designed Christian Tradition.

Teaching Methods: *Computers:* Internet, real-time chat, electronic classroom, e-mail, CD-ROM, newsgroup, LIST-SERV. *Other:* independent study, individual study.

Credits Granted for: experiential learning, portfolio assessment, extrainstitutional learning, examination (CLEP, ACT-PEP, DANTES, GRE).

Admission Requirements: *Graduate:* Nursing GRE exam for masters, undergraduate degree from accredited institution.

On-Campus Requirements: None.

Tuition and Fees: *Undergraduate:* $185/credit. *Graduate:* $225/credit. *Application Fee:* $25/$50.

Financial Aid: Federal Stafford Loan, Federal Perkins Loan, Federal PLUS Loan, Federal Pell Grant, Federal Work-Study, VA, Maine resident programs.

Accreditation: New England Association of Schools and Colleges, National League for Nursing.

Description: Saint Joseph's College (1912) was founded by the Sisters of Mercy. Our distance education program is 25+ years old and we are continuing to grow by introducing new programs and new technology. The beautiful campus is located on Sebago Lake in Maine.

Saint Mary-of-the-Woods College

Guerin Hall	Phone: (800) 926-7692
Saint Mary-of-the-Woods, IN 47876	(812) 535-5106
	Fax: (812) 535-4900

Division(s): Women's External Degree Admission
Web Site(s): http://www.smwc.edu
E-mail: wedadms@smwc.edu

Undergraduate Degree Programs:
Associate in Arts/Associate in Science in:
  Early Childhood Education
  General Business
  Gerontology
  Humanities
  Paralegal Studies
Bachelor of Arts/Bachelor of Science in:
  Accounting
  Business Administration
  Computer Information Systems
  Education, including:
    Early Childhood
    Kindergarten-Primary

Elementary Education
Special Education
Secondary Education:
  English
  Mathematics
  Social Studies
English
Gerontology
Human Resource Management
Human Services
Humanities
Journalism
Marketing
Mathematics
Paralegal Studies
Psychology
Social Science and History
Theology

Graduate Degree Programs:
Master of Arts in Pastoral Theology
Master of Arts in Earth Literacy

Certificate Programs: Computer Information Systems, Gerontology, Paralegal Studies, Theology.

Class Titles: Almost all courses for above majors and general studies may be taken individually at a distance.

Teaching Methods: *Computers:* Internet, real-time chat, electronic classroom, e-mail, CD-ROM. *Other:* audiotapes, independent study, individual study.

Credits Granted for: experiential learning, portfolio assessment, extrainstitutional learning, examination (CLEP, DANTES).

Admission Requirements: *Undergraduate:* high school diploma/GED, academic history/work experience considered. Education majors must reside within 200 miles of campus. *Graduate:* bachelor's degree. *Certificate:* English Composition required if not previously taken.

On-Campus Requirements: Minimal residency each semester. Education majors must reside within 200 miles of campus.

Tuition and Fees: *Undergraduate:* $265/credit. *Graduate:* $300/credit. *Application Fee:* $30. *Credit by:* semester.

Financial Aid: Federal Stafford Loan, Federal Perkins Loan, Federal PLUS Loan, Federal Pell Grant, Federal Work-Study, Indiana resident programs.

Accreditation: North Central Association of Colleges and Schools.

Description: Since 1973, the Women's External Degree program at Saint Mary-of-the-Woods College (1840) has provided the curriculum for contemporary adult women who juggle multiple responsibilities yet need or want a college degree. This structured but flexible independent study program of 5-month semesters leads to a degree in one of more than 20 majors. Beginning with an in-person appointment, faculty and students communicate by telephone, voice mail, e-mail, and postal service. (Computers with modems are required only for accounting and CIS majors, but computer/word processor access is strongly recommended.) Full-time faculty members serve as academic advisers, and WED staff provide additional support, advocacy, registration assistance, and information, including a quarterly newsletter for distance learners. Students may also take on-campus, independent study courses with intensive weekend seminars.

Saint Peter's College

2641 Kennedy Boulevard	Phone: (201) 915-9022
Jersey City, NJ 07643	Fax: (201) 432-4997

Division(s): Academic Affairs
Web Site(s): http://www.spc.edu
E-mail: surrey_d@spcvxa.spc.edu

Certificate Programs: Master of Urban Education

Class Titles: several undergraduate introductory courses, graduate education courses, courses in MBS/MIS program.

Teaching Methods: *Computers:* Internet, real-time chat, electronic classroom, e-mail, LISTSERV. *TV:* videotape, satellite broadcasting. *Other:* interactive TV, fax, correspondence, independent study, individual study, learning contracts.

Credits Granted for: experiential learning, portfolio assessment, extrainstitutional learning.

Admission Requirements: *Undergraduate:* honors high school senior or college freshman, resident of New Jersey. *Graduate:* BA or BS, New Jersey resident, GRE for Education or Miller Analogies test.

On-Campus Requirements: 9 hours in workshops for graduate education courses; undergraduate students meet live with professor at their sites or the college several times/semester.

Tuition and Fees: *Undergraduate:* $455/credit or $300/special course. *Graduate:* $477/credit or $425/special course. *Application Fee:* $30. *Credit by:* semester.

Financial Aid: Federal Stafford Loan, Federal Perkins Loan, Federal PLUS Loan, Federal Pell Grant, Federal Work-Study, VA, New Jersey resident programs.

Accreditation: Middle States Association of Colleges and Schools.

Description: Saint Peter's College (1876) is a Jesuit college dedicated to *cura personalis* in an urban environment. Traditionally the typical undergraduate student has been a first-generation student, although recently the entering classes are more of a cross-section. The graduate programs usually attract professionals already in the field. Saint Peter's

entered the field of Distance Learning in 1991 under a state Challenge Grant via satellite delivery. Since then the college has expanded its efforts to include interactive TV, Web pages, videotape, satellite, fax, correspondence, independent study, individual study, and learning contracts. The on-campus requirements reflect the college's determination to maintain *cura personalis* in whatever teaching methodology is utilized.

Salve Regina University

100 Ochre Point Avenue	Phone: (800) 637-0002
Newport, RI 02840	Fax: (401) 849-0702

Division(s): Extension Study
Web Site(s): http://www.salve.edu (general University site)
http://www.salve.edu/geshome.html (graduate extension study)
http://www.salve.edu/undergrad-ext.html (for undergraduate)
E-mail: mistol@salve.edu or sruexten@salve.edu

Undergraduate Degree Programs:
Bachelor of Arts in Liberal Studies
Bachelor of Science in Business

Graduate Degree Programs:
Master of Arts in Human Development
Master of Arts in International Relations
Master of Science in Management

Certificate Programs: Management, Correctional Administration

Class Titles: Undergraduate classes are listed at http://www.salve.edu/undergrad-ext.html; graduate classes are listed at http://www.salve.edu/geshome.html.

Teaching Methods: *Computers:* Internet, e-mail. *Other:* fax, correspondence, independent study, individual study.

Credits Granted for: portfolio assessment, examination (CLEP, ACT-PEP, DANTES, GRE)

Admission Requirements: *Undergraduate:* 45 earned credits in undergraduate work. *Graduate:* BA/BS; GRE or MAT scores.

On-Campus Requirements: minimum of 4 days.

Tuition and Fees: *Undergraduate:* $700/course. *Graduate:* $900/course. *Application Fee:* $25 (undergraduate), $35 (graduate). *Other Costs:* $100 commitment fee. *Credit by:* semester.

Financial Aid: Federal Stafford Loan, Federal Perkins Loan, Federal PLUS Loan, Federal Pell Grant, VA, Rhode Island resident programs.

Accreditation: New England Association of Schools and Colleges.

Description: Salve Regina University (1934) was founded by the Religious Sisters of Mercy as an independent institution of higher education in the Catholic tradition. The university acquired property in Newport in 1947 and welcomed its first class of 58 students. Salve Regina now serves 2,200 men and women from 40 states and 24 foreign countries and boasts more than 10,000 alumni. The university has always sought to address the needs of adult learners by offering programs in the liberal arts and professional development through evening or convenient, off-campus courses. In 1984 SRU added an extension study program with detailed study guides, prepared by faculty members, that provide a structured, step-by-step approach to learning while allowing students flexibility in time and place of study. The process involves a one-on-one relationship with instructors who guide the student's learning via written comments, telephone conversations, and electronic mail.

San Antonio College

1300 San Pedro Avenue	Phone: (210) 733-2045
San Antonio, TX 78212	(210) 733-2181
	Fax: (210) 785-6494

Division(s): Distance Education Unit

Class Titles: General Biology, Child Growth/Development, Freshman Composition, American Government-National, American Government-Problems/Policy, History of U.S., Child Psychology, Sociology, Marriage/Family, Conversational Spanish, Nutrition, Mass Communication, Psychology, Business, Astronomy, Geography of World, Earth Sciences, Geographic Information Systems, Architectural Design, Data Communications, Criminal Justice, Legal/Research, Management, Public Administration, American/Texas Government, Crime in America, British Literature, American Literature, Reading in World Literature, Philosophy, Humanities.

Teaching Methods: *Computers:* Internet, real-time chat, electronic classroom, e-mail, newsgroup, LISTSERV. *TV:* videotape, cable program, satellite broadcasting, PBS. *Other:* videoconferencing, educational on-site contracts with business and industry.

Credits Granted for: extrainstitutional learning, examination (CLEP, ACT-PEP, DANTES, GRE).

Admission Requirements: *Undergraduate:* contact Admissions for information.

On-Campus Requirements: most students register for combined courses: telecourses, Internet, and on-campus courses.

Tuition and Fees: *Undergraduate:* contact school for complete tuition and fee information. *Credit by:* By semester 16 weeks and flex term semesters.

Financial Aid: Federal Stafford Loan, Federal Perkins Loan, Federal PLUS Loan, Federal Pell Grant, Federal Work-Study, VA, Texas resident programs.

Accreditation: Southern Association of Colleges and Schools.

Description: San Antonio College (1925), a college of the Alamo Community College District, began Distance Education courses in the 1980s by offering telecourses. In 1992, the college expanded its off-campus course offerings to area businesses, and the surrounding cities of Seguin, New Braunfels, and Kerrville. In 1996, a Distance Education Director was hired and several off-campus coordinators were hired to coordinate and manage course offerings at various off-campus sites. The Distance Education Program at San Antonio College has been expanded since 1996 to include: telecourses, Internet courses, off-campus courses in area high schools and at military bases, interactive videoconferencing, contract education (on-site education at area businesses), and dual credit instruction (eligible high school students earn high school and college credit for approved courses). These flexible instructional delivery methods are available at 13 off-campus sites. The Distance Education Program serves approximately 3,000 distance education students per fall/spring semesters. San Antonio College has an annual enrollment of approximately 21,500 students (which includes the distance learners) and approximately 18,000 continuing education students. The mission of Distance Education is to provide high quality academic courses/programs to students when and where they want it using time-and-place independent learning options.

San Diego City College

| 1313 12th Avenue | Phone: (619) 230-2534 |
| San Diego, CA 92101-4787 | Fax: (619) 230-2063 |

Division(s): Office of Distance Education
Web Site(s): http://sdccd.cc.ca.us
E-mail: cmccarty@sdccd.cc.ca.us

Undergraduate Degree Programs:
Associate of Arts
Associate of Science

Certificate Programs: Certificate of Achievement

Class Titles: Cultural Anthropology, Descriptive Astronomy, Business, Business Mathematics, Business Law/Legal Environment, Child Development, Computer Science, Economics, Cultural Geography, Geology, Health/Life Style, U.S. History, Mass Communications, Photography, Politics of Change/Revolution, General Psychology.

Teaching Methods: *Computers:* Internet, electronic classroom, e-mail. *TV:* videotape, cable program, satellite broadcasting, PBS. *Other:* videoconferencing, independent study, individual study, learning contracts.

Credits Granted for: experiential learning, portfolio assessment, examination (CLEP, ACT-PEP, DANTES, GRE).

Admission Requirements: *Undergraduate:* high school diploma, California high school proficiency exam certification, 45 GED, OR provisional status for age 18 or emancipated minors without high school diploma/equivalent, OR "special part-time" status for age 15 in high school beyond ninth grade. Persons not meeting one of the above admission criteria will not be admitted under any circumstances.

On-Campus Requirements: 20–22 hours in traditional classroom.

Tuition and Fees: *Undergraduate:* $13/credit. *Credit by:* semester.

Financial Aid: Federal PLUS Loan, Federal Pell Grant, Federal Work-Study, VA, Federal Supplemental Educational Opportunity Grant, Federal Direct Loan (subsidized), Federal Direct Loan (unsubsidized), Cal Grant B and C, Student Emergency Loans, Board of Governors Waiver.

Accreditation: Western Association of Schools and Colleges, Office of Private Postsecondary Education for Veteran Training, and U.S. Department of State and U.S. Immigration Service for International Student Education.

Description: San Diego City College (1994) is a public, 2-year community college whose mission is to provide accessible, high-quality learning experiences to meet the community's diverse educational needs. To fulfill this role, the college strives to provide instruction for those not traditionally served. Instruction includes the broadcast telecourse, the best-tested and most widely used educational telecommunications medium in California. The college offered 6 telecourses in 1994 and now offers 17 with another 2 in the planning stages. The distance education program continues to grow.

San Diego Community College District City, Mesa, and Miramar Colleges

3375 Camino del Rio South	Phone: (619) 584-6965
San Diego, CA 92108-3883	Fax: (619) 584-6523

Division(s): Instructional Services
Web Site(s): http://www.sdccd.cc.ca.us
E-mail: kfawson@sdccd.cc.ca.us

Class Titles: Cultural Anthropology, Descriptive Astronomy, Business, Business Law/Legal Environment, Business Math, Principles of Child Development, Computer Science, Economics, Geography, Psychology, Health/Life Style, History of U.S., Mass Communications, Photography.

Teaching Methods: *Computers:* Internet, electronic classroom, e-mail, CD-ROM, newsgroup, LISTSERV. *TV:* videotape, cable program, satellite broadcasting, PBS. *Other:* radio broadcast, videoconferencing, audioconferencing, individual study, learning contracts.

Credits Granted for: examination (CLEP, ACT-PEP, DANTES, GRE).

Admission Requirements: *Undergraduate:* ability to benefit.

On-Campus Requirements: for orientation.

Tuition and Fees: *Undergraduate:* $12/credit. *Credit by:* semester.

Financial Aid: Federal Stafford Loan, Federal Perkins Loan, Federal PLUS Loan, Federal Pell Grant, Federal Work-Study, VA, California resident programs.

Accreditation: Associate of Community and Junior Colleges (Western Association of Schools and Colleges).

Description: The San Diego Community College District (1970) serves 100,000 students each semester through 3 two-year colleges and 6 continuing education centers. The colleges—San Diego City (1914), Mesa (1964), and Miramar (1969)—offer associate degrees and certificates in occupational programs that prepare students for entry-level jobs, plus arts and sciences programs that transfer to 4-year colleges and universities. The Continuing Education Centers allow adults to renew their learning experiences through noncredit vocational, basic skills, life skills, and enrichment classes at sites throughout the city. Shared governance activities involve faculty, students, and staff in the development of solutions to key policy and budget issues.

San Diego State University

5250 Campanile Drive	Phone: (619) 594-5152
San Diego, CA 92182	Fax: (619) 594-7080

Division(s): College of Extended Studies
Web Site(s): http://www.ces.sdsu.edu
E-mail: extended.std@sdsu.edu

Class Titles: World Music, Music, Kinesiology, Human Physiology, Jazz History/Appreciation.

Teaching Methods: *Computers:* Internet, e-mail. *TV:* videotape, cable program, satellite broadcasting, PBS. *Other:* None.

Credits Granted for: completion of course work as outlined in class syllabus.

Admission Requirements: *Undergraduate:* for details, go to http://www.ces.sdsu.edu

On-Campus Requirements: None.

Tuition and Fees: *Undergraduate:* varies with each class, go to www.ces.sdsu.du for fee information. *Credit by:* semester.

Accreditation: Western Association of Schools and Colleges.

Description: The College of Extended Studies (1897) serves as the principal university liaison with the adult community and provides a wide variety of traditional and nontraditional, credit and noncredit, quality educational experiences designed to fit the lifestyle and expectations of mature adults. In addition, it provides a range of academic and special programs for students and groups during the summer months, in the evenings, and between semesters. Under the direction of the Dean of the College, programs are developed and carried out within 5 divisions: Special Sessions and Extension, Professional Development, American Language Institute, International Training Center, and Administrative Services. The majority of the programs are operated on a self-support basis since state funds are not provided for continuing education activities. The College of Extended Studies offered its first distance learning via ITFS in 1984 and has expanded delivery of a variety of classes via satellite, compressed video, cable, and the Internet.

San Joaquin Delta College

5151 Pacific Avenue　　　　**Phone: (209) 954-5039**
Stockton, CA 95207　　　　　**Fax: (209) 954-5600**

Division(s): Instructional Development and Regional Education
Web Site(s): http://www.sjdccd.cc.ca.us
E-mail: kcampbell@sjdccd.cc.ca.us

Class Titles: Accounting, Business, Advertising, Transportation, Chinese, Study Skills, English, Human Development, Algebra, Sociology, Computer Science.

Teaching Methods: *Computers:* Internet, real-time chat, electronic classroom, e-mail, CD-ROM, newsgroup, LISTSERV. *TV:* videotape, microwave broadcasting. *Other:* videoconferencing.

Credits Granted for: experiential learning, examination (CLEP).

Admission Requirements: *Undergraduate:* assessment/placement for first-time students.

On-Campus Requirements: None.

Tuition and Fees: *Undergraduate:* $12/credit residents, $121/credit nonresidents/international. *Credit by:* semester.

Financial Aid: Federal Pell Grant, Federal Work-Study, VA, California resident programs.

Accreditation: Western Association of Schools and Colleges.

Description: San Joaquin Delta is a public, 2-year community college founded in 1935. Its 165-acre campus is in Stockton, with other centers in nearby communities. The college operates a 157-acre educational farm, a 93-acre forestry field study area, and conducts evening classes in most district communities. Since its founding, San Joaquin has provided distance education to surrounding communities. The college televised its first distance courses over local channels in the early 1970s and has offered open broadcast telecourses since 1977. In 1985 Delta began offering 4 courses each semester over an Instructional Television Fixed Service System to several off-campus sites. In 1997 the college offered its first Internet courses. The 5-year distance education plan includes more Internet and televised courses, plus distance certificate programs.

San Jose State University

One Washington Square　　　**Phone: (408) 924-2636**
San Jose, CA 95192-0169　　　　　　　**(408) 924-2678**
　　　　　　　　　　　　Fax: (408) 924-2881/2616

Division(s): Technology Education Network (video), University Continuing Education (online)
Web Site(s): http://www.sjsu.edu/dept/TEN/
http://conted.sjsu.edu
E-mail: lelvin@email.sjsu.edu
szlotolo@conted.sjsu.edu

Class Titles: Business, Counselor Education, Special Education, Teacher Education, Environmental Studies, Geology, History, Nursing, Master of Occupational Therapy Courses Online, Instructional Technology.

Teaching Methods: *Computers:* Internet, real-time chat, electronic classroom, e-mail, newsgroup, LISTSERV. *TV:* videotape. *Other:* videoconferencing.

Credits Granted for: examination (CLEP, ACT-PEP, GRE).

Admission Requirements: *Undergraduate:* refer to SJSU's Web page for information on admission. *Graduate:* requirements on the CSU Web page: prospective students http://info.sjsu.edu, general campus information http://www.sjsu.edu.

On-Campus Requirements: depending on the program residence credit is required.

Tuition and Fees: *Undergraduate:* $676/1–6.0 units, $1,009/6.1+ units. *Application Fee:* $55. *Credit by:* semester.

Financial Aid: Federal Stafford Loan, Federal Perkins Loan, Federal PLUS Loan, Federal Pell Grant, Federal Work-Study, VA, California resident programs.

Accreditation: Western Association of Schools and Colleges.

Description: San Jose State University (1857) is California's oldest institution of public higher education. It was named the California State Normal School in 1862 and moved to San Jose in 1871. Today SJSU is a large master's university serving more than 27,000 students. Today, the multi-ethnic student body prepares for careers in the professions, business, social work, engineering, science, technology, education, social science, the arts, and the humanities. The university offers baccalaureate and master's degrees and professional credentials in more than 150 disciplines. The university has been involved in distance education since 1985. Line-of-sight microwave has been the main technology used, but over the past 5 years we have developed a student body using videoconferencing and now online learning.

San Juan College

4601 College Boulevard
Farmington, NM 87402

Phone: (505) 599-0231
Fax: (505) 599-0385

Division(s): Distance Education
Web Site(s): http://sjc.cc.nm.us
E-mail: golden@sjc.cc.nm.us

Undergraduate Degree Programs:
Associate of Science
Associate of Arts

Class Titles: Math, English, ECON, Child Care.

Teaching Methods: *Computers:* Internet, electronic classroom, e-mail. *TV:* videotape, cable program, satellite broadcasting. *Other:* videoconferencing.

Credits Granted for: experiential learning, corporate or professional association seminars/workshops, examination (CLEP, ACT-PEP, DANTES, GRE).

Admission Requirements: *Undergraduate:* GED or high school graduate.

On-Campus Requirements: No

Tuition and Fees: *Undergraduate:* $15/credit. *Application Fee:* $10. *Credit by:* semester.

Financial Aid: Federal Stafford Loan, Federal Perkins Loan, Federal PLUS Loan, Federal Pell Grant, Federal Work-Study, VA, programs for New Mexico residents and Indian Tribes.

Accreditation: North Central Association of Colleges and Schools.

Description: San Juan College (1965) serves northwestern New Mexico and the surrounding Four Corners region by providing a quality 2-year education at minimal cost. The college's mission is to provide educational opportunities and supportive services to its regional citizens to increase the productivity and efficiency of the surrounding business area.

Sandhills Community College

2200 Airport Road
Pinehurst, NC 28374

Phone: (910) 692-6185
Fax: (910) 695-1823

Division(s): Curriculum Instruction
Web Site(s): http://normandy.sandhills.cc.nc.us/indexj.html
E-mail: swansonr@email.sandhills.cc.nc.us

Undergraduate Degree Programs:
Associate in Arts

Class Titles: Most freshman/sophomore general education courses.

Teaching Methods: *Computers:* Internet, real-time chat, electronic classroom, e-mail, CD-ROM. *TV:* videotape, PBS. *Other:* videoconferencing, independent study.

Credits Granted for: experiential learning, examination (CLEP).

Admission Requirements: *Undergraduate:* high school diploma, placement exam.

On-Campus Requirements: None.

Tuition and Fees: *Undergraduate:* $20/credit in-state, $163/credit out-of-state. *Credit by:* semester.

Financial Aid: Federal Stafford Loan, Federal PLUS Loan, Federal Pell Grant, Federal Work-Study, VA, North Carolina resident programs, state/local scholarships.

Accreditation: Southern Association of Colleges and Schools.

Description: Sandhills Community College is a 2-year, public, postsecondary educational institution founded in 1963. Offering 53 technical/vocational programs and 3 for transfer degrees, Sandhills also offers the state's only Landscape Gardening program. Several programs, such as Hotel/Restaurant Management and Turf Management, are designed to support the area's golf and hospitality industries. Sandhills has delivered distance courses for 15 years and continues to develop accessible, flexible higher education.

Santa Fe Community College

6401 Richards Avenue
Santa Fe, NM 87505

Phone: (505) 428-1301
Fax: (505) 428-1237

Division(s): Instructional Technology
Web Site(s): http://www.santa-fe.cc.nm.us
E-mail: areed@santa-fe.cc.nm.us

Class Titles: Sociology, Technical Writing, Spanish, Medical Terminology, Contemporary Math (all are 100–200 level).

Teaching Methods: *Computers:* Internet, real-time chat, electronic classroom. *TV:* TV, videotape, cable program. *Other:* None.

Credits Granted for: examination (CLEP, ACT).

Admission Requirements: *Undergraduate:* open-admission.

On-Campus Requirements: midterms/finals in some courses.

Tuition and Fees: *Undergraduate:* $20–$45/credit, depending on residency. *Other Costs:* $20 Flex Lab. *Credit by:* semester.

Financial Aid: Federal Stafford Loan, Federal Pell Grant, Federal Work-Study, district aid.

Accreditation: North Central Association of Colleges and Schools.

Description: Santa Fe Community College has grown rapidly in enrollments and campus expansion since its founding in 1983. Today the college serves 12,000 students each semester. Distance learning programs will soon expand into the Internet and cable TV.

Saskatchewan Indian Federated College of the University of Regina

2nd Floor, 25-11th Street E	Phone: (306) 763-0066
Prince Albert, Saskatchewan, Canada	Fax: (306) 764-3511

Division(s): Northern Campus and Extension Department
Web Site(s): http://www.sifc.edu
E-mail: LAlexson@tansi.sifc.edu

Undergraduate Degree Programs:
University Entrance Program

Graduate Degree Programs:
Education (Elementary)
Administration
Arts and Science

Certificate Programs: Nations Language, Diploma in First Nations Inter-Disciplinary Studies in Justice, Indian Career and Community Counseling, Social Work.

Class Titles: Linguistics, Ojibway, English, Indian Studies, Indian Art History, Cree, Administration, Computer Science.

Teaching Methods: *Computers:* Internet, e-mail, CD-ROM, newsgroup. *TV:* videotape, cable program, satellite broadcasting, PBS. *Other:* radio broadcast, audioconferencing, videoconferencing, audiographics, audiotapes, fax, correspondence, independent study, individual study, learning contracts.

Credits Granted for: some transfer credits. Contact school for information.

Admission Requirements: *Undergraduate:* international applicants from other countries seeking admission must submit both a completed Application for Admission form and original documents covering their present academic standing and should write to Admissions, Office of the Registrar for detailed information concerning admission requirements for the faculty to which they seek admission. If the academic documents are not in English they must be accompanied by the certified copies of an English translation.

On-Campus Requirements: for 4-year BA, at least half your program and at least half the required hours in your major must consist of University of Regina courses; other programs also have restrictions.

Tuition and Fees: *Undergraduate:* these costs are estimates only, the actual cost may vary from program to program and with the actual courses in which the student is enrolled. Course fees are charged on the basis of which faculty is teaching the course. Administration: $14/3-hour course, Arts: $14, Education: $22, Engineering: $29, Fine Arts: $29, Journalism: $29, Physical Activities Studies: $14, Social Work: $22. *Application Fee:* $50. *Credit by:* semester.

Accreditation: Association of Universities and Colleges of Canada.

Description: In May 1976, the Federation of Saskatchewan Indian Nations entered into a federation agreement with the University of Regina, creating the Saskatchewan Indian Federated College. The agreement provides for an independently administered university college, the mission of which is to serve the academic, cultural, and spiritual needs of First Nations students. The College also accepts non-First Nations students. The College's Board of Governors is appointed by the Chiefs of Saskatchewan. Programs are academically integrated with the University of Regina, and the college follows all university regulations respecting admissions and the development of new programs. All SIFC programs are fully accredited through the University of Regina. The college has close to 60 full-time faculty and offers students a unique Indian curriculum. The SIFC has developed degree and certificate programs in a variety of faculties and disciplines: the Bachelor of Arts in Indian Studies was approved in 1976 and in 1977 Indian Art, Indian Languages, Indian Education, and Indian Social Work were added. In 1978 a program in Indian Management and Administration began, and Indian Communication Arts, Indian Health Careers, and the Special Case Master's programs were established in the early 1980s. In 1987 the Department of Science was established; in 1989 the School of Business and Public Administration came into being and, in 1995 the First Nations MBA was established in conjunction with the University of Saskatchewan.

Sauk Valley Community College

173 Illinois Route 2	Phone: (815) 288-5511
Dixon, IL 61021	Fax: (815) 288-5958

Division(s): Instructional Deans
Web Site(s): http://www.svcc.edu
E-mail: ullrics@svcc.edu

Undergraduate Degree Programs:
Associate of Science
Associate of Arts

Class Titles: English, Humanities, Math, Criminal Justice.

Teaching Methods: *Computers:* Internet, real-time chat, e-mail, CD-ROM, LISTSERV. *TV:* videotape. *Other:* videoconferencing, audioconferencing, audiotapes, fax, correspondence, independent study.

Credits Granted for: experiential learning, examination (CLEP, ACT-PEP, DANTES, GRE).

Admission Requirements: *Undergraduate:* open policy.

On-Campus Requirements: some classes have test requirements that must be taken on campus or proctored.

Tuition and Fees: *Undergraduate:* $46/credit. *Other Costs:* out-of-state Internet $78/hour. *Credit by:* semester

Financial Aid: Federal Stafford Loan, Federal Perkins Loan, Federal PLUS Loan, Federal Pell Grant, Federal Work-Study, VA, Illinois resident programs.

Accreditation: North Central Association of Colleges and Schools.

Description: Sauk Valley Community College (1965) provides opportunities in the traditional transfer areas, plus vocational-technical, adult and continuing education, community service, and career education. Sauk has taken a lead role in Internet classes and is teamed with the University of Illinois for the Illinois Virtual Campus. SVCC is authorized to confer the associate of arts, associate of science, associate of engineering science, and associate of fine arts degrees to students completing requirements in the university transfer programs. The college confers the associate of applied science degree and certificates to students completing requirements in career education programs. The associate of liberal studies degree is available to students desiring a nonspecialized degree.

Saybrook Graduate School and Research Center

| 450 Pacific Avenue, Third Floor | Phone: (415) 433-9200 |
| San Francisco, CA 94133 | Fax: (415) 433-9271 |

Division(s): Entire School
Web Site(s): http://www.saybrook.org
E-mail: mmeyers@igc.org

Graduate Degree Programs:
Master of Arts
Doctor of Philosophy

Class Titles: All classes available if taken singly as a non-matriculated student.

Teaching Methods: *Computers:* Internet, electronic classroom, e-mail. *Other:* correspondence, independent study, individual study.

Credits Granted for: portfolio assessment.

Admission Requirements: *Graduate:* accredited bachelor's degree, 3.0 GPA (some exceptions possible), degrees completed in under 7 years. *Doctoral:* same as graduate.

On-Campus Requirements: 3-day orientation to begin, 2 one-week conferences yearly.

Tuition and Fees: *Graduate:* $11,750/year (1998/99). Students pay for a year's worth of course work, irregardless of the number of courses they take. If a student pays out of pocket, there is an 8-payment plan; payment from loans is 2 times/year (February and August). *Other Costs:* varies for books (the average/year is $700); $400 Orientation Conference fee (includes workshops, food, room—the student pays for travel expenses); $600–$800 for each of other 2 required conferences/year, depending on number of meals bought and whether a room is shared or not (students pay travel arrangements). *Credit by:* credits awarded/class.

Financial Aid: Federal Stafford Loan, VA.

Accreditation: Western Association of Schools and Colleges.

Description: Saybrook Graduate School and Research Center (1971) offers master's and doctoral degrees in Psychology and Human Science, based in a humanistic tradition. Areas of concentration include Clinical Inquiry, Consciousness Studies, Creativity/the Arts, Health Studies, Humanistic/Transpersonal Studies, Organizational Systems Inquiry, Peace/Conflict Resolution Studies, and Social Philosophy/Political Psychology. Saybrook's programs, designed for adult professionals, blend the humanistic and transpersonal psychology studies in consciousness and spirituality with critical and creative methods of inquiry. Using learning guides, students complete course work in independent study encouraged and evaluated by faculty who communicate by phone, letter, fax, or computer. Saybrook faculty serve as advisors, mentors, and tutors rather than as traditional "teachers." While much of the student's intellectual work is done independently, the relationship between faculty and student allows for support, commentary, and analysis that exceed traditional classroom situations.

Schoolcraft College

18600 Haggerty Road	Phone: (734) 462-4532
Livonia, MI 48152	(734) 462-4801
	Fax: (734) 462-4589

Division(s): Instruction
Web Site(s): http://www.schoolcraft.cc.mi.us/
E-mail: edoinidi@schoolcraft.cc.mi.us

Undergraduate Degree Programs:
Associate of Arts
Bachelor of Science in Business Administration

Graduate Degree Programs:
Master of Science in Business Administration
(online degrees offered in connection with Madonna University)

Class Titles: Cultural Anthropology, Nutrition, Business, Business Math, Business Statistics, Business Management, Marketing, Child Development, Computer Systems, Office '95 Szabo, Speech, Economics, Composition, Literature/Short Fiction, Literature/Poetry, French, World Geography, Ancient World, Early Modern World, Early America (U.S. History), Contemporary America (U.S. History), Humanities through Arts, Math, Philosophy, Ethical Problems, Astronomy, Survey of American Government, Psychology, Child Psychology, Sociology, Spanish.

Teaching Methods: *Computers:* Internet, electronic classroom, e-mail, CD-ROM. *TV:* videotape, PBS. *Other:* audioconferencing, videoconferencing, audiotapes, fax, independent study.

Credits Granted for: examination (CLEP, ACT-PEP, DANTES, GRE).

Admission Requirements: *Undergraduate:* high school and college transcripts, ACT or placement tests in math, reading, and English.

On-Campus Requirements: None.

Tuition and Fees: *Undergraduate:* $51/credit (in-district) plus $20 fee, $180/credit online degree program (includes materials). *Application Fee:* $25. *Other Costs:* laboratory/course fees. *Credit by:* semester.

Financial Aid: Federal Stafford Loan, Federal PLUS Loan, Federal Pell Grant, Federal Work-Study, VA, Michigan resident programs.

Accreditation: North Central Association of Colleges and Schools.

Description: Schoolcraft College is a fully-accredited community college founded in 1961 and located in northwestern Wayne County. Schoolcraft strongly emphasizes service to the community conducive to pursuing a quality education. The college provides corporate training programs and business services for companies exploring new world markets through its prototype "export resource center." The continued demand for excellence will lead us to monitor, improve, and expand to all markets.

Seabury-Western Theological Seminary

2122 Sheridan Road	Phone: (847) 328-9300 x26
Evanston, IL 60201	Fax: (847) 328-9624

Division(s): Academic Affairs
Web Site(s): http://www.swts.nwu.edu
E-mail: swts@nwu.edu

Graduate Degree Programs:
Master of Divinity
Master of Theological Studies
Doctor of Ministry

Certificate Programs: Study, Advanced Study

Teaching Methods: *Computers:* Internet, electronic classroom, e-mail, CD-ROM, LISTSERV. *TV:* videotape, cable program, satellite broadcasting, PBS. *Other:* audiotapes, fax, correspondence, independent study, individual study, learning contracts.

Admission Requirements: *Graduate:* bachelor's degree. *Certificate:* bachelor's degree and/or first professional degree.

On-Campus Requirements: 4 quarters/degree, 3 quarters/certificate.

Tuition and Fees: *Graduate:* $1,150/credit. *Application Fee:* $25. *Other Costs:* room/board, insurance, books. *Credit by:* quarter.

Financial Aid: Federal Stafford Loan, Federal Perkins Loan, Federal PLUS Loan, Federal Pell Grant, Federal Work-Study, VA, Illinois resident programs.

Accreditation: North Central Association of Colleges and Schools, Association of Theological Schools.

Description: Seabury-Western Theological Seminary is one of 11 accredited seminaries of the Episcopal Church. It was created in 1933 by merging Seabury Divinity School (1858) and Western Theological Seminary (1883). Since its initial fusion of Evangelical and Anglo-Catholic traditions, Seabury-Western has continued to respect and nurture the historic and evolving diversities in the Episcopal Church and Anglican Communion. In 1994 the seminary created the Seabury Institute ministry as a partnership with parishes exercising leadership for Church mission. The seminary's mission is to educate priests and lay leaders for Episcopal Church ministry. To that end, Seabury-Western is committed to all aspects of technology for enhanced teaching and learning. Beginning with e-mail and the Internet, Seabury now uses electronic reserves in most classes and offers at least one Internet class/year with e-mail and LISTSERV.

Seattle Central Community College

1701 Broadway, BE1144	Phone: (206) 587-4060
Seattle, WA 98122	(800) 510-1724
	Fax: (206) 287-5562

Division(s): Distance Learning Program
Web Site(s):
http://seaccd.sccd.ctc.edu/central/virtcoll/index.html
E-mail: dislrn@sccd.ctc.edu

Undergraduate Degree Programs:
Associate of Arts

Class Titles: Cultural Anthropology, Composition, Literature, Geography, Pacific Century, Intercultural Communication, American Cinema, Ethics in America, American National Government, General Psychology, Developmental Psychology, Abnormal Psychology, Women Studies, Mass Media, Poetry, Astronomy, Environmental Issues/Problems, Spanish, Business/Economic Statistics.

Teaching Methods: *TV:* videotape, cable program, correspondence. *Other:* None.

Credits Granted for: work experience, examination (CLEP, ACT-PEP, ASSET, DANTES, GRE).

Admission Requirements: *Undergraduate:* age 18 or high school graduate (special consideration may be given to persons not meeting these conditions); application; all official transcripts from high school and any higher-education schools; placement tests. To qualify for in-state (resident) tuition, you must have lived in Washington state, for reasons other than educational purposes, for one full year prior to the first day of the quarter in which you claim the right to pay resident fees.

On-Campus Requirements: None.

Tuition and Fees: *Undergraduate:* depending on number of credits registered: for in-state students, $370/5-credit class plus supplemental materials for out-of-state students. *Other Costs:* varies for supplemental materials. *Credit by:* quarter.

Financial Aid: Federal Pell Grant, Federal Supplemental Educational Opportunity Grant, Washington State Need Grant (state residency status required).

Accreditation: Northwest Association of Schools and Colleges.

Description: In its 30-year history, Seattle Central Community College (1968) has established a reputation for educational excellence and innovation. It is one of the largest colleges in Washington state, with an enrollment of 10,000 students. More than 60% of Seattle Central's students are taking freshman- and sophomore-level classes with plans to complete a bachelor's degree. Each year, the college transfers one of the largest number of students in the state to 4-year institutions.

Seattle Pacific University

3307 Third Avenue W	Phone: (800) 482-3848
Seattle, WA 98119	Fax: (206) 281-2662

Division(s): Continuing Studies
Web Site(s): http://www.spu.edu/dcs
E-mail: erikafox@spu.edu

Class Titles: Art Instruction for Elementary Classroom, Old Testament, New Testament, Romans, Behavior is Language, Motivating At-Risk Learners, Problem Behaviors in Elementary School, Proactive Classroom Management, Anger Control for Children/Teens, Advanced School Counseling, Emotional Intelligence, Moving from Teaching to Learning, Linking Language/Arts/Mathematics, Transformational Teaching, Standards-Based Teaching, Teaching Early Literacy, Language Study, Medieval Europe, Great War/Shaping of 20th Century, U.S. History Since 1877, Civil War, History of Pacific Northwest, Values/Faith/Social Issues, Politics, U.S. Government/Politics, Disabilities, Classroom Strategies, Building Classroom Programs, Gifted Students, Strategies for ADD/Active Learners, One-Computer Classroom, Native American Art of Pacific Northwest Coast, Washington History, History of Puget Sound, Media Literacy, Impact of TV/Video, Assessment Literacy, Integrated Teaching, Survival Kit for New Elementary Teachers.

Teaching Methods: *Computers:* some software programs. *TV:* videotape, PBS. *Other:* audiotapes, correspondence, extensive course study guides, textbooks.

Admission Requirements: *Undergraduate:* high school graduate. *Graduate:* bachelor's degree, no formal admission or requirements. Teachers take most graduate-level, professional development courses.

On-Campus Requirements: None.

Tuition and Fees: *Graduate:* approximately $65/credit. *Other*

Costs: $10–$100 course materials. *Credit by:* quarter.

Accreditation: Washington State Board of Education, Northwest Association of Schools and Colleges, National Council for Accreditation of Teacher Education. SPU credits recognized by various regional association members and leading graduate schools throughout the country.

Description: For more than a decade, Seattle Pacific University's (1891) distance learning program has served 2 primary audiences: adult learners seeking to complete an undergraduate degree, and K–12 educators desiring quality professional development course work. SPU does not currently offer a complete degree program via distance learning. However, many individual courses may apply toward undergraduate or graduate degree requirements or toward fulfilling school district, endorsement-related, or other professional development needs.

Seminary Extension

901 Commerce Street, Suite 500	Phone: (615) 242-2453
Nashville, TN 37203-3631	Fax: (615) 782-4822

Division(s): Independent Study Institute
Web Site(s): None.
E-mail: seisi@compuserve.com

Class Titles: Theology, Pastoral Ministries, Religious Education, Biblical Study

Teaching Methods: *Computers:* Internet, real-time chat, e-mail. *TV:* videotape. *Other:* audiotapes, fax, correspondence, independent study, individual study.

Credits Granted for: extrainstitutional learning.

Admission Requirements: *Undergraduate:* age 16.

On-Campus Requirements: None.

Tuition and Fees: *Undergraduate:* Cost on course by course basis. Course cost variable according to cost of textbooks. *Credit by:* semester.

Accreditation: Distance Education and Training Council; course transfer credit recommended by American Council on Education (ACE).

Description: Seminary Extension (1951) has been offering quality distance education for more than 45 years. Courses in Theology, Christian Education, Biblical Studies, Pastoral Ministry, Church History, Music, and Church Growth are offered for those who feel the call to ministry. Class offerings have grown over the years and continue to grow today. We strive to provide a quality education at a very affordable price. Beginning with a few students taking courses through correspondence, Seminary Extension has grown to more than 5,000 students taking courses either through independent study or through a classroom network in more than 450 locations in the continental U.S. and abroad. We are expanding into online computer classes and currently deliver about 10 courses in this manner.

Seton Hall University

Koslowski Hall	Phone: (973) 275-2721
South Orange, NJ 07079	Fax: (973) 275-2187

Division(s): College of Education and Human Services
Web Site(s): http://www.shu.edu
E-mail: brookmse@shu.edu

Graduate Degree Programs:
Master of Arts in Education

Certificate Programs: Information Technology
Supervision and Administration

Class Titles: All courses in degree program/certification may be taken individually.

Teaching Methods: *TV:* interactive television courses, cable program, satellite broadcasting, PBS. *Other:* videoconferencing.

Admission Requirements: *Graduate:* BA/BS degree, MAT, or GRE exams. *Certificate:* enrolled in the MA program in Education

On-Campus Requirements: one 3-credit course on campus in Graduate Research Methods.

Tuition and Fees: *Undergraduate:* Call school. *Graduate:* call Office of Continuing Professional Education. *Credit by:* semester.

Accreditation: Middle States Association of Colleges and Schools.

Description: Seton Hall University (1986) initiated their distance learning program in response to educators who wanted convenient locations to complete MA degree in Education.

Shasta College

11555 Old Oregon Trail	Phone: (530) 225-4814
Redding, CA 96049	Fax: (530) 225-4983

Division(s): Extended Education and Telecommunications
Web Site(s): http://www.shastacollege.edu
E-mail: jpoulsen@shastacollege.edu

Class Titles: Physical Sciences, Natural Sciences, Math, English, Psychology, Sociology, Political Science, History, Speech.

Teaching Methods: *Computers:* Internet, real-time chat, electronic classroom, e-mail, CD-ROM, newsgroup, LIST-SERV. *TV:* videotape, cable program, PBS. *Other:* videoconferencing, audioconferencing, audiographics, audiotapes, fax, correspondence, independent study, individual study, learning contracts.

Credits Granted for: examination (CLEP, ACT-PEP, DANTES, GRE).

Admission Requirements: *Undergraduate:* high school graduate or age 18.

On-Campus Requirements: None.

Tuition and Fees: *Undergraduate:* $12/credit. *Credit by:* semester.

Financial Aid: Federal Stafford Loan, Federal Perkins Loan, Federal PLUS Loan, Federal Pell Grant, Federal Work-Study, VA, California resident programs.

Accreditation: Western Association of Schools and Colleges.

Description: Shasta College (1948) is one of 107 community colleges serving the educational needs of students. Programs are offered for the first 2 years of work designed for transfer to a college or university, vocational programs, and remedial education. Located in the far northern part of California surrounded by lakes, streams, and mountains, the college serves a geographical area of 10,000 square miles. Due to the rural nature of the college district, Shasta College has been involved in distance education for many years.

Shawnee Community College

8364 Shawnee College Road	Phone: (618) 634-2242
Ullin, IL 62992	Fax: (618) 634-9711

Division(s): Learning Resources/Instructional Services
Web Site(s): http://www.shawnee.cc.il.us
E-mail: deeb@shawnee.cc.il.us

Class Titles: Accounting-Financial Concepts, Accounting-Managerial Concepts, Abnormal Psychology, Advanced Medical Terminology, Microsoft Access, Microsoft Excel, Word Perfect, American Literature, Anthropology, Art Appreciation, Bookkeeping, Business/Law, Business Organization, Calculus for Business/Social Science, Career Development, Algebra, Developmental Math, Dynamics, Economics (micro/macro), Exceptional Children, Composition, Finite Mathematics, French, Zoology, Government, Health, Human Growth/Development, Astronomy, Biology, Circuit Analysis, Health Information, Literature, Psychology, Sociology, Math for Liberal Arts, Medical Terminology, Modern Fiction, Nutrition, Microsoft Word, Physical Science–Physics, Management, Reading Improvement, Thermodynamics, Trigonometry, World Literature, Business Management, Astronomy.

Teaching Methods: *Computers:* Internet, e-mail. *TV:* videotape, PBS. *Other:* videoconferencing, fax, correspondence, independent study.

Credits Granted for: all courses are for college credit.

Admission Requirements: *Undergraduate:* open-door policy for high school diploma/GED, with preference given to District #531 residents.

On-Campus Requirements: Class participation at designated sites for interactive video, on-campus midterm/finals for telecourses.

Tuition and Fees: *Undergraduate:* $37/hour, plus applicable fees, for in-district students. *Other Costs:* lab fees. *Credit by:* semester.

Financial Aid: Federal Pell Grant, Federal Work-Study, VA, Illinois resident programs, institutional scholarships.

Accreditation: North Central Association of Colleges and Schools.

Description: The main campus of Shawnee Community College (1967) is located 7 miles east of the Interstate 57 Ullin exit, southern Illinois. SCC operates extension centers in Anna, Cairo, and Metropolis, Illinois. The college entered into distance learning by offering telecourses. In 1994, SCC installed interactive video classrooms at the Ullin campus and the Metropolis extension center. This video network now includes 9 classrooms located at extension centers, high schools, and in one business in the Shawnee Community College district. Through participation in the Southern Illinois Telecommunications Network, SCC students can access classes offered by other state community colleges, colleges, and universities. SCC offers English Composition and Microsoft application software courses online.

Shoreline Community College

16101 Greenwood Avenue N	Phone: (206) 546-4663
Shoreline, WA 98133	Fax: (206) 546-4604

Division(s): Library Media Center
Web Site(s): http://oscar.ctc.edu/shoreline
E-mail: lcheng@ctc.edu

Class Titles: History, Math, Geology, Physics, Psychology, English, Library Science/Music, Biology, Business, Communications, French, Spanish, Wellness, Social Sciences, Geography, Applied News Writing, Women of Power, Information Competency, others.

Teaching Methods: *Computers:* Internet, real-time chat, electronic classroom, e-mail, CD-ROM, newsgroup, LISTSERV. *TV:* videotape, cable program, satellite broadcasting, PBS, Coast, Dallas, Jones, Thompson. *Other:* videoconferencing (Interactive TV), audioconferencing, audiotapes, fax, correspondence, independent study, individual study, learning contracts.

Credits Granted for: experiential learning, portfolio assessment, extrainstitutional learning, examination (CLEP, ACT-PEP, DANTES, GRE).

Admission Requirements: *Undergraduate:* accredited high school graduate or GED or age 18. *Certificate:* same as undergraduate.

On-Campus Requirements: up to 3 for telecourses.

Tuition and Fees: *Undergraduate:* $101/1–2 credits, $151/3 credits, $202/4 credits, $505/full-time (10–18 credits), residents. *Application Fee:* $10 nonrefundable. *Other Costs:* $30 lab fees if student wants to use Shoreline's computer lab for Internet access. *Credit by:* quarter.

Financial Aid: Federal Stafford Loan, Federal Perkins Loan, Federal PLUS Loan, Federal Pell Grant, Federal Work-Study, VA, Washington resident programs.

Accreditation: Northwest Association of Schools and Colleges.

Description: Shoreline Community College (1964) offers excellent academic, professional/technical, and work force training programs to meet the lifelong learning needs of its community. Dedicated faculty and staff are committed to the educational success of all students. Located 10 miles north of downtown Seattle, Shoreline is one of the most strikingly beautiful college campuses in the state. Twenty-seven buildings constitute the 83-acre campus. These include a state-of-the-art automotive training center and visual arts building, computer centers, laboratories, a student center, theater, a well-equipped gymnasium, child care center, a state-of-the-art multimedia center, and a library/media center. Shoreline's satellite, the Northshore Center, is conveniently located in Bothell and provides academic transfer courses and customized training. The college is a member of the American Association of Community Colleges and the Association of Community College Trustees.

Sierra Community College

5000 Rocklin Road	Phone: (916) 789-2638
Rocklin, CA 95677	Fax: (916) 789-2992

Division(s): Multimedia and Distance Learning
Web Site(s): http://www.sierra.cc.ca.us
E-mail: DAVENPORT_SU@email.sierra.cc.ca.us

Undergraduate Degree Programs:
Associate of Arts

Class Titles: Statistics, Algebra, Physical Geography, Computing, Computer Programming, Object-Oriented Programming Using JAVA, Psychology, Alcohol/Drugs/Society, U.S. History, Administration of Justice, Physical Anthropology, Sociology, Composition, Literature, Shakespeare, Modern Art History, American Government, Visual Communication, Theater, Economics, College Study Skills, Environment/Human Impact, Music, Biology.

Teaching Methods: *Computers:* Internet, e-mail. *TV:* Interactive cable program and low-power television. *Other:* videoconferencing, fax.

Admission Requirements: *Undergraduate:* high school diploma, age 18 (high school students may apply through Academic Enrichment Program).

On-Campus Requirements: Must take all exams/quizzes at

on-campus Testing Center. Televised courses must be viewed live.

Tuition and Fees: *Undergraduate:* $13/credit residents, $138/credit nonresidents, $143/credit foreign. *Graduate:* $10 degree petition. *Other Costs:* $10 health fee. *Credit by:* semester.

Financial Aid: Federal Stafford Loan, Federal Perkins Loan, Federal PLUS Loan, Federal Pell Grant, Federal Work-Study, VA, California resident programs.

Accreditation: Western Association of Schools and Colleges.

Description: Located near the Sierra, Nevada foothills, Sierra Community College (1914) serves 16,000 students each semester. Its Distance Learning Program began in 1988 with televised cable channel courses to assist nontraditional students with their educational goals. Today Sierra College operates a cable channel through a large network in Placer and Nevada counties with plans to begin a second channel and offer Internet courses by fall of 1999. Sierra is deeply committed to serving its distance students through instructional technologies.

Simpson College

701 North C Street	Phone: (800) 362-2454 x1614
Indianola, IA 50125	Fax: (515) 961-1498

Division(s): Adult Learning
Web Site(s): http://www.simpson.edu/dal
E-mail: adultlrn@simpson.edu

Undergraduate Degree Programs:
Bachelor of Arts

Class Titles: Criminal Justice, Communications.

Teaching Methods: *Computers:* Internet, electronic classroom, e-mail, LISTSERV. *Other:* None.

Credits Granted for: experiential learning, portfolio assessment, extrainstitutional learning, examination (CLEP, ACT-PEP, DANTES, GRE).

Admission Requirements: *Undergraduate:* contact school.

On-Campus Requirements: the majority of our studies are in-class. A limited number of courses are offered online or in a combination of online and in person.

Tuition and Fees: *Undergraduate:* $185/credit. *Graduate:* $200/credit. *Other Costs:* $50 admission fee. *Credit by:* semester.

Financial Aid: Federal Stafford Loan, Federal Perkins Loan, Federal PLUS Loan, Federal Pell Grant, Federal Work-Study, VA, Iowa resident programs.

Accreditation: North Central Association of Colleges and Schools.

Description: Simpson College (1860) is a private, selective liberal arts college located in the Des Moines area. We have

1,300 full-time students and 650 part-time students who are served by the Division of Adult Learning. Simpson has served adult students for more than 20 years with adapted class schedules and locations.

Sinclair Community College

444 West Third Street	Phone: (937) 512-2354
Dayton, OH 45402	Fax: (937) 512-2891

Division(s): Distance Learning Division
Web Site(s): http://www.sinclair.edu/academic/distance
E-mail: pfalkens@sinclair.edu

Undergraduate Degree Programs:
Associate of Arts in Liberal Arts/Sciences
Associate of Science in Business Administration

Class Titles: Art Appreciation, Women Artists, Business of Art, Biology, Business Ownership, Business Management, International Business, Business Law, Microsoft Office, Internet, DC/AC Circuits, Electronics, Engineering Technology Economics, Experience-Based Education, U.S. History, Humanities, Personal Law, Allied Health Informatics, Health Information Management, Medical Terminology, Abnormal Psychology, General Psychology, Stress Management, Psychology of Aging, Adult/Adolescent Psychology, Life Span Development, Child Development, Developmental Reading, General Sociology, Comparing Cultures, American Racial/Ethnic Groups, Rural Communities, Accounting, Automotive Systems, Intercultural Groups, Accounting, Intercultural Communication, Food/Nutrition, Economics, Quality Engineering, Astronomy, English Composition, Business Communication, American Cinema, Quality Management, Marketing, Mathematics, Physics.

Teaching Methods: *Computers:* Internet, asynchronous chat, electronic classroom, e-mail, CD-ROM. *TV:* videotape, cable program, PBS. *Other:* audioconferencing, videoconferencing, audiotapes, fax, correspondence, independent study, individual study, learning contracts.

Credits Granted for: experiential learning, portfolio assessment, extrainstitutional learning, examination (CLEP, ACT-PEP, DANTES, GRE).

Admission Requirements: *Undergraduate:* English/math placement test.

On-Campus Requirements: None.

Tuition and Fees: *Undergraduate:* $31/credit Montgomery County, $50/credit outside Montgomery County in-state, $83/credit out-of-state. *Application Fee:* $10. *Other Costs:* shipping. *Credit by:* quarter.

Financial Aid: Federal Stafford Loan, Federal Perkins Loan, Federal PLUS Loan, Federal Pell Grant, Federal Work-Study, VA, Ohio resident programs.

Accreditation: North Central Association of Colleges and Schools.

Description: Sinclair Community College is a comprehensive, 2-year, public institution offering educational opportunities to Miami Valley citizens for more than 100 years. Sinclair is Dayton's largest institution of higher education, serving 21,000 students and accounting for one-third of local enrollment. It is also among the 20 largest, single-campus, community colleges in the U.S., with 1,400 courses in 1,000 disciplines and 46 association degrees in 25 areas. Not only does Sinclair prepare students for transfer into upper division baccalaureate university programs and technical schools, but it also offers them extensive opportunities to update technical knowledge needed in today's global economy. The college first offered distance learning in 1979 through local public service TV programs. Sinclair quickly realized that these nontraditional courses were helping the working population, with career and family commitments, acquire a college education.

Skagit Valley College

2405 East College Way	Phone: (360) 416-7603 or 7770
Mount Vernon, WA 98273-5899	Fax: (360) 416-7838

Division(s): Distance Education
Web Site(s): http://www.svc.ctc.edu
E-mail: keeler@skagit.ctc.edu

Undergraduate Degree Programs:
Associate in Arts University and College Transfer

Certificate Programs: Microcomputers

Class Titles: Technical Writing, Math, Employer/Employee Roles/Perspectives, Computer Science C++, Computer Science Visual BASIC, Cultural Anthropology, Business, Chemical Concepts, Geology, Composition, History of World Civilization, Arts in Humanities, Literature, Film, Basic Arithmetic, Algebra, Applied Mathematics, Contemporary Mathematics, Probability/Statistics, Environmental Science, Nutrition, Ethics, Wellness for Life, Physical Fitness, General Psychology, Abnormal Psychology, Career Development, Sociology, Job Search Techniques, Spanish, Interpersonal Communication, Art/Craft of Social Structures, Perceptions of Earth's Geological Influences on Human Behavior, Information Age, Computer Science, Visual BASIC Programming, Microcomputers, Using Windows 95, Spreadsheets, Databases, Internet, Creating Web Pages, Microsoft Word, Wordperfect, Integrated Software Basics, Presentation Software.

Teaching Methods: *Computers:* Internet, electronic classroom, e-mail, newsgroup, LISTSERV. *TV:* videotape, satellite broadcasting, PBS. *Other:* audioconferencing, videoconferencing, audiotapes, fax, correspondence, independent study, individual study.

Credits Granted for: experiential learning, portfolio assessment, examination (DANTES).

Admission Requirements: *Undergraduate:* high school graduate or more than age 18.

On-Campus Requirements: for testing purposes only.

Tuition and Fees: *Undergraduate:* $46/credit. *Other Costs:* $25/course telecourses fee, $30/course tape rental fee rented during a specific quarter (optional), $25/quarter network user fee (mandatory for students taking computer-based courses). *Credit by:* quarter.

Financial Aid: Federal Stafford Loan, Federal PLUS Loan, Federal Pell Grant, Federal Work-Study, VA, Washington resident programs.

Accreditation: Northwest Association of Schools and Colleges.

Description: Skagit Valley College (1926) is the 2nd oldest, 2-year community college in the state, operating in Skagit, Island, and San Juan counties. In 1955 a 35-acre site was purchased and a complex of 6 buildings was soon completed. SVC now operates campuses in Mount Vernon, Oak Harbor, Clinton (South Whidbey Center), and Friday Harbor (San Juan Center). The college has taken an ever-increasing role in meeting the educational needs of the community. SVC enrolls more than 7,000 students, with full-time equivalents of 4,150. A strong international program attracts students from more than a dozen countries. Distance education is helping a growing number of students overcome the obstacles of time and geography. Half of the students attend SVC transfer to 4-year colleges or universities, while another one-third pursue vocational and technical training in 24 programs.

Skidmore College

815 North Broadway	Phone: (518) 580-5450
Saratoga Springs, NY 12866	Fax: (518) 580-5449

Division(s): University Without Walls
Web Site(s): http://www.skidmore.edu (Click on UWW)
E-mail: uww@skidmore.edu

Undergraduate Degree Programs:
Individualized studies in many disciplines/fields.

Class Titles: Varies.

Teaching Methods: *Computers:* Internet, real-time chat, electronic classroom, e-mail, LISTSERV. *Other:* fax, correspondence, independent study, individual study.

Credits Granted for: experiential learning, portfolio assessment, extrainstitutional learning, examination (CLEP, ACT-PEP, DANTES, GRE).

On-Campus Requirements: 3 visits for admissions interview, advising/enrollment, and degree plan/final project.

Tuition and Fees: *Undergraduate:* $475/3-credit independent study course. *Application Fee:* $40. *Other Costs:* $2,600 annual enrollment fee. *Credit by:* semester.

Financial Aid: Federal Stafford Loan, Federal PLUS Loan, Federal Pell Grant, VA, New York resident programs.

Accreditation: Middle States Association of Colleges and Schools.

Description: Founded in 1911, Skidmore College began its distance learning program, the University Without Walls, in 1971. More than 275 students use UWW's flexible framework to develop individually tailored undergraduate degree programs. UWW shapes its programs to fit accessibility options of students throughout the country and overseas. UWW students may earn a BA or BS on campus, via the Web, through classes at nearby colleges and universities, in distance courses at major universities, or in internships.

Solano Community College

4000 Suisun Valley Road	Phone: (707) 864-7000
Suisun City, CA 94585	Fax: (707) 864-0361

Division(s): Learning Resources
Web Site(s): http://www.solano.cc.ca.us
E-mail: dkirkori@solano.cc.ca.us
dsee@solano.cc.ca.us

Undergraduate Degree Programs:
Associate of Arts
Associate of Science

Certificate Programs: not for distance learning.

Class Titles: Business, Management, Health Education, Child Development, Sociology, Psychology, Music Appreciation.

Teaching Methods: *TV:* videotape, cable program, satellite broadcasting, PBS. *Other:* videoconferencing.

Admission Requirements: *Undergraduate:* high school graduate or equivalent, or age 18 and can benefit from instruction.

On-Campus Requirements: orientation session; 5–10 class meetings.

Tuition and Fees: *Undergraduate:* $12/unit. *Credit by:* semester.

Financial Aid: Federal Stafford Loan, Federal PLUS Loan, Federal Pell Grant, Federal Work-Study, VA.

Accreditation: Western Association of Schools and Colleges.

Description: Solano Community College (1945) is a tradition in Solano County. The 192-acre campus opened in 1971 with 5,000 students. Today the college's 11,000 students are part of California's public community college system of 106 campuses in 70 districts. Solano's flexible scheduling includes transferable year-round classes and occupational training offered during the day, evening, or on Saturdays—on or off the campus—in traditional, short-term, or open-entry/exit formats. SCC's distance learning program began in 1975 and includes TV, video, and home and travel study. In addition, CSU Sacramento is offering upper-division courses at Solano via 2-way, interactive TV.

South Mountain Community College

7050 South 24th Street	Phone: (602) 243-8000
Phoenix, AZ 85050	Fax: (602) 243-8329

Division(s): None.
Web Site(s): http://www.smc.maricopa.edu
E-mail: admissions@smc.maricopa.edu

Undergraduate Degree Programs:
Associate of Arts
Associate of General Studies
Associate of Applied Science

Certificate Programs: Computer Programming, Microcomputer Applications, Microcomputer Systems Maintenance/Repair, Office Automation Systems, Call Center Supervision, Telecommunications Technology, Call Center Customer Service Representative, Early Childhood Development, Wholesale Food Management, Supervision/Management, Supermarket Management, Quality Process Leadership, Quality Customer Service, Organizational Leadership, Import/Export Trade, International Business.

Teaching Methods: *Computers:* CD-ROM, LISTSERV, electronic forum. *Other:* videoconferencing.

Credits Granted for: examination (CLEP).

Admission Requirements: *Undergraduate:* open-admission. *Certificate:* open-admission.

On-Campus Requirements: contact school for requirements.

Tuition and Fees: *Undergraduate:* $39/credit for county residents. *Credit by:* semester.

Financial Aid: Federal Pell Grant, Federal Work-Study.

Accreditation: North Central Association of Colleges and Schools.

Description: South Mountain Community College (SMCC) (1979) is a small, public, commuter, 2-year community college which has a diverse student body. SMCC offers a complete liberal arts program leading to an associate degree for transfer to a university and employment. Located in urban Phoenix, Arizona, the college is one of the 10 Maricopa County Community Colleges. SMCC has a variety of student support services, student clubs, athletics and activities, and small classes to help make students successful.

Southeast Arkansas College

1900 Hazel Street	Phone: (870) 543-5900
Pine Bluff, AR 71603	Fax: (870) 543-5927

Division(s): Dean of Instruction, General Studies Coordinator
Web Site(s): http://seark.org
E-mail: bscruggs@stc.seark.tec.ar.us

Class Titles: Statistics, English Composition, U.S. History to

1865, U.S. History Since 1865, U.S. Government, Geography, Personal Health/Safety, Art Appreciation, Sociology, Psychology, Anthropology, Small Business Management.

Teaching Methods: *TV:* videotape, cable program, satellite broadcasting, PBS. *Other:* None.

Credits Granted for: experiential learning, portfolio assessment, extrainstitutional learning (corporate or professional association seminars/workshops), examination (CLEP, locally developed challenge exams).

Admission Requirements: *Undergraduate:* Please contact school for details.

On-Campus Requirements: Orientation, midterm, final. Access to videotaped broadcast during 8- to 16-week schedule.

Tuition and Fees: *Undergraduate:* $30/credit. *Other Costs:* $20 Telecourse, $5 Assessment. *Credit by:* semester.

Financial Aid: Federal Stafford Loan, Federal PLUS Loan, Federal Pell Grant, Federal Work-Study, VA, JTPA.

Accreditation: North Central Association of Colleges and Schools.

Description: Southeast Arkansas College was transformed from a vocational-technical school to a 2-year comprehensive technical college in 1992. Previously, SeArk College was the state's oldest vocational-technical school. Enrollment has grown 148%, with course offerings at the Associate of Arts and Associate of Applied Science degree levels. SeArk has offered telecourses since 1994, compressed interactive video since 1998, and leads the state in number of courses offered and students enrolled. These courses help students maintain flexible hours around work, family, and classtime.

Southeast Community College

8800 O Street	Phone: (402) 437-2705
Lincoln, NE 68520	Fax: (402) 437-2704

Division(s): Academic Education
Web Site(s): http://www.college.sccm.cc.ne.us
E-mail: rhiatt@sccm.cc.ne.us

Class Titles: Business, Small Business Management, Principles of Management, Composition, Nutrition, Physical Geology, American History, Psychology, Sociology, Diversity, Geography.

Teaching Methods: *Computers:* electronic classroom, Internet, telecourses. *TV:* videotape, cable program, satellite broadcasting, PBS. *Other:* videoconferencing, independent study, individual study.

Admission Requirements: *Undergraduate:* Under age 16 with permission, COMPASS assessment for Composition.

On-Campus Requirements: None.

Tuition and Fees: *Undergraduate:* $29/quarter credit in-state, $34 out-of-state; $41/semester credit in-state, $49 out-of-state. *Other Costs:* Student Fees: $1/quarter credit, $4/semester credit. *Credit by:* Beatrice campus is semester, Lincoln campus is quarter.

Financial Aid: Federal Stafford Loan, Federal Perkins Loan, Federal PLUS Loan, Federal Pell Grant, Federal Work-Study, VA.

Accreditation: North Central Association of Colleges and Schools.

Description: Southeast Community College (1973) is a 2-year institution offering academic transfer and vocational programs. It provides distance learning through telecourses, NEB*SAT (Nebraska Educational Television), Internet, and a fiber optic network in southeast Nebraska.

Southeast Missouri State University

One University Plaza	Phone: (573) 651-2189
Cape Girardeau, MO 63701	Fax: (573) 651-2827

Division(s): Office of Extended Learning
Web Site(s): http://www.semo.edu
E-mail: sschapman@semovm.semo.edu

Undergraduate Degree Programs:
Business
Nursing
Elementary Education
Criminal Justice

Graduate Degree Programs:
Educational Administration
Elementary and Secondary Education
Educational Counseling

Teaching Methods: *Computers:* Internet, real-time chat, e-mail. *TV:* videotape, ITV. *Other:* videoconferencing, fax.

Credits Granted for: examination (CLEP), early college credit.

Admission Requirements: *Undergraduate:* High school diploma or equivalent, ACT score if within 3 years of high school graduation, ASSET scores (administered locally) for returning adult learners. *Graduate:* Accredited BA/BS degree with 3.0 GPA cumulative, GRE score in upper 50%, letters of recommendation, plus additional requirements/department.

On-Campus Requirements: Approved undergraduate degree completion programs may by completed entirely via off-campus courses including those delivered by electronic means; other undergraduate programs and graduate programs require that 50% of work be completed on campus, however, ITV and Web-based courses will apply.

Tuition and Fees: *Undergraduate:* approximately $104/credit. *Graduate:* approximately $113/credit. *Application Fee:* $20 for undergraduates. *Software:* varies. *Other Costs:* varied lab and course support fees. *Credit by:* semester.

Financial Aid: Federal Stafford Loan, Federal Perkins Loan, Federal PLUS Loan, Federal Pell Grant, Federal Work-Study, VA, Missouri resident programs.

Accreditation: North Central Association of Colleges and Schools.

Description: Southeast Missouri State University (1873) was a teacher's college and a state college before becoming a university in 1972. Southeast is a regional institution of higher education serving the interests of the nation and Missouri while maintaining a strong focus on the needs of the 25 counties of southeast Missouri. The university achieves its multipurpose goals by offering programs at the associate, bachelor's, master's, and specialist levels. As an institution with a large, mostly rural service region, Southeast has a keen interest in developing and maintaining an innovative distance learning program. In addition to an expanding evening program on campus, the university operates off campus via fixed-site centers and temporary sites, utilizing on-site instruction, ITV delivery, and a growing number of Web-based courses.

Southeastern Community College

1015 South Gear Avenue	Phone: (319) 752-2731 x8261
West Burlington, IA 52655-0605	Fax: (319) 752-4957

Division(s): Distance Education
Web Site(s): http://www.secc.cc.ia.us
E-mail: cchrisman@secc.cc.ia.us

Class Titles: Psychology, German, Biology, Chemical Dependency, National Government, French, Industrial Maintenance, Electrical Apprenticeship, Limited Practice Radiology, Emergency Medical Technician. (Important: these classes are only available to Iowa Communication Networks.)

Teaching Methods: *Computers:* Internet, e-mail, LISTSERV. *TV:* videotape, cable program, satellite broadcasting, PBS. *Other:* videoconferencing, fax.

Admission Requirements: *Undergraduate:* open-door policy.

On-Campus Requirements: None.

Tuition and Fees: *Undergraduate:* $53 resident, $79 out-of-state. *Other Costs:* $10/credit, $11/credit out-of-state. *Credit by:* semester.

Financial Aid: Federal Stafford Loan, Federal Perkins Loan, Federal PLUS Loan, Federal Pell Grant, Federal Work-Study, VA, Iowa resident programs.

Accreditation: North Central Association of Colleges and Schools.

Description: Burlington Junior College (1920) and Keokuk Community College (1953) merged to become the North and South campuses of today's Southeastern Community College

(1965). Southeastern is dedicated to the philosophy that individuals should have access to educational opportunities from which they can appropriately benefit. As an integral part of the regional society, the college has a major responsibility to support the economic and social development of the area. The college dedicates its resources to the realization of this philosophy by providing educational opportunities and services that promote personal, intellectual, economic, and social growth. SCC offers courses in 30 academic programs and 20 occupational disciplines. Southeastern offers a full range of credit courses that, if satisfactorily completed, will lead to a diploma or an associate degree. In addition, the college's Center for Business and Industry Services provides customized training for the region.

Southern Arkansas University Tech

100 Carr Road	Phone: (870) 574-4495
Camden, AR 71701	Fax: (870) 574-4538

Division(s): Continuing Education
Web Site(s): http://www.sautech.edu
E-mail: sraney@sautech.edu

Undergraduate Degree Programs:
Under development.

Certificate Programs: Under development.

Class Titles: Composition, Business, History to 1876, Philosophy, Computers.

Teaching Methods: *Computers:* Internet, real-time chat, electronic classroom, e-mail, CD-ROM, newsgroup, LISTSERV. *TV:* videotape, cable program, satellite broadcasting, PBS. *Other:* videoconferencing, fax, correspondence, independent study, individual study.

Credits Granted for: experiential learning, portfolio assessment, corporate or professional association seminars/workshops, examination (CLEP, ACT-PEP, DANTES, GRE).

Admission Requirements: *Undergraduate:* contact admissions for details.

On-Campus Requirements: Orientation, midterms, and finals.

Tuition and Fees: *Undergraduate:* $35/credit. *Other Costs:* $12/credit up to 12 hours, $15 one-time transcript fee. *Credit by:* semester.

Financial Aid: Federal Stafford Loan, Federal PLUS Loan, Federal Pell Grant, Federal Work-Study, VA, Arkansas resident programs, Arkansas Institutional Scholarship, Foundational Scholarship.

Accreditation: North Central Association of Colleges and Schools.

Description: Since 1967, when the Brown Foundation donated 70 acres and 6 buildings, Southern Arkansas University Tech has grown from a residential, dorm-filled, 2-

year technical campus to a diversified technical and university-parallel campus serving 2 groups of students: local students who enroll in a combination of technical and college programs, and statewide students who participate in high-tech degree and advanced certificate programs. Today SAU Tech is the state's technical/junior college and leader in high tech education. It is Arkansas' member of the Consortium for Manufacturing Competitiveness of the Southern Technology Council, and the Arkansas Business Council designated it as the Technical Center of Excellence in Computer Integrated Manufacturing. The university's mission is to educate students for productive and fulfilling lives by providing opportunities for intellectual growth, individual enrichment, skill development, and meaningful career preparation. Further, the university believes in the worth of the individual and that it has a responsibility for developing in its students those values and competencies essential for effective citizenship in an ever-changing, free, and democratic society.

Southern Christian University

1200 Taylor Road	Phone: (800) 351-4040
Montgomery, AL 36117-3553	Fax: (334) 271-0002

Division(s): Extended Learning Department
Web Site(s): http://www.southernchristian.edu
E-mail: scuniversity@mindspring.com

Undergraduate Degree Programs:
Bachelor of Arts in Biblical Studies
Bachelor of Science in General Studies
Bachelor of Science in Biblical Studies

Graduate Degree Programs:
Master of Arts in Biblical Studies
Master of Science in:
 Ministry
 Clinical Counseling
 Marriage and Family Therapy
 Pastoral Counseling
Master of Divinity

Doctoral Degree Programs:
Doctor of Ministry

Certificate Programs: Applied Christian Ministry

Class Titles: Examples include Foundation Studies, Research Studies, Old Testament Studies, New Testament Studies, Professional Studies, Theological/Historical Studies, Missions Studies, Counseling Studies, Clinical Counseling, Pastoral Counseling, Marriage/Family Therapy, Doctor of Ministry courses. Visit http://www.southernchristian.edu for complete listing.

Teaching Methods: *Computers:* Web-based. *TV:* videotape, PBS. *Other:* None.

Credits Granted for: experiential learning, examination (CLEP, DANTES) on the undergraduate level.

Admission Requirements: *Undergraduate:* Standardized Bible Placement Evaluation. *Graduate:* Bachelor's degree, MAT or GRE score.

On-Campus Requirements: None.

Tuition and Fees: *Undergraduate:* $220/semester hour. *Graduate:* $220/semester hour. *Application Fee:* $35. *Other Costs:* $55/quarter hour Extended Learning Fee. *Credit by:* semester.

Financial Aid: Federal Stafford Loan, Federal Perkins Loan, Federal PLUS Loan, Federal Pell Grant, Federal Work-Study, VA, scholarship program.

Accreditation: Southern Association of Colleges and Schools.

Description: The primary purpose of Southern Christian University (1967) is to educate Christian ministers, leaders, teachers, and scholars to use their gifts and knowledge in proclaiming the gospel and in Christian service. To accomplish this, SCU uses academic and practical studies to prepare students for ministerial professions and voluntary service. The university offers undergraduate- and graduate-level programs, along with continuing education for non-degree students. These programs are biblical in orientation, scholarly in intellectual preparation, and relevant in application to contemporary life. They strongly emphasize biblical studies, supported by biblical languages, church history, systematic theology, homiletics and communication, religious education, professional ministerial studies, missionology, and counseling. A secondary purpose of SC University is to help churches, church-related organizations, and Christian leaders to conduct research, obtain advice, and acquire training and assistance for their work. Entire degrees are available via SCU's Extended Learning Program. Weekly 3-hour classes are professionally videotaped daily and delivered priority mail to you. After viewing the tapes, you are encouraged to call toll-free or e-mail the faculty. In fact, faculty often refer to distance students by name during classes. You have the same time to complete assignments as on-campus students, and exams are proctored through local libraries.

Southern Illinois University, Edwardsville

Campus Box 1084	Phone: (618) 650-3210
Edwardsville, IL 62026-1084	Fax: (618) 650-2629

Division(s): Office of Continuing Education
Web Site(s): http://www.siue.edu/CE/
E-mail: coned@siue.edu

Undergraduate Degree Programs:
Bachelor of Science in Nursing
Bachelor of Science in Business Administration

Graduate Degree Programs:
Master of Business Administration

Teaching Methods: *Computers:* Internet, e-mail, LISTSERV. *TV:* real-time interactive compressed video and audio—closed consortium network, videotape. *Other:* fax, independent study.

Credits Granted for: examination (CLEP, DANTES) Advanced Placement.

Admission Requirements: *Undergraduate:* For a recent high school graduate, completed application 3 weeks prior to term, official transcripts, certified high school graduating rank, ACT (preferred) or SAT. The SIUE Undergraduate Catalog online at http://www.admis.siue.edu/97-99catalog/index.html) outlines additional requirements including high school courses and admission of nontraditional and international students. *Graduate:* Application deadline for classified (degree-seeking) students is one month prior to term; unclassified deadline is 5 working days. Degree program applicants must be accepted by the Graduate School and by the academic unit offering the program. All students must submit official transcripts of bachelor's degree and all graduate work. Other requirements, including admission tests, test scores, grades, interviews, etc., vary according to program (send for SIUE's Graduate Catalog, or view online at www.siue.edu/GRADUATE/catalog.html).

On-Campus Requirements: Distance learning classes meet in specially equipped classrooms at off-campus sites (usually community colleges) in southern Illinois.

Tuition and Fees: *Undergraduate:* $84/credit plus an off-campus delivery fee of $72/course. *Graduate:* $90/credit plus an off-campus delivery fee of $72/course. *Application Fee:* Undergraduate $0, Graduate $25 (additional application fee for MBA program $35). *Software:* varies. *Other Costs:* course-specific fees vary. *Credit by:* semester.

Financial Aid: Federal Stafford Loan, Federal Perkins Loan, Federal PLUS Loan, Federal Pell Grant, Federal Work-Study, VA, Illinois resident programs, various institutional scholarships.

Accreditation: North Central Association of Colleges and Schools, National League for Nursing, American Assembly of Collegiate Schools of Business.

Description: Southern Illinois University, Edwardsville, established in 1957, is located 18 miles from downtown St. Louis on a 2,660-acre campus. SIUE is a major, public university, offering a broad choice of degrees and programs ranging from career-oriented fields to the more traditional, liberal arts. Students have an opportunity to interact with outstanding teachers and scholars, as well as with other students from all parts of the U.S. and the world. They enjoy the excellent facilities of a new and growing campus, including extensive research laboratories, specialized equipment for professional preparation, and comfortable, spacious classrooms. In addition, academic services help students meet the demands of university life. Through its participation in regional, higher education consortia, SIUE utilizes the facilities of a dedicated, real-time, interactive, audio/video instructional network to deliver instruction at off-campus sites in southern Illinois.

Southern Illinois University, Carbondale

Morris Library, Mailcode 6632
Carbondale, IL 62901-6632

Phone: (618) 453-1018
Fax: (618) 453-3010

Division(s): Interactive Learning Program
Continuing Education, Individualized Learning Program
WSIU/WUSI Broadcasting Service
Interactive Learning Program (ILP)
Continuing Education (CE):
Phone: (618) 536-7751
Fax: (618) 453-5668
Broadcasting Service (BS):
Phone: (618) 453-4343
Fax: (618) 453-6186
Web Site(s): http://www.lib.siu.edu/dlearn (ILP)
http://www.siu.edu/~conted/ilp.htm (CE)
http://www.wsiu.org (BS)
E-mail: hgreer@lib.siu.edu (ILP)
ilpdce@siu.edu (CE)
candis_isberner@wsiu.pbs.org (BS)

Undergraduate Degree Programs:
Electrical Engineering
University Studies

Class Titles: Accounting, Aerospace Studies, Agribusiness Economics, Court Reporting, Educational Psychology, Electrical Engineering, Electronics Management, Information Systems Technologies, Radiologic Sciences, Rehabilitation, Social Work, Special Education, Workforce Education/Development, Core Curriculum, Administration of Justice, Advanced Technical Careers, Allied Health Careers, Art, Biology, General Agriculture, Finance, Journalism, Management, Marketing, Mathematics, Philosophy, Political Science, Russian, Spanish, Education, Business, Science, Social Science, Health, Psychology.

Teaching Methods: *Computers:* Internet, real-time chat, bulletin board, e-mail, CD-ROM, newsgroup, LISTSERV, online testing, electronic reserve materials, Web-based audio and video lecture presentations. *TV:* videotape, telecourses. *Other:* videoconferencing, fax, audiotapes, correspondence, independent study, individual study.

Credits Granted for: experiential learning, portfolio assessment, extrainstitutional learning, examination (CLEP, ACT, DANTES), Capstone Program.

Admission Requirements: *Undergraduate:* Interactive Distance Learning courses are taken in 2-way interactive video classrooms in southern Illinois. Acceptance into interactive distance learning courses does not admit one to a degree program. *Degree Students:* Admission for distance learning students seeking entry to a SIUC degree program is the same as for on-campus students. A formal application and all academic credentials including transcripts must be submitted to the Office of Admissions and Records. *Nondegree Students:* special admission is available for nondegree distance learning students. Persons possessing a high school diploma or GED certificate, anyone enrolled in another university, or anyone who already holds a college degree can take courses through the Individual Learning Program. Enrollment in an ILP course does not constitute admission to an SIUC program. *Graduate:* Distance courses taken in interactive video classrooms in southern Illinois. Students allowed one off-campus semester prior to graduate school registration. For unclassified registration, bachelor's degree and $20 application fee. For degree program on campus, full admission packet available at each department, all official transcripts, $20 application fee. For more details, see http://www.siu.edu/gradschl.

On-Campus Requirements: At the master's degree level, one-half of the course work must be taken on campus. At the doctoral level, the residency requirement is satisfied by completion of 24 semester hours of graduate credit on campus.

Tuition and Fees: *Undergraduate:* $93/credit for Interactive Distance Learning Program, $91/credit for Individualized Learning Program. *Graduate:* $99/credit. *Doctoral:* $99/credit. *Other Costs:* vary for textbooks/study guides. *Credit by:* semester.

Financial Aid: Federal Stafford Loan, Federal Perkins Loan, Federal PLUS Loan, Federal Pell Grant, Federal Work-Study, VA, Illinois resident programs, various institutional scholarships.

Accreditation: North Central Association of Colleges and Schools.

Description: Southern Illinois University (1869) is one of the most diverse and affordable in Illinois. Located a short drive from the Shawnee National Forest, the Carbondale campus is internationally acclaimed as the second-largest comprehensive university in the state. With 22,000 students, SIU offers a big-school, educational experience in a small town setting. In 1982 the Individualized Learning Program began offering Correspondence Courses to distance students. Today, ILP offers some courses both via the Web and with traditional, print-based materials for undergraduate credit only. In 1992 the university joined with the Illinois Board of Higher Education and the Illinois Community College Board to assist underserved areas and address workforce issues. To accomplish this, SIU uses 2-way, interactive video and audio technology to offer courses off campus in southern Illinois. SUIC's online courses and programs may be viewed through college and faculty Web sites. Visit the SIUC Campus Directory at http://www.siu.edu/siuc/jiffy.

Southern Methodist University, School of Engineering and Applied Science

| PO Box 750335 | Phone: (214) 768-3232 |
| Dallas, TX 75275-0335 | Fax: (214) 768-3778 |

Division(s): Distance Education
Web Site(s): http://www.seas.smu.edu

E-mail: sdye@seas.smu.edu

Graduate Degree Programs:
Master of Science in:
  Telecommunications
  Software Engineering
  Engineering Management
  Systems Engineering
  Computer Science
  Electrical Engineering
  Hazardous and Waste Materials Management
  Manufacturing Systems Management
  Mechanical Engineering

Certificate Programs: Telecommunications

Teaching Methods: *TV:* videotape, satellite broadcasting. *Other:* None.

Credits Granted for: Up to 6 transfer credits of previous graduate study.

Admission Requirements: *Graduate:* appropriate bachelor's degree; 3.0 GPA; GRE for Computer Science, Electrical Engineering, Mechanical Engineering. *Certificate:* 60 semester hours with 2.0 GPA; 3 years of related work experience; courses in differential/integral calculus, physics, or electronics; programming, preferably in assembly language.

On-Campus Requirements: None.

Tuition and Fees: *Graduate:* $662/credit, $1,986/course. *Application Fee:* $25. *Credit by:* semester.

Financial Aid: Call Financial Aid Office (800) 323-0672.

Accreditation: Southern Association of Colleges and Schools.

Description: Southern Methodist University was founded in 1911, and its School of Engineering and Applied Science has been a national pioneer in graduate distance education for more than 30 years. SEAS offers its distance master's programs nationally and internationally via videotape and, in north Texas, via closed-circuit TV. The Master of Science in Telecommunications is available through the National Technological University satellite network. SEAS offers Master of Science programs in several professional areas and in traditional engineering disciplines.

Southern Oregon University

| 1250 Siskiyou Boulevard | Phone: (541) 552-6331 |
| Ashland, OR 97520 | Fax: (541) 552-6047 |

Division(s): Extended Campus Programs
Web Site(s): http://www.sou.edu/ecp
E-mail: huftill@sou.edu

Undergraduate Degree Programs:
Bachelor of Science in:
  Business, Degree Completion (Medford, Grants Pass)
  Nursing (Oregon Health Sciences, Southern Oregon)
  Interdisciplinary Social Science, Human Services (Medford, Ashland)

Graduate Degree Programs:
Master of Science in Education
Master of Science in Management (Medford, Ashland)

Certificate Programs: Oregon Standard Teacher's License

Teaching Methods: *Computers:* e-mail, LISTSERV. *TV:* Most courses are delivered via 2-way interactive satellite broadcast to downlink sites in Gold Beach, Grants Pass, Lakeview, Medford, Klamath Falls, Roseburg in Southern Oregon. *Other:* None.

Credits Granted for: professional association seminars/workshops—preapproved, CLEP, IB, some military experience.

Admission Requirements: *Undergraduate:* application. *Graduate:* undergraduate degree. *Certificate:* Contact university for details.

On-Campus Requirements: One visit for some courses. Master's in Education completion courses during summer.

Tuition and Fees: *Undergraduate:* $249/3-credit course. *Graduate:* $444/3-credit class. *Software:* varies. *Other Costs:* Internet Service Provider, nonresident tuition for full load. *Credit by:* quarter.

Financial Aid: Federal Stafford Loan, Federal Perkins Loan, Federal PLUS Loan, Federal Pell Grant, Federal Work-Study, VA.

Accreditation: Northwest Association of Schools and Colleges.

Description: Founded in 1869, Southern Oregon University is one of eight institutions in the Oregon University System. In 1956 it transitioned from a teacher education institution to a regional liberal arts college. Then in 1997 it became Southern Oregon University to reflect its role as a regional multipurpose institution serving the state through instruction, research, and public service. The university began distance learning in 1984 through regional public broadcasting and PBS video courses. In 1991 SOU received a Title III grant that funded a 2-way interactive video system at sites throughout southwestern Oregon. As technology advances, so does SOU's multimodality outreach via 2-way video, cable, LISTSERV, the Internet, and CD-ROM.

Southern Polytechnic State University

1100 South Marietta Parkway
Marietta, GA 30060

Phone: (770) 528-5531
Fax: (770) 528-7490

Division(s): Extended University
Web Site(s): http://www.spsu.edu/oce/ocehome.html
E-mail: dramsey@spsu.edu

Undergraduate Degree Programs:
Industrial Distribution

Graduate Degree Programs:
Master of Science in:

Computer Science
Electrical Engineering Technology
Quality Assurance
Technical Communications

Certificate Programs: Web Development

Class Titles: Based on prerequisites, all classes.

Teaching Methods: *Computers:* Internet, real-time chat, electronic classroom, e-mail, newsgroup, LISTSERV. *Other:* videoconferencing, individual study, learning contracts.

Credits Granted for: examination (CLEP).

Admission Requirements: *Undergraduate:* 450 verbal, 430 math SAT; 2.0 high school GPA; all college prep courses completed. *Graduate:* GRE score, 4-year degree, 3.0 GPA (these requirements may vary by program).

On-Campus Requirements: None, with MSQA as an exception.

Tuition and Fees: *Undergraduate:* $72/credit. *Graduate:* $83/credit. *Application Fee:* $20. *Other Costs:* *$38 activity fee, $51 for Wellness Center, $23 health service, $48 athletic fee (*may not apply for distance learning students). *Credit by:* semester.

Financial Aid: Federal Stafford Loan, Federal Perkins Loan, Federal PLUS Loan, Federal Pell Grant, Federal Work-Study, VA, Georgia resident programs.

Accreditation: Southern Association of Colleges and Schools.

Description: Southern Polytechnic State University (1948) provides the residents of Georgia with university-level education in technology, engineering technology, arts and sciences, architecture, management, and related fields. SPSU is a senior institution in the University System of Georgia. The school began providing distance learning opportunities in 1995.

Southern Utah University

351 West Center Street
Cedar City, UT 84720

Phone: (435) 586-7850
Fax: (435) 865-8087

Division(s): Continuing Education
Web Site(s): http://www.suu.edu
E-mail: freeman@suu.edu

Undergraduate Degree Programs:
Contact Southern Utah University for more information

Teaching Methods: *Computers:* Internet, real-time chat, e-mail, LISTSERV *Other:* fax, correspondence, independent study, individual study, learning contracts

Credits Granted for: examination (CLEP, ACT-PEP, DANTES, GRE).

Admission Requirements: *Undergraduate:* application, official high school and/or college transcripts, ACT/SAT scores. For transfer students, 2.25 GPA. See online information at Web site.

On-Campus Requirements: All online classes are self-contained.

Tuition and Fees: *Undergraduate:* $74/credit. *Graduate:* $92/credit. *Doctoral:* $92/credit. *Application Fee:* $30. *Software:* To be established. *Credit by:* semester.

Financial Aid: Federal Pell Grant, Federal Work-Study, VA, Utah resident programs.

Accreditation: Northwest Association of Schools and Colleges.

Southern Vermont College

| Monument Avenue | Phone: (802) 447-6304 |
| Bennington, VT 05201 | Fax: (802) 447-4695 |

Division(s): None.
Web Site(s): http://svc.edu
E-mail: admis@svc.edu

Class Titles: varies; has included financial accounting, managerial accounting, Lotus 1-2-3.

Teaching Methods: *Computers:* Internet, e-mail, lecture, and problem analysis. *Other:* fax, correspondence, independent study, individual study, learning contracts.

Credits Granted for: portfolio assessment, corporate or professional association seminars/workshops, examination (CLEP, ACT-PEP, DANTES, GRE).

Admission Requirements: *Undergraduate:* contact school for admission requirements. Students must matriculate after earning 15 credits.

On-Campus Requirements: some exams.

Tuition and Fees: *Undergraduate:* $380. *Application Fee:* $25 *Other Costs:* books and classroom materials. *Credit by:* semester.

Financial Aid: Federal Stafford Loan, Federal Perkins Loan, Federal PLUS Loan, Federal Pell Grant, Federal Work-Study, VA, Vermont resident programs.

Accreditation: New England Association of Schools and Colleges.

Description: Southern Vermont College (1926) is a small, private, career-oriented liberal arts institution located in the heart of the Green Mountains. At SVC, students have an opportunity to experience a close personal interchange with faculty. The college's unique faculty structure permits the degree program coordinators to teach in their area of specialization and also to serve as advisors for those degree program students. Plus, the student/faculty ratio of 9:1 enables students to express their ideas, give feedback, and grow intellectually and socially within a supportive environ-

ment. The college offers expanding curriculum choices and an aggressive approach to career planning and placement. SVC also provides a diverse and growing schedule of campus and athletic events (NCAA Division III). All faculty and staff, including the president, believe in an "open door" policy.

Southern West Virginia Community and Technical College

| Dempsey Branch Road | Phone: (304) 792-7098 |
| Mt. Gay, WV 25637 | Fax: (304) 792-7028 |

Division(s): Instructional Technology
Web Site(s): http://www.southern.wvnet.edu/
E-mail: JPO@southern.wvnet.edu

Undergraduate Degree Programs:
Associate of Arts in:
    Communications
    Criminal Justice
    Elementary Education
    General Studies
    Liberal Arts
    History
    Psychology/Sociology
Associate of Science in:
    General Business
    Chemistry
    Physics
    Computer Science
Associate of Applied Science
Allied Health Programs:
    Medical Laboratory Technology
    Nursing
    Radiologic Technology
Business Programs:
    Business Accounting
    Computer Information Systems
    General Business-Small Business
        Management
    Office Information Technology
        Administrative Option
        Legal Option
        Medical Option
Criminal Justice Programs:
    Corrections
    Law Enforcement
Technology Programs:
    Automotive Power Technology
    Drafting and Design Technology
    Electrical Engineering Technology
    Environmental Technology
    Welding Technology

Certificate Programs: Criminal Justice, Long Term Health Care, Secretarial Science.

Teaching Methods: *Computers:* Internet, real-time chat, electronic classroom, e-mail, CD-ROM, newsgroup, LIST-

SERV. *TV:* satellite broadcasting, PBS. *Other:* videoconferencing, independent study.

Credits Granted for: experiential learning, portfolio assessment, extrainstitutional learning, examination (CLEP, ACT-PEP, DANTES, GRE).

Admission Requirements: *Undergraduate:* high school diploma or GED, if within last 5 years. Degree-seeking students planning to enroll for 12 or more credit hours or those who have successfully completed 30 hours or less from an accredited institution must submit ACT score reports. Admission to Southern does not imply eligibility for, nor admission to, any specific program for which more stringent entrance requirements are established. *Certificate:* same as above.

On-Campus Requirements: currently no degree program can be completed without coming to a campus location.

Tuition and Fees: *Undergraduate:* contact school for all tuition and fee information. *Credit by:* semester.

Financial Aid: Federal Stafford Loan, Federal Perkins Loan, Federal PLUS Loan, Federal Pell Grant, Federal Work-Study, VA, West Virginia resident programs.

Accreditation: North Central Association of Colleges and Schools.

Description: Southern West Virginia Community and Technical College (1971) was established as an open-door comprehensive community college by combining 2 existing branches of Marshall University. As the student population increased, the need for larger facilities became evident. In 1982 the Southern West Virginia Community College Foundation purchased a building in Madison to house the Boone County Center. In 1986 property was purchased at Saulsville, West Virginia for the new site of the Wyoming County Center. In January of 1992 the Board of Directors designated the centers in Wyoming and Boone counties as campuses. As a result of the legislative action in March 1995 the name of the college was officially changed to Southern West Virginia Community and Technical College and the district was again increased to include all of Lincoln and McDowell counties as well as a portion of Raleigh County.

Southwest Missouri State University

901 South National Avenue	Phone: (417) 836-4128
Springfield, MO 65804-0089	Fax: (417) 836-6016

Division(s): Academic Outreach
Web Site(s): http://ce.smsu.edu
http://smsuonline.smsu.edu
http://ccpe.smsu.edu
http://www.mscis.smsu.edu
E-mail: dianagarland@mail.smsu.edu

Graduate Degree Programs:
Master of Administrative Studies
Master of Business Administration
Master of Science in Elementary Education
Master of Science in Computer Information Systems (Internet Based program)

Certificate Programs: a variety of Professional Development Certificates for nonacademic credit

Class Titles: Undergraduate: Anthropology, Astronomy, Biology, Chemistry, Communications, Consumer/Family Studies, Economics, Finance/General Business, Health Care Management, History, Media, Middle School Education Management, Music, Mythology, Nursing, Physics, Political Science, Reading, Religious Studies, Spanish, Substance Abuse, Technology, Theater, Vocational Education. Graduate: Accounting, Communications, Computer Information Systems, Early Childhood Education, Educational Administration, Elementary Education, Marketing Management, Reading, Religious Studies, Secondary Education.

Teaching Methods: *Computers:* Internet, real-time chat, electronic classroom. *TV:* videotape, cable program, satellite broadcasting, interactive video. *Other:* videoconferencing, audioconferencing, audiotapes, fax.

Credits Granted for: examination (CLEP, ACT-PEP, DANTES, GRE).

Admission Requirements: *Undergraduate:* call Admissions at (800) 492-7900 for current policy and for special limited-hour policies for nondegree-seeking undergraduate, transfer, and adult students. *Graduate:* contact Graduate College at (417) 836-5335 for details and catalog. Students with bachelor's degree not wishing to pursue additional degree may be admitted in limited-hour postbaccalaureate status. *Doctoral:* for information on statewide cooperative EdD in Educational Leadership, call Educational Administration at (417) 836-5392. *Certificate:* variable by program. Contact The Center for Continuing and Professional Education at (417) 836-6660 or Academic Outreach at (888) 879-7678 for information.

On-Campus Requirements: A one-week on-campus session is required for the MS in CIS program each semester for 4 semesters; contact mscis@mail.smsu.edu or http://www.mscis.smsu.edu for more information.

Tuition and Fees: *Undergraduate:* $98/credit. *Graduate:* $110/credit. *Software:* $15 undergraduate, $25 graduate. *Other Costs:* $32 for course materials fee for Internet-based instruction *Credit by:* semester.

Financial Aid: Federal Stafford Loan, Federal Perkins Loan, Federal PLUS Loan, Federal Pell Grant, Federal Work-Study, VA, Missouri resident programs.

Accreditation: North Central Association of Colleges and Schools.

Description: Southwest Missouri State University (1905) is a state-supported, comprehensive institution. SMSU first offered distance learning courses in 1974. In 1997–1998, it offered 65 courses at a distance. In the fall of 1998, 1,125 students enrolled in distance learning courses.

Southwest Texas State University

601 University Drive
San Marcos, TX 78666-4616

Phone: (512) 245-2322
Fax: (512) 245-8934

Division(s): Office of Correspondence and Extension Studies
Web Site(s): http://www.ideal.swt.edu/correspondence
E-mail: dp01@a1.swt.edu

Class Titles: Art, Biology, Career/Technology Education, Computer Science, Criminal Justice, English, Family/Consumer Sciences, Geography, Health Information Management, History, Long-term Care Administration, Marketing, Mathematics, Music, Philosophy, Political Science, Psychology, Sociology, Spanish, Theater Arts.

Teaching Methods: *Computers:* Internet, e-mail. *TV:* videotape. *Other:* audiotapes, fax, correspondence.

Credits Granted for: examination (CLEP, ACT-PEP, DANTES, GRE).

Admission Requirements: *Undergraduate:* Completion time is 45 days to 12 months, with one extension up to 6 more months. Some courses have prerequisites. *Graduate:* same as undergraduate.

On-Campus Requirements: None.

Tuition and Fees: *Undergraduate:* $57/credit. *Graduate:* $95/credit. *Other Costs:* Variable for services such as course extensions, transfers, drops, and required textbooks. *Credit by:* semester.

Financial Aid: Federal Stafford Loan, Federal Perkins Loan, Federal PLUS Loan, Federal Pell Grant, Federal Work-Study, VA, Texas resident programs.

Accreditation: Southern Association of Colleges and Schools.

Description: Southwest Texas State University (1903) is a comprehensive, public university committed to providing an intellectually stimulating and socially diverse climate for its students, faculty, and staff. SWT offers effective undergraduate and master's-level instruction dedicated to teaching, advancing knowledge and artistic expression, and serving as a resource for the surrounding regions. The Office of Correspondence and Extension Studies began in 1953 and helps students reach their educational goals regardless of time, place, or other constraints preventing them from attending on-campus classes. Courses are delivered to distance learners in a variety of formats determined by content and learner resources.

Southwestern Adventist University

100 Hillcrest Drive
Keene, TX 76059

Phone: (800) 433-2240 x204
Fax: (817) 556-4742

Division(s): Adult Degree Program
Web Site(s): http://www.swau.esu
E-mail: philbeckl@swau.esu

Undergraduate Degree Programs:
Bachelor of Science in:
  Business Administration
  Accounting
  Computer Science
  Communication
  English
  Education
  Mathematics
  Office Administration
  Psychology
  Religion
  Social Science
  Theology
  Criminal Justice

Teaching Methods: *Computers:* Internet, real-time chat, e-mail. *TV:* videotape. *Other:* fax, correspondence, independent study, individual study.

Credits Granted for: experiential learning, portfolio assessment, extrainstitutional learning, examination (CLEP, ACT-PEP, DANTES, GRE).

Admission Requirements: *Undergraduate:* age 22, application, official high school transcript or GED if fewer than 12 transferable hours, any college transcripts, SAT/ACT scores, 2.0 GPA.

On-Campus Requirements: attend 6-day seminar offered 3 times/year.

Tuition and Fees: *Undergraduate:* $293/credit. *Credit by:* semester.

Financial Aid: Federal Stafford Loan, Federal Perkins Loan, Federal PLUS Loan, Federal Pell Grant, VA, Texas resident programs.

Accreditation: Southern Association of Colleges and Schools.

Description: Southwestern Adventist University (1893) is a private, Christian coeducation institution with 1,100 students, 260 of whom are distance learners. The school entered distance learning in 1971.

Southwestern Assemblies of God University

1200 Sycamore St.	Phone: (972) 937-4010
Waxahachie, TX 75165	Fax: (972) 923-0488

Division(s): School of Distance Education
Web Site(s): http://sagu.edu/sde
E-mail: sde@sagu.edu

Undergraduate Degree Programs:
Associate of Arts, Bachelor of Arts, or Bachelor of Science in:
Church Ministries
Pastoral Ministries
Church Music Ministries
Church Business Administration
General Ministries
Urban Ministries
Children's Ministries
Christian Education
Biblical Studies
Pastoral Counseling
Counseling Psychology
Elementary Education
Secondary Education
Accounting
General Business
Business Administration
Music
Professional Development

Graduate Degree Programs:
Master of Science in Practical Theology

Certificate Programs: Biblical Studies

Teaching Methods: *Computers:* Internet, e-mail, LISTSERV. *TV:* videotape. *Other:* audioconferencing, videoconferencing, audiographics, audiotape, fax, correspondence, independent study, individual study, learning contracts.

Credits Granted for: experiential learning, portfolio assessment, examination (CLEP, ACT-PEP)

Admission Requirements: *Undergraduate:* age 23, ACT scores or transfer credit. *Graduate:* GRE test.

On-Campus Requirements: Courses are opened on campus where faculty meet face to face with their students.

Tuition and Fees: *Undergraduate:* $175/hour for less than 14 hours, summer; $175/hour for less than 14 hours. *Graduate:* $175/hour. *Application Fee:* $35 undergraduate, $50 graduate. *Other Costs:* prorated general fee for 11 hours and below; $250 general fee for 12 hours and above. $20/class with a maximum of $60 for Telecommunications/Media. *Credit by:* semester.

Financial Aid: Federal Stafford Loan, Federal Perkins Loan, Federal PLUS Loan, Federal Pell Grant, Federal Work-Study, VA, Texas resident programs.

Accreditation: Southern Association of Colleges and Schools, Accrediting Association of Bible Colleges.

Description: Southwestern Assemblies of God University (1927) is a church-based institution of higher learning, self-described as a "Bible University for Theological and Professional Studies." All degree-seeking students earn a major in Bible in addition to their chosen field. SAGU's parent body is the Assemblies of God. The school resulted from a merger of institutes in the first half of the 20th century and formerly included a high school and a junior college. It now offers AA, BA, BS, and MS degrees. SAGU established its distance education program in 1984.

Southwestern Michigan College

58900 Cherry Grove Street	Phone: (616) 782-1369
Dowagiac, MI 49047	Fax: (616) 782-8414

Division(s): Community and Technical Services
Web Site(s): http://www.smc.cc.mi.us
E-mail: isheffer@smc.cc.mi.us

Undergraduate Degree Programs:
Associate of Arts
Associate of Science

Class Titles: Art Appreciation, Sociology, Human Communications, Psychology.

Teaching Methods: *Computers:* Internet, real-time chat, e-mail. *TV:* videotape, cable program, satellite broadcasting, PBS. *Other:* independent study, individual study.

Credits Granted for: examination (CLEP, ACT-PEP, DANTES).

Admission Requirements: *Undergraduate:* application; e-mail nmartin@smc.cc.mi.us *Certificate:* see undergraduate.

On-Campus Requirements: orientation.

Tuition and Fees: *Undergraduate:* $45/credit in-state. *Other Costs:* $4/credit technology fee, $5/credit registration fee. *Credit by:* semester.

Financial Aid: Federal Stafford Loan, Federal Perkins Loan, Federal PLUS Loan, Federal Pell Grant, Federal Work-Study, VA, Michigan resident programs.

Accreditation: North Central Association of Colleges and Schools.

Description: Southwestern Michigan College (1964) is a public, 2-year community college located on a 240-acre, tree-studded campus that showcases Michigan's 4 seasons. SMC offers affordable one- and two-year degrees in business, nursing, technology, and transfer programs. In addition, Ferris State University operates an extension site at the college, allowing students to earn a bachelor's degree in business management, business administration, computer information systems, or nursing, with all classes held on the SMC campuses in Dowagiac and Niles. SMC students come from the Michigan area, all over the U.S., and many foreign countries. Cultural experiences include the SMC Museum, the Starlight Series, and the Art Gallery. Distance learning began in 1995 through a grant from the W.K. Kellogg Foundation. Southwestern Michigan College: "Excellence with a Personal Touch."

Southwestern Oregon Community College

| 1988 Newmark Avenue | Phone: (541) 888-7339 |
| Coos Bay, OR 97420 | Fax: (541) 888-7247 |

Division(s): Extended Learning and Community Education
Web Site(s): http://www.southwestern.cc.or.us
E-mail: cscott@southwestern.cc.or.us

Class Titles: Writing, Math, Prior Learning Resume, History, Sociology, Psychology, Library Skills, Hospitality/Management, Computer Information Systems, Lifetime Wellness, Personal Health, Nutrition, General Science, Physical Education, Human Development/Family Studies, Human Services.

Teaching Methods: *Computers:* Internet, e-mail, LISTSERV. *TV:* videotape, cable program, satellite broadcasting, PBS. *Other:* None.

Credits Granted for: extrainstitutional learning, credit by examination (CLEP, AP, military credit).

Admission Requirements: *Undergraduate:* contact school. *Certificate:* contact school.

On-Campus Requirements: some instructors require students to test on campus.

Tuition and Fees: *Undergraduate:* variable. *Application Fee:* $20. *Other Costs:* varies for books, etc., must have Internet access. *Credit by:* quarter.

Financial Aid: institutional grants and loans, Federal Pell Grant, Federal Work-Study, VA, Oregon resident programs.

Accreditation: Northwest Association of Colleges and Schools.

Description: Southwestern Oregon Community College (1961) is located within 2 miles of the Pacific Ocean in an area of scenic beauty and mild climate. The 153-acre institution lies completely within the city of Coos Bay and is bordered on the east and north by the city of North Bend. Southwestern Oregon Community College was formed in a May 1961 tax district election. It included Coos and western Douglas counties. On July 1, 1995, Curry County joined the College District. The district now encompasses 3648 square miles with a population of more than 92,000. The college is the only public postsecondary institution in the region. Enrollment has grown from 266 to 13,000 students. Staff size has grown from 15 to 70 full-time faculty and from 11 to 275 part-time instructors. Cultural and athletic events at the college attract

20,000 men, women and children each year. Throughout the college's years, a comprehensive instructional program has evolved. Instructional offerings include 2-year transfer programs, one- and two-year professional-technical programs, short-course occupational programs, adult basic education, high school diploma program, and adult enrichment courses.

Spokane Falls Community College

| 3410 West Fort Wright Drive | Phone: (509) 533-3420 |
| Spokane, WA 99224 | Fax: (509) 533-3433 |

Division(s): Distance Education
Web Site(s): http://www.sfcc.spokane.cc.wa.us
E-mail: mariannek@sfcc.spokane.cc.wa.us

Undergraduate Degree Programs:
Associate of Arts

Teaching Methods: *Computers:* Internet, real-time chat, electronic classroom, e-mail, LISTSERV. *TV:* videotape, cable program. *Other:* audioconferencing, videoconferencing, audiotapes, fax.

Credits Granted for: portfolio assessment, examination (CLEP, ACT-PEP, DANTES, GRE).

Admission Requirements: *Undergraduate:* entrance exams.

On-Campus Requirements: None.

Tuition and Fees: *Undergraduate:* $50/credit resident, $199/credit nonresident. *Application Fee:* $10. *Credit by:* quarter.

Financial Aid: Federal Stafford Loan, Federal Perkins Loan, Federal PLUS Loan, Federal Pell Grant, Federal Work-Study, VA, Washington resident programs.

Accreditation: Northwest Association of Schools and Colleges.

Description: Spokane Falls Community College (1967) strives for excellence in education by creating and encouraging dedication to learning for all people within the community, regardless of economic status or educational background. The college further strives to foster the love and pursuit of knowledge and truth by offering students the means to achieve personal fulfillment and resources for living responsibly as members of the world community. The college's mission is to be a primary provider of a comprehensive liberal arts college transfer program. In addition, the college offers professional/technical programs that enable students to enter the job market successfully, basic skills courses that enable students to succeed in college-level courses, continuing education that enables students to upgrade job skills and enrich their personal lives, and a comprehensive distance learning program that enables students to balance their educational endeavors with work, family, time, and distance considerations. SFCC has been providing distance education since 1976.

Spoon River College

23235 North County Highway 22	Phone: (309) 647-4645
Canton, IL 61520	Fax: (309) 649-6235

Division(s): Academic Services
Web Site(s): None.
E-mail: swrenn@src.cc.il.us

Undergraduate Degree Programs:
Individual classes

Certificate Programs: Associate of Arts
Associate of Applied Sciences
Associate of General Studies
Associate Degree Nursing
Associate of Science

Class Titles: Composition, Health Science, Math, Art, History, Education, Religion, Philosophy, English.

Teaching Methods: *Computers:* electronic classroom, CD-ROM. *TV:* videotape, satellite broadcasting. *Other:* videoconferencing, independent study.

Credits Granted for: examination (CLEP, department proficiency).

Admission Requirements: *Undergraduate:* open admissions.

On-Campus Requirements: 15 credit hours from Spoon River College.

Tuition and Fees: *Undergraduate:* $50/credit. *Credit by:* semester.

Financial Aid: Federal Stafford Loan, Federal Perkins Loan, Federal PLUS Loan, Federal Pell Grant, Federal Work-Study, VA, Illinois resident programs, institutional scholarships and grants.

Accreditation: North Central Association of Colleges and Schools.

Description: Spoon River College (1959) is a multifaceted community college dedicated to providing students with a quality education. Students have a variety of educational goals, and SRC is positioned to meet the needs of all these students by providing the first 2 years of college and preprofessional courses in 30 college majors, 30 career and technical programs, and continuing education. Spoon River serves 4,000 credit students per year in a 1,400-square-mile area including Fulton, McDonough, Mason, and Schuyler counties. SRC is a member of the Western Illinois Educational Consortium and began providing distance learning in 1994. SRC graduates who transfer to other colleges and universities traditionally achieve higher GPAs than students who begin their college careers at other transfer institutions. The college also participates in the Illinois Articulation Initiative, a statewide agreement that allows transfer of the completed Illinois General Education Core Curriculum between participating institutions.

St. Charles County Community College

4601 Mid Rivers Mall Drive	Phone: (314) 922-8470
St. Peters, MO 63376-0975	Fax: (314) 922-8433

Division(s): Instructional Resources
Web Site(s): http://www.stchas.edu/academics/distance/dlmain.htm
E-mail: arandazzo@scccc.stchas.edu

Class Titles: Anthropology, Art, Biology, Business, Criminal Justice, English, History, Health, Psychology, Sociology, Theater.

Teaching Methods: *Computers:* Internet, e-mail, LISTSERV. *TV:* videotape, PBS. *Other:* interactive video.

Credits Granted for: experiential learning, portfolio assessment, examination (CLEP, ACT-PEP, DANTES, GRE).

Admission Requirements: *Undergraduate:* high school diploma or a GED certificate, age 18 and demonstrate the ability to benefit through the student assessment process. *Certificate:* same as undergraduate.

On-Campus Requirements: None.

Tuition and Fees: *Undergraduate:* $43/credit in-district, $63/credit out-of-district in-state; $97/credit out-of-state/international. *Other Costs:* $5/credit service fee, $38/video/telecourse. *Credit by:* semester.

Financial Aid: Federal Stafford Loan, Federal Pell Grant, Federal Work-Study, VA, Missouri resident programs, A+, SCOG, VR, JTPA.

Accreditation: North Central Association of Colleges and Schools.

Description: St. Charles County Community College (1986) is an open-admission institution dedicated to providing accessible postsecondary educational programs and community services at a reasonable cost. By incorporating academic excellence and technological advancements, we prepare our students to achieve their educational, professional, and personal goals and enhance their cultural experiences. The college began offering courses through distance learning in 1992.

St. Francis Xavier University

West Street	Phone: (902) 867-3906
Antigonish, NS, Canada B2G 2W5	Fax: (902) 867-5154

Division(s): Extension
Web Site(s): http://www.stfx.ca
E-mail: cjones@stfx.ca

Undergraduate Degree Programs:
Bachelor of Science in Nursing
Interdisciplinary Studies in Aquatic Resources

Certificate Programs: Real Property Appraisal and Assessment, Diploma in Ministry.

Class Titles: Biology, Microbiology, Human Physiology, Anatomy (nonlab courses).

Teaching Methods: *TV:* online. *Other:* correspondence.

Admission Requirements: *Undergraduate:* high school certification, registered nurse certification. *Certificate:* high school certification.

On-Campus Requirements: None.

Tuition and Fees: *Undergraduate:* contact school. *Credit by:* semester.

Accreditation: Association of Universities and Colleges of Canada.

Description: St. Francis Xavier University (1853) is a small liberal-arts institution in Atlantic Canada, highly ranked among Canadian universities for academic quality. Its distance education programs are learner-centered, with a strong emphasis on student support systems.

St. Petersburg Junior College

9200 113th Street North	Phone: (727) 394-6116
Seminole, FL 33772	Fax: (727) 394-6124

Division(s): Telecourses and Online Courses, Seminole Campus
Web Site(s): http://tech.spjc.cc.fl.us/seminole/virtual/Class room.html
E-mail: womerl@mail.spjc.cc.fl.us

Undergraduate Degree Programs:
Associate of Arts
Associate of Science in Veterinary Technology

Class Titles: Online/Internet courses: Biological Science, Biological Issues, Composition, Motion Picture Writing, Motion Picture Writing East-West Synthesis of Humanities, Developmental Mathematics, Algebra, Studies in Applied Ethics, Statistics, Emergency Management, Public Policy in Emergency Management, Emergency Technical Applications, EM Leadership, Disaster Recovery Operations, the entire Veterinary Technology Program. Telecourses: History of U.S., Cultural Anthropology, Accounting, Understanding Art, Universe: Infinite Frontier, Biological Science, Criminal Justice, Constitutional Law/Rules, Computer Concepts, Child Development, Principles of (Macro) Economics, Composition, Western Civilization, Environmental Science, Personal Finance, French, Business, Earth Revealed, Personal Wellness, Personal/Community Health, Western Humanities, Earth Science/Planet Earth, College Algebra, Small Business Management, Principles of Management, Principles of Marketing, Salesmanship, Oceanography, Applied Ethics, American National Government, General Psychology, Public Speaking, Spanish, Statistics, Sociology, Marriage/Family.

Teaching Methods: *Computers:* Internet, real-time chat, electronic classroom, e-mail, CD-ROM, LISTSERV. *TV:* videotape, cable program, satellite broadcasting, PBS. *Other:* videoconferencing.

Credits Granted for: experiential learning, examination (CLEP).

Admission Requirements: *Undergraduate:* completed application, high school graduate with certain criteria or college can assist (or GED), eligible transfer students, early admission and dual-credit students, credit bank students, nondegree students not intending to pursue a formal degree, transient students, or students from other countries who have been admitted or are contemplating admittance to the U.S. to pursue their education (international students please call for details).

On-Campus Requirements: Presently, students may obtain an entire associate of arts degree through our telecourse program. On-campus requirements include an orientation session, a midterm review session, a midterm exam, a final review session, and a final exam.

Tuition and Fees: *Undergraduate:* $43/credit (in-state resident), $142/credit (out-of-state resident). *Application Fee:* $25. *Other Costs:* lab fees vary by course. *Credit by:* semester.

Financial Aid: Federal Stafford Loan, Federal Perkins Loan, Federal PLUS Loan, Federal Pell Grant, Federal Work-Study, VA, Federal Supplemental Educational Opportunity Grant, Student Assistant Program, Florida resident programs.

Accreditation: Southern Association of Colleges and Schools.

Description: St. Petersburg Junior College (1927) is recognized as one of America's best community colleges. Until 1942, SPJC was a private, nonprofit institution in downtown St. Petersburg, but today its campuses span Pinellas County. College sites now include 3 traditional campuses in Clearwater, St. Petersburg, and Tarpon Springs, plus a health education center in Pinellas Park and corporate and criminal justice/law enforcement training facilities in St. Petersburg. A new Seminole campus opened in the fall of 1998. In addition, SPJC offers classes at various offsite locations as well as via TV and computer. The Telecourse program, which began in 1980, is the largest in the Florida Community College system.

State Center Community College District

PO Box 1910	Phone: (209) 683-3940
Oakhurst, CA 93644	Fax: (209) 683-4193

Division(s): None.
Web Site(s): None.
E-mail: hoffman_r@scccd.cc.ca.us

Class Titles: Health Science, Cultural Geography, Office

Technology (Legal/Medical), Linguistics, Natural Resources, Child Development, Criminal Justice, Accounting, Art Appreciation.

Teaching Methods: *Other:* audioconferencing, videoconferencing, 2-way, interactive, live.

Admission Requirements: *Undergraduate:* open admission.

On-Campus Requirements: None.

Tuition and Fees: *Undergraduate:* $12/unit *Other Costs:* $11/semester health fee *Credit by:* semester

Financial Aid: Federal Stafford Loan, Federal Perkins Loan, Federal PLUS Loan, Federal Pell Grant, Federal Work-Study, VA, California resident programs.

Accreditation: Western Association of Schools and Colleges.

Description: The State Center Community College District (1963) provides day, evening, and Saturday classes. Operated on an 18-week semester system, the college offers a fall and spring term as well as 4/6/8/12-week summer sessions. The district operates 8 satellite locations.

State University of New York College at Oswego

| 43 Swetman Hall | Phone: (315) 341-2270 |
| Oswego, NY 13126 | Fax: (315) 341-3078 |

Division(s): Division of Continuing Education
Web Site(s): http://oswego.edu
E-mail: ameigh@oswego.edu

Class Titles: Broadcasting/Cable, Broadcast Newswriting, Media Economics, Telecommunications, Eastern Religious Traditions, Data Communications/Networks, Personnel Management, Vocational Curriculum Development, Evaluation of Instruction, Fundamentals of Administration, Curriculum Facilitation.

Teaching Methods: *Computers:* Internet, electronic classroom, e-mail. *TV:* videotape, cable program. *Other:* videoconferencing, independent study, individual study, learning contracts.

Credits Granted for: experiential learning, portfolio assessment, extrainstitutional learning, examination (CLEP, ACT-PEP, GRE).

Admission Requirements: *Undergraduate:* high school diploma. *Graduate:* acceptance by Dean of Graduate Studies. *Certificate:* acceptance by Program Coordinator.

On-Campus Requirements: Must have a minimum of 30 hours of State University of New York, Oswego credit; 122 hours total credit required for undergraduate degree.

Tuition and Fees: *Undergraduate:* $137/credit. *Graduate:* $213/credit. *Application Fee:* $30. *Other Costs:* $273 fee/term undergraduate, $191 graduate. *Credit by:* semester.

Financial Aid: Federal Stafford Loan, Federal Perkins Loan, Federal PLUS Loan, Federal Pell Grant, Federal Work-Study, VA, New York resident programs.

Accreditation: Middle States Association of Colleges and Schools.

Description: While maintaining its high standards as a former teachers' college, the State University of New York, College at Oswego (1861) broadened its academic perspective in 1962 when it became one of the colleges of arts and science in the State University system. Collectively these colleges are now called the University Colleges of the State University of New York. SUNY Oswego first offered distance learning courses over cable TV in 1995, adding ISDN-based videoconferencing in 1996 and Internet courses in 1997. Plans are underway to provide undergraduate and graduate distance degree options in the near future.

State University of New York Institute of Technology, Utica/Rome

| PO Box 3050 | Phone: (315) 792-7500 |
| Utica, NY 13504 | Fax: (315) 792-7837 |

Division(s): School of Business/School of Arts and Sciences
Web Site(s): http://www1.sunyit.edu
E-mail: admissions@sunyit.edu

Undergraduate Degree Programs:
None.

Graduate Degree Programs:
Master of Science in Accountancy

Class Titles: classes in Health Services Management and in Political Science, courses toward a graduate degree in Health Services Management. Classes vary each semester, fall 1998: 1998 Elections, Health Care Delivery, Health Policy, Advanced Income Tax, Advanced Financial Theory, Accounting.

Teaching Methods: *Computers:* Internet, real-time chat, electronic classroom (in progress), e-mail, newsgroup, LISTSERV. *TV:* videotape. *Other:* videoconferencing, fax, correspondence, independent study, individual study, learning contracts.

Credits Granted for: extrainstitutional learning, examination (CLEP, ACT-PEP, DANTES, GRE).

Admission Requirements: *Undergraduate:* generally 56 credits, minimum 2.5 GPA, offer only junior and senior level courses. *Graduate:* 3.0+ GPA undergraduate, GMAT exam, completed application (students without an undergraduate degree in Business, Accounting for MS Accountancy should call for more information).

On-Campus Requirements: None.

Tuition and Fees: *Undergraduate:* New York State: $137/credit, out-of-state: $346/credit. *Graduate:* New York State:

$213/credit, out-of-state: $351/credit. *Application Fee:* $30 undergraduate, $50 graduate. *Other Costs:* miscellaneous fees. *Credit by:* semester.

Financial Aid: Federal Stafford Loan, Federal Perkins Loan, Federal PLUS Loan, Federal Pell Grant, Federal Work-Study, VA, New York resident programs.

Accreditation: Middle States Association of Colleges and Schools.

Description: SUNY Institute of Technology at Utica/Rome (1966) is a college for transfer students established as SUNY's only upper division college. It was created to meet the needs of 2-year college graduates who wanted to extend their professional and technical educations.

State University of New York College of Technology at Canton

34 Cornell Drive	Phone: (315) 386-7102
Canton, NY 13617	Fax: (315) 386-7928

Division(s): Extended Studies/Academic Affairs
Web Site(s): http://www.canton.edu
E-mail: PerryLM@Scanva.Canton.Edu

Class Titles: Criminal Justice, Psychology, Sociology, Government, Literature, Veterinary Technology.

Teaching Methods: *Computers:* Internet, real-time chat, electronic classroom, e-mail. *TV:* videotape. *Other:* videoconferencing, fax, correspondence.

Credits Granted for: experiential learning, examination (CLEP, ACT-PEP, DANTES, GRE).

Admission Requirements: *Undergraduate:* variable. *Certificate:* GED or high school diploma.

On-Campus Requirements: None.

Tuition and Fees: *Undergraduate:* $99/credit off-campus; $128/credit on-campus. *Other Costs:* $85 college fee; $2/credit tech fee. *Credit by:* semester.

Financial Aid: Federal Stafford Loan, Federal Perkins Loan, Federal PLUS Loan, Federal Pell Grant, Federal Work-Study, VA, New York resident programs.

Accreditation: Middle States Association of Colleges and Schools.

Description: The State University of New York College of Technology at Canton (1906) is a tax-assisted, 2- and 4-year residential college located on a spacious campus along the banks of the Grasse River. SUNY Canton shares the commitment of the university to provide educational opportunities for New York state residents. Students number 2,000 and are taught by faculty who have both outstanding academic credentials and sound technical experience. Most have on-the-job professional experience, are licensed in their fields, and currently practice in their professions. The effective student-faculty ratio is 18:1.

State University of New York, Buffalo

128 Parker Hall	Phone: (716) 829-3131
Buffalo, NY 14214-3007	Fax: (716) 829-2475

Division(s): Millard Fillmore College
Web Site(s): http://www.mfc.buffalo.edu
E-mail: mfc@msmail.buffalo.edu

Undergraduate Degree Programs:
Bachelor of Science in Nursing

Graduate Degree Programs:
Master of Science in Engineering in:
Aerospace/Aeronautical
Civil
Electrical
Mechanical
Industrial
Master of Science in Nursing

Certificate Programs: Computing and Network Management; Civil, Structural, and Environmental Engineering; Electrical and Computer Engineering/Controls, Communications, and Software; Mechanical and Aerospace Engineering—Computer-Aided Design.

Class Titles: Computing, English, Nutrition, Media Study, Psychology.

Teaching Methods: *Computers:* Internet, real-time chat, electronic classroom, e-mail, CD-ROM, newsgroup, LIST-SERV. *TV:* videotape, cable program. *Other:* videoconferencing.

Credits Granted for: experiential learning, portfolio assessment, extrainstitutional learning, examination (CLEP, ACT-PEP, DANTES, GRE), program-specific.

Admission Requirements: *Undergraduate:* variable—see online catalog(s). *Graduate:* BA, variable—see online catalog(s). *Certificate:* variable—see online catalog(s).

On-Campus Requirements: None.

Tuition and Fees: *Undergraduate:* $137/credit in-state, $346/credit out-of-state. *Graduate:* $213/credit in-state, $351/credit out-of-state. *Application Fee:* $30–$35. *Other Costs:* variable. *Credit by:* semester.

Financial Aid: Federal Stafford Loan, Federal Perkins Loan, Federal PLUS Loan, Federal Pell Grant, Federal Work-Study, VA, New York resident programs.

Accreditation: Middle States Association of Colleges and Schools.

Description: The University of New York at Buffalo (1846) is New York's premier public center for graduate and professional education and the state's largest and most comprehensive public university. As the only public member in New York and New England of the prestigious Association of American Universities, the University at Buffalo stands in the first rank among the nation's research-intensive public universities. The university was a private institution from 1846 until 1962; during that time, 11 of its 12 professional schools were founded. After merging with the State University of New York in 1962, the already mature University at Buffalo was a direct beneficiary of New York's aggressive investment in public higher education and grew in size and ambition at a remarkable pace. This private-public heritage has endowed the University at Buffalo with a special character. The University at Buffalo first began offering distance learning courses in 1994. Currently, courses are delivered through telecourses, synchronous (interactive video), and asynchronous (Web-based). Noncredit, undergraduate, and graduate degree programs will be expanded over the next few years. Millard Fillmore College, the continuing education and evening division of the university, is the point-of-contact for UB's distance learning programs.

State University of New York, Morrisville

Eaton Street	Phone: (315) 684-6059
Morrisville, NY 13408	Fax: (315) 684-6249

Division(s): Instructional Communication Services
Web Site(s): http://www.morrisville.edu
E-mail: matthet@morrisville.edu

Undergraduate Degree Programs:
Bachelor of Science in Computer Information Technology

Class Titles: Agriculture, Business, Math, Science, Health, Technology, General Studies.

Teaching Methods: *Computers:* Internet, electronic classroom, e-mail, CD-ROM. *TV:* videotape, cable program, satellite broadcasting, PBS. *Other:* radio broadcast, videoconferencing, audioconferencing, audiotapes, fax correspondence, independent study, individual study.

Credits Granted for: examination (CLEP, ACT-PEP, GRE).

Admission Requirements: *Undergraduate:* open-enrollment.

On-Campus Requirements: None.

Tuition and Fees: *Undergraduate:* $99/credit. *Credit by:* semester.

Financial Aid: Federal Direct Loan, Federal Perkins Loan, Federal PLUS Loan, Federal Pell Grant, Federal Work-Study, VA, New York resident programs, New York State Tuition Assistance Program.

Accreditation: Middle States Association of Colleges and Schools.

Description: The State University of New York, College of Agriculture and Technology at Morrisville (1908) is located in a rural community in central New York state. The college is dedicated to providing access to quality postsecondary education in residential and off-campus settings. SUNY Morrisville started offering distance learning courses in August 1996. In September 1996, we were designated as the coordination site for the 5 University Colleges of Technology. Over the past 2 years, the 5 colleges have developed 46 distance learning courses and degree programs that are offered through our compressed video network and the Internet.

State University of New York, New Paltz

75 South Manheim Boulevard, Suite 9	Phone: (914) 257-2900
New Paltz, NY 12561-2443	Fax: (914) 257-2899

Division(s): Continuing and Professional Education
Web Site(s): http://www.newpaltz.edu/continuing_ed/
E-mail: edl@newpaltz.edu

Class Titles: vary each semester; undergraduate liberal arts courses, some graduate education courses.

Teaching Methods: *Computers:* Internet, electronic classroom, e-mail, newsgroup, LISTSERV. *TV:* videotape. *Other:* videoconferencing.

Credits Granted for: experiential learning, portfolio assessment, examination (CLEP).

Admission Requirements: *Undergraduate:* open-enrollment for distance learning courses. *Graduate:* open-enrollment for distance learning courses.

On-Campus Requirements: Distance learning courses fulfill the residency requirement.

Tuition and Fees: *Undergraduate:* $137/credit resident, $346/credit out-of-state. *Graduate:* $213/credit resident, $351/credit out-of-state. *Credit by:* semester.

Financial Aid: Federal Stafford Loan, Federal Supplemental Educational Opportunity Grant, Federal Perkins Loan, Federal PLUS Loan, Federal Pell Grant, New York resident programs.

Accreditation: Middle States Association of Colleges and Schools.

Description: The State University of New York at New Paltz (1828) is a comprehensive and selective public university located in the mid-Hudson region of New York. Admission standards for its 7,500 full- and part-time students have established SUNY New Paltz as among the most selective colleges in the Northeast and are reflective of its commitment to diversity. The college is committed to the primacy of undergraduate and graduate teaching, an ethnically and culturally diverse campus population, and international studies. SUNY New Paltz provides more than 100 undergraduate and 50 advanced degree programs, in addition to a variety of continuing and professional education offerings.

State University of West Georgia

Honors House, 1600 Maple Street
Carrollton, GA 30118

Phone: (770) 836-4647
Fax: (770) 836-4666

Division(s): Distance Education Center
Web Site(s): http://www.westga.edu/~distance
E-mail: mhill@westga.edu

Certificate Programs: Distance Education

Class Titles: Graduate courses in Research, Media, Technology, English to Speakers of Other Languages, Public Administration, Business Administration, Nursing, Counseling/Educational Psychology.

Teaching Methods: *Computers:* Internet, real-time chat, electronic classroom, e-mail, CD-ROM, LISTSERV. *TV:* videotape. *Other:* videoconferencing.

Credits Granted for: examination (CLEP, ACT-PEP, DANTES, GRE).

Admission Requirements: *Undergraduate:* SAT or ACT, high school GPA, college preparatory curriculum. *Graduate:* bachelor's degree, appropriate admission test, 3 letters of recommendation. *Doctoral:* PhD in Education—undergraduate GPA 2.6 or higher, GRE of 1,000 or higher. *Certificate:* see master's degree; see graduate.

On-Campus Requirements: varies among courses.

Tuition and Fees: *Undergraduate:* $840/12 hours or more if resident; if nonresident, add tuition of $2,231. *Graduate:* $617/12 hours or more if resident; if nonresident, add tuition of $1,640. *Doctoral:* see graduate. *Application Fee:* $15. *Other Costs:* $60 undergraduate, $40 graduate health fee; $135 undergraduate, $90 graduate athletic fee; $9 undergraduate, $6 graduate transportation fee. *Credit by:* semester.

Financial Aid: Federal Stafford Loan, Federal Perkins Loan, Federal PLUS Loan, Federal Pell Grant, Federal Work-Study, VA, Georgia resident programs

Accreditation: National Council for Accreditation of Teacher Education, American Assembly of Collegiate Schools of Business, National League for Nursing, National Association of Schools of Music, National Association of Schools of Public Affairs and Administration, American Chemical Society Consortium for Diversified Psychology Programs.

Description: The State University of West Georgia (1933) originated as the 4th District Agricultural and Mechanical School. In 1956, the institution was authorized to confer the BS degree in Education, making it a 4-year, senior college in the University System of Georgia. During the following years, the college became one of the fastest-growing institutions of higher learning in the South, maturing into a university in 1996. The Distance Learning program began in 1995 following the passing of the Distance Learning and Telemedicine Act of 1992 by the Georgia legislature.

Stenotype Institute of Jacksonville, Inc.

500 9th Avenue N
Jacksonville Beach, FL 32250

Phone: (904) 246-7466
Fax: (904) 246-0129

Division(s): None.
Web Site(s): None.
E-mail: jaxsteno@aol.com

Certificate Programs: Court Reporting.

Teaching Methods: *Other:* radio broadcast, videoconferencing, audioconferencing, audiographics, audiotapes, fax, correspondence, independent study, individual study, learning contracts.

Credits Granted for: experiential learning, extrainstitutional learning.

Admission Requirements: *Undergraduate:* high school diploma or GED, entrance exam.

On-Campus Requirements: None.

Tuition and Fees: *Undergraduate:* $100/month, maximum $4,500. *Application Fee:* $150.

Financial Aid: Pell Grants and Stafford Loans available for qualified resident students, but not for home study students.

Accreditation: Distance Education and Training Council.

Description: The Stenotype Institute of Jacksonville, Inc. (1940), is the only court-reporting school in the U.S. with an accredited resident program approved by the National Court Reporters Association and an accredited home-study program. This latter program was founded in 1967 and has a current enrollment of 160 students. The Stenotype Institute has always maintained academic and skill requirements a cut above the minimum standards set by the national association. The Institute's 97.5% accuracy requirement, while higher than the association's 95%, should make it easier to pass the national exam to become a Registered Professional Reporter.

Stephens College

1211 East Broadway
Columbia, MO 65215

Phone: (800) 388-7579
(573) 876-7125
Fax: (573) 876-7248

Division(s): School of Graduate and Continuing Education
Web Site(s): http://www.stephens.edu
E-mail: sce@wc.stephens.edu

Undergraduate Degree Programs:
Bachelor of Arts in:
  Business Administration
  Early Childhood Education
  Elementary Education
  English
  Philosophy
  Law and Rhetoric

Psychology
Health Care (and second area)
Health Science (and second area)
Bachelor of Science in Health Information Management

Graduate Degree Programs:
Master of Business Administration with emphasis in:
Management
Entrepreneurial Studies
Clinical Information Systems Management

Certificate Programs: Health Information Management, Elementary Education, Early Childhood Education.

Teaching Methods: *Computers:* Internet, e-mail, CD-ROM, newsgroup, LISTSERV. *Other:* fax, correspondence, independent study, individual study, learning contracts.

Credits Granted for: experiential learning, portfolio assessment, extrainstitutional learning, examination (CLEP, ACT-PEP, DANTES, GRE).

Admission Requirements: *Undergraduate:* age 23, high school diploma or GED, personal essay, college transcripts, Liberal Studies Seminar. *Graduate:* accredited bachelor's degree, 3.0 GPA, GMAT, 3 letters of recommendation, essay, interview. *Certificate:* bachelor's degree, personal essay, college transcripts.

On-Campus Requirements: Liberal Studies Seminar for undergraduate students, offered in 7-day or double-weekend format, worth 3.0 Humanities credits.

Tuition and Fees: *Undergraduate:* $650/course, $500/course mid-Missouri residents. *Graduate:* $230/credit. *Application Fee:* $50 undergraduate, $25 graduate. *Other Costs:* Internet/e-mail access, $5 transcript requests. *Credit by:* semester.

Financial Aid: Federal Stafford Loan, Federal Perkins Loan, Federal PLUS Loan, Federal Pell Grant, Federal Work-Study, VA, Missouri resident programs.

Accreditation: North Central Association of Colleges and Schools.

Description: Stephens College began offering traditional courses in 1833. Its School of Graduate and Continuing Education offers programs designed to address the content and logistics needs of nontraditional students. The staff is attuned to the complications of maintaining jobs, handling family responsibilities, and completing degrees, because many teachers have been nontraditional students themselves. With a curriculum that emphasizes concerns of women and ethnic minorities, the program also strives to promote and enhance personal and professional development, personal empowerment, and leadership skills.

Stevens Institute of Technology

Castle Point on Hudson	Phone: (201) 216-5229
Hoboken, NJ 07030	Fax: (201) 216-8044

Division(s): The Graduate School
Web Site(s): http://www.stevens-tech.edu/
E-mail: jmoeller@stevens-tech.edu

Graduate Degree Programs:
Master of Science in:
Management
Telecommunications Management
Project Management
Computer Science
Master of Engineering in Concurrent Engineering

Certificate Programs: Graduate; areas noted above.

Class Titles: All courses in disciplines listed above.

Teaching Methods: *Computers:* Internet, e-mail, LISTSERV. *Other:* videoconferencing.

Credits Granted for: extrainstitutional learning (corporate or professional association seminars/workshops), regular class enrollment and participation.

Admission Requirements: *Graduate:* bachelor's degree, letters of recommendation, transcript. *Doctoral:* master's degree, letters of recommendation, transcript. *Certificate:* bachelor's degree, letters of recommendation, transcript.

On-Campus Requirements: For interactive video instruction, student must attend at remote video site.

Tuition and Fees: *Graduate:* $650/credit. *Doctoral:* $650/credit. *Application Fee:* $45. *Credit by:* semester.

Financial Aid: Federal Stafford Loan, Federal Perkins Loan, Federal PLUS Loan, Federal Pell Grant, Federal Work-Study, VA, New Jersey resident programs.

Accreditation: Middle States Association, Accreditation Board for Engineering and Technology, Computer Science Accreditation Board.

Description: Stevens Institute of Technology (1870) is a private university dedicated to academics and research. Stevens' traditions of expert problem-solving, depth in the humanities, superior technical breadth, personal integrity, and an unsurpassed work ethic play a dramatic role in educating the best engineers, scientists and managers in the country and helping the U.S. restore the environment and improve industrial competitiveness and education. Of the 110 scientists and managers (full-time faculty), 95% hold doctoral degrees. Core courses in the 4 undergraduate programs—engineering, science, computer science, humanities—stress a multidisciplinary understanding of engineering and scientific principles and an appreciation of the humanities. Stevens also offers highly successful preprofessional programs in dentistry, law, and medicine. Graduate programs include engineering, science, computer sciences and management and lead to one of 44 advanced degrees from the certificate of special study to master's and doctorates. Stevens maintains 8 industrial interdisciplinary alliances focused on solving key technological problems facing industry. Applied research programs address automated concurrent engineering to improve manufacturing processes, environmental remediation and pollution control technologies, telecommunications, surface-engineering materials, coastal erosion, and precollege mathematics and science education. Stevens has earned numerous accreditations and is one of only a few universities to hold both general engineering and specialized engineering accreditations in 7 disciplines from the Accreditation Board for Engineering and Technology.

Strayer University

PO Box 487	Phone: (703) 339-1850
Newington, VA 22122	(800) 422-8055
	Fax: (703) 339-1852

Division(s): Distance Learning
Web Site(s): http://www.strayer.edu
E-mail: mlb@strayer.edu

Undergraduate Degree Programs:
Associate of Arts in:
    Accounting
    Business Administration
    Computer Information Systems
    Economics
    Marketing
    General Studies
Bachelor of Science in:
    Accounting
    Business Administration
    Computer Information Systems
    Economics

Graduate Degree Programs:
Master of Science in:
    Business Administration
    Information Systems
    Professional Accounting

Certificate Programs: Computer Information Systems Diploma

Class Titles: 200 courses, including Business, Organizational Behavior, Management, International Business Environment, Business Ethics, Human Resource Management, Business Policy, Financial Management, Business Law, Computer Information Systems, Microcomputer Applications in Business, Computer Programming Design, Using/Programming Access, UNIX Operating System, Networking, Data Communication Technologies, Computer Architectures, Distributed Communication Systems, Computer Operating Systems, Systems Analysis/Design, Software Engineering, Database Management Systems, Management Information Systems,

Accounting, Managerial Accounting

Teaching Methods: *Computers:* Internet, real-time chat, electronic classroom. *Other:* None.

Credits Granted for: experiential learning, portfolio assessment, extrainstitutional learning, examination (CLEP, ACT-PEP, DANTES, GRE).

Admission Requirements: *Undergraduate:* high school graduate or GED, placement tests. *Graduate:* accredited bachelor's degree. *Certificate:* see undergraduate.

On-Campus Requirements: None.

Tuition and Fees: *Undergraduate:* $180/credit full-time, $190/credit part-time. *Graduate:* $250/credit. *Doctoral:* $25. *Credit by:* quarter (4.5 credits/course).

Financial Aid: Federal Stafford Loan, Federal Perkins Loan, Federal PLUS Loan, Federal Pell Grant, Federal Work-Study, VA, Strayer University Education Loan Program.

Accreditation: Middle States Association of Colleges and Universities.

Description: Strayer University, founded in 1892, offers undergraduate and graduate degree programs to 9,400 students at 9 campuses in Washington, DC, Virginia, and Maryland. Strayer also provides distance learning through Internet online courses. The university attracts working students by offering computer and business programs, convenient campus locations, online courses, flexible class schedules, information technology courses, and an experienced teaching faculty. A pilot program for online courses (Strayer Online) began in 1996, and a year later all programs received online approval. Online courses are synchronous, with classes meeting weekly. Students may access a chat room and are in conversation mode with the instructor and other class members.

Suffolk County Community College

533 College Road	Phone: (516) 451-4174
Selden, NY 11784	Fax: (516) 451-4681

Division(s): Office of Academic Affairs/Central Administration
Web Site(s): http://www.sunysuffolk.edu
E-mail: kania@sunysuffolk.edu

Class Titles: English, History, Business, Psychology, Health/Nutrition, Geology, Sociology, Science, Fine Arts, Women's Studies.

Teaching Methods: *Computers:* Internet, electronic classroom. *TV:* videotape, cable program, PBS. *Other:* independent study, contract learning.

Credits Granted for: experiential learning, portfolio assessment, examination (CLEP, ACT-PEP, DANTES, GRE).

Admission Requirements: *Undergraduate:* may be prerequisites for upper-level courses. *Certificate:* may be prerequisites for upper-level courses.

On-Campus Requirements: for telecourses, 5 required on-campus sessions (7 for lab courses).

Tuition and Fees: *Undergraduate:* $94/credit for county residents; $188/credit for nonresidents. *Application Fee:* $30. *Other Costs:* $40 telecourse fee. *Credit by:* semester.

Financial Aid: Federal Stafford Loan, Federal Pell Grant, Federal Work-Study, VA, New York resident programs.

Accreditation: Middle States Association of Colleges and Schools.

Description: Suffolk County Community College (1959) is a 3-campus community college of more than 20,000 students located in Suffolk County, Long Island, New York. The college has been offering telecourses via cable TV or through videocassette loans for more than 10 years. It is presently offering its first 2 Web-based courses, one in atmospheric science and one in English. It will offer its first 3 synchronous courses among the 3 campuses in spring 1999.

Sul Ross State University

| Alpine, TX 79832 | Phone: (915) 837-8368 |
| | Fax: (915) 837-8382 |

Division(s): School of Arts and Sciences
Web Site(s): http://www.sulross.edu
E-mail: bglasrud@sulross.edu
rcullins@sulross.edu

Class Titles: contact school.

Teaching Methods: *Computers:* Internet, electronic classroom, e-mail. *TV:* videotape. *Other:* audioconferencing, videoconferencing, fax, independent study, individual study.

Credits Granted for: portfolio assessment, examination (CLEP, ACT-PEP, DANTES, GRE).

Admission Requirements: *Undergraduate:* contact school.

On-Campus Requirements: None.

Tuition and Fees: *Undergraduate:* $222/3-credit course. *Graduate:* same as undergraduate. *Credit by:* semester.

Financial Aid: Federal Stafford Loan, Federal Perkins Loan, Federal PLUS Loan, Federal Pell Grant, Federal Work-Study, VA, Texas resident programs.

Accreditation: Southern Association of Colleges and Schools.

Description: Sul Ross State University (1917) is a comprehensive regional institution of higher education in west Texas. SRSU is a Hispanic-serving institution committed to excellence in teaching, to a "student centered" philosophy, and to serving the needs of the broad community. Set in the midst of a vast, sparsely populated region, the university offers distance learning courses to serve the needs of the remote peoples of this area.

Sussex County Community College

| 1 College Hill | Phone: (973) 300-2136 |
| Newton, NJ 07860 | Fax: (973) 300-2277 |

Division(s): Academic Affairs
Web Site(s): http://www.Sussex.cc.nj.us
E-mail: Thomasi@Sussex.cc.nj.us

Undergraduate Degree Programs:
Associate of Arts
Associate of Science

Certificate Programs: Legal Assistant

Teaching Methods: *Computers:* Internet, e-mail. *TV:* videotape, cable program. *Other:* fax, correspondence, independent study, individual study, learning contracts.

Credits Granted for: portfolio assessment, examination (CLEP, ACT-PEP, DANTES, GRE).

Admission Requirements: *Undergraduate:* open-access. *Certificate:* open-access.

On-Campus Requirements: To get a degree, students have to take courses on campus in addition to distance education courses.

Tuition and Fees: *Undergraduate:* $68/credit. *Credit by:* semester.

Financial Aid: Federal Stafford Loan, Federal Perkins Loan, Federal PLUS Loan, Federal Pell Grant, Federal Work-Study, VA, New Jersey resident programs.

Accreditation: Middle States Association of Colleges and Schools.

Description: Sussex County Community College (1982) is an open-access, exit-standard, 2-year public institution.

Syracuse University

700 University Avenue	Phone: (315) 443-3480
Syracuse, NY 13244	(800) 442-0501 (USA only)
	Fax: (315) 443-4174

Division(s): Continuing Education
Web Site(s): http://www.suce.syr.edu/ISDP
http://www.suce.syr.edu/ONLINE
E-mail: suisdp@syr.edu

Undergraduate Degree Programs:
Associate of Arts in Liberal Studies
Bachelor of Arts in Liberal Studies

Graduate Degree Programs:
Master of Arts in Advertising Design or Illustration
Master of Business Administration
Master of Library Science
Master of Science in:
Communications Management

Information Resources Management
Nursing
Telecommunications and Network Management
Master of Social Science

Class Titles: Writing, Philosophy, Psychology, Speech, Biology.

Teaching Methods: *Computers:* Internet, real-time chat, electronic classroom, e-mail, LISTSERV. *Other:* videoconferencing, fax, correspondence, independent study.

Credits Granted for: experiential learning, portfolio assessment, extrainstitutional learning, examination (CLEP, ACT-PEP, DANTES, GRE) undergraduate only.

Admission Requirements: *Undergraduate:* Associate/Bachelor in Liberal Studies—TOEFL of 550; high school degree; 2.5 GPA for transfer students; January, May, or August admission. *Graduate:* program-specific; contact school.

On-Campus Requirements: 2–4 weeks/year in residence on campus or at other sites.

Tuition and Fees: *Undergraduate:* $336/credit. *Graduate:* $555/credit. *Application Fee:* $40. *Other Costs:* room and board (approximately $50–$100/day), books (approximately $35/credit course), Internet costs (vary). *Credit by:* semester.

Financial Aid: Federal Stafford Loan, Federal Perkins Loan, Federal Pell Grant, Federal Work-Study, Unsubsidized Federal Stafford Loan, UC Institutional Graduate Tuition Award.

Accreditation: Middle States Association of Colleges and Schools, Association of American Universities.

Description: Syracuse University (1870) is a major private research university in central New York State, with 14,500 residential and 5,000 part-time, adult students. The institution is organized into 13 schools and colleges, each offering a variety of bachelor's, master's, and doctoral degrees. Syracuse has excellent research facilities, including sophisticated computer networks and a library with more than 2.4 million volumes. The university is ranked by *U.S. News and World Report* as one of the top 50 universities in the U.S. and is one of few universities selected for membership in the prestigious Association of American Universities. In 1966 the university pioneered its nontraditional Independent Study Degree program, one of the three oldest external degree programs in the U.S. Offered through 9 of the university's academic units, the programs reflect the university's response to the demands for creative educational techniques in a constantly changing society.

Taft College

29 Emmons Park Drive   **Phone:** (805) 763-7700
Taft, CA 93268   **Fax:** (805) 763-7705

Division(s): Instruction
Web Site(s): http://www.taft.cc.ca.us

E-mail: bell@taft.org

Class Titles: Chemistry, Computer Sciences, English, History, Humanities, Library Skills, Math.

Teaching Methods: *Computers:* Internet, real-time chat, electronic classroom, e-mail, CD-ROM, LISTSERV. *TV:* videotape, cable program. *Other:* fax, correspondence, independent study, individual study.

Admission Requirements: *Undergraduate:* variable.

On-Campus Requirements: None.

Tuition and Fees: *Undergraduate:* $12. *Credit by:* semester.

Financial Aid: Federal Pell Grant, Federal Work-Study, VA, California resident programs.

Accreditation: Western Association of Schools and Colleges.

Description: Taft College (1922) was originally established as a junior college. In 1956 it expanded into a new campus with new facilities.

Tarleton State University

Box T-0810   **Phone:** (254) 968-9050
Stephenville, TX 76402   **Fax:** (254) 968-9540

Division(s): Academic Departments or
Center for Distance Learning and Instructional Technology
Web Site(s): http://www.tarleton.edu
E-mail: ross@tarleton.edu

Class Titles: classes vary. Call for catalog or check Web site at http://www.tarleton.edu/catalog/.

Teaching Methods: *Computers:* Internet, real-time chat, electronic classroom, e-mail, newsgroup, LISTSERV. *Other:* videoconferencing, independent study, individual study.

Admission Requirements: *Undergraduate:* request catalog for details. *Graduate:* request catalog for details.

On-Campus Requirements: state-mandated requirements. Contact school for complete information.

Tuition and Fees: *Undergraduate:* $60/credit, $120 minimum, $272/credit nonresident. Check catalog for current information and full details. *Graduate:* $70/credit, $120 minimum, $272/credit nonresident. *Other Costs:* $12/credit student services fee, $44 other. *Credit by:* semester.

Financial Aid: Federal Stafford Loan, Federal Perkins Loan, Federal PLUS Loan, Federal Pell Grant, Federal Work-Study, VA, Texas resident programs, departmental and other grants and scholarships.

Accreditation: Southern Association of Colleges and Schools.

Description: Tarleton State University (1899) offers a wide variety of major programs in agriculture, business administration, and teacher education. Other strong degree programs exist for allied health and community services, the fine arts, social sciences, physical and biological sciences, humanities, mathematics, and technology. The university functions as an educational, scientific, and cultural center for the Crosstimbers region of Texas through its 3-fold mission of teaching, research, and service. Instruction by interactive videoconferencing began in the spring of 1992. Internet courses began in the fall of 1998.

Tarrant County Junior College

5301 Campus Drive	Phone: (817) 515-4532
Fort Worth, TX 76119	Fax: (817) 515-4400

Division(s): Center for Distance Learning
Web Site(s): http://www.tcjc.cc.tx.us
E-mail: keason@tcjc.cc.tx.us

Undergraduate Degree Programs:
Associate of Arts in Liberal Arts

Teaching Methods: *Computers:* Internet, real-time chat, e-mail, CD-ROM. *TV:* videotape, cable program, satellite broadcasting, PBS. *Other:* None.

Credits Granted for: examination (CLEP, ACT-PEP, DANTES, GRE).

Admission Requirements: *Undergraduate:* Official, accredited, high school graduation or GED; college transfers; or individual approval. Plus, mandatory Texas Academic Skills Program competency test in reading, writing, and math. Any deficiencies necessitate appropriate remediation. TASP exemptions for students with 3 college credits prior to the fall, 1989 semester; students from specific private or out-of-state institutions; senior citizens; certain noncitizens; students with accredited baccalaureate degrees or higher; and for students with board-established ACT, SAT, or TAAS scores. Call Registrar's Office for details: (817) 515-5291.

On-Campus Requirements: Yes, for some courses that require laboratory experiences, such as Biology and Geology. In addition, all courses offer on-campus orientation sessions and some courses offer enrichment seminars throughout the semester.

Tuition and Fees: *Undergraduate:* $22/semester hour with a $100 minimum, $12/semester hour out-of-district, $140/semester hour with a $200 minimum out-of-state; $140/semester hour with a $200 minimum nonresident alien. *Application Fee:* $10, $30 foreign processing/evaluation fee. *Other Costs:* $5/semester hour, $24 laboratory fee, $2 student services fee, other fees may apply such as returned check fee, graduation fee, transcript fee. *Credit by:* semester.

Financial Aid: Federal Stafford Loan, Federal PLUS Loan, Federal Pell Grant, Federal Work-Study, VA, Texas resident programs, Federal SEOG, Federal SSIG, State Work-Study, institutional scholarships, and short term loans.

Accreditation: Southern Association of Colleges and Schools

and approved by the Texas Higher Education Coordinating Board and the Texas Education Agency. Memberships are also held in the Texas Association of Community Colleges, Association of Texas Colleges and Universities, Southern Association of Community Colleges and the American Association of Community Colleges.

Description: Tarrant County Junior College (1966) is a comprehensive community college dedicated to providing quality education to the people of Tarrant County. Distance learning began in 1973 with Instructional TV and has since expanded to include Internet/computer delivered instruction. The full-time faculty are dedicated to providing positive learning experiences for students, who may contact instructors by phone or e-mail. Included in the 54 Internet/CDI and 30 ITV courses offered in the fall, 1998 semester are accounting, business, computer science, English, math, government, history, psychology, sociology, biology, geology, music, office occupations, speech, Spanish, French, economics, and religion.

Taylor University World Wide Campus

1025 West Rudisill Boulevard	Phone: (800) 845-3149
Fort Wayne, IN 46807-2197	(219) 456-2111 x32225
	Fax: (219) 456-2118

Division(s): Institute of Extended Learning
Web Site(s): http://www.wwcampus.tayloru.edu
http://www.tayloru.edu/~iel
E-mail: wwcampus@tayloru.edu or ielearn@tayloru.edu

Undergraduate Degree Programs:
Associate of Arts in:
    Biblical Studies
    General Studies (Liberal Arts)
    Justice Administration (Public Policy concentration)
    Justice Administration (Ministry concentration)

Certificate Programs: Christian Worker, Justice and Ministries

Class Titles: New Testament Greek, Old Testament Hebrew, Old Testament Survey, New Testament Survey, Historical Books, Genesis, Matthew, Inductive Study of Bible, Gospel of John, Romans, Pentateuch, Acts/Early Church, Pauline Epistles, Hebrews/General Epistles, Gospels, Poetic/Wisdom Literature, Urban Ministry, Ministry to Children, Ministry to Youth, Ministry to Adults, Leadership Development, American Religious History, Early Christianity Through Medieval Times, Reformation Christianity, European Christianity: 1650–Present, Public Speaking, Journalistic Writing, Criminal Justice, Correctional Chaplaincy, Restorative Justice, Educational Psychology, Art, Music Fundamentals, Music Appreciation, World History, U.S. History, Orientation to Distance Learning, Foundations of Christian Thought, American Literature, British Literature, Finite Mathematics, Modern Cults, Perspectives on

World Christian Movement, World Religions, Cross-Cultural Evangelism, Biological Science Survey, Physical Geography, Physical Science Survey, Worship, Evangelism/Discipleship, Pastoral Theology, Preaching, Philosophy, Logic, Contemporary Issues, Apologetics, Psychology, Research in Psychology, Abnormal Psychology, Integration of Psychology/Christianity, Theories of Personality, Counseling, Social Problems, Cultural Anthropology, Theology.

Teaching Methods: *Computers:* Internet, e-mail, CD-ROM, newsgroup. *TV:* videotape. *Other:* audiotapes, fax, correspondence, independent study, individual study.

Credits Granted for: examination (CLEP, ACT-PEP, DANTES, GRE).

Admission Requirements: *Undergraduate:* high school diploma or GED, 2.5 high school GPA, SAT/ACT or OTIS test scores, personal reference, signed Code of Conduct statement. No requirements if nondegree-seeking.

On-Campus Requirements: Justice and Ministries Certificate and Associate of Arts degree in Justice Administration (Ministry Concentration) require 2 one-week intensive summer sessions on the Fort Wayne, Indiana campus (this requirement may be waived with petition).

Tuition and Fees: *Undergraduate:* $99/credit, correspondence study; $199/credit, online study. *Credit by:* semester.

Accreditation: North Central Association of Colleges and Schools.

Description: Taylor University (1846) is an evangelical, independent, interdenominational, Christian, liberal arts college where faith and learning are integrated. Taylor has a rural campus in Upland, Indiana, an urban campus in Fort Wayne, and a virtual campus known as the World Wide Campus. Under the direction of the College of Adult and Lifelong Learning, Taylor University's World Wide Campus provides undergraduate-level, credit courses through alternate delivery systems to a wide variety of individuals by offering a current, Christ-centered curriculum in liberal arts and professional disciplines. Since 1938, the World Wide Campus (known previously as the Fort Wayne Bible College Institute of Correspondence Studies) has provided distance learning opportunities to 35,000 students.

Technical College of the Lowcountry

921 Ribaut Road	Phone: (843) 525-8204
Beaufort, SC 29902	Fax: (843) 525-8330

Division(s): Instruction
Web Site(s): http://www.tcl-tec-sc-us.org
E-mail: fseitz@tcl.tec.sc.us

Class Titles: Teleclasses/telecourses support certificates, diplomas, and degrees in Business, Criminal Justice, Office System Technology, Paralegal (Legal Assistant), Environmental Technology, Pharmacy Technician (MTC), Medical Records Coder (MTC), and the Transfer Program (Associate of Arts/Associate of Science). Classes include Business, Accounting, Criminal Justice, Paralegal, Office Systems Technology, Chemistry, Environmental Technology, Pharmacy Technician (MTC), Medical Records Coder (MTC), English, Mathematics, History, Government, Speech.

Teaching Methods: *Computers:* Internet, e-mail (support for teleclasses). *TV:* videotape, satellite broadcasting. *Other:* videoconferencing (ISDN).

Credits Granted for: experiential learning, portfolio assessment, examination (CLEP, DANTES).

Admission Requirements: *Undergraduate:* open admission. *Certificate:* open admission.

On-Campus Requirements: None.

Tuition and Fees: *Undergraduate:* $42/credit in-state, $63/credit out-of-state, $80/credit international. *Application Fee:* $10. *Credit by:* semester.

Financial Aid: Federal Stafford Loan, Federal Perkins Loan, Federal PLUS Loan, Federal Pell Grant, Federal Work-Study, VA, South Carolina resident programs.

Accreditation: Southern Association for Colleges and Schools.

Description: Technical College of the Lowcountry traces its roots to the Mather School, which began in 1868 to educate the daughters of newly freed slaves. Today it is one of 16 technical and comprehensive 2-year colleges of the South Carolina Technical College System. To better serve the needs of its 2,858 square-mile rural service area of small towns and sea islands, TCL began its distance learning program in 1996 with help from a USDE Title III grant. Teleclasses are offered via the SCETV 32-channel digital satellite system and via ISDN teleconferencing. TCL also receives teleclasses from other institutions, including graduate courses from Clemson University. Shared programs include Pharmacy Technician and Medical Records Coder. The Pharmacy Technician program is supported by a state-of-the art laboratory at the H. Mungin Center. Most teleclasses originate on the Beaufort Campus. The SCETV system has 1,500 receive sites, primarily on Hilton Head Island and in Varnville. Telecourses (videotape-based) and independent study courses are also available throughout the state of South Carolina.

Télé-université, Université du Québec

2600 Boulevard Laurier	
Tour de la Cité, 7th Level	Phone: (418) 657-2262
Sainte-Foy, PQ G1V 4V9	Fax: (418) 657-2094

Division(s): Anne Marrec
Web Site(s): http://www.teluq.uquebec.ca
E-mail: INFO@teluq.uquebec.ca

Undergraduate Degree Programs:
Contact school for complete listing.

Graduate Degree Programs:
Contact school for complete listing.

Teaching Methods: *Computers:* Internet, e-mail, CD-ROM, newsgroup. *TV:* videotape, cable program. *Other:* videoconferencing, audioconferencing, individual study.

Credits Granted for: experiential learning, portfolio assessment, extrainstitutional learning, examination (CLEP, ACT-PEP, DANTES, GRE).

Admission Requirements: *Undergraduate:* age 21.

On-Campus Requirements: None.

Tuition and Fees: *Undergraduate:* $56 (Canadian). *Graduate:* $56 (Canadian). *Credit by:* semester.

Accreditation: Association of Universities and Colleges of Canada.

Description: Télé-université (1972) is the only French language university in North America that offers educational training entirely at a distance. It was founded in 1972, and is a Université du Québec School of Higher Learning. Télé-université's mandate is to provide university education using the distance education mode, as well as carry out research. Programs and courses are made available to Canadian citizens as well as to foreign students directly or though local universities. Télé-université admits more than 10,000 students per year. Since its creation, it has awarded 12,000 degrees. Registered students receive their course materials by mail or via a telematic medium. Pedagogic support is provided through telephone or telematic tutoring. A variety of communications media and technologies are used as part of the courseware; these include print, audiovisuals, multimedia, telematics, teleconferencing, videoconferencing, and the Information Superhighway. The university offers programs and courses in Administration, Communications, Computer Science, Languages, General and Applied Sciences, Social Sciences and Humanities, broken down as follows: 2 Bachelor of Arts degrees, 19 certificates, 17 short programs, more than 200 courses that make up the different programs. It also offers graduate programs. Two diplomas are currently available: the Diploma in Distance Education and the Diploma in Business Financing. Two other programs are in preparation—a master's degree in distance education and a doctorate in cognitive computing. Some programs are developed with the collaboration of other universities. For the 1995–1996 year, Tele-universite received about $3 million in research grants, of which more than half went to the LICEF Research Center (a laboratory for cognitive computing applied to training environments). The center focuses mainly on integrating information and communication technologies in the distance education setting, using multimedia, hypermedia, and the virtual classroom for teaching purposes.

Temple Baptist Seminary

1815 Union Avenue
Chattanooga, TN 37404

Phone: (423) 493-4221
(800) 553-4050 x4221
Fax: (423) 493-4471

Division(s): Seminary Office

Graduate Degree Programs:
Master of:
Ministry
Arts in Biblical Studies
Religious Education

Doctoral Degree Programs:
Doctor of Ministry

Certificate Programs: Biblical Studies.

Teaching Methods: *TV:* videotape. *Other:* audiotapes, independent study, individual study.

Credits Granted for: examination, institutionally developed/course.

Admission Requirements: *Graduate:* bachelor's degree of 120 hours, 3 recommendations, application. *Doctoral:* for Doctor of Ministry: Master of Divinity or equivalent, 3.0 GPA, active in ministry. *Certificate:* 2 years of college and 2 years of ministry.

On-Campus Requirements: Not currently. The catalog for 2000–2002 will require CM 829 Research Design/Procedures be taken on campus.

Tuition and Fees: *Graduate:* $135. *Application Fee:* $25–$35. *Other Costs:* registration fee $25–$50/semester, student activity fee $15/semester, comprehensive fee $0–$50/semester, audiotapes $80/course, videotapes $130/course. *Credit by:* semester.

Financial Aid: VA.

Accreditation: Candidate with Transnational Association of Christian Colleges and Schools.

Description: Temple Baptist Seminary (1948) is a ministry of Highland Park Baptist Church, an independent Baptist Church. From the outset, the seminary has been committed to upholding the biblical faith historically believed by fundamental Baptists. In addition, there has been a strong emphasis upon Bible teaching, Christian education, evangelism, and ministry endeavor. With the theme of "Preparing for Leadership," Temple Baptist Seminary continues to expand its efforts to equip church leaders and laypersons for the work of the ministry. In recent years, a program of fall, winter, and summer modular classes has been initiated. That program has become very popular with resident and out-of-town students. In 1993, snow during a modular week prevented many students from attending. The class was taped for those who had looked forward to coming. From that beginning, modular classes have been taped for use in the External Studies program.

Tennessee State University

330 Tenth Avenue N
Nashville, TN 37203

Phone: (615) 963-7004
Fax: (615) 963-7007

Division(s): Center for Extended Education
Web Site(s): http://www.tnstate.edu
E-mail: scollier@harpo.tnstate.edu

Class Titles: Psychology, Education, English, History, Nursing, Art, Public Administration

Teaching Methods: *Computers:* Internet, e-mail, LISTSERV. *TV:* videotape, satellite broadcasting, PBS. *Other:* videoconferencing.

Credits Granted for: examination (CLEP, ACT-PEP, DANTES, GRE).

Admission Requirements: *Undergraduate:* see TSU Web page at www.tnstate.edu.

On-Campus Requirements: cee TSU catalog at www.tnstate.edu.

Tuition and Fees: *Undergraduate:* $90/credit in-state, $294 out-of-state. *Graduate:* $135/credit in-state, $336 out-of-state. *Application Fee:* $15 undergraduate, $25 graduate. *Other Costs:* $6/credit technology fee. *Credit by:* semester.

Financial Aid: Federal Stafford Loan, Federal Perkins Loan, Federal PLUS Loan, Federal Pell Grant, Federal Work-Study, VA.

Accreditation: Southern Association of Colleges and Schools.

Description: Tennessee State University, an 1890 land-grant institution, is a major state-supported, urban and comprehensive university governed by the Tennessee Board of Regents. This unique combination of characteristics—land-grant, urban, and comprehensive—differentiates the university from all others in the state and distinctively shapes its instructional, research, and public service programs. In carrying out its diverse mission, the university serves the City of Nashville and Middle Tennessee, the state, the nation, and the international community. As an 1890 land-grant institution, Tennessee State University provides instructional programs, statewide cooperative extension services, cooperative agricultural research, and food and agricultural programs of an international dimension. As a comprehensive institution, Tennessee State University provides programming in agriculture, allied health, arts and sciences, business, education, engineering and technology, home economics, human services, nursing, and public administration. The institution is broadly comprehensive at the baccalaureate and master's levels. While doctoral programs are focused in education and public administration, future doctoral programs will continue to address the needs of an urban population. As a major urban institution located in the capital city, Tennessee State University provides both degree and nondegree programs (day, evening, weekend, and at off-campus sites) that are appropriate and accessible to a working urban population.

Tennessee Technological University

5 William L. Jones Drive
PO Box 5073, TTU
Cookeville, TN 38505-0001

Phone: (931) 372-3394
Fax: (931) 372-3499

Division(s): Extended Education
Web Site(s): http://www.tntech.edu
E-mail: jgalloway@tntech.edu

Class Titles: Accounting, Algebra, Chemistry, Education, English, History, Industrial Technology, Nursing.

Teaching Methods: *Computers:* Internet, e-mail, CD-ROM. *TV:* videotape, cable program, satellite broadcasting, PBS, compressed video, full-motion video. *Other:* videoconferencing, fax.

Credits Granted for: examination (CLEP, ACT-PEP, DANTES, GRE), educational experience in the Armed Forces.

Admission Requirements: *Undergraduate:* age 16, physical examination, high school graduate or GED, 2.35 high school GPA, ACT composite of 19, and assessment tests. *Graduate:* accredited bachelor's or master's, exam score (GRE, AMAT, MAT, etc.), recommendation letter.

On-Campus Requirements: None.

Tuition and Fees: *Undergraduate:* $85/hour resident, $211/hour out-of-state. *Graduate:* $129. *Application Fee:* $25 graduate, $15 undergraduate. *Other Costs:* $9/hour technology access fee. *Credit by:* semester.

Financial Aid: Federal Stafford Loan, Federal Perkins Loan, Federal Pell Grant, Federal Work-Study, VA, Tennessee resident programs, Tennessee student assistant awards.

Accreditation: Southern Association of Colleges and Schools.

Description: Tennessee Technological University (1915) originally opened its doors to students at the high school and junior-college levels. By 1929 the first class of 4-year graduates received BS degrees. In 1949 the administrative structure was expanded into 5 schools consisting of Arts/Sciences, Agriculture/Home Economics, Business Administration, Education, and Engineering. The Specialist in Education was authorized in 1970, the Doctor of Philosophy in 1971, the MBA in 1976, and the BS in Nursing and Bachelor of Fine Arts in 1980. The BS in Technical Communication and the Bachelor of Music were added in 1986 and 1994, respectively. The first distance learning courses were offered through telecourse delivery in 1980. Interactive TV became available in 1992, and Web courses were added to distance learning delivery in 1998.

Tennessee Temple University

1815 Union Avenue   Phone: (423) 493-4288
Chattanooga, TN 37404   Fax: (423) 493-4497

Division(s): School of External Studies
Web Site(s): http://www.tntemple.edu
E-mail: delmottd@tntemple.edu

Undergraduate Degree Programs:
Associate of Arts in Biblical Studies
Bachelor of Science in Biblical Studies

Teaching Methods: *TV:* videotape. *Other:* audiotapes, correspondence.

Credits Granted for: examination (CLEP, ACT-PEP, DANTES, GRE).

Admission Requirements: *Undergraduate:* high school diploma, written testimony of faith in Christ.

On-Campus Requirements: 3 hours of speech, residentially (here or transfer); 2 hours of church ministries.

Tuition and Fees: *Undergraduate:* $75/credit. *Application Fee:* $25. *Other Costs:* $100/course for materials and enrollment fee. *Credit by:* semester.

Financial Aid: Not available right now to distance education students.

Accreditation: American Association of Bible Colleges.

Description: Tennessee Temple University (1946) began as the higher education ministry of Highland Park Baptist Church. The school has alumni worldwide as missionaries, preachers, school teachers, and business and professional people. Included are an academy, Bible school (2-year), university, and seminary.

Terra State Community College

2830 Napoleon Road   Phone: (419) 334-8400
Fremont, OH 43420   Fax: (419) 334-9035

Division(s): Educational Catalyst Center
Web Site(s): http://www.terra.cc.oh.us/
E-mail: teishen@terra.cc.oh.us
cmichael@terra.cc.oh.us
(online registration form provided on Web site)

Class Titles: AutoCAD, CAD Designer, College Composition, Economics, Technical/Business Writing, Humanities, Small Business Management, Principles of Buying.

Teaching Methods: *Computers:* Internet, Web-based assignments, Web-board with chat rooms and virtual office hours, e-mail. *TV:* videotapes. *Other:* audiotapes, fax, phone, correspondence.

Admission Requirements: *Undergraduate:* high school transcript or GED certificate. Applicants with previous college

work should also submit official college transcripts to Terra's Records Office. Students currently in the senior year of high school, age 16 or older, are eligible to earn college credit by taking day or evening courses, with written approval from their high school counselor or principal. International students are welcomed at Terra. Because the entrance requirements are based on state and federal regulations that sometimes change, international students seeking admission to Terra Community College should contact the Admissions Office for the latest information. Prerequisites: check the online college catalog for course prerequisites. Restrictions: the distance learning courses are completed during the quarter.

On-Campus Requirements: each instructor has set up the distance education courses differently. Some courses require that exams be taken on campus.

Tuition and Fees: *Undergraduate:* Terra's online catalog (http://www.terra.cc.oh.us/catalog.html) provides a section on fees which includes a table for tuition fees for a state resident and non-Ohio residents. *Other Costs:* $25 security deposit for videos and audios that are checked out to the student. *Credit by:* quarter.

Financial Aid: Federal Stafford Loan, Federal Perkins Loan, Federal PLUS Loan, Federal Pell Grant, Federal Work-Study, VA, Ohio resident programs.

Accreditation: North Central Association of Colleges and Schools.

Description: The mission of Terra College (1968) is to provide the opportunity for quality learning experiences. To support this mission, Terra, formerly a technical college for 26 years, became a state community college in 1994. Terra was then able to grant the Associate of Arts and Associate of Science degrees, as well as the Associate Degree in Applied Business and the Associate Degree in Applied Science. The college is accredited by the North Central Association of Colleges and Schools and holds memberships in many professional and service associations. To meet the students' educational needs, Terra began offering video-based distance learning courses 2 years ago. Just as the college continues to increase its offerings of distance learning courses, the modalities on which the courses are delivered are also expanding. Terra currently offers courses that incorporate audiocassettes and/or videotapes, text and Web-based assignments, and others that are conducted entirely online via the Internet.

Texas A&M University, Commerce

PO Box 3011   Phone: (903) 886-5511
Commerce, TX 75429   Fax: (903) 886-5991

Division(s): Instructional Technology
Web Site(s): http://www.tamu-commerce.edu/ntep/
E-mail: Candy_Mathews@tamu-commerce.edu

Class Titles: Accounting, Biology, Chemistry, Computer Science, Counseling, Early Childhood Education, Economics, Educational Administration, Educational Technology, Elementary Education, English, Finance, Business, Health Education, Health/Physical Education, History, Journalism, Management, Marketing, Math, Physics, Psychology, Reading, Recreation, Secondary/Higher Education, Sociology, Special Education, Technology.

Teaching Methods: *Computers:* Internet, real-time chat, electronic classroom, e-mail, CD-ROM, newsgroup, LIST-SERV. *Other:* videoconferencing, audioconferencing, audiographics, audiotapes, fax, correspondence, independent study, individual study, learning contracts.

Credits Granted for: examination (CLEP), ACT/SAT subject assessments, Advanced Placement passing scores.

Admission Requirements: *Undergraduate:* application, ACT or SAT scores, transcripts. *Graduate:* application, transcripts, GRE or other. *Doctoral:* application, transcripts, GRE or other. *Certificate:* application, transcripts.

On-Campus Requirements: some for most degree programs.

Tuition and Fees: *Undergraduate:* $293/3 credits Texas resident, $1,023/12 credits resident, $920/3 credits nonresident, $3,579/12 credits nonresident. *Graduate:* $359/3 credits resident, $1,287/12 credits resident, $985/3 credits nonresident, $3,843/12 credits nonresident. *Doctoral:* same as graduate. *Software:* variable. *Credit by:* semester.

Financial Aid: Federal Stafford Loan, Federal Perkins Loan, Federal PLUS Loan, Federal Pell Grant, Federal Work-Study, VA, Texas resident programs.

Accreditation: Southern Association of Colleges and Schools.

Description: Texas A&M University, Commerce (1889) became part of the Texas A&M System in 1996. The first distance learning video classes were offered in 1993 using a compressed video system connecting 3 sites. There are now 12 sites and classrooms on the system, 2 connections with the Texas A&M System's Trans-Texas Video Network, and an ISDN connection. In 1995 a full-motion fiber optic system became operational, linking the university with 11 rural schools in northeast Texas. The university typically offers 35–40 courses each semester via 2-way, interactive video. In 1998, Web-based courses were initiated, with 11 offered during the fall. The university is also exploring the feasibility of offering a doctoral degree program in the Department of Psychology and Special Education focusing on cognitive learning and the use of technology to improve student learning.

Texas Tech University

15th Street and Akron Avenue	Phone: (800) 692-6877 (A)
Box 42191	(806) 742-2352 (A)
Lubbock, TX 79409-2191	(806) 742-2501 (B)
MS 3091	(806) 742-3451 (C)
Lubbock, TX 79409-3091 (B)	Fax: (806) 742-2318 (A)
MS 3103	Fax: (806) 742-0989 (B)
Lubbock, TX 79409-3101 (C)	Fax: (806) 742-3493 (C)

Division(s): Outreach and Extended Studies (A)
Department of English (B)
College of Engineering (C)
Web Site(s): http://www.dce.ttu.edu (A)
http://english.ttu.edu/tc/dl (B)
http://aln.coe.ttu.edu/ (C)
E-mail: distlearn@ttu.edu (A)
Rude@ttu.edu (B)
BGuinn@coe.ttu.edu (C)

Undergraduate Degree Programs:
Bachelor of General Studies
Bachelor of Business Administration

Graduate Degree Programs:
Master of Arts in Technical Communication
Master of Engineering

Certificate Programs: C/C++ Programming, Java, PowerBuilder 6.0, UNIX System Administration Training, End-User Certification for Microsoft Office Products and Windows '95 or '98, Comprehensive End-User Overview of Lotus Notes Release 4, High-Level Overview of Establishing and Maintaining Web Sites, Web End-User/Publisher, Microsoft Certified Systems Engineer, Microsoft Certified Solution Developer, Novell Certified NetWare Engineer.

Class Titles: Elementary Accounting, Agricultural Economics, Agricultural Science, Agronomy, Anthropology, Business Law, Counselor Education, Economics, Educational/Instructional Technology, Educational Psychology/Leadership, Thermodynamics, English, Family Studies, Finance, Food/Nutrition, Geography, History, Human Development, Information Systems/Quantitative Sciences, Spanish, Management, Marketing, Mass Communications, Analytical Geometry, Calculus, Algebra, Statistical Methods, Mathematical Analysis, Music, Philosophy, Political Science, Psychology, Restaurant/Hotel/Institutional Management, Technical Writing. Master of Engineering Program offers 85 graduate-level courses in the following engineering disciplines: Civil Engineering, Chemical Engineering, Computer Science, Electrical Engineering, General Engineering, Industrial Engineering, Mechanical Engineering, Petroleum Engineering.

Teaching Methods: *Computers:* Internet, e-mail. *TV:* videotape. *Other:* correspondence, independent study, individual study, audiotape.

Admission Requirements: *Graduate:* bachelor's degree (Technical Communication Program); bachelor's degree in engineering or equivalent (Engineering Program), GRE and

GPA scores specified by the department and Graduate School.

On-Campus Requirements: None.

Tuition and Fees: *Undergraduate:* $53/semester hour. *Graduate:* $554/3-hour course in state, $1,178/3-hour course out of state (Technical Communication Program); $895/3-hour course in state, $1,525/3-hour course out of state (Engineering Program). *Other Costs:* $20/course administrative fee, $50 for admission in external degree program. *Credit by:* semester.

Accreditation: Southern Association of Colleges and Schools.

Description: Texas Tech University (1923) began offering graduate instruction through extension and correspondence in 1927 to serve the rural population of western Texas. Today, TTU is classified as a major research university with a resident student population of 25,000 and a distance learning population of 70,000. The Division of Extended Learning grew from extension and correspondence programs for college credit to its current offerings of high school, middle school, and elementary credit courses; college credit courses; college credit courses offered in extension; personal, professional, and enrichment courses; external degrees; and certificate programs.

Texas Wesleyan University

1201 Wesleyan	Phone: (800) 254-9656
Fort Worth, TX 76105	Fax: (310) 394-6017

Division(s): School of Education
Web Site(s): None.
E-mail: janl@canterweb.com

Graduate Degree Programs:
Master of Education (Distance Learning Degree Program)

Class Titles: High-Performing Teacher, Succeeding With Difficult Students, Psychological Dimensions in Education—Motivating Today's Learner, Models of Effective Teaching, Including Students with Special Needs in Classroom, Technology/Learning in Today's Classroom.

Teaching Methods: *Other:* The course content is presented through multiple learning modalities. Using videotaped presentations of nationally known educational experts and computer technology, we have designed a program that offers high quality graduate education in the convenience of your own home or school. Collegial study teams (overseen by a faculty mentor) coupled with individual work assignments, provides the student with the teamwork skills and personal experience necessary for a successful teaching career. Faculty are available to you via a toll-free number, e-mail, and TENET to provide support, assistance, and encouragement.

Admission Requirements: *Graduate:* accredited bachelor's,

3.0 college GPA in last 60 hours (if below 3.0, need 900 on GRE), one year experience as Teacher of Record.

On-Campus Requirements: None.

Tuition and Fees: *Graduate:* $275/credit. *Application Fee:* $40 (nonrefundable). *Other Costs:* materials $70/course, general university fee $25/hour, transcript fee $5/semester, teacher tuition scholarship of $60/semester hour are available. *Credit by:* semester.

Financial Aid: Teacher Tuition Scholarship, Federal Loans (817) 531-4458, Veteran's Assistance (817) 531-4420.

Accreditation: Southern Association of Colleges and Schools.

Description: Texas Wesleyan University (1890) is located on 4 acres, only 4 miles southeast of downtown Fort Worth.

Texas Woman's University

PO Box 425649	Phone: (940) 898-3415
Denton, TX 76204-5649	Fax: (940) 898-3412

Division(s): Graduate School
Web Site(s): http://www.dl.twu.edu
E-mail: dl@twu.edu

Graduate Degree Programs:
Master of Library Science
Master of Science in Speech-Language Pathology

Certificate Programs: Learning Resources Endorsement

Class Titles: In addition to degree programs, TWU offers via distance technologies upper division undergraduate and graduate-level courses in Family Sciences, Health Studies, Nursing, Occupational Therapy, Physical Therapy, Psychology, Women's Studies.

Teaching Methods: *Computers:* Internet, real-time chat, electronic classroom, e-mail, newsgroup, LISTSERV. *TV:* videotape. *Other:* audioconferencing, videoconferencing, fax, correspondence, independent study, individual study.

Admission Requirements: *Undergraduate:* accredited high school graduate or equivalent, SAT (910 combined) or ACT (19), 2.0 GPA, 22 credits of the new, recommended Texas High School Graduation Program. First-time freshman admitted if graduated in top 25% from regionally accredited, Texas high school within last 2 years. NOTE: Students entering Texas public institutions of higher learning or educator preparation programs must pass Texas Academic Skills Program test for reading, math, and writing, with remediation required for deficiencies. *Graduate:* accredited bachelor's degree, GRE (scores vary by department), B average on graduate and final 60 undergraduate hours, official college transcripts.

On-Campus Requirements: None.

Tuition and Fees: *Undergraduate:* $36/credit with a minimum of $120 plus fees. Fees vary according to arrangements made. Contact school for details. *Graduate:* $56/credit with a minimum of $120 plus fees. Fees vary according to arrangements made. Contact school for details. *Credit by:* semester.

Financial Aid: Federal Stafford Loan, Federal Perkins Loan, Federal PLUS Loan, Federal Pell Grant, VA, Texas resident programs.

Accreditation: Southern Association of Colleges and Schools.

Description: Texas Woman's University (1901) is a comprehensive public institution located just 35 miles north of the Dallas-Fort Worth metroplex. TWU has centers in Dallas and Houston offering upper-level undergraduate and graduate-level studies in allied health fields. The university will proudly celebrate its centennial in 2001. Of TWU's 9,400 students, 4,200 are in graduate programs. Although TWU is primarily for women, qualified applicants may enroll in all programs of the General Divisions, Institute of Health Sciences, and the Graduate School. Nearly 100 major fields can lead to bachelor's, master's, and doctoral degrees. As an urban university with a mission that is statewide and beyond, TWU recognizes that distance education plays a significant role in serving its varied, often place-bound constituencies. The university began distance programs in 1994, and offerings throughout Texas and the region continue to expand.

Thomas College

180 West River Road	Phone: (207) 877-0102
Waterville, ME 04901	Fax: (207) 877-0114

Division(s): Continuing Education
Web Site(s): http://www.thomas.edu
E-mail: CED@Thomas.edu

Graduate Degree Programs:
Master of Science in Computer Technology Education

Teaching Methods: *Computers:* Internet, real-time chat, electronic classroom, e-mail, CD-ROM, newsgroup, LIST-SERV. *Other:* None.

Admission Requirements: *Graduate:* Contact school.

On-Campus Requirements: None.

Tuition and Fees: *Graduate:* $510/class. *Software:* $100/year. *Credit by:* trimester.

Financial Aid: Federal Stafford Loan, Federal Perkins Loan, Federal PLUS Loan, Federal Pell Grant, Federal Work-Study, VA, Maine resident programs.

Accreditation: New England Association of Schools and Colleges.

Description: Thomas College (1893) gives students a remarkably well-balanced blend of those skills that will be required in society and in the business world of the 21st century, combined with something far more important: the ability to learn new skills and acquire new knowledge. Thomas' graduates are lifelong learners and are thus well-prepared for a future shaped by people who take this approach to work and to life.

Thomas Edison State College

101 West State Street	Phone: (609) 984-1150
Trenton, NJ 08608-1176	Fax: (609) 984-8447

Division(s): Office of Admissions
Web Site(s): http://www.tesc.edu
E-mail: admissions@call.tesc.edu

Undergraduate Degree Programs:
Associate of Arts
Associate of Applied Science in Radiologic Technology
Associate of Management
Associate of Science in:
    Natural Sciences and Mathematics
    Public and Social Science
    Applied Science and Technology
Bachelor of Arts
Bachelor of Science in:
    Business Administration
    Applied Science and Technology
    Human Services
    Nursing

Graduate Degree Programs:
Master of Science in Management

Certificate Programs: Accounting, Administrative Office Management, Computer Aided Design, Computer Science, Data Processing, Electronics, Finance, Labor Studies, Marketing, Human Resources Management, Operations Management, Public Administration.

Class Titles: refer to catalog and/or registration bulletin.

Teaching Methods: *Computers:* Internet, e-mail. *TV:* videotape. *Other:* independent study, individual study, learning contracts.

Credits Granted for: experiential learning, portfolio assessment, extrainstitutional learning (ACE College Credit Recommendation Service, corporate or professional association seminars/workshops), examination (CLEP, ACT-PEP, DANTES, TECEP), transfer credits.

Admission Requirements: *Undergraduate:* student must live or work in New Jersey for BS in Nursing. *Graduate:* bachelor's degree in any disciple and/or 3–5 years of managerial/supervisory experience. No GRE or GMAT required.

On-Campus Requirements: None.

Tuition and Fees: *Undergraduate:* There are 2 different ways that adults may pay for their undergraduate education at Thomas Edison. Under the first plan, adult students may take unlimited Thomas Edison tests, portfolios, and courses to apply toward their undergraduate degree for $2,200/year in-state (and military) or $3,150/year out-of-state, full- or part-time. Under the second plan, students who prefer to pay for ways of learning as they use them may choose instead to pay enrollment and technology services fees each year and then pay for methods of earning credit (e.g., tests) individually. Undergraduate annual fees in this second plan total $605 in-state (and military), $1,040 out-of-state and $1,400 for international students (based on FY99 tuition and fee structure). In addition, students using this second plan pay for tests, portfolio, courses, and other ways of learning as they use them (e.g., $66/credit for guided study courses, $42 for portfolio assessment, etc.). *Graduate:* $289/credit. *Application Fee:* $75. *Other Costs:* vary; refer to catalog or prospectus. *Credit by:* semester for DIAL courses.

Financial Aid: VA, New Jersey resident programs.

Accreditation: Middle States Association of Colleges and Schools.

Description: Thomas Edison State College (1972) is a worldwide community of adult learners. Cited as "one of the brighter stars of higher learning" by *The New York Times* and named one of the nation's Top 20 Cyber-Universities by *Forbes Magazine,* Thomas Edison provides adults from every state and 86 other countries with unparalleled flexibility and many ways to complete a quality degree. Originally founded to provide distance education exclusively to adults, this world-renowned institution offers 12 associate, bachelor's, and master's degrees in more than 100 areas. The college's convenient programs enable adult learners to pursue their educational goals while attending to the challenges and priorities of adult life. Thomas Edison State College offers a distinguished academic program for the self-motivated adult learner.

Thunderbird
The American Graduate School
of International Management

15249 North 59th Avenue	**Phone: (602) 978-7210**
Glendale, AZ 85306	**Fax: (602) 439-5432**

Division(s): Thunderbird Admissions Office
Web Site(s): http://www.t-bird.edu
http://www.ruv.itesm.mx/programs/maestrial/mimla
E-mail: t-bird@t-bird.edu

Graduate Degree Programs:
Master of International Management for Latin America

Teaching Methods: *Computers:* Internet, electronic classroom, computer conferencing e-mail, CD-ROM. *TV:* interactive TV, videotape, cable program, satellite broadcasting. *Other:* audioconferencing, videoconferencing, audiotapes, fax, correspondence, independent study, individual study.

Credits Granted for: examination (CLEP, ACT-PEP, DANTES).

Admission Requirements: *Graduate:* prerequisites, bachelor's degree, GMAT, TOEFL, 2 letters of recommendation, resume, copy of birth certificate.

On-Campus Requirements: A 2-day orientation and a one-week seminar at Thunderbird in Glendale, AZ; a one-week seminar at the end on the ITESM campus in Monterrey, Mexico.

Tuition and Fees: *Graduate:* $20,000/year. *Application Fee:* $50. *Other Costs:* $70 testing fee at ITESM. *Credit by:* semester.

Financial Aid: private loans and scholarships available for MIMLA.

Accreditation: Satisfies standards specified by the American Assembly of Collegiate Schools of Business for a master's degree in business. ITESM is in the process of applying.

Description: Thunderbird, The American Graduate School of International Management (1946), is a private, nonprofit, graduate school for men and women who want to be leaders in the global arenas of business, government, or not-for-profit. Thunderbird's outstanding reputation has stood the test of time for 50 years in the world's most important organizations. The degree is offered through a strategic alliance with the Instituto Tecnologico y de Estudios Superiores de Monterrey (ITESM) in Mexico. ITESM has been involved in education and research since its founding 50 years ago when Eugenio Garza Sada led a group of Mexican businessmen in creating a school to provide the country with professionals educated at the highest academic levels. Thunderbird and ITESM each bring certain strengths to the MIMLA program. *U.S. News and World Report* has ranked Thunderbird the top program in international business for 3 consecutive years. ITESM has acquired considerable expertise in distance learning education and has a virtual university infrastructure at its disposal. Initially, the MIMLA program will be offered at the ITESM campuses in Mexico. Recognizing that ITESM's satellite signal footprint covers all of Latin America, other countries are expected to be added to the network in the future to include Argentina, Chile, Colombia, Peru, Puerto Rico, and Venezuela. The combination of satellite broadcasts and local classes, offered in a 20-course, lock-step format, provides for a virtual campus environment that encourages students to interact with others in different locales, and with their faculty on a regular basis.

Tidewater Community College

121 College Place	**Phone: (757) 822-1065**
Norfolk, VA 23510	**Fax: (757) 822-1060**

Division(s): Dean, Instruction and Student Services
Web Site(s): http://www.tc.cc.va.us/
E-mail: tcswags@tc.cc.va.us

Class Titles: Astronomy, Meteorology, Psychology, English Composition, Mythology in Literature/Arts, Technology/Liberal Arts.

Teaching Methods: *Computers:* Internet, real-time chat, electronic classroom, e-mail, CD-ROM, newsgroup, LISTSERV. *TV:* videotape, cable program, PBS. *Other:* Compressed video within the state of Virginia.

Credits Granted for: experiential learning, portfolio assessment, examination (CLEP, ACT-PEP, DANTES, GRE).

Admission Requirements: *Undergraduate:* open admission. Must be age 18 or show ability to benefit.

On-Campus Requirements: Online computer-based courses are via computer, compressed video courses meet in a classroom at one of Virginia's 23 community colleges, and telecourses meet on campus at least twice/semester.

Tuition and Fees: *Undergraduate:* $55/credit. *Credit by:* semester.

Financial Aid: Federal Stafford Loan, Federal PLUS Loan, Federal Pell Grant, Federal Work-Study, VA, Virginia resident programs.

Accreditation: Southern Association of Colleges and Schools.

Description: Tidewater Community College (1968) is a comprehensive community college that offers both transfer and occupational/technical programs and courses. The college offers distance education courses through three formats: (1) telecourses, (2) compressed video within Virginia, and (3) online, computer-based courses.

Towson University

8000 York Road	Phone: (410) 830-3467
Towson, MD 21252	Fax: (410) 830-2032

Division(s): Extended Learning
Web Site(s): http://www.towson.edu
E-mail: gwilliams@towson.edu

Class Titles: contact school.

Teaching Methods: *Computers:* Internet, e-mail. *TV:* videotape. *Other:* videoconferencing, fax, independent study, individual study.

Credits Granted for: experiential learning, extrainstitutional learning, examination (CLEP, ACT-PEP, DANTES, GRE).

Admission Requirements: *Undergraduate:* contact school.

On-Campus Requirements: None.

Tuition and Fees: *Undergraduate:* $139/credit in-state, $322/credit out-of-state. *Graduate:* $187/credit in-state, $364/credit out-of-state. *Other Costs:* $39/credit university fee. *Credit by:* semester.

Financial Aid: Federal Stafford Loan, Federal Perkins Loan, Federal PLUS Loan, Federal Pell Grant, Federal Work-Study, VA.

Accreditation: Middle States Association of Colleges and Schools.

Description: The institution known today as Towson University (1866) has undergone a number of changes in name and status. The university's 320-acre campus, home of the institution since 1915, boasts an impressive blend of traditional and modern architecture. With the original mission of preparing teachers for Maryland's public school system, Towson's new status recognizes its development and growth into a metropolitan university. Contrasting with its first class of 11 students, the university today enrolls 10,000 full-time and 2,800 part-time undergraduates, plus 2,000 graduate students. Thirty academic departments offer 40 majors and 60 concentrations leading to bachelor's degrees. The departments are grouped into 6 subdivisions: the colleges of Liberal Arts, Natural and Mathematical Sciences, Fine Arts and Communication, Education, Health Professions, and Business and Economics. In addition, the Graduate School offers 26 master's degree programs.

Trinidad State Junior College

600 Prospect Street	Phone: (800) 621-8752
Trinidad, CO 81082-2396	Fax: (719) 846-5667

Division(s): Instruction
Web Site(s): http://www.tsjc.cccoes.edu
E-mail: Frank.Armijo@tsjc.cccoes.edu

Undergraduate Degree Programs:
Associate of Applied Science in Business
Associate of Applied Science in Occupational Safety and Health

Certificate Programs: Business.

Class Titles: Sociology, Anthropology, English, Spanish.

Teaching Methods: *Computers:* Internet, real-time chat, electronic classroom, e-mail, CD-ROM, LISTSERV. *TV:* videotape. *Other:* videoconferencing, audioconferencing, fax, correspondence, independent study.

Credits Granted for: experiential learning, portfolio assessment, examination (CLEP, ACT-PEP, DANTES, GRE).

On-Campus Requirements: None.

Tuition and Fees: *Undergraduate:* Colorado $54, nonresidents $189, WICHE $81. *Other Costs:* registration fee $9/semester, campus fee $1/credit, student union/student activity $1/credit, band $5/credit up to 15 credits. *Credit by:* semester.

Financial Aid: Federal Stafford Loan, Federal Perkins Loan, Federal PLUS Loan, Federal Pell Grand, Federal Work-Study, VA, Colorado resident programs.

Accreditation: North Central Association of Colleges and Schools.

Description: Trinidad State Junior College (1925), the oldest public 2-year college in Colorado, can look back on almost 75 years of service to the community of Trinidad and its surrounding area. In its first years, the school offered regular first-year college courses leading to the Arts and Science degree, and several teacher training courses. In the fall of 1932, course offerings were increased to encompass 2 years of college-level study. Today the college continues to offer traditional, quality programs of study in academic/transfer and vocational/technical areas, as well as providing opportunities for part-time day and evening students. TSJC's distance learning technology, which includes OPTEL, PictureTel, and the Internet, has recently sent nursing and occupational safety technology classes to students in Colorado and beyond.

Trinity International University

| 2065 Half Day Road | Phone: (800) 417-9999 |
| Deerfield, IL 60015 | Fax: (847) 317-6509 |

Division(s): Extension and Affiliated Education Division of Open Studies
Web Site(s): http://www.tiu.edu
E-mail: extension@tiu.edu

Graduate Degree Programs:
Master of Arts in Religion
Master of Arts in Religion/Urban Ministries

Certificate Programs: Biblical Studies

Class Titles: Old Testament, New Testament, Theology, Church History, Missions, Christian Education, Pastoral Ministry.

Teaching Methods: *TV:* videotape. *Other:* audiotapes, print media, independent study, on-site lectures.

Admission Requirements: *Graduate:* bachelor's degree, GPA 2.5. *Certificate:* bachelor's degree, mature learners: 60 semester hours of undergraduate credit.

On-Campus Requirements: Master of Arts in Religion: 4 semester hours of on-campus residency.

Tuition and Fees: *Graduate:* $225/credit. *Application Fee:* $25. *Credit by:* semester.

Accreditation: North Central Association of Colleges and Schools, The Association of Theological Schools in the U.S. and Canada.

Description: Trinity International University (1897) consists of Trinity Evangelical Divinity School, Trinity College of Arts and Sciences, Trinity Graduate School, and Trinity Law School. Through Trinity's Division of Open Studies, Trinity provides educational services that are accessible to learners whose life situations are characterized by being rooted in communities other than Deerfield, Illinois. Trinity has extension sites around the U.S., affiliated programs with parachurch organizations, occasional courses in various places and times, and independent study courses. Trinity International University is affiliated with the Evangelical Free Church of America.

Triton College

| 2000 5th Avenue | Phone: (708) 456-0300 |
| River Grove, IL 60171 | Fax: (708) 583-3121 |

Division(s): Arts and Sciences
Web Site(s): http://www.triton.cc.il.us
E-mail: cthayer-@triton.cc.il.us

Class Titles: Anthropology, Business, Economics, Electronics, English, Fine Arts, Health, History, Mathematics, Music, Political Science, Psychology, Real Estate, Sociology, Statistics.

Teaching Methods: *Computers:* Internet, e-mail. *TV:* videotape, cable program, microwave. *Other:* interactive TV.

Credits Granted for: experiential learning, portfolio assessment, examination (CLEP, ACT-PEP, DANTES, GRE).

Admission Requirements: *Undergraduate:* high school graduate or GED. *Certificate:* high school graduate or GED.

On-Campus Requirements: None.

Tuition and Fees: *Undergraduate:* $43/credit in-district. *Other Costs:* $4/credit Student Fees ($42 max), $5 part-time or $10 full-time Registration Fee. *Credit by:* semester.

Financial Aid: Federal Stafford Loan, Federal Perkins Loan, Federal PLUS Loan, Federal Pell Grant, Federal Work-Study, VA, Illinois resident programs.

Accreditation: North Central Association of Colleges and Schools.

Description: Triton College (1964) is a comprehensive community college that serves the near-western suburbs of Chicago. Triton is recognized for its attractive 100-acre campus, its diverse and innovative programs, and its quality faculty. Currently, the college enrolls more than 18,000 students each semester and offers more than 150 degree and certificate programs. Triton began offering Distance Education courses in 1979 through videotape classes. Currently, the college enrolls 700 students in 60 videotape classes each semester. In addition, Triton now offers a small but growing number of courses via Internet. The college is a member of northern Illinois' West Suburban Postsecondary Consortium, a partnership of more than 20 institutions of higher education that share courses via 2-way, interactive TV.

Troy State University

| 81 Beal Parkway, Suite 2A | Phone: (850) 301-2150 |
| Fort Walton Beach, FL 32548 | Fax: (850) 301-2179 |

Division(s): University College-Florida Region
Web Site(s): http://www.tsufl.edu
E-mail: distlearn@tsufl.edu

Undergraduate Degree Programs:
Associate of Science in General Education
Associate of Science in Business Administration

Bachelor of Applied Science in Resource Management
Bachelor of Science in Management

Graduate Degree Programs:
Master of Science in International Relations
Master of Public Administration

Class Titles: Principles of Accounting, Cultural Anthropology, Criminal Justice, Principles of Macroeconomics, English Composition, Western Civilization, U.S. Diplomatic History, French Revolution/Napoleonic Period, Contemporary Europe, Legal Environment, Principles of Management/Organization Behavior, Principles of Marketing, College Algebra, Math for General Studies, Music in Individual Development, American National Government, Contemporary American Foreign Policy, American Political Processes, Survey of International Relations, Business Statistics, Sociology for General Studies, Race/Ethnic Relations, Family Relations, Social Foundations of American Education, Contemporary Europe, Survey of Business Concepts, Survey of Public Administration, Organizational Behavior, Latin America in World Affairs.

Teaching Methods: *Computers:* Internet, e-mail, discussion groups, LISTSERV. *TV:* videotape. *Other:* audiotape.

Credits Granted for: examination (CLEP, DANTES).

Admission Requirements: *Undergraduate:* admission form. *Graduate:* admission form.

On-Campus Requirements: None.

Tuition and Fees: *Undergraduate:* $100/quarter hour. *Graduate:* $150/quarter hour. *Application Fee:* $30 undergraduates and graduates. *Credit by:* quarter.

Financial Aid: VA.

Accreditation: Southern Association of Colleges and Schools.

Description: Troy State University (1887) has developed a rigorous academic review of its courses and faculty in its 100-year history. Student requirements in the distance learning courses are subjected to similar standards. TSU faculty are responsible for presenting their courses to facilitate the best possible learning experience for each student.

Troy State University, Montgomery

PO Drawer 4419
Montgomery, AL 36103-4419

Phone: (800) 355-8786
(334) 241-9553
Fax: (334) 240-7320

Division(s): Distance Learning and Extended Academic Services
Web Site(s): http://www.tsum.edu/DL
E-mail: jmacey@tsum.edu

Undergraduate Degree Programs:
Associate of Science in General Education with concentrations in:

Business Administration
Child Care
History
Political Science
Psychology
Social Science
Bachelor of Science in Professional Studies
Bachelor of Arts in Professional Studies
Bachelor's degrees are offered with academic concentrations in:

Resource Management (Business)
English
History
Political Science
Psychology
Social Science

Class Titles: over 90 courses offered; visit Web site at http://www.tsum.edu/DL/learningcontracts/index.htm.

Teaching Methods: *Computers:* Internet, electronic classroom, e-mail, LISTSERV. *TV:* videotape, cable program, satellite broadcasting, PBS. *Other:* audioconferencing, videoconferencing, audiotapes, fax, correspondence, independent study, individual study, learning contracts.

Credits Granted for: experiential learning, portfolio assessment, extrainstitutional learning, examination (CLEP, ACT-PEP, DANTES, GRE).

Admission Requirements: *Undergraduate:* high school graduate.

On-Campus Requirements: students who reside within the state of Alabama are required to attend an on-campus orientation at the outset of their program. The orientation is conducted the last Monday morning of each month. Further, all students pursuing a bachelor's degree are required to defend their senior project at the end of their program. Generally, this defense is conducted on campus; however, in those instances where this is impractical, e.g., physical disability, incarceration, single parent with minor children, etc., arrangements can be made to conduct the defense via teleconferencing/videotaping.

Tuition and Fees: *Undergraduate:* $57/credit in-state, $80/credit out-of-state. Most courses are 5 (quarter) credit hours. *Application Fee:* $65 ($50 for students previously enrolled in one of the Troy State University System institutions). *Other Costs:* $10 administrative fee/each enrollment in a learning contract course; $50–$75/course for materials. *Credit by:* quarter; scheduled to convert to semester in 2000.

Financial Aid: VA, Alabama resident programs.

Accreditation: Southern Association of Colleges and Schools.

Description: Troy State University, Montgomery (1887), a public, coeducational institution, is dedicated to providing excellence in traditional and nontraditional educational opportunities for mature students of all races and ethnic backgrounds. The university's uniqueness centers on its status as Alabama's only university devoted exclusively to the education of mature students. The typical student is a working adult with family and community responsibilities. The integration of military personnel into its regular programs is evidence of the university's strong commitment to meeting the needs of military as well as civilian learners.

Truckee Meadows Community College

7000 Dandini Boulevard	Phone: (702) 673-7148
Reno, NV 89512-3999	Fax: (702) 673-7242

Division(s): Distance Education
Web Site(s): http://www.tmcc.edu
E-mail: lokken_fred@tmcc.edu

Class Titles: Anthropology, Art, Criminal Justice, Political Science, Psychology, Economics, Math, Hotel/Restaurant Management.

Teaching Methods: *Computers:* Internet, e-mail. *TV:* videotape, cable program, PBS. *Other:* videoconferencing, fax, independent study, individual study.

Credits Granted for: experiential learning, portfolio assessment, examination (CLEP, DANTES), extrainstitutional learning.

Admission Requirements: *Undergraduate:* open-door policy, age 18, high school graduate or equivalent, U.S. citizens or immigrants. High school students, international students, and nonimmigrants may also be eligible. Admission to Health Science Programs: The health science programs include Dental Assisting, Nursing, Paramedic and Radiologic Technology. Admission to any of these programs is limited and requires special procedures. To be admitted into English classes or Math 096 or higher, students must have taken the course prerequisites within the last 3 years with a minimum grade of C, or have qualifying scores on the CPT. The ACT or SAT scores will also be accepted. TMCC will accept credit from a variety of training and educational programs toward an associate degree and/or certificate of achievement. The maximum number of credits allowed for transfer from all sources is 45 credits per degree. The maximum number of credits possible in each category is: (1) advanced standing from other colleges and universities: 45 credits total, (2) advanced standing from credit by examination: 30 credits, (3) advanced standing from nontraditional sources: 15 credits. for more information, contact: TMCC Admissions and Records at (702) 673-7042 or visit our Web site: http://www.tmcc.edu

On-Campus Requirements: None.

Tuition and Fees: *Undergraduate:* $40/credit Nevada residents, $60/credit if student lives in neighboring county in California; $60/credit for less than 7 credits plus $1,919/semester out-of-state, $40/credit for 7 or more credits plus

$1,919/semester out-of-state. *Application Fee:* $5. *Software:* varies. *Credit by:* semester.

Financial Aid: Federal Stafford Loan, Federal Perkins Loan, Federal PLUS Loan, Federal Pell Grant, Federal Work-Study, VA, Nevada resident programs.

Accreditation: Northwest Association of Schools and Colleges.

Description: Truckee Meadows Community College (1971), an institution of the University and Community College System of Nevada, is located in Reno, Nevada. TMCC recently celebrated its 25th anniversary and has experienced strong growth in enrollments and program offerings. Currently, 11,000 students are served, with the campus offering classes and degrees in 40 career fields as well as a full university transfer associate degree program. TMCC's Distance Education program is in its third year and offers credit instruction in several formats including: Interactive TV, Cablecast courses, Going the Distance with PBS/Channel 5 and Internet instruction.

Tulsa Community College

909 South Boston Avenue	Phone: (918) 595-7143
Tulsa, OK 74119	Fax: (918) 595-7306

Division(s): Office of Distance Learning
Web Site(s): http://www.tulsa.cc.ok.us/dl
E-mail: rdomingu@tulsa.cc.ok.us

Undergraduate Degree Programs:
Associate in Liberal Arts

Certificate Programs: various.

Teaching Methods: *Computers:* Internet, e-mail, CD-ROM, LISTSERV. *TV:* videotape, cable program, PBS. *Other:* videoconferencing.

Credits Granted for: examination (CLEP, APP, PEP).

Admission Requirements: *Undergraduate:* Demonstrated proficiency in English, math, and science. ACT scores, CPT scores, and college transcripts can be used to demonstrate proficiency. *Certificate:* Demonstrated proficiency in English, math, and science.

On-Campus Requirements: None.

Tuition and Fees: *Undergraduate:* $42/credit in-state. *Application Fee:* $15. *Other Costs:* Lab fees vary. *Credit by:* semester.

Financial Aid: Available for persons who qualify, through grants, scholarships, loans and part-time employment, from federal, state, institutional, and private sources.

Accreditation: North Central Association of Colleges and Schools, Oklahoma State Regents for Higher Education.

Description: Tulsa Junior College (1970) became Tulsa

Community College in May, 1996. Although TCC has only served Tulsa and the surrounding communities since 1970, the college has established a tradition of offering students a personal approach to a practical and useful higher education. When the college first opened its doors, initial enrollment was 2,800 students. Since that time, TCC has provided quality educational services to 300,000 persons. TCC Distance Learning now offers up to 30 telecourses, several Interactive TV courses, and 25 Internet courses each semester.

Tyler Junior College

East 5th Street	Phone: (903) 510-2200
Tyler, TX 75711	Fax: (903) 510-2634

Division(s): Academic Dean's Office
Web Site(s): http://www.tyler.cc.tx.us
E-mail: klew@tjc.tyler.cc.tx.us

Class Titles: Biology, Environmental Science, Business, Chemistry, Computers, Macro/Micro Economics, Composition/Rhetoric, American Government, American State Government, U.S. History, Psychology, Sociology, Spanish, Speech Communication, Financial Accounting, Managerial Accounting, Art Appreciation, Design, Drawing, Accounting, Legal Environment in Business, Computer Literacy, Computer Programming: QUICK BASIC, PASCAL, C, COBOL, Business Computer Applications, DOS/Windows, Spreadsheet Concepts, Computer Programming Logic, Networking, Software Applications, Data Structures, Object Oriented Programming, Data Base Concepts, Current Computer Science Topics, Creative Writing, World Literature, Legal Ethics, Algebra, Astronomy, Wildlife Management, Survey of New Testament, Criminal Justice, Crime in America, Agriculture Economics/Finance, Health Professions, TASP Math Review, Trigonometry, Precalculus, Calculus with Analytic Geometry, Medical Terminology, German.

Teaching Methods: *Computers:* Internet, electronic classroom, CD-ROM. *TV:* videotape, cable program, satellite, PBS. *Other:* videoconferencing, audiotapes, independent study, individual study.

Credits Granted for: examination (CLEP, ACT-PEP, DANTES, GRE).

Admission Requirements: *Undergraduate:* high school graduate or GED, TASP required before class placement.

On-Campus Requirements: None.

Tuition and Fees: *Undergraduate:* contact school for all tuition and fee information. *Credit by:* semester.

Financial Aid: Federal Stafford Loan, Federal PLUS Loan, Federal Pell Grant, Federal Work-Study, VA, Texas resident programs.

Accreditation: Southern Association of Colleges and Schools.

Description: Tyler Junior College (1926) is the largest single-campus community college in the state of Texas, enrolling approximately 8,000 students in credit instruction each fall. Tyler Junior College is a comprehensive community college committed to meeting the needs of East Texas by providing excellence in an environment which broadens the mind, challenges the spirit, and maximizes human potential.

UC Raymond Walters College

9555 Plainfield Road	Phone: (513) 745-5776
Cincinnati, OH 45236-1096	Fax: (513) 745-8315

Division(s): Outreach and Continuing Education
Web Site(s): http://www.rwc.uc.edu (click on Distance Learning)
E-mail: janice.kagrisje@uc.edu

Class Titles: Economics, English Composition, Small Business Management, Sales, Sociology of Family, Chemistry, Health, Physics.

Teaching Methods: *Computers:* Internet, real-time chat, e-mail, CD-ROM, LISTSERV. *TV:* videotape, PBS. *Other:* fax, independent study, individual study.

Credits Granted for: experiential learning, portfolio assessment in selected departments, extrainstitutional learning, examination (CLEP, ACT-PEP, DANTES, GRE).

Admission Requirements: *Undergraduate:* high school transcript/GED, placement exam if seeking degree. *Certificate:* varies.

On-Campus Requirements: A couple of sessions for all classes.

Tuition and Fees: *Undergraduate:* $99/credit. *Application Fee:* $30. *Software:* $6 (optional). *Other Costs:* $50 matriculation. *Credit by:* quarter.

Financial Aid: Federal Stafford Loan, Federal Perkins Loan, Federal PLUS Loan, Federal Pell Grant, Federal Work-Study, VA, Ohio residents (OIG).

Accreditation: North Central Association of Colleges and Schools.

Description: Since its founding in 1967, UC Raymond Walters College has strived to provide high quality general education to create informed citizenry who can think critically, communicate effectively, and solve problems. The college provides lifelong learning opportunities for job preparation and mobility, the pursuit of higher education, and personal enrichment. To maintain quality, the college engages in comprehensive assessment of its programs, courses, and services.

UCLA Extension

10995 LeConte Avenue, Suite 639
Los Angeles, CA 90024

Phone: (310) 825-2648
Fax: (310) 206-5006

Division(s): Distance Learning Programs
Web Site(s): http://www.unex.ucla.edu
http://www.onlinelearning.net
E-mail: dstlrng@unex.ucla.edu or enroll@unex.ucla.edu

Certificate Programs: College Counseling, Technical Communications, Online Teaching, General Business Studies, CTC Cross-Cultural Language and Academic Development, Professional Skills Development, Teaching English as a Foreign Language, Teaching English to Speakers of Other Languages.

Class Titles: Architecture, Area/Ethnic/Cultural Studies, American Studies, Asian Studies, Biological/Life Sciences, Business, Accounting, Business Administration/Management, Business Communications, Finance, Hospitality Services Management, Human Resources Management, International Business, Investments/Securities, Management Information Systems, Marketing, Organizational Behavior Studies, Real Estate, Journalism, Public Relations, Computer/Information Sciences, Computer Programming, Information Sciences/Systems, Education, Continuing Education, Curriculum/Instruction, Instructional Media, Special Education, Student Counseling, Teacher Education, Engineering, Creative Writing, English as Second Language, Composition, Technical Writing, Foreign Languages/Literature: European, Spanish Language/Literature, Health/Physical Education/Fitness, Health Professions/Related Sciences, Math, Algebra, Philosophy/Religion, Ethics, Physical Sciences, Astronomy/Astrophysics, Psychology, Cognitive Psychology, Counseling Psychology, Social Sciences, Economics, Visual/Performing Arts, Design, Film Studies.

Teaching Methods: *Computers:* Internet, real-time chat, virtual classrooms, audio. *Other:* videoconferencing, independent study.

Admission Requirements: *Undergraduate:* open admissions or specific to degree. *Graduate:* same as undergraduate. *Certificate:* TOEFL score, BA degree-specific to each certificate.

On-Campus Requirements: prerequisites specific to each program.

Tuition and Fees: *Application Fee:* already built into the course fees. *Other Costs:* graduate courses carry individual course fees, vary for text/materials; contact school for course fee information. *Credit by:* quarter.

Financial Aid: Federal Stafford Loan, Federal Perkins Loan, Federal PLUS Loan, Federal Pell Grant, Federal Work-Study, VA, California resident programs, Life Long Learning Taxpayer Relief Program.

Accreditation: Western Association of Schools and Colleges.

Description: UCLA Extension (1917) is the nation's—and probably the world's—largest urban, single-campus, continu-ing higher education program, enrolling 110,000 annually. The particular province of extension—continuing higher education—advances the interconnected assigned missions of the University of California. These are: to conduct and disseminate basic research; to provide instruction to the bachelor's, master's, and doctoral levels; and to be of public service. To find innovative ways to reach our student population, a new platform evolved—education through distance learning. From the first pioneering steps in 1996 to the present, UCLA Extension has enjoyed substantial growth, presently offering 250 courses to 2,000 students annually. The implications of this growth were best described by Chancellor Camesale: "Knowledge is exploding at an ever-increasing pace, but so too are the capabilities of the new information technology systems. I have no doubt that we are in the midst of a true technological revolution in this domain—one that will change fundamentally the ways in which universities carry out their missions."

Ulster County Community College

Cottekill Road
Stone Ridge, NY 12484

Phone: (914) 687-5040
Fax: (914) 687-5083

Division(s): Vice President of Academic Affairs
Web Site(s): None.
E-mail: makowsp@synyUlster.edu
slnetw@ulster.edu

Class Titles: Environmental Biology, Interpreting Statistics, Latin America 21st Century, Library Information Literacy.

Teaching Methods: *Computers:* Internet, real-time chat, electronic classroom, e-mail, CD-ROM. *TV:* videotape, cable program, satellite. *Other:* correspondence, independent study, individual study.

Credits Granted for: experiential learning, portfolio assessment, extrainstitutional learning, examination (CLEP, ACT-PEP, DANTES, GRE).

Admission Requirements: *Undergraduate:* open admission. *Graduate:* open admission. *Doctoral:* open admission. *Certificate:* open admission.

On-Campus Requirements: None.

Tuition and Fees: *Undergraduate:* $89/credit in-state, $178/credit out-of-state. *Other Costs:* $200/credit cost enrollment fee, subject to change. *Credit by:* Semester.

Financial Aid: Federal Stafford Loan, Federal Perkins Loan, Federal PLUS Loan, Federal Pell Grant, Federal Work-Study, VA, New York resident programs.

Accreditation: The Commission of Higher Education of the Middle States Association.

Description: Ulster County Community College (1962) has grown rapidly. It began its first academic year in September 1963. Classes were held at a temporary campus in the historic Ulster Academy building made available through the corporation of the Board of Education of Kingston City Schools Consolidated. Two years later, 48 students received their degrees at the college's first graduation. The college has now conferred in excess of 11,000 degrees. Ulster County Community College began offering Internet courses through the SUNY Learning Network in 1996. Ulster plans to offer an Associate in Science Degree in individual states pending approval of the State Education Department and the Commission for the Middle States Association.

UNET: University of Maine System Network for Education and Technology Services

46 University Drive	**Phone: (207) 621-3408**
Augusta, ME 04330	**Fax: (207) 621-3420**

Division(s): Education Services
Web Site(s): http://www.unet.maine.edu
E-mail: teleservice@enm.maine.edu

Undergraduate Degree Programs:
Associate of Art in Liberal Arts (UMA)
Associate of Art in Social Services (UMA)
Associate of Science in:
General Studies (UMA)
Business Administration (UMA)
Library and Information Technology (UMA)
Educational Technician (KVTC)
Law Enforcement Technology (SMTC)
Bachelor of Art in Behavioral Sciences (UMFL, UMM, UMPI)
Bachelor of Science in:
Business Administration (UMA)
Mental Health and Human Services (UMA)
Bachelor of University Studies (UM)
Registered Nursing to Bachelor of Science Nursing (USM)

Graduate Degree Programs:
Master of Art in Liberal Studies (UM)
Master of Science in Health Policy and Management (USM)
Degree programs available in Maine only; Internet courses available everywhere.

Certificate Programs: undergraduate: Classical Studies, Maine Studies; graduate: Health Policy and Management, Community Planning and Development, Nonprofit Management, Mental Health Rehabilitation Technician, Child and Family Services.

Class Titles: contact school.

Teaching Methods: *Computers:* Internet. *TV:* videotape, satellite broadcasting. *Other:* audioconferencing, videoconferencing, audiographics, audiotapes, fax, correspondence, independent study, individual study, learning contracts.

Credits Granted for: experiential learning, portfolio assess-

ment, extrainstitutional learning, examination (CLEP, ACT-PEP, DANTES, GRE).

Admission Requirements: *Undergraduate:* contact individual campus. *Graduate:* contact individual campus. *Certificate:* contact individual campus.

On-Campus Requirements: attendance at Maine center/site for ITV courses. Most online courses have none.

Tuition and Fees: *Undergraduate:* contact individual campus. *Graduate:* contact individual campus. *Credit by:* semester.

Financial Aid: Federal Stafford Loan, Federal Perkins Loan, Federal PLUS Loan, Federal Pell Grant, Federal Work-Study, VA, Maine resident programs.

Accreditation: UMS universities are accredited by the New England Association of Schools and Colleges.

Description: UNET, begun in 1989, serves 3,000 students each semester through 100 courses from 21 degree and certificate programs at the associate, bachelor's, and master's levels. A nationally-recognized service of the University of Maine System, UNET was one of the nation's first to implement distance learning to geographically dispersed rural students. In 1989 UNET delivered its courses via interactive TV. Today, faculty use a variety of technology, based on course content and learning objectives, to deliver distance courses. Interactive TV courses are available only in Maine, while Internet classes may be accessed from students' homes or at dozens of convenient sites in-state. Also, UNET's Teleservice Center allows students to register, add or drop courses, receive assistance with institutional forms, obtain referral to appropriate support services, and request information about the institution and its services.

Union Institute

440 East McMillan Street	**Phone: (513) 861-6400**
Cincinnati, OH 45206	**(800) 486-3116**
	Fax: (513) 861-9026

Division(s): College of Undergraduate Studies, Center for Distance Learning
Web Site(s): http://tui.edu
E-mail: tmott@tui.edu

Undergraduate Degree Programs:
Bachelor of Arts
Bachelor of Science

Teaching Methods: *Computers:* Internet, real-time chat, e-mail, newsgroup. *Other:* audioconferencing, fax, correspondence, independent study, individual study, learning contracts.

Credits Granted for: experiential learning, examination (CLEP, ACT-PEP, DANTES), transfer credit from other regionally accredited colleges.

Admission Requirements: *Undergraduate:* college-level

learning ability, interview with faculty advisor, application essay, 2 letters of recommendation, official college transcripts (if applicable).

On-Campus Requirements: Weekend seminar each semester.

Tuition and Fees: *Undergraduate:* $248/credit. *Application Fee:* $50. *Credit by:* semester.

Financial Aid: Federal Stafford Loan, Federal Perkins Loan, Federal PLUS Loan, Federal Pell Grant, Federal Work-Study, VA (some states), Ohio, Florida, California (possibly others) resident programs.

Accreditation: North Central Association of Colleges and Schools.

Description: The Union Institute was founded in 1964 to provide educational opportunities to working adults through innovative and flexible delivery systems. The undergraduate distance learning program originated in 1993 to expand access to the College of Undergraduate Studies' bachelor's program to adult learners located throughout the country.

United States Sports Academy

One Academy Drive	Phone: (800) 223-2668
Daphne, AL 36526	(334) 626-3303
	Fax: (334) 621-1149

Division(s): Distance Learning
Web Site(s): http://www.sport.ussa.edu
E-mail: academy@ussa-sport.ussa.edu

Graduate Degree Programs:
Master of Sport Science in:
 Sport Management
 Sport Medicine
 Sport Coaching
 Sports Medicine, emphasis in Exercise Physiology
dual majors also available

Certificate Programs: Sport Coaching, Sport Management, Sports Medicine, Exercise Physiology, Sport Conditioning, Bodybuilding, Personal Training, Travel and Tourism.

Teaching Methods: *Computers:* e-mail. *Other:* audiotapes, fax, correspondence, telephone conferences, independent study.

Admission Requirements: *Graduate:* application; 2.75 undergraduate GPA; 800 GRE, 27 MAT, or 400 GMAT scores; 3 recommendation letters; written personal statement of goals, resume.

On-Campus Requirements: comprehensive examination at conclusion of course requirements. Offered at end of each semester.

Tuition and Fees: *Undergraduate:* $75/CEU (4 CEUs/class) for

certification. *Graduate:* $350/credit (3 credits/class). *Application Fee:* $59. *Other Costs:* $100 one-time computer fee. *Credit by:* semester.

Financial Aid: available after payment of initial course. Federal Stafford Loans available.

Accreditation: Southern Association of Colleges and Schools.

Description: The United States Sports Academy has been in service since 1972, providing training for the sport professional with a sports specific curriculum. The role of the academy in higher education is to prepare men and women for sport professions in the areas of sport management, sports medicine, and sport coaching.

Université de Moncton

Taillon Building, room 345	Phone: (506) 858-4121
Moncton, NB, Canada E1A 3E9	Fax: (506) 858-4489

Division(s): Continuing Education, faculty departments
Web Site(s): http://www.umoncton.ca
E-mail: blancha@umoncton.ca

Undergraduate Degree Programs:
Bachelor in Science in Nursing
Bachelor in Adult Education

Graduate Degree Programs:
Master of Business Administration
Master in Education
Diploma of Graduate Studies in Professional Counseling

Certificate Programs: Cooperative Studies, Alcoholism and Toxicology, Professional Counseling, Adult Education.

Teaching Methods: *Computers:* Internet, real-time chat, electronic classroom, e-mail, CD-ROM, newsgroup, LISTSERV. *TV:* videotape, satellite broadcasting, PBS. *Other:* videoconferencing, audioconferencing, audiographics, audiotapes, fax, independent study, individual study.

Credits Granted for: experiential learning, portfolio assessment, extrainstitutional learning.

Admission Requirements: *Undergraduate:* high school graduate or age 18. *Graduate:* program-specific. *Doctoral:* bachelor's degree, others program-specific. *Certificate:* program-specific.

On-Campus Requirements: None.

Tuition and Fees: *Undergraduate:* $94/credit. *Graduate:* $94/credit. *Doctoral:* $110/credit. *Credit by:* credit system.

Financial Aid: Federal Loan

Accreditation: Association of Universities and Colleges of Canada.

Description: The Université de Moncton (1963) has offered distance education courses since 1984.

University College of Cape Breton

PO Box 5300
Sydney, NS, Canada B1P 6L2

Phone: (902) 563-1423
Fax: (902) 563-1449

Division(s): Extension and Community Affairs
Web Site(s): http://www.uccb.ns.ca
E-mail: jpino@uccb.ns.ca

Undergraduate Degree Programs:
Bachelor of Arts Community Studies
Bachelor of Technology Environmental Studies (postdiploma)

Graduate Degree Programs:
Diploma in Education (Curriculum)
Certificate in Education (Technology)

Certificate Programs: Public Administration

Class Titles: Business Administration, Economics, Education, English, Environmental Studies, Problem-Centered Studies, Political Science, Psychology.

Teaching Methods: *Computers:* Internet, electronic classroom, e-mail, LISTSERV. *Other:* videoconferencing, audiographics, correspondence, independent study.

Credits Granted for: experiential learning, portfolio assessment, extrainstitutional learning.

Admission Requirements: *Undergraduate:* High school graduates with 60% overall average, OR approved transfers, OR "nontraditional learners" out of high school for 2 years who have completed Grade 10 and are age 20. Admission is subject to space and program restrictions, and specific programs may have additional requirements. *Graduate:* undergraduate degree.

On-Campus Requirements: None.

Tuition and Fees: *Undergraduate:* $365/3-credits, $730/6-credits. *Graduate:* $808. *Application Fee:* $20. *Other Costs:* $50/course Distance Fees. *Credit by:* semester.

Accreditation: Association of Universities and Colleges of Canada, Association of Canadian Community Colleges, Association of Atlantic Universities, Associate Member of the Association of Commonwealth Universities.

Description: Located near Sydney on beautiful Cape Breton Island, the University College of Cape Breton (1974) is Canada's first university college. UCCB offers an innovative blend of degree, diploma, and certificate programs. The college also supports community economic development and applied research and provides technical assistance to business and industry. Its mission is to ensure continued emphasis on, and commitment to, meaningful, relevant, and accessible programs that build upon a unique blend of educational traditions. For many years, UCCB has enjoyed a reputation for providing flexible credit and noncredit distance learning opportunities. The school's network of electronic, audiographic classrooms facilitates course delivery throughout Nova Scotia. Correspondence courses began in 1996, and Web-delivered courses recently added to the broad range of options available to students studying at a distance.

University College of the Cariboo

900 College Drive
Kamloops, BC, Canada V2C 5N3

Phone: (250) 371-5667
Fax: (250) 371-5771

Division(s): Distance Education in the Sciences and Health Sciences
Web Site(s): http://www.cariboo.bc.ca/schs/dist_ed.htm
E-mail: daly@cariboo.bc.ca

Undergraduate Degree Programs:
Bachelor of Health Science (Respiratory Therapy)

Certificate Programs: Anesthesia Technology, Cardiovascular Perfusion, Animal Welfare, Medical Laboratory Assistant, Asthma Educator, Executive Diplomas in: General Management, Human Resource Management, Management and Training.

Class Titles: Animal Welfare, Animal Care, Safety in Workplace, Workplace Hazardous Management, Information Systems, Electrocardiogram Analysis, Medical Terminology, Applied Science, Anatomy/Physiology, Laboratory Procedures, Blood Gas Analysis, Veterinary Hospital Safety, Pathophysiology, Pharmacology, Forest Ecology, Respiratory Therapy Procedures, Anesthesia Technology, Neonatology, Hemodynamic/Physiological Monitoring, Emergency Cardiac Care, Asthma Educators, Elementary Science Teacher.

Teaching Methods: *Computers:* Internet, real-time chat, electronic classroom, e-mail, CD-ROM, LISTSERV, newsgroup. *TV:* interactive TV, videotape, satellite broadcasting, PBS. *Other:* radio broadcast, videoconferencing, audioconferencing, audiotapes, fax, correspondence, independent study, individual study, learning contracts.

Admission Requirements: *Graduate:* Executive Diploma: undergraduate degree and/or several years of management/supervisory experience. *Certificate:* diploma in Allied Health.

On-Campus Requirements: a 5-day residency is required for the Executive Diploma Programs. These will be held at UCC and at key locations within North America. Anesthesia and Cardiovascular Perfusion have clinical practicums.

Tuition and Fees: *Undergraduate:* $150–$350 Canadian/course. *Other Costs:* Participants are responsible for all computer hardware/software costs. *Credit by:* semester.

Accreditation: Association of Universities and Colleges of Canada.

Description: University College of the Cariboo (1970) has offered distance learning opportunities for more than a decade to thousands of professional students across the country and, indeed, around the world. We note with pride that UCC has been recognized by the League of Innovation in Community Colleges as having one of the 20 best distance learning programs in North America. Distance learning students are able to take immediate advantage of UCC's extensive experience and services. We have completion rates in our Health Science distance education programs hovering around the 80% mark. We attribute our high completion rate to several critical factors: type of program, target audience, quality of contact between learner and tutor, and ongoing evaluation.

University of Akron

Akron, OH 44325	Phone: (330) 972-6400
	Fax: (330) 972-5636

Division(s): Off-Campus
Web Site(s): http://www.uakron.edu
E-mail: InfoReq@uakron.edu

Graduate Degree Programs:
Master of Education
Master of Social Work

Class Titles: English, Math, Sociology, Japanese, Anthropology, general studies courses.

Teaching Methods: *Computers:* Internet, real-time chat, electronic classroom, e-mail, CD-ROM, newsgroup, LISTSERV. *TV:* videotape, cable program. *Other:* radio broadcast, audioconferencing, videoconferencing, audiographics, audiotapes, fax.

Credits Granted for: examination (CLEP).

Admission Requirements: *Undergraduate:* high school diploma or equivalent, pass state competency exam. *Graduate:* 2.75 GPA. *Doctoral:* 2.0 GPA. *Certificate:* 2.0 GPA.

On-Campus Requirements: cohort advising.

Tuition and Fees: *Undergraduate:* $139/credit resident, $338/credit nonresident. *Graduate:* $168/credit resident, $321/credit nonresident. *Doctoral:* same as undergraduate. *Application Fee:* $25. *Credit by:* semester.

Financial Aid: Federal Stafford Loan, Federal Perkins Loan, Federal PLUS Loan, Federal Pell Grant, Federal Work-Study, VA, Ohio resident programs.

Accreditation: North Central Association of Colleges and Schools.

Description: The University of Akron (1870) has an open-admission policy for its 9 degree-granting colleges. Degrees are offered from the associate level through the PhD. Distance learning in social work began 3 years ago, and other programs have since been added. A fiber optic system for distance learning is now in operation, and the university plans to expand its distance systems throughout the area it serves. In the fall of 1998, the College of Business began offering graduate courses on the Web.

University of Alabama

127 Martha Parham West	Phone: (205) 348-9278
PO Box 870388	(800) 452-5971
Tuscaloosa, AL 35487-0388	Fax: (205) 348-0249

Division(s): College of Continuing Studies
Distance Education Division
Web Site(s): http://ua1ix.ua.edu/~disted
E-mail: disted@ccs.ua.edu

Graduate Degree Programs:
Master of Science in:
    Aerospace Engineering
    Environmental Engineering
    Civil Engineering
    Electrical Engineering
    Mechanical Engineering
    Engineering
    Engineering, Engineering Management emphasis
Master of Arts in:
    Health Studies
    Advertising and Public Relations
    Rehabilitation Counseling
Master of Law and Taxation

Doctoral Degree Programs:
Educational Specialist Degree in Educational Leadership

Certificate Programs: Criminal Justice

Class Titles: undergraduate credit through written correspondence: Astronomy, Athletic Coaching, Biology, Chemical Engineering, Classics, Computer Science, Consumer Science, Counselor Education, Criminal Justice, Economics, English, Finance, Geography, German, Health Education, History, Human Development/Family Studies, Human Nutrition/Hospitality Management, Journalism, Library Studies, Management, Mass Communication, Math, Music Academics, Philosophy, Physics, Political Science, Psychology, Religious Studies, Sociology, Spanish, Statistics, Telecommunication/Film, Theater; undergraduate credit via online computer: Athletic Coaching, Educational Computer Technology, English, Engineering, Health; undergraduate/graduate credit by videotape: Engineering, Nursing, Commerce/Business Administration, Human Environmental Sciences, College of Education; undergraduate/graduate credit through videoconferencing, including: Education, Nursing, Material Science, Engineering, Communications, Law, Library Studies, Math, Business; noncredit courses through written correspondence: Bail Bond, Citizenship.

Teaching Methods: *Computers:* Internet, real-time chat, electronic classroom, e-mail. *TV:* videotape, satellite. *Other:* videoconferencing, audiotapes, fax, written correspondence, independent study.

Admission Requirements: *Undergraduate:* varies. *Graduate:* University of Alabama Graduate School admittance. *Doctoral:* varies. *Certificate:* no restrictions.

On-Campus Requirements: None.

Tuition and Fees: *Undergraduate:* varies. *Graduate:* varies. *Doctoral:* varies. *Application Fee:* varies. *Software:* varies. *Other Costs:* varies. *Credit by:* semester.

Financial Aid: Federal Stafford Loan, Federal Perkins Loan, Federal PLUS Loan, Federal Pell Grant, Federal Work-Study, VA, Alabama resident programs.

Accreditation: Southern Association of Schools and Colleges, appropriate accreditation agencies for individual academic divisions.

Description: Established in 1831, the University of Alabama is a dynamic center of learning, rich with diverse opportunities for people of varied interests. Roughly one-third of its 19,000 students come from outside the state, and the university has a growing international enrollment with students representing 80 countries. Though a traditionally residential campus, the university reaches out through Distance Education to meet the educational needs of citizens of the state, nation, and globe. UA offers distance learning in a variety of formats, including written correspondence, videotape, live videoconferencing, satellite, and the Internet. The University of Alabama Division of Distance Education extends its academic resources to people who seek college credit toward a degree but who cannot attend classes on campus.

The University of Alabama at Birmingham

Holley-Mears Building
924 19th Street S
Birmingham, AL 35294

Phone: (205) 934-3295
Fax: (205) 934-8251

Division(s): UAB Options/Services for Adult Students
Web Site(s): http://www.uab.edu/conted
E-mail: bdi@cec.conteduc.uab.edu

Class Titles: varies from term to term. Contact school for complete class listing.

Teaching Methods: *Computers:* e-mail. *Other:* videoconferencing.

Credits Granted for: portfolio assessment, extrainstitutional learning, examination (CLEP, ACT-PEP, DANTES, GRE).

Admission Requirements: *Undergraduate:* admission criteria varies depending on the applicant's educational background. A high school graduate with no college course work must have at least a 2.0 (C) grade point average in high school academic subjects in grades 9–12 (including a minimum of 2.0 in both English and mathematics courses). If high school graduation was within 3 years of the date for which entry to UAB is sought, the applicant must also have a minimum composite score of 20 on the ACT Assessment or a combined SAT score of 950. An applicant who has not graduated from high school and has no college work must be at least age 19 and have a score of at least 52 on the General Education Development (GED) test. Minimum grade point average of 2.0 on all previous college work attempted. Applicants from outside the U.S. must have the academic, linguistic, and financial resources to complete their educational objectives successfully at UAB. International students can obtain information and application materials from the Office of Undergraduate Admissions. *Graduate:* each graduate program sets its own minimum standards for admission. The graduate school has established guidelines for admission to master's degree programs. These guidelines are (1) a B average (computed overall, or alternatively computed over the last 60 semester hours or earned credit) in undergraduate work, (2) evidence of a bachelor's degree from a regionally accredited university or college in the U.S., (3) a score of at least 500 on each section of the Graduate Record Examination General Test (some programs require or accept other national tests), and (4) previous academic work appropriate to the academic area to which application is being made. *Doctoral:* same as graduate. Note that some programs also require a master's degree before admission to the doctoral program. Because of guidelines set by external accreditation authorities, the requirements for application and admission to certain graduate programs may differ from the above, particularly in the standard test required. *Certificate:* UAB only offers noncredit certificates. No admission requirements.

On-Campus Requirements: at least 32 of the 128 semester hours required for graduation, including 12 of the last 18, must be taken at UAB. Credit for unconventional academic course work may not be used to satisfy this requirement. At least 9 of the hours required for the major must be completed at UAB.

Tuition and Fees: *Undergraduate:* $87/credit in-state, $174/credit out-of-state for courses taken in schools other than Health Related Professions, Nursing, or Public Health. For courses taken in the School of Health Related Professions: $107 in-state, $214 out-of-state. For courses taken in the School of Nursing: $97 in-state, $194 out-of-state. *Graduate:* $99/credit in-state, $198/credit out-of-state for courses taken in schools other than Health Related Professions, Nursing, or Public Health. For courses taken in the School of Health Related Professions: $129/credit in-state, $258/credit out-of-state. For courses taken in the School of Public Health: $102/credit in-state, $204/credit out-of-state. *Doctoral:* same as Graduate. *Application Fee:* $25 undergraduate, $35 graduate. *Other Costs:* $23/quarter plus $4/credit student service fee; $17/quarter plus $3/credit building fee in schools other than HRP, NUR or PUH; $17 building fee in HRP, NUR, or PUH; $35 lab fee for A&H, BUS, EDU, HRP, SBS, PUH; $50 lab fee for EGR, NSM; $35 group music fees; $50 private music fees; $9/credit learning resources fee in BUS, EDU, EGR, PUH; $7/credit learning resources fee in NUR, HRP; $4/credit learning resources fee in A&H, SBS, NSM. *Credit by:* semester.

Financial Aid: Federal Stafford Loan, Federal Perkins Loan,

Federal Pell Grant, Federal Work-Study, Federal Supplemental Educational Opportunity Grant, Federal Direct Parent Loan, VA, Alabama resident programs.

Accreditation: Southern Association of Colleges and Schools.

Description: During the first half of the 20th century the University of Alabama in Tuscaloosa (1969) began offering educational opportunities to residents in urban communities throughout Alabama. An extension center offering both day and evening classes was established in Birmingham. This center evolved into a new university campus, serving the working community as well as its traditional students. The IITS program (videoconferencing network) began as a way to share resources as well as expand the course offerings to students located all over Alabama.

The University of Alabama, Huntsville

301 Sparkman Drive
Technology Hall, Room N136
Huntsville, AL 35899

Phone: (256) 890-6075
Fax: (256) 890-6608

Division(s): Industrial and Systems Engineering and Engineering Management
Web Site(s): http://www.eb.uah.edu
E-mail: utley@ebs330.eb.uah.edu.

Graduate Degree Programs:
Master of Science in Engineering in:
    Manufacturing Systems
    Quality Engineering
    Systems Engineering
    Engineering Management
    Environmental Engineering

Doctoral Degree Programs:
Doctor of Philosophy in Industrial and Systems Engineering, Engineering Management emphasis
Systems Engineering emphasis
Quality Engineering emphasis

Teaching Methods: *Computers:* e-mail, Internet. *TV:* videotape, cable programming, satellite broadcasting. *Other:* videoconferencing, fax, correspondence, independent study.

Credits Granted for: previous graduate work.

Admission Requirements: *Graduate:* 1,500 on GRE or UAH waiver; accredited engineering degree, related experience in U.S.-based firm (2 years or holding full-time engineering position for master's; 5 years for PhD). *Doctoral:* see graduate criteria.

On-Campus Requirements: Oral final exam for certificate. For PhD, 2 consecutive, full-time semesters (9 hours/semester) satisfy residency. This can still be met through the Distance Learning program, however, 2 PhD courses, one in the fall and one in the spring, meet 5 Mondays/semester on campus.

Tuition and Fees: *Graduate:* $192–$300/credit, depending on student location. *Application Fee:* $20. *Software:* varies. *Other Costs:* $50–$150/semester books. *Credit by:* semester.

Financial Aid: Federal Stafford Loan, Federal Perkins Loan, Federal PLUS Loan, Federal Pell Grant, Federal Work-Study, VA, Alabama resident programs (Normally, companies sponsor their full-time employee students).

Accreditation: Accreditation Board for Engineering and Technology (undergraduate level).

Description: The University of Alabama in Huntsville is a research campus offering a variety of degree programs since its founding in 1961. It has offered degrees in Industrial and Systems Engineering and Engineering Management for 25 years. An extensive distance learning program began in 1992 and has grown to 200 MSE students and 50 PhD students.

University of Alaska, Fairbanks

PO Box 756700
Fairbanks, AK 99775

Phone: (907) 474-5353
Fax: (907) 474-5402

Division(s): Distance Education and Independent Learning
Web Site(s): http://www.dist-ed.uaf.edu
E-mail: racde@uaf.edu

Undergraduate Degree Programs:
Associate of Arts
Associate of Applied Science in:
    Community Health
    Early Childhood Development
    Human Service Technology
    Microcomputer Support Specialist
Bachelor of Arts in Rural Development
Bachelor of Arts in Social Work

Certificate Programs: Community Health, Early Childhood Development, Microcomputer Support Specialist.

Teaching Methods: *Computers:* Internet, e-mail, CD-ROM. *TV:* videotape, satellite broadcasting, PBS. *Other:* radio broadcast, audioconferencing, videoconferencing, audiographics, audiotapes, fax, correspondence, independent study, individual study, learning contracts.

Credits Granted for: experiential learning, portfolio assessment, extrainstitutional learning, examination (CLEP, ACT-PEP, DANTES, GRE).

Admission Requirements: *Undergraduate:* age 18, high school diploma/GED, SAT/ACT.

On-Campus Requirements: None.

Tuition and Fees: *Undergraduate:* $73/credit lower division, $81/credit upper division. *Graduate:* $100/credit 500-level. *Doctoral:* $162/credit 600-level. *Application Fee:* $35. *Other Costs:* $20/course service/handling, average $75/course materials. *Credit by:* semester.

Financial Aid: Federal Stafford Loan, Federal Perkins Loan,

Federal PLUS Loan, Federal Pell Grant, VA, Alaska resident programs.

Accreditation: Northwest Association of Schools and Colleges.

Description: In 1922, just 20 years after the discovery of gold in the heart of the Alaskan wilderness, the Alaska Agricultural College and School of Mines opened with 6 faculty members and 6 students. Today UAF has branches in Bethel, Dillingham, Kotzebue, Nome, and the Interior/Aleutians, in addition to the main campus in Fairbanks. UAF is the state's land-, sea-, and space-grant institution. Its College of Rural Alaska has the primary responsibility for Alaska Native education and study, and UAF remains the state's only university offering doctoral degrees. UAF's colleges and schools offer 70 fields of study and a variety of technical and vocational programs. The university developed a Correspondence Study Program in the late 1950s, then created its Center for Distance Education and Independent Learning in 1987. The center supports 200 distance-delivered courses for certificate, degree, and master's programs, and the Independent Learning Program serves 3,400 students worldwide each year.

University of Alaska Southeast, Juneau Campus

11120 Glacier Highway	Phone: (907) 465-6353
Juneau, AK 99801	Fax: (907) 465-6549

Division(s): Distance Programs, Novatney Hall
Web Site(s): http://www.jun.alaska.edu
E-mail: jnsdg@uas.alaska.edu

Undergraduate Degree Programs:
Associate of Applied Science in Business Administration
Bachelor of Business Administration, Management emphasis
Bachelor of Business Administration, General emphasis

Graduate Degree Programs:
Master of Public Administration
Master of Education in Early Childhood Education

Certificate Programs: Credential Endorsement in Early Childhood Education, Credential Endorsement in Elementary Education

Class Titles: Wildlife Biology: Bears/Eagles/Whales, Microsoft Applications (Access, Excel), Microcomputer Concepts/Operations.

Teaching Methods: *Computers:* Internet, electronic classroom, e-mail, CD-ROM, LISTSERV. *TV:* videotape, satellite broadcasting. *Other:* audioconferencing, audiotapes, fax, correspondence.

Credits Granted for: examination (CLEP, ACT-PEP, DANTES, GRE).

Admission Requirements: *Undergraduate:* AAS only at Alaska military sites. For AAS and BBA, high school diploma or GED. For MPA, accredited bachelor's degree, 3.0 GPA, official transcripts, economics/statistics in past 5 years or competency test, GRE or GMAT in 50th percentile, 500 word writing sample specifying reasons for seeking admission. For MED, bachelor's degree in education or credential endorsement in education, official transcripts, 3.0 GPA, 3 current letters of recommendation, summary of educational experiences, description of professional goals and statement how graduate program will help attain those goals. For credential programs, same requirements as MED, except a 2.5 GPA.

On-Campus Requirements: For MED, several weeks during summer session.

Tuition and Fees: *Undergraduate:* $73/credit lower division, $81/credit upper division. *Graduate:* $162/credit. *Application Fee:* $35. *Other Costs:* $40–$75 distance fee. *Credit by:* semester.

Financial Aid: Federal Stafford Loan, Federal Perkins Loan, Federal PLUS Loan, Federal Pell Grant, Federal Work-Study, VA, Alaska resident programs.

Accreditation: Northwest Association of Schools and Colleges.

Description: The University of Alaska Southeast's Juneau campus is located in Alaska's beautiful capital city with the world famous Mendenhall Glacier in clear view from the main campus. The Southeastern Senior College (1972) and the Juneau-Douglas Community College (1956) were merged in 1980 to form the current campus. Today the Juneau campus continues to be the center for undergraduate and graduate education in the region.

University of Alaska Southeast, Sitka Campus

1332 Seward Avenue	Phone: (907) 747-6653
Sitka, AK 99835	Fax: (907) 747-3552

Division(s): Distance Education Office
Web Site(s): http://www.jun.alaska.edu/uas/sitka/index.html
E-mail: TNDMB@acad1.alaska.edu

Undergraduate Degree Programs:
Associate of Arts
Associate of Applied Science in:
    Computer Information Office Systems
    Early Childhood Education
    Environmental Technology
    Health Information Management
    Human Services Technology
    Microcomputer Support Specialist

Certificate Programs: Environmental Technology, Microcomputer Support Specialist, Administrative Office Support, Computer Application, Desktop Publishing Graphics, Medical

Office Procedures, Web Publishing, Networking Essentials.

Teaching Methods: *Computers:* Internet, e-mail, CD-ROM, LISTSERV. *TV:* videotape, cable program, satellite broadcasting, PBS. *Other:* radio broadcast, audioconferencing, videoconferencing, audiotapes, fax, correspondence, individual study, learning contracts.

Credits Granted for: experiential learning, portfolio assessment, extrainstitutional learning, examination (CLEP, ACT-PEP, DANTES, GRE).

Admission Requirements: *Undergraduate:* high school diploma or GED.

On-Campus Requirements: None.

Tuition and Fees: *Undergraduate:* $73/credit. *Graduate:* $81/credit. *Doctoral:* $162/credit. *Application Fee:* $35. *Other Costs:* $40/course Distance Fee. *Credit by:* semester.

Financial Aid: Federal Stafford Loan, Federal Perkins Loan, Federal PLUS Loan, Federal Pell Grant, Federal Work-Study, VA, Alaska resident programs.

Accreditation: Northwest Association of Schools and Colleges.

Description: The Sitka campus, founded as Sitka Community College in 1962, shares Sitka's heritage of being the former capital of Russian America. Sitka is rich in history and a popular tourist attraction. Mount Edgecumbe, known as Alaska's Mount Fuji, dominates the horizon across the water from the city. The Sitka campus awards certificates of completion and associate degrees. Since restructuring to include the Juneau and Ketchikan campuses, the Sitka campus has assumed administrative responsibility for the university's outreach programs. In addition, the Sitka campus and Sheldon Jackson College share cross-registration and Sheldon's library.

University of Arizona

| 888 North Euclid Avenue | Phone: (520) 626-2071 |
| Tucson, AZ 85721-0158 | Fax: (520) 621-3269 |

Division(s): Extended University
Web Site(s): http://www.arizona.edu/~uaextend/dist
E-mail: mham@u.arizona.edu

Certificate Programs: Reliability and Quality Engineering

Class Titles: Aerospace/Mechanical Engineering, Electrical Engineering, Library Science.

Teaching Methods: *Computers:* Internet, e-mail, CD-ROM, LISTSERV. *TV:* videotape, satellite broadcasting through National Technological University. *Other:* videoconferencing, fax, correspondence.

Credits Granted for: examination (GRE), transfer credit from other accredited universities and colleges.

Admission Requirements: *Undergraduate:* vary by department; consult with department advisor. *Graduate:* vary by

department; consult with department advisor. *Doctoral:* vary by department; consult with department advisor. *Certificate:* bachelor's degree in engineering, math or physics. A university-level introductory course in probability and statistics within the past 5 years is highly recommended.

On-Campus Requirements: vary by department.

Tuition and Fees: *Undergraduate:* vary by program. *Graduate:* vary by program. *Doctoral:* vary by program. *Application Fee:* varies by program. *Credit by:* semester.

Accreditation: North Central Association of Colleges and Schools.

Description: The University of Arizona (1972) is committed to distance learning. If the student can't come to the campus, the campus will come to the student. Courses are taught by top faculty members who incorporate the latest research and technological developments. Students can choose the distance learning course and format that best meet their needs. UA offers classes on videotape and via satellite in a wide range of engineering fields. Students can work toward a technical degree in Aerospace/Mechanical Engineering, Electrical/Computer Engineering, Optical Sciences, Reliability/Quality Engineering, or Systems/Industrial Engineering. A professional certificate program is also available in Reliability and Quality.

University of Arkansas, Little Rock

| 2801 South University Avenue | Phone: (501) 569-3003 |
| Little Rock, AR 72204 | Fax: (501) 569-8538 |

Division(s): Off-Campus Credit Program and Computing Services
Web Site(s): http://www.ualr.edu/~occp
E-mail: drsmith@ualr.edu

Class Titles: Anthropology, Geography, Gender Studies, History, Journalism, Political Science, Psychology, Radio/TV/Film, Rhetoric/Writing, Sociology, Criminal Justice, Adult Education, Criminal Justice, Economics, English, Finance, hundreds of off-campus courses.

Teaching Methods: *Computers:* Internet, real-time chat, e-mail, CD-ROM, LISTSERV. *TV:* videotape, cable program, satellite broadcasting, PBS, telecourse. *Other:* radio broadcast, audiotapes, fax, independent study, compressed video. These teaching methods are all used at UALR, but mostly as supplements to traditional lecture only.

Credits Granted for: some military/law enforcement service, some occupational programs, examination (CLEP).

Admission Requirements: *Undergraduate:* application, high school transcript or GED scores, official ACT or SAT scores, immunization record. *Graduate:* application, official transcript, entrance exam scores (vary by program), immunization record. *Doctoral:* application, official transcript, immunization record.

On-Campus Requirements: variable.

Tuition and Fees: *Undergraduate:* $109/credit. *Graduate:* $149/credit. *Doctoral:* $149/credit. *Software:* variable. *Other Costs:* Nonresidents are charged more for tuition. *Credit by:* semester.

Financial Aid: Federal Stafford Loan, Federal Perkins Loan, Federal PLUS Loan, Federal Pell Grant, Federal Work-Study, VA, Arkansas resident programs, scholarships, campus employment.

Accreditation: North Central Association of Colleges and Schools.

Description: The University of Arkansas at Little Rock (1927) became part of the University of Arkansas system in 1969. UALR achieved a combined semester headcount of 28,034 in the 1997–1998 academic year, with 14% from the Off-Campus Credit (OCC) Program. OCC initiated distance learning at UALR by offering off-campus classes at various locations in central Arkansas. The program has grown to 408 sections in the past year, with the cooperation of 44 academic units, at 35 sites, in 20 counties statewide. Two sections were offered outside the state, with one outside the country. As the definition of "Distance Education" has changed, so has OCC, with the introduction of telecourses in the late 1980s, compressed video in the early 1990s, and the most recent addition of Web-based courses.

University of Baltimore

1420 North Charles Street	Phone: (887) ApplyUB
Baltimore, MD 21201-5779	(410) 837-4777
	Fax: (410) 837-4793

Division(s): Admissions Office
Web Site(s): http://www.ubalt.edu
E-mail: admissions@ubmail.ubalt.edu

Graduate Degree Programs:
Master of Business Administration

Class Titles: Business, Communications Design, Criminal Justice, Government/Public Policy.

Teaching Methods: *Computers:* Internet, real-time chat, electronic classroom, e-mail, LISTSERV. *TV:* interactive video classroom. *Other:* individual study.

Credits Granted for: examination (ACT-PEP, DANTES, GRE).

Admission Requirements: *Undergraduate:* 56 credits and minimum 2.0 GPA, now accepting limited number of students with sophomore status (24+ credits) meeting specified GPA levels. *Graduate:* some programs may require GMAT or GRE, contact school for more information.

On-Campus Requirements: no for Web MBA, yes for courses taught in interactive video classroom.

Tuition and Fees: *Undergraduate:* $157 resident, $351 out-of-state *Graduate:* $239 resident, $356 out-of-state, $1,225/ course for Web MBA program (flat rate). *Application Fee:* $35. *Other Costs:* $17/credit fee undergraduate and graduate. *Credit by:* semester.

Financial Aid: Federal Stafford Loan, Federal Perkins Loan, Federal PLUS Loan, Federal Pell Grant, Federal Work-Study, VA, Maryland resident programs, Merit Scholarships, special scholarships, student employment, emergency loans.

Accreditation: Middle States Association of Colleges and Secondary Schools, Maryland State Board of Education, American Assembly of Collegiate Schools of Business, National Association of Schools of Public Affairs and Administration, American Bar Association.

Description: The University of Baltimore (1925) holds a unique role in Maryland's higher education system as the state's only upper-division university, offering junior and senior years of bachelor study as well as distinct graduate programs in business, law, and liberal arts. As of fall 1998, UB is authorized to admit a limited number of qualified sophomores. The university's emphasis on professional education attracts students with strong career objectives. Courses in Communication Design, Criminal Justice, Government/Public Policy, and Business have been offered via interactive video classroom to sites around Maryland since 1994. Beginning in January 1999, the University of Baltimore will offer its Web MBA, a fully online Master of Business Administration, taught by faculty of UB's Merrick School of Business, an AACSB-accredited program provider. A unique model, emphasizing student cohorts enrolled in 2 courses in 10-week sessions across the academic year, allows students to complete their MBA, conveniently and with collegial support, in 2 years.

University of Bridgeport

126 Park Avenue	Phone: (203) 576-4851
Bridgeport, CT 06601	Fax: (203) 576-4672

Division(s): Distance Education
Web Site(s): http://www.bridgeport.edu
E-mail: gmichael@cse.bridgeport.edu

Graduate Degree Programs:
Master of Science in Human Nutrition

Certificate Programs: International Finance, Computer Science.

Teaching Methods: *Computers:* Internet, real-time chat, electronic classroom, e-mail, CD-ROM, newsgroup. *Other:* None.

Admission Requirements: *Graduate:* undergraduate degree.

On-Campus Requirements: None.

Tuition and Fees: *Graduate:* $340/credit. *Application Fee:* $40. *Credit by:* semester.

Financial Aid: Federal Stafford Loan

Accreditation: New England Association of Schools and Colleges.

Description: The University of Bridgeport, founded in 1927, is an independent, nonsectarian, comprehensive university offering a variety of undergraduate, graduate, and professional degree programs through its several colleges and schools. The university's mission is to teach, search for new knowledge, and discover solutions to social and natural problems. To this end, it offers a high-quality, central liberal arts experience with accredited scientific, technical, business, legal, professional, and liberal arts programs, as well as lifelong learning opportunities. UB's distance learning program is committed to the larger social mission of worldwide education. The program began in 1997 with 8 courses in the Master's of Science in Human Nutrition program. This convenient online program allows students to communicate with instructors and classmates from the convenience of home or office with just a computer, modem, and Internet access. Students have access to many online tools, including e-mail, newsgroups, class conferences, informal chat rooms, textbooks, and specially produced software. Distance learning students also have access to the traditional student resources of the library, counselors, registration, and financial aid through the school's Virtual Campus.

University of British Columbia

2329 West Mall, Room 1170	Phone: (604) 822-6565 or 6500
Vancouver, BC Canada V6T 1Z4	(800) 754-1811
	Fax: (604) 822-8636

Division(s): Distance Education and Technology, Continuing Studies
Web Site(s): http://det.cstudies.ubc.ca
E-mail: det@cstudies.ubc.ca

Certificate Programs: Technology-Based Distributed Learning (see the Web site at http://itesm.cstudies.ubc.ca/info/)

Class Titles: Credit courses toward degrees are offered through 12 faculties: Agricultural Sciences, Applied Sciences, Arts, Commerce, Dentistry, Education, Forestry, Law, Medicine, Pharmaceutical Sciences, Science. Graduate studies are offered presently in Education/Watershed Management. More graduate programs in the areas of social work and forestry are under development.

Teaching Methods: *Computers:* Internet, electronic classroom, e-mail, CD-ROM. *TV:* videotape, cable program: Knowledge Network. *Other:* audioconferencing, videoconferencing, audiotapes, fax, correspondence, independent study, individual study.

Credits Granted for: variable according to the academic program and policies administered by the UBC Registrar's Office; phone (604) 822-5544 for details.

Admission Requirements: *Undergraduate:* variable; call (604) 822-5544. *Graduate:* variable; call (604) 822-5544 or contact UBC Registrar's office. *Doctoral:* variable; call (604) 822-5544 or contact Distance Education and Technology. *Certificate:* variable; call (604) 822-5544.

On-Campus Requirements: Usually UBC's distance education programs do not require on-campus class and lab work, but students should check with their appropriate faculty adviser for exceptions.

Tuition and Fees: *Undergraduate:* $77/credit. *Graduate:* There is no per-credit rate, graduate students pay via lump sum payments. *Doctoral:* Fees vary according to the academic program. *Application Fee:* $45. *Credit by:* semester.

Financial Aid: UBC's endowment fund endows undergraduate scholarships, undergraduate and graduate bursaries, and graduate fellowships. Please call the Awards and Financial Aid office at (604) 822-5111 for more information.

Accreditation: Association of Universities and Colleges of Canada.

Description: The University of British Columbia (1915) is one of the largest universities in Canada and is recognized as a global center of research and learning. Under Continuing Studies at UBC, Distance Education and Technology (DE&T) develops and delivers programs, courses, and learning materials for individuals and clients who require cost-effective, quality education delivered in flexible formats. Faculty and off-campus organizations pool their expertise to develop interdisciplinary programs on local, national, and international levels. In this way, DE&T serves learners unable to attend the UBC campus regularly. Since 1949, UBC distance programs have focused on the needs of lifelong learners wishing to complete degrees, update their knowledge and skills, or change careers. DE&T serves these learners in collaboration with all 12 UBC faculties and the various program areas of Continuing Studies.

University of Calgary

| 2500 University Drive NW | Phone: (403) 220-7346 |
| Calgary, AB, Canada T2N 1N4 | Fax: (403) 777-1959 |

Division(s): Distance Learning
Web Site(s): http://www.ucalgary.ca
E-mail: ikirek@ucalgary.ca

Undergraduate Degree Programs:
Bachelor of Nursing Post Diploma
Bachelor of Community Rehabilitation

Graduate Degree Programs:
Master of Education in:
    Adult, Community and Higher Education
    Teaching and Learning
    Educational Technology
    Educational Leadership

Master of Continuing Education
Master of Education, Pan Canadian Collaborative Degree in Community Rehabilitation
Master of Strategic Studies

Certificate Programs: Teacher Assistant, Adult Learning.

Teaching Methods: *Computers:* Internet, real-time chat, electronic classroom, e-mail, CD-ROM, newsgroup, LIST-SERV. *TV:* videotape, satellite broadcasting. *Other:* audioconferencing, videoconferencing, fax, independent study, learning contracts.

Credits Granted for: extrainstitutional learning, examination (CLEP, ACT-PEP, DANTES, GRE).

Admission Requirements: *Undergraduate:* 65% average high school. *Graduate:* 3.0 GPA.

On-Campus Requirements: one graduate program has a 3-week on-site requirement.

Tuition and Fees: *Undergraduate:* $176/half course. *Graduate:* $497/credit. *Application Fee:* $60. *Credit by:* semester.

Financial Aid: Provincial Federal Student Loan Program.

Accreditation: Association of Universities and Colleges of Canada.

Description: The University of Calgary (1966) shares the youth and energy of the city and province with which it has grown. Combining the best of long-established university traditions with Calgary's entrepreneurial spirit, the U of C offers a dynamic learning experience and the opportunity to study with leading academic explorers. The institution is the most research-intensive university in Alberta and among the top 10 in Canada.

University of California Irvine Extension

Pereira Drive, West of East Peltason
PO Box 6050
Irvine, CA 92616-6050

Phone: (949) 824-5414
Fax: (949) 824-2090

Division(s): Engineering and Information Technologies
Web Site(s): http://www.unex.uci.edu/academic/tech
E-mail: unex@uci.edu

Certificate Programs: specializing in certificate programs and courses only.

Class Titles: Visual Basic, Visual C++, Visual J++.

Teaching Methods: *Computers:* Internet. *Other:* None.

Credits Granted for: experiential learning, extrainstitutional learning (corporate or professional association seminars/workshops), examination (SAT, GMAT, GRE).

Admission Requirements: *Certificate:* students must meet one of the following: (1) bachelor's degree in engineering, computer science, math, physics, or business and 2 years of relevant work experience; (2) associate degree in relevant discipline and 4 years of work experience in computer and/or software engineering; or (3) equivalent work experience with the consent of the program director.

On-Campus Requirements: None.

Tuition and Fees: *Doctoral:* $540/3-unit certificate course. *Application Fee:* $50 certificate candidacy fee. *Software:* downloaded from online classroom provider. *Credit by:* quarter.

Financial Aid: Citibank Assist Student Loan Program.

Accreditation: Western Association of Schools and Colleges, National University Continuing Education Association.

Description: UC Irvine Extension (1963) is the continuing education branch of the University of California, Irvine. For more than 30 years, we have offered quality continuing education courses taught by UCI faculty members and industry experts from business and the professions. All classes are open to the public. There is no lengthy application process, and a college degree is not required for most courses. We currently offer more than 1,800 courses in 40 certificate programs and specialized studies each year. Classes are located on the UC Irvine campus, at the UCI Learning Center in Orange, California. Most courses are offered at night and on weekends. We currently offer 3 online courses in Windows programming. New courses are developed each quarter to meet the changing needs of professionals.

University of California Extension

2000 Center Street, Suite 400
Berkeley, CA 94704

Phone: (510) 642-4124
Fax: (510) 643-9271

Division(s): Center for Media and Independent Learning
Web Site(s): http://www-cmil.unex.berkeley.edu and http://learn.berkeley.edu
E-mail: askcmil@uclink4.berkeley.edu

Certificate Programs: Hazardous Materials Management, Computer Information Systems.

Class Titles: Ancient Egyptian Art, Drawing, Publication Design, Graphic Design, Art of Film, Screenwriting, Classics of Children's Literature, Multicultural Literature, Women Writers, Shakespeare, English Language, Mystery Fiction, English Novel, U.S. Fiction, Writing, Business Writing Review, ESL Grammar/Composition, Grammar for Editors, Composition/Literature, Technical Writing, Editorial Workshop, Writing/Revising Short Story, Popular Forms of Fiction, Marketing/Publishing Fiction, Nonfiction Writing, Creative Nonfiction, Magazine Article Writing, Advanced Article Writing, Poetry Writing, World Civilization: Neolithic Age–Renaissance, World Civilization: 1500–Present, U.S. History, Cultural Diversity in U.S., Cyberculture Studies, Chinese, French, Italian, Spanish, Spanish for Professions,

Music Appreciation, Musics of World, History of Western Philosophy, History of Buddhist Philosophy, World Religions, Administrative Accounting, Financial Accounting, Managerial Accounting, Accounting, Cost Accounting, Auditing, Electronic Data Processing/Operational Auditing, Governmental Accounting Information Systems, Federal Income Tax (Individuals/Partnerships/Corporations), Business Law, Investment Management, Human Resources, Labor Relations/Collective Bargaining, International Business, Cultural Diversity within Organization, Information Resource Management, Business Organization/Management, Small Business Management, Managing Production/Operations, Project Management, Quality Management, Cultural Diversity/New Business Opportunities, Marketing, Public Relations, Purchasing, Real Estate, Information Systems, Database Management Systems, Systems Analysis/Design, Information Resource Management, Online Searching/Electronic Research, UNIX System, Programming: BASIC XII/PASCAL/C/C++/Java, Data Communications/Networks, Digital Telecommunications, Computer Networks, Digital Integrated Circuits, Modern Plague: HIV/AIDS, HMOs/Managed Care, Nutrition, Radiologic Technology, Algebra, Precalculus, Calculus, Math for Electronics, Statistics, Astronomy, Physics, Biology, Biology of Cancer, Human Physiology, Molecular Cell Biology, Genetics, Marine Biology, Plant Life in California, Chemistry, Organic Chemistry, Biochemistry, Environmental Issues, U.S. Environmental/Cultural History, Earthquakes, Physical Geology, Geology of California, Hazardous Materials Management, Environmental Regulatory Framework, Toxicology/Risk Assessment for Environmental Decision Making, Environmental Behavior of Pollutants, Treatment Disposal/Remediation of Hazardous Wastes, Hazardous Materials Emergency Management, Pollution Prevention/Waste Minimization, Environmental Auditing/Assessment, Pest Control-Prevention Control Corrections/Repairs, Poetry of Self: Writer Within, Managing Stress/Conflict in Workplace, Time Management, Psychological/Social Health, Managing Major Life Changes, Physical Anthropology, Social/Cultural Anthropology, Exploring Contemporary Culture through Film, Economics (macro/micro), U.S. Politics, Psychology, Critical Thinking, Abnormal Psychology, Developmental Psychology, Adolescence, Psychology of Communication, Sociology, Crime/Society.

Teaching Methods: *Computers:* Internet, real-time chat, electronic classroom, e-mail. *Other:* audiotapes, fax, correspondence, independent study.

Admission Requirements: *Undergraduate:* Course completion in one year for independent study courses; 6 months for online courses. *Certificate:* 4 year completion.

On-Campus Requirements: None.

Tuition and Fees: *Undergraduate:* approximately $415/course. *Application Fee:* $60 certificate programs. *Other Costs:* $50 Online Resource Fee/online course. *Credit by:* semester.

Financial Aid: VA.

Accreditation: Western Association of Schools and Colleges.

Description: The University of California is one of the largest and most acclaimed institutions of higher education in the world. The Center for Media and Independent Learning is the distance learning division of University of California Extension, the continuing education arm of UC. CMIL was established more than 85 years ago to expand university resources throughout the community, state, and nation. CMIL offers 150 college and professional courses at a distance, including 50 courses online.

University of Central Oklahoma

100 North University, Box 192	Phone: (405) 974-5395
Edmond, OK 73034	Fax: (405) 974-3835

Division(s): Information Technology Consulting
Web Site(s): http://www.ucok.edu/Cyber
http://libweb.ucok.edu:10020/Cyber
E-mail: smartin@ucok.edu

Undergraduate Degree Programs:
Bachelor of Arts in Criminal Justice

Graduate Degree Programs:
Master of Arts in Criminal Justice

Class Titles: Psychology of Grief, Administration of Justice, Women Artists, Vocational Student Organizations, Methods of Teaching Occupational/Technical Education, History of Teaching Occupational/Technical Education, Instructional Development, Art History, Survey of Art History, Medical Terminology, Business, Business Statistics, Legal Aspects of Business Environment, Personal Finance, Business Finance, Financial Statement Analysis, Salesmanship, Marketing, Marketing Research, Sales Management, Organic Chemistry, Economics (macro/micro), Educational Psychology, Child Psychology, Adolescent Psychology, Grammar, Composition, Human Geography, American National Government, State/Local Government, Wellness/Positive Life, Oklahoma History, Nutrition, College Algebra for Business, College Algebra, Math/Analysis for Business, Math for Elementary Teachers, History of Mathematics, Sociology, Social Problems, Social Psychology, Juvenile Delinquency, Minorities/American Society, Sociology/Health/Medicine, Family, Criminology, Organizational Behavior, Human Behavior/Sociological Environment, Sociological Theory, Police Administration/Organization, Police Community Relations, Innovations of Corrections/Penology, Administration of Correctional Institutions.

Teaching Methods: *Computers:* Internet, e-mail, LISTSERV. *TV:* TV transmission, videotape, One-Net Fiber Optics System. *Other:* fax, correspondence, videoconferencing, telephone, interactive TV, videocassette, audioconferencing.

Credits Granted for: experiential learning, portfolio assessment, extrainstitutional learning, examination (CLEP, ACT-PEP, DANTES, GRE).

Admission Requirements: *Undergraduate:* high school

diploma, transcripts, ACT, application fee. *Graduate:* bachelor's degree in Criminal Justice or related field, college transcripts, application fee.

On-Campus Requirements: Undergraduate Criminal Justice program: 2 6-hour visits (beginning and end of program). Graduate Criminal Justice program: same as undergraduate plus comprehensive exam.

Tuition and Fees: *Undergraduate:* $47/credit in-state, $87/ credit out-of-state. *Graduate:* $62/credit in-state, $102/ credit out-of-state. *Application Fee:* $15. *Credit by:* semester.

Financial Aid: Federal Stafford Loan, Federal Perkins Loan, Federal PLUS Loan, Federal Pell Grant, Federal Work-Study, VA, Oklahoma resident programs.

Accreditation: North Central Association of Colleges and Schools.

Description: Educating students to succeed in life is the primary mission of the University of Central Oklahoma (1890). UCO adheres to the philosophy that education is the key that allows us to fulfill our potential and to be of service to others. However, it also believes in one other very important concept—that everyone should have access to the benefits of higher education without going broke in the process.

University of Charleston

2300 MacCorkle Avenue SE	Phone: (304) 357-4714
Charleston, WV 25304	Fax: (304) 357-4769

Division(s): Special Programs
Web Site(s): http://www.uchaswv.edu
E-mail: jhoyer@uchaswv.edu

Class Titles: Interpersonal Communication, Leadership Development, Microsoft Applications, Novell.

Teaching Methods: *Computers:* Internet, real-time chat, electronic classroom, e-mail, CD-ROM, newsgroup, LISTSERV. *Other:* fax, correspondence, independent study, individual study, learning contracts.

Credits Granted for: experiential learning, portfolio assessment, extrainstitutional learning, examination (CLEP, ACT-PEP, DANTES, GRE).

Admission Requirements: *Undergraduate:* 2.25 GPA, 18 on ACT or 850 on SAT.

On-Campus Requirements: None.

Tuition and Fees: *Undergraduate:* $255/credit distance learning. *Credit by:* semester.

Financial Aid: Federal Stafford Loan, Federal Perkins Loan, Federal PLUS Loan, Federal Pell Grant, Federal Work-Study, VA, West Virginia resident programs.

Accreditation: North Central Association of Colleges and Schools.

Description: Founded in 1988, the University of Charleston has offered self-paced courses since the 1980s. In 1997 it began awarding credit for CBT courses offered through various employers.

University of Cincinnati

PO Box 210019	Phone: (513) 556-9154
Cincinnati, OH 45221-0019	Fax: (513) 556-6380

Division(s): College of Evening and Continuing Education
Web Site(s): http://www.uc.edu/
http://www/cece/
E-mail: melody.clark@uc.edu

Undergraduate Degree Programs:
Bachelor of Science in Nursing—College of Nursing/Health
Bachelor of Science in Fire Science Administration—College of Applied Science

Class Titles: Social Sciences, Business/Management, Humanities.

Teaching Methods: *Computers:* Internet, electronic classroom, e-mail, CD-ROM. *TV:* videotape, cable program, satellite broadcasting, PBS. *Other:* videoconferencing, audiotapes, fax, correspondence, independent study, individual study, learning contracts.

Credits Granted for: experiential learning, portfolio assessment, examination (CLEP, ACT-PEP, DANTES, GRE).

On-Campus Requirements: yes for telecourses (individual courses), no for fire science and nursing.

Tuition and Fees: *Undergraduate:* $132/credit resident, $341/ credit out-of-state. *Graduate:* $187/credit resident, $352/credit out-of-state. *Application Fee:* $30. *Credit by:* quarter.

Financial Aid: Federal Stafford Loan, Federal Perkins Loan, Federal PLUS Loan, Federal Pell Grant, Federal Work-Study, VA, Ohio resident programs.

Accreditation: North Central Association of Colleges and Schools.

Description: The University of Cincinnati (1819) traces its origins to Cincinnati College and the Medical College of Ohio. Located on 5 campuses, the university today serves 34,000 students through 17 colleges and divisions offering 450 degree programs from the associate to the doctoral level. The University of Cincinnati has established a continuing reputation for excellence in graduate and undergraduate education, cultural services, and basic and applied research. Since its founding, UC has been the source of many contributions to society, including the oral polio vaccine, the first program of cooperative education, the first electronic organ, the first safe antiknock gasoline, and the first antihistamine. The College of Evening and Continuing Education has offered telecourses for 20 years.

University of Colorado, Boulder

Campus Box 435	Phone: (303) 492-6331
Boulder, CO 80309-0435	Fax: (303) 492-5987

Division(s): Center for Advanced Training in Engineering and Computer Science (CATECS)
Web Site(s): http://www.colorado.edu/CATECS/
E-mail: catecs-info@colorado.edu

Graduate Degree Programs:
Master of Science in:
   Aerospace Engineering
   Electrical and Computer Engineering
   Telecommunications
Master of Engineering in:
   Aerospace Engineering
   Computer Science
   Electrical and Computer Engineering
   Engineering Management
   Telecommunications

Certificate Programs: Engineering Management

Class Titles: Any of the 150 CATECS classes may be taken without degree program admission.

Teaching Methods: *Computers:* Internet, e-mail, LISTSERV. *TV:* videotape, ITFS (microwave). *Other:* videoconferencing, fax, correspondence, independent study, individual study.

Admission Requirements: *Graduate:* accredited bachelor's degree in engineering or technical science, 3.0 GPA, possibly GRE. Most departments allow completion time of 4 years for MS degree, 6 years for Master of Engineering. *Certificate:* For Engineering Management, 2 years of professional experience, undergraduate degree, 3.0 GPA, demonstrated writing proficiency.

On-Campus Requirements: defense of final thesis/project for some programs.

Tuition and Fees: *Graduate:* $332/credit. *Application Fee:* $40. *Software:* varies. *Other Costs:* textbooks. *Credit by:* semester.

Financial Aid: Contact Financial Aid Office (303) 492-5091.

Accreditation: North Central Association of Colleges and Schools, Accreditation Board for Engineering and Technology.

Description: For 15 years, the School of Engineering and Applied Science at the University of Colorado (1876) has been a leader in graduate distance learning courses. The Center for Advanced Training in Engineering and Computer Science allows professionals to continue their education or pursue degrees at the work site via live transmission or videotape. Past courses are available for rent or purchase on videotape through the CATECS Tape Library. Created in 1983 in response to the needs of business, industry, and government leaders, CATECS enrolls 1,600 annually from 250 job sites worldwide. Students pursuing master's degrees or professional development receive the best of both worlds through CATECS: the convenience of distance education and University of Colorado academic quality.

University of Dallas
Graduate School of Management

1845 East Northgate Drive	Phone: (972) 721-4008
Irving, TX 75062-4736	Fax: (972) 721-4009

Division(s): Distance Learning Coordinator
Web Site(s): http://gsm.udallas.edu
E-mail: kpotwark@gsm.udallas.edu

Graduate Degree Programs:
Master of Business Administration in Health Services and Telecommunications
Master of Management in Health Services and Telecommunications

Certificate Programs: Telecommunications, Health Services Management.

Teaching Methods: *Computers:* Internet, electronic classroom, e-mail. *TV:* videotape, satellite broadcasting. *Other:* videoconferencing, independent study, individual study.

Admission Requirements: *Graduate:* GMAT, transcripts for evaluation. *Certificate:* bachelor's degree.

On-Campus Requirements: None.

Tuition and Fees: *Graduate:* $380/credit. *Credit by:* trimester.

Financial Aid: Federal Stafford Loan, Federal Perkins Loan, Federal PLUS Loan, Federal Pell Grant, Federal Work-Study, VA, Texas resident programs.

Accreditation: Southern Association of Colleges and Schools.

Description: The University of Dallas was founded in 1956 as an independent Catholic university dedicated to excellence in its educational programs. In its short history, UD has become one of the nation's leading Catholic universities. The Graduate School of Management, with an enrollment of 1,450 students, has become the largest MBA-granting institution in the Southwest. The school was founded in 1966 with a distinctive mission: to make a professionally sound MBA program accessible to individuals employed in business and the professions. Since then, the graduate school's scope has broadened to serve a wider clientele, including students from 50 countries, but serving the employed professional remains a primary emphasis. More than 75% of GSM students work full-time and pursue their studies part-time.

University of Denver

2211 South Josephine Street
Denver, CO 80210

Phone: (303) 871-3354
(800) 347-2042
Fax: (303) 871-3305

Division(s): University College
Web Site(s): http://www.distance-education.org
http://du.edu
E-mail: Telecommunications Department: bpruter@du.edu
Environment Policy/Management: jsnyder@du.edu
General inquiries: ucolinfo@du.edu

Graduate Degree Programs:
Master of Telecommunications
Master of Environmental Policy and Management

Certificate Programs: Telecommunications:
Network Analysis/Design
Environmental Policy and Management:
Management of Hazardous Materials
Environmental Regulatory Compliance
Ecotourism Management
Environmental Management

Teaching Methods: *Computers:* Internet, real-time chat, electronic classroom, e-mail, CD-ROM, newsgroup, LIST-SERV, bulletin boards *TV:* videotape *Other:* audiotapes, fax, US mail, overnight mail.

Credits Granted for: Credit is only awarded for classes taken at an accredited college or university.

Admission Requirements: *Graduate:* accredited undergraduate degree, acceptable GPA, writing sample, 2 letters of recommendation, no GRE or GMAT needed. *Certificate:* no undergraduate degree needed; course work may be applied to a degree.

On-Campus Requirements: None.

Tuition and Fees: *Graduate:* $310/credit. *Application Fee:* $25. *Software:* generally no special software is required that is not free off the Internet; Internet access is required. *Other Costs:* $4/credit additional technology fee applied to all courses taken for credit. *Credit by:* quarter

Financial Aid: Some financial aid programs are available to assist students who are unconditionally admitted to master's degree programs. Certificate candidates in approved programs may also be eligible for financial aid upon verification of an approved bachelor's degree by the Admissions Office. The University of Denver's Office of Student Financial Services handles all application for financial aid. Call (303) 871-4900 between 8:00 A.M. to 4:30 P.M.

Accreditation: North Central Association of Colleges and Schools.

Description: The University of Denver (1864) is the oldest independent institution of higher education in the Rocky Mountain West. More than 8,500 students from 50 states and 90 countries are enrolled. The student body is evenly divided into undergraduate, traditional graduate, and nontraditional adult continuing education students. The University College specializes in adult education that is career oriented, industry specific, and immediately applicable in the workplace. Courses, degrees, and certificates have been offered by the UC via distance education since 1996. Currently 2 master's degrees, 6 certificates, and more than 60 individual courses are available via the Internet. The UC tailors its programs to adult learners and has separate registration, finance, and advising functions dedicated to its adult student body.

University of Guam

2nd Floor Computer Center/MARC Bldg.
303 University Drive
Mangilao, GU 96923

Phone: (671) 735-2600
Fax: (671) 734-1233

Division(s): Center for Continuing Education and Outreach Programs
Web Site(s): http://uog2.uog.edu/cceop
E-mail: jrrider@uog9.uog.edu

Class Titles: Tourism (planned for future), cooperative program with Toranomon Accounting School in Japan to prepare Japanese accountants to take the American CPA examination, cooperative program with Asia International University for AIU graduates who already have an MBA but who want to pursue an American MBA. Health Assessment, Communications/Critical Thinking for Health Care Providers, Transitional Nursing Concepts, Pathophysiology, Nutrition for Health Professionals, Leadership Management for Health Professionals, Communication/Mental Health.

Teaching Methods: *Computers:* Internet, e-mail, newsgroup, LISTSERV. *TV:* videotape, cable program, satellite radio broadcasting (PEACESAT). *Other:* radio broadcast, audio-conferencing, fax.

Credits Granted for: experiential learning.

Admission Requirements: *Undergraduate:* 12 years of formal education or GED of 45, application, placement exam for English and Math, MMR vaccination, PPD test for tuberculosis. Residency established after 12 months. Request catalog for more admission details. *Graduate:* application, 2 copies of official transcripts, 2 letters of recommendation, letter of intent, GRE/GMAT, meet English language requirements, MMR vaccination, PPD test for tuberculosis. Residency established after 12 months. Request catalog for more admission details.

On-Campus Requirements: program specific.

Tuition and Fees: *Undergraduate:* $66/credit resident, $198/credit nonresident. *Graduate:* $90/credit resident, $224/credit nonresident. *Application Fee:* $37, $62 international. *Other Costs:* $155, $187 international for student fees. *Credit by:* semester.

Financial Aid: Federal Stafford Loan, Federal Perkins Loan, Federal PLUS Loan, Federal Pell Grant, Federal Work-Study, VA, Guam resident programs.

Accreditation: Western Association of Schools and Colleges.

Description: The University of Guam (1952) is the major institution of higher education in the Western Pacific. It is a land-grant institution. The campus is located on a gently sloping, 100-acre site minutes from the Guam capital of Agana. It overlooks Pago Bay and commands a breathtaking view of the Pacific Ocean. On the shoreline is the UOG Marine Lab. On-campus, student resident facilities are available.

University of Guelph

160 Johnston Hall	Phone: (519) 824-4120 x6776
Guelph, ON, Canada N1G 2W1	Fax: (519) 824-1112

Division(s): Office of Open Learning
Web Site(s): http://www.open.uoguelph.ca
E-mail: info@open.uoguelph.ca

Undergraduate Degree Programs:
Bachelor of Arts

Certificate Programs: Food Science

Class Titles: Plants/Human Use, Economics (macro/micro), English Writers, Human Development, French, Geology, Science/Society Since 1500, History of Cultural Form, Music, Nutrition/Society, Physics, World Politics, Behaviour, Dynamics of Behaviour, Spanish, Humans in Natural World, Calculus (nondegree), Cell Biology, Personal/Financial Management, Biology of Plant Pests, Apiculture, Contemporary Cinema, Economic Growth/Environmental Quality, Business Economics, Couple/Family Relationships, Human Sexuality, Exceptional Child in Family, Infant Development, Food Science, Food Processing, British Isles—1066–1603, Canadian Business Management, 5,000 Days, Meteorology, History of Jazz, Family/Community Nutrition, Philosophy of Environment, Canadian Government, Social Psychology, Personality, Soil Science, Environmental Stewardship, Statistics for Business Decisions, Aquatic Environments, Nature Interpretation, Finance, Equity Markets, Communication, Technology, Adolescent Development, German for Professionals, Celtic Britain/Ireland to 1066, Witchcraft/Popular Culture: Scotland 1560–1700, Celtic Britain/Ireland Since 1603, Scotland in Age of Immigration, Beyond 5,000 Days, Planning Recreation/Tourism, Disease, Environmental Policy Formation/Administration, Occupational Health Psychology, Psychological Measurement, Industrial-Organizational Psychology, Psychology of Death/Dying, Mental Retardation, Soil/Water Conservation/Reclamation, Forest Ecology (graduate).

Teaching Methods: *Computers:* Internet, Web-based conferencing, electronic classroom, e-mail, CD-ROM, newsgroup, LISTSERV, quizzes on disk. *TV:* videotape. *Other:* audiotapes, audio CDs, microfiche, fax, correspondence.

Admission Requirements: *Undergraduate:* varies.

On-Campus Requirements: None.

Tuition and Fees: *Undergraduate:* $346/credit Canadian. *Other Costs:* $65 Canadian/credit Distance Education Resource Fee. *Credit by:* semester.

Financial Aid: Federal Stafford Loan, Federal Perkins Loan, Federal PLUS Loan, Federal Pell Grant, Federal Work-Study, VA, Ontario resident programs.

Accreditation: Association of Universities and Colleges of Canada.

Description: University of Guelph roots go back to the 1964 union of Ontario Agricultural College, Ontario Veterinary College, and Macdonald Institute in this historic city of 95,000 people, 60 miles west of Toronto and 75 miles northwest of Niagara Falls. This union now includes physical and biological sciences, arts, social sciences, and family and consumer studies. Also, the school's 100 years of tradition and its progressive outlook to the future make it one of Canada's leading research institutions. The Office of Open Learning continues the university's long tradition of outreach, offering short courses, workshops, seminars, conferences, and degree-credit distance education courses. Distance courses serve nondegree and degree students, who generally complete courses on-campus and via distance.

University of Hawaii System

2532 Correa Road, Building 37	Phone: (808) 956-5023
Honolulu, HI 96822	Fax: (808) 956-9966

Division(s): Information Technology Services: Distance Learning and Instructional Technology
Web Site(s): http://www2.hawaii.edu/dlit
E-mail: hae@hawaii.edu

Undergraduate Degree Programs:
Associate of Arts
Bachelor of Arts in Liberal Studies
Bachelor of Arts in Professional Studies
Bachelor of Education in Elementary Education
Bachelor of Education in Secondary Education
Bachelor of Science in Computer Science

Graduate Degree Programs:
Master of Science in:
    Computer Science
    Counseling and Guidance
    Educational Administration
    Library Studies
    Nursing
    Public Administration
    Public Health
    Social Work

Telecommunication and Information Resource Management
Professional Education Diploma

Certificate Programs: Counseling and Guidance, Professional Education Diploma, Special Education, Telecommunication and Information Resource Management.

Teaching Methods: *Computers:* Internet, real-time chat, electronic classroom, e-mail, CD-ROM, newsgroup, LIST-SERV. *TV:* videotape, cable program. *Other:* audioconferencing, videoconferencing, fax, independent study, individual study.

Credits Granted for: experiential learning, examination (CLEP, ACT-PEP, DANTES, GRE).

Admission Requirements: *Undergraduate:* Must be age 18 for AA degree. Others must be high school graduate with SAT-I or ACT. *Graduate:* accredited bachelor's degree, appropriate graduate exams.

On-Campus Requirements: Depending on program due to the specialized resources needed for the program.

Tuition and Fees: *Undergraduate:* $122/credit residents, $392/credit nonresidents. *Graduate:* $163/credit residents, $410/credit nonresidents. *Application Fee:* $25. *Credit by:* semester.

Financial Aid: Federal Stafford Loan, Federal Perkins Loan, Federal PLUS Loan, Federal Pell Grant, Federal Work-Study, VA, Hawaii resident programs.

Accreditation: Western Association of Schools and Colleges.

Description: The University of Hawaii (1907) is a postsecondary education system composed of 10 campuses throughout the 50th state. In addition to the flagship campus at Mano, it includes the University of Hawaii at Hilo on the island of Hawaii and the smaller University of Hawaii-West Oahu, which offers an upper division program on the leeward side of Oahu. The UH community college system has 4 campuses on Oahu and one each on Maui, Kauai, and Hawaii. The university began systemwide delivery of distance learning in 1990 through the Hawaii Interactive TV System, a microwave network with 2-way video and audio instruction between all campuses. UH currently uses multiple technologies to provide access.

University of Houston

4242 South Mason Road	Phone: (800) 687-8488
Katy, TX 77450	Fax: (281) 395-2629

Division(s): Distance and Continuing Education
Web Site(s): http://www.uh.edu/uhdistance
E-mail: nherron@uh.edu

Undergraduate Degree Programs:
Bachelor of Arts in:

Earth Science
English
History
Psychology
Bachelor of Science in:
Psychology
Hotel and Restaurant Management
Computer Drafting Design Technology
Industrial Supervision Technology

Graduate Degree Programs:
Master of Hospitality Management
Master of Science in Occupational Technology, Training and Development
Master of Science in Computer Science
Master of Education, Reading Specialist Certificate
Master of Education, Reading and Language Arts
Master of Electrical Engineering (Computer/Electronics)
Master of Industrial Engineering (Engineering Management)

Certificate Programs: Curriculum and Instruction-Information Processing Technologies, Curriculum and Instruction-Master of Education with an endorsement in Gifted and Talented Education, Curriculum and Instruction-Master of Education in Reading, Language Arts, and Literature Education, Educational Psychology-Master of Education with a major emphasis in Individual Differences in the Classroom, Technology-Industrial Distribution.

Teaching Methods: *Computers:* Internet, real-time chat, electronic classroom, e-mail, CD-ROM, newsgroup, LIST-SERV. *TV:* videotape, cable program, PBS, interactive TV. *Other:* face-to-face, videoconferencing.

Admission Requirements: *Undergraduate:* application, application fee, official high school/college transcripts. *Graduate:* graduate application, reference letters, official test scores (requirements vary/program), 2 official transcripts from each institution; refer to Graduate and Professional Studies catalog or consult major department before applying. *Certificate:* see undergraduate and graduate admission requirements.

On-Campus Requirements: None.

Tuition and Fees: *Undergraduate:* $337/3 hours residents, $961/3 hours nonresidents. *Graduate:* $397/3 hours residents, $961/3 hours nonresidents. *Application Fee:* $30 for undergraduates, varies by college for graduates. *Other Costs:* $50/semester off-campus fee. *Credit by:* semester.

Financial Aid: Federal Stafford Loan, Federal Perkins Loan, Federal PLUS Loan, Federal Pell Grant, Federal Work-Study, VA, Texas resident programs.

Accreditation: Southern Association of Colleges and Schools, Middle States Association of Colleges and Schools, New England Association of Schools and Colleges, North Central Association of Colleges and Schools, Northwest Association of Schools and Colleges, Western Association of Schools and Colleges.

Description: University of Houston (1927) began distance education in 1980 with 2 off-campus institutes, adding live, closed-circuit, televised classes in 1984. UH began delivering complete distance degrees in 1993. Students may now complete their degrees at neighborhood sites, in the workplace, or at home. UH Distance Education delivers selected degree programs and courses to students via TV (cable and PBS), live videoconferencing, videotape, online to 4 off-campus sites and to 13 community colleges. The university offers more upper-division, resident, credit courses and degree programs and has higher enrollment than any other upper-level institution in Texas. UH DE offers 85 junior, senior, and graduate credit courses each semester enabling students to complete degrees in 14 fields. This translates to 6,500 enrollments annually, with numbers growing every semester. In 1996 the University Continuing Education Association honored UH with an award for Outstanding Distance Education Credit Program in the nation. UH DE also received the 1997 UCEA awards for Outstanding Instructor and Outstanding Promotional Video, plus a 1998 Innovative Distance Education award and 2 Outstanding Faculty awards.

University of Houston, Clear Lake

2700 Bay Area Boulevard	Phone: (281) 283-7600
Houston, TX 77058-1098	Fax: (281) 283-2530

Division(s): Associate Vice-President of Academic Affairs and Associate Deans in each college
Web Site(s): http://www.cl.uh.edu/courses/courses.html
http://www.cl.uh.edu/
E-mail: visit Web site for addresses.

Graduate Degree Programs:
Master of Science in:
    Software Engineering
    Instructional Technology

Class Titles: Software Project Management, Software Construction, Software Engineering Processes, Internet Exploration, Educational Applications of Technology, Environmental Economics, Healthcare Productivity/Quality Assessment, Multicultural Education, Educational Statistics/Measurement, Research Design/Analysis, Literature of Future.

Teaching Methods: *Computers:* Internet, electronic classroom, e-mail, real-time chat, CD-ROM, LISTSERV. *TV:* videotape, cable program, satellite broadcasting. *Other:* audioconferencing, videoconferencing, fax.

Credits Granted for: if approved for the program, up to 18 hours of earned correspondence, extension, or CLEP credit may apply as lower-level credit toward an undergraduate degree.

Admission Requirements: *Undergraduate:* successful completion of college algebra or higher math, 54 hours of college credit with grades of C or better or conferral of an associate degree from an approved regionally accredited institution,

eligibility to return to the last institution attended, Texas Academic Skills Program test or proof of exemption. Admission for degree program candidacy is accomplished by completion of an approved Candidate Plan of Study. All upper level requirements should be completed within 7 years. *Graduate:* an appropriate bachelor's degree from an approved regionally accredited institution and be eligible to return to last institution. Degree-seeking students must also submit GRE, GMAT or other scores as required by the program and establish candidacy by filing an approved Candidate Plan of Study. All degree requirements should be completed within 5 years.

On-Campus Requirements: some classes require attendance on-campus to take exams or participate in class assignments. Others, such as software engineering, may be completed entirely off-campus but in a designated location that can provide an electronic classroom and proctored examinations.

Tuition and Fees: *Undergraduate:* contact school for complete tuition and fee information. *Credit by:* semester.

Financial Aid: Federal Stafford Loan, Federal Perkins Loan, Federal PLUS Loan, Federal Pell Grant, Federal Work-Study, VA, Texas resident programs.

Accreditation: Southern Association of Colleges and Schools; some programs are additionally accredited.

Description: The University of Houston, Clear Lake (1974) is an upper-level education institution which emphasizes (1) learning through teaching, research, scholarship, and professional and community service; (2) the advancement of knowledge; (3) delivery of educational opportunities through new instructional technologies and through distance learning; (4) a commitment to high academic standards; (5) sensitivity to the needs of the students and communities served by the institution; and (6) above all, integrity in all institutional functions. Undergraduate, graduate, and professional programs are available. The university serves a diverse student population from the state, the nation and abroad, particularly from the Houston-Galveston metropolitan area by offering programs on and off campus. Located adjacent to the National Aeronautics and Space Administration's Johnson Space Center, UHCL is situated in the heart of Clear Lake's high-technology community. The first degrees completed entirely off campus were Master of Science degrees awarded in 1997 in the program of Software Engineering.

University of Idaho, Engineering Outreach

University of Idaho	Phone: (208) 885-6373
Moscow, ID 83844-1014	(800) 824-2889
	Fax: (208) 885-6165

Division(s): Engineering Outreach
Web Site(s): http://www.uidaho.edu/evo
E-mail: outreach@uidaho.edu

Graduate Degree Programs:
Master of Arts in Teaching Mathematics
Master of Engineering in:
    Biological/Agricultural Engineering
    Civil Engineering
    Computer Engineering
    Electrical Engineering
    Engineering Management
    Geological Engineering
    Mechanical Engineering
    Metallurgical Engineering
    Mining Engineering
Master of Science in:
    Biological/Agricultural Engineering
    Civil Engineering
    Computer Engineering
    Computer Science
    Electrical Engineering
    Geological Engineering
    Psychology with emphasis in Human Factors

Doctoral Degree Programs:
Doctorate in Computer Science
Doctorate in Electrical Engineering

Teaching Methods: *Computers:* Internet, real-time chat, electronic classroom, e-mail, newsgroup, LISTSERV. *TV:* primary delivery is by videotape; satellite broadcasting. *Other:* videoconferencing, audioconferencing.

Credits Granted for: experiential learning, portfolio assessment, extrainstitutional learning, examination (CLEP, ACT-PEP, DANTES, GRE).

Admission Requirements: *Graduate:* accredited bachelor's degree, 2.8+ GPA, GRE, letters of reference, or a letter of intent. Departments have different requirements. Contact the University of Idaho College of Graduate Studies.

On-Campus Requirements: some on-campus component for PhD programs.

Tuition and Fees: *Graduate:* $341/credit ($314/credit for nondegree-seeking students). *Doctoral:* $341/credit. *Application Fee:* $35. *Other Costs:* lab course fees. *Credit by:* semester.

Financial Aid: Federal Stafford Loan, Federal Perkins Loan, Federal PLUS Loan, Federal Pell Grant, Federal Work-Study, VA, Idaho resident programs.

Accreditation: Northwest Association of Schools and Colleges. Member of National Association of State Universities and Land-Grant Colleges, National Commission on Accrediting. All Engineering Outreach credits are official University of Idaho credits, NOT just correspondence or "distance learning" credits.

Description: The University of Idaho founded the Engineering Outreach program in 1976. As part of the University of Idaho College of Engineering, the Engineering Outreach program uses videotape, interactive videoconferencing, electronic mail, the World Wide Web, and print materials to deliver graduate-level courses to distant students. The program delivers more than 90 courses per semester to about 400 students in 200+ locations and has awarded more than 200 graduate degrees. As it grows, the Engineering Outreach proudly maintains a committed faculty and dedicated staff who seek to meet the individual needs of the students it serves.

University of Illinois, Springfield

PO Box 19243   Phone: (217) 206-6600
Springfield, IL 62794-9243   (800) 252-8533
                                  Fax: (217) 206-6620

Division(s): (1) Office of Technology-Enhanced Learning, (2) Library Media Services
Web Site(s): http://www.uis.edu
E-mail: long.diane@uis.edu

Undergraduate Degree Programs:
Bachelor of Science in Nursing (Illinois Valley College only)

Graduate Degree Programs:
Master of Science in Management Information Systems

Certificate Programs: Career Specialist

Class Titles: Communications, Computer Science, Constitution, Electronic Commerce—Internet, Nursing and Career Specialist courses. No lower-division classes.

Teaching Methods: *Computers:* Internet, real-time chat, electronic classroom, e-mail, CD-ROM, newsgroup, LISTSERV. *TV:* videotape, cable program, satellite broadcasting, PBS. *Other:* videoconferencing, fax, correspondence, independent study, individual study, learning contracts.

Credits Granted for: experiential learning, portfolio assessment, extrainstitutional learning (corporate or professional association seminars/workshops), CLEP examination.

Admission Requirements: *Undergraduate:* accredited 45 semester hours, 2.0 GPA. *Graduate:* accredited bachelor's degree, 2.5 GPA.

On-Campus Requirements: Varies.

Tuition and Fees: *Undergraduate:* $90/credit residents, $271/credit nonresidents. *Graduate:* $99/credit residents, $297/credit nonresidents. *Other Costs:* $30–96 fees. *Credit by:* semester.

Financial Aid: Federal Stafford Loan, Federal Perkins Loan, Federal PLUS Loan, Federal Pell Grant, Federal Work-Study, Federal Supplemental Educational Opportunity Grant, VA, Illinois resident programs, institutional need-based grants, institutional scholarship program.

Accreditation: North Central Association of Colleges and Schools.

Description: Established as Sangamon State University in 1969, the campus joined UI in 1995 and became the University of Illinois at Springfield. The first of 2 senior-level institutions in Illinois, the Springfield campus responds to the community college system and provides new means for individuals to enter upper-division and graduate study. With its interest in innovative education, the campus is involved in the many forms of distance learning.

University of Illinois, Urbana-Champaign

302 East John Street, Suite 1406	Phone: (217) 333-1321
Champaign, IL 61820	Fax: (217) 333-8524

Division(s): Division of Guided Individual Study and Division of Extramural Programs
Web Site(s): http://www.extramural.uiuc.edu/gis/
http://www/extramural.uiuc.edu/
E-mail: GISinfor@c3po.ceps.uiuc.edu

Graduate Degree Programs:
Master of Science in:
    General Engineering
    Electrical Engineering
    Mechanical Engineering
    Theoretical and Applied Mechanics
    Library and Information Science

Class Titles: Accounting, Advertising, Advertising Creative Strategy, Advertising in Contemporary Society, Anthropology Human Origins/Culture, Archaeology of Illinois, Archaeology, Purchasing/Materials Management, Business/Administrative Communication, Technical/Scientific Communication, Marketing, Management, Contemporary Health, Drug Use/Abuse, Health Behavior, Human Sexuality, Health Program Development, Epidemiology, Economics (macro/micro), Economic Statistics, Public Finance, History of Economic Thought, Educational Psychology, Drama, Film, Masterpieces of English Literature, Masterpieces of American Literature, Shakespeare, Modern Short Story, British Novel, American Fiction, French, Engineering Graphics, Physical Geography–Atmospheric Environment, Physical Geography, German, Western Civilization Antiquity–1660, Western Civilization 1660–Present, History of U.S. to 1877, History of U.S. 1877–Present, Latin, Latin Literature, Algebra, Trigonometry, Calculus/Analytical Geometry, Finite Math, Linear Algebra with Applications, Calculus for Social Scientists, Differential Equations/Orthogonal Functions, Linear Transformations/Matrices, Political Science, American Government Organization/Powers, Comparative Politics, Emerging Nations, Political Theory, International Relations, Psychology, Social Psychology, Child Psychology, Cognitive Psychology, Perception/Sensory Processes, Descriptive Statistics, Inferential Statistics, Statistics, Industrial Psychology, Psychology of Learning/Memory, Psychology of Personality, Modern Viewpoints in Psychology, Composition, Russian, 19th Century Russian Literature, Sociology, Modern Africa, Stratification/Social Classes, Juvenile Delinquency, Crowds/Social Movements/ Violence, Alcohol/Society, Family Violence, Spanish, Reading/Writing Spanish.

Teaching Methods: *Computers:* Internet, real-time chat, e-mail. *TV:* videotape. *Other:* videoconferencing, audioconferencing, audiographics, audiotapes, fax, correspondence, independent study, undergraduate credit/placement for prerequisites.

Credits Granted for: examination (CLEP).

Admission Requirements: *Graduate:* contact school for details.

On-Campus Requirements: None.

Tuition and Fees: *Undergraduate:* $83/semester hour. *Graduate:* $155/credit hour, $198/credit hour for graduate engineering, out-of-state tuition for graduation engineering degrees is higher. *Application Fee:* $20 for undergraduate *Other Costs:* $23/course for undergraduate course instructional material fee. *Credit by:* open system with rolling enrollment period; semester hours of credit for undergraduates. Semester hours and graduate units (one unit plus 4 semester hours) for graduates.

Financial Aid: VA, Illinois resident programs.

Accreditation: North Central Association of Colleges and Schools.

Description: Since its founding in 1867, the University of Illinois at Urbana-Champaign (UIUC) has earned a reputation of international stature. As a land-grant institution, it serves 36,000 full-time students by providing undergraduate and graduate education in more than 150 fields of study. In addition, another 75,000 Illinois residents participate in conferences, institutes, credit and noncredit courses, and workshops each year. These nontraditional programs are offered statewide and nationally at public and corporate sites. The university's more significant resource is its talented and highly respected faculty, which includes Nobel laureates and Pulitzer Prize winners. The campus's academic resources are among the finest in the world.

University of Iowa

116 International Center	Phone: (800) 272-6430
Iowa City, IA 52242-1802	(319) 335-2575
	Fax: (319) 335-2740

Division(s): Center for Credit Programs
Web Site(s): http://www.uiowa.edu/~ccp
E-mail: credit-programs@uiowa.edu

Undergraduate Degree Programs:
Bachelor of Liberal Studies

Class Titles: academic subject areas—African American World Studies, African Studies, Aging, American Studies, Anthropology, Art/Art History, Asian Languages/Literature,

Center for Book, Classics, Communication, Dance, Economics, Education, Counselor Education, Curriculum/Instruction, Psychological/Quantitative Foundations, Nonfiction Writing, Creative Writing, Exercise Science, French, Geography, German, History, American History, European History, Journalism/Mass Communication, Linguistics, Math, Medicine, Nursing, Political Science, Psychology, Religion, Rhetoric, Social Work, Sociology, Spanish, Sport/Health/Leisure/Physical Studies, Statistics, Theater Arts, Women's Studies.

Teaching Methods: *Computers:* Internet, e-mail. *TV:* videotape. *Other:* audiotapes, fax, guided correspondence.

Credits Granted for: extrainstitutional learning (corporate or professional association seminars/workshops), examination (limited CLEP).

Admission Requirements: *Undergraduate:* 24 transferable semester hours, 2.25 GPA.

On-Campus Requirements: None.

Tuition and Fees: *Undergraduate:* $84/credit Guided Correspondence. *Graduate:* $84/credit Guided Correspondence. *Application Fee:* $20. *Other Costs:* $15/course correspondence fee, books, materials. *Credit by:* semester.

Financial Aid: limited.

Accreditation: North Central Association of Colleges and Schools.

Description: The University of Iowa opened in 1847 and first offered correspondence study in 1916. Its Guided Correspondence Study allows independent, self-paced learning and personalized instruction. The flexibility of the 160 GCS courses makes it excellent for students with work or family obligations. UI also provides distance education courses through interactive TV and as telecourses, but these are limited to in-state audiences.

University of Kansas

Continuing Education Building	**Phone: (785) 864-4440**
Lawrence, KS 66045-2606	**Fax: (785) 864-7895**

Division(s): Academic Outreach Programs, Continuing Education
Web Site(s): http://www.kumc.edu/kuce/isc
E-mail: ssh@falcon.cc.ukans.edu

Class Titles: Black Experience in Americas, American Society, General Anthropology, Fundamentals of Physical Anthropology, Cultural Anthropology, Myth/Legend/Folk Belief in East Asia, Fundamentals of Physical Anthropology, Meteorology, Unusual Weather, Sign Variations/Research, Principles of Biology, Principles of Human Physiology, Human Sexuality, Greek/Roman Mythology, Word Power: Greek/Latin Elements in English, Organizational Communication, Loving Relationships, Myth/Legend/Folk Belief in East Asia, Economics, Composition, Composition/Literature, Composition/Literature: Literature of Sports, Fiction, Poetry, American Literature, Recent Popular Literature, Shakespeare, Writing Fiction, Grammar/Usage for Composition, Business Writing, Technical Writing, Literature for Children, Directed Study: Willa Cather, Directed Study: Ernest Hemingway, Kansas Literature, Principles of Environmental Studies, French for Reading Knowledge, Principles of Physical Geography, Human Geography, History of Earth, German, World History, History of U.S. through Civil War, History of U.S. after Civil War, America/World War II, Hitler/Nazi Germany, Imperial Russia/Soviet Union, History of American Indian, History of Kansas, Art History, Impressionism, Principles of Environmental Design/Family, Child Behavior/Development, Principles of Nutrition/Health in Development, Marriage/Family Relationships, Adult Development/Aging, Children/TV, Western Civilization, Latin, Latin Reading/Grammar, Virgil's Aeneid, Math, Algebra, Trigonometry, Precalculus Mathematics, Mathematics for Elementary Teachers, Calculus, Statistics, Philosophy, Reason/Argument, U.S. Politics, Comparative Politics, Public Administration, U.S. Government/Politics, General Psychology, Statistics in Psychological Research, Cognitive Psychology, Child Psychology, Social Psychology, Brain/Behavior, Mind, Children/TV, Human Sexuality, Psychology/Law, Psychology of Adolescence, Psychology of Families, Living Religions of West, Understanding Bible, Loving Relationship, Elements of Sociology, Social Problems/American Values, Sociology of Families, Principles of Sociology, American Society, Sociology of Sex Roles, Sociology of Aging, Spanish Reading, Spanish, Survey of Communication Disorders, History of American Sound Film, Coaching of Basketball, Personal/Community Health, Principles of Health/Nutrition, Communicable/Degenerative Diseases, Drugs in Society, Environmental Health, Career/Life Planning: Decision Making for College Students, Principles of Human Learning, Psychology/Education of Exceptional Children/Youth, Design/Delivery of Instruction Using Educational Communications, Managing Behavior Problems: Concepts/Applications, Curriculum Development for Exceptional Children/Youth, Teaching Reading in Content Areas, Teaching Literature for Young Adults (Grades 7–12), Foundations of Education, Foundations of Curriculum/Instruction, History/Philosophy of Education, Design/Delivery of Instruction Using Educational Communications, Curriculum Planning for Educational Settings, Jazz, Mainstreaming/Inclusion in Music Education, Reporting, Managing Stress: Principles/Techniques for Coping/Prevention/Wellness. Options for High School Students: American Government, Career Planning, Project Self-Discovery, Short Story for Reluctant Readers.

Teaching Methods: *Computers:* Internet, real-time chat, electronic classroom, e-mail, CD-ROM, newsgroup, LISTSERV. *TV:* videotape. *Other:* fax, correspondence, independent study.

Admission Requirements: *Undergraduate:* contact school. *Graduate:* contact school.

On-Campus Requirements: None.

Tuition and Fees: *Undergraduate:* $91/credit. *Graduate:* $132/credit. *Other Costs:* $45 for materials, handling and postage; $15–$45 audio/video user fees. *Credit by:* semester.

Financial Aid: Federal Stafford Loan, Federal Pell Grant, VA, Kansas resident programs.

Accreditation: North Central Association of Colleges and Schools.

Description: The University of Kansas (1865) has been involved in distance education since 1891. The university is the premier research institution in Kansas and serves a wide variety of educational and professional groups.

University of La Verne

1950 3rd Street   Phone: (800) 695-4858 x5301
La Verne, CA 91750   Fax: (909) 981-8695

Division(s): ULV On-Line
Web Site(s): http://www.ulv.edu/dlc/dlc.html
E-mail: harrisoa@ulv.edu

Class Titles: Biology, Chemistry, Core General Education, Education, English, History, Humanities, Political Science, Psychology.

Teaching Methods: *Computers:* Internet, real-time chat, e-mail, LISTSERV. *TV:* videotape. *Other:* audiotapes, fax, correspondence, independent study, individual study.

Credits Granted for: experiential learning, portfolio assessment, extrainstitutional learning, examination (CLEP, ACT-PEP, DANTES, GRE).

Admission Requirements: *Undergraduate:* 2.0 GPA. *Graduate:* accredited bachelor's degree, 2.5 GPA in last 60 undergraduate semester hours, 3 positive references, demonstrated graduate writing ability.

On-Campus Requirements: Not for the individual courses currently being offered, except for one lab session in Biology.

Tuition and Fees: *Undergraduate:* $275/credit plus lab fees in certain lab courses. *Graduate:* $335/credit. *Application Fee:* $25. *Other Costs:* $10/course for academic services (library). *Credit by:* semester.

Financial Aid: Federal Stafford Loan, Federal Perkins Loan, Federal PLUS Loan, Federal Pell Grant, VA, California resident programs. These are available for matriculated students only.

Accreditation: Western Association of Schools and Colleges.

Description: University of La Verne (1891) is an independent, nonsectarian university with a strong liberal arts curriculum and recognized professional programs in business, communications, counseling, education, educational management, health services management, law, and public administration. It offers bachelor's and master's degrees in several fields and doctoral degrees in educational management, law, psychol-

ogy, and public administration. In 1969 the university began offering programs off its central campus; currently it has campuses or centers in Alaska; Athens, Greece; and at several locations in California. Building upon this solid foundation, La Verne began offering undergraduate general education, graduate business, and graduate professional courses over the Internet in 1996 and is preparing to offer its first Web-based degree programs in 1998.

University of Louisville

First and Brandeis Streets
School of Education   Phone: (502) 852-6421
Louisville, KY 40292   Fax: (502) 852-3976

Division(s): Special Education
Web Site(s): http://www.louisville.edu/edu/edsp/distance/
E-mail: d0edge01@athena.louisville.edu

Graduate Degree Programs:
Master of Education in:
    Special Education
    Visual Impairment

Certificate Programs: Special Education for Teachers, Visual Impairment for Teachers.

Class Titles: Mental Retardation, Learning Disabilities, Autism, Assistive Technology, Inclusion.

Teaching Methods: *Computers:* video-streaming, Internet, real-time chat, electronic classroom, e-mail, LISTSERV. *TV:* videotape, cable program, satellite broadcasting. *Other:* audioconferencing, videoconferencing, audiographics, audiotapes, fax, correspondence, independent study, individual study, learning contracts.

Credits Granted for: transfer credits.

Admission Requirements: *Graduate:* BA, GRE, transcripts. *Certificate:* BA, transcripts.

On-Campus Requirements: The Program in Visual Impairment requires student teaching which is offered at the Kentucky School for the Blind during the summer. Special arrangements may be made at an institution near the student.

Tuition and Fees: *Graduate:* $175/credit Kentucky residents, $500/credit out-of-state. *Application Fee:* $25. *Other Costs:* books. *Credit by:* semester.

Financial Aid: Kentucky resident programs, other state programs; check with your Director of Special Education in your school district.

Accreditation: Southern Association of Colleges and Schools, National Council Accreditation of Teacher Education.

Description: The University of Louisville (1798) is a state institution originally established as Jefferson Seminary. Five years ago, in response to a critical shortage of teachers in visual impairment, the Department of Special Education developed a distance learning program. Since that time, the Distance Education Program has won 3 national awards from the U.S. Distance Learning Association for the Best Distance Learning Programs in the Nation in Higher Education. We currently offer 20 courses and enroll 500 students annually. UL is committed to offering its distance students the same quality of education and access to resources as students studying on campus.

University of Maine

5713 Chadbourne Hall, Room 122	Phone: (207) 581-3143
Orono, ME 04469-5713	Fax: (207) 581-3141

Division(s): Continuing Education Division
Web Site(s): http://www.maine.edu/~ced/lifelongtop.html
E-mail: CEDSS@Maine.edu

Undergraduate Degree Programs:
Bachelor of University Studies

Graduate Degree Programs:
Master of Arts in Liberal Studies

Certificate Programs: Maine Studies, Classical Studies.

Teaching Methods: *Computers:* Internet, real-time chat, electronic classroom, e-mail, CD-ROM, newsgroup, LIST-SERV. *TV:* videotape, cable program, PBS. *Other:* audioconferencing, videoconferencing, audiographics, audiotapes, fax, correspondence, independent study, individual study, learning contracts.

Credits Granted for: experiential learning, portfolio assessment, extrainstitutional learning, examination (CLEP, ACT-PEP, DANTES, GRE).

Admission Requirements: *Undergraduate:* SAT I or ACT, TOEFL for international applicants whose native language is not English. See university catalog for more details. *Graduate:* see university catalog for details. *Doctoral:* see university catalog for details. *Certificate:* see university catalog for details.

On-Campus Requirements: Both degree programs above may require students to attend one or more classes at a particular campus or center.

Tuition and Fees: *Undergraduate:* $129/credit for Maine residents, $365/credit for nonresidents. *Graduate:* $194/credit for Maine residents, $548/credit for nonresidents. *Doctoral:* $188/credit for Maine residents, $531/credit for nonresidents. *Application Fee:* $25 undergraduate, $50 graduate. *Software:* $5/credit technology fee. *Other Costs:* $30 nonrefundable summer session registration fee, $25 undergraduate or $18 graduate activity fee, $10 communication fee, $13 recreation fee, $208 semester comprehensive fee for 12 or more hours, $104 semester comprehensive fee for 7–11 hours, no semester comprehensive fee assessed for 1–6 hours. *Credit by:* semester.

Financial Aid: Federal Stafford Loan, Federal Perkins Loan, Federal PLUS Loan, Federal Pell Grant, Federal Work-Study, VA, Maine resident programs, Terry Loans.

Accreditation: New England Association of Schools and Colleges.

Description: The University of Maine (1862) is situated 35 miles west of the rocky coast of Maine and on the edge of the Maine North Woods. The institution opened in 1868 with 12 students and 2 faculty members, and by 1872 it admitted women students. Schools of Business Administration, Forestry, Home Economics, and Nursing opened in 1958; Engineering Technology and Performing Arts began in 1975; and the College of Forest Resources opened in 1982. In 1996, 5 new colleges were created: Business-Public Policy and Health, Education and Human Development; Engineering, Liberal Arts and Sciences, and Natural Sciences-Forestry and Agriculture. These colleges create a shared commitment to the liberal arts foundation of UMaine's curriculum, highlight opportunities for Bachelor of Arts students, promote areas of excellence in graduate education and research, strengthen the mandate for research, and increase the school's institutional commitment to diversity and multicultural approaches.

University of Maine, Machias

9 O'Brien Avenue	Phone: (207) 255-1200
Machias, ME 04654	Fax: (207) 255-1376

Division(s): Behavioral Science
Web Site(s): http://www.umm.maine.edu/BEX
E-mail: jlehman@acad.umm.maine.edu or bcook@acad.umm.maine.edu

Undergraduate Degree Programs:
Behavioral Science External Degree Program

Class Titles: Behavioral Science in Information Age, Psychological Models, Sociocultural Models, Research Methods/Design, Ethical Dimensions. Course descriptions at http://www.umm.maine.edu/BEX/Courses.

Teaching Methods: *Computers:* Internet, real-time chat, electronic classroom, e-mail, newsgroup, LISTSERV. *TV:* videotape. *Other:* videoconferencing, fax, correspondence, independent study, individual study, learning contracts, internships.

Credits Granted for: experiential learning, portfolio assessment (maximum credits: 3).

Admission Requirements: *Undergraduate:* AA, AS, or 45 accredited hours.

On-Campus Requirements: None.

Tuition and Fees: *Undergraduate:* $101/credit. *Application Fee:* $25. *Other Costs:* $35 Orientation, $6/credit (to $62) Student Activity, $5 Technology, $5 handling for ITV classes. *Credit by:* semester.

Financial Aid: Federal Stafford Loan, Federal Perkins Loan, Federal PLUS Loan, Federal Pell Grant, Federal Work-Study, VA, Maine resident programs.

Accreditation: New England Association of Schools and Colleges.

Description: The Behavioral Science External Degree Program is a BA completion program offered by the Tri-Campus Consortium represented by the campuses of the University of Maine at Fort Kent, Machias, and Presque Isle. Through the Tri-Campus Consortium, these universities are creating a new model for distance bachelor's programs within the state. Students matriculate through the University of Maine at Machias, which is the easternmost university in the U.S. and is a public undergraduate institution chartered in 1909. UMM's personal approach in its excellent programs in liberal arts, natural and behavioral sciences, teacher education, and recreation management prepares graduates to succeed in their chosen fields, to dedicate themselves to lifelong learning, and to become responsible citizens.

University of Manitoba

Room 188, Continuing Education Complex	Phone: (204) 474-8012
Winnipeg, MB, Canada R3T 2N2	Fax: (204) 474-7661

Division(s): Continuing Education
Web Site(s): http://www.umanitoba.ca/ConEd/de
E-mail: stusvcs_ced@umanitoba.ca

Undergraduate Degree Programs:
Bachelor of Arts
Bachelor of Social Work
Baccalaureate Nursing Program for Registered Nurses

Certificate Programs: Education Post-Baccalaureate, others available (e.g. Prairie Horticulture, Management); see Web site.

Class Titles: Human Origins/Antiquity, Cultural Anthropology, Greek/Roman Culture/Civilization, Economics, Microeconomic Theory/Its Applications, Macroeconomic Theory/Its Applications, Representative Literary Works, Canadian Literature (Pre-1967), Canadian Literature (Post-1967), Roman Canadienne Française, Human Geography, Physical Geography, Geography of Canada, Geography of U.S., Geography of Cultural Landscape, Geography of Social Landscape, Urban Geography, History of Western Civilization, History of Canada from 1534, History of U.S. from 1607, 20th-Century World, Historical Method, Modern Canada: 1921–Present, History of Canadian-American Relations, Philosophy, Logic, Ethics/Society, Politics, Canadian Government, European Union in World Politics, Great Political Thinkers, Foreign Policy, Canadian Foreign Policy, Research Design/Measurement, Psychology, Psychology of Sex Differences, Social Psychology, Behavior Modification, Psychology Behavior Modification Applications, Dyadic Relations, Psychology of Personality, Abnormal Psychology, Psychology of Sport, World Religions, Bible, Sociology, Research Methods, Social Psychology in Sociological Perspective, Criminology, Sociology of Criminal Justice/Corrections, Sociology of Aging, Education Measurement/Evaluation, Theories/Issues in School Counseling, Secondary School Counseling, Psychology of Exceptional Children, Diagnosis/Programming in Special Education, History of Educational Ideas, School Organization, Cross-Cultural Education, Recent Developments in Educational Administration, Problems in Cross-Cultural Education, Adult Education, Organizational Planning/Development in Education, Health Assessment of Individuals, Theoretical Basis of Nursing, Nursing Individuals/Families with Long-Term Illness/Disability, Community Health Nursing, Nursing of Individuals with Mental Illness/Their Families, Assessing Health of Communities, Issues/Trends in Nursing/Health Care, Leadership in Nursing Practice, Teaching/Learning Process in Nursing, Law/Ethics in Nursing Practice, Theoretical/Practical Applications Regarding Promotion of Health in First Nations Communities, Concepts of Recreation/Leisure, Recreational Program Planning, Biology, Earth/Planetary Science, Dynamic Earth, Environmental Geology, Energy/Mineral Resources, Vector Geometry/Linear Algebra, Calculus, Microbiology, Statistical Analysis, Social Welfare Policy, Interpersonal Communication Skills, Human Behavior/Social Work Practice, Emergence of Canadian Social Welfare State, Systemic Inquiry in Social Work, Contemporary Canadian Social Work, Social Work Practice, Field Instruction, Field/Focus of Social Work Practice, Feminist Perspectives on Social Work/Social Welfare Policy, Aboriginal People/Social Work, Problem Seminar, physical education courses, graduate education courses.

Teaching Methods: *Computers:* Independent Study Program: Print-based course package, textbook(s), and interaction with the instructional staff over the phone on a one-to-one basis. Assignments can be submitted by mail, fax, or e-mail. Media supports for Independent Study may include printed reading manuals, audiotapes, and/or videotapes. Bookstore and library supports provided for all distance education students through mail, fax, and expanding Internet support. Group-Based Program: starts with the Independent Study material and adds group interaction using a limited number of scheduled audioconferencing sessions from student's home phone. Net-Based Program: Includes correspondence, restricted access to Web-based course materials, interaction and assignments/submission/return process. First Year Distance Education Program: Involves using audiographics. Software program used is I-Linc, a WindowsNT-based system. Video capture and transmission, WWW access, and ability to run software packages during class are possible with the system. Communications link is through the Internet. *Other:* None.

Credits Granted for: Transfer of credits potential.

Admission Requirements: *Undergraduate:* variable; please consult Distance Education Program Guide for details. *Certificate:* variable. Please consult Distance Education Program Guide for details.

On-Campus Requirements: None.

Tuition and Fees: *Undergraduate:* $261/3-credit course, $721/6-credit course (1998 costs); variable by program and academic year. *Graduate:* part of regular graduate fee. *Application Fee:* by faculty, one-time fee. *Software:* variable by delivery method and course; see Distance Education Calendar. *Other Costs:* long-distance telephone costs for group-based study courses. *Credit by:* semester.

Financial Aid: Canada Student Loans

Accreditation: Association of Universities and Colleges of Canada.

Description: The University of Manitoba (1877) was established on the model of the University of London, as an examining and degree-conferring body, with instruction given in affiliated colleges. In 1898 the university received a land grant of 150,000 acres from the dominion government, and in 1900 it was given power to offer instruction. In 1929, having outgrown its Winnipeg city buildings, the university was removed to a permanent rural site with ample space for expansion. The university's Correspondence Program was established around that time and now offers opportunities for personal development, job upgrading/certification, and credit toward degrees.

University of Mary

7500 University Drive	Phone: (701) 255-7500
Bismarck, ND 58504	Fax: (701) 255-7687

Division(s): Registrar's Office or Coordinator of Adult Learning Services
Web Site(s): http://umary.edu
E-mail: jhilsend@umary.edu

Class Titles: Liberal Arts, Humanities, Social Sciences, Math/Science, Philosophy/Theology.

Teaching Methods: *Computers:* Internet, e-mail, CD-ROM *TV:* videotape. *Other:* fax, correspondence, independent study, individual study, learning contracts.

Credits Granted for: experiential learning, portfolio assessment, extrainstitutional learning, examination (CLEP, ACT-PEP, DANTES, GRE).

Admission Requirements: *Undergraduate:* 2.0 GPA. *Graduate:* 2.5 GPA and accredited bachelor's degree. *Certificate:* BS or BA.

On-Campus Requirements: 32 semester hours at University of Mary, 16 semester hours in student's major area, 8 semester hours in the student's minor.

Tuition and Fees: *Undergraduate:* $250/credit. *Graduate:* $265/credit. *Application Fee:* $25 *Other Costs:* $55/course for videocourse rental. *Credit by:* semester.

Financial Aid: Federal Stafford Loan, Federal Perkins Loan, Federal PLUS Loan, Federal Pell Grant, Federal Work-Study, VA, North Dakota resident programs.

Accreditation: North Central Association of Colleges and Schools.

Description: The University of Mary (1955), the only private Catholic university in North Dakota, was founded as the 2-year Mary College by the Benedictine Sisters of Annunciation Monastery. It became a 4-year, degree-granting institution in 1959 and achieved university status in 1986. The university continues to expand its curricular offerings and maintain excellence in its programs. The opening of the Butler Center for Lifelong Learning in 1982, and more recently the Fargo Center, has added much needed sites for adult classes and service to the local area. In the fall of 1996, the university began offering 2 accelerated degrees, a BS in Management and a Master's in Management. An Applied Management minor and several liberal arts classes are also offered in the accelerated format.

University of Maryland University College

SFSC 3237	
University Boulevard at Adelphi Road	Phone: (800) 283-6832
College Park, MD 20742	Fax: (301) 985-4615

Division(s): Office of Distance Education
Web Site(s): http://www.umuc.edu/distance
E-mail: umucinfo@nova.umuc.edu

Undergraduate Degree Programs:
Accounting
Behavioral and Social Sciences
Business and Management
Communication Studies
Computer and Information Science
Computer Studies
English
Fire Science
Humanities
Management
Management Studies
Paralegal Studies
Technology and Management

Graduate Degree Programs:
Master of Science in:
    Computer Systems Management
    Technology Management
    Management
    Environmental Management
Master of International Management

Certificate Programs: Paralegal Studies

Class Titles: Any distance course may be taken once student is admitted.

Teaching Methods: *Computers:* asynchronous learning via WWW and client-server software. *TV:* videotape, cable program, closed-circuit within Maryland. *Other:* supporting technologies include voice mail, videoconferencing, audiotapes, CD-ROM, e-mail, fax.

Credits Granted for: *Undergraduate:* prior learning course-challenge examinations, EXCEL program portfolio assessments, Cooperative Education on-the-job learning, professional and military training and experience evaluated by the American Council on Education (CREDIT formerly known as PONSI, National Guide), standardized examination (CLEP, CLEP-ACT, DANTES/SST). *Graduate:* visit http://www.umuc.edu/gsmt.

Admission Requirements: *Undergraduate:* high school diploma or equivalent (225 GED, no score below 40 on any test), 2.0 GPA on all college-level work, official transcript from each institution (if admission is for degree). TOEFL score of 213 or higher on the computerized format/550 or higher on the written test is required. International students may contact the school. *Graduate:* visit http://www.umuc.edu/gsmt.

On-Campus Requirements: None.

Tuition and Fees: *Undergraduate:* $183/credit in-state, $222/credit out-of-state. *Graduate:* $277/credit in-state, $367/credit out-of-state. *Application Fee:* $30 undergraduate, $50 graduate. *Other Costs:* voice mail courses require $5/course charge. *Credit by:* semester.

Financial Aid: Federal Direct Stafford Loan, Federal Direct PLUS Loan, Federal Perkins Loan, Federal Pell Grant, Federal Work-Study, institutional grants, private and institutional scholarships, VA, Maryland resident programs.

Accreditation: Middle States Association of Colleges and Schools.

Description: University of Maryland University College (1947) is one of 11 degree-granting institutions in the University System of Maryland. For more than 50 years, it has fulfilled its principal mission: to serve adult, part-time students through high-quality, educational opportunities. Classroom sites can be found throughout Maryland; the Washington, DC, metropolitan area; and at hundreds of locations overseas. Students also can "attend class" at a distance from anywhere in the world that can be connected electronically—even places as remote as Antarctica. UMUC's place at the forefront of higher education worldwide has inspired a motto that expresses the scope of this innovative institution: "The sun never sets on the University of Maryland [University College]."

University of Maryland at College Park

2105 Engineering Classroom Building	Phone: (301) 405-4910
College Park, MD 20742	Fax: (301) 314-9639

Division(s): Instructional Television System
Web Site(s): http://www.glue.umd.edu/itv/
E-mail: el23@umail.umd.edu

Graduate Degree Programs:
Professional Master of Engineering with concentration in:
   Electrical Engineering
   Civil Engineering
   Mechanical Engineering (available locally)
   Reliability Engineering (available out-of-state)

Certificate Programs: Reliability Engineering

Teaching Methods: *Computers:* Internet, e-mail. *TV:* ITFS microwave (one-way video/2-way audio) in the Maryland, D.C. area; videotape. *Other:* None.

Admission Requirements: *Graduate:* contact ITV. *Certificate:* contact ITV.

On-Campus Requirements: None.

Tuition and Fees: *Undergraduate:* $170/credit. *Graduate:* $400/credit. *Application Fee:* $50. *Credit by:* semester.

Financial Aid: Federal Stafford Loan, Federal Perkins Loan, Federal PLUS Loan, Federal Pell Grant, Federal Work-Study, VA, Maryland resident programs.

Accreditation: Middle States Association of Colleges and Schools.

Description: The Instructional Television System was established by the University of Maryland's College of Engineering in 1976. We are an innovative broadcast network that provides high-quality graduate-level distance courses leading to master's degrees in engineering.

University of Maryland, Baltimore County

1000 Hilltop Circle	Phone: (410) 455-2797
Baltimore, MD 21250	Fax: (410) 455-1115

Division(s): Department of Education, Professional Programs
Web Site(s): http://research.umbc.edu/~eholly/ceduc/isd/
E-mail: connect@umbc.edu

Graduate Degree Programs:
Master of Arts

Certificate Programs: Distance Education

Class Titles: Distance Education, Online Classroom, Corporate Distance Training, Interactive Video/Conferencing.

Teaching Methods: *Computers:* Internet, real-time chat, electronic classroom, e-mail, newsgroup, mailing lists. *Other:* audioconferencing, videoconferencing, audiographics, audiotapes, fax, correspondence, learning contracts, Web-based instruction, self-reflection.

Admission Requirements: *Graduate:* bachelor's degree, 3.0 GPA, GRE. *Certificate:* bachelor's degree, 3.0 GPA.

On-Campus Requirements: None.

Tuition and Fees: *Graduate:* $260/credit in-state, $468/credit out-of-state. *Application Fee:* $40. *Other Costs:* $28/credit miscellaneous fees. *Credit by:* semester.

Financial Aid: Federal Stafford Loan, Federal Perkins Loan, VA, Maryland resident programs.

Accreditation: Middle States Association of Colleges and Schools.

Description: The University of Maryland, Baltimore County is a midsize research university in the Baltimore-Washington corridor offering graduate students advanced study in 27 traditional master's and doctoral programs. UMBC offers a Letter of Certification in Distance Education through the Instructional Systems Development Training Systems graduate program. This 9-credit certificate program, first offered in 1996, is available online, with courses applicable to the on-site Master of Arts program in ISD Training Systems.

University of Massachusetts, Amherst

113 Marcus Hall, PO Box 35115	Phone: (413) 545-0063
Amherst, MA 01003-5115	Fax: (413) 545-1227

Division(s): Video Instructional Program
Web Site(s): http://www.ecs.umass.edu/vip/
E-mail: vip@vip.ecs.umass.edu

Graduate Degree Programs:
Master of Science in:
    Computer Science
    Electrical and Computer Engineering
    Engineering Management

Doctoral Degree Programs:
Students may begin a PhD in Electrical and Computer Engineering, or Engineering Management; however, at least one year's academic residency is required.

Class Titles: Chemical Engineering, Math

Teaching Methods: *Computers:* Internet, e-mail. *TV:* videotape, satellite broadcasting, National Technological University. *Other:* audioconferencing, videoconferencing, fax, correspondence, independent study.

Admission Requirements: *Undergraduate:* completed application and fees, 2.75 GPA, accredited bachelor's degree, all official college transcripts, 2 letters of recommendation, general GRE. *Graduate:* same as undergraduate.

On-Campus Requirements: None.

Tuition and Fees: *Graduate:* $1,225/3-credit course for domestic U.S. students, $1,425/3-credit course for international students. *Application Fee:* $20/semester. *Software:* $15–$45. *Other Costs:* international shipping. *Credit by:* semester.

Financial Aid: For financial aid information contact Financial Aid Services at the University of Massachusetts, phone (413) 545-0801. Federal Stafford Loan, Federal Perkins Loan, Federal PLUS Loan, Federal Pell Grant, Federal Work-Study, Massachusetts resident programs.

Accreditation: New England Association of Schools and Colleges.

Description: The College of Engineering at the University of Massachusetts, Amherst (1863), in conjunction with industry partners, developed the Video Instructional Program in 1974. As a distance learning facility, the VIP addresses continuing education and advanced degree needs. The VIP videotapes and broadcasts courses as they are taught by resident, graduate, faculty members before an on-campus, student audience. The videotapes are then delivered to VIP students across the country and the world—the quality of a university education without the sacrifice in time.

University of Massachusetts, Lowell

One University Avenue	Phone: (978) 934-2464
Lowell, MA 01854	Fax: (978) 934-3043

Division(s): Continuing Education
Web Site(s): http://cybered.uml.edu
http://www.uml.edu/DCE
E-mail: Steven_Tello@uml.edu
Katherine_Galaitsis@uml.edu

Undergraduate Degree Programs:
Undergraduate CyberEd courses can be applied to both the Associate and Bachelor of Science Degree in Information Systems.

Certificate Programs: UNIX, Computer Proficiency.

Class Titles: American Cinema, Business Writing, C Programming, C++ Programming, Dynamic HTML, Psychology, Data Structures, Perl, Sociology, UNIX, Java Programming, JavaScript, Math, Purchasing Materials, Relational Database Concepts, TCP/IP Programming, Network Architecture, Technical/Scientific Communication, UNIX Shell Programming, Visual Basic, Writing for Interactive Media.

Teaching Methods: *Computers:* Internet, LISTSERV, real-time chat, discussion forums. *TV:* videoconferencing, PBS, telecourses. *Other:* None.

Credits Granted for: examination (CLEP, DANTES, GRE), transfer credit.

Admission Requirements: *Undergraduate:* high school graduate or equivalent; applications for all programs are accepted on a rolling admissions basis.

On-Campus Requirements: None.

Tuition and Fees: *Undergraduate:* $555/3-credit course. *Credit by:* semester.

Financial Aid: depends on matriculation status of student; see DCE Web site (http://www.uml.edu/DCE).

Accreditation: New England Association of Schools and Colleges, Accreditation Board for Engineering Technology, American Association of Colleges and School of Business.

Description: The University of Massachusetts, Lowell (1895) is a comprehensive university committed to providing students with the education and skills they need for continued success throughout their lives. Specializing in applied science and technology, the university conducts research and outreach activities that add great value to the Northeast Region. The Division of Continuing Education at UMass Lowell is one of the largest continuing education operations in New England. Our focus in developing distance learning programs is to ensure a quality, interactive experience for our students, increasing their access to science and technology education.

University of Memphis

376 Administration Building
Campus Box 526649
Memphis, TN 38152-6649

Phone: (901) 678-3807
Fax: (901) 678-5112

Division(s): Extended Programs
Web Site(s): http://www.extended.memphis.edu/extended2.html
E-mail: sowens@memphis.edu

Graduate Degree Programs:
Master's courses in Journalism and Journalism Administration

Class Titles: Anthropology, Communication, Consumer Science, Geology, Geography, Journalism, Math, Sociology, English, Health/Fitness.

Teaching Methods: *Computers:* Internet, real-time chat, electronic classroom, e-mail, newsgroup, LISTSERV. *TV:* videotape, cable program, PBS. *Other:* videoconferencing, independent study.

Credits Granted for: experiential learning, portfolio assessment, examination (CLEP, ACT-PEP, DANTES, GRE).

Admission Requirements: *Undergraduate:* high school diploma or GED, ACT/SAT. *Graduate:* bachelor's degree, entrance exam (GRE, GMAT, MAT).

On-Campus Requirements: None.

Tuition and Fees: *Undergraduate:* $127/credit, residents; $340/credit, nonresidents. *Graduate:* $166/credit, residents; $379/credit, nonresidents. *Application Fee:* $10 undergraduate, $25 graduate. *Other Costs:* $75–$200/course for books, software, video rental, etc. *Credit by:* semester.

Financial Aid: Federal Pell Grant, Federal Supplemental Educational Opportunity Grant, Federal PLUS Loan, Federal Perkins Loan, Federal Direct Loan Program (subsidized and unsubsidized), Federal Work-Study, VA, Tennessee resident programs.

Accreditation: Southern Association of Colleges and Schools.

Description: From the opening of its doors as a normal school for training teachers to its present status as one of Tennessee's 2 comprehensive universities, the University of Memphis (1912) has been thrust forward by the growth of Memphis and the Mid-South. The metropolitan and regional requirements for more highly trained university graduates have, of necessity, caused the university to expand all its offerings and to enhance its delivery methods to include distance learning options.

University of Michigan

837 Greene Street
Ann Arbor, MI 48104-3213

Phone: (734) 764-5300
Fax: (734) 936-7736

Division(s): Academic Outreach
Web Site(s): http://www.outreach.umich.edu
E-mail: ao-courses@umich.edu

Class Titles: Arabic Literature in Translation, Asia through Fiction, Economics, Contemporary Novel, Hemingway/Fitzgerald, French: Special Reading Course, German: Special Reading Course, Environment/Citizen, Psychology of Aging, Behavior Therapy, Women's Studies, Gender/Society, Women in Literature/Arts.

Teaching Methods: *Other:* correspondence.

On-Campus Requirements: None.

Tuition and Fees: *Undergraduate:* $255/credit. *Graduate:* $524/credit. *Other Costs:* $185 infrastructure maintenance fee. *Credit by:* semester.

Financial Aid: Federal Stafford Loan, Federal Perkins Loan, Federal Pell Grant, VA, Michigan resident programs.

Accreditation: North Central Association of Colleges and Schools.

Description: The University of Michigan (1817) is a large public research institution that has offered correspondence courses for more than 80 years.

University of Minnesota

101 Wesbrook Hall
77 Pleasant Street SE
Minneapolis, MN 55455

Phone: (612) 625-3333
(800) 234-6564
Fax: (612) 626-7900

Division(s): University College
Web Site(s): http://www.cee.umn.edu/dis/
http://www.cee.umn.edu/dis/bulletin/active
http://www.cee.umn.edu/couns/
http://www.cee.umn.edu/bab/
E-mail: CEEADV@mail.cee.umn.edu

Undergraduate Degree Programs:
Bachelor of Applied Business

Class Titles: Historical Perspectives/Contemporary Business Challenges, Problem Solving, Communicating for Results, Accessing/Using Information Effectively, Project Management, Accounting/Finance for Managers, Management/Human Resource Practices, Business Proposal, Financial Reporting, Management Accounting, African Literature, Issues in Sustainable Agriculture, American Indian History, American Cultures, Understanding Cultures, Human Origins, Ecological Anthropology, Psychological Anthropology, Farm Management, Visual Arts, Art of India, Financial Fundamentals, Ethics/Stakeholder Management, International Business, Biocatalysts, Biology, Heredity/Human Society, Environmental Studies, Genetics, Cell Biology, C++ in Embedded Systems, Computer-Based Instructional Design, Second Languages for Young Children, Magic/Witchcraft, Mythology, Greek/Latin Terminology, Madness–Greek/Rome, European Folktales, Gender Communication, Child Psychology, Infancy, Social Development, Adolescent Psychology, Processes of Social Development, Computer Systems Performance Analysis, Drafting, Retail Merchandising, Religions of East Asia, Economics (micro/macro), Money/Banking, Creating Social Studies Curriculum Materials, Digital Signal Processing, Computer Systems Performance Analysis, Ecology, Preparatory Writing Practice, Writing about Literature, Writing for Humanities, Writing for Arts, Writing for Social Sciences, Writing for Science, Read/Writing for Management, Technical Writing for Engineers, Writing for Business, American Literature, Modern Poetry, Modern Drama, Science Fiction/Fantasy, Literature American Minorities, Techniques for Literature Study, Survey of English Literature, Shakespeare, Fitzgerald/Hemingway, American Literature to 1850, American Literature 1850–1900, American Literature 1900–1945, American Short Story, English Language, Origin of English Words, Celtic World, D.H. Lawrence/Freud, Modern Women Writers, Women Writers of 19th Century, Hemingway, 20th Century English Novel, Pirandello to Pinter, James Joyce, American Poetry 1890–1940, Deformable Body Mechanics, Fiction Writing—Short Story, Poetry Writing, Journaling Fiction, Journal/Memoir Writing, Professional Editing, Knowing/Learning/Thinking, Psychology of Student Learning, Integrative Career Planning, Counseling Procedures, Finnish, Reading French, French, Nutrition, Human Sexual Behavior, Family Systems, Racial/Ethnic Diversity in Families, Math, Plane Geometry, Algebra, Solar System Astronomy, Stellar Astronomy, Chemistry, Law in Society, Psychology of Human Development, U.S. Literature, Reading Short Stories, Statistics, Business/Society, Small Business, Practical Law, Accounting, Marketing, Marketing—Management, Microcomputer Applications, Parent-Child Relations, African-American Literature, Asian-American Literature, Genetics, Geology, Historical Geology, World Around Us, Geography of U.S./Canada, Geography of Minnesota, Geography of Latin America, Russia/Environs, Environmental Problems, German, Heinrich B-F611 (in English), World History, American History, Cultural Pluralism in American History, Ancient Asia, Latin American History to 1800, Latin American History 1800–1929, Latin American History 1929–Present, Ancient Asia, Columbus, Peter the Great, Civil War/Reconstruction, U.S. in 20th Century 1890–1917, U.S. 1932–1960, American Indian History, History of American Foreign Relations 1760–1865, History of American Foreign Relations 1865–1945, History of American Foreign Relations 1945–1995, American Immigration 1884–1984, Constitutional History, Landscape Gardening/Design, Humanities/West, European Heritage–Greece, European Heritage–Rome, C++ in Embedded Systems, Teaching Labor Relations, Collective Bargaining, Italian, Mass Communications, Media in American History/Law, Magazine Writing, Information for Mass Communications, Communications/Public Opinion, History of Journalism, Literature Aspects of Journalism, Judaism, Latin, Latin Literature, Latin Prose/Poetry, Cicero, Virgil's Aeneid, Nature of Human Language, Sociolinguistics, Trigonometry, College Algebra/Analytic Geometry, Short Calculus, Precal culus, One Variable Differential/Integral Calculus, Linear Algebra/Differential Equations, Multivariable Differential Calculus, Multivariable Integral Calculus, Entrepreneurship/Smaller Enterprise, Biocatalysts, Marketing, Music, Avant-Garde, 20th Century American Music, Norwegian, Conservation of Natural Resources, Life Span Growth/Development, Logic, Philosophy, Ethics, Physical World, Change in Physical World, Physics, Physics w/Calculus, Occupational Therapy, American Government/Politics, Contemporary Political Ideologies, U.S. Congress, Judicial Process, Understanding War, American Political Parties, Psychology, Biological Psychology, Personality, Abnormal Psychology, Stress Management, Dying/Death in Contemporary Society, Religions of South Asia, Judaism, Managing Information— Internet, Writing in Your Profession, Corporate Video, Document Design, Audience Analysis, Media Selection, Russian, Russian Literature—Middle Ages to Dostoyevsky in Translation, H. C. Andersen, Ingmar Bergman, Sociology/ Social Problems, Criminology, Women—Muslim Sociology, Social Psychology, Reading Spanish, Spanish, Ever Present Past in Spanish/Portuguese Culture, Topics in Spanish/Port uguese Civilization/Culture, Communication in Organizations, Ideas Statistics, American Social Welfare/Community Services, Child Abuse Prevention, Social Work with

Involuntary Clients, Swedish, Readings in Swedish Literary Texts, Theater, Play Writing, Northern Minnesota Women: Myths/Realities, Women in World Cultures.

Teaching Methods: *Computers:* Internet, e-mail, CD-ROM, newsgroup, LISTSERV. *TV:* videotape. *Other:* audiotapes, fax, correspondence, independent study.

Admission Requirements: *Undergraduate:* university admission not required to take distance learning courses. Bachelor of Applied Business admission is required to obtain the degree, but not to take BAB classes.

On-Campus Requirements: None.

Tuition and Fees: *Undergraduate:* $90/credit (variable). *Graduate:* $250/credit (variable). *Other Costs:* varies for textbooks, $60 ($30 refundable) videotape rental, $40 materials fee. *Credit by:* quarters converting to semesters beginning fall, 1999.

Financial Aid: University College Tuition Assistance Grant Program, Remington Scholarship, VA, Minnesota Work Force, Rehabilitation Branch funds, employer assistance. Students admitted to a University of Minnesota-Twin Cities degree or certificate program may be eligible for Minnesota State Grant or Federal Pell Grant, but details have not yet been finalized—call UC Counseling, (612) 625-2500. Correspondence credits are not counted in enrollment for Federal Supplemental Educational Opportunity Grant, Federal Work-Study, State Work-Study, federal and state educational loan programs, and other University of Minnesota grants, loans, and scholarships administered by the Office of Scholarships and Financial Aid.

Accreditation: North Central Association of Colleges and Schools.

Description: The University of Minnesota (1851) is regarded as one of the finest public land-grant universities in the country. It is also among the largest, with 4 campuses and more than 40,000 day students enrolled. The University College, the continuing education area of the institution, was established in 1913. The mission of the college has always been to extend the resources of the university to adult and nontraditional students, statewide, nationwide, and even worldwide.

University of Minnesota, Crookston

2900 University Avenue	Phone: (218) 281-6510
Crookston, MN 56716	(800) 862-6466
	Fax: (218) 281-8050

Division(s): Office of Continuing Education and Outreach
Web Site(s): http://www.crk.umn.edu
E-mail: klemmerm@mail.crk.umn.edu

Undergraduate Degree Programs:
Bachelor of Applied Health

Certificate Programs: Hotel, Restaurant, and Institutional Management

Class Titles: Finance/Regulatory Compliance in Health Care Management Comparative Systems, Global Issues/Trends in Health Care Management, Health Law/Biomedical Ethics Management, Leadership/Health Care Planning, Managed Care, Quality Assurance/Utilization Review/Risk Management, Food Preparation, Sanitation/Safety, Menu Design/Analysis, Hospitality Selection/Procurement, Food/Beverage/Labor Control, Global Tourism, Hospitality Marketing/Sales, Hospitality Law, Food Technology, Global Food Systems, Facilities Engineering, Food Manufacturing Operations, Management, College Algebra/Analytical Geometry, Topics in Industrial Math, Trigonometry, Short Calculus, Composition, Human Anatomy/Physiology, Microbiology, Psychology, Developmental Psychology, Speech, Nutrition, Marketing, Local Area Networking, Wide Area Networking, Microcomputer Operating Systems, Systems Architecture, Object-Oriented Programming, Project Management in Information Technology, Equine Nutrition.

Teaching Methods: *Computers:* Internet, real-time chat, electronic classroom, e-mail, CD-ROM, newsgroup, LISTSERV, Internet voice and video, proprietary voice and video. *TV:* videotape, satellite broadcasting, PBS. *Other:* videoconferencing, audioconferencing, fax, independent study, individual study, learning contracts.

Credits Granted for: experiential learning, portfolio assessment, extrainstitutional learning, examination (CLEP, DANTES, College Board Advanced Placement Program).

Admission Requirements: *Undergraduate:* accredited high school graduate or GED, ACT.

On-Campus Requirements: 30 of the last 90 credits must be UMC credits.

Tuition and Fees: *Undergraduate:* $72/lower division credit plus base tuition rate, resident. $78/upper division credit plus base tuition rate, resident. $196/credit, nonresident. Reciprocity agreements exist with Manitoba, North Dakota, South Dakota, Wisconsin. *Application Fee:* $25. *Other Costs:* $320 technology access fee for students taking 12 or more credits, $180 for students taking 8–11 credits, and $50 for students taking 3–7 credits. *Credit by:* quarters, converting to semesters.

Financial Aid: Federal Direct Stafford Loan, Federal Perkins Loan, Federal PLUS Loan, Federal Pell Grant, Federal Work-Study, VA, Minnesota resident programs.

Accreditation: North Central Association of Colleges and Schools.

Description: Nationally recognized as a leader in technology-enhanced education, the University of Minnesota, Crookston (1905) is part of the University of Minnesota system. UMC is a 4-year, public, coeducational institution of 1,650 full- and part-time students with a focus on polytechnic education.

UMC's mission is to provide teaching, research, and outreach with a focus on applied undergraduate instruction in agriculture; business; early childhood education; natural resources; equine industries; health management; hotel, restaurant, and institutional management; food processing management; information networking management; scientific and technical communication; sport and recreation management; and appropriate interdisciplinary studies. In 1993 UMC became the first campus in the nation to issue notebook computers to all students. UMC is committed to lifelong learning and has offered Web-based courses in its distance education program since 1995. UMC responds to the demands of the information age by offering technology-enhanced curricula that prepare students for careers of tomorrow.

University of Minnesota, Rochester Center

855 30th Avenue SE	Phone: (507) 280-2828
Rochester, MN 55904	(800) 947-0117
	Fax: (507) 280-2839

Division(s): University College
Web Site(s): http://www.roch.edu/umrc/index.html
E-mail: bbesonen@mail.cee.umn.edu

Undergraduate Degree Programs:
Bachelor of Arts or Bachelor of Science in self-designed area of study through the Program for Individualized Learning (PIL)

Graduate Degree Programs:
Master of Science in:
    Computer Engineering
    Computer/Information Sciences
    Electrical Engineering
    Mechanical Engineering
    Nursing with emphasis on Public Health or Psychiatric
    Mental Health
Master of Social Work

Certificate Programs: Child Abuse Prevention Studies.

Class Titles: Biomedical Engineering, Control Science/Dynamical Systems, Health Informatics, Industrial Engineering/Operations Research, Mathematics, Chemical Engineering/Materials Science.

Teaching Methods: *Computers:* Internet/classroom, real-time chat, electronic classroom, e-mail, LISTSERV. *TV:* videotape, satellite broadcasting, interactive television classroom (both 2-way audio/one-way video and 2-way audio/2-way video). *Other:* correspondence, independent study, individual study.

Credits Granted for: classroom study, some experiential learning by arrangement with instructor/department.

Admission Requirements: *Undergraduate:* contact school for information. *Graduate:* contact school for information. *Certificate:* contact the School of Social Work for information.

On-Campus Requirements: None.

Tuition and Fees: *Undergraduate:* $101–107/credit. *Graduate:* $250–$260/credit. *Application Fee:* $25 undergraduate, $40 graduate. *Other Costs:* students in the Computer/Information Sciences, Electrical Engineering, Mechanical Engineering, and Computer Engineering Masters may need to connect to a UNIX Lab and pay a quarterly rate of approximately $110/ every other quarter, and campus fee: $1/credit to a maximum of $15. *Credit by:* quarter (currently) or semester in the fall of 1999.

Financial Aid: available through the University of Minnesota Minneapolis campus on a limited basis.

Accreditation: North Central Association of Colleges and Schools, Accrediting Board for Engineering and Technology for engineering programs.

Description: The University of Minnesota Rochester Center (1966) extends the educational resources of the University of Minnesota to southeastern Minnesota. In the mid-1980s, the U of M Institute of Technology began sending IT classes to Rochester via UNITE (one-way video and 2-way audio). In 1992, with a move to the University Center Rochester campus, ITV class offerings were expanded to include 2-way audio and 2-way video.

University of Mississippi

E.F. Yerby Conference Center	
University Avenue at Grove Loop	
PO Box 879	Phone: (601) 232-7282
University, MS 38677	Fax: (601) 234-8744

Division(s): Continuing Studies
Web Site(s): http://umdl.olemiss.edu
http://www.olemiss.edu
E-mail: umdl@olemiss.edu

Class Titles: Management, Marketing, Finance, Education, Paralegal, Law, Engineering, English, Philosophy, Political Science, Economics, Health Safety, History.

Teaching Methods: *Computers:* Internet, e-mail. *Other:* videoconferencing, correspondence, independent study.

Admission Requirements: *Undergraduate:* contact Institute for Continuing Studies, e-mail cstudies@olemiss.edu

On-Campus Requirements: None.

Tuition and Fees: *Undergraduate:* $83/credit in-state. *Graduate:* $111/credit in-state. *Doctoral:* $111/credit in-state. *Credit by:* semester.

Financial Aid: Federal Stafford Loan, Federal Perkins Loan, Federal PLUS Loan, Federal Pell Grant, Federal Work-Study, VA, Mississippi resident programs.

Accreditation: Southern Association of Colleges and Schools.

Description: The University of Mississippi (1848) offers more than 100 programs that lead to careers in engineering, business, telecommunications, politics, journalism, pharmacy, law, medicine, teaching, and more. The university also has outstanding pre-med, pre-law, and pre-pharmacy programs. A long-standing support system helps ensure success for Ole Miss students. In our School of Engineering, which offers 8 majors, small classes mean you'll be more than a face in the crowd to professors. Personal attention and daily interaction with faculty are tangible benefits of the Ole Miss program. The schools of Business Administration and Accountancy recently moved into a new $18 million facility with a dozen state-of-the-art classrooms, a 170-seat multimedia auditorium, and expanded computer labs, in which you can prepare to lead top-performing companies or start your own. If you want to teach high school, you can get on the fast track to a career with a bachelor's degree, plus just 9 hours of designated education courses and a few other requirements. This alternate route to teacher certification is available for 15 different subjects. An undergraduate degree from The University of Mississippi is also excellent preparation for graduate study in any field.

University of Missouri

136 Clark Hall	Phone: (800) 609-3727
Columbia, MO 65211-4200	(573) 882-2491
	Fax: (573) 882-6808

Division(s): Independent Study
Web Site(s): http://indepstudy.ext.missouri.edu
E-mail: indstudy@missouri.edu

Class Titles: Abnormal Psychology, Accounting, Programs for Children/Families, Adolescent Development, Adolescent Psychology, Affective Development of Gifted Students, African-American Literature, Aging, America 1945–Present, America Since 1865, American Constitution, American Foreign Relations, American Government, American Health Care, American History to 1877, American Literary Masterpieces, American Literature, Analytic Geometry/Calculus, Animal Behavior, Applied Nutrition, Art Activities in Elementary School, Home Horticulture, Career Planning, Child Development, Child Psychology, Mythology, Cognitive Psychology, Algebra, Computer Application, Congress/Legislative Policy, Congressional Politics, Corrections, Cosmic Evolution/Astronomy, Fiction Writing, Poetry Writing, Earth Science, French, German, Russian, Spanish, Statistics, Health Education, Engineering Mechanics: Dynamics, Engineering Mechanics: Statics, Environmental Psychology, Ethics/Professions, Exposition/Argumentation, Finite Math, Formal Logic, Educational/Psychological Measurement, Logic/Scientific Method, Philosophy, Teaching Adults, Management, Anthropology, Biology, Genetics, Psychology, Geography of Missouri, Geometric Concepts for Teachers, High School Journalism, History of Missouri, History of Modern Europe, History of Science, History of American South, Horse Production, Human Learning, Human Resource Management, Industrial Psychology, Insects in Environment, Latin, Intercultural Communication, International Relations, BASIC, British Litera-

ture, British Masterpieces, Criminology/Criminal Justice, Educational Statistics, Folklore, Leisure Studies, Mental Retardation/Severe Handicaps, Philosophy, Political Science, Sociology, Special Education, Special Education for Regular Educators, American Economy, Meteorology, Issue/Trends in Reading Instruction, Learning/Instruction, Literary Types, Literature of New Testament, Literature of Old Testament, Logic/Language, Major Questions in Philosophy, Making of Modern Britain, Mathematical Logic, Mechanical Universe, Modern Western Civilization, Money/Banking/Monetary Theory, Multicultural Study of Children/Families, Music Appreciation, Number Systems/Applications, Operation of Therapeutic Recreation, Organizational Analysis in Higher/Adult Continuing Education, Organizational Theory, Perception, Personal/Family Finance, Photography for Teachers, Physical Geography, Physical Geology, Politics of Third World, Finance, Geology, Marketing, Psychology/Education of Exceptional Individuals, Psychology of Sensation/Perception, Public Administration, Regions/Nations of World, Revolutionary America 1754–1789, Rights of Offender, Rural Sociology, Secondary School Curriculum, Teaching Reading Comprehension, Social Inequalities, Social Organization of City, Social Policy/Service Delivery in Social Work, Social Psychology, Symbolic Logic, Surface Water Management, Teaching of Reading, Teaching Reading in Content Areas, British Literature to 1784, Technical Writing, Theory/Concepts of Plant Pathology, Thinking/Cognition, Trigonometry, Urban/Rural Sociology, Western Civilization Since 1600, Special Topics: Changing World/Changing Classroom: Dealing with Critical Situation in School, New Approach to Discipline: Democratic Classroom, Cooperative Classroom Management, Coping with Student Problems in Classroom—Dealing in Discipline, Dealing with Teacher Stess/Burnout, Developing Personal System of Discipline, Educating Gifted, Preventing School Failure, Shakespeare, Teaching Students Optimism, Teaching Tolerance to Students, Working with Students at Risk; Topics: American Poetry, Experiencing American Cultures in Contemporary Novel, Gothic Fiction, Shakespeare, Twilight of Sioux, War in Vietnam/the U.S., Women in Popular Culture, Women in Modern Fiction, European Civilization 1715–Present, Health Services Management: Principles of Economics for Health Care Executives.

Teaching Methods: *Computers:* Internet, e-mail. *TV:* videotape. *Other:* audiotapes, correspondence, independent study.

Admission Requirements: *Undergraduate:* Students may enroll in Independent Study courses anytime, with 9 months' completion time, but enrollment does not constitute university admission. *Graduate:* same as undergraduate.

On-Campus Requirements: None.

Tuition and Fees: *Undergraduate:* $129/credit. *Graduate:* $163/credit. *Other Costs:* $10 handling/enrollment. *Credit by:* semester.

Accreditation: North Central Association of Colleges and Secondary Schools.

Description: The University of Missouri Center for Independent Study was established in 1911. Today it is one of the nation's largest distance learning programs, with 15,000 annual enrollments. The center has earned a solid reputation based on providing quality courses and superior service to its students worldwide. Current efforts are focused on utilizing the latest technology in all program areas. By accessing the Web site, students can get up-to-date course information, enroll in courses, request exams, and submit lessons for courses. In addition, the center is developing a number of online courses; all lessons and instructions for these Web courses are on the Internet.

University of Missouri, Kansas City

301 Fine Arts Building
5100 Rockhill Road
Kansas City, MO 64110

Phone: (816) 235-1096
Fax: (816) 235-1170

Division(s): Interactive Video Network
Web Site(s): http://www.umkc.edu
E-mail: CarnettJ@smtpgate.umkc.edu

Undergraduate Degree Programs:
Bachelor of Science in Nursing

Graduate Degree Programs:
Master of Science in Nursing

Teaching Methods: *Computers:* Internet, real-time chat, electronic classroom, e-mail. *TV:* videotape, cable program, satellite broadcasting. *Other:* radio broadcast, audioconferencing, videoconferencing.

Admission Requirements: *Undergraduate:* department-specific.

On-Campus Requirements: None.

Tuition and Fees: *Undergraduate:* contact school. *Graduate:* contact school. *Credit by:* semester.

Financial Aid: Federal Stafford Loan, Federal Perkins Loan, Federal PLUS Loan, Federal Pell Grant, Federal Work-Study, VA, Missouri resident programs.

Accreditation: North Central Association of Colleges and Schools.

Description: The fundamental purpose of the University of Missouri, Kansas City (1933) is to provide enlightened and able graduates who have the potential to provide leadership in the economic, social, and cultural development of the state and nation. The university has well-defined admission requirements that ensure a high probability of academic success for its students. The university is committed to the principles of academic freedom, equal opportunity, diversity, and to protecting the search for truth and its open expression.

University of Montana, Missoula

32 Campus Drive
Missoula, MT 59812

Phone: (406) 243-2900
Fax: (406) 243-2047

Division(s): Continuing Education
Web Site(s): http://www.umt.edu/ccesp/
E-mail: http://www.umt.edu/registrar/homepage.html

Undergraduate Degree Programs:
Bachelor of Arts in Liberal Studies

Graduate Degree Programs:
Master of Business Administration
Master of Education

Doctoral Degree Programs:
Doctorate of Education
Pharmacy Doctorate (PharmD)

Class Titles: extensive list in areas of Business, Education, Forestry, Pharmacy, etc.; contact Registrar for details.

Teaching Methods: *Computers:* Internet, real-time chat, electronic classroom, e-mail, CD-ROM, newsgroup, LIST-SERV. *TV:* videotape, cable program, satellite broadcasting, PBS. *Other:* radio broadcast, audioconferencing, videoconferencing, audiographics, audiotapes, fax, correspondence, independent study, individual study, learning contracts.

Credits Granted for: examination (CLEP, ACT-PEP, DANTES, GRE).

Admission Requirements: *Undergraduate:* some restrictions as to location within Montana. *Graduate:* some restrictions as to location within Montana.

On-Campus Requirements: some programs require a limited residency.

Tuition and Fees: *Undergraduate:* $175–$250/credit. *Graduate:* $175–$275/credit. *Application Fee:* $30. *Software:* varies. *Other Costs:* program specific. *Credit by:* semester.

Financial Aid: Federal Stafford Loan, Federal Perkins Loan, Federal PLUS Loan, Federal Pell Grant, Federal Work-Study, VA, Montana resident programs.

Accreditation: Northwest Association of Schools and Colleges.

Description: The University of Montana (1893) is a comprehensive, graduate level one institution of 12,000 students in a community of 80,000. Comprehensive undergraduate and graduate programs include professional schools of business, fine arts, forestry, journalism, pharmacy, law, and education. Master's degrees are granted in more than 20 fields and doctoral degrees in 12 fields. Additionally, a College of Technology, located in Missoula, is part of the University of Montana, Missoula.

University of Nebraska, Lincoln

33rd and Holdrege Streets	Phone: (402) 472-4321
Lincoln, NE 68583-9800	Fax: (402) 472-4317

Division(s): Continuing Studies
Web Site(s): http://www.unl.edu/conted
E-mail: unldde1@unl.edu

Graduate Degree Programs:
Master of Arts in Journalism and Mass Communication
Master of Business Administration
Master of Science in:
> Industrial and Management Systems Engineering (with option for specialization in Engineering Management)
> Manufacturing Systems Engineering
> Interdepartmental Human Resources and Family Sciences

Doctoral Degree Programs:
Doctorate in Administration, Curriculum, and Instruction (Cohort Recruitment and Admission) (K–12 Specialization: Educational Leadership or Teaching, Curriculum and Instruction)
Doctorate in Administration, Curriculum and Instruction (Specialization: Educational Leadership and Higher Education)

Certificate Programs: Educational Technology (K–12 instructional technology training).

Class Titles: Accounting, Agricultural Law, Art History, Ecology, Broadcasting, Broadcast Writing, Scientific Greek/Latin, Teaching Social Studies in Elementary School, Economics (micro/macro), Statistics, International Economics, Composition, 20th-Century Fiction, Shakespeare, Business Writing, Human Development/Family, Insurance, Finance, Real Estate Principles/Practices, Real Estate Finance, Economic Geography, Human Geography, Physical Geography, Geography of U.S., Health, Western Civilization, Latin American History, East Asian History, American History, History of Middle Ages, History of Early Modern Europe, Nebraska History, Engineering Economy, Elementary Quantitative Methods, Operations/Resource Management, Personnel/Human Resource Management, International Management, Business Policies/Strategies, Marketing, Geometry, Algebra, Trigonometry, Calculus, Pathophysiology, Evaluating Nursing Research, Nutrition, Logic/Critical Thinking, Modern Logic, Philosophy of Religion, Elementary Physics, Calculus-based Physics, American Government, Contemporary Foreign Governments, International Relations, Public Administration, Psychology, Psychosocial Aspects of Alcoholism, Real Estate Management, Real Estate Investments, Real Estate Appraisal, Sociology, Social Problems, Sociology of Crime, Marriage/Family, Technical Writing, Computer Science, Electrical Engineering, courses from College of Agriculture/Natural Resources.

Teaching Methods: *Computers:* Internet, real-time chat, electronic classroom, e-mail, CD-ROM, newsgroup, LISTSERV. *TV:* videotape, cable program, satellite broadcasting. *Other:* audioconferencing, videoconferencing, audiographics, audiotapes, fax, correspondence, independent study, individual study.

Credits Granted for: experiential learning, portfolio assessment, extrainstitutional learning, examination (CLEP, ACT-PEP, DANTES, GRE). See an UNL academic advisor.

Admission Requirements: *Undergraduate:* independent study courses: prerequisites are listed with courses; students have one year to complete a semester course, with a one-year extension possible. *Graduate:* application, 2 copies of all official transcripts (including bachelor's degree completion), 6-year completion limit, GMAT for MBA, TOEFL for international students. *Doctoral:* GRE for doctoral program in Curriculum and Instruction.

On-Campus Requirements: Doctoral Programs require 2–10 week summer sessions on campus at UNL.

Tuition and Fees: *Undergraduate:* $94/credit independent study, $105/credit nursing courses, $165/credit Engineering and MBA distance education courses, $125/credit all other distance education courses. *Graduate:* $110/credit independent study, $219/credit Engineering and MBA distance education courses, $164/credit all other distance education courses. *Doctoral:* $164/credit Doctoral Programs through Teachers College. *Application Fee:* $35 Graduate School. *Other Costs:* $21 shipping and handling, $50 extension for independent study courses, vary for books, special library resource requests (interlibrary loans, etc.). *Credit by:* semester.

Financial Aid: Federal Stafford Loan, Federal Perkins Loan, Federal PLUS Loan, Federal Pell Grant, Federal Work-Study, VA, Nebraska resident programs. Contact UNL Financial Aid Office, restrictions apply.

Accreditation: North Central Association of Colleges and Schools.

Description: The Lincoln campus of the University of Nebraska (1869) is the state's land-grant university and the only comprehensive university in Nebraska. Through its 3 primary missions of teaching, research, and outreach, the University of Nebraska has been recognized by the state legislature as the primary research and doctoral-degree granting institution in the state. NU is one of a select group of research universities that holds membership in the American Association of Universities (1909), and is classified as a Research I University by the Carnegie Foundation. In 1997 the institution moved up to the second tier in *U.S. News and World Report's* 11th annual "America's Best Colleges" issue. The University of Nebraska boasts 22 Rhodes Scholars and 2 Nobel laureates among its alumni. The university began offering courses at a distance in 1909 and currently uses almost every distance instructional technology available. The mission of the Division of Continuing Studies is to extend the resources of the university to promote lifelong learning. Each year we serve 87,000 people with our programs that reach people in all 93 counties of Nebraska, all 50 states, and 135 countries.

University of Nevada, Reno

PO Box 14429
Reno, NV 89507

Phone: (702) 784-4652
Fax: (702) 784-4801

Division(s): Correspondence Study
Web Site(s): http://www.dce.unr.edu/istudy/
E-mail: istudy@scs.unr.edu

Class Titles: Over 100 undergraduate, graduate, and high school correspondence classes.

Teaching Methods: *Computers:* Internet, e-mail, LISTSERV. *TV:* videotape. *Other:* audiotapes, fax, correspondence, independent study.

Credits Granted for: experiential learning, examination (CLEP, ACT-PEP, DANTES, GRE).

Admission Requirements: *Undergraduate:* age 15+. *Graduate:* graduate status.

On-Campus Requirements: None.

Tuition and Fees: *Undergraduate:* $70/credit. *Graduate:* $90/credit. *Application Fee:* $40 graduate. *Other Costs:* books, materials, handling. *Credit by:* semester.

Financial Aid: VA, Nevada resident programs.

Accreditation: Northwest Association of Schools and Colleges.

Description: The University of Nevada was founded in 1867 and has offered Correspondence Study to Nevada and the world since 1944. In addition to its 100 classes from high school to graduate level, the university is developing many new Internet courses. UNR wants to put you in a class all your own!

University of New Brunswick

Continuing Education Centre
6 Duffie Drive
Fredericton, NB, Canada E3A 5A3

Phone: (506) 453-4646
Fax: (506) 453-3572

Division(s): Extension and Summer Session
Web Site(s): http://www.unb.ca/coned/
E-mail: coned@unb.ca

Class Titles: Applied Mechanics, Electrical Engineering, Economics (micro/macro), Economics (Money/Banking), English–Prose Narrative, Psychology, Technology Management in Entrepreneurial Environment. Available inside Canada: Human Physiology for Nurses, Pathophysiology, Shakespeare/His Contemporaries, Survey of English Literature–Beginnings to Late 18th Century, Survey of English Literature–Romantics, Development of Western Thought, Elementary Statistical Techniques.

Teaching Methods: *Computers:* Internet, e-mail, CD-ROM, newsgroup, LISTSERV. *TV:* satellite broadcasting. *Other:* audioconferencing, videoconferencing, audiographics, audiotapes, correspondence, independent study, individual study.

Admission Requirements: *Undergraduate:* 6 months to complete a 3-credit course; 12 months for a 6-credit course.

On-Campus Requirements: None.

Tuition and Fees: *Undergraduate:* approximately Cdn $330/3-credit course. *Software:* varies; see http://www.unb.ca/web/coned/de/ocrsof.html. *Other Costs:* varies; see http://www.unb.ca/web/coned/de/ocrsof.html. *Credit by:* semester.

Financial Aid: limited to Canadian citizens and landed immigrants only.

Accreditation: Association of Universities and Colleges of Canada.

Description: The University of New Brunswick (1785) values academic success. *Maclean's* 1997 Annual Ranking of Canada's Universities gave UNB "top marks for going the distance" with its students. It is the only university in New Brunswick that puts student success and achievement first. UNB strives to be known for its excellence in teaching by providing students with the highest possible quality instruction, library and laboratory resources appropriate for both undergraduate and graduate learning, and an environment conducive to the development of the whole person.

University of New England

716 Stevens Avenue
Portland, ME 04103

Phone: (207) 797-7261 x4381
(800) 339-0155
Fax: (207) 878-2434

Division(s): Distance Learning
Web Site(s): http://www.une.edu/cpcs/msedhm.html
E-mail: MSED@mailbox.une.edu

Graduate Degree Programs:
Master of Science in Education

Class Titles: Technology/Learning in Today's Classroom, Helping Students Become Self-Directed Learners, Learning Differences: Effective Teaching with Learning Styles/Multiple Intelligences, Building Your Repertoire of Teaching Strategies, Including Students with Special Needs in Regular Classroom, Motivating Today's Learner, Teaching Students to Get Along, Strategies for Preventing Conflict/Violence, Succeeding with Difficult Students, High Performing Teacher, How to Get Parents on Your Side, Assertive Discipline/Beyond.

Teaching Methods: *TV:* videotape. *Other:* texts and printed study guide.

Admission Requirements: *Graduate:* official college transcript, accredited bachelor's degree, teaching certificate or evidence of teaching experience, minimum one year teaching experience, 2 letters of reference, personal goal statement.

On-Campus Requirements: 3-credit summer seminar.

Tuition and Fees: *Graduate:* $235/credit. *Application Fee:* $40. *Other Costs:* $60/course Materials Fee, $55 General Service Fee. *Credit by:* term.

Financial Aid: Federal Stafford Loans, VA.

Accreditation: New England Association of Schools and Colleges.

Description: The University of New England is a comprehensive, private, independent institution originally founded in 1978. However, in 1996 the university merged with Portland's small, liberal arts Westbrook College, so UNE now recognizes Westbrook's 1831 charter date as its own. The UNE Master of Science in Education program, begun in 1995, allows experienced teachers to study, reflect, and practice skills based on the most recent educational research and instructional techniques. The curriculum is presented through multiple learning modalities. Each course includes videotaped presentations featuring nationally recognized education experts. Study guides help students apply the concepts in the video lessons; textbooks and selected articles provide additional information. Courses are provided in sequence, building on previous courses, to ensure students are exposed to a comprehensive curriculum relevant to contemporary classroom teachers. Students submit work to and communicate with faculty via toll-free telephone, e-mail, fax, or correspondence.

University of New Hampshire

6 Garrison Avenue	Phone: (603) 862-1937
Durham, NH 03824	Fax: (603) 862-1113

Division(s): Continuing Education
Web Site(s): http://www.learn.unh.edu
E-mail: learn.dce@unh.edu

Graduate Degree Programs:
Master of Science/Communication Disorders

Certificate Programs: Real Estate Recertification, Surveying/Land Use Planning (both noncredit).

Class Titles: Environmental Conservation, Neuropathologies, Organic Pathologies in Children, Diagnostic Methods in Speech Pathology, Microcomputer Technology, Manufacturing Tooling/Processes, Stuttering, Land Records (noncredit), Real Estate Salespersons/Brokers Recertification (noncredit).

Teaching Methods: *Computers:* Internet, real-time chat, electronic classroom, e-mail, CD-ROM, LISTSERV. *TV:* videotape, T1 compressed video. *Other:* videoconferencing, fax, independent study, individual study, learning contracts.

Credits Granted for: extrainstitutional learning, examination (CLEP, ACT-PEP, DANTES, GRE).

Admission Requirements: *Graduate:* program-specific, accredited college degree.

On-Campus Requirements: None.

Tuition and Fees: *Undergraduate:* $176/credit. *Graduate:* $205/credit. *Application Fee:* $40. *Other Costs:* $15 registration, special course fees where applicable. *Credit by:* semester.

Financial Aid: Federal Stafford Loan, Federal Perkins Loan, Federal PLUS Loan, Federal Pell Grant, Federal Work-Study, VA, New Hampshire resident programs.

Accreditation: New England Association of Schools and Colleges.

Description: The University of New Hampshire's (1866) community includes more than 12,000 undergraduate and graduate students as well as nearly 1,000 full- and part-time faculty. In its 133rd year, UNH is committed to excellence in education and to supporting the best in scholarship and research while also contributing to economic opportunity and the quality of life in New Hampshire.

University of New Orleans Metropolitan College

Education Building, Room 122	
University of New Orleans	Phone: (504) 280-7100
New Orleans, LA 70148	Fax: (504) 280-7317

Division(s): Metropolitan College
Web Site(s): http://metrocollege.uno.edu
E-mail: bmcdonal@uno.edu

Certificate Programs: Clinical Supervision, ASTD, Computer Training.

Class Titles: Personal Enrichment, Academic Preparation, Personal Development, Career Assessment, Ethics/International Politics, Conflict/Diplomacy.

Teaching Methods: *Computers:* Internet, real-time chat, electronic classroom, e-mail, CD-ROM, newsgroup, LISTSERV. *TV:* videotape, cable program, satellite broadcasting, PBS. *Other:* radio broadcast, audioconferencing, videoconferencing, audiographics, audiotapes, fax, correspondence, independent study, individual study, learning contracts.

Admission Requirements: *Undergraduate:* students need not supply previous transcripts or test scores, and up to 30 semester hours earned in this nondegree status may apply towards a degree later from the University of New Orleans. *Graduate:* students who have a bachelor's and do not wish to pursue a graduate degree from the University of New Orleans may apply for admissions to the Metropolitan College as a nondegree seeking student. A student may apply up to 20 semester hours earned. *Doctoral:* same as graduate.

On-Campus Requirements: Tests will be proctored by an administrator at your host institution.

Tuition and Fees: *Undergraduate:* approximately $1,181 for full-time students, contact school for details. *Graduate:* contact school for details. *Application Fee:* $20 admission application fee for first-time students. *Other Costs:* $30 nonrefundable late registration fee, $17 extended payment plan option, $40 international student fee, $45 off-campus registration fee (except for graduate students), $5/credit ($75 max.) technology fee, $10–$100 special fees depending on course *Credit by:* semester.

Financial Aid: Federal Stafford Loan, Federal Perkins Loan, Federal PLUS Loan, Federal Pell Grant, Federal Work-Study, VA, Louisiana resident programs.

Accreditation: Southern Association of Colleges and Schools.

Description: The University of New Orleans (1958) provides its undergraduate students equality of access to educational opportunities, and seeks to nurture in them scholarship, academic excellence, the ability to work productively with others, and qualities of leadership.

The University of North Carolina at Charlotte

9201 University City Boulevard	Phone: (704) 547-2424
Charlotte, NC 28223	Fax: (704) 547-3158

Division(s): Continuing Education, Summer Programs and Extension
Web Site(s): http://www.uncc.edu/conteduc/
E-mail: dmlockli@email.uncc.edu

Undergraduate Degree Programs:
Bachelor of Science in Engineering Technology

Graduate Degree Programs:
Master of Education, Special Education

Certificate Programs: Supported Employment and Transition

Teaching Methods: *Computers:* Internet, real-time chat, electronic classroom, e-mail, CD-ROM, newsgroup, LIST-SERV. *TV:* videotape, cable program, satellite broadcasting, PBS. *Other:* audioconferencing, videoconferencing, audiotapes, fax.

Credits Granted for: examination (CLEP, ACT-PEP, DANTES, GRE).

Admission Requirements: *Undergraduate:* AAS in Electrical or Electronic Engineering Technology, 2.2 GPA, prerequisite courses. This is a cohort program that began in 1997 and is not currently scheduled to be repeated. *Graduate:* bachelor's degree, 2.75 GPA, official transcripts, GRE/GMAT/MAT. This is a cohort program that began in 1997 and is not currently scheduled to be repeated. Students can be admitted for individual courses for licensure. Course work ends spring of 1999.

On-Campus Requirements: Special Education classes are held at 3 community college sites in Dallas, Salisbury, and Statesville, NC. Students attend classes at the UNC Charlotte campus during summer. Engineering Technology classes are held at 3 community college sites in Dallas, Winston-Salem, and Raleigh, NC. Students at Dallas and Winston-Salem attend labs on the UNC Charlotte campus during summer.

Tuition and Fees: *Undergraduate:* $246 tuition and fees for 7 hours of credit as a NC resident in 1998 spring semester. *Graduate:* $359 tuition and fees for 6 hours of credit as a state resident for 1998 spring semester. *Application Fee:* $35. *Credit by:* semester.

Financial Aid: Federal Stafford Loan, Federal Perkins Loan, Federal PLUS Loan, Federal Pell Grant, Federal Work-Study, VA, North Carolina resident programs.

Accreditation: Southern Association of Colleges and Schools.

Description: The University of North Carolina at Charlotte (1945) subsumes the College of Arts and Sciences and 5 professional colleges: Architecture, Business Administration, Education, Engineering, and Nursing and Health Professions. Enrollment has passed 15,800 and is expected to reach 25,000 within the next 12 years. Located in the 33rd-largest city, UNC Charlotte serves one of the nation's most dynamic regions, with 5,500,000 people in a 100-mile radius. UNC Charlotte participates in 2 statewide, interactive-video networks that "broadcast" courses from the Charlotte campus to other institutions of higher education, community colleges, high schools, hospitals, and other sites throughout the state. Distance education will soon include a major portion of a master's degree in Special Education and a bachelor's completion program in Engineering Technology.

University of North Carolina, Chapel Hill

CB# 1020 The Friday Center	Phone: (800) 862-5669
Chapel Hill, NC 27599-1020	(919) 962-1134
	Fax: (919) 962-5549

Division(s): Continuing Education
Web Site(s): http://www.fridaycenter.unc.edu
E-mail: stuserv.ce@mhs.unc.edu

Class Titles: Accounting, Economics, Business, African Studies, Art, Biology, Chemistry, Classics, Communication Studies, Computer Science, Drama, Education, English, Environmental Sciences, French, Geography, Geology, Health Administration, History, Interdisciplinary Studies, Italian, Journalism, Latin, Library Science, Math, Music, Nursing, Nutrition, Philosophy, Physics, Planning, Political Science, Poultry Science, Psychology, Religious Studies, Russian, Sociology, Spanish, Statistics.

Teaching Methods: *Computers:* Internet, e-mail, CD-ROM, asynchronous discussion forum. *TV:* videotape. *Other:* audiotapes, correspondence, independent study.

On-Campus Requirements: None.

Tuition and Fees: *Undergraduate:* $80/credit, correspondence courses; $390/online course. *Credit by:* semester.

Financial Aid: not specifically for distance education students. Requests are handled on individual basis.

Accreditation: Southern Association of Colleges and Schools.

Description: University of North Carolina-Chapel Hill (1793) is a major teaching and research institution that consistently receives high rankings for the quality of its instruction. The university's 14 colleges and schools provide instruction in a hundred fields. The Division of Continuing Education was established in 1913 and began offering correspondence courses that same year. Print-based distance instruction has been offered continually since then; online instruction for distance students was added in 1997. Since the mid-1970s, UNC-Chapel Hill has provided administrative support for all University of North Carolina campuses offering correspondence courses.

University of North Dakota

Box 9021   Phone: (701) 777-2661
Grand Forks, ND 58202   Fax: (701) 777-4282

Division(s): Continuing Education
Web Site(s): http://www.und.nodak.edu/dept/conted/learn.htm
E-mail: dorine_houck@mail.und.nodak.edu

Undergraduate Degree Programs:
Bachelor of Business Administration in Management
Corporate Engineering Degree Program with a Bachelor of Science in:
  Electrical Engineering
  Mechanical Engineering
  Chemical Engineering
Bachelor of Science in Occupational Therapy

Graduate Degree Programs:
Master of Business Administration
Master of Education in:
  Elementary Education
  General Studies
  Education Leadership
Master of Public Administration
Master of Social Work
Master of Science with specialties in:
  Rural Health Nursing
  Space Studies
  Medical Technician

Teaching Methods: *TV:* videoconferencing, interactive video network system within North Dakota. *Other:* correspondence.

Credits Granted for: examination (CLEP, ACT/PEP, DANTES, GRE).

Admission Requirements: *Undergraduate:* contact admissions office. *Graduate:* contact admissions office. *Doctoral:* contact admissions office.

On-Campus Requirements: distant students do not have residency requirements except in North Dakota, Canada, Montana, South Dakota, Minnesota.

Tuition and Fees: *Undergraduate:* contact school. *Graduate:* contact school. *Credit by:* semester.

Financial Aid: Federal Stafford Loan, Federal Perkins Loan, Federal PLUS Loan, Federal Pell Grant, Federal Work-Study, VA, North Dakota resident programs.

Accreditation: North Central Association of Colleges and Schools.

Description: The University of North Dakota (1883) existed 6 years before North Dakota became a state. Unlike most state institutions of higher education west of the Mississippi, UND did not begin as an agricultural school or a teachers college. Organized initially as a College of Arts and Sciences, with a Normal School for the education of teachers, UND soon evolved into a full-fledged multipurpose university. The instruction of graduate students (the first master's degree was awarded in 1895) and the conducting of research were underway before the end of the 19th century. Depressions, drought, wars, and financial crises have more than once threatened UND's future, but the university has been able to withstand these challenges and to prosper as an institution of national caliber. Extended Degree programs are only available in the North Dakota area via the interactive video network system. The master's degree in Space Studies is available internationally via the Internet and videotapes.

University of Northern Iowa

124 SHC   Phone: (319) 273-2123
Cedar Falls, IA 50614-0223   Fax: (319) 273-2872

Division(s): Continuing Education
Web Site(s): http://www.uni.edu/contined/gcs
E-mail: contined@uni.edu

Undergraduate Degree Programs:
Bachelor of Liberal Studies

Class Titles: A variety of undergraduate and graduate-level courses in Business, Communication Studies, Family/Consumer Sciences, Education, Social Sciences.

Teaching Methods: *Computers:* Internet, e-mail, CD-ROM. *TV:* videotape, PBS. *Other:* videoconferencing, correspondence, independent study. Primarily a print-based correspondence study program.

Credits Granted for: examination (Credit by Examination, ACE military).

Admission Requirements: *Undergraduate:* for BLS, 62 transferable, semester credits, college transcripts, 2.0 GPA.

On-Campus Requirements: None.

Tuition and Fees: *Undergraduate:* $84/credit (correspondence study courses). *Graduate:* $84/credit (correspondence study courses). *Application Fee:* $30 to apply for admission to Bachelor of Liberal Studies. *Other Costs:* $13 enrollment fee for each course. *Credit by:* semester.

Financial Aid: VA.

Accreditation: North Central Association of Colleges and Schools.

Description: The University of Northern Iowa (1876) has a long and distinguished history of distance education. As early as 1914 college credit courses were offered off-campus to provide opportunities for teachers, most of whom did not have bachelor's degrees. While traditional methods of on-site, off-campus teaching and print-based correspondence study will continue, courses delivered over the Iowa Communications Network and the Internet are likely to increase, driven by both the supply and the demand.

University of Notre Dame

| 126 College of Business Administration | Phone: (800) 631-3622 |
| Notre Dame, IN 46556 | Fax: (219) 631-6783 |

Division(s): Executive Programs
Web Site(s): http://www.nd.edu/~execprog/
E-mail: Rita.A.Gong.1@nd.edu

Graduate Degree Programs:
Executive Master of Business Administration

Certificate Programs: Executive Management, Supervisory Development (plus some custom programs).

Teaching Methods: *TV:* videoconferencing. *Other:* None.

Admission Requirements: *Graduate:* 5 years of meaningful management responsibilities, undergraduate degree or GMAT, registrar's transcript of previously completed college level education.

On-Campus Requirements: August 6-day residency.

Tuition and Fees: *Graduate:* $24,900/year. *Application Fee:* $50. *Credit by:* semester.

Accreditation: North Central Association of Colleges and Schools, American Assembly of Collegiate Schools of Business.

Description: Founded by a Catholic priest in 1842, the University of Notre Dame has enjoyed constant and planned growth as an institution of higher education. Its programs have successfully combined moral, ethical, and spiritual considerations with educating students to meet the requirements of contemporary industrial, commercial, social, and technological systems. Recognition of its quality, through the success of its graduates and the esteem of alumni, has generated worldwide respect for the Notre Dame degree. The College of Business Administration traces its origin to 1913, when 6 students enrolled in a series of commercial courses. The Executive MBA program began in 1982 and launched its distance education program in 1995. Its videoconferencing classrooms are equipped with tracking cameras, wireless microphones, large display monitors, and many other multimedia devices for instruction and presentation. Live, 2-way, interactive videoconferencing is offered to remote sites in Indianapolis, Toledo, and in Hoffman Estates, Illinois.

University of Oklahoma

| 1600 South Jenkins, Room 101 | Phone: (405) 325-1921 |
| Norman, OK 73071 | Fax: (405) 325-7687 |

Division(s): Independent Study
Web Site(s): http://www.occe.ou.edu
E-mail: lbergeron@cce.occe.ou.edu

Class Titles: Accounting, Anthropology, Astronomy, Business, Chemistry, Chinese, Classical Culture, Drama, Economics, Education, Engineering, English, Finance, French, Geography, Geology, German, Greek, Health/Sport Sciences, History, Human Relations, Japanese, Journalism/Mass Communication, Latin, Library/Information Studies, Management, Marketing, Math, Music, Philosophy, Political Science, Psychology, Russian, Sociology, Spanish.

Teaching Methods: *Computers:* Internet, real-time chat, electronic classroom, e-mail, CD-ROM, newsgroup, LISTSERV. *Other:* videotape, audiotapes, correspondence.

Credits Granted for: Check with OU Admissions and Records Office.

Admission Requirements: *Graduate:* check with Admissions Office. *Doctoral:* check with Admissions Office. *Certificate:* check with Admissions Office.

On-Campus Requirements: None.

Tuition and Fees: *Undergraduate:* $70/credit. *Other Costs:* $7 records fee, variable materials fee, book/kits fee. *Credit by:* semester.

Accreditation: North Central Association of Colleges and Schools, Commission on Colleges and Universities.

Description: The University of Oklahoma (1890) was established 17 years before Oklahoma became a state. Today the university is a major national research university that serves the educational, cultural, and economic needs of the state, region, and nation. The university's 25,400 students are enrolled in 19 colleges. In addition, a wide variety of courses and programs are offered through the College of Continuing Education.

University of Oregon

1277 University of Oregon
Eugene, OR 97403-1277

Phone: (541) 346-0696
(800) 824-2714
Fax: (541) 346-0689

Division(s): Continuation Center
Web Site(s): http://de.uoregon.edu
http://center.uoregon.edu
http://cep.uoregon.edu
E-mail: dasst@continue.uoregon.edu

Class Titles: Astronomy, Economics, Geology, Physics, Political Science.

Teaching Methods: *Computers:* Internet, e-mail. *TV:* satellite broadcasting. *Other:* individual study.

Credits Granted for: examination.

On-Campus Requirements: None.

Tuition and Fees: *Undergraduate:* $390/class. *Software:* $10 selected classes. *Credit by:* quarter.

Financial Aid: Federal Stafford Loan, Federal Perkins Loan, Federal PLUS Loan, Federal Pell Grant, Federal Work-Study, VA, Oregon resident programs available only to admitted students who are enrolled half-time or more.

Accreditation: Association of American Universities, Northwest Association of Schools and Colleges, Western Interstate Commission for Higher Education.

Description: The University of Oregon (1876) is a comprehensive research university that serves its students and the people of Oregon, the nation, and the world through the creation and transfer of knowledge in the liberal arts, the natural and social sciences, and the professions. It is the Association of American Universities' flagship institution of the Oregon University System. Distance Education courses were first offered in 1996, and additional offerings are being developed each year.

University of Phoenix Online Campus

100 Spear Street, Suite 110
San Francisco, CA 94105

Phone: (800) 388-5463
Fax: (415) 541-7832

Division(s): Distance Education
Web Site(s): http://www.uophx.edu/online
E-mail: online@apollogrp.edu

Undergraduate Degree Programs:
Associate of Arts in General Studies
Bachelor of Science in:
    Business/Administration
    Business/Information Systems
    Business/Management
    Business/Marketing
    Business/Project Management

Graduate Degree Programs:
Master of Arts in Organizational Management
Master of Business Administration
Master of Business Administration in Global Management
Master of Business Administration in Technology Management
Master of Science in Computer Information Systems

Teaching Methods: *Computers:* Internet, electronic classroom, conferencing, e-mail, CD-ROM. *Other:* None.

Credits Granted for: experiential learning, portfolio assessment, examination (CLEP, ACT-PEP, DANTES, GRE).

Admission Requirements: *Undergraduate:* high school diploma or equivalent, age 23, current employment or access to organizational environment to apply classroom concepts to workplace, TOEFL of 580 for non-native speakers of English. *Graduate:* accredited undergraduate degree with 2.5 cumulative GPA, 3.0 cumulative GPA (plus transcripts) for all graduate work, 3 years of full-time, post-high-school work experience with exposure to organizational systems and management processes, TOEFL of 580 for non-native speakers of English, current employment or access to organizational environment to apply classroom concepts to workplace.

On-Campus Requirements: None.

Tuition and Fees: *Undergraduate:* $365/credit. *Graduate:* $460/credit. *Application Fee:* $58. *Software:* $102. *Other Costs:* textbooks. *Credit by:* tract system.

Financial Aid: Federal Stafford Loan, Federal PLUS Loan, Federal Pell Grant, VA.

Accreditation: North Central Association of Colleges and Schools.

Description: The University of Phoenix Online Campus (1976) is a leader in time- and place-independent, group-based education and training. We offer a highly effective learning environment, bringing geographically diverse faculty and students together through technology. We serve motivated working adults interested in expanding their practical skills and knowledge to meet their personal and professional goals. The Online Campus provides students a structured classroom and the individual flexibility to attend when and where it is most convenient so they can meet academic responsibilities as well as the obligations of home and work; creates a unique learning dynamic that fosters reflective, substantive, and articulate expressions of ideas in which each class member has equal access for participation and for sharing knowledge; and offers access to an unlimited pool of accomplished faculty professionals selected for their education, work experience, and skill at facilitating asynchronous learning.

University of Regina

Room 211, College Building
Regina, SK, Canada S4S 0A2

Phone: (306) 585-5803
Fax: (306) 585-5779

Division(s): University Extension
Web Site(s): http://www.uregina.ca
E-mail: offcamp@uregina.ca

Class Titles: Astronomy, Biology, Cree, English, French, Geology, Human Justice, Psychology, Religious Studies, Women's Studies, Genealogy.

Teaching Methods: *Computers:* Web-based. *TV:* satellite broadcasting. *Other:* videoconferencing, audioconferencing.

Admission Requirements: *Undergraduate:* Saskatchewan Grade 12 standing or equivalent with specified averages in designated courses. Those age 21 without regular admission requirements may be admitted to the University Entrance Program. *Graduate:* 4-year degree with an average of 70% in undergraduate work. *Doctoral:* master's degree or equivalent. *Certificate:* same as undergraduate.

On-Campus Requirements: traditionally instructed labs for biology courses.

Tuition and Fees: *Undergraduate:* $94/credit. *Graduate:* $94/credit. *Doctoral:* $94/credit. *Application Fee:* $50. *Other Costs:* $32 (0–8 credits) service fees, $6–$13/credit course fees. *Credit by:* semester.

Financial Aid: Canada Student Loans

Accreditation: Association of Universities and Colleges of Canada.

Description: The University of Regina (1925) is a dynamic institution with a heritage going back 80 years. It has a reputation for innovative academic programming and continually seeks to provide new, nontraditional programs in response to public demand. The university is recognized as a national leader in the areas of aboriginal education, cooperative work/study education, teacher training, the fine arts, systems engineering, journalism, computer science, and training for human service careers. University Extension extends learning opportunities off campus through traditional face-to-face courses and distance education. Distance education courses are primarily offered through satellite broadcast (one-way video and 2-way audio) on the Saskatchewan Communication Training Network. Other modes of delivery for distance education courses include: Internet-based courses, computer-mediated conferencing, audioconferencing, and videoconferencing.

University of Sarasota

5250 17th Street
Sarasota, FL 34235

Phone: (941) 379-0404
(800) 331-5995
Fax: (941) 379-9464

Division(s): Admissions
Web Site(s): http://www.sarasota.edu
E-mail: univsar@compuserve.com

Graduate Degree4 Programs:
Master of Arts in:
   Mental Health Counseling
   Guidance Counseling
Master of Business Administration

Doctoral Degree Programs:
Educational Specialist in:
   Educational Leadership
   Curriculum/Instruction
   School Counseling
Doctor of Education in:
   Educational Leadership
   Curriculum/Instruction
   Organizational Leadership
   Counseling Psychology
   Pastoral Community Counseling
Doctor of Business Administration

Certificate Programs: Advanced Graduate Business, Professional Graduate Business, Basic Graduate Business.

Teaching Methods: *Computers:* Internet, e-mail. *TV:* videotape. *Other:* fax, correspondence, independent study.

Credits Granted for: transfer credit from another college.

Admission Requirements: *Graduate:* accredited bachelor's degree, previous and sustained 3.0 GPA, possible interview, personal statement of professional and educational goals, online and e-mail access, program completion within 4 years, TOEFL of 500 (173 computer-based) for applicants whose native language is not English. *Doctoral:* EdS: accredited master's degree, previous and sustained 3.0 GPA, possible interview, personal statement of professional and educational goals, 3 current professional recommendations, online and e-mail access, TOEFL of 550 (213 computer-based) for all applicants whose native language is not English. For EdS in School Counseling ONLY: Teaching experience in either a public or private K–12 school, program completion within 3 years. Doctorates: accredited master's degree, possible interview, resume, 3 current professional recommendations, personal statement of professional and educational goals, program completion within 7 years (within 5 years for Pastoral Community Counseling), TOEFL of 550 (213 computer-based) for applicants whose native language is not English. *Certificate:* Advanced Graduate Business Certificates: admission as a student-at-large and must meet all requirements for Doctor of Business Administration program. Professional and Basic Graduate Business Certificates:

admission as a student-at-large and must meet all requirements for MBA program.

On-Campus Requirements: Doctor of Education/Doctor of Business Administration on-campus requirement is 8 courses (24 credits). Educational Specialist on-campus requirement is 5 courses (15 credits). Master of Arts/Master of Business Administration on-campus requirement is 6 courses (18 credits).

Tuition and Fees: *Graduate:* $353/credit. *Application Fee:* $50. *Software:* $11/course. *Credit by:* semester.

Financial Aid: Federal Stafford Loan

Accreditation: Southern Association of Colleges and Schools.

Description: University of Sarasota (1969) was established to serve the graduate educational needs of adult working professionals. As relevant technologies emerged, they were incorporated into the university's flexible delivery systems. The state of Florida granted licensure to the university in 1976 to offer the Doctorate in Education (EdD). Two years later, the state authorized the university to offer the Master of Arts in Education (MAEd). In 1980, the university received additional approval to offer the Master of Business Administration (MBA). In 1990, the university was accredited by the Commission on Colleges of the Southern Association of Colleges and Schools to offer master's and doctoral degrees. In 1994, the Doctor of Business Administration (DBA) program was established. The university has also gained approval to award bachelor's and educational specialist degrees.

University of Saskatchewan

Room 326 Kirk Hall
117 Science Place
Saskatoon, SK, Canada S7N 5C8

Phone: (306) 966-5563
Fax: (306) 966-5590

Division(s): Extension Credit Studies
Web Site(s): http://www.extension.usask.ca
E-mail: extcred@usask.ca

Certificate Programs: Education and Arts and Science courses, including Adult and Continuing Education, Agriculture, Prairie Horticulture, Teaching English as a Second Language.

Class Titles: Most first-year degree courses.

Teaching Methods: *Computers:* Internet, e-mail, CD-ROM, LISTSERV. *TV:* videotape, satellite broadcasting. *Other:* audioconferencing, audiotapes, fax, correspondence, independent study, individual study, learning contracts.

Credits Granted for: portfolio assessment.

Admission Requirements: *Undergraduate:* high school diploma/matriculation. *Certificate:* high school diploma/matriculation or equivalent.

On-Campus Requirements: None.

Tuition and Fees: *Undergraduate:* $100/credit, $72–$115/equivalent credit unit for certificate programs. *Application Fee:* $50 for ACE Certificate. *Other Costs:* $50 admission. *Credit by:* term (2/year).

Financial Aid: part-time student loans (federal/provincial).

Accreditation: Association of Universities and Colleges of Canada.

Description: Since 1907 the University of Saskatchewan has provided a blend of liberal, professional, and applied education and research. In 1929 the university first delivered correspondence courses. Distance education courses today still use print-based material but also may incorporate audio, video, satellite, or computer technologies.

University of South Carolina

915 Gregg Street
Columbia, SC 29208

Phone: (800) 922-2577
Fax: (803) 777-6264

Division(s): Distance Education and Instructional Support
Web Site(s): http://www.sc.edu/deis/student.services
E-mail: question@gwm.sc.edu

Graduate Degree Programs:
Master of Science in:
 Engineering
 Business

Class Titles: Astronomy, Library Science, Education, English, French, History, Marine Science, Nursing, Anthropology, Social Work, Business Administration, Journalism, Engineering.

Teaching Methods: *Computers:* Internet, real-time chat, electronic classroom, e-mail, CD-ROM, LISTSERV. *TV:* videotape, satellite broadcasting, audioconferencing, videoconferencing, audiotapes. *Other:* correspondence, independent study, individual study, learning contracts.

Credits Granted for: examination (CLEP, ACT-PEP, DANTES, GRE).

Admission Requirements: *Undergraduate:* call Distance Education and Instructional Support. *Graduate:* call Distance Education and Instructional Support.

On-Campus Requirements: some sessions for some departments; department-specific.

Tuition and Fees: *Undergraduate:* program-specific, around $144/credit. *Other Costs:* program-specific, around $4/credit technology fee. *Credit by:* semester.

Financial Aid: Federal Stafford Loan, Federal Perkins Loan, Federal PLUS Loan, Federal Pell Grant, Federal Work-Study, VA, South Carolina resident programs.

Accreditation: Southern Association of Colleges and Schools.

Description: The University of South Carolina (1801) was the first higher education institution funded entirely by a state. Faculty included Francis Lieber, author of Civil Liberty and Self Government, scientists John and Joseph LeConte, and chemist William Eller, who produced the first daguerreotype in the U.S. The voluntary enlistment of all students in the Army of the Confederacy forced the college to close during the Civil War. It was rechartered to offer "the largest and best work in education that time and place and conditions render possible." In addition to the Columbia campus, there are two 4-year campuses and five 2-year regional campuses, with a total enrollment of 35,000. While correspondence study has been offered at USC for more than 70 years, the university's commitment to televised instruction began in 1969 through the state's closed-circuit system. Today the distance education program, utilizing satellite, video/audiocassettes, and correspondence study, is a vital part of the university's commitment to providing alternative educational opportunities to students.

University of Southern California School of Engineering

Olin Hall of Engineering, Room 108 School of Engineering, MC 1455 Los Angeles, CA 90089-1455	Phone: (213) 740-0115 Fax: (213) 749-3289

Division(s): Instructional TV Network for the School of Engineering

Web Site(s):
http://www.usc.edu/dept/engineering/Distance_Learning
E-mail: collins@mizar.usc.edu

Graduate Degree Programs:
Master of Science in:
Computer Science
Computer Engineering
Electrical Engineering
Systems Architecting and Engineering
Aeronautics

Certificate Programs: Aerospace Engineering (specialization in Astronautics).

Teaching Methods: *Computers:* Internet, e-mail, newsgroup. *TV:* videotape, satellite broadcasting, ITFS. *Other:* videoconferencing.

Credits Granted for: Regular live courses only, GRE required for admission (see below).

Admission Requirements: *Graduate:* Accredited bachelor's degree, GRE, undergraduate GPA of 3.0, completion in 7 years.

On-Campus Requirements: It is best in the program that the student watch a "live" broadcast of a course in the company classroom. The student is able to ask questions and receive an immediate response.

Tuition and Fees: *Undergraduate:* $706/credit. *Graduate:* $716/credit. *Doctoral:* $716/credit. *Application Fee:* $55. *Other Costs:* $35/semester Unix account, $100/unit for local ITV Surcharge, $750/course + tuition for satellite site. *Credit by:* semester.

Financial Aid: Most companies reimburse 100%.

Accreditation: ABET.

Description: The goals of the University of Southern California School of Engineering (1906) are (1) to provide undergraduate and graduate engineering degree programs for qualified students; (2) to extend the frontiers of engineering knowledge by encouraging and assisting faculty to pursue and publish research; (3) to stimulate and encourage in its students those qualities of scholarship, leadership, and character that mark the true academic and professional engineer; (4) to serve the industrial community of Southern California in providing for the continuing education of engineering and scientific personnel; and (5) to provide professional engineering leadership in solving community, regional, national, and global problems.

University of Southern Colorado

2200 Bonforte Boulevard Pueblo, CO 81001-4901	Phone: (800) 388-6154 (719) 549-2316 Fax: (719) 549-2438

Division(s): Continuing Education
Web Site(s): http://www.uscolo.edu/coned
E-mail: coned@uscolo.edu

Undergraduate Degree Programs:
Bachelor of Science in Social Science

Certificate Programs: Legal Investigation, Victim Advocacy, Legal Secretary.

Class Titles: Accounting, Art, Biology, Business, Chemistry, Economics, Education, English, Geography, History, Management, Marketing, Nursing, Political Science, Psychology, Social Science, Sociology, Social Work.

Teaching Methods: *Computers:* Internet, e-mail. *TV:* videotape. *Other:* audiotapes, fax, correspondence, independent study.

Credits Granted for: experiential learning, CLEP, DANTES, military, transfer credit.

Admission Requirements: *Undergraduate:* ACT, high school transcripts if fewer than 30 semester college credits.

On-Campus Requirements: must complete 32 semester credits through correspondence, television or online.

Tuition and Fees: *Undergraduate:* $75/credit. *Graduate:* $85/credit. *Application Fee:* $125. *Other Costs:* $75 videotapes (if course requires). *Credit by:* semester.

Financial Aid: Company- and military-sponsored assistance, DANTES.

Accreditation: North Central Association of Colleges and Schools.

Description: The University of Southern Colorado has served the changing needs of students for more than 60 years. USC's 275-acre campus crowns the north end of a historically and culturally rich city of 100,000 in the colorful Pikes Peak region. USC's 4,000 students from the state, nation, and several foreign countries represent a diversity of age groups and backgrounds. The institution's mission includes emphasizing career-oriented, technological, and applied programs while maintaining strong liberal arts programs; engaging in basic and applied research for the benefit of society; and functioning as the major educational resource for cultural, industrial, and economic growth in southeastern Colorado.

University of Southern Indiana

8600 University Boulevard	Phone: (800) 813-4238
Evansville, IN 47712	Fax: (812) 465-7061

Division(s): Distance Education Programming
Web Site(s): http://www.usi.edu/distance
E-mail: arose.ucs@smtp.usi.edu

Undergraduate Degree Programs:
Associate of Science in Communications
Bachelor of Science in Nursing
Bachelor of Science in Health Services

Class Titles: Business, Advertising, Public Relations, Radio/TV, Theater, Interpersonal/Organizational, Mass Media, Mass Communications Law, Journalism, Education, English, Mythology, Humanities, Nursing, Political Science, Psychology, Health Services.

Teaching Methods: *Computers:* Internet, real-time chat, electronic classroom, e-mail, CD-ROM, newsgroup, LISTSERV. *TV:* videotape, cable program, satellite broadcasting, PBS. *Other:* audioconferencing, videoconferencing, fax, correspondence.

Credits Granted for: examination (CLEP, ACT-PEP, DANTES, GRE).

Admission Requirements: *Undergraduate:* SAT or ACT (no specific score required), application, official high school and college (if any) transcripts.

On-Campus Requirements: None.

Tuition and Fees: *Undergraduate:* $88/credit state resident, $215/credit nonresident. *Graduate:* $129/credit state resident, $260/credit nonresident. *Doctoral:* $25. *Other Costs:* No service fee for 0–3 hours, $23 for 4–7 hours, $30 for 8+ hours (applicable for off-campus as well as on-campus students). These are only in fall and spring; for summer, it is $8/session regardless of hours taken. *Credit by:* semester. The fall and spring semesters are 16 weeks each, and the 3 summer sessions are 5 weeks each.

Financial Aid: Federal Stafford Loan, Federal Perkins Loan, Federal PLUS Loan, Federal Pell Grant, Federal Work-Study, VA, Indiana resident programs, scholarships, other aid. Students can contact the Student Financial Assistance office at (812) 464-1767 for details.

Accreditation: North Central Association of Colleges and Schools.

Description: The University of Southern Indiana (1965) is a general, multipurpose, public-supported, coeducational institution of higher education offering programs of instruction, research, and service. The 60 undergraduate programs offered through the university's 5 schools are grounded in a liberal arts and science foundation. Programs are available in Business, Education and Human Services, Liberal Arts, Nursing and Health Professions, and Science and Engineering Technology. Master's degrees are conferred in Business Administration, Industrial Management, Liberal Studies, and Education. Noncredit courses, business training programs, certificate programs, continuing education, and programs for K–12 teachers and students are available. Through all its programs, the university seeks to serve the academic, cultural, and career needs of the student body. As a public institution, it counsels and assists business, industry, and social, educational, governmental, and health agencies. As a university, it seeks to support education, social and economic growth, and civic and cultural awareness in southwestern Indiana, devoting itself primarily to preparing students to live wisely. USI's Learning Network enables Indiana students to enroll in distance courses that fit their time or travel needs. Courses may be delivered by videotape, CD-ROM, electronic mail, TV, or other media. Some courses meet at learning centers in Evansville or locations throughout Indiana.

University of St. Augustine for Health Sciences

1 University Boulevard	Phone: (800) 241-1027
St. Augustine, FL 32086	(904) 826-0084
	Fax: (904) 826-0085

Division(s): None.
Web Site(s): http://www.usa.edu
E-mail: info@usa.edu

Graduate Degree Programs:
Postprofessional Master of Science in Physical Therapy
Postprofessional Distance Education or Clinical Residency

Doctoral Degree Programs:
Doctor of Physical Therapy

Class Titles: Manual Therapy, Primary Care, Adult Neurology, Integrated Orthopaedics, Industrial Rehabilitation, Sports Physical Therapy.

Teaching Methods: *TV:* videotapes. *Other:* printed study guides, resident instruction. Graduate credit earned through the combination of attending seminars for clinical hands-on instruction and successfully completing home study courses.

Credits Granted for: experiential learning, portfolio assessment, extrainstitutional learning, examination, by petition and review.

Admission Requirements: *Graduate:* BS in Physical Therapy, licensed in the U.S. *Doctoral:* MS in Physical Therapy, licensed in the U.S. *Certificate:* open to all appropriately licensed physical therapists. Credit for these seminars can later be applied to the distance education, postprofessional degree programs. Select seminars are open to licensed occupational therapists. International/foreign students considered for all university programs.

On-Campus Requirements: Master's students spend two 3-week, on-campus, academic residencies, with a possible third residency of 1–3 weeks. Distance education doctoral students attend on-campus Entry Colloquium (6 days), Medical Ethics (5 days), and Behavioral Psychology (5 days). This same colloquium is not required for the clinical residency DPT program.

Tuition and Fees: *Graduate:* contact school for more information. *Other Costs:* Tuition for seminars varies, home study credit assignment tuition is $225/course with the exception of Independent Study/Clinical Residency fees, which are $195/credit, $295/2 credits, $395/3 credits, etc. *Credit by:* semester.

Financial Aid: Postprofessional division programs: TFC Loan Program, TERI Continuing Education Loan, Nellie Mae's GradEXCEL Loan, Key Career Loan, DANTES, PLATO Career Education Loan; postprofessional scholarships: Stanley G. Paris Commonwealth Scholarship and Faculty Development Scholarship.

Accreditation: The Florida State Board of Independent Colleges and Universities (SBICU), Florida Department of Education, Tallahassee, Florida, license the University of St. Augustine for Health Sciences to offer its degree programs. This licensure includes the postprofessional advanced Master of Science in Physical Therapy and the Doctor of Physical Therapy; Distance Education and Training Council.

Description: The University of St. Augustine for Health Sciences (1966) has taught continuing professional distance education to physical therapists since its founding. The university offers appropriately licensed health care professionals seminars and clinical certifications in 6 areas. In addition, the university offers physical therapists the postprofessional MS in Physical Therapy and the distance education track or clinical residency track for the Doctor of Physical Therapy. These distance programs are designed to assist therapists in improving their clinical skills through seminars and home study courses that require minimal time away from home and practice. The university offers 2 campus-based first professional degrees—Master of Occupational Therapy and Master of Physical Therapy—for those interested in becoming occupational or physical therapists.

University of St. Francis

500 Wilcox
Joliet, IL 60435

Phone: (815) 740-3400
(800) 735-7500
Fax: (815) 740-4285

Division(s): Health Arts, Graduate Studies, Registrar
Web Site(s): http://www.stfrancis.edu
E-mail: admissions@stfrancis.edu

Undergraduate Degree Programs:
Health Arts

Graduate Degree Programs:
Health Services Administration
Master of Business Administration

Class Titles: Health Services Administration, Business, Health Arts, various courses including areas of Registered Nursing, Radiology, Dental Hygiene.

Teaching Methods: *Computers:* Internet, electronic classroom, e-mail. *TV:* videotape. *Other:* off-campus sites (19 states), videoconferencing, independent study, individual study, learning contracts.

Credits Granted for: experiential learning, portfolio assessment, extrainstitutional learning, examination (CLEP, ACT-PEP, DANTES, GRE).

Admission Requirements: *Undergraduate:* ACT/SAT, top 50% of class, 16 hours of certain units from high school curriculum; or transfer with 30 semester credits. *Graduate:* bachelor's degree, 2.75 GPA, computer competence, program-specific.

On-Campus Requirements: program-specific.

Tuition and Fees: *Undergraduate:* $285/credit. *Graduate:* $370/credit. *Application Fee:* $20. *Other Costs:* $100 full-time fees. *Credit by:* semester.

Financial Aid: Federal Stafford Loan, Federal Perkins Loan, Federal PLUS Loan, Federal Pell Grant, Federal Work-Study, Illinois resident programs.

Accreditation: North Central Association of Colleges and Schools.

Description: The University of St. Francis (1920) is a 4-year institution offering undergraduate and graduate programs. The university serves 1,000 students at its main campus in Joliet, Illinois, and 3,000 students at off-campus sites throughout the country. The university is a career-oriented school of liberal arts and sciences. Conscious of its Catholic heritage, the university offers a liberal education with religious dimensions. Through the efforts of each student and graduate, the university desires to renew society in wisdom, justice, and charity.

University of St. Thomas

2115 Summit Avenue	Phone: (612) 962-6800
St. Paul, MN 55105	Fax: (612) 962-6816

Division(s): Instructional Support Services, Mail 5048
Web Site(s): http://www.iss.stthomas.edu
E-mail: prprifrel@stthomas.edu

Graduate Degree Programs:
Master of Business Administration
Master of Science in Manufacturing Systems
Master of Science in Health Management

Teaching Methods: *Computers:* Internet, e-mail, CD-ROM. *Other:* videoconferencing.

Admission Requirements: *Undergraduate:* application, high school and/or college transcripts, GPA, ACT/SAT. *Graduate:* department-specific.

On-Campus Requirements: with some programs—contact school.

Tuition and Fees: *Undergraduate:* $1,912/course, contact UST for complete information. *Other Costs:* variable. *Credit by:* semester.

Financial Aid: Federal Perkins Loan, Federal Stafford Loan, Federal Plus Loan, Self Loan, Federal Work-Study, Minnesota resident programs. Consult with a UST financial aid counselor for information.

Accreditation: North Central Association of Colleges and Schools.

Description: The University of St. Thomas (1885) was founded by Archbishop John Ireland. What began as the St. Thomas Aquinas Seminary, with 62 students and 5 faculty, has grown into Minnesota's largest independent university, with 10,000 students on 4 campuses.

The University of Tennessee, Knoxville

1534 White Avenue, Room A118	Phone: (800) 670-8657
Knoxville, TN 37996-1525	(423) 974-5134
	Fax: (423) 974-4684

Division(s): Distance Education and Independent Study
Web Site(s): http://www.ce.utk.edu/deis/
E-mail: indstudy@gateway.ce.utk.edu or distance-ed@gateway.ce.utk.edu

Graduate Degree Programs:
Master of Science in Industrial Engineering
Master of Science in Information Sciences

Class Titles: Undergraduate correspondence: Accounting, Agricultural Economics, Anthropology, Business Management, Chemistry, Child/Family Studies, Criminal Justice, Curriculum/Instruction, Economics, Education, English, French, Geography, German, Health, History, Library Service, Math, Nutrition, Philosophy, Political Science, Psychology, Religious Studies, Safety, Sociology, Spanish, Special Education; graduate videotape: Civil Engineering, Environmental Engineering.

Teaching Methods: *Computers:* e-mail, computer conferencing. *TV:* videotape, compressed/interactive video. *Other:* correspondence.

Admission Requirements: for correspondence. *Graduate:* GRE, undergraduate GPA.

On-Campus Requirements: None.

Tuition and Fees: *Undergraduate:* $88/credit. *Graduate:* $150/credit in-state, $408/credit out-of-state. *Other Costs:* possibly multimedia materials (disks, audio/videotapes), $11 postage/handling for correspondence, $100 Access Fee for videotape courses, $25 admission. *Credit by:* semester.

Financial Aid: VA.

Accreditation: Southern Association of Colleges and Schools.

Description: Founded in 1794, the University of Tennessee is the official land-grant institution for the state. UT Knoxville is the state's oldest, largest, and most comprehensive institution, offering 300 degree programs to its 25,000 students. The university entered distance education in 1923 with correspondence courses, and has offered TV and videotape classes since the early 1970s.

University of Texas, Austin

3001 Lake Austin Boulevard	Phone: (512) 471-0226
Austin, TX 78703	Fax: (512) 471-7853

Division(s): Distance Education is decentralized in the schools and colleges. Continuing Education & Extension offers distance education through the Distance Education Center. This report is based on their offerings.
Web Site(s): http://www.utexas.edu/dce/eimc
E-mail: jryahola@mail.utexas.edu

Certificate Programs: Purchasing Management

Class Titles: courses that prepare students to take the Microsoft and Novell certification exams, American Studies, Anthropology, Art Education, Art History, Astronomy, Curriculum/Instruction, Czech, Economics, Educational Psychology, English, French, Geography, German, Government, Greek, History, Kinesiology/Health Education, Latin, Literature, Math, Nursing, Nutrition, Philosophy, Physics, Psychology, Writing, Radio-TV-Film, Sociology, Spanish, Women's Studies, Zoology, End User, Programming/System Administration, Computer-Based Training.

Teaching Methods: *Computers:* Internet, real-time chat, e-mail, CD-ROM, LISTSERV, Web. *TV:* videotape. *Other:* audioconferencing, videoconferencing, audiotapes, fax, correspondence, independent study, individual study, telephony, voice mail.

Admission Requirements: *Undergraduate:* enrollment is open to all persons. UT admission is not required. Students enrolled at UT Austin must have dean's signature before submitting enrollment form. Nonexempt, degree-seeking students entering Texas public colleges and universities are required by law to take the Texas Academic Skills Program test.

On-Campus Requirements: None.

Tuition and Fees: *Undergraduate:* $65/credit, $79/half-credit high school course. *Other Costs:* $20 enrollment fee, other fees to fax in lessons ($20), transfer from one course to another, or extend time. Check each catalog listing for course fee. This fee includes all materials, the textbook (and audiotapes or videotapes), needed to complete the course. *Credit by:* Each course represents a semester's work; however, the student may enroll at any time and has 9 months to complete the course.

Financial Aid: Reimbursement for fees and tuition exemptions are available on a limited basis for qualified students. In general, such aid is administered through government agencies to military personnel and persons with disabilities. All federal financial aid programs require that students be enrolled in programs leading to a degree, a certificate, or some other educational credential in order to be considered for assistance. If you think you might be eligible for one of the following benefit programs, call our supervisor of student services (1-888-Be A Grad) for more information. Active Military Personnel: Education officer at military installations can provide information about possible tuition reimbursement for distance education study. Student with Disabilities: If you are age 16 or older and have specific disabilities, you may be exempt from certain fees, or you may be eligible for financial assistance. Contact the local district office of the Texas Rehabilitation Commission or the Texas Commission for the Blind.

Accreditation: Southern Association of Colleges and Schools; high school courses approved by the Texas Education Agency.

Description: The University of Texas at Austin (1909) is the flagship research university of Texas. The university began serving Texans with correspondence and extension courses through its Continuing Education & Extension center. As instructional technology advanced, UT-Austin courses incorporated the best to provide high-quality courses to students anytime, anyplace. Today UT-Austin offers 200 courses in a variety of delivery modes. Continuing Education & Extension believes in "the power of education to change lives" and in its mission to provide quality education anytime, anyplace.

University of Texas of the Permian Basin

4901 East University
Odessa, TX 79762

Phone: (915) 552-2870
Fax: (915) 552-2871

Division(s): REACH Program Center
Web Site(s): http://www.utpb.edu/
E-mail: REACH@utpb.edu

Certificate Programs: Early Childhood Endorsement.

Class Titles: Psychology, Physical Education, Education, English, Math, Computer Science, Marketing, Management, Decision Science, Accounting, Finance, Theater, Criminal Justice Administration, History, Political Science, Art.

Teaching Methods: *Computers:* Internet, real-time chat, e-mail. *Other:* videoconferencing.

Credits Granted for: examination (CLEP, AP).

Admission Requirements: *Undergraduate:* high school diploma, SAT/ACT score (sliding scale), specific list of high school courses. *Graduate:* undergraduate degree, GRE, minimum GPA. *Doctoral:* undergraduate degree.

On-Campus Requirements: None.

Tuition and Fees: *Undergraduate:* $73/credit Texas resident, $286/credit nonresident. *Graduate:* $87/credit Texas resident, $286/credit nonresident. *Doctoral:* $73/credit Texas resident, $286/credit nonresident. *Other Costs:* $70, any number of hours. *Credit by:* semester.

Financial Aid: Federal Stafford Loan, Federal Perkins Loan, Federal PLUS Loan, Federal Pell Grant, Federal Work-Study, VA, Texas resident programs, various scholarships.

Accreditation: Southern Association of Colleges and Schools.

Description: University of Texas of the Permian Basin (1973) is a comprehensive university serving a mostly nonresidential student body in a vast area of western Texas. Some UTPB students commute from communities as far as 100 miles from the main campus. The university offers undergraduate and master's degrees in a variety of disciplines. For the first 18 years of its existence, UTPB was an upper-division and graduate-only institution. The first lower-division students entered in the fall of 1991. UTPB began its distance learning program in 1996, sharing courses via an interactive (compressed) video network linking UT System components and area community colleges. Web-based courses were offered for the first time in the spring of 1998. Although many distance courses are offered, no full degree programs are currently available through distance learning.

University of Toledo

SeaGate Campus
401 Jefferson Avenue
Toledo, OH 43604-1005

Phone: (419) 321-5130
Fax: (419) 321-5147

Division(s): Distance Learning
Web Site(s):
http://www.utoledo.edu/colleges/ucollege/dislrn.htm
UT's Virtual Campus: http://www.uol.com/utoledo
E-mail: krhoda@utnet.utoledo.edu

Certificate Programs: OSHA Fundamentals of Lab Safety, Geographic Information Systems.

Class Titles: a wide variety of courses and expanding, including English, Economics, History, Philosophy, Psychology, Sociology, Political Science, Medical Terminology, Africana Studies Program, Chemistry, Nutrition, Physics, Legal Assisting Program, Leadership Skills, Special Education, Exploring College Careers, Criminal Law Practice, Information Systems, Portfolio Development.

Teaching Methods: *Computers:* Internet, real-time chat, electronic classroom, e-mail, CD-ROM, LISTSERV. *TV:* videotape, cable program, PBS. *Other:* videoconferencing, fax.

Credits Granted for: portfolio assessment, corporate or professional association seminars/workshops, examination (CLEP, ACT-PEP, DANTES, GRE).

Admission Requirements: *Undergraduate:* variable; contact Adult Student Assistance Center, (419) 530-4137. *Graduate:* contact Adult Student Assistance Center, (419) 530-4137. *Doctoral:* contact Adult Student Assistance Center, (419) 530-4137. *Certificate:* contact Continuing Education, (419) 321-5139.

On-Campus Requirements: None.

Tuition and Fees: *Undergraduate:* $140/credit in-state. *Graduate:* $212/credit in-state. *Doctoral:* $263/credit in-state—Law College. *Application Fee:* $30. *Other Costs:* $20 special status application for graduation. *Credit by:* semester.

Financial Aid: Federal Stafford Loan, Federal Perkins Loan, Federal PLUS Loan, Federal Pell Grant, Federal Work-Study, VA, Ohio resident programs.

Accreditation: North Central Association of Colleges and Schools.

Description: The University of Toledo's (1872) Division of Distance Learning's mission is to promote learning without time or space barriers to encourage outreach and lifelong-learning. UT's Division of Distance Learning facilitates innovative delivery of high-quality, university instruction to meet the educational needs of students, whatever their location. Distance Learning offers a variety of state-of-the-art technologies to deliver credit and noncredit education taught by skilled, enthusiastic faculty.

University of Utah

1901 East South Campus Drive
Annex Room 2180
Salt Lake City, UT 84112-9364

Phone: (801) 581-8801
(800) 467-8839
Fax: (801) 581-6267

Division(s): Continuing Education
Web Site(s): http://ulearn.utah.edu
E-mail: inthing@admin.dce.utah.edu

Class Titles: Anthropology, Art, Biology, Chemistry, Civil Engineering, Communication, Communication Disorders, Economics, Educational Psychology, Educational Studies, English, Family/Consumer Studies, Finance, Foods/Nutrition, Geography, Gerontology, Health Education, History, Management, Math, Meteorology, Music, Pharmacology/Toxicology, Physics, Political Science, Psychology, Special Education, Writing.

Teaching Methods: *Computers:* Internet, real-time chat, electronic classroom, e-mail, CD-ROM, newsgroup, LISTSERV. *TV:* videotape, cable program, satellite broadcasting, PBS. *Other:* radio broadcast, audioconferencing, videoconferencing, audiographics, audiotapes, fax, correspondence, independent study, individual study, learning contracts.

Admission Requirements: *Undergraduate:* enrollment does not constitute admission.

On-Campus Requirements: Some.

Tuition and Fees: *Undergraduate:* $85/credit. *Other Costs:* $15 text, manual. *Credit by:* semester.

Financial Aid: Federal Stafford Loan, Federal Perkins Loan, Federal PLUS Loan, Federal Pell Grant, Federal Work-Study, VA, Utah resident programs—matriculated.

Accreditation: Northwest Association of Schools and Colleges.

Description: The University of Utah has been the flagship institution of higher education in the Intermountain West since its founding in 1850. As a public urban research and teaching institution, the U of U allows students to pursue academic disciplines on the undergraduate and graduate level. The Distance Education unit extends the university's resources to a diverse student population that requires creative course delivery. This unit serves 6,400 students annually in broadcast and correspondence courses, most available on the Internet. The courses fulfill many general education requirements, with a cluster of courses specifically designed for teacher recertification.

University of Vermont

460 South Prospect Street
Burlington, VT 05401-3534

Phone: (802) 656-8019
Fax: (802) 656-1347

Division(s): Continuing Education Distance Learning Network
Web Site(s): http://uvmce.uvm.edu:443/
E-mail: sreed@zoo.uvm.edu

Certificate Programs: Gerontology

Class Titles: variable, usually a course or 2 in Nursing, Education, Gerontology, Business, Engineering, Math, Public Administration, Advanced Placement high school courses in English Literature/Composition.

Teaching Methods: *Computers:* Internet, real-time chat, e-mail, LISTSERV. *TV:* videotape, satellite broadcasting, 2-way audio/video interactive TV network. *Other:* audioconferencing, videoconferencing, fax, correspondence.

Credits Granted for: examination (CLEP, GRE).

Admission Requirements: *Undergraduate:* high school graduation or GED, official high school transcripts, SAT I/ACT. The following are also considered: overall academic performance, class rank, standardized test scores, and essays. Contact department for high school classes required and program specifics. *Graduate:* accredited bachelor's degree (unaccredited degrees must include both general and advanced subject GRE scores). Completion limits: 3 years for full-time, 5 years for part-time. Accelerated Master's Programs available for some programs. Contact department for program specifics. *Doctoral:* up to 24 appropriate UVM graduate credits may be applied to a UVM PhD (the same credits cannot apply to 2 degrees). Contact department for program specifics. *Certificate:* Gerontology: for professionals currently working in fields related to aging and others interested in such fields, 6 credits from required courses and 12 from a list of electives. Admission granted through UVM's Center for the Study of Aging. Computer Programming: the Department of Computer Science and Electrical Engineering offers several tracks requiring 5 courses (15 credits) in approved computer courses at UVM. Contact school for program specifics.

On-Campus Requirements: labs for some classes.

Tuition and Fees: *Undergraduate:* $245/distance learning credit for nondegree students, both resident and nonresident. Total tuition and associated fees, including an estimate for books: resident/year $7,032, nonresident $17,580. Resident tuition/credit $293 through 11.5 hours. From 12–18 credits, tuition cost is $3,516/semester plus $293/credit for each hour in excess of 18 hours. Nonresident tuition/credit $733 through 11.5 hours. From 12–18 credits, tuition cost is $8,790/semester plus $732/credit for each hour in excess of 18 hours. *Graduate:* tuition/credit is same as above. Associated fees include comprehensive fee based on number of credit hours taken. Cost can range from $44–$200. Transportation fee $48, student health fee $118. Student accident and sickness insurance is optional. Advanced degree fee is charged to each advanced degree recipient as follows: doctorate $25, master's with thesis $20, master's without thesis $10. *Doctoral:* same tuition as above. *Application Fee:* $45 undergraduate. *Credit by:* semester.

Financial Aid: Federal Stafford Loan, Federal Perkins Loan, Federal Pell Grant, Federal Work-Study, VA, Vermont Scholars Program.

Accreditation: New England Association of Schools and Colleges.

Description: The University of Vermont (1791) was chartered the same year Vermont became the 14th state in the union. The campus is located in the state's largest city, Burlington, population 39,000. The university blends the academic heritage of private institution with the service missions in the land grant tradition. UVM directs its resources toward the provision of excellence in instruction, innovation in research, and public service to the citizens of the state, nation, and world. To extend its land grant mission of service, the university's Distance Learning Network was established in 1995. Credit courses, certificate programs, and Advanced Placement high school courses are offered to 50 locations across the state, with outreach capabilities to New England, the U.S., and beyond. Technology includes the Internet, satellite, videoconferencing, and interactive TV. Distance students have access to UVM faculty, libraries, student advisors, and each other via computer.

University of Virginia

104 Midmont Lane
Charlottesville, VA 22903

Phone: (804) 982-5254
Fax: (804) 982-5270

Division(s): Continuing Education
Web Site(s): http://uvace.virginia.edu
E-mail: jpayne@virginia.edu

Graduate Degree Programs:
Master of Science in Engineering

Teaching Methods: *Other:* videoconferencing.

Admission Requirements: *Graduate:* contact Televised Graduate Engineering Program Office, (804) 924-4051 [or call collect: (804) 924-4075].

On-Campus Requirements: courses are synchronously delivered and require attendance at remote sites.

Tuition and Fees: *Graduate:* (for all sites except Northern Virginia) $257/credit ($771/course) in-state, $447/credit ($1,341/course) out-of-state; (for Northern Virginia Center) $262/credit ($786/course) in-state, $453/credit ($1,359/course) out-of-state. Registrants at the Northern Virginia Center in Falls Church also pay an additional "Facilities Fee" of $10/credit. NOTE: Students must register for classes before the third class session. There are no refunds after tuition is paid. Students may drop without academic penalty at any time up to the final exam by submitting written notice explaining reasons for request. *Credit by:* semester.

Accreditation: Southern Association of Colleges and Schools, member of Association of American Universities.

Description: The leading universities in the Commonwealth of Virginia have combined to make master's degrees in several engineering disciplines easily available to qualified engineers. At the center of the system is the graduate engineering program of the University of Virginia (1819). This nationally ranked university televises regular master's courses via Net.Work.Virginia from a special classroom on campus to sites in Virginia as well as out-of-state. The classes are received live, and students are able to participate fully in all classroom discussions. Classes are scheduled in late afternoon and early evening hours. This program is directed by Dr. George L. Cahen, Jr. The administrator of the program is Rita F. Kostoff. The University of Virginia and Virginia Polytechnic Institute and State University, in cooperation with Virginia Commonwealth University, Old Dominion University, and George Mason University, deliver televised graduate engineering courses to areas in the Commonwealth of Virginia, as well as some out-of-state sites. Beginning in fall 1998, lectures will be delivered via an asynchronous transfer mode on Net.Work.Virginia within the state and via videoconferencing equipment to out-of-state sites. This means that classes are 2-way video and 2-way audio. It should be noted that on-grounds students at the University of Virginia also take these courses in the studio classroom as they are delivered to the off-site campuses. The primary intent is to provide engineers and other qualified individuals with strong backgrounds in the sciences an opportunity to pursue a program in graduate studies leading to a master's degree in engineering. However, courses may also be taken on a nondegree, continuing education basis. This effort is in response to one of the State Council of Higher Education's objectives to expand technical education opportunities for Virginians.

University of Washington

5001-25th NE	Phone: (206) 543-2350
Seattle, WA 98105	(800) 543-2320 x4
	Fax: (206) 543-0887

Division(s): Program Support Services
Web Site(s): http://www.outreach.washington.edu
E-mail: distance@u.washington.edu

Undergraduate Degree Programs:
90 distance learning credits may count toward undergraduate degrees.

Certificate Programs: For credit: Graduate Public Health Practice, Aging, School Library Media, Teaching/Learning Technology, Facilities Management; noncredit: C Programming, C++ Programming, Java Programming, Fiction Writing, Project Management, Data Resource Management, Data Communications.

Class Titles: 110 undergraduate courses in Humanities, Social Sciences, Physical Sciences, Business.

Teaching Methods: *Computers:* Internet, electronic classroom, e-mail, LISTSERV. *TV:* videotape. *Other:* telephone conferencing, audiotapes, fax, print, traditional correspondence.

Admission Requirements: *Undergraduate:* math/accounting courses may have some. *Certificate:* varies.

On-Campus Requirements: None for most course work.

Tuition and Fees: *Undergraduate:* $80/credit. *Graduate:* $189/credit. *Application Fee:* $40 certificate programs. *Credit by:* quarter.

Accreditation: Northwest Association of Schools and Colleges.

Description: Established in 1912, University of Washington Distance Learning offers a broad range of courses and educational programs that extend the university's resources worldwide. Courses are delivered by print, video, or computer and typically consist of assigned texts, study guides, assignments, and exams. Formal university admission is not required for Distance Learning enrollment. Up to 90 Distance Learning credits may apply to a bachelor's degree, and grades are recorded on official University of Washington transcripts.

University of Waterloo

200 University Avenue West	Phone: (519) 888-4050
Waterloo, ON, Canada, N2L 3G1	Fax: (519) 746-6393

Division(s): Distance and Continuing Education Office
Web Site(s): http://dce.uwaterloo.ca/
E-mail: distance@uwaterloo.ca
Undergraduate Degree Programs:
Bachelor of Art
Bachelor of Science
Bachelor of Environmental Studies

Graduate Degree Programs:
Master in Management of Technology (MOT) by distance education to students residing in Canada or the continental U.S. The rest of the information in this profile does not pertain to the MOT program. Contact the Department of Management Sciences at (519) 888-4799, e-mail mot@iir.uwaterloo.ca, or http://innovate.uwaterloo.ca/mot-de/info.html.

Certificate Programs: Classical Studies or Classical Languages, General Social Work, Social Work (Child Abuse).

Class Titles: Accounting, Actuarial Science, Anthropology, Applied Mathematics, Arts, Biology, Canadian Studies, Chemistry, Classical Studies, Combinatorics/Optimization, Computer Science, Croatian, Dutch, Earth Sciences, Economics, English, Environmental Studies, French, Geography, German, Gerontology, Greek, Health Studies, History, Interdisciplinary Social Science, Jewish Studies, Kinesiology, Latin, Mathematics, Native Studies, Nutrition, Peace/Conflict Studies, Philosophy, Physics, Planning, Polish, Psychology, Recreation, Religious Studies, Russian, Science, Social Work, Sociology, Spanish, Statistics, Studies in Personality/Religion, Women's Studies.

Teaching Methods: *Computers:* Internet, conferencing, electronic classroom, e-mail, CD-ROM, newsgroup, LIST SERV. *TV:* videotape. *Other:* audiographics, audiotapes, print material, correspondence, independent study.

Admission Requirements: *Undergraduate:* Ontario Secondary School Diploma (OSSD) with 6 Ontario Academic Course credits (minimum of 70% average) or equivalent. Request information about other countries' OSSD equivalencies. Distance courses are normally available to students residing in Canada or the continental U.S. "Mature Student" applications may be accepted without OSSDs.

On-Campus Requirements: None.

Tuition and Fees: *Undergraduate:* $399 CDN/half-credit course for Canadian citizens/permanent residents. $1,217 CDN/half-credit course for others. *Other Costs:* materials and deposits. *Credit by:* semester.

Financial Aid: available for Canadian citizens/permanent residents. Other students should investigate their eligibility.

Accreditation: Canadian Provincial Legislation, member of Association of Universities and Colleges of Canada and of Association of Commonwealth Universities.

Description: The University of Waterloo is one of Canada's leading comprehensive universities, with undergraduate and graduate programs in Applied Health Sciences, Arts, Engineering, Environmental Studies, Mathematics, and Science. On-campus classes began in 1957; in 1968 UW offered its first distance courses. Entire degree programs are now available by distance study (see above), with 250 courses covering more than 40 subjects. UW pioneered audiotaped lectures, and as it strives to improve its "anytime, anywhere" study opportunities, the university is exploring new technologies to supplement print- and audio-based courses. Such innovations as the Web and computer conferencing will improve interaction for students and instructors. Through distance education, UW's resources are available to thousands of busy people for whom a university education might otherwise be impossible. Though academic deadlines exist, the flexibility of distance study allows you to study when and where it is most convenient.

The University of Western Ontario

1151 Richmond Street N	Phone: (519) 661-3982
London, ON, Canada N6A 5B8	Fax: (519) 661-3615

Division(s): Office of the Registrar
Web Site(s): http://www.registrar.uwo.ca
E-mail: reg-admissions@julian.uwo.ca

Undergraduate Degree Programs:
General Bachelor of Arts (3-year). Not all subjects are offered strictly through distance studies as course offerings change on an annual basis.

Teaching Methods: *Computers:* Internet, electronic classroom and conference, e-mail, CD-ROM, newsgroup, LISTSERV. *TV:* videotape, audiotapes, correspondence. *Other:* None.

Admission Requirements: *Undergraduate:* vary depending upon student's status (i.e., Canadian resident, international, mature). Students registered full-time with the university may take a distance studies course at any time without special requirements. Please consult the Admission Office.

On-Campus Requirements: attendance on campus is only required if students wish to pursue a 4-year honors degree, a Bachelor of Science degree or any Bachelor of Arts program that does not offer all degree requirement courses through distance.

Tuition and Fees: *Undergraduate:* $778/full-course credit, $427/half-course credit. *Application Fee:* $80 Canadian, $90 international. *Other Costs:* up to $100/half-course for books/materials, $75 program-related fee for all distance studies courses. *Credit by:* 4 terms (fall/winter, spring/summer)

Financial Aid: contact Financial Aid Services for loan eligibility, (519) 661-3775.

Accreditation: Association of Universities and Colleges of Canada, Association of Commonwealth Universities, International Association of Universities.

Description: The University of Western Ontario (1878) is now a long-established academic community. The university is a vibrant center of learning with 24,000 undergraduate and graduate students and 1,250 faculty members. Founded in 1878, Western is one of Canada's oldest and most prestigious universities. Western offers daytime and evening courses in various subjects, and 20 subjects may be taken through distance education.

University of Windsor

401 Sunset Avenue	Phone: (519) 253-3000 x3470
Windsor, ON, Canada N9B 3P4	Fax: (519) 973-7038

Division(s): Continuing Education
Web Site(s): http://www.uwindsor.ca/coned
E-mail: coned@uwindsor.ca

Undergraduate Degree Programs:
Bachelor of Commerce
Bachelor of Business Studies, General (Accounting Track Degree)
Bachelor of Commerce for University Graduates
Bachelor of Science for Medical Laboratory Technician

Certificate Programs: Business Administration

Class Titles: Arts, Social Science.

Teaching Methods: *Computers:* Internet, e-mail, CD-ROM. *TV:* TVOntario broadcasts, videotapes. *Other:* correspondence, independent study, audiotapes.

Admission Requirements: *Undergraduate:* high school graduate. *Certificate:* high school graduate.

On-Campus Requirements: only attendance at a final exam is required at an institution near student's home.

Tuition and Fees: *Undergraduate:* $425/credit plus books. *Application Fee:* $25. *Other Costs:* $40 for evaluation of prior credits toward degree program. *Credit by:* semester.

Financial Aid: provincial (OSAP) and Canada student loans, bursaries.

Accreditation: Association of Universities and Colleges of Canada.

Description: In 1963 the new, nondenominational University of Windsor (1857) inherited Assumption College, an educational complex developed since 1870 by the Basilian Fathers (the Congregation of St. Basil) and expanded to independent university status in 1953. This unprecedented transition from a historically Roman Catholic university to a nondenominational institution began in 1956 with the affiliation of Essex College, the first provincially-assisted public institution of higher education. During 1963–1964, affiliation agreements were also made with Holy Redeemer College, Canterbury College, and the new Iona College (United Church of Canada). UW assumed control of the campus in 1963 and soon became a member of the International Association of Universities. Distance education courses were first offered in 1989.

University of Winnipeg

515 Portage Avenue	Phone: (204) 786-9849
Winnipeg, MB, Canada R3B 2E9	Fax: (204) 783-3116

Division(s): Learning Technologies
Web Site(s):
http://www.uwinnipeg.ca/academic/clt/tele/uwin_sched.htm
E-mail: darelene.frederickson@uwinnipeg.ca

Undergraduate Degree Programs:
Bachelor of Arts
Bachelor of Science
Bachelor of Education
Bachelor of Theology

Graduate Degree Programs:
Master of Arts
Master of Public Administration
Master of Divinity
Master of Marriage and Family Therapy
Master of Sacred Theology

Teaching Methods: *Computers:* Internet, real-time chat, electronic classroom, e-mail (for northern students only). *TV:* cable program (urban Winnipeg and selected rural communities). *Other:* None.

Credits Granted for: experiential learning, portfolio assessment (both under consideration).

Admission Requirements: *Undergraduate:* completion of university-track secondary program or mature status.

On-Campus Requirements: courses needed to complete degree.

Tuition and Fees: *Undergraduate:* $330/3 credits plus incidental fees. *Application Fee:* $35. *Other Costs:* varies for textbooks, etc. *Credit by:* semester.

Accreditation: Association of Universities and Colleges of Canada.

Description: The University of Winnipeg (1871) is a liberal arts undergraduate institution offering some master's programs. The university views both excellence and accessibility as important goals and values academic freedom, self-governance, and community service. The Centre for Learning Technologies has been offering limited distance education opportunities to northern students for 10 years via live satellite, teleconference and now real-time Internet-based computer programs; and in the last 5 years to urban Winnipeg and southern rural community students via cable TV.

University of Wisconsin, Eau Claire

105 Garfield Avenue	Phone: (715) 836-6006
Eau Claire, WI 54701	Fax: (715) 836-6001

Division(s): Media Development Center
Web Site(s): http://www.uwec.edu
E-mail: scleidd@uwec.edu

Undergraduate Degree Programs:
Collaborative Nursing

Teaching Methods: *Computers:* classroom computers, Internet, e-mail, CD-ROM, PowerPoint. *TV:* videotape, cable program, satellite broadcasting, PBS, NTU, PBS/ALSS, 2-way distance education networks, laser disk players, slide-to-video converters. *Other:* audioconferencing, videoconferencing, audiographics, audiotapes, fax, correspondence, independent study, individual study, ITFS.

Credits Granted for: examination (CLEP, DANTES), AP, 1B, some military experience.

Admission Requirements: *Undergraduate:* accredited high school diploma or equivalent, upper 50% of class OR 110 composite SAT I (22 on ACT). *Graduate:* college transcript, letter of recommendation, interview, essay, GMAT, GRE, 2.75 GPA, additional requirements per specific program.

On-Campus Requirements: None.

Tuition and Fees: *Undergraduate:* $126/credit residents, $387/credit nonresidents. *Graduate:* $203/credit residents, $628/credit nonresidents. *Application Fee:* $35. *Credit by:* semester.

Financial Aid: Federal Stafford Loan, Federal Perkins Loan, Federal PLUS Loan, Federal Pell Grant, Federal Work-Study,

VA, Wisconsin resident programs.

Accreditation: North Central Association of Colleges and Schools.

Description: University of Wisconsin, Eau Claire, which celebrated its 75th anniversary in 1991, is one of the nation's leading regional public universities offering the opportunities of a larger school and the personal attention and academic distinction of a private college. Its innovative baccalaureate program combines liberal arts and sciences with practical training for 21st-century careers. In 1986 the UW-Eau Claire School of Nursing established an off-campus, distance education, baccalaureate program in cooperation with Saint Joseph's Hospital. In 1992 UW-Eau Claire and LacCourte Oreilles Ojibwa Community College collaborated on a Bachelor of Science in Nursing degree for Native American students. Nursing faculty and administrators from UW in Eau Claire, Green Bay, Madison, Milwaukee, and Oshkosh agreed in 1995 to develop a collaborative program for registered nurses. The most common distance technologies include audiographic conferencing and full-motion, 2-way video.

University of Wisconsin, La Crosse

1705 State Street, FWCC 162	Phone: (608) 785-8048
La Crosse, WI 54601	Fax: (608) 785-8825

Division(s): Media Services/Educational Television Center
Web Site(s):
http://www.uwlax.edu/InfoTech/Media/DistanceEd.html
E-mail: schumach@mail.uwlax.edu

Class Titles: Clinical Hematology, Muscle Physiology, Principles of Insurance, International Accounting, Immunohematology, Intermediate Russian, Organizational Management Foundations, Microeconomics, Macroeconomics, Children's Literature, Woman/Poverty.

Teaching Methods: *Computers:* Internet, real-time chat, electronic classroom, e-mail, CD-ROM, newsgroup, LISTSERV. *TV:* videotape, cable program, satellite broadcasting, PBS. *Other:* videoconferencing, audioconferencing, audiographics, fax, correspondence, independent study, individual study.

Credits Granted for: extrainstitutional learning, examination (CLEP, DANTES, GRE), local department credit by exam, international bachelor's degree.

Admission Requirements: *Undergraduate:* class rank and ACT scores for new students. *Graduate:* undergraduate degree, GPA, specific program requirements, nontraditional waivers may apply, GPA and good standing for transfer students.

On-Campus Requirements: minimum of 30 credits must be earned in residence. For residence, credit means credits registered for and earned through UW-La Crosse.

Tuition and Fees: *Undergraduate:* approximately $140/credit

Graduate: approximately $210/credit *Application Fee:* $35 undergraduate, $45 graduate. *Other Costs:* graduate students must purchase textbooks. *Credit by:* semester.

Financial Aid: Federal Stafford Loan, Federal Perkins Loan, Federal Pell Grant, Federal Work-Study, VA.

Accreditation: North Central Association of Colleges and Secondary Schools, American Assembly of Collegiate Schools of Business, American Chemical Society, American Physical Therapy Association, American Society of Microbiology, Commission on Accreditation of Allied Health Education Programs, Council on Accreditation of the National Recreation and Parks Association/American Association for Leisure and Recreation, Council on Education for Public Health, Council on Social Work Education, National Association of Schools of Music, National Council for Accreditation of Teacher Education, Medical Laboratory Sciences and Nuclear Medical Technology are accredited through affiliated hospitals.

Description: The University of Wisconsin, La Crosse (1909), one of 13 University of Wisconsin System universities, is nestled in a small town of 50,000 bordered by towering bluffs in the Mississippi River Valley. The university is comprised of 4 colleges: Business Administration, Liberal Studies, Science and Allied Health, and the Alliance for Human Development Programs. UW-L entered distance education in 1995 and currently has capabilities in compressed video, full-motion DS-3 video, audiographics, and Web-based instruction. The campus has 2 distance education rooms, with a third to be completed in 1999. UW-La Crosse is a member of the WONDER and CESA 4 WELEARN networks.

University of Wisconsin, Milwaukee

161 West Wisconsin Avenue #6000	Phone: (414) 227-3223
Milwaukee, WI 53203	Fax: (414) 227-3396

Division(s): Distance Learning and Instructional Support
Web Site(s):
http://www.uwm.edu:80/Dept/DOCE/deuwm/Facultyfocus
E-mail: susansim@uwm.edu
jll@dcs.uwm.edu

Class Titles: Social Welfare, Library Science, Foreign Language, Nursing, Business, Healthcare.

Teaching Methods: *Computers:* Internet, real-time chat, electronic classroom, e-mail, LISTSERV. *TV:* cable program, satellite broadcasting, PBS. *Other:* videoconferencing, audioconferencing, audiographics, fax, correspondence.

Credits Granted for: varies by department

Admission Requirements: *Undergraduate:* for more detailed information see: http://www.uwm.edu/UWM/Student/UGBulletin/Admission.html. *Certificate:* graduation from a recognized high school; or a high school equivalency certificate or diploma based on the General Educational Development (GED) exam, or a Wisconsin High School Equivalency exam.

All new freshman applicants who are Wisconsin residents and under age 21 as of September 1 of the fall term in which they intend to enroll must submit ACT scores prior to final admission to the university. (Out-of-state applicants may submit SAT scores.) Additional testing and a personal interview may be required. Some UWM schools and colleges have additional requirements and recommendations. Normally, students with an overall C (2.0 GPA on a 4.0 scale) average on 12 or more attempted credits at a previous accredited institution(s) shall be admissible to UWM. If the student does not wish to enter a specific school they may be admitted as a nondegree candidate or "Special Student." The following materials are required for application processing: (1) A completed and signed application form. (2) A $28 state-required application fee and a $25 processing fee (if non-U.S. academic credentials are submitted). These are nonrefundable fees and are not applicable to any other university fee or bill. Fees are subject to change. (3) Original or officially certified copies of all grade reports for all secondary and higher school studies, as well as original or officially certified copies of all academic diplomas, certificates, and national or other major examination results. Official records must be submitted in the native language and must be accompanied by an official English translation. Notarized copies will not be accepted. Official records should be sent to OISP Admissions directly from the institution. (4) Concrete evidence of the applicant's ability in the English language. Testimonial letters are not sufficient. Most applicants must take the Test of English as a Foreign Language (TOEFL).

On-Campus Requirements: None.

Tuition and Fees: *Undergraduate:* for in-state tuition requirements see the Department of Enrollment Services at: http://des.uwm.edu/Dept/undergrad/resident.html. *Graduate:* See specific program information at http://www.uwm.edu/Dept/Grad_Sch/Services/. *Credit by:* semester.

Financial Aid: Federal Stafford Loan, Federal Perkins Loan, Federal PLUS Loan, Federal Pell Grant, Federal Work-Study, VA, Wisconsin resident programs. For more information see: http://www.uwm.edu/Dept/FINAID/.

Accreditation: North Central Association of Colleges and Schools.

Description: The University of Wisconsin, Milwaukee (1956) traces its origin to the Milwaukee State Normal School, which was founded in 1885 and subsequently became Wisconsin State College. Its establishment in 1956 came with the merger of Wisconsin State College and the University of Wisconsin Extension Division in Milwaukee, to become University of Wisconsin, Milwaukee. The University of Wisconsin, Milwaukee is Wisconsin's premier urban university located in the economic and cultural heart of the state. Distance learning delivers instruction to students at locations and times convenient for them. To accomplish this, University of Wisconsin, Milwaukee faculty, staff, and students may use a variety of technologies such as satellite, ITFS, broadcast TV, computers, telephone and compressed video. Each University of Wisconsin, Milwaukee school or college has an appointed Distance Education Liaison (DEL) who is the primary contact for instructors considering using these instructional technologies. Contact your dean's office for the name of your DEL representative.

University of Wisconsin, River Falls

410 South Third Street River Falls, WI 54022

Phone: (715) 425-3256 Fax: (715) 425-0624

Division(s): Continuing Education Extension/Outreach
Web Site(s): http://www.uwrf.edu/distance-ed/welcome.htm

Class Titles: Agriculture, Business, Education, Liberal Arts.

Teaching Methods: *Computers:* e-mail, LISTSERV, Web pages. *TV:* compressed video (ISDN) fiberoptic 2-way interactive audio/video. *Other:* audioconferencing, audiographics, fax.

Credits Granted for: examination (CLEP general examinations, challenge).

Admission Requirements: *Undergraduate:* high school diploma with 22 ACT, OR top 40% with 18 ACT. Transfer students, 2.6 GPA. *Graduate:* varies.

On-Campus Requirements: Most degree programs completed on campus.

Tuition and Fees: *Undergraduate:* $102/credit residents, $106/credit reciprocity residents, $261/credit nonresidents. *Graduate:* $183/credit residents, $183/credit reciprocity residents, $425/credit nonresidents. *Application Fee:* $35. *Other Costs:* $15/credit distance education fee. *Credit by:* semester credit.

Financial Aid: Federal Stafford Loan, Federal Perkins Loan, Federal PLUS Loan, FSEOG, Federal Pell Grant, Federal Work-Study, VA, Wisconsin resident programs.

Accreditation: North Central Association of Colleges and Secondary Schools.

Description: Founded in 1874, University of Wisconsin-River Falls consists of the College of Agriculture, Food, and Environmental Sciences, the College of Arts and Sciences, the College of Education and Graduate Studies, and the School of Business and Economics. It offers 40 majors, 60 minors, and several preprofessional programs. UW-RF has offered varied types of distance education for many years; interactive TV courses began in 1994.

University of Wisconsin, Stevens Point

1101 Reserve Street	Phone: (715) 346-2647
Stevens Point, WI 54481	Fax: (715) 346-3998

Division(s): University Telecommunications and Distance Learning Resources
Web Site(s): http://www.uwsp.edu
E-mail: pkonkol@uwsp.edu

Graduate Degree Programs:
Master of Science in Education

Class Titles: Russian, Education, Music, Sociology, Business, Economics, Natural Resources, Communication.

Teaching Methods: *Computers:* Internet, e-mail, LISTSERV. *TV:* videotape, satellite broadcasting, PBS. *Other:* audioconferencing, videoconferencing, audiographics.

Credits Granted for: experiential learning, portfolio assessment, examination (GRE).

Admission Requirements: *Undergraduate:* ACT. *Graduate:* GRE.

On-Campus Requirements: None.

Tuition and Fees: *Undergraduate:* $114/credit in-state, $389/credit nonresident. *Graduate:* $215/credit in-state, $617/credit nonresident. *Application Fee:* $100. *Other Costs:* $80/class for certain distance education courses. *Credit by:* semester.

Financial Aid: Federal Stafford Loan, Federal Perkins Loan, Federal PLUS Loan, Federal Pell Grant, Federal Work-Study, VA, Wisconsin resident programs.

Accreditation: North Central Association of Colleges and Schools.

Description: University of Wisconsin at Stevens Point (1894) has a long and proud academic tradition. Since opening its doors as a teacher training school to 300 students, the university has undergone several name changes and expanded its programs. It is now one of 13 units in the University of Wisconsin System, with 8,400 undergraduate and graduate students. Nearly 80% of the 600 full- and part-time teaching staff have doctorate or equivalent degrees. Distance Learning efforts started with ITFS and cable; moved to statewide public TV wrap-around audioconferencing; and now include Internet classes.

University of Wisconsin, Whitewater

800 West Main Street	Phone: (414) 472-5247
Whitewater, WI 53190	Fax: (414) 472-5210

Division(s): Continuing Education
Web Site(s): http://www.uww.edu
http://academics.uww.edu/business/gradprog/gradprog.htm
E-mail: gibbsk@uwwvax.uww.edu
zahnd@uwwvax.uww.edu

Graduate Degree Programs:
Online Master of Business Administration

Class Titles: varies by semester. Examples: Worlds of Childhood, Whole Child, School Finance/Accounting, School Auxiliary Services Management, Collective Negotiations in Education, Strategies for Full Inclusion, Classroom Behavior Management, Internet for Speech, Language/Hearing Professionals, Feminist Theories.

Teaching Methods: *Computers:* Internet, electronic classroom, e-mail, LISTSERV, newsgroup, CD-ROM. *TV:* PBS. *Other:* audioconferencing, videoconferencing, independent study, individual study.

Credits Granted for: portfolio assessment, examination (CLEP, CEEB, IB, departmental, DANTES).

Admission Requirements: *Graduate:* bachelor's degree, 2.75 GPA, GMAT composite score of 1,000, TOEFL: 550, 7 years to complete.

On-Campus Requirements: None.

Tuition and Fees: *Graduate:* Current resident and nonresident graduate business fees for online courses will apply. Contact zahnd@uwwvax.uww.edu for specific information. *Application Fee:* $45. *Credit by:* semester.

Financial Aid: Federal Stafford Loan, Federal Perkins Loan, Federal PLUS Loan, Federal Pell Grant, Federal Work-Study, Supplemental Educational Opportunity Grant, Indian Grant (state and federal), VA, Wisconsin resident programs: Talent Incentive Program, Lawton Retention Grant for Minority Students, Division of Vocational Rehabilitation, Wisconsin Handicapped Program.

Accreditation: National Council on Accreditation of Teacher Education, American Assembly of Collegiate Schools of Business.

Description: The University of Wisconsin, Whitewater (1868), a public institution, is part of a 26-campus university system. UW-Whitewater is committed to the goal of achieving "Excellence for the 21st Century" where faculty teaching is the first and foremost responsibility of every faculty member. UW-Whitewater enrolls 10,500 students and offers 42 undergraduate and 14 graduate degree programs in the Colleges of Arts and Communication, Business and Economics, Education, and Letters and Sciences. The Whitewater campus is nationally recognized for serving disabled students. UW-Whitewater ranked in the first tier among 123 Midwestern comprehensive colleges and universities in the *1999 College Guide of America's Best Colleges,* published by *U.S. News and World Report* magazine. UW-Whitewater entered the field of distance education 2 decades ago when it began offering teacher education courses over the statewide Educational Teleconference Network and the SEEN network (audio and freeze frame video images). In the past 3 years, a number of interactive video courses have been offered in the areas of teacher education, women's studies, and school business management and, more recently, the online MBA has been launched.

University System of Georgia Independent Study

Georgia Center for Continuing Education	
Suite 193	Phone: (706) 542-3243
University of Georgia	(800) 877-3243
Athens, GA 30602-3603	Fax: (706) 542-6635

Division(s): USGIS courses are offered by academic departments located at senior institutions of higher education within the University System of Georgia. Faculty of the academic departments develop the courses offered and grade lessons submitted by students to satisfy requirements of the courses. The office of University System of Georgia Independent Study is located at the University of Georgia Center for Continuing Education.

Web Site(s): http://www.gactr.uga.edu/usgis/

E-mail: usgis@arches.uga.edu

Class Titles: Agribusiness Management, Principles of Accounting, Taxation, Anthropology, Art Appreciation, Ecology, Environmental Conservation, Development Within Family, Child Development, Development of Interpersonal Relationships, Family, Greek Culture, Roman Culture, Classical Mythology, Medical Terminology, Turfgrass Management, Office Management, Ecological Bases of Environmental Issues, Environment/Humans, Ecology, Principles of Macroeconomics, Principles of Microeconomics, Economic Development of U.S., Economics of Human Resources, Career/Life Planning, Foundations of Education, English Composition, English Lit: Beginnings–1700, English Lit: 1700–Present, Writing for Business, American Literature, 19th Century Brit Lit: Romantics, Medieval Literature, Modern Southern Literature, Prose: Modern Novel, People of Paradox: American Colonial Voices, African American Literature, Children's Literature, Learning/Development in Education, Child/Adolescent Development for Education, Human Nutrition/Food, French, Outdoor Recreation/Environmental Awareness, German, Human Geography, Physical Geography, Physical Geography Lab, Economic Geography, Meteorology, Earth Processes/Environments, General Physical Geology/Lab, American History to 1865, American History Since 1865, History of Western Society to 1500, History of Western Society Since 1500, History of Georgia, Vietnam War, Horticultural Science, Fruit Crops, Effects of Drug Use/Abuse, Newswriting/Reporting, Journalism in Secondary Schools, Latin, Golden Age Latin Literature, Vergil's Aeneid, Ovid, Management of Organizations and Individuals, Integrated Resource Management, Human Resource Management, Mathematical Modeling, College Algebra, Trigonometry, Precalculus, Calculus, Statistics, Marketing, Advertising, Retailing, Philosophy, Logic/Critical Thinking, Ethics, Symbolic Logic, American Government, Comparative Politics, International Politics/Issues, Political Parties/Elections, Public Administration, Criminal Justice Administration, Russia/Eastern Europe in Post Cold War Era, Presidency, Environmental Policy, Politics of Middle East, Politics of Modern Africa, Contemporary American Foreign Policy, Psychology, Psychology of Adjustment, Psychology in Work Place, Abnormal Psychology, Psychology of Sex/Sexual Deviations, Social/Personality Development, Theories of Personality, Outdoor Rec/Environmental Awareness, Judaism/Christianity/Islam, Religions of India/China/Japan, West Religious Thought, World Religions, Comparative Religion, Sociology, Social Problems, Juvenile Delinquency, Personality/Social Structure, Sociology of Occupations, Spanish, Oral Decision Making, Communication Strategies in Social Movements, Persuasion, Clinical Medicine, Women's Studies.

Teaching Methods: *Computers:* Web courses (real-time chat, electronic classroom, e-mail, bulletin boards), electronic course guides, e-mail lesson submission courses. *TV:* videotapes. *Other:* audiotapes, independent study (all available as correspondence-based courses via postal service and fax).

Credits Granted for: course completion including final exam at an official college/university test site.

Admission Requirements: *Undergraduate:* USGIS registration does not constitute college/university admission and, therefore, does not necessitate admission tests, high school/college transcripts, or college/university enrollment (except for high school and home-school students). Registration and catalog available online (http://www.gactr. uga.edu/usgis/).

On-Campus Requirements: None.

Tuition and Fees: *Undergraduate:* $96/semester credit. *Other Costs:* $30 drop/add fee plus $10/lesson submitted for grading prior to drop/add (eligible for drop/add within 53 calendars of registration); $60 extension fee to extend the course for an additional 3 months if the extension fee is received prior to the course expiration date. International airmail costs (for receipt of course guide and student packet and return of graded lessons): $25/initial course material package (includes course guide), $6/lesson, $8/mid-term examination (where applicable), $8/final examination. $40 within the U.S. and $65 international lesson fax fee (return of graded lessons); $30 course guide or e-guide replacement fee. Textbooks and instructional materials: students purchase textbooks and other course materials through the University of Georgia's University Bookstore. All materials listed on the title page of the independent study course guide are required, unless otherwise indicated. Contact the University Bookstore at (706) 542-3171, fax (706) 542-7243 for current price information. An instructional materials order form may be found in the catalog and in all student packets. *Credit by:* semester.

Financial Aid: Eligibility to receive financial aid or scholarships must be cleared with the financial aid office of the student's institution prior to registration for an independent study course. Students receiving financial aid (e.g., loans, grants, tuition reimbursements, or scholarships) must pay tuition fees in full at the time of registration.

Accreditation: Southern Association of Colleges and Schools.

Description: University System of Georgia Independent Study's (1932) mission is to increase access to higher education by transcending barriers of geography and time while meeting the highest academic standards, encouraging academic rigor, and requiring equivalent levels of student achievements regardless of delivery format. USGIS permits students to register at any time and take several courses simultaneously with up to a year for course completion. Academic credit is recorded permanently in the University of Georgia Registrar's Office and, with institutional approval, may be transferable.

Upper Iowa University

608 Washington	
PO Box 1861	Phone: (319) 425-5251
Fayette, IA 52142	Fax: (319) 425-5353

Division(s): External Degree Program
Web Site(s): http://www.uiu.edu
E-mail: extdegree@uiu.edu

Undergraduate Degree Programs:
Associate of Arts
Bachelor of Science

Class Titles: Art, Accounting Principles, Marketing Principles, Economics (Macro/Micro), Management Information Systems, Business Ethics, Business Law, Sales Management, Financial Accounting, Federal Taxation, Corporate Financial Management, Consumer Behavior, Human Resources Management, Supervision, Advertising, Entrepreneurship/Small Business Management, Training/Development, Business Communication, Marketing Management, Compensation/Benefits Management, Complex Organizations, Personnel Selection/Evaluation, Labor Relations, Managerial Cost Accounting, International Marketing, Auditing, Operations Management, Accounting for Not-for-Profit Organizations, Contemporary Topics in Management, Marketing Research, Strategic Management, Economics of International Business, Environmental Biology, General Physical Science, Computer Applications, Interpersonal Communications, Composition, Literature, American Civilization, American History, American Economic History, College Algebra, Quantitative Methods, Statistics, Public Administration, Cases in Public Administration, Public Budgeting Process, Administrative Law, U.S. Government, State/Local Government, American Constitution Law, General Psychology, Human Services, Substance Abuse, Abnormal Psychology, Research Methods, Social Welfare Programs/Policies, Industrial Psychology, Issues/Ethics in Helping Professions, Special Project, Social Problems, Cultural/Racial Minorities, Spanish.

Teaching Methods: *Computers:* Internet, e-mail. *TV:* videotape. *Other:* fax, correspondence, independent study, individual study.

Credits Granted for: experiential learning, portfolio assessment, extrainstitutional learning, examination (CLEP, ACT-PEP, DANTES).

Admission Requirements: *Undergraduate:* high school graduate, GED.

On-Campus Requirements: None.

Tuition and Fees: *Undergraduate:* $145/credit. *Application Fee:* $35. *Other Costs:* $60/semester hour experiential learning credit. *Credit by:* semester.

Financial Aid: Federal Stafford Loan, Federal Pell Grant, VA.

Accreditation: North Central Association of Colleges and Schools.

Description: Upper Iowa University was established in Fayette in 1857. Numerous off-campus centers now serve working adults in civilian and military communities. In addition to completing degrees, External Degree courses may supplement degrees at on-site locations, helping students pursuing degrees at other institutions or seeking personal/professional development. UIU's External Degree Program, established in 1973, was one of the country's first independent study degree completion programs. Through progressive transfer policies, students may combine Bachelor of Science experience with majors in Accounting, Business, Human Resources Management, Public Administration (also with Police Science and Fire Science emphases), Management, Social Science, Marketing, and Human Services. Students may use toll-free numbers to register, seek advising, and order textbooks, and qualified staff provide individualized instruction for independent study courses. Many courses have video supplements, and students may submit assignments via e-mail, fax, or regular mail. Students may enroll anytime, with a 6-month initial enrollment period and two 3-month extensions. With no minimum completion time for courses, the program is self-paced and flexible.

Utah State University

Merrill Library Room 208	Phone: (800) 233-2137
3080 Old Main Hill	(435) 797-2137
Logan, UT 84322-3080	Fax: (435) 797-1399

Division(s): Independent and Distance Education
Web Site(s): http://www.ext.usu.edu/distance
E-mail: http://www.de-info@ext.usu.edu

Undergraduate Degree Programs:
Bachelor of:
Accounting
Business Administration
Business Information Systems
Computer Science
Psychology

Graduate Degree Programs:
Master of:
Business Information Systems
Computer Science

Educational Technology
Elementary Education
Human Resource Management
Human Environments/Home Economics Education
School Counseling
Technical Writing (WWW)
Minor: Anthropology

Certificate Programs: Administrative Supervisory Endorsement, Child Development Associate, Library Media.

Teaching Methods: *Computers:* Internet, real-time chat, electronic classroom, e-mail, CD-ROM. *TV:* cable program, satellite broadcasting, televideo. *Other:* radio broadcast, videoconferencing, audioconferencing, audiotapes, fax, correspondence, independent study.

Credits Granted for: portfolio assessment, extrainstitutional learning, examination.

Admission Requirements: *Undergraduate:* new applicants: application and fees, high school transcript, and ACT (preferred) or SAT. Former students (returning after one or more semesters): must reapply plus $10 fee. Contact school for more information.

On-Campus Requirements: yes, depending on individual degree/program requirements.

Tuition and Fees: *Undergraduate:* $248. *Graduate:* $251. *Application Fee:* $35. *Credit by:* semester.

Financial Aid: Federal Stafford Loan, Federal Perkins Loan, Federal PLUS Loan, Federal Pell Grant, Federal Work-Study, VA, Utah resident programs, alternative loans.

Accreditation: Northwest Association of Schools and Colleges.

Description: Utah State University (1888) integrates teaching, research, extension, and service to meet its unique role as Utah's land grant university. USU provides high-quality undergraduate and graduate instruction, excellent general education, and specialized academic and professional degree programs. The university's distance education program traces its beginnings to 1911 when correspondence study served the needs of off-campus students who could enroll for the modest sum of $2. Today, Independent Study, with 3,000 enrollments in 120 courses, remains the backbone of USU's distance education programs. Bachelor's and master's degrees are offered to students unable to attend USU because of time, distance, work, or family constraints. USU's new digital satellite broadcast system provides full-motion video and 2-way audio to each of its receiver sites.

Valley City State University

101 College Street	Phone: (701) 845-7302
Valley City, ND 58072	Fax: (701) 845-7121

Division(s): Interactive Active Video Coordinator
Web Site(s): http://vcsu.nodak.edu
E-mail: Jan_Drake@mail.vcsu.nodak.edu

Class Titles: Federal Tax, Sociology, Gerontology, Women in U.S. History, Spanish, Auditing, Geography of Europe.

Teaching Methods: *Computers:* Internet, chat, electronic classroom, e-mail, CD-ROM, LISTSERV. *TV:* videotape. *Other:* videoconferencing, fax, correspondence, independent study, individual study, learning contracts.

Credits Granted for: experiential learning, portfolio assessment, extrainstitutional learning, examination (CLEP, ACT-PEP).

Admission Requirements: *Undergraduate:* ACT for high school graduates from 1993; 4 English, 3 math, 3 science, and 3 social science high school classes; verification of measles or immunization if born after 1954; GED of 45.

On-Campus Requirements: None.

Tuition and Fees: *Undergraduate:* $76/credit. *Application Fee:* $25. *Other Costs:* $4/credit technology fee, $36/credit notebook computer fee. *Credit by:* semester.

Financial Aid: Federal Stafford Loan, Federal Perkins Loan, Federal PLUS Loan, Federal Pell Grant, Federal Work-Study, VA, North Dakota resident programs.

Accreditation: North Central Association of Colleges and Schools, National Council for Accreditation of Teacher Education "Exemplary Practices".

Description: Valley City State University (1888) is a small liberal arts college located in the heart of the Sheyenne River Valley. About 50% of its 1,000 students live on campus. The school's distance education, offered through the Outreach Campus, has evolved into an interactive video program available throughout the state, with plans for future expansion.

Ventura College

4667 Telegraph Road	Phone: (805) 654-6455
Ventura, CA 93003	Fax: (805) 654-6466

Division(s): Student Development
Web Site(s): None.
E-mail: lmacconnaire@vcccd.cc.ca.us

Undergraduate Degree Programs:
Associate of Arts, General Liberal Arts/Sciences
Associate of Science

Certificate Programs: Yes.

Teaching Methods: *Computers:* videotape, cable program, satellite broadcasting, PBS. *Other:* None.

Admission Requirements: *Undergraduate:* high school graduate or GED, age 18, high school students with permission. *Certificate:* Same.

On-Campus Requirements: For our TV classes, students meet on campus with the instructor at least 4 times/semester, 3 hours each time.

Tuition and Fees: *Undergraduate:* $13/unit, $12/unit starting fall 1998 *Application Fee:* residents $0, nonresidents $13/unit. *Other Costs:* nonresident tuition is $117/unit, health fee $10, parking (optional) $30/semester. *Credit by:* semester.

Financial Aid: Federal Perkins Loan, Federal Pell Grant, Federal Work-Study.

Accreditation: Western Association of Schools and Colleges.

Description: Ventura College (1925) traces its beginnings back to the early 1900s when a junior college department was added to Ventura Union High School. Between the years of 1929–1955, Ventura evolved to its present configuration of offering the freshman and sophomore years of college education. In 1955 the college was moved from the high school to its present 112-acre hillside campus a few miles from sandy beaches. Current enrollment is 11,000 day, evening, and off-campus students. Ventura is part of a 3-college district providing educational opportunities for all of Ventura County. The college has been offering distance learning classes for 15 years and is presently exploring developing courses to be offered over the Internet.

Vermont College of Norwich University

36 College Street	Phone: (800) 336-6794
Montpelier, VT 05602	Fax: (802) 828-8855

Web Site(s): http://www.norwich.edu/vermontcollege
E-mail: vcadmis@norwich.edu

Undergraduate Degree Programs:
Adult Degree Program, New College

Graduate Degree Programs:
Master of Arts
Master of Arts in Art Therapy
Master of Education
Master of Fine Arts in:
    Visual Art
    Writing (poetry, fiction, nonfiction)
    Writing for Children

Certificate Programs: Advanced graduate studies in education and integrated studies.

Class Titles: Postgraduate semester or one-year intensive study in the MFA in Writing programs.

Teaching Methods: *Computers:* Internet, electronic classroom, real-time chat, e-mail. *Other:* audiotapes, fax, correspondence, independent study, individual study, learning contracts.

Credits Granted for: experiential learning, portfolio assessment, extrainstitutional learning, examination (CLEP, ACT-PEP, DANTES, GRE).

Admission Requirements: *Undergraduate:* high school diploma, letters of recommendation. *Graduate:* accredited bachelor's degree.

On-Campus Requirements: 2 residencies each year that vary in length from 9–12 days; weekend options in ADP and the graduate program meet one weekend each month; online option also available in the graduate program.

Tuition and Fees: *Undergraduate:* Adult Degree Program: $4,225/semester (6 months, 15 credits), New College: $4,500/semester (18 weeks, 15 credits). *Graduate:* $4,485–4,676/semester, $5,460/semester (15 credits/semester, MFA in Visual Art), $4,850/semester (6 months, 16 credits, MFA in Writing and in Writing for Children), $7,200/semester (12 weeks, 13–15 credits, summer residency for MA in Art Therapy), $6,100 (35 weeks, 17 credits, Practicum for MA in Art Therapy), $4,975/semester (12 credits, Certificate of Advanced Graduate Studies). *Application Fee:* $35 undergraduate, $50 graduate. *Other Costs:* variable—international surcharge, professional development, thesis writing extensions, etc. *Credit by:* semester.

Financial Aid: Federal Stafford Loan, Federal Perkins Loan, Federal PLUS Loan, Federal Pell Grant, Federal Work-Study, VA, Vermont resident programs.

Accreditation: New England Association of Schools and Colleges.

Description: Norwich University's (1819) Vermont College programs are the oldest brief-residency adult degree programs in the U.S., having been in existence since 1963. Based on the progressive education philosophy of John Dewey and employing the mentoring model used by Oxford and other European universities, these programs put the student's learning first. Each individual designs his or her own study in collaboration with a faculty mentor. Residencies bring students together in cohesive learning communities; directed, independent study during 6-month semesters focuses on the particular needs of each student.

Victor Valley Community College

18422 Bear Valley Road	Phone: (760) 245-4271
Victorville, CA 92392	Fax: (760) 245-9744

Division(s): Dean of Instruction, Academic Programs
Web Site(s): http://www.victor.cc.ca.us

Class Titles: Not all these classes are offered every semester: Reserve Level III Academy Nondesignated Reserve Peace

Officers (includes labs), Physical Anthropology, Principles of Management, Legal Environment of Business, General Biology, Chemistry, Computer Literacy, Internet, Cultural Geography, History of World to 1500, World History Since 1500, History of Indians of U.S., History of U.S. to 1876, History of U.S. Since 1876, Philosophy, American Government/Politics, General Psychology, Developmental Psychology.

Teaching Methods: *Computers:* Internet, real-time chat, electronic classroom, e-mail, CD-ROM, newsgroup, LISTSERV. *TV:* videotape, cable program, satellite broadcasting, PBS. *Other:* None.

Credits Granted for: examination (CLEP, AP, DANTES, Department Exam, Military).

Admission Requirements: *Undergraduate:* Resident, accredited high school graduates with acceptable California Proficiency Exam or GED scores; returning students in good standing who did not attend another college or university; transfer students eligible to return to previous college or university; apprentices as defined in Labor Code Section 3077; nonresident high school graduates; foreign students meeting their requirements and deadlines; residents age 18 who did not graduate or pass high school proficiency or GED (these students must have training, work experience, or assessment results demonstrating they would benefit from attending). *Certificate:* same as for undergraduate. Also the same for Individual Class.

On-Campus Requirements: varies. Telecourses require students to attend 3 mandatory and 2 optional sessions/semester. Videocassette lecture/lab courses require attendance at one class session of 4 hours weekly for lab. Online courses require either no classroom attendance or 3/semester.

Tuition and Fees: *Undergraduate:* $13/credit for residents; $124/credit for nonresident. *Graduate:* same as for undergraduate. *Doctoral:* same as for undergraduate. *Other Costs:* $1/credit (maximum of $10/year) student center fee. *Credit by:* semester.

Financial Aid: Board of Governors Fee Waiver, William D. Ford Federal Direct Loan Program, Federal Supplemental Educational Opportunity Grant, Federal Pell Grant, Federal Work-Study, VA, Bureau of Indian Affairs, California resident programs (Cal Grants).

Accreditation: Western Association of Schools and Colleges.

Description: Victor Valley Community College (1960) is committed to excellence in educational programs and services accessible to a diverse student population. It is a public, 2-year community college with 9,000 students representing 26 ethnic cultures. VVC is situated in the High Desert region of the Mohave Desert and serves a population of 250,000 in many rural, desert community areas of more than 2,200 square miles. It is among the most modern of the 106 community colleges in California. The Victor Valley is separated from metropolitan areas of southern California by mountain ranges that isolate the region. Distance education through telecourses has been offered since the early 1980s, and social sciences faculty recently pioneered online courses.

Virginia Commonwealth University Medical College of Virginia Campus

1008 East Clay Street
PO Box 980203
Richmond, VA 23298-0203

Phone: (804) 828-0719
Fax: (804) 828-1894

Division(s): Department of Health Administration
Web Site(s): http://www.had.vcu.edu
E-mail: shavasy@hsc.vcu.edu

Graduate Degree Programs:
Master of Science in Health Administration (Executive Program)

Teaching Methods: *Computers:* Internet, e-mail, CD-ROM, newsgroup, streaming audio. *TV:* videotape. *Other:* audioconferencing, audiotapes, fax, correspondence, independent study, individual study, learning contracts, focus on asynchronous learning.

Admission Requirements: *Graduate:* 5 years of health care experience—preferably administrative—and an undergraduate degree from accredited college, GRE/GMAT (may be waived for advanced degrees), 2.75 GPA.

On-Campus Requirements: 5 on-campus sessions, 9–14 days each.

Tuition and Fees: *Undergraduate:* $3,737/semester in-state and academic common market participants, $7,583 out-of-state. *Doctoral:* $30. *Software:* $169. *Other Costs:* multimedia computer/Internet access, travel/lodging for on-campus sessions, books. *Credit by:* semester.

Financial Aid: Scholarship, grant, and loan programs.

Accreditation: Southern Association of Colleges and Schools, Accrediting Commission on Education for Health Services Administration.

Description: The Master of Science Health Administration can be completed in 2 years by U.S. residents working full-time. It is designed for physicians and other clinicians, mid-level managers, and health care executives seeking graduate education in management. The Department of Health Administration at VCU enjoys a strong national reputation. It also offers preparation leading to the Master of Health Administration and Doctor of Philosophy degrees. Through its David G. Williamson, Jr., Institute for Health Studies, the department conducts major research, outreach, service, and consultation programs. The MCV campus has a 1,058-bed teaching hospital and 5 schools of clinical and basic sciences. More than 1,700 alumni provide an extensive professional development and career placement network.

Virginia Commonwealth University

West Hospital
1200 East Broad Street
Richmond, VA 23219

Phone: (804) 282-7247
Fax: (804) 828-8656

Division(s): School of Allied Health Professions
Web Site(s): http://views.vcu.edu/sahp/phd/
E-mail: mlwhite@hsc.vcu.edu

Graduate Degree Programs:
Master of Science in Health Administration (Executive Program)

Doctoral Degree Programs:
Doctorate in Health Related Sciences

Teaching Methods: *Computers:* Internet, real-time chat, electronic classroom, e-mail, CD-ROM, newsgroup, LIST-SERV. *TV:* videotape. *Other:* audioconferencing, videoconferencing, audiographics, audiotapes, fax, correspondence, independent study.

Credits Granted for: examination (CLEP, ACT-PEP, DANTES, GRE).

Admission Requirements: *Graduate:* GRE or GMAT, 5 years of progressive work experience and related undergraduate degree from an accredited college. *Doctoral:* GRE or MAT, related master's degree.

On-Campus Requirements: One week at beginning and end of semester.

Tuition and Fees: *Graduate:* $260/credit in-state; $687/credit out-of-state. *Doctoral:* same as gradauate. *Application Fee:* $30. *Software:* $300–$350. *Other Costs:* $1,326 master's program fee, $1,750 ($200/credit hour) doctoral program fee; travel, subsistence, lodging for on-campus sessions. *Credit by:* semester.

Financial Aid: Federal Stafford Loan, Federal Perkins Loan, Federal PLUS Loan, Federal Pell Grant, Federal Work-Study, VA, Virginia resident programs.

Accreditation: Southern Association of Colleges and Schools.

Description: Virginia Commonwealth University christened the Medical College of Virginia in 1838. VCU is the major urban university in the state and is classified as a Carnegie Foundation Research University I institution. The university is a public state-supported institution with 22,000 undergraduate, graduate, and health professional students. VCU's administration understands the critical role of distance learning for the next century. Distance learning began at VCU in 1988 with the Master of Science in Health Administration program. In the fall of 1998, the university began its new doctoral program in Health Related Sciences, an interdisciplinary, distance learning, Internet-based program.

Virginia Polytechnic Institute and State University

Old Security Building (0445)
Blacksburg, VA 24061-0445

Phone: (540) 231-4199
Fax: (540) 231-5922

Division(s): The Office of Distance and Distributed Learning
Web Site(s): http://www.vt.edu
http://www.vto.vt.edu
http://www.dl.vt.edu
E-mail: vtwebreg@vt.edu

Graduate Degree Programs:
Master of Science in:
  Civil Engineering
  Electrical Engineering
  Industrial/Systems Engineering
  Systems Engineering
Master of Arts in:
  Health/Physical Education
  Instructional Technology
  Political Science
MBA Business Administration

Certificate Programs: Administration of Community-Based Services for Older Adults (graduate)

Class Titles: Biology, Communications, Computer Science, English, Entomology, Geography, Math, Political Science, Sociology, Spanish, Family/Child Development.

Teaching Methods: *Computers:* Internet, real-time chat, electronic classroom, e-mail, CD-ROM, newsgroup, LIST-SERV. *TV:* videotape, cable program, satellite broadcasting. *Other:* videoconferencing, audiographics.

Admission Requirements: *Undergraduate:* see Web site (http://www.vt.edu). *Graduate:* see Web site (http://www.rgs.vt.edu). *Doctoral:* see Web site (http://www.vt.edu). *Certificate:* see Web site (http://www.vt.edu).

On-Campus Requirements: variable.

Tuition and Fees: *Undergraduate:* in-state: $438/3 credit course, out-of-state: $1,340. *Graduate:* in-state: $687/3 credit course, out-of-state: $1,227. *Application Fee:* $25. *Credit by:* semester.

Financial Aid: Federal Direct Stafford Loan, Federal Direct Perkins Loan, Federal Direct PLUS Loan, Federal Pell Grant, Federal Work-Study, Virginia Guaranteed Assistance Program (VGAP-VA), Commonwealth Award (VA Grant), College Scholarship Assistance Program (CSAP-VA and federal funds combined).

Accreditation: Southern Association of Colleges and Schools.

Description: Virginia Polytechnic Institute and State University (1872), a land grant university dedicated to instruction, research, and outreach, offers more than 200 degree programs and is the largest university in Virginia. It is also one of the nation's leading research institutions. Virginia Tech is a model for the development and use of sophisticated instructional technologies in the classroom. The 26,000 students (on and off campus) are enrolled in one of 7 undergraduate colleges, the Graduate School, or the Virginia-Maryland Regional College of Veterinary Medicine. Virginia Tech has been actively involved in distance learning since 1983 when it began offering televised graduate engineering courses via satellite. Currently Virginia Tech offers 8 master's degree programs, one certificate, and numerous individual courses through a variety of distance learning technologies.

Walden University

155 Fifth Avenue S	Phone: (612) 338-7224
Minneapolis, MN 55401	Fax: (612) 338-5092

Division(s): Academic Affairs
Web Site(s): http://www.waldenu.edu
E-mail: request@waldenu.edu

Graduate Degree Programs:
Master of Science

Doctoral Degree Programs:
Doctorate in Psychology

Certificate Programs: Professional Postdoctoral Psychology, various certificates within the Psychology and Education programs.

Teaching Methods: *Computers:* Internet, real-time chat, electronic classroom, e-mail, CD-ROM, newsgroup, LIST-SERV. *TV:* videotape, cable program, satellite broadcasting, PBS. *Other:* audioconferencing, videoconferencing, audiotapes, fax, correspondence, independent study, individual study, learning contracts.

Admission Requirements: *Graduate:* accredited bachelor's degree, additional criteria may apply depending upon program. *Doctoral:* accredited master's degree, 3 years of relevant professional experience, additional criteria may apply depending upon program.

On-Campus Requirements: brief, flexible residency for doctoral study. To graduate, doctoral students must complete 32 residency units. Numerous options are available including dispersed weekend residencies offered at convenient locations across the U.S. All doctoral students must complete a 2-week summer session at the Bloomington campus of Indiana University.

Tuition and Fees: *Graduate:* $220/credit (1997/98 tuition). *Doctoral:* $3,040/quarter (1997/98 tuition). *Application Fee:* $50. *Software:* full Internet access is required with a mail program like Eudora, a Web browser like Netscape, and a Telnet program. *Other Costs:* additional fees include residency and graduation fees. *Credit by:* credits are awarded quarterly for course-based programs. Doctoral students in many programs progress by completing the required Knowledge Area Modules (or KAMs). There are 7 KAMs in addition to a

dissertation and students are awarded credit for the successful completion of each KAM research paper. Continuous enrollment is required.

Financial Aid: Federal Stafford Loan, VA. Financial assistance is also available through group enrollment discounts, spousal assistance, and in the form of Higher Education Professional Development Fellowships.

Accreditation: North Central Association of Colleges and Schools.

Description: Walden University (1970) provides high-quality distance graduate education. Students have considerable flexibility in shaping their course of study, enabling them to apply what they learn directly to their professions. Walden students engage in self-directed research, and they schedule classes in consultation with their faculty mentor, or in interaction with other residency students, using today's technology. MS degrees in Psychology and Education can be completed in as little as 18 months and are delivered completely online. Most doctoral students earn their PhD within 3 years in Management, Psychology, Education, Health Services, and Human Services. Currently the university enrolls 1,200 students from all 50 states and 20 foreign countries, and one-third of the students are from minority groups. Walden has 2 office locations: The Office of Academic Affairs in Minneapolis, Minnesota, and the Office of Administration and Finance in Bonita Springs, Florida.

Walla Walla Community College

500 Tausick Way	Phone: (509) 527-4583
Walla Walla, WA 99362	Fax: (509) 527-4572

Division(s): Distance Learning
Web Site(s): http://www.ww.cc.wa.us/dl
E-mail: wwcc-dl@po.ww.cc.wa.us

Undergraduate Degree Programs:
Associate of Arts

Certificate Programs: Microcomputer Applications Specialist, Unix Systems Administrator.

Class Titles: Principles of Electronics, Computer Technology, Microcomputer Applications, Technical Writing, Physical Geography, Solar System Astronomy, Windows, Microsoft Office, MS Word, MS Excel, MS Access, MS PowerPoint, Internet, Windows NT Workstation.

Teaching Methods: *Computers:* Internet, electronic classroom, e-mail, CD-ROM. *TV:* videotape, cable program. *Other:* videoconferencing, correspondence, independent study, individual study, learning contracts.

Credits Granted for: examination (course challenge, CLEP).

Admission Requirements: *Undergraduate:* open to all students, ASSET placement tests for English and math for all degree-seeking students, additional fees for out-of-state students. *Certificate:* same as undergraduate.

On-Campus Requirements: None.

Tuition and Fees: *Undergraduate:* $52/credit Washington resident, $59/credit Oregon and Idaho residents. *Application Fee:* $40. *Other Costs:* $3/credit (maximum of 10 credits) technology fees. *Credit by:* quarter.

Financial Aid: Federal Stafford Loan, Federal Perkins Loan, Federal PLUS Loan, Federal Pell Grant, Federal Work-Study, VA, Washington resident programs.

Accreditation: Northwest Association of Schools and Colleges.

Description: Walla Walla Community College (1967) serves a 4-county region of southeastern Washington state that is largely rural and diverse. In spite of having a service area 150 miles wide and 80 miles long, WWCC is proud to maintain one of the highest service levels per capita among the community and technical colleges in the state. Distance learning is a focus and a priority as a means to continue offering college, continuing, and community education opportunities to our district and beyond. WWCC is proud of its partnerships with John Deere, Cisco Systems, and Microsoft, among others, and is looking to distance learning to extend these partnerships and create new ones in turf management, irrigation technology, agriculture, computer science, and the sciences.

Washington State University

Van Doren 204/PO Box 645220	Phone: **(509) 335-3557**
Pullman, WA 99164-5220	**(800) 222-4978**
	Fax: **(509) 335-4850**

Division(s): Extended Degree Programs/Extended University Services
Web Site(s): http://www.eus.wsu.edu/edp/
E-mail: edp@wsu.edu

Undergraduate Degree Programs:
Bachelor of Arts in:
    Social Sciences
    Human Development
    Business Administration (at selected pilot sites)
    Criminal Justice (beginning spring semester 1999)

Certificate Programs: Professional Writing

Teaching Methods: *Computers:* Internet, real-time chat, electronic classroom, e-mail, CD-ROM, LISTSERV. *TV:* videotape, cable program, satellite broadcasting. *Other:* videoconferencing, audiotapes, fax, correspondence, independent study, individual study.

Credits Granted for: examination (CLEP, ACT-PEP, DANTES, GRE).

Admission Requirements: *Undergraduate:* Must have 27

semester (40 quarter) accredited, transferable, college credits with a 2.0 GPA.

On-Campus Requirements: None.

Tuition and Fees: *Undergraduate:* $170/semester credit in-state, $255/semester credit out-of-state, $90/semester credit flexible enrollment courses tuition in- or out-of-state. *Other Costs:* $35 admission fee, additional charges for textbooks, audiotapes, and/or videotapes and required course guides vary by course, $40/course charge for foreign mailing. *Credit by:* semester.

Financial Aid: Federal Stafford Loan, Federal Perkins Loan, Federal PLUS Loan, Federal Pell Grant, Federal Work-Study, VA, Washington resident programs.

Accreditation: Northwest Association of Schools and Colleges.

Description: Washington State University (1890), the state's land grant university, is dedicated to the preparation of students for productive lives and professional careers, to basic and applied research in various fields, and to the dissemination of knowledge. The heart of the WSU system is the Pullman campus with its 17,000 students. The university became multicampus in 1989 with extensions in Spokane, the Tri-Cities, and Vancouver, with 2,000 students attending these branches. Established in 1992, the Extended Degree Program has utilized a variety of technologies to help hundreds of distance students earn bachelor's degrees without attending classes on campus, and individuals anywhere can do likewise. EDP began with just one degree offered at 4 sites to 50 students. Since then, WSU's social science degree has attracted more than 1,000 degree-seeking students. By the spring of 1999, EDP anticipates offering 3 more degree programs: human development, business administration (at selected pilot sites), and criminal justice.

Waukesha County Technical College

800 Main Street	Phone: **(414) 691-5594**
Pewaukee, WI 53072	Fax: **(414) 691-5047**

Division(s): Business Occupations Division
Web Site(s): http://www.waukesha.tec.wi.us
E-mail: lrevoy@waukesha.tec.wi.us

Undergraduate Degree Programs:
Associate Degree in:
    Real Estate Brokerage
    Property Management
    Property Appraisal/Assessment
    Mortgage Lending
    Financial Planning

Certificate Programs: Wisconsin Residential Appraisal Certification, Wisconsin General Appraisal Certification.

Teaching Methods: *Computers:* Internet, real-time chat, electronic classroom, e-mail. *TV:* videotape, cable program. *Other:* None.

Credits Granted for: experiential learning, portfolio assessment, extrainstitutional learning, examination (CLEP, ACT-PEP, DANTES, GRE).

Admission Requirements: *Undergraduate:* Asset test.

On-Campus Requirements: None.

Tuition and Fees: *Undergraduate:* $67/credit. *Application Fee:* $25. *Other Costs:* Internet access. *Credit by:* semester.

Financial Aid: Federal Stafford Loan, Federal PLUS Loan, Federal Pell Grant, Federal Work-Study, VA, Wisconsin resident programs, various scholarships.

Accreditation: North Central Association of Colleges and Schools.

Description: Waukesha County Technical College has undergone many changes since its vocational school status in 1919. Today it touts formal athletic programs and clubs along with its 40 associate degree programs. Distance learning began with local TV courses in 1993 and included full degrees via the Internet by 1995. Since July 1998 all WCTC required courses are available worldwide through Virtual Degree programs.

Wayne County Community College

| 801 West Fort Street | Phone: (313) 496-2602 |
| Detroit, MI 48226 | Fax: (313) 496-0451 |

Division(s): Distance Learning
Web Site(s): http://www.wccc.edu
E-mail: citcdf@admin.wccc.edu

Undergraduate Degree Programs:
Associate of Arts
Associate of General Studies

Class Titles: Anthropology, English, Humanities, Sociology, Psychology, Geology, Geography, Business, Management, Marketing, Computer/Information Systems, Political Science, History, Philosophy.

Teaching Methods: *TV:* videotape, cable program, PBS, Interactive TV (ITV). *Other:* None.

Credits Granted for: experiential learning, examination (CLEP, ACT-PEP, DANTES, GRE).

Admission Requirements: *Undergraduate:* age 18.

On-Campus Requirements: Telecourse requires attendance at 4-6 on-campus sessions for each course. ITV is on campus.

Tuition and Fees: *Undergraduate:* $54 in-district, $70/other MI residents, $89/out-of-state. *Application Fee:* $10. *Other Costs:* $20 one-time testing fee, $25/registration fee, $2/credit

activity fee. *Credit by:* semester.

Financial Aid: Federal Stafford Loan, Federal Pell Grant, Federal Work-Study, VA, Michigan resident programs, Michigan Adult Part-time Grant, Michigan College Work-Study, Michigan Educational Opportunity Grant, Michigan Tuition Incentive Program.

Accreditation: North Central Association of Colleges and Schools.

Description: Wayne County Community College District (1967) first offered courses in rented facilities throughout Wayne County. Today the district is comprised of 5 comprehensive campuses. Three telecourses were first offered in the fall of 1978. Since that time, the distance learning program has expanded to include 30 telecourses, allowing students to complete Associate of Arts or Associate of General Studies degrees exclusively through telecourse instruction. Interactive TV courses were introduced in the winter of 1997 and are offered at 2 of our 5 campuses. Satellite downlink capabilities are also available at one of our campuses.

Wayne State College

1111 Main Street	Phone: (800) 228-9972 x7217
Wayne, NE 68787	(402) 375-7217
	Fax: (402) 375-7204

Division(s): Office of Regional Education and Distance Learning
Web Site(s): http://www.wsc.edu
E-mail: extcampus@wscgate.wsc.edu

Graduate Degree Programs:
Master of Business Administration
Master of Science in Education

Class Titles: Business, English, Biology, Math, Chemistry, Education, Art, Music, Wellness, Physics, Political Science, Criminal Justice, Sociology, History, Geography, Vocational Education, Industrial Technology, German, Spanish, Literature, Communication.

Teaching Methods: *Computers:* Internet, real-time chat, electronic classroom, e-mail, CD-ROM, newsgroup, LISTSERV. *TV:* satellite broadcasting, PBS. *Other:* audioconferencing, videoconferencing, independent study, individual study, learning contracts.

Credits Granted for: extrainstitutional learning, examination (CLEP, ACT-PEP, DANTES, GRE).

Admission Requirements: *Undergraduate:* open-admission, high school diploma or GED, ACT test scores preferred, high school transcripts as proof of graduation, and a one-time admission fee must accompany admission application. Nebraska resident status determined by length of time in state (>6 months) or may be obtained by special authorization—contact Admissions Office. *Graduate:* open-admission, undergraduate transcripts for all degree-seeking graduate students, GMAT or GRE scores and references for degree programs, and a one-time application fee must accompany application for graduate admission (fee waived if paid as an undergraduate). Nebraska resident status determined by length of time in state (>6 months) or may be obtained by special authorization—contact Admissions Office.

On-Campus Requirements: None.

Tuition and Fees: *Undergraduate:* $60/credit resident, $119/credit nonresident. *Graduate:* $75/credit resident, $149/credit nonresident. *Application Fee:* $10 one-time fee. *Other Costs:* $3/credit facilities fee, $10/credit extended campus fee. *Credit by:* semester.

Financial Aid: Federal Stafford Loan, Federal Perkins Loan, Federal PLUS Loan, Federal Pell Grant, Federal Work-Study, VA, Nebraska resident programs.

Accreditation: North Central Association of Colleges and Schools, National Council for Accreditation of Teacher Education.

Description: Wayne State College (1891) serves 4,000 students from several states and several foreign countries. Students can major in 40 programs, with an average of 50% graduating in the arts and sciences, 30% in education, and 20% in business. Wayne State is a regional public college and is a part of a 3-school state college system geographically positioned to serve rural Nebraska. The 3 colleges, supported by the Nebraska Educational TV system and the University of Nebraska, have joined together to provide distance learning programming across the system and to isolated rural communities. The Nebraska State College System has been producing satellite-based and videoconferencing-based programming for most of the past decade. The system has recently added Internet-based course work to supplement the other programs and add flexibility for the nontraditional students across the region.

Weber State University

4005 University Circle	Phone: (800) 848-7770 x6785
Ogden, UT 84408-4005	(801) 626-6785
	Fax: (801) 626-8035

Division(s): Office of Distance Learning
Web Site(s): http://www.weber.edu
and http://www.wsuonline.weber.edu
E-mail: dist-learn@weber.edu

Undergraduate Degree Programs:
Associate of Science in Respiratory Therapy
Associate of Applied Science in Respiratory Therapy
Bachelor of Science in:
   Health Services Administration
   Health Promotion
   Health Information Management
   Clinical Laboratory Science

Radiologic Sciences
Respiratory Therapy

Certificate Programs: Radiologic Sciences, Respiratory Therapy.

Class Titles: Survey of Accounting, Anthropology, Plants in Human Affairs, Business/Society, Chemistry, Human Development, Mass Communication, Mass Media/Society, Criminal Justice, Writing, Blueprint Reading, Developmental Writing, Technical Writing, Creative Writing, Literature, Personal Finance, Meteorology, Gerontology, Healthy Lifestyles, Human Sexuality, Nutrition, Medical Terminology, Biomedical Core Lecture/Lab, Biomedical Principles: Certificate of Completion for Paramedics, Pathophysiology, World History to 1500 C.E., World History: 1500 C.E. to Present, American Civilizations, U.S. Diplomatic History, 20th-Century U.S. Since 1945, Far Eastern History, Middle Eastern History, History of Africa, History of Utah, 20th-Century Europe, Design for Living, Algebra, Organizational Behavior/Management, Music, Diet Therapy, Philosophy, Fitness for Life, American National Government, International Politics, Public Administration, Psychology, Psychology of Adjustment, Interpersonal Relationships, Biopsychology, Conditioning/Learning, Theories of Personality, Social Psychology, General Psychology, Counseling Theories, Selling Techniques, Retail Merchandising/Buying Methods, Distribution Principles, Fashion Merchandising, Credit/Collection Methods, Advertising Methods, Customer Service Techniques, Ethical Sales/Service, Principles of Supervision, Principles of Sociology, Social Problems.

Teaching Methods: *Computers:* Internet, real-time chat, e-mail, CD-ROM. *TV:* videotape. *Other:* videoconferencing, audiotapes, fax, correspondence, independent study, individual study, learning contracts.

Credits Granted for: extrainstitutional learning, examination (CLEP, ACT-PEP, DANTES, GRE).

Admission Requirements: *Undergraduate:* high school graduation or GED; ACT, SAT, or placement test. ARRT certification for bachelor's or certificate in Radiologic Science. Clinical Laboratory Science students must be working clinical laboratory technician.

On-Campus Requirements: None.

Tuition and Fees: *Undergraduate:* $95/semester credit. *Application Fee:* $30 ($45 international). $10 more for degree- or certificate-seeking students. *Other Costs:* books. *Credit by:* semester.

Financial Aid: Federal Stafford Loan, Federal Perkins Loan, Federal PLUS Loan, Federal Pell Grant, Federal Work-Study, VA.

Accreditation: Northwest Association of Schools and Colleges.

Description: Weber State University was founded in 1889 and is situated in the foothills of the Wasatch Mountains overlooking Ogden. With a current student body of 15,000, Weber is recognized as a metropolitan university providing programs for students with varied interests and educational goals. Continuing Education developed the distance learning program for people who cannot attend regularly scheduled university courses. Through this self-paced, individualized program, students can meet degree requirements, enhance their professional skills, and achieve their personal goals. Weber State is committed to offering its students quality courses through correspondence, providing excellent customer service, and developing lasting relationships among students, faculty, and staff.

West Hills College

300 Cherry Lane	Phone: (209) 935-0801 x3353
Coalinga, CA 93210	Fax: (209) 935-5655

Division(s): Learning Resources
Web Site(s): http://www.westhills.cc.ca.us
E-mail: DavisLL@whccd.cc.ca.us

Class Titles: Health Education, Computer Information Systems, Geography, Math, Agriculture, Psychology, Business, History, Biology, Philosophy, Journalism, Sociology, Art.

Teaching Methods: *Computers:* Internet, e-mail, newsgroup, LISTSERV. *TV:* videotape, cable program, PBS. *Other:* videoconferencing, fax, correspondence, independent study, learning contracts.

On-Campus Requirements: For TV courses only, students are required to meet at one of 3 campus sites for 3 hours on 5 different dates during a semester.

Tuition and Fees: *Undergraduate:* $12/credit residents, $100/credit U.S. residents outside of California, $140/credit international students. *Credit by:* semester.

Financial Aid: Federal Stafford Loan, Federal Perkins Loan, Federal PLUS Loan, Federal Pell Grant, Federal Work-Study, VA, California resident programs.

Accreditation: Western Association of Schools and Colleges.

Description: West Hills College (1933) is a public community college providing certificate programs in vocational majors and Associate of Arts and Associate of Science degrees in transfer majors. With its main campus in Coalinga and education centers in Lemoore and Firebaugh, the college serves more than 4,000 students in central California. In response to student requests for greater schedule flexibility, West Hills began offering distance education classes via TV and cable broadcasts in 1995. The college has since expanded the program to include Internet-based courses.

West Valley College

14000 Fruitvale Avenue	Phone: (408) 741-2065
Saratoga, CA 95070	Fax: (408) 741-2134

Division(s): Instructional Development/Distance Learning
Web Site(s): http://www.westvalley.edu/wvc/dl/DL.HomePage
E-mail: steve_peltz@westvalley.edu

Undergraduate Degree Programs:
Associate of Arts
Associate of Science

Certificate Programs: 66 different programs across the curriculum.

Class Titles: Anthropology, Art Appreciation, Astronomy, Biology, Business Law, Management, Sales, General Business, Marketing, Page Layout, Child Growth/Development, English Composition, French, Spanish, Geology, Health, Nutrition, Physical Fitness, Film Studies, Digital Photography, Oceanography, Political Science, History, Sociology, Web Authoring.

Teaching Methods: *Computers:* Internet, real-time chat, electronic classroom, e-mail, CD-ROM, newsgroup, LISTSERV. *TV:* videotape, cable program, PBS. *Other:* videoconferencing, audiotapes, fax, correspondence, independent study, individual study, learning contracts.

Credits Granted for: extrainstitutional learning, Advanced Placement Program (CEEB), examination (CLEP), Military credit, credit for Certified Professional Secretary rating.

Admission Requirements: *Undergraduate:* Application, high school graduate or age 18 and can profit from instruction, including those who have passed the High School Proficiency Exam or GED. Student must declare a classification: new, continuing, returning (former), new transfer, international, or nonresident. Residency is specifically defined in the college catalog.

On-Campus Requirements: None.

Tuition and Fees: *Undergraduate:* $12/credit California resident, $120/credit out-of-state, $125/credit international. *Application Fee:* $50 for international students. *Other Costs:* $17/semester assorted basic fees. *Credit by:* semester.

Financial Aid: Federal Stafford Loan, Federal Perkins Loan, Federal PLUS Loan, Federal Pell Grant, Federal Work-Study, VA, California resident programs.

Accreditation: Western Association of Schools and Colleges.

Description: West Valley College (1963) is a public community college open to those seeking advanced educational opportunities. Our primary purpose is to facilitate successful learning. We are committed to educating the individual and fostering the economic development of the communities we serve. WVC provides students with opportunities to participate in a wide spectrum of educational experiences designed to fulfill their academic and career needs, enrich the quality of their lives, and develop job skills and other competencies necessary to function and succeed in contemporary society. We have offered distance learning courses for 22 years.

West Virginia Northern Community College

1704 Market Street	Phone: (304) 233-5900
Wheeling, WV 26003-3699	Fax: (304) 233-8132

Division(s): Learning Resource Center
Web Site(s): http://www.northern.wvnet.edu
E-mail: tdanford@northern.wvnet.edu

Undergraduate Degree Programs:
Associate in Science
Associate in Business Administration, transfer option

Class Titles: Biology, Computer Science, English, Economics, Business Administration, Psychology, Sociology, Politics/American Government, Health Science.

Teaching Methods: *Computers:* Internet, real-time chat, electronic classroom, e-mail, CD-ROM, newsgroup, LISTSERV, MOO. *TV:* videotape, satellite broadcasting, PBS. *Other:* audiotapes, fax, correspondence, independent study, individual study, learning contracts.

Credits Granted for: examination (CLEP), GED.

Admission Requirements: *Undergraduate:* high school diploma or GED. *Certificate:* same as undergraduate.

On-Campus Requirements: limited on-campus meetings for instructional TV.

Tuition and Fees: *Undergraduate:* $59/credit. *Software:* variable. *Other Costs:* $6 student assessment. *Credit by:* semester.

Financial Aid: Federal Stafford Loan, Federal Perkins Loan, Federal PLUS Loan, Federal Pell Grant, Federal Work-Study, VA, West Virginia resident programs.

Accreditation: North Central Association of Colleges and Schools.

Description: West Virginia Northern Community College (1972), located in the northern panhandle of West Virginia, is a tri-campus comprehensive community college, offering associate degrees and certificates. Northern began distance education efforts in 1988 with the installation of a 2-way, interactive compressed video system and electronic classrooms connecting 2 campuses 35 miles apart. Distance education expanded during a Title III Technology Across the Curriculum grant from 1992 until 1995. Most recently, a PBS Going the Distance associate degree in business administration, transfer option, has been initiated.

Westchester Community College

75 Grasslands Road AD-207	Phone: (914) 785-6658
Valhalla, NY 10595	Fax: (914) 785-6129

Division(s): Continuing Education
Web Site(s): http://www.westchestercc.org
E-mail: tkk1@wccmail.co.westchester.ny.us

Class Titles: Art, Economics (Macro/Micro), World Geography, Western Civilization: Rome–1648, 20th Century U.S. History, American Government/Issues, American Politics/Policies, Psychology, Abnormal Psychology, Developmental Psychology, Sociology, Marriage/Family, Criminalistics, State/Local Government, Criminal Justice Systems, Telecom, Electrical Circuits, Computer Applications.

Teaching Methods: *Computers:* Internet, real-time chat, electronic classroom, e-mail, CD-ROM, newsgroup, LISTSERV. *TV:* videotape, cable program, satellite broadcasting, PBS. *Other:* videoconferencing.

Admission Requirements: *Undergraduate:* open-enrollment. *Certificate:* open-enrollment.

On-Campus Requirements: depends on the course.

Tuition and Fees: *Undergraduate:* $98/credit in-county, $98/credit out-of-county with certificate of residency, $245/credit out-of-county, out-of-state. *Other Costs:* tuition and fees subject to change. *Credit by:* semester.

Financial Aid: Federal Stafford Loan, Federal Perkins Loan, Federal PLUS Loan, Federal Pell Grant, Federal Work-Study, VA, New York resident programs.

Accreditation: Middle States Association of Colleges and Schools.

Description: In the academic year 1996–97, Westchester Community College (1946) celebrated 50 years of excellence. It enrolls 11,000 full-time and part-time credit students each semester as well as 8,500 noncredit students. Westchester Community College offers distance learning courses as regular credit courses and through the State of New York Learning Network.

Western Baptist College

5000 Deer Park Drive S	Phone: (503) 375-7590
Salem, OR 97301-9392	(800) 764-1383
	Fax: (503) 375-7583

Division(s): Adult Studies, Biblical Studies
Web Site(s): http://www.wbc.edu
E-mail: rtaylor@wbc.edu

Undergraduate Degree Programs:
Management and Communications

Class Titles: Missiology, Christian Evidence, Christian Theology.

Teaching Methods: *Computers:* Internet, electronic classroom, e-mail. *Other:* audioconferencing, fax, correspondence, independent study, individual study, learning contracts.

Credits Granted for: experiential learning, portfolio assessment, life-learning papers, extrainstitutional learning, Professional Schools and Training, examination (CLEP, DANTES, American Council of Education).

Admission Requirements: *Undergraduate:* employed, 62 transferable semester hours that satisfy lower-division requirements, basic computer literacy, writing sample, professional and church references.

On-Campus Requirements: For the management and communication degree completion program, a 3-day orientation at the school is required. For individual courses, there is no residency requirement.

Tuition and Fees: *Undergraduate:* $280/credit. *Other Costs:* $100 class reservation deposit, $40 late applicant processing fee. *Credit by:* semester.

Financial Aid: Federal Stafford Loan, Federal Perkins Loan, Federal Pell Grant, VA, Oregon resident programs.

Accreditation: Northwest Association of Schools and Colleges.

Description: Western Baptist College (1935) has existed in Salem for the past 27 years as a Christian college offering majors in liberal arts and professional studies. The school originated in Phoenix, Arizona, as a Bible institute. In 1991 Western began offering alternatively formatted, adult degree programs (one night per week) and, building on the success of campus-based programs, expanded into modified (limited residency) distance programs in 1993. Western plans to continue expanding nontraditional, educational opportunities for its wide constituency of Christian young adults and midcareer professionals.

Western Montana College of the University of Montana

710 South Atlantic Street	Phone: (406) 683-7537
Dillon, MT 59725	Fax: (406) 683-7493

Division(s): Outreach
Web Site(s): http://www.wmc.edu
E-mail: v_lansing@wmc.edu

Class Titles: extension courses (one credit each): Behavior is Language: Strategies for Managing Disruptive Behavior, Behavior is Language: More Strategies for Managing Disruptive Behavior, Classroom Collaboration Using Internet, Learning Basic Internet Skills; 3-credit course: Young Adult Literature Via Internet.

Teaching Methods: *Computers:* Internet, electronic classroom, e-mail, LISTSERV. *Other:* None.

On-Campus Requirements: None.

Tuition and Fees: *Undergraduate:* $80/extension credit; 3-credit course: $360 resident degree student, $935 nonresident degree student, $335 junior or senior resident, $910 junior or senior nonresident, $310 lower-division resident, $886 lower-division nonresident. *Other Costs:* $65/each Behavior is Language course. *Credit by:* semester.

Financial Aid: Federal Stafford Loan, Federal Perkins Loan, Federal PLUS Loan, Federal Pell Grant, Federal Work-Study, VA, Montana resident programs.

Accreditation: Northwest Association of Schools and Colleges, National Council for the Accreditation of Teacher Education.

Description: Western Montana College of the University of Montana was founded in 1893. It is located in Dillon, Montana, a town of 5,000 situated in the beautiful Beaverhead Valley. Only 4 distance learning courses are offered at present.

Western Nevada Community College

160 Campus Way	Phone: (702) 423-5847
Fallon, NV 89406	Fax: (702) 423-8029

Division(s): Off Campus Programs
Web Site(s): http://scs.unr.edu/wncc
E-mail: scharman@fs.scs.unr.edu

Undergraduate Degree Programs:
Associate of Arts
Associate of Science
Associate of General Studies
Associate of Applied Science
    Nursing
    General Business
    Criminal Justice
    Early Childhood Education

Certificate Programs: Practical Nursing, Early Childhood Education, Criminal Justice, General Business.

Class Titles: Criminal Justice, Math, Political Science, Art Appreciation, Using Internet, History, Anthropology, English, Biology, Western Traditions, Early Childhood Education, Education.

Teaching Methods: *Computers:* Internet, real-time chat, electronic classroom, e-mail, CD-ROM. *TV:* videotape, cable program, satellite broadcasting, PBS. *Other:* videoconferencing, audioconferencing, audiotapes, fax, correspondence, independent study, individual study.

Credits Granted for: extrainstitutional learning, examination (CLEP, ACT-PEP, DANTES, GRE).

Admission Requirements: *Undergraduate:* age 15 or older and have a high school diploma or GED. *Certificate:* same as undergraduate.

On-Campus Requirements: None.

Tuition and Fees: *Undergraduate:* $40/credit. *Application Fee:* $5. *Other Costs:* $15/credit for interactive video classes, $20/class for Internet and telecourses. *Credit by:* Semester.

Financial Aid: Federal Stafford Loan, Federal PLUS Loan, Federal Pell Grant, Federal Work-Study, VA, Nevada Residency Grant.

Accreditation: Northwest Association of Schools and Colleges.

Description: Western Nevada Community College (1971) is one of 4 community college is the state of Nevada. WNCC is governed by the University and Community College System of Nevada Board of Regents. The main campus is located in Carson City, with satillite campuses in Fallon and Gardnerville/Minden. The 19,971 square mile service area is spotted with 7 other instructional centers in Yerington, Hawthorne, Lovelock, Fernley, Virginia City, South Lake Tahoe, and Dayton. The college first began its distance education efforts in 1993 when, with a grant from the Nevada Rural Hospital Project, it started it 2-year Registered Nursing program via interactive video. Since that humble beginning, WNCC now offeres more than 18 classes per semester via interactive video joining as many as 9 interactive video classrooms with college courses. In the fall of 1998, the college will begin its first efforts in Internet "online" courses and telecourse "public access" courses. In the spring 1998 semester, more than 400 student registered for distance education courses through Western Nevada Community College.

Western Oregon University

345 North Monmouth Avenue	Phone: (503) 838-8483
Monmouth, OR 97361	Fax: (503) 838-8473

Division(s): Extended and Summer Studies
Web Site(s): http://www.wou.edu/DESS
E-mail: disted@wou.edu

Undergraduate Degree Programs:
Bachelor of Arts/Bachelor of Science in Fire Services Administration

Class Titles: Writing, Psychology, Anthropology, Education.

Teaching Methods: *Computers:* Internet, real-time chat, electronic classroom, e-mail, CD-ROM, newsgroup, LISTSERV. *TV:* videotape, satellite broadcasting, PBS. *Other:* videoconferencing, fax, correspondence, independent study, individual study.

Credits Granted for: examination.

Admission Requirements: *Undergraduate:* call Admissions. *Graduate:* call Admissions.

On-Campus Requirements: None.

Tuition and Fees: *Undergraduate:* $90/credit. *Graduate:*

$120/credit. *Application Fee:* TBA. *Software:* TBA. *Other Costs:* TBA. *Credit by:* quarter.

Financial Aid: Federal Stafford Loan, Federal Perkins Loan, Federal PLUS Loan, Federal Pell Grant, Federal Work-Study, VA, Oregon resident programs.

Accreditation: Northwest Association of Schools and Colleges, National Council on Accreditation of Teacher Education, American Association of Colleges for Teacher Education, National Association of Schools of Music, Council on Rehabilitation Education, Council on Education of the Deaf, Oregon Teacher Standards and Practices Commission.

Description: With a tradition of excellence since its founding, Western Oregon University (1856) is a comprehensive liberal arts institution offering a variety of programs leading to bachelor's and master's degrees. WOU provides a comprehensive higher education experience including teaching and research activities, personal growth and cultural opportunities, and public service. Campus-based outreach and continuing education programs prepare students to make personal and professional contributions to the economy, culture, and society of Oregon, the nation, and the world. Responding to the challenges Oregonians face in career changes, life transitions, and in adapting to new technologies, WOU provides a multitude of lifelong learning and professional growth opportunities. Distance education has been integral to WOU since the mid-1970s via videotape-based learning, correspondence study, and, most recently, Internet-based courses.

Western Seminary

5511 SE Hawthorne Boulevard	Phone: (800) 547-4546
Portland, OR 97215	Fax: (503) 239-4216

Division(s): Center for Lifelong Learning
Web Site(s): http://www.westernseminary.edu
E-mail: admiss@westernseminary.edu
jlraible@westernseminary.edu

Graduate Degree Programs:
Master of Arts
Master of Christian Leadership
Master of Divinity

Doctoral Degree Programs:
Doctor of Ministry
Doctor of Missiology

Certificate Programs: Theological Studies, Biblical Studies, Church Ministries, Diploma in Theological Studies, Diploma in Ministerial Studies, Pastoral Care to Women (advanced certificate).

Class Titles: Biblical Literature, Theology, Church History, New Testament Greek.

Teaching Methods: *Computers:* Internet, real-time chat, electronic classroom, CD-ROM, e-mail. *TV:* videotape. *Other:* audiotapes, correspondence, fax, independent study, individual study.

Credits Granted for: examination.

Admission Requirements: *Graduate:* accredited bachelor's degree, 2.5 GPA for MDiv, 3.0 for MA. *Doctoral:* 3.0 GPA, accredited MDiv or equivalent.

On-Campus Requirements: Up to one-third of a degree may be earned through external study; the remainder must be completed at one of our campuses (Portland, Oregon; Seattle, Washington; or northern California sites at San Jose or Sacramento).

Tuition and Fees: *Graduate:* $300/credit. *Application Fee:* $40. *Credit by:* semester.

Financial Aid: Federal Stafford Loan, Federal Perkins Loan, Federal PLUS Loan, Federal Work-Study, VA, Oregon resident programs.

Accreditation: Northwest Association of Schools and Colleges, Association of Theological Schools.

Description: Western Seminary (1927) is a transdenominational graduate school of ministry with branch campuses in San Jose, Sacramento, and Seattle. Our mission statement accurately describes Western as "nurturing for the church godly leaders who are committed to, and competent for, the redemptive purpose of Christ throughout the world." Western is a convictionist institution and believes in the inerrancy of the Scriptures in the original autographs. The seminary has students from 30 major denominations and from many nations of the world studying for ministry. The distance education program began in 1981 and has traditionally served students with video courses. Western is now moving aggressively into online, Internet-mediated courses to increase student interaction with their instructors.

Western University of Health Sciences

309 East Second Street   Phone: (909) 409-5541
Pomona, CA 91766-1854   Fax: (909) 469-5570

Division(s): College of Graduate Nursing
Web Site(s): http://www.westernu.edu
E-mail: admissions@westera.edu

Graduate Degree Programs:
Master of Science/Family Nurse Practitioner

Teaching Methods: *Computers:* Internet, real-time chat, electronic classroom, e-mail, online discussion. *Other:* independent study.

Credits Granted for: portfolio assessment, transcripts of work experience on a case by case evaluation.

Admission Requirements: *Graduate:* Bachelor of Science in Nursing, Master's Degree in Nursing, Master of Public Health

degree, or Doctorate Degree in Nursing. *Certificate:* contact school.

On-Campus Requirements: seminar weekends 8 times/year.

Tuition and Fees: *Graduate:* $17,150/year. *Application Fee:* $60. *Other Costs:* $100 graduation fee, $1,500 textbooks (one-time fee), $450 physical exam equipment (one-time fee), approximately $1,850 computer, $550/year lodge/meals (semester weekends). *Credit by:* semester.

Financial Aid: Federal Stafford Loan, Federal Perkins Loan, Federal Work-Study, VA, California resident programs.

Accreditation: Western Association of Schools and Colleges, National League of Nursing, American Association of Colleges of Nursing, California Board of Registered Nurses (approval in process).

Description: Western University (1977) is a nonprofit, accredited, independent academic health center, whose main campus is located on 15 acres in Pomona, California. Founded as the College of Osteopathic Medicine of the Pacific, a 4-year medical school educating osteopathic physicians, the institution has expanded its mission by offering primary care-focused educational programs in the allied health professions, pharmacy, and advanced nursing. In 1996 the institution officially became a university and changed its name to Western University of Health Sciences. WesternU's distance learning Family Nurse Practitioner (FNP) program began in January 1997 at the university's Chico, California, satellite campus. WesternU recently expanded that program into the College of Graduate Nursing (CGP), to be based at the main campus and which will continue to offer the distance learning FNP program. WesternU's 3 other colleges are: the College of Osteopathic Medicine of the Pacific (COMP); the College of Allied Health Professions; and the College of Pharmacy.

Western Washington University

                              Phone: (360) 650-3650
Bellingham, WA 98225-5293   Fax: (360) 650-6858

Division(s): University Extended Programs
Web Site(s): http://www.ac.wwu.edu/~extended/ilearn.html
E-mail: ilearn@cc.wwu.edu

Class Titles: Cultural Anthropology, Religion/Culture, Sex/Gender in Culture, Joseph Campbell: Transformation of Myth Through Time, Peoples of Sub-Saharan Africa, Childhood/Culture, Canadian Studies, Ancient Greek Literature, East Asia: Political/Material Aspects, East Asia: Religious/Philosophic/Literary Aspects, Japanese Literature in Translation, Traditional Chinese Medicine, Economics (micro/macro), Money/Banking, Canadian Economic History, Foundations of Education, Elementary Classroom Management/Discipline, School-Home-Community Relationships, Expository Writing, American Literature, Greek/Roman Literature, Romantic through Modern Literature, British Literature: Romantic, American

Literature 1860–1940, Post-Colonial Literatures, Women/ Literature, Poetry Writing, English Language Studies, Literature of Ireland, Advanced Poetry Writing, Structure of English, Cultural History of English, Language/Gender, Environmental Studies, Environmental History/Ethics, American History to 1865, American History Since 1865, Western Civilization 476–1713, East Asian Civilization, Gods/Demigods: Yao to Mao, Chinese Economy: Stone Age to Mao's Age, Human Economic Action in Unconstrained Market, Human Action in Constrained Market, History of Pacific Northwest, Black History in Americas: Slavery Era, Civil War, Renaissance/Reformation, Great European Witch Craze, Women/ Men in Transition, Work/Human Services, Myth/Folklore, Sociolinguistics, Function/Algebraic Methods, Mathematical Reasoning/Applications, Calculus/Analytical Geometry, Algebra in Business/Economics, Calculus in Business/Economics, Statistics, Listening to Music, Psychology, Abnormal Psychology, Developmental Psychology, Evolution of Society, Youth/Social Justice, Advanced Topics in Family, Technology Safety Education, Vocational Education, Community/Industrial Resources, Occupational Analysis, Women Studies, Elementary French.

Teaching Methods: *Computers:* e-mail. *TV:* videotapes. *Other:* CD-ROM, audiotapes, fax, correspondence, individual study, learning contracts.

On-Campus Requirements: None for above classes. Degrees mandate 45 credits on campus.

Tuition and Fees: *Undergraduate:* $65/credit. *Other Costs:* $15/course registration fee, books/materials. *Credit by:* quarter.

Financial Aid: Not available for individual courses listed above. For on-campus students: Federal Stafford Loan, Federal Perkins Loan, Federal PLUS Loan, Federal Pell Grant, Federal Work-Study, VA, Washington resident programs.

Accreditation: Northwest Association of Schools and Colleges.

Description: Western Washington University began in 1893 by preparing teachers for rural assignments. The institution evolved into a degree-granting institution in 1933 and a university in 1977. Correspondence courses began in 1912, but WWU currently offers certificates and degrees only on campus. Some students combine WWU correspondence courses with their other on-campus programs to achieve their educational goals.

Westlawn Institute of Marine Technology

733 Summer Street	**Phone: (203) 359-0500**
Stamford, CT 06901	**Fax: (203) 359-2466**

Division(s): School of Yacht Design
Web Site(s): http://westlawn.org
E-mail: westlawn@aol.com

Certificate Programs: Yacht Design

Teaching Methods: *Computers:* Internet, e-mail *Other:* fax, independent study, individual study

Admission Requirements: *Undergraduate:* high school or equivalent, 2 years of math (algebra, trigonometry).

On-Campus Requirements: None.

Tuition and Fees: *Undergraduate:* $3,200 first term, $1,600 second term. *Software:* approximately $400.

Accreditation: Distance Education and Training Council.

Description: Westlawn (1930) is the leading yacht design correspondence course in the world. In this course, topics such as hydrostatics, resistance, hull lines, arrangements, fiberglass and aluminum construction, systems, and equipment are studied to provide the student with a sound understanding of production yacht design. Westlawn graduates and advanced students are working within the production boat industry as designers and design department heads. Other graduates are employed with independent design firms. Refer to the Westlawn Internet site for more information on the courses offered.

Westmoreland County Community College

400 Armbrust Road	**Phone: (724) 925-4000**
Youngwood, PA 15697	**(724) 836-1600**
	Fax: (724) 925-1150

Division(s): Learning Resources
Web Site(s): http://www.westmoreland.cc.pa.us
E-mail: stubbsms@wccc.westmoreland.cc.pa.us

Undergraduate Degree Programs:
Associate of Arts
Associate of Applied Science

Certificate Programs: available in a number of programs, contact school for more information.

Class Titles: Allied Health, Anthropology, Art, Banking/ Finance, Biology, Business, Computer Technology, Criminal Justice, Early Childhood Education, Earth Science, Economics, English, Environmental Science, Fire Science, Food Service, French, Geography, Geology, Health/Physical Education, History, Human Services, Humanities, Legal Assisting, Mathematics, Multimedia Technology, Philosophy, Physics, Political Science, Psychology, Real Estate, Sociology, Speech Communication.

Teaching Methods: *Computers:* Internet, real-time chat, electronic classroom, e-mail. *TV:* videotape. *Other:* videoconferencing, independent study.

Credits Granted for: experiential learning, portfolio assessment, extrainstitutional learning, examination (CLEP, ACT-PEP, DANTES, GRE).

Admission Requirements: *Undergraduate:* age 18; high school graduate or GED.

On-Campus Requirements: None.

Tuition and Fees: *Undergraduate:* $46/credit Westmoreland County residents, double for out-of-county, triple for out-of-state. *Credit by:* semester.

Financial Aid: Federal Stafford Loan, Federal Perkins Loan, Federal PLUS Loan, Federal Pell Grant, Federal Work-Study, VA, Pennsylvania state programs.

Accreditation: Middle States Association of Colleges and Schools.

Description: Westmoreland County Community College (1970) began telecourses in 1987, interactive videoconferencing in 1996, and online courses in 1998.

Whatcom Community College

237 West Kellogg Road	Phone: (360) 676-2170 x3371
Bellingham, WA 98226	Fax: (360) 676-2171

Division(s): Extended Learning
Web Site(s): http://www.whatcom.ctc.edu
E-mail: chagman@whatcom.ctc.edu

Undergraduate Degree Programs:
Associate of Arts

Class Titles: Math, Science, Social Science, Fine Arts, Humanities.

Teaching Methods: *Computers:* Internet, electronic classroom. *TV:* videotape. *Other:* learning contracts.

Credits Granted for: experiential learning, portfolio assessment, extrainstitutional learning, examination (CLEP, ACT-PEP, DANTES, GRE).

Admission Requirements: *Undergraduate:* assessment tests for math and English, high school degree or GED.

On-Campus Requirements: None.

Tuition and Fees: *Undergraduate:* $50/credit resident, $192/credit nonresident. *Other Costs:* $52/online course. *Credit by:* quarter.

Financial Aid: Federal Stafford Loan, Federal Perkins Loan, Federal PLUS Loan, Federal Pell Grant, Federal Work-Study, VA, Washington resident programs.

Accreditation: Northwest Association of Schools and Colleges.

Description: Whatcom Community College (1967) is a comprehensive community college, part of the Washington Community and Technical College System. In fall of 1998 WCC enrolled 6,000 students, with 200 in various distance education classes. WCC is a charter member of Washington Online, a consortium of Washington Community Colleges which offers an AA degree via the Internet. In the fall of 1998

WAOL offered 9 classes, 2 of which were offered by Whatcom faculty. 106 students enrolled for WAOL classes through WCC.

Wilfrid Laurier University

75 University Avenue W	Phone: (519) 884-1970
Waterloo, Ontario, Canada N2L 3C5	Fax: (519) 884-0181

Division(s): Continuing Education
Web Site(s): http://www.wlu.ca/~wwwconte/
E-mail: distance@mach1.wlu.ca

Undergraduate Degree Programs:
Sociology
Geography

Class Titles: general fields of Anthropology, Business, Canadian Studies, Economics, English, Geography, Geology, German, History, Philosophy, Political Science, Psychology, Religion/Culture, Science, Social Welfare, Sociology. Web site—http://www.wlu.ca/~wwwconte/.

Teaching Methods: *Computers:* Internet, real-time chat, e-mail, LISTSERV. *TV:* videotape. *Other:* audiotapes, fax, correspondence, individual study.

Admission Requirements: *Undergraduate:* age 21, worked for 2 years. *Certificate:* age 21, worked for 2 years.

On-Campus Requirements: None.

Tuition and Fees: *Undergraduate:* $796/credit. *Application Fee:* $30. *Other Costs:* $24–32 (depending on course) Administrative fee for course material. *Credit by:* Term.

Financial Aid: OSAP and/or bursaries may be available.

Accreditation: Association of Universities and Colleges of Canada.

Description: Wilfrid Laurier University (1911) opened its doors as the Evangelical Lutheran Seminary of Canada for pretheological education. Facilities soon moved to Waterloo College School and added courses leading to senior matriculation. By 1924, WCS offered courses in postsecondary education in a 4-year program, later offering honors degree programs in the arts. In 1973 Waterloo became Wilfrid Laurier University, one of Ontario's provincially assisted universities, after Royal Assent was given by the Lieutenant Governor.

Winthrop University

Thurmond Building	Phone: (803) 323-2409
Rock Hill, SC 29733	Fax: (803) 323-2539

Division(s): College of Business Administration
Web Site(s): http://www.cba.winthrop.edu/programs/gradprog.htm
E-mail: hagerp@mail.winthrop.edu

Graduate Degree Programs:
Master of Business Administration
Master of Business Administration, Accounting

Teaching Methods: *Computers:* Internet, real-time chat, electronic classroom, e-mail, LISTSERV. *TV:* videotape, satellite broadcasting. *Other:* videoconferencing, audiotapes, fax, correspondence, independent study.

Credits Granted for: examination (CLEP).

Admission Requirements: *Graduate:* undergraduate degree and Graduate Management Admission Test.

On-Campus Requirements: No, however, will transfer only 12 hours from another institution.

Tuition and Fees: *Graduate:* $164/credit in-state, $294/credit out-of-state. *Application Fee:* $35. *Other Costs:* Books. *Credit by:* semester.

Financial Aid: Federal Stafford Loan, Federal Perkins Loan, Federal PLUS Loan, Federal Pell Grant, Federal Work-Study, VA, South Carolina resident programs.

Accreditation: American Assembly of Collegiate Schools of Business.

Description: Winthrop University (1886) is a comprehensive teaching university committed to being a model of excellence in higher education. Winthrop's distinctive mission is to offer challenging academic programs of national caliber to its 5,500 high-achieving, culturally diverse, socially responsible students in a contemporary physical environment of exceptional beauty and historic character only 20 miles south of Charlotte. In keeping with a technology emphasis, Winthrop began distance education in 1994. With seating for 40, the school's state-of-the-art distance learning facility is equipped for fully interactive, 2-way video and audio (utilizing T1 transmission), and more services are in development. It delivers MBA courses to Coastal Carolina University and dual-credit courses to 3 local high schools.

Wisconsin Indianhead Technical College

505 Pine Ridge Drive	Phone: (715) 468-2815
Shell Lake, WI 54871	Fax: (715) 468-2819

Division(s): Instructional Services and Continuing Education
Web Site(s): http://witc.tec.wi.us
E-mail: bczyscon@witc.tec.wi.us
sgilbert@witc.tec.wi.us
sgingras@witc.tec.wi.us
enowak@witc.tec.wi.us

Class Titles: many in areas of Computers, Child Care, Medical Transcription, Business, Accounting, Finance.

Teaching Methods: *Computers:* Internet, electronic classroom, e-mail, CD-ROM, LISTSERV. *TV:* videotape. *Other:*

audiotapes, fax, correspondence, independent study, individual study.

Credits Granted for: experiential learning, portfolio assessment, extrainstitutional learning.

Admission Requirements: *Undergraduate:* ASSET or COMPASS assessment, counselor interview, in-state/out-of-state tuition, ability to benefit. *Certificate:* same as undergraduate.

On-Campus Requirements: 25 credits.

Tuition and Fees: *Undergraduate:* $57/credit in-state, $441/credit out-of-state. *Application Fee:* $25. *Credit by:* semester and open-entry/open-exit.

Financial Aid: Federal Stafford Loan, Federal Perkins Loan, Federal PLUS Loan, Federal Pell Grant, Federal Work-Study, VA, Wisconsin resident programs.

Accreditation: North Central Association of Colleges and Schools.

Description: Wisconsin Indianhead Technical College (1912) is a public postsecondary educational institution that serves the communities of the college district and their residents by providing comprehensive educational programming and support services for meaningful career preparation and personal effectiveness. As a dynamic organization dedicated to lifelong learning, WITC seeks to improve the quality of life for individuals and enhance the economic potential of their communities. One of 16 districts in the Wisconsin Technical College System, WITC began serving northwest Wisconsin 85 years ago in Superior, and now has campuses in Ashland (since 1920), New Richmond (since 1967), and Rice Lake (since 1941). The administrative office is located in Shell Lake (since 1973).

Worcester Polytechnic Institute

100 Institute Road	Phone: (508) 831-5220
Worcester, MA 01609-2280	Fax: (508) 831-5881

Division(s): Advanced Distance Learning Network
Web Site(s): http://www.wpi.edu/Academics/ADLN
E-mail: adln@wpi.edu

Graduate Degree Programs:
Civil and Environmental Engineering
Fire Protection Engineering
Management

Certificate Programs: customized graduate certificates in Management, Fire Protection Engineering, Civil and Environmental Engineering.

Class Titles: All classes offered through ADLN may be taken individually. Subject areas include: Accounting, Business Administration/Management, Business Communications, Finance, International Business, Management Information

Systems, Marketing, Organizational Behavior Studies, Civil Engineering, Engineering/Industrial Management, Environmental Engineering, Industrial Engineering, Fire Protection Engineering, Business Law.

Teaching Methods: *Computers:* World Wide Web, Internet, real-time chat, electronic classroom, e-mail, CD-ROM, newsgroup, LISTSERV. *TV:* videotape. *Other:* videoconferencing, fax, correspondence, independent study, individual study.

Credits Granted for: some courses have waiver exams.

Admission Requirements: *Graduate:* GRE optional (GMAT for Management), TOEFL for international students, college transcripts, essay or personal statement, letters of recommendation. *Certificate:* all graduate certificate credits earned from WPI, GRE optional (GMAT for Management), TOEFL for international students, college transcripts, essay or personal statement, letters of recommendation.

On-Campus Requirements: None.

Tuition and Fees: *Graduate:* $636/credit for FY99. *Application Fee:* $50. *Other Costs:* possible shipping fees for students outside continental U.S. *Credit by:* semester.

Financial Aid: Loans possible for half- or full-time students.

Accreditation: New England Association of Schools and Colleges.

Description: Worcester Polytechnic Institute, the nation's third-oldest private university of engineering, science, and management, has been a pioneer in technological higher education since its founding in 1865. Its mission is to educate talented men and women for careers of professional practice, civic contribution, and leadership. WPI awarded its first advanced degree in 1893. Since then, the university has earned a reputation for excellence in technological education, for practical application to marketplace challenges, and for a faculty of renowned academicians and industry experts who are practitioners in their fields. Today, most departments offer master's and doctoral programs and support leading-edge research in a broad range of fields. In 1979 WPI's commitment to lifelong learning prompted the creation of the Advanced Distance Learning Network. ADLN programs empower working professionals to grow in their chosen fields without making repeated trips to the WPI campus in Worcester, Massachusetts.

York Technical College

452 South Anderson Road	Phone: (803) 981-7044
Rock Hill, SC 29730	Fax: (803) 981-7193

Division(s): Distance Learning
Web Site(s): http://www.yorktech.com
E-mail: mcbride@york.tec.sc.us

Certificate Programs: Entrepreneurial, Accounting Clerk.

Class Titles: Accounting, History, Sociology, Psychology, English, Math, Business, Economics, Office Systems.

Teaching Methods: *Computers:* Internet, real-time chat, electronic classroom, e-mail, CD-ROM. *TV:* videotape, cable program, live 2-way interactive ATM, T1 classes. *Other:* independent study, textbased telecourses.

Credits Granted for: experiential learning, examination (CLEP).

Admission Requirements: *Undergraduate:* age 18, admissions application, $10 nonreturnable fee, admissions test or placement test, interview with admissions counselor, admission into a program. *Certificate:* same as undergraduate.

On-Campus Requirements: 25% of the credit hours need to be completed with York Technical College classes.

Tuition and Fees: *Undergraduate:* $42/credit in-county, $51/credit out-of-county, $128/credit out-of-state. *Application Fee:* $10. *Credit by:* semester.

Financial Aid: Federal Stafford Loan, Federal Perkins Loan, Federal PLUS Loan, Federal Pell Grant, Federal Work-Study, VA, South Carolina resident programs.

Accreditation: Southern Association of Colleges and Schools.

Description: York Technical College (1964) opened as a Technical Education Center with 60 students enrolled in 7 programs housed in one building. The college's enrollment has grown in the past 3 decades to 3,600 credit-students in 50 programs. In 1974 York County Technical Education Center became York Technical College.

York University, Atkinson College

4700 Keele Street	Phone: (416) 736-5831
Toronto, ON, Canada M3J 1P3	Fax: (416) 736-5439

Division(s): Centre for Distance Education
Web Site(s): http://www.atkinson.yorku.ca/cde/
E-mail: amalias@yorku.ca

Undergraduate Degree Programs:
Bachelor of Administrative Studies
Bachelor of Arts
Bachelor of Science

Class Titles: Administrative Studies, Economics, English, Geography, History, Humanities, Music, Natural Science, Nursing, Philosophy, Political Science, Psychology, Social Science, Sociology, Urban Studies, Women's Studies.

Teaching Methods: *Computers:* Internet, real-time chat, electronic classroom, e-mail, CD-ROM, newsgroup, LISTSERV, Real Audio. *TV:* videotape. *Other:* audiotapes, fax, correspondence.

Admission Requirements: *Undergraduate:* if over 21, can be admitted as a "mature student" without high school diploma;

if under 21, need 6 Ontario Academic Credits or equivalent. Must have C average for any postsecondary experience.

On-Campus Requirements: Final exams are sometimes written on-campus or at off-campus locations.

Tuition and Fees: *Undergraduate:* Canadian $137/credit (half course 3 credits–$410, full course 6 credits–$823). *Application Fee:* $60. *Software:* variable. *Credit by:* semester.

Financial Aid: Ontario Student Assistance Program

Accreditation: Association of Universities and Colleges of Canada, International Association of Universities, Association of Commonwealth Universities.

Description: York University, Atkinson College (1962) is the part-time studies faculty of York University, whose mission is to reach out and improve access to university study for those with distance, time, and commitment demands. The year-round college provides high-quality, university-level education from full-time, devoted faculty. Atkinson's unique philosophy emphasizes the needs of the part-time, adult student by recognizing that contemporary society requires constant learning with flexible choices, and therefore embraces the challenge of providing lifelong learning opportunities. Students can choose from a wide range of degree and certificate programs in the liberal arts, fine arts, sciences, and in professional studies. In 1994 the college enhanced its learning opportunities to a wider range of students by offering distance learning courses, with Internet courses added in 1996. Atkinson's Centre for Distance Education continues to expand the offerings available by both correspondence and the Internet. We are proud of our satisfied students and their successes.

Yuba College

2088 North Beale Road
Marysville, CA 95901

Phone: (530) 741-6754
Fax: (530) 741-6824

Division(s): Learning Resources
Web Site(s): http://yubalib.yuba.cc.ca.us/disedu.htm
E-mail: jobryan@mail2.yuba.cc.ca.us
Undergraduate Degree Programs:

Associate of Arts
Transfer Program

Certificate Programs: In development.

Teaching Methods: *TV:* videotape, cable program, satellite broadcasting, PBS, ITFS. *Other:* videoconferencing, correspondence, independent study, individual study.

Admission Requirements: *Undergraduate:* call for details.

On-Campus Requirements: None.

Tuition and Fees: *Undergraduate:* $12/credit resident, $125/credit nonresident. *Other Costs:* $4 student services. *Credit by:* semester.

Financial Aid: Federal Stafford Loan, Federal Pell Grant, Federal Work-Study, VA, California resident programs.

Accreditation: Western Association of Schools and Colleges.

Description: Yuba College is an institution of higher education that prepares students to meet the intellectual, occupational, and technological challenges of a complex world. Since 1927 the primary mission of Yuba College has been to provide rigorous, high-quality degree and certificate curricula in lower division arts and sciences and in vocational and occupational fields. Yuba has offered distance education courses since 1975 and today delivers 100 hours/week of degree-bound and certificate courses.

Index by State and Province

Index by On-Campus Requirements

Some degree and certificate programs require that students take certain classes or seminars in a traditional classroom setting either on the university's campus or in an off-campus location. If you live a long distance from the campus, this on-campus time requirement becomes a very important part of your decision-making process. The amount of time required on campus varies by school, program, and class. For example, some schools require time on campus for certain types of degree programs and not for others. Attendance might be necessary only for examinations or orientations. Always check with the individual college or university about its on-campus requirements, and remember that attendance requirements are sometimes negotiable.

The following colleges and universities have some type of on-campus requirement:

Index by Fields of Study
Undergraduate Degree Programs

(A) = Associate Degree
(B) = Bachelor's Degree

New College of California (B), 294
North Iowa Area Community College (A), 303
Northwest Iowa Community College (A), 307
Ohio University (A), 313
Open Learning Agency (B), 315
Owens Community College (A), 319
Palomar Community College (A), 321
Pasadena City College (A), 323
Penn State University (A), 323
Richland Community College (A), 338
Rio Salado College (A), 339
San Diego City College (A), 348
San Juan College (A), 351
Sandhills Community College (A), 351
Sauk Valley Community College (A), 352
Schoolcraft College (A), 353
Seattle Central Community College (A), 354
Sierra Community College (A), 357
Simpson College (B), 358
Skagit Valley College (Transfer) (A), 359
Solano Community College (A), 360
South Mountain Community College (A), 360
Southwestern Michigan College (A), 370
Spokane Falls Community College (A), 371
St. Petersburg Junior College (A), 373
Sussex County Community College (A), 380
Thomas Edison State College (A)(B), 389
Union Institute (B), 397
University of Alaska, Fairbanks (A), 402
University of Alaska Southeast, Sitka Campus (A), 403
University of Guelph (B), 412
University of Hawaii System (A), 412
University of Manitoba (B), 420
University of Waterloo (B), 446
University of Winnipeg (B), 442
Upper Iowa University (A), 453
Walla Walla Community College (A), 458
Wayne County Community College (A), 460
West Valley College (A), 462
Western Nevada Community College (A), 464
Westmoreland County Community College (A), 467
Whatcom Community College (A), 468
York University, Atkinson College (B), 470
Yuba College (transfer) (A), 471

AUDIOVISUAL COMMUNICATIONS TECHNOLOGY

Inter-American University of Puerto Rico (A), 232

AUTOMOTIVE STUDIES

Community College of Philadelphia (A), 163
Mount Wachusett Community College (A), 288
Northwestern College, Lima (A), 308
Southern West Virginia Community and Technical College (A), 367

AVIATION

Henderson State University (B), 219

Business Administration Major
Embry-Riddle Aeronautical University (A), 190

Flight Technology Major
Indiana College Network (A), 228

BEHAVIORAL SCIENCES

Concordia University, Austin (B), 166
Indiana College Network (A), 228
Linfield College (B), 260
UNET: University of Maine System Network for Education and Technology Services (UMFL, UMM, UMPI) (B), 397
University of Maine, Machias (B), 419

BIOLOGY

Centralia College (A), 138
Henderson State University (B), 219
Inter-American University of Puerto Rico (B), 232

Microbiology, Public Health, and Environmental Majors
Inter-American University of Puerto Rico (B), 232

BOTANY

Centralia College (A), 138

BROADCASTING

Centralia College (A), 138
Mount Wachusett Community College (A), 288

BUSINESS

Andrew Jackson University (B), 100
Baker University (A), 110
Blackfeet Community College (B), 116
Bucks County Community College (A), 122
California College for Health Sciences (A)(B), 125
Casper College (A), 133
Champlain College (B), 141
Clarkson College (B), 148
Community College of Philadelphia (A), 163
Concordia-New York (B), 166
Concordia University, Austin (B), 166
Eastern Oregon University (B), 186
Edison Community College, Piqua (A), 188
Greenville Technical College (A), 215
Lafayette College (A), 248
Lake Tahoe Community College (A), 250
Lakeland Community College (A), 251
Liberty University (B), 258
Loyola College, Maryland (B), 263
Madonna University (B), 266
Mott Community College (A), 287
New Hampshire College (pending) (B), 295
North Central Technical College (A), 300
Northwest Missouri State University (B), 307
Oklahoma City University (B), 314
Otero Junior College (A), 318
Pitt Community College (B), 327
Presentation College (B), 330
Pueblo Community College (CCC Online) (A), 331
Red Rocks Community College (A), 334
Regents College (A)(B), 336
Saint Joseph's College (B), 345
Saint Mary-of-the-Woods College (A), 346
Salve Regina University (B), 347
Southeast Missouri State University (B), 361
Southern Oregon University (degree completion) (Medford, Grants Pass) (B), 365
Southern West Virginia Community and Technical College (A), 367
Southwestern Assemblies of God University (A)(B), 370
Trinidad State Junior College (A), 391
University of Maine, Machias (B), 419
University of Minnesota (B), 425
University of Windsor (B), 447
Western Nevada Community College (A), 464

Communication Major
JEC College Connection (B), 238
Lewis-Clark State College (B), 257

Education Major
East Carolina University (B), 183

Management Major
Anne Arundel Community College (A), 102
Columbus State Community College (A), 162
Fort Peck Community College (B), 198

Marylhurst University (B), 269
Newman University (B), 299
Prince George's Community College (A), 331
Roger Williams University (B), 341
University of Maine, Machias (B), 419

Project Management Major
University of Phoenix Online Campus (B), 436

Small Business Major
Southern West Virginia Community and Technical College (A), 367

Technology Major
Barstow College (A), 111

BUSINESS ADMINISTRATION

Anne Arundel Community College (transfer) (A), 102
Arkansas State University (B), 104
Baker College (A)(B), 109
Baker University (B), 110
Barstow College (June 2029) (A), 111
Brookdale Community College (A), 121
Caldwell College (B), 119
California National University for Advanced Studies (B), 126
Central Washington University (B), 137
Centralia College (A), 138
City University (B), 145
Eastern New Mexico University (completion program) (B), 186
Fitchburg State College (B), 194
Franklin University (completion degree) (B), 200
Graceland College (B), 211
Henderson State University (B), 219
Indiana College Network (A), 228
Inter-American University of Puerto Rico (A), 232
Ivy Tech State College (B), 235
J. Sargeant Reynolds Community College (A), 236
JEC College Connection (B), 238
Kirtland Community College (transfer) (A), 246
Lake Superior State University (B), 249
Lehigh Carbon Community College (A), 255
Marist College (B), 268
Marshall University (B), 268
Mississippi State University (B), 280
Mount St. Vincent University (B), 288
Mount Wachusett Community College (A), 288
New Mexico State University, Alamogordo (B), 296
New York Institute of Technology (B), 298
North Iowa Area Community College (B), 303
Northern Virginia Community College (A), 306
Northwestern College, Lima (A), 308
Northwood University (B), 311
Open Learning Agency (B), 315
Oral Roberts University (B), 316
Penn State University (A), 323
Rogers State University (A), 342
Saint Mary-of-the-Woods College (B), 346
Schoolcraft College (B), 353
Sinclair Community College (A), 358
Southern Illinois University, Edwardsville (B), 363
Southwestern Assemblies of God University (A)(B), 370
Stephens College (B), 377
Strayer University (A)(B), 379
Texas Tech University (B), 387
Thomas Edison State College (B), 389
Troy State University (A), 392
Troy State University, Montgomery (A), 393
UNET: University of Maine System Network for Education and Technology Services (UMA) (A)(B), 397
University of Alaska Southeast, Juneau Campus (A), 403

University of Phoenix Online Campus (B), 436
Utah State University (B), 453
Washington State University (selected sites) (B), 459
West Virginia Northern Community College (transfer) (A), 463
York University, Atkinson College (B), 470

Accounting Major
The College of West Virginia (A)(B), 156
Inter-American University of Puerto Rico (B), 232

Business Administration Minor
California State University, Chico, 127

Computer Management Information Systems Major
Inter-American University of Puerto Rico (B), 232

Finance Major
Indiana Institute of Technology (A)(B), 229

Financial Planning Major
Marywood University (B), 269

General Business
The College of West Virginia (A)(B), 156
New Mexico State University (B), 296
University of Alaska Southeast, Juneau Campus (B), 403

Health Administration Major
Alaska Pacific University (B), 96
Athabasca University (B), 106

Human Resources Major
Indiana Institute of Technology (B), 229
Inter-American University of Puerto Rico (B), 232

Industrial Relations Major
Athabasca University (B), 106

Management Major
Adelphi University (pending New York state approval) (B), 95
Athabasca University (B), 106
The College of West Virginia (A)(B), 156
Indiana College Network (A), 228
Indiana Institute of Technology (A)(B), 229
Inter-American University of Puerto Rico (B), 232
Marywood University (B), 269
University of Alaska Southeast, Juneau Campus (B), 403
University of North Dakota (B), 434

Managerial Economics Major
Inter-American University of Puerto Rico (B), 232

Marketing Major
Indiana Institute of Technology (B), 229
Inter-American University of Puerto Rico (B), 232
Marywood University (B), 269

Office Management Major
The College of West Virginia (A)(B), 156
Lake Tahoe Community College (A), 250

Organization Major
Athabasca University (B), 106

Public Administration Major
Athabasca University (B), 106
Open Learning Agency (B), 315

Restaurant Management Major
Indiana College Network (A), 228

CANADIAN STUDIES
Athabasca University (B), 106

CERTIFICATES
Achievement
Metropolitan Community College, 274
Business
Technical College of the Lowcountry, 383

Criminal Justice
Technical College of the Lowcountry, 383
Environmental Technology
Technical College of the Lowcountry, 383
Medical Records Coder (MTC)
Technical College of the Lowcountry, 383
Office System Technology
Technical College of the Lowcountry, 383
Paralegal (Legal Assistant)
Technical College of the Lowcountry, 383
Pharmacy Technician (MTC)
Technical College of the Lowcountry, 383
Technical
Ivy Tech State College, Central Indiana, 236
Unspecified
University of Missouri, 428

CHEMICAL
Engineering Major
University of North Dakota (B), 434
Technology Major
Community College of Philadelphia (A), 163

CHEMISTRY
Centralia College (A), 138
Henderson State University (B), 219
Southern West Virginia Community and Technical College (A), 367

CHILD CARE
Concordia University, St. Paul (B), 167
Henderson State University (A), 219
Mount Wachusett Community College (A), 288
Troy State University, Montgomery (A), 393
University of Alaska, Fairbanks (A), 402

CHIROPRACTIC
Centralia College (pre-chiropractic) (A), 138

CHURCH BUSINESS STUDIES
Home Study International (B), 224
Southwestern Assemblies of God University (A)(B), 370

CHURCH MINISTRY
North Central Bible College (A)(B), 300
North Central University (B), 302
Oral Roberts University (B), 316
Southwestern Assemblies of God University (A)(B), 370
Children's Major
Southwestern Assemblies of God University (A)(B), 370
Intercultural Major
Northwestern College, St. Paul (A), 309
Pastoral Major
Mid-America Bible College (B), 276
Southwestern Assemblies of God University (A)(B), 370
Urban Major
Southwestern Assemblies of God University (A)(B), 370
Youth Major
Mid-America Bible College (B), 276

CHURCH MUSIC
Conducting Major
Concordia University, Austin (B), 166

Ministry Major
Southwestern Assemblies of God University (A)(B), 370
Organ Major
Concordia University, Austin (B), 166

CINEMA STUDIES
Burlington College (B), 123

CIVIL ENGINEERING
Centralia College (A), 138

COMMERCE
Athabasca University (B), 106
University of Windsor (university graduates also) (B), 447

COMMUNICATION
Andrew Jackson University (B), 100
Henderson State University (B), 219
University of Maryland University College (B), 421
Disorders Major
Eastern New Mexico University (completion program) (B), 186
Organizational Major
Marist College (B), 268
Marylhurst University (B), 269

COMMUNICATIONS
Athabasca University (B), 106
Caldwell College (B), 119
California State University, Stanislaus (B), 129
Concordia University, Austin (B), 166
Indiana College Network (A), 228
Marylhurst University (B), 269
Oakland University (B), 312
Southern West Virginia Community and Technical College (A), 367
University of Southern Indiana (A), 440
Western Baptist College (B), 463
Technology Major
Inter-American University of Puerto Rico (B), 232

COMMUNITY STUDIES
Native American Educational Services College (A), 293
University College of Cape Breton (B), 399
University of Alaska, Fairbanks (A), 402
University of Calgary (rehabilitation) (B), 406

COMPUTER APPLICATIONS
Business Major
Community College of Philadelphia (A), 163
Inter-American University of Puerto Rico (B), 232
Northwestern College, Lima (A), 308
Scientific Major
Inter-American University of Puerto Rico (B), 232

COMPUTER ENGINEERING
Grantham College of Engineering (A), 213

COMPUTER OCCUPATIONS TECHNOLOGY
Mott Community College (A), 287

COMPUTER SCIENCE
Barstow College (A), 111
California National University for Advanced Studies (B), 126
California State University, Chico (for employees of participating companies) (B), 127

Community College of Philadelphia (A), 163
Franklin University (B), 200
Grantham College of Engineering (A), 213
Henderson State University (business or math) (B), 219
Lehigh Carbon Community College (A), 255
Mercy College (B), 274
Nova Southeastern University (campus-based) (B), 311
Rogers State University (A), 342
Southern West Virginia Community and Technical College (A), 367
University of Hawaii System (B), 412
Utah State University (B), 453

COMPUTER SOFTWARE
Capitol College (B), 131

Internet Applications Major
Capitol College (B), 131

Programming Major
Champlain College (B), 141
Community College of Philadelphia (A), 163

COMPUTER SUPPORT
Inter-American University of Puerto Rico (A), 232
University of Alaska, Fairbanks (A), 402
University of Alaska Southeast, Sitka Campus (A), 403

COMPUTING
Athabasca University (B), 106
Capitol College (B), 131
Lake Tahoe Community College (A), 250
University of Maine, Machias (B), 419

CONSTRUCTION TECHNOLOGY
Community College of Philadelphia (A), 163

CONSUMER SCIENCES
Henderson State University (B), 219

COUNSELING
Christian Major
Oral Roberts University (B), 316

Pastoral Major
Southwestern Assemblies of God University (A)(B), 370

Psychology Major
Southwestern Assemblies of God University (A)(B), 370

CRIMINAL JUSTICE
Andrew Jackson University (B), 100
Athabasca University (B), 106
Bemidji State University (A)(B), 114
Caldwell College (B), 119
Christopher Newport University (B), 143
Graceland College (B), 211
Greenville Technical College (A), 215
JEC College Connection (B), 238
Kirtland Community College (transfer) (A), 246
Lake Superior State University (B), 249
Lake Tahoe Community College (A), 250
Lehigh Carbon Community College (A), 255
Loyola University, New Orleans (B), 263
Mount Wachusett Community College (A), 288
New York Institute of Technology (B), 298
Roger Williams University (B), 341
Saint Joseph's College (B), 345
Southeast Missouri State University (B), 361
Southern West Virginia Community and Technical

College (A), 367
University of Central Oklahoma (B), 409
Washington State University (B), 459
Western Nevada Community College (A), 464

CRIMINOLOGY
Arkansas State University (B), 104

CULINARY ARTS
Greenville Technical College (A), 215

Chef Major
Community College of Philadelphia (A), 163

Chef Apprenticeship Major
Community College of Philadelphia (A), 163

CULTURE, SCIENCE AND TECHNOLOGY
Community College of Philadelphia (A), 163

DENTISTRY
Centralia College (pre-dentistry) (A), 138
Community College of Philadelphia (hygiene) (A), 163

DESIGN
Open Learning Agency (B), 315

DIESEL EQUIPMENT TECHNOLOGY
Centralia College (A), 138

DIETETIC STUDIES
Community College of Philadelphia (A), 163
Kansas State University (B), 243
Penn State University (A), 323

DIPLOMAS
Banking Management
Leicester University, 256

Business
Technical College of the Lowcountry, 383

Computer Science
Laval University, 254

Criminal Justice
Technical College of the Lowcountry, 383

Environmental Technology
Technical College of the Lowcountry, 383

Finance Management
Leicester University, 256

Food Science and Quality Food Merchandising
Laval University, 254

Horticulture and Landscape Management
Laval University, 254

Human Resource Management
Leicester University, 256

Medical Records Coder (MTC)
Technical College of the Lowcountry, 383

Ministry
ICI University, 226

Office System Technology
Technical College of the Lowcountry, 383

Paralegal (Legal Assistant)
Technical College of the Lowcountry, 383

Personal Financial Planning
Laval University, 254

Pharmacy Technician (MTC)
Technical College of the Lowcountry, 383

Technical
Fox Valley Technical College, 199

Theological Studies
Central Baptist Theological Seminary, 134
ICI University, 226

Training and Development
Leicester University, 256

DRAFTING AND DESIGN TECHNOLOGY
Community College of Philadelphia (A), 163
Indiana College Network (CAD) (A), 228
Ivy Tech State College (B), 235
Mount Wachusett Community College (A), 288
Southern West Virginia Community and Technical College (A), 367
University of Houston (B), 413

DRAMATIC ARTS
Centralia College (A), 138

EARTH SCIENCES
Centralia College (A), 138
University of Houston (B), 413

ECONOMICS
Eastern Oregon University (B), 186
Marylhurst University (B), 269
Strayer University (A)(B), 379

EDUCATION
Central Washington University (B), 137
Community College of Philadelphia (A), 163
Concordia-New York (B), 166
Goddard College (B), 206
Great Basin College (B), 214
Lehigh Carbon Community College (A), 255
New River Community College (A), 297
University of Winnipeg (B), 442

Adult Major
Université de Moncton (B), 398

Christian Major
Mid-America Bible College (B), 276
North Central University (A)(B), 302
Oral Roberts University (elementary) (B), 316
Southwestern Assemblies of God University (A)(B), 370

Early Childhood Major
California College for Health Sciences (A), 125
Centralia College (A), 138
Community College of Philadelphia (A), 163
Concordia University, Austin (B), 166
Lake Tahoe Community College (A), 250
Saint Mary-of-the-Woods College (A)(B), 346
Stephens College (B), 377
University of Alaska Southeast, Sitka Campus (A), 403
Western Nevada Community College (A), 464

Elementary Major
Arkansas State University (B), 104
Blackfeet Community College (B), 116
Concordia University, Austin (B), 166
Fort Peck Community College (B), 198
Graceland College (B), 211
Henderson State University (B), 219
Saint Mary-of-the-Woods College (B), 346
Southeast Missouri State University (B), 361
Southern West Virginia Community and Technical College (A), 367
Southwestern Assemblies of God University (A)(B), 370
Stephens College (B), 377
University of Hawaii System (B), 412

Religious Major
Home Study International (B), 224
ICI University (B), 226

Physical Education Major
Centralia College (A), 138
Eastern Oregon University (B), 186
Henderson State University (B), 219
Lake Tahoe Community College (plus dance) (A), 250

Secondary Major
Concordia University, Austin (B), 166
Saint Mary-of-the-Woods College (B), 346
Southwestern Assemblies of God University (A)(B), 370
University of Hawaii System (B), 412

Special Major
Saint Mary-of-the-Woods College (B), 346

Vocational Business Major
Henderson State University (B), 219

Youth Development Major
Concordia University, St. Paul (B), 167

ELECTRICAL ENGINEERING
Capitol College (B), 131
Inter-American University of Puerto Rico (B), 232
Iowa State University (B), 234
Rochester Institute of Technology (B), 340
Southern Illinois University, Carbondale (B), 364
Southern West Virginia Community and Technical College (A), 367
University of North Dakota (B), 434

ELECTRONICS
Computer Major
Capitol College (B), 131

Technology Major
Central Missouri State University (B), 136
Centralia College (A), 138
Indiana College Network (B), 228
Mount Wachusett Community College (A), 288

ELECTRONICS ENGINEERING TECHNOLOGY
Cleveland Institute of Electronics (A)(B), 149
Community College of Philadelphia (A), 163
Grantham College of Engineering (A), 213

Biomedical Major
Community College of Philadelphia (A), 163

Digital Communications Major
Community College of Philadelphia (A), 163

EMERGENCY STUDIES
Management Major
Rochester Institute of Technology (B), 340

Medical Services Major
American College of Prehospital Medicine (A)(B), 97
Lima Technical College (A), 259

ENGINEERING
California National University for Advanced Studies (B), 126
Centralia College (A), 138
College of DuPage (A), 153
Community College of Philadelphia (A), 163
Greenville Technical College (A), 215
Lehigh Carbon Community College (A), 255
Northern Virginia Community College (A), 306
Richland Community College (A), 338
The University of North Carolina at Charlotte (B), 433

Management Major
Lake Superior State University (B), 249

ENGLISH
Athabasca University (B), 106
Caldwell College (B), 119
Concordia University, Austin (B), 166
Henderson State University (B), 219
Lake Tahoe Community College (A), 250
Saint Mary-of-the-Woods College (B), 346
Stephens College (B), 377
Troy State University, Montgomery (B), 393
University of Houston (B), 413
University of Maryland University College (B), 421

English Minor
Queen's University, 333

Literature Major
Burlington College (B), 122
Centralia College (A), 138

Rhetoric Major
Stephens College (B), 377

Writing Major
Burlington College (B), 122
Centralia College (A), 138

ENVIRONMENTAL STUDIES
Clinton, Muscatine and Scott Community Colleges (A), 150
The College of West Virginia (A), 156
Community College of Philadelphia (A), 163
Concordia University, Austin (B), 166
Marylhurst University (B), 269
Rochester Institute of Technology (B), 340
Southern West Virginia Community and Technical College (A), 367
University College of Cape Breton (post-diploma) (B), 399
University of Alaska Southeast, Sitka Campus (A), 403
University of Waterloo (B), 446

FAMILY STUDIES
Henderson State University (B), 219
Penn State University (A), 323

FINANCE
Community College of Philadelphia (A), 163
Waukesha County Technical College (A), 459

FINE ARTS
Beaver College (B), 112
Burlington College (B), 122
Carl Sandburg College (A), 132
Centralia College (A), 138
Corcoron School of Art (B), 168
Kirtland Community College (transfer) (A), 246
Lake Tahoe Community College (A), 250
Lehigh Carbon Community College (A), 255
Open Learning Agency (B), 315

FIRE SCIENCE AND PREVENTION
Cogswell Polytechnical College (B), 152
Community College of Philadelphia (A), 163
Lake Tahoe Community College (A), 250
Mount Wachusett Community College (A), 288
Oklahoma State University, Oklahoma City (A), 315
University of Cincinnati (B), 409
University of Maryland University College (B), 421

FIRE SERVICES ADMINISTRATION
Eastern Oregon University (B), 186
Western Oregon University (B), 465

FOREIGN LANGUAGES
Centralia College (A), 138

FORESTRY TECHNOLOGY
Centralia College (A), 138

FRENCH
Athabasca University (B), 106

Translation Major
College Universitaire de Saint-Boniface (B), 157

GENERAL STUDIES
Anne Arundel Community College (transfer) (A), 102
Athabasca University (B), 106
Carl Sandburg College (A), 132
Citrus Community College (A), 144
City University (A)(B), 145
Clinton, Muscatine and Scott Community Colleges (A), 150
Coconino Community College (A), 151
College for Lifelong Learning (A)(B), 153
College of DuPage (A), 153
The College of West Virginia (A), 156
Columbia Basin College (A), 159
Community College of Southern Nevada (A), 164
Edison Community College, Ft. Myers (B), 187
Emporia State University (B), 191
Fitchburg State College (B), 194
Grays Harbor College (A), 214
Indiana College Network (A)(B), 228
Indiana University (A)(B), 229
Kansas City, Kansas Community College (A), 242
Labette Community College (A), 247
Laney College (A), 252
Liberty University (A), 258
Montgomery County Community College (A), 283
Mott Community College (A), 287
Mount Wachusett Community College (A), 288
New River Community College (A), 297
Northampton Community College (B), 304
Northeast Louisiana University (A), 304
Northern Virginia Community College (A), 306
Oakland University (B), 312
Open Learning Agency (B), 315
Pikes Peak Community College (A), 326
Prince George's Community College (A), 331
Rio Salado College (A), 339
South Mountain Community College (A), 360
Southern Christian University (B), 361
Southern West Virginia Community and Technical College (A), 367
Strayer University (A), 379
Texas Tech University (B), 387
UNET: University of Maine System Network for Education and Technology Services (UMA) (A), 397
Troy State University (A), 392
University of Nevada, Reno (B), 431
University of Phoenix Online Campus (A), 436
Wayne County Community College (A), 460
Western Nevada Community College (A), 464

Business Major
Lansing Community College (A), 252

Cross-Cultural Relations Major
Andrews University (B), 100

Human Organization and Behavior Major
Andrews University (B), 100

Humanities Major
Andrews University (B), 100

Medical Office, Lab Technology Major
City University (A), 145

University of Alaska Southeast, Sitka Campus (office) (A), 403

Management Major
Franklin University (B), 200

INTEGRATIVE STUDIES
Clayton College and State University (A), 148

INTERDISCIPLINARY STUDIES
Chadron State College (B), 141
Hamilton College (A), 216
Lewis-Clark State College (B), 257
New York Institute of Technology (B), 298

INTERIOR DESIGN
Community College of Philadelphia (A), 163

INTERNATIONAL BUSINESS
Caldwell College (B), 119
Community College of Philadelphia (A), 163
Linfield College (B), 260
Mercy College (B), 274

INTERNATIONAL STUDIES
City University (B), 145
Christopher Newport University (B), 143

INTERPRETER EDUCATION
Community College of Philadelphia (A), 163
Oklahoma State University, Oklahoma City (A), 315

JOURNALISM
City University (B), 145
Saint Mary-of-the-Woods College (B), 346

JUSTICE ADMINISTRATION
Community College of Philadelphia (A), 163

Ministry Major
Indiana College Network (A), 228
Taylor University World Wide Campus (A), 382

Public Policy Major
Indiana College Network (A), 228
Taylor University World Wide Campus (A), 382

LABOR STUDIES
Athabasca University (B), 106
Indiana College Network (A)(B), 228
Indiana University (A)(B), 229

LAW
Marist College (B), 268
Stephens College (B), 377

LAW ENFORCEMENT
Centralia College (A), 138
Indiana College Network (A), 228
Southern West Virginia Community and Technical College (A), 367
UNET: University of Maine System Network for Education and Technology Services (SMTC) (A), 397

LEGAL OFFICE STUDIES
Brevard Community College (A), 119
Centralia College (A), 138
Southern West Virginia Community and Technical College (A), 367

LIBERAL ARTS
Bucks County Community College (A), 122
Camden County College (A), 131
Centralia College (A), 138

Concordia-New York (B), 166
Concordia University, Austin (B), 166
J. Sargeant Reynolds Community College (A), 236
Lake Tahoe Community College (A), 250
Lehigh Carbon Community College (A), 255
Lewis-Clark State College (A), 257
Mercy College (A), 274
Mount Wachusett Community College (A), 288
New School (B), 297
Oklahoma City University (B), 314
Regents College (A)(B), 336
Rockland Community College (A), 341
Rogers State University (A), 342
Sinclair Community College (A), 358
Southern West Virginia Community and Technical College (A), 367
Tarrant County Junior College (A), 382
Tulsa Community College (A), 394
UNET: University of Maine System Network for Education and Technology Services (UMA) (A), 397

General Major
Community College of Philadelphia (A), 163
Cumberland County College (A), 171
Indiana College Network (A), 228
Taylor University World Wide Campus (A), 382
Ventura College (A), 454

Global Studies Major
Mount Wachusett Community College (A), 288

Humanities Major
Community College of Philadelphia (A), 163

International Studies Major
Community College of Philadelphia (A), 163

Liberal Studies Major
Mount Wachusett Community College (A), 288

Pre-Engineering Major
Mount Wachusett Community College (A), 288

Social-Behavioral Science Major
Community College of Philadelphia (A), 163

Theatre Arts Major
Mount Wachusett Community College (A), 288

LIBERAL STUDIES
Brookdale Community College (A), 121
Eastern Oregon University (B), 186
Elmhurst College (B), 190
Laurentian University (B), 253
Montgomery County Community College (A), 283
Oral Roberts University (B), 316
Porterville College (B), 328
Richland Community College (A), 338
Salve Regina University (B), 347
Syracuse University (A)(B), 380
University of Hawaii System (B), 412
University of Iowa (B), 416
University of Montana, Missoula (B), 429
University of Northern Iowa (B), 434

LIBRARY STUDIES
Rose State College (A), 343
UNET: University of Maine System Network for Education and Technology Services (UMA) (A), 397

LIFE PLANNING
Marylhurst University (B), 269

Career and Life Planning Minor
California State University, Chico, 127

MANAGEMENT
Baker University (B), 110
Barstow College (June 2029) (A), 111

Caldwell College (B), 119
Centralia College (A), 138
Champlain College (B), 141
City University (A)(B), 145
Community College of Philadelphia (A), 163
Concordia University, Austin (B), 166
Hamilton College (A), 216
J. Sargeant Reynolds Community College (A), 236
Linfield College (B), 260
Rochester Institute of Technology (B), 340
Southern West Virginia Community and Technical College (A), 367
Thomas Edison State College (A), 389
Troy State University (B), 392
University of Maryland University College (B), 421
University of Phoenix Online Campus (B), 436
Western Baptist College (B), 463

MANUFACTURING ENGINEERING
Michigan Technological University (B), 276

MARKETING
Caldwell College (B), 119
Centralia College (A), 138
City University (B), 145
Community College of Philadelphia (A), 163
Northwestern College, St. Paul (A), 309
Saint Mary-of-the-Woods College (B), 346
Strayer University (A), 379
University of Phoenix Online Campus (B), 436

MASS COMMUNICATIONS
City University (B), 145
Henderson State University (B), 219

MATHEMATICS
Centralia College (A), 138
Henderson State University (B), 219
Inter-American University of Puerto Rico (B), 232
Lehigh Carbon Community College (A), 255
Marylhurst University (B), 269
Saint Mary-of-the-Woods College (B), 346
Thomas Edison State College (A), 389

MECHANICAL ENGINEERING
Inter-American University of Puerto Rico (B), 232
Rochester Institute of Technology (B), 340
University of North Dakota (B), 434

Design Major
Michigan Technological University (B), 276

Technology Major
Lehigh Carbon Community College (A), 255

MEDICAL OFFICE STUDIES
Centralia College (A), 138
Community College of Philadelphia (A), 163
Lake Tahoe Community College (A), 250
Mount Wachusett Community College (A), 288
Northwestern College, Lima (A), 308
Southern West Virginia Community and Technical College (A), 367

MEXICAN AMERICAN STUDIES
Concordia University, Austin (B), 166

MIDDLE SCHOOL
Cambridge Academy, 130

MILITARY
American Military University (B), 99

Index by Fields of Study
Graduate Degree Programs

ACCOUNTING
Elmhurst College, 190
State University of New York Institute of Technology, Utica/Rome, 374
Strayer University, 379
Winthrop University, 468

ACQUISITION MANAGEMENT
American Graduate University, 98

ADMINISTRATIVE STUDIES
Southwest Missouri State University, 368

ADVERTISING/MARKETING
Michigan State University, 275
Syracuse University, 380
University of Alabama, 400

AEROSPACE/AERONAUTICAL
Auburn University, 107
Embry-Riddle Aeronautical University, 190
Oklahoma State University, 314
State University of New York, Buffalo, 375
University of Alabama, 400
University of Colorado, Boulder, 410
University of North Dakota, 434
University of Southern California School of Engineering, 442

AGRICULTURAL ENGINEERING
Colorado State University, 158
Iowa State University, 234
Kansas State University, 243
University of Idaho, Engineering Outreach, 414

APPLIED LINGUISTICS
Leicester University, 256

APPLIED MECHANICS
University of Illinois, Urbana-Champaign, 416

ANTHROPOLOGY
Utah State University, 453

ARCHEOLOGY
Leicester University, 256

ART/ART THERAPY
Henderson State University, 219
Vermont College of Norwich University, 455

ARTS ADMINISTRATION
Goucher College, 210

AVIATION
Central Missouri State University, 136

BIBLICAL STUDIES
Dallas Theological Seminary, 174
ICI University, 226
Reformed Theological Seminary, 335
Southern Christian University, 363
Temple Baptist Seminary, 384

BIOLOGY
Henderson State University, 219

BUSINESS
Blackfeet Community College, 116
Regent University, 335

BUSINESS ADMINISTRATION
Andrew Jackson University, 100
Athabasca University, 106
Auburn University, 107
Baker College, 109
Baker University, 110
Bellevue University, 114
California National University for Advanced Studies, 126
California State University, Fullerton, 128
California State University, Stanislaus, 129
Capitol College, 131
City University, 145
Colorado State University, 158
Concordia University Wisconsin, 167
Dalhousie University, 173
Duquesne University, 181
Eastern New Mexico University, 186
Fuqua School of Business at Duke University, 202
Heriot-Watt University, 220
Henderson State University, 219
Hope International University, 224
Indiana College Network, 228
Indiana Wesleyan University, 231
ISIM University, 235
JEC College Connection, 238
Lake Superior State University, 249
Lehigh University, 255
Leicester University, 256
Loyola College, Maryland, 263
Madonna University, 266
Maharishi University of Management, 266
Marist College, 268
Marshall University, 268
Marylhurst University, 269
Mississippi State University, 280
National University, 293
New Hampshire College, 295
New York Institute of Technology, 298
North Dakota State University, 302
Northwood University, 311
Oklahoma State University, 314

Porterville College, 328
Rensselaer Polytechnic Institute, 337
Saskatchewan Indian Federated College of the University of Regina, 352
Schoolcraft College, 353
Southern Illinois University, Edwardsville, 363
Southwest Missouri State University, 368
Stephens College, 377
Strayer University, 379
Syracuse University, 380
Université de Moncton, 398
University of Baltimore, 405
University of Montana, Missoula, 429
University of Nebraska, Lincoln, 430
University of North Dakota, 434
University of Notre Dame, 435
University of Phoenix Online Campus, 436
University of Sarasota, 437
University of South Carolina, 438
University of St. Francis, 441
University of St. Thomas, 442
University of Wisconsin, Whitewater, 451
Virginia Polytechnic Institute and State University, 457
Wayne State College, 460
Winthrop University, 468

BUSINESS COMMUNICATION
JEC College Connection, 238
Regent University, 335

CHEMICAL ENGINEERING
Auburn University, 107
Colorado State University, 158
Kansas State University, 243
Lehigh University, 255
Michigan State University, 275
Mississippi State University, 280
National Technological University, 292

CHEMISTRY
Lehigh University, 255

CHRISTIAN SCHOOL ADMINISTRATION AND TEACHING
Oral Roberts University, 316
Western Seminary, 465

CIVIL ENGINEERING
Auburn University, 107
Colorado State University, 158
Kansas State University, 243
Mississippi State University, 280
State University of New York, Buffalo, 375
University of Alabama, 400
University of Idaho, Engineering Outreach, 414

University of Maryland at College Park, 422
Virginia Polytechnic Institute and State University, 457
Worcester Polytechnic Institute, 469

COMMUNICATIONS
Syracuse University, 380

COMMUNICATIVE DISORDERS
California State University, Northridge, 128
Eastern New Mexico University, 186
University of New Hampshire, 432

COMMUNITY SERVICES
Michigan State University, 275

COMPUTER ENGINEERING
Grantham College of Engineering, 213
Iowa State University, 234
Kansas State University, 243
National Technological University, 292
University of Idaho, Engineering Outreach, 414
University of Minnesota, Rochester Center, 427
University of Southern California School of
  Engineering, 442

COMPUTER SCIENCE
Auburn University, 107
California State University, Chico, 127
Colorado State University, 158
Columbus State University, 162
Grantham College of Engineering, 213
Indiana College Network, 228
Knowledge Systems Institute, 246
Michigan State University, 275
National Technological University, 292
Northeastern University, 305
Nova Southeastern University, 311
Oklahoma State University, 314
Rensselaer Polytechnic Institute, 337
Southern Methodist University, School of Engineering
  and Applied Science, 365
Southern Polytechnic State University, 366
Stevens Institute of Technology, 378
University of Colorado, Boulder, 410
University of Hawaii System, 412
University of Houston, 413
University of Idaho, Engineering Outreach, 414
University of Massachusetts, Amherst, 423
University of Minnesota, Rochester Center, 427
University of Southern California School of
  Engineering, 439
Utah State University, 453

COMPUTER SYSTEMS
City University, 145
Elmhurst College, 190
University of Maryland University College, 421

COUNSELING
Beaver College, 112
Covenant Theological Seminary, 170
Gonzaga University, 208
Henderson State University, 219
Liberty University, 258
Southern Christian University, 363
Université de Moncton, 398
University of Alabama, 400
University of Hawaii System, 412
University of Sarasota, 437
Utah State University, 453

CRIMINAL JUSTICE
Andrew Jackson University, 100
Central Missouri State University, 136
Leicester University, 256
Michigan State University, 275
University of Central Oklahoma, 408

DIGITAL COMMUNICATION TECHNOLOGY
East Carolina University, 183

DISTANCE EDUCATION
Athabasca University, 106
Florida State University, 196
Texas Wesleyan University, 388

DIVINITY
Central Baptist Theological Seminary, 134
Covenant Theological Seminary, 170
Luther Seminary, 264
Lutheran Theological Seminary at Philadelphia, 265
Reformed Theological Seminary, 335
Regent University, 335
Seabury-Western Theological Seminary, 354
Southern Christian University, 363
University of Winnipeg, 448
Western Seminary, 465

EARTH LITERACY
Saint Mary-of-the-Woods College, 346

EDUCATION
Arkansas State University, 104
Ashland Community College, 105
Atlantic Union College, 107
Baker University, 110
Beaver College, 112
Blackfeet Community College, 116
Central Methodist College, 135
City University, 145
Cleveland State University, 149
College of St. Scholastica, 155
Concordia University, Austin, 166
Concordia University, St. Paul, 167
Concordia University Wisconsin, 167
Dakota State University, 172
Dalhousie University, 173
Eastern New Mexico University, 186
Eastern Oregon University, 186
Elmhurst College, 190
Emporia State University, 191
Fitchburg State College, 194
Goddard College, 207
Gonzaga University, 208
The Graduate School of America, 212
Henderson State University, 219
Herkimer County Community College, 221
Indiana College Network, 228
Indiana University, 229
JEC College Connection, 238
Lesley College, 257
Loyola College, Maryland, 263
Michigan State University, 275
Mississippi State University, 280
Montana State University, 282
Mount St. Vincent University, 288
New Mexico State University, 296
Newman University, 299
Northwest Missouri State University, 307
Nova Southeastern University, 311
Oklahoma State University, 314
Regent University, 335
Rosemont College, 343

Saskatchewan Indian Federated College of the
  University of Regina, 352
Seton Hall University, 356
Southern Oregon University, 365
Southwest Missouri State University, 368
Thomas College, 389
Université de Moncton, 398
University College of Cape Breton, 399
University of Akron, 400
University of Alaska Southeast, Juneau Campus, 403
University of Calgary, 406
University of Hawaii System, 412
University of Houston, 413
University of Louisville, 418
University of Montana, Missoula, 429
University of New England, 431
The University of North Carolina at Charlotte, 433
University of North Dakota, 434
University of Wisconsin, Stevens Point, 451
Utah State University, 453
Vermont College of Norwich University, 455
Virginia Polytechnic Institute and State University, 457
Wayne State College, 460

EDUCATION ADMINISTRATION/MANAGEMENT
Arkansas State University, 104
Concordia University Wisconsin, 167
East Carolina University, 183
George Washington University, 205
Gonzaga University, 208
Henderson State University, 219
Michigan State University, 275
North Dakota State University, 302
University of Hawaii System, 412

ELECTRICAL ENGINEERING
Arizona State University, 103
California State University, Fullerton, 128
Cleveland Institute of Electronics, 149
Colorado State University, 158
Grantham College of Engineering, 213
Indiana College Network, 228
Iowa State University, 234
Kansas State University, 243
Michigan State University, 275
Mississippi State University, 280
National Technological University, 292
Northeastern University, 305
Oklahoma State University, 314
Rensselaer Polytechnic Institute, 337
Southern Methodist University, School of Engineering
  and Applied Science, 365
Southern Polytechnic State University, 366
State University of New York, Buffalo, 375
University of Alabama, 400
University of Colorado, Boulder, 410
University of Houston, 413
University of Idaho, Engineering Outreach, 414
University of Illinois, Urbana-Champaign, 416
University of Massachusetts, Amherst, 423
University of Minnesota, Rochester Center, 427
University of Southern California School of
  Engineering, 439
Virginia Polytechnic Institute and State University, 457

ENERGY MANAGEMENT
New York Institute of Technology, 298

ENGINEERING
Arizona State University, 103

California National University for Advanced Studies, 126
Kansas State University, 243
Kettering University, 244
Purdue University, 332
Rensselaer Polytechnic Institute, 337
Stevens Institute of Technology, 378
University of Alabama, 400
University of Illinois, Urbana-Champaign, 416
University of Maryland at College Park, 422
University of South Carolina, 438
University of Virginia, 445

ENGINEERING MANAGEMENT
Colorado State University, 158
Kansas State University, 243
Milwaukee School of Engineering, 279
National Technological University, 292
New Mexico State University, 296
Southern Methodist University, School of Engineering and Applied Science, 365
University of Alabama, 400
The University of Alabama, Huntsville, 402
University of Colorado, Boulder, 410
University of Houston, 413
University of Idaho, Engineering Outreach, 414
University of Massachusetts, Amherst, 423
University of Nebraska, Lincoln, 430

ENGLISH
Eastern New Mexico University, 186
Henderson State University, 219
Northwestern State University of Louisiana, 310

ENVIRONMENTAL ENGINEERING
Colorado State University, 158
University of Alabama, 400
The University of Alabama, Huntsville, 402
Worcester Polytechnic Institute, 469

ENVIRONMENTAL MANAGEMENT
Duquesne University, 181
East Carolina University, 183
National Technological University, 292
Rochester Institute of Technology, 340
University of Denver, 411
University of Maryland University College, 421

FAMILY STUDIES
Iowa State University, 234
Michigan State University, 275

FINANCE AND FINANCIAL PLANNING
City University, 145
College for Financial Planning, 152
Golden Gate University, 208
Leicester University, 256

FIRE PROTECTION
Worcester Polytechnic Institute, 469

FORENSICS
Leicester University, 256

FORESTRY
Lakehead University, 250

GEOLOGICAL ENGINEERING
University of Idaho, Engineering Outreach, 414

GOVERNMENT
Regent University, 335

HAZARDOUS AND WASTE MATERIALS MANAGEMENT
Southern Methodist University, School of Engineering and Applied Science, 365

HEALTH CARE ADMINISTRATION/MANAGEMENT
California National University for Advanced Studies, 126
College of St. Scholastica, 155
Oklahoma State University, 314
Rochester Institute of Technology, 340
UNET: University of Maine System, 397
University of Dallas Graduate School of Management, 410
University of St. Francis, 441
University of St. Thomas, 442
Virginia Commonwealth University Medical College of Virginia Campus, 456
Virginia Commonwealth University, 457

HEALTH SCIENCES/ARTS
Beaver College, 112
California National University for Advanced Studies, 126
Clarkson College, 148
Goddard College, 207
National Technological University, 292
Rosemont College, 343
Saint Joseph's College, 345
University of Alabama, 400

HISTORIC PRESERVATION
Goucher College, 210

HOTEL/RESTAURANT MANAGEMENT
Auburn University, 107
University of Houston, 413

HUMAN AND COMMUNITY DEVELOPMENT
California School of Professional Psychology, Fresno, 126
Pacific Oaks College, 320
Salve Regina University, 347

HUMAN NUTRITION
University of Bridgeport, 405

HUMAN RESOURCE DEVELOPMENT AND MANAGEMENT
California National University for Advanced Studies, 126
Colorado State University, 158
Indiana College Network, 228
Leicester University, 256
New York Institute of Technology, 298
Ottawa University, Kansas City, 318
University of Nebraska, Lincoln, 430
Utah State University, 453

HUMAN SERVICES
Blackfeet Community College, 116
The Graduate School of America, 212

INDIVIDUALIZED STUDY
City University, 145
Goddard College, 207

INDUSTRIAL ENGINEERING
Auburn University, 107
Colorado State University, 158
Indiana College Network, 228
Mississippi State University, 280

Rensselaer Polytechnic Institute, 337
State University of New York, Buffalo, 375
University of Nebraska, Lincoln, 430
The University of Tennessee, Knoxville, 442
Virginia Polytechnic Institute and State University, 457

INDUSTRIAL HYGIENE
Colorado State University, 158

INFORMATION MANAGEMENT
ISIM University, 235
Nova Southeastern University, 311
Syracuse University, 380
University of Illinois, Springfield, 415

INFORMATION SYSTEMS
City University, 145
Dakota State University, 172
Ferris State University, 193
Florida State University, 196
ISIM University, 235
Northeastern University, 305
Nova Southeastern University, 311
Rensselaer Polytechnic Institute, 337
Rochester Institute of Technology, 340
Southwest Missouri State University, 368
Strayer University, 379
University of Phoenix Online Campus, 436
The University of Tennessee, Knoxville, 442
Utah State University, 453

INSTRUCTIONAL/PERFORMANCE TECHNOLOGY
Boise State University, 118
East Carolina University, 183
Mississippi State University, 280
University of Houston, Clear Lake, 414
Virginia Polytechnic Institute and State University, 457

INTERDISCIPLINARY ARTS
Goddard College, 207

INTERDISCIPLINARY ENGINEERING
Indiana College Network, 228

INTERNATIONAL DEVELOPMENT/MANAGEMENT
Hope International University, 224
National Technological University, 292
Salve Regina University, 347
Thunderbird, The American Graduate School of International Management, 390
Troy State University, 392
University of Maryland University College, 421

JEWISH EDUCATION
Hebrew College, 219

JEWISH STUDIES
Hebrew College, 219

JOURNALISM
University of Memphis, 424
University of Nebraska, Lincoln, 430

LAW
Leicester University, 256
Regent University, 335
University of Alabama, 400

LEADERSHIP
Bellevue University, 114

Index by Fields of Study
Doctoral Degree Programs

Index by Fields of Study
Certificate and Diploma Programs

College for Financial Planning, 152
Dalhousie University, 173
Florida Atlantic University, 195
Florida State University, 196
Golden Gate University, 208
ISIM University, 235
Laval University, 254
Leicester University, 256
Palo Alto College, 320
Thomas Edison State College, 389
University of Bridgeport, 405

FIRE SCIENCE/TECHNOLOGY
Coconino Community College, 151
Cogswell Polytechnical College, 152
Dalhousie University, 173
East Central College, 183
Kansas City, Kansas Community College, 242
Lake Tahoe Community College, 250
Oklahoma State University, 314
Worcester Polytechnic Institute, 469

FLORIST/FLORAL ARRANGEMENT
Lifetime Career Schools, 259

FOOD SCIENCE AND QUALITY FOOD MERCHANDISING
Laval University, 254

FOREIGN POLICY/INTERNATIONAL
American Military University, 99
South Mountain Community College, 360

FORENSICS
The Graduate School of America, 212

FRENCH
Athabasca University, 106
Lock Haven University of Pennsylvania, 260
Mount St. Vincent University, 288

GEMOLOGICAL STUDIES
Gemological Institute of America, 204

GENERAL OFFICE
Blackfeet Community College, 116
Centralia College, 138
Coconino Community College, 151
The College of West Virginia, 156
Community College of Philadelphia, 163
Diablo Valley College, 179
East Central College, 183
Fond du Lac Tribal and Community College, 197
Grays Harbor College, 214
Lehigh Carbon Community College, 255
Lifetime Career Schools, 259
Marywood University, 269
Midland College, 278
Palo Alto College, 320
Southern West Virginia Community and Technical College, 367
University of Alaska Southeast, Sitka Campus, 403

GENERAL STUDIES
Indiana College Network, 228
Lock Haven University of Pennsylvania, 260
Open Learning Agency, 315
Reformed Theological Seminary, 335
UNET: University of Maine System, 397
University of Maine, 419
University of Waterloo, 446

GEOGRAPHY
Lock Haven University of Pennsylvania, 260

GERMAN
Lock Haven University of Pennsylvania, 260

GERONTOLOGY
California College for Health Sciences, 125
The College of West Virginia, 156
Community College of Philadelphia, 163
The Graduate School of America, 212
Kansas City, Kansas Community College, 242
Laurentian University,
Lehigh Carbon Community College, 255
Mount St. Vincent University, 288
Mount Wachusett Community College, 289
Penn State University, 323
Saint Joseph's College, 345
Saint Mary-of-the-Woods College, 346
Southern West Virginia Community and Technical College, 367
University of Vermont, 444
University of Washington, 446
Virginia Polytechnic Institute and State University, 457

GOVERNMENT
Dalhousie University, 173

HEALTH ADMINISTRATION/MANAGEMENT
Athabasca University, 106
Beaver College, 112
College for Lifelong Learning, 153
Golden Gate University, 208
Pitt Community College, 327
Rochester Institute of Technology, 340
Stephens College, 377
UNET: University of Maine System, 397
University of Dallas Graduate School of Management, 410
University of New Orleans Metropolitan College, 432

HEALTH/HEALTH SCIENCES
Beaver College, 112
California College for Health Sciences, 125
Grays Harbor College, 214
Johns Hopkins School of Hygiene and Public Health, 240
Lock Haven University of Pennsylvania, 260
Mount St. Vincent University, 288
Mount Wachusett Community College, 289
New Hampshire College, 295
North Central Technical College, 301
Polytechnic University, 328
Rensselaer Polytechnic Institute, 337
Saint Joseph's College, 345
University of Alaska, Fairbanks, 402
University of Washington, 446

HORTICULTURE
Diablo Valley College, 179
Laval University, 254
Midland College, 278
University of Saskatchewan, 438

HOTEL/RESTAURANT MANAGEMENT
Champlain College, 141
Coconino Community College, 151
Diablo Valley College, 179
East Central College, 183
Hospitality Training Center, 225
University of Minnesota, Crookston, 426

HUMAN RESOURCES
California State University, Bakersfield, 127
Dalhousie University, 173
Florida Atlantic University, 195
JEC College Connection, 238
Leicester University, 256
Linfield College, 260
Mount St. Vincent University, 288
New Hampshire College, 295
North Carolina State University, 300
Penn State University, 323
Thomas Edison State College, 389
University College of the Cariboo, 399

HYPNOTHERAPY
Hypnosis Motivation Institute, 226

INDUSTRIAL AUTOMATION/ROBOTICS
Lehigh Carbon Community College, 255

INDUSTRIAL/POWER PLANT
Centralia College, 138
Columbia State Community College, 160
Greenville Technical College, 215

INFORMATION SYSTEMS
Anne Arundel Community College, 102
Athabasca University, 106
Beaver College, 112
California State University, Bakersfield, 127
Cerro Coso Community College, 140
City University, 145
Diablo Valley College, 179
East Central College, 183
Grays Harbor College, 214
Highline Community College, 221
ISIM University, 235
Judson College, 241
Knowledge Systems Institute, 246
Linfield College, 260
Marist College, 268
Midland College, 278
Mount Wachusett Community College, 289
New York University, 299
Nova Southeastern University, 311
Polytechnic University, 328
Rensselaer Polytechnic Institute, 337
Saint Mary-of-the-Woods College, 346
Seton Hall University, 356
Strayer University, 379
Texas Tech University, 387
University of California Extension, Berkeley, 407
University of Toledo, 444

INTERNET
Bellevue Community College, 113
Carroll College, 132
Lansing Community College, 252
Northeastern University, 305
Southern Polytechnic State University, 366
Texas Tech University, 387
University of Alaska Southeast, Sitka Campus, 403

ISLAMIC STUDIES
Luther Seminary, 264

JEWELRY
Highline Community College, 221

JEWISH STUDIES
Hebrew College, 219

Index by Fields of Study
Individual Classes

Please note that the colleges and universities responding to the survey were asked to provide listings of representative classes, so this listing is not exhaustive. Some schools requested that prospective students call for a complete listing of available classes. Therefore, you should not eliminate a school from consideration just because their name does not appear under a category in which you are interested. Check the school's Web site or call for a current catalog.

ABNORMAL PSYCHOLOGY
(see Psychology, Abnormal)

ACCOUNTING AND BOOKKEEPING

ADMINISTRATIVE AND SECRETARIAL SERVICES

ADULT LEARNING AND DEVELOPMENT

ADVERTISING

AEROSPACE, AERONAUTICAL ENGINEERING
(see Engineering)

AFRICAN-AMERICAN STUDIES
(see Area, Ethnic, and Cultural Studies)

AGING
(see Gerontology and Sociology)

AGRICULTURE
Bismarck State College, 116
Butte Community College, 123
Carl Sandburg College, 132
Connors State College, 168
Edison Community College, Ft. Myers, 187
Kansas State University, 243
Montana State University, 282
Murray State University, 290
Open Learning Agency, 315
Southern Illinois University, Carbondale, 364
State University of New York, Morrisville, 376
Texas Tech University, 387
Tyler Junior College, 395
University of British Columbia, 406
University of Guelph, 412
University of Minnesota, 425
University of Nebraska, Lincoln, 430
The University of Tennessee, Knoxville, 442
University of Wisconsin, River Falls, 450
University Systems of Georgia Independent Study, 452
West Hills College, 462

AIR CONDITIONING REPAIR
(see Mechanical Repair)

ALGEBRA AND CALCULUS
(see also Mathematics)
Bay Mills Community College, 112
Bismarck State College, 116
Centralia College, 138
Chabot College, 140
Chadron State College, 141
Citrus Community College, 144
Clark College, 147
Dallas TeleCollege, 173
De Anza College, 176
Delaware Technical and Community College, 177
Eastern Kentucky University, 184
Florence-Darlington Technical College, 194
Fort Scott Community College, 198
Genesee Community College, 205
Hillsborough Community College, 222
Ivy Tech State College, 235
Jacksonville State University, 237
Jefferson College, 238
Kankakee Community College, 242
Kansas State University, 243
Kellogg Community College, 244
Lake Land College, 248
Lima Technical College, 259
Mid-Plains Community College, 277
Murray State University, 290
North Carolina State University, 300
Northeastern University, 305
Northern State University, 306
Northwest Technical College, 308
Open Learning Agency, 315
Otero Junior College, 318
Pensacola Junior College, 324
Peralta Community College District, 324
Piedmont College, 325
Pierce College, 325
Pikes Peak Community College, 326
Portland State University, 329

Pueblo Community Colleges, 332
Rogers State University, 342
San Joaquin Delta College, 350
Shawnee Community College, 356
Sierra Community College, 357
St. Petersburg Junior College, 373
Tennessee Technological University, 385
Texas Tech University, 387
Troy State University, 392
Tyler Junior College, 395
UCLA Extension, 396
University of California Extension, Berkeley, 407
University of Central Oklahoma, 408
University of Guelph, 412
University of Illinois, Urbana-Champaign, 416
University of Kansas, 417
University of Manitoba, 420
University of Minnesota, 425
University of Minnesota, Crookston, 426
University of Missouri, 428
University Systems of Georgia Independent Study, 452
Upper Iowa University, 453
Weber State University, 461
Western Washington University, 466

ALTERNATIVE THERAPIES
(see also Medicinal Herbs)
American Academy of Nutrition, 97
Bastyr University, 111
University of St. Augustine for Health Sciences, 440
Western Washington University, 466

AMERICAN CINEMA AND FILM STUDIES
Camden County College, 131
Clark College, 147
College of San Mateo, 154
College of the Canyons, 155
Fullerton College, 202
Genesee Community College, 205
Governors State University, 210
Lake Tahoe Community College, 250
Lakeland Community College, 251
Lamar University, 251
Marylhurst University, 269
Nassau Community College, 291
Open Learning Agency, 315
Pueblo Community Colleges, 332
Seattle Central Community College, 354
Sinclair Community College, 358
Skagit Valley College, 359
St. Petersburg Junior College, 373
UCLA Extension, 396
University of Alabama, 400
University of Arkansas, Little Rock, 404
University of California Extension, Berkeley, 407
University of Guelph, 412
University of Illinois, Urbana-Champaign, 416
University of Kansas, 417
University of Massachusetts, Lowell, 423
West Valley College, 462

ANATOMY
American Academy of Nutrition, 97
Dalhousie University, 173
De Anza College, 176
Hamilton College, 216
Hocking College, 223
Parkland College, 322
Pierce College, 325
Pueblo Community Colleges, 332
Rancho Santiago Community College District, 334

Rogers State University, 342
St. Francis Xavier University, 372
University College of the Cariboo, 399
University of Minnesota, Crookston, 426

ANTHROPOLOGY
Athabasca University, 106
Blinn College, 117
Brookdale Community College, 121
Burlington County College, 123
Butte Community College, 123
Cabrillo Community College, 123
California State University, Stanislaus, 129
Camden County College, 131
Chabot College, 140
Charter Oak State College, 142
Citrus Community College, 144
Clackamas Community College, 146
Coastline Community College, 150
College of the Canyons, 155
Columbia Basin College, 159
Community College of Philadelphia, 163
Dallas TeleCollege, 173
Delaware County Community College, 176
Edison Community College, Ft. Myers, 187
El Camino College, 189
Florida Community College, Jacksonville, 195
Front Range Community College, 200
Galveston College, 203
Genesee Community College, 205
Governors State University, 210
Green River Community College, 215
Harrisburg Area Community College, 218
Houston Community College, 225
Hutchinson Community College, 225
Indiana University, 229
Jacksonville State University, 237
Johnson County Community College, 240
Kellogg Community College, 244
Kirkwood Community College, 245
Lafayette College, 248
Lake Land College, 248
Laney College, 252
Laramie County Community College, 253
Las Positas College, 253
Madison Area Technical College, 265
Montgomery County Community College, 286
Mt. San Antonio College, 290
North Dakota State University, 302
North Iowa Area Community College, 303
Northwestern Community College, 309
Northwestern Michigan College, 309
Ohlone College, 313
Open Learning Agency, 315
Palomar Community College, 321
Pasadena City College, 323
Peralta Community College District, 324
Pierce College, 325
Rancho Santiago Community College District, 334
Rio Salado College, 339
Riverside Community College, 339
Saddleback College, 345
San Diego City College, 348
San Diego Community College District, 349
Schoolcraft College, 353
Seattle Central Community College, 354
Shawnee Community College, 356
Sierra Community College, 357
Skagit Valley College, 359
Southeast Arkansas College, 360
Southwest Missouri State University, 368
St. Charles County Community College, 372

BEHAVIOR AND DRUGS
(see also Psychology)
Acadia University, 95
Fitchburg State College, 194
Fond du Lac Tribal and Community College, 197
Governors State University, 210
Lower Columbia College, 262
North Central Technical College, 301
Sierra Community College, 357
Southeastern Community College, 362
Southwest Missouri State University, 368
University of Illinois, Urbana-Champaign, 416
University of Nebraska, Lincoln, 430
University Systems of Georgia Independent Study, 452

BEHAVIORAL SCIENCE
Andrews University, 100
Arizona State University, 103
Black Hills State University, 116
Bluefield State College, 117
Bridgewater State College, 120
California State University, Stanislaus, 129
Centralia College, 138
Chabot College, 140
Citrus Community College, 144
College for Lifelong Learning, 153
Columbus State Community College, 162
Delaware Technical and Community College, 177
Florence-Darlington Technical College, 194
Fond du Lac Tribal and Community College, 197
Governors State University, 210
Ivy Tech State College, 235
John Tracy Clinic, 239
Lakeland Community College, 251
Mercy College, 274
Middle Tennessee State University, 277
Milwaukee School of Engineering, 279
North Central Technical College, 301
University of Guelph, 412
University of Illinois, Urbana-Champaign, 416
University of Maine, Machias, 419
University of Manitoba, 420
University of Michigan, 424
University of Minnesota, 425
Upper Iowa University, 453
Western Montana College of The University of Montana, 464
Worcester Polytechnic Institute, 469

BIBLE STUDIES
(see also Religious Studies)
Andrews University, 100
Church Divinity School of the Pacific, 143
Columbia International University, 159
Gordon-Conwell Theological Seminary, 209
Grace University, 211
Grand Rapids Baptist Seminary, 213
Hope International University, 224
Indiana Wesleyan University, 231
Lutheran Theological Seminary at Philadelphia, 265
Mid-America Bible College, 276
Notre Dame College, 311
Seattle Pacific University, 355
Seminary Extension, 355
Southern Christian University, 363
Taylor University World Wide Campus, 382
Trinity International University, 392
Tyler Junior College, 395
University of Kansas, 417
University of Manitoba, 420

University of Missouri, 428
Western Baptist College, 463
Western Seminary, 465

BIOLOGY
American River College, 99
Athabasca University, 106
Auburn University, 107
Barstow College, 111
Burlington County College, 123
California State University, Stanislaus, 129
Central Virginia Community College, 137
Charter Oak State College, 142
Clayton College and State University, 148
Coastline Community College, 150
The College of West Virginia, 156
Columbia Union College, 161
Community College of Rhode Island, 164
Dallas TeleCollege, 173
De Anza College, 176
Eastern Kentucky University, 184
Edison Community College, Ft. Myers, 187
Florida Community College, Jacksonville, 195
Front Range Community College, 200
Genesee Community College, 205
Great Basin College, 214
Greenville Technical College, 215
Harrisburg Area Community College, 218
Highline Community College, 221
Hillsborough Community College, 222
Indiana University, 229
J. Sargeant Reynolds Community College, 236
Jefferson College, 238
Johnson County Community College, 240
Joliet Junior College, 241
Kingwood College, 245
Laney College, 252
Laramie County Community College, 253
Lewis-Clark State College, 257
Lock Haven University of Pennsylvania, 260
Long Beach City College, 261
Marylhurst University, 269
New River Community College, 297
North Carolina State University, 300
Northwestern Michigan College, 309
Open Learning Agency, 315
Palo Alto College, 320
Pasadena City College, 323
Peralta Community College District, 324
Pikes Peak Community College, 326
Pitt Community College, 327
Pueblo Community Colleges, 332
Rancho Santiago Community College District, 334
Rio Salado College, 339
Roger Williams University, 341
San Antonio College, 348
Shawnee Community College, 356
Shoreline Community College, 357
Sierra Community College, 357
Sinclair Community College, 358
Southeastern Community College, 362
Southwest Missouri State University, 368
Southwest Texas State University, 369
St. Francis Xavier University, 372
St. Petersburg Junior College, 373
Syracuse University, 380
Taylor University World Wide Campus, 382
Texas A&M University, Commerce, 386
Tyler Junior College, 395
Ulster County Community College, 396
University of Alabama, 400

University of California Extension, Berkeley, 407
University of Kansas, 417
University of La Verne, 418
University of Manitoba, 420
University of Minnesota, 425
University of Missouri, 428
University of North Carolina, Chapel Hill, 433
University of Regina, 437
University of Southern Colorado, 439
University of Utah, 444
University of Waterloo, 446
Upper Iowa University, 453
Victor Valley Community College, 455
Virginia Polytechnic Institute and State University, 457
Wayne State College, 460
West Hills College, 462
West Valley College, 462
West Virginia Northern Community College, 463
Western Nevada Community College, 464
Westmoreland County Community College, 467

BIOLOGY, HUMAN
American Academy of Nutrition, 97
Burlington County College, 123
Centralia College, 138
Hocking College, 223
Montana State University, College of Technology, 283
University of California Extension, Berkeley, 407
University of Minnesota, 425

BIOLOGY AND LIFE SCIENCES
(Includes Zoology, Apiculture, and Wildlife Studies)
Burlington County College, 123
California State University, Stanislaus, 129
Centralia College, 138
Charter Oak State College, 142
Coastline Community College, 150
Community College of Rhode Island, 164
Community College of Vermont, 165
Dallas TeleCollege, 173
Delaware County Community College, 176
Dodge City Community College, 181
Florida Community College, Jacksonville, 195
Great Basin College, 214
Green River Community College, 215
Indiana University, 229
J. Sargeant Reynolds Community College, 236
Jefferson College, 238
Middle Tennessee State University, 277
Mississippi State University, 280
Monroe Community College, 282
Montgomery County Community College, 286
Murray State University, 290
North Dakota State University, 302
Open Learning Agency, 315
Shawnee Community College, 356
Southern Illinois University, Carbondale, 364
St. Charles County Community College, 372
UCLA Extension, 396
University College of the Cariboo, 399
University of Alaska Southeast, Juneau Campus, 403
University of California Extension, Berkeley, 407
University of Guelph, 412
University of Missouri, 428
University of North Carolina, Chapel Hill, 433
University of Texas, Austin, 442

BIOPHYSICS
(see Physiology and Biophysics)

Dallas TeleCollege, 173
Davenport Educational System, Inc., 175
Delaware Technical and Community College, 177
D'Youville College, 182
El Camino College, 189
Emporia State University, 191
Hocking College, 223
Lima Technical College, 259
McGill University, 271
Pueblo Community Colleges, 332
Sinclair Community College, 358
Southwest Missouri State University, 368
Southwest Texas State University, 369
State Center Community College District, 373
State University of New York Institute of Technology, Utica and Rome, 374
University of Houston, Clear Lake, 414
University of Minnesota, Crookston, 426
University of Minnesota, Rochester Center, 427
University of Missouri, 428
University of North Carolina, Chapel Hill, 433
University of St. Francis, 441

HEALTH EDUCATION
(see Education, Health, and Physical Education)

HEALTH, OCCUPATIONAL AND SAFETY
McGill University, 271
Montana Tech of the University of Montana, 284
San Jose State University, 350
Texas Woman's University, 388

HEALTH PROFESSION AND CAREERS
Boise State University, 118
Brookdale Community College, 121
Cabrillo Community College, 123
California State University, Stanislaus, 129
Central Florida Community College, 135
Chadron State College, 141
Christopher Newport University, 143
Clackamas Community College, 146
Clark College, 147
Cleveland State University, 149
Coastline Community College, 150
College for Lifelong Learning, 153
College of San Mateo, 154
College of St. Scholastica, 155
College of the Canyons, 155
The College of West Virginia, 156
Columbia Union College, 161
Columbus State Community College, 162
Cuesta College, 170
Dakota State University, 172
Dalhousie University, 173
Danville Area Community College, 174
Danville Community College, 175
De Anza College, 176
Delaware Technical and Community College, 177
Delgado Community College, 178
Dodge City Community College, 181
D'Youville College, 182
Hocking College, 223
Lima Technical College, 259
Mansfield University, 267
Pitt Community College, 327
Professional Career Development Institute, 331
The Richard Stockton College of New Jersey, 338
Southeastern Community College, 362
Southern Illinois University, Carbondale, 364
Technical College of the Lowcountry, 383
Texas Woman's University, 388
Tyler Junior College, 395

UCLA Extension, 396
University College of the Cariboo, 399
University of California Extension, Berkeley, 407
University of St. Francis, 441
University of Wisconsin, Whitewater, 451

HEALTH SCIENCES
American River College, 99
Barstow College, 111
Bluefield State College, 117
Boise State University, 118
Brookdale Community College, 121
Bucks County Community College, 122
Cabrillo Community College, 123
Calhoun State Community College, 124
California State University, Northridge, 128
Camden County College, 131
Carl Sandburg College, 132
Central Florida Community College, 135
Central Virginia Community College, 137
Centralia College, 138
Chabot College, 140
Chadron State College, 141
Christopher Newport University, 143
Clackamas Community College, 146
Clark College, 147
Clayton College and State University, 148
Coastline Community College, 150
College for Lifelong Learning, 153
College of San Mateo, 154
College of the Canyons, 155
Columbia Union College, 161
Columbus State Community College, 162
Dakota State University, 172
Dalhousie University, 173
Danville Area Community College, 174
Danville Community College, 175
Delaware Technical and Community College, 177
Delgado Community College, 178
Dodge City Community College, 181
East Central Community College, 184
Eastern Kentucky University, 184
Eastern Washington University, 187
Edison Community College, Ft. Myers, 187
Garland County Community College, 203
Genesee Community College, 205
Green River Community College, 215
Harrisburg Area Community College, 218
Houston Community College, 225
Iowa Wesleyan College, 234
Johnson County Community College, 240
Kutztown University, 247
Lake Land College, 248
Lake-Sumter Community College, 249
Lakeland Community College, 251
Lima Technical College, 259
Lock Haven University of Pennsylvania, 260
Mansfield University, 267
Michigan State University, 275
Montana Tech of the University of Montana, 284
Montgomery County Community College, 286
Moraine Park Technical College, 286
Mount Hood Community College, 288
Murray State University, 290
Nassau Community College, 291
New Mexico State University, Alamogordo, 296
New River Community College, 297
Northwest Technical College, 308
Open Learning Agency, 315
Peralta Community College District, 324
Pierce College, 325
Pitt Community College, 327

Porterville College, 328
The Richard Stockton College of New Jersey, 338
Rio Salado College, 339
San Diego City College, 348
San Diego Community College District, 349
Shawnee Community College, 356
Shoreline Community College, 357
Southeast Arkansas College, 360
Southern Illinois University, Carbondale, 364
Southwestern Oregon Community College, 371
Spoon River College, 372
St. Charles County Community College, 372
St. Petersburg Junior College, 373
State Center Community College District, 373
State University of New York, Morrisville, 376
Texas Woman's University, 388
Triton College, 392
UC Raymond Walters College, 395
University College of the Cariboo, 399
University of Alabama, 400
University of British Columbia, 406
University of California Extension, Berkeley, 407
University of Guam, 411
University of Illinois, Urbana-Champaign, 416
University of Kansas, 417
University of Manitoba, 420
University of Memphis, 424
University of Minnesota, Crookston, 426
University of Mississippi, 427
University of Southern Indiana, 440
University of St. Francis, 441
The University of Tennessee, Knoxville, 442
University of Waterloo, 446
University of Wisconsin, La Crosse, 449
University of Wisconsin, Milwaukee, 449
Weber State University, 461
West Valley College, 462
West Virginia Northern Community College, 463
Westmoreland County Community College, 467

HEARING LOSS AND SPECIAL NEEDS
John Tracy Clinic, 239

HERBS
(see Medicinal Herbs)

HISTORY, AFRICAN
California State University, Stanislaus, 129
Eastern Washington University, 187
Governors State University, 210
Indiana University, 229
Metropolitan State College of Denver, 274
New School, 297
University of Iowa, 416
University of North Carolina, Chapel Hill, 433
Weber State University, 461
Western Washington University, 466

HISTORY, ASIAN
California State University, Stanislaus, 129
College of San Mateo, 154
Governors State University, 210
Open Learning Agency, 315
Pierce College, 325
UCLA Extension, 396
University of Iowa, 416
University of Kansas, 417
University of Minnesota, 425

HISTORY, CANADIAN
Acadia University, 95
Open Learning Agency, 315

HISTORY, WORLD AND WESTERN CIVILIZATION

HOLISTIC HEALTH
(see Alternative Therapies)

HOME ECONOMICS AND FAMILY SCIENCES

HORTICULTURE

MECHANICAL ENGINEERING
(see Engineering, Mechanical)

MECHANICAL REPAIRS

MEDICAL
(see Health Sciences)

MEDICAL TERMINOLOGY

MEDICINAL HERBS

MENTAL HEALTH
(see also Psychology)

METEOROLOGY

PSYCHOLOGY, PHYSIOLOGICAL

SPANISH LANGUAGE
(see Language, Spanish)

SPECIAL EDUCATION
(see Education, Special)

SPEECH COMMUNICATIONS

SPEECH PATHOLOGY

SPORTS STUDIES AND MEDICINE
(see also Nutrition, Sports Clinical)

STATISTICS

Texas Tech University, 387
Triton College, 392
Troy State University, 392
Ulster County Community College, 396
University of Alabama, 400
University of California Extension, Berkeley, 407
University of Central Oklahoma, 408
University of Guelph, 412
University of Illinois, Urbana-Champaign, 416
University of Iowa, 416
University of Kansas, 417
University of Manitoba, 420
University of Minnesota, 425
University of Missouri, 428
University of Nebraska, Lincoln, 430
University of North Carolina, Chapel Hill, 433
University of Waterloo, 446
University Systems of Georgia Independent Study, 452
Western Washington University, 466

STRESS MANAGEMENT
Acadia University, 95
Bellevue Community College, 113
Chabot College, 140
Fullerton College, 202
Monroe Community College, 282
Mount Hood Community College, 288
University of Minnesota, 425

SUPERMARKET AND CONVENIENCE STORES
Cornell University, 169

SWEDISH LANGUAGE
(see Language, Swedish)

TEACHER EDUCATION
(see Education, Teacher)

TECHNICAL WRITING
(see also Creative Writing and Business Communications)
Blinn College, 117
Brookdale Community College, 121
California State University, Stanislaus, 129
Citrus Community College, 144
Clark College, 147
Columbia Basin College, 159
Columbus State Community College, 162
Delaware Technical and Community College, 177
Eastern Oregon University, 186
Edison Community College, Piqua, 188
Fitchburg State College, 194
Genesee Community College, 205
Green River Community College, 215
Hocking College, 223
Johnson County Community College, 240
Juniata College, 241
Lake Tahoe Community College, 250
Lima Technical College, 259
Milwaukee School of Engineering, 279
Mount Hood Community College, 288
New School, 297
Northwestern Michigan College, 309
Park College, 322
Pikes Peak Community College, 326
Polytechnic University, 328
Santa Fe Community College, 351
Skagit Valley College, 359
Terra State Community College, 386
UCLA Extension, 396
University of California Extension, Berkeley, 407

University of Kansas, 417
University of Massachusetts, Lowell, 423
University of Minnesota, 425
University of Nebraska, Lincoln, 430
University of Utah, 444
Walla Walla Community College, 458
Weber State University, 461

TECHNOLOGY
Cerritos College, 140
Dodge City Community College, 181
Duquesne University, 181
Edison Community College, Ft. Myers, 187
Emporia State University, 191
Essex Community College, 192
George Washington University, 205
Lesley College, 257
Montana State University, 282
Murray State University, 290
Northern State University, 306
Pitt Community College, 327
Roger Williams University, 341
San Jose State University, 350
Southwest Missouri State University, 368
State University of New York, Morrisville, 376
State University of West Georgia, 377
Texas A&M University, Commerce, 386
Texas Tech University, 387
Tidewater Community College, 390
University of Houston, Clear Lake, 414
Western Washington University, 466
Westmoreland County Community College, 467

TELECOMMUNICATIONS
Boise State University, 118
Butte Community College, 123
Champlain College, 141
George Washington University, 205
Golden Gate University, 208
Illinois Eastern Community Colleges, 227
Indiana University, 229
Lesley College, 257
Michigan State University, 275
North Central Technical College, 301
Seattle Pacific University, 355
State University of New York College at Oswego, 374
Texas Tech University, 387
University of Alabama, 400
University of California Extension, Berkeley, 407

TEXTILES
North Carolina State University, 300

THEATER AND PERFORMING ARTS
Arizona State University, 103
Boise State University, 118
Brookdale Community College, 121
Burlington County College, 123
Calhoun State Community College, 124
Chadron State College, 141
Crowder College, 170
Eastern Kentucky University, 184
Edison Community College, Ft. Myers, 187
Lewis-Clark State College, 257
Lock Haven University of Pennsylvania, 260
Mansfield University, 267
Monroe Community College, 282
Queen's University, 333
Rio Salado College, 339
Roger Williams University, 341
Sierra Community College, 357

Southwest Missouri State University, 368
Southwest Texas State University, 369
St. Charles County Community College, 372
University of Alabama, 400
University of Illinois, Urbana-Champaign, 416
University of Iowa, 416
University of Minnesota, 425
University of North Carolina, Chapel Hill, 433
University of Oklahoma, 435
University of Southern Indiana, 440
University of Texas of the Permian Basin, 443

THEATER APPRECIATION
Calhoun State Community College, 124

THEOLOGICAL STUDIES
Church Divinity School of the Pacific, 143
Cincinnati Bible College and Seminary, 144
Columbia International University, 159
Columbia Union College, 161
Concordia University, 165
Franciscan University of Steubenville, 199
Fuller Theological Seminary, 202
Grace University, 211
Grand Rapids Baptist Seminary, 213
Hope International University, 224
Jewish Theological Seminary, 239
Lutheran Theological Seminary at Philadelphia, 265
Mid-America Bible College, 276
Seminary Extension, 355
Southern Christian University, 363
Taylor University World Wide Campus, 382
Trinity International University, 392
University of Mary, 421
Western Baptist College, 463
Western Seminary, 465

TRANSLATOR AND TRANSLATION COURSES
College Universitaire de Saint-Boniface (in French), 157

TRAVEL INDUSTRY
The College of West Virginia, 156
International Aviation and Travel Academy, 233
Monroe Community College, 282
Professional Career Development Institute, 331
University of Guam, 411

TUTOR TRAINING
American River College, 99

VETERINARIAN STUDIES
Carroll Community College, 133
Essex Community College, 192
Kansas State University, 243
Murray State University, 290
Professional Career Development Institute, 331
St. Petersburg Junior College, 373
State University of New York College of Technology at Canton, 375
University College of the Cariboo, 399
University of Minnesota, Crookston, 426
University of Missouri, 428

VISUAL AND PERFORMING ARTS
Auburn University, 107
Boise State University, 118
The Richard Stockton College of New Jersey, 338
UCLA Extension, 396
University of Minnesota, 425